BIBLIOGRAPHIES IN AMERICAN HISTORY

BIBLIOGRAPHIES IN AMERICAN HISTORY

GUIDE TO MATERIALS FOR RESEARCH

BY

HENRY PUTNEY BEERS, Ph. D.

OCTAGON BOOKS

A DIVISION OF FARRAR, STRAUS AND GIROUX

New York   1973

LIBRARY OF CONGRESS CATALOG CARD NUMBER: 78-159167
ISBN 0-374-90515-0

Printed in USA by
Thomson-Shore, Inc.
Dexter, Michigan

To

GRACE, HARRY, CHARLES, and MARY BEERS

PREFACE TO THE SECOND REPRINT OF
THE SECOND EDITION

The enlarged, revised edition of this compilation was originally published by the H. W. Wilson Company in 1942. A reprint issued by Pageant Books, Inc. in 1959 has been out of print for several years. To meet the demand which still exists for copies of this work, this second reprint is issued. During research carried on in the last 30 years the compiler has assembled an extensive collection of additional titles which will be expanded for an additional volume that he hopes will be ready at an early date.

H.P.B.

Arlington, Va.
Sept. 14, 1972

PREFACE TO THE REPRINT OF
THE SECOND EDITION

This compilation was originally published by the H. W. Wilson Company in 1942 and has been out of print for a number of years. To meet the demand which still exists for copies of the work, it has seemed desirable to bring out a reprint by the photo-offset method. No changes or additions have been made in the text. To include bibliographic titles which have appeared in the past seventeen years would expand the collection beyond the capacity of a single volume of the same format. Much of the research carried on by the compiler during the intervening years has been of a bibliographical character, and he has assembled a considerable collection of additional titles, most of which are new but some of which were published prior to 1942. The bibliographic output of institutions and individuals has been on the increase, especially, in the fields of archives and manuscripts which have been stimulated by the establishment of national, state, and local archival and manuscript depositories and by the activities of associations composed largely of the staffs of those institutions. It is planned by the compiler to publish a supplement later in a separate volume.

H.P.B.

Arlington, Va.
August 3, 1959

PREFACE TO THE FIRST EDITION

The present compilation is an attempt at a comprehensive collection of bibliographical materials for research in American history. As the table of contents indicates, the words history and bibliography have been broadly interpreted, but no more broadly than historians have been interpreting them for some time past.

Foremost among the libraries in which research has been pursued is the Library of Congress with its special bibliography collection, and the Union Catalogue, comprising 8,500,000 author entries from over 700 American libraries. From his table on the bibliography deck, the writer has had within sight and reach many of the titles listed in the present compilation. The Union Catalogue not only facilitated research, but brought to light many new titles. Miss Florence S. Hellman, Acting Chief of the Division of Bibliography, has been particularly obliging in extending the facilities of her division. In addition to providing advice on various points, Miss Grace Gardner Griffin kindly permitted the use of the proof sheets and cards of her *Writings on American History* for 1931 to 1933.

Besides government departmental and bureau libraries, use has been made in Washington of the libraries of the Bureau of Railway Economics and the Carnegie Endowment for International Peace, whose staffs the compiler wishes to take this opportunity to thank.

The early work on this compilation was carried on in Philadelphia libraries. To Mr. C. Seymour Thompson and the staff of the University of Pennsylvania Library, the author is grateful for their uniformly courteous service. Mr. Layton B. Register, of the Biddle Law Library of the University of Pennsylvania, graciously permitted the use of that special library. Mr. Franklin H. Price, librarian of the Free Library of Philadelphia, afforded access to a special collection on bibliography in that library. Among other libraries in this city the writer is indebted to the staffs of the Historical Society of Pennsylvania, the Library Company of Philadelphia, and the American Philosophical Society. Use was also made of the Mercantile Library and the Commercial Museum Library.

For assistance of various kinds and for advice, the compiler wishes to make acknowledgment to a number of individuals. Mr. Waldo G. Leland, Secretary of the American Council of Learned Societies, examined and criticised portions of the manuscript. Miss Winifred Gregory kindly permitted the use of a bibliographical collection of titles on American newspapers.   Dr. Solon J. Buck, Director of Publications of The National Archives, supplied for examination a collection of several hundred titles compiled for a bibliography of guides to materials for research by Franklin F. Holbrook for the Joint Committee on Research of the American Council of Learned Societies and the Social Sciences Research Council, and a collection compiled by himself in connection with his studies of government historical publications.   His assistant, Mr. Herbert E. Angel, proffered the use of titles relating to government publications gathered from the library of the Superintendent of Documents.   The compiler is indebted to the staff of The H. W. Wilson Company for a revision of the index and for other editorial services.   For the copying of many titles he is indebted to his parents.

H. P. B.

Washington, D.C
July 28, 1937

PREFACE TO THE SECOND EDITION

This compilation, like the first edition, is intended to list titles relating to the United States of America, no matter where published. Many titles have been included which deal primarily with foreign countries, but they are included because they contain matter relating to the United States.

About 4,000 titles have been added to the second edition of this work. These include numerous publications which appeared before the first edition was published and all publications discovered since that time up to the end of 1941. Besides published matter, compilations in progress and manuscript bibliographies have been listed, as in the first edition. The additions include several hundred cartographical titles. Part of these are grouped together in Chapter XV, while others are classified under many subjects.

Courtesies and privileges extended by various individuals have been of considerable assistance. Miss Grace Gardner Griffin and Mrs. Dorothy M. Louraine kindly permitted the use of *Writings on American History* for 1936-1938. Catalogs of map lists and bibliographies were placed at the service of the compiler by Mrs. Clara Egli Le Gear, of the Division of Maps, Library of Congress, and Mr. Herman R. Friis, of the Division of Maps and Charts, The National Archives. Doctors Luther H. Evans and W. J. Wilson made arrangements for the use of the Bibliography of American History being compiled by the Historical Records Survey in the Library of Congress. Mr. Sargent B. Child, director of the Historical Records Survey, supplied lists of the publications of that organization. My thanks are due to The National Archives Library staff for its uniform courtesy. My parents have again assisted in various ways, as has my wife.

H. P. B.

The National Archives
November 10, 1941

CONTENTS

Chapter I

GENERAL AIDS

Chapter II

COLONIAL PERIOD, REVOLUTION, CONFEDERATION

Chapter III

THE UNITED STATES

Chapter IV

DIPLOMATIC HISTORY

Chapter V

ECONOMIC HISTORY

Chapter VI

EDUCATION

Chapter VII

POLITICAL SCIENCE, CONSTITUTIONAL, LEGAL

Chapter VIII

ARMY AND NAVY

Chapter IX

RACES

Chapter X

RELIGIOUS HISTORY

Chapter XI

SOCIAL, CULTURAL, SCIENTIFIC

Chapter XII

BIOGRAPHY AND GENEALOGY

Chapter XIII

TERRITORIES, POSSESSIONS, DEPENDENCIES

Chapter XIV

STATES

Chapter XV
Cartography

ABBREVIATIONS

acad.	academy	govt.	government	planog.	planographed
add.	addresses	Hisp.	Hispanic	pol.	political
Am.	American	hist.	historical,	pr.	press
Amer.	America		history	prep.	prepared
ann.	annals	inst.	institute	priv.	privately
antiq.	antiquarian	jour.	journal	proc.	proceedings
arch.	archeological	lib.	library	pt.	part
asso.	association	lithog.	lithographed	ptd.	printed
autog.	autographed	lithop.	lithoprinted	ptg.	printing
bibliog.	bibliographical	mag.	magazine	pub.	public, publi-
biog.	biographical,	mim.	mimeographed		cation, pub-
	biography	misc.	miscellaneous		lished
bul.	bulletin	MS., ms.	manuscript	quar.	quarterly
chron.	chronicles	MSS., mss.	manuscripts	rec.	record
co.	company	multig.	multigraphed	reg.	register
col.	collections	n.d.	no date	rep.	report
com.	committee	n.p.	no place, no	reprod.	reproduced
comm.	commission		publisher	rev.	review
comp.	compiled	n.s.	new series	ser.	serial, series
dept.	department	no.	number	so.	south
doc.	document	off.	office	soc.	society
dup.	duplicated	o.p.	out of print	south.	southern
econ.	economics	p.	page, pages	stud.	studies
ed.	edited	pap.	paper, papers	trans.	transactions
geneal.	genealogical	photo.	photolithograp-	typ.	typewritten
geog.	geography		hed	univ.	university
geol.	geological	photop.	photoprinted	unpag.	unpaged

Bibliographies in American History

CHAPTER I

GENERAL AIDS

BIBLIOGRAPHIES OF BIBLI-OGRAPHIES

General

American Council of Learned Societies Devoted to Humanistic Studies. Catalogue of current bibliographies in the humanistic sciences; avant-projet présenté à l'union académique international. Wash. D.C. Am. Council of Learned Societies. 1931. 73p. **1**

American Library Association. Board on Surveys. Directory of union catalogs in the United States. Chicago. In progress **1a**

Bennett, Whitman. A practical guide to American book-collecting. N.Y. The Bennett Book Studios, Inc. 1941. 254p. **1b**

Berthold, Arthur. Union catalogues; a selective bibliography. Phila. Union Library Catalog of the Philadelphia Metropolitan Area, N.Y. H. W. Wilson. 1936. 70p. planog. **1c**

Besterman, Theodore. A world bibliography of bibliographies. London. Printed for the author at the University Press, Oxford. 1939-40. 2v. **1d**

Bibliographic index, a cumulative bibliography of bibliographies. v. I-, March 1938-N.Y. H.W. Wilson. 1938- **1e**

Bibliographical Society of America. Index to the publications of the Bibliographical Society of America, and of the Bibliographical Society of Chicago, 1899-1931. Chicago. Univ. of Chicago Press. 1931. 43p. **2**

—— The news sheet, no. 1- 1926- (Contains data about bibliographies published and in progress) **2a**

Bibliographie des bibliotheks- und buchwesens. 1-9 jahrg. 1904-12; 1922-25. Leipzig. O. Harrassowitz. 1905-27. 13v. **3**

Bibliographies, American and English. *In* The annual literary index, 1892-1906; The annual library index, 1907-10; The American library annual, 1911/12-1917/18. N.Y. Publishers' Weekly. 1893-1918 **4**

Bishop, William Warner. Union catalogs. Chicago. (pub. ?) 1937 [72]p. **4a**

Bradley, I. S. Bibliographies published by historical societies of the United States. Bibliog. Soc. of Amer. pap. I. pt. 2. p146-57. 1907 **5**

Buck, Solon J. The status of historical bibliography in the United States. International Federation for Documentation, XIVth conference, Oxford-London, 1938, trans. I. p46-9. 1938 (Also reprinted, and republished in Pa. mag. hist. LXIII. p390-400. Jan. 1939) **5a**

Cannon, Carl Leslie. American book collectors and collecting, from colonial times to the present. N.Y. H.W. Wilson. 1941. 391p. **5b**

Cannons, H. G. T. Bibliography of library economy; a classified index to the professional periodical literature in the English language relating to library economy, printing, methods of publishing, copyright, bibliography, etc. from 1876 to 1920. Chicago. Am. Lib. Asso. 1927. 680p. **6**

Caspar, Carl N. J. M. Directory of the antiquarian booksellers and dealers in second-hand books of the United States. Milwaukee. C.N. Caspar. 1885. 276p. **6a**

Conference of College and University Libraries of Southern California. Bibliography of bibliographies in the libraries of Southern California. Claremont, Calif. Claremont College Lib. In progress **6b**

Coulter, Edith M. and Gerstenfeld, Melanie. Historical bibliographies; a systematic and annotated guide. Berkeley, Calif. Univ. of California Press. 1936. 206p. **7**

Courtney, William Prideaux. A register of national bibliography, with a selection of the chief bibliographical books and articles printed in other countries. London. Constable. 1905. 2v. **8**

Cutter, C. A. List of printed catalogues of public libraries in the United States, arranged by date of publication. *In* Public libraries in the United States of America. (Department of Interior. Bureau of Educ. Special report. pt. I) Wash. Govt. Ptg. Off. 1876. p576-622 **9**

Downs, Robert B. Notable materials added to American libraries, 1938-39, 1939-1940. Lib. quar. X. p157-91 (April 1940); XI. p257-301 (July 1941) **9a**

Ford, Paul Leicester. Check list of bibliographies, catalogues, reference-lists, and lists of authorities of American books and subjects. Brooklyn, N.Y. 1889. 64p. (Based on Reference list to bibliographies, catalogues, and reference lists on America in Library Journal. XIII. Feb.-Oct. 1888)   **10**

Hirsch, Rudolph. A list of recent bibliographies. N.Y. Pub. Lib. bul. XLII. p109-32 (Feb. 1938); XLIII. p323-32, 493-512, 548-62 (April, June, July 1939)   **10a**

Internationale bibliographie des buch- und bibliothekswesens mit besonderer Berücksichtigung der bibliographie. neue folge 1- jahrgang. 1926- Leipzig. O. Harrassowitz. 1928-   **11**

Josephson, Aksel G. S. Bibliographies of bibliographies, chronologically arranged with occasional notes and an index. Chicago. Bibliog. Soc. of Chicago. 1913. 38p. (Reprinted from the Bibliog. Soc. of Amer. bul. II, p21-4, 53-6. 1900; III. p23-4, 50-3. 1911; IV. p23-7. 1912; Bibliog. Soc. of Amer. pap. VII. p33-40, 115-24. 1912-13)   **12**

League of Nations. Committee on Intellectual Cooperation. Index bibliographicus international; catalogue of sources of current bibliographical information (periodicals and institutions). Arranged and edited by Marcel Godet. Geneva. 1925. 233p. (Second edition in French. 1931. 420p.)   **13**

Medina, José Toribio. Bio-bibliografía. *In* Catálogo breve de la biblioteca Americana que obsequia a la nacional de Santiago. Santiago de Chile. Imprenta Universitaria. 1926. I. p1-26   **14**

Morsch, Lucile M. Library literature, 1921-1932; a supplement to Cannons' bibliography of library economy 1876-1920. Comp. by the Junior members round table of the American Library Association. Chicago. Am. Lib. Asso. 1934. 430p.   **15**

Mudge, Isadore G. Guide to reference books. Chicago. Am. Lib. Asso. 1936. 504p. Supplement. 1939. 69p.   **16**

Munsell, J. Catalogue of American and foreign books in bibliography and other departments of literature . . . rare works relating to printing, voyages and travels, etc. Albany. J. Munsell. 1857. 74p.   **17**

New York. State Library School. Selected national bibliographies. New York State Lib. School. bul. no. 436, Dec. 1, 1908. 35p.   **18**

Northrup, Clark S. and others. A register of bibliographies of the English language and literature. New Haven. Yale Univ. Press. 1925. 507p.   **19**

Polk, Prudence McNeal. Book trade bibliographies in the Nashville libraries. Comp. for the Nashville Library Club under the direction of Irene May Doyle. Nashville, Tenn. 1933. 12p. mim.   **20**

Providence (R.I.) Public Library. Index to reference lists published by libraries. Bulletin of Bibliog. II- Oct. 1904-   **21**

Sabin, Joseph. A bibliography of bibliography; or a handy book about books which relate to books, being an alphabetical catalogue of the most important works descriptive of the literature of Great Britain and America, and more than a few relative to France and Germany. N.Y. J. Sabin. 1877. cl p.   **22**

Shores, Louis. Basic reference books; an introduction to the evaluation, study, and use of reference materials, with special emphasis on some 300 titles. Chicago. Am. Lib. Asso. 1939. 472p.   **22a**

Stein, Henri. Manuel de bibliographie générale. Paris. Alphonse Picard et Fils. 1897. 895p.   **23**

Stillwell, Margaret Bingham. Incunabula and Americana, 1450-1800; a key to bibliographical study. N.Y. Columbia Univ. Press. 1931. 483p.   **24**

Union list of literature on library science and bibliography up to 1935. Comp. by a Com. of the union list of literature on library science and bibliography in the League of young librarians. Osaka. League of young librarians. 1938. 255p.   **24a**

U.S. Library of Congress. Union catalog. Card file of subject bibliographies. Wash. D.C. In progress   **24b**

—— —— —— Catalogs and lists which have been incorporated in the union catalog. Wash. Govt. Ptg. Off. 1933. 7p.   **25**

Vail, Robert W. G. The literature of book collecting; a selective bibliography prepared for the Washington Square college book club of New York University. N.Y. N. Y. Univ. priv. print. for the Book club. 1936. 50p.   **26**

Van Hoesen, Henry Bartlett and Walter, Frank Keller. Bibliography: practical, enumerative, historical; an introductory manual. N.Y., London. Scribners. 1928. 519p. (Bibliog. appendix, p425-502)   **27**

Van Male, John. Union card catalogs in the United States, a preliminary list. Denver. Bibliographical Center for Research. 1938. 9p.   **27a**

Webber, Winslow Lewis. Books about books: a bio-bibliography for collectors. Boston. Hale, Cushman & Flint. 1937. 168p.   **27b**

Winchell, Constance M. Locating books for inter-library loan, with a bibliography of printed aids which show location of books in American libraries. N.Y. H.W. Wilson. 1930. 170p.   **28**

—— Reference books of 1938-1940. Chicago. Am. Lib. Asso. 1941   **28a**

Winsor, Justin. Americana in libraries and bibliographies. *In* Narrative and critical history of America. Boston, N.Y. Houghton Mifflin. 1889. I. p i-xix   **29**

Wroth, Lawrence C. Recent bibliographical work in America. The library. 4th ser. IX. p59-85 (June 1928)   **30**

Special

Alexander, Carter. Educational research; suggestions and sources of data with special reference to administration. N.Y. Columbia Univ., Teachers College, Bureau of publications. 1931. 115p. **31**

Baker, Blanch M. Bibliography of bibliographies (Indexes, lists, catalogs, etc.). *In* Dramatic bibliography; an annotated list of books on the history and criticism of the drama and stage and on the allied arts of the theatre. N.Y. H.W. Wilson. 1933. p246-63 **32**

Barrow, John Graves. A bibliography of bibliographies in religion, with a critical study of bibliographies dealing with American Protestant missions to foreign lands. (Yale Univ. Ph.D. thesis) c1930. MS. (Not available for use; compiler intends to publish) **33**

Beal, W. H. and Ogden, E. L. The contribution of the U.S. Department of Agriculture to the bibliography of science. Bibliog. Soc. Amer. pap. II. p135-52. 1907-08 **34**

Boston. Public Library. Bibliographies of special subjects originally published in the Bulletins of the library, no. 5; a catalogue of the bibliographies of special subjects in the Boston public library, together with an index to notes upon books and reading to be found in library catalogues, in periodical and other publications. Comp. by James L. Whitney. Boston. Rockwell & Churchill, city printers. 1890. 71p. (*Also in* Boston Public Lib. Handbook for readers in the Boston Public Lib. Boston. 1890. p28-262; and in Boston Public Lib. bul. n.s. II. p135-203. April 1890) **35**

—— —— Indexes to periodicals, etc. *In* Handbook for readers in the Boston Public Library. Boston. Pub. by the Trustees. 1890. p263-321 **35a**

Brown, Karl and Haskell, Daniel C. A bibliography of union lists of newspapers. *In* American newspapers, 1821-1936; a union list of files available in the United States and Canada. Ed. by Winifred Gregory. N.Y. H. W. Wilson. 1937. p787-9 **35b**

Brown, Stephen J. An introduction to Catholic booklore. (Catholic bibliog. series no. 4) London. Burns, Oates & Washbourne. 1933. 105p. **36**

Bureau of Railway Economics. Library. Railroad bibliographies—a trial check-list, Aug. 1938. [Wash. D.C. 1938] 71p. mim. **36a**

Carnegie Endowment for International Peace. Library. Bibliographies and catalogs of international law. M. Alice Matthews, librarian. Wash. D.C. 1931. 3p. typ. **37**

Cross, Tom Peete. A list of books and articles chiefly bibliographical designed to serve as an introduction to the bibliography and methods of English literary history (with an index). Chicago. Univ. of Chicago Press. [1925] 56p. **38**

Culver, Dorothy Campbell. Methodology of social science research; a bibliography. (Publications of the Bureau of Public Administration, Univ. of Calif.) Berkeley, Calif. Univ. of Calif. Press. 1936. 159p. **39**

Dunbar, Clarence Peckham. Bibliography of bibliographies on subjects related to national defense. (Louisiana State Univ. Bureau of Educational Research. Bibliog. ser., no. 1) University, La. 1941. 12p. reprod. typ. **39a**

Edwards, Everett E. An annotated bibliography on the materials, the scope, and the significance of American agricultural history. Agricultural hist. VI. p38-43 (Jan. 1932) **40**

Elliott, Richard R. Indian bibliographies. Am. Catholic quar. rev. XVIII. p698-719; XIX. p545-61; XX. p238-65, 721-49 (1893-95) **41**

Federal Writers' Project, New York (city). A trial bibliography of bibliographies relating to labor; a preliminary check list. [N.Y. 1937] 45,8,8,5 p. mim. **41a**

Friend, W. L. jr. A survey of Anglo-American legal bibliography. Law lib. jour. XXXIII. p1-18 (Jan. 1940) **41b**

Growoll, Adolf. American book clubs; their beginnings and history, and a bibliography of their publications. N.Y. Dodd, Mead. 1897. 423p. **42**

—— Book trade bibliography in the United States in the nineteenth century. N.Y. E.B. Hackett, The Brick Row Book Shop, Inc. [1939] 79p. **42a**

Guernsey, R. S. Legal bibliography; the catalogue of the New York law institute. Reprinted from the N. Y. daily register March, 27, 1874. 7p. **43**

Guthrie, Anna L. Library work cumulated, 1905-1911; a bibliography and digest of library literature. Minneapolis. H.W. Wilson. 1912. 409p. **43a**

Haskell, Daniel C. A bibliography of union lists of serials. *In* Union list of serials in the United States and Canada. Ed. by Winifred Gregory. N.Y. H.W. Wilson. 1927. p1581-8 **44**

Hayes, Alice. A list of bibliographies on woman suffrage. Bul. of bibliog. VIII. p194-5 (July 1915) **45**

Jackson, James. Liste provisoire de bibliographies géographiques spéciales. Paris. Société de Géog. 1881. 340p. **46**

John Crerar Library. A bibliography of union lists of serials. By Aksel G. S. Josephson. Chicago. 1906. 28p. **47**

—— A list of bibliographies on special subjects. Chicago. Printed by order of the board of directors. 1902. 503p. **48**

—— A list of reference indexes, special bibliographies and abstract serials, in the John Crerar Library. By H. Einar Mose (Reference list nos. 4, 9, 20) Chicago. 1930, 1932. 3 pts. typ. **49**

Keitt, Lawrence. An annotated bibliography of bibliographies of statutory materials of the United States. (Harvard series of legal bibliographies, ed. by Eldon R. James, II) Cambridge, Mass. Harvard Univ. Press. 1934. 191p.   **50**

Library literature, 1933/35- ; an author and subject index-digest to current books, pamphlets and periodical literature relating to the library profession. N.Y. H.W. Wilson. 1936-   **50a**

Margerie, Emmanuel de. Catalogue des bibliographies géologiques. Paris. Gauthier-Villars et fils. 1896 (Amérique de Nord, p596-651)   **50b**

Mathews, E. B. Catalogue of published bibliographies in geology, 1896-1920. National Research Council bul. no. 36. v. 6. pt. 5. Oct. 1923. 228p.   **51**

Monroe, Walter S. and Asher, Ollie. A bibliography of bibliographies. (Univ. of Illinois. bul. v. 24. no. 44. Bureau of educational research. Bul. no. 36) Urbana. Univ. of Illinois. 1927. 60p. (Bibliographies in education)   **52**

Monroe, Walter S., Hamilton, Thomas T. and Smith, V. T. Bibliography of bibliographies. *In* Locating educational information in published sources. (Univ. of Illinois. Bureau of educational research. bul. no. 50) Urbana. 1930. p58-130   **53**

Monroe, Walter S. and Shores, Louis. Bibliography and summaries in education to July 1935: a catalog. N.Y. H.W. Wilson. 1936. 470p.   **54**

National Education Association of the United States. Research division. Index to certain bibliographies available in printed, typewritten or mimeographed form. [Wash.] Jan. 1933. 45p. mim.   **55**

Newberry Library. Book arts, bibliography, printing, bookbinding, publishing & bookselling, national & local bibliography. Chicago. 1919-20. multig. as MS. 2v.   **56**

Palfrey, Thomas R. and Coleman, Henry E. Guide to bibliographies of theses, United States and Canada. Chicago. Am. Lib. Asso. 1940. 54p. planog.   **56a**

Schaefer, Victor A. A register of Catholic bibliographies. In progress   **56b**

Sellin, Johan Thorsten and Shalloo, Jeremiah P. A bibliographical manual for the student of criminology. Phila. 1935. 41p.   **57**

Shunami, Shlomo. Bibliography of Jewish bibliographies. Jerusalem. [Hebrew] Univ. Press. 1936. 399p.   **58**

Smith, Wilbur M. A list of bibliographies of theological and biblical literature published in Great Britain and America, 1595-1931, with critical, biographical and bibliographical notes. Coatesville, Pa. Priv. print. 1931. 62p.   **59**

Society of Industrial Engineers and Engineering Societies Library. Committee on research. A list of bibliographies on industrial engineering and management

(Society of Industrial Engineers. Publication. III. no. 6. May 1920) [N.Y. 1920] 23p.   **60**

Sohon, Julian Arell and Schaaf, William L. A reference list of bibliographies, chemistry, chemical technology and chemical engineering published since 1900. N.Y. H.W. Wilson. 1924. 100p.   **61**

U.S. Department of Agriculture. Library. List of manuscript bibliographies and indexes in the Department of Agriculture, including serial mimeographed lists of current literature. Comp. by E. Lucy Ogden and Emma B. Hawks (Bibliog. contributions no. 11) Wash. Jan. 1926. 38p. mim.   **62**

U.S. Library of Congress. Division of bibliography. A bibliography of bibliographies of trade unions. Comp. by Helen F. Conover. Oct. 1937. 20p. mim.   **62a**

—— —— —— Crime and criminal justice; a bibliography of bibliographies and a selected list of recent books, 1937-1939. Comp. by Helen F. Conover. June 29, 1940. 52p. mim.   **62b**

—— —— —— List of bibliographies on accounting. March 4, 1918. 2p. typ.   **63**

—— —— —— List of bibliographies on automobiles. Nov. 16, 1922. 4p. mim.   **64**

—— —— —— List of bibliographies on coal. Sept. 16, 1920. 11p. mim.   **65**

—— —— —— List of bibliographies on commerce. June 3, 1921. 20p. mim.   **66**

—— —— —— List of bibliographies on commercial education. Aug. 5, 1920. 3p. typ.   **67**

—— —— —— List of bibliographies on crime and criminals. Feb. 1, 1922. 21p. mim.   **68**

—— —— —— List of bibliographies on foreign commerce. 1934. 46p. mim.   **69**

—— —— —— List of bibliographies on home economics. Oct. 26, 1922. 11p. mim.   **70**

—— —— —— List of bibliographies on the housing problem. Sept. 16, 1925. 7p. typ.   **71**

—— —— —— List of bibliographies on military and naval art and science. Sept. 9, 1921. 23p. typ.   **73**

—— —— —— List of bibliographies on petroleum. March 11, 1921. 7p. typ.   **74**

—— —— —— A list of bibliographies on propaganda. Comp. by Grace H. Fuller. Nov. 22, 1940. 6p. mim.   **74a**

—— —— —— List of bibliographies on public utilities, including regulation, valuation, and municipal ownership. Jan. 10, 1921. 11p. mim.   **75**

—— —— —— A list of bibliographies on questions relating to national defense. Comp. by Grace H. Fuller. June 24, 1941. 25p. processed   **75a**

—— —— —— List of bibliographies on the regulation of public utilities. June 10, 1916. 4p. typ. (Additional references. Sept. 15, 1926. 1p. typ.)   **76**

—— —— —— List of bibliographies on retailing. May 26, 1916. 2p. typ.   **77**

—— —— —— List of bibliographies on social, political and economic sciences. March 30, 1918. 8p. typ. (Additional references. Sept. 22, 1933. p9-10) **78**

—— —— —— List of bibliographies on social surveys. Aug. 13, 1920. 3p. typ. **79**

—— —— —— List of bibliographies on strikes. June 5, 1922. 5p. mim. **80**

—— —— —— List of bibliographies on thrift and savings. Aug. 27, 1926. 4p. typ. **81**

—— —— —— A list of bibliographies on U.S. national defense. March 3, 1941. 7p. typ. **81a**

—— —— —— List of bibliographies on vocational guidance. Sept. 11, 1922. 4p. mim. (Additional references. Sept. 24, 1925. p5-6) **82**

—— —— —— List of bibliographies on voyages and travel. Oct. 31, 1916. 7p. typ. **83**

—— —— —— List of bibliographies on wages and salaries, with a section on bonus and profit-sharing systems. April 23, 1921. 9p. mim. **84**

—— —— —— List of bibliographies on woman suffrage. April 24, 1922. 4p. typ. **85**

—— —— —— Select list of references to bibliographies of the American Indians. June 3, 1910. 3p. typ. **85a**

—— —— —— A selected list of recent bibliographies on employment management. Comp. by Grace Hadley Fuller. 1938. 8p. mim. **85b**

U.S. Superintendent of Documents. Bibliographic material from U.S. Government publications up to about 1895. Collected by Adelaide R. Hasse (MS. in Office of the Supt. of Documents) **86**

U.S. Works Progress Administration. New York (city). Selected list of bibliographies on the polar regions, parts I and II. N.Y. 1938, 1939. 41, 27p. mim. **86a**

Valle, Rafael Heliodoro. Bibliography of American anthropology, 1936-1937. Boletín bibliográfico de antropología americana. I. no. 4, p267-87. 1937 **86b**

Wagner, W. H. A bibliography of bibliographies applicable to transportation, etc. ICC practitioner's jour. IV. p308-20 (March 1937) **86c**

Witherington, Aubrey Milton. A bibliography of bibliographies of interest to administrators. (George Peabody College for Teachers. Master's thesis) Nashville. Tenn. 1928. 152p. MS. **87**

Work, Monroe N. A bibliography of bibliographies on the Negro in the United States. *In* A bibliography of the Negro in Africa and America. N.Y. H.W. Wilson. 1928. p630-6 **88**

Wright, John Kirtland. Aids to geographical research, bibliographies and periodicals. (Am. Geog. Soc. Research series. no. 10. ed. by W. L. G. Joerg) N.Y. Am. Geog. Soc. 1923. 243p. **89**

Wright, Joseph. Bibliographies relating to municipal government. National municipal rev. III. p430-49 (April 1914) **90**

Places and Periods

Beers, Henry Putney. Pennsylvania bibliographies. Pennsylvania hist. II. p104-8, 178-82, 239-43; III. p46-56 (April 1935-Jan. 1936) (Also extracted) **91**

Bump, Charles Weathers. Bibliographies of the discovery of America. (Johns Hopkins Univ. Studies in historical and political science. X) Balt. Johns Hopkins Univ. Press. 1892. p519-32 **92**

Chapin, Howard Millar. Bibliography of Rhode Island bibliography. (Contributions to Rhode Island bibliog. no. 1) Providence, R.I. Rhode Island Hist Soc. 1914. 11p. **93**

John Crerar library. Bibliographical guides, directories, and authority lists for studying the New Deal. (Reference list no. 31. comp. by John K. Wilcox) Chicago. 1935. 11p. typ. **94**

Johnson, Maude E. A bibliography of New Jersey bibliographies. N.J. Hist. Soc. Proc. 3d ser. IX-X. p61-2 (April 1915) **95**

Jones, Cecil K. Hispanic American bibliographies. Hisp. Am. hist. rev. III. p414-42, 603-34 (Aug., Nov. 1920); IV. p126-56, 523-52 (Feb., Aug. 1921); VI. p100-33 (Feb.-Aug. 1926); XI. p397-410 (Aug. 1931); XIII. p380-402 (Aug. 1933); XIV. p531-44 (Nov. 1934); XVII. p111-38 (Feb. 1937); XVIII. p403-23 (Aug. 1938). (Earlier portions reprinted: Balt. 1922. 200p.) **96**

Josephson, Aksel G. S. Bibliographies of the Philippine Islands; chronological check list. Bul. of bibliog. II. p10-12 (Oct. 1899). (Reprinted as Bul. of bibliog. pamphlets no. 7. Boston. Boston Book Co. 1899. 8p) **97**

Kaiser, John Boynton. The national bibliographies of the South American republics. (Bul. of bibliog. pamphlets no. 21) Boston. Boston Book Co. 1913. 19p. (Reprinted from the Bul. of bibliog. VII. no. 6. July 1913) **98**

Keniston, Hayward. List of works for the study of Hispanic-American history. N.Y. Hispanic Soc. of Amer. 1920. 451p. **99**

Léon, Nicolás. Bibliografía bibliográfica mexicana, primera parte. Mexico. Talleres graficos del Museo Nacional de Arqueología, Historia y Etnografía. 1923. 66p. **100**

McGill University. Library School. A bibliography of Canadian bibliographies. Comp. by the 1929 and 1930 classes in bibliography of the McGill University library school under the direction of Marion V. Higgins (McGill Univ. publications. ser. VII. Lib. no. 20) Montreal. 1930. 45p. **101**

Pan American Union. Columbus Memorial Library. Bibliographies pertaining to Latin America in the Columbus Memorial Library of the Pan American Union. Comp. by Charles E. Babcock. Wash. D.C. 1928. 34p. mim. **102**

Ring, Elizabeth. A bibliography of Maine bibliographies. no place, no pub. Jan. 1937. 18p. typ. **102a**

Smith, Robert L. Some bibliographies of the European war and its causes. Bul. of bibliog. X. p49-52 (July-Aug.-Sept. 1918) **103**

Trelles, C. M. Bibliografía antillana. Hisp. Am. hist. rev. IV. p324-8 (May 1921) **104**

U.S. Library of Congress. Division of bibliography. List of bibliographies on the European war. June 18, 1919. 31p. mim. **105**

—— —— —— List of bibliographies on Maine. Dec. 29, 1919. 3p. typ. **106**

—— —— —— List of bibliographies on the New England states. Aug. 3, 1915. 4p. typ. **107**

Wallace, W. S. The bibliography of Canadiana. Canadian hist. rev. V. p4-8 (March 1924) **108**

Waters, Willard O. California bibliographies. Cal. Hist. Soc. quar. III. p245-58 (Oct. 1924) **109**

Wilgus, Alva Curtis. Bibliographical activities in the United States concerning Latin America. Pan Amer. Inst. Geog. Hist. proc. 1937. p268-78 **109a**

—— Some bibliographies in English dealing with Hispanic America. Pan-Am. mag. XLIII. p162-4 (Sept. 1930) **110**

INDEXES TO PERIODICALS

Agricultural index: subject index to a selected list of agricultural periodicals and bulletins, 1916- . N.Y. H.W. Wilson. 1919- **111**

Annual magazine subject-index; a subject-index to a selected list of American and English periodicals and society publications, 1907- . Boston. F. W. Faxon. 1908- **112**

Art index; a cumulative author and subject index to a selected list of fine arts periodicals and museum bulletins, 1929- . N.Y. H. W. Wilson. 1930- **113**

Bibliographie der fremdsprachigen zeitschrift-literatur. Répertoire bibliographique international des revues, etc. International index to periodicals, etc. 1- 1911- Gautzsch b Leipzig. Felix Dietrich. 1911- **114**

Catholic periodical index; a guide to Catholic magazines, 1930-1931. Scranton. National Cath. Education Asso.; N.Y. H.W. Wilson. 1930. 1931. 2v. **116**

Catholic periodical index; a cumulative author and subject ·index to a selected list of Catholic periodicals 1930/33- . Ed. by Laurence A. Leavey. N.Y. Published for the Catholic Lib. Asso. by The H.W. Wilson Company. 1930- **116a**

Construction materials index, 1934/5- . San Francisco Construction Materials Research Co. 1934- **117**

Cooperative index to periodicals, 1883-1891. Ed. by W. I. Fletcher with the cooperation of the members of the American Library Association. N.Y. 1884-92. 9v. (1885-87 appeared as supplement to the Lib. jour. Superseded by the Annual literary index) **118**

Cumulative index to a selected list of periodicals, 1896-June 1903. Cleveland. Cumulative Index Co. 1897-1903. 8v. **119**

Current events index; a guide to material in the daily press, December, 1907-first quarter, 1910. [Madison, Wis.] Wisconsin Free Lib. Com. 1907-10. 4v. (Continued in the Readers' guide) **120**

Current magazine contents, I, no. 1-II, no. 8, April 1928-Nov. 1929. Wichita, Kan. Wichita Pub. Co. 1928-29. 2v. (Monthly index to current periodicals) **121**

Day, Katharine B. Check list of cumulative indexes to current Anglo-American legal periodicals. Law lib. jour. XXXII. p35-39 (May 1939) **121a**

Education index, Jan. 1929- . N.Y. H.W. Wilson. 1929- **122**

Engineering index [A descriptive monthly index to the leading articles published currently in the American, British and continental engineering journals, 1891-1918]. *In* The Engineering mag. 1892-1918. v. I-LVI **123**

Engineering index, 1-4, 1884/91-1901/05. N.Y., London. Engineering mag. 1892-1906. 4v. (Material in v. 1-2 appeared in the Jour. of the Asso. of Engineering Soc. Continued as Engineering index annual) **124**

Engineering index. . . . N.Y. Pub. by the Am. Soc. of Mechanical Engineers, 1907-1934; Engineering Index, Inc. 1934- (Title varies: 1906-18 Engineering index annual. Comp. from the Engineering index pub. monthly in the Engineering mag. [1917-1918 Industrial management] Continuation of the Engineering index, 1884-1905) **125**

Hasid's index to periodicals and booklist; a bibliography of current magazine articles and new books on the vital aspects of Jewish life. N.Y. Jewish Statistical Bureau. 1932- **126**

Index medicus; a monthly classified record of current medical literature of the world. N.Y. F. Leypoldt, 1873-1903; Wash. D.C. Carnegie Inst. 1903- **127**

Index of twentieth century artists. Pub. (monthly) by the Research Inst. of the College Art Asso. I. no. 1, Oct. 1933- **128**

Index to labor articles. N.Y. Rand School of Social Science, Labor Research Dept. 1926- mim. **129**

Index to legal periodical literature. Boston. 1888-1924; Indianapolis, 1933- (Pub. v. 1. Boston. C. C. Soule 1888; v. 2-3. Boston. The Boston Book Co. 1899-1919; v. 4. Boston. The Chipman Law Pub. Co. 1924. v. 5. Indianapolis. Bobbs-Merrill Co. 1933- Comp. 1-2 by L. A. Jones; 3- by F. E. Chipman) **130**

Index to legal periodicals and Law library journal, 1908- . Madison, Wis. Am. Asso. of Law Libraries; N.Y. H.W. Wilson. 1909- (Law library journal dropped beginning January 1936) **131**

Industrial arts index; subject index to a selected list of engineering, trade and business periodicals, books and pamphlets, 1913- . N.Y. H.W. Wilson. 1914- **132**

International index to periodicals, devoted chiefly to the humanities and pure science, 1907/15- . N.Y. H.W. Wilson. 1916- (Vols. 1-2, 1907-19 issued under title: Readers' guide to periodical literature) **133**

Loyola educational index; a reader's guide to education and psychology, I, Dec. 1928. Ed. by Augustin G. Schmidt. Chicago. Loyola Univ. Press. 1928 **134**

New York. Public Library. A check list of cumulative indexes to individual periodicals in the New York Public Library. Comp. by Daniel C. Haskell. N.Y. N.Y. Pub. Lib. MS. **134a**

Poole's index to periodical literature, 1800-1906. Ed. by William Frederick Poole, William I. Fletcher, and Mary Poole. Boston., N.Y. Houghton Mifflin. 1893-1908. 6v. **135**

Poole's index to periodical literature; abridged edition covering the contents of thirty-seven important periodicals, 1815-1899. By William I. Fletcher and Mary Poole. Boston, N.Y. Houghton Mifflin. 1901. 843p. **136**

Population literature. I. no. 1, Jan. 20, 1935- **137**

Psychological index; an annual bibliography of the literature of psychology and cognate subjects, 1894- . Princeton. Psychological Rev. Co. 1895- **138**

Public affairs information service. Bul. of the Public affairs information service, 1915- White Plains, N.Y., N.Y. 1915- **139**

Quarterly cumulative index medicus. I, Jan. 1927- Chicago. Am. Medical Asso. 1927- **140**

Readers' guide to periodical literature, 1900- . [Minneapolis, 1900-13, White Plains, N.Y. 1914-16] N.Y. 1917- H. W. Wilson (An Abridged readers' guide started Sept. 1935) **141**

Review of reviews; index to the periodicals of 1890-1902. London, N.Y. Rev. of rev. 1891-1903. 13v. **142**

Richardson, Ernest Cushing. Periodical articles on religion, 1890-1899, author index. N.Y. Scribner's. 1911. 876p. **143**

Richardson, Ernest Cushing and others. An alphabetical subject index and index encyclopaedia to periodical articles on religion, 1890-1899. N.Y. For the Hartford Seminary Press by Scribner's. [1907] 1168, 876p. 2v. **144**

Roys, Margaret. Cumulative indexes to individual periodicals. *In* Bibliographic index; a cumulative bibliography of bibliographies. 1938. N.Y. H.W. Wilson [1939] p333-44 **144a**

—— Separate indexes to individual periodicals. *In* International index to periodicals, 1924-27, Jan. 1928-June 1931, July 1931-June 1934. N.Y. H.W. Wilson. 1929, 1931, 1934. p v-x, v-xi, v-xiv **144b**

Street's pandex of the news and cumulative index to current history, 1903-1904, 1908-1917. Chicago. The Pandex Co. 1903-19? **145**

U.S. Library of Congress. Division of aeronautics. Subject index to aeronautical periodical literature and reports, 1938- Issued in cooperation with the Institute of the Aeronautical Sciences. [N.Y.] 1939- mim. **145a**

U.S. Works Progress Administration. American periodical index. N.Y. Washington Square College, N. Y. Univ. In progress (A card index to 339 periodicals and 7,000 books, 1728-1870, mostly material not in Poole's Index) **145b**

Weekly bulletin of newspaper and periodical literature, July 25, 1891-April 29, 1893. Boston. B.R. Tucker. 1891-93 **146**

PERIODICALS

Allen, Charles A. American little magazines, 1900-1940. Iowa City, Ia. Univ. of Iowa. In progress **146a**

American Federation of Labor. Trade unions official journals and labor papers received at headquarters of American Federation of Labor, Sept. 1905- . Wash. D.C. 1905- **147**

American Library Association. Committee on Resources of Southern Libraries. Serials currently received in southern libraries: a union list. Ed. by Alma S. Skaggs. Chapel Hill. 1936. 194p. mim. **147a**

Associated Business Papers, Inc. The Blue book of the Associated business papers, inc. N.Y. 1937- **147b**

Australia. Council for Scientific and Industrial Research. Catalogue of the scientific and technical periodicals in the libraries of Australia. By Ernest R. Pitt. Melbourne. H. J. Green, govt. printer. [1930] 1208p. **148**

Beer, William. Checklist of American periodicals, (1741-1800). Am. Antiq. Soc. proc. XXXII. n.s. pt. 2. p330-45 (Oct. 1922) **149**

Births and deaths; a record of new titles, changed titles, and deaths in the periodical world. *In* Bul. of bibliog. III-Oct. 1902- **149a**

Bolton, Henry Carrington. A catalogue of scientific and technical periodicals, 1665-1895; together with chronological tables and a library checklist (Smithsonian miscellaneous collections. XL. no. 514). Wash. D.C. 1898. 1247p. **150**

Boston. Public Library. Guide to serial publications founded prior to 1918 and now or recently current in Boston, Cambridge, and vicinity. Comp. and ed. by Thomas Johnston Homer. Boston. The Trustees. 1922. **151**

Boston. Public Library. A list of periodicals, newspapers, transactions and other serial publications currently received in the principal libraries of Boston and vicinity. Boston. The Trustees. 1897. 143p. (Also in Boston Public Lib. bul. XII. p37-85. April 1893. supplementary list. p128-36. July 1893)   **152**

Brody, Fannie M. The Hebrew periodical press in America, 1871-1931; a bibliographical survey. Am. Jewish Hist. Soc. pub. no. 33. p127-70. 1934   **153**

Bucks County Historical Society. Library. A check list of American and foreign periodicals in the library of the Bucks County Historical Society. Doylestown, Pa. The Bucks County Hist. Soc. 1940. 118, [15]p.   **153a**

Buffalo. Public Library. Union catalog of serials in Buffalo libraries. Buffalo, N.Y. Cards   **153b**

Bunnell, Ada. Medical serials with bibliography of medical jurisprudence by W. Burt Cook, Jr. N.Y. State Lib. bul. bibliog. 47. 1910. 153p.   **153c**

Bureau of Railway Economics. A check list of railway periodicals showing files in the library of the Bureau of Railway Economics. Wash. D.C. 1924. 112p.   **154**

Cairns, William B. Later magazines. *In* The Cambridge history of American literature. Ed. by William P. Trent and others. N.Y. Putnam's. 1921. III. p299-318; IV. p774-9   **155**

—— Magazines, annuals, and gift-books, 1783-1850. *In* The Cambridge history of American literature. Ed. by William P. Trent and others. N.Y. Putnam's. 1918. II. p160-75, 511-18   **156**

—— On the development of American literature from 1815 to 1833 with especial reference to periodicals (Bul. of the Univ. of Wisconsin, Philology and literature series. I. no. 1). Madison, Wis. Pub. by the Univ. March 1898. 87p.   **157**

California. University. Classified index of all philosophical periodicals. Berkeley. WPA project   **157a**

—— —— Library. Cooperative list of periodical literature in libraries of central California. (Lib. bul. no. 1) Berkeley [State Ptg. Off. Sacramento] 1902. 130p.   **158**

—— —— —— List of serials in the University of California Library. (Lib. bul. no. 18) Berkeley, Calif. 1913. 266p.   **159**

California Library Association. Southern district. Union list of serials in libraries of southern California. Comp. by S.E.R.A. and W.P.A. workers, with the advice and direction of Dorothy H. Thompson. (Publication, no. 3) Santa Monica, Calif. The Asso. 1939. 504p.   **159a**

Cannons, H. G. T. Classified guide to 1700 annuals, directories, calendars & year books. London. Grafton. 1923. 196p.   **160**

Catholic University of America. Library. Periodicals and serials in the library of the Catholic University of America, 1910. Wash. D.C. Cath. Univ. of Amer. 1910. 113p.   **161**

Clark, Alvan Whitcombe. Checklist of indexed periodicals. N.Y. H. W. Wilson. 1917. 59p.   **162**

Columbia University. Law Library. Serials of an international character; tentative list. Prep. . . by F. C. Hicks (Inst. of International Education. Bul. 2d ser. no. 3) N.Y. 1921. 60p.   **163**

—— Library. List of theological periodicals currently received in the libraries of New York City, June, 1913. N.Y. Columbia Univ. 1913. 15p.   **164**

Commonwealth College. Library. A check list of American Socialist, Communist, and Populist periodicals published since the Civil War. Mena, Ark. ms.   **164a**

—— —— Radical periodicals: their place in the library. Comp. by Henry Black. Mena, Ark. 1937. 11p. mim.   **164b**

Conat, Mabel L. A list of periodical publications relating to municipal affairs. Special libraries. VI. p129-39 (Oct. 1915)   **165**

Davis, E. Jeffries and Taylor, E. G. R. Guide to periodicals and bibliographies dealing with geography, archaeology, and history. London. Pub. for the Hist. Asso. by G. Bell and Sons. 1938. 22p.   **165a**

Davis, Sheldon E. List of educational periodicals. *In* Educational periodicals during the nineteenth century (U.S. Bureau of Education. Bul. 1919. no. 28) Wash. Govt. Ptg. Off. 1919. p92-125   **166**

Duke University. Library. A checklist of scientific periodicals and of selected serials in the libraries of Duke University. Ed. by Marjorie Gray Wynne. Durham, N.C. 1939. 110p.   **166a**

Educational Press Association of America. Classified list of educational periodicals. Wash. D.C. 1938. 23p.   **166b**

Emory University. Union list of serials in the Atlanta district. Emory University, Ga.   **166c**

Engineering Societies Library. Catalogue of technical periodicals (in the) libraries in the city of New York and vicinity. Comp. by Alice Jane Gates (Bibliog. contributions no. 1) N.Y. 1915. 110p.   **167**

Faxon, F. W., Company. Indexed periodicals; an alphabetical list of over 2000 American and foreign periodicals, showing how often and in what months issued, and giving index, title-page, and volume records . . . indicating in which of the general periodical indexes each magazine is included, 1938- . [Boston] F.W. Faxon. 1938-   **167a**

Foik, Paul Joseph. Pioneer Catholic journalism. (U.S. Cath. Hist. Soc. Monograph series. XI) N.Y. U.S. Cath. Hist. Soc. 1930. 221p.   **168**

Ford, Paul Leicester. Check-list of American magazines printed in the eighteenth century. Brooklyn, N.Y. 1889. 12p. **169**

Fort Benning. Card index to military periodicals. Fort Benning, Ga. **169a**

Freidus, A. S. A list of Jewish periodicals published in the United States. (Jewish Pub. Soc. of Amer. The American Jewish year book, 1899-1900) Phila. 1899. p271-82 **170**

Garwood, Irving. American periodicals from 1850 to 1860. Macomb, Ill. W. Ill. State Teachers College. 1931. 83p. **171**

Gates, Paul W. Historical periodicals in the college libraries of Pennsylvania. Soc. stud. XXV. p10-11 (Jan. 1934) **171a**

Gee, Pauline E. Anglo-American legal periodicals; births, deaths and changes since 1933. [Wash. D.C. Library Press. 1937] 12p. (Reprinted from the Law lib. jour. XXX. Sept. 1937. Supplementing appendix IX in Hicks. Materials and methods of legal research. 1933. p492-543. Continued in Law lib. jour.) **171b**

George Washington University. Library. Periodicals currently received in the university libraries. [1935- Wash. D.C. 1935-] mim. **172**

Gilmer, Gertrude C. Checklist of southern periodicals to 1861. Boston. F.W. Faxon. 1934. 128p. **173**

Gohdes, Clarence L. F. The periodicals of American Transcendentalism. Durham, N.C. Duke Univ. Press. 1931. 264p. **174**

Heindel, Richard H. The Anglo-American press. Anglo-Am. news. Dec. 1937 **174a**

Historical Foundation of the Presbyterian and Reformed Churches. Union list of serials of the Presbyterian and Reformed Churches in the principal Presbyterian and Reformed theological seminaries and other large libraries of the United States and Canada. Montreat, N.C. ms. **174b**

Hohenhoff, Elsa von. Bibliography of journals, books and compilations (American and foreign) which list and abstract patents. Baltimore. Baltimore Spec. Lib. Asso. 1936. 70p. **174c**

Illinois. University. List of serials in the University of Illinois Library, together with those in other libraries in Urbana and Champaign. Comp. by Francis K. W. Drury (Univ. of Illinois. Bul. IX. no. 2) Urbana. 1911. 233p. **175**

International Committee of Historical Sciences. World list of historical periodicals and bibliographies. Ed. by Pierre Caron and Marc Jaryc. Oxford. International Committee of Historical Sciences. 1939. 387p. **175a**

Iowa. University. Library. A list of serial publications in the libraries of the university. Iowa City. The Univ. 1911. 32p. **176**

Jacobsen, Edna L. American archival journals. Am. archivist. II. p37-45 (Jan. 1939) **176a**

John Crerar Library. A list of current periodicals. Chicago. Printed by order of the Board of trustees. 1924. 236p. **177**

—— A list of current periodicals. Chicago. 1938. 91p. **177a**

—— Supplement to the list of serials in public libraries of Chicago and Evanston. Ed. by C. W. Andrews. Chicago. 1906. 220p. **178**

Kentucky. University. Union lists of periodicals in Louisville and Lexington libraries. Lexington, Ky. ms. **178a**

Lamberton, John P. A list of serials in the principal libraries of Philadelphia and its vicinity. Phila. Lib. Co. Bul. 1908. 309p. (Supplement. 1910) **179**

Lee, James Melvin. History of American journalism. Boston, N.Y. Houghton Mifflin. 1917. 462p. **180**

Leland Stanford Junior University. Library. List of serials in the Leland Stanford Junior University Library. [Palo Alto, Calif.] Stanford Univ. 1916. 169p. **181**

List of Catholic periodicals, magazines and newspapers in the United States (December 31, 1920). Cath. hist. rev. I. p72-9 (April 1921) **181a**

Litchfield, Dorothy Hale. Classified list of 4800 serials currently received in the libraries of the University of Pennsylvania and of Bryn Mawr, Haverford, and Swarthmore colleges. Ed. . . . for the Board of graduate education and research. Phila. Univ. of Pa. Press. 1936. 411p. **182**

Lutrell, Estelle and Guild, Mabel A. A list of serials in the University of Arizona Library, with a check list of the University of Arizona publications. Univ. of Arizona. Record. XI. no. 2. Lib. bibliog. no. 4. Tucson. 1918. 46p. **183**

Lyle, Guy R. and Trumper, Virginia M. Classified list of periodicals for the college library. Boston. F.W. Faxon. 1940. 95p. reprod. typ. **183a**

McLean, Elliott Hall. Periodicals published in the South before 1880. (Univ. of Virginia. MS. 1928) **184**

Manley, Marian C. Business magazines classified by subject. . . . Newark, N.J. Free Pub. Lib. 1933. 31p. **184a**

Margoshes, Joseph. A list of Jewish periodicals published in New York city previous to 1917. *In* The Jewish communal register of New York city, 1917-1918. Ed. by the Kehillah (Jewish Community) N.Y. 1918. p619-32 **185**

Matthews, Albert Carlos. Lists of New England magazines, 1743-1800. Cambridge. J. Wilson. 1910 (Reprinted from Colonial Soc. Mass. pub. XIII. p69-74. Jan. 1910) **186**

Middleton, Thomas C. Catholic periodicals published in the United States from the earliest in 1809 to the close of the year 1892. Phila. 1908. 24p. (Supplements following title; reprinted from Am. Cath. Hist. Soc. rec. XIX. p18-41. March 1908) **187**

Middleton, Thomas C. A list of Catholic and semi-Catholic periodicals published in the United States from the earliest years down to the close of the year 1892. Am. Cath. Hist. Soc. rec. IV. p213-42. 1893
188

Mims, Edwin. Southern magazines. *In* The south in the building of the nation. Richmond, Va. The Southern Hist. Soc. 1909. VII. p437-69
189

Missouri. University. Library. List of periodicals currently received by the University library 1926. By Henry O. Severance. Check list of student publications. By John H. Dougherty (Univ. of Missouri. Bul. XXVII. no. 48. Lib. series no. 14) Columbia. 1926. 54p.
190

Missouri Library Association. Committee on cooperative acquisitions. Union list of serials in the libraries of Missouri. Columbia. 1935. 228p. mim.
191

Mott, Frank Luther. American magazines, 1865-1880. (Univ. of Pa. Ph.D. thesis) Iowa City, Iowa. Midland Press. 1928. 95p.
192

—— A history of American magazines, 1741-1885. I. N.Y. Appleton. 1930. 848p.; II-III. Cambridge. Harvard Univ. Press. 1938
193

National Industrial Conference Board. Employee magazines in the United States. N.Y. National Industrial Conference Board. 1925. 8p.
194

New York. Public Library. Economic and sociological periodicals in the New York Public Library. N.Y. Pub. Lib. bul. XXVII-XXXI. 1923-27
194a

—— Latin-American periodicals current in the reference department. N.Y. 1920. 7p. (Reprinted from the Bul. Sept. 1920)
195

—— Periodicals, collections and society publications relating to American history and genealogy, in the New York Public Library and Columbia University Library. N.Y. Pub. Lib. bul. II. p120-58 (Jan. 1908)
196

New York Library Club. Union list of periodicals currently received by the New York and Brooklyn libraries. N.Y. 1887. 58p.
197

New York Special Libraries Association. Union list of periodicals in special libraries of the New York metropolitan district. Ed. by Ruth Savord and Pearl M. Keefer. N.Y. H.W. Wilson. 1931. 238p.
198

New York University. Washington Square College. Library. An annotated list of 100 education serials. N.Y. New York Univ. 1936. 24p.
199

Newark, N.J. Free Public Library. Business magazines classified by subject. Comp. by Marian C. Manley under the direction of Beatrice Winser. Newark Pub. Lib 1933. 31p.
200

Ohio Library Association. College and University Section. Regional list of serials in the college and university section of the Ohio Library Association. Ann Arbor, Mich. Edwards Brothers, inc. 1936. 205p.
200a

Pan American Union. Columbus Memorial Library. Current Latin American periodicals relating to economic subjects in the Library of the Pan American Union. (Bibliographic series, no. 20) Wash. D.C. July 1, 1938. 35p. mim.
200b

Payne, George Henry. History of journalism in the United States. N.Y. Appleton. 1920. 453p.
201

Phelps, Edith M. and Ball, Eleanor E. Periodicals of international importance; a selection of 600 useful in libraries everywhere. N.Y. H.W. Wilson. 1926. 28p.
202

Philadelphia. Free Library. List of periodicals currently received. Phila. The Lib. 1937. 102p.
202a

—— Union list of serials in the libraries of Philadelphia. (MS. catalogue in the library)
203

Pittsburgh. Carnegie Library. Periodicals and other serials currently received by the Carnegie Library of Pittsburgh. Pittsburgh. Carnegie Lib. 1915. 42p.
204

Postage and the Mailbag, inc. A directory of house magazines 1931. Brooklyn. Postage and the Mailbag, inc. 1931. 56p.
205

Redford, Edward H. Bibliography on high school journalism. Wash. D.C. Nat. Asso. of Student Editors. 1936
206

Redman, Aletha Burnett. A classified list of current periodicals in the fields of athletics, health, physical education, and sports, published in the United States and Canada. Ann Arbor, Mich. 1935 (Reprinted from the Research quar. VI. no. 1. March 1935)
207

Richardson, Ernest Cushing. A list of religious periodicals currently taken by Union, Princeton, Yale and Hartford theological seminaries. Wash. D.C. n.p. 1934. 31p.
208

Richardson, Lyon N. A history of early American magazines, 1741-1789. N.Y. Nelson. 1931. 414p.
209

Robbins, Roy Marvin. A bibliography of American periodicals found in the libraries of Cleveland and Oberlin, Ohio, to the year 1900. Cleveland, Graduate School of Western Reserve Univ. 1935. 58p. mim.
210

Rochester, N.Y. Public Library. Union list of serials in the libraries of Rochester, including periodicals, newspapers, annuals, publications of societies and other books published at intervals. Rochester. Rochester Pub. Lib. 1917. 147p.
211

Roorbach, Orville Augustus. List of periodicals published in the United States. *In* Bibliotheca Americana; catalogue of American publications, including reprints and original works, from 1820 to 1852. N.Y. Peter Smith. 1939. p644-52 **211a**

Rutherford B. Hayes and Lucy Webb Hayes Foundation. An index and list of the pamphlets and periodicals collected by Rutherford Birchard Hayes. Columbus. Ohio State Arch. and Hist. Soc. 1935. 45p. **211b**

Salmon, Lucy M. The Justice collection of material relating to the periodical press in Vassar College Library. [Poughkeepsie, N.Y.] 1925. 20p. **212**

Scudder, Samuel H. Catalogue of scientific serials of all countries including the transactions of learned societies in the natural, physical and mathematical sciences, 1633-1876 (Lib. of Harvard Univ. Special publications. I). Cambridge. 1879. 358p. **213**

Serials not now received in southern libraries, based upon Skagg's Serials currently received in southern libraries: a union list, 1936: selection of titles from Ulrich's Periodicals directory, 1935. Chapel Hill. 1937. 104p. mim. **213a**

Severance, Henry Ormal. A guide to the current periodicals and serials of the United States and Canada. Ann Arbor, Mich. George Wahr. 1931. 432p. **214**

Shearer, Augustus Hunt. American historical periodicals. Am. Hist. Asso. rep. 1916. I. p469-84 **215**

Smith, Oma. Union list of serials in Maine libraries. (Maine bul. xxxix, no. 8; Univ. of Maine studies, 2nd ser., no. 40) Orono, Univ. of Maine Press. 1937. 267p. **215a**

Special Libraries Association. Cincinnati chapter. Union list of periodicals currently received by libraries in Cincinnati, 1934. Comp. by Louise G. Prichard and Katherine B. Strong. [Cincinnati] Cincinnati chapter, Special Libraries Asso. 1934. 95p. **216**

—— Pittsburgh chapter. Union list of periodicals in some of the special libraries of Pittsburgh. Pittsburgh. Special Lib. Asso. Pittsburgh chapter, 1934. 139p. mim. **217**

—— San Francisco Bay Region Chapter. Union list of serials of the San Francisco Bay region. Stanford University, Calif. Stanford Univ. Press; London. H. Milford, Oxford Univ. Press. 1939. 283p. photop. **217a**

Steiger, E. The periodical literature of the United States of America with index and appendices. N.Y. E. Steiger. 1873. 139p. **218**

Stephens, Ethel. American popular magazines; a bibliography. Bul. of bibliog. IX. p7-10, 41-3, 69-70. 95-8 (Jan.-Oct. 1916) **219**

Stock, Leo F. A list of American periodicals and serial publications in the humanities and social sciences (Am. Council of Learned Societies. Bul. no. 21. March 1934) Wash. D.C. 1934. 130p. **220**

Swan, Gustavus N. Swedish-American literary periodicals. (Augustana Historical Society publications, VI) Rock Island, Ill. Augustana Hist. Soc. 1936. 91p. **220a**

Tassin, Algernon. The magazine in America. N.Y. Dodd, Mead. 1916. 374p. **221**

Tucker, Gilbert Milligan. American agricultural periodicals; an historical sketch. Albany, N.Y. Priv. print. 1909. 79p. **222**

Ulrich, Carolyn F. Periodicals directory; a classified guide to a selected list of current periodicals foreign and domestic. 2d ed. rev. and enl. N.Y. Bowker. 1935. 371p. **223**

Union list of serials for the Atlanta district. With supplemental titles and holdings from some other Georgia libraries. [Emory Univ. 1938] 146p. mim. **223a**

Union list of serials in libraries of the United States and Canada. Ed. by Winifred Gregory. N.Y. H.W. Wilson. 1927. 1588p. **224**

Union list of serials in libraries of the United States and Canada; supplements, January 1925-June 1931; July 1931-December 1932. Ed. by Gabrielle E. Malikoff. N.Y. H.W. Wilson. 1931, 1933. 2v. **225**

U.S. Bureau of Agricultural Economics. Periodicals relating to shipping. Comp. by Esther M. Colvin and Nellie G. Larson (Economic lib. list, no. 6) Wash. D.C. The Bureau. 1939. 13p. **225a**

—— —— Library. Business and banking periodicals, reviewing the business situation; a selected list compiled from the periodicals received in the libraries of the U.S. Department of Agriculture and the Federal Farm Board. Comp. by Mamie I. Herb under the direction of Mary G. Lacy (Agricultural economics bibliog. no. 34) Wash. D.C. Aug. 1931. 21p. **226**

—— —— —— List of periodicals containing prices, and other statistical and economic information on fruits, vegetables and nuts. Comp. by Esther M. Colvin (Agricultural economics bibliog. no. 55) Wash. D.C. 1935. 238p. mim. **227**

—— —— —— Periodicals received currently in the library of the U.S. Bureau of Agricultural Economics. Comp. by Vajen E. Hitz under the direction of Mary G. Lacy. Wash. D.C. 1932. 195p. mim. **228**

—— —— —— Periodicals relating to dairying in the United States. Comp. by Muriel F. Wright under the direction of Mary G. Lacy (Agricultural economics bibliog. no. 16) Wash. D.C. June 1926. 147p. mim. **229**

U.S. Commissioner of Education. List of college and student periodicals currently received by the libraries in the District of Columbia. (Rep. 1909) Wash. Govt. Ptg. Off. 1909. p551-6 **230**

U.S. Department of Agriculture. Library. Catalogue of the periodicals and other serial publications (exclusive of U.S. government documents) in the library of the U.S. Dept. of Agriculture. Prepared under the direction of Josephine A. Clark (Bul. no. 37) Wash. D.C. 1901. 362p. (Supplement. no. 1. 1901-05. Wash. D.C. 1907. 217p.) **231**

U.S. Department of Agriculture. Library. List of periodicals currently received in the library of the U.S. Department of Agriculture (Library bul. no. 75) Wash. Govt. Ptg. Off. 1909. 72p.   **232**

U.S. Department of Labor. Library. Labor and industry; list of periodicals and newspapers in U.S. Department of Labor Library. Wash. D.C. 1919. 23p. mim.   **233**

—— —— —— List of labor papers and journals and other periodicals featuring labor matters received currently in the Department of Labor Library. Monthly labor rev. VIII. p334-53 (June 1919)   **234**

U.S. Farm Credit Administration. Cooperative division. Periodicals issued by farmers' marketing and purchasing associations. Comp. by Chastina Gardner. Wash. D.C. 1937. 17p. mim.   **234a**

U.S. Forest Service. Library. A union checklist of forestry serials. [Wash. D.C. 1936] 146p. mim.   **235**

U.S. Library of Congress. Want list of American historical serials. Wash. Govt. Ptg. Off. 1909. 37p.   **236**

—— —— **Division of aeronautics.** Aeronautical periodicals and serials in the Library of Congress. Wash. D.C. 1937-   **236a**

—— —— —— Aeronautical periodicals received currently by the Division of aeronautics of the Library of Congress. N.Y. 1933. p111-13 (Reprinted from Air law review. no. 1)   **237**

—— —— **Division of bibliography.** List of works relating to the history of the periodical press. 1906. 19p. typ.   **238**

—— —— —— Union list of periodicals, transactions, and allied publications currently received in the principal libraries of the District of Columbia. Comp. under the direction of A. P. C. Griffin. Wash. Govt. Ptg. Off. 1901. 315p.   **239**

—— —— **Periodical division.** Want list of periodicals. Wash. Govt. Ptg. Off. 1909. 241p.   **240**

U.S. Office of Education. Preliminary bibliography of current periodicals, quarterlies, yearbooks, and bulletins in business education. (Vocational division, Miscellaneous 2221) Wash. D.C. 1939. 33p. mim.   **240a**

U.S. Surgeon-General's Office. Library. Classification of periodicals, Army Medical Library. Wash. D.C. 1928. 55p. mim.   **240b**

—— —— —— Periodicals currently received in Army medical library, Washington, D.C. April 1, 1936. [Wash. 1936] 42p. mim.   **240c**

—— —— —— Periodicals currently received in Army Medical Library. Wash. 1936. 42p. mim.   **240d**

U.S. Tariff Commission. Index of foreign commercial and economic periodicals currently received in departmental and other institutional libraries located at Washington, D.C. Comp. by Carlton C. Rice. Wash. Govt. Ptg. Off. 1926. 88p.   **241**

U.S. Work Projects Administration. Wisconsin. Union list of periodicals in Milwaukee. Milwaukee. 1939. 240p. reprod. typ.   **241a**

Venable, William H. Literary periodicals of the Ohio Valley (1819-1860). Ohio Arch. and Hist. Soc. quar. I. p201-5 (Sept. 1887)   **242**

World list of scientific periodicals published in the years, 1900-1933. London. Oxford Univ. Press, Humphrey Milford. 1934. 780p.   **243**

NEWSPAPERS

Alden, Edwin, Company. The Edwin Alden Co's American newspaper catalogue, including lists of all newspapers and magazines published in the United States and the Canadas. . . . Cincinnati. E. Alden Co's Advertising Co. 1883?   **244**

The **American labor press;** an annotated directory. Comp. by the University of Wisconsin, Work Projects Administration, official work project no. 9422. Wash. D.C. Am. Council on Pub. Affairs [1940] 120p.   **244a**

American newspapers, 1821-1936; a union list of files available in the United States and Canada. Ed. by Winifred Gregory under the auspices of the Bibliographical Society of America. N.Y. H.W. Wilson. 1937. 791p.   **244b**

American Press Association. The complete directory of country newspaper rates, 1923-. N.Y. Am. Press Asso. 1923-   **245**

—— Democratic daily and weekly newspapers of the United States that use plate matter; a complete and accurate list. Comp. by the American Press Asso. for the convenience of national and state publicity committees. [Wash. D.C. 1916] 20p.   **246**

—— Independent daily and weekly newspapers of the United States that use plate matter; a complete and accurate list. Comp. by the American Press Asso. for the convenience of national and state publicity committees. [Wash. D.C. 1916] 24p.   **247**

Ander, O. Fritiof. Swedish-American political newspapers; a guide to the collections in the Royal Library, Stockholm and the Augustana College Library, Rock Island. Uppsala. [Almqvist & Wiksells boktryckeri-A.-B.] 1936. 28p.   **248**

An **annotated** bibliography of journalism subjects in American magazines. Jour. quar. VII. June 1930-   **248a**

Ayer, firm, Philadelphia. N. W. Ayer & Son's directory of newspapers and periodicals; a guide to publications printed in the United States and possessions, the Dominion of Canada, Bermuda, Cuba and the West Indies. Phila. N.W. Ayer & Son. 1880- **249**

Barnhart, Thomas F. The weekly newspaper: a bibliography (1925-41). Minneapolis, Minn. Burgess Pub. Co. 1941. 107p. reprod. typ. **249a**

Barton, Albert Olaus. The beginnings of the Norwegian press in America. State Hist. Soc. of Wisconsin. Separate no. 174, from the Proc. of the soc. for 1916. p186-212 **250**

Batten, George, Company. Batten's agricultural directory; a directory of the agricultural press of the United States and Canada, together with detailed reports of farm products and values by states and provinces. N.Y. George Batten Co. 1908. 212p. **251**

Baumgartner, Apollinaris W. Catholic journalism; a study in its development in the United States, 1789-1930. N.Y. Columbia Univ. Press. 1931. 113p. **252**

Belisle, Alexandre. Histoire de la presse franco-américaine. Worcester, Mass. Ateliers typographiques de "L'Opinion publique." 1911. 434p. **253**

Benjamin, S. G. W. A group of pre-revolutionary editors: beginnings of journalism in America. Mag. of Am. hist. XVII. p1-28 (Jan. 1887) **254**

— Notable editors between 1776 and 1800; influence of the early American press. Mag. of Am. hist. XVII. p97-127 (Feb. 1887) **255**

Bömer, Karl. Vereinigten staaten von Amerika. *In* Internationale bibliographie des zeitungswesens. Leipzig. O. Harrassowitz. 1932. p285-302 **256**

Brigham, Clarence S. Bibliography of American newspapers, 1690-1820. Am. Antiq. Soc. proc. n.s. XXIII-XXXV. 1913-1926. (Analyzed under the section on "States." A revision of this is in preparation) **256a**

Cannon, Carl L. Journalism: a bibliography. N.Y. N.Y. Pub. Lib. 1924. 360p. **257**

Casey, Ralph D. and Barnhart, Thomas F. An annotated bibliography of journalism subjects in American magazines, January 1930-. Journalism quar. VII- June 1930- **258**

Caspar, Carl N. J. M. Caspar's directory of the American book, news and stationery trade, wholesale and retail, comprising [also the] theory and practice of the book trade and kindred branches; hints and suggestions; trade bibliographies, trade journals, etc. . . . Milwaukee. C.N. Caspar; N.Y. The Publishers' Wkly. 1889. 1434p. **258a**

Chicago. University. Library. Newspapers in libraries of Chicago; a joint check list. Prepared by the University of Chicago libraries, Document section. Chicago. 1936. 257p. mim. **258b**

Chicago Historical Society. Library. A check list of the Kellogg collection of "patent inside" newspapers of 1876. Prep. for exhibit at the Centennial Exposition at Philadelphia, and now preserved in the library of the Chicago Historical Society. Chicago. Historical Records Survey. 1939. 99p. mim. **258c**

Coggeshall, William Turner. The newspaper record, containing a complete list of newspapers and periodicals in the United States, Canadas, and Great Britain, together with a sketch of the origin and progress of printing. . . . Phila. Lay and Brother. 1856. 194p. **259**

Cook, Elizabeth Christine. Colonial newspapers and magazines, 1704-1775. *In* The Cambridge history of American literature. Ed. by William P. Trent and others. N.Y. Putnam's. 1917. I. p111-23, 452-4 **260**

Dauchy co.'s newspaper catalogue; a list of the newspapers and periodicals published in the United States and territories, and Canada, with date of establishment, frequency or day of issue, politics, denomination, nationality or special character, etc. N.Y. Dauchy. 1891- **261**

Demaree, Albert L. The American agricultural press, 1819-1860. (Columbia Univ. stud. in the hist. of American agriculture, no. 8) N.Y. Columbia Univ. Press. 1941. 430p. **261a**

Desmond, Robert W. List of books and periodicals valuable for newspaper libraries. *In* Newspaper reference methods. Minneapolis. Univ. of Minnesota Press. 1933. p139-96 **262**

Deutsche presse in den Vereinigten Staaten. Der Deutsche pionier, erinnerungen aus dem pionier; leben der Deutschen in Amerika. VIII. p289-320 (Oct. 1876) **263**

Dieserud, Juul. Den norske presse i Amerika; en historisk oversigt. Normands-Forbundet, 3dje hefte April 1912. 5te aargang. p153-82 **264**

Dill, William A. The first century of American newspapers; a graphic check list of periodicals published from 1690 to 1790 in what was to become the United States. (Bul. of the Dept. of journalism in the Univ. of Kansas. Sept. 1925) [Lawrence, Kan. 1925] 23p. **265**

Dodd, firm, Boston. Advertisers' newspaper manual, containing a list of American newspapers . . . published in the United States, Dominion of Canada and Newfoundland. . . . Boston. Dodd's Advertising & Checking Agency. 1895. 378p. **266**

Drury, Clifford M. Presbyterian journalism on the Pacific Coast. Pacific hist. rev. IX. p461-9 (Dec. 1940) **266a**

Duke University. Library. A checklist of United States newspapers (and weeklies before 1900) in the general library. Comp. by Mary Wescott and Allene Ramage. (Bibliog. contributions of the Duke Univ. libraries Part I-VI) Durham, N.C. Duke Univ. 1932-37. 6pts. in 3v.   **267**

Educational Press Association of America. America's educational press; a classified list of educational publications issued in the United States with a limited listing of foreign journals. *In* Year book, 1st- . 1925- . Wash. D.C. 1925-   **267a**

Faÿ, Bernard. Notes on the American press at the end of the eighteenth century. N.Y. Grolier Club. 1927. 29p.   **268**

Ford, Edwin H. A bibliography of literary journalism in America. Minneapolis, Minn. Burgess Pub. Co. 1937. 68p.
                                                              268a

—— History of journalism in the United States; a bibliography of books and annotated articles. Minneapolis, Minn. Burgess Pub. Co. 1938. 42p.   **268b**

Foreign Language Information Service. Foreign language publications in the United States. N.Y. 1926-30. 2v.   **269**

Gavit, Joseph. American newspaper reprints. N.Y. N.Y. Pub. Lib. 1931. 16p. (Reprinted from the Bul. XXXV. p212-23. April 1931)   **270**

Goddard, Delano Alexander. Newspapers and newspaper writers in New England, 1787-1815. Read before the New England Hist. and Geneal. Soc. Feb. 4, 1880. Boston. A. Williams. 1880. 39p.   **271**

Graham, Robert Xavier. A bibliography in the history and backgrounds of journalism; history, biography, analyses of the press, adventure and reminiscence. [Pittsburgh] 1940. 16p.   **271a**

Gregory, Winifred. Union list of newspapers in the libraries of the United States. Lib. of Congress. (In press) **272**

Guild, C. H., & Co., Boston. Advertising in New England; a complete handbook for 1896-97, containing a carefully prepared catalogue and complete description of all newspapers and periodicals published in New England. . . . Boston. Guild. 1896. 324p.   **273**

Hamilton, Milton Wheaton. Anti-Masonic newspapers. Reading, Pa. Albright College. In progress   **273a**

—— Anti-masonic newspapers, 1826-1834. Portland, Me. The Southworth-Anthoensen Press. 1939. p71-97 (Separate from the Bibliog. Soc. of Amer. pap. XXXII, 1938. List of newspapers, 1826-1834, New York, 78-97)   **273b**

Henry, Edward A. The Durrett collection, now in the library of the University of Chicago. Chicago. 1914. 38p. (Newspapers on various states)   **274**

Hewett, Daniel. Daniel Hewett's list of newspapers and periodicals in the United States in 1828. Worcester, Mass. 1935. (Reprinted from the Am. Antiq. Soc.

pub. n.s. XLIV. pt. 2. p365-82. Oct. 17, 1934. Pub. originally in the "Traveller and monthly gazetteer" for June 1828)   **275**

Hudson, Frederic. Journalism in the United States, from 1690 to 1872. N.Y. Harper. 1873. 789p.   **276**

Hudson, I. N. and Menet, A. List of newspapers published in the United States and Canada. N.Y. 1870   **277**

Kellogg, A. N., Newspaper Company. Kellogg's lists, 1908, family weekly newspapers of the better class. Chicago. 1908. unpag.   **278**

Kenny, Daniel J. The American newspaper directory and record of the press, containing an accurate list of all the newspapers, magazines, reviews, periodicals, etc., in the United States & British provinces of North America. N.Y. Watson. 1861. 123p.   **279**

Larson, Cedric. American army newspapers in the world war. Jour. quar. XVII. p121-32 (June 1940)   **279a**

Levermore, Charles H. The rise of metropolitan journalism, 1800-1840. Am. hist. rev. VI. p446-65. (April 1901)   **280**

Lincoln, Waldo. List of newspapers of the West Indies and Bermuda in the library of the American Antiquarian Society. Am. Antiq. Soc. proc. n.s. XXXVI. p130-56. (April 1926)   **281**

Lord & Thomas and Logan pocket directory of the American press . . . a complete list of newspapers, magazines, farm journals, religious papers, trade and class journals, foreign language publications, and other periodicals published in the United States, Canada, Yukon territory, Newfoundland, Cuba, Porto Rico, Hawaiian, Philippine and Virgin islands, 1890-1927. Chicago. Lord & Thomas. 1890-1927. 26v.   **282**

Meehan, Thomas F. Early Catholic weeklies. U.S. Cath. Hist. Soc. rec. XXVIII. p237-55. 1937   **282a**

Meier, J. H. Catholic press directory for 1923- with a complete list of Catholic papers and periodicals published in the United States. Chicago. J. H. Meier. 1923-   **283**

Merwin, Fred E. and Smith, Henry L. Press and communications; an annotated bibliography of journalistic subjects in American magazines, November, December, January, 1936-1937. Journalism quar. XIV. p64-80 (March 1937)   **283a**

Minnesota. University. Division of library instruction. American newspapers 1719-1934 in the University of Minnesota library. (Bibliographical projects no. 2, March 1935) [Minneapolis] 1935. 12p.
                                                              283b

Morse, Lucius B. The daily court newspapers of the United States. (Univ. of Pennsylvania. Graduation thesis, Research in journalism) Phila. Wharton School. 1929. 56p.   **284**

Mott, Frank Luther. American journalism; a history of newspapers in the United States through 250 years, 1690 to 1940. N.Y. Macmillan. 1941. 772p.   **284a**

Nafziger, Ralph O. International news and the press; communications, organization of newsgathering, international affairs and the foreign press; an annotated bibliography. N.Y. H.W. Wilson. 1940. 193p. **284b**

National Advertising Service. 876 college newspapers. N.Y. 1937. 17p. **284c**

Negro newspapers and periodicals in the United States, 1937. Wash. D.C. U.S. Bureau of the Census. 1938. 18p. **284d**

Nelson, William. American newspapers of the eighteenth century, chronology and history; list of files, and libraries in which they may be found; with some notices of the first printing and the first newspaper in each state. *In* Archives of the state of New Jersey, first series, XI, ix-cxxvi; XII, cxxvii-cclxviii; XIX, vii-lxxviii. Paterson, N.J. Press Print. and Pub. Co. 1894-97 **285**

—— The American newspapers of the eighteenth century as sources of history. Am. Hist. Asso. rep. 1908. I. p211-22 **286**

—— Notes toward a history of the American newspaper. Volume I. Containing the history of newspapers in Alabama . . . to New Hampshire. (Heartman's hist. series. no. 31) N.Y. Charles F. Heartman. 1918. 644p. **287**

New York. Public Library. Checklist of newspapers and official gazettes in the New York Public Library. By Daniel C. Haskell. N.Y. N.Y. Pub. Lib. 1915. 579p. (Reprinted from the Bul. XVIII. p683-722, 793-826, 905-38, 1079-110, 1261-94, 1467-80; XIX. p553-69. (July 1914-July 1915)) **288**

New York Times. New York times index, 1- 1913-. N.Y. N.Y. Times Co. 1913- **289**

New York Tribune. New York daily tribune index, 1875-1906. N.Y. Tribune Asso. 1876-1907. 31v. **290**

Norcross, Grenville Howland. Southern newspapers printed on wall paper. Massachusetts Hist. Soc. proc. XLVI. p241-3 (Nov. 1912) **290a**

North, S. N. D. History and present condition of the newspaper and periodical press of the United States, with a catalogue of the publications of the census year. *In* U.S. Bureau of the Census. Tenth census. v. 8. Wash. Govt. Ptg. Off. 1884. 446p. **291**

Osada, Stanislaw. Prasa i publicystyka Polska w Ameryce, w treściwym referacie opracowanym z okazje dwochsetnego jubileiszu prasy w polsce i sześćdziesieciolecia w Ameryce. Pittsburgh, Pa. Nakłodem i drukiem "Pittsburczanina." 1930. 96p. (Polish-American newspapers) **292**

Pacific states newspaper directory. San Francisco. Palmer & Rey. 1888 **293**

Palmer & Rey. Pacific states newspaper directory. . . . San Francisco. 1888-95. 5v. **293a**

Pan American Union. Columbus Memorial Library. Catalogue of newspapers and magazines in the Columbus Memorial Library of the Pan American Union. (Bibliog. series no. 6) Wash. D.C. 1931. 112p. mim. **294**

Pettingill, firm, Boston. National newspaper directory and gazetteer, containing a complete classified directory of the newspapers and periodicals published in the United States, 1877-1900. Boston. Pettingill. 1877-99. 5v. **295**

Purcell, George W. A survey of early newspapers in the middle western states. Indiana mag. hist. XX. p347-63. (Dec. 1924) **296**

Rand School of Social Science. Labor research department. American labor press directory. N.Y. 1925. 82p. **297**

Redford, Edward H. Bibliography of secondary school journalism; a comprehensive compilation of journalistic source material. Chicago. Northwestern Univ., Quill and Scroll Foundation. 1941. 80p. **297a**

—— Bibliography on high school journalism. Prep. . . . for the National Association of Student Editors. Wash. D.C. 1935? 50p. **297b**

Remington brothers' newspaper manual; a complete catalogue of the newspapers of the United States, Canada, Porto Rico, Cuba, and Hawaii. . . . N.Y. Remington Brothers' Newspaper Advertising. 1892- **298**

Rowell's American newspaper directory, containing a description of all the newspapers and periodicals published in the United States and territories, Dominion of Canada and Newfoundland. . . 1869-1908. N.Y. G.P. Rowell. 1869-1908. 40v. in 61 **299**

Rusk, Ralph L. Newspapers and magazines. *In* The literature of the middle western frontier. N.Y. Columbia Univ. Press. 1925. I. p131-203; II. p145-84 **300**

Schwegmann, George A., Jr. Preliminary checklist of newspapers on microfilm. Jour. doc. reprod. IV. p122-34 (June 1941) **300a**

Scott, Frank W. Newspapers, 1775-1860. *In* The Cambridge history of American literature. Ed. by W. P. Trent and others. N.Y. Putnam's. 1918. II. p176-95, 518-24 **301**

—— Newspapers since 1860. *In* The Cambridge history of American literature. Ed. by William P. Trent and others. N.Y. Putnam's. 1921. III. p319-36; IV. p779-82 **302**

Smith, Culver H. Bibliographical guide to the history of the American newspaper press. Jan. 1932. 8p. (Typ. MS. (carbon) in Lib. of Congress. Periodical division) **303**

—— Guide to the opinion-forming press of the United States. Chattanooga Univ. (In progress) **304**

Stockholm. Kongl. Bibliotekets sam lingar. Svenska tidningar och tidskrifter, utgifna inom Nord-Amerikas Förenta Stater. Bibliografisk öfversigt of Bernhard Lundstedt. Stockholm. Kongl. Boktryckeriet. 1886. 53p. (A guide to the Swedish-American newspapers and periodicals in the Royal Library, Stockholm) **305**

Stuntz, Stephen Conrad. List of American agricultural journals. MS. in U.S. Department of Agriculture, Wash. D.C. **305a**

Thwaites, Reuben Gold. The Ohio Valley press before the war of 1812-15. Worcester, Mass. Am. Antiq. Soc. 1909 (Reprinted from the Proc. of the Am. Antiq. Soc. ns. XIX. p309-68. April 1909) **306**

Tobias Brothers' German newspaper directory, containing a . . . list of all the German newspapers published in the United States, territories and Dominion of Canada . . . also a separate list of religious newspapers. N.Y. Tobias Brothers. 1885, 1890. 2v. **307**

U.S. Bureau of Foreign and Domestic Commerce. Domestic commerce division. Small business section. A list of Negro newspapers, magazines, trade journals, and press services in the United States. Comp. by James Jackson. Wash. D.C. 1930. 8p. **308**

U.S. Dept. of Labor. Library. List of American trade union journals and labor papers currently received by the Library. Wash. D.C. The Lib. 1939. 29p. mim. **308a**

U.S. Library of Congress. Division of bibliography. Journalism; a list of recent books. July 22, 1931. 12p. typ. **309**

—— —— **Periodical division.** A checklist of American eighteenth century newspapers in the Library of Congress. Originally compiled by John Van Ness Ingram, new ed. rev. and enl. under the direction of Henry S. Parsons. Wash. Govt. Ptg. Off. 1936. 401p. **310**

—— —— —— A check list of American newspapers in the Library of Congress. Comp. under the direction of Allan B. Slausson. Wash. Govt. Ptg. Off. 1901. 292p. **311**

—— —— —— A check list of foreign newspapers in the Library of Congress. Newly compiled under the direction of Henry S. Parsons. Wash. Govt. Ptg. Off. 1929. 209p. **312**

—— —— —— Want list of American eighteenth century newspapers, 1909. Wash. Govt. Ptg. Off. 1909. 43p. **313**

United States daily. Annual index, 1926-32. Wash. D.C. U.S. Daily Publishing Co. 1927-32 **314**

Walker, Norman. The southern press. *In* The South in the building of the nation. Richmond, Va. Southern Hist. Pub. Soc. 1909. VII. p402-36 **315**

Wall, Alexander J. Early newspapers, with a list of the New York Historical Society's collection of papers published in California, Oregon, Washington, Montana and Utah. N. Y. Hist. Soc. quar. bul. XV. p39-66. (July 1931) **316**

Watson, Elmo Scott. A check list of Indian war correspondents, 1866-1891. Jour. quar. XVII. p310-12 (Dec. 1940) (Includes names of newspapers) **316a**

Western Pennsylvania Historical Survey. Inventory of files of American newspapers in Pittsburgh and Allegheny County, Pennsylvania. (Bibliog. contributions no. 2) Pittsburgh. Hist. Building. Aug. 1933. 34p. Printed by offset process **317**

Wheeling, Katherine Eleanor. Bibliography for student publications: a list of books covering the several aspects of school press activities. N.Y. The Columbia Scholastic Press Asso. 1940. 60p. **317a**

Wieder, Collie. Daily newspapers in the United States. (Practical bibliographies) N.Y. H.W. Wilson. 1916. 56p. **318**

Willigan, Walter Luke. A bibliography of the Irish American press, 1691-1835. [Brooklyn? 1934] 21p. typ. **319**

Winship, George Parker. French newspapers in the United States from 1790 to 1800. Bibliog. Soc. Am. pap. XIV. pt. II. p82-91. 1920 **320**

Wisconsin. State Historical Society. Library. Annotated catalogue of newspaper files in the library of the State Historical Society of Wisconsin. Madison. The Soc. 1911. 591p. **320a**

—— —— Supplementary catalogue of newspaper files in the Wisconsin Historical Library, listing the papers acquired during the years 1911-1917. Prepared by Lillian J. Beecroft and Marguerite Jenison (Bul. of information no. 93) Madison, Wis. 1918. 91p. **320b**

Wolseley, Roland Edgar. The journalist's bookshelf; a bibliography of American journalism. Minneapolis, Minn. Burgess Pub. Co. 1939. 51p. **320c**

Yale University Library. A list of newspapers in the Yale University Library. (Yale hist. publications. Miscellany. II) New Haven. Yale Univ. Press. 1916. 216p. **321**

Yenawine, W. S. Checklist of CCC camp newspapers. Urbana. Univ. of Illinois Lib. School. In progress **321a**

DISSERTATIONS AND FACULTY PUBLICATIONS

General

American Economic Association. Doctoral dissertations in political economy in progress in American universities and colleges. Am. econ. rev. I- March 1911- **322**

—— List of doctoral dissertations in political economy in progress in American universities and colleges, January 1, 1905-January 1, 1910. Publications of the Am. Econ. Asso. 3d ser. VI. no. 2 (May 1905); VII. no. 3. supplement. p43-8 (Aug. 1906); VIII. no. 2, supplement. p42-7 (1907); Bul. of the Am. Econ. Asso. April 1908. p69-75; April 1909. p16-23; March 1910. p12-20   **323**

American Historical Association. List of doctoral dissertations in history now in progress at universities in the United States and the Dominion of Canada, with an appendix of other research projects in history now in progress in the United States and in Canada, December 1939, December 1940. Am. hist. rev. supplements to XLV. April 1940; XLVI. April 1941. 104, 54p.   **323a**

American Political Science Association. Doctoral dissertations in political science in preparation at American universities. Am. pol. science rev. IV- Nov. 1910- (None pub. 1915-19, 1921, 1923, 1924) **324**

Association of Collegiate Schools of Business. Academic histories of faculty members of The Associated Collegiate Schools of Business with bibliographies of their publications. Bloomington, Ind. 1925. 204p.   **325**

Bibliography of American Rhodes scholars. Am. oxonian. XIX. no. 1. Jan. 1932. 159p.   **326**

Browne, A. D. Classification of completed theses and selected subjects written in various colleges and universities in the United States. Am. Physical Education Asso. research quar. II. p119-51. 1931   **326a**

Carnegie Institution of Washington. List of doctoral dissertations in history now in progress at the chief American universities, 1918 [-1938] Wash. D.C. 1918-39   **326b**

China Institute in America. Theses and dissertations by Chinese students in America. N.Y. China Institute in Amer. 1927. 42p.   **326c**

Current research projects. Am. jour. of sociology. XXXIV. no. 4- Jan. 1929- **327**

Derring, Clara Esther. Lists and abstracts of master's theses and doctor's dissertations in education. Teachers College rec. XXIV. p490-502. 1933   **327a**

Dissertations in geography accepted by universities in the United States for the degree of doctor of philosophy, as of May, 1935. Asso. of Am. geog. annals. XXV. p211-37. 1935   **327b**

Doctorates conferred by American universities, 1897/98-1914/15. Science. n.s. VIII-XLII (1898-1915)   **327c**

Eby, Frederick and Frost, S. E., Jr. Graduate theses and dissertations written in the field of education at Baylor University, Southern Methodist University,

Texas Christian University, Texas Technological College, The University of Texas, Texas State Teachers College. Austin. Univ. of Texas. 1934. 77p. **328**

Fort Hays Kansas State College. A partial list of titles of essays written by candidates for the master's degree in colleges and universities of the United States, 1929-30. Current problems in research. bul. no. 1. Fort Hays Kansas State College bul. XXI. no. 3 (Jan. 1931) **328a**

Gilchrist, Donald B. Doctoral dissertations accepted by American universities, 1933/1934- . Comp. for The National Research Council and The Am. Council of Learned Societies by The Asso. of Research Libraries. N.Y. H.W. Wilson. 1934- **329**

Gloss, G. M. Bibliography of master's theses and doctoral studies in the field of recreation. Am. Asso. Health phys. educ. and recreation research quar. XI. p150-63 (March 1940) **329a**

Good, Carter V. Doctoral dissertations in the field of educational law, 1918-1935. Yearbook of school law, 1937, p138-44; 1938, p133-47; 1939, p166-96; 1940, p157-82 **329b**

—— Doctors' theses under way in education, 1930-1940. Jour. of educational research. XXIII. p85-112; XXV. p56-80; XXVI. p381-400; XXVII. p380-400; XXVIII. p376-99; XXIX. p384-406; XXX. p370-96; XXXI. p377-400; XXXII. p371-400; XXXIII. p374-400 (1931-40) **330**

Gray, Ruth A. Recent theses in education. School life. XVIII. 1933- **330a**

Heyl, Lawrence. Sources of information covering research in progress and university dissertations. School and soc. XXIX. p808-10 (June 22, 1910) **331**

Hiss, Priscilla. Research in fine arts in the colleges and universities of the United States. N.Y. Carnegie Corp. 1934. 223p. (Contains: List of master's essays and doctor's theses written in the colleges and universities of the United States. p181-97) **332**

Hunter, William L. Abstracts of graduate theses and dissertations in industrial arts education and vocational-industrial education accepted by institutions of higher learning in Pennsylvania, 1921-33. Ames. Iowa State College, Industrial Arts Dept. 1934. mim. **332a**

Jameson, J. Franklin. List of doctoral dissertations in history now in progress at the chief American universities, 1901-11. (Pamphlets to 1911; 1912 in Hist. teachers' mag. IV. p8-15 (Jan. 1913); 1913-17 in Am. hist. rev. XIX. p450-66; XX. p484-502; XXI. p421-40; XXII. p486-508; XXIII. p486-504 **333**

Kirk, Grayson L. Doctoral dissertations in political science in preparation at American universities. Am. pol. sci rev. XXVIII. p766-78 (Aug. 1934) **333a**

Leisy, Ernest E. List of dissertations and articles, and of Americana in libraries. *In* Foerster, Norman. The reinterpretation of American literature. N.Y. Farrar and Rinehart. 1928. appendix B. p237-71 (Brings up to date the list pub. in Stud. in philology. XXIII and XXIV) **334**
—— A list of research in progress supplementary to that given in The reinterpretation of American literature. Am. literature. I. no. 1- March, 1929- **334a**
Leisy, Ernest E. and Hubbell, Jay B. Doctoral dissertations in American literature. Durham, N.C. Duke Univ. Press. 1933. p419-65 (Reprinted from Am. literature. IV. no. 4. Jan. 1933) **335**
Manual Arts Conference. Special research committee. Annotated list of 800 graduate theses and dissertations in industrial arts education and vocational-industrial education accepted in institutions of higher learning in the United States, 1892-1933. Comp. by a Special research com. for the twenty-fourth Manual arts conference [1933] [Ames, Ia. Industrial arts dept., Iowa State College. 1933] 89p. mim. **336**
Merrill, R. M. American doctoral dissertations in the romance field, 1876-1926. N.Y. Columbia Univ. Press.; London. Milford. 1927. 87p. **337**
Monroe, Walter S. Titles of masters' and doctors' theses in education accepted by colleges and universities in the United States between January 1917, and October 15, 1927. Urbana. College of Education, Univ. of Illinois. Bureau of educational research. 1920-28. mim. **338**
National Education Association of the United States. Department of secondary school principals. Abstracts of unpublished masters' theses in the field of secondary-school administration. (Bulletins nos. 24, 34, 36, 39, 43, 47) Berwyn, Ill. 1929- (Theses of the Univ. of Chicago, Univ. of Southern Calif., George Peabody College for Teachers, and the Univ. of Minn.) **338a**
National Research Council. Research information service. Doctorates conferred in the sciences by American universities, 1919/20- . (Reprint and circular ser. of the National Research Council) Wash. D.C. National Research Council. 1920- **339**
Oregon State Agricultural College. Library. Theses submitted for advanced degrees in forestry in the following institutions: University of California, Harvard University, University of Idaho, Michigan State College, University of Michigan, University of Montana, Oregon State Agricultural College, University of Washington, Yale University. n.p. June 1935. unpag. typ. **340**
Pan American Union. Columbus Memorial Library. Theses on Pan American topics prepared by candidates for degrees in universities and colleges in the United States. (Bibliog. ser. no. 5) Wash. D.C. 1933. 113p. mim. **341**

—— **Division of intellectual cooperation.** Latin American studies in American institutions of higher learning; academic year 1938-1939. Wash. D.C. 1940. 96p. mim. **341a**
Pfankuchen, L. Doctoral dissertations in political science. Am. pol. sci. rev. XXXIII. p732-47 (Aug. 1939) **341b**
Students' dissertations in sociology. Am. jour. of sociology. XXI. 1916- **342**
Thesis guide. Chicago. National Collegial Soc. Oct. 1935- **342a**
Tonne, Herbert A. Studies in business education. Jour. of business education. VII. p23-4, 25-7 (Feb.-March 1932) **342b**
U.S. Library of Congress. Catalogue division. A list of American doctoral dissertations printed in 1912- . Wash. Govt. Ptg. Off. 1913- **343**
U.S. Office of Education. Bibliography of secondary education research, 1920-1925. (Bul. 1926, no. 2) Wash. Govt. Ptg. Off. 1926. Same. (Bul. 1927, no. 27) Wash. Govt. Ptg. Off. 1928 **343a**
—— —— Doctors' theses in education; a list of 797 theses deposited with the Office of Education and available for loan. (Office of Education. Pamphlet no. 60) Wash. Govt. Ptg. Off. 1935. 69p. **344**
—— —— **Library.** Recent theses in education; an annotated list of 242 theses deposited with the Office of Education and available for loan. Wash. Govt. Ptg. Off. 1932. 41p. **345**
West, Clarence J. and Hull, Callie. Doctorates conferred in the arts and sciences by American universities, 1921/1922. School and soc. XVII. p57-63, 106-9, 132-9. 1923 **345a**

Institutional

Alabama. University. Bibliographies of the members of the faculty of the University of Alabama. University, Ala. 1935. unpag. typ. **346**
—— —— **Graduate school.** Bibliography of master's theses, University of Alabama, 1925-1937. (Univ. of Alabama. Bul. n.s. no. 161. April 1, 1937) [University, Ala.] 1937. 32p. **346a**
American Bankers' Association. Graduate school of banking. Cumulative catalogue of theses, 1937-1940. N.Y. 1940. 65p. **346b**
American University. Degrees conferred in course by the American University [1916-1931]. The Am. Univ. bul. catalogue no. for 1933-34 session; The Graduate School and School of Political Science. VIII. no. 3 (June 1933) **346c**
Arizona. University. Abstracts of theses for higher degrees, 1933- and lists of all theses for higher degrees as catalogued in the University library. (Univ. of Ariz. Bul. IV. no. 5. July 1, 1933. General bul. no. 1) Tucson, Ariz. Univ. of Ariz. 1933- **347**

Baylor University. Graduate work in Baylor University: presented by the University committee on research work. The Baylor bul. XXVIII. no. 4 (Dec. 1925)
347a

Boston College. Graduate School. Subject of theses submitted in partial fulfillment of requirements for degrees. Chestnut Hill, Mass. June 1931. unpag. 348

Bowdoin College. Publications of the presidents and faculty of Bowdoin College, 1802-1876. Brunswick, Me. A.G. Tenney. 1876. 35p. 349

Brown University broadsides. By George Parker Winship. Providence, R.I. 1913. 7p. (Reprinted from Brown alumni monthly. May 1913) 350

California. University. Abstracts of doctor's theses in education at the University of California, 1898 to March 1933. By Arnold E. Joyal. [Los Angeles. Frank Wiggins Trade School. 1933] 104p. 351

—— —— Digest of theses accepted in partial fulfillment of the requirements for higher degrees in education at the University of California, December 1931-[May 1933]. By E. S. Edwards. Univ. High School jour. XI. p14-19; XII. p46-50, 221-6; XIII. p23-5 (1931-33) 352

—— —— **Graduate division.** Record of theses submitted in partial fulfillment of the requirements for the degree of doctor of philosophy at the University of California, 1885-1926. [Berkeley] Univ. of Calif. 1926. 132p. (Supplement. 1926-31, 1932. 83p.) 353

Catholic University of America. A decade of research at the Catholic University of America; list of research projects and writings of professors and students, the Catholic University of America, during the past decade, 1921-1930. Comp. by Maurice S. Sheehy. Wash. D.C. Cath. Univ. of Amer. 1931. 202p. 354

—— Dissertations in American church history, (1889-1932). (Am. church history seminar bulletins no. 1) Wash. D.C. Priv. print. 1933. 27p. 355

—— Doctoral dissertations published by the students of the Catholic University of America, 1897-1928. Wash. D.C. The Univ. 1928. 15p. 356

—— Summaries of dissertations accepted in partial fulfillment of the requirements for degrees, I, 1937-. Wash. D.C. 1937-
356a

—— **Graduate School.** Final examinations for the degree of doctor of philosophy, May 1932-July 1932; Jan.-July 1933. Wash. D.C. 1932-33 357

Chicago. University. Abstracts of theses, humanistic series, I, 1922-. Chicago. Univ. of Chicago Press. 1925- 358

—— —— Annotated list of graduate theses and dissertations, the department of education, the University of Chicago, 1900-1931. Chicago. Univ. of Chicago. 1933. 119p. mim. 359

—— —— Publications of the members of the University, 1902-1916. Chicago. Univ. of Chicago Press. 1917. 518p. 360

—— —— Register number. Doctors of philosophy, June 1893-April 1931. (The Univ. of Chicago. Announcements. XXXI, no. 19. May 15, 1931) Chicago. Univ. of Chicago Press. 1931. 174p. 361

—— —— Register of doctors of philosophy, June, 1893-April, 1938. (Announcements, v. 38, no. 14) Chicago. Univ. of Chicago Press. 1938. 207p. 361a

—— —— The report of the president; publications of the members of the university. (The decennial publications. First ser. II) Chicago. Univ. of Chicago Press. 1904. 185p. 362

—— —— Theses of the University of Chicago doctors of philosophy, June 1893-September 1921. Chicago. 1922. 96p. 363

Cincinnati. University. Bibliographical record; The Graduate School, 1900-1910. Univ. of Cincinnati rec. Ser. I. v. VII. no. 2. Nov. 1910. 36p. 364

—— —— Teachers College. Abstracts: graduate theses in education, 1927-1931. By Carter V. Good and others. Cincinnati. Teachers College, Univ. of Cincinnati. 1931 (cont. 1931-36. 1937-39. Cincinnati. 1936. 1940) 365

—— **Teachers College.** Master of arts in education and doctor of philosophy in education, 1924-1931. Cincinnati. Teachers College, Univ. of Cincinnati. 1931
365a

Clark University. Clark University thesis abstracts of dissertations and theses, 1932-1934. Worcester, Mass. 1932-35. 3v. 365b

—— Degrees conferred, 1921 to February 1, 1926. *In* Administrative report of the president, 1920-1925. Clark Univ. bul. April 1926 365c

—— List of degrees granted at Clark University and Clark College, 1889-1920. Comp. by Louis N. Wilson (Publications of the Clark Univ. Lib. VI. no. 3) Worcester. Clark Univ. Press. 1920. 76p.
366

—— Papers published by past and present members of the staff, fellows and scholars. *In* Decennial celebration. Worcester. Pub. for the Univ. 1899. p459-564 367

—— Thesis abstracts, 1929- . Worcester. 1930- 368

—— **Library.** Report on research work, with selected bibliographies of the faculty of Clark University. (Publications of the Clark Univ. Lib.) Worcester. 1932. 92p. 369

Colorado. University. Abstracts of theses for higher degrees, 1929- . Univ. of Colorado stud. XVII. 1929- 369a

—— —— Writings and addresses by officers of the University of Colorado, 1877-1913. Comp. by C. Henry Smith (Univ. of Colorado stud. XIV. no. 4) Boulder, Colo. April 1914. 141p. 370

Columbia University. A bibliography of the faculty of political science of Columbia University, 1880-1930. N.Y. Columbia Univ. Press. 1931. 365p. 371

Columbia University. A catalogue of the publications of the Columbia studies in history, economics and public law, 1917. N.Y. Columbia Univ. 1917. 55p. **372**

—— Digests of dissertations submitted by candidates for the degree of doctor of philosophy, September 1925-December 1931. N.Y. Teachers College, Columbia Univ. n.d. **372a**

—— List of theses submitted by candidates for the degree of doctor of philosophy in Columbia University, 1872-1910. (Columbia Univ. Bul. of information. tenth ser. no. 26, July 10, 1910) N.Y. 1910. 51p. **373**

—— **Library.** Masters essays, 1891-1917. N.Y. Columbia Univ. [1917] 347p. **374**

—— —— Masters essays, 1918- . N.Y. Columbia Univ. 1918- **375**

—— —— University bibliography, 1909-. N.Y. Columbia Univ. 1910- (Continuation of the Univ. bibliog. previously published in the March number of the Columbia Univ. quar.) **376**

—— **Teachers College.** Catalog of publications, Teachers College, Columbia University. N.Y. Teachers College, Columbia Univ. 1917. 28p. **377**

—— —— Register of doctoral dissertations accepted in partial fulfillment of the requirements for the degree of doctor of philosophy . . . v. 1- 1899/1936- N.Y. 1937- **377a**

—— —— Register of Teachers College doctors of philosophy, 1899-1928. N.Y. Teachers College, Columbia Univ. 1929 (Supplements pub. 1931-34) **378**

Contributions to education. Peabody reflector and alumni news. V. no. 7 (July 1932) (George Peabody College for Teachers) **379**

Cornell University. Abstracts of theses accepted in partial satisfaction of the requirements for the doctor's degree, 1937. Ithaca, N.Y. Cornell Univ. Press. 1938 **379a**

—— Recent publications by officers of Cornell University. Library bul. I-II (April 1884-June 1895) **379b**

Fisk University. Library. Fisk University theses, 1917-1939, available for inter-library loan. Nashville, Tenn. 1940. 18p. mim. **379c**

Florida. University. Library. Graduate theses and dissertations, 1906-1938. (Lib. bul. VIII, nos. 5 & 6, May-Aug. 1939) Gainesville, Fla. Library, Catalog Dept., Univ. of Florida. 1939. 35p. mim. **379d**

Fordham University. Dissertations accepted for higher degrees in the graduate school. N.Y. Fordham Univ. 1935- **379e**

George Peabody College for Teachers. Abstracts of unpublished masters' theses in the field of secondary education: theses completed and prepared at George Peabody College for Teachers. National Education Asso., Dept. of Secondary School Principals bul. no. 43. 1932 **379f**

George Washington University. Bibliography; titles of books, monographs, papers, etc., published by members of the faculties, doctors of philosophy and doctors of civil law. Wash. D.C. The Univ. 1934. 59p. (Supplements in The George Wash. Univ. publications, bibliog. ser.) **380**

—— A list of theses written by candidates whose degrees were granted February 22, 1932- . Wash. D.C. George Wash. Univ. Lib. 1932- mim. **380a**

—— Summaries of doctoral theses, 1925/28- . Wash. The Univ. 1931- **381**

Goucher College. Library. Publications of the faculty; a bibliography of the publications of the Goucher College faculty of 1929-30. (Bul. of Goucher College. June 1930) Balt. 1930. 39p. **382**

Harvard Law School Association. Legal writings by teachers at the Harvard Law School. *In* Harvard Law School Association. The Centennial history of the Harvard Law School, 1817-1917. [Cambridge] 1918. p290-343 **383**

Harvard University. Doctors of philosophy and doctors of science who have received their degree in course from Harvard University, 1873-1926, with the titles of their theses. Cambridge. Harvard Univ. 1926. 199p. **384**

—— **Graduate School of Arts and Sciences.** Summaries of theses accepted in partial fulfilment of the requirements for the degree of doctor of philosophy, 1925-. Cambridge. Harvard Univ. Press. 1928- **385**

—— **Graduate School of Education.** Publications of the Graduate School of Education. Harvard University. Cambridge. Harvard Univ. Press. 1932. 27p. **386**

—— **Library.** Harvard College; the class of 1828 with a bibliography of the publications of its members. By Justin Winsor. (Bibliog. contributions. no. 46) Cambridge. John Wilson. 1892. 28p. **387**

—— —— List of publications of Harvard University and its officers, 1870-1892. By William Hopkins Tillinghast. (Bibliog. contributions. no. 12, 23, 28, 33, 38, 41, 44, 47) Cambridge. John Wilson. 1881-93 **388**

Historical Records Survey. North Dakota. Bibliography of theses prepared at the University of North Dakota. Bismarck, N.D. 1940. 68p. reprod. typ. **388a**

Illinois. University. Annotated bibliography of graduate theses in education at the University of Illinois. By Russell T. Gregg and Thomas T. Hamilton, jr. (Univ. of Illinois. Bul. XXVIII. no. 40. June 2, 1931) Urbana. 1931. 80p. **389**

—— —— Books and articles published by the corps of instruction, University of Illinois, May 1, 1914. Urbana. 1915- **390**

—— —— Title of articles and books published by the corps of instruction, University of Illinois between May 1, 1905 and May 1, 1906. By Katherine L. Sharp. (Univ. of Illinois. Bul. III. no. 16. May 15, 1906) Urbana. 1906. p85-96 **391**

—— —— **Bureau of educational research.**
Masters' and doctors' theses in education
accepted between January 1917 and June
1919. Urbana. 1920. 66p. mim. **392**

—— —— **Graduate School.** Final examination[s] . . . for the degree of doctor of
philosophy, May 1926-May 1932. Urbana.
1926-32 **393**

Indiana. University. Abstracts of theses
and dissertations in education at Indiana
University, approved in June and October,
1931, 1932 and 1933. (Phi Delta Kappa,
Alpha chapter bul. no. 6, 1932; no. 7,
1934) Bloomington. Indiana Univ. Book
Store. 1932-34 **393a**

—— —— Abstracts of theses presented to
the School of Education at Indiana University, 1926-1930. Phi Delta Kappa,
Alpha chapter. Indiana Univ. News letter. Jan. 1927; Jan. 1928; March 1929;
Feb. 1930; April 1931. mim. **393b**

—— Bibliography of publications by present and former members of the faculty,
students and alumni. (Indiana Univ. Bul.
II. no. 6) Bloomington. 1905. 152p. (Reprinted from Indiana Univ. 1820-1904. ed.
by Samuel B. Harding. Indiana Univ.
1904) **394**

—— Bibliography of publications by present members of the graduate school and
of graduate students since January 1904,
by departments. (Indiana Univ. Stud.
VIII. Dec. 1921) Bloomington. 1921. p17-
133 **395**

—— List of theses submitted to date, October 1931. Bloomington. Indiana Univ.
1931. mim. **395a**

Iowa. University. Abstracts in history from
dissertations for the degree of doctor of
philosophy as accepted by the Graduate
College of the State University of Iowa,
1922-1937. Ed. by Louis Pelzer. Iowa
City. 1932-37 **396**

—— —— A bibliography of the publications of the University and its members
(1868-99). (State Univ. of Iowa. Bul. n.s.
no. 8. March 1900) Iowa City. 1900.
64p. **397**
1900-1912. By Malcolm G. Wyer
(State Univ. of Iowa. Bul. n.s. no. 67.
July 1913) Iowa City. 1913. 74p. **398**
1913-1916. By Jane E. Roberts (State
Univ. of Iowa. Monographs. first ser.
no. 9) Iowa City. 1917. 41p. **399**
1917. (State Univ. of Iowa. Monographs. first ser. no. 20) Iowa City. 1918.
20p. **400**
1918-1920. (State Univ. of Iowa. Stud.
first ser. no. 49) Iowa City. 1921. 32p.
401

—— —— Check list and price list of university studies. (State Univ. of Iowa. Bul.
n.s. no. 803. Aug. 3, 1935) Iowa City.
1935. 31p. **402**

—— —— Dissertations in history and English. (Univ. of Iowa stud., no. 85, Jan.
15, 1925; 183, July 15, 1930) Iowa City.
1925, 1930 **402a**

—— —— Doctoral theses in education.
(Univ. of Iowa stud., no. 267, Jan. 15,
1934; 272, April 1, 1934; 296, Jan. 1935;
368, 1939) Iowa City. 1934, 1935, 1939
402b

—— —— Programs announcing candidates
for higher degrees, 1917- . Iowa City.
1917- **403**

—— —— Schedule of dissertations of approved candidates for advanced degrees,
with major and minor subjects. Univ. of
Iowa stud. no. 4, 14, 27, 30, 46, 60 (1917-
22) **403a**

—— —— **Graduate School.** Graduate
theses, including schedule of dissertations
of approved candidates for advanced degrees, with major and minor subjects.
Univ. of Iowa stud. no. 75- Feb. 1, 1924-
404

**Iowa State College of Agriculture and
Mechanic Arts.** Abstracts of doctoral
theses, 1931- . Ames. Iowa State College. 1932- (Reprinted from Iowa State
College jour. of science. VI-) **405**

—— List of publications of members of the
staff of Iowa State College. . ., 1920-.
Ames. Iowa State Col. Lib. 1928- **406**

—— Roster of doctors of philosophy, 1916-
1934. Ames, Iowa. 1934. 44p. **406a**

—— Theses pertaining to industrial arts
education, Iowa State College, 1922-1935.
Comp. by William L. Hunter. Ames.
Iowa State College. 1935. 18p. mim.
406b

—— Titles of master's theses accepted at
Iowa State College in the department
of vocational education, home economics
education and industrial arts, 1921-1931.
Ames. Iowa State College. 1931. mim.
407

John B. Stetson University. Summaries of
masters' theses. (John B. Stetson Univ.
bul. XXXIV, no. 6, Dec. 1934) Deland,
Fla. 1934 **407a**

Johns Hopkins University. Doctors' dissertations, 1878-1919. (Johns Hopkins Univ.
circular, no. 321, Jan. 1920) Baltimore.
1920 **407b**

—— Herbert B. Adams; tributes of friends,
with a bibliography of the department of
history, politics and economics of the
Johns Hopkins University, 1876-1901.
(Johns Hopkins univ. Stud. in hist. and
pol. science. ser. 20. extra no.) Balt.
Johns Hopkins Univ. Press. 1902. 160p.
408

—— Publications of members and graduates of the departments of history, political economy and political science, 1901-
1915. (Johns Hopkins Univ. Circular.
n.s. no. 10) Balt. Johns Hopkins Univ.
Press. 1915. 112p. **409**

—— **Library.** List of dissertations submitted in conformity with the requirements for the degree of doctor of philosophy, doctor of engineering and doctor of
science in hygiene in the Johns Hopkins
University, 1876-1926. (Johns Hopkins
Univ. Circular. n.s. 1926. no. 8) Balt.
Johns Hopkins Univ. Press. 1926. 85p.
410

Kansas. State Teachers College. Annotated bibliography of dissertations accepted for the master of science degree, Kansas State Teachers College of Emporia, 1929-1939. By E. J. Brown, H. E. Schrammel and Irene Niles. (Bul. of information XIX, no. 9) Emporia, Kans. 1939. 61p.
410a

Kansas. University. Titles and authors of theses written for graduate degrees in education, 1922-30. (Univ. of Kansas. Bul. of education, II, no. 2, Dec. 1928; III, no. 2, Dec. 1930) Lawrence. 1929-30 **410b**

—— —— Titles of theses presented in partial fulfillment of the requirements for advanced degrees in the Graduate School. Lawrence. Univ. of Kansas. 1920. 43p. Same. 1921-32. 1932 **411**

—— —— **Library.** List of publications. Comp. by Mary Maud Smelser. Pub. by the University, Lawrence, 1935. Topeka. Printed by Kansas State Ptg. Plant, W.C. Austin, state printer. 1935. 127p. **411a**

Kansas State Teachers Association. Research studies in Kansas; brief abstracts of theses developed at the graduate schools of the state. Kansas teacher and western school jour. XLII. p24-5, 24; XLIII. p15, 17, 13 (Feb.-April, June, Sept. 1936) **411b**

Kentucky. University. Theses in education. University of Kentucky. Lexington. 1937. 32p. **411c**

—— —— Theses in education. Bul. of the Bureau of school service, College of Education. V. no. 4 (June 1933). Same. January 1, 1933 to January 1, 1935. Lexington. Univ. of Kentucky. 1935. mim. **411d**

—— —— **Graduate School.** Theses and dissertations; presented in partial fulfillment of the requirements for advanced degrees at the University of Kentucky during the years 1925-1937 inclusive. [Lexington, Ky.] The Graduate School of the Univ. of Kentucky. 1938. 59p.
411e

Leland Stanford Junior University. Library. Abstracts of dissertations for the degree of doctor of philosophy and doctor of education, with the titles of theses accepted for the degree of master of arts and engineers, 1924/1926- . Stanford University, Calif. The Univ. 1927- **412**

—— —— Degrees conferred by Stanford University, June 1892-June 1924, doctors of philosophy, masters of arts, engineers, with the titles of their theses. Stanford University, Calif. Univ. press. 1928. 100p.
413

—— —— University bibliography for the academic year . . . 1938/39- . Stanford University, Calif. 1939- **413a**

List of publications of members of the faculty of the University of New Mexico issued prior to June 1939. By Mary Elizabeth Brindley and Lloyd Spencer Tireman. (University of New Mexico bul. Catalog ser. vol. 53, no. 5. Whole no. 362) Albuquerque, N.M. Univ. of New Mexico Press. 1940. 54p. **413b**

Louisiana. State University. Abstracts of theses, 1935-36-[1936-37]. (Louisiana State Univ. Bul., n.s. XXVIII, no. 12; n.s. XXX, no. 3) University, La. Louisiana State Univ. Press. 1936-38. 2v. **413c**

Maryland. University. Graduate School. Abstracts of theses for the degree of doctor of philosophy, with the titles of theses accepted for the master's degree, for the academic years 1938-1939 and 1939-1940. College Park, Md. 1940. 55p. **413d**

Michigan. University. Bibliography of publications by members of the several faculties of the University of Michigan. . . . , 1907/09- Ann Arbor. 1909-
414

—— —— **Library.** University of Michigan publications containing material of a scientific or learned character. Comp. by Esther Anne Smith. Ann Arbor. 1922. 99p. **415**

—— —— **School of Education. Bureau of educational reference and research.** Abstracts of dissertations and theses in education at the University of Michigan, 1917-1931. Monograph no. 1- Ann Arbor. Univ. of Michigan. 1932- **415a**

Minnesota. University. Abstracts of master's and doctor's theses in education, 1928/29-[1930/31]. Minneapolis. Eta chapter, Phi Delta Kappa. Univ. of Minnesota. 1931-32. 3v. **415b**

—— —— Masters' and doctors' theses in education, 1912-1928. Comp. by Fred Engelhardt and Henry J. Otto. Minneapolis. Univ. of Minnesota Press. 1929. 32p. **416**

—— —— Publications of the faculties, 1928-1930 (Univ. of Minnesota. Bul. XXXIII. no. 43, Sept. 15, 1930) 146p. (1931-32 in Bul. XXXV. no. 65, Dec. 3, 1932. 127p.; 1933-34 in Bul. XXXVIII. no. 1. Jan. 8, 1935. 148p.) **417**

—— —— A register of the Ph.D. degrees conferred by the University of Minnesota, 1888-1932. Minneapolis. Univ. of Minnesota Press. 1932. 177p. **418**

—— —— Register of Ph.D. degrees conferred by the University of Minnesota, 1888 through June 1938. (Bul. v. 42, no. 31) Minneapolis. 1939. 276p. **418a**

—— —— **Library.** The scientific publications of the University of Minnesota, including the publications of the Geological and natural history survey. Minneapolis. 1915- **419**

Missouri. University. Degree of doctor of philosophy in education conferred by the University of Missouri. Columbia. Univ. of Missouri. 1931. **419a**

—— —— Partial bibliography and index of the publications of the College of Agriculture and the Agricultural Experiment Station. (The Univ. of Missouri. Bul. lib. ser. II. no. 1) Columbia. July 1912. 19p. **420**

—— —— **Library.** Check list of the official serial publications of the university. (Univ. of Missouri. Bul. XXVII. no. 16. lib. ser. no. 12) Columbia, Mo. 1926. 63p. **421**

Montana. University. List of theses of the department and school of education . . . accepted for the master of arts degree, 1922-1932. Missoula. 1932 **421a**

Nebraska. University. Bibliographical contributions from the library of the University of Nebraska. VI. 1926; VIII. 1932; IX. 1934. Lincoln. 1926-34. 3v. **421b**

—— —— **Library.** The learned and scientific publications of the University of Nebraska (1871-1926). (Bibliog. contributions. VI) Lincoln. Univ. of Nebraska. 1926. 130p. **422**

—— —— —— List of publications by members of the University of Nebraska, January 1925 to June 1931. Comp. by Clara L. Craig and Ruby C. Wilder (Bibliog. contributions. VIII) Lincoln. Univ. of Nebraska. 1932. 147p. (July 1931 to June 1933 in Bibliog. contributions. IX. 92p.; 1933-1935. Univ. of Nebraska bul. ser. XLI. no. 8. 1936. 72p.; 1935-1937. *ibid.* ser. XLIII. no. 5. 1938. 76p.) **423**

New Hampshire. University. Summaries of doctoral dissertations and masters' theses accepted during 1936. (Publication no. 121. Education monograph, no. 10) Lincoln. 1937 **423a**

New Mexico. University. Abstracts of masters' theses, 1917-1928. Univ. of New Mexico bul. XLII. no. 2 (March 1929). 26p. **423b**

—— —— A catalog of publications of the University. (Bul. Catalog ser. LIII, no. 4, whole no. 361. Oct. 1, 1940) Albuquerque, Univ. of New Mexico Press. 1940. 31p. **423c**

—— —— A catalogue of publications of the university. (Bul. catalogue ser. XLVII. no. 1. Jan. 1, 1934) Albuquerque. Univ. of New Mexico Press. 1934. 14p. **424**

New York. State College for Teachers. Masters' theses: titles of theses, 1914-1931; abstracts of theses, June 1932. Official register of the N.Y. State College for Teachers. XVII. no. 3. 1932. 35p. **424a**

New York (city). College of the City of New York. Annotated bibliography and topical index of master of science in education theses, 1923-31. [N.Y.] College of the City of New York, School of Education. 1931. mim.
Supplement. nos. 1-2. 1932-34. mim. **424b**

—— —— **School of Education.** Abstracts of theses for the degree of master of science in education, 1923-1939. N.Y. 1939. 118p. **424c**

New York. State University. Bibliography of research studies in education pertaining to New York state. Albany. Educational Research Division, Univ. of the State of New York Press. 1932 **424d**

New York University. Graduate theses in business education, 1925-1930. N.Y. Univ. research bul. in commercial education. II. p17-20 (Dec. 1930) **424e**

—— Index of dissertations of the School of Education, New York University. Prepared by Herbert A. Tonne. N.Y. Pub. by the Rho chapter of Phi Delta Kappa, School of Education, N.Y. Univ. 1932. 48p. **425**

—— List of graduates, with titles of their theses, to whom the degrees of doctor of philosophy and doctor of science had been given, 1887-1914. N.Y. Univ. bul. 1915/16. N.Y. N.Y. Univ. 1915 **425a**

—— University bibliography, 1929/30- N.Y. Univ. bul. 1930- **426**

—— **School of Education.** Abstracts of theses submitted in partial fulfillment of the requirements for the degree of doctor of philosophy in the School of Education of New York University. [N.Y. N.Y. Univ. Press.] 1930- **426a**

—— **Washington Square College. Library.** List of doctors' and masters' theses in education, New York University, 1890-June 1936. Comp. under the direction of Nouvart Tashjian. N.Y. Rho Chapter, Phi Delta Kappa, School of Education, New York Univ. 1937. 117p. photop. **426b**

North Carolina. University. Research in progress, 1918- . Chapel Hill. Univ. of North Carolina.]1920-] **426c**

—— —— Scientific investigation at the university, 1795-1910. (The Univ. of North Carolina rec. no. 86, Nov. 1910) Chapel Hill. Univ. Press. 1910. 60p. **427**

Northwestern University. Abstracts of masters' theses in education . . . in 1931 and 1932. (Contributions to education, School of Education ser. no. 10) Evanston. Northwestern Univ., School of Education. 1933. 129p. **427a**

—— A list of doctoral dissertations submitted at Northwestern University, 1896-1934. Chicago and Evanston. 1935. 27p. **428**

—— **Graduate School.** Summaries of Ph.D. dissertations, 1933- . Chicago and Evanston. 1933- **429**

Notre Dame. University. A summary of masters' degrees in education done at the University of Notre Dame from 1918-1935. By Brother Justin Dwyer. South Bend, Ind. 1936 **429a**

Ohio. State University. Abstracts of theses presented by candidates for the master's degree, . . . 1929- . Columbus. Ohio State Univ. Press. 1929- **429b**

—— —— Annual list of publications, 1929- . Columbus. Ohio State Univ. Press. 1929- **430**

—— —— Information concerning persons granted the degree of doctor of philosophy by the Ohio State University, [1890-1930]. Columbus. Ohio State Univ. 1930 **430a**

—— —— Publications of the teaching staff, 1907- . (Ohio State Univ. Bul. XII-) Columbus. The Univ. 1908- **431**

Ohio. State University. Graduate School. Abstracts of dissertations presented by candidates for the degree of doctor of philosophy, 1929- . Columbus. Ohio State Univ. Press. 1929-   **432**

Oklahoma. Agricultural and Mechanical College. List of theses for the M.A. and M.S. degree at Oklahoma Agricultural and Mechanical College. By Josephine Plunkett. Stillwater, Okla. 1938. MS. **432a**

—— —— Summaries of theses submitted in partial fulfillment of the requirements for the degrees of master of science and master of arts, spring and summer, 1935 [-1939]. Stillwater, Okla. 1935-39 **432b**

Oklahoma. University. Abstracts of theses for higher degrees in the Graduate School. 1930, with an appendix giving the titles of theses presented prior to 1930. (Univ. of Oklahoma. Bul. n.s. no. 501, Feb. 14, 1931) Norman. Univ. of Oklahoma. 1931. (Supplements) **432c**

—— —— List of publications of faculty members of the University of Oklahoma from May 1927 to May 1929. Comp. under the auspices of the Oklahoma chapter of the American Association of University Professors (Univ. of Oklahoma. Bul. n.s. 432. March 2, 1929) Norman. The Univ. 1929. 16p. **433**

—— —— A list of theses in the University of Oklahoma Library. Norman. Univ. of Oklahoma Lib. 1929. mim. **434**

Oregon. University. Graduate theses of the Oregon system of higher education. (Oregon state system of higher education. Leaflet ser. no. 167, pt. 2) Eugene. Oregon State Board of Higher Education. 1939 **434a**

—— —— Publications of the University of Oregon, 1878-1937. Comp. by George N. Belknap. Eugene. Univ. of Oregon. 1938. 48p. **434b**

Pennsylvania. State College. Abstracts of doctoral dissertations submitted in partial fulfillment of the requirements for the degrees of doctor of education and doctor of philosophy, 1938. State College, Pa. 1938 **434c**

—— —— Abstracts of studies in education at the Pennsylvania State College . . . 1931-35- . By Charles C. Peters and others. (Pennsylvania State College stud. in education) State College, Pa. School of Education, Pennsylvania State College. 1931-35- **434d**

—— **Library.** Graduate theses and dissertations, 1892-1937. State College, Pa. The College. 1937. 100p. **434e**

Pennsylvania. University. Doctors of philosophy of the Graduate School, 1889-1927. Phila. The Univ. 1927. 128p. **435**

Pittsburgh. University. Graduate School. Abstracts of doctors' dissertations, 1925- . (Univ. of Pittsburgh. Bul. XX. no. 8. April 1, 1926) Pittsburgh. Univ. of Pittsburgh. 1926- **436**

—— —— **Mellon Institute of Industrial Research.** A list of the books, bulletins, journal contributions, and patents by members of Mellon Institute of Industrial Research, 1911-1927. By Lois Heaton (Bibliog. ser. Bul. no. 2) Pittsburgh [The Eddy Ptg. Corp.] 1927. 80p. (Supplements. 1928-34) **437**

—— —— **School of Education.** Annotations of theses and dissertations in education. Pittsburgh. Xi chapter of Phi Delta Kappa. 1934. 56p. **438**

Princeton University. Abstracts of theses presented for the degree of doctor of philosophy, September 1931-June 1932. Princeton, N.J. 1932 **438a**

Purdue University. A bibliography of the more important contributions by the faculty of Purdue University for the past ten years; also a list of bulletins published by the United States Experiment Station from December 1884 to November 1898. An appendix to the Twenty-fourth annual report of Purdue University, October 1898. [Lafayette. 1898] 18p. (Published at intervals since 1898) **439**

Radcliffe College. Graduate School of Arts and Sciences. Summaries of theses accepted in partial fulfillment of the requirements for the degree of doctor of philosophy, 1931-1934[-1935-1938] Cambridge. Harvard Univ. Press. 1935-38. 2v. **440**

Rochester. University. Check lists of masters' and doctors' theses accepted by the University of Rochester, 1897-1933. [Rochester, N.Y.] Univ. Lib. Staff. Sept. 1933 **441**

St. Louis University. Publications of the faculty and graduate students of St. Louis University in the five years, 1923-1927. (St. Louis Univ. Bul. XXV. special no.) St. Louis. 1929. 102p. **442**

Smith College. Development of history and government in Smith College, 1875-1920, with a list of publications of the faculty and alumnae. By Mary B. Fuller. (Smith College. Stud. in hist. V, no. 3. April 1920) Northampton, Mass. Smith College. 1920. p143-73 **442a**

—— Smith College studies in social work, I, September 1930. (Abstracts of theses submitted) **442b**

South Carolina. University. Abstracts of theses of higher degrees, 1930/31-1931/32. (Bul. of the Univ. of South Carolina) Columbia. Farrell Print. Co. 1931-32 **443**

—— —— Faculty research and productive scholarship: language and literature, social science, natural science and mathematics, professional schools, bulletins of the University of South Carolina. (Univ. of South Carolina bul. no. 211. pt. 1. March 1, 1931) Columbia. The State Co. 1931. 58p. **444**

—— —— Graduate School of the University of South Carolina, 1929. (Univ. of South Carolina bul. no. 208. Oct. 15, 1929) p52-101 **445**

Southern California. University. Abstracts of dissertations for the degree of doctor of philosophy, with the titles of theses accepted for masters' degrees, 1936-1940. Los Angeles. Univ. of Southern California Press. 1938-40. 5v. **445a**

—— —— Annotated index of theses and dissertations in education. By Frederick J. Weersing and Benjamin R. Haynes. Los Angeles. Univ. of South. Calif. 1936. 133p. **445b**

—— —— Trends in scholarship, annotations of theses and dissertations accepted by The University of Southern California, 1910-1935. (Univ. of South. Calif. Publications, Univ. chronicles ser. no. 4) Los Angeles. Univ. of South. Calif. Press. 1936. 133p. **445c**

Southern Methodist University. Abstracts of all masters' theses accepted by Southern Methodist University, 1915-1926. (Bul. XII. no. 3. July 1927) Dallas. Southern Methodist Univ. 1927 **445d**

—— Abstracts of theses: masters' degrees in the Graduate School, 1932-33. Dallas. Southern Methodist Univ. 1934 **445e**

Springfield College. Selected bibliography of graduate theses, Springfield College, 1929-1934. Am. Physical Education Asso. research quar. VI. no. 2. supplement. p126-8 (May 1935) **446**

Stanford University. Abstracts of dissertations for the degrees of doctor of philosophy and doctor of education, with the titles of theses accepted for the degrees of master of arts and engineer, October 1924-June 1926. Stanford University, Calif. Stanford Univ. Press. 1927. Same. 1926-34. 8v. **446a**

—— Degrees conferred by Stanford University, June 1892-June 1924; doctors of philosophy, masters of arts, engineers, with titles of their theses. Stanford University, Calif. Stanford Univ. Press. 1927 **446b**

Temple University. Studies in education and psychology: abstracts of doctoral dissertations. By George E. Walk and others. (Temple Univ. bul. I) Phila. Temple Univ. 1934 **446c**

—— **Library.** Bibliography of research studies at Temple University, 1935-38 (supplement to A list of theses and dissertations, 1908-35) By Maurice F. Tauber. Phila. Temple Univ. In progress **446d**

—— —— Graduate theses and dissertations, 1894-1940. Comp. by J. Periam Danton and Maurice F. Tauber. (Sullivan Memorial Library stud.) Phila. 1940. 94p. **446e**

—— —— Index of theses and dissertations prepared at Temple University, 1908-1935. Comp. by Maurice E. Tauber. Phila. Temple Univ. 1935. 44p. mim. **446f**

Texas. East State Teachers College. Graduate studies, 1939. By H. M. Lafferty. (Bul. XXII. no. 4) Commerce, Texas. 1939 **446g**

Texas. University. Notes on publications by the faculty, 1912/13.-. (Univ. of Texas. Bul. no. 294. Official ser. no. 90. Sept. 8, 1913) Austin. 1913- (Continued from The Record) **447**

—— —— Publications of the University of Texas, 1882-1914; list of bulletins, with index and index to the University of Texas record. (Univ. of Texas. Bul. no. 379. Official ser. no. 113. Dec. 25, 1914) Austin. 1915. 103p. **448**

Texas. West State Teachers College. The number of master of arts degrees conferred by the institution, 1932-34. Canyon, Texas. 1934 **448a**

Trinity College, Hartford. Bibliography of official publications, 1824-1905. (Trinity College. Bul. II. no. 4) Hartford, Conn. Sept. 1905. 42p. **449**

Tulane University. Theses on Louisiana. (Louisiana Library Association. Bul. I. no. 3. Dec. 1932) [New Orleans] 1932 **449a**

—— **Graduate school.** Titles of theses, 1885-1937. New Orleans. The School. 1939. 31p. **449b**

Utah. University. Scientific or professional books, monographs, and articles in professional magazines by faculty members of the University of Utah (published during 1926-1931). Bul. XXII. no. 2. Dec. 1931) Salt Lake City. 1932. 20p. **450**

—— —— Scientific or professional books, monographs, and articles in professional magazines by faculty members of the University of Utah (published from January 1, 1932 to June 30, 1939) (Bul. v. 30, no. 10) Salt Lake City. Univ. of Utah. 1940. 34p. **450a**

Vanderbilt University. Abstract of theses, 1931- . Vanderbilt Univ. bul. XXXII. Sept. 15, 1932- **450b**

Virginia. University. Abstracts of dissertations, 1931/32-[1933/34]. Nos. 179-236. [Charlottesville. Dept. of graduate stud. Univ. of Virginia, 1933-35] 3v. in 1 **450c**

—— —— Abstracts of dissertations accepted in partial fulfillment of the requirements for the degree of doctor of philosophy, 1935. Charlottesville. The Univ. 1935. (Complete list of doctoral dissertations, 1885-1935, in appendix, p49-64) **450d**

—— —— Bibliography of the University of Virginia, 1826-1921. Univ. of Virginia alumni bul. 3d ser. XVI-XVII (April 1923-Oct. 1924) **451**

—— —— Research at the University of Virginia, 1919-1922. Univ. of Virginia alumni bul. 3d ser. XV. p275-320 (July-Aug. 1922) **452**

—— —— Publications and research, 1922-. Univ. of Virginia rec., extension ser. IX. Sept. 1924- (1922-26 entitled Univ. bibliog.) **452a**

Virginia Polytechnic Institute. Research and publications, 1923/25-[1929/31]. Blacksburg. Virginia Polytechnic Inst. 1927-32. 3v. **453**

Washington. University. Abstracts of theses and faculty bibliography [1936-37]. (Univ. of Washington. Publications. Theses ser. II. Aug. 1937) [Seattle] 1937. (Cont. in Univ. of Washington. Publications. Theses ser. III, IV. Dec. 31, 1938. Nov. 25, 1939. Seattle. 1938-39) **453a**

—— —— Digests of theses, 1914-1931. (Univ. of Wash. Publications. I. Dec. 1931) Seattle. Univ. of Wash. Press. 1931 **454**

—— —— Library. A list of University of Washington publications. Comp. by the lib. staff (Univ. of Wash. Bul. general ser. no. 210. Oct. 15, 1927) Seattle. 1927. 30p. **455**

—— —— —— Publications of the University of Washington faculty, November 4, 1861-March 31, 1936. Compiled by Clara J. Kelly, with assistance from the library staff. Seattle, Wash. The Univ. of Washington. 1937. 316p. (Publications of the University of Washington. Library series. no. 1) **455a**

Washington University, St. Louis. Annual bibliography; books and articles published by the corps of instruction of Washington University, 1923/25- . (Wash. Univ. Stud. n.s.) St. Louis. 1925- **455b**

West Virginia University. Bibliography of West Virginia University, its faculty and graduates, 1867-1907. By P. W. Leonard. Morgantown, W.Va. 1907. 62p. **456**

Western Reserve University. Bibliography and index of publications of Western Reserve University for the years 1822-1936. Comp. by W. T. Brahm. (Bul. n.s. v. 40. no. 8) Cleveland. The Univ. 1937. 83p. **456a**

—— Bibliography of theses 1927-1937. Graduate School, Western Reserve University. [Cleveland. 1938] mim. Supplement. 1938-39. 1940. mim. **456b**

Wichita. University. Dissertations accepted for higher degrees in the Graduate School, June 1929-June 1935. (Municipal Univ. of Wichita bul. X. no. 12) Wichita. Univ. of Wichita. 1935 **456c**

—— —— Graduate School. Dissertations accepted for higher degrees in the Graduate school. (Municipal Univ. of Wichita. Bul. X. no. 12) [Wichita] The Univ. 1935. 11p. **456d**

Williams College. Publications of the president and professors of 1793-1876. North Adams, Mass. J. T. Robinson. 1876. 19p. **457**

Wisconsin. University. Abstracts of theses submitted in partial fulfillment of the requirements for the degree of doctor of philosophy, 1917- . Madison. 1917- **458**

—— —— Checklist of publications of the University of Wisconsin, 1911- . Madison. The Univ. 1911- **459**

—— —— Summaries of doctoral dissertations, University of Wisconsin, submitted to the graduate school in partial fulfill-ment of the requirements for the degree of doctor of philosophy, July, 1935 [-June, 1939]. I [-IV] Madison. 1937 [-40] **459a**

Wyoming. University. Graduate students who have received advanced degrees, with the titles of theses, 1897-1933. Univ. of Wyoming bul. XXX. no. 4. p49-56 (June 1933) **459b**

Yale University. Bibliographies of the present officers of Yale University, together with a bibliography of the late President Porter. New Haven. Tuttle, Morehouse & Taylor. 1893. 160p. **460**

—— Graduate School. Doctors of philosophy of Yale University with the titles of their dissertations, 1861-1927. New Haven. Graduate School, Yale Univ. 1927. Supplement. 1928-30 (Bul. of Yale Univ. April 1, 1931) New Haven, Conn. Yale Univ. 1931. Supplement. 1928-30. New Haven, Conn. 1931 **461**

GENERAL BIBLIOGRAPHIES

American bookfinder and, serially, American book prices current, I- April 2, 1937- N.Y. R.R. Bowker. 1937- **461a**

American book-prices current; a record of books, manuscripts and autographs sold in the principal auction rooms of the United States. N.Y. Dodd, Mead. 1895-1917; E.P. Dutton. 1918-28; R.R. Bowker. 1930- . Index to American book prices current, 1916-1922. Comp. by P.S. Goulding and H.P. Goulding. N.Y. E.P. Dutton. 1925. 1397p. A priced index, 1923-1932. Comp. by Eugenia Wallace and Lucie E. Wallace. N.Y. R.R. Bowker. 1936. 1007p. Index, 1933-1940. N.Y. 1941. 765p. **461b**

Anderson Galleries. Extraordinary collection of Americana consigned by Henry E. Huntington. N.Y. Anderson Galleries. 1917. 114p. **462**

Aspinwall, Thomas. Catalogue of books relating to America. Paris. 1832? 66p. **463**

Baginsky, Paul H. German works relating to America, 1493-1800; a list compiled from the collections of the New York Public Library. N.Y. Pub. Lib. bul. XLII. p909-18 (Dec. 1938); XLIII. 140-4, 349-58, 523-8, 575-80, 622-30, 671-86, 760-78, 921-46 (Feb., April, June-Oct., Dec. 1939); XLIV. 39-56 (June 1940) **464**

Barringer, George A. Catalogue de l'his-toire de l'Amérique. Paris. Bibliothèque nationale. 1903-11. 5v. **464a**

Barros Arana, Diego. Notas para una bib-liografía de obras anónimas i seudónimas sobre la historia, la jeografía i la litera-tura de America. Santiago de Chile. Im-prenta nacional. 1882. 171p. **465**

Bibliotheca Americana; being a choice col-lection of books relating to North and South America and the West-Indies, in-cluding voyages to the southern hemi-sphere, maps, engravings, and medals. Paris. 1831 **465a**

Bibliotheca Americana; or, a chronological catalogue of the most curious and interesting books, pamphlets, state papers, etc. upon the subject of North and South America, from the earliest period to the present, in print and manuscript .... London. J. Debrett. 1789. 271p. (Attributed to Arthur Homer, Mr. Reid, J. Debrett and to Alexander Dalrymple) **466**

Bonaventure, E. F. The bibliopole; catalogue of rare and fine books. N.Y. The author. 1890. 94p. **466a**

Boon, Edward P. Catalogue of books and pamphlets principally relating to America. N.Y. 1870. 597p. **467**

Boston Athenaeum. Catalogue of the library of the Boston Athenaeum, 1807-1871. Boston. 1874-82. 5v. **468**

Brinley, George. Catalogue of the American library of the late Mr. George Brinley, of Hartford, Conn. Hartford. Case, Lockwood & Brainard. 1878-93. 5v. (Index comp. by W. I. Fletcher pub. separately the same year in 80p.) **469**

Brown, John Carter. Bibliographical notices of rare and curious books relating to America, printed in the XVth and XVIth centuries (1482-1700) in the library of the late John Carter Brown of Providence, R.I. By John Russell Bartlett. Providence. Printed for private distribution by H.O. Houghton. Cambridge. 1875-82. 2v. **470**

—— Bibliotheca Americana; a catalogue of books relating to North and South America in the library of the late John Carter Brown of Providence, R.I. . . . With notes by John Russell Bartlett. Providence. [Printed by H.O. Houghton. Cambridge] 1865-71. 3pts. in 4v. **471**

—— Bibliotheca Americana; a catalogue of books relating to North and South America in the library of the late John Carter Brown of Providence, R.I. . . . With notes by John Russell Bartlett. Providence. Printed by H.O. Houghton. Cambridge. 1875-82. 2v. (A second edition of pts. I-II first pub. in 1865-66) **472**

Christie-Miller, Sydney Richardson. Catalogue of the magnificent series of early works relating to America from the renowned library at Britwell Courts, Burnham, Bucks, the property of S.R. Christie-Miller, esq. . . . London. Dryden Press, J. Davy. 1916. 122p. **473**

Church, E. D. A catalogue of books relating to the discovery and early history of North and South America, forming a part of the library of E.D. Church. Comp. by George Watson Cole. N.Y. Dodd, Mead. 1907. 5v. **474**

Clarke, firm, booksellers. Bibliotheca Americana, 1886. Catalogue of a valuable collection of books and pamphlets relating to America with a descriptive list of Robert Clarke & Co's historical publications. Cincinnati. Robert Clarke. 1886. 280' 51p. **475**

Clements, William L. Uncommon, scarce and rare books relating to American history during the discovery and colonial periods, together with other Americana from the library of William L. Clements. Bay City, Mich. 1914. unpag. **476**

—— The William L. Clements Library of Americana at the University of Michigan. Ann Arbor. The Univ. 1923. 228p. **477**

Colón, Fernando. Catalogue of the library of Ferdinand Columbus. Reproduced in facsimile from the unique MS. in the Columbine Library of Seville by Archer M. Huntington. N.Y. 1905. unpag. **478**

Cooke, J. J. Catalogue of the library of the late Joseph J. Cooke of Providence, Rhode Island; Part the third, Americana; books relating to America. . . . Geo. A. Leavitt & Co., auctioneers. N.Y. 1883. 401p. **479**

Court, J. Catalogue de la précieuse bibliothèque de feu M. le Docteur J. Court, comprenant une collection unique de voyageurs et d'historiens relatifs à l'Amérique. Paris. Ch. Leclerc. 1884. 2v. **480**

Edwards, Francis, firm, booksellers, London. Edwards's American catalogue. Catalogue of books, pamphlets, maps, views, &c., relating to the geography and history of the American continent. . . . London. Edwards. [1904-06] 409p. **481**

Fabyan, Francis Wright. Illustrated catalogue of Americana rarissima from the private library of Francis W. Fabyan, esq., of Boston, including a remarkable collection of works by Increase and Cotton Mather. . . . N.Y. Am. Art Asso. 1920. 70p. **482**

Fischer, Augustin. Bibliotheca Mejicana, catalogue of books and manuscripts relating to the history and literature of North and South America, particularly Mexico. . . . London. Puttick & Simpson. 1869. **483**

Ford, Worthington Chauncey. The Society's photostat, 1925-1929. Mass. Hist. Soc. proc. LXII. p87-110. 1928-29 (Photostats of Americana) **484**

Grolier Club. Catalogue of early printed books relating to America, exhibited at the Grolier Club. . . . N.Y. 1888. 20p. **485**

Guild, Charles Henry. Catalogue of the . . . collection of books and pamphlets relating to America, belonging to Charles H. Guild . . . consisting of New England, New York, and western local history . . . genealogies . . . privately printed books . . . Washingtoniana. . . . Boston. C.F. Libbie. 1887. 344p. **486**

Harper, Francis P. Bibliotheca Americana; priced catalogue of a remarkable collection of scarce and out-of-print books relating to the discovery, settlement and history of the western hemisphere. . . . N.Y. Harper. 1903. 224p. **487**

Harper, Lathrop C. Priced catalogue of a remarkable collection of scarce and out-of-print books relating to the discovery, settlement, and history of the western hemisphere. . . . N.Y. Harper. 1914. 219p. **488**

Heartman, Charles F. Americana. Rare books and pamphlets and a few choice autographs. . . Metuchen, N.J. 1930. 42p. **489**

—— Rare Americana, printed and in manuscript, including the fine collection by Foster Stearns, of Hancock, N.H. . . . Metuchen, N.J. [1932] 585p. **490**

—— Six hundred pamphlets, broadsides, and a few books written in the English language and relating to America issued prior to eighteen hundred, bibliographically, historically and sometimes sentimentally described. . . N.Y. Heartman. 1919. 119p. **491**

Henkels, Stan V. Catalogue of the valuable private library of Mr. Charles Henry Hart . . . peculiarly rich in Americana and works on the fine arts. . . Phila. 1893. 158p. **492**

Hiersemann, Karl W. Catalogue 394. Americana. I. The United States, Canada, Arctic regions. Leipzig. Hiersemann. 1911. 96p. **493**

—— Katalog 179-182. Bibliotheca Americana relating to North and South America. Leipzig. Hiersemann. 1897. **494**

Historical Records Survey. Bibliography of American broadsides. Douglas C. McMurtrie. 950 Michigan Ave. Evanston, Ill. In progress **494a**

Hubbard, Lucius Lee. The valuable private library of Lucius L. Hubbard, of Houghton, Michigan, consisting almost wholly of rare books and pamphlets relating to American history. . . [N.Y. S. L. Parsons. 1914] 345p. **495**

Huntington, Henry E. Catalogue of rare Americana from the library of Mr. Henry E. Huntington. . . N.Y. D. Taylor. 1917. 104p. **496**

Jaray, Gabriel-Louis. Les principaux livres sur l'histoire de l'Amérique septentrionale de 1534 à 1803. France-Amérique. XXVII. p233-47. 1936 **496a**

John Carter Brown Library. Bibliotheca Americana; catalogue of the John Carter Brown Library in Brown University, Providence, Rhode Island. Providence. The Library. 1913-31. 3v. **497**

Jones, Herschel V. Adventures in Americana, 1492-1897; the romance of voyage and discovery from Spain to the Indies, the Spanish Main, and North America; inland to the Ohio country; on toward the Mississippi, through to California, over Chilkoot Pass to the gold fields of Alaska. . . . N.Y. W. E. Rudge. 1928. 142+300p. **498**

—— Americana collection of Herschel V. Jones, a check-list (1473-1926). Comp. by Wilberforce Eames. N.Y. Priv. print. by W. E. Rudge's sons. 1938. 220p. **498a**

Kelly, James. The American catalogue of books (original and reprints), published in the United States from Jan. 1861, to Jan. 1871, with date of publication, size, price, and publisher's name. N.Y. J. Wiley & Sons; London. N. Trubner & Co. 1866-71. 2v. (Reprinted N.Y. Peter Smith. 1938. 2v. Continuation of Roorbach's Bibliotheca Americana, 1820-1860; continued by the American catalogue, 1876-1910) **498b**

Kennett, White. Bibliotheca Americana primordia; an attempt towards laying the foundation of an American library. . . . London. Printed for G. Churchill, at the Black Swan in Paternoster Row. 1713. 275p. **499**

Leavitt, George A. & Co., auctioneers. Catalogue of the magnificent library of the late Hon. Henry C. Murphy, of Brooklyn, Long Island, consisting almost wholly of Americana or books relating to America. . . . N.Y. Leavitt. 1884. 434p. **500**

Leavitt, Strebeigh & Co. Bibliotheca Americana; catalogue of a private library . . . rare and valuable books relating to America, also local histories. . . . N.Y. 1870. 172p. **501**

—— Catalogue of an extraordinary collection of works relating to America. N.Y. Bradstreet Press. 1868. 140p. **502**

Leclerc, Charles. Bibliotheca Americana; catalogue raisonné d'une très précieuse collection de livres anciens et modernes sur l'Amérique et les Philippines classés par ordre alphabétique de noms d'auteurs. Paris. Maisonneuve et Cie. 1867. 424p. **503**

—— Bibliotheca americana; histoire, géographie, voyages, archéologie et linguistique des deux Amériques et des îles Philippines. Rédigée par Ch. Leclerc. Paris. Maisonneuve et Cie. 1878. 737p. (Supplement no. 1. Nov. 1881. 102p.; no. 2. 1887. 127p.) **504**

Lefferts, Marshall Clifford. Americana; books and autographs chiefly from the collection of Mr. Marshall C. Lefferts. . . . N.Y. Geo. H. Richmond. 1902. 66p. **505**

—— Catalogue of the remaining portion of the valuable collection of Americana formed by Marshall C. Lefferts, esq., of New York. . . . London. Dryden Press, J. Davy. 1902. 60p. **506**

Leiter, Levi Ziegler. The Leiter library; a catalogue of the books, manuscripts and maps relating principally to America collected by the late Levi Ziegler Leiter. With collations and bibliographical notes by Hugh Alexander Morrison. Wash. Priv. print. 1907. 533p. **507**

Libbie, C. F. & Co. Catalogue of the valuable private library of the late Charles Deane, LL.D., historian, comprising a fine collection of rare Americana, including early voyages and discoveries. . . . Boston. Libbie Show Print. [1898] 392p. **508**

McKay, George L. American book auction catalogues, 1713-1934, a union list. N.Y. N.Y. Pub. Lib. 1937. 540p. (Reprinted with additions from the N.Y. Pub. Lib. bul. XXXIX-XL. 1935-36) **509**

Maggs Brothers, bookseller. An illustrated catalogue raisonné of one hundred and six original manuscripts, autographs, maps, and printed books, illustrating the discovery & history of America, from 1492 to 1814. . . . Leamington Spa. Courier Press. 1929. 232p. **510**

—— Bibliotheca Americana. London. Maggs Brothers. 1922-30. 9v. **511**

Martin-Chabot, Eugène. Amérique Latine. *In* Histoire et historiens depuis cinquante ans. Paris. 1927. II. p473-88 **511a**

Medina, José Toribio. Catálogo breve de la Biblioteca Americana que obsequia á la nacional de Santiago. Santiago de Chile. Imprenta universitaria. 1926. 2v. **512**

Moore, George Henry. Catalogue of the library of the late George H. Moore, LL.D., for many years librarian of the N.Y. Historical Society, and superintendent of the Lenox Library. . . to be sold. . . by Bangs & Co. [N.Y. 1893-94] 2v. **513**

Muller, Frederik. Books on America; early voyages. Catalogue of books, maps, plates on America, and of a remarkable collection of early voyages . . . and presenting an essay towards a Dutch-American bibliography. . . . Amsterdam. Frederik Muller. 1872. 288p. **514**

—— Catalogue of books and pamphlets, atlases, maps, plates and autographes (sic) relating to North and South America, including the collections of early voyages by de Bry, Hulsius, Hartgers, etc. . . . Amsterdam. Frederik Muller. 1877. 218p. **515**

—— Catalogue of books relating to America; including a large number of rare works printed before 1700 amongst which a nearly complete collection of the Dutch publications on New Netherland from 1612 to 1820. Amsterdam. Frederik Muller. 1850. 104p. **516**

Murphy, Henry C. A catalogue of an American library, chronologically arranged. Brooklyn. Priv. print. 1853? 58p. **517**

'Museo Mitre.' Catálogo de la Biblioteca Ministerio de Justicia é Instrucción Publica. Buenos Aires. 1907. 704p. **517a**

Norton, Chas. B. Catalogue of a large and valuable collection of books, relating chiefly to America. N.Y. John A. Gray. 1862. 138p. **518**

O'Halloran, T. P. A bibliography of South America. Buenos Aires. Mackern; London. T.F. Unwin. 1912. 55p. **518a**

Palma, Ricardo. Catálogo de los libros que existen en el Salon América. Lima. Biblioteca Nacional. 1891. 217p. **518b**

Pan American Institute of Geography and History. Library. Catálogo de la biblioteca (1930-1939). Preparado por su director, Jorge A. Vivó (Publicación núm. 47) Tacubaya, D.F. 1940. 412p. **518c**

Paris. Bibliothèque Nationale. Inventaire des livres et documents relatifs à l'Amérique, recueillis et légués à la Bibliothèque Nationale par M. Angrand. Paris. 1887. 75p. **518d**

Parsons, Wilfrid. Early Catholic Americana; a list of books and other works by Catholic authors in the United States, 1729-1830. N.Y. Macmillan. 1939. 282p. **518e**

—— Researches in early Catholic Americana. Bibliog. Soc. Am. pap. XXXIII. p55-68. 1939 **518f**

Pinart, Alphonse Louis et L'Abbé Brasseur de Bourbourg. Catalogue de livres rares et precieux manuscrits et imprimés principalement sur l'Amérique et sur les langues du monde entier. Composant la bibliothèque de M. Alph.-L. Pinart et . . . la bibliothèque Mexico-Guatémalienne de M. L'Abbé Brasseur de Bourbourg. Paris. Vve. Adolphe Labitte. Libraire de la Bibliothèque nationale. 1883. 248p. **519**

Porrúa Hermanos, booksellers. Catálogo de libros impresos en América o que tratan de América y de algunos otros raros o curiosos de la librería de Porrúa hermanos. México, D.F. 1931. 208p. **519a**

Power, Eugene B. Source materials for the study of American culture. Jour. doc. reprod. III. p192-7 (Sept. 1940) (Microfilm collections of American periodicals, 1741-1799 and 250 books on America, 1493-1800) **519b**

Puttick and Simpson, auctioneers. Bibliotheca Americana. A catalogue of books relating to the history and literature of America. . . . London. 1861. 273p. **520**

Quaritch, Bernard, firm. A catalogue of works dealing with geography, voyages and travels, chiefly concerning America, Africa and Australia, with some books on the natural history & languages of those continents. London. Bernard Quaritch. 1915. 156p. **521**

Rich, Obadiah. Bibliotheca Americana nova; or, a catalogue of books in various languages, including voyages to the Pacific and round the world, and collections of voyages and travels printed since the year 1700. Compiled principally from the works themselves. London. Rich. 1846. 2v. **522**

—— A catalogue of books relating principally to America, arranged under the years in which they were printed (1500-1700). London. 1832. 129p. **523**

Robinson, William H., Ltd. Books relating to America. . . . Birmingham, England. F. Juckes, Ltd., printers. 1933. 115p. **524**

Rosenbach Company, firm, booksellers. A catalogue of an exhibition of memorable documents in American history from Columbus to Hoover. . . . N.Y. Rosenbach. 1931. 107p. **525**

Sabin, Joseph. Bibliotheca Americana; a dictionary of books relating to America from its discovery to the present time. Begun by Joseph Sabin, continued by Wilberforce Eames, and completed by R.W.G. Vail for the Bibliog. Soc. of Amer. N.Y. v. 1. N.Y. J. Sabin. 1868. v. 2-11. N.Y. J. Sabin & sons. 1869-79. v. 12-13. N.Y. J. Sabin's sons. 1880-81. v. 14-19. N.Y. Sabin. 1884-91. v. 20-26. N.Y. Bibliog. Soc. of Amer., W. E. Rudge. 1892-1936. v. 27-29. Bibliog Soc. of Amer., The Southworth-Anthoensen Press. Portland, Me. 1936 **526**

—— Catalogue of the books, manuscripts and engravings belonging to William Menzies of New York. N.Y. [Press of Joel Munsell. Albany, N.Y.] 1875. 473p. **527**

Santiago de Chile. Biblioteca Nacional. Cátalogo de la Sección Américana; América en general. Santiago de Chile. Imprenta universitaria. 1902. 152p. **527a**

Silber, Mendel. America in Hebrew literature. New Orleans. Steeg. 1928. 104p. (Article with same title in Am. Jewish Hist. Soc. pub. no. 22. p101-37. 1914) **528**

Skiff, Frederick Woodward. Adventures in Americana; recollections of forty years collecting books.... Portland, Ore. Metropolitan Press. 1935. 366p. (Particularly useful for the Pacific Northwest and Oregon) **528a**

Smith, Alfred Russell. Bibliotheca Americana; a catalogue of a valuable collection of books and pamphlets, illustrating the history & geography of North & South America and the West Indies. London. Smith. 1874. 733p. **529**

Smith, John Russell. Bibliotheca Americana; a catalogue of a valuable collection of books, pamphlets, mss., maps, engravings and engraved portraits, illustrating the history and geography of North and South America, and the West Indies. . . . London. 1865. 308p. **530**

Stevens, Henry. Bibliotheca Americana; a catalogue of books relating to the history and literature of America. London. Puttick and Simpson. 1861. 273p. **531**

—— Bibliotheca geographica & historica; or, a catalogue of . . . (3,109 lots) illustrative of historical geography and geographical history. . . . London. H. Stevens. 1872. 361p. **532**

—— Bibliotheca historica; or, a catalogue of 5000 volumes of books and manuscripts relating chiefly to the history and literature of North and South America. . . . Boston. Houghton. 1870. 234p. **533**

—— Catalogue of the American books in the library of the British museum at Christmas MDCCCLVI. London. Chiswick Press. 1866. 4 pts in 1v. **534**

—— Historical nuggets; Bibliotheca Americana, or, a descriptive account of my collection of rare books relating to America. London. Whittingham & Wilkins. 1862-85. 3v. **535**

Stevens, Henry. Schedule of two thousand American historical nuggets taken from the Stevens diggings in September, 1870, and set down in chronological order of printing from 1490 to 1800 (1776), described and recommended as a supplement to my printed Bibliotheca Americana. London. Priv. print. 1870. 20p. **536**

—— Steven's historical collection; catalogue of the first portion of the extensive & varied collections of rare books and manuscripts relating chiefly to the history and literature of America, comprising the great collections of voyages & travels of De Bry (in Latin and German) Hulsius Thevenot Purchas and Hakluyt with early separate voyages of the Dutch, English and French navigators. . . . London. Sotheby, Wilkinson & Hodge. 1881, 1886. 2 pts. 229, 84p. **537**

Stevens, Henry, son, and Stiles, firm, London. Rare Americana; a catalogue of historical and geographical books & pamphlets relating to America, with numerous annotations bibliographical and descriptive. . . . [London. Dryden Press. 1927] 575p. **538**

Ternaux Compans, Henri. Bibliothèque américaine; ou catalogue des ouvrages relatifs à l'Amérique qui ont paru depuis sa découverte jusqu'à l'an 1700. Paris. Arthus Bertrand. 1837. 191p. **539**

Trömel, Paul Friedrich. Bibliothèque Américaine; catalogue raisonné d'une collection de livres précieux sur l'Amérique, parus depuis sa découverte jusqu'à l'an 1700. . . . Leipzig. Brockhaus. 1861. 133p. **540**

Valle, Rafael Heliodoro. Bibliografía de historia de America, 1937-1938. Rev. hist. amer. I. no. 1, p113-41, no. 2, 125-51, no. 3, 136-64, no. 4, 161-209. 1938 (to be cont.) **540a**

Vicuña Mackenna, Benjamín. Bibliografía americana; estudios i catálogo completo i razonadado de la biblioteca americana coleccionada por el Sr. Gregorio Beéche. Valparaiso. 1879. 795p. **540b**

—— Catálogo completo de la biblioteca americana, compuesta de mas de 3,000 volumenes que posee Don Benjamín Vicuña Mackenna. Valparaiso. Impr. y libreria del Mercurio. 1861. 60p. **540c**

Warden, David B. Bibliotheca Americana, being a choice collection of books relating to North and South America and the West Indies, including voyages to the southern hemisphere. Paris. 1840. 124p. **541**

—— Bibliotheca Americo-septentrionalis; being a choice collection of books in various languages, relating to the history, climate, geography, produce, population, agriculture, commerce, arts, sciences, etc., of North America, from its discovery to its present existing government . . . with all the important official documents published . . . by the authority of Congress. Paris. Nouzou. 1820. 147p. **542**

Whitney, James Lyman. Catalogue of the Spanish library and of the Portuguese books bequeathed by George Ticknor to the Boston Public Library, together with the collection of Spanish and Portuguese literature in the general library. Boston. The Trustees. 1879. 476p. **543**

Woodward, William Elliot. Bibliotheca Americana; catalogue of the library of W. Elliot Woodward of Boston Highlands, Mass. Boston. L.B. Webster. 1869. 668p. **544**

Wright, J. O. Catalogue of the American library of Samuel Latham Mitchell Barlow. N.Y. n.p. 1889. 450p. **545**

Yarmolinsky, Avrahm. Early Polish Americana; a bibliographical study. With an appendix: A legendary predecessor of Columbus. N.Y. N. Y. Pub. Lib. 1937. 79p. (Reprinted with revisions and additions from the N. Y. Pub. Lib. bul. April 1934; March, July, Dec. 1935; May 1936) **545a**

—— Studies in Russian Americana. N. Y. Pub. Lib. bul. XLIII. p539-43, 895-900 (July, Dec. 1939) **545b**

ANTIQUITIES

Ambrosetti, Juan Bautista. Antigüedad del Nuevo mundo. (Crítica al doctor Latouche-Treville á propósito de su artículo titulado "L'antiquité du nouveau monde l'Amérique avant Colomb") Buenos Aires. J. Peuser. 1903. 16p. (Extracto de la Revista de derécho, historia y letras) **546**

Archaeological news and discussions; notes on recent archaeological excavations, summaries of original articles chiefly in current publications. Am. jour. arch. I. no. 1. 1897- **547**

Collins, Varnum Lansing. Index to the American journal of archaeology, volumes I-X, with an appendix for volume XI. Princeton. Princeton Univ. Press. 1890. 166p. **548**

Fewkes, Jesse W. Commemoration of the fourth centenary of the discovery of America. Columbian Historical Exposition, Madrid. Catalogue of the Hemenway collection in the Historico-American Exposition of Madrid. From the report of the Madrid Commission. 1892. Wash. Govt. Ptg. Off. 1895. p279-327 (Includes a list of The Bandelier collection of copies of documents relative to the history of New Mexico and Arizona. p305-26) (Antiquities of the Southwest) **549**

Haven, Samuel F. Archaeology of the United States; or. sketches, historical and bibliographical of the progress of information and opinion respecting vestiges of antiquity in the United States. N.Y. Putnam. 1856. 168p. (Also in Smithsonian contributions to knowledge. VIII. p 1-168. Wash. D.C. Smithsonian Inst. 1856) **550**

Merrill, William Stetson. Archaeological Institute of America. Index to publications, 1879-1889. Cambridge. John Wilson, Harvard Univ. Press. 1891. 89p. **552**

Paton, Lucy Allen. American journal of archaeology, second series, The Journal of the Archaeological Institute of America, index to volumes I-X, 1897-1906. N.Y. Macmillan. 1908. 285p. **553**

A preliminary archaeological bibliography of the eastern United States—parts one and two. Archaeol. Soc. of Conn. bul. IX. p1-68 (Oct. 1939); X. p. 1-32 (Jan. 1940) **553a**

Rivet, Paul and others. Bibliographie Américaniste. Journal de la Société des Américanistes de Paris, n.s. XII- Paris. Au siège de la société. 1920- (Also extracted. 1925-) **554**

Sabin, Joseph. Catalogue of the library of E.G. Squier. . . . N.Y. C.C. Shelly. 1876. 277p. (Contains: A list of books, pamphlets, and more important contributions to periodicals, etc., by E. George Squier. N.Y. 1876. 8p.) **555**

Sellards, E. H. Early man in America: index to localities and selected bibliography. Geol. Soc. of Amer. bul. LI. p373-432 (March 1940) **555a**

Société des Américanistes de Paris. Bulletin critique. Journal de la Société des Américanistes de Paris. n.s. I-XII. Paris. Au siège de la société. 1903-20 (Reviews of books) **556**

U.S. Library of Congress. Division of bibliography. List of references on mounds and mound-builders. June 29, 1923. 12p. typ. **557**

—— —— —— List of references on pre-Columbian art in America. May 24, 1926. 21p. typ. **558**

Winsor, Justin. [Bibliography of American Indians—antiquities, industries and trade —American linguistics—myths and religions—archaeological museums and periodicals]. *In* Narrative and critical history of America. Boston, N.Y. Houghton Mifflin. 1889. I. p413-44 **559**

—— The progress of opinion respecting the origin and antiquity of man in America. *In* Narrative and critical history of America. Boston, N.Y. Houghton Mifflin. 1889. I. p369-412 **560**

CHAPTER II

COLONIAL PERIOD, REVOLUTION, CONFEDERATION

DISCOVERY

Adams, Randolph G. The case of the Columbus letter. N.Y. N. Y. Univ. Book Store. 1939. 35p. (A bibliographical summary of the 15th century editions) **560a**

Asher, Adolf. Bibliographical essay on the collection of voyages and travels published by Levinus Hulsius, at Nuremberg and Francfort, from 1598 to 1660. Berlin. A. Asher. 1839. 118p. **561**

Batalha-Reis, J. The supposed discovery of South America before 1448, and the critical methods of the historians of geographical discovery. Geog. jour. IX. p185-210 (Feb. 1897) **561a**

Bibliographical account of the voyages of Columbus. Hist. mag. V. p33-8 (Feb. 1861) **562**

Binayán, Narciso. Henry Harrisse; ensayo biobibliográfico. [Buenos Aires. Universidad nacional] Publicaciones del Instituto de investigaciones historicas, no. XVI) Buenos Aires. Talleres s.a. Casa Jacobo Perser. 1923. 36p. **562a**

Boston. Public Library. America before Columbus. Boston Pub. Lib. bul. III. p65-9 (April 1876) **563**

—— —— Arctic regions and Antarctic regions. Boston Pub. Lib. bul. V. p21-49 (April 1894) **564**

—— —— Columbus: a list of the writings of Christopher Columbus, and of the works relating to him in the possession of the Public Library of the city of Boston. Boston Pub. Lib. bul. XI. p221-33 (Oct. 1892) **565**

—— —— Discoveries in America—Early historians and later collections. Boston Pub. Lib. bul. III. p207-9 (April 1877) **566**

—— —— Early English explorations in America. Boston Pub. Lib. bul. III. p241-4 (July 1877) **567**

—— —— Early explorations in America. Boston Pub. Lib. bul. III. p103-6, 136-41 (July-Oct. 1876) **568**

Boucher de la Richarderie, Gilles. Bibliothèque universelle des voyages. Paris. Treuttel et Wurtz. 1908 (Cinquième partie. Voyages en Amérique, et descriptions de cette partie du monde. v. V-VI) **569**

British Museum. Department of printed books. Catalogue of printed books, Colombo (Cristoforo). London. 1886. (From the Catalogue of printed books, pt. Colm-Comly. 1886, p55-63) **570**

Budinger, Max. Zur Columbus literatur. Vienna. 1889. (Article from Mitt. der K. K. Geog. Gesell. 1889. Vienna Acad. of Sciences) **571**

Camus, A. G. Mémoire sur la collection des grands et petits voyages, et sur la collection Thevenot. Paris. Baudouin, Imprimeur de l'Institut national. 1802. 401p. **572**

Cancellieri, Francesco Girolamo. Dissertazioni epistolari bibliografiche di Francesco Cancellieri sopra Cristoforo Colombo. . . . Roma. F. Bovrlie. 1809. 415p. **573**

Channing, Edward. Critical essay on the sources of information—The companions of Columbus. *In* Narrative and critical history of America. Ed. by Justin Winsor. Boston, N.Y. Houghton Mifflin. 1884. II. p204-16 **574**

Cole, George Watson. De Bry's collection of great and small voyages. *In* Church, E.D. A catalogue of books relating to the discovery and early history of North and South America. . . . N.Y. Dodd, Mead. 1907. I. p316-478; II. p478a-580 **575**

Cordier, Henri. Bibliographie. *In* Henry Harrisse, 1830-1910. Chartres. Durand. 1910? p9-39 **576**

Cutter, Charles A. A bibliographical description of the collection of "Grand voyages" of De Bry translated from Brunet's "Manuel du librarie." N.Y. Priv. print. 1869. 61p. **577**

Dawson, Samuel Edward. The voyages of the Cabots; latest phases of the controversy. Royal Soc. of Canada. Trans. III. p139-268. 1897 **577a**

Deane, Charles. Critical essay on the sources of information—The voyages of the Cabots. *In* Narrative and critical history of America. Ed. by Justin Winsor. Boston, N.Y. Houghton Mifflin. 1884. III. p7-58 **578**

DeCosta, Benjamin F. Bibliography of Verrazano. Mag. of Am. hist. VI. p68-70 (Jan. 1881) **579**

—— Critical essay on the sources of information—Norumbega and its English explorers. *In* Narrative and critical history of America. Ed. by Justin Winsor. Boston, N.Y. Houghton Mifflin. 1884. III. p184-98   580

Dexter, George. Critical essay on the sources of information—Cortereal, Verrazano, Gomez, Thevet. *In* Narrative and critical history of America. Ed. by Justin Winsor. Boston, N.Y. Houghton Mifflin. 1884. IV. p12-32   581

Farinelli, Arturo. Viájes por España y Portugal desde la edad media hasta el siglo XX. Divagaciones bibliográficas. Madrid. n.p. 1920. 511p.   582

Fischer, Joseph. The discoveries of the Norsemen in America, with special relation to their early cartographical representation. London. H. Stevens, Son & Stiles; St. Louis. B. Herder. 1903. 130p.   582a

Fumagalli, Giuseppe and Amat di S. Filippo, Pietro. Bibliografia degli scritti italiani o stampati in Italia sopra Cristoforo Colombo, la scoperta del Nuovo Mondo e i viaggi degli Italiani in America. (Commissione Colombiana. Raccolta di documenti e studi. Parte VI. v.I) Roma. Ministero della pubblica istruzione. 1893. 217p. (Bibliografica Italo-Americana della geografia di America on p113-217)   583

Genoa. Biblioteca Berio. Catalogo delle opere componenti la raccolta Colombiana esistente nella cinica Biblioteca Berio de Genova. Genova. Fratelli Pagano. 1906. 126p.   584

Geoffroy, Atkinson. La littérature géographique française de la Renaissance: répertoire bibliographique. Paris. August Picard. 1927. 565p.   585

Growoll, Adolf. Henry Harrisse, biographical and bibliographical sketch. N.Y. Dibdin Club. 1899. 16p.   586

Haebler, Konrad. Die neuere Columbusliteratur. Historische zeitschrift, Der Ganzen Reihe. LVII. neue folge. XXI. p222-34. 1887   587

—— Sur quelques incunables espagnols relatifs à Christophe Colomb. Besançon. Imprimerie et lithographie de Paul Jacquin. 1900. 24p. (Extrait du Bibliographie moderne. III. p365-86. 1899) 588

Hakluyt Society. The Hakluyt Society (founded 1846) prospectus and list of members, with a list of publications and maps. London. Printed for the Soc. at the Bedford Press. 1934. lv p.   589

Harrisse, Henry. Bibliotheca americana vetustissima; a description of works relating to America published between the years 1492 and 1551. N.Y. Geo. P. Philes. 1866. 519p. (Additions to this published in Paris. 1872. 199p.)   590

—— Christophe Colomb et ses historiens espagnols, 12 Octobre, 1892. Paris [Le Puy, Imp. Marchesson fils] 1892. 19p. (Extrait de la Revue critique d'histoire et de littérature) (This is a critique of Asenio's work on Columbus.)   591

—— The discovery of North America; a critical, documentary, and historic investigation, with an essay on the early cartography of the new world, including descriptions of two hundred and fifty maps or globes, existing or lost, constructed before the year 1536. Paris. H. Welter; London. H. Stevens and Son; [Rochdale, England. J. Clegg. print. Aldine Press] 1892. 802p.   591a

—— The early Paris editions of Columbus's first "epistola." Extract from the Centralblatt für bibliothekswesen. Leipzig. Otto Harrassowitz. 1893. 6p.   592

—— Excerpta Colombiana: bibliographie de quatre cents pièces gothiques, françaises, italiennes et latines du commencement du XVIᵉ siècle, non décrites jusqu'ici. Précédée d'une histoire de la bibliothèque Colombine et de son fondateur. Paris. H. Welter. 1887. 315p. 593

—— D. Fernand Colon, historiador de su padre. Ensayo critico. Sevilla. R. Tarascó. 1871. 220p. Paris. Tross. 1872. 230p.   594

—— Jean et Sebastien Cabot, leur origine et leurs voyages. Étude d'histoire critique, suivie d'une cartographie, d'une bibliographie et d'une chronologie des voyages au Nord-Ouest, de 1497 à 1559. . . . Paris. E. Leroux. 1882. 400p.   595

—— Notes on Columbus. N.Y. Priv. print. 1866. 227p. (Includes maps)   596

—— Opera minora; Christophe Colomb et des academiciens espagnols; notes pour servir à l'histoire de la science en Espagne au XIXᵉ siècle. . . . Paris. H. Welter. 1894. 157p.   597

Henry, William Wirt. Critical essay on the sources of information—Sir Walter Raleigh: settlements at Roanoke and voyages to Guiana. *In* Narrative and critical history of America. Ed. by Justin Winsor. Boston. Houghton Mifflin. 1884. III. p121-6   598

Hermannsson, Halldór. Bibliography of the Eddas (Islandica, XIII). Ithaca, N.Y. Cornell Univ. Lib. 1920. 95p.   599

—— Bibliography of the Icelandic sagas and minor tales (Islandica, I). Ithaca, N.Y. Cornell Univ. Lib. 1908. 126p. 600

—— Bibliography of the mythical-heroic sagas (Islandica, V). Ithaca, N.Y. Cornell Univ. Lib. 1912. 73p.   601

—— Bibliography of the sagas of Norway and related sagas and tales (Islandica, III). Ithaca, N.Y. Cornell Univ. Lib. 1910. 75p.   602

—— The Northmen; a contribution to the bibliography of the subject in America (Islandica, II). Ithaca, N.Y. Cornell Univ. Lib. 1909. 94p.   603

—— Old Icelandic literature; a bibliographical essay (Islandica, XXIII). Ithaca, N.Y. Cornell Univ. Lib. 1933. 50p.   604

—— Sagas of the kings (konunga sögur) and the mythical-heroic sagas (fornaldar sögur). (Islandica, v. 26) Ithaca. Cornell Univ. Press. 1937. 72p.   604a

Hessels, J. H. Essai sur les éditions de la première lettre de Colomb imprimées avant 1500. Bibliophile Belge. 6e année. p93-121. 1871   **605**

Humboldt, Alexander, freiherr von. Examen critique de l'histoire de la géographie du nouveau continent et des progrès de l'astronomie nautique aux 15me et 16me siècles. Paris. Gide. 1836-39. 5v.   **605a**

Kretschmer, Konrad. Die literatur zur geschichte der erdkunde vom mittelalter an (1907-25). Geographisches jahrbuch. XLI. p122-92. 1926   **605b**

Lenox Library, New York. Contributions to a catalogue of The Lenox Library, no. 1. Voyages of Hulsius, etc. N.Y. Printed for the Trustees. 1878. 24p.   **606**

Lollis, Cesare de. Cristoforo Colombo nella leggenda e nella storia. Milano, Roma. Soc. editrice "La cvltvra." 1931. 425p.   **606a**

Ludovic, Earl of Crawford and Balcarres. Bibliotheca Lindesiana. Collations and notes, no. 3. Grands et petits voyages of De Bry. London. Bernard Quaritch. 1884. 215p.   **607**

Major, Richard Henry. The bibliography of the first letter of Christopher Columbus, describing his discovery of the New World. London. Ellis & White. 1872. 61p.   **608**

Marcellino, da Civezza. Saggio di bibliografia geografica storica etnografica sanfrancescana. Prato. R. Guasti. 1879. 698p.   **608a**

Markham, Albert Hastings. An enumeration of the works on the art of navigation previous to and during the age of Elizabeth. *In* The voyages and works of John Davis, the navigator (Works issued by the Hakluyt Soc. LIX. p339-67) London. 1880   **609**

Medina, José Toribio. Bibliografía hispanocabotiana. *In* El veneziano Sebastian Caboto, al servício de España y especialeménte de su proyectada viaje á las Molucas por el Estrecho de Magallanes y al reconocimiénto de la costa del continente hasta la gobernacion de Pedrarias Davila. Santiago de Chile. Impr. y encuadernacion universitaria. 1908. I. p551-608   **610**

Merrill, William Stetson. Bibliography of the Vinland voyages of the Norsemen. In progress   **610a**

—— The Catholic contribution to the history of Norse discovery of America. Cath. hist. rev. VII. p589-619 (Jan. 1928)   **610b**

Modena. R. Biblioteca Estense. Mostra Colombiana e Americana della R. Biblioteca Estense; documenti e edizioni a stampa esposti del R. archivio di stato e dalla R. Biblioteca estense di Modena nell'anniversario della scoperta dell'America. Modena. Società tipografica Modenese, Antica tipografia Soliani. 1925. 108p.   **611**

Murphy, H. C. Lijst van stukken betreffende Niew Nederland verschenen in Amerikaansche mengelwerken. n.p. n.p. n.d. 12p.   **612**

New York. Public Library. Catalogue of the De Bry collection of voyages in the New York Public Library. N.Y. Pub. Lib. bul. VIII. p230-43 (May 1904) (Reprinted, 1909)   **613**

Packard, Alpheus Spring. Bibliography of books and articles relating to the geography and civil and natural history of Labrador. *In* The Labrador coast; a journal of two summer cruises to that region. N.Y. Hodges. 1891. p475-501 **614**

Parks, George Bruner. Richard Hakluyt and the English voyages. (Am. Geog. Soc. Special publication. no. 10) N.Y. Am. Geog. Soc. 1928. 289p. (Contains: A list of Hakluyt's writings, p260-8; and A list of English books on geography and travel to 1600, p269-77)   **615**

Petherick, Edward Augustus, comp. Catalogue of the York Gate Library formed by Mr. S. William Silver; an index to the literature of geography, maritime and inland discovery, commerce and colonisation. London. John Murray. 1886 (Section on America and the West Indies, p284-324)   **616**

Proctor, Robert George Collier. Jan van Doesborgh, printer at Antwerp; an essay in bibliography. (Bibliog. Soc. Monograph no. 2. Dec. 1894) London. 1894. 101p. (Contains material on a letter of Vespucius to Lorenzo de'Medici)   **617**

Purchas, Samuel. Index. Hakluytus posthumus; or, Purchas his pilgrimes, contayning a history of the world in sea voyages and lande travells by Englishmen and others. Glasgow. James MacLehose and Sons. 1907. XX. p139-415   **618**

Putnam, Herbert. A Columbus codex. Critic. XLII. p244-51 (March 1903) **618a**

Quaritch, Bernard. A catalogue of geography, voyages, travels, Americana. London. 1895. 200p.   **619**

Real Academia de la Historia. Bibliografía Colombina; enumeración de libros y documentos concerniéntes á Cristobal Colón y sus viajes, obra que publica La Real Academia de la Historia. Madrid. Fortanet. 1892. 680p.   **620**

Royal Empire Society. Voyages and travels, Arctic and Antarctic regions. *In* Subject catalogue of the library of the Royal Empire Society, formerly Royal Colonial Institute. By Evans Lewin. London. The Royal Empire Soc. 1931. II. p573-664   **621**

Sabin, Joseph. A list of printed editions of the works of Fray Bartolomé de Las Casas, Bishop of Chiapa. N.Y. J. Sabin & Sons. 1870. 27p. (Extracted from Sabin's Dictionary of books relating to America)   **622**

Santarem, Manuel, Le Vicomte de. Recherches historiques, critiques et bibliographiques sur Améric Vespuce et ses voyages. Paris. Arthus Bertrand. 1842. 335+19p. (Trans. by E. V. Childe. Boston. C. C. Little. 1850. 221p.) **623**

Serrano y Sanz, Manuel. El archivo colombino de la Cartuja de las Cuevas; estudio histórico y bibliográfico. Madrid. Tip. de archivos. 1930. 215p. **624**

Servano Arbolé y Farando. Bibliotheca Colombina. Catálogo de sus libros impresos publicado por primera vez en virtud de acuerdo del excmo é ilmo. . . . Sevilla. Imp. de E. Rasco, Bastos Tavera. 1888-94. 3v. **625**

Shea, John G. Critical essay on the sources of information—Ancient Florida. *In* Narrative and critical history of America. Ed. by Justin Winsor. Boston, N.Y. Houghton Mifflin. 1884. II. p283-98 **626**

Stevens, Henry. Historical and geographical notes on the earliest discoveries in America, 1453-1530, with comments on the earliest charts and maps; the mistakes of the early navigators & the blunders of the geographers. New Haven, Conn. Am. Jour. of Sci. 1869. 54p. **626a**

Thacher, Joseph Boyd. The continent of America; its discovery and its baptism. An essay on the nomenclature of the old continents. A critical and bibliographical inquiry into the naming of America, and into the growth of the cosmography of the New World. N.Y. W.E. Benjamin. 1896. 270p. **626b**

Tiele, Pieter Anton. Mémoire bibliographique sur les journaux des navigateurs Néerlandais, réimprimés dans les collections de le Bry et de Hulsius, et dans les collections hollandaises du XVIIᵉ siècle et sur les anciennes éditions hollandaises des journaux de navigateurs étrangers. . . . Amsterdam. F. Muller. 1867. 372p. **627**

—— Nederlandsche bibliographie van landen volkenkunde. Amsterdam. F. Muller. 1884. 288p. **628**

Tillinghast, William H. Critical essay on the sources of information—Notes—The geographical knowledge of the ancients considered in relation to the discovery of America. *In* Narrative and critical history of America. Ed. by Justin Winsor. Boston, N.Y. Houghton Mifflin. 1889. I. p33-58 **629**

Travaux de la Commission des grands voyages et des grandes découvertes—bibliographie. International Com. of Hist. Science. bul. VII. pt. iv. no. 29. p363-445 (Dec. 1935) (Books and articles pub. from 1912-31. Amérique. p409-18; Christophe Colomb, p419-29; Amérique (par régions) p429-37) **629a**

U.S. Library of Congress. Division of bibliography. List of books in English on Greenland. Oct. 19, 1931. 7p. typ. **630**

Vignaud, Henry. Bibliografia della polemica concernente Paolo Toscanelli e Cristoforo Colombo originata dalle comunicazioni di Gonzalez de la Rosa e di Enrico Vignaud al Congresso degli Americanisti tenuto a Parigi nel settembre del 1900. Napoli, Tocco-Salvietti, 1905. 36p. **631**

—— Bibliography of Toscanelli-Columbus correspondence. *In* Toscanelli and Columbus: letters to Sir Clements R. Markham . . . and to C. Raymond Beazley. London. Sands & Co. 1903. p5-14 (Cont. in the author's Toscanelli and Columbus: a letter from Sir Clements R. Markham. . . . 1903. p5-6, and in his La route des Indes et les indications que Toscanelli aurait fournies a Colomb. 1903. p5-6) **631a**

—— A critical study of the various dates assigned to the birth of Christopher Columbus, the real date, 1451, with a bibliography of the question. London. H. Stevens Son & Stiles. 1903. 121p. **631b**

—— Henry Harrisse. Étude biographique et morale avec la bibliographie critique de ses écrits. Paris. Librairie Ch. Chadenat. 1912. 83p. **632**

—— Histoire critique de la grande entreprise de Christophe Colomb; comment il aurait conçu et formé son projet, sa présentation à différentes cours, son acceptation finale, sa mise a exécution—son véritable caractère. Paris. H. Welter. 1911. 2v. **632a**

—— La maison d'Albe et les archives Colombiennes, avec un appendice sur les manuscrits que possédait Fernan Colomb et un tableau généalogique. [Paris] Aux siège de la Société. 1904. 17p. (Extrait du Journal de la Société des américanistes de Paris, t. 1, no. 3) **632b**

Wallace, W. S. The literature relating to the Norse voyages to America. Canad. hist. rev. XX. p8-16 (March 1939) **632c**

Watson, Paul Barron. Bibliography of the pre-Columbian discoveries of America. Lib. jour. VI. p227-44 (Aug. 1881) (Also in Rasmus B. Anderson's America not discovered by Columbus. Chicago. S.C. Griggs. 1883. p121-64) **633**

Wilgus, A. Curtis. Some sixteenth century histories and historians of America. Pan Am. Union bul. LXVII. p558-65, 741-9 (July 1933) **634**

Willis, William. A bibliographical essay on the early collections of voyages to America. New England hist. and geneal. reg. XV. p97-104, 205-16 (April, July 1861) **635**

Winship, George Parker. Cabot bibliography, with an introductory essay on the careers of the Cabots based upon an independent examination of the sources of information. N.Y. Dodd, Mead. 1900. 180p. (Shorter list appeared in the Providence Pub. Lib. bul. III. p137-57. June 1897, which was also reprinted) **636**

Winsor, Justin. The bibliography of Pomponius Mela, Solinus, Vadianus, and Apianus. *In* Narrative and critical history of America. Boston; N.Y. Houghton Mifflin. 1886. II. p181-6   **636a**
—— A bibliography of Ptolemy's geography. (Lib. of Harvard Univ. Bibliog. contributions. no. 18) Cambridge. Harvard Univ. Press, John Wilson and son. 1884. 42p. (Republished from the Bul. of Harvard Univ. nos. 24-9. Jan. 1883-Oct. 1884) **637**
—— Critical and bibliographical notes on Vespucius and the naming of America. *In* Narrative and critical history of America. Boston, N.Y. Houghton Mifflin. 1884. II. p153-79   **638**
—— Critical essay on the sources of information—Notes—Columbus and his discoveries. *In* Narrative and critical history of America. Boston, N.Y. Houghton Mifflin. 1886. II. p24-92   **639**
—— Critical notes on the sources of information—Pre-Columbian explorations. *In* Narrative and critical history of America. Boston, N.Y. Houghton Mifflin. 1889. I. p76-116   **640**
—— The early descriptions of America and collective accounts of the early voyages thereto. *In* Narrative and critical history of America. Boston, N.Y. Houghton Mifflin. 1891. I. p.xix-xxxvii   **641**
—— Sources, and the gatherers of them—biographers and portraitists. *In* Christopher Columbus and how he received and imparted the spirit of discovery. Boston. Houghton Mifflin. 1891. p1-70   **643**
Yarmolinsky, Avrahm. Bibliographical studies in early Polish Americana. N.Y. Pub. Lib. bul. XXXIX. March 1935-   **644**

SPANISH INFLUENCE

Altamira y Crevea, Rafael et Capdequi, José María Oto. Bibliographie d'histoire coloniale (1900-1930) Espagne. Premier congrès international d'histoire coloniale Paris, 1931. Paris. Société de l'Histoire des Colonies Françaises. 1932. 69p. **645**
Arana, Enrique. Catálogo razonado; libros, folletos y mapas en su mayoria referentes a Hispano America, historia, derecho, bibliografía, imprenta, viajeros, ingleses, etc., pertenecientes a la biblioteca de Enrique Arana. Buenos Aires. 1935 **645a**
Bancroft, Hubert Howe. The early American chroniclers. San Francisco. A.L. Bancroft. 1883. 45p. **646**
Barros Arana, Diego. Estudios histórico-bibliográficos. (Obras completas. Tom. 6, 8-11) Santiago de Chile. Imprenta Cervantes. 1909-11. 5v. **646a**
Beristan de Souza, José Mariano. Biblioteca hispano americana septentrional. . . . Mexico [A. Valdés] 1816-21. 3v. (A second edition was published in 1883; an additional volume in 1897, and another in 1898.) **646b**

Brevoort, J. C. Spanish-American documents printed or inedited. Mag. Am. hist. III. p175-8 (Jan. 1879) **646c**
Buenos Aires. Biblioteca Nacional. Catálogo cronológico de reales cédulas, órdenes, decretos, provisiones, etc., referentes a América, 1508-1810. Seguido de un índice alfabético de [nombres de persona y otro auxiliar de lugares, instituciones, órdenes religiosas, pueblos indígenas, mitos, animales y cosas. Buenos Aires. Imprenta de la Biblioteca Nacional. 1938. 302p. **646d**
California. University. Library. Spain and Spanish America in the libraries of The University of California; a catalogue of books. Berkeley, Calif. 1928, 1930. 2v. **647**
Carbonell, Diego. Historiadores de Indias. Anales de la Universidad central de Venezuela. XXVI. p54-107. 1938 **647a**
Casteneda, Carlos Eduardo. A report on the Spanish archives in San Antonio, Texas. San Antonio. Yanaguana soc. 1937 **647b**
Dunne, Peter M. The literature of the Jesuits of New Spain. Cath. hist. rev. XX. p248-59 (Oct. 1934) **647c**
Ellis, George E. Critical essay on the sources of information—Editorial note—Las Casas, and the relation of the Spaniards to the Indians. *In* Narrative and critical history of America. Ed. by Justin Winsor. Boston, N.Y. Houghton Mifflin. 1884. II. p331-48 **648**
Griffin, George Butler. A brief bibliographical sketch of the "Recopilacion de Indias"—or Spanish India code—and other collections of Spanish laws relating to the Indies, compiled during the sixteenth, seventeenth and eighteenth centuries. Hist. Soc. South. Calif. annual publications. I. p36-45. 1887 **648a**
Hanke, Lewis. Some studies in progress in Spain on Hispanic American history. Hisp. Am. hist. rev. XV. p105-13 (Feb. 1935) **649**
Haynes, Henry W. Critical essay on the sources of information—Editorial note—Early explorations of New Mexico. *In* Narrative and critical history of America. Ed. by Justin Winsor. Boston, N.Y. Houghton Mifflin. 1884. II. p473-504 **650**
Hispanic Society of America. Bibliographie Hispanique. N.Y. Putnam's. 1905-17 **651**
—— List of printed books in the library of The Hispanic Society of America. N.Y. [The De Vinne Press] 1910. 20v. **652**
—— **Library.** List of books printed 1601-1700, in the library of the Hispanic Society of America. Comp. by Clara Louise Penney. N.Y. 1938. 972p. **652a**
Hodge, Frederick W. Bibliography of Fray Alonso de Benavides. (Museum of the Am. Indian, Heye Foundation. Indian notes and monographs, III. no. 1) N.Y. 1919. 39p. **653**

Kilger, Laurenz. Systematisch-analytisches verzeichnis der abhandlungen, beiträge und rundschauen sowie der besprechungen und der bibliographie. Zeitschrift für missionswissenschaft und religionswissenschaft. XXV. p307-418, 1935 (Guide to the material in the first twenty-five volumes of that publication for the years 1910-35 on Spanish mission activity of the colonial period) **653a**

Lewis, T.H. The chroniclers of De Sota's expedition. *In* A symposium on the place of discovery of the Mississippi River by Hernando de Sota. (Miss. Hist. Soc. publications. Special bul. no. 1. ed. by Dunbar Rowland) Jackson, Miss. 1927. p1-10 **654**

—— The chroniclers of De Sota's expedition (through the Gulf states). Miss. Hist. Soc. publications. VII. p379-87. 1903 **655**

Librería Española e Hispañoamericana. Catálogo general de la Librería Española e Hispañoamericana; años 1901-1930; autores. Madrid. 1932-35. 3v. **656**

MacNutt, Francis Augustus. Bartholomew de Las Casas, his life, his apostolate, and his writings. N.Y., London. Putnam's. 1909. 472p. **656a**

Major, H. A. With the Spanish records of West Florida. East and West Baton Rouge hist. soc. proc. II. p60-4. 1917-1918 **656b**

Martin, Percy Alvin. Notes on recent books and articles in the Hispanic American field. Hisp. Am. hist. rev. XVII. p242-59 (May 1937) **656c**

Mecham, J. Lloyd. The northern expansion of New Spain, 1522-1822; a selected descriptive bibliographical list. Hisp. Am. hist. rev. VII. p233-76 (May 1927) **657**

Medina, José Toribio. Biblioteca hispano-Americana, 1493-1810. Santiago de Chile. El autor. 1898-1907. 7v. **658**

—— Noticias bio-bibliográficas de los Jesuítas expulsos de America en 1767. Santiago de Chile. Elzeviriana. 1914. 327p. **659**

Navarrete, Martin Fernandez de. Biblioteca marítima Española. . . . Madrid. Impr. de la Viúda de Calero. 1851. 2v. **660**

O'Hara, John F. The Benavides memorials. Cath. hist. rev. III. p76-7 (April 1917) (Catholic church in the southwest) **660a**

Palau y Dulcet, Antonio. Manuel del librero hispano-Americano; inventario bibliográfico de la producción científica y literaria de España y de la America latina desde de invención de la imprenta hasta nuestros dias, con el valor comercial de todos los articulos descritos. Barcelona. Librería anticuaria. 1923-27. 7v. **661**

Praesent, Hans. Ibero-Amerikanische bibliographie, I- . Berlin and Bonn. 1930/31- . 4 nos. (Beiläge zu "Ibero-amerikanisches archiv." V. p1-4) **662**

Puente y Olea, Manuel de la. Estudios españoles; los trabajos geográficos de la Casa de contratacion. . . . Seville. Escuela tipográfica y librería Salesianas. 1900. 451p. **662a**

Reid, Dorcas and Reid, John T. An annotated bibliography of books on Spanish South America and the West Indies. Hispania. XX. p313-26. 1937 **662b**

Roth, H. Ling. Bibliography and cartography of Hispaniola. Royal Geog. Soc. Supplementary pap. pt. 1. p41-97. 1889 **663**

Sánchez Alonso, Benito. Fuentes de la historia española e hispañoamericana; ensayo de bibliografía sistemática de impresos y manuscritos que ilustran la história política de España y sus antiquas províncias de ultramár. Madrid. Impr. clásica española. 1927. 2v. in 1 **664**

Smith, Carleton S. Seventeenth century bibliography of Latin America. N.Y. (In progress) **665**

Steere, Elizabeth B. Hispanic American bibliography of the colonial period. Univ. of Michigan. (In progress) **666**

Toro, Josefina del. A bibliography of the collective biography of Spanish America. (Univ. of Puerto Rico. bul. ser. 9, no. 1) Rio Piedras, P.R. 1938. 140p. **666a**

U.S. Library of Congress. Division of bibliography. List of references on the buccaneers and pirates of the Spanish Main. Oct. 16, 1923. 8p. typ. **667**

Vance, John Thomas. The background of Hispanic-American law; legal sources and juridical literature of Spain. Wash. D.C. Catholic Univ. of Am. 1937. 280p. **667a**

Vasquez, Alberto and Rose, R. Seldon, eds. Algunas cartas de Don Diego Hurtado de Mendoza. New Haven. Yale Univ. Press. 1940. 430p. **667b**

Vindel, Francisco. Manuel gráfico-descriptívo del bibliófilo hispano-americano (1475-1850). Madrid. F. Vindel. 1930-34. 12v. **668**

Vindel, Pedro. Biblioteca ultramarína; manuscrítos muchos de ellos origináles e inéditos referentes á América, China, Filipinas, Japón y otras países. . . . Madrid. [P. Vindel] 1917. p169-324 **669**

Wagner, Henry R. Bibliography of printed works in Spanish relating to those portions of the United States which formerly belonged to Mexico. Santiago de Chile. 1917. 43p. (Supplement. Berkeley, Calif. 1918. 8p.) **670**

—— The Spanish Southwest, 1542-1794; an annotated bibliography. [Quivira Society. Pub. v. VII) Albuquerque. The Quivira Soc. 1937. 2v. **671**

—— Suplemento al Bibliografía Mexicana del siglo XVI de Joaquin García Icazbalceta. In progress **671a**

Wilgus, Alva Curtis. Histories and historians of Hispanic America; a bibliographical essay. (Inter-Am. bibliog. and lib. publications. ser. I. 2) Wash. D.C. Inter-Am. Bibliog. and Lib. Asso. 1936. 113p. **672**

Wilgus, Alva Curtis. The historiography of Hispanic America. George Wash. Univ. (In progress) **672a**
—— Index to source material in English dealing with Latin America. Wash. D.C. George Washington Univ. In progress **672b**
—— Selected biographies of early explorers in America. Pan Am. mag. XLIII. p252-3 (Oct. 1930) **673**
—— A survey of investigations, in progress and contemplated, in the field of Hispanic American history. Hispanic Am. hist. rev. VII. p361-74 (Aug. 1927); XI. p411-24 (Aug. 1931); XV. p390-402 (Aug. 1935); XIX. p407-22 (Aug. 1939) **674**

Winship, George Parker. List of titles of documents relating to America contained in volumes I-CX of the Colección de documentos inéditos para la historia de España. [Boston. 1894] 14p. (Reprinted from the Boston Pub. Lib. bul. XIII. Oct. 1894; also in Inst. investigaciones hist. bol. IV. no. 27. p308-18, no. 28. p439-67, Jan., April 1926) **674a**
—— List of works useful to the student of the Coronado expedition. (U.S. Bureau of Ethnology. 14th annual report. 1892-93) Wash. Govt. Ptg. Off. 1896. p599-613. (Also reprinted in advance. Wash. D.C. 1896) **675**

Winsor, Justin. Bibliographical notes on the West Indies and the Spanish Main. *In* Narrative and critical history of America. Boston, N.Y. Houghton Mifflin. 1889. VIII. p270-94 **676**
—— Critical essay on the sources of information—Spanish North America. *In* Narrative and critical history of America. Boston, N.Y. Houghton Mifflin. 1889. VIII. p246-70 **677**
—— Discoveries on the Pacific coast of North America. *In* Narrative and critical history of America. Boston, N.Y. Houghton Mifflin. 1884. II. p431-72 **678**
—— Documentary sources of early Spanish-American history. *In* Narrative and critical history of America. Boston; N.Y. Houghton Mifflin. 1886. II. p i-ix **678a**

Wyllys, Rufus Kay. A short bibliography of works in English on the Spanish missions of the Southwest. Ariz. hist. rev. IV. p58-61 (Jan. 1932) **679**

FRENCH RÉGIME

Acadia University. Library. A catalogue of the Eric R. Dennis collection of Canadiana in the library of Acadia University. Prep. by Helen D. Beals. Wolfville, Nova Scotia. 1938. 212p. **679a**
André, Louis. Les sources de l'histoire de France: XVII° siècle (1610-1715). v. VI. Histoire maritime et coloniale, histoire religieuse (Manuels de bibliographie historique) Paris. Auguste Picard. 1932. 462p. **680**

Andrieux, Georges. Important livres et manuscrits relatifs aux Amériques et à la guerre d'indépendance, très précieux documents originaux sur la découverte et colonisation du Canada et de la Louisiane, manuscrits autographes de La Pérouse, Rochambeau, etc. vente à Paris. . . . Abbeville, Imprimerie F. Paillart. 130p. **680a**

Backer, Augustin de. Bibliothèque de la Compagnie de Jésus, Première partie: Bibliographie par les pères Augustin et Aloys de Backer. Seconde partie: Histoire par le père Auguste Carayon. Nouvelle édition par Carlos Sommervogel, S.J. . . . Bruxelles. Oscar Schepens; Paris. Alphonse Picard. 1890-1909. 10v. **681**

Bertrand, Louis. Bibliothèques Sulpicienne ou histoire littéraire de la Compagnie de Saint-Sulpice. Paris. Alphonse Picard. 1900. 3v. **682**

Bibaud, Maximilien (François Marie Uncas Maximilien). Bibliothèque canadienne, ou Annales bibliographiques. Montréal. Imprimé par Cérat et Bourguignon. 1858. 52p. **683**

Biggar, Henry Percival. Canada. *In* Histoire et historiens depuis cinquante ans. Paris. 1927. II. p489-99 **683a**
—— The Public Archives at Ottawa. Bul. of the Inst. of Hist. Research. II. p66-79; III. p38-44 (Feb., June 1925) **684**
—— The sources—introduction, official—narrative—anonymous. *In* Early trading companies of New France; a contribution to the history of commerce and discovery in North America. Toronto. Univ. of Toronto Lib. 1901. p171-296 **684a**

Boimare, A. L. Notes bibliographiques et raisonnées sur les principaux ouvrages publiés sur La Floride et l'ancienne Louisiane depuis leur découverte jusqu'à l'époque actuelle. . . . Paris. Priv. lithographed, 1855. 60p. (Reprinted in Louisiana hist. quar. I. p9-78. Sept. 1917) **685**

Bond, D. F. and others. Anglo-French and Franco-American studies; a current bibliography. Roman rev. XXXI. p133-46 (April 1940) **685a**

Bourgeois, Émile and André, Louis. Les sources de l'histoire de France, XVII° siècle (1610-1715) (Manuels de bibliographie historique III. Les sources de l'histoire de France depuis les origines jusqu'en 1815. . . 3. ptie) Paris. A. Picard. 1913-35. 8v. **685b**

Bourinot, John George. Historical and descriptive account of the Island of Cape Breton and of its memorials of the French régime: with bibliographical, historical and critical notes. (p123-64) Montreal. W. F. Brown. 1892. 183p. (Reprinted from the Transactions of the Royal Soc. of Canada. 1891) **686**
—— The library of the late Sir John Bourinot containing rare books, pamphlets, and maps relating to the progress of geographical discovery and the history

of Canada, including many relating to the American Revolution and the history of America in colonial times. N.Y. Anderson Auction Co. 1906. 176p.   **687**

Bowe, Forrest. Translations from French printed in America before 1821. N.Y. St. John's Univ. In progress   **687a**

Brault, Lucien. Cartier bibliography. Bul. des recherches historique. XLI. p724-35 (Dec. 1935)   **687b**

Brown, Charles Raynor. Bibliography of Quebec or Lower Canada laws. Reprinted from Law lib. jour. v. 19. no. 4. Jan. 1927. 22p.   **688**

Bryce, George. Critical essay on the sources of information—Canada from 1763 to 1867. *In* Narrative and critical history of America. Ed. by Justin Winsor. Boston, N.Y. Houghton Mifflin. 1889. VIII. p170-87   **689**

Buffalo Historical Society. The Peter A. Porter collection [on Louis Hennepin]. *In* Babcock, Louis A. The war of 1812 on the Niagara frontier. (Buffalo Hist. Soc. Publications. XXIX. p321-30) Buffalo, N.Y. Buffalo Hist. Soc. 1927   **690**

Burpee, Lawrence J. Historical activities in Canada. Miss. valley hist. rev. II. p225-60 (Sept. 1915); III. p203-18 (Sept. 1916); IV. p209-26 (June 1917); VI. p236-59 (Sept. 1918)   **691**

Burpee, Lawrence J. and Doughty, Arthur G. Index and dictionary of Canadian history. (The Makers of Canada, ed. by D. C. Scott and others. v. XXI) Toronto. Morang. 1911. 446p.   **692**

Butterfield, Consul W. Bibliography of Jean Nicolet. State Hist. Soc. Wis. colls. VI. p23-5. 1888   **693**

Canada. Archives. Catalogue of pamphlets in the Public Archives of Canada, 1493-1877, with index. Prepared by Magdalen Casey (Publications of the Public Archives of Canada. no. 13) Ottawa. F. A. Acland, printer to the King. 1931-32. 2v.   **694**

—— —— Index to Reports of Canadian Archives from 1872 to 1908. Published by authority of the minister of agriculture under the direction of the Archivist (Publications of the Canadian Archives. no. 1) Ottawa. Printed by C. H. Parmelee. 1909. 231p.   **695**

Canada. Parliament. Library. Alphabetical catalogue of the library of Parliament; being an index to classified catalogues printed in 1857, 1858 and 1864, and to the books and pamphlets since added to the library, up to 1st October, 1867. Printed by authority. Ottawa. Printed by G. E. Desbarats. 1867. 496p.   **696**

—— —— —— Catalogue of books relating to the history of America, forming part of the library of the Legislative assembly of Canada. Quebec. Print. at W. Cowan & Son. 1845. 29p.   **696a**

—— —— —— Catalogue of the Library of Parliament. . . . Ottawa. Maclean, Roger & Co. 1879-80. 2v.   **697**
Annual supplement. . . Classified list of all books and pamphlets added to the lib. 1864, 79, 82-Feb. 1886, Dec. 1895-Jan. 1908, Dec. 1909-Dec. 1915, Jan. 1918-Dec. 1934. Ottawa. 1865-1935   **698**

Canadian catalogue of books published in Canada, books about Canada, as well as those written by Canadians. Comp. by the Toronto Public Library. Toronto. Dept. of Education of Ontario, Pub. Lib. Branch. 1923-   **698a**

Canadian historical review. New series of the review of historical publications relating to Canada. I. no. 1- March 1920- Toronto. Univ. of Toronto Press. 1920- (Contains section on Recent publications relating to Canada)   **699**

Canadian periodical index, 1928-1932. Windsor, Ont. Pub. Lib. 1928-32. 5v.   **700**

Carayon, Auguste. Bibliographie historique de la Compagnie de Jésus, ou catalogue des ouvrages relatifs a l'histoire des Jésuites depuis leur origine jusqu'à nos jours. Paris. Auguste Durand; London. Barthes and Lowell; Leipzig. A. Franck'sche buchhandlung. 1864. 609p.   **701**

Catalogue, Canadian historical exhibition. . . . Victoria College, Queen's Park, Toronto under the patronage of his excellency the governor general and the Countess of Minto, June 14th to 28th, 1899. Toronto. William Briggs. 1899. 154p.   **701a**

Chinard, Gilbert. L'Amérique et le rêve exotique dans la littérature française au XVIIe et au XVIIIe siècle. Paris. Hachette. 1913. 448p. (Influence of America upon philosophic thought)   **701b**

Chronicles of Canada series. Ed. by George M. Wrong and H. H. Langton. Toronto. Glasgow, Brook. 1914-16. 32v. (Bibliographical note in each vol.)   **701c**

Clements, William Lawrence. Jesuit relations in the library of William L. Clements, Bay City, Michigan. Corrected to August 1921. . . . [Bay City, Mich. 1921?] 6p.   **701d**

Cole, Arthur H. The Bancroft collection on the South Sea Bubble. Bus. Hist. Soc. bul. IX. p93-6. 1935, and Harvard alumni bul. XXXVIII. p376-8 (Dec. 13, 1935) (Hugh Bancroft collection of printed and ms. material on the South Sea Bubble)   **701e**

Davis, Andrew McFarland. Critical essay on the sources of Louisiana history. *In* Narrative and critical history of America. Ed. by Justin Winsor. Boston, N.Y. Houghton Mifflin. 1887. V. p63-78   **702**

Davis, Samuel M. Hennepin as discoverer and author. Minn. Hist. Soc. colls. IX. p233-40. 1901   **703**

DeCosta, Benjamin F. Critical essay on the sources of information—Jacques Cartier and his successors. *In* Narrative and critical history of America. Ed. by Justin Winsor. Boston, N.Y. Houghton Mifflin. 1884. IV. p62-80   **704**

Delanglez, Jean. Hennepin's Description of Louisiana; a critical essay. Mid-America. XXIII. p3-24 (Jan. 1941)   **704a**

Detroit. Public Library. Antoine de la Mothe Cadillac and Detroit before the conspiracy of Pontiac: a bibliography. Detroit. Pub. Lib. 1912. 30p.   **705**

Dionne, Narcisse Eutrope. Hennepin; ses voyages et ses oeuvres. Quebec. Raoul Renault. 1897. 40p.   **706**

—— Inventaire chronologique des cartes, plans, atlas, relatifs à la Nouvelle-France et à la Province de Québec, 1508-1908. Quebec. 1909. 124p. (Also published in Royal Soc. of Canada. Proc. & trans. 3d ser. II, pt. II, 1908)   **706a**

—— Inventaire chronologique des livres, brochures, journaux, et revues, publiés en langue anglaise dans la province de Québec, depuis l'établissement de l'imprimerie en Canada jusqu'à nos jours, 1764-1906. Québec. n.p. 1907. Tome III. 228p.   **707**

—— Inventaire chronologique des livres, brochures, journaux, et revues, publiés en langue française dans la province de Québec depuis l'établissement de l'imprimerie au Canada jusqu'à nos jours, 1764-1905. Québec. n.p. 1905. 175p. (Also in Royal Soc. of Canada proc. and trans. 2d ser. X. supplementary volume)   **708**

—— Québec et Nouvelle France, bibliographie; inventaire chronologique des ouvrages publiés à l'étranger en diverses langues sur Québec et la Nouvelle France depuis la découverte du Canada jusqu'à nos jours. Québec. n.p. 1906. Tome II. 155p.   **709**

Doughty, Arthur G. and Trotter, Reginald G. Bibliography. *In* The Cambridge history of the British empire. v. VI. Canada and Newfoundland. Ed. by J. Holland Rose and others. N.Y. Macmillan. 1930. p813-85   **710**

Duff, Louis Blake. The printer of the Jesuit "Relations" (overrun from The Colophon, n.s. no. 1, II. 33-41, 1936). (Concerning Sebastian Cramoisy)   **710a**

Ellis, George E. and Winsor, Justin. Critical essay on the sources of information —The Red Indian of North America in contact with the French and English. *In* Narrative and critical history of America. Ed. by Justin Winsor. Boston, N.Y. Houghton Mifflin. 1889. I. p316-28   **711**

Faribault, Georges Barthélemi. Catalogue d'ouvrages sur l'histoire de l'Amérique, et en particulier sur celle du Canada, de la Louisiane, de l'Acadie, et autres lieux, ci-devant connus sous le nom de Nouvelle-France; avec des notes bibliographiques, critiques, et littéraires, en trois parties. Quebec. W. Cowan. 1837. 207p.   **712**

Fauteux, Aegidius. Bibliographie de l'histoire canadienne. Montreal. 1926   **713**

—— The introduction of printing into Canada; a brief history. Montreal. Rolland. 1930. 178p.   **714**

—— An inventory of the early printed books, pamphlets and broadsides in Canada, down to 1820. McGill Univ. (In Progress)   **715**

Fernow, Berthold. The papers of Father Bruyas, Jesuit missionary to Canada. Mag. Am. hist. III. p250-60 (March 1879)   **715a**

Ford, Worthington C. French royal edicts, etc., on America. Mass. Hist. Soc. proc. LX. p250-304 (April 1927)   **716**

Fortier, Alcée. French literature of Louisiana. *In* Library of southern literature. Ed. by Edwin Alderman, and others. N.Y. Martin & Hoyt. 1907. IV. p1739-50   **717**

French, Benjamin Franklin. Bibliographical notice of the works of Father Louis Hennepin, a Recollect of the province of St. Anthony, in Artois. *In* Historical collections of Louisiana. N.Y. Wiley and Putnam. 1852. pt. 4, p99-106   **717a**

Froidevaux, Henri. L'histoire des colonies françaises à l'Exposition cartographique de la Bibliothèque nationale. Rev. hist. colonies franç. IIe ann. p77-104. 1914   **717b**

—— L'histoire des colonies françaises d'Amérique dans la bibliothèque de Sir Thomas Phillipps. Soc. Amér. Paris jour. n.s. XII. p257-62. 1920   **717c**

Gagnon, Philéas. Essai de bibliographie canadienne; inventaire d'une bibliothèque comprenant imprimés, manuscrits, estampes, etc., relatifs à l'histoire du Canada et des pays adjacent, avec des notes bibliographiques. Québec. L'auteur. 1895-1913. 2v.   **718**

—— Notes bibliographiques sur les écrits de Champlain, manuscrits et imprimés. Société de géographie de Québec. Bul. Juillet 1908. p55-77   **719**

Galinée, Bréhant de. Explorations of the Great Lakes, 1669-1670, by Dollier de Casson and de Bréhant de Gallinée; Galinée's narrative and map with an English version, including all the map-legends; illustrated with portraits, maps, views, a bibliography, cartography and annotations. Translator and editor James H. Coyne. (Ontario Hist. Soc. pap. and rec. IV) Toronto. 1903. 89p.   **719a**

Ganong, William F. The cartography of the gulf of St. Lawrence, from Cartier to Champlain. Royal Soc. of Canada. trans. VIII. section II. p17-58. 1889   **719b**

—— Crucial maps in the early cartography and place-nomenclature of the Atlantic coast of Canada. Royal Soc. of Canada. trans. n.s. XXIII. section II. p135-75. 1929; XXIV. section II. p135-87. 1930; XXV. section II. p169-203. 1931; XXVI. section II. p125-79. 1932   **719c**

Graduate theses in Canadian history, and related subjects. Canad. hist. rev. VIII-. March 1927-   **719d**

Griffin, Appleton Prentiss Clark. Bibliography of the discovery and explorations of the Mississippi Valley. *In* Knox College, Galesburg, Ill., Library. An annotated catalogue of books belonging to the Finley collection on the history and romance of the Northwest. Galesburg, Ill. Knox College. 1924. p47-67 **720**

—— Discovery of the Mississippi, with bibliographical account of the travels of Nicolet, Alloüez, Marquette, Hennepin, and LaSalle in the Mississippi Valley. Mag. of Am. hist. IX. p190-9, 273-80. 1883. (List with same title in: Joutel, Henri. Joutel's journal of LaSalle's last voyage. Albany. 1906. p221-39) **721**

Ham, Edward B. The library of the Union St.-Jean-Baptiste d'Amérique. Franco-Am. rev. I. p271-5. 1937 **721a**

Harrisse, Henry. Notes pour servir à l'histoire à la bibliographie et à la cartographie de la Nouvelle-France et des pays adjacents, 1545-1700. Paris. Librairie Tross. 1872. 367p. **722**

Hughes, Thomas Aloysius. Register and notices of the sources. *In* History of the Society of Jesus in North America, colonial and federal. N.Y. Longmans, Green. 1907. I. p1-45 **723**

Hugolin, Père. Bibliographie des bibliographies du P. Louis Hennepin, Récollet. (Notes bibliographiques pour servir à l'histoire des Récollets du Canada. 4) Montreal. 1933 **724**

—— Bibliographie des travaux édités ou imprimés en Europe sur les Récollets du Canada. Royal Soc. Canada. trans. 3d ser. XXVII. section 1. p87-109. 1933 **725**

—— Bibliographie du Tiers-Ordre seculier de Saint François au Canada (province de Québec). Montreal. A. Menard. 1921. 149p. Supplément pour les années 1921 à 1931. 1932. 348p. **726**

—— Notes bibliographiques pour servir à l'histoire des Récollets du Canada. Montreal. Imp. des Franciscains. 1932. 51+xxviii+38+23p. 3pts. **727**

Isnard, Albert. Joseph-Nicholas Delisle, sa biographie et sa collection de cartes géographiques à la Bibliothèque Nationale. *In* France. Ministère de l'Instruction Publique et des Beaux-arts. Comité des travaux historiques et scientifiques. Bulletin de la section de géographie. XXX. p34-168. 1915 **727a**

Jaray, Gabriel Louis. Les principaux livres sur l'histoire de l'Amérique septentrionale de 1534 à 1803. France-Amérique. XXXI (300) 233-47 (Dec. 1936) **727b**

Jean-Baptiste-Louis Franquelin, un hydrographe du roi au pays de Nouvelle-France. Soc. géog. Québec bul. XV. p127-82 (May 1921) **727c**

Kenney, James T. Historical activities in Canada. Miss. Valley hist. rev. I. p190-206 (Sept. 1918) **728**

King, Grace. Baron Marc de Villiers du Terrage. La. hist. quar. V. p287-97 (July 1922) **728a**

Kingsford, William. Canadian archaeology: an essay. Montreal. W. Drysdale. 1886. 118p. (Concerns the sources of Canadian history, especially archives) **729**

—— The early bibliography of the province of Ontario, Dominion of Canada, with other information. Toronto. Rowsell & Hutchison. 1892. 140p. **730**

Kingston, Ont., Queen's University. Library. Canadiana, 1698-1900, in the possession of the Douglas Library, Queen's University, Kingston, Ontario. Comp. by Janet S. Porteous and revised, checked and typed by Lillian Houghtling. Kingston. 1932. 86p. **731**

Lanctot, Gustave. A list of all official documents of the kings of France relating to New France, 1540-1780. McGill Univ. (In progress) **732**

Leland, Waldo Gifford. Classified list of ms. maps relating to North America and the West Indies [in the Bibliothèque Nationale, Département des imprimes, cartes et plans]. *In* Guide to materials for American history in the libraries and archives of Paris. (Carnegie Inst. of Wash. Publication no. 392) Wash. D.C. 1932. I. p221-37 **732a**

Lenox Library, New York. Contributions to a catalogue of the Lenox Library, No. 2. The Jesuit relations. N.Y. Printed for the Trustees. 1879 **733**

Livingston, Luther S. The works of Father Hennepin; a catalogue of the collection brought together by Peter A. Porter of Niagara Falls, N.Y. N.Y. Dodd & Livingston. 1910. 13p. **733a**

McCoy, James Comly. Canadiana and French Americana in the library of J. C. McCoy; a hand-list of printed books. Grasse. France. 1931. 87p. **734**

McMurtrie, Douglas C. Les premières impressions françaises à Détroit. Paris. L. Giraud-Badin. 1932. p350-74. (Extrait du Bulletin du bibliophile. Août-Septembre, 1932) **735**

Maggs Bros. (London). The French colonisation [sic] of America as exemplified in a remarkable collection of French administrative acts (1581-1791) mainly from the library of Cardinal E. C. de Loménie de Brienne . . . offered for sale by Maggs Bros., Paris. [Abbeville and Paris. Print. by F. Paillart] 1936. 139p. **735a**

Marcel, Gabriel. Cartographie de la Nouvelle France; supplément à l'ouvrage de M. Harrisse, publié avec des documents inédits. Paris. Maisonneuve Frères et Ch. Leclerc. 1885. 41p. (Also in Revue de géographie. XVI. p186-94, 282-9, 359-65, 442-7; XVII. p50-7. 1885) **735b**

Massicotte, E. Z. Inventaire des cartes et plans de l'île et de la ville de Montréal. Bul. recherche hist. XX. p33-41, 65-73 (Feb., March 1914) **735c**

Morgan, Henry James. Bibliotheca Canadensis; or manual of Canadian literature. Ottawa. G.E. Desbarats. 1867. 411p. **736**

Munro, William Bennett. Bibliographical appendix. *In* The seignorial system in Canada; a study in French colonial policy. (Harvard hist. stud. XIII) N.Y. Longmans, Green. 1907. p253-75 **737**

Munro, William Bennett. The Jesuit relations; their value as historical material. Reprinted from Queen's quar. July 1905. 10p.   **738**

Neill, Edward D. The writings of Louis Hennepin, Récollet Franciscan missionary. Prepared for the monthly meeting of the Department of Am. hist., Minn. Hist. Soc. . . . Minneapolis. 1880. 10p.   **739**

Neill, Edward D. and Winsor, Justin. Critical essay on the sources of information—Discovery along the Great Lakes. *In* Narrative and critical history of America. Ed. by Justin Winsor. Boston; N.Y. Houghton Mifflin. 1884. IV. p196-200   **740**

New France. Conseil supérieur de Québec. Inventaire des jugements et deliberations du Conseil supérieur de la Nouvelle-France de 1717 à 1760. Par Pierre-Georges Roy (Archives de la province de Québec). Beauceville, Québec. L' "Eclaireur." 1932-34. 5v.   **741**

New York. Commissioners of the state reservation at Niagara. Bibliography of La Salle (1697-1893). Ninth annual rep. IX. p76-80. 1893   **742**

New York. Public Library. Canada; an exhibition commemorating the four-hundreth anniversary of the discovery of the Saint Lawrence by Jacques Cartier, 1534-1535; a catalogue with notes. N.Y. Pub. Lib. 1935. 59p. (Reprinted from the Bul. July and Aug. 1935)   **743**

O'Callaghan, Edmund Bailey. Jesuit relations of discoveries and other occurrences in Canada and the northern and western states of the union, 1632-1672. . . . N.Y. Press of the Hist. Soc. 1847. 22p. (From N.Y. Hist. Soc. proc. Nov. 1847)   **744**

Ontario. Department of Education. Catalogue of the books relating to Canada: historical and biographical, in the library of the Education Department for Ontario, arranged according to topics and in alphabetical order. Toronto. Warwick. 1890. 122p.   **745**

Paltsits, Victor Hugo. Bibliographical data. *In* Hennepin, Father Louis. A new discovery of a vast country in America. Ed. by R. G. Thwaites. Chicago. A. C. McClurg. 1903. I. p. xlv-lxiv (Bibliog. reprinted as: Bibliography of the works of Father Louis Hennepin. Chicago. A. C. McClurg. 1903)   **746**

—— A bibliography of the writings of Baron Lahontan; separate from the reprint of Lahontan's "New voyages to North America." Ed. by R. G. Thwaites. Chicago. A. C. McClurg. 1905. I. p. li-xciii   **747**

—— Contribution to the bibliography of the "Lettres édifiantes." Cleveland. Imperial Press. 1900. 41p. (Reprinted from v. LX of The Jesuit relations and allied documents. Ed. by Reuben G. Thwaites)   **748**

Parker, David W. A guide to the documents in the manuscript room at the Public Archives of Canada. Vol. I (Publications of the Archives of Canada. no. 10) Ottawa. Govt. Ptg. Bur. 1914. 318p.   **749**

Pease, Theodore E. The French regime in Illinois, a challenge to historical scholarship. Ill. State Hist. Soc. trans. 1936. p69-79   **749a**

Peloux, Vicomte Charles du. Répertoire générale des ouvrages modernes relatifs au dix-huitième siècle français (1715-1789). Paris. E. Grund. 1926. 306p.   **749b**

Porter, Peter Augustus. The works of Father Hennepin; a catalogue of the collection brought together by Peter A. Porter of Niagara Falls, N.Y. N.Y. Dodd & Livingston. 1910. 13p.   **750**

Recent publications relating to Canada. Canad. hist. rev. I- (March 1920-)   **750a**

Remington, Cyrus Kingsbury. The shipyard of the Griffon, a brigantine built by René Robert Cavelier, sieur de la Salle, in the year 1679 above the falls of the Niagara. . . Together with the most complete bibliography of Hennepin. . . . Buffalo, N.Y. J.W. Clement. 1891. p51-78 (Also in Ninth annual rep. of the Commissioners of the state reservation at Niagara. IX. p55-75. 1893)   **751**

Renault, Raoul. Champlain, ses oeuvres et ses historiens, essai bibliographique. Le courrier du livre. III. p143-62 (Sept. 1898)   **752**

Répertoire bibliographique de l'histoire de France, I. 1920/1921. Paris. A. Picard. 1923-   **752a**

Review of historical publications relating to Canada, volume I-XXII, 1896-1918. Comp. by George M. Wrong, Hugh H. Langton, and William S. Wallace. Toronto. Univ. of Toronto. 1896-1918. 22v.   **752b**

Rivière, Ernest M. Corrections et additions à la bibliothèque de la Compagnie de Jésus. Supplément du "De Backer-Sommervogel." Toulouse. L'auteur. 1911-17. 4pts. 907p.   **753**

Roy, Antoine. L'oeuvre historique de Pierre-Georges Roy; bibliographie analytique. Paris. Jouve et cie. 1928. 268p.   **753a**

Roy, Francis A. Bibliography of translations from French into English published in the United Colonies and in the United States from 1639 to 1800. Tucson. Univ. of Arizona. In progress. Also A bibliography of books published in French in this country during the same period.   **753b**

Roy, J. Edmund. Le baron de Lahontan. Royal Soc. of Canada proc. and trans. 1894. XII. Mémoires section. I. p63-192   **754**

Roy, Pierre Georges. Inventaire des concessions en fief et seigneurie, fois et hommages et aveux et dénombrements, conservées aux archives de la province de Québec. (Collection des archives de la province de Québec) Beauceville. 1927-29. 6v.   **754a**

—— Inventaire des insinuations de conseil souverain de la Nouvelle-France de 1663 à 1758. (Collection des archives de la province de Québec) Beauceville. 1921. 326p. **754b**

—— Inventaire des jugements et délibérations du conseil supérieur de la Nouvelle-France, de 1717 à 1760. (Collection des archives de la province de Québec) Beauceville. 1932-33. 3v. **754c**

—— Inventaire des ordonnances des intendants de la Nouvelle-France, conservées aux archives provinciales de Québec. (Collection des archives de la province de Québec) Beauveville. 1919. 4v. **754d**

—— Inventaire des proces-verbaux des grands voyers, conservées aux archives de la province de Québec. (Collection des archives de la province de Québec) Beauceville. 1923-32. 6v. **754e**

—— Inventaire des registres de l'état civil, conservées aux archives judiciaires de Québec. (Collection des archives de la province de Québec) Beauceville. 1921. 364p. **754f**

—— Inventaire d'une collection de pièces judiciaires notariales, etc., etc., conservées aux archives judiciaires de Québec. (Collection des archives de la province de Québec) Beauceville. 1917. 2v. **754g**

Royal Empire Society. Subject catalogue of the Library of the Royal Empire Society, formerly Royal Colonial Institute. By Evans Lewin. v. III. The Dominion of Canada, and its provinces, The Dominion of Newfoundland, The West Indies, and colonial America. London. Royal Empire Soc. 1932. 822p. **755**

Sabin, Joseph. A list of the editions of the works of Louis Hennepin and Antonio de Herrera. Extracted from a Dictionary of books relating to America. N.Y. J. Sabin. 1876. 16p. **756**

Scott, S. Morley. Material relating to Quebec in the Gage and Amherst papers. Canad. hist. rev. XIX. p378-86 (Dec. 1938) **756a**

Shea, John Gilmary. Critical essay on the sources of information—The Jesuits, Récollets, and the Indians. *In* Narrative and critical history of America. Ed. by Justin Winsor. Boston, N.Y. Houghton Mifflin. 1884. IV. p290-4 **757**

Slafter, Edmund F. Critical essay on the sources of information—Champlain. *In* Narrative and critical history of America. Ed. by Justin Winsor. Boston, N.Y. Houghton Mifflin. 1884. IV. p130-4 **758**

Smith, Charles C. Critical essay on the sources of information—Acadia. *In* Narrative and critical history of America. Ed. by Justin Winsor. Boston, N.Y. Houghton Mifflin. 1887. IV. p149-62 **759**

Stewart, George, Jr. Critical essay on the sources of information—Editorial notes—Frontenac and his time. *In* Narrative and critical history of America. Ed. by Justin Winsor. Boston, N.Y. Houghton Mifflin. 1884. IV. p356-68 **760**

Stewart, Sheila I. A catalogue of the Akins collection of books and pamphlets, compiled under the direction of D. C. Harvey. (Publications of the Public Archives of Nova Scotia. no. 1) Halifax. Imperial Publishing Co. 1933. 206p. **761**

Sulte, Benjamin. The historical and miscellaneous literature of Quebec, 1764 to 1830. Royal Soc. of Canada. proc. 2d ser. III. p269-78. 1897 **761a**

Thwaites, Reuben Gold, ed. The Jesuit relations and allied documents, travels, and explorations of the Jesuit missionaries in New France, 1610-1791. . . . Cleveland. Burrows. 1896-1901. 73v. (Bibliog. data appended to some volumes; v. 72-3 consist of an index to the series, which is also the work of James Alexander Robertson) **762**

Toronto. Public Library. A bibliography of Canadiana; being items in the Public Library of Toronto, Canada, relating to the early history and development of Canada. Ed. by Frances M. Staton and Marie Tremaine, with an introduction by George H. Locke. Toronto. Pub. Lib. 1934. 828p. **763**

—— —— Canadian books; a study outline for the people. Toronto. Dept. of Education, pub. lib. branch. 1923. 20p. **764**

—— —— The Canadian catalogue of books published in Canada, as well as those written by Canadians, 1921/22-. Comp. by the Public Library, Toronto, George H. Locke, chief librarian. Toronto. Pub. Lib. of Toronto. 1923- **765**

Toronto. University. Review of historical publications relating to Canada. Ed. by George M. Wrong and H. H. Langton. v. I-XXII. 1896-1917/18. (Univ. of Toronto. Stud. in hist.) Toronto. 1897-1919 (With indexes to v. I-X and XI-XX) **766**

Trotter, Reginald George. Canadian history; a syllabus and guide to reading. N.Y. Macmillan. 1934. 193p. **767**

Union Saint-Jean-Baptiste d'Amérique. Bibliothèque. Catalogue de la Bibliothèque de l'Union Saint-Jean-Baptiste d'Amérique. Collection Mallet. Deuxième édition. Woonsocket, R.I. 1935. 302p. (Books, mss. and brochures on Canada and the United States and their relations with France) **767a**

Upham, Warren. Bibliography. *In* Groseilliers and Radisson. The first white men in Minnesota, 1655-56, and 1659-60, and their discovery of the Upper Mississippi River. Minn. Hist. Soc. colls. X. pt. 2. p568-94. 1905 **768**

Webster, John Clarence. Catalogue of the John Clarence Webster Canadiana collection (pictorial section) New Brunswick Museum. (Catalogue no. 1) Saint John. The New Brunswick Museum. 1939. 371p. **768a**

Windsor, Ontario, Public Library. Canadian periodical index, 1931-. First annual cumulation. Windsor, Ont. 1932- **769**

Winsor, Justin. Baron La Hontan, a bibliographical and critical note by the editor. *In* Narrative and critical history of America. Boston, N.Y. Houghton Mifflin. 1884. IV. p257-62 **770**

—— Cartography of Louisiana and Mississippi basin, under the French dominion. *In* Narrative and critical history of America. Boston; N.Y. Houghton Mifflin. 1887. V. p79-86 **770a**

—— Father Louis Hennepin and his real or disputed discoveries (bibliographical). *In* Narrative and critical history of America. Boston, N.Y. Houghton Mifflin. 1884. IV. p247-56 **771**

—— The Jesuit relations and other mission records—a chronological bibliography by the editor. *In* Narrative and critical history of America. Boston, N.Y. Houghton Mifflin. 1884. IV. p295-316 **772**

—— Joliet, Marquette and La Salle: historical sources and attendant cartography. *In* Narrative and critical history of America. Boston, N.Y. Houghton Mifflin. 1884. IV. p201-46 **773**

—— The maps of the seventeenth century, showing Canada. *In* Narrative and critical history of America. Boston; N.Y. Houghton Mifflin. 1884. IV. p377-94 **773a**

Wood, William. The new provincial archives of Quebec. Canadian hist. rev. II. p126-54 (June 1921) **774**

Wroth, Lawrence C. The Jesuit relations from New France. Bibliog. Soc. Am. pap. XXX. p110-49. 1936 **774a**

Wroth, Lawrence C. and Annan, Gertrude L. Acts of French royal administration concerning Canada, Guiana, the West Indies, and Louisiana prior to 1791. N. Y. Pub. Lib. bul. XXXIII. p789-800, 868-93 (Oct., Dec. 1929); XXXIV. p21-55, 87-126, 155-93 (Jan.-March 1930) (Reprinted, N.Y. N. Y. Pub. Lib. 1930. 151p.) **775**

BRITISH RELATIONS

Abbott, Wilbur Cortez. A bibliography of Oliver Cromwell; a list of printed materials relating to Oliver Cromwell, together with a list of portraits and caricatures. Cambridge. Harvard Univ. Press. 1929. 540p. **776**

Adair, Edward Robert. The sources for the history of the Council in the sixteenth & seventeenth centuries. (Helps for students of hist. no. 51) London. Soc. for Promoting Christian Knowledge. 1924. 96p. **777**

Allen, Frederick J. A topical outline of English history, including references for literature, for the use of classes in high schools and academies. Boston. Heath. 1897. 71p. **778**

Bateson, Frederick Wilse. The Cambridge bibliography of English literature. N.Y. Macmillan; Cambridge, England. University Press. 1941. 4v. **778a**

Beazley, Charles Raymond. Documents mainly illustrating the English career of John and Sebastian Cabot—Cabot literature. *In* John and Sebastian Cabot; the discovery of North America. N.Y. Longmans, Green. 1898. p265-91 **778b**

Books relating to the Hudson's Bay Company. Beaver. CCLXV. p55-60. 1934 **778c**

Briggs, Gordon. The archives of the Hudson's Bay Company. Canadian chartered accountant. XXXII. p116-20 (Feb. 1938) **778d**

British Museum. Department of printed books. Map room. Sir Francis Drake's voyage round the world, 1577-1580; two contemporary maps. London. 1927. 11p. **778e**

—— **Library.** Catalogue of the pamphlets, books, newspapers & manuscripts relating to the Civil War, the Commonwealth and Restoration, collected by George Thomason, 1640-1661. London. 1908. 2v. **779**

Brushfield, T. N. A bibliography of Sir Walter Raleigh, Knt. Exeter. James G. Commin. 1908. 181p. **780**

Canada. Archives. Bouquet collection. *In* Report on Canadian archives. 1889. Ottawa. 1890. 337p. (Henry Bouquet papers, 1756-1765) **780a**

—— —— Calendar of Shelburne correspondence. *In* Report on Canadian archives, 1921. Ottawa. 1922. Appendix C, p229-81 **780b**

—— —— Haldiman collection, calendar. *In* Report on Canadian archives, 1884-1889. Ottawa. 1885-1890. 1884, 136p.; 1885, p137-382; 1886, p383-741, 1-84; 1887, p85-564; 1888, p565-1028, 1-52; 1889, p53-299. (Sir Frederick Haldiman, British army officer in America, 1756-1784) **780c**

—— —— The Northcliffe collection; presented to the government of Canada by Sir Leicester Harmsworth, Bt., as a memorial to his brother, the Right Honourable Alfred Charles William Harmsworth, viscount Northcliffe. Ottawa. F.A. Acland. 1926. 464p. (Calendar of the papers of Gen. Robert Monckton and Brig. Gen. Townshend concerning the capture of Quebec) **781**

Cannon, Henry L. Reading references for English history. Boston. Ginn. 1910. 559p. **782**

Chicago University. Library. Eckels collection. Cromwelliana and English civil war books in library of George M. Eckels. Aug. 1, 1912. [Chicago. 1912?] 215p. typ. **783**

Cole, Arthur H. Finding list of royal commissions that have functioned in the British self-governing colonies and the several state or provinces thereof. Cambridge. Harvard Univ. In progress **783a**

Cole, George Watson. Elizabethan Americana. *In* Bibliographical essays; a tribute to Wilberforce Eames. Cambridge. Harvard Univ. Press. 1924. p161-78 **784**

Cowley, John D. A bibliography of abridgments, digests, dictionaries and indexes of English law to the year 1800. London. Quaritch. 1932. 196p.   **785**

Crane, R. S. and Kaye, F. B. A census of British newspapers and periodicals, 1620-1800. Chapel Hill. Univ. of North Carolina Press. 1927. 205p.   **786**

Craven, Wesley Frank. Bibliographical article—Historical study of the British empire. Jour. of modern hist. VI. p40-69 (March 1934)   **787**

Crawford, Clarence Cory. A guide to the study of the history of English law and procedure. Toronto. Carswell. 1923. 83p.   **788**

Davenport, Frances Gardiner. Materials for English diplomatic history, 1509-1783, calendared in the Report of the Historical Manuscripts Commission, with reference to similar manuscripts in the British Museum. (Great Britain. Hist. Manuscripts Comn. 18th rep.) London. 1917. p357-402   **789**

Davies, Godfrey. Bibliography of British history, Stuart period, 1603-1714. Oxford. Clarendon Press. 1928. 459p.   **790**

De Puy, Henry F. A bibliography of the English colonial treaties with the American Indians, including a synopsis of each treaty. N.Y. Printed for the Lenox Club. 1917. unpag.   **791**

Dictionary of national biography. Ed. by Leslie Stephen and Sidney Lee. vol. I-LXIII and supplement vol. I-III. N.Y. Macmillan; London. Smith, Elder. 1885-1901. 66v. 2d-[4th] supplement. London. Oxford Univ. Press, H. Milford, etc. 1912-[37] 5v.   **791a**

Doughty, Arthur G. and Parmelee, G. W. Bibliography of the siege of Quebec, with a list of plans of Quebec by Philip Lee Phillips. *In* The siege of Quebec and the battle of the Plains of Abraham. Quebec. Dussault & Proulx. 1901. VI. p153-313   **792**

Eames, Wilberforce. A bibliography of Sir Walter Raleigh. N.Y. 1886. 35p. (Reprinted from Sabin's Bibliotheca Americana. XVI. p250-82. 1886)   **793**

Ford, Paul Leicester. List of some briefs in appeal causes which relate to America, tried before the Lords commissioners of appeals of prize causes of His Majesty's Privy Council, 1736-1758. Brooklyn, N.Y. 1889. 20p.   **794**

Fryer, C. E. Further pamphlets for the Canada-Guadeloupe controversy. Miss. Valley hist. rev. IV. p227-30 (Sept. 1917)   **794a**

Gabler, Anthony J. Checklist of English newspapers and periodicals before 1801 in the Huntington library. Cambridge. Harvard Univ. Press. 1931. 66p. (Reprinted from the Huntington Lib. bul. no. 2. November 1931)   **795**

Gardiner, Samuel R. and Mullinger, J. Baes. Introduction to the study of English history. London. Kegan, Paul, Trench, Trübner. 1894. 468p.   **796**

Gerould, James Thayer. Sources of English history of the 17th century, 1603-1689 in the University of Minnesota Library. (Research publications of the Univ. of Minnesota, bibliog. ser. no. 1) Minneapolis. Univ. of Minnesota. 1921. 565p.   **797**

Great Britain. Admiralty Library. Subject catalogue of printed books. Part I. Historical section. London. Eyre and Spottiswoode. 1912. 374p.   **798**

Great Britain. Parliament. House of Commons. Catalogue of papers printed by order of the House of Commons, 1731-1800, in the custody of the Clerk of the journals. London. 1807. 101p.   **799**

—— —— —— Catalogue of parliamentary reports and a breviate of their contents, arranged under heads according to their subject, 1696-1834. (House of Commons. 1834. rep. 626) London. 1836. 221p.   **800**

—— —— —— General index to the reports from committees of the House of Commons, 1715-1801, forming the series of 15 volumes of reports. Ordered by the House of Commons to be printed, 1803. London. 1803. 380p.   **801**

Great Britain. Public Record Office. An alphabetical guide to certain war office and other military records preserved in the Public Record Office. (Lists and indexes no. LIII) London. H.M. Stationery Off. 1931. 530p.   **802**

—— —— List of admiralty records, preserved in the Public Record Office. (Lists and indexes no. XVIII) London. Printed for H.M. Stationery Off. by Mackie & Co., Ltd. 1904   **803**

—— —— List of colonial office records, preserved in the Public Record Office. (Lists and indexes no. XXXVI) London. Printed for H.M. Stationery Off. 1911. 337p.   **804**

Grose, Clyde Leclare. A select bibliography of British history, 1660-1760. Chicago. Univ. of Chicago Press. 1939. 507p.   **804a**

—— Thirty years' study of a formerly neglected century of British history, 1660-1760. Jour. of modern hist. II. p448-71 (Sept. 1930)   **805**

Hall, Edward E. Critical essay on Drake's Bay. *In* Narrative and critical history of America. Ed. by Justin Winsor. Boston, N.Y. Houghton Mifflin. 1884. III. p74-8   **806**

Haller, William. The rise of Puritanism; or, The way to the New Jerusalem as set forth in pulpit and press from Thomas Cartwright to John Lilburne and John Milton, 1570-1643. N.Y. Columbia Univ. Pr. 1938. p405-40   **806a**

Henry E. Huntington Library and Art Gallery. Checklist or brief catalogue of the library of Henry E. Huntington (English literature to 1640). Comp. under the direction of George Watson Cole. N.Y. 1919. 482p. (Lists voyages of Capt. John Smith and other English books relating to America)   **807**

Higgs, Henry. Bibliography of economics, 1751-1775. Cambridge, England. Univ. Press. 1935. 742p. **808**

Historical Association. Annual bulletin of historical literature, no. 1- . 1911- . London. [1912- **808a**

Holdsworth, William Searle. The historians of Anglo-American law. N.Y. Columbia Univ. Press. 1928. 175p. **808b**

—— Sources and literature of English law. Oxford. Clarendon Press. 1925. 247p. **809**

Hudson's Bay Company. List of books relating to Hudson's Bay Company, incorporated 2nd May, 1670. (London. Hudson's Bay Company) 1935. 13p. **809a**

Kellogg, Louise P. The mission of Jonathan Carver. Wis. mag. of hist. XII. p127-45 (Dec. 1928) **810**

Laprade, W. T. Bibliographical article— The present state of the history of England in the eighteenth century. Jour. of modern hist. IV. p581-603 (Dec. 1932) **811**

Lee, John Thomas. A bibliography of Carver's travels. Madison, Wis. State Hist. Soc. of Wis. 1910. p143-83 (Reprinted from the Proc. of the State Hist. Soc. of Wis. 1909) **812**

Lomas, S. C. The state papers of the early Stuarts and the Interregnum. Royal Hist. Soc. trans. n.s. XVI. p97-132. 1902. **813**

Lydekker, John W. The archives of the Society for the propagation of the gospel. Internat. rev. of missions. XXV. p371-7 (July 1936) **813a**

McCutcheon, Roger P. Americana in English newspapers, 1648-1660. Col. Soc. Mass. pub. XX. p84-96. 1920 **813b**

Malcolm, Harcourt. List of documents relating to the Bahama Islands in the British museum and Record office. London, Nassau. The Nassau guardian. 1910. 50p. **814**

Manwaring, G. E. A bibliography of British naval history; a biographical and historical guide to printed and manuscript sources. London. Routledge. 1929. 163p. **815**

Medley, Dudley J. and Pargellis, Stanley M. Bibliography of British history, eighteenth century. In progress **815a**

Moore, Margaret Findlay. Two select bibliographies of mediaeval historical study. I. A classified list of works relating to the study of English palaeography and diplomatics. II. A classified list of works relating to English manorial and agrarian history from the earliest times to the year 1660. London. Constable. 1912. 185p. **816**

Morgan, William Thomas. A bibliography of British history, (1700-1715), with special reference to the reign of Queen Anne. (Indiana Univ. stud. XVIII-XIX. Dec. 1931-March 1932. Stud. no. 94-5; XXIII-XXIV; Stud. no. 114-18; XV. Stud. no. 119-22) Bloomington, Ind. 1934. 3v. **817**

—— A guide to the study of English history. N.Y. Knopf. 1926. 222p. **818**

Mowat, Charles L. Material relating to British East Florida in the Gage papers and other manuscript collections in the William L. Clements Library. Fla. hist. quar. XVIII. p46-60 (July 1939) **818a**

Museum Book Store, London. Political economy; rare books and pamphlets of great value for the study of social and political science. London. Museum Book Store. 1930. 194p. **819**

New York. Public Library. A checklist of acts relating to the Americas and the West Indies, 1692-1808, to be found in: Great Britain. Statutes; a collection of the public general statutes; London, 1692-1808. N.Y. 1937. 29p. typ. **819a**

New York (city). Union Theological Seminary Library. Catalogue of the McAlpin collection of British history and theology. Comp. and ed. by Charles Ripley Gillett. N.Y. [Plimpton Press. Norwood, Mass.] 1927-30. 5v. (Contains titles of 15,000 books printed before 1700) **820**

Newton, Arthur P. An introduction to the study of colonial history. (Helps for students of history no. 16) London. Soc. for Promoting Christian Knowledge; N.Y. Macmillan. 1918. 46p. **821**

—— A list of selected books relating to the history of the British empire overseas suitable for the use of schools and students. (Hist. Asso. publications. no. 46) London. 1929. 32p. **822**

Pargellis, Stanley M. and Cuthbert, Norma B. Loudoun papers. (a) Colonial, 1756-58. (b) French colonial, 1742-53. Huntington lib. bul. no. 3. p97-107 (Feb. 1933) **822a**

Penson, Lillian M. General bibliography. *In* The old empire from the beginnings to 1783. (The Cambridge hist. of the British empire. Ed. by J. Holland Rose, A. P. Newton, and E. A. Benians, v. I) N.Y. Macmillan; Cambridge, England. Univ. Press. 1929. p824-88 **823**

Phillips, P. Lee. List of books relating to America in the register of the London Company of Stationers from 1562 to 1638. Am. Hist. Asso. rep. 1896. I. p1249-61 (Also reprinted) **824**

Pittsburgh. Carnegie Library. Expeditions of Colonel Bouquet to the Ohio country, 1763 and 1764. Monthly bul. of the Carnegie Lib. of Pittsburgh. XIV. p603-13 (Dec. 1909) **825**

—— —— List of references on Braddock's expedition. Monthly bul. of the Carnegie Lib. of Pittsburgh. XI. p497-507 (Nov. 1906) **826**

—— —— List of references on the expedition of General Forbes against Fort Duquesne. Monthly bul. of the Carnegie Lib. of Pittsburgh. XIII. p351-65 (June 1908) (Reprinted. 1908. 20p.) **827**

Power, Eileen Edna. The industrial revolution 1750-1850, a select bibliography, compiled for the Economic History Society. London. Economic Hist. Soc. 1927. 30p. **828**

Ragatz, Lowell Joseph. A guide for study of British Caribbean history, 1763-1834. Wash. Govt. Ptg. Off. 1933. 725p. (Also as Am. Hist. Asso. rep. 1930. v. III)
829

Read, Conyers. Bibliography of British history Tudor period, 1485-1603. Oxford. Clarendon Press. 1933. 467p.
830

Reed, Susan Martha. British cartography of the Mississippi Valley in the eighteenth century. Miss. Valley hist. rev. II. p213-24 (Sept. 1915)
830a

Roberts, Richard Arthur. The reports of the Historical MSS. Commission. (Helps for students of history, no. 22) London. Soc. for Promoting Christian Knowledge; N.Y. The Macmillan Company. 1920. 91p.
830b

Royal Empire Society. Subject catalogue of the library of the Royal Empire Society formerly Royal Colonial Institute. v. I. The British empire generally, and Africa. By Evans Lewin. London. Royal Empire Soc. 1930. 582, cxxiii p.
831

Royal Historical Society. Writings on British history, 1934- ; a bibliography of books and articles on the history of Great Britain from about 450 A.D. to 1914, published during the year . . . with an appendix containing a select list of publications . . . on British history since 1914. . . Comp. by Alexander Taylor Milne. London. J. Cape. 1937-
831a

Stauffer, Donald A. The art of biography in eighteenth century England: bibliographical supplement. Princeton. Princeton Univ. Press. 1941. 293p.
831b

Stewart, Irene. List of references on the expedition of General Forbes against Fort Duquesne. *In* Letters of General John Forbes relating to the expedition against Fort Duquesne in 1758. Pittsburgh. Allegheny County Com. 1927. p77-88
832

Sweet & Maxwell, Ltd., London. A bibliography of English law to 1932. Volumes 1-2 of Sweet & Maxwell's complete law book catalogue. Comp. by W. Harold Maxwell. London. Sweet & Maxwell. 1925-33. 3v.
833

The Times, London. Tercentenary handlist of English & Welsh newspapers, magazines & reviews. London. The Times. 1920. 324, xxxv p.
834

U.S. Library of Congress. Division of bibliography. Select list of references on Braddock's campaign against Fort Duquesne. 1908. 8p. typ.
835

——— ——— Division of manuscripts. List of the Vernon-Wagner manuscripts in the Library of Congress. Comp. under the direction of Worthington Chauncey Ford. Wash. Govt. Ptg. Off. 1904. 148p. (Relate to the West Indies during the French and Indian war)
836

Waldon, Freda F. Queen Anne and "The four kings of Canada"; a bibliography of contemporary sources. Canad. hist. rev. XVI. p266-75 (Sept. 1935) (Visit of four Indian chiefs to England in 1710)
836a

Williams, Judith Blow. A guide to the printed materials for English social and economic history, 1750-1850. (Records of civilization: Sources and stud. ed. by J. T. Shotwell) N.Y. Columbia Univ. Press. 1926. 2v.
837

Winfield, Percy H. The chief sources of English legal history. Cambridge. Harvard Univ. Press. 1925. 374p.
838

Winsor, Justin. Editorial notes on the sources of information—Hawkins and Drake. *In* Narrative and critical history of America. Boston; N.Y. Houghton Mifflin. 1884. III. p78-84
839

——— English publications on America, and other notes. *In* Narrative and critical history of America. Boston; N.Y. Houghton Mifflin. 1884. III. p199-218
840

——— The maps and bounds of Acadia. *In* Narrative and critical history of America. Boston; N.Y. Houghton Mifflin. 1887. V. p472-82
840a

Wolf, Edwin, 2d. Check list of the earliest English Americana. Bibliog. Soc. Am. pap. XXXIII. p49-54. 1939
840b

CONTINENTAL COLONIES

Source Materials

Adams, Randolph Greenfield. William Hubbard's "Narrative" 1677; a bibliographical study. Portland, Me. Southworth Press. 1939. p25-39 (Reprineted from the Bibliog. Soc. Am. pap. XXXIII. p25-39. 1939) (Concerns A narrative of the troubles with the Indians in New England. Boston. 1677)
840c

American Antiquarian Society. Exhibition of American almanacs, October, 1925, in honor of the gift to the society from Samuel L. Munson of his notable collection of almanacs. Lists and notes compiled by Charles L. Nichols (Worcester? 1925) 11p.
840d

Amherst College. Plimpton Collection. The Plimpton Collection of French and Indian war items. Presented to Amherst College and exhibited at the Lord Jeffrey Inn, Amherst, Massachusetts. Described by J. C. Long. Amherst. Amherst College. 1934. 39p. (Includes manuscript letters)
841

Andrews, Charles M. List of reports and representations of the plantation councils, 1660-1674, The Lords of Trade, 1675-1696, and The Board of Trade, 1696-1782, in the Public Record Office. Am. Hist. Asso. rep. 1913. I. p321-406
842

——— List of the commissions, instructions, and additional instructions issued to the royal governors and others in America. Am. Hist. Asso. rep. 1911. I. p393-528
843

——— List of the journals and acts of the councils and assemblies of the thirteen original colonies, and the Floridas, in America, preserved in the Public Record Office, London. Am. Hist. Asso. rep. 1908. I. p399-509
844

Bancroft, George. Lists of letters and documents dealing with American affairs, seventeenth and eighteenth centuries, being Bancroft's memoranda, mostly in his own handwriting, of material in the British and other archives; line titles and dates, with brief indications of the character of the documents. (MS. in the Bancroft collection in the N.Y. Pub. Lib.) 250p. **845**

Basye, Arthur H. Abstract of commissions and instructions to colonial governors in America, 1740. Am. Hist. Asso. rep. 1919. I. p327-49 **846**

Benedict, Russell. Illustrated catalogue of acts and laws of the colony and state of New York and of the other original colonies and states, constituting the collections made by Hon. Russell Benedict. . . . N.Y. The American Art Galleries. 1922. unpag. **847**

Benson, Adolph B. Pehr Kalm's writings on America; a bibliographical review. Scandinavian stud. and notes. XII. p89-98. 1933 **847a**

Boston. Public Library. Prince Collection. The Prince library; a catalogue of the collection of books and manuscripts which formerly belonged to the Reverend Thomas Prince, and was by him bequeathed to the Old South Church, and is now deposited in the Public Library of the city of Boston. Boston. A. Mudge & Son. 1870. 160p. **847b**

Brigham, Clarence S. An account of American almanacs and their value for historical study. Reprinted from the Proc. of the Am. Antiq. Soc. for Oct. 1925. Worcester, Mass. The Soc. 1925. 25p. **848**

—— Report of the librarian. Am. Antiq. Soc. proc. n.s. XXXV. p190-218. 1926 (p195-209 is a summary of the collection of American almanacs presented to the Society by Samuel Lyman Munson) **848a**

Charlemagne Tower collection of American colonial laws. Priv. print. for The Hist. Soc. of Pennsylvania. [Phila. Lippincott] 1890. 298p. **849**

Cox, John H. Compilations of colonial imports and exports on film. Jour. doc. reprod. II. p198-201 (Sept. 1939) **849a**

Fitts, James H. The [Isaiah] Thomas almanacs. Essex Institute historical collections. XII. p243-70 (Oct. 1874) **849b**

Gay, Frederick Lewis. A rough list of a collection of transcripts relating to the history of New England, 1630-1776. Brookline, Mass. Priv. print. 1913. 273p. **850**

Green, Samuel Abbott. A list of early American imprints belonging to the library of the Massachusetts Historical Society. Cambridge. John Wilson & Son. 1895. 137p. (Reprinted from the Mass. Hist. Soc. proc. 2d ser. IX. p410-540. 1894) (A supplementary list. 1898. 46p. Reprinted from the Mass. Hist. Soc. proc. 2d ser. XII. p273-86. June 1898. A sec-

ond supplement. 1899. 70p. Reprinted from the Mass. Hist. Soc. proc. 2d ser. XII. p380-423. Jan. 1899. A third supplement. 1903. 67p. Reprinted from the Mass. Hist. Soc. proc. 2d ser. XVII. p13-75. Jan. 1903) **851**

Greene, Evarts B. and Morris, Richard Brandon. A guide to the principal sources for early American history (1600-1800) in the city of New York. N.Y. Columbia Univ. Press. 1929. 357p. **852**

Griffin, Appleton P. C. Bibliography of the historical publications issued by the New England states. Reprinted from The Publications of The Colonial Soc. of Mass. v. III. Cambridge. John Wilson. Univ. Press. 1895. 47p. **853**

Haraszti, Zoltan. Harvard tercentenary exhibit. More books: Boston pub. lib. bul. XI. p257-76 (Sept. 1936) (Manuscripts and books relative to New England in the Boston Public Library) **853a**

Hasse, Adelaide Rosalie. Materials for a bibliography of the public archives of the thirteen original states, covering the colonial period and the state period to 1789. Am. Hist. Asso. rep. 1906. II. p239-561 **854**

Henry E. Huntington Library and Art Gallery. A century of conflict in America; catalogue of a collection of tracts and manuscripts from Walker's expedition against Quebec in 1711 to the War of 1812. London. The Museum Book Store. 1925. 79p. **855**

—— Check list of American laws, charters, and constitutions of the seventeenth and eighteenth centuries in the Huntington Library. Comp. by Willard Waters (Huntington Lib. lists no. 1) San Marino, Calif. 1936. 140p. **856**

Higham, C. S. S. The colonial entry books (Helps for students of history, no. 45) London. Soc. for Promoting Christian Knowledge. 1921. 48p. **857**

Jameson, J. Franklin. Colonial assemblies and their legislative journals. Am. Hist. Asso. rep. 1897. p405-53 **858**

—— Guide to the items relating to American history in the reports of the English historical manuscripts commission and their appendices. Am. Hist. Asso. rep. 1898. p611-700 **859**

Kane, Hope F. Colonial promotion literature; a critical and bibliographical study. Providence, R.I. In progress **859a**

Lancour, A. Harold. Passenger lists of ships coming to North America, 1607-1825, a bibliography. N.Y. New York Pub. Lib. 1938. 26p. (Also N.Y. Pub. Lib. bul. XLI. p389-410. May 1937) **859b**

Lincoln, Charles Henry. A list of additional manuscripts of the French and Indian war in the library of the society. Am. Antiq. Soc. proc. n.s. XIX. p255-301 (Oct. 1908) **860**

McMurtrie, Douglas C. A bibliography of eighteenth century broadsides. Filson Club hist. quar. X. p23-30 (Jan. 1936) **860a**

Massachusetts Historical Society. Continuation of the narrative of newspapers published in New England, from 1704 to the Revolution. Mass. Hist. Soc. colls. ser. 1. VI. p64-77. 1800. (Reprinted, 1846)   **861**
—— A narrative of the newspapers printed in New England. Mass. Hist. Soc. colls. ser. 1. V. p208-16. 1798 (Reprinted in 1816 and 1835   **862**
Morris, Richard B. The sources of early American law: colonial period. W. Va. law quar. XL. p212-23 (April 1934) (Documentary series and archival sources)   **862a**
New York. Public Library. The Albany Congress of 1754. N.Y. Pub. Lib. bul. I. p76-81 (March 1897) (Calendar of the Emmet collection of printed and manuscript material)   **862b**
Paine, Nathaniel. A list of early American broadsides, 1680-1800, belonging to the library of the American Antiquarian Society. Worcester, Mass. 1897. 64p. (Reprinted from the Am. Antiq. Soc. proc. n.s. XI. p455-516)   **863**
—— A list of early American imprints, 1640-1700, belonging to the library of the American Antiquarian Society. Worcester. Press of Charles Hamilton. 1896. 80p. (Reprinted from the Am. Antiq. Soc. proc. n.s. X. p281-350. Oct. 1895)   **864**
Pantle, Alberta. Early American almanacs in the library of the Long Island Historical Society. Long Island Hist. Soc. quar. II. p99-108 (Oct. 1940)   **864a**
Sherwood, George. American colonists in English records; first series; a guide to direct references in authentic records, passenger lists, not in "Hotten," &c. London. George Sherwood. 1932. 99p.   **865**
Smithsonian Institution. Some account of a collection of several thousand bills, accounts and inventories, illustrating the history of prices between the years 1650 and 1750, presented to the Smithsonian Institution by James O. Halliwell. [Washington?] Brixton Hill, printer. 1852. 120p.   **866**
Swan, Robert T. Bibliographical: New England town records. Am. hist. rev. I. p581-4, 771-2 (April-July 1896)   **867**
Tuttle, Julius H. Early manuscript maps of New England. Col. Soc. Mass. pub. XVII. p112-15. 1915   **867a**
U.S. Library of Congress. Preliminary check list of American almanacs, 1639-1800. Comp. by Hugh A. Morrison. Wash. Govt. Ptg. Off. 1907. 160p.   **868**

Secondary Works

Ames, William Homer. A selected list of books dealing with the American colonial and revolutionary periods. . . . Phila.? 1926. 16p.   **869**
Bibliography—articles on the history of New England in periodical publications, January-October, 1927-date. Comp. by

Allyn B. Forbes, 1929-date. The New England quar.; an hist. rev. of New England life and letters. I. no. 1. Jan. 1928-   **870**
Bird, Henry C. & Co. Catalogue of books, chiefly relating to the history of New England, comprising a complete collection of the local histories of Massachusetts, also of Vermont; and, with few exceptions those of New Hampshire, Connecticut, and Rhode Island. . . . Boston. Rand, Avery & Co. 1872. 58p.   **871**
Black, George F. List of works in the New York Public Library relating to witchcraft in the United States. N.Y. Pub. Lib. bul. XII. p658-75 (Sept. 1908)   **872**
Boston. Public Library. Catalogue of a collection of early New England books made by the late John Allen Lewis and now in the possession of the Boston Public Library. Boston. The Trustees. 1892. 31p. (Reprinted from the Bul. XI. p151-79. July 1892)   **873**
—— New England; a selected list of works in the Public Library of the city of Boston (Brief reading lists, no. 16, Aug. 1920). Boston. The Trustees. 1920. 38p.   **874**
Butler, James David. American pre-revolutionary bibliography. Bibliotheca sacra. XXXVI. p72-104 (Jan. 1879)   **875**
Chitwood, Oliver Perry. Bibliographical notes. *In* A history of colonial America. N.Y. London. Harper. 1931. p708-90   **876**
Connecticut Historical Society. Maine, New Hampshire and Vermont local histories in the Connecticut Historical Society's Library. Conn. Hist. Soc. pap. and rep. 1898. p27-33   **877**
Dannappel, E. Die literatur der Salzburger emigration (1731-35), verzeichniss der deutschen und in Deutschland gedruckten schriften, welche aus anlass der Salzburgischen emigration erschienen sind. Stuttgart. Hoffmann'schen Buchdruckerie. 1886. 23p.   **878**
Deane, Charles. Critical essay on the sources of information—New England. *In* Narrative and critical history of America. Ed. by Justin Winsor. Boston, N.Y. Houghton Mifflin. 1884. III. p340-79   **879**
Drake, S. G. A catalogue of rare, useful and curious books, and tracts, chiefly historical (relating principally to New England). . . . Boston. 1864. 91p.   **880**
Eames, Wilberforce. Bibliographic notes on Eliot's Indian Bible and on his other translations and works in the Indian language of Massachusetts, extract from a Bibliography of the Algonquian languages. [by James C. Pilling] Wash. Govt. Ptg. Off. 1890. 58p.   **881**
—— Early New England catechisms: a bibliographical account of some catechisms published before the year, 1800, for use in New England. Am. Antiq. Soc. proc. n.s. XII. p76-182. 1897-98 (Also pub. separately. Worcester. 1898. 111p.)   **882**

Edwards, Everett Eugene. References on American colonial agriculture. (Bibliographical contributions, no. 33) Wash. U.S. Dept. of Agriculture Lib. 1938. 101p. mim.   **882a**

Ellis, George E. Critical essay on the sources of information—The religious element in the settlement of New England. *In* Narrative and critical history of America. Ed. by Justin Winsor. Boston, N.Y. Houghton Mifflin. 1884. III. p244-56   **883**

Evans, Charles. American bibliography; a chronological dictionary of all books, pamphlets and periodical publications printed in the United States of America from the genesis of printing in 1639 down to and including the year 1820 with bibliographical and biographical notes. Chicago. Printed for the author by the Blakeley Press; Hollister Press; Columbia Press. 1903-34. 12v. (Latest volume comes down to 1799. Cf. Munger, John C. Evans's American bibliography; tentative check list of the library location symbols. N.Y. Pub. Lib. bul. XL. p665-8. Aug. 1936. Being completed by the American Antiquarian Society)   **884**

Fernow, Berthold. Critical essay on the sources of information—Editorial notes—The middle colonies. *In* Narrative and critical history of America. Ed. by Justin Winsor. Boston, N.Y. Houghton Mifflin. 1887. V. p231-58   **885**

Fernow, Berthold and Winsor, Justin. Cartography and boundaries of the middle colonies. *In* Winsor, Justin, ed. Narrative and critical history of America. Boston; N.Y. Houghton Mifflin. 1887. V. p233-40   **885a**

Ford, Paul Leicester. The New England primer; a history of its origin and development, with a reprint of the unique copy of the earliest known edition. N.Y. Dodd, Mead. 1897. 354p.   **886**

Harper, Laurence A. A bibliography of colonial trade and commerce. Berkeley, Calif. University of California. In progress   **886a**

Harrisse, Henry. Bibliotheca Barlowiana. N.Y. 1864. 35p. (Originally printed in the N.Y. world. Descriptive catalogue of the Samuel L. M. Barlow-Aspinwall collection on Virginia and New England history during 17th century)   **887**

Harvard University. Library. Antinomian controversy in New England, 1636, etc. Harvard Univ. Lib. bul. I. no. 11. p287-8 (Feb.-March 1879)   **888**

Haven, Samuel F. Catalogue of publications in what is now the United States, prior to the Revolution of 1775-76. *In* Thomas, Isaiah. The history of printing in America. Transactions of the Am. Antiq. Soc. VI. p309-666. 1874   **889**

Heartman, Charles F. The New England primer issued prior to 1830; a bibliographical checklist for the more easy attaining the true knowledge of this book. . . . N.Y. Heartman. 1922. 192p.   **890**

Henry E. Huntington Library and Art Gallery. American imprints, 1648-1797, in the Huntington Library, supplementing Evans' American bibliography. Comp. by Willard O. Waters. Huntington Lib. bul. no. 3. 1933. 95p. (Reprinted, Harvard Univ. Press. 1933)   **891**

Keen, Gregory B. Note on New Albion. *In* Narrative and critical history of America. Ed. by Justin Winsor. Boston, N.Y. Houghton Mifflin. 1884. III. p457-68   **892**

Libbie, C. F. & Co. Catalogue of the valuable collection of books and pamphlets relating to America, forming the library of E. N. Coburn, Esq., of Charlestown, Mass., consisting of Massachusetts local history, genealogy, New England state histories, reprints, newspapers, travels, works by the Mathers, and other New England Divines. . . . Boston. Libbie. 1888. 180p.   **893**

Littlefield, George Emery. Catalogue of New England histories. Boston. 1881 **894**

—— Early schools and schoolbooks of New England. Boston. Club of Odd Volumes. 1904. 354p.   **895**

Love, William De Loss. Bibliography. *In* The fast and thanksgiving days of New England. Boston, N.Y. Houghton Mifflin. 1895. p515-602   **896**

Merrill, William Stetson. Catholic authorship in the American colonies before 1784. Wash. D.C. 1917. 18p. (Reprinted from the Cath. hist. rev. III. p308-25. Oct. 1917)   **897**

Meyers, Charles Lee. Bibliography of colonial costume. Comp. for The Society of Colonial Wars in the state of New Jersey. [N.Y. 1923] 36p.   **898**

Morris, Richard Brandon. Historiography of America, 1600-1800, as represented in the publications of Columbia University Press. N.Y. Columbia Univ. Press. 1933. 30p.   **899**

New England historical and genealogical register. Index of persons, volumes 1-50. Boston. New England Hist. and Geneal. Soc. [1905]-07. 3v.   **900**

—— Index of places, volumes 1-50. Boston. New England Hist. and Geneal. Soc. 1911. 123p.   **901**

—— Index of subjects, volumes 1-50. Boston. New England Hist. and Geneal. Soc. 1908. 296p.   **902**

Nijhoff, Martinus. Biblioteca historico-Neerlandica; histoire des Pays-Bas; catalogue systematique de livres anciens et modernes en vente aux prix marques chez Martinus Nijhoff. La Haye. M. Nijhoff. 1899. 471p.   **903**

—— The Hollanders in America; a choice collection of books, maps and pamphlets relating to the early colonization, voyages, exploration, etc., by the Hollanders, in different parts of North and South America. The Hague. M. Nijhoff. 1925. 91p.   **904**

Parker, John W. Catalogue of the private library of the late John Wells Parker, esq., of Roxbury, containing many New England publications . . . and also the private library of F. V. Marissal. . . . Boston. W. F. Brown. 1882. 91p. **905**

Parrington, Vernon Louis. The Puritan divines, 1620-1720. *In* The Cambridge history of American literature. Ed. by William P. Trent and others. N.Y. Putnam's. 1917. I. p31-56, 385-425 **906**

Pierce, William. A select bibliography of the Pilgrim fathers of New England. Congregational Hist. Soc. trans. VIII. p16-23, 59-68 (Feb.-Aug. 1920) **907**

Presbyterian Historical Society. Library. Short title list of books printed in America before 1800. Library of the Department of history (Presbyterian Historical Society) of the Presbyterian church in the United States of America. Comp. by Thomas C. Pears and Margaret Forman. [Phila.] 1937. 141p. mim. **907a**

Ragatz, Lowell Joseph. A bibliography of articles, descriptive, historical and scientific, on colonies and other dependent territories, appearing in American geographical and kindred journals through 1934. London. Arthur Thomas. [1935] 2v. 122,92p. **907b**

—— Colonial studies in the United States during the twentieth century. London. Arthur Thomas. 1932. 48p. **908**

—— A list of books and articles on colonial history and overseas expansion published in the United States, 1900-1930. Ann Arbor, Mich. Edwards Brothers, Inc. 1939. 45p. photop. **908a**

—— A list of books and articles on colonial history and overseas expansion published in the United States in 1931 and 1932. Toronto. W. Miller. [1934]. 41p. **909**

—— A list of books and articles on colonial history and overseas expansion published in the United States in 1933, 1934 and 1935. London. Arthur Thomas. [1936] 91p. **909a**

Reinsch, Paul Samuel. A short bibliography of American colonial law. *In* Association of American Law Schools. Select essays in Anglo-American legal history. Boston. Little, Brown. 1908. II. p164-8 **910**

Riley, Woodbridge. Philosophers and divines, 1720-1789. *In* The Cambridge history of American literature. Ed. by William P. Trent and others. N.Y. Putnam's. 1917. I. p72-89, 438-42 **911**

Robinson, William H., Ltd., Booksellers. Books and manuscripts relating to America, arranged in chronological order, including the library of George Grenville (1712-1770) the promoter of the famous Stamp act. . . London. [Birmingham. The Press of F. Juckes. 1940] 224p. **911a**

Rutherford, Livingston. John Peter Zenger, his press, his trial, and a bibliography of Zenger imprints, also a reprint of the first edition of the trial. N.Y. Dodd, Mead. 1904. 275p. **912**

Sanders, Jennings Bryan. Introductory bibliography. *In* Early American history (1492-1789) political, social, economic. N.Y. Prentice-Hall. 1938. p633-76 **912a**

Shurtleff, Nathaniel B. Catalogue of the library of Dr. N. B. Shurtleff. . . . Boston. W. F. Brown. 1875. 92p. (Books relating to New England) **913**

Slafter, Edmund F. A bibliography of the controversy in America relating to Episcopacy, conducted by the Puritan divines and the clergy of the Church of England, 1719-1774. *In* John Checkley, or the evolution of religious tolerance in Massachusetts Bay (The publications of the Prince Soc.) Boston. John Wilson. 1897. II. p225-98 **914**

Thomas, Isaiah. Catalogue of booksellers in the colonies from the first settlement of the country to the commencement of the Revolutionary war, in 1775. *In* Thomas, Isaiah. The history of printing in America. Transactions of the Am. Antiq. Soc. VI. p205-43. 1874 **915**

Trumbull, J. Hammond. Origin and progress of the Indian missions in New England with a list of books in the Indian language printed at Cambridge and Boston, 1653-1721. From the Report of the Council of the Am. Antiq. Soc. presented at the annual meeting held in Worcester, Oct. 22, 1873. Worcester, Mass. 1874. p33-50. (Also in Am. Antiq. Soc. proc. V. p45-62. 1873) **916**

U.S. Library of Congress. Division of bibliography. List of memoirs, etc., depicting the social life of colonial America, 1660-1775. 1904. 10p. typ. **917**

—— —— —— List of references on Acadia. n.d. 7p. typ. **918**

—— —— —— List of references on the commercial and economic conditions in the colonies. Sept. 8, 1914. 4p. typ. **919**

—— —— —— List of references on the Pilgrim fathers. July 14, 1920. 5p. mim. **920**

—— —— —— List of references on the customs, etc., of colonial times. 1903. 4p. typ. **921**

Vail, R. W. G. A check list of New England election sermons. Am. Antiq. Soc. 1936. 36p. (Preprint from the Am. Antiq. Soc. proc. n.s. Oct. 1935) **922**

Welch, Jane M. A finding list; English settlements in America, series no. 2, pt. I. Buffalo. The Courier Co. 1894. 24p. **923**

Wilson, Minnie C. Reading list, colonial New England. N.Y. state lib. bul. bibliog. no. 2. p17-33 (April 1897) **924**

Winship, George Parker. The earliest American imprints. Milwaukee. The E. Keogh Press. 1899. 10p. (Reprinted from Am. book-lore. July 1899) **925**

—— The Eliot Indian tracts. *In* Bibliographical essays; a tribute to Wilberforce Eames. Cambridge. Harvard Univ. Press. 1924. p179-92. (Reprinted separately. 1925) **926**

Winsor, Justin. Authorities on the French and Indian wars of New England and Acadia, 1688-1763. *In* Narrative and critical history of America. Boston; N.Y. Houghton Mifflin. 1887. V. p420-72   **927**

—— The cartography of the northeast coast of North America, 1535-1600. *In* Narrative and critical history of America. Boston; N.Y. Houghton Mifflin. 1884. IV. p81-102   **927a**

—— Critical essay on the sources of information—The Carolinas. *In* Narrative and critical history of America. Boston; N.Y. Houghton Mifflin. 1887. V. p335-56   **928**

—— Critical essay on the sources of information—Maryland and Virginia. *In* Narrative and critical history of America. Boston; N.Y. 1887. V. p270-84   **929**

—— Critical essay on the sources of information—New England, 1689-1763. *In* Narrative and critical history of America. Boston; N.Y. Houghton Mifflin. 1887. V. p156-88   **930**

—— Critical essay on the sources of information—The struggle for the great valleys of North America. *In* Narrative and critical history of America. Boston; N.Y. Houghton Mifflin. 1887. V. p560-622   **931**

—— The earliest printed sources of New England history, 1602-1629. Cambridge. John Wilson. 1894. 14p. (Reprinted from Mass. Hist. Soc. proc. 2d ser. IX. p181-92. Nov. 1894)   **932**

—— Literature of witchcraft in New England. Am. Antiq. Soc. proc. n.s. X. p351-73 (Oct. 1895) (Reprinted. Worcester. 1897. 25p.)   **933**

—— Maps of the eastern coast of North America, 1500-1535, with the cartographical history of the sea of Verrazano. *In* Narrative and critical history of America. Boston; N.Y. Houghton Mifflin. 1884. IV. p33-46   **933a**

—— The New-England Indians, 1630-1700. Mass. Hist. Soc. proc. X. p327-59. 1895-96. (Reprinted. Cambridge. 1895)   **934**

Wroth, Lawrence Counselman. An American bookshelf, 1755. Phila. Univ. of Pennsylvania Press. 1934. 191p.   **935**

—— The colonial printer. N.Y. The Grolier Club. 1931. 271p.   **936**

—— Williams Parks, printer and journalist of England and colonial America, with a list of the issues of his several presses. . . (The William Parks Club. publication no. 3) Richmond. Appeals Press. 1926. 70p. (Presses located at Annapolis and Williamsburg)   **937**

REVOLUTION AND CONFEDERATION

Source Materials

Abbott, Wilbur Cortez. An introduction to the documents relating to the international status of Gibraltar, 1704-1934. N.Y. Macmillan. 1934. 112p.   **938**

Adams, Randolph G. A new library of American revolutionary records. Current hist. XXXIII. p234-8 (Nov. 1930) (William L. Clements Lib., Univ. of Michigan)   **939**

—— The papers of Lord George Germain; a brief description of the Stopford-Sackville papers now in the William L. Clements Library. (Univ. of Michigan. William L. Clements Lib. Bul. no. 18) Ann Arbor. Wm. L. Clements Lib. 1928. 46p.   **940**

Alvord, Clarence W. The Shelburne manuscripts in America. Inst. of Hist. Research bul. I. p77-80 (Feb. 1924)   **941**

Bourne, Edward Gaylord. The authorship of the Federalist. *In* Essays in historical criticism. N.Y. Scribner's. 1901   **941a**

Calkin, Homer L. Pamphlets and public opinion during the American revolution. Pa. mag. hist. LXIV. p22-42 (Jan. 1940)   **941b**

Campbell, William J. Unknown issues of the journals of the Continental Congress. The Am. collector. III. p114-16 (Dec. 1926)   **942**

Canada. Archives. Calendar of Shelburne correspondence. *In* Report of the public archives for the year 1921. Ottawa. King's printer. 1922. p229-81 (Covers vols. 13-217 of the Shelburne or Lansdowne correspondence relating to the period 1763 to 1783)   **942a**

—— —— Report on manuscript lists in the archives relating to the United Empire Loyalists with reference to other sources. Prep. by Wilfrid Campbell. [Ottawa] Print. for the use of the Archives Branch. 1909. 30p.   **943**

Carter, Clarence E. Notes on the Lord Gage collection of manuscripts. Miss. Valley hist. rev. XV. p511-19 (March 1929)   **944**

Chapin, Howard Millar. Calendrier française pour l'année 1781 and the printing press of the French fleet in American waters during the revolutionary war. (Contributions to Rhode Island bibliog. II) Providence. 1914. 9p.   **945**

Clark, Hollis Chenery. Report on publication of revolutionary military records. Am. Hist. Asso. rep. 1915. p191-9   **946**

Craft, Rev. David. List of journals, narratives, etc. of the western expedition—1779. Mag. of Am. hist. III. pt. 2. p673-5 (Nov. 1879)   **947**

Doniol, Henri. Index analytique de l'ouvrage. *In* Histoire de la participation de la France à l'établissement des États-Unis d'Amérique, correspondence diplomatique et documents. Paris. Imprimerie nationale. 1892. VI. p627-721   **948**

Draper, Mrs. Amos G. Rejected pension papers discovered. Daughters of Am. revolution mag. LXIV. p78-82, 142-7 (Feb.-March 1930) (Rejected applications of revolutionary soldiers in Boston)   **949**

Draper, Lyman Copeland. An essay on the autographic collections of the signers of the Declaration of Independence and of the Constitution. From vol. Xth. Wisconsin Hist. Soc. colls. N.Y. Burns & Son. 1889. 117p. **950**

Farrand, Max. The records of the Federal convention. Am. hist. rev. XIII. p44-65 (Oct. 1907) **951**

Flick, Alexander C. New sources on the Sullivan-Clinton campaign in 1779. N.Y. State Hist Asso. quar. jour. X. p185-224, 265-317 (July-Oct. 1929) **952**

Ford, Paul Leicester. The authorship of the Federalist. Am. hist. rev. II. p675-82 (July 1897) **952a**

—— A list of editions of "The Federalist." Brooklyn, N.Y. 1886. 25p. (Reprinted from the author's Bibliotheca Hamiltoniana. 1886. pt. I. p13-35) **953**

—— Some materials for a bibliography of the official publications of the Continental Congress, 1774-1789. Brooklyn, N.Y. 1888. 57p. (Also Boston Pub. Lib. Bibliographies of special subjects no. 6. Boston. 1890. 31p., and Boston Pub. Lib. bul. VIII-X. Sept. 1888-July 1891) **954**

Friedenwald, Herbert. The journals and papers of the Continental Congress. Am. Hist. Asso. rep. 1896. I. p83-135 **955**

Frothingham, Richard. Maps and plans of the battle of Bunker Hill. Mass. Hist. Soc. proc. XIV. p53-9. 1876 **955a**

Greenough, Chester N. New England almanacs, 1766-1775, and the American revolution. Am. Antiq. Soc. proc. XLV. p288-316 (Oct. 16, 1935) **955b**

Hartley, David. A catalogue of a valuable . . . collection of manuscripts and autograph letters, chiefly relating to America. . . . sold by auction. . . . [London. 1859] 18p. **956**

Henkels, Stan V. An unique collection of Revolutionary broadsides. . . Phila. 1915. 11p. **957**

Historical Records Survey. District of Columbia. Calendar of the letters and documents of Peter Force on the Mecklenburg declaration of independence in the Loomis collection, Washington, D.C. Wash. D.C. April 1940. 35p. mim. **957a**

Index to army returns of the revolution, from the Washington manuscripts (Force copies), originals in the Adj-Gen'ls. office —War Department, Washington, D.C. (Seven bound volumes in the MSS. division of the Lib. of Congress) **958**

Jameson, J. Franklin. The action of the states [and journals and debates of the state conventions]. *In* Studies in the history of the Federal convention of 1787. Am. Hist. Asso. rep. 1902. I. p161-7 **959**

Jenkins, Charles F. The completed sets of the signers of the Declaration of Independence, 1925. Pa. mag. hist. XLIX. p231-49 (July 1925) **959a**

Kellar, Charles Roy and Pierson, George Wilson. A new Madison manuscript relating to the Federal convention of 1787. Am. hist. rev. XXXVI. p17-30 (Oct. 1930) **959b**

Lapham, Ruth. Checklist of American revolutionary war pamphlets in the Newberry Library. Chicago. Newberry Lib. 1922. 115p. **960**

McIlwaine, H. R. The revolutionary war material in the Virginia State Library. Mag. of hist. X. p143-50 (Sept. 1909) **961**

Maggs Bros. (London). The American war for independence as related in the unpublished manuscript journals and plans of Alexander Berthier, staff officer to General Comte de Rochambeau during the American campaign, later Napoleon's favorite marshal and created by him Prince of Wagram and Prince of Neuchatel. London. Maggs Bros. Ltd. 1936. 36p. **961a**

Michigan. University. William L. Clements Library of American history. British headquarters maps and sketches used by Sir Henry Clinton while in command of the British forces operating in North America during the war for independence, 1775-1782; a descriptive list of the original manuscripts and printed documents now preserved in the William L. Clements Library at the University of Michigan. Comp. by Randolph G. Adams. Ann Arbor. 1928. 144p. **961b**

—— —— British maps of the American Revolution; a guide to an exhibition in the William L. Clements Library. (Bul. XXIV) Ann Arbor. 1936. 23p. **961c**

—— —— Exhibition of some interesting papers from the archives of Sir Henry Clinton, commander-in-chief of the British army in North America, 1778-1782. (Bul. no. 13) Ann Arbor. 1926. 4p. **961d**

—— —— The headquarters papers of the British army in North America during the war of the American revolution; a brief description of Sir Henry Clinton's papers in the William L. Clements Library. By Randolph G. Adams. (Bul. no. 14) Ann Arbor. 1926. 47p. **961e**

—— —— Papers from the archives of Sir Henry Clinton. (Univ. of Michigan. William L. Clements Lib. bul. no. 13) Ann Arbor. Wm. L. Clements Lib. 1926. 4p. **961f**

—— —— Report on the Sir John Vaughan papers in the William L. Clements Library. (Bul. XIX) Ann Arbor. 1929. 37p. **961g**

Mitchell, James Tyndale. Collection of engraved portraits of officers in the army and navy of the War of the Revolution, the second war with Great Britain, and the Mexican war; also views of land and naval battles belonging to Hon. James T. Mitchell, Chief Justice of Pennsylvania. Catalogue compiled and sale conducted by Stan. V. Henkels at the auction rooms of Davis & Harvey, Philadelphia. (Nov. and Dec. 1906) Phila. 1906. 131p. **961h**

Moore, Jacob B. Maps in the DeWitt collection. *In* Journals of the military expedition of Major General John Sullivan against the Six Nations of Indians in 1779. Ed. by Frederick Cook. Auburn, N.Y. Knapp, Peck and Thomson. 1887. p291-5 (MS. surveys by Robert Erskine, geographer to the American army, in the New York Historical Society)   961i

Moore, John Bassett. The diplomatic correspondence of the American revolution. Pol. science quar. VIII. p33-47 (March 1893) (Concerning Sparks's compilation)   963

Paltsits, Victor Hugo. A plan of the Yorktown campaign. N.Y. Pub. Lib. bul. XXVI. p855-8 (Oct. 1922)   963a

Pennsylvania. Historical commission. List of Sullivan expedition manuscripts and published material. (MS. in possession of the comn.)   964

Revolutionary war manuscripts in possession of the Marblehead Historical Society. Essex Inst. hist. coll. LXXV. p15-22 (Jan. 1939)   964a

Rosenbach, Abraham Simon Wolf. The Declaration of independence, July 4, 1776; its inception and history, illustrated by original documents, including memorable autographs of all the signers . . . Phila. 1937. 30p.   964b

Rosenbach Company. 1776 Americana; a catalogue of autograph letters and documents relating to the Declaration of Independence and the Revolutionary War. Phila. Rosenbach. 1926. 95p.   965

Stockbridge, J. C. Pamphlets in the John Carter Brown Library relating to the Revolutionary War. Mag. of Am. hist. VI. p310-14 (April 1881)   966

Thomas, William S. American revolutionary diaries; also journals, narratives, autobiographies, reminiscences and personal memoirs, catalogued and described with an index to places and events. N.Y. Hist. Soc. bul. VI. p32-5, 61-71, 101-7 (April-Oct. 1922)   967

U.S. Congress. House. Committee on military affairs. Compilation of revolutionary war records; report to accompany S. 271. March 20, 1912. House report 431, 62 Cong. 2 sess. Serial 6130. 6p.   968

—— —— **Senate. Committee on military affairs.** Compilation of revolutionary war records; report to accompany S. 271. Jan. 15, 1912. Senate report 176, 62 Cong. 2 sess. Serial 6120. 5p.   968a

U.S. Department of State. Catalogue of the papers of the Continental Congress; miscellaneous index; appendix: Documentary history of the Constitution. . . . (Bureau of rolls and library. Bul. no. 1) Wash. D.C. 1893. 102, 46p. (Appendix reissued as first 46 pages of Documentary history of the Constitution of the United States of America. 1894)   968b

—— —— Documentary history of the revolution . . . on the subject of the contract entered into by Edward Livingston, late secretary of state, with Matthew St. Clair Clarke and Peter Force, for the collection and publication of the documentary history of the American Revolution. House document no. 36. 23 Congress. 2 session. Dec. 24, 1834. 98p.   968c

—— —— Preliminary index to correspondence and topics in introduction and notes. *In* The revolutionary diplomatic correspondence of the United States. Edited by Francis Wharton. Wash. Govt. Ptg. Off. 1889. I. p1-243   963d

U.S. Library of Congress. Division of bibliography. List of memoirs, diaries, journals, etc., of French officers, in the Revolutionary War 1781-1783. 1903. 8p. typ.   969

—— —— —— List of the more important official or semi-official publications which contain registers or rosters of the revolutionary soldiers. 1912. 3p. typ.   970

—— —— **Division of manuscripts.** Bibliographical notes. *In* Journals of the Continental Congress, 1774-1789. Ed. by Worthington C. Ford, Gaillard Hunt, John C. Fitzpatrick, and Roscoe R. Hill. Wash. Govt. Ptg. Off. 1904-36 (Completed to 1787 in 33v.)   971

—— —— —— Naval records of the American revolution, 1775-1788. Prepared from the originals in the Library of Congress by Charles Henry Lincoln. Wash. Govt. Ptg. Off. 1906. 549p.   971a

Winsor, Justin. Maps of the revolutionary period. *In* The memorial history of Boston. Boston. J.R. Osgood & Co. 1881. III, pi-xii   972

Secondary Works

Adams, Randolph G. The cartography of the British attack on Fort Moultrie in 1776. *In* Essays offered to Herbert Putnam by his colleagues and friends on his thirtieth anniversary as librarian of Congress, 5 April 1929. Ed. by William W. Bishop and Andrew Keogh. New Haven. Yale Univ. Press. 1939. p35-46   972a

Anderson Galleries. Memorial exhibition Thaddeus Kosciuszko, revered Polish and American hero, his patriotism, vision, and zeal revealed in a collection of autograph letters . . . oil paintings, medals, engravings, books, broadsides, and other relics, being the collection formed by Dr. & Mrs. Alexander Kahanowicz. . . . N.Y. Anderson Galleries, 1927. 72p.   973

Bement, Clarence Sweet. A valuable collection of rare and scarce Americana and early American imprints, including . . . an extraordinary collection of pamphlets on the Stamp Act, and on the American Revolutionary War. Phila. Bicking. 1896. 50p.   974

Boston. Public Library. Literature of 1776. Boston Pub. Lib. bul. III. p31-4, 172-7 (Jan. 1876, Jan. 1877)   975

Campbell, Charles A. Bibliography of Major André. Mag. of Am. hist. VIII. p61-72 (Jan. 1882)   976

Carnegie Endowment for International Peace. Library. Bibliography of Count de Grasse (Grasse-Tilly, François Joseph Paul, marquis de, 1723-1788). M. Alice Matthews, librarian. Wash. D.C. 1931. 4p. typ. **977**

Chamberlain, Mellen. Critical essay on the sources of information—Editorial notes— The revolution impending. *In* Narrative and critical history of America. Ed. by Justin Winsor. Boston, N.Y. Houghton Mifflin. 1887. VI. p62-111 **978**

Channing, Edward. Critical essay on the sources of information—The war in the southern department. *In* Narrative and critical history of America. Ed. by Justin Winsor. Boston, N.Y. Houghton Mifflin. 1887. VI. p507-55 **979**

Cullum, George W. Critical essay on the sources of information—Editorial notes— The struggle for the Hudson. *In* Narrative and critical history of America. Ed. by Justin Winsor. Boston, N.Y. Houghton Mifflin. 1887. VI. p315-66 **980**

Davis, Andrew McFarland. Critical essay on the sources of information—The Indians and the border warfare of the revolution. *In* Narrative and critical history of America. Ed. by Justin Winsor. Boston, N.Y. Houghton Mifflin. 1887. VI. p647-84 **981**

Egerton, Helen Merrill. United Empire loyalist literature. The United Empire Loyalist Asso. of Canada. annual trans. 1917-26. p15-18. (Reprinted from the Toronto mail and empire) **982**

Ellis, George E. Critical essay on the sources of information—Editorial notes— The sentiment of independence, its growth and consummation. *In* Narrative and critical history of America. Ed. by Justin Winsor. Boston, N.Y. Houghton Mifflin. 1887. VI. p252-74 **983**

Faÿ, Bernard. Bibliographie critique des ouvrages français relatifs aux États-Unis, (1770-1800). (Bibliothèque de la revue de littérature comparés, dirigée par Fernand Baldensperger et Paul Hazard. VII. pt. 2) Paris. Champion. 1925. 108p. **984**

Fisher, Sidney George. The legendary and myth-making process in histories of the American revolution. Am. Phil. Soc. proc. LI. p53-76. 1912 (Reprinted in Hist. teach. mag. IV. p63-71. 1913) **984a**

Ford, Paul Leicester. Josiah Tucker and his writings; an eighteenth century pamphleteer on America. Chicago. Univ. of Chicago Press. 1894. 18p. (Reprinted from the Jour. of pol. economy. no. 1. March 1894) **985**

Gottlieb, Theodore D. The origin and evolution of the Betsy Ross flag; legend or tradition. Newark, N.J. 1938. 8p. **985a**

Gottschalk, Louis R. Lafayette. [Bibliography] Jour. of modern hist. II. p281-7 (June 1930) **986**

Green, Fletcher Melvin. Heroes of the American Revolution; an outline for individual and group study. (North Carolina. Univ. extension division. Univ. of North Carolina extension bul. XI. no. 5. Jan. 1932) Chapel Hill, N.C. Univ. of North Carolina Press. 1932. 55p. **987**

Halsey, R. T. Haines. "Impolitical prints." The American revolution as pictured by contemporary English caricaturists; an exhibition. N.Y. Pub. Lib. bul. XLIII. p795-829 (Nov. 1939) **987a**

Hays, Isaac Minis. A contribution to the bibliography of the Declaration of Independence. [Phila. 1900] 11p. (Reprinted from Am. Phil. Soc. proc. XXXIX. p69-78. Jan. 1900) **988**

Heartman, Charles F. The cradle of the United States, 1765-1789; five hundred contemporary broadsides, pamphlets, and a few books pertaining to the history of the Stamp act, the Boston massacre and other pre-revolutionary troubles, the war for independence and the adoption of the federal constitution, alphabetically arranged with index to items issued anonymously but listed under author's name, bibliographically, historically and sometimes sentimentally described by the owner. Perth Amboy, N.J. [Charles F. Heartman] 1922-23. 126+112p. **989**

—— Rare Americana; books relating to the American Revolution. N.Y. Charles F. Heartman. 1917. 35p. **990**

Ingalsbe, Grenville Mellen. A bibliography of Sullivan's Indian expedition. Hudson Fall, N.Y. The author. 1914. 36p. (Also in N. Y. State Hist. Asso. proc. VI. p37-70. 1906) **991**

Jackson, Stuart W. La Fayette, a bibliography. N.Y. William Edwin Rudge. 1930. 226p. **992**

Jay, John. Critical essay on the sources of information—Editorial notes—The peace negotiations of 1782-1783. *In* Narrative and critical history of America. Ed. by Justin Winsor. Boston, N.Y. Houghton Mifflin. 1888. VII. p165-84 **993**

Libby, Orin Grant. A critical examination of William Gordon's history of the American revolution. Am. Hist. Asso. rep. 1899. I. p367-88 **993a**

—— Ramsay as a plagiarist. Am. hist. rev. VII. p697-703 (July 1902) (David Ramsay, American revolution) **993b**

Lodge, Henry Cabot. Bibliography of the "Federalist." *In* The works of Alexander Hamilton. N.Y., London. Putnam's. 1904. XI. p. xxi-xl **994**

Lossing. Davidson, Alexander, Jr. How Benson J. Lossing wrote his "field books" of the revolution, the war of 1812 and the civil war. Bibliog. Soc. Am. pap. XXXII. p57-64. 1938 **994a**

Lowell, Edward J. Critical essay on the sources of information—Notes—The United States of America, 1775-1782, their political struggles and relations with

Lowell, E. J. Critical essay—*Continued*
Europe. *In* Narrative and critical history of America. Ed. by Justin Winsor. Boston, N.Y. Houghton Mifflin. 1888. VII. p73-88 **995**

MacDonald, William. American political writing, 1760-1789. *In* The Cambridge history of American literature. Ed. by William P. Trent and others. N.Y. Putnam's. 1917. I. p124-49, 454-7 **996**

Nelson, William. The controversy over the proposition for an American episcopate, 1767-1774: a bibliography of the subject. Paterson, N.J. Paterson Hist. Club. 1909. unpag. **997**

New York. Public Library. The Declaration of Independence. N.Y. Pub. Lib. bul. I. p351-64 (Nov. 1897) (Calendar of the Emmet collection of printed and manuscript material) **997a**

—— —— Exhibition commemorating the 150th anniversary of the adoption of the Declaration of Independence, 1776-1926. Arranged by Charles F. McCombs and Ernest L. Hettick, described by E. L. Hettick. N. Y. Pub. Lib. bul. XXXI. p807-25, 904-59 (Oct.-Nov. 1927) **998**

—— —— The members of the Continental Congress, 1774-1789. N.Y. Pub. Lib. bul. I. p159-72, 191-200, 227-36, 257-67, 289-99 (June-Oct. 1897) (Calendar of the Emmett collection of printed and manuscript material) **998a**

Northrop, Everett H. Burgoyne's invasion, 1777; a select list of published sources, both primary and secondary. Syracuse, N.Y. Syracuse Univ. In progress **998b**

Reuss, Jeremias David. Alphabetical register of all the authors actually in Great-Britain, Ireland and in the United provinces of North-America, with a catalogue of their publications, from the year 1770 to the year 1790. Berlin and Stettin. Nicolai. 1791. Supplement and continuation from the year 1790 to the year 1803. Berlin and Stettin. Nicolai. 1804. 3v. **999**

Salley, A. S., Jr. The Mecklenberg declaration: the present status of the question. Am. hist. rev. XIII. p16-43 (Oct. 1907) **999a**

Salley, A. S., Jr. and Ford, Worthington C. Dr. S. Millington Miller and the Mecklenberg declarations. Am. hist. rev. XI. p548-58 (April 1906) **999b**

Seitz, Don C. Bibliography. *In* Paul Jones; his exploits in English seas during 1777-1780. N.Y. E.P. Dutton. 1917. p167-327 **1000**

Smith, Lloyd P. A bibliography of that ancient and honourable order The Society of the Cincinnati. Phila. For private distribution. 1885. 18p. (Reprinted from the Bul. of the Lib. Co. of Phila. n.s. no. 15. p47-58 (July 1885)) **1001**

Stevens, Henry, son and Stiles, firm, booksellers. The American War of Independence; its history, origin, and progress as revealed by contemporary books, pamphlets, manuscripts, maps and plans

with numerous notes, bibliographical and descriptive, together with an introduction by Dr. Randolph G. Adams. London. H. Stevens, son and Stiles. 1931. 139p. **1002**

Thornton, Mary Lindsay. The battle of King's Mountain: a bibliography. North Carolina Lib. bul. VII. p275-6 (June 1930) **1003**

Tyler, Moses Coit. The writers of history—Bibliography. *In* The literary history of the American Revolution. N.Y., London. Putnam's. 1897. II. p383-429, 429-83 **1004**

U.S. Library of Congress. Division of bibliography. Causes of the American Revolution; a list of writings. Aug. 19, 1936. 3p. typ. **1005**

—— —— —— Count Kazimierz (Casimir) Pulaski, 1748-1779; a bibliographical list. Aug. 16, 1929. 8p. typ. **1006**

—— —— —— List of references on Detroit in the Revolution. March 27, 1917. 4p. typ. **1007**

—— —— —— List of references on pre-constitutional period of the diplomatic history and policy of the United States. Nov. 30, 1921. 13p. typ. **1008**

—— —— —— List of references on the battle of Lexington. March 16, 1925. 8p. typ. **1009**

—— —— —— List of references on the Continental Congress. Feb. 12, 1916. 6p. typ. **1010**

—— —— —— List of references on the Declaration of Independence. March 26, 1925. 3p. typ. (Supplement. April 7, 1933. 4p. typ.) **1011**

—— —— —— List of references on the Loyalists of the American Revolution. Nov. 13, 1920. 9p. typ. **1012**

—— —— —— List of references on the Marquis de Lafayette. (Supplementing those appearing in our printed list of works relating to the French alliance in the Am. Revolution) Aug. 19, 1919. 4p. typ. (List of recent references. June 11, 1931. 8p. typ.) **1013**

—— —— —— List of references on the Mecklenburg declaration of independence. May 21, 1915. 4p. typ. **1014**

—— —— —— List of works relating to the French alliance in the American Revolution. Comp. under the direction of A. P. C. Griffin. Wash. Govt. Ptg. Off. 1907. 40p. **1015**

—— —— —— Military activities of the American Loyalists in the American Revolution; a list of selected references. April 18, 1936. 13p. typ. **1016**

—— —— —— The Saratoga campaign 1777: a bibliographical list. Comp. by Florence S. Hellman. Feb. 2, 1940. 26p. typ. **1016a**

—— —— —— Select list of references on Thaddeus Kosciusko. Dec. 2, 1913. 8p. typ. **1017**

Utica, N.Y. Public Library. Bibliography of Sullivan's expedition against the Six nations in 1779. Utica, N.Y. 1929. 22p. **1017a**

Whitney, James L. The nineteenth of April in literature. *In* Proceedings at the Centennial celebration of the Concord fight, April 19, 1875. Concord. Pub. by the town. 1876. p165-73. (Also separately pub.)   **1018**

Williams, George Clinton Fairchild. The fine historical library of Dr. George C. F. Williams, Hartford, Conn. . . . N.Y. Anderson Galleries. 1926. 208p. (Books, pamphlets, broadsides, autographs, manuscripts and documents on the American Revolution)   **1019**

Winsor, Justin. Critical essay on the sources of information—editorial notes—The conflict precipitated. *In* Narrative and critical history of America. Boston, N.Y. Houghton Mifflin. 1887. VI. p172-230   **1020**

—— Editorial notes on events in the North, 1779-1781. *In* Narrative and critical history of America. Boston, N.Y. Houghton Mifflin. 1887. VI. p555-62   **1021**

—— Editorial notes on the sources of information—The struggle for the Delaware. *In* Narrative and critical history of America. Boston, N.Y. Houghton Mifflin. 1887. VI. p403-47   **1022**

—— The literature of Bunker Hill, with its antecedents and results. *In* Boston City Council. Celebration of the centennial anniversary of the battle of Bunker Hill. Boston. Printed by order of the City Council. 1875. p151-74 (Reprinted from the Boston Pub. Lib. bul. no. 34. July 1875)   **1023**

—— The reader's handbook of the American Revolution, 1761-1783. Boston; N.Y. Houghton Mifflin. 1879. 328p.   **1024**

—— Special editorial notes—The naval history of the American Revolution. *In* Narrative and critical history of America. Boston; N.Y. Houghton Mifflin. 1887. VI. p589-604   **1025**

—— The treason of Arnold; a critical study of the authorities by the editor. *In* Narrative and critical history of America. Boston; N.Y. Houghton Mifflin. 1887. VI. p447-68   **1026**

Woodward, C. L. Catalogue of tidbits relating to the American revolution. N.Y. 1877   **1027**

CHAPTER III

THE UNITED STATES

PUBLIC DOCUMENTS

Handbooks and Guides

Albertson, George H. Geologic index of the publications of the United States Geological Survey. Denver. Geol. Publishing Co. 1931. 420p. (Supplement. 1932. 25p.) **1027a**

Austin, O. P. Use of statistical publications of the government in working out problems of commercial investigation. Administration. III. p433-6 (April 1922) **1028**

Bemis, Samuel Flagg and Griffin, Grace Gardner. Remarks on the sources— Printed states papers. *In* Guide to the diplomatic history of the United States, 1775-1921. Wash. Govt. Ptg. Off. 1935. p807-36 **1028a**

Blanchard, Edwin C. Docket-citator to reported formal complaint decisions and ex parte investigations of the Interstate Commerce Commission, vol. 1-100 inclusive [1887-1925] except finance and valuation opinions. Wash. D.C. 1925. 40p. **1028b**

Blanchard, Edwin C. and Heid, Fred W. Consolidated index to the reported decisions of the Interstate Commerce Commission, vols. 1-85 [1887-1923] inclusive, except finance and valuation decisions. Wash. D.C. Capital Traffic Service Bureau. 1925. 292p. (Supplement no. 1. v. 86 to 96. 1923-25. Wash. D.C. 1925. 365p. multig.) **1028c**

Boyd, Anne Morris. United States government publications as sources of information for libraries. N.Y. H. W. Wilson. 1931. 329p. o.p. **1029**

Briggs, Samuel W. Regulation of interstate commerce; history of bills and resolutions introduced in Congress respecting federal regulation of interstate commerce by railways, etc., from the thirty-seventh Congress to the sixty-second Congress, inclusive, 1862-1913. Wash. Govt. Ptg. Off. 1913. 168p. **1030**

Carter, Clarence Edwin. The United States and documentary historical publication. (Senate doc. 33, 76th Cong. 1st sess.) Wash. Govt. Ptg. Off. 1939 (Reprinted form the Miss. Valley hist. rev. June 1938) **1030a**

Childs, James Bennett. An account of government document bibliography in the United States and elsewhere. Wash. Govt. Ptg. Off. 1930. 57p. **1031**

—— The current recording of United States government publications. Wash. 1937. (Reprinted for private distribution from the Communications to the World Congress of Universal Documentation, Paris, August 16-21, 1937) **1031a**

Clark, A. Howard. What the United States government has done for history. Am. Hist. Asso. rep. 1894. p549-61 **1032**

Clarke, Edith E. Guide to the use of the United States government publications. Boston. Boston Book Co. 1918. 308p. **1033**

Colegrove, Kenneth W. Expansion of the publications of the Department of State. Am. pol. sci. rev. XXIII. p69-77 (Feb. 1929) **1034**

Dennett, Tyler. Governmental publications for the study of international law. Am. Soc. of Inter. Law proc. XXIII. p55-62. 1929 **1035**

—— The publication policy of the Department of State. Foreign affairs. p301-5 (Jan. 1930) **1036**

Everhart, Elfrida. A handbook of United States public documents. Minneapolis. H. W. Wilson. 1910. 320p. **1037**

Falkner, R. P. A list of bibliographies published in official documents of the United States. May 1902-April 1903, inclusive. Lib. jour. XXVIII. p775-6 (Nov. 1903) **1038**

Fassig, Oliver Lanard. Bibliography of meteorology, classed catalogue of printed literature of meteorology from origin of printing to close of 1881, with supplement to close of 1887 and another index. Wash. D.C. Signal Off. 1889-91. 4pts. **1039**

Finch, George Augustus. Present interest in foreign affairs and the State Department's publication facilities. Am. Jour. of International law. XXIII. p121-6. 1929 **1040**

Fitzgerald, Roy G. (Historical sketch of efforts to codify the laws of the United States). *In* Congressional record, Feb. 27, 1931. Wash. Govt. Ptg. Off. 1931. LXXIV. p6312-17 **1040a**

Ford, Paul Leicester. A list of treasury reports and circulars issued by Alexander Hamilton, 1789-1795. Brooklyn. 1886. 47p. (Reprint of pt. 2 of the author's Bibliotheca Hamiltoniana. 1886) **1041**

Ford, Worthington C. Publication of historical material by the United States government. *In* Report of the Librarian of Congress, 1904. Wash. Govt. Ptg. Off. 1904. p171-82 **1042**

Graske, Theodore Wesley. Federal reference manual; a complete guide to all federal departments, administrations . . . systems, committees . . . having legal or quasi-legal status, and courts: with official publications. Wash. D.C. National Law Book Co. 1939. 601p. **1042a**

Griffith, William. Catalogue of "Federal" law books. *In* Annual register of the laws of the United States. Burlington, N.J. David Allinson. 1822. IV. p1445-8 **1043**

Guerrier, Edith. The federal executive departments as sources of information for libraries. (U.S. Bureau of Education. Bul. 1919. no. 74) Wash. Govt. Ptg. Off. 1919. 204p. **1044**

Hadley, Arthur T. Facilities for study and research in the offices of the United States government. (U.S. Bureau of Education. Bul. 1909. no. 1) Wash. Govt. Ptg. Off. 1909. 73p. **1045**

Hill, David Spence. Libraries of Washington. Chicago. American Library Association. 1936. 296p. **1045a**

Hill, Joseph A. The historical value of the census records. Am. Hist. Asso. rep. 1908. I. p197-208 **1046**

Index and review, all about government publications. v. 1-2. March 1901-April 1903. Wash. D.C. W.J. Young, C.H. Ferrell. 1901-03. 2v. in 1 **1047**

Jameson, J. Franklin. Gaps in the published records of United States history. Am. hist. rev. XI. p817-31 (July 1906) **1048**

Keiser, Alonzo Harold. Readers modern guide; books for the asking! Vincennes, Ind. Readers Modern Guide Publication Co. c1934. 102p. (U.S. government publications) **1049**

Kleist, Esther Ellen. The bibliographical work of the United States government with a selected annotated list of important bibliographies from January 1920 to January 1934. (Univ. of Illinois. M.A. thesis) Urbana. 1935. 210p. typ. carbon **1050**

Lane, Lucius Page. Aids to the use of government publications. Am. Statistical Asso. quar. pub. VII. no. 49. p40-58 (March, June 1900) **1051**

Larson, Cedric. Uncle Sam; printer, publisher and literary sponsor. [Mount Vernon, N.Y. Walpole Ptg. Off. 1939] [16]p. (Printed for the Colophon, graphic ser. pt. 1) **1051a**

Lathrop, Olive C. Federal and state check lists. Law lib. jour. XXXIII. p289-93 (Sept. 1940) **1051b**

Lawyers' Cooperative Publishing Co. Index to notes in U.S. Supreme Court reports, lawyers' edition. [Rochester, N.Y. Lawyers' Cooperative Publishing Co. 1929] p1093-164 **1051c**

Lowery, Woodbury. Index-digest to the decisions of the Supreme Court of the United States in patent causes, including those adjudged during October term 1896, and containing references to the concurrent reports. . . . Wash. D.C. J. Byrne. 1897. 445p. **1051d**

Miller, Clarence A. United States public documents as law books. Law lib. jour. XVIII. p7-44 (April 1925) **1052**

Miller, David Hunter. Secret statutes of the United States; a memorandum. Wash. Govt. Ptg. Off. 1918. 44p. **1052a**

Miller, Kathryn Naomi. The selection of United States serial documents for liberal arts colleges. N.Y. The H.W. Wilson Company. 1937. 364p. **1052b**

Moore, Charles C. The United States revised statutes, supplements, and statutes at large. *In* Federal statutes annotated. Northport, Long Island, N.Y. 1903. I. pcxxv-cxxx **1052c**

Mullinix, Frederick Charles. Index to the bankruptcy opinions of the Supreme Court of the United States, rendered since passage of the act of 1898. Jonesboro, Ark. Sammons. 1927. 112p. **1052d**

Myer, William G. An index to the reports of the Supreme Court of the United States embracing all the reported decisions of the Court from its organization to the present date. St. Louis. W.J. Gilbert. 1878. 537p. **1052e**

Myers, Denys D. Secrets of state. Hist. outlook. XVIII. p361-9 (Dec. 1927) (U.S. foreign relations) **1053**

New York. Public Library. Check list of American federal documents relating to finance in the New York Public Library. N.Y. Pub. Lib. bul. VI. p287-92 (Aug. 1902) **1054**

—— Documents of the first and second Congresses of the United States in the New York Public Library. N.Y. Pub. Lib. bul. III. p462-9 (Nov. 1899) **1055**

Northrop, Everett H. Check list of U.S. administrative decisions to January 1, 1941. Law lib. jour. XXXIV. p29-32 (Jan. 1941) **1055a**

Northwest Publishers, Aberdeen, S.D. An index to educational material available to teachers. Aberdeen, S.D. Northwest Pub. c1935. 39p. (U.S. government publications) **1056**

Noyes, Frederick K. Teaching material in government publications. (U.S. Bureau of Education. Bul. 1913. no. 47) Wash. Govt. Ptg. Off. 1913. 61p. **1057**

Powell, Sophy H. Checklist of papers bearing the designation "executive order," to January 1, 1937. [Wash. D.C.] School of Government, George Washington Univ. MS. **1057a**

Prime, Frederick. A catalogue of official reports upon geological surveys of the United States and territories, and of British North America. Phila. Sherman & co. 1879. 71p. (Supplement. 1881. 13p. Reprinted from Am. Inst. of Mining Engineers trans. 1879-81. VII-IX) **1057b**

Ronald, James H. Publication of federal administrative legislation. George Washington Univ. law rev. VII. p52-92 (Nov. 1938) **1057c**

Saville, Mahala. A descriptive list of the periodical publications of the United States government. (Univ. of Illinois. M.A. thesis) Urbana. 1935. 161p. typ. **1058**

Schmeckebier, Laurence F. The government printing office; its history, activities and organization. (Inst. for Govt. Research. Service monograph of the U.S. govt. no. 36) Balt. Johns Hopkins Univ. Press. 1925. 143p. **1059**

—— Government publications and their use. (The Inst. for Govt. Research of The Brookings Inst. Stud. in administration no. 33) Wash. D.C. The Brookings Inst. 1939. 479p. **1060**

—— The statistical work of the national government. (Inst. for Govt. Research. Stud. in administration. XI) Balt. Johns Hopkins Univ. Press. 1925. 574p. **1061**

Schram, Jennie L. Press releases of the United States government bureaus. Chicago. Illinois Chamber of Commerce, Research dept. 1927. 27p. mim. **1062**

Science Advisory Board. Report of the committee on mapping services of the Federal Government. *In* Second report of the Science Advisory Board, September 1, 1934 to August 31, 1935. Wash. Govt. Ptg. Off. Sept. 1, 1935. p129-306 **1062a**

Social Science Research Council. Committee on government statistics and information services. Government statistics; a report. . . . (Soc. Sci. Research Council bul. 26) N.Y. 1937. 174p. **1062b**

Spaulding, E. Wilder and Blue, George Verne. The Department of State of the United States. (U.S. Departme. t of State. Publication 878) Wash. Govt. Ptg. Off. 1936. 65p. **1062c**

Special Libraries Association. Bibliography committee. Descriptive list for use in acquiring and discarding United States government periodical mimeographed statements; including advance press releases, preliminary and informal reports issued at frequent intervals, with notes indicating the permanent documents in which the data appear if republished. Providence, R.I. Special Libraries Asso. 1929. 76p. **1063**

Sullivan, Lawrence. Government by mimeograph. Atlantic mthly. CLXI. p306-15 (March 1938) . **1063a**

Swanton, Walter I. Guide to United States government publications. (U.S. Bureau of Education. Bul. 1918. no. 2) Wash. Govt. Ptg. Off. 1918. 206p. **1064**

Swem, Earl G. Virginia editions of acts and journals of Congress. The Am. collector. II. 309 (May 1926) **1065**

Tisdel, Alton P. Recent trends in the publication and distribution of United States documents. *In* American Library Association. Public documents; state, municipal, federal, foreign . . . 1933. . . . Chicago. Am. Lib. Asso. 1934. p106-51 **1066**

—— United States documents—recent trends in publication and distribution. Wash. Govt. Ptg. Off. 1934. 7p. **1067**

U.S. Bureau of Efficiency. Statistical work, United States government. (House document no. 394. 67 Cong. 2 sess. Ser. 8084) Wash. Govt. Ptg. Off. 1922. 405p. **1068**

U.S. Committee on department methods. Message from the President of the United States, transmitting a report . . . on the documentary historical publications of the United States government, together with a draft of a proposed bill providing for the creation of a permanent commission on national historical publications. (Senate document. no. 714. 60 Cong. 2 sess.) Wash. Govt. Ptg. Off. 1909. 45p. **1069**

U.S. Federal Reserve Board. Preliminary list of publications of the federal government's emergency agencies. (Agencies, except Reconstruction Finance Corp., not in existence before March 3, 1933) Wash. D.C. 1934. 14p. mim. **1070**

U.S. Laws, statutes, etc. Tables, showing the comparative chaptering in various editions of the laws of the United States, and exhibiting lists of the acts of Congress, from 1789 to 1845 inclusive, relating to the judiciary, imports and tonnage, public lands, and post-office. *In* Statutes at large. Boston. Little, Brown. 1853. I. pxli-cxxii **1070a**

U.S. Library of Congress. Division of Documents. Popular names of federal statutes; a tentative list based on records of American law section, legislative reference service, Library of Congress. Revised June 1926 under the direction of James B. Childs. Wash. Govt. Ptg. Off. 1926. 19p. **1071**

U.S. Office of Education. Government publications showing the work of the government. (Circular no. 78) Wash. D.C. 1933. 7p. **1072**

—— —— United States government publications on the work of the government. Comp. by G. S. Wright. Wash. D.C. 1937. 14p. **1072a**

U.S. Office of Government Reports. National defense and neutrality: proclamations, executive orders, military orders and presidential administrative orders and regulations, July 1, 1939-March 19, 1941. Wash. D.C. 1941. 32p. processed **1072b**

U.S. President's Commission on Economy and Efficiency. Bibliography of congressional inquiries into the conduct of the business of executive departments other than by standing committees of Congress, 1789-1911. *In* The need for a national budget; message from the president of the United States. . . . Wash. Govt. Ptg. Off. 1912. p477-85 **1073**

U.S. Superintendent of Documents [Publishes free price lists of government publications on: Alaska and Hawaii, American history and biography, animal industry, Army and militia, census publications, Children's bureau and other publications relating to children, commerce and manufactures, proceedings of Congress, education, farm management, finance, foreign relations, forestry, geography and explorations, Geological survey, government periodicals, health, immigration, Indians, insular possessions, Interstate commerce commission and Federal communications commission, irrigation, drainage, water power, labor laws, maps, mines, Navy, Marine corps and Coast guard, Pacific states, political science, public domain, tariff and taxation, transportation] **1074**

—— Classified list of United States government publications issued in series or of a miscellaneous character available for selection of depository libraries. Wash. Govt. Ptg. Off. 1932. 19p. **1075**

—— Documents due depositories. . . . a list of annual and serial public documents that should be regularly supplied to the designated depository libraries. . . . Wash. Govt. Ptg. Off. 1907. 39p. **1076**

Wilcox, Jerome K. Guide to the official publications of the New Deal administrations. (Mim. and printed) Chicago. Am. Lib. Asso. 1934. 113p. (Supplement. April 15, 1934-December 1, 1935. 1936. 184p. Second supplement. December 1, 1935-January 1, 1937. 1937. 190p.) **1077**

—— Mimeographed, multigraphed, and other near print publications of the Federal government; their origin, distribution, indexing and other problems. *In* American Library Association. Public documents, state, municipal, federal, foreign; policies and problems concerning issuance, distribution and use. . . . 1933. Chicago. Am. Lib. Asso. 1934. p160-93. Same. 1935. 1936. p25-44 **1078**

—— N R A: the New Deal for business and industry; a bibliography, May-August 1933, together with a list of official publications of other new governmental agencies. Comp. for The John Crerar Lib. Chicago. Am. Lib. Asso. 1933. 78p. reprod. typ. **1079**

—— Unemployment relief documents; guide to the official publications and releases of F.E.R.A. and the 48 state relief agencies. N.Y. H. W. Wilson. 1936. 95p. **1079a**

—— United States reference publications; a guide of the current reference publications of the Federal government. Boston. F.W. Faxon. 1931. 96p. (Supplement. 1932. 135p.) **1080**

Willoughby, William F. Statistical publications of the United States government. Am. Acad. of Pol. and Social Science, ann. II. p92-104. 1891 **1081**

Wright, Quincy. Publications of the Department of State. Iowa law rev. XIX. p301-11 (Jan. 1934) **1082**

Wroth, Lawrence C. A description of federal public documents. White Plains, N.Y. H.W. Wilson. 1915. **1083**

Wyer, J. I. U.S. government documents, federal, state and city. Chicago. Am. Lib. Asso. 1933. 56p. **1084**

Wynne, Cyril. Publications of the Department of state. Federal Bar Asso. jour. II. p103-8 (Nov. 1934) **1085**

Young, Charles Nelson. Accident statistics of the Federal government. Prep. for the Central Statistical Board. Wash. D.C. 1937. 141p. reprod. **1085a**

Indexes

Alden, Timothy John Fox. Index to the reports of the decisions of the Supreme Court of the United States. From Dallas to 14 Howard inclusive. [1790-1852.] Phila. G. Charles. 1854. 3v. **1085b**

Ames, John G. Comprehensive index to the publications of the United States government, 1881-1893. Wash. Govt. Ptg. Off. 1905. 2v. **1086**

—— Finding list, showing where in the set of Congressional documents the individual volumes of certain series of government publications are found. Wash. Govt. Ptg. Off. 1892. 52p. **1087**

—— List of Congressional documents from the fifteenth to the fifty-first Congress, and of government publications containing debates and proceedings of Congress from the first to the fifty-first Congress, together with miscellaneous lists of public documents with historical and bibliographical notes. Wash. Govt. Ptg. Off. 1892. 120p. **1088**

Anglim, James & Co. Monthly bulletin of the publications of the U.S. government. Wash. D.C. 1883-? **1089**

Burch, Samuel. General index to the laws of the United States of America, from March 4th, 1789, to March 3d, 1827. Wash. D.C. 1828. 331p. **1089a**

Burke, Edmund. List of patents for inventions and designs, issued by the United States, from 1790 to 1847. Wash. D.C. J. and G. S. Gideon. 1847. 608p. **1089b**

Campbell, Grace. A study of the extent to which existing printed government indexes and catalogues can replace the card catalogue in making the contents of federal documents available. (Oklahoma Agricultural and Mechanical College bul. v. 36, no. 17, Library bul. no. 7) [Stillwater, Okla. 1939] 30p. **1089c**

Church, Alonzo Webster and Smith, Henry H. Tables showing the contents of the several volumes comprising the Annals of Congress, Congressional debates, Congressional globe, Congressional record, statutes at large, Supreme Court reports, and succession of Supreme Court justices arranged by years and congresses. Comp. originally for the Senate library. Wash. Govt. Ptg. Off. 1889. 19p. **1090**

Claussen, Martin P. and Friis, Herman R.
Descriptive catalog of maps published by Congress 1817-1843. P.O. Box 4672. Wash. D.C. 1941. 104p.   **1090a**

The **Code** of federal regulations of United States of America, having general applicability and legal effect in force June 1, 1938. Index. Pub. by the Division of the Federal Register, The National Archives. Wash. Govt. Ptg. Off. 1939. 513p.   **1090b**

Greely, Adolphus Washington. Public documents of the early Congresses, with special reference to Washington's administration, supplemented by a bibliographical list of all official journals, documents, and reports of the first and second Congresses, 1789-1793. Am. Hist. Asso. rep. 1896. p1109-1248 (Issued also as House document. no. 353, 54 Cong. 2 sess. Ser. 3550[1])   **1091**

—— Public documents of the first fourteen Congresses, 1789-1817; papers relating to early Congressional documents. (Senate document. no. 428. 56 Cong. 1 sess. Ser. 3879) Wash. Govt. Ptg. Off. 1900. 903p.   **1092**

—— Public documents of the first fourteen Congresses, 1789-1817. Am. Hist. Asso. rep. 1903. I. p343-406. (Supplements list in Senate document 428)   **1093**

Hasse, Adelaide Rosalie. A list of United States public documents published as serials of the 61st, 62d, 63d, and 64th Congress . . . 1909-1917. N.Y. N.Y. Pub. Lib.. 1918. 37p.   **1093a**

Hickcox, John H. United States government publications; a monthly catalogue. Wash. D.C. The editor, W.H. Lowdermilk. 1885-94. 10v. (Succeeded by the Superintendent of Documents' Monthly catalogue)   **1094**

List of United States public documents published as serials of the 61st, 62d, 63d, and 64th Congresses . . . 1909-1917. Comp. under the direction of Adelaide R. Hasse, Chief of the economics division, N.Y. Public. Lib. 1918. Printed for the use of the Joint com. on ptg. Wash. Govt. Ptg. Off. 1918. 37p.   **1095**

McKee, T. H. [Index to] Reports of the committee on accounts, House of Representatives, from the fourteenth Congress, 1815 to the forty-ninth Congress, 1887, inclusive. Wash. Govt. Ptg. Off. 1887. 6p.   **1096**

—— Reports of the committee on American ship-building, House of Representatives, from the forty-first Congress, 1870, to the forty-ninth Congress, 1887, inclusive. Wash. D.C. 1887. 6p.   **1096a**

—— Reports of the committee on appropriations, House of Representatives, from the organization of the committee, March 2, 1865, to the close of the forty-ninth Congress, 1887. Wash. D.C. 1887. 7p.   **1096b**

—— Reports of the committee on appropriations, United States Senate, from the organization of the committee, March 6, 1867, to the close of the forty-ninth Congress, 1887. Wash. D.C. 1887. 8p.   **1096c**

—— Reports of the committee on banking and currency, House of Representatives, from the organization of the committee, March 2, 1865, to the close of the forty-ninth Congress, 1887. Wash. D.C. 1887. 8p.   **1096d**

—— Reports of the committee on claims, House of Representatives, from the fourteenth Congress, 1815, to the forty-ninth Congress, 1887, inclusive. Wash. D.C. 1887. 79p.   **1096e**

—— Reports of the committee on the District of Columbia, House of Representatives, from the fourteenth Congress, 1815, to the forty-ninth Congress, 1887, inclusive. Wash. D.C. 1887. 14p.   **1096f**

—— Reports of the committee on education, House of Representatives, from the organization of the committee, March 21, 1867, to the close of the forty-ninth Congress, 1887. Wash. D.C. 1887. 6p.   **1096g**

—— Reports of the committee on education and labor, United States Senate, from the organization of the committee, January 28, 1869, to the close of the forty-ninth Congress, 1887. Wash. D.C. 1887. 7p.   **1096h**

—— Reports of the committee on expenditures in Department of Justice, House of Representatives, from the organization of the committee, January 16, 1874, to the close of the forty-ninth Congress, 1887. Wash. D.C. 1887. 7p.   **1096i**

—— Reports of the committee on expenditures in Interior Department, House of Representatives, from the organization of the committee, March 16, 1860, to the close of the forty-ninth Congress, 1887. Wash. D.C. 1887. 5p.   **1096j**

—— Reports of the committee on expenditures in Navy Department, House of Representatives, from the fourteenth Congress, 1826, to the forty-ninth Congress, 1887, inclusive. Wash. D.C. 1887. 6p.   **1096k**

—— Reports of the committee on expenditures in Treasury Department, House of Representatives, from the fourteenth Congress, 1816, to the forty-ninth Congress, 1887, inclusive. Wash. D.C. 1887. 5p.   **1096l**

—— Reports of the committee on expenditures in War Department, from the fourteenth Congress, 1815, to the forty-ninth Congress, 1887, inclusive. Wash. D.C. 1887. 6p.   **1096m**

—— Reports of the committee on finance, United States Senate, from the organization of the committee, December 10, 1816, to the close of the forty-ninth Congress, 1887. Wash. D.C. 1887. 18p.   **1096n**

—— Reports of the committee on foreign affairs, House of Representatives, from the organization of the committee, March 13, 1822, to the close of the forty-ninth Congress, 1887. Wash. D.C. 1887. 19p.
1096o

—— Reports of the committee on foreign relations, United States Senate, from the organization of the committee, December 10, 1816, to the close of the forty-ninth Congress, 1887. Wash. D.C. 1887. 19p.
1096p

—— Reports of the committee on internal improvements, House of Representatives, from the twentieth Congress, 1828, to the twenty-second Congress, 1832, inclusive. Wash. D.C. 1887. 6p.
1096q

—— Reports of the committee on invalid pensions, House of Representatives, from the organization of the committee, January 10, 1831, to the close of the forty-ninth Congress, 1887. Wash. D.C. 1887. 108p.
1096r

—— Reports of the committee on judiciary, House of Representatives, from the fourteenth Congress, 1815, to the forty-ninth Congress, 1887, inclusive. Wash. D.C. 1887. 29p.
1096s

—— Reports of the committee on the judiciary, United States Senate, from the fifteenth Congress, 1816, to the forty-ninth Congress, 1887, inclusive. Wash. D.C. 1887. 35p.
1096t

—— Reports of the committee on labor, House of Representatives, from the organization of the committee, December 23, 1883, to the close of the forty-ninth Congress, 1887. Wash. D.C. 1887. 6p.
1096u

—— Reports of the committee on levees and improvements of Mississippi River, House of Representatives, from the organization of [the] committee, December 10, 1875, to the close of the forty-ninth Congress, 1887, inclusive. Wash. D.C. 1887. 6p.
1096v

—— Reports of the committee on the library, House of Representatives, from the fourteenth Congress, 1815, to the forty-ninth Congress, 1887, inclusive. Wash. D.C. 1887. 7p.
1096w

—— Reports of the committee on the library, United States Senate, from the organization of the committee, December 10, 1822, to the close of the forty-ninth Congress, 1887. Wash. D.C. 1887. 8p.
1096x

—— Reports of the committee on mileage, House of Representatives, from the organization of [the] committee, September 15, 1837, to the close of the forty-ninth Congress, 1887. Wash. D.C. 1887. 5p.
1096y

—— Reports of the committee on military affairs, House of Representatives, from the fourteenth Congress, 1815, to the forty-ninth Congress, 1887, inclusive. Wash. D.C. 1887. 50p.
1096z

—— Reports of the committee on military affairs, United States Senate, from the organization of the committee, December 10, 1816, to the close of the forty-ninth Congress, 1887. Wash. D.C. 1887. 53p.
1096aa

—— Reports of the committee on the militia, House of Representatives, from the organization of [the] committee, December 10, 1835, to the close of the forty-ninth Congress, 1887. Wash. D.C. 1887. 6p.
1096bb

—— Reports of the committee on mines and mining, House of Representatives, from the organization of the committee, December 19, 1865, to the close of the forty-ninth Congress, 1887. Wash. D.C. 1887. 5p.
1096cc

—— Reports of the committee on naval affairs, House of Representatives, from the organization of the committee, March 13, 1822, to the close of the forty-ninth Congress, 1887. Wash. D.C. 1887. 26p.
1096dd

—— Reports of the committee on naval affairs, United States Senate, from the organization of the committee, March 13, 1822, to the close of the forty-ninth Congress, 1887. Wash. D.C. 1887. 37p.
1096ee

—— Reports of the committee on ordnance, and ordnance and war-ships, United States Senate, from the fortieth Congress, 1867, to the close of the forty-ninth Congress, 1887. Wash. D.C. 1887. 6p.
1096ff

—— Reports of the committee on Pacific railroads, House of Representatives, from the organization of the committee, March 2, 1865, to the close of the forty-ninth Congress, 1887. Wash. D.C. 1887. 7p.
1096gg

—— Reports of the committee on Pacific Railroads, United States Senate, from the organization of the committee, March 8, 1865, to the close of the forty-ninth Congress, 1887. Wash. D.C. 1887. 6p.
1096hh

—— Reports of the committee on patents, House of Representatives, from the organization of the committee, September 15, 1837, to the forty-ninth Congress, 1887, inclusive. Wash. D.C. 1887. 12p. **1096ii**

—— Reports of the committee on patents, United States Senate, from the organization of the committee, September 7, 1837, to the close of the forty-ninth Congress, 1887. Wash. D.C. 1887. 20p. **1096jj**

—— Reports of the committee on pensions, bounty, and back pay, House of Representatives, from the organization of the committee, May 16, 1879, to the close of the forty-eighth Congress, 1885. Wash. D.C. 1887. 6p.
1096kk

—— Reports of the committee on pensions, House of Representatives, from the fourteenth Congress, 1815, to the forty-ninth Congress, 1887, inclusive. Wash. D.C. 1887. 47p.
1096ll

McKee, T. H. Reports of the committee on pensions, United States Senate, from the organization of the committee, December 10, 1816, to the close of the forty-ninth Congress, 1887. Wash. D.C. 1887. 80p. **1096mm**

—— Reports of the committee on printing, House of Representatives, from the fourteenth Congress, 1815, to the forty-ninth Congress, 1887, inclusive. Wash. D.C. 1887. 10p. **1096nn**

—— Reports of the committee on printing, United States Senate, from the organization of the committee, December 15, 1841, to the close of [the] forty-ninth Congress, 1887. Wash. D.C. 1887. 7p. **1096oo**

—— Reports of the committee on private land claims, House of Representatives, from the fifteenth Congress, 1816, to the forty-ninth Congress, 1887, inclusive. Wash. D.C. 1887. 20p. **1096pp**

—— Reports of the committee on private land claims, United States Senate, from the organization of the committee, December 27, 1826, to the close of the forty-ninth Congress, 1887. Wash. D.C. 1887. 25p. **1096qq**

—— Reports of the committee on privileges and elections, United States Senate, from the organization of the committee, March 10, 1871, to the close of the forty-ninth Congress, 1887. Wash. D.C. 1887. 12p. **1096rr**

—— Reports of the committee on public expenditures, House of Representatives, from the fourteenth Congress, 1815, to the forty-ninth Congress, 1887, inclusive. Wash. D.C. 1887. 7p. **1096ss**

—— Reports of the committee on public lands, House of Representatives, from the fourteenth Congress, 1815, to the forty-ninth Congress, 1887, inclusive. Wash. D.C. 1887. 42p. **1096tt**

—— Reports of the committee on public lands, United States Senate, from the organization of the committee, December 10, 1816, to the close of the forty-ninth Congress, 1887. Wash. D.C. 1887. 35p. **1096uu**

—— Reports of the committee on railroads, United States Senate, from the organization of the committee, December 4, 1873, to the close of the forty-ninth Congress, 1887. Wash. D.C. 1887. 7p. **1096vv**

—— Reports of the committee on railways and canals, House of Representatives, from the organization of the committee, December 15, 1831, to the close of the forty-ninth Congress, 1887. Wash. D.C. 1887. 11p. **1096ww**

—— Reports of the committee on railways and canals, United States Senate, from the fourteenth Congress, 1815, to the close of the Thirty-fourth Congress, 1815 [*sic*, 1857] Wash. D.C. 1887. 10p. **1096xx**

—— Reports of the committee on reforms in civil service, House of Representatives, from the organization of the committee, December 6, 1875, to the close of the forty-ninth Congress, 1887. Wash. D.C. 1887. 6p. **1096yy**

—— Reports of the committee on retrenchment, House of Representatives, from the organization of the committee, December 31, 1828, to the close of the forty-ninth Congress, 1873. Wash. 1887. 7p. **1096zz**

—— Reports of the committee on revision of laws, House of Representatives, from the organization of [the] committee, July 25, 1868, to the close of the forty-ninth Congress, 1887. Wash. D.C. 1887. 6p. **1096aaa**

—— Reports of the committee on revolutionary claims, United States Senate, from the organization of the committee, December 28, 1832, to its discontinuance, 1883. Wash. D.C. 1887. 12p. **1096bbb**

—— Reports of the committee on rivers and harbors, House of Representatives, from the organization of the committee, December 19, 1883, to the close of the forty-ninth Congress, 1887. Wash. D.C. 1887. 6p. **1096ccc**

—— Reports of the committee on rules, House of Representatives, from the fourteenth Congress, 1815, to the forty-ninth Congress, 1887, inclusive. Wash. D.C. 1887. 7p. **1096ddd**

—— Reports of the committee on rules, United States Senate, from the organization of the committee, December 9, 1874, to the close of the forty-ninth Congress, 1887. Wash. D.C. 1887. 6p. **1096eee**

—— Reports of the committee on territories, House of Representatives, from the organization of the committee, December 13, 1825, to the close of the forty-ninth Congress, 1887. Wash. D.C. 1887. 11p. **1096fff**

—— Reports of the committee on the territories, United States Senate, from the organization of the committee, March 25, 1844, to the close of the forty-ninth Congress, 1887. Wash. D.C. 1887. 10p. **1096ggg**

—— Reports of the committee on transportation routes to the seaboard, United States Senate, from the organization of the committee, March 19, 1879, to the close of the forty-ninth Congress, 1887. Wash. D.C. 1887. 6p. **1096hhh**

—— Reports of the committee on ways and means, House of Representatives, from the fourteenth Congress, 1815, to the forty-ninth Congress, 1887, inclusive. Wash. D.C. 1887. 21p. **1096iii**

—— Reports of the committee on woman suffrage, United States Senate, from the organization of the committee, December 5, 1882, to the close of the forty-ninth Congress, 1887. Wash. D.C. 1887. 5p. **1096jjj**

—— Reports of the committee to audit and control the contingent expenses, United States Senate, from the fourteenth Congress, 1815, to the close of the forty-ninth Congress, 1887. Wash. D.C. 1887. 7p. **1096kkk**

—— Reports of the select and special committees, House of Representatives, from the fourteenth Congress, 1815, to the forty-ninth Congress, 1887, inclusive. Wash. D.C. 1887. 34p. **1096lll**

—— Reports of the select and special committees, United States Senate, from the fourteenth Congress, 1815, to the forty-ninth Congress, 1887, inclusive. Wash. D.C. 1887. 29p. **1096mmm**

McPherson, Edward. Consolidated index of the executive documents of the House of Representatives, from the twenty-sixth to the fortieth Congress, inclusive. (House miscellaneous documents. 40 Cong. 3 sess. Ser. 1387) Wash. Govt. Ptg. Off. 1870. 393p. **1097**

—— Consolidated index of the reports of the committees, of the House of Representatives, from the twenty-sixth to the fortieth Congress, inclusive. (House miscellaneous documents. 40 Cong. 3 sess. Ser. 1386) Wash. Govt. Ptg. Off. 1869. 158p. **1098**

—— An index of bills presented in the House of Representatives, from the first to the forty-second congress, inclusive, relating to banks, currency, public debt, tariff, and direct taxes, showing the title of the bill, name of person introducing, nature of report, and disposition of the bill. House miscellaneous document. no. 92. 43 Cong. 2 sess. 1875. 183p. Ser. 1654 **1099**

Ordway, Albert. General index of the Journals of Congress from the first to the sixteenth congress, inclusive, being a synoptical subject-index of the proceedings of Congress on all public business from 1789 to 1821, with references to the debates, documents and statutes connected therewith. House rep. no 1776. 46 Cong. 2 sess.; House rep. no. 1559. 47 Cong. 1 sess. 1880, 1883. 2v. Ser. 1939, 2071 **1100**

—— General personal index of the Journals of Congress from the first to the sixteenth congress, inclusive, being an index of the personal record of members of Congress from 1789 to 1821. House rept. no. 2692. 48 Cong. 2 sess.; House rep. no. 3475. 49 Cong. 1 sess. 1885, 1887. 134,191p. Ser. 2331, 2446 **1101**

Poore, Ben Perley. A descriptive catalogue of the government publications of the United States, September 5, 1774-March 4, 1881. (Senate miscellaneous document. no. 67. 48 Cong. 2 sess.) Wash. Govt. Ptg. Off. 1885. 1392p. **1102**

Rice, David Hall and Rice, Lepine C. Digest of the decisions of law and practice in the Patent Office from 1869 to 1880. Boston. G.B. Reed. 1880. 475p. Same. 1880-1890. By Edward S. Beach. 1890. 203p. Same. 1890-1900. By Lepine Hall Rice. 1900. 404p. **1102a**

Scott, George Winfield, Beaman, Middleton G. and others. Index analysis of the federal statutes together with a table of repeals and amendments, 1789-1907. Prepared under the direction of the Librarian of Cong. Wash. D.C. 1908, 1911. 2v. **1103**

Shepard, Frank, Co. A table of federal acts which have been cited by popular names, to January 1931. N.Y. Shepard. 1931. 77p. (Supplement. Jan. 1, 1931 to Dec. 1, 1934. 14p.) **1104**

Thomas, Edward. A digest of process and composition and allied decisions in patent cases. Phila. John C. Winston. 1908. 66 coll. **1104a**

Underwood, Lineas D. and others. A list of adjudicated patents arranged by number and by subject matter or title of invention. Wash. D.C. J. Bryne. 1907. 325p. "Cumulative" supplement vol. 1, no. 1; Underwood's list of adjudicated patents and disclaimers. Wash. D.C. Card Digest Co. 1909- **1104b**

U.S. Bureau of Agricultural Economics. Library. Measures of major importance enacted by the 73d Congress, March 9 to June 16, 1933 and January 3 to June 18, 1934. Comp. by Vajen E. Hitz under the direction of Mary G. Lacy. (Agricultural economics bibliog. no. 54) Wash. D.C. Nov. 1934. 55p. mim. **1105**

U.S. Bureau of Insular Affairs. Index of government documents relating to the Philippines. (MS. in the Bureau) **1106**

U.S. Congress. Congressional record index, 1873-. Wash. Govt. Ptg. Off. 1874- **1106a**

—— —— **House of Representatives.** Calendars of House of Representatives and history of legislation. (Issued for official use only) (Indexes and lists bills and resolutions) **1106b**

—— —— —— Consolidated index of claims reported by the commissioners of claims to the House of Representatives from 1871 to 1880. Comp. under the supervision of J. B. Holloway and Walter H. French. Wash. Govt. Ptg. Off. 1892. 262p. **1107**

—— —— —— A digested index to the executive documents, and reports of committees of the House of Representatives, from the eighteenth to the twenty-first Congress, both included. (House documents. 21 Cong. 2 sess. Ser. 209²) Wash. Duff Green. 1832. 152p. **1108**

—— —— —— Digested summary and alphabetical list of private claims which have been presented to the House of Representatives from the first to the fifty-first Congress, inclusive, exhibiting the action of Congress on each claim, with references to the journals, reports, bills, &c. elucidating its progress. House miscellaneous document. 32 Congress. 1 sess. 1853. Ser. 653-5: House miscellaneous document no. 109. 42 Cong. 3 sess. 1873. Ser. 1574; House miscellaneous document no. 53. 47 Cong. 1 sess. 1882. Ser. 2036; House miscellaneous document no. 213. 53 Cong. 2 sess. 1896. Ser. 3268. 6v. **1109**

U.S. Congress. House. General personal index of the journals of Congress from the first to eighth Congress, inclusive, being an index of the personal record of members of Congresses from 1789 to 1805. House rep. no. 2692. 48 Cong. 2 sess. 1885. 134p. Ser. 2331   **1110**

—— —— —— History of bills and resolutions. *In* Journal of the House of Representatives   **1111**

—— —— —— Index to the executive communications made to the House of Representatives from December 3d, 1817, to March 3d, 1823, 15th, 16th & 17th Congress. (House documents. 17th Cong. 2 sess. Ser. 85²) Wash. Gales & Seaton. 1823. 129p.   **1112**

—— —— —— Index to the executive communications made to the House of Representatives from the commencement of the present form of government until the end of the fourteenth Congress, inclusive, also, an index to all the printed committee reports, alphabetically arranged. House document. no. 163. 18th Cong. 1 sess. 1824. 247p. Ser. 104   **1113**

—— —— —— Index to reports of committees of the House of Representatives. Comp. under the direction of the Joint com. on ptg. by T.H. McKee. Wash. Govt. Ptg. Off. 1887. 58 v. in 1 (Index to reports, 14th-49th Congress, inclusive, classified by committees)   **1114**

—— —— —— Index to the executive documents and reports of committees of the House of Representatives from the twenty-second to the twenty-fifth Congress, both included, commencing December 1831, and ending March 1839. (House documents. Ser. 350) Wash. S. D. Langtree. 1840? 380p.   **1115**

—— —— —— List of documents (2268 volumes of papers) transferred from House of Representatives office building to Library of Congress, Nov.-Dec. 1929. (MS. in Lib. of Cong. MSS. division) 24p.   **1116**

—— —— —— **Clerk.** Reports to be made to Congress. Jan. 3, 1936. House document. no. 359. 74 Cong. 2 sess. 20p.   **1117**

—— —— —— **Committee on claims.** History of legislation, with general alphabetical index showing nature and final status of all bills and resolutions before the committee; members' index; committee rules and procedure; statistics; and general information concerning the prosecution of claims against the United States. Seventyfourth- .Congress ... v. [I- .] [Wash. Govt. Ptg. Off.] 1936-   **1117a**

—— —— —— **Committee on judiciary.** Index to reports of the Committee on the judiciary, House of Representatives, 54th-62d Congresses. [Wash.] 1913. 93p.   **1118**

—— —— —— **Library.** Congressional committee hearings; an index of those prior to Jan. 3, 1919 in the Library of the U.S. House of Representatives. Comp. by W. Perry Miller. Wash. Govt. Ptg. Off. 1939. 609p.   **1118a**

—— —— —— —— Index to Congressional committee hearings prior to January 3, 1939 in the library of the United States House of Representatives. Comp. by W. Perry Miller. Wash. Govt. Ptg. Off. 1939. 609p.   **1118b**

U.S. Congress. Senate. Alphabetical list of private claims which were brought before the Senate of the United States . . . from March 4, 1891 to March 4, 1905. Senate document. no. 499. 56 Cong. 1 sess. 2v.; Senate document. no. 221. 57 Cong. 2 sess. 197p.; Senate document. no. 3. 59 Cong. 1 sess. 709p. 1900, 1903, 1905   **1119**

—— —— —— General index to all reports of receipts and expenditures of the secretaries of the Senate from 1823 to January 31, 1900. (Senate doc. 290, 56 Cong. 1 sess.) Wash. Govt. Ptg. Off. 1900. 349p.   **1119a**

—— —— —— History of bills and resolutions introduced in the United States Senate. (Issued for official use only)   **1119b**

—— —— —— History of bills and resolutions. *In* Journal of the Senate   **1119c**

—— —— —— Index to reports of committees of the Senate. Comp. under the direction of the Joint com. on ptg by T. H. McKee. Wash. Govt. Ptg. Off. 1887   **1120**

—— —— —— List of private claims brought before the Senate of the United States from the . . . fourteenth Congress to the . . . close of the fifty-first Congress. (Senate miscellaneous document. no. 14. 46 Cong. 3 sess. 2v.; Senate miscellaneous document. no. 266. pts. 1-3. 53 Cong. 2 sess.) Wash. Govt. Ptg. Off. 1881-95   **1121**

—— —— —— **Library.** Catalogue of the library of the United States Senate. Comp. and printed under the direction of George A. Sanderson . . . by Edward C. Goodwin. Wash. [Govt. Ptg. Off.] 1924. 1210p. (Contents: list of hearings before committees before 1923, publications of departments in Congressional documents, list of Senate and House documents and reports from 1789 to 1923)   **1122**

—— —— —— Finding list to important serial documents published by the government in the library of the United States Senate. Prepared under the direction of Charles G. Bennett, by James M. Baker. (Senate document. no. 238. 56 Cong. 2 sess.) Wash. Govt. Ptg. Off. 1901. 281p.   **1123**

—— —— —— Index of congressional committee hearings (not confidential in character) prior to January 3, 1935 in the United States Senate library. Wash. Govt. Ptg. Off. 1935. Supplement. January 3, 1935-January 5, 1937. 1937. 148p. **1123a**

—— —— —— —— Index of congressional hearings (not confidential in character) prior to January 3, 1935 in the United States Senate. Rev. by James D. Preston. Wash. Govt. Ptg. Off. 1935. 1056p. **1124**

U.S. Department of Commerce and Labor. Departmental index, being an alphabetical arrangement of subjects in the statutes relating to the executive departments in general. Prepared under the direction of the Secretary of Commerce and Labor. Wash. Govt. Ptg. Off. 1905. 60p. **1125**

U.S. Department of the Interior. List of congressional documents from the twentieth to the forty-sixth Congress, inclusive. Wash. Govt. Ptg. Off. 1882. 63p. **1126**

U.S. Laws, Statutes, etc. Consolidated index to statutes at large, March 4, 1789 to March 3, 1903. Wash. D.C. 1906. 4v. **1126a**

—— —— A synoptical index to the laws and treaties of the United States of America, from March 4, 1789 to March 3, 1851, with references to the edition of the laws published by Bioren and Duane, and to the statutes at large, published by Little and Brown under the authority of Congress. Prepared under the direction of the secretary of the Senate. Boston. C.C. Little and J. Brown. 1852. 747p. **1127**

U.S. Library of Congress. Sources of information on legislation, 1937-1938; a supplementary list of published material reporting legislative enactments of 1937 and 1938, received in the Library of Congress since publication of State law index, Special report no. 1, and prior to January 1, 1940. Comp. by Jacob Lyons. Wash. D.C. 1940. 56p. mim. **1127a**

—— —— **Division of bibliography.** Sources of information on legislation of 1937-1938; a bibliographical list of published material reporting legislative bills and enactments of 1937 and 1938. Comp. by Jacob Lyons. Wash. Govt. Ptg. Off. 1938. 38p. **1127b**

—— —— **Legislative reference service.** Digest of public general bills with index, seventy-fourth Congress, [first-　] session, January 18, 1936-　. no. 1-　. Wash. Govt. Ptg. Off. 1936-　 **1127c**

—— —— —— Index to the federal statutes, 1874-1931; general and permanent law contained in the revised statutes of 1874 and volumes 18-46 of the statutes at large. Revision of the Scott and Beaman Index analysis of the federal statutes, by Walter H. McLenon and Wilfred C. Gilbert. Wash. Govt. Ptg. Off. 1933. 1432p. **1128**

U.S. Superintendent of Documents. Catalogue of publications issued by the government of the United States during the month of January 1895-. Wash. Govt. Ptg. Off. 1895- **1129**

—— —— Catalogue of the public documents of the fifty-third Congress and of all departments of the government, March 4, 1893-. Wash. Govt. Ptg. Off. 1896- (Commonly cited as Document catalogue) **1130**

—— —— Checklist of United States public documents, 1789-1909. Congressional: to the close of the sixtieth Congress; departmental: to end of calendar year 1909. v. I. Lists of congressional departmental publications. Wash. Govt. Ptg. Off. 1911. 1707p. **1131**

—— —— Index to the reports and documents of the 54th Congress, 1st session— 72d Congress, 2d session, Dec. 2, 1895— March 4, 1933, with numerical lists and schedule of volumes; being no. 1-43 of the "Consolidated index" provided for by the act of January 12, 1895. Wash. Govt. Ptg. Off. 1897-1933. 43v. **1132**

—— —— [A list of original prints of the publications of the first fourteen Congresses]. (Cards in the Office of the Supt. of Documents) 1909 **1133**

—— —— List of United States public documents and reports relating to construction of new navy; also references to debates in Congress on the subject, 1880-1901. Wash. Govt. Ptg. Off. 1902. 18p. **1134**

—— —— Numerical lists and schedule of volumes of the reports and documents of the 73d Congress, 1st and 2d sessions, 1933/1934- . Wash. Govt. Ptg. Off. 1934- **1135**

—— —— Numerical tables and schedule of volumes of the documents and reports of the 59th Congress, 2d session. December 3, 1906-March 4, 1907. Wash. Govt. Ptg. Off. 1908. 124p. **1136**

—— —— Weekly list of selected United States government publications issued by the Superintendent of Documents. Wash. Govt. Ptg. Off. July 11, 1928- **1137**

U.S. Supreme Court. Indexed digest of the United States Supreme Court reports; supplement, all decisions of the October terms, 1894-1901, volumes 155-186. Rochester, N.Y. Lawyers' Co-operative Pub. Co. 1903. 596p. **1137a**

Weaver, Jesse Conrad. Digest of the customs reports covering decisions of the United States Court of Customs and Patent Appeals contained in volumes 1 to 22, inclusive, of the Customs reports. Chicago. Callaghan. 1936. 538p. **1137b**

—— Patent and trade-mark digest of the decisions of the United States Court of Customs and Patent Appeals, covering volumes 17 to 22, inclusive, of the patent reports. Chicago. Callaghan. 1936. 218p. **1137c**

Departmental Publications

DEPARTMENT OF AGRICULTURE

Barnett, Claribel R. Near-print publications of the U.S. Department of Agriculture. *In* American Library Association. Public documents, 1938. Chicago. Am. Lib. Asso. 1938. p411-19 **1137d**

U.S. Agricultural Adjustment Administration. List of informative material issued by the Agricultural Adjustment Administration, May 12, 1933 to May 1, 1935. Prepared in the Correspondence, records and printing section, Division of information. [Wash. Govt. Ptg. Off.] 1935. 4p. **1138**

—— —— List of publications and other printed material of the Agricultural Adjustment Administration, May 12, 1933 to June 1, 1934. Prepared in the Division of information, correspondence, records and printing. Wash. Govt. Ptg. Off. 1934. 25p. **1139**

—— —— Division of information. List of publications, May 12, 1933 through July 31, 1940. Wash. D.C. 1940. 16p. processed **1139a**

U.S. Agricultural Marketing Service. Printed publications. Wash. D.C. March 1940. 18p. processed **1139b**

—— —— Publications relating to cotton available in the Agricultural Marketing Service. Wash. D.C. April 1, 1940. 10p. mim. **1139c**

U.S. Bureau of Agricultural Economics. Inventory of reports and research studies completed and in progress relating to adjustments of population to resources in the northern great plains states. Comp. by N.W. Johnson and O.E. Goodsell. Wash. D.C. Jan. 1940. 86p. mim. **1139d**

—— —— Printed publications issued by the Bureau. . . . Wash. D.C. 1938. 28p. manifold copy **1139e**

—— —— Printed publications issued by the Bureau of Agricultural Economics. Wash. D.C. Aug. 1939. 28p. processed **1139f**

—— —— Division of economic information. List of agricultural economic reports and services of the Bureau of Agricultural Economics. Wash. D.C. n.p. 1931- mim. **1140**

—— —— Grain division. List of publications prepared by the Grain division, arranged alphabetically by subjects. Comp. by C. Louise Phillips. [Wash. D.C. n.p. 1936] 14p. mim. **1141**

—— —— Library. Economic reports and services. Wash. D.C. 1938. 62p. mim. **1141a**

U.S. Bureau of Biological Survey. Index to papers relating to the food habits of birds by members of the Biological Survey in publications of the United States Department of Agriculture, 1885-1911. By Waldo Lee McAtee (Biological Survey. Bul. no. 43) Wash. Govt. Ptg. Off. 1913. 69p. **1142**

—— —— List of publications of the Biological Survey. Comp. in the editorial office. Wash. D.C. 1928. 29p. **1143**

U.S. Bureau of Chemistry and Soils. Index of publications . . . 75 years-1862-1937. Vol. I. List of titles and authors. Prep. by H. P. Holman, V. A. Pease, K. Smith, M. T. Reid, A. Crebassa, under the direction of W. W. Skinner. Wash. D.C. 1939. 546p. mim. **1143a**

—— —— List of articles from the Fertilizer investigations unit, Bureau of Chemistry and Soils, published in scientific and technical journals. [Wash. D.C. n.p. 1935] 32p. mim. **1143b**

—— —— List of articles from the fixed nitrogen research laboratory in scientific and technical journals, chronologically arranged to date. [Wash. D.C. n.p. 1928] 14p. Autog. from typ. copy **1144**

—— —— Publications relating to sugar cane soil investigations, 1920-1930. Comp. by Oswald Schreiner and R.B. Deemer. Wash. D.C. n.p. 1931. 74p. mim. **1145**

U.S. Bureau of Crop Estimates. Statistical data compiled and published by the Bureau of Crop Estimates, 1863-1920. (Dept. of Agriculture. Circular 150) Wash. Govt. Ptg. Off. 1921. 64p. **1146**

U.S. Bureau of Dairy Industry. Library. List of publications of the Bureau of Dairy Industry from July 1, 1924 to Dec. 31, 1928. Wash. D.C. n.p. 1929. 26p. mim. **1147**

U.S. Bureau of Entomology. Index to bulletins nos. 1-30 (n.s.) (1896-1901) of the Division of Entomology. By Nathan Banks. (U.S. Dept. of Agriculture. Division of Entomology. Bul. n.s. 36) Wash. Govt. Ptg. Off. 1902. 64p. **1148**

—— —— List of entomological publications of personnel of cereal and forage investigations, U.S. Bureau of Entomology, 1904-1928, inclusive. Comp. by Joseph S. Wade. Wash. D.C. The Bureau. 1929. 46p. mim. **1149**

U.S. Bureau of Entomology and Plant Quarantine. List of publications of the Division of insecticide investigations, July 1, 1937-June 30, 1938. Wash. D.C. The Bureau. 1938. 10p. mim. **1149a**

U.S. Bureau of Home Economics. Publications of the Bureau of Home Economics, U.S. Dept. of Agriculture, July 1923-January 1930, arranged by subjects. . . . [Wash. D.C. n.p. 1930] 16p. mim. **1150**

U.S. Bureau of Markets. Library. Selected list of publications on the marketing of farm products. Wash. D.C. n.p. 1918. 29p. mim. **1151**

U.S. Bureau of Plant Industry. Contents of and index to bulletins of the Bureau of Plant Industry, nos. 1 to 100, inclusive. Comp. by Julius Ensign Rockwell. (Bureau of Plant Industry. Bul. 101) Wash. Govt. Ptg. Off. 1907. 102p. **1152**

—— —— Index to papers relating to plant industry subjects in the Yearbooks of the United States Department of Agriculture. Comp. by Julius Ensign Rockwell. (Bureau of Plant Industry. Circular 17) Wash. Govt. Ptg. Off. 1908. 55p. **1154**

—— —— List of publications relating to the activities of the Division of western irrigation agriculture, October 1932. [Wash. D.C. n.p. 1933] 13p. **1155**

U.S. Bureau of Plant Quarantine. Cumulative index to service and regulatory announcements nos. 1 to 117, 1914-33, Bureau of Plant Quarantine. Comp. by Horace S. Dean. [Wash. Govt. Ptg. Off. June 1934. 68p. **1156**

U.S. Cooperative Extension Work in Agriculture and Home Economics. 4-H club and older youth studies: some findings, bibliography and studies in progress. Comp. by B. D. Joy, and Lucinda Crile. (Extension service circular 339) Wash. D.C. Aug. 1940. 53p. processed **1156a**

U.S. Department of Agriculture. A general index of the agricultural reports of the Patent Office, for twenty-five years, from 1837 to 1861; and of the Department of Agriculture, for fifteen years, from 1862 to 1876. Wash. Govt. Ptg. Off. 1879. 225p. Supplement . . . 1877 to 1885, inclusive. Wash. Govt. Ptg. Off. 1886. 113p. **1157**

—— —— Index to Farmers' bulletins, nos. 1-1000. Prepared by C. H. Greathouse. Wash. Govt. Ptg. Off. 1920. 811p. **1158**

—— —— Index to Farmers' bulletins, nos. 1001-1500. By Mabel G. Hunt. Wash. Govt. Ptg. Off. 1929. 371p. **1158a**

—— —— Index to technical bulletins nos. 1-500. By Mabel G. Hunt. Wash. Govt. Ptg. Off. 1937. 249p. **1158b**

—— —— List of available publications of the United States Department of Agriculture, January 2, 1940; arranged by subjects. Comp. by Fred L. Zimmerman and Phyllis R. Read. (Miscellaneous publication no. 60, revised) Wash. D.C. 1940. 212p. **1158c**

—— —— List of publications of the United States Department of Agriculture from January 1901 to December 1925, inclusive. Comp. by comparison with the originals by Mabel G. Hunt, supplementary to bul. 6, Division of publications issued in 1902. (Miscellaneous publication 9) Wash. Govt. Ptg. Off. 1927. 182p. **1159**

—— —— List of the publications of the United States Department of Agriculture from January 1926 to December 1930, inclusive. Comp. by comparison with the originals by Mabel G. Hunt, supplementary to Miscellaneous publication 9 (Miscellaneous publication 153) Wash. Govt. Ptg. Off. 1932. 46p. Same. January 1931 to December 1935 (Miscellaneous publication 252) 1936. 64p. **1160**

—— —— **Division of publications.** Index to authors with titles of their publications, appearing in the documents of the United States Department of Agriculture, 1841 to 1897. By George F. Thompson. (Bul. no. 4) Wash. Govt. Ptg. Off. 1898. 303p. **1161**

—— —— —— Index to literature relating to animal industry in the publications of the Department of Agriculture, 1837 to 1898. By George Fayette Thompson. (Bul. 5) Wash. Govt. Ptg. Off. 1900. 676p. **1163**

—— —— —— Index to publications of the United States Department of Agriculture, 1926-1930. By Mary A. Bradley. Wash. Govt. Ptg. Off. 1935. 694p. Same. 1931-1935. 1937. 518p. **1164**

—— —— Index to the annual reports of the U.S. Department of Agriculture for the years 1837 to 1893, inclusive. comp. by George F. Thompson (Bul. 1) Wash. Govt. Ptg. Off. 1896. 252p. **1165**

—— —— Index to the Yearbooks of the United States Department of Agriculture, 1894-1910. Prepared by Charles H. Greathouse. (Buls. no. 7, 9, 10) Wash. Govt. Ptg. Off. 1902-13. 3v. **1166**

—— —— Index to the yearbooks of the United States Department of Agriculture, 1911-1915. Prepared by Charles H. Greathouse under the supervision of John L. Cobbs, Jr. Wash. Govt. Ptg. Off. 1922. 178p. **1167**

—— —— List by titles of publications of the United States Department of Agriculture from 1840 to June 1901, inclusive. By R. B. Handy and Minna A. Cannon (Bul. 6) Wash. Govt. Ptg. Off. 1902. 216p. **1168**

—— —— Monthly list of publications, March 1896-July 1929. Wash. [Govt. Ptg. Off. 1896-1929] **1169**

—— —— Synoptical index of the reports of the statistician, 1863-1894. By George F. Thompson. (Bul. 2) Wash. Govt. Ptg. Off. 1897. 258p. **1170**

—— —— **Library.** Check list of publications issued by the Bureau of Plant Industry, 1901-20, and by the divisions and offices which combined to form this bureau, 1862-1901. (Bibliog. contributions no. 3) Wash. D.C. 1921. 127p. mim. **1170a**

—— —— —— A classified list of soil publications of the United States and Canada. (Bibliog. contributions no. 13) Wash. D.C. 1927. 549p. mim. **1171**

—— —— —— Cotton and cottonseed, a list of publications of the United States Department of Agriculture, including early reports of the United States Patent Office. By Rachel P. Lane and Emily L. Day. (Dept. of Agriculture. Miscellaneous publication 203) Wash. D.C. 1934. 149p. **1172**

—— —— —— List of publications of the U.S. Department of Agriculture from 1841 to June 30, 1895, inclusive. By Adelaide R. Hasse. (Bul. 9) Wash. Govt. Ptg. Off. 1896. 76p. **1173**

—— —— **Office of information.** Publications of the U.S. Department of Agriculture. Comp. by Doris Stockdale. Wash. Govt. Ptg. off. 1926- **1174**

—— —— —— **Division of publications.** Index to department bulletins nos. 1-1500. By Mabel G. Hunt. Wash. Govt. Ptg. Off. 1936. 384p. **1175**

—— —— —— —— Index to publications of the United States Department of Agriculture, 1901-1925. By Mary A. Bradley assisted by Mabel G. Hunt. Wash. Govt. Ptg. Off. 1932. 2689p. **1176**

U.S. Dept. of Agriculture. Office of information. Division of publications. Special administrative list of publications of the United States Department of Agriculture available free to agricultural administrators for their official use. Comp. by M. A. Downes. Wash. Govt. Ptg. Off. 1934. 20p. **1177**

—— —— **Office of the Solicitor.** Index of the opinions of the solicitor, March 1, 1916-. [Wash. D.C. 1917-] **1178**

—— —— —— Index to legislative history of acts of Congress involving the United States Department of Agriculture. Prepared . . . by Mr. Otis H. Gates. Wash. Govt. Ptg. Off. 1912. 53p. **1179**

U.S. Extension Service. Publications of the extension service. (Extension service circular 323) Wash. D.C. Jan. 1940. 25p. processed **1179a**

U.S. Farm Security Administration. List of available publications. Wash. D.C. Sept. 1, 1940. 6p. processed **1179b**

U.S. Forest Service. Branch of research. Division of silvics. Library. Complete List of Forest Service publications, Feb. 16, 1936. [Wash. D.C. 1936] 122p. mim. **1180**

—— —— **Forest products laboratory, Madison, Wis.** List of Forest Service publications, logging, manufacture, distribution, and use of timber, lumber, and other wooden products. Prepared by section of industrial investigations. Madison. 1923. 36p. **1181**

—— —— —— List of publications January 1, to June 30, 1940. 1940. 6p. processed **1181a**

U.S. Office of Experiment Stations. General index to Experiment station record, vols. I to XII, 1889-1901 and to Experiment station bulletin no. 2, the latter a digest of the annual reports of the experiment stations for 1888. Wash. Govt. Ptg. Off. 1903. 671p. **1182**

—— —— General index to Experiment station record, vols. XIII to XXV, 1901-1911. Prepared by M. D. Moore and William Henry. Wash. Govt. Ptg. Off. 1913. 1159p. **1183**

—— —— General index to Experiment station record, vols. XXVI to [LX] 1912-[1929]. Prepared by Martha C. Gundlach. Wash. Govt. Ptg. Off. 1926-32. 3v. **1184**

—— —— List of bulletins of the agricultural experiment stations in the United States from their establishment to the end of 1920. (Bul. no 1199) Wash. Govt. Ptg. Off. 1924. 186p. **1185**

—— —— List of bulletins of the agricultural experiment stations for the calendar years, 1921-. By Catherine E. Pennington. Wash. Govt. Ptg. Off. 1924- **1186**

—— —— List of publications of the agricultural experiment stations in the United States [to June 30, 1906]. (Bul. no. 180) Wash. Govt. Ptg. Off. 1907. 104p. **1187**

—— —— List of publications on irrigation and drainage. Wash. Oct. 25, 1907. 12p. **1188**

—— —— **Library.** List of station publications received by the Office of Experiment Stations during Nov. 1903-. Wash. Govt. Ptg. Off. 1904- **1189**

U.S. Superintendent of Documents. Experiment stations office. Bulletins, circulars, experiment station record, and reports of Colonial experiment stations. Wash. Govt. Ptg. Off. 1911. 29p. **1190**

—— —— Farmers' bulletins, department bulletins, circulars, agricultural yearbooks, statistical bulletins; series list of above agricultural publications. Wash. Govt. Ptg. Off. 1926. 65p. **1191**

—— —— List of publications of the Agriculture Department, 1862-1902, with analytical index. (Bibliog. of U.S. public documents. Dept. list 1) Wash. Govt. Ptg. Off. 1904. 622p. **1192**

—— —— Publications of the Weather Bureau, Agriculture Department, U.S.A. and of the Signal office, War Department. Wash. Govt. Ptg. Off. 1911. 11p. **1193**

U.S. Weather Bureau. Library. Checklist of Library of Congress printed catalog cards for Weather Bureau publications. Wash. Govt. Ptg. Off. 1917. 39p. **1194**

DEPARTMENT OF COMMERCE

Ellsworth, Henry L. A digest of patents, issued by the United States, from 1790 to January 1, 1839. Wash. D.C. 1840. 672p. Digest . . . 1839, 1840 and 1841. Wash. D.C. 1842 **1194a**

Fenning, Karl. Cumulative digest of . . . the United States . . . decisions relating to patents . . . July 1, 1935 to June 30, 1938. Wash. D.C. 1938. 779p. **1194b**

U.S. Bureau of Air Commerce. Aeronautic publications. [Wash. Govt. Ptg. Off. 1927-] **1195**

U.S. Bureau of Fisheries. An analytical subject bibliography of the publications of the Bureau of Fisheries, 1871-1920. By Rose MacDonald. Wash. Govt. Ptg. Off. 1921. 306p. (Appendix V to the Rep. of the U.S. commissioner of fisheries for 1920. Bureau of fisheries document 899) **1196**

—— —— List of publications of the Bureau of Fisheries available for distribution. Wash. Govt. Ptg. Off. 1907-15 **1197**

—— —— List of publications of the United States Commission of fish and fisheries from its establishment in February 1871, to February 1896. By Charles W. Scudder. (U.S. Comn. of fish and fisheries. Rep. of the commissioner for 1894) Wash. Govt. Ptg. Off. 1896. p617-706 **1198**

—— —— Publications of the United States Commission of fish and fisheries available for distribution, 1897-1903. (U.S. Comn. of fish and fisheries. Rep. of the commissioner for 1896-1903) Wash. Govt. Ptg. Off. 1898-1905 **1199**

U.S. Bureau of Foreign and Domestic Commerce. Government publications relating to textiles. Wash. Govt. Ptg. Off. 1931. 101p. **1200**

—— —— List of selected publications issued by the Bureau of Foreign and Domestic Commerce. Wash. Govt. Ptg. Off. 1941. 27p. **1200a**

—— —— Publications of the Bureau of Foreign and Domestic Commerce, October 1931. Wash. Govt. Ptg. Off. 1931. 133p. **1201**

—— **Division of commercial laws.** Index to publications of Division of commercial laws. [Wash. D.C.] July 25, 1936. 54p. processed **1202**

U.S. Bureau of Foreign Commerce. Index to the consular reports, nos. 1-239, 1880-1900. Wash. Govt. Ptg. Off. 1887-1901. 5v. **1203**

U.S. Bureau of Home Economics. Selected list of government publications on housing and equipment. Comp. by Ruth Van Deman. (Home economics bibliog. no. 2) [Wash. D.C.] May 1928. 16p. mim. **1204**

U.S. Bureau of Standards. Publications of the Bureau of Standards, complete from establishment of bureau 1901 to June 30, 1925. (Circular 24) Wash. Govt. Ptg. Off. 1925. 271p. (Supplementary list. 1925-31, 1932. 214p. Jan. 1, 1932-June 30, 1936. 1936) **1205**

—— —— Publications of the Bureau of Standards, 1907-. Wash. Govt. Ptg. Off. 1907- **1206**

—— —— Publications on paper and paper research. . . . Wash. D.C. April 1937. v p. mim. **1206a**

—— —— Publications relating to textiles. . . . (Letter circular LC-396 superseding LC-143) Wash. 1933. 63p. mim. **1207**

—— **Division of building and housing.** Publications of the Bureau of Standards relating to building materials, home building, home ownership, city planning and zoning. (Letter circular no. 290) Wash. D.C. 1930. 58p. **1208**

U.S. Bureau of the Census. Census of business: 1935; business census publications. [Wash. Govt. Ptg. Off. 1937] 16p. photop. **1208a**

—— —— Census publications available for distribution by the Bureau of the Census, Feb. 1, 1921. Wash. Govt. Ptg. Off. 1921. 16p. **1209**

—— —— Circular of information concerning census publications, 1790-1916. (Circular of information 2) Wash. Govt. Ptg. Off. 1917. 124p. **1210**

—— —— List of publications, tenth, eleventh and twelfth censuses, and permanent bureau. Wash. Govt. Ptg. Off. 1905. 8p. **1211**

—— —— List of reports and publications relating to vital statistics. Wash. D.C. 1938. 4p. **1211a**

—— —— Topical index of population census reports, 1900-30. By Olive M. Riddleberger. Wash. 1934. 76p. processed **1212**

U.S. Census. Key to the publications of the United States census, 1790-1887. By Edward C. Lunt. Am. Statistical Asso. publication, n.s. I. p63-125 (March 1888) **1214**

U.S. Civil Aeronautics Authority. List of publications. Feb. 15, 1940. Wash. 1940. processed **1214a**

U.S. Coast and Geodetic Survey. Bibliography; descriptive catalogue of publications relating to the U.S. Coast and Geodetic Survey, 1807 to 1896 and to U.S. Standard weights and measures, 1790 to 1896. (Special publication no. 2) Wash. Govt. Ptg. Off. 1898. 118p. (Earlier list in U.S. Coast and Geodetic Survey. Report for 1891. Appendix XI. pt. 2. p365-474) **1215**

—— —— Catalogue of charts . . . (numerous editions) **1215a**

—— —— List and catalogue of the publications issued by the U.S. Coast and Geodetic Survey, 1816-1902. By E.L. Burchard. Wash. Govt. Ptg. Off. 1902. 239p. (Reprinted 1908 with a supplement [by R.N. Brown] in 44p. covering 1903-08) **1216**

—— —— List of all unpublished maps on file. MS. **1216a**

U.S. Department of Commerce. List of publications of the Department of Commerce, May 1908-1935. Wash. Govt. Ptg. Off. 1908-35. 15v. **1217**

—— —— Monthly list of publications, no. 1, July 1914-. Wash. Govt. Ptg. Off. 1914- **1218**

—— —— **Division of publications.** List of publications available for distribution by the issuing offices of the department and its field agencies or from the Superintendent of documents and agents of his office. Wash. Govt. Ptg. Off. 1934. 144p. **1219**

—— —— —— List of publications of the Department of Commerce pertaining to the shipping industry. April 1, 1920. Wash. Govt. Ptg. Off. 1920. 27p. **1220**

U.S. Department of State. Letter from the Secretary of State transmitting a list of all patents granted by the United States. (House. doc. 50, 21 Cong. 2 sess.) Wash. D.C. 1831. 504p. **1220a**

U.S. Patent Office. [Annual index to] Official gazette. Wash. Govt. Ptg. Off. 1872- **1220b**

—— —— Subject-matter index of patents for inventions issued by the United States Patent Office from 1790 to 1873, inclusive. Comp. by M. D. Leggett. Wash. Govt. Ptg. Off. 1874. 3v. **1220c**

—— —— Women inventors to whom patents have been granted by the United States Government, 1790 to July 1, 1888 and appendix no. 1-2. Wash. Govt. Ptg. Off. 1888-95. 3v. in 1 **1220d**

U.S. President's commission on economy and efficiency. Publications of the Patent Office. In Report of the investigations of the United States Patent Office made by the President's commission on econ-

U.S. President's comm. on economy and efficiency. Publications of the Patent Office—*Continued*
omy and efficiency. December 1912. House document no. 1110. 62 Cong. 3 sess. 1912. p477-95 **1221**

U.S. Superintendent of documents. Census publications. Wash. Govt. Ptg. Off. 1930. 38p. **1221a**

DEPARTMENT OF THE INTERIOR

U.S. Bureau of Education. See U.S. Office of Education

U.S. Bureau of Mines. Bibliography of the United States Bureau of Mines investigations on coal and its products, 1910-1935. By A.C. Fieldner and M.W. von Bernewitz. (Technical paper no. 576) Wash. Govt. Ptg. Off. 1937. 145p. **1229**

—— —— Index of Bureau of Mines papers published in the technical press, July 1, 1910 to December 31, 1930. Comp. by H. C. Carroll. Wash. D.C. 1931. 2 pts in 1 v. reprod. from typ. copy **1230**

—— —— Index of Bureau of Mines publications, 1922-1927. Wash. Govt. Ptg. Off. 1922-27. 6v. **1231**

—— —— Index of Bureau of Mines reports of investigations and information circulars, December 31, 1926. Comp. by Harry E. Tufft. Wash. D.C. July 1927. 93p. mim. **1232**

—— —— List and index of Bureau of Mines, reports of investigations and information circulars, issued during the calendar year 1927. Wash. D.C. May 1928. 27p. mim. **1233**

—— —— List of publications, Bureau of Mines, complete from establishment of Bureau 1910 to June 30, 1937, with subject and author index. Wash. Govt. Ptg. Off. 1938. 356p. (Cont.) **1234**

—— —— A selected list of Bureau of Mines publications and motion picture films dealing with petroleum, natural gas, helium, oil shale, and allied subjects. (Prepared with assistance of WPA project O.P. no. 65-2-65-346) Petroleum experimental station, Bartlesville, Oklahoma, April, 1940, in cooperation with the state of Oklahoma. [Bartlesville, Okla. 1940.] 129p. reprod. **1234a**

—— —— Selected list of Bureau of Mines publications covering safety studies and activities of the electrical section. By L.C. Ilsley. (Information circular. 6310) Wash. D.C. 1930. 9p. processed **1235**

U.S. Bureau of Pensions. Subject-matter index and ready reference to the rulings of the Commissioner of Pensions. Wash. D.C. 1887. 24p. **1235a**

U.S. Bureau of Reclamation. Index: First to twentieth annual reports of the Reclamation service. *In* Twentieth annual report of the Reclamation service, 1920-21. Wash. Govt. Ptg. Off. 1921. p583-642 **1236**

—— —— List of engineering articles. Wash. Govt. Ptg. Off. 1915- **1237**

—— —— Publications of the Bureau of Reclamation; price list no. 10. Wash. Govt. Ptg. Off. 1908- **1238**

U.S. Commission to the Five Civilized Tribes. Index to the annual reports of the Commission to the Five Civilized Tribes for the years 1894 to 1905, inclusive. Wash. Govt. Ptg. Off. 1906. 136p. **1239**

U.S. Department of the Interior. List of books, reports, documents, and pamphlets published by the Department of the Interior, and its several bureaus and offices [from 1789 to 1881] (Senate executive document no. 182. 47 Cong. 1 sess. Ser. 1991) 1882. 76p. **1240**

U.S. General Land Office. Circulars and regulations of the General Land Office with reference tables and index... Wash. Govt. Ptg. Off. 1930. 1696p. **1240a**

—— —— Index to circulars and publications of the General Land Office. Wash. Govt. Ptg. Off. 1928. 48p. **1241**

—— —— Index to circulars and regulations of the General Land Office, issued since January 1930. Comp. by C. G. Fisher. Wash. Govt. Ptg. Off. 1932. 13p. **1242**

—— —— List of military bounty land warrants, cancelled and suspended by the Commissioner of pensions, corrected and complete to date, October 13, 1850. Wash. D.C. C. Alexander. 1850. 45p. **1243**

U.S. Geological and Geographical Survey of the Territories. Catalogue of the publications of the U.S. Geological and Geographical Survey of the Territories. F. V. Hayden, U. S. geologist. Wash. Govt. Ptg. Off. 1879. 54p. **1244**

U.S. Geological Survey. Bibliographic review and index of papers relating to underground waters published by the United States Geological Survey, 1879-1904. By Myron L. Fuller. (Water-supply paper. 120) Wash. Govt. Ptg. Off. 1905. 128p. **1245**

—— —— Bibliographic review and index of underground water literature published in the United States in 1905. By Myron L. Fuller and others. (Water-supply paper. 163) Wash. Govt. Ptg. Off. 1906. 130p. **1246**

—— —— Bibliography and index of the publications of the United States Geological Survey, relating to ground water. By Oscar E. Meinzer. (Water-supply paper. 427) Wash. Govt. Ptg. Off. 1918. 169p. **1247**

—— —— Catalogue and index of the publications of the Hayden, King, Powell, and Wheeler surveys, namely Geological and Geographical survey of the territories, Geographical exploration of the fortieth parallel, Geographical and geological surveys of the Rocky mountain region, Geographical surveys west of the one hundredth meridian. By Laurence F. Schmeckebier. (Bul. 222) Wash. Govt. Ptg. Off. 1904. 208p. (Also House document no. 606. 58 Cong. 2 sess. Ser 4684) **1248**

U.S. Geological Survey. Catalogue and index of the publications of the United States Geological Survey, 1880-1901. By Philip C. Warman. (Bul. 177) Wash. Govt. Ptg. Off. 1901. 858p. (Also House document no. 535. 56 Cong. 2 sess. Ser. 4187) **1249**

—— —— Catalogue and index of the publications of the United States Geological Survey, 1901 to 1903. By Philip C. Warman. (Bul. no. 215) Wash. Govt. Ptg. Off. 1903. 234p. (Also House document no. 471. 57 Cong. 2 sess) **1250**

—— —— Gaging stations maintained by the United States Geological Survey, 1888-1910 and Survey publications relating to water resources. By Mrs. Beatrice (Dawson) Wood. (Water-supply paper 280) Wash. Govt. Ptg. Off. 1912. 102p. **1251**

—— —— Index to the hydrographic progress reports of the United States Geological Survey, 1888-1903. By John C. Hoyt and B. D. Wood. (Water-supply and irrigation paper 119) Wash. Govt. Ptg. Off. 1905. 253p. **1252**

—— —— Preliminary index to river surveys made by the United States Geological Survey and other agencies. By Benjamin E. Jones and Randolph O. Helland. (Water-supply paper. 558) Wash. Govt. Ptg. Off. 1926. 108p. **1252a**

—— —— Publications of the United States Geological Survey (not including topographic maps) Wash. D.C. issued annually **1252b**

—— —— U.S. Geological Survey publications, 1901-1914, on the oil fields of the United States. (Geol. survey. Mineral resources of the U. S. 1914. pt. II) Wash. Govt. Ptg. Off. 1916. p1093-8 **1252c**

—— —— Water-supply papers. 1926. p89-120 **1252d**

—— —— The publications of the United States Geological Survey relating to water resources, July 1910. Wash. Govt. Ptg. Off. 1910. 31p. **1252e**

U.S. Office of Education. Bulletins of the Bureau of Education, 1906-1927, with index by author, title, and subject. By Edith A. Wright and Mary S. Phillips. (Bul. 1928. no. 17) Wash. Govt. Ptg. Off. 1928. 65p. **1253**

—— —— Government publications of interest to home economics teachers and students. (Home economics circular 5) Wash. D.C. 1923. 15p. **1254**

—— —— Government publications useful to teachers. By Eustace E. Windes. Bul. 1924. no. 23) Wash. Govt. Ptg. Off. 1924. 34p. **1255**

—— —— Index to the reports of the commissioner of education, 1867-1907. (Bul. 1909. no. 7. whole no. 407) Wash. Govt. Ptg. Off. 1909. 103p. **1256**

—— —— List of bulletins of the Bureau of Education, 1906-1922. By Edith A. Wright. (Bul. 1923. no. 35) Wash. Govt. Ptg. Off. 1923. 52p. **1257**

—— —— List of publications of the Office of Education, 1910-1936, including those of the former Federal Board for Vocational Education for 1917-1933, with author and subject indexes. Wash. Govt. Ptg. Off. 1937. 158p. **1257a**

—— —— List of publications of the United States Bureau of Education, 1867-1910 (Bul. 1910. no. 3. whole no. 439) Wash. Govt. Ptg. Off. 1910. 55p. (List for 1867 to 1890 was reprinted from chapter XXXV of the Report of the Commissioner of education for 1888-89, p1453-1551. 1867-1895 in *ibid.* 1894-95, II, p1821-8. 1867-1907 in Bureau of Education. Bul. 1908. no. 2. 69p.) **1257b**

—— —— List of publications of the United States Bureau of Education, available for free distribution, September 1912. (Bul. 1912. no. 25. whole no. 497) Wash. Govt. Ptg. Off. 1912. 37p. **1258**

—— —— Mimeographed circulars of the Office of Education [Wash. D.C.] Jan. 1934. 5p. processed **1259**

—— —— Publications of the Federal Office of Education during 1930-33; bulletins, pamphlets, leaflets. [Wash. D.C.] n.d. 9p. processed **1260**

—— —— Publications of the . . . Office of Education, 1930-38. Wash. D.C. Jan. 1939. 18p. processed **1260a**

—— —— United States publications on education, 1931-. Wash. D.C. 1931- **1261**

U.S. Office of Indian Affairs. Subject index of Indian office circulars nos. 160 to 1000 from July 8, 1907, to June 25, 1915. Wash. Govt. Ptg. Off. 1916. 39p. **1262**

DEPARTMENT OF JUSTICE

Morse, L. W. Historical outline and bibliography of attorneys general reports and opinions from their beginnings through 1936. Law lib. jour. XXX. p239-47 (April 1937) **1262a**

U.S. Department of Justice. Federal anti-trust decisions; index-digest (volumes 1-6) 1890-1917, with tables of reported and cited cases, including also an appendix containing the federal anti-trust laws. Prep. by John L. Lott and Roger Shale. (Federal anti-trust decisions, VII) Wash. Govt. Ptg. Off. 1918. 513p. **1262b**

—— —— The federal anti-trust laws with amendments; list of cases instituted under or relating thereto. Wash. Govt. Ptg. Off. 1922. 158p. **1262c**

—— —— Index to the opinions of the attornies general of the United States. As printed by the House of Representatives in executive document no. 55. 2d sess. 31st Cong. Wash. D.C. C. Alexander. 1852. 194p. **1263**

—— —— List of publications (March 4, 1789 to March 4, 1881) (Senate executive document no. 109. 47 Cong. 1 sess. Ser. 1990) 1881. 12p. **1264**

DEPARTMENT OF LABOR

U.S. Bureau of Labor Statistics. Bulletins and articles published by Bureau of Labor Statistics; a selected list of references. Comp. by Elizabeth A. Johnson. (Bul. 614) Wash. Govt. Ptg. Off. 1935. 19p.   **1265**

—— —— Index of all reports issued by Bureaus of labor statistics in the United States prior to March 1, 1902. Prepared under the direction of Carroll D. Wright. Wash. Govt. Ptg. Off. 1902. 287p. **1266**

—— —— A selected list of the publications of the Bureau of Labor Statistics. Comp. by Elizabeth A. Johnson. Wash. Govt. Ptg. Off. 1935-   **1266a**

—— —— Subject index of the Monthly labor review, vols. I-XI, July 1915 to December 1920. By Karoline Klager and Elsie M. Pursglove. Wash. Govt. Ptg. Off. 1923. 176p.   **1267**

—— —— Subject index of the publications of the United States Bureau of Labor Statistics up to May 1, 1915. (Bul. 174. miscellaneous ser. no. 11) Wash. Govt. Ptg. Off. 1915. 233p. (Also issued as House document 1707. 63 Cong. 2 sess.) **1268**

U.S. Children's Bureau. Publications. . . . Wash. Govt. Ptg. Off. 1920-   **1269**

U.S. Department of Labor. Publications of the Department of Labor. . . . Wash. Govt. Ptg. Off. 1914-   **1270**

—— —— **Consumers' project.** A selected list of government publications of interest to consumers. Wash. D.C. [1937] 14p.
                                              1270a

—— —— **Division of publications and supplies.** Publications of the Department of Labor, November 15, 1937. Wash. D.C. 1937. 52p.   **1270b**

DEPARTMENT OF THE NAVY

U.S. Bureau of Ordnance (Navy). Index [to] Ordnance pamphlets with notes relative to their use and distribution. [Nov. 1905. 13th revision] Wash. D.C. June 1928] 67p.   **1271**

U.S. Department of the Navy. A cumulative index to court-martial orders for the years 1916 to 1937. Wash. Govt. Ptg. Off. 1940. 840p   **1271a**

—— —— General orders and circulars issued by Navy Department 1863 to 1887, with an alphabetical index of subjects, also index of bureau and Marine corps circulars, general court-martial orders and special death notices. Comp. by M.S. Thompson. Wash. Govt. Ptg. Off. 1887. 353p.   **1272**

—— —— Index [alphabetical] to general orders, circulars, &c., issued by the department, Jan. 10, 1863-June 30, 1881. Comp. by P. A. Webster. Wash. 1881
                                              1273

—— —— . . . List of books, &c. published by the Secretary of the Navy and the bureaus of the Navy Dept. [From March 4, 1789 to March 4, 1881] (Senate executive document no. 37. 47 Cong. 1 sess. Ser. 1987) 1882. 15p.   **1274**

—— —— Official records of the Union and Confederate navies in the war of the rebellion—General index. By Dudley W. Knox. Wash. Govt. Ptg. Off. 1927. 457p. (Also pub. as House document 113. 69 Cong. 1 sess.)   **1275**

—— —— United States Navy registers. Wash. D.C. Navy Dept. 1891. 3p. **1276**

—— —— **Office of naval war records.** Naval war records, office memoranda no. 9; Index of official records of the Union and Confederate navies in the war of the rebellion, series I, volumes 1-13. Wash. Govt. Ptg. Off. 1902 **1277**

U.S. Hydrographic Office. Catalogue of charts, plans, sailing direction issued. . . . (numerous editions)   **1277a**

—— —— General catalogue of mariners' and aviators' charts and books. Wash. Govt. Ptg. Off. 1931. 258p.   **1278**

U.S. Judge advocate general's department (Navy) Index of court martial orders, 1924-1932. Wash. Govt. Ptg. Off. 1925-33. 9v.   **1279**

U.S. Naval Observatory. List of publications issued by the United States Naval Observatory, 1845-1908. By William D. Horigan (Publications of the U.S. Naval Observatory. 2d ser. VI. appendix III) Wash. Govt. Ptg. Off. 1911. pD1-D36 (Also issued separately)   **1280**

—— —— A subject index to the publications of the United States Naval Observatory, 1845-1875. By Edward Singleton Holden. (U.S. Naval Observatory. Wash. astronomical observations for 1876. Appendix I) Wash. Govt. Ptg. Off. 1879. 74p.   **1281**

DEPARTMENT OF STATE

U.S. Congress. House. Committee on Appropriations. Foreign relations, International law digest and other State department publications. (Dept. of state. Publication 1151) Wash. Govt. Ptg. Off. 1938. p93-123   **1281a**

—— —— —— —— The Foreign relations volumes and other Department of State publications. (Dept. of State. Pub. 1005) Wash. Govt. Ptg. Off. 1937. p68-93
                                              1281b

—— —— —— —— Peace conference records and other State department publication projects. (Dept. of State. Publication 1343) Wash. Govt. Ptg. Off. 1939. p36-43, 69-102, 108-12, 272-94   **1281c**

U.S. Department of State. Contents of and index to the first twenty-six and a half numbers of the reports from the consuls of the United States on the commerce, manufactures, etc., of their consular districts. (House miscellaneous document 39. 47 Cong. 2 sess. Ser. 2127) May 1883. 118p.   **1282**

—— —— The Department of State bulletin. Wash. Govt. Ptg. Off. 1940- (Supersedes its Press releases and Treaty information series) **1282a**

—— —— General index to the published volumes of the diplomatic correspondence and foreign relations of the United States, 1861-99. Wash. Govt. Ptg. Off. 1902. 945p. **1283**

—— —— Index to consular reports, nos. 60 to 111 (Vols. 18 to 31) 1886-1889. (House miscellaneous document no. 233. 51 Cong. 1 sess. Ser. 2784) 1890. 192p. **1284**

—— —— Index to press releases. Wash. Govt. Ptg. Off. 1930-39. 20v. **1284a**

—— —— Index to treaty information bulletins. (In preparation) **1285**

—— —— Publications, available documents, and archives of the Department of State. By Cyril Wynne. Press releases. no. 234. March 24, 1934. publication no. 571. p164-9 **1286**

—— —— Publications of the Department of State; a list cumulative from October 1, 1929, July 1, 1935. Wash. Govt. Ptg. Off. 1935. 26p. **1287**

—— —— Publications of the Department of State; a quarterly list, April 1930-July 1936. (Publication no. 58, 87, 116, 150, 177, 205, 239, 269, 305, 336, 377, 415, 443, 535, 547, 578, 612, 652, 686, 761, 790, 825, 861) Wash. Govt. Ptg. Off. 1930-36 **1288**

—— —— Status of the foreign relations and the Miller treaty volumes. (Dept. of State. Publication no. 864) Wash. Govt. Ptg. Off. p46-8 **1289**

—— —— Treaty information, cumulative index, bulletins 1-69, inclusive, October 1929-June 1935. Wash. Govt. Ptg. Off. 1937. 133p. **1289a**

Wynne, Cyril. Progress of the State Department's publication program. (U.S. Dept. of State. Pub. 1280) Wash. Govt. Ptg. Off. 1939. 19p. **1289b**

—— Publications of the Department of State. (U.S. Dept. of State. Pub. 1170) Wash. Govt. Ptg. Off. 1938. 19p. **1289c**

DEPARTMENT OF THE TREASURY

U.S. Bureau of Internal Revenue. Citator of internal revenue; treasury decisions, regulations, and miscellaneous published office rulings, showing where treasury decisions (internal revenue) nos. 1-4264 and other decisions are cited, amended reversed, etc., December 29, 1899-March 31, 1929. Wash. Govt. Ptg. Off. 1930. 270p. (Supplements. no. 1. April 1, 1929 to March 31, 1930. 67p.; no. 2. April 1, 1930 to March 31, 1931. 69p.) **1290**

U.S. Comptroller of the Currency. Digest of decisions relating to national banks, 1864-1926. Wash. Govt. Ptg. Off. 1927- **1290a**

U.S. Department of the Treasury. Index to decisions made by the Secretary of the Treasury as to the assessment of duty on imported goods under the tariff act of March 3, 1883, to January 1, 1890, including index to decisions under acts of Congress relating to Alaska; to the restriction and exclusion of Chinese; to the prevention of the importation of adulterated and spurious teas, etc., covering the period from March, 1883, to January, 1890. Wash. Govt. Ptg. Off. 1890. 135p. **1290b**

—— —— Index to synopses of the decisions of the Treasury Department and the Board of United States general appraisers on the construction of the tariff, navigation, and other laws, January 1, 1890, to December 31, 1895. Wash. Govt. Ptg. Off. 1896. cccix p. **1291**

—— —— Periodical publications of the Treasury Department, revised to February 1, 1928, and summary of tabular material in the Annual reports of the Secretary of the Treasury from 1914 to 1927. Wash. Govt. Ptg. Off. 1928. 20p. **1292**

—— —— Synopsis of executive documents, letters, reports, etc., upon banking, coinage, currency, finance, etc., submitted to Congress by secretaries of Treasury from the 1st Congress to 1st session of 53d Congress inclusive. Wash. Govt. Ptg. Off. 1893. 73p. **1293**

—— —— **Research and statistics division.** Publications of the Treasury Dpartment. as of July 1, 1935. [Wash. D.C. 1935] 19p. mim. **1294**

U.S. Office of Internal Revenue. Index to mimeographs nos. 1717 to 3299, from January 8, 1918 to April 10, 1925, inclusive, and collectors' circulars nos. 1 to 616, from July 7, 1920 to March 21, 1925. Wash. Govt. Ptg. Off. 1925. 153p. **1295**

U.S. Public Health Service. Public health service publications; a list of publications issued during the period, 1922- . Wash. Govt. Ptg. Off. 1923- **1296**

WAR DEPARTMENT

U.S. Adjutant General's Office. Analytical index of general orders, Adjutant General's Office, 1861-1876. Wash. Govt. Ptg. Off. 1878. 127p. **1297**

—— —— Index of general court-martial orders, Adjutant General's Office, 1878-1881. Wash. 1879-82. 4v. in 1 **1298**

—— —— Index to army regulations including all regulations and changes promulgated prior to January 1, 1935. Wash. Govt. Ptg. Off. 1935. 433p. **1299**

—— —— List of War Department documents, issued by the Adjutant General of the army with their distribution. Prepared in the office of the Adjutant general. (War dept. Document no. 1008) Wash. Govt. Ptg. Off. 1920. 20p. **1300**

—— —— Subject index of general orders of the War Department, January 1, 1809 to December 31, 1860. Comp. under the direction of Brigadier General Richard C. Drum . . . by Jeremiah C. Allen. Wash. Govt. Ptg. Off. 1886. 192p. **1301**

U.S. Adjutant General's Office. Subject index of the general orders from January 1, 1861 to December 31, 1880. Comp. under the direction of Brigadier General Richard C. Drum . . . by Jeremiah C. Allen. Wash. Govt. Ptg. Off. 1882. 506p. **1302**

—— —— Subject index to the general orders and circulars of the War department and the headquarters of the army. Adjutant general's office, from January 1, 1860 to December 31, 1880. Wash. Govt. Ptg. Off. 1913. 266p. **1302a**

—— —— Same. January 1, 1881 to December 31, 1911. Wash. Govt. Ptg. Off. 1912. 650p. **1303**

—— —— The different editions of army regulations. [By James B. Fry. N.Y. n.p. 1876] 7p. **1303a**

U.S. Air Corps. Materiel' division. Numerical index of air corps technical reports, Jan. 1927-. [Wash. D.C.] 1927- **1304**

U.S. Engineer Department. Index of general orders and circulars, headquarters Corps of engineers, and circulars, office of Chief of Engineers, 1868-82, with copies of important orders and circulars issued during that period. n.p. n.d. 44, 99p. **1305**

—— —— [Index to] preliminary examinations surveys, projects, and appropriations, for rivers and harbors. (House document no. 1491. 63 Cong. 3 sess. Ser. 6805) 1916 (Contents: List of preliminary examinations and survey reports made prior to and including March 4, 1915, p7-197; List of projects in force on March 4, 1915, p198-385; List of appropriations by localities, p394-583; List of appropriations by states, p583-94) **1306**

—— —— Index to the reports of The Chief of Engineers, U.S. Army (including the reports of the Isthmian Canal Commission, 1899-1914) 1866-1912. Completed under the direction of Brig. Gen. Dan C. Kingman, Chief of engineers . . . by Colonel George A. Zinn, Corps of engineers. John McClure, compiler. Volume I. Rivers and harbors. Volume II. Fortifications, bridges, Panama canal, etc. (House document no. 740. 63 Cong. 2 sess. ser. 6617) Wash. Govt. Ptg. Off. 1915-16 **1307**

—— —— Index to the reports of the Chief of Engineers, U.S. Army, 1913-1917; supplemental to index, 1866-1912, including the reports of the governor of the Panama canal, 1915-1917; professional papers of the Corps of engineers, U.S. Army; professional memoirs, Corps of engineers, U.S. Army and Engineer Department at Large; and congressional documents relating to works of river and harbor improvements, 1905-1917. Comp. under the direction of the Chief of Engineers, U.S. Army, by Lieut. Col. William B. Ladue, Corps of Engineers. Claude Lindsey compiler. (House document no. 724. 66 Cong. 2 sess.) Wash. Govt. Ptg. Off. 1921. 455p. vol. III. **1308**

—— —— List of publications of the Engineer Department, U.S. Army, including reports on explorations, &c. conducted under other branches of the Department of War, exhibited at The International Exhibition, 1876 at Philadelphia. Wash. Govt. Ptg. Off. 1876. 27p. **1309**

—— —— List of reports and maps of the United States geographical surveys west of the 100th meridian. By George M. Wheeler. Wash. Govt. Ptg. Off. 1878. 36p. **1310**

—— —— Lists and indexes of documents and reports on rivers and harbors, 1900- (A special compilation available in the Engineer Department and in the Public Documents Library) **1310a**

—— —— Orders and regulations, Corps of engineers, U.S. Army; general index. Wash. Govt. Ptg. Off. 1935. 117p. **1311**

U.S. Engineer School. List of publications printed by the Battalion Press, Willets Point, New York harbor and by the Engineer School Press, Washington Barracks, D.C. Comp. by Henry E. Haferkorn. (Occasional pap. Engineer School, U.S. Army. no. 43) Wash. Barracks, D.C. 1910. 10p. **1312**

U.S. General Staff. War plans division. List of War Department pamphlets on military training. Prepared in the War plans division, General Staff. Wash. Govt. Ptg. Off. 1920. 19p. **1313**

U.S. Geographical Surveys West of the 100th Meridian. Lists of reports and maps of the United States Geographical Surveys West of the 100th Meridian. George M. Wheeler . . . in charge. Wash. Govt. Ptg. Off. 1881. 74p. **1314**

U.S. Judge Advocate General's Department. Consolidated index of published volumes of opinions and digests of opinions of Judge Advocate General of the Army, 1912-24, inclusive. Wash. Govt. Ptg. Off. 1926. 352p. **1315**

—— —— Cumulative index of the monthly digest of opinions of the Judge, Advocate General of the Army, January 1 to September 30, 1919. Wash. Govt. Ptg. Off. 1920. 76p.

Same. Jan. 1 to Dec. 31, 1921. 1923. 24p. **1316**

—— —— A digest of opinions of the Judge Advocates General of the Army. Wash. Govt. Ptg. Off. 1912. 1103p. Supplements published 1932 and 1937 **1316a**

U.S. Lake Survey. Catalogue of charts of the Great Lakes, Lake Champlain, New York canals, Lake of the Woods, Rainy Lake, distributed by U.S. Lake Survey Office, Detroit, Mich. [Detroit, Mich. 1939] 14p. **1316b**

U.S. Mississippi River Commission. Index to reports of the Mississippi River Commission, 1879-95. Wash. D.C. 1896. 100p. Same. 1895-1909. St. Louis. 1911. 120p. **1317**

U.S. National Guard Bureau. Index to National guard regulations, War Department. [Wash. D.C.] Feb. 1, 1936. 49p. **1318**

U.S. Office of the Chief of the Air Corps.
Index to U.S. Army Air Corps information circulars, June 1917- . (Air corps information circular no. 1. June 1917-) [Wash. D.C.] 1917- **1319**

—— —— Index to unrestricted U.S. Army Air Corps information circulars. (Air corps information circular. VI. no. 600. May 15, 1928) Wash. D.C. 1928. 40p. **1320**

—— —— Supplement to index to unrestricted U.S. Army Air Corps information circulars nos. 601-657 inclusive. (Air corps information circular. VI. no. 600. supplement Jan. 15, 1931) Wash. D.C. 1931 **1321**

U.S. Ordnance Department. Index of ordnance notes (nos. 1 to 357, inclusive), vols. I to XII. From the Ordnance Office, War Department, Washington, D.C. 1873-84. [Wash. Govt. Ptg. Off. 1884] 73p. **1322**

—— —— Index to general war plans of the Ordnance Department, United States Army, general orders no. 3 of 1913 and nos. 2, 3, 4, 5, 6, and 11 of 1912, Office of the Chief of Ordnance. Wash. Govt. Ptg. Off. 1914. 4p. **1323**

—— —— Index to ordnance circulars, 1863 to 1873. n.p. n.p. n.d. 25p. **1324**

—— —— Index to reports of tests of metals and other materials made with the United States testing machine at Watertown arsenal, and to reports of United States board for tests of metals from 1881-1912, both inclusive. Wash. Govt. Ptg. Off. 1913. 240p. **1325**

—— —— Index to the reports of the Chief of Ordnance, United States Army, 1864-1912. Prep. under the direction of the Chief of Ordnance. Wash. Govt. Ptg. Off. 193p. **1326**

U.S. Panama Canal. Washington office.
Congressional history of the Panama canal [index]. [Wash. D.C. 1919] unpag. typ. **1327**

U.S. Signal Office. Report of [O. L. Fassig] bibliographer and librarian [on publications of the U.S. Signal Service from 1861 to July 1, 1891]. *In* Annual report of the Secretary of War, 1891. Wash. Govt. Ptg. Off. 1892. IV. p387-409 **1328**

U.S. Surgeon General's Office. Classified list of special medical reports, Surgeon General's Office and Council of National Defense. Wash. D.C. 1918. 22p. **1329**

U.S. War Department. Index to general orders and bulletins. War department 1917-1926 both years inclusive. Wash. Govt. Ptg. Off. 1928. 12p. **1329a**

—— —— Index to general orders (with synopsis of same) affecting the volunteer forces of the United States for 1861, 1862, and part of 1863. St. Louis. G. Knapp. 1863. 58p. **1330**

—— —— Index to numbered circulars; War Department, 1918-1929, both years inclusive. Wash. Govt. Ptg. Off. 1930. 26p. **1331**

—— —— Index to opinions of the Judge Advocate General of the Army and the Attorney General and decisions of the Comptroller of the Treasury and courts as digested and published in the War Department bulletins, no. 12, August 8, 1912, to no. 9, March 13, 1915. Wash. Govt. Ptg. Off. 1915. 52p. **1332**

—— —— [Index to] special orders, War Department, Adjutant General's Office. Wash. D.C. 1909-15. 17v. **1333**

—— —— Index to the general orders amendatory of the U.S. Army regulations, together with index to the circulars, rulings, and decisions of the War Department to January 1, 1887. By William Baird. Wash. D.C. Chapman. 1887. 108p. **1334**

—— —— . . . Reports of the publications, &c. of the respective bureaus of the War Department from March 4, 1789 to March 4, 1881. (Senate executive document no. 47. 47 Cong. 1 sess. Ser. 1987) 1882. 19p. **1335**

—— —— Training publications; list of training regulations, technical regulations, and training manuals published to date and distribution thereof. (Training regulations no. 1-10. Jan. 2, 1936) Wash. D.C. Supt. of Documents. 1936. 15p. **1336**

—— —— The war of the rebellion; a compilation of the official records of the Union and Confederate navies; general index and additions and corrections. Wash. Govt. Ptg. Off. 1901. 1242p. (Also issued as House document 558. 56 Cong. 2 sess.) **1337**

U.S. War Records Office. The war of the rebellion; official records of the Union and Confederate armies, series I; index to battles, campaigns, etc. Wash. Govt. Ptg. Off. 1899. 76p. **1338**

Publications of Independent Establishments

Federal Writers' Project. Catalog of publications, Federal Writers' Project, Works Progress Administration. Wash. Govt. Ptg. Off. 1938. 31p. **1338a**

International Joint Commission. (U.S. and Canada). List of decisions, reports, etc. of International joint commissions. Wash. Govt. Ptg. Off. 1916. 11p. **1339**

—— List of documents of the International Joint Commission. Ottawa. J. de Labroquerie Taché. 1919. 14p. **1340**

U.S. Bureau of American Ethnology. General index, Annual reports of the Bureau of American Ethnology, volumes 1 to 48 (1879 to 1931). Comp. by Biren Bonnerjea. (Forty-eighth annual rep. 1931-32) Wash. Govt. Ptg. Off. 1933. p25-1220 **1341**

—— —— List of publications of the Bureau of American Ethnology, with index to authors and titles. Wash. Govt. Ptg. Off. 1923. 45p. **1342**

U.S. Civil Service Commission. List of publications. Wash. Govt. Ptg. Off. 1923- **1343**

U.S. Civilian Conservation Corps. Civilian conservation corps bibliography; a list of references on the United States Civilian conservation corps. Wash. D.C. 60p. mim. **1343a**

U.S. Commodity Exchange Administration. Commodity exchange administration literature, Jan. 1938- **1343b**

—— —— List of publications issued by the Commodity Exchange Administration. Wash. D.C. June 1940. 7p. processed **1343c**

U.S. Federal Emergency Administration of Public Works. Bibliography of PWA publications and official documents pertaining to PWA. [Wash. 1938] 23p. mim. **1343d**

U.S. Federal Emergency Relief Administration. Index of the Monthly reports of the Federal Emergency Relief Administration, June 1933 through June 1936. Wash. Govt. Ptg. Off. 1937. 20, 25, 26, 15p. **1343e**

—— —— Index to bulletins (May 31, 1933-Sept. 15, 1934). [Wash. D.C.] 1935. 27p. mim. **1344**

—— —— Index to policies, reports, and other publications (May 31, 1933-Dec. 31, 1934). [Wash. D.C. 1935] 55p. mim. **1345**

—— —— Subject index of research bulletins and monographs issued by Federal Emergency Relief Administration and Works Progress Administration, Division of Social Research. [Wash.) 1936. 119p. mim. **1345a**

—— —— **Publications division.** Index to bulletins (May 31, 1933-Sept. 15, 1934). Wash. D.C. 1934. 27p. **1346**

U.S. Federal Power Commission. [Subject] index to 1st to 10th annual reports. [Wash. D.C. 1932] 81p. mim. **1347**

U.S. Federal Reserve Board. Index-digest, Federal Reserve bulletin, volumes I-VI, inclusive, 1914-1920, inclusive. By Charles S. Hamlin. Wash. Govt. Ptg. Off. 1921. 249p. **1348**

—— —— Index to regulations [now in effect, with list of currently effective regulations]. Wash. 1940. 71p. **1348a**

U.S. General Accounting Office. Index to the published decisions of the accounting officers of the United States with statutes, decisions and opinions, cited therein, also cross references, 1894-1929. Wash. Govt. Ptg. Off. 1931. 857p. **1349**

U.S. Government Printing Office. Index to annual reports of Public printer. 1921/1928-. [Wash.] 1929- **1350**

U.S. Housing Authority. Publications of the United States Housing Authority. Wash. Supt. of Doc. 1938-1939. 2v. **1350a**

U.S. Interstate Commerce Commission. Consolidated index to the reported decisions (except finance and valuated decisions) Wash. D.C. Capital Traffic Service Bureau. 1925-33. 4v. in 2 **1350b**

—— —— General index of laws and annotations. *In* Interstate commerce acts annotated; compilation of federal laws relating to the regulation of carriers subject to the Interstate Commerce act. . . Prepared by and under the direction of Clyde B. Aitchison. Wash. Govt. Ptg. Off. 1930. V. p4059-432 **1353**

—— —— Index of commodities—decisions of the Interstate Commerce Commission relative to propriety of classification, together with decisions bearing upon principles embodied in the rules of the consolidated freight classification, Interstate Commerce Commission reports, vols. 1-54; inclusive. Comp. for the official, southern and western classification committees. Chicago. Hawkins & Loomis. 1920. 65p. **1353a**

—— —— An index-digest of decisions under the federal safety appliance acts. Prep. by Otis Beall Kent. Wash. D.C. 1910. 294p. **1353b**

—— —— Interstate Commerce Commission cases in the federal courts, 1887 to 1927. Bureau of administration, Section of indices. Wash. Govt. Ptg. Off. 1927. 152p. **1354**

—— —— Table of cases on the formal docket of the Interstate Commerce Commission from April 1887, to August 28, 1906, not disposed of in the printed reports. Wash. Govt. Ptg. Off. 1910. 90p. **1354a**

—— —— Tables of cases and opinions of the Interstate Commerce Commission; decisions under original acts and subsequent amendments from April 1887 to June 1913, vols. I-XXVII, inclusive, I.C.C. reports, Division of indices. Wash. Govt. Ptg. Off. 1914. 168p. Supplement no. 1, June 1913-July 1915, vols. XXVII-XXXV, inclusive, 1915. 88p. Supplement no. 2, July 1915-December 1921, vols. XXXVI-LXIV, inclusive, 1922. 297p. **1354b**

U.S. Isthmian Canal Commission. General index—Minutes of meetings of the Isthmian Canal Commission, March 1904 to March 1907, inclusive. Wash. Govt. Ptg. Off. 1908. 121p. **1357**

U.S. Library of Congress. Publications issued by the library since 1897. Wash. Govt. Ptg. Off. 1961- **1357a**

—— —— **Division of bibliography.** Trial check list of the publications of the U.S. Food Administration. n.d. 6p. mim. **1358**

U.S. National Academy of Sciences. Publications of the National Academy of Sciences of the United States of America (1915-1926). Pt. I. Index to the first ten volumes of the proceedings (1915-1924). Pt. II. List of other publications of the Academy from 1863-1926. Pt. III. List of publications of the National Research Council from 1916-1925. Proc. XIII. Jan. 1927. 197p. **1359**

U.S. National Advisory Committee for Aeronautics. List of reports, with prices. Wash. D.C. Jan. 1938. 65p. **1359a**

—— —— List of reports, with prices. Wash. D.C. Dec. 1939. 70p. **1359b**

U.S. National Labor Relations Board. List of references on National labor relations board. Wash. D.C. The Board. 1939. 26p. **1359c**

U.S. National Museum. A list of the publications of the United States National Museum (1875-1900) with index to titles. By Randolph I. Geare (Bul. 51) Wash. Govt. Ptg. Off. 1902. 168p. **1360**

—— —— A list of publications of the United States National Museum, 1901-06, with index to titles. By Randolph I. Geare (Bul. 51. Supplement 1) Wash. Govt. Ptg. Off. 1906. 40p. **1361**

—— —— Publications issued by the United States National Museum from 1906 to 1912. Wash. Govt. Ptg. Off. 1914. 41p. **1362**

U.S. National Recovery Administration. Index to the hearings on the codes of fair competition held under the National Recovery Act. Prepared by T. R. Schellenberg, executive secretary Joint committee on materials for research of the American Council of Learned Societies and the Social Science Research Council. Wash. D.C. 1934. 77p. mim. **1363**

U.S. National Resources Committee. Reference list of publications of the National Resources Committee. [Wash. D.C. 1938] 10p. mim. **1363a**

—— —— Subject index of reports by the National Planning Board, National Resources Board, National Resources Committee. Wash. Govt. Ptg. Off. 1940. 76p. **1363b**

U.S. National Resources Planning Board. Reference list of publications of the National Resources Planning Board and its predecessors, National Resources Committee, National Planning Board and National Resources Board and National Planning Board. Wash. D.C. 1939. 12p. processed **1363c**

U.S. National Youth Administration. Index to bulletins and other publications issued to state administrators. . . . [Wash. D.C.] 1935. 49p. mim. **1364**

U.S. Railroad Administration. Index to United States Railroad Administration documents. March 1, 1920. (MS. copy in the Lib. of Cong.) **1365**

U.S. Railroad Labor Board. Cumulative index to decisions of the United States Railroad Labor Board, to January, 1, 1925, including a cumulative index to regulations of the Railroad Labor Board, and court and administrative decisions and regulations of the Interstate Commerce Commission in respect to Title III of the Transportation act, 1920, volumes I-V (inclusive). Decisions nos. 1 to 2773. Wash. Govt. Ptg. Off. 1925. 188p. (Printed as a supplement to vol. V, Railroad Labor Board decisions, 1924) **1365a**

—— —— Index-digest of decisions of the United States Railroad Labor Board (cumulative) including an index-digest of all regulations of the Railroad Labor Board, and court and administrative decisions and regulations of the Interstate Commerce Commission in respect to Title III of the Transportation act, 1920. To July 1, 1923 (decisions nos. 1 to 1870) Wash. Govt. Ptg. Off. 1923. 403p. **1366**

U.S. Shipping Board. List of current publications issued by U.S. Shipping Board. Wash. D.C. 1932 **1367**

U.S. Smithsonian Institution. Catalogue of publications of the Smithsonian Institution, (1846-1882), with an alphabetical index of articles in the Smithsonian contributions to knowledge, miscellaneous collections, annual reports, bulletins and proceedings of the U.S. National Museum, and report of the Bureau of Ethnology. (Smithsonian miscellaneous collections. XXVII. no. 478) Wash. D.C. Smithsonian Inst. 1882. 328p. (A catalogue covering 1846-86 by Rhees appears in Annual report of the Smithsonian Institution. 1886. p485-867) **1368**

—— —— Classified list of Smithsonian publications available for distribution. . . April 1904-. Wash. D.C. Smithsonian Inst. 1904- **1369**

—— —— List of publications of the Smithsonian Institution, 1846-1903. By William Jones Rhees. Wash. D.C. Smithsonian Inst. 1903. 99p. (No. 18 in volume lettered Smithsonian Institution. Lists of publications, 1862-1904. Also issued as Smithsonian miscellaneous collections. 44, no. 1376) **1370**

—— —— Lists of publications, 1862-1904. Wash. D.C. Smithsonian Inst. 1862-1904 **1371**

U.S. Superintendent of Documents. Publications of the Interstate Commerce Commission. Wash. Govt. Ptg. Off. 1930. 19p. **1372**

U.S. Supreme Court. Indexed digest of the United States Supreme Court reports; supplement, all decisions of the October terms, 1894-1901, volumes 155-186, federal court rules. Rochester, N.Y. Lawyers' Cooperative Publishing Co. 1903. 596p. **1373**

U.S. Surplus Marketing Administration. Publications of the Dairy Division. Wash. D.C. Aug. 1, 1940. 8p. processed **1373a**

U.S. Tariff Commission. List of principal subjects investigated and reported upon by the United States Tariff Commission. Wash. Govt. Ptg. Off. 1928. 38p. **1376**

—— —— List of publications of the United States Tariff Commission. Wash. Govt. Ptg. Off. 1920- **1377**

—— —— Publications of the Tariff Commission. Wash. D.C. 1939. 132p. reprod. **1377a**

—— —— Subject index of Tariff Commission publications. Wash. Govt. Ptg. Off. 1934. 57p. **1378**

—— —— Subject index to tariff information surveys and reports. (Tariff information ser. 17) Wash. Govt. Ptg. Off. 1920. 25p. **1379**

U.S. Tennessee Valley Authority. Library. A bibliography of the Tennessee Valley Authority. Prepared by Harry C. Bauer. [Knoxville, Tenn. 1934] 25p. mim. (Supplements. Jan.-June, 1935. 10p. mim.; July-December 1935. 9p. mim.)   **1380**
—— —— —— An indexed bibliography of the Tennessee Valley Authority. Knoxville, Tenn. 1936. 60,viii p. processed. Supplements Jan. 1, 1939. 53p.; July 1, 1939. 10p.; Jan. 1, 1940. 8p. mim.   **1381**
—— —— —— A selected list of books, theses, and pamphlets on TVA. Comp. by Ernest I. Miller. Knoxville, Tenn. 1940. 7p. mim.   **1381a**
U.S. Works Progress Administration. Catalog of research and statistical publications. [Wash. D.C.] 1941. 25p.   **1381b**
—— —— Catalog of research bulletins issued by Research section, Division of research, statistics, and finance, Federal Emergency Relief Administration and Division of social research, Works Progress Administration. [Wash. D.C.] 1937. 22p. mim.   **1381c**
—— —— Index of research projects. Wash. Govt. Ptg. Off. 1938-   **1381d**
—— —— Subject index of research bulletins and monographs issued by Federal Emergency Relief Administration and Works Progress Administration, Division of social research. September 1937. Wash. D.C. 1937. 110p.   **1381e**
Work of the Federal Writers' Project of WPA. Publishers' wkly. CXXXV. p1130-5 (March 18, 1939)   **1381f**

United States Archives

Allen, Andrew Henry. The historical archives of the Department of State. Am. Hist. Asso. rep. 1894. p281-98   **1383**
Allison, William Henry. Inventory of unpublished material for American religious history in Protestant church archives and other repositories. (Carnegie Inst. of Wash. Publication no. 137) Wash. D.C. Carnegie Inst. of Wash. 1910. 254p.   **1384**
American Historical Association. Public archives commission. Report [1900]-1917, 1918/22, 1st-19th. *In* Am. Hist. Asso. rep. 1900-17, 1922 (The contents of these reports are listed under the states)   **1384a**
Bartlett, Richard. Remarks and documents relating to the preservation and keeping of the public archives. Concord, Mass. Asa M'Farland. 1837. 72p.   **1385**
Beers, Henry Putney. The archives of the territorial acquisitions of the United States. Arlington, Va. In progress   **1385a**
Bemis, Samuel Flagg and Griffin, Grace Gardner. Remarks on the sources—Manuscript sources: archival collections in the United States and abroad. *In* Guide to the diplomatic history of the United States, 1775-1921. Wash. Govt. Ptg. Off. 1935. p855-942   **1385b**
Boyd, Julian P. Recent activities in relation to archives and historical manuscripts in the United States. Read at the

Conference of archivists called to found The Society of American Archivists, Providence, R.I., Dec. 29, 1936. n.p. n.p. n.d. 20p. processed   **1385c**
Brown, Everett S. Archives of the Food Administration as historical sources. Am. Hist. Asso. rep. 1917. p124-35   **1386**
Burnett, Edmund C. A list of printed guides to and descriptions of archives and other repositories of historical manuscript. Am. Hist. Asso. rep. 1896. I. p481-512   **1387**
Claussen, Martin P. The archives of the Civil War. Wash. D.C. The National Archives. In progress   **1387a**
Evans, Luther. The historical records survey. Am. pol. science rev. XXX. p133-5 (Feb. 1936)   **1388**
Foik, Paul J. Catholic archives of America. Cath. hist. rev. I. p63-4 (April 1915) **1388a**
Ford, Worthington C. Public records in our dependencies. Am. Hist. Asso. rep. 1904. p131-47   **1389**
Foreman, Grant. A survey of tribal records in the archives of the United States government in Oklahoma. Chronicles Oklahoma. XI. p625-34 (March 1933) (Reprinted 1934? 10p.)   **1390**
Gregory, Carl L. Survey of motion picture, photographic, and sound recording archives. (Survey of Federal Archives, memo. 77) [Wash. D.C.] June 25, 1936. 10p. processed   **1390a**
Grover, Wayne C. Research facilities and materials at The National Archives. Am. pol. sci. rev. XXXIV. p976-83 (Oct. 1940)   **1390b**
Guthrie, Chester L. The United States Grain Corporation records in The National Archives. Agric. hist. XII. p347-54 (Oct. 1938)   **1390c**
Hagen, Fred E. Early military records and memoranda. The quartermaster rev. XV. p30-40 (Sept.-Oct. 1935) (Schuylkill arsenal, Phila.)   **1391**
Hamer, Philip M. Federal archives outside of the District of Columbia. Soc. Am. archivists proc. 1936-37. p83-9   **1391a**
Hanna, A. J. Diplomatic missions of the United States to Cuba to secure the Spanish archives of Florida. Rollins College, Winter Park, Florida. In progress **1391b**
Hill, Roscoe R. Los Archivos Nacionales en Washington. Congreso International de Historia de América, 2d, Buenos Aires, 1937, Publications. V. p137-44. 1938 **1391c**
Hoar, George F. [Material for historical study in Washington]. Am. Antiq. Soc. proc. n.s. II. p118-35 (Oct. 1882)   **1392**
Holdcamper, Forrest R. Registers, enrollments and licenses in the National Archives. Am. neptune. I. p275-94 (July 1941)   **1392a**
Hunt, Gaillard. Calendar of applications and recommendations for office during the presidency of George Washington. Prepared from the files of the Bureau of Appointments, Department of State. Wash. D.C. 1901. 146p.   **1393**

Ingram, Augustus E. When was this consulate first opened? Am. for. ser. jour. XVII. p522-6 (Sept. 1940). (Discussion of early records of State Department and existing indexes to establish early data on posts) **1393a**

Irvine, Dallas D. Old records division, The Adjutant General's Office. [Wash. D.C.] The National Archives. May 1936. 183p. typ. **1393b**

Jameson, John Franklin. The archives of the United States of America. Royal Hist. Soc. trans. 4th ser. II. p37-40. 1919 **1393c**

Joerg, W. L. G. The internal improvement maps (1825-1835) In The National Archives. Asso. Am. Geog. ann. XXVIII. p52 (March 1938) **1393d**

Kahn, Herman. The National Archives, storehouse of national park history. Regional rev. IV. p13-17 (Feb. 1940) **1393e**

Kemp, Edwin C. Archives and romance. Am. for. service jour. XIII. p265-7, 299-304 (May 1936) (Material relating to American shipping in the archives of the consulate at Havre, France) **1393f**

Knox, Dudley W. Our vanishing history and traditions. U.S. Naval Inst. proc. LII. p15-25 (Jan. 1926) (Concerns our naval archives) **1394**

—— The vanishing naval history of the Revolution. Daughters of the Am. Revolution mag. LX. p477-80 (Aug. 1926) **1395**

Kuhlman, Augustus F. The next steps in the collection, organization, and preservation of source materials in the South. [Nashville, Tenn. 1938?] 15p. typ. **1395a**

Larson, Cedric and Mock, James R. The lost files of the Creel Committee of 1917-19. Pub. opin. quar. III. p5-29 (Jan. 1939) **1395b**

Leland, Waldo G. The accessibility of foreign archives—XXIX United States of America. Inst. Hist. Research bul. VI. p156-66 (Feb. 1929) **1395c**

—— The archives of the federal government. Columbia Hist. Soc. rec. XI. p71-100. 1908 **1396**

—— The archives of the war. Am. Hist. Asso. rep. 1917. p117-23 **1397**

Leland, Waldo Gifford and Mereness, Newton Dennison. Introduction to the American official sources for the economic and social history of the World War. (Carnegie Endowment for International Peace. Division of economics and history. Economic and social history of the World War. American series) New Haven. Yale Univ. Press. 1926. 532p. **1398**

McCain, William D. Development of archival institutions in Alabama and the South. Paper read before the Society of American Archivists, Montgomery, Ala., Nov. 11, 1940. [Jackson, Miss. Miss. Dept. of Archives and Hist.] 1940. 23p. typ. **1398a**

McLaughlin, Andrew Cunningham. Report on the diplomatic archives of the Department of State, 1789-1840. (Carnegie Inst. of Wash. Publication no. 22) Wash. D.C. 1906. 73p. **1399**

Mereness, Newton D. Calendar of material in the Federal archives in Washington relating to the Upper Mississippi Valley. (250,000 cards listing documents found among the records of the Senate and of the State, War, Post Office, and Interior Departments. Sets of the cards are in the possession of the University of Illinois and the state historical agencies of Ohio, Indiana, Michigan, Wisconsin, Iowa, and Minnesota. A microfilm copy is available in The National Archives.) **1399a**

—— Historical material in Washington of value to the state. Miss. Valley hist. rev. X. p47-53 (June 1923) **1400**

Miller, Hunter. Transfer to the Department of State of the older archives of certain American embassies, legations, and consulates. Am. hist. rev. XXXIX. p184-5 (Oct. 1933) **1401**

Mock, James R. The national archives with respect to the records of the negro. Jour. negro hist. XXIII. p49-56 (Jan. 1938) **1401a**

Newsome, A. R. Recent surveys of state and local archives in the United States. Paper read before the Joint conference of historical societies and archivists, Dec. 28, 1934. 19p. typescript **1402**

—— Unprinted public archives of the post colonial period; their availability. Am. hist. rev. XXXIX. p682-9 (July 1934) **1403**

Paltsits, Victor Hugo. An historical resume of the Public Archives Commission from 1892 to 1921. Am. Hist. Asso. rep. 1922. p152-63 **1403a**

Parker, David W. Calendar of papers in Washington archives relating to the territories of the United States (to 1783). (Carnegie Inst. of Wash. Publication no. 148) Wash. D.C. 1911. 476p. **1404**

Pumphrey, Lowell. Material in The National Archives of especial interest to economists. Am. econ. rev. XXXI. p344-5 (June 1941) **1404a**

Report of a board of inquiry into the causes of the Interior Department fire. Oct. 17, 1877. House ex. doc. 2, 45 Cong., 1 sess. Serial 1773. 15p. **1404b**

Report of the librarian of Congress upon the American archives, or documentary history of the American revolution. May 15, 1879. Senate misc. doc. 34, 46 Cong. 1 sess. 3p. Ser. 1873 **1404c**

Riepma, Siert F. Portrait of an adjutant general: the career of Major General Fred C. Ainsworth. Jour. Am. Mil. Inst. II. p26-35 (Spring 1938) (Service records of The War Department) **1404d**

Roberts, Martin Arnold. Records of the Copyright office deposited by the United States district courts covering the period, 1790-1870. Wash. Govt. Ptg. Off. 1939. 19p. (Also Bibliog. Soc. Am. pap. XXXI. p81-101. 1937) **1404e**

Salado Álvarez, Victoriano. Breve noticia de algunos manuscritos de interés histórico para México, que se encuentran en los archivos y bibliotecas de Washington, D.C. México. Impr. del Museo nacional. 1908. 24p. (Extractado del t. I de la tercera época de los "Anales del Museo nacional") **1404f**

Schellenberg, Theodore R. Federal records on cotton growing. Paper read before the Society of American Archivists, Montgomery, Ala., Nov. 11, 1940. [Wash. D.C. The National Archives] 1940. 16p. typ. **1404g**

Sena, José D. Archives in the office of the cadastral engineer at Santa Fe. El Palacio. XXXVI. p113-21. 1934 **1405**

Stimson, Julia C. Records in the nursing division of the Surgeon General's Office. Military surgeon. LXXVIII. p307-9 (April 1936) **1406**

Sweet, William W. Church archives in the United States. Church hist. VIII. (March 1939) **1406a**

U.S. Army War College. Historical Section. Index C-in-C report file, A.E.F. records. Comp. by Lt. Col. W. C. Koenig. [Wash. D.C.] A.E.F. Record section. 1935. 24p. typ. **1406b**

—— —— —— War Department repositories of historical records in and near District of Columbia. Prepared by R. S. Thomas and others. [Wash. D.C. Army War College] Dec. 1935. 12p. mim. **1407**

U.S. Bureau of Rolls and Library. [Miscellaneous index to the several classes of papers deposited in the Bureau of Rolls and Library]. Bul. of the Bureau of Rolls and Lib. no. 1. p25-102; no. 3. p24-134; no. 5. p18-138; no. 7. p12-126; no. 9. p7-36. Wash. D.C. 1893-95 **1408**

U.S. Coast and Geodetic Survey. List of original topographic and hydrographic sheets, geographically arranged, registered in the archives of the United States Coast and Geodetic Survey, from January, 1834, to December 31, 1895. *In* U.S. Coast and Geodetic Survey. Report... 1895. Wash. Govt. Ptg. Off. 1896. pt. II, appendix no. 11, p399-516 **1408a**

U.S. Congress. House. Committee on military affairs. Publication of World War records; hearings before the Committee on military affairs, House of Representatives, seventieth Congress, second session, on H. J. res. 359, Feb. 28, 1929. Wash. Govt. Ptg. Off. 1929. 33p. **1408b**

—— —— —— —— Publication of World War records; hearings before the Committee on military affairs, House of Representatives, seventy-first Congress, second session, on H.J. res. 34, March 25, 1930. Wash. Govt. Ptg. Off. 1930. 37p. **1408c**

—— —— —— **Committee on the library.** Transfer of certain records of House of Representatives to National archives ... Report [to accompany H. Res. 222] (75th Cong., 1st sess. House report 917) [Wash. Govt. Ptg. Off. 1937] 17p. **1408d**

U.S. Department of the Navy. Alphabetical index to records of the secretary's office, Navy Department from its organization to 1880. Wash. Govt. Ptg. Off. 1882. 75p. **1409**

—— —— List of log-books of U.S. vessels, 1861-1865, on file in the Navy Department. (Bureau of navigation) (Office of naval war records. Office memoranda no. 5) Wash. Govt. Ptg. Off. 1898. 49p. **1410**

U.S. Department of State. Calendar of the miscellaneous letters received by the Department from the organization of the government to 1820. Wash. Govt. Ptg. Off. 1897. 557p. **1411**

—— —— Catalogue of manuscript books; being records of the proceedings of Congress; the domestic and foreign correspondence thereof; military letters, reports of the boards of war, finance, admiralty, &c., with miscellaneous letters and papers relating to the War of the Revolution, and of the Confederacy, from 1774 to 1789. Wash. D.C. A.O.P. Nicholson. 1855. 72p. **1412**

—— —— Catalogue of records of territories and states. (Bul. of Bureau of Rolls. no. 7) Wash. Dept. of State. 1895. 126p. **1413**

—— —— Catalogue of the papers of the Continental Congress. (Bul. of the Bureau of Rolls and Lib. of the Dept. of State. no. 1. September 1893) Wash. D.C. Dept. of State. 1893. p1-22 **1414**

—— —— Documentary history of the American revolution; letter from the secretary of state on the contract entered into by Edward Livingston, late secretary of state, with Matthew St. Clair Clarke and Peter Force, for the collection and publication of the documentary history of the American revolution. (Ex. docs. 36, 23 Cong., 2 sess) Wash. D.C. Gales & Seaton. 1834? Ser. 272. 98p. **1414a**

—— —— Letter from the Secretary of State, reporting the results of an examination of the revolutionary archives, except military records, in pursuance of the act of Congress, approved August 18, 1894. (Senate executive document no. 22. 53 Cong. 3 sess. Ser. 3275) 1895. 12p. **1415**

—— —— A list of papers chiefly relative to claims of the United States against foreign governments and of citizens of foreign nations against the United States on file in Bureau of Rolls and Library, Department of State, August 1, 1887. [Wash. Govt. Ptg. Off. 1887] 61p. **1416**

—— —— List of the manuscript volumes in the Department of State containing the records of and papers of the Revolution. Am. Hist. Asso. rep. 1894. p554-61. (Reprinted from Senate executive document no. 22. 53 Cong. 2 sess. Ser. 3160) **1417**

—— —— Report of the Secretary of State, accompanied by copies of printed documents containing the information desired respecting the historical archives deposited in the Department of State. May 16, 1896. Senate doc. 262, 54 Cong., 1 sess. 5p. Ser. 3354 **1417a**

—— —— Results of examination of revolutionary archives, except military records. Jan. 4, 1895. Senate ex. doc. 22, 53 Cong. 3 sess. 12p. Ser. 3275 **1417b**

U.S. Library of Congress. Archives of government offices outside of the city of Washington. (House document no. 1443. 62 Cong. 3 sess. Ser. 6501) Wash. Govt. Ptg. Off. 1913. 219p. **1418**

—— —— **Division of bibliography.** A selected list of references on the administration and care of public archives in the United States. Nov. 19, 1934. 18p. typ. **1419**

U.S. National Archives. Annual report of the Archivist of the United States, 1934/35-. Wash. Govt. Ptg. Off. 1936- **1420**

—— —— The archives of the United States government; a documentary history, 1774-1934. Comp. by Percy Scott Flippin. Wash. D.C. 1938. 24v. MS. (The contents in v. 24, 87p., constitutes a bibliography of the scattered material brought together in this compilation. The index in 77p. is also useful bibliographically.) **1420a**

—— —— Bibliography of archival administration, archives and manuscripts. Cards in the Division of Reference, The National Archives, Wash. D.C. **1420b**

—— —— Civil war pardon papers; War Department and Department of Justice. [Wash. D.C.] April 5, 1938. typ. **1420c**

—— —— Classification scheme of the documents and records from the archive of the Food Administration, Washington office, 1917-1919. Prep. by the Division of Classification. [Wash. D.C.] 1940? typ. **1420d**

—— —— Classification scheme; records of the Council of National Defense. Prep. by the Division of Classification. [Wash. D.C.] 1940. xxvi, 94, 14p. typ. **1420e**

—— —— Classification scheme; records of the Senate of the United States of America, 1st-74th Congresses. Prep. by the Division of Classification. Wash. D.C. 1940. 877p. typ. **1420f**

—— —— Classification scheme; records of the United States Food Administration, field offices, 1917-1919. Prep. by the Division of Classification. [Wash. D.C.] 1941 **1420g**

—— —— The National Archives. Classification scheme; records of the Committee on public information, 1917-1919. Prep. by the Division of classification, Roscoe R. Hill, chief. Frank Hardee Allen, classifier. [Wash.] 1938. 78p. photop. **1420h**

—— —— The National Archives. Classification scheme. Records of the National commission on law observance and enforcement [Wickersham commission]

Prep. by the Division of classification, Roscoe R. Hill, chief. David C. Duniway, classifier. [Wash. D.C. 1938] 36p. photop. **1420i**

—— —— Guide to the material in The National Archives. Wash. Govt. Ptg. Off. 1940. 303p. (This is kept up to date by lists in the Annual reports of the Archivist of the United States and by quarterly lists of National Archives accessions, January 1-March 31, 1940-) **1420j**

—— —— Guide to the materials in The National Archives, June 30, 1937. In Third annual report of the Archivist of the United States. Wash. Govt. Ptg. Off. 1938. p111-68 **1420k**

—— —— Material in The National Archives relating to individuals—personal history. [Wash. D.C.] n.d. typ. **1420l**

—— —— Pre-federal records in The National Archives. [Wash. D.C.] n.d. typ. **1420m**

—— —— Preliminary inventory of the War Industries Board records. (Preliminary inventory, no. 1) Wash. D.C. 1941. 134p. **1420n**

—— —— President's Commission on Economy and Efficiency, 1910-1933—PCEE—scheme of classification for its papers. Devised by Raphael L. Shanafelt; revised and arranged by William D. McCain, classifier. [Wash. D.C.] 1937. 58p. typ. **1420o**

—— —— Report upon the climatological records transferred from the Weather Bureau, Department of Agriculture as part of accession 22 and 293 and from the Smithsonian Institution as part of accession 357. Prep. by Lewis J. Darter, Jr. [Wash. D.C.] July 17, 1940. 403p. typ. **1420p**

U.S. Surgeon General's Office. Reports on the extent of materials available for preparation of medical and surgical history of the rebellion. Phila. J.B. Lippincott. 1865. 166p. **1421**

U.S. War Department. List of records and files of the War Department arranged by offices and divisions, with names of the clerks in each division; also a statement of the subject-matter recorded and filed, and date of the commencement and termination of each series of records. . . . Wash. Govt. Ptg. Off. 1890. 145p. **1422**

U.S. Works Progress Administration. Survey of federal archives outside of Washington. [This is a survey of the records of all federal offices outside of Washington sponsored by The National Archives, where the reports of the Survey will be deposited] **1423**

Van Tyne, Claude Halstead and Leland, Waldo Gifford. Guide to the archives of the government of the United States in Washington. (Carnegie Inst. of Wash. Publication no. 92) Wash. D.C. 1907. 327p. **1424**

Wright, Almon R. Food and society: wartime archives of the U.S. Food Administration. Am. scholar. VII. p243-6 (Spring 1938) **1424a**

Wright, Almon R. Records of the Food Administration: new field for research. Pub. opin. quar. III. p278-84 (April 1939) **1424b**

Manuscripts

[**Account** of places of deposit of the unpublished papers of the presidents] Congressional record. LXXXIV. pt. 8. p9043-4 (July 13, 1939) **1424c**

Adams, Randolph G. The papers of Lord George Germain; a brief description of the Stopford-Sackville papers now in the William L. Clements Library. (William L. Clements Lib. Bul. no. 18) Ann Arbor. 1928. 46p. **1424d**

Agricultural records in the Baker Library. Bus. hist. soc. bul. IX. p60-3 (June 1935) (MSS. on the period 1762-1925) **1424e**

American Antiquarian Society. A guide to the resources of the American Antiquarian Society, a national library of American history. Worcester, Mass. 1937. 98p. **1424f**

American Historical Association. Historical manuscripts commission. Items respecting historical manuscripts. A. Libraries and archives. B. MSS. in private hands. Am. Hist. Asso. rep. 1898. p573-90; 1900. I. p595-607 **1425**

American Philosophical Society. Calendar of manuscripts. In progress **1426**

—— **Library.** Calendar of the correspondence relating to the American Revolution of Brigadier-General George Weedon, Hon. Richard Henry Lee, and Major-General Nathanael Greene in the Library of the American Philosophical Society. Phila. 1900. 255p. **1426a**

—— —— A catalogue of manuscript and printed documents chiefly Americana, selected from the archives and manuscript collections of the American Philosophical Society, held at Philadelphia for promoting useful knowledge, and placed upon exhibition in the library of the society, December 28-31, 1937, on the occasion of the annual meeting of the American Historical Association and the Societies gathering concurrently. Phila. 1937. 38p. **1426b**

Association for the Study of Negro Life and History, Washington, D.C. Detailed inventory of 2,520 manuscripts relating to Negro history collected by the association and deposited in the Library of Congress. (57 typ. pages) (In a reprint of the Asso. in possession of the Social Science Research Council) **1427**

Bancroft, George. Chronological index to the American correspondence in the Bancroft collection, 1742-1789. (MS. in the N.Y. Pub. Lib.) 2v. **1428**

Barck, Dorothy C. New York Historical Society. Business hist. soc. bul. VIII. p1-5 (Jan. 1934) (Material for business history) **1428a**

Barth, Arthur August. Guide to materials for the history of Indian missions of the trans-Mississippi west ... in the archives of Saint Louis University. (St. Louis Univ. Master's thesis, 1936-37) St. Louis, Mo. **1428b**

Beard, William E. Letters to a president of the United States. Tenn. hist. mag. IX. p143-65 (Oct. 1925, issued May 1928) (Unofficial letters to President Polk) **1428c**

Berkeley, Francis L., Jr. A checklist of bound business records in the manuscript collections of the Alderman Library, University of Virginia. In Virginia. University. Library. Eighth annual report of the archivist. [Chalottesville, Va.] Univ. of Virginia. 1938. p17-45 **1428d**

Bishop, Elsie Hight. The business man as a business historian. Bus. Hist. Soc. bul. XII. p17-24 (April 1938) (Survey of the Heard papers in the Baker Library) **1428e**

Bispham, Clarence W. New Orleans, a treasure house for historians. Louisiana hist. quar. II. p237-47 (July 1919) **1429**

Boston. Public Library. Brief description of the Chamberlain collection of autographs; collection formed by Hon. Mellen Chamberlain and now deposited in the Boston Public Library. Boston. 1897. 65p. **1429a**

Briggs, Gordon. The archives of the Hudson's Bay Company. Canadian chartered accountant. XXXII. p116-20 (Feb. 1938) **1429b**

Brigham, Clarence S. New England's most precious book; records of the "Council for New England" recently found. Boston? 1912? 1p. (MS. records of meetings from May 1622 to June 29, 1623. Reprinted from the Boston transcript, Dec. 21, 1912) **1429c**

—— The records of the Council for New England. Am. Antiq. Soc. proc. n.s. XXII. p237-47. 1912 **1429d**

Brown, Lloyd A. Manuscript maps in the William L. Clements Library. Am. neptune. I. p141-8 (April 1941) **1429e**

Buffalo Historical Society. Rough list of manuscripts in the library of the Buffalo Historical Society. Buffalo Hist. Soc. Publications, XIV. p421-85. 1910. (Reprinted Buffalo. 1910. 65p.) **1430**

Burton, Clarence Monroe. The Burton historical collection of the public library, Detroit. Bibliog. Soc. Am. pap. XVI. p10-16. 1922 **1430a**

Butler, Ruth L. List of manuscript maps in the Ayer collection. Newberry Lib., Chicago. In progress **1430b**

Calendar of Shelburne correspondence. In Canada. Archives. Report of the public archives for the year 1921. Ottawa. King's Printer. 1922. p229-81 **1430c**

Chicago. University. Library. A descriptive catalogue of manuscripts in the libraries of the University of Chicago. Prepared by Edgar J. Goodspeed, with the assistance of Martin Sprengling. Chicago. Univ. of Chicago Press. 1912. 128p. **1431**

Clark, Robert C. The archives of the Hudson's Bay Company. Pacific northw. quar. XXIX. p3-15 (Jan. 1938) **1431a**

Cleland, Robert G. The research facilities of the Huntington Library: Americana. Huntington Lib. quar. III. p135-41 (Oct. 1939) (MSS.) **1431b**

Columbia University. Library. Lists of the more important personal papers in the MS. collection of the Library of Columbia University. 1916. (MS. in the lib.) **1432**

Comstock, H. Brooklyn museum's manuscripts. Internat. studio. LXXXV. p44-8 (Nov. 1926) **1432a**

Conklin, Edwin G. The American Philosophical Society and the founders of our government. Pa. hist. IV. p235-40 (Oct. 1937) (MSS. on the colonial, revolutionary, and confederation periods) **1432b**

Corning, Howard. The Essex Institute of Salem. Business Hist. Soc. bul. VII. no. 5. p1-5 (Oct. 1933) (Source material in the Essex Institute on maritime history, shipping and other businesses) **1433**

Cutter, Charles A. Catalogue of the library of Jared Sparks, with a list of the historical manuscripts collected by him and deposited in the library of Harvard University. Cambridge, Mass. Riverside Press. 1871. 230p. **1435**

Detroit. Public Library. The Burton historical collection of the Detroit Public Library [Detroit. 1928?] 16p. **1435a**

Domínguez Bordona, Jesús. Manuscritos de América. Ed. Patrimonio de la república. (Catálogo de la Biblioteca de Palacio, IX) Madrid. 1935. 250p. **1435b**

Duniway, David C. A calendar of English California manuscripts in the Bancroft Library of the University of California with additional material from the San Francisco Bay Region. In progress **1435c**

East Indiamen and clipper ships. (The Gordon Dexter collection) Bus. Hist. Soc. bul. II. p3-9 (May 1928) (MS. papers of Samuel Appleton and Co., Boston, Mass., 1840's and 1850's) **1435d**

Edwards, Everett Eugene. Agricultural records; their nature and value for research. Agric. hist. XIII. p1-12 (Jan. 1939) **1435e**

Eliot, Margaret Sherburne. Inventories and guides to historical manuscript collections. In Archives and libraries, 1940. Ed. by A.F. Kuhlman. Chicago. American Library Association. 1940. p26-35 **1435f**

—— The manuscript program of the Historical Records Survey. In Public documents, 1938. Ed. by Jerome K. Wilcox. Chicago. Am. Lib. Asso. 1938. p317-26 **1435g**

Foglesong, Hortense. The Charles G. Slack collection of manuscripts, Marietta College. Ohio Valley Hist. Asso. rep. 1909. II. p20-5 **1435h**

Ford, Worthington Chauncey. Manuscripts on American history in England. Mass. Hist. Soc. proc. XLVI. p475-8. 1913 **1435i**

Friedenwald, Herbert. Historical manuscripts in the Library of Congress. Am. Hist. Asso. rep. 1898. p35-45 **1435j**

Great Britain. Historical Manuscripts Commission. Guide to the reports of the Royal Commission on historical manuscripts, 1870-1911. Part II—Index of persons. Ed. by Francis Bickley. First section. A-Lever; second section. Lever-Z. London. H.M. Stationery Off. 1935. 1938. 2v. **1435k**

—— —— Report on the manuscripts of Mrs. Stopford-Sackville, of Drayton house, Northamptonshire. London. H.M. Stationery Off. 1904-10. 2v. (MSS. of Lord George Sackville; the 2d vol. is devoted to America, Canada, and the West Indies) **1435l**

Griffin, Appleton P. C. An account of the manuscripts in the Boston Athenaeum. Boston Athenaeum report, 1896. 2p. **1435m**

Harvard University. Graduate School of Business Administration. Baker Library. List of business manuscripts in Baker Library. Comp. by Margaret Ronzone Cusick. Cambridge, Mass. The Lib. 1932. 112p. **1436**

—— **Library.** Calendar of the Sparks manuscripts in the Harvard College Library, with an appendix showing other manuscripts. By Justin Winsor. (Bibliog. contributions. no. 22) Cambridge, Mass. 1889. 88p. (Republished from the Bul. of Harvard Univ.) **1437**

Heaton, Herbert. Some sources for northwest history: business records. Minn. hist. XX. p165-8 (June 1939) **1437a**

Heindel, Richard H. Historical manuscripts in the Academy of Natural Sciences, Philadelphia. Pa. hist. V. p30-2 (Jan. 1938) **1437b**

Henry E. Huntington Library and Art Gallery. Huntington Library collections. Cambridge. Harvard Univ. Press. 1931. p33-106 (Reprinted from The Huntington Lib. bul. no. 1. May 1931, comp. by George Sherburn and others) **1438**

—— **North Carolina.** Guide to the manuscript collections in the Duke University Library. Raleigh, N.C. June 1939. 165p. mim. **1438a**

—— —— Guide to the manuscripts in the Southern Historical Collection of the University of North Carolina. (The James Sprunt stud. in hist. and pol. sci. v. 24, no. 2) Chapel Hill. Univ. of North Carolina Press. 1941. 204p. **1438b**

Historical Records Survey. Southern California. Calendar of the Major Jacob Rink Snyder collection of the Society of California pioneers. San Francisco, Calif. 1940. 107p. reprod from typ. copy **1438c**

—— —— Inventory of the Bixby collection in the Palos Verdes Library and Art Gallery. Los Angeles, Calif. Oct. 1940. 43p. mim. **1438d**

—— —— List of the letters and documents of rulers and statesmen in the William Andrew Clark Memorial Library. (University of California at Los Angeles) Los Angeles, Calif. Jan. 1941. 16p. mim. **1438e**

Historical Records Survey. Southern California. List of the letters and manuscripts of musicians in the William Andrews Clark Memorial Library, University of California at Los Angeles. Los Angeles. May 1940. 12p. mim. **1438f**

Hussey, Roland D. Manuscript Hispanic Americana in the Ayer collection of the Newberry Library, Chicago. Hispanic Am. hist. rev. X. p113-18 (Feb. 1930) (MSS. relating to California, Louisiana, etc.) **1439**

—— Manuscript Hispanic Americana in the Harvard College Library. Hisp. Am. hist. rev. XVII. p259-77 (May 1937) **1439a**

Illinois. University. Department of history. Materials for historical research afforded by the University of Illinois. (Univ. of Illinois. Bul. XX. no. 1) Urbana. Univ. of Illinois. 1922. 56p. **1440**

Johansen, Dorothy O. The Simeon G. Reed collection of letters and private papers. Pacific northw. quar. XXVII. p54-65 (Jan. 1936) (MSS. concerning transportation, industry, and agriculture in the Pacific northwest) **1440a**

Johnston, Henry P. The Franklin, Rochambeau, and Force papers. Mag. of Am. hist. VIII. p346-50 (May 1882) **1441**

Jones, Cecil Knight. Hispano-Americana in the Library of Congress. Hispanic Am. hist. rev. II. p96-104 (Feb. 1919) **1442**

Jones, Fred M. The collection of business records at the University of Illinois. Bus. Hist. Soc. bul. XIII. p94-5 (Dec. 1939) **1442a**

Kellar, Herbert A. Organization and preservation of manuscript collections in the McCormick Historical Association Library. *In* Public documents, 1938. Ed. by Jerome K. Wilcox. Chicago. Am. Lib. Asso. 1938. p357-64 **1442b**

Kendall, John S. Historical collections in New Orleans. North Carolina hist. rev. VII. p463-76 (Oct. 1930) **1443**

Leland Stanford Junior University. Library. Hoover library on war, revolution and peace. Special collections in the Hoover Library on War, Revolution, and Peace. Prep. by Nina Almond and H.H. Fisher. Stanford University, Calif. 1940. 111p. **1443a**

Leveson-Gower, R. H. G. The archives of the Hudson's Bay Company. Beaver. CCLXIV. no. 3. p40-2; CCLXV. no. 1. p19-21, 66, no. 3. p37-9; CCLXVI. no. 2. p22-4. 1933-35 **1444**

Lincoln, Charles Henry. The manuscript collections of the American Antiquarian Society. Bibliog. Soc. Amer. pap. IV. p59-72. 1909 **1444a**

Lutz, Ralph H. The Hoover war library; the great international archives at Stanford University. Army ordnance. X. p331-5 (March 1930) **1444b**

—— The World war in history; a survey of source materials in the Hoover War Library. Am. Mil. Inst. jour. I. p18-21 (Spring 1937) **1444c**

The McCormick Historical Association. Bus. Hist. Soc. bul. X. p76-8. 1936 (General survey of materials for research) **1444d**

Martin, Thomas P. Sources of negro history in the manuscript division of the Library of Congress. Jour. negro hist. XIX. p72-6 (Jan. 1934) **1444e**

Metzdorf, Robert F. Catalogue of the autograph collection of the University of Rochester. Rochester, N.Y. Univ. of Rochester Lib. 1940. 176p. **1444f**

Michigan. University. William L. Clements Library. Guide to the manuscript collections in the William L. Clements Library. Comp. by Howard H. Peckham. Ann Arbor. In progress **1444g**

Minnesota Historical Society. Guide to the personal papers in the manuscript collections of the Minnesota Historical Society. By Grace Lee Nute and Gertrude W. Ackerman. St. Paul, Minn. Hist. Soc. 1935. 146p. **1445**

Morison, Samuel E. The very essence of history. N.Y. times mag. March 19, 1939. p4, 5, 22 (Concerns the papers of presidents of the U.S. and the projected Franklin D. Roosevelt Lib.) **1445a**

Morton, A. S. The business methods and the archives of the Hudson's Bay Company. Canadian Hist. Asso. rep. May 1938. p134-44 **1445b**

New York. Public Library. Calendar of the Emmet collection of manuscripts, etc. relating to American history. Presented to the New York public library by John S. Kennedy. N.Y. N.Y. Pub. Lib. 1900. 563p. (Pages 1-267 first appeared in the Bul. I-III. 1897-99. Includes MSS. on the colonial, revolutionary and national periods) **1446**

—— Manuscript collections in the New York Public Library. N.Y. Pub. Lib. bul. V. p306-36 (July 1901) **1447**

—— —— Manuscript Division accessions [1935-] N.Y. Pub. Lib. bul. XLI. Feb. 1936- **1447a**

Newberry Library. List of manuscript maps in the Edward E. Ayer collection. Comp. by Clara A. Smith. Chicago. 1927. 101p. **1447b**

—— Edward E. Ayer Collection. A check list of manuscripts in the Edward E. Ayer collection. Comp. by Ruth Lapham Butler. Chicago. The Newberry Lib. 1937. 295p. **1447c**

Nitzsche, George E. Pennsylvania's historical treasures. General mag. and hist. chron. XXXV. p86-98. 1932 (MSS. and books dealing with colonial and early American history in the University of Pennsylvania) **1447d**

Nute, Grace Lee. The Mississippi Valley from Prairie du Chien to Lake Pepin; a survey of unpublished sources. Minn. hist. VII. p32-41 (March 1926) (Minn. Hist. Soc. MSS.) **1448**

Ohio State Archaeological and Historical Society. Hayes memorial library. Annual report, 1937/38- Fremont, Ohio. 1938- **1448a**

Paine, Nathaniel. Remarks on the manuscripts in the library of the American Antiquarian Society. Worcester, Mass. C. Hamilton. 1903. (From the Rep. of the council, presented April 29, 1903) **1449**

Paltsits, Victor Hugo. Manuscript division accessions during 1934-[35]. N.Y. Pub. Lib. bul. XXXIX. p97-100 (Feb. 1935); XL. p103-12 (Feb. 1936) **1450**

—— The manuscript division in the New York Public Library. N.Y. Pub. Lib. bul. XIX. p135-65 (Feb. 1915) **1451**

Paris. Bibliothèque Nationale. Section de géographie. Quatrième centenaire de la découverte de l'Amérique; catalogue des documents géographiques exposées à la Section des cartes et plans de la Bibliothèque Nationale. Paris. J. Maisonneuve. 1892. 77p. **1451a**

Parkman, Francis. Early unpublished maps of the Mississippi and the Great Lakes. *In* France and England in North America. Boston. Little, Brown & Co. 1879. p449-58 **1451b**

Patterson, Margetta. The Garcia library, a nucleus of Latin-American collection. Bunker's mthly. XXII. p82-8 (July 1928) **1451c**

Peckham, Howard P. Military papers in the Clements library. Am. Mil. Inst. jour. II. p126-30 (Fall 1938) **1451d**

Pennington, Edgar Legare. The General Convention and the preservation of our church's historical material. P.E. Church hist. mag. IX. p171-93 (Sept. 1940) **1451e**

—— Manuscript sources of our church history (colonial period). P.E. church hist. mag. I. p19-31 (March 1932) **1451f**

Pike, Charles B. Chicago Historical Society. Business hist. soc. bul. VIII. p37-41 (1934) (Collections for business history) **1451g**

Putnam, Herbert. The manuscript sources for American history. *In* N. Am. Rev. 178:527-38 (April 1904) (Important material on the history of the archives) **1451h**

Qualey, Carlton C. A hunt for Norwegian-American records. Norwegian-Am. stud. and rec. VII. p95-120. 1933 **1452**

Quenzel, Carrol H. West Virginia University collection of manuscripts. Bus. Hist. Soc. bul. VIII. p21-3. 1934 (Review of the economic and business mss. in the collection) **1452a**

Rich, E. E. The Hudson's Bay Company's activities; forthcoming publication of documents by Hudson's Bay Record Society. Pacific hist. rev. VII. p267-73 (Sept. 1938) **1452b**

Roberts, Richard Arthur. The reports of the historical mss. commission. (Helps for students of history, no. 22) London. Soc. for Promoting Christian Knowledge. 1920. 91p. **1452c**

Rodríguez Moñino, A. R. Catálogo de los manuscritos de América existentes en la "Collección de jesuítas," de la Academia de la historia. Badajoz. 1935. 90p. **1452d**

Rosenbach, A. S. W. Address of the president. Am. Jewish Hist. Soc. pub. no. 33. p1-9. 1934 (Describes the Gratz papers relating to Jewish life in America from the Revolution to the Civil War) **1452e**

Rothert, Otto A. Shane, the western collector. The Filson Club hist. quar. IV. p1-16 (Jan. 1930) (Material on the Mississippi Valley, particularly Kentucky and Tennessee, now in the State Hist. Soc. of Wis., and the Presbyterian Hist. Soc. of Phila.) **1453**

Sabin, Joseph F. The library of the late Hon. George Bancroft; a sketch of the historical manuscripts; memoranda concerning the books and pamphlets. N.Y. 1891? 101p. **1454**

St. Louis. Mercantile Library Association. Manuscripts relating to Louisiana territory and Missouri. (Reference list no. 1. pt. 2) St. Louis. 1898. p17-22 **1455**

Schafer, Joseph. The Draper collection of manuscripts. Madison. 1922. (Separate no. 221, from State Hist. Soc. of Wis. proc. 1922. p51-68) **1456**

Secretary's column—acquisitions. Bus. Hist. Soc. bul. I-. June 1926- **1456a**

Seris, Homero. The libraries and archives of Madrid. *In* Coral Gables, Fla. University of Miami. Hispanic-American Institute. Lectures (Hispanic-American stud. no. 1) 1939. p89-107 **1456b**

Severance, Henry O. A survey of the resources of the University of Missouri Library for research work. (Univ. of Missouri bul. XXXVIII, no. 16, lib. ser. no. 19) Columbia, Mo. 1937. 30p. **1456c**

The shipping papers of James Hunnewell. Business hist. soc. bul. VIII. p63-6 (June 1934) **1456d**

Smith, Charles W. A union list of manuscripts in libraries of the Pacific northwest. Seattle. Univ. of Wash. Press. 1931. 57p. **1457**

Sparks, Jared. Catalogue of the library of Jared Sparks; with a list of the historical manuscripts collected by him and now deposited in the library of Harvard University. Cambridge, Mass. Riverside Press. 1871. 230p. **1458**

Stillé, Charles J. Archivum Americanum in the consistory court of the archbishop of Upsala. Pa. mag. hist. XV. p481-5. 1891 (MSS. relating to the Swedish emigration to the shores of the Delaware during the 18th century) **1458a**

Texas. University. Library. Guide to the Archives Collection of the Texas University Library. Austin, Texas. In progress **1458b**

—— —— —— Guide to the Latin American manuscripts in the University of Texas Library. Ed. for the University of Texas and the Committee on Latin American studies of the American Council of Learned Societies by Carlos E. Castaneda and Jack Autrey Dabbs. Cambridge, Mass. Harvard Univ. Press. 1939. 217p. **1458c**

Tilton, Asa C. House miscellaneous papers in the Library of Congress. State Hist. Soc. of Wis. proc. 1912. p228-45   **1459**

True, Rodney H. Some pre-revolutionary agricultural correspondence. Agric. hist. XII. p107-17 (April 1938) (Collection of letters written to Jared Eliot (1749-1769) of Kenilworth, Conn. now in the Yale Univ. Lib.)   **1459a**

Tulane University. Library. Manuscripts in the Department of Middle American Research. New Orleans. Tulane Univ. 1933. p221-97   **1459b**

Turner, Morris K. The Baynton, Wharton, and Morgan manuscripts. Miss. Valley hist. rev. IX. p236-41 (Dec. 1922)   **1459c**

Tuttle, Julius Herbert. Catalogue of the library and collection of autograph letters, papers, and documents bequeathed to the Massachusetts Historical Society by the Rev. Robert Waterston. Boston. 1906. 479p. (Lists papers of early presidents, Lincoln, and others)   **1459d**

U.S. Department of State. List indicating the arrangement of the papers of Madison, Jefferson, Hamilton, Monroe, and Franklin. (Bul. of the Bureau of Rolls and Lib. no. 5. May 1894) Wash. D.C. Dept. of State. 1894. p1-14   **1460**

U.S. Library of Congress. Division of manuscripts. Accessions of manuscripts, broadsides and British transcripts. Wash. Govt. Ptg. Off. Lib. branch. 1922- (For earlier years see Reports of the Librarian of Congress)   **1461**

—— —— —— Checklist of collections of personal papers in historical societies, university and public libraries, and other learned institutions in the United States. Wash. Govt. Ptg. Off. 1918. 87p.   **1462**

—— —— —— Handbook of manuscripts in the Library of Congress. Wash. Govt. Ptg. Off. 1918. 750p.   **1463**

—— —— —— List of manuscript collections in the Library of Congress to July, 1931. By Curtis Wiswell Garrison. Wash. Govt. Ptg. Off. 1932. p123-249 (Reprinted from the Annual rep. of the Am. Hist. Asso. 1930)   **1464**

—— —— —— List of manuscript collections received in the Library of Congress, July 1931 to July 1938. Comp. by C. Percy Powell. Wash. Govt. Ptg. Off. 1939. 33p. (Reprinted from the Annual report of the Am. hist. asso. 1937)   **1464a**

—— —— —— Manuscripts in public and private collections in the United States. Wash. Govt. Ptg. Off. 1924. 98p.   **1465**

—— —— —— The present collections: manuscripts. *In* Report of the librarian of Congress, 1901. Wash. Govt. Ptg. Off. 1901. p335-44   **1465a**

U.S. National Archives. Annual report of the archivist of the United States as to the Franklin D. Roosevelt Library, Hyde Park, N.Y.... 1st- . 1939/40- . Wash. Govt. Ptg. Off. 1941-   **1465b**

Upton, Eleanor S. The location of seventeenth-century documents described in the first nine reports of the Historical Manuscripts Commission. Inst. Hist. Research bul. XV. p73-8 (Nov. 1937) **1465c**

Utley, George B. Source material for the study of American history in the libraries of Chicago. Bibliog. Soc. of Amer. pap. XVI. pt. I. p17-46. 1922. (Also reprinted. 46p.)   **1466**

Vail, R. W. G. The American Antiquarian Society. Business Hist. Soc. bul. VII. no. 6. p1-5 (Dec. 1933) (MSS. on economic history)   **1467**

Vallée, Léon. Notice des documents exposés à la section des cartes. . . Bibliothèque Nationale. Paris. 1912. 65p. **1467a**

Vedeler, Harold C. Historical materials at the southern branch of the University of Idaho. Pacific northw. quar. XXVII. p174-5 (April 1936) (Source materials for the history of the Pacific northwest) **1467b**

Wall, Alexander J. The Landauer lottery collection. N.Y. Hist. Soc. bul. XVI. p87-91. 1931 (Description of a collection of lottery cards and advertisements from many states)   **1467c**

Wentz, A. R. Collections of the Lutheran Historical Society. Pa. hist. III. p66-9 (Jan. 1936) (Books and mss. at Gettysburg Theological Seminary)   **1467d**

Western Pennsylvania Historical Survey. Inventory of the manuscripts and miscellaneous collections of the Historical Society of Western Pennsylvania. (Bibliog. contributions no. 1) Pittsburgh. Jan. 1933. 11p. multig.   **1468**

Winsor, Justin. Manuscript sources of American history; the conspicuous collections extant. Mag. of Am. hist. XVIII. p20-34 (July 1887); Am. Hist. Asso. pap. III. no. 1. p9-27. 1877   **1469**

—— The manuscript sources of the history of the United States of America with particular reference to the American Revolution. *In* Narrative and critical history of America. Boston, N.Y. Houghton, Mifflin. 1889. VIII. p412-68   **1470**

Wisconsin. State Historical Society. Descriptive list of manuscript collections of the State Historical Society of Wisconsin; together with reports on other collections of manuscript material for American history in adjacent states. Ed. by Reuben Gold Thwaites. Madison. Pub. by the Soc. 1906. 197p.   **1471**

Woodson, Carter G. Historical materials in the hands of Negroes. Wash. D.C. (In progress)   **1472**

Foreign Archives

Aiton, Arthur S. and Mecham, J. Lloyd. The archivo general de Indias. Hisp. Am. hist. rev. IV. p553-67 (Aug. 1921) **1472a**

Altolaguirre y Duvale, Angel de and Bonilla y San Martín, Adolfo. Indice general de los papeles del Consejo de Indias, publicado en virtud de acuerdo de la Real academia de la historia. (Coleccion de documentos inéditos relativos al descubrimiento, conquista y organizacion de los antiguos posesiones españoles de ultramar. 2 serie. t. XIV-XIX) Madrid. Tip. de la "Revista de archivos, biblioteca y museos." 1923-26. 6v. **1472b**

André, Louis and Bourgeois, Émile. Les sources de l'histoire de France, XVIIe siècle (1610-1715). Paris. A. Picard. 1913-35. 8v. **1472c**

Andrews, Charles M. Guide to the materials for American history to 1783, in the Public Record Office of Great Britain. (Carnegie Inst. of Wash. Publication no. 90-A) Wash. D.C. 1912. 2v. **1473**

—— Materials in British archives for American history. Am. hist. rev. X. p325-49 (Jan. 1905) **1474**

—— The story of the transcripts. *In* Essays offered to Herbert Putnam by his colleagues and friends on his thirtieth anniversary as Librarian of Congress, 5 April, 1929. New Haven. Yale Univ. Press. 1929. p47-56 **1475**

Andrews, Charles M. and Davenport, Frances C. Guide to the manuscript materials for the history of the United States to 1783, in the British Museum, in minor London archives, and in the libraries of Oxford and Cambridge. (Carnegie Inst. of Wash. Publication no. 90) Wash. D.C. 1908. 499p. **1476**

Angulo íñiguez, Diego. Planos de monumentos arquitectonicos de América y Filipinas existentes en el Archivo de Indias; catálogo. [Sevilla] Laboratorio de arte. 1933-34. 2v. **1476a**

Archivo de protocolos, Sevilla. Catálogo de los fondos americanos del Archivo de protocolos de Sevilla, t.v. siglos XV y XVI. (Publicación del Instituto hispanocubano de historia de América (Fundación Rafael G. Abreu) Wash [Imprenta de la Gavidia] 1937. 564p. **1476b**

Baird, Charles W. A month among the records in London. Mag. Am. hist. II. p321-33 (June 1878) **1476c**

Baumgarten, Paul M. The Vatican. Catholic encyclopedia. XV. p276-302. 1912 (Section VIII, The palace as a scientific institute, p286-97 treats of the Vatican Archives and the Vatican Library) **1476d**

Bell, Herbert C., Parker, David W. and others. Guide to British West Indian archive materials, in London, and in the Island, for the history of the United States. (Carnegie Inst. of Wash. Publication no. 372) Wash. D.C. 1926. 435p. **1477**

Bemis, Samuel Flagg and Ford, Worthington C. Rockefeller grants. Project A. Acquisition of source material for American history. *In* Report of the Librarian of Congress, 1928, 228-37; 1929, 75-96; 1930, 95-106; 1931, 87-99; 1932, 60-72. Wash. Govt. Ptg. Off. 1928-32. (Bemis, 1928-29; Ford, 1930-32) (Transcripts from European archives) **1478**

Biggar, Henry P. The public archives at Ottawa. Inst. of Hist. Research bul. II. p66-79 (Feb. 1925); III. p38-44 (June 1925) **1478a**

Bloom, Herbert I. The Dutch archives, with special reference to American Jewish history. Am. Jewish Hist. Soc. publications. no. 32. p7-21. 1931 **1479**

Bolton, Herbert Eugene. Guide to materials for the history of the United States in the principal archives of Mexico. (Carnegie Inst. of Wash. Publication no. 163) Wash. D.C. 1913. 553p. **1480**

—— Some materials for southwestern history in the Archivo general de Mexico. Texas State Hist. Asso. quar. VI. p103-12 (Oct. 1902) **1481**

Bordier, Henri L. Les archives de la France, ou histoire des archives de l'empire, des archives des ministères, des départements, des communes, des hôpitaux, des greffes, des notaires, etc., contenant l'inventaire d'une partie de ces dépôts. Paris. Dumomulin. 1855. 412p. **1481a**

Brom, Gisbert. Guide aux archives du Vatican. Rome. Loescher & co. (W. Regenberg) 1911. 104p. **1481b**

Brown, George W. Provincial archives in Canada. Canad. hist. rev. XVI. p1-18 (March 1935) **1481c**

Campillo, Miguel Gómez del. Index to material in the Archivo Histórico Nacional at Madrid for the history of the United States to 1800. Typescript copy in the Library of Congress **1481d**

—— Madrid archives, chronological statement of papers and documents relative to Louisiana in the National historical archives of Madrid (1740-1832). Louisiana Hist. Soc. publications. IV. p122-44. 1908 **1482**

Canada. Archives. Abstracts of political correspondence relating to the United States (1778-1780) in the ministry of foreign affairs, France. *In* Report on Canadian archives, 1912. Ottawa. 1913. Appendix L, p162-214. Same. 1780-1781. *In* Report. . . 1913. Appendix H, p152-226 **1482a**

—— —— Calendar of papers relating to Nova Scotia [1603-1801] *In* Report on Canadian archives, 1894. Ottawa. 1895. 573p. **1482b**

—— —— Calendar of series C.O. 42 [1761-1821]. *In* Report of the public archives, 1921. Ottawa. 1922. Appendix D, p283-359 **1482c**

—— —— Catalogue of maps, plans, and charts in the maps room of the Dominion Archives. Comp. by H.R. Holmden. (Publications of the Canadian Archives, no. 8) Ottawa. Govt. Ptg. Bur. 1912. 685p. **1482d**

—— A guide to the documents in the manuscript room at the Public archives of Canada. v. I. Prepared by David W. Parker. Published by authority of the Secretary of State under the direction of the archivist. (Publications of the Archives of Canada. no. 10) Ottawa. Govt. Ptg. Bureau. 1914. 318p. **1483**

Canada. Archives. Report of Mr. Edouard Richard [on material in the Ministère des Colonies, Paris relating to Canada] *In* Report on Canadian archives, 1899, supplement. Ottawa. 1901. 548p.   **1483a**

—— —— Report of the public archives, 1881- . Ottawa. 1882- (The reports for 1872-1880 were included in the reports of the minister of agriculture. These reports contain much information concerning Canadian archives and accessions of mss. and maps, etc.)   **1483b**

—— —— Summary of documents in Paris. *In* Report on Canadian archives, 1905. Ottawa. 1906. I, pt. 6, 661p.   **1483c**

—— —— Summary of documents in Paris, made by the late M. Edouard Richard, with index. *In* Report on Canadian archives, 1904. Ottawa. 1905. 357p.   **1483d**

—— —— Synopsis of papers in the Public Record Office, London. *In* Report on Canadian archives, 1883. By Douglas Brymner. Ottawa. MacLean, Roger. 1884. p18-73   **1483e**

—— —— Synopsis of papers, in the state departements, Paris. By Joseph Marmette. *In* Reports on Canadian archives, 1883, 1885, 1886, 1887. Ottawa. MacLean, Roger. 1884-88. p120-59, xxii-lxxix, xxxi-cl, cxxxv-cccxcviii   **1483f**

Carnegie Institution of Washington. Guides to materials for American history in the archives of Norway, Sweden, Denmark, Netherlands and Scotland. MS. in the Carnegie Institution of Washington, Wash. D.C.   **1483g**

Chapman, Charles Edward. Catalogue of materials in the Archivo general de Indias for the history of the Pacific coast and the American southwest. (Univ. of Calif. Publications in hist. VIII). Berkeley. Univ. of Calif. Press. 1919. 755p.   **1484**

—— A description of certain legajos in the Archivo general de Indias. Hispanic Am. hist. rev. I. p209-30, 352-71 (May, Aug. 1918) (Relating to the U.S. and Mexico)   **1485**

Corwin, E. T. Recent ecclesiastical researches in Holland. Jour. of the Presbyterian Hist. Soc. I. p161-88 (Dec. 1901) (Church records relating to New York)   **1486**

[Cuban archives copied for the Texas State Library and other libraries by Miss Elizabeth H. West, July 1914, in Havana] Texas State Hist. Asso. quar. XVIII. p337 (Jan. 1915)   **1486a**

De Boer, Louis P. The archives of the Netherlands and their importance for American genealogy. Nation. Geneal. Soc. quar. XVI. p33-7 (Sept. 1928)   **1486b**

Desdevises du Dézert, Georges Nicolas. Les sources manuscrites de l'histoire de l'Amérique latine à la fin du XVIIIᵉ siècle, 1760-1807. (Nouvelle archives des missions scientifiques et littéraires. n.s. fasc. XII) Paris. Imprimerie nationale. 1914. 64p. (Spanish archives)   **1486c**

Doré, Robert. État des inventaires et répertoires des archives nationales, départementales, communales et hospitalières de la France à la date du 1ᵉʳ décembre 1919. Paris. É. Champion. 1919. 60p. (Extrait de la Revue des bibliothèques, nos. 7-9)   **1486d**

Doughty, Arthur G. The Canadian archives and its activities. Ottawa. F.A. Acland. 1924. 88p.   **1486e**

—— Sources for the history of the Catholic church in the public archives of Canada. Cath. hist. rev. XIX. p148-66 (July 1933)   **1486f**

Edwards, Joseph Plimsoll. The public records of Nova Scotia, their history and present condition. Halifax, N.S. Commissioner of Pub. Works & Mines, King's Printer. 1920. 20p.   **1486g**

Esteve Barbá, F. Los manuscritos americanos de la Biblioteca pública de Toledo. III. Anales de la Universidad de Madrid. III. p94-109. 1934   **1486h**

Faust, Albert Bernhardt. Guide to the materials for American history in Swiss and Austrian archives. (Carnegie Inst. of Wash. Publication no. 220) Wash. D.C. 1916. 299p.   **1487**

Fish, Carl Russell. American history in Roman archives. Catholic world. XCI. p657-67 (Aug. 1910)   **1487a**

—— Guide to the materials for American history in Roman and other Italian archives. (Carnegie Inst. of Wash. Publication no. 128) Wash. D.C. 1911. 289p.   **1488**

France, Archives de la Guerre. Catalogue général des manuscrits des bibliothèques publiques de France: Archives de la Guerre. Par Louis Tuetey. Paris. Plon, Nourrit et cⁱᵉ. 1912-20. 3v.   **1488a**

France. Archives de la Marine. État sommaires des archives de la marine antérieures à la révolution. Paris. L. Baudoin. 1898. 694p.   **1488b**

—— Inventaire des Archives de la Marine; series B; service général. Paris. L. Baudoin. 1885-1904. 6v.   **1488c**

France. Archives des Affaires Étrangères. Archives du Ministère des Affaires Étrangères; inventaire sommaire de la correspondence politique, États-Unis [1775-1835]. 1935. 64p. (Photostat in the Lib. of Cong. MSS. division)   **1489**

France. Archives Nationales. Catalogue des manuscrits conservés aux archives nationales. Paris. E. Plon, Nourrit et cⁱᵉ. 1892. 532p.   **1489a**

—— —— Inventaire sommaire et tableau méthodique des fonds conservés aux Archives Nationales. 1 partie. Régime antérieur à 1789. Paris. Imprimerie Nationale. 1871-75. 2v.   **1489b**

France. Ministère des Affaires Étrangères. Abstracts of political correspondence relating to United States (1778-1780) in the Ministry of foreign affairs. France [v. I-XI] *In* Canada. Archives. Report of the work of the Archives branch for the year 1912. Ottawa. C. H. Parmelee. 1913. p162-214   **1489c**

Giesecke, Albert A. Report on materials on commerce in the various public depositories in London. (Typ. MS. in the Univ. of Pennsylvania Lib., and the Dept. of hist. of the Carnegie Inst. of Wash.) Oct. 1905. 78p. **1490**

Gilbert, John T. The history, position, and treatment of the public records of Ireland. London. 1864. 204p. **1490a**

Golder, Frank A. Guide to materials for American history in Russian archives. (Carnegie Inst. of Wash. Publication no. 239) Wash. D.C. 1917, 1937. 177, 55p. **1491**

Great Britain. Colonial Office. Catalogue of maps, plans, and charts in the library of the Colonial Office. 1910 (A special compilation of excerpts from printed lists of maps of America, Canada, and the North American colonies) **1491a**

—— List of maps at the Record office [relating to North America]. *In* Canada. Archives. Report concerning Canadian archives, 1905. Ottawa. 1906. II. p vii-xv **1491b**

Great Britain. Historical Manuscripts Commission. Report on American manuscripts in the Royal Institution of Great Britain; presented to Parliament by command. (Rep. on hist. MSS. unnumbered ser.) London. H.M. Stationery Off. by Mackie & Co. 1904-09. 4v. (Headquarters papers of British commanders in chief in the American revolution) **1492**

Great Britain. Public Record Office. An alphabetical guide to certain war office and other military records. (Lists and indexes no. LIII) London. H.M. Stationery Off. 1931. 530p. **1492a**

—— —— Annual report of the deputy keeper of the public records, 1839/40-. London. 1840- **1492b**

—— —— Calendar of state papers, Colonial series, America and the West Indies, 1574-[1733] London, 1860-[1939] v. 1, 5, 7, 9-[40] (In progress) **1492c**

—— —— Colonial office records; list of documents in the Public Record Office [relating to colonial matters] on 1st July 1876. London. H.M. Stationery Off. 1876. 279p. **1492d**

—— —— A guide to the various classes of documents preserved in the Public Record Office. By S. R. Scargill-Bird. London. H.M. Stationery Off. 1908. 460p. **1492e**

—— —— List of colonial office records, preserved in the Public Record Office. (Lists and indexes, no. XXXVI) London. Print. for H.M. Stationery Off. 1911. 337p. **1492f**

Griffin, Grace G. Foreign American history mss. copies in Library of Congress. Jour. doc. reprod. III. p3-9 (March 1940) **1492g**

Hall, Hubert. A discussion on the exploration of Anglo-American archives. Royal Hist. Soc. of Great Britain trans. ser. 4. XVI. p55-68. 1933 **1493**

—— A repertory of British archives. London. Royal Hist. Soc. 1920 **1493a**

Haskins, Charles H. The Vatican archives. Am. hist. rev. II. p40-58 (Oct. 1896) **1493b**

Higham, C. S. S. The colonial entry-books; a brief guide to the colonial records in the Public Record Office before 1696. (Helps for students of history, no.45) London. Soc. for Promoting Christian Knowledge; N.Y. Macmillan. 1921. 48p. **1493c**

Hill, Roscoe R. Los archivos Españoles y los investigadores Americanos. *In* Coleccion de estudios, históricos, jurídicos, pedagógicos y literarios. Madrid, Bermejo, 1936 **1493d**

—— Descriptive catalogue of the documents relating to the history of the United States in the Papeles procedentes de Cuba deposited in the Archivo general de Indias at Seville. (Carnegie Inst. of Wash. Publication no. 234) Wash. D.C. 1916. 594p. **1494**

—— Sources of American history in Spanish archives. *In* Pan American Institute of Geography and History. Proceedings of the second general assembly. Wash. 1937. p257-67. Also reprinted in part from Boletín de la Union Panamericana for April 1936 as "Fuentes de historia americana en los archivos españoles" in Revista geografica americana, VI. p70-3 (July 1936) **1495**

Jameson, J. Franklin. Notes from the archives of Scotland concerning America. Am. Hist. Asso. rep. 1930. I. p97-122 **1496**

Johnson, Charles. The Public Record Office. (Helps for students of history, no. 4) London. Soc. for Promoting Christian Knowledge. 1932. 47p. **1496a**

Karpinski, Louis Charles. Manuscript maps relating to American history in French, Spanish, and Portuguese archives. Am. hist. rev. XXXIII.p328-30 (Jan. 1928) **1496b**

Kenney, James F. The public records of the Province of Quebec, 1763-1791. Inter-American Bibliog. and Lib. Asso. proc. 1939. p252-66 **1496c**

Langlois, Charles V. and Stein, H. Les archives de l'histoire de France. Paris. A. Picard. 1891. [1893] 1000p. **1496d**

Larrabure y Uñanue, Eugenio. Les archives des Indes et la Bibliothèque Colombine de Séville; renseignements sur leurs richesses bibliographiques et sur l'exposition d'anciens documents relatifs à l'Amérique. Paris. Hemmerlé. 1914. 88p. **1497**

Learned, Marion Dexter. Guide to the manuscript materials relating to American history in German state archives. (Carnegie Inst. of Wash. Publication no. 150) Wash. D.C. 1912. 352p. **1498**

Leland, Waldo Gifford. French sources of American history. *In* Essays offered to Herbert Putnam by his colleagues and friends on his thirtieth anniversary as Librarian of Congress, 5 April 1929. New Haven. Yale Univ. Press. 1929. p288-301 **1499**

Leland, Waldo Gifford. Guide to material for American history in French archives. Am. Council of Learned Societies, Wash. D.C. In progress   **1499a**

—— Guide to materials for American history in the libraries and archives of Paris. Vol. 1. Libraries. (Carnegie Inst. of Wash. Publication no. 392) Wash. D.C. 1932. 343p.   **1500**

—— Notes on material in the French archives relating to the history of the Mississippi Valley. State Hist. Soc. of Wisconsin. proc. LVI. p42-6. 1909   **1501**

—— Report on the catalogue of documents in French archives relating to the history of the Mississippi Valley. Am. Hist. Asso. rep. 1912. p202-5   **1502**

—— Report on transcription of documents from French archives. *In* Report of the Librarian of Congress, 1921. Wash. Govt. Ptg. Off. 1921. p177-86   **1503**

—— Les sources de l'histoire américaine (période de la colonisation française) à Paris. Rev. hist. moderne. III. p297-9 (juillet-août 1928)   **1504**

Lista de planos y descripciones de Luisiana y Florida, Archivo de Indias, Papeles de Luisiana, [Indiferente general] Est. 145. Cajón 7. Leg. 9. Boletín del Museo Nacional de Arqueología, Historia y Etnografía (Mexico). 5 ser. II. p85-8. 1933   **1504a**

Liste des documents concernant la Louisiana conservé aux Archives Coloniales (Ministère des colonies, Pavillon de Flore, Paris) La. Hist. Soc. pubs. II, pt. 4. p9-12. 1902   **1504b**

Livingstone, H. Guide to · the public records of Scotland, deposited in H.M. Register House, Edinburgh. Edinburgh. H.M. Register House. 1905. 233p. **1504c**

Martin, Thomas P. Spanish archive materials and related materials in other national archives, copied for the Library of Congress, project "A" gift fund, 1927-1929. Hispanic Am. hist. rev. X. p95-8 (Feb. 1930)   **1505**

—— Transcripts, facsimiles, and manuscripts in the Spanish language in the Library of Congress, 1929. Hispanic Am. hist. rev. IX. p243-6 (May 1929)   **1506**

Martín-Granizo, León. Aportaciones bibliográficas viajeros y viajes de españoles, portugueses é hispano-americanos. Rev. geog. col. y. merc. XX. p275-92, 305-26, 369-96 (Aug., Sept., Nov. 1923); XXI. p81-101, 145-66, 217-31 (March-July 1923)   **1506a**

Matteson, David Maydole. List of manuscripts concerning American history preserved in European libraries and noted in their published catalogues and similar printed lists. (Carnegie Inst. of Wash. Publication no. 359) Wash. D.C. 1925. 203p.   **1507**

Montero, Juan. Guía histórica y descriptiva del Archivo general de Simancas. Madrid. Revista de archivos. 1920. 245p. **1507a**

Nabholz, Hans P. K. International archivführer. Zürich, Rascher. 1936. 110p. (A guide to research in various national and departmental archives of the world)
                    1507b

Nasatir, Abraham P. and Liljegren, Ernest R. Materials relating to the history of the Mississippi Valley from the minutes of the Spanish Supreme Councils of State, 1787-1797; ·a calendar. La. hist. quar. XXI. p5-75 (Jan. 1938)   **1507c**

New York. State Library. Descriptive list of French manuscripts copied for New York State Library from National Archives and National Library at Paris, 1888. N. Y. State Lib. bul. 57. hist. 5. p319-82. 1902   **1508**

Newhall, Beatrice. The Miranda archives. Pan Am. Union Bul. LXVII. p491-6 (June 1933)   **1509**

Nova Scotia. Public Archives. A calendar of official correspondence and legislative papers, Nova Scotia, 1802-15. Comp. by Margaret Ells under the direction of D. C. Harvey, archivist. (Public Archives of Nova Scotia. Publication no. 3) Halifax, N.S. 1936. 354p.   **1509a**

Nussbaum, Frederick Louis. A check list of film copies of archival material in the University of Wyoming Library from the Public Record Office, the India Office, the British Museum in London, the Archives Nationales in Paris. [Laramie, Wyo. Univ. of Wyoming. 1936] [p213]-43 (Univ. of Wyo. pub. II, Dec. 1, 1936)
                    1509b

Ots Capdequi, José María, ed. Catálogo de los fondos Americanos del archivo de protocolos de Sevilla. (Colleción de documentos ineditos para la historia de Hispano-America, VIII) Madrid. Compañia Ibero-Americana de publicaciones. 1930. 561p.   **1509c**

Pares, Richard. Public records in British West India islands. Inst. Hist. Research bul. VII. p149-57 (Feb. 1930) (Jamaica, Barbadoes, Antigua, and St. Kitts) **1509d**

Paris. Bibliothèque nationale. Département des manuscrits. Catalogue des manuscrits américains de la Bibliothèque nationale. Paris. Bibliothèque nationale, département des manuscrits. 1925. 25p. (Extrait de la Revue des bibliothèques. nos. 1-6. 1925)   **1510**

Parker, David W. Guide to the material for United States history in Canadian archives. (Carnegie Inst. of Wash. Publication no. 172) Wash. D.C. 1913. 339p.   **1511**

Paullin, Charles O. and Paxson, Frederic L. Guide to the materials in London archives for the history of the United States since 1783. (Carnegie Inst. of Wash. Publication no. 90-B) Wash. D.C. 1914. 642p.   **1512**

Paz, Julián. Catálogo de manuscritos de América existentes en la Biblioteca nacional. Madrid. Tip. de archivos. 1933. 724p.   **1513**

Perez, L. M. Guide to the materials for American history in Cuban archives. (Carnegie Inst. of Wash. Publication no. 83) Wash. D.C. 1907. 142p. **1514**

Read, Benjamin M. Chronological digest of the "documentos ineditos del archivo de las Indias." Albuquerque, N. Mex. Albright & Anderson. 1914. 161p. **1515**

Robertson, James Alexander. List of documents in Spanish archives relating to the history of the United States, which have been printed or of which transcripts are preserved in American libraries. (Carnegie Inst. of Wash. Publication no. 124) Wash. D. C. 1910. 368p. **1516**

Rosengarten, Joseph G. German archives as sources of German-American history. [Phila.] 1907. 15p. (Reprinted from German American ann. n.s. V. p357-69 (Nov. 1907)) **1516a**

Roussier, Paul. Le dépôt des papiers de colonies. Rev. hist. mod. IV. p241-62 (July 1929) **1516b**

—— Les origines du dépôt des papiers public des colonies; le dépot de Rochefort (1763-1790). Rev. hist. colonies Franç. XXXI. (no. 49) p21-50. 1925 **1516c**

Roy, J.-Edmond. Rapport sur les archives de France relatives à l'histoire du Canada; publié avec l'autorisation de ministère de l'agriculture, sous la direction de l'archiviste. (Publications des Archives du Canada. no. 6) Ottawa. Imprimeur de son très excellent majesté le Roi. 1911. 1093p. **1517**

Rubio y Moreno, Luis. Inventario general de registros cedularios del archivo general de Indias de Sevilla presentado por el autor en el congreso de historia y geografía celebrado en 1921, siendo subjefe del archivo general de Indias. (Colección de documentos inéditos para la historia de Hispano-América, tomo V) Madrid. Compañia Ibero-Americana de publicaciones, S.A. 1928. 454p **1518**

—— Pasajeros a Indias; catálogo metodologico de las informaciones y licencias de los que allé pasaron, existentes en el archivo general de Indias—siglo primero de la colonización de América, 1492-1592. (Colección de documentos inéditos para la historia de Hispano-América, tomo VIII [i.e. IX]) Madrid. Compañia Ibero-Americana de publicaciones, S.A. 1930? 2v. **1519**

Sharp, Henry A. The preservation of historical records in Holland. Lib. world. Jan. 1914. p185-96 **1519a**

Shepherd, William R. Guide to the materials for the history of the United States in Spanish archives. (Carnegie Inst. of Wash. Publication no. 91) Wash. D.C. 1907. 107p. **1520**

—— The Spanish archives and their importance for the history of the United States. Am. Hist. Asso. rep. 1903. I. p145-83 **1521**

Sluiter, Engel. The Dutch archives and American historical research. Pacific hist. rev. VI. p21-36 (March 1937) (Reprinted: The Hague. M. Nijhoff. 1938 **1521a**

Spain. Archivo General de Indias. Archivo general de Indias; catálogo; cuadro general de la documentación. Por Pedro Torres Lanzas y Latorre y Satén, Germán. (Publicaciones del Centro oficial de estudios americanistas de Sevilla. Biblioteca colonial americana. t. I) Sevilla. Tip. Zarzuela. 1918. 165p. **1521b**

—— —— Catálogo de la sección 1a; real patronado. Redactado por Vicente Llorens Asenio. (Centro de estudios americanistas de Sevilla. Biblioteca colonial americana. t. 12) Sevilla. Tip. Zarzuela. 1924- t. 1- **1521c**

—— —— Catálogo de legajos del Archivo General de Indias; secciones primera y segunda; patronato y contaduría del Consejo de Indias. Por Pedro Torres Lanzas. (Publicaciones del Centro oficial de estudios americanistas de Sevilla. Biblioteca colonial americana. II) Sevilla. Tip. Zarzuela. 1919. 203p. **1521d**

—— —— Catálogo de legajos del Archivo General de Indias; sección tercera: Casa de la contratación de Indias. Por Pedro Torres Lanzas. (Publicaciones del Centro de estudios americanistas de Sevilla. Biblioteca colonial americana. t. VI) Sevilla. Tip. Zarzuela. 1921-22. 4v. in 2 **1521e**

—— —— Indice de documentos de Nueva España existentes en el Archivo de Indias de Sevilla. (Monografias bibliograficas mexicanas. núm. 12, 14) Mexico. Imprenta de la secretaria de relaciones exteriores. 1928-29. 2v. **1521f**

Spain. Archivo de Protocolos. Catálogo de los fondos americanos del Archivo de Protocolos de Sevilla. Siglo XVI. Con XX apéndices documentales. (Colección de documentos inéditos para la historia de Hispano-América, tomo VIII [i.e. X, XI,XIV]) Madrid, Buenos Aires. Compañia Ibero-Americana de publicaciones, S.A. 1930-37. 3v. **1522**

Spain. Cuerpo Facultativo de Archiveros, Bibliotecarios y Arqueólogos. Guia histórica y descriptiva de los archivos, bibliotecas y museos arqueológicos de España que están a Cuerpo facultativo del ramo, publicado bajo la dirección del Excmo Francisco Rodriguez Marin. Madrid. Tip. de la "Revista de archivos, bibliotecas y museos." 1916- [i.e. 1921-] **1522a**

Spain. Depósito de la Guerra. Catálogo general del archivo de mapas, planos y memorias del Depósito de la Guerra. Madrid. Imp. y lit. del mismo. 1900. 2v. **1522b**

Stevens, Benjamin Franklin. American manuscripts in European archives. N.Y.? 1887? 18p. **1523**

Stevens, Benjamin Franklin. Catalogue index of manuscripts in the archives of England, France, Holland, and Spain relating to America, 1763-1783. (MS. in the Lib. of Cong.) London. 1870-1902 **1524**

—— Chronological arrangement of the documents, nos. 1 to 2107 contained in volumes I to XXIV of B. F. Stevens's Facsimiles of manuscripts in European archives relating to America, 1773-1783. London. 1898. 82p. (In the Ford collection in the N.Y. Pub. Lib.) **1525**

—— Facsimiles of manuscripts in European archives relating to America, 1773-1783. Vol. XXV. Index. London. Cheswick Press. 1898. 351p. **1526**

—— Introduction to the catalogue index of manuscripts in the archives of England, France, Holland and Spain relating to America, 1763 to 1783; compiled in three divisions in each of which all of the 161,000 documents enumerated are cited. London, England, 1870 to 1902. *In* Fenn, George M. Memoir of Benjamin Franklin Stevens. London. 1903. p195-304 **1526a**

Surrey, Nancy Maria (Miller). Calendar of manuscripts in Paris archives and libraries relating to the history of the Mississippi Valley to 1803. Wash. D.C. Carnegie Inst. of Wash. 1926, 1928. 2v. planog. **1527**

—— History of the calendar of documents in the archives of Paris relating to the Mississippi Valley. Louisiana hist. quar. VII. p551-63 (Oct. 1924) **1528**

Torre Revello, José. El Archivo general de Indias de Sevilla; historia y clasificacion de sus fundos. (Buenos Aires. Universidad nacional] Publicaciones del Instituto de investigaciones historicas. no. L) Buenos Aires. Talleres s.s. Casa Jacobo Peuser. 1929. 214p. **1528a**

Torres y Lanzas, Pedro. Archivo general de Indias, Sevilla; clasificacion de sus fondos. Bol. centro estud. Am. Seville, año III. p1-8, 64-78, 27-34, 33-42, 22-32, 25-34 (May, June, July, Sept., Oct., Nov., Dec. 1915) **1528b**

—— Relación descriptiva de los mapas, planos, etc. de Filipinas existentes en el archivo general de Indias. *In* Retana y Gamboa, Wenceslao Emilio. Archivo del bibliófilo general de Indias. Madrid. Imp. de la viuda de M. Minuesa de los Rios. 1897. III. p443-97 **1528c**

—— Relación descriptiva de los mapas, planos, etc., de México y Floridas existentes en el archivo general de Indias. Sevilla. Imp. de El Mercantil. 1900. 2v. **1528d**

The **unedited** documents of the Indies at Seville, Spain. Pan Am. union bul. XLIV. p465-77 (April 1917) **1528e**

U.S. Library of Congress. Division of manuscripts. Memorandum of index of documents in Madrid archives furnished to the Library of Congress by Miss Irene A.

Wright. October 27, 1926. (Photostat in the Division of manuscripts in two volumes. Contents: Material in the Archivo historico nacional at Madrid consisting of the dispatches of the Spanish diplomatic representative in America, 1807-1823. From this selections were made for photostats. There is also a supplementary index by Miss Wright of Expedientes extracted from the dispatches of the Spanish diplomatic representative in America from 1807 to 1823, March 25, 1927) **1529**

—— —— **European historical mission. German staff.** Supplements, corrections and new inventory-lists to be added to M. D. Learned's guide to the manuscript materials relating to American history in the German state archives. 1929-32 (Typescript in the Lib. of Cong.) 2v. **1530**

Van den Eynde, Damian. Calendar of Spanish documents in John Carter Brown library. Hisp. Am. hist. rev. XVI. p564-607 (Nov. 1936) (Includes material on New Spain, Pensacola, New Mexico and Texas) **1530a**

Vaux de Foletier, F. de. Les sources de l'histoire coloniale aux archives de la Charente-Inferieure. Rev. hist. colonies. XXVIII. p49-64. 1935 **1530b**

Weidmann, P. Deutsch archivmaterial z. nordamerik geschichte. *In* Hamburg-Amerika-Post Band 2. p76-83. 1930 **1530c**

Wright, Irene A. Further research work in Seville, Spain. *In* Year book of the Louisiana society Sons of the American revolution for 1919-1920. New Orleans, La. p83-102 (Research work carried on for the Society in the Archivo general de Indias) **1530d**

—— The General archives of the Indies at Seville, Spain. National hist. mag. LXXIX. p4-6. 1938 **1530e**

SECONDARY WORKS

General

Adams, Charles Kendall. A manual of historical literature, comprising brief descriptions of the most important histories in English, French and German, together with practical suggestions as to methods and courses of historical study. N.Y. Harper. 1882 (Histories of the United States on p530-93) **1531**

Adams, Herbert B. and others. Seminary notes on recent historical literature. (Johns Hopkins Univ. Stud. in hist. and pol. science. eighth ser. XI-XII) Balt. Johns Hopkins Press. 1890. 105p. **1532**

American Historical Association. The American historical review. General index to volumes I-[XXX]. Comp. by David M. Matteson. N.Y. Macmillan. 1906, 1916, 1926. 3pts. **1533**

—— General index to papers and annual reports of the American Historical Association, 1884-1914. Comp. by David M. Matteson. Am. Hist. Asso. rep. 1914. Wash. Govt. Ptg. Off. 1918. 793p. (Also pub. as House document 818. 64 Cong. 2 sess.) **1534**

—— List of research projects in history exclusive of doctoral dissertations, now in progress in the United States and the Dominion of Canada. (Am. hist. rev. Supplement to v. XXXIX. no. 3. April 1934) Richmond, Va., N.Y. Macmillan. 1934. 54p. **1535**

American nation: a history. Ed. by Albert Bushnell Hart. N.Y. Harper. 1904-08. 27v. (Contents: Cheyney, E. P. European background of American history; Farrand, L. Basis of American history; Bourne, E. G. Spain in America; Tyler, L. G. England in America; Andrews, C. M. Colonial self-government; Greene, E. B. Provincial America; Thwaites, R. G. France in America; Howard, G. E. Preliminaries of the Revolution; Van Tyne, C. H. The American Revolution; McLaughlin, A. C. The constitution and the confederation; Bassett, J. S. The federalist system; Channing, E. The Jeffersonian system; Babcock, K. C. The rise of American nationality; Turner, F. G. Rise of the new West; MacDonald, W. Jacksonian democracy; Hart, A. B. Slavery and abolition; Garrison, G. P. Westward extension; Smith, T. C. Parties and slavery; Chadwick, F. E. Causes of the Civil war; Hosmer, J. K. The appeal to arms; Hosmer, J. K. Outcome of the Civil war; Dunning, W. A. Reconstruction, political and economic; Sparks, E. E. National development; Dewey, D. R. National problems; Latané, J. H. America as a world power; Hart, A. B. National ideals historically traced; Ogg, F. A. National progress. (Ogg's is a supplementary volume published in 1918. Vol. XXVII is an Analytic index by David M. Matteson) **1536**

Among the current magazines. The Social stud., continuing The Hist. outlook. XXV. no. 7- Nov. 1934- **1537**

Barnes, Viola F. The history of the writing of American history, 1660 to the present. Mount Holyoke College. In progress **1538**

Baxter, James P. III, Merk, Frederick, Morison, Samuel E. and Schlesinger, Arthur M. Guide to the study and reading of American history (Revision of no. 1541 below; in progress) **1538a**

Bibliografía de historia de América, 1937/1938. Revista de historia de América. I. 1938- **1538b**

Bolton, Herbert E. History of the Americas: a syllabus with maps. Boston. Ginn. 1935. 314p. **1539**

Brainerd, Ira Hutchinson. Index and list of authorities. *In* Von Holst, H. The constitutional history of the United States. Chicago. Callaghan. 1892. VIII. 356p. **1540**

Callegari, Guido Valeriano. Bibliografía Americana, 1906-1936. Trento. Tipografía editrice mutilati e invalidi. 1936. 21p. **1540a**

Channing, Edward, Hart, Albert Bushnell and Turner, Frederick Jackson. Guide to the study and reading of American history. Boston. Ginn. 1912. 650p. **1541**

Chatelain, Verne E. A new national program for the preservation of historic sites in the United States. Pan Am. Inst. Geog. and Hist. 2d general assembly 1935, proc. 415-20. 1937 **1541a**

Chronicles of America. Ed. by Allen Johnson. New Haven. Yale Univ. Press. 1918-21. 50v. (Contents: Huntington, E. The red man's continent; Richman, I. B. The Spanish conquerors; Wood, W. C. H. Elizabethan sea-dogs; Munro, W. B. Crusaders of New France; Johnston, Mary. Pioneers of the old south; Andrews, C. M. The fathers of New England; Goodwin, M. W. Dutch and English on the Hudson; Fisher, S. G. The Quaker colonies; Andrews, C. M. Colonial folk-ways; Wrong, G. M. The conquest of New France; Becker, C. L. The eve of the Revolution; Wrong, G. M. Washington and his comrades; Farrand, Max. The fathers of the constitution; Ford, H. J. Washington and his colleagues; Johnson, Allen. Jefferson and his colleagues; Corwin, E. S. John Marshall and the constitution; Paine, R. D. The fight for a free sea; Skinner, C. L. Pioneers of the old southwest; Ogg, F. A. The old northwest; Ogg, F. A. The reign of Andrew Jackson; Hulbert, A. B. The paths of inland commerce; Skinner, C. L. Adventurers in Oregon; Bolton, H. E. The Spanish borderlands; Stephenson, N. W. Texas and the Mexican war; White, S. E. The forty-niners; Hough, Emerson. The passing of the frontier; Dodd, W. E. The cotton kingdom; Macy, J. The anti-slavery crusade; Stephenson, N. W. Abraham Lincoln and the union; Stephenson, N. W. The day of the Confederacy; Wood, W. C. H. Captains of the Civil war; Fleming, W. L. The sequel of Appomattox; Slosson, E. E. The American spirit in education; Perry, Bliss. The American spirit in literature; Orth, S. P. Our foreigners; Paine, R. D. The old merchant marine; Thompson, Holland. The age of invention; Moody, J. The railroad builders; Hendrick, B. J. The age of big business; Orth, S. J. The armies of labor; Moody, J. The masters of capital; Thompson, Holland. The new south; Orth, S. J. The boss and the machine; Ford, H. J. The Cleveland era; Buck, S. J. The agrarian crusade; Fish, C. R. The path of empire; Howland, H. J. Theodore Roosevelt and his times; Seymour, Charles. Woodrow Wilson and the World war; Skelton, O. D. The Canadian rebellion; Shepherd, W. R. Hispanic nations of the new world) **1542**

Commager, Henry Steele. The literature of American history, 1934-[1935]. The Social stud. XXVI. p233-53 (April 1935); XXVII. p251-68 (April 1936)   **1543**

Coulomb, Charles A. Books on history and government published in the United States. The Hist. outlook; a jour. for readers and teachers of hist. and the social stud. continuing The hist. teachers' mag. II-XXV (Jan. 1911-May 1934) (Mag. changed to The Social stud. in 1934)   **1544**

Current publications received. The Social stud. continuing The Hist. outlook. XXV. no. 6- Oct. 1934-   **1545**

Danforth, George Flavel. Bibliography of books reviewed in leading American periodicals. Bloomington, Ind. Index Publishing Co. 1902-03. 2v.   **1546**

Eberhardt, Fritz. Amerika-literatur; die wichtigsten seit 1900 in deutscher sprache erschienenen werke über Amerika. Leipzig. Verlag von Koehler & Volckmar. 1926. 335p.   **1547**

Foster, W. E. References to the history of presidential administrations, 1789-1885. (Economic tracts no. XVII) N.Y. The Soc. for Pol. Education. 1885. 58p.   **1548**

Gordy, W. F. and Twitchell, W. I. A pathfinder in American history. Boston. Lee and Shepard. 1893. 261p.   **1549**

Grafton index of the titles of books and magazine articles on history, genealogy and biography printed in the United States on American subjects during the year 1909, comprising the quarterly installments published in The Grafton magazine of history and genealogy arranged under one alphabet. N.Y. The Grafton Press. 1910. 68p.   **1550**

Hart, Albert Bushnell. Manual of history, diplomacy, and government of the United States for class use. Cambridge. Harvard Univ. 1908. 554p.   **1551**

Hazen, David W. American history shelves. Portland, Oregon. Priv. printed. 1929. 142p.   **1552**

History of American life. Ed. by Arthur M. Schlesinger and Dixon Ryan Fox. N.Y. Macmillan. 1927- (Contents: Priestley, H. I. The coming of the white man; Wertenbaker, T. J. The first Americans; Adams, J. T. Provincial society; Fish, C. R. The rise of the common man; Cole, A. C. The irrepressible conflict; Nevins, A. The emergence of modern America; Schlesinger, A. M. The rise of the city, 1878-1898; Faulkner, H. U. The quest for social justice; Tarbell, Ida M. The nationalizing of business, 1878-1898)   **1553**

Holt, W. Stull. American historiography. Johns Hopkins Univ. (In progress)   **1554**

Humphrey Press, Inc., W.F. Americana; catalogue of the famous Abbatt reprints. Geneva, N.Y. W. F. Humphrey Press, Inc. 1936. 31p. (Reprints ed. and pub. by William Abbatt and called "Extra numbers" of the Magazine of history)   **1554a**

Institute of International Education. A bibliography on the United States for foreign students. (Bul. 3d ser., no. 3) N.Y. 1922. 50p.   **1554b**

International bibliography of historical sciences, 1926- Ed. for the International Committee of Historical Sciences. Paris, Berlin, London, N.Y. 1930-   **1554c**

Jahresberichte der geschichtswissenschaft, 1878-1913; im auftrage der Historischen gesellschaft zu Berlin herausgegeben. Berlin. E. S. Mittler. 1880-1916. 36 v. in 48.   **1554d**

Jernegan, Marcus Wilson. United States. *In* Guide to historical literature. Ed. by George Matthew Dutcher and others. N.Y. Macmillan. 1931. p 997-1050   **1555**

Johnston, W. Dawson and Mudge, Isadore G. Special collections in libraries in the United States. (U.S. Bureau of Education. Bul. 1912. no. 23) Wash. Govt. Ptg. Off. 1912. 140p.   **1556**

Leland, Waldo Gifford. Descriptive and critical summary of publications dealing with United States history, issued in 1904-5. Berlin. Weidmannsch Buchhandlung. 1907 (Reprinted from the Jahresberichte der geschichtswissenschaft. XXVIII. p213-39)   **1556a**

Lingelbach, William E., ed. Approaches to American social history. N.Y. D. Appleton-Century. 1937. 101p. (Appraisals by Roy F. Nichols, Bernard De Voto, and John A. Krout of the History of American life series edited by Arthur M. Schlesinger and Dixon Ryan Fox)   **1556b**

Literature of American history; a bibliographical guide. Ed. by Joseph N. Larned. Boston. Pub. for the Am. Lib. Asso. by Houghton Mifflin. 1902. 588p. (Supplement for 1900 and 1901. Ed. by Philip P. Wells. 1902. 37p.)   **1557**

Martin, Thomas P. List of references on the history of the United States. Austin, Tex. Univ. of Texas Press. 1924. unpag.   **1558**

Minnesota. University. Survey of materials for research in American history in the Twin cities area. (Prepared by the Hist. dept. unpublished)   **1559**

Nelson, Ernesto. Bibliografía general de las obras referentes a Estados Unidos publicados en dicho país hasta 1933. Buenos Aires. Instituto cultural Argentino Norteamericano. 1934. 160p.   **1560**

New England History Teachers' Association. Historical sources in schools. Report to the New England History Teachers' Association by a select committee. N.Y. Macmillan. 1902. 299p.   **1561**

Pasquet, D. Histoire des États-Unis; bibliographie, ouvrages généraux et période coloniale. Rev. hist. CXXXIX. p232-59 (March 1922)   **1561a**

Préclin, E. Histoire des États-Unis des origines à 1787. Rev. hist. CLXXIV. p269-303, 519-74 (Sept.-Oct., Nov.-Dec. 1934)   **1561b**

Roorbach, Orville, A. ed. Bibliotheca americana; catalogue of American publications, including reprints and original works from 1820 to 1860 inclusive, together with a list of periodicals published in the United States. N.Y. Roorbach. 1852-60. 4v. **1562**

Roos, Jean Carolyn. Background readings for American history; a bibliography for students, librarians and teachers of history. N.Y. H.W. Wilson. 1935. 48p. **1563**

Shaw, Charles B. History—United States. *In* A list of books for college libraries. Chicago. Am. Lib. Asso. 1931. p430-55. Supplement pub. 1940 **1564**

Short, John Thomas. Historical reference lists for the use of students in the Ohio State University. Columbus, Ohio. Smythe. 1882. 96p. **1565**

Sparks, Edwin Erle. Topical reference lists in American history with introductory lists in English constitutional history. Columbus, Ohio. Smythe. 1900. 96p. **1566**

Stock, Leo F. Historical articles in current periodicals. The Hist. outlook. X-XXV (May 1919-May 1934) **1567**

Trübner, Nikolas. Trübner's bibliographical guide to American literature. London. Trübner & Co. 1859. 554p. **1567a**

U.S. Works Progress Administration. Historical records survey. Annotated bibliography of writings in American history. (In preparation) **1567b**

Vincent, John Martin. Contributions toward a bibliography of American history, 1888-92, adopted from reports to the "Jahresbericht der geschichtswissenschaft" of Berlin. Am. Hist. Asso. rep. 1893. p501-72 **1568**

Waldman, Milton. Americana; the literature of American history. N.Y. Holt. 1925. 271p. **1569**

Ward, A. W. and others, eds. General bibliography. *In* The United States. (The Cambridge modern hist. v. VII) N.Y., London. Macmillan. 1903. p753-834 **1570**

Winsor, Justin. Comprehensive printed authorities upon the general and upon some special phases of the history of the United States, 1776-1850. *In* Narrative and critical history of America. Boston, N.Y. Houghton Mifflin. 1889. VIII. p469-508 **1571**

Writings on American history, 1902; an attempt at an exhaustive bibliography of books and articles on United States history published during the year 1902 and some memoranda on other portions of America. Comp. by Ernest Cushing Richardson and Anson Ely Morse. Princeton, N.J. The Lib. Book Store. 1904. 294p. **1572**

Writings on American history, 1903. A bibliography of books and articles on United States history published during the year 1903, with some memoranda on other portions of America. Prepared by Andrew Cunningham McLaughlin, William Adams Slade and Ernest Dorman Lewis. (Carnegie Inst. of Wash. Publication no. 38) Wash. D.C. 1905. 172p. **1573**

Writings on American history, 1906-1936. A bibliography of books and articles on United States and Canadian history published during the years, 1906-36, with some memoranda on other portions of America. Comp. by Grace Gardner Griffin. N.Y. Macmillan. 1908-10 (for years 1906-08); Wash. Govt. Ptg. Off. 1911-13 (years 1909-11 in Am. Hist. Asso. reports. 1909-11); New Haven. Yale Univ. Press. 1914-19. (for years 1912-17); Wash. Govt. Ptg. Off. 1921- (years 1918- in Am. Hist. Asso. reports as supplements) (A general index for the volumes is being compiled by David M. Matteson) **1574**

Periods

BEFORE THE WORLD WAR

Billington, Ray Allen. The literature of Anti-Catholicism. *In* The Protestant crusade, 1800-1860; a study of the origins of American nativism. N.Y. Macmillan. 1938. p345-79 **1574a**

Cuba. Archivo nacional. Inventario general del archivo de la delegacion del Partido revolucionario cubano en Nueva York (1892-1898). Havana. Imp. "El siglo XX" Sociedad editorial Cuba contemporanea. 1921 (Also published in the Boletin del archivo nacional, XVI-XXIX. July-Aug. 1917-Jan.-June 1920) **1574b**

Hacker, Louis Morton and Kendrick, Benjamin B. Bibliography. *In* The United States since 1865. N.Y. Crofts. 1932. p737-62 **1575**

Harkness, Madge E. A selected list of references on the Federal Trade Commission and its activities. George Washington law rev. VIII. p671-707 (Jan., Feb. 1940) **1575a**

Savage, William Sherman. The controversy over the distribution of abolition literature, 1830-1860. Wash. D.C. Association for the Study of Negro Life and History, Inc. 1938. 141p. **1575b**

Simms, Henry H. A critical analysis of abolition literature, 1830-1840. Jour. south. hist. VI. p368-82 (Aug. 1940) **1575c**

U.S. Library of Congress. Division of bibliography. Brief list of references on treasury surplus, 1885-1889. March 15, 1923. 3p. typ. **1576**

—— —— —— List of references on alien and sedition laws, 1798. Feb. 6, 1925. 11p. **1577**

—— —— —— List of references on censorship of the press during the Civil war. March 12, 1917. 3p. typ. **1578**

—— —— —— List of references on finance and taxation during the Civil war. April 23, 1917. 10p. typ. **1579**

U.S. Library of Congress. Division of bibliography. List of references on illegal trade between citizens of the United States and Great Britain during the war of 1812. Jan. 29, 1915. 4p. typ.   **1580**

—— —— —— List of references on soldiers' and sailors' homestead legislation after the Civil war. Nov. 27, 1917. 4p. typ.   **1581**

—— —— —— List of references on the deflation of the currency after the Civil war. July 12, 1920. 3p. typ.   **1582**

—— —— —— List of references on the Hayes-Tilden electoral commission. n.d. 3p. typ.   **1583**

—— —— —— List of references on the [old] Ku Klux Klan. July 25, 1924. 8p. typ.   **1584**

—— —— —— List of references on the social effects of the Civil war. June 24, 1918. 2p. typ.   **1585**

—— —— —— A list of references to material dealing with instances of alleged corruption in governmental affairs, 1861-1921. February 16, 1924. 5p. typ.   **1586**

—— —— —— Select list of references on the Sherman antitrust act of 1890. March 19, 1912. 9p. typ. (Additional references. Jan. 25, 1913. 2p.)   **1587**

WORLD WAR

Allen, Lafon. Lafon Allen collection of posters of the World war. Yale Univ. Lib. gaz. XII. p1-16 (July 1937)   **1587a**

Boston. Public Library. A selected list of references on the reconstruction and re-education of disabled soldiers and sailors in the public library of the city of Boston. (Brief reading lists no. 5. June 1918) Boston. The Trustees. 1918. 22p.   **1587b**

Bureau of Railway Economics. Library. The Railroads' war board; a brief list of references. Wash. D.C. 1925. 13p. typ.   **1588**

Chicago. Public Library. Rehabilitation, mental, physical, vocational, of crippled and disabled soldiers; select list of references to books and periodicals in the Chicago Public Library. Chicago. Chicago Pub. Lib. 1919. 19p.   **1589**

Esterquest, Ralph Theodore. War literature and libraries; the role of the American library in promoting interest in and support of the European war, 1914-1918. (Univ. of Illinois. M.A. thesis) Urbana, Ill. Univ. of Ill. 1940. typ.   **1589a**

Johnson, Ethel M. Women: war time occupations and employment; list of references. Special libraries. IX. p12-16 (Jan. 1918)   **1590**

Koch, Theodore Wesley. Books in the war; the romance of library war service. Boston, N.Y. Houghton Mifflin. 1919. 388p.   **1591**

Leland Stanford Junior University. Library. Hoover library on war, revolution and peace. Annual report, 1928/29-1929/30-Stanford University, Calif. Stanford Univ. Press. 19-   **1591a**

Lutz, Ralph Haswell. La documentation de guerre aux États-Unis. Rev. hist. guerre mondiale. XII. p1-39. 1934   **1591b**

McMurtrie, Douglas C. Abstract—Catalogue of literature on the war blinded. Comp. with the assistance of Alexander Gourvich. (Publications of the Red Cross Inst. for the Blind. ser. 1. no. 5. July 1, 1919) Balt. 1919. 82p.   **1592**

—— A bibliography of the war cripple. N.Y. The Red Cross Inst. for Crippled and Disabled Men. 1918. 41p.   **1593**

Mereness, Newton Dennison. American historical activities during the World war. Am. Hist. Asso. rep. 1919. I. p137-293   **1594**

National Security League. Committee on patriotism through education. America at war; a handbook of patriotic education references. Ed. by Albert Bushnell Hart. N.Y. George H. Doran. 1918 (Bibliog. material on p1-70)   **1595**

New York. Public Library. The war and after. N.Y. Pub. Lib. bul. XXIII-XXIV (Jan. 1919-Dec. 1920)   **1596**

Nims, Marion R. Woman in the war. Wash. Govt. Ptg. Off. 1918. 77p.   **1597**

Princeton University. Library. War posters collection; alphabetical finding list, Jan. 20, 1919. [Princeton. 1919]   **1597a**

Smith, Munroe. War books by American diplomatists. Pol. sci. quar. XXXV. p94-125 (March 1920)   **1597b**

U.S. Housing Corporation. Selected bibliography of industrial housing in America and Great Britain during and after the war. Preprint from War emergency construction (Housing war workers) Rep. of the U.S. Housing Corp. Wash. Govt. Ptg. Off. 1919. p xix (*Also in* U.S. Housing Corporation. War emergency construction (Housing war workers) Rep. of the U.S. Housing Corp. Wash. Govt. Ptg. Off. 1920. II. p. i-xix   **1598**

U.S. Library of Congress. Division of bibliography. Armistice day; a bibliographical list. Nov. 8, 1927. 6p. typ.   **1601**

—— —— —— Brief list of references on the effect of war on contracts (with special reference to the European war). March 13, 1919. 5p. typ.   **1604**

—— —— —— Brief list of references on the hospitalization of soldiers and sailors of the United States in the World war. April 4, 1922. 5p. mim.   **1605**

—— —— —— Brief list of references on the moral effects of the European war. Jan. 29, 1923. 3p. typ.   **1606**

—— —— —— Brief list of references on the response of America to the World war. Feb. 18, 1920. 6p. typ. (Additional references. Nov. 26, 1923. 2p.)   **1607**

—— —— —— Conscription of wealth in time of war; a bibliographical list. Oct. 22, 1927. 4p. typ.   **1608**

—— —— —— List of references on armed merchant vessels. March 7, 1916. 7p. typ.   **1609**

—— —— —— List of references on nursing in the European war and training of nurses for war service. Aug. 24, 1917. 7p. typ. **1610**

—— —— —— List of references on trading with the enemy. June 27, 1917. 5p. typ. **1611**

—— —— —— List of references on trading with the enemy act. Jan. 16, 1923. 8p. mim. **1612**

—— —— —— List of references on warsaving, thrift and business as usual (with reference to the European war). April 22, 1918. 15p. typ. (Additional references. 1918. 3p.) **1613**

—— —— —— List of references on woman's work in the European war (exclusive of Red Cross activities). Jan. 10, 1918. 15p. typ. (Supplement. Nov. 2, 1918. 13p. typ.) **1614**

—— —— —— List of references on the attitude of the United States towards the war. July 15, 1919. 3p. typ. **1615**

—— —— —— List of references on the commerce in munitions of war between the United States and European belligerents, 1914-1915. Oct. 29, 1915. 5p. typ. **1616**

—— —— —— List of references on the cost of the European war. 1918. 12p. dupl. **1617**

—— —— —— List of references on the effect of the entrance of the United States into the war on the financial affairs of the country. Nov. 7, 1917. 3p. typ. **1618**

—— —— —— List of references on the financial influence of the European war, especially on the United States. Sept. 8, 1915. 4p. typ. **1619**

—— —— —— List of references on the financing of private enterprises by the government in war time. May 13, 1918. 6p. typ. **1620**

—— —— —— List of references on the mobilization and control of industries for national defense. April 5, 1917. 12p. typ. (Additional references. June 14, 1917. 2p. typ.) **1621**

—— —— —— List of references on the mobilization of farm labor for war service. Feb. 23, 1918. 9p. dupl. **1622**

—— —— —— List of references on the relief of dependent families and sailors (with special reference to the European war). May 11, 1917. 8p. dupl. **1622a**

—— —— —— List of references on the return of alien property. April 3, 1925. 4p. typ. **1622b**

—— —— —— List of references on the trade of the United States as affected by the war (Supplementary to lists published in Special libraries for Dec. 1914 and Sept. 1916, and the typewritten list of Oct. 5, 1917). Sept. 30, 1921. 7p. typ. **1623**

—— —— —— List of references on the training and rehabilitation of disabled or injured men. July 19, 1917. 8p. dupl. (Supplement. Oct. 21, 1918. 13p. dupl.) **1624**

—— —— —— List of references on the universities and colleges and the war. May 22, 1918. 8p. dupl. **1524a**

—— —— —— List of references on the War Finance Corporation. Dec. 6, 1921. 6p. typ. **1625**

—— —— —— List of references on the work of the Red Cross in the European war. April 3, 1917. 7p. typ. **1626**

—— —— —— Select list of references on war finance with special reference to loans and war taxes, etc. Aug. 30, 1918. 8p. mim. **1627**

—— —— —— The War Industries Board: a bibliographical list. Jan. 12, 1932. 16p. typ. **1628**

—— —— —— The War Trade Board: a bibliographical list. June 25, 1934. 4p. typ. **1629**

SINCE THE WORLD WAR

Beardsley, Arthur S. A selected bibliography of legal and other materials relating to the National industrial recovery act. Law lib. jour. XXVII. p15-31 (April 1934) **1630**

Beardsley, Arthur S. and Orman, Oscar C. Bibliography of selected materials relating to the legislation of the New Deal. Seattle, Wash. Univ. Book Store. 1935. 111p. mim. **1631**

Blegen, Theodore C. Some aspects of historical work under the New Deal. Miss. Valley hist. rev. XXI. p195-206 (Sept. 1934) (C.W.A. surveys and other historical activities) **1632**

California. University. Bureau of public administration. Labor under the New Deal: a selected bibliography, including analyses of labor organization periodicals. Comp. by Dorothy Campbell Culver. Berkeley. 1934. 58p. mim. **1633**

Cam, Gilbert Arthur. The social security act; a selected reading list. New York Pub. Lib. bul. XLI. p292-8 (April 1937) **1633a**

Carnegie Endowment for International Peace. Library. Conscription of men, material resources and wealth in time of war; with select references on war profiteering. Comp. by Mary Alice Matthews. Wash. D.C. 1940. 15p. **1633b**

Culver, Dorothy Campbell. Administration and organization in wartime in the United States: a bibliography. (Public Administration Service. Publication no. 71) Chicago. Public Admin. Service. 1940. 17p. **1633c**

—— Selected descriptive list of sources for the study of federal administration. (?) 1935 **1634**

George, John J. Literature of the New Deal. National municipal rev. XXIII. p340-2 (June 1934) **1635**

Lincoln, Mildred E. Foundations of NYA guidance, including bibliographies and annotated references. . . National Youth Administration, New York state (exclusive of New York City). . . June 1, 1937. [Albany. 1937] 100p. reprod. **1635a**

McClellan, Corbett. Bibliography of legal problems attending recovery legislation. Indiana law jour. IX. p570-81 (June 1934)
1636

Owen, Thomas M., Jr. The American legion —a bibliography. The National Archives, Wash. D.C. In progress   **1636a**

Perry, Donald. A bibliography on the constitutional aspects of the recovery program. Law lib. jour. XXVIII. p9-27 (Jan. 1935)   **1637**

Rugg, Harold Ordway. Study guide to national recovery; an introduction to economic problems. N.Y. John Day. 1933. 48p.   **1638**

St. Louis. Public Library. After the war; a selected reading list on peace and reconstruction. By Margaret L. Pilcher. St. Louis. St. Louis Pub. Lib. 1919. 20p. (Reprinted from St. Louis Pub. Lib. monthly bul. n.s. XVII. no. 2. p57-75. Feb. 1919)   **1639**

Stern, B. W. List of references on National Labor Relations Board. . . [Wash. D.C. 1937] 11p. reprod.   **1639a**

Turner, Mrs V. B. List of references on reconstruction. Monthly labor rev. VII. 1529-61 (Dec. 1918)   **1640**

U.S. Bureau of Agricultural Economics. Library. Agricultural relief: a selected and annotated bibliography. Comp. under the direction of Margaret T. Olcott. (Agricultural economics bibliog. no. 50) Wash. D.C. 1933. 382p. mim.   **1641**

—— —— —— The domestic allotment plans for the relief of agriculture: selected references. Comp. by Louise O. Bercaw under the direction of Mary G. Lacy. (Agricultural economics bibliog. no. 41) Wash. D.C. 1933. 48p. mim.   **1642**

—— —— —— Farmers' strikes and riots in the United States, 1932-1933; a list of references in the library, Bureau of Agricultural Economics, U.S. Department of Agriculture. Wash. D.C. 1933. 30p. mim.   **1643**

U.S. Department of Labor. Library. The Public contracts (Walsh-Healey) act; selected references. Comp. by Eleanor M. Mitchell. Wash. D.C. Oct. 1940. 16p. processed   **1643a**

U.S. Farm Credit Administration. Library. A selected list of references on the Farm Credit Administration. Comp. by Robert Haven Willey . . . under the direct supervision of Miriam C. Vance. Wash. D.C. 1935. 56p. photoprinted   **1644**

U.S. Geological Survey. Library. References on The federal emergency administration of public works and its work including The Public works housing division. Comp. by James T. Rubey and William H. Heers. (Bibliog. list. no. 2) Wash. D.C. March 1, 1936. mim.   **1645**

U.S. Library of Congress. Division of bibliography. The banking situation, 1933, including the banking act, 1933. October 25, 1933. 4p. typ.   **1646**

—— —— —— The business situation, 1929-1931, and its recovery, a select list of references. October 12, 1931. 31p. mim.
1647

—— —— —— Citations to debates in Senate and House of Representatives on the soldiers' bonus, 1918-1930. May 29, 1933. 15p. typ.   **1648**

—— —— —— Economic conditions in the United States: a list of recent references. Sept. 19, 1932. 32p. mim.   **1649**

—— —— —— Index to remarks (as printed in the Congressional record) relating to veterans affairs. (73 Cong. 1st sess.) July 19, 1933. 31p.   **1650**

—— —— —— A list of recent books on contemporary American history and politics. July 21, 1924. 6p. typ.   **1651**

—— —— —— A list of references on distribution and the N.R.A. June 1, 1934. 16p. typ.   **1652**

—— —— —— A list of references on N.R.A. and the lumber industry. July 22, 1935. 15p. typ.   **1653**

—— —— —— A list of references on priorities. Comp. by Grace H. Fuller. Oct. 26, 1940. 16p. processed   **1653a**

—— —— —— List of references on soldiers' bonus. Jan. 10, 1922. 10p. mim. (Supplement. Nov. 3, 1923. 14p. mim.)
1654

—— —— —— List of references on soldiers' bonuses. Dec. 29, 1920. 4p. multig.
1655

—— —— —— A list of references on the bituminous coal conservation acts of 1935 and 1937. Supplement. Comp. by Florence S. Hellman. Jan. 11, 1938. 18p. typ.
1655a

—— —— —— A list of references on the Guffey-Snyder bituminous coal conservation act of 1935. March 16, 1936. 11p. typ. (Supplement. Jan. 11, 1938. 18p. mim.)   **1656**

—— —— —— List of references on the Knights of the Ku Klux Klan (exclusive of the original Ku Klux Klan, but including Night Riders). Feb. 16, 1923. 6p. typ.   **1657**

—— —— —— A list of references on the Ku Klux Klan. July 24, 1924. 9p. typ.
1658

—— —— —— A list of references on the Robinson-Patman Price Discrimination Act. Comp. by Ann Duncan Brown. [Wash. D.C. 1937] 29p. reprod. (Supplement. 1938. 22p. mim.)   **1658a**

—— —— —— A list of references on the Securities act of 1933. March 5, 1935. 12p. typ.   **1659**

—— —— —— A list of references on the Securities exchange act of 1934. July 10, 1935. 6p. typ.   **1660**

—— —— —— List of references on the settlement of soldiers and sailors on the land. March 26, 1919. 11p. mim.   **1661**

—— —— —— List of references on the Teapot Dome oil controversy. Sept. 26, 1923. 3p. typ.   **1662**

—— —— —— A list of references on the transportation act of 1920 (Supplementary to the list compiled by the library of the Interstate Commerce Commission, July 18, 1923). Dec. 26, 1923. 10p. typ. **1663**

—— —— —— A list of references on the United States Civilian Conservation Corps. March 4, 1936. 26p. mim. (Supplement. June 1937. 13p. reprod.) **1664**

—— —— —— List of speeches as printed in the Congressional record on the accomplishment of the Harding administration and Congress. April 10, 1923. 3p. typ. **1665**

—— —— —— List of United States documents relating to the relief and rehabilitation of soldiers, sailors and marines of the World war. Jan. 6, 1923. 12p. mim. **1666**

—— —— —— Select list of references on economic reconstruction, including reports of the British Ministry of Reconstruction. Wash. Govt. Ptg. Off. 1919. 47p. **1667**

—— —— —— A selected list of references on the New Deal. Comp. by Florence S. Hellman. June 14, 1940. 71p. mim. **1667a**

—— —— —— The Tennessee Valley authority: a bibliographical list of references. Dec. 6, 1933. 13p. typ. **1668**

—— —— —— War relief organizations in the United States relating to the European war, 1939—: pamphlets and articles in periodicals. Comp. by Ann D. Brown. April 30, 1941. 17p. typ. **1668a**

—— —— —— Youth movements in the United States and foreign countries, including a section on the National Youth Administration. June 12, 1936. 46p. mim. **1669**

—— —— **Legislative reference service.** Acts of Congress, executive orders, and proclamations from March 4, 1933, relating to money and monetary policy. N.Y. Pub. Affairs Information Service. 1935. 5p. typ. **1670**

—— —— **Reading room.** List of recent references on business recovery with special reference to the National industrial recovery act, 1933. By James T. Rubey. Aug. 10, 1933. 13p. typ. (Supplements. Sept. 1, 1933. 18p.; April 15, 1934. 71p.) **1671**

U.S. Social Security Board. Library. A brief reading list on the Social Security Act, including references on the amendments of 1939. (Informational service circular 33) Wash. Govt. Ptg. Off. 1939. 12p. **1671a**

U.S. Superintendent of Documents. List of United States government emergency agency publications available for selection by depository libraries. Wash. D.C. 1934. 8p. **1672**

U.S. Work Projects Administration. Library. Chronology of federal relief legislation, 1932-1939. Wash. D.C. Dec. 1939. **15p.** **1672a**

CHAPTER IV

DIPLOMATIC HISTORY

SOURCES

Hasse, Adelaide Rosalie. Index to United States documents relating to foreign affairs, 1828-1861. Wash. D.C. Carnegie Inst. of Wash. 1914-21. 3v. **1673**

Index to claimants before the Court of Commissioners of Alabama Claims. Wash. D.C. 1877. 180p. **1673a**

Miller, David Hunter. Bibliography of United States treaty collections—List of documents in the edition—List of the treaty series—Chronological list of proclamations affecting treaty relations—Classified list of proclamations affecting treaty relations. *In* Treaties and other international acts of the United States of America. Wash. Govt. Ptg. Off. 1931. I (short print) p39-173 **1674**

—— Writings cited. *In* Treaties and other international acts of the United States of America. Wash. Govt. Ptg. Off. 1931-37. II. p. xxiii-xxix; III. p. xiii-xxiv; IV. p. xiii-xxvi; V. p. xiii-xxxii **1675**

Myers, Denys Peter. Manual of collections of treaties and of collections relating to treaties. Cambridge. Harvard Univ. Press; London. Humphrey Milford. 1922. 685p. **1676**

United States. Alphabetical list of the documents and correspondence submitted with the cases and counter cases of the United States and of Great Britain to the Tribunal of arbitration at Geneva. [Geneva? 1872] 3,259,34,24p. **1676a**

U.S. Congress. Senate. List of arbitration treaties and conventions submitted to and acted upon by the United States Senate. Senate document no. 373. 62 Cong. 2 sess. 1912. Ser. 6175. 7p. **1677**

U.S. Court of Commissioners of Alabama Claims. Alphabetical index to the list of claims of the Court of Commissioners of Alabama Claims. N.Y. Trow's. 1883. 31p. **1677a**

U.S. Department of State. Catalogue of treaties, 1814-1918. Wash. Govt. Ptg. Off. 1919. 716p. **1678**

—— —— Index to the United States treaty series from March 4, 1923 to February 28, 1929, nos. 667-777. Comp. in the Dept. of State. Wash. D.C. 1929. 74p. autog. from typ. copy **1679**

—— —— A list of commercial treaties and conventions and agreements effected by exchange of notes or declarations, in force between the United States and other countries. Corrected to August 1, 1928. Am. jour. of international law.

XXII. supplement. p196-203. 1928 (Also issued separately autog. from typ. copy) **1680**

—— —— A list of consular conventions and articles concerning consular officers in treaties other than consular conventions in force between the United States and other countries. Corrected to November 1, 1926 [Wash. D.C. 1926] 9p. autog. from typ. copy **1681**

—— —— List of papers concerning foreign relations, printed by order of Congress. . . *In* Register of the Department of State, 1882-1903. Wash. Govt. Ptg. Off. 1882-1903 **1682**

—— —— List of so-called Bryan peace treaties. Wash. D.C. 1924. 5p. mim. **1683**

—— —— A list of treaties and other international acts of the United States of America in force December 31, 1932. (Treaty information, Dec. 31, 1932, supplement to bul. no. 39) Wash. Govt. Ptg. Off. 1933. 172p. **1683a**

—— —— List of treaties, conventions, exchanges of notes, and other international agreements in force between the United States and other powers in relation to China. Wash. Govt. Ptg. Off. 1925. 7p. **1684**

—— —— List of treaties submitted to the Senate, 1789-1931 which have not gone into force, October 1, 1932. (Publication no. 382) Wash. Govt. Ptg. Off. 1932. 25p. **1685**

—— —— List of treaties submitted to the Senate, 1789-1934. (Dept. of State. Publication no. 765) Wash. Govt. Ptg. Off. 1936. 138p. **1686**

—— —— List of treaties submitted to the Senate, 1935; procedure during 1935 on, and status of, certain treaties submitted to the Senate, 1923-1934. (Dept. of State. Publication no. 817) Wash. Govt. Ptg. Off. 1936. 7p. (cont.) **1687**

—— —— Revised list of claims filed with the Department of State, growing out of the acts committed by the several vessels, which have given rise to the claims generically known as the Alabama claims. Wash. Govt. Ptg. Off. 1872. 399p. **1687a**

—— —— Subject index of the treaty series and the executive agreement series, July 1, 1931. Wash. Govt. Ptg. Off. 1932. 214p. **1688**

—— —— A tentative list of treaty collections. Wash. Govt. Ptg. Off. 1919. 103p. **1689**

GENERAL

American Association for International Conciliation. Monthly bulletin of books, pamphlets, and magazine articles dealing with international relations, April, 1908-April, 1913. N.Y. 1908-13 **1690**

Barnes, Harry E. and Langer, William L. Some recent books on international affairs. Foreign affairs. I- Sept. 15, 1922- **1691**

Bemis, Samuel Flagg, ed. Bibliographical notes. *In* The American Secretaries of State. N.Y. Knopf. 1927-29. 10v. **1692**

Bemis, Samuel Flagg and Griffin, Grace Gardner. Guide to the diplomatic history of the United States, 1775-1921. Wash. Govt. Ptg. Off. 1935. 979p. **1693**

Bradley, Phillips. Literature of international relations and political ideas, 1939 and 1940. Soc. educ. V. p204-12 (March 1941) **1693a**

Brooks, Arthur A. Foreign affairs; an American quarterly review. Index, volumes 1-10, September, 1922-July, 1932. N.Y. Foreign affairs. 1934. 182p. **1694**

Carnegie Endowment for International Peace. Library. The Department of State; with supplement concerning treaties between the United States and other powers. (Comp. by Mary Alice Matthews. (Select bibliographies no. 6) Wash. D.C. 1936. 9p. mim. **1695**

—— —— Diplomacy, select list of works in English on diplomacy, diplomatic and consular practice, and foreign office organization. Comp. by M. Alice Matthews. (Select bibliographies no. 4. March 5, 1936) Wash. D.C. 1936. 15p. mim. **1696**

—— —— Hoover-Stimson doctrine (nonrecognition policy). (Reading list. miscellaneous no. 53) Wash. D.C. 1934. 2p. typ. **1697**

—— —— Neutrality and American policy on neutrality, with select references on contraband of war, embargo on arms, and freedom of the seas. M. Alice Matthews, librarian. (Brief reading list. no. 5) Wash. D.C. 1935. 11p. mim. **1698**

—— —— Some American statesmen and world peace. (Reading lists. miscellaneous no. 50) Wash. D.C. 1933. 7p. typ. **1699**

Council on Foreign Relations. Recent books on international relations, April 1938. N.Y. 1938. 19p. **1699a**

—— Business branch. Selected bibliography. *In* The United States in world affairs; an account of American foreign relations, 1931- . N.Y. Harper. 1932- **1700**

Fish, Carl Russell. An introduction to the history of American diplomacy. (Helps for students of history no. 19. ed. by C. Johnson and J. P. Whitney) London. Society for Promoting Christian Knowledge; N.Y. Macmillan. 1919. 63p. **1701**

Great Britain. Foreign Office. Library. Catalogue of printed books in the library of the Foreign Office. London. H.M. Stationery Off. 1926. 1587p. **1702**

Hart, Albert Bushnell. A trial bibliography of American diplomacy. Am. hist. rev. VI. p848-66 (July 1901) (*Also in* The foundations of American foreign policy. N.Y. Macmillan. 1901. p241-93) **1703**

Langer, William L. and Armstrong, Hamilton Fish. Foreign affairs bibliography; a selected and annotated list of books on international relations, 1919-1932. N.Y., London. Pub. by Harper for Council on Foreign Relations, Inc. 1933. 551p. **1704**

Recent books on international relations. Foreign affairs. I-. (Sept. 15, 1922-) **1704a**

Research Center on International Affairs and by the International Institute of Intellectual Cooperation. Bulletin bibliographique de documentation internationale contemporaine, Bibliographical bulletin of international affairs, Jan./Feb. 1926-Dec. 1928. Paris. Les presses universitaires de France. 1926-28. Issued by the Research Center on International Affairs and by the European center of the Carnegie Endowment for International Peace, Jan. 1929- (Preceded by Bulletin de l'Office de documentation internationale contemporaine 1925 and by Bulletin de documentation internationale contemporaine, 1922-1924, pub. by the Bibliothèque musée de la guerre) **1705**

Savord, Ruth. Directory of American agencies concerned with the study of international affairs. N.Y. Council on Foreign Relations, Inc. 1931. 138p. **1706**

Schmeckebier, Laurence F. International organizations in which the United States participates. (The Inst. for Govt. Research. Stud. in administration. no. 30) Wash. D.C. The Brookings Inst. 1935. 370p. **1707**

Sturdy, Henry Francis. A collection of nuclear bibliographies of the dynamic problems in world affairs for general line course students. [Annapolis. 1927] 18p. **1708**

U.S. Bureau of Rolls and Library. A list of books, pamphlets, and maps received at the library of the Department of State, by purchase, exchange, and gift. . ., with reference to articles in periodicals relating to the law of nations; diplomacy, history and political science; supplemented by a list of newspapers and periodicals received. Wash. D.C. 1893-1906. nos. 1-32 **1709**

—— —— A list of books received at the library of the Department of State. . . with references to international treaties and articles on subjects relative to the law of nations and diplomacy in magazines, no. 1-11, July 1886-Sept. 1887. Wash. D.C. 1886-87. 11v. in 1 **1710**

U.S. Library of Congress. Division of bibliography. Brief list of references on the ratification of treaties by a majority of the Senate instead of by two-thirds. Jan. 5, 1922. 3p. typ. **1712**

U.S. Library of Congress. Division of bibliography. Democratic control of foreign affairs: a bibliographical list. Oct. 28, 1927. 22p. mim. **1713**

—— —— Foreign relations of the United States; a bibliographical list. May 21, 1929. 24p. mim. (List of recent references. April 1935. 23p. mim.; Dec. 5, 1940. 55p. mim.) **1714**

—— —— —— List of articles in recent periodicals and newspapers on the present foreign policy of the United States and its relationship with other governments. Dec. 15, 1922. 6p. mim. **1715**

—— —— —— List of references on American diplomacy. Feb. 26, 1925. 6p. typ. **1716**

—— —— —— List of references on diplomacy. May 25, 1923. 17p. typ. **1717**

—— —— —— A list of the references on the diplomacy of the United States, 1789-1823. April 1, 1924. 14p. typ. **1718**

—— —— —— List of references on the international relations of the United States from a historical viewpoint. Jan. 5, 1921. 5p. multig. **1719**

—— —— —— List of references on the treaty-making power. Comp. under the direction of H. H. B. Meyer. Wash. Govt. Ptg. Off. 1920. 219p. **1719a**

—— —— —— A list of references on the treaty-making power as regards revenue. 1908? 9p. typ. **1720**

—— —— —— List of references on the United States consular service, with appendix on consular systems of foreign countries. Wash. Govt. Ptg. Off. 1905. 27p. **1721**

—— —— —— List of references on the United States diplomatic and consular service, 1913-1920. Jan. 18, 1921. 9p. multig. **1722**

—— —— —— Powers of the president of the United States, with special reference to foreign relations; a brief list. Oct. 9, 1929. 3p. typ. **1723**

—— —— —— References for use in connection with a study club programme on international problems of the United States. June 27, 1929. 46p. typ. **1724**

—— —— —— Revision of treaties; a bibliographical list. June 15, 1931. 7p. typ. **1725**

—— —— —— Select list of recent references on the consular service. Feb. 1, 1913. 8p. typ. **1726**

Ware, Edith E. The study of international relations in the United States; survey for 1934. Published for the American national committee on intellectual cooperation of The League of nations. N.Y. Columbia Univ. Press. 1934. 503p. Survey for 1937. 1938. 540p. **1727**

Winsor, Justin. Editorial notes on the sources of information—The diplomacy of the United States. *In* Narrative and critical history of the United States. Boston; N.Y. Houghton Mifflin. 1888. VII. p513-28 **1728**

World Peace Foundation. International books news, Jan. 1928-. Boston. 1928- **1729**

—— International relations publications available from a group of American organizations. Boston. 1927. 71p. **1730**

Wriston, Henry Merritt. Agents to international conferences. *In* Executive agents in American foreign relations. Balt. Johns Hopkins Univ. Press; London. Humphrey Milford, Oxford Univ. Press. 1929. p572-618 **1731**

AFRICA

Ashbee, Henry Spencer. A bibliography of Tunisia from the earliest times to the end of 1888 (in two parts) including Utica and Carthage, the Punic Wars, the Roman occupation, the Arab conquest, the expeditions of Louis IX and Charles V and the French protectorate. London. Dulau & Co. 1889. 144p. **1732**

Ceccherini, Ugo. Bibliografia della Libia (in continuazione all "Bibliografia della Libia" di F. Minutilli). Roma. Tipografia nazionale di G. Bertero e c 1915. 204p. **1733**

Minutilli, Federico. Bibliografia della Libia; catalogo alfabetico e metodico di tutte le pubblicazioni . . . confinanti regioni del deserto. Torino. Fratelli Bocca editori. 1903. 136p. **1734**

Playfair, Sir R. Lambert. A bibliography of Algeria from the expedition of Charles V in 1541 to 1887. (Royal Geog. Soc. Supplementary pap. II. pt. 2. London. John Murray. 1889. p129-430 (Supplement to 1895. London. 1898. 321p.) **1735**

—— The bibliography of the Barbary states, pt. I: Tripoli and the Cyrenaica. Royal Geog. Soc. Supplementary. pap. II. p557-614. 1889 **1736**

Playfair, Sir R. Lambert and Brown, Robert. A bibliography of Morocco, from the earliest times to the end of 1891. (Royal Geog. Soc. Supplementary pap. III. pt. 3) London. John Murray. 1893. p201-476 **1737**

Rouard de Card, Edgard. Livres français des XVIIe & XVIIIe siècles concernant les États Barbaresques; regences d'Alger, de Tunis, de Tripoli, et empire de Maroc. Paris. A. Pedone. 1911. 36p. (Supplément. . . Paris. A. Pedone. 1917. 24p.) **1738**

U.S. Engineer School. Library. The South African War, 1899-1902; a bibliography of books and articles in periodicals with an index to authors and titles. Prepared by Henry E. Haferkorn. Wash. Barracks, D.C., Fort Humphreys, Va. 1924. 72p. **1739**

U.S. Library of Congress. Division of bibliography. List of books in the Library of Congress on the Boer war. *In* U.S. General staff, 2d division. Selected translations pertaining to the Boer war. Wash. Govt. Ptg. Off. 1905. p207-31 **1740**

—— —— —— List of books on Liberia in the Library of Congress. n.d. 11p. typ. (Additional references. Aug. 3, 1914. 3p.) **1741**

CANADA

Canada. Archives. Bibliography of materials at the Public Archives of Canada relating to the rebellion of 1837-38. *In* Report of the public archives, 1939. Ottawa. 1940. p63-113 **1741a**

—— —— Inventory of the military documents in the Canadian archives. Prepared by Lieut. Col. Cruikshank. Published by authority of the minister of agriculture under the direction of the archivist. (Publications of the Canadian archives no. 2) Ottawa. Govt. Ptg. Bureau. 1910. 370p. **1742**

Hasse, Adelaide Rosalie. The northeastern boundary; references to (selected) maps, documents, reports and other papers in the New York Public Library relating to the north eastern boundary controversy. N.Y. Pub. Lib. bul. IV. p391-411 (Dec. 1900) **1743**

Long, Robert J. Bibliography of Nova Scotia. Orange, N.J. 1918. 312p. **1744**

MacFarlane, W. G. New Brunswick bibliography; the books and writers of the province. St. John, N.B. 1895. 98p. **1745**

Severance, Frank H. Contributions towards a bibliography of the Niagara region; the Upper Canada rebellion of 1837-'38; being an appendix to volume five. Buffalo Hist. Soc. publications. V. p427-95. 1902 **1746**

Staton, Frances M. Some unusual sources of information in the Toronto Reference Library on the Canadian rebellions of 1837-38. Ontario Hist. Soc. pap. and rec. XVII. p58-73. 1919 **1747**

Toronto. Public Library. The rebellion of 1837-38; a bibliography of the sources of information in the public reference library of the city of Toronto, Canada. Toronto. 1924. 81p. **1748**

U.S. Library of Congress. Division of bibliography. Brief list of references on Canadians in the United States. June 19, 1925. 4p. typ. **1749**

—— —— List of books on reciprocity with Canada. Comp. under the direction of A.P.C. Griffin. Wash. Govt. Ptg. Off. 1907. 14p. (Additional references. Comp. under the direction of H.H.B. Meyer. 1911. 44p.) **1750**

—— —— List of references on the arbitration of Canadian fisheries disputes. Nov. 29, 1920. 19p. typ. **1751**

—— —— A list of references on the tariff relations between the United States and Canada. Feb. 14, 1931. 6p. typ. **1752**

—— —— Select list of reference on the annexation of Canada to the United States. 1907. 8p. typ. **1753**

—— —— —— Select list of references on the commercial and treaty relations of the United States and Canada, with special references to the Great Lakes. 1910? 4p. typ. **1754**

EUROPE

Allied and associated powers. Treaty with Germany, June 28, 1919. Index to the treaty of peace between the Allied and associated powers and Germany, signed at Versailles, June 28, 1919. (Great Britain. Foreign Office. Treaty ser. 1920. no. 1) London. H.M. Stationery Off. 1920. 59p. **1755**

Almond, Nina and Lutz, Ralph Haswell. An introduction to a bibliography of the Paris Peace Conference; collections of sources, archive publications and source books. (Hoover War Lib. Bibliog. ser. II) Stanford Univ. Stanford Univ. Press; London. Humphrey Milford, Oxford Univ. Press. 1935. 32p. **1756**

American Library in Paris. Reference service on international affairs. Official publications of European governments. Paris. 1926. 283p. mim. **1757**

Angell, Pauline K. Some of the more recent books and articles dealing with the problems of the settlement. *In* Balch, Emily Greene. Approaches to the great settlement. . . Published for the American union against militarism. N.Y. B.W. Huebsch. 1918. p315-51 **1758**

Binkley, Robert C. Ten years of peace conference' history. Jour. of modern hist. I. p607-29 (Dec. 1929) **1759**

Boston. Public Library. French spoliations. Boston Pub. Lib. bul. VI. p393-402 (May 1885) **1760**

—— —— A league of nations; selected references to recent books and magazines in the public library of the city of Boston. (Brief reading list no. 7. Feb. 1919) Boston. The Trustees. 1919. 22p. **1761**

Bouglé, Célestin C. A. Le guide de l'étudiant en matière de Société des nations: livres-revues-écoles. Paris. Marcel Rivière. 1933. 131p. **1762**

Carnegie Endowment for International Peace. Library. Anglo-American alliance. Comp. by Mary A. Matthews. Wash. 1938. 5p. mim. **1762a**

—— —— Anglo-American relations, 1776 to 1934. M. Alice Matthews, librarian. (Brief reference list no. 4) Wash. D.C. 1935. 4p. mim. **1763**

—— —— League of nations covenant. (Reading list no. 1a) Wash. D.C. 1928 **1764**

—— —— Multilateral treaty for renunciation of war. M. Alice Matthews, librarian. (Reading list no. 26) Wash. D.C. 1929. 10p. mim. **1765**

—— —— War debt problems, with special reference to France. (Reading list no.10) Wash. D.C. 1927. 9p. mim. **1766**

Childs, James Bennett. Foreign government publications; survey of the more important accessions during the fiscal year ended June 30, 1927. Wash. D.C. 1928. 9p.   **1767**

Davenport, Frances Gardiner and Paullin, Charles Oscar. European treaties bearing on the history of the United States and its dependencies [1455-1815]. Wash. D.C. Carnegie Inst. of Wash. 1917-37. 4v. (A bibliography precedes each treaty)   **1767a**

DeWolf, Francis Colt. General synopsis of treaties of arbitration, conciliation, judicial settlement, security and disarmament, actually in force between countries invited to the disarmament conference. Wash. D.C. Carnegie Endowment for International Peace. 1933. 201p. **1768**

Gooch, George Peabody. Recent revelations of European diplomacy. London, N.Y. Longmans, Green. 1930. 218p. **1769**

Great Britain. Index to the case, counter-case, and argument or summary, and to the seven volumes of appendix, presented on the part of the government of Her Britannic Majesty. [London. 1872?] 69p. (Alabama claims)   **1769a**

Great Britain. Historical Manuscripts Commission. Report on the manuscripts of Earl Bathurst preserved at Cirencester Park. London. H.M. Stationery Off. printed by T.B. Hart, ltd. 1923. 788p.   **1770**

Great Britain. Public Record Office. List of Foreign office records to 1878, preserved in the Public Record Office. (Lists and indexes no. LII) London. H.M. Stationery Off. 1929 (U.S. material on p5-23)   **1771**

Gregory, Winifred. List of the serial publications of foreign governments, 1815-1931. Ed. for the Am. Council of Learned Societies. Am. Lib. Asso., National Research Council. N.Y. H. W. Wilson. 1932. 720p.   **1772**

Kircheisen, Frederic M. Bibliographie du temps de Napoléon, comprenant l'histoire des États-Unis. Paris. Honoré Champion; Genève. F. M. Kircheisen; London. Sampson Low, Marston. 1908, 1912. 2v.   **1773**

League of Nations. Secretariat. Library. Books on the work of the League of Nations catalogued in the library of the secretariat. Geneva. 1928. 274p. **1774**

—— —— —— List of works relating to the mandates system and the territories under mandate catalogued in the library of the League of Nations. Geneva. 1930. 106p.   **1775**

—— —— —— Monthly list of books catalogued in the library. Geneva. 1928-32. 5v.   **1776**

Leland Stanford Junior University. Library. Hoover library on war, revolution and peace. A catalogue of Paris Peace Conference delegation propaganda in the Hoover War Library. (Stanford Univ.

publications. Hoover War Lib. Bibliog. ser. I) Stanford Univ. Stanford Univ. Press. 1926. 96p.   **1777**

Lingelbach, William Ezra. Historical investigation and the commercial history of the Napoleonic era. Am. hist. rev. XIX. p257-81 (Jan. 1914)   **1778**

Lutz, Ralph Haswell. Bibliographical article—Studies of World war propaganda, 1914-33. Jour. modern hist. V. p496-516 (Dec. 1933)   **1779**

Moon, Parker Thomas. Syllabus on international relations. N.Y. Macmillan. 1925. 276p.   **1780**

National Board for Historical Service. Peace and reconstruction; preliminary bibliography. *In* A League of nations, II, Special number. Boston. World Peace Foundation [1919] 37p. (Also in Hist. outlook. X. p151-67. March 1919)   **1781**

New York. Public Library. Armenia and the Armenians; a list of references in the New York Public Library. Comp. by Ida A. Pratt under the direction of Richard Gottheil. N.Y. 1919. 96p. (Reprinted with additions from the Bul. XXIII. p124-43. March-May 1919)   **1782**

—— —— Diplomatic history of the European war; a list of references in the New York Public Library. Comp. by Rollin A. Sawyer, Jr. N.Y. 1917. 21p. (Reprinted from the Bul. XXI. p413-31. June 1917)   **1783**

Pittsburgh. Carnegie Library. Pan-Germanism. Monthly bul. XXII. p786-91 (Dec. 1917)   **1784**

Rockwell, William W. Armenia; a list of books and articles. White Plains, N.Y. H. W. Wilson. 1916. 8p.   **1785**

Sawyer, Rollin A., Jr. The Bank for international settlements; a list of references. N.Y. Pub. Lib. bul. XXXVI. p229-42 (April 1932)   **1786**

Sveistrup, Hans. Die schuldenlast des weltkrieges; quellen- und literatur-nachweis zu den interalliierten kriegsschulden, den reparationen und dem Dawesplan, 1918-1930. Im auftrage der Preussischen Staatsbibliothek bearbeitet von Hans Sveistrup. Berlin. Struppe & Winckler. 1929-31. 2v.   **1787**

Temperley, Harold W.H. and Penson, Lillian M. A century of diplomatic blue books, 1814-1914. Cambridge, England. The Univ. Press. 1938. 600p.   **1787a**

U.S. Library of Congress. Division of bibliography. Anglo-American relations; some recent writings. Jan. 18, 1927. 3p. typ.   **1788**

—— —— Bibliography on the causes of the World war. MS. (Card bibliography kept up to date)   **1789**

—— —— Brief list of references on the Anglo-French-American alliance. Jan. 23, 1920. 2p. typ.   **1790**

—— —— Brief list of references on the attitude of the United States toward the neutrality of the Dardanelles. Feb. 6, 1923. 2p. typ.   **1791**

—— —— —— Brief list of references on the cancellation of the allied war debt. Feb. 29, 1924. 3p. mim. (Additional references. Nov. 30, 1926. 3p.) **1792**

—— —— —— Brief list of references on the United States as mandatory for Armenia. May 27, 1920. 3p. typ. **1793**

—— —— —— Check list of documents relating to the Paris Peace Conference, 1919. March 16, 1922. 6p. typ. **1794**

—— —— —— The inter-allied debt to the United States; a bibliographical list (with special reference to cancellation and the moratorium). Nov. 12, 1931. 20p. mim. (Supplements. June 9, 1933. 15p. typ.; Feb. 6, 1934. 17p. mim.; Jan. 8, 1936. 12p. typ.) **1795**

—— —— —— The Lausanne Conference and reparations treaty, 1932; a list of references. Oct. 21, 1932. 8p. typ. **1796**

—— —— —— List of recent references on the reparations problem. Oct. 24, 1932. 41p. mim. **1797**

—— —— —— List of recent references on the reparations problem, with special references to the Dawes plan. Feb. 4, 1925. 9p. mim. **1798**

—— —— —— List of references on a League of nations. Oct. 7, 1918. 18p. mim. (Supplements. March 3, 1919. 13p. mim.; March 26, 1920. 32p. mim.; Nov. 24, 1922. 29p. mim.; Dec. 6, 1924. 4p. typ.; Jan. 20, 1928. 7p. typ.; Jan. 23, 1929. 9p. typ.; April 10, 1930. 8p. mim.; June 22, 1933. 46p. mim.) **1799**

—— —— —— List of references on Europe and international politics in relation to the present issues. Comp. under the direction of H.H.B. Meyer. Wash. Govt. Ptg. Off. 1914. 144p. **1800**

—— —— —— List of references on French spoliation claims. (Supplementary to Boston Pub. Lib. list. May 1885) Jan. 27, 1922. 3p. typ. **1801**

—— —— —— List of references on refunding of foreign debts. Dec. 17, 1921. 6p. mim. (Supplement. Jan. 8, 1924. 7p. typ.; Feb. 17, 1926. 19p. typ.) **1802**

—— ——. —— List of references on Talleyrand's diplomatic relations with the United States. Dec. 13, 1919. 4p. typ. **1803**

—— —— —— List of references on the debts of foreign countries to the United States (with special reference to their cancellation). Dec. 27, 1921. 6p. mim. Oct. 20, 1921. 5p. typ. **1804**

—— —— —— List of references on the Declaration of Paris. May 4, 1916. 4p. typ. **1805**

—— —— —— List of references on the international relations between the United States and Russia. Dec. 7, 1915. 7p. typ. **1806**

—— —— —— List of references on the neutrality of the United States in the European war. April 7, 1917. 3p. typ. **1807**

—— —— —— List of references on the Russian policy of the United States. March 14, 1922. 13p. mim. **1808**

—— —— —— List of references on the Treaty of Versailles, June 28, 1919. March 9, 1922. 15p. typ. **1809**

—— —— —— List of works relating to collections of debts of foreign countries. 1907. 25p. typ. **1810**

—— —— —— References on the British debt funding agreement. Dec. 28, 1926. 4p. typ. **1811**

—— —— —— References on the French debt funding agreement. Dec. 29, 1926. 4p. typ. **1812**

—— —— —— Select list of references on Anglo-Saxon interests. Comp. under the direction of A.P.C. Griffin. Wash. Govt. Ptg. Off. 1906. 22p. (Supplement. Nov. 2, 1916. 3p. typ.) **1813**

—— —— —— Select list of references treating of the international relations of Great Britain and the United States. Oct. 20, 1913. 12p. typ. (Recent references. Dec. 29, 1920. 7p. multig.) **1814**

—— —— —— Selected list of recent references on the relations between the United States and Great Britain. 1938. 7p. mim. **1814a**

—— —— —— A selected list of references on the diplomatic and trade relations of the United States with the Union of Soviet Socialist Republics, 1919-1935. Nov. 5, 1935. 29p. mim. **1815**

—— —— —— United States foreign relations with France and Russia during 1853-1857. Feb. 10, 1914. 4p. typ. **1816**

—— —— **Reading room.** A list of references on reparations of the European war, 1914-1918. Prepared by Donald G. Patterson and James T. Ruby. Wash. D.C. June 3, 1932. 136p. typ. (Supplement. July 1, 1933. Prepared by James T. Ruby. p137-47. typ.) **1817**

Wegerer, Alfred von. Bibliographie zur vorgeschichte des weltkrieges. Berlin. Quaderverlag G. m. b. 1934. 136p. **1818**

Williams, R. Hodder. The literature of the peace conference. Canadian hist. rev. II. p155-71 (June 1921) **1819**

Winsor, Justin. The cartographical history of the northeastern boundary controversy between the United States and Great Britain. Cambridge, Mass. J. Wilson and Sons. 1887. 24p. (Reprint from Mass. Hist. Soc. proc. Oct. 1887) **1819a**

LATIN AMERICA

General

Bibliografía hispanoamericana. Revista hispánica moderna. A. 1. no. 1. Oct. 1934- **1820**

Bibliographical section—recent publications. Hisp. Am. hist. rev. I- . (Feb. 1918-) **1820a**

Boggs, Ralph S. Card bibliography of 100,000 titles of Spanish and Spanish American books. Univ. of North Carolina, Chapel Hill, N.C. **1820b**

Bradley, Phillips. A bibliography of the Monroe doctrine 1919-1929. (Stud. in economics and pol. science no. 7) Letchworth. Printed by the Garden City Press. London. Pub. by the London School of Economics. 1929. 39p. **1821**

Brooks, Janeiro. A bio-bibliography of works by Latin Americans on the Monroe Doctrine. (George Wash. Univ. M.A. thesis) (In progress) **1822**

Carnegie Endowment for International Peace. Library. Intellectual and cultural relations between the United States and Latin America. Comp. by Mary Alice Matthews (Reading list no. 35) Wash. D.C. 1935. 17p. mim. **1823**

—— International American conferences. (Reading list no. 25) Wash. D.C. 1928. 20p. mim. **1824**

—— —— Intervention, with special reference to protection of foreign loans and investments. (Reading list no. 18) Wash. D.C. 1927. 11p. mim. **1825**

—— —— The Monroe doctrine; with special reference to its modern aspects. Comp. by Mary Alice Matthews. (Select bibliographies, no. 5) Wash. D.C. 1936. 15p. mim. **1825a**

Childs, James B. Hispanic American government documents in the Library of Congress. Hispanic Am. hist. rev. VI. p134-41 (Feb.-Aug. 1926) (Also reprinted) **1826**

Fogg, George W. Latin America; social, economic, political, historical (more than 900 references including analytics of several series, references to special maps and biographical material regarding the Latin American countries). (Monographs in bibliography, I, no. 3) Wash. D.C. 1941 **1826a**

Goldsmith, Peter H. A brief bibliography of the books in English, Spanish and Portuguese, relating to the republics commonly called Latin America, with comments. N.Y. Macmillan. 1915. 107p. **1827**

Hanke, Lewis. Handbook of Latin American studies; a guide to the material published in 1935- on anthropology, archaeology, economics, geography, history, law, and literature. By a number of scholars, ed. by Lewis Hanke. Cambridge. Harvard Univ. Press. 1936-. 250p. **1828**

Hispanic American historical review. Bibliographical section. I. no. 1. Feb. 1918- **1829**

Inter-American Book Exchange. Index to Latin-American books, 1938-. I-. By Raoul d'Eça. Wash. D.C. 1940- **1829a**

Johnson, Elvera Ethel. The good neighbor policy, 1933-1938: a selected bibliography. Madison. Univ. of Wis. Lib. School. 1938. 63p. typ. **1829b**

Kelchner, Warren H. Inter-American conferences, 1926-1933; chronological and classified lists. (The Dept. of State. Conference ser. no. 16) Wash. Govt. Ptg. Off. 1933. 34p. **1830**

Key Ayala, Santiago. Series hemero-bibliográficas: L. ser. Bolivariana. Caracas. Tipografía americana. 1933. 202p. (Simon Bolivar) **1830a**

Leavitt, Sturgis E. Hispano-American literature in the United States; a bibliography of translations and criticisms. Cambridge. Harvard Univ. Press. 1932. 54p. **1831**

Library table. The Pan Am. mag. I. 1900- (Book reviews) **1832**

McCutcheon, Lydia M. Bibliography on the subject resolved: that the Monroe Doctrine should be discontinued. Seattle. Univ. of Wash. 1916. 15p. **1833**

Manning, William R. The Mexican foreign office archives. Pan Am. union bul. XXXVII. p657-61 (Nov. 1913) **1833a**

Newhall, Beatrice. The Miranda archives. Pan Am. union bul. LXVII. p491-6. 1933 (MSS. of Francisco de Miranda) **1833b**

Pan American book shelf. v. 1-. March 1937-. Wash. D.C. Pan American Union. 1937- **1833c**

Pan American Union. Columbus Memorial Library. Bibliography. on the Monroe Doctrine; documentary material, secondary material in the library of the Pan American Union. Wash. D.C. Oct. 10, 1924. 23p. autog. from typ. copy **1834**

—— —— The histories of Hispanic America; a bibliographical essay. By Alva Curtis Wilgus. (Bibliog. ser. no. 9) Wash. D.C. 115p. mim. **1835**

—— —— Recent trends in inter-American relations; a bibliography. (Bibliog. ser. no. 21) Wash. D.C. 1939. 52p. mim. **1835a**

—— —— Selected list of books and magazine articles on hemisphere defense. (Bibliog. ser. no. 24) Wash. D.C. 1941. 14p. mim. **1835b**

—— —— Selected list of books and magazine articles on inter-American relations. (Bibliog. ser. no. 7) Wash. D.C. 1934. 20p. mim. **1836**

Recent publications. Hispanic Am. hist. rev. I- 1918- **1837**

Trelles y Govin, Carlos M. Estudio de la bibliografía cubana sobre la Doctrina de Monroe. Havana. Imp. "El Siglo XX." 1922. 234p. **1838**

—— Study of Cuban bibliography relative to the Monroe Doctrine. Hispanic Am. hist. rev. V. p107-15 (Feb. 1922) **1839**

U.S. Bureau of Foreign and Domestic Commerce. Latin American division. List of selected titles referring to the petroleum industry in Latin America. Wash. D.C. 1920. 20p. mim. **1840**

U.S. Library of Congress. List of references on international American conferences, 1826-1914. March 22, 1917. 18p. typ. **1841**

—— —— Division of bibliography. League of American republics (Bibliography). May 1915. 6p. typ. **1842**

——— ——— ——— List of references on the Monroe Doctrine. Comp. under the direction of H.H.B. Meyer. Wash. Govt. Ptg. Off. 1919. 122p. **1843**

Wilgus, A. Curtis. A bibliography of source materials, readings and contemporary accounts in English dealing with Hispanic American affairs. George Wash. Univ. In progress **1844**

——— Index of articles relating to Hispanic America published in the National geographic magazine, volumes I-LXI, inclusive (1888-1932). Hispanic Am. hist. rev. XII. p491-502 (Nov. 1932) **1845**

——— List of articles relating to Hispanic America published in the periodicals of the American Geographical Society, 1852-1933, inclusive. Hispanic Am. hist. rev. XIV. p114-30 (Feb. 1934) **1846**

——— List of government publications concerning Hispanic America. Hisp. Am. hist. rev. XVIII. p127-41, 272-84, 437-43 (Feb.-Aug. 1938) (From the Monthly catalogue United States public documents) **1846a**

——— Source material and special collections dealing with Latin America in libraries of the United States. Wash. D.C. Pan Am. Union. 1934. 22p. **1847**

World Peace Foundation. Books recommended for reading, study and reference [in the new Pan Americanism]. (Pamphlet ser. VI. no. 2. p111-15. April 1916) Boston. 1916 **1848**

Wright, Almon R. Archival sources for the study of war-time relations of Latin America with the United States, 1917-1920: illustrations of their use. Inter-Am. bibliog. rev. I. p23-35 (Spring 1941) **1848a**

Central America

Baker, James M. List of . . . Congressional documents . . . relating to interoceanic canals and especially to the Maritime Canal Company of Nicaragua. Senate document no. 26. 55 Cong. 3 sess. Dec. 12, 1898. Ser. 3725. 9p. **1849**

Bancroft, Hubert Howe. Authorities quoted. *In* History of Central America. San Francisco. A. L. Bancroft. 1882. I. p. xxv-lxxii **1850**

Bandelier, Adolph Francis Alphonse. Notes on the bibliography of Yucatan and Central America. Am. Antiq. Soc. proc. n.s. I. p82-118 (Oct. 1880) **1851**

Childs, James B. The memorias of the republics of Central America and the Antilles. Wash. Govt. Ptg. Off. 1932. 170p. **1852**

De Kalb, Courtenay. A bibliography of the Mosquito coast of Nicaragua. Am. Geog. Soc. jour. XXVI. p241-8. 1894 **1853**

Frank, John C. American interoceanic canals; a list of references in the New York Public Library. N.Y. 1916. 90p. (Reprinted from the Bul. XX. p11-81. Jan. 1916) **1854**

Martinez Alomia, Gustavo. Historiadores de Yucatan; apuntes biográficos y bibliograficos de los historiadores de esta peninsula desde su descubrimiento hasta fines del siglo XIX. Campeche. Tip. El Fenix. 1906. 360p. **1855**

Minor, Van Lieu. A brief classified bibliography relating to the United States intervention in Nicaragua. Hispanic Am. hist. rev. XI. p261-77 (May 1931) **1856**

Pan American Union. Columbus Memorial Library. Bibliography . . . on the relations between the United States and Panama. [Wash. D.C.] 1924. 4p. **1857**

Phillips, P. Lee. A list of books, magazine articles, and maps relating to Central America, including the republics of Costa Rica, Guatemala, Honduras, Nicaragua, and Salvador, 1800-1900. Comp. for the International Bureau of the American Republics. 1902. 109p. **1858**

U.S. Library of Congress. Division of bibliography. List of books and of articles in periodicals relating to interoceanic canal and railway routes (Nicaragua, Panama, Darien, and the Valley of the Atrato; Tehuantepec and Honduras; Suez Canal). By Hugh A. Morrison. With appendix: Bibliography of U.S. public documents. Prepared in Office of Superintendent of Documents. Wash. Govt. Ptg. Off. 1900. 174p. (Also Senate document 59. 56 Cong. 1 sess. Ser. 3848) **1859**

——— ——— ——— List of references on acquisition of the Panama Canal Zone by the United States, and the Columbian treaties. March 15, 1917. 11p. typ. **1859a**

——— ——— ——— List of references on Nicaragua (with special reference to her relations with the United States). Sept. 3, 1921. 11p. typ. (Supplement. Aug. 1, 1927. 9p. typ.) **1860**

——— ——— ——— List of references on Panama Canal tolls. Sept. 26, 1921. 25p. mim. **1861**

——— ——— ——— List of references on the Panama Canal and the Panama Canal Zone. Prepared under the direction of H. H. B. Meyer. Wash. Govt. Ptg. off. 1919. 21p. **1862**

——— ——— ——— List of references on the revolution in Panama. April 14, 1914. 4p. typ. (Additional references. 1915. 1p.) **1863**

——— ——— ——— Recent references on Nicaragua (with special reference to her relations with the United States). Wash. D.C. Feb. 25, 1927. 7p. (Supplement. Oct. 25, 1927. 9p. mim.) **1864**

——— ——— ——— Select list of recent references on the Panama Canal. 1910. 63p. typ. **1865**

——— ——— ——— Select list of references on Nicaragua Canal. 1906. 5p. typ. **1866**

——— ——— ——— Select list of references on the international status of the Panama Canal and similar waterways. Jan. 26, 1911. 16p. typ. **1867**

U.S. Library of Congress. Division of bibliography. Select list of references on the sanitation of Panama and other tropical regions controlled by the United States. June 9, 1913. 12p. typ.   **1868**

Mexico

Alessio Robles, Vito. Bibliografía de Coahuila, histórica y geográfica. (Mexico. Monografias bibliográficas Mexicanas, núm. 10) [Mexico. Imp. de la Secretaría de Relaciones exteriores] 1927. 450p.   **1870**
Bancroft, Hubert Howe. Authorities quoted. *In* The history of Mexico. San Francisco. The Hist. Co. 1890. I. p. xxi-cxii   **1871**
Castillo, Ignaçio B. del. Bibliografía de la imprenta de la Cámara de Diputados para servir a los historiadores de la época de Madero, Huerta y la convencion, 1912-1915. *In* Iguiniz, Juan B. Concurso de bibliografía y biblioteconomia convocado por la Biblioteca nacional. . . 1918, II. Mexico. Oficina impresora de hacienda Departamento de Comunicaciones. 1918. 48p.   **1872**
—— Bibliografía de la revolución mexicana de 1910-1916; historia, legislación, literatura, cuestiones sociales, políticas y económicas documentos, etc., marzo de 1908 a junio de 1916. *In* Iguíniz, Juan B. Concurso de bibliografía y biblioteconomia convocado por la Biblioteca nacional estudios premiados dados. . . . Mexico. Talleres graficos de la Secretaría de Comunicaciones. 1918. 92p.   **1873**
Jones, Cecil Knight. Bibliography of the Mexican revolution. N.Y. 1919. p311-14 (Reprinted from the Hispanic Am. hist. rev. II. May 1919)   **1874**
Nelson, Edward W. Bibliography of Lower California. *In* Lower California and its natural resources, Memoirs of the National Academy of Sciences, XVI, first memoir. p147-171. 1922   **1875**
New York. Public Library. List of works in the New York Public Library relating to Mexico. N.Y. Pub. Lib. bul. XIII. p622-62, 675-737, 748-829 (Oct.-Dec. 1909)   **1876**
Pan American Union. Columbus Memorial Library. Bibliography . . . on relations between the United States and Mexico. [Wash. D.C. 1924] 6,14p. autog. from typ. copy   **1877**
Ramos, Roberto. Bibliografía de la revolución mexicana (hasta mayo de 1931). (Monográfias bibliográficos mexicanas numero 21) México. Imp. de la Secretaría de Relaciones exteriores. 1931. 530p.   **1878**
Rippy, J. Fred. The diplomatic monographs of the Mexican government. Hispanic Am. hist. rev. X. p247-54 (May 1930)   **1879**
Spell, Lota M. The Anglo-Saxon press in Mexico, 1846-1848. Am. hist. rev. XXXVIII, p20-32 (Oct. 1932)   **1880**

U.S. Library of Congress. Division of bibliography. Brief list of references on the recognition of the government of Mexico by the United States. Jan. 19, 1923. 3p. typ.   **1881**
—— —— —— List of references on intervention in Mexico by the United States. Feb. 7, 1920. 7p. typ.   **1882**
—— —— —— List of references on the American punitive expedition into Mexico, 1916. Oct. 8, 1921. 8p. typ.   **1883**
—— —— —— Lower California; a bibliographical list. Aug. 15, 1931. 13p. typ. Supplement. Dec. 23, 1938. 9p. photo.   **1884**
—— —— —— References to speeches, etc., in the Congressional record on intervention in Mexico. Feb. 23, 1916. 4p. typ.   **1885**
—— —— —— United States relations with Mexico and Central America, with special reference to intervention. Nov. 13, 1928. 30p. mim.   **1886**
U.S. War Department. Library. Index of publications, articles, and maps relating to Mexico in the War Department Library. Wash. Govt. Ptg. Off. 1896. 120p.   **1887**
Valle, Rafael Heliodoro. Mexico in United States and British periodicals. Hispanic Am. hist. rev. XV. p126-42 (Feb. 1935)   **1888**

South America

Bealer, Lewis W. Contribution to a bibliography, on Artigas and the beginnings of Uruguay, 1810-1820. Hispanic Am. hist. rev. XI. p108-34 (Feb. 1931)   **1889**
Clavery, Edouard. Les archives de Miranda à Caracas. Revue de l'Amérique latine. XVII. p113-19 (1er janvier 1929)   **1890**
Medina, José Toribio. Dos obras de viajeros norte-americanos traducidas al castellano. Hispanic Am. hist. rev. I. p106-14 (Feb. 1918)   **1891**
Pan American Union. Columbus Memorial Library. Bibliography of the liberator, Simon Bolivar. . . . (Bibliog. ser. no. 1 (rev. and enl.) [Wash. D.C.] 1933. 107p.   **1892**
—— —— Bibliography . . . on the relations between the United States and Colombia. [Wash. D.C. 1924] 5,4p. autog. from typ. copy   **1893**
Robertson, William Spence. The lost archives of Miranda. Hispanic Am. hist. rev. VII. p229-32 (May 1927)   **1894**
U.S. Library of Congress. Division of bibliography. List of references on the Tacna-Arica question. April 18, 1919. 8p. typ. (Supplement. March 26, 1926. 7p. typ.)   **1895**
—— —— —— Select list of references on the Venezuelan boundary, 1895-1896. Nov. 8, 1912. 9p. typ.   **1896**

West Indies

Annexation of Cuba, and independence of the Philippines. (Univ. of Wisconsin. Bul. 1911) Madison. 1912. 16p. **1897**

Boston College. Library. Catalogue of books, manuscripts, etc. in the Caribbeana section (specializing in Jamaicana) of the Nicholas M. Williams memorial ethnological collection. Chestnut Hill, Mass. 1932. 133p. **1898**

Brooklyn. Public Library. A list of books on the West Indies and the Bermuda Islands in the Brooklyn Public Library. Brooklyn, N.Y. 1904. 12p. **1899**

Cotts, Grace Winifred. The United States and Haiti, and historical development of our possessions in the Caribbean; a selected bibliography. Madison, Univ. of Wisconsin. 1931. 49,39p. photostat reproduction **1900**

Cundall, Frank. Bibliography of the West Indies (excluding Jamaica). Kingston. The Inst. of Jamaica. 1909. 179p. **1901**

New York. Public Library. List of works in the New York Public Library relating to the West Indies. N.Y. 1912. 392p. (Reprinted from the Bul. XVI. Jan.-Aug. 1912) **1902**

Pan American Union. Columbus Memorial Library. Bibliography . . . on relations between the United States and Haiti. [Wash. D.C. 1924] 3,5p. autog. from typ. copy **1903**

—— —— Bibliography . . . on the relations between the United States and Dominican Republic. [Wash. D.C. 1924] 3,6p. autog. from typ. copy **1904**

Perez, Luis Marino. Bibliografía de la revolución de Yara; folletos y libros impresos de 1868 a 1908, historia y política, biografías, masonería, asuntos eclesiástico-políticos, esclavitud, asuntos económicos, asuntos administrativos, literatura patriótica. Habana, Cuba. Imp. Advisador commercial. 1908. 73p. **1905**

Phillips, P. Lee. A list of books, pamphlets, articles and maps relating to Cuba. Comp. for the International Bureau of American Republics. Wash. Govt. Ptg. Off. 1903. 110p. **1906**

Stuart, Graham H. Cuba and its international relations. (Inst. of International Education. International Relations Clubs. Syllabus no. XIV) N.Y. 1923. 46p. **1907**

Trelles y Govín, Carlos M. Bibliografía cubana del siglo XIX. Matanzas. Quiros y Estrada. 1911-15. 8v. **1908**

—— Bibliografía cubana del siglo XX, 1900-1916. Matanzas. Imp. de la vda. de Quiros y Estrada. 1916-17. 2v. **1909**

U.S. Library of Congress. Division of bibliography. List of books relating to Cuba (including references to collected works and periodicals). By A.P.C. Griffin. With a bibliography of maps by P. Lee Phillips. Senate document no. 161. 55 Cong. 2 sess. 1898. Ser. 3600. 61p. (Includes: A synoptical catalog of manuscripts in the Library of Congress, relating to Cuba, p58-61) **1910**

—— —— —— List of references between the United States and Haiti and the Dominican Republic. Dec. 19, 1918. 3p. typ. (Additional references. April 10, 1919. 5p. typ.) **1911**

—— —— —— List of references on annexation of Cuba. March 4, 1912. 3p. typ. **1912**

—— —— —— List of references on Haiti and Santo Domingo. Aug. 15, 1921. 14p. typ. **1913**

—— —— —— List of references on the Platt amendment, including references on conditions in Cuba. Jan. 3, 1934. 11p. typ. **1914**

—— —— —— List of writings relating to the Santo Domingo question, 1904-1906. 1906. 7p. typ. **1915**

PACIFIC AREA

Allen, Percy S. Bibliography of works on the Pacific Islands. *In* Stewart's handbook of the Pacific Islands. Sydney, Australia. McCarron, Stewart & Co. 1921. p491-534 **1916**

Boston. Public Library. The United States and Japan; selected references to books and periodicals in the Public Library of the city of Boston. (Brief reading lists no. 22. Nov. 1921) Boston. The Trustees. 1921. 19p. **1917**

Buell, Raymond Leslie. Problems of the Pacific; a brief bibliography. Prepared for the American group of the Institute of Pacific Relations. (World Peace Foundation. Pamphlets. VIII. no. 1) Boston. 1925. 34p. **1918**

Claremont Colleges. Library. Materials on the Pacific area, in the Oriental Library and in the libraries of Pomona College and Scripps College, Claremont, California. Claremont, Calif. 1939. 141p. mim. **1918a**

Condliffe, John Bell. A Pacific bibliography. Honolulu, Hawaii. 1927. 83p. **1919**

Cowan, Robert E. and Dunlap, Boutwell. Bibliography of the Chinese question in the United States. San Francisco. A.M. Robertson. 1909. 68p. **1920**

Gardner, Charles S. A union list of selected western books on China in American libraries. Wash. D.C. Am. Council of Learned Societies. 1932. 48p. **1921**

Hussey, Roland Dennis. Pacific history in Latin American periodicals. Pacific hist. rev. I. p470-6 (Dec. 1932) **1922**

Institute of Pacific Relations. Publications on the Pacific, 1936; catalogue of the Institute of Pacific Relations and its national councils. N.Y. Publications Office [of the Inst. 1936] 42p. **1923**

—— Some publications on Pacific problems; a list of available papers and books published by or in cooperation with The Institute of Pacific Relations, May 1932. Honolulu. Inst. of Pacific Relations. [1932] 24p. **1924**

Institute of Pacific Relations. American Council. Current research projects dealing with subjects relating to the Pacific area, 1937-1938. N.Y. 1939. 37p.   **1924a**

—— —— List of current research projects dealing with China, Hawaii, Japan, Philippine Islands, Russia and/or the Pacific Islands and miscellaneous subjects of importance to the Pacific area. N.Y. Amer. council, Inst. of Pacific Relations. 1936. 27p. Reprod.   **1924b**

—— —— The Pacific area in American research: a list of current research projects, Spring, 1940. San Francisco, N.Y. The Inst. 1940. 32p. mim.   **1924c**

Jore, Léonce Alphonse Noël Henri. Essai de bibliographie du Pacifique. Paris. Éditions Duchartre. 1931. 233p.   **1925**

Kerner, Robert J. Russian expansion to America; its bibliographical foundations. Bibliog. Soc. of Amer. pap. XXV. p111-29. 1931   **1926**

—— Slavic Europe; a selected bibliography in the western European languages, comprising history, languages and literatures. Cambridge. Harvard Univ. Press. 1918. 402p.   **1927**

Latourette, Kenneth S. Japan; suggested outlines for a discussion of Japan, her history, culture, problems and relations with the United States. N.Y. Japan Soc., Inc. 1921. 39p.   **1928**

Leebrick, R. C. Recent books on the Pacific area. Pol. science quar. XLV. p259-72 (June 1930)   **1929**

MacFadden, Clifford H. A bibliography of Pacific area maps. (Studies of the Pacific, no. 6) N.Y. American Council, Inst. of Pacific Relations. 1940. 123p.   **1929a**

Miller, Dorothy Purviance. Japanese-American relations; a list of works in the New York Public Library. N.Y. 1921. 67p. (Reprinted from the Bul. XXV. Jan.-May 1921)   **1930**

New York. Public Library. List of works in the New York Public Library relating to Japan. N.Y. N.Y. Pub. Lib. 1906. 79p. (Reprinted from the Bul. X. p383-423, 439-77. Aug.-Sept. 1906)   **1931**

Nugent, Donald R. and Bell, Reginald. The Pacific area and its problems: a study guide. N.Y. Inst. of Pacific Relations. 1936. 234p.   **1931a**

Pacific house bibliographies. . . . San Francisco, Calif. Dept. of the Pacific Area, Golden Gate International Exposition [1938-] 3v. (v. I. Our debt to the Pacific. v. II. Exploring the Pacific. v. III. America and the Pacific)   **1931b**

Paris. Bibliothèque nationale. Département des imprimés. Catalogue de l'histoire de L'Océanie. Par George A. Barringer. Paris. 1912. 169p.   **1932**

Quigley, Harold S. An introductory syllabus on Far Eastern diplomacy. Chicago. Pub. for the Am. Council, Inst. of Pacific Relations. 1931. 40p.   **1933**

Robertson, James A. The Far East, with special reference to China; its culture, civilization and history; an outline for indvidual and group study. (North Carolina. Univ. Extension division. Univ. of North Carolina extension bul. XI. no. 2) Chapel Hill, N.C. 1931. 87p.   **1934**

Royal Empire Society. Library. Subject catalogue of the library of the Royal Empire Society formerly Royal Colonial Institute; Volume two. The Commonwealth of Australia, The Dominion of New Zealand, The South Pacific, general voyages and travels, and Arctic and Antarctic regions. Comp. by Evans Lewin. London. 1931. 761p.   **1935**

Taylor, Louise M. Catalogue of books on China in the Essex Institute. Salem, Mass. The Essex Inst. 1926   **1936**

U.S. Bureau of Foreign and Domestic Commerce. Division of regional information. A selected bibliography on the Far East. Comp. by J. H. Nunn (Special circular no. 213. Far Eastern ser. no. 97) Wash. D.C. 1930. 62p. mim.   **1937**

U.S. Library of Congress. Division of bibliography. Brief list of references on the island of Yap. Jan. 12, 1922. 3p. typ.   **1938**

—— —— —— List of references on the open door policy in China. Dec. 2, 1921. 14p. typ.   **1939**

—— —— —— List of references on the relations of the United States with the Orient and the Barbary states from 1781-1789. Nov. 18, 1921. 6p. typ.   **1940**

—— —— —— List of references on the Shantung question. Nov. 19, 1919. 6p. typ.   **1941**

—— —— —— Select list of books (with reference to periodicals) relating to the Far East. Comp. under the direction of A. P. C. Griffin. Wash. Govt. Ptg. Off. 1904. 74p.   **1942**

—— —— —— Select list of references on relations between the United States and China, 1900-1912; supplementary to Chinese immigration, 1904, and Far East, 1904. May 1, 1912. 12p. typ. (Supplement. Jan. 1, 1934. 8p. typ.)   **1943**

—— —— —— U.S. interference in foreign affairs, with special reference to China and Japan. Nov. 17, 1931. 3p.   **1944**

—— —— Reading room. A list of recent references in the Sino-Japanese dispute with special reference to the action of the League of Nations. Comp. by James T. Rubey. May 20, 1933. 22p. typ.   **1945**

Windeyer, Margaret. China and the Far East, 1889-99; contribution toward a bibliography. N.Y. State Lib. bul. LIX. Bibliog. 25. p563-679. 1901   **1946**

DISARMAMENT

Boston. Public Library. Disarmament and substitutes for war; selected references to books and periodicals in the Public Library of the City of Boston. (Brief reading lists no. 21. Nov. 1921) Boston. The Trustees. 1921. 17p. **1947**

Carnegie. Endowment for International Peace. Library. Disarmament and security; select list of recent books, pamphlets and periodical articles. Comp. by Mary Alice Matthews (Reading list no. 32) Wash. D.C. 1931. 31p. **1948**

—— —— The Permanent court of arbitration; select list of references on arbitrations before the Hague tribunals and the International Commissions of Enquiry, 1902-1928. (Reading list no. 30) Wash. D.C. 1931. 29p. **1949**

Douma, Jean. Bibliographical list of official and unofficial publications concerning the Permanent Court of International Justice, [no. 1]—*In* Hague. Permanent Court of International Justice. Publications, ser. E. no. 1- Annual rep. Leyden. [1925-] (Also reprinted) **1950**

League of Nations. Secretariat. Library. Annotated bibliography on disarmament and military questions. Geneva. 1931. 163p. **1951**

U.S. Library of Congress. Division of bibliography. Brief select list of references on disarmament. Aug. 10, 1920. 5p. typ. **1952**

—— —— —— Conference on the limitation of naval armaments, Geneva, 1927. (The Three-power conference; a bibliographical list) Dec. 16, 1929. 13p. typ. **1953**

—— —— —— Disarmament, with special reference to naval limitation; a bibliographical list. Dec. 1929. 40p. mim. (Recent references. 1934. 42p. mim.) **1954**

—— —— —— The League of Nations and disarmament; a bibliographical list. Dec. 18, 1929. 18p. mim. **1955**

—— —— —— List of references on limitation of armaments (supplementing list in list of references on international arbitration, printed in 1908). Feb. 10, 1921. 10p. typ. **1956**

—— —— —— List of references on naval disarmament, with special reference to Great Britain, Japan, and the United States. March 30, 1921. 5p. typ. **1957**

—— —— —— List of references on the Washington conference on the limitation of armament, 1921-1922. Dec. 27, 1922. 24p. typ. (Supplements. Feb. 28, 1925. 14p. typ.; May 18, 1927. 3p. typ.; Dec. 17, 1929. 5p. typ.) **1958**

—— —— —— London naval conference, 1930; a bibliographical list. May 1930. 19p. mim. **1959**

—— —— —— Select list of references on the limitation of armaments. Sept. 30, 1921. 7p. mim. **1960**

INTERNATIONAL LAW

American journal of international law. An analytical index to the American journal of international law and supplements, volumes I-XIV (1907-20) and the Proceedings of the American Society of International Law. Prepared by George A. Finch. Wash. D.C. The Soc. 1921. 321p. **1963**

Bibliography, Jan. 1, 1919-. *In* British year book of international law, 1920/21- . London. Oxford Univ. Press. 1920- **1964**

Boston. Public Library. Freedom of the seas; selected references to recent books and magazines. . . (Brief reading lists no. 6) Boston. 1919. 12p. **1965**

Calvo, Carlos. Histoire du droit des gens. *In* Le droit international théorique et pratique précédé d'un exposé historique des progrès de la science du droit des gens. Paris. Rousseau. 1896. I. p101-37. (Esquisse historique des progrès du droit international théorique et pratique appears in v. VI. p. xxix-lxi) **1966**

Carnegie Endowment for International Peace. Library. The American Institute of International Law and the codification of international law. Comp. by Mary Alice Matthews (Selected bibliographies no. 2) Wash. D.C. 1933. 17p. mim. **1967**

—— —— Codification of international law; a select list of references. M. Alice Matthews, librarian (Reading list. miscellaneous no. 51) Wash. D.C. 1934. 4p. mim. **1968**

—— —— International law; select list of works in English on public international law; with collections of cases and opinions. Comp. by Mary Alice Matthews (Select bibliographies no. 3) Wash. D.C. 1936. 21p. mim. **1969**

—— —— Intervention; select list of references on intervention in its relation to international law and the protection of foreign loans and investments. Comp. by Mary Alice Matthews. (Reading list no. 18) Wash. D.C. The Endowment. 1938. 14p. mim. **1969a**

—— —— Munitions of war and embargo on arms. M. Alice Matthews, librarian (Brief reference list no. 3) Wash. D.C. 1934. 10p. mim. **1970**

Cuba. Congreso. Cámara de Representantes. Biblioteca. Catálogo de las obras que formen su bibliotéca derecho internacional. Havana. Imp. "El siglo XX" de A. Miranda. 1917. 72p. **1971**

Edward Fry Library of International Law, London. Catalogue of the books, pamphlets, and other documents in the library, together with other works bearing on the subject of international law contained in the library of the London School of Economics. Comp. and ed. by B. M. Headicar. London. St. Clements Press. 1923. 174p. (First supplement. London. St. Clements Press. 1925. 54p. **1972**

Finch, George A. Public documents relating to international law. Am jour. international law. IV-XVIII (Oct. 1910-July 1924) **1973**

Foster, John Watson. America's contribution to the literature of international law and diplomacy. (International law pamphlets. I. no. 4) n.p. [1904] [12]p. **1974**

Grotius Society, London. Library. Catalogue of the books in the library of the society. Arranged according to subjects by Wyndham A. Bewes. London. Sweet & Maxwell, Ltd. 1923. 65p. **1975**

Havana. Bibliotéca nacional. Donativo Bustamante. Catálogo de derecho internacional. I- . Havana. Imp. de la Bibliotéca nacional. 1917- **1976**

Holtzendorff, Franz de et Rivier, Alphonse. Introduction au droit des gens; recherches philosophiques, historiques et bibliographiques. Hambourg. J. F. Richter. 1889. 524p. **1977**

Hudson, Manley O. Twelve casebooks in international law. Am. jour. internat. law. XXXII. p447-56 (July 1938) **1977a**

Indianapolis. Public Library. List of books and magazine articles on international extradition. . . . Indianapolis. Press of Central Ptg. Co. 1903. 6p. **1978**

International Law Association. Library. A forty years' catalogue of the books, pamphlets and papers in the library of the International Law Association, comprising an index to the papers read at its conferences (1874-1914). Arranged in a systematic classification by the honorary general secretaries. London. R. Flint. 1915. 70p. **1979**

Ketcham, Earl Hoyt. Preliminary select bibliography of international law. Syracuse? N.Y. 1937? 69p. mim. **1979a**

Moore, John Bassett. Digest of international law, as embodied in diplomatic discussions, treaties, and other international agreements, international awards, the decisions of municipal courts, and the writings of jurists, and especially in documents, published and unpublished, issued by presidents and secretaries of states of the United States, the opinions of the attorneys general, and the decisions of courts, federal and state. Wash. Govt. Ptg. Off. 1906. 8 v. (Also published as House doc. 551. 56 Cong. 2 sess., serials 4202-6 List of authorities. v.I. p. ix-xxx) **1979b**

—— Fifty years of international law. Harvard law rev. L. p395-448 (Jan. 1937) **1979c**

—— History and digest of international arbitrations to which United States have been a party together with appendices containing the treaties relating to such arbitrations, and historical and legal notes. (House miscellaneous document. no. 39. 53 Cong. 2 sess.) Wash. Govt. Ptg. Off. 1898. 6v. **1980**

Nijhoff, Martinus. A selected list of books on private international law. The Hague. M. Nijhoff. 1916. 40p. **1981**

—— A systematical catalogue of the principal books on public international law. The Hague. M. Nijhoff. 1924. 106p. **1982**

Nys, Ernest. Les États-Unis et le droit des gens. Brussels. Bureau de la Revue de Droit international. 1909. 166p. (Extrait de la Droit international et de législation comparée. deuxième série. tome XI. 1909. 41e année) **1983**

Oficina Panamericana de la República de Cuba. Catálogo de obras de derecho internacional e historia de América que el gobierno cubano pone á disposición, para su consulta, de los señores delegados a la sexta conferencia internacional Americana. Havana. Montalvo y Cardenas. 1928. 429p. **1984**

Olivart, Ramón de Dalman y de Olivart, Marqués de. Bibliographie du droit international . . . catalogue d'une bibliothèque de droit international et sciences auxiliaires. . . . Paris. A. Pedone. 1905-10. 1278p. **1985**

Periodical literature of international law. Am. jour. internat. law. I-. (Jan. 1907-) **1985a**

Princeton University. Library. An alphabetical subject index to some recent periodical articles on international law, being an index to the more recent volumes of certain periodicals from the Pitney collection in the Princeton University Library loaned to the American Commission to Negotiate Peace. Comp. and ed. by Charles R. Arrott. Princeton. The Univ. Lib. 1919. 207p. (Index to Revue de droit international, 1894-; Questions diplomatiques, 1900- ; Clunet, 1900-)**1986**

Select list of relations on public international law for college students. Bul. of bibliog. XI. p64-7, 86-7, 101-5, 124, 162-4 (Jan. 1921-Dec. 1922) **1987**

Stoerk, Felix. Die litteratur des internationalen rechts, 1884 bis 1894. Leipzig. J. C. Hinrichs. 1896 **1989**

Strupp, Karl. Bibliographie du droit des gens et des relations internationales. Leyde, Hollande. A.W. Sijthoff. 1938. 521p. **1989a**

U.S. Department of State. Digest of international law. By Green Haywood Hackworth. Wash. Govt. Ptg. Off. 1940- v. I- **1989b**

—— —— Library. Catalogue of works relating to the law of nations and diplomacy in the library of the Department of State. Part I. October 1897, A-Bryn. Wash. D.C. 1897. 110p. (No more published) **1990**

U.S. Library of Congress. Division of bibliography. The freedom of the seas; a bibliographical list. Jan. 1930. 37p. mim. (Additional references. July 23, 1936. 3p. mim.; Earlier lists. Feb. 19, 1917. 4p. typ.; March 2, 1917. 6p. typ.; Dec. 26, 1918. 12p. typ.) **1991**

—— —— —— International law; a list of books. Feb. 21, 1929. 11p. typ. **1992**

—— —— —— A list of recent references on American policy on neutrality. Feb. 14, 1936. 10p. typ. **1993**

—— —— —— List of references on armed neutrality. March 3, 1917. 9p. mim. **1994**

—— —— —— List of references on international arbitration. Comp. under the direction of A. P. C. Griffin. Wash. Govt. Ptg. Off. 1908. 151p. **1995**

—— —— —— List of references on international extradition. Aug. 25, 1914. 12p. typ. (Additional references. 1931. 3p.) **1996**

—— —— —— List of references on maritime law in war, with special reference to the Declaration of London. Aug. 14, 1914. 5p. typ. (Supplement. 2p.) **1997**

—— —— —— List of references on recognition in international law and practice. Wash. Govt. Ptg. Off. 1904. 18p. **1998**

—— —— —— List of references on the codification of international law. May 25, 1923. 8p. mim. (Supplement. June 3, 1924. 5p. mim.) **1999**

—— —— **Law division.** The bibliography of international law and continental law. By Edwin M. Borchard. Wash. Govt. Ptg. Off. 1913. 93p. **2000**

U.S. Naval War College. Newport. General index to international law situations, topics, discussions, documents, and decisions, volumes I to XXX, 1901-1930. Wash. Govt. Ptg. Off. 1933. 332p. **2001**

Wright, Quincy. Research in international law since the war; a report to the International Relations Committee of the Social Science Research Council. (Pamphlet ser. of the Carnegie Endowment for International Peace, Division of international law no. 51) Wash. D.C. 1930. 58p. **2002**

PEACE

Brooklyn. Public Library. International peace; a list of books, with reference to periodicals. . . . Brooklyn, N.Y. 1908. 53p. **2003**

Carnegie Endowment for International Peace. List of publications of the endowment. *In* Carnegie Endowment for International Peace. Yearbook. 1932. Wash. D.C. 1932. p193-219 **2004**

—— **Library.** Education for world peace, the study and teaching of international relations and international law; select list of books, pamphlets and periodical articles with annotations. Comp. by Mary Alice Matthews. (Reading list no. 33) Wash. D.C. 1932. 37p. **2005**

—— —— Peace and the peace movement; select list of references. Comp. by Mary Alice Matthews. Wash. D.C. 1924. 28p. mim. **2006**

—— —— Peace education; select list of references on international friendship, for the use of teachers and goodwill books for children. Comp. by Mary Alice Matthews. (Reading list no. 38) Wash. D.C. 1939. 24p. **2006a**

—— —— Peace forces of today; select list of recent books and articles on various aspects of the peace movement, with annotations. Comp. by Mary Alice Matthews. Wash. D. C. 1938. 54p. **2007**

—— —— The peace movement; select list of references on the work of national and international organizations for the advancement of peace; with special attention to the movement in the United States. Comp. by Mary Alice Matthews. (Reading list no. 39) [Wash. D.C. 1940] 67p. **2007a**

—— —— Peace projects; select list of references on plans for the preservation of peace from medieval times to the present day. Comp. by Mary Alice Matthews. (Reading list no. 36) Wash. D.C. 1936. 60p. **2008**

—— —— The Permanent Court of International Justice and the relation of the United States to the court; select list of books, pamphlets and periodicals. Comp. by Mary Alice Matthews. (Reading list no. 28) Wash. D.C. 1931. 17p. **2009**

Hague. Palace of Peace. Library. Catalogue. Par P. C. Molhuysen and E. R. Oppenheim. Leyde. A. W. Sijthoff. 1916. 1576col. Premier supplément du catalogue (1916). Par P. C. Molhuysen et D. Albers. Leyde. A. W. Sijthoff. 1922. 1042col. Deuxieme supplément (1929) au catalogue (1916). Par Jacob ter Meulen et Arnoldus Lysen. Leyde. A. W. Sijthoff. 1930. 1554col. Index alphabétique du catalogue (1916) et du supplément (1922). Leyde. A. W. Sijthoff. 1922. 790col. Index alphabétique par noms d'auteurs ou mots d'ordre du catalogue (1916) et des suppléments (1922 et 1929) Leyde. A. W. Sijthoff. 1932. 1466col. Index sommaire par ordre alphabétique des matières du catalogue (1916) et des suppléments (1922 et 1929). Leyde. A. W. Sijthoff. 1933. 76col. Troisième supplément. (Acquisitions; 1828/29-1936) Par Jacob ter Meulen et Arnoldus Lysen. Leyde. A. W. Sijthoff. 1937. 2742col. Index alphabétique par noms propres du troisième supplément. Leyde. A. W. Sijthoff. 1937. 79p. **2010**

Huntsman, M. H. Peace bibliography. London. The National Peace Council. 1910. 10p. (Reprinted from the Peace year book. 1910) **2011**

Jordan, David Starr. For international peace; list of books, reviews, and other articles in the interest of peace, friendship, and understanding between nations. . . 1898 to 1927. Stanford Univ. Stanford Univ. Press. 1927. 24p. **2012**

King, Gertrude Elizabeth (Nelson). World friendship; a bibliography; sources of educational material. Boston. Chapman & Grimes [1935] p9-81 **2013**

Mead, Edwin Doak. The literature of the peace movement. (World Peace Foundation. Pamphlet ser. no. 7. pt. IV) Boston. 1912. 14p. **2014**

Metz, J. R. Peace literature of the war, material for the study of international polity. (International conciliation. Special bul. Jan. 1916) N.Y. 1916 **2015**

Root, R. C. Bibliographies on international peace topics. n.p. 1914. 16p. **2016**

U.S. Library of Congress. Division of bibliography. List of references on international courts with special reference to the Permanent Court of International Justice. Oct. 10, 1923. 27p. mim. **2017**

—— —— —— List of references on the Bok peace award. April 7, 1924. 5p. typ. **2018**

—— —— —— List of references on the Permanent Court of International Justice. Oct. 25, 1923. 21p. mim. (Supplements. Jan. 13, 1926. 31p. mim.; June 18, 1928. 26p. mim.; June 5, 1929. 10p. mim.; May 29, 1930. 16p. mim.; June 29, 1931. 14p. mim.; April 25, 1932. 15p. mim.; April 26, 1933. 19p. mim.; April 28, 1934. 9p. mim.; May 24, 1935. 14p. mim.; May 5, 1936. 9p. mim.; May 6, 1937. 8p. mim.) **2019**

—— —— —— Permanent Court of International Justice; references supplementing previous lists. 1937. 8p. **2019a**

MISCELLANEOUS

American Foreign Service Journal. Bibliography of foreign service study. Wash. D.C. 1931. 4p. (Reprinted from Am. For. ser. jour. VIII. p34-7. Jan. 1931) **2019b**

Borchard, Edwin Montefiore. (General and national bibliographies on the law of aliens). In The diplomatic protection of citizens abroad; or, The law of international claims. N.Y. Banks Law Publishing Co. 1928. p865-927 **2020**

Cam, Gilbert Arthur. United States neutrality resolutions of 1935, 1936, and 1937, a selected list. New York Pub. Lib. bul. XLI. p417-26 (May 1937) **2020a**

Carnegie Endowment for International Peace. Library. Isolation and economic nationalism. (Brief reference list, no. 14) Wash. D.C. The Endowment. 1939. 5p. mim. **2020b**

—— —— Neutrality; select list of references on neutrality and the policy of the United States in the World war and post war periods. Comp. by Mary Alice Matthews. (Reading list no. 37) Wash. D.C. 1938. 36p. **2020c**

—— —— Traffic in arms, munitions, and implements of war and control of their manufacture; select list of books, pamphlets and periodical articles with annotations. Comp. by Mary Alice Matthews. (Reading list no. 34) Wash. D.C. 1933. 22p. **2021**

Council on Foreign Relations. The Council on Foreign Relations; a record of fifteen years, 1921-1936. N.Y. 1937. 56p. **2021a**

Doré, Robert. Essai d'une bibliographie des Congrès internationaux. Paris. Edouard Champion. 1923. 56p. (Reprinted from Revue des bibliothèques. 32ᵉ année. 1922. nᵉˢ 10-12. octobre-décembre. p389-444) **2022**

Heatley, D. P. The literature of international relations. In Diplomacy and the study of international relations. Oxford. Clarendon Press. 1919. p85-115 **2023**

Hicks, Frederick Charles. Internationalism; a selected list of books, pamphlets and periodicals. (International conciliation. . . no.64) N.Y. Am. Asso. for International Conciliation. 1913. 30p. **2024**

Hyde, Marguerite R. Good references on educating for international understanding. (U.S. Office of Education. Bibliography no. 16) Wash. Govt. Ptg. Off. 1938. 16p. **2024a**

International conciliation. Index to International conciliation, April 1907-December 1906 (nos. 1-325) including Special bulletins (S.B.) dated but not numbered. N.Y. Carnegie Endowment for International Peace. [1937?] 22p. **2024b**

International congresses and conferences, 1840-1937; a union list of their publications available in libraries of the United States and Canada. Ed. by Winifred Gregory under the auspices of the Bibliographical Society of America. N.Y. H.W. Wilson. 1938. 229p. **2024c**

Jordan, David Starr and Krehbiel, Edward B. Syllabus of lectures on international conciliation given at Leland Stanford Junior University. Boston. World Peace Foundation. 1912. 180p. **2025**

Laughlin, J. Laurence and Willis, H. Parker. Bibliography; list of references on reciprocity and allied subjects. In Reciprocity. N.Y. Baker & Taylor. 1903. p439-71 **2026**

National Council for Prevention of War. A selected list of recent articles on international affairs, no. 1-107, Oct./Nov. 1923-Sept./Oct. 1932. Comp. by Mary P. Webster. Wash. D.C. 1923-32. 107 nos. in 4v. **2027**

Newark, N.J. Free Public Library. Aids to international understanding; a book list with notes (with supplement). Madison, N.J. The New Jersey Federation of Womens Clubs, com. on international relations. [1927, 1929] 2pts. in 1v. **2028**

Pinson, Koppel S. A bibliographical introduction to nationalism. N.Y. Columbia Univ. Press. 1935. 70p. **2029**

Royal Institute of International Affairs, London. Catalogue of publications on international affairs. . . . London. 1933- **2030**

—— —— Consolidated index to the Survey of international affairs, 1920-1930, and supplementary volumes. Comp. by Miss M. Franklin. London. Oxford Univ. Press. 1932. 214p. **2031**

Stumke, Hans. Bibliographie der internationalen Kongresse und Verbände in der Preussischen Staatsbibliothek. Band I: Medizin. Leipzig. Otto Harrassowitz. 1939. 281p. **2031a**

U.S. Bureau of Agricultural Economics. Library. America must choose; a brief list of references relating to nationalism, internationalism and a planned middle course. N.Y. "America must choose" dept., Foreign Policy Asso., Inc., World Peace Foundation. 1934. 11p. **2032**

U.S. Department of Justice. Compilation of references to federal statutes relating to neutrality, espionage, sabotage, sedition and kindred national defense laws. Prep. by the Special Defense Unit, L.M.C. Smith, Chief. Wash. D.C. March 1941. 108p. mim. **2032a**

U.S. Library of Congress. Division of bibliography. A list of recent references on neutrality. Comp. by Florence S. Hellman. Sept. 23, 1939. 19p. mim. **2032b**

—— —— —— List of recent references on women in international affairs. Nov. 16, 1926. 6p. typ. **2032c**

—— —— —— List of references on alien enemies (exclusive of trading with the enemy). March 20, 1918. 15p. typ. **2033**

—— —— —— List of references on international agreements as distinguished from more formal treaties. Dec. 18, 1917. 7p. mim. **2034**

—— —— —— List of references on international loans and their influence on international politics. Dec. 29, 1919. 6p. typ. **2035**

—— —— —— A list of references on mandates. May 10, 1924. 31p. mim. **2036**

—— —— —— A list of references on petroleum in world relations. Nov. 1, 1923. 7p. typ. **2037**

—— —— —— List of references on reciprocity. Comp. under the direction of A. P. C. Griffin (1st edition. 1902) and H. H. B. Meyer (2d edition) Wash. Govt. Ptg. Off. 1910. 137p. **2038**

—— —— —— List of references on secret diplomacy and a more democratic control of foreign policy. April 29, 1916. 2p. typ. **2039**

—— —— —— List of references on the most-favored nation clause (supplementary to list of reference on reciprocity, 1910). May 23, 1918. 3p. typ. **2040**

—— —— —— List of references on the outlawry of war. June 5, 1925. 6p. mim. **2041**

—— —— —— A list of references on the privileges and immunities of public officers including ambassadors, consuls, and members of legislative bodies. Nov. 28, 1923. 8p. mim. **2042**

—— —— —— List of references on the recall or dismissal of foreign representatives by the executive. April 28, 1916. 6p. typ. **2043**

—— —— —— List of speeches, addresses, etc. on neutrality as printed in the Congressional record, 1937-1939. Comp. by Anne L. Baden, under the direction of Florence S. Hellman. 1939. 42p. mim. **2043a**

—— —— —— Nationalism; a selected list of writings since 1918, with a section on economic nationalism. June 14, 1934. 22p. mim. **2044**

—— —— —— Renunciation of war; a bibliographical list. Sept. 20, 1928. 10p. typ. **2045**

—— —— —— A selected list of recent references on foreign indebtedness to the United States. Comp. by Grace H. Fuller. May 15, 1939. 14p. mim. **2045a**

—— —— —— Selected list of recent writings on internationalism (super-state). Aug. 8, 1933. 30p. mim. **2046**

World Congress of Universal Documentation, Paris, 1937. Texte des communications. Berichte. Communications. Paris. Secrétariat. 1937. 344p. (Bibliography of congresses) **2046a**

CHAPTER V

ECONOMIC HISTORY

GENERAL

American Economic Association. General contents and index of volumes I to XI, 1886-1896. (Am. Economic Asso. Publications. v. XI) N.Y. Pub. for the Am. Economic Asso. by the Macmillan Co. 1896. 52p. **2048**

—— Reviews and new books. The Am. economic rev. I. March 1911- **2049**

Batson, Harold Edward. A select bibliography of modern economic theory, 1870-1929, with an introduction by Lionel Robbins. (Stud. in economics and pol. science. no. 6. in the ser. of bibliographies by writers connected with the London School of Economics and Pol. Science) London. Routledge. 1930. 224p. **2050**

Book reviews and titles of new books. Am. econ. rev. I.- . (March 1911-) **2050a**

Booth, Mary J. Material on geography, including commercial products, industries, transportation and education exhibits which may be obtained free at small cost. Charleston, Ill. The Compiler. 1927. 101p. **2051**

Bowker, R. R. and Iles, George. The reader's guide in economic, social and political science, being a classified bibliography, American, English, French and German, with descriptive notes, author, title and subject-index, courses of reading, college courses, etc. N.Y. Putnam's. 1891. 169p. **2052**

Brace, Maria Clark. A selected list of books on proposed roads to prosperity. Balt.? Columbian Lib. Asso. 1933. 7p. **2053**

Chicago. University. Bibliography of economics for 1909; a cumulation of bibliography appearing in the Journal of political economy, from February, 1909 to January, 1910, inclusive. Ed. by the University of Chicago. Faculty of the Department of political economy. Chicago. Univ. of Chicago Press. 1910. 282p. **2054**

Cochran, Thomas C. A bibliography of American economic history since the Civil War. N.Y. New York Univ. In progress **2054a**

Doriot, Georges F. and McNair, M. P. Selected list of references on economics, finance, manufacturing and marketing. (Supplement to the Bul. of the Harvard Business School Alumni Asso. Nov. 1929) **2055**

Dunbar, Charles F. Economic science in America, 1776-1876. N. Am. rev. CXXII. p124-54 (Jan. 1876) **2055a**

Edwards, Everett E. A list of American economic histories. (U.S. Department of Agriculture. Library. Bibliog. contributions no. 27) Wash. D.C. 1939. 43p. mim. **2055b**

—— References on economic history as a field of research and study. (U.S. Department of Agriculture. Library. Bibliog. contributions no. 31) Wash. D.C. 1936. 83p. **2055c**

Gordon, R. A. Selected bibliography of the literature of economic fluctuations, 1936-37. Rev. econ. statis. XX. p120-7 (Aug. 1938) **2055d**

—— A selected bibliography of the literature on economic fluctuations, 1930-36. Rev. econ. statist. XIX. p37-86. 1937 **2055e**

Gough, W. A. Bibliotheca politica. Part I. Being a collection of books and pamphlets relating to the economic, social and political development of America. N.Y. 1916. 32p. **2056**

Gras, Norman Scott Brien. Books and articles on the economic history of the United States and Canada. Economic hist. rev. VI. p247-55 (April 1936); VII. p258-66 (May 1937) **2056a**

Great Britain. Board of Trade. Library. Catalogue of library, 1912. London. H. M. Stationery Off., Darling & Son. 1913. 467p. **2057**

Harvard University. List of references in economics 2; economic history of Europe since 1800, and of the United States. By Edmond E. Lincoln. Cambridge. Pub. by Harvard Univ. 1920. 145p. **2058**

Hollander, Jacob H. The economic library of Jacob H. Hollander, Ph.D., professor of political economy in the Johns Hopkins University. Comp. by E. A. G. Marsh. Baltimore. Priv. print. 1937. 324p. **2058a**

Homan, Paul T. Economic planning; the proposals and the literature. Quar. jour. of economics. XLVII. p102-22 (1932-33) **2059**

Laing, Graham A. Economics in a changing world; a guide for studying economic change and how it affects human lives. Wash. D.C. Am. Assoc. of Univ. Women. 1936 **2059a**

McClurg, A. C., firm, booksellers, Chicago. A classified catalogue of works on economics and politics, including political economy and sociology, finance, the tariff, trade and labor, the land question, railways, and kindred subjects. Chicago. McClurg. 1895. 50p. **2060**

AGRICULTURE

General

Nickles, John M. Annotated bibliography of economic geology. Prepared under the auspices of the National Research Council. Lancaster, Pa. Economic Geol. Publishing Co. 1928. 380p. **2061**

Osaka University of Commerce. The Institute for Economic Research. Bibliography of economic science. Tokyo. Maruzen Co., Ltd. 1934-39. 4v. **2061a**

The Quarterly journal of economics. (Indexes). Index, 1886-1936. Cambridge, Mass. Harvard Univ. Press; London. H. Milford, Oxford Univ. Press. 1936. 138p. **2061b**

Rand, Benjamin. A bibliography of economics. Cambridge, Mass. John Wilson. 1895. 88p. (Also in Selections illustrating economic history since the Seven years war. Cambridge, Mass. J. Wilson. 1895) **2062**

Recent publications. Quar. jour. econ. I-1886- **2062a**

Silvin, Edward. Index to periodical literature on socialism. Santa Barbara, Calif. Rogers & Morley. 1909. 45p. **2063**

Taussig, Frank William. Topics and references in economics 6, [Harvard College], the economic history of the United States. Cambridge, Mass. 1901? **2064**

Thompson, Laura A. National economic councils; a list of references. Monthly labor rev. XXXII. p1249-58 (May 1931) **2065**

U.S. Department of Agriculture. Library. A list of American economic histories. By Everett Eugene Edwards (Bibliog. contributions no. 27) Wash. D.C. Nov. 1935. 25p. mim. **2066**

U.S. Library of Congress. Division of bibliography. Economic councils and economic planning; a list of recent references. Sept. 13, 1932. 10p. mim. (Supplement. Sept. 10, 1933. 15p. mim.) **2067**

———— ———— Select list of references on functional representation including national economic councils. Oct. 28, 1932 8p. typ. **2068**

———— ———— A selected list of recent references on economic planning, with a section on economic councils. Oct. 24, 1935. 39p. mim. **2069**

———— Reading room. A list of references on economic planning. Wash. D.C. July 12, 1933. 23p. mim. **2070**

Verwey, Gerlof and Renooij, D. C. The economist's handbook; a manual of statistical sources. Amsterdam. The economist's handbook. 1934. 460p. (Section on the U. S. p385-415) **2071**

Virginia. State Library. Economics (General), economic history, economic theory. Virginia State Lib. bul. III. p29-96 (Jan., April, July 1910) **2072**

Arents, George. Books, manuscripts and drawings relating to tobacco from the collection of George Arents, jr., on exhibition at the Library of Congress, Washington, D.C., April 1938. [Wash. Govt. Ptg. Off. 1938] 113p. **2072a**

———— Books, manuscripts and drawings relating to tobacco from the collection of George Arents, on exhibition at Duke University Library, Durham, North Carolina, April 28th to June 2nd 1941. [Durham N.C. 1941] 60p. **2072b**

———— Early literature of tobacco. So. Atlantic quar. XXXVII. p97-107 (April 1938) **2072c**

Bidwell, Percy W. and Falconer, John I. Classified and critical bibliography. In History of agriculture in the northern United States, 1620-1860. (Carnegie Inst. of Wash. Publication no. 358) Wash. D.C. 1925. p454-92 **2073**

Bitting, Clarence R. Bibliography on sugar. n.p. Priv. print. 1937. 72p. **2073a**

Brooks, Jerome E. Tobacco: its history illustrated by the books, manuscripts and engravings in the library of George Arents, Jr. N.Y. The Rosenbach Company. 1937 **2073b**

California. University. College of agriculture. Agricultural experiment station. Rural land economics, 1936: outstanding references relating to rural land economics, especially to the present national land policy (supplementing Rural land economics 1933-1935). Comp. by Orpha Cummings. Berkeley. 1937. 93p. **2073c**

Current writings on American agricultural history. Agric. hist. I- . (Jan. 1917-) **2073d**

Davis, Joseph S. The literature of the agricultural situation once more. Quar. jour. economics. XLIV. p138-59 (Nov. 1929) **2074**

———— Recent books on the agricultural situation. Quar. jour. economics. XLIII. p532-43 (May 1929) **2075**

Day, Mary B. Selected reading list of interest to students in the field of agricultural history and allied subjects in the Museum library. (Reading list no. 5, 1939 rev. ed.). Chicago. Lib. Mus. of Sci. and Industry. 1939. 14p. mim. **2075a**

Dewees, Anne. Selected list of agricultural history publications arranged to show the development of agricultural history research in the U.S. Department of Agriculture. . . . Wash. D.C. Bur. of Agricul. Econ. May 20, 1939. 11p. processed **2075b**

Edwards, Everett E. A bibliography of the history of agriculture in the United States. (U.S. Department of Agriculture. Miscellaneous publications no. 84) Wash. Govt. Ptg. Off. 1930. 307p. **2076**

Edwards, Everett E. A guide for courses in the history of American agriculture. (U.S. Department of Agriculture. Library. Bibliog. contributions no. 35) Wash. D.C. 1939. 192p.   **2076a**
—— References on agricultural history as a field for research. (U.S. Department of Agriculture. Library. Bibliog. contributions no. 32) Wash. D.C. 1937. 41p. **2076b**
—— References on agriculture in the life of the nation. (U.S. Department of Agriculture. Library. Bibliog. contributions no. 34) Wash. D.C. 1938. 73p. mim. **2076c**
—— Selected references on the history of agriculture in the United States. (U.S. Department of Agriculture. Library. Bibliog. contributions no. 26 (ed. 2)) Wash. D.C. 1939. 43p. mim.   **2076d**
Gray, Lewis Cecil and Thompson, Esther Katherine. Bibliography. *In* History of agriculture in the southern United States to 1860. (Carnegie Inst. of Wash. Publication no. 430) Wash. D.C. 1933. II. p945-1016   **2077**
Hamilton, Schuyler. Bibliography on all matter printed in the United States concerning the cultivation of grape vines in America and the production of American wine. 50 East 72nd St. N.Y. Planned **2077a**
List of books on farming, homemaking and rural life for farmers and homemakers. (Bul. v. 36, no. 41) Urbana. Univ. of Ill. 1939. 31p.   **2077b**
Schmidt, Louis Bernard. Topical studies and references on the history of American agriculture. Ames, Dept. of history and government. Iowa State College. 1940. 123p.   **2078**
Stryker, Roy E. The Farm Security Administration collection of photographs and its value for agricultural history. Address at the 1940 annual meeting of the Agricultural History Society **2078a**
Taylor, Raymond G. Some sources for Mississippi Valley agricultural history. Miss. Valley hist. rev. VII. p142-5 (Sept. 1920)   **2079**
Texas. University. Department of extension. A selected classified list of free publications on agriculture and allied subjects for use in the school and home. (Bul. of the Univ. of Texas. 1915. no. 16. March 15, 1915) Austin. The Univ. 1916. 32p.   **2080**
Trimble, William J. Introductory manual for the study and reading of agrarian history. Fargo, N.D. Agricultural College Book Store. 1917. 47p.   **2081**
True, Rodney Howard. Beginnings of agricultural literature in America. Am. Lib. Asso. pap. and proc. Colorado Springs Conference bul. 14. no. 4. p186-94 (July 1920)   **2082**
U.S. Agricultural Adjustment Administration. Consumers' bookshelf; a bibliography of publications on commodity buying and other consumer problems. Comp. by B. S. Yane and R. S. Hadsell. (Consumers' counsel ser., pub. no. 4) Wash. Govt. Ptg. Off. 1938. 100p. **2082a**

U.S. Bureau of Agricultural Economics. Library. Agricultural economics; a selected list of references. Comp. by Mary G. Lacy (Agricultural economics bibliog. no. 1. rev. 1929) Wash. D.C. Feb. 1929. 18p. mim.   **2083**
—— —— Agricultural economics; selected list of references. Comp. by Mary G. Lacy. Wash. D.C. 1938. 31p. mim. **2083a**
—— —— —— Agricultural economics literature, I, Jan. 1927- . Wash. D.C. 1927- **2084**
—— —— —— Agricultural labor in the United States, 1915-1935; a select list of references. Comp. by Esther M. Colvin and Josiah C. Folsom, under the direction of Mary G. Lacy. (Agricultural economics bibliog. no. 64) Wash. D.C. 1935. 493p.   **2084a**
—— —— Agricultural labor in the United States, 1936-1937; a selected list of references. Comp. by Esther M. Colvin and Josiah C. Folsom. Wash. D.C. 1938. 205p. mim.   **2084b**
—— —— —— Agricultural relief measures relating to the raising of farm prices. 74 Cong., Jan. 3, 1935-June 20, 1936. Comp. by Marion E. Wheeler. (Agricultural economics bibliog. no. 84) Wash. D.C. April 1940. 75p. mim.   **2084c**
—— —— —— Agricultural relief measures relating to the raising of farm prices. 75 Cong., Jan. 5, 1937 to June 16, 1938. Comp. by Marion E. Wheeler and Mamie I. Herb. (Agricultural economics bibliog. no. 76) Wash. D.C. Feb. 1939. 109p. mim.   **2084d**
—— —— —— Anthropology and agriculture; selected references on agriculture in primitive cultures. Comp. by Kenneth MacLeish and Helen E. Hennefrund. (Agricultural economics bibliog. no. 89) Wash. D.C. Nov. 1940. 134p. processed **2084e**
—— —— —— Corn in the development of the civilization of the Americas; a selected and annotated bibliography. Comp. by Louise O. Bercaw, Annie M. Hannay, and Nellie G. Larson. (Agricultural economics bibliog. no. 87) Wash. D.C. Sept. 1940. 195p. processed **2084f**
—— —— —— Cotton linters; selected references in English, 1900-July 1940. Comp. by Emily L. Day. (Agricultural economics bibliog. no. 88) Wash. D.C. Oct. 1940. 39p. processed **2084g**
—— —— —— Cotton picking machinery; a short list of references. Comp. by Emily L. Day. (Economic library list no. 9) Wash. D.C. March 1940. 19p. processed **2084h**
—— —— —— Food and cotton stamp plans; a selected list of references. Comp. by Mamie I. Herb. (Economic library list no. 18) Wash. D.C. Nov. 1940. 25p. processed **2084i**
—— —— —— Large scale and corporation farming. (Agricultural economics bibliog. no. 69) Wash. D.C. 1937. 121p. mim.   **2084j**

—— —— —— Long-time agricultural economics in the United States—national, regional, and state. Comp. by Mary G. Lacy (Agricultural economics bibliog. no. 5) Wash. D.C. June 1925. 20p. mim. **2085**

—— —— —— Part-time farming in the United States; a selected list of references. Comp. by Helen E. Hennefrund. (Agricultural economics bibliog. no. 77) Wash. D.C. Feb. 1939. 272p. mim. **2085a**

—— —— —— Price fixing by government in the United States, 1926-1939; a selected list of references on direct price fixing of agricultural products by the federal and state governments. Comp. by Louise O. Bercaw. (Agricultural economics bibliog. no. 79) Wash. D.C. July 1939. 214p. mim. **2085b**

—— —— —— References on agricultural history as a field of research and study. Comp. by Everett E. Edwards. [Wash. D.C.] Nov. 1934. 6p. mim. **2086**

—— —— —— References on the history of agriculture in the United States. Comp. by Everett E. Edwards. [Wash. D.C.] Sept. 1934. 13p. mim. **2087**

—— —— —— Research in rural economics and rural sociology in the southern states since 1920; a list of published, unpublished and current studies. Comp. under the direction of Mary G. Lacy (Agricultural economics bibliog. no. 10) Wash. D.C. Jan. 1926. 44p. mim. **2088**

—— —— —— Rural psychology; a partial list of references. (Agricultural economics bibliog. no. 78) Comp. by M. T. Olcott. Wash. D.C. March 1939. 76p. mim. **2088a**

—— —— —— Sea island cotton; selected references. Comp. by Emily L. Day. (Economic library list no. 8) Wash. D.C. Nov. 1939. 13p. processed **2088b**

—— —— —— The soybean industry; a selected list of references on the economic aspects of the industry in the United States, 1900-1938. Comp. by Helen E. Hennefrund and Esther M. Colvin, under the direction of Mary G. Lacy. (Agricultural economics bibliog. no. 74) Wash. D.C. Oct. 1938. 474p. mim. **2088c**

—— —— —— Storage of grain in the United States; selected references to publications issued 1931-1937. Comp. by Helen E. Hennefrund. Wash. D.C. Feb. 1, 1938. 35p. typ. **2088d**

—— —— —— Uses and products made of corn; abstracts and references. Comp. by C. L. P. Corbett and E. G. Boerner. Wash. D.C. March 1937. 64p. mim. **2088e**

U.S. Bureau of Agricultural Engineering. Agricultural engineering; a selected bibliography. Comp. by Dorothy W. Graf. Wash. D.C. 1937. 373p. mim. (Lists principally publications of the U.S. Dept. of Agriculture, the state agricultural experiment stations and the state extension services from their beginning through 1935) **2088f**

—— —— Bibliography on combine harvester-threshers. (A selected list of references) Comp. by Dorothy W. Graf. Wash. D.C. 1935. 23p. Reprod. **2088g**

—— —— Library. Card catalog on agricultural engineering. Wash. D.C. **2088h**

U.S. Bureau of Plant Industry. Library. Agronomy; current literature, v. 1-9, Jan., 1926-Dec. 22, 1934. Wash. D.C. 1926-34. mim. **2089**

—— —— —— Index catalog of literature on plant industry. Wash. D.C. MS. **2089a**

U.S. Commodity Exchange Administration. Library. Futures trading in agricultural commodities; a selected list of references. Comp. by C. Louise Phillips-Corbett. Wash. D.C. Aug. 1938. 65p. mim. **2089b**

—— —— Futures trading in agricultural commodities; a selected list of references to publications issued prior to 1920. Comp. by C. Louise Phillips-Corbett. Wash. D.C. Feb. 1939. 11p. mim. **2089c**

U.S. Department of Agriculture. The influence of weather on crops: 1900-1930; a selected and annotated bibliography. Comp. by A. M. Hannay. (Miscellaneous publications no. 118) Wash. D.C. 1931 **2089d**

—— —— List of bulletins of the agricultural experiment stations for the calendar years, 1937 and 1938. Comp. by C. E. Pennington. (Miscellaneous publications no. 362) Wash. D.C. Jan. 1940. 91p. **2089e**

—— —— Library. Agricultural library notes, I- . Jan. 1926- . [Wash. D.C.] 1926- **2090**

—— —— —— Selected list of American agricultural books. Wash. D.C. Oct. 1940. 37p. processed **2090a**

U.S. Farm Credit Administration. Cooperation in agriculture; a selected and annotated bibliography with special reference to marketing, purchasing and credit. Comp. by Chastina Gardner. (Cooperative division. Bul. no. 4) Wash. D.C. 1936. 214p. **2091**

—— —— Library. Reference material in library of Farm Credit Administration, including periodicals, house organs, newspapers, bulletins, reports, law books, etc. Wash. D.C. 1934. 39p. mim. **2092**

U.S. Federal Emergency Relief Administration. Office of specialist in workers education. Education division. The farm problem; suggested readings on the problems facing the American farm population and proposed solutions. Wash. D.C. Oct. 1934. 29p. mim. **2093**

U.S. Library of Congress. Division of bibliography. A list of references on the present agricultural situation in the United States. Feb. 1924. 17p. mim. **2094**

U.S. Office of Experiment Stations. Some books on agriculture and agricultural science, published 1893-1896. (Office of Experiment Stations. Circular no. 31) Wash. Govt. Ptg. Off. 1896. 176p. **2095**

U.S. Office of Experiment Stations. Some books on agriculture and sciences related to agriculture. (Office of Experiment Stations. Circular no. 38) Wash. Govt. Ptg. Off. 1898. 45p.   **2096**

U.S. Works Progress Administration. National research project on reemployment opportunities and recent changes in industrial techniques. Selected references on practices and use of labor on farms. Comp. by W. A. Newman and L. K. Macy. Phila. 1937. 284p.   **2096a**

Virginia. State Library. Finding list of books in agriculture. Comp. under the direction of Earl G. Swem. Virginia State Lib. bul. IV. p236-304 (April-Oct. 1911)   **2097**

Warner, Marjorie F. and Brown, Janice S. Checklist of sixteenth, seventeenth, and eighteenth century gardening books. Wash. D.C. U.S. Bureau of Plant Industry. In progress   **2097a**

Animal Industry, Dairying, Poultry

Hawks, Emma B. A bibliography of poultry. U.S. Dept. of Agriculture. Bul. XVIII (Oct. 1897) 32p.   **2098**

Malin, James C. Notes on the historical literature of the range cattle industry. Kansas hist. quar. I. p74-6 (Nov. 1931)   **2099**

Plumb, Charles S. A partial index to animal husbandry literature. Columbus, Ohio. Plumb. 1911. 94p.   **2100**

Schmidt, P. Marcus. The dairy industry in America: its status and development; a selected bibliography. Madison. Univ. of Wisconsin Lib. School. 1938. 33p. typ.   **2100a**

U.S. Bureau of Agricultural Economics. Library. The dairy industry in the United States, 1932 and 1933; a selected list of references. Comp. by Margaret Harrison and Louise O. Bercaw. [Wash. D.C. Dec. 21, 1933] 23p. typ.   **2101**

—— —— —— The dairy industry in the United States; selected references on the economic aspects of the industry. Comp. by Louise O. Bercaw. (Economic library list no. 11) Wash. D.C. July 1940. 59p. processed   **2101a**

—— —— —— List of periodicals containing prices and other statistical and economical information on dairy products. Comp. by Esther M. Colvin. (Agricultural economics bibliog. no. 71) Wash. D.C. Oct. 1937. 114p.   **2101b**

—— —— —— Livestock financing in the United States; selected references to material published, 1915-1935. Comp. by Katherine Jacobs under the direction of Mary G. Lacy (Agricultural economics bibliog. no. 62) Wash. D.C. 1935. 57p. mim.   **2102**

—— —— —— The meat industry in the United States; a selected list of references on the economic aspects of the industry, including meat packing published since 1918. Comp. by Minna Gill and Lillian Crans. Wash. D.C. Dec. 17, 1928. 24p.   **2103**

—— —— —— The poultry industry; a selected list of references on the economic aspects of the industry, 1920-1927. Comp. by Louise O. Bercaw under the direction of Mary G. Lacy (Agricultural economics bibliog. no. 24) Wash. D.C. Feb. 1928. 104p. mim.   **2104**

U.S. Bureau of Animal Industry. Library. Card catalog of animal industry. Wash. D.C.   **2104a**

—— —— —— Card catalog of veterinary literature. Wash. D.C.   **2104b**

U.S. Bureau of Dairy Industry. Library. Dairy card catalog. Wash. D.C.   **2104c**

U.S. Department of Agriculture. Library. Cattle, sheep and goat production in the range country; a selected list of publications issued by the U.S. Dept. of Agriculture and the Agricultural colleges, experiment stations and departments of agriculture of the seventeen range states. Comp. by Emma B. Hawks and Earl W. McComas (Bibliog. contributions no. 19) Wash. D.C. 1928. 78p. mim.   **2105**

—— —— —— Partial list of publications on dairying issued in the United States 1900 to June, 1923. Comp. by Carrie B. Sherfy. (Bibliog. contributions no. 6) Wash. D.C. Aug. 1923. 236p. mim.   **2106**

U.S. Forest Service. A selected bibliography on management of western ranges, livestock and wildlife. By F. G. Renner and others. (U.S. Dept. of Agriculture. Miscellaneous publications no. 281) Wash. D.C. 1938. 468p.   **2106a**

U.S. Library of Congress. Division of bibliography. A list of references on the history of the horse in America. 1938. 10p.   **2106b**

—— —— —— Select list of references on cattle ranches, fencing, etc. 1907. 13p. typ. (Additional references. 1911. 1p.)   **2107**

—— —— —— Select list of references on Texas fever in cattle. Jan. 30, 1913. 13p. typ.   **2108**

Forestry

Averell, James L. American forest literature from a bibliography point of view. Jour. of forestry. XXX. p197-9 (Feb. 1932)   **2109**

Boston. Public Library. Codman collection. The Codman collection of books on landscape gardening; also a list of books on trees and forestry. Boston Pub. by the Trustees. 1899. 26p. (Reprinted from the Monthly bul. Oct.-Nov. 1898)   **2110**

Brooklyn. Public Library. Trees, forestry and lumbering; a list of books and of references to periodicals in the Brooklyn Public Library. Brooklyn, N.Y. 1911. 40p.   **2111**

New York State. Forest Commission. Bibliography of forestry; a list of books and publications on forests and tree culture. Annual rep. 1885. p161-204   **2112**

—— —— Bibliography of forestry and kindred topics. Annual rep. 1888. p77-122 **2113**

Pittsburgh. Carnegie Library. Trees and forestry; a selected list of the more important books in the library. Pittsburgh. Carnegie Lib. 1917. 18p. (Reprinted from the Monthly bul. May 1917) **2114**

Schuette, H. A. and Schuette, Sybil C. Maple sugar: a bibliography of early records. Wis. acad. sci. trans. XXIX. p207-36. 1935 **2114a**

Society of American Foresters, Washington, D.C. Appalachian section. Cumulated index for proceedings of the Society of American Foresters, volumes 1-11, May, 1905-October, 1916; Forest quarterly, volumes 1-14, October, 1902-December, 1916; Journal of forestry, volumes, 15-27, January, 1917-December, 1929. Wash. D.C. 1930. 111p. **2115**

U.S. Department of Agriculture. Library. Catalogue of publications relating to forestry in the library of the United States Department of Agriculture. Prepared in the library of the Department with the cooperation of the Forest Service (Bul. no. 76) Wash. Govt. Ptg. Off. 1912. 302p. **2116**

U.S. Forest Service. A bibliography on artificial reforestation. Comp. by D. S. Olson, W. B. Apgar, and Florence R. Caswell. Wash. D.C. 1931. 83p. mim. **2117**

—— —— Community forests, a bibliography of publications and literature relating to community forests. Issued by the Division of state cooperation. Wash. D.C. March 1, 1938. 14p. mim. **2117a**

—— —— Forest economics bibliography. Wash. D.C. 1929. 31p. **2118**

—— —— A selected bibliography of North American forestry. Comp. by E. N. Munns. (U.S. Department of Agriculture. Miscellaneous publications no. 364) Wash. Govt. Ptg. Off. 1940. 1142p. **2118a**

—— —— **Division of forest economics.** Rural assessment with special reference to forests; a bibliography (general and by states). Comp. by Alf Z. Nelson. Wash. D.C. July 1, 1940. 29p. mim. **2118b**

—— —— **Library.** Channels of publication for articles by members of the Forest Service. Wash. D.C. Feb. 15, 1940. 62p. processed (Periodicals and farm journals) **2118c**

—— —— —— Cooperative marketing of forest products: a bibliography. Wash. D.C. Nov. 1, 1939. 22p. mim. **2118d**

—— —— —— Effects of fire on forests: a bibliography. Wash. D.C. Sept. 15, 1938. 130p. mim. **2118e**

—— —— —— Forestry; current literature, Jan., 1928-. Wash. D.C. 1928- mim. (For previous publication of this list see Schmeckebier. U.S. government publications. p9-70) **2119**

Land and Irrigation

California. University. Bureau of Public Administration. Land utilization; a bibliography. Comp. by Dorothy Campbell Culver. Berkeley, May 15, 1935 (Reissued, with typographical corrections, November 15, 1937) [Berkeley, 1937] 222p. mim. **2120**

Ellis, Arthur J. The divining rod; a history of water witching with a bibliography. (U.S. Geol. Survey. Water-supply paper. 416) Wash. D.C. 1917. p26-53. **2121**

Gaul, John J. Reclamation, 1902-1938, a supplemental bibliography. (Bibliographical Center for Research, Regional checklist no. 6) Denver, Colo. Denver Pub. Lib. and State Dept. of Education. 1939. 98p. mim. **2121a**

Hedrick, Ellen A. List of references to publications relating to irrigation and land drainage. (U.S. Dept. of Agriculture. Bul. no. 41) Wash. Govt. Ptg. Off. 1902. 181p. **2122**

Minneapolis. Board of Education. A selected and annotated bibliography of conservation literature. Prep. with the assistance of Work Projects Administration, project 61-1-71-221 (3). [Minneapolis] 1940. 132p. reprod. **2122a**

Publication notes. U.S. Bureau of Agricultural Economics, Land policy circular, June 1935- **2122b**

Shaw, Charles Frederick and Baldwin, Mark. Bibliography of soil series. (MC—3) Wash. D.C. U.S. Bureau of Chemistry and Soils. 1938. 167p. mim. **2122c**

U.S. Bureau of Agricultural Economics. Land economics division. Digest of outstanding federal and state legislation affecting rural land use. (Bul. no. 55) Wash. D.C. May 1, 1940. 27p. mim. **2122d**

—— —— **Library.** Bibliography of land utilization, 1918-36. Comp. by Louise O. Bercaw and Annie M. Hannay under the direction of Mary G. Lacy, and in cooperation with the Land utilization division, Resettlement Administration. (U.S. Dept. of Agriculure. Miscellaneus publications no. 284) Wash, D.C. 1938 **2122e**

—— —— —— Indirect flood damages; a list of references. Comp. by Louise O. Bercaw. (Economic library list no. 13) Wash. D.C. Aug. 1940. 15p. processed **2122f**

—— —— —— Land classification; a selected bibliography. Comp. by Orval E. Goodsell and Walter M. Rudolph. (Agricultural economics bibliog. no. 83) Wash. D.C. March 1940. 95p. processed **2122g**

—— —— —— Land utilization and land policies in the United States; a preliminary list of references. Comp. by Louise O. Bercaw under the direction of Mary G. Lacy. Wash. D.C. May 1936. 34p. mim. **2123**

—— —— —— Soil erosion and its prevention (A partial list of references, 1900-1934). Comp. by Dorothy W. Graf. [Wash. D.C.] 1935. 91p. **2124**

U.S. Bureau of Agricultural Engineering. Library. Irrigation, a selected bibliography. Comp. by Dorothy W. Graf. Wash. D.C. 1938. 631p. mim.   **2124a**

U.S. Bureau of Chemistry and Soils. Soil erosion; a partial bibliography. H. H. Bennett, in charge, Soil erosion investigations. Wash. D.C. 1933. 82p. mim.
2125

U.S. Department of Agriculture. Bibliography on land settlement, with particular reference to small holdings and subsistence homesteads. Comp. by Louise O. Bercaw, A. M. Hannay, and Esther M. Colvin, under the direction of Mary G. Lacy. (Miscellaneous publications no. 172) Wash. Govt. Ptg. Off. 1934. 492p.
2126

U.S. Forest Service. Library. Forest recreation: a bibliography. Wash. D.C. 1938. 129p. mim.   **2126a**

U.S. Geological Survey. Irrigation literature. (Geol. Survey. Eleventh annual rep. 1889-90. pt. 2) Wash. Govt. Ptg. Off. 1891. p345-88   **2127**

—— —— Selected bibliography on erosion and silt movement. (Water supply paper 797) Wash. D.C. 1937. 91p.   **2127a**

U.S. Library of Congress. Division of bibliography. List of references on water rights and the control of waters. Comp. under the direction of H. H. B. Meyer. Wash. Govt. Ptg. Off. 1914. 111p. (Supplementary. July 15, 1931. 26p.)   **2128**

—— —— —— Select list of references on the conservation of natural resources in the United States. Comp. under the direction of H. H. B. Meyer. Wash. Govt. Ptg. Off. 1912. 110p. (Supplements. Oct. 24, 1913. 5p.; Feb. 9, 1921. 5p. typ.; Aug. 4, 1924. 15p. mim.; 1934. 65p. mim.; 1938. 72p. mim.)   **2128a**

U.S. Soil Conservation Service. Bibliography on soil conservation. Comp. by Lillian H. Wieland, 1935, revised by June Henderson, 1936. [Wash. D.C.] July 1936. 179p. mim.   **2129**

—— —— Bibliography on soil erosion and soil and water conservation. Comp. by Stanley E. Gaines; with abstracts by Francesca Vincent, Marion Bloom and James F. Carter. (U.S. Department of Agriculture. Miscellaneous publications no. 312) Wash. Govt. Ptg. Off. 1938. 651p.
2129a

—— —— Economic aspects of soil conservation; references to the literature on the subject. Comp. by Mildred Benton. Wash. D.C. Sept. 26, 1940. 12p. processed   **2129b**

—— —— Publications on national, regional, state, and farm planning for soil and water conservation, wildfire conservation, and flood control. Wash. D.C. 1937. 29p. mim.   **2129c**

—— —— Publications on planning for soil, water, and wildlife conservation, flood control, and land utilization. Comp. by Etta G. Rogers and Zelma E. McIlvain. Wash. D.C. Aug. 1939. 119p. processed **2129d**

—— —— Selected annotated bibliography on sedimentation as related to soil conservation and flood control. Comp. by Carl B. Brown and Farrell F. Barnes. [Wash. D.C. 1939] 40p. mim.   **2129e**

—— —— Social aspects of soil conservation; references to literature on the subject. Comp. by Mildred Benton. Wash. D.C. Dec. 4, 1940. 7p. processed **2129f**

—— —— Wind erosion and sand dune control; a selected list of references. Comp. by Ruby W. Moats. (Soil conservation bibliography no. 1) Wash. D. C. June 1940. 66p. processed   **2129g**

—— —— **Library.** Soil conservation literature, Jan.-Feb. 1937- Wash. D.C. 1937-
2129h

Williams, G. R. and others. Selected bibliography on erosion and silt movement. U.S. Geological Survey water-supply paper 797. p6-45. 1937   **2129i**

Rural Life

Bercaw, Louise Oldham. The southern sharecropper; a selected list of references. [Wash. D.C. April 23, 1935] 15p. typ.   **2130**

Illinois. University. College of Agriculture. A list of books on farming, homemaking and rural life; for farmers and homemakers. (Bul. v. XXXVI, no. 41) Urbana, Ill. 1939. 31p.   **2130a**

Landis, Benson Y. A guide to the literature of rural life. N.Y. Dept. of research and education of Federal Council of Churches of Christ in America. 1939. 15p.   **2131**

Literature on rural life. Rural America
2131a

President's conference on home building and home ownership, Washington, D.C., 1931. Committee on Farm and village housing. Annotated lists of references on rural housing. Comp. by Josiah C. Folsom. Wash. D.C. 1931. 5pts. in 1. reprod. from typ. copy   **2132**

—— —— Farm and village home building and ownership; a selected bibliography. Comp. by Josiah C. Folsom. Wash. D.C. 1931. 21p. reprod. from typ. copy   **2133**

President's conference on home building and home ownership, Washington, D.C., 1931. Committee on Farm and village housing. Housing in labor camps; a bibliography. Comp. by Josiah C. Folsom. Wash. D.C. 1931. 16p. reprod. from typ. copy   **2134**

—— —— Housing of Mexicans and Indians; a bibliography. Comp. by Josiah C. Folsom. Wash. D.C. 1931. 12p. reprod. from typ. copy   **2135**

—— —— Housing of migratory agricultural laborers; a bibliography. Comp. by Josiah C. Folsom. Wash. D.C. 1931. 21p. reprod. from typ. copy   **2136**

U.S. Bureau of Agricultural Economics. Library. Advantages and disadvantages of country life; selected references. Comp. by Louise O. Bercaw under the direction of Mary G. Lacy (Agricultural economics bibliog. no. 37) Wash. D.C. May 1932. 27p. mim. **2137**

—— —— —— A beginning of a bibliography of rural life. Comp. by Mary G. Lacy (Agricultural economics bibliog. no. 3) Wash. 1924. 20p. mim. **2138**

—— —— —— Farm tenancy in the United States, 1925-1935; a beginning of a bibliography. Comp. by Louise O. Bercaw and Helen E. Hennefrund (Agricultural economics bibliog. no. 59) Wash. D.C. 1935. 86p. mim. **2139**

—— —— —— Farm tenancy in the United States, 1937-1939; a selected list of references. Comp. by John M. McNeill. (Agricultural economics bibliog. no. 85) Wash. D.C. April 1940. 160p. processed **2139a**

—— —— —— Relocation of farm families; selected references on settler relocation. Comp. by Louise O. Bercaw. (Economic library list no. 14) Wash. D.C. Sept. 1940. 46p. processed **2139b**

—— —— —— Rural standards of living; a selected bibliography. Comp. by Louise O. Bercaw under the direction of Mary G. Lacy (Agricultural economics bibliog. no. 32) Wash. D.C. Aug. 1930. 121p. mim. **2140**

—— —— —— Rural zoning: a list of references. Wash. D.C. June 30, 1937. 12p. mim. **2140a**

—— —— —— Valuation of real estate, with special reference to farm real estate. Comp. by Margaret T. Olcott and Helen E. Hennefrund under the direction of Mary G. Lacy (Agricultural economics bibliog. no. 60) Wash. D.C. 1935. 350p. mim. **2141**

U.S. Bureau of Agricultural Engineering. Bibliography relating to farm structures. By Guy Ervin (Miscellaneous publications no. 125) Wash. D.C. 1931. 43p. **2142**

—— —— **Library.** Electricity on the farm (a partial list of references). Comp. by Dorothy W. Graf. Wash. D.C. 1932. 31p. mim. **2143**

U.S. Department of Agriculture. Rural standards of living; a selected bibliography. Comp. by Louise O. Bercaw under the direction of Mary G. Lacy. (Miscellaneous publications no. 116) Wash. Govt. Ptg. Off. 1931. 84p. **2144**

U.S. Library of Congress. Division of bibliography. A list of books dealing with social, economic and religious aspects of country life. March 12, 1924. 6p. typ. **2145**

—— —— —— List of references on state aid to farm and home ownership. Nov. 8, 1921. 5p. mim. **2146**

U.S. Office of Education. List of references on rural life and culture. (Lib. leaflet. no 26) Wash. Govt. Ptg. Off. 1924. 12p. **2147**

Miscellaneous

American Association of Economic Entomologists. Index to the literature of American economic entomology, 1905-1924. Comp. by Nathan Banks (1905-14), and Mabel Colcord (1915-24) (Special publication 1-3) Melrose Highlands, Mass. 1917-25. 4v. **2148**

Arents, George, Jr. Tobacco; its history illustrated by the books, manuscripts and engravings in the library of George Arents, Jr., together with an introductory essay, a glossary and bibliographic notes by Jerome E. Brooks. N.Y. The Rosenbach Co. 1937- **2148a**

Barnett, Claribel R. References to the literature of the sugar beet, exclusive of works in foreign languages. U.S. Dept. of Agriculture. Lib. Bul. XVI (June 1897) 9p. **2149**

Bragge, William. Bibliotheca nicotiana; a catalogue of books about tobacco. Birmingham, England. Priv. printed. 1880. 251p. **2150**

Canada. Honorary Advisory Council for Scientific and Industrial Research. Bibliography on wool. Prepared by M. R. Whalley. Ottawa. 1927. 174p. **2151**

Evans, Mary. Garden books, old and new, selected, classified and with annotations. Phila. The Pennsylvania Horticultural Soc. 1926. 86p. **2152**

Frazer, Persifor. Bibliography of injuries to vegetation by furnace gases, 1907. Am. Inst. of Mining Engineers trans. XXXVIII. p520-55. 1908 **2153**

Garner, W. W. Selected bibliography on tobacco. Wash. D.C. Pan Am. Union, Division of agricultural cooperation. 1933. 25p. mim. **2154**

Mann, B. Pickman. Bibliography of some of the literature concerning destructive locusts. (U.S. Entomological Comn. Second rep. 1878-79) Wash. Govt. Ptg. Off. 1881. p33-56 **2155**

Massachusetts Agricultural College. List of references on women in agriculture. Special libraries. X. p138-45 (June 1919) **2156**

Montana. Agricultural Experiment Station. Publications and reports; a bibliography of publications and reports representing the results of research projects in which the Work Projects Administration has participated. Bozeman, Mont. [1940] 17p. reprod. typ. **2156a**

New England Research Council on Marketing and Food Supply. Tentative bibliography of published and unpublished research in agricultural economics, farm management and rural sociology in the New England states. Boston. 1928. 37p. mim. **2157**

New York. Public Library. Check list of works on landscape gardening and parks in the New York Public Library. N.Y. Pub. Lib. bul. III. p506-17 (Dec. 1899) **2158**

New York. Public Library. Gardens and gardening; a selected list of books. Prepared by The Garden Club of America, The Horticultural Society of New York, The New York Public Library. N.Y. N.Y. Pub. Lib. 1927. 48p. (Reprinted from the bul. XXXI. p163-77. 384-410. 1927) **2159**

Peterson, Merriam Henrietta. Standardization of agricultural products by government brands and standards, 1930-1938: a selected bibliography. Madison. Univ. of Wisconsin Lib. School. 1938. 32p. typ. **2159a**

Roth, H. Ling. A guide to the literature of sugar; a book of reference for chemists, botanists, librarians, manufacturers and planters, with comprehensive subject-index. London. K. Paul, Trench, Trübner. 1890. 159p. **2160**

U.S. Bureau of Agricultural Economics. Selected list of references on grain sorghums, grass sorghums, and broom corn. Comp. by C. Louise Phillips (Agricultural economics bibliog. no. 9) Wash. D.C. 1925. 9p. mim. **2161**

—— —— **Grain division.** Futures trading; selected references, including United States congressional documents, on futures trading in commodities, with particular reference to grain and cotton. Comp. by C. Louise Phillips. Wash. D.C. April 1934. 29,17p. typ. **2162**

—— —— **Library.** Agricultural relief; a selected and annotated bibliography. Comp. by Esther M. Colvin under the direction of Mary G. Lacy (Agricultural economics bibliog. no. 27) Wash. June 1929. 51p. mim. **2163**

—— —— —— The American farm problem; a selected list of books and pamphlets on the economic status of the farmer and measures for his relief since 1920. Comp. under the direction of Mary G. Lacy (Agricultural economics bibliog. no. 52) Wash. D.C. 1934. 13p. **2164**

—— —— —— The apple industry in the United States; a selected list of references on the economic aspects of the industry together with some references on varieties. Comp. by Louise O. Bercaw, under the direction of Mary G. Lacy (Agricultural economics bibliog. no. 19) Wash. D.C. June 1927. 168p. mim. **2165**

—— —— —— Bounties on agricultural products; a selected bibliography. Comp. by A. M. Hannay under the direction of Mary G. Lacy. (Agricultural economics bibliog. no. 20) Wash. D.C. July 1927. 126p. mim. **2166**

—— —— —— Cherry industry in the United States; a selected list of references on the economic aspects of the industry, 1925 to date. Comp. by Lillian Crans. Wash. D.C. Oct. 9, 1931. 13p. typ. **2167**

—— —— —— Consumption of fruits and vegetables in the United States; an index to some sources of statistics. Comp. by Mamie I. Herb under the direction of Mary G. Lacy (Agricultural economics bibliog. no. 56) Wash. D.C. 1935. 125p. mim. **2168**

—— —— —— Control of production of agricultural products by governments. Comp. by A. M. Hannay under the direction of Mary G. Lacy (Agricultural economics bibliog. no. 23) Wash. D.C. Dec. 1927. 85p. mim. **2169**

—— —— —— Cotton surplus relief plans, some references to comment on the subject, 1930. Comp. by Mildred C. Benton. Wash. D.C. Jan. 26, 1932. 11p. **2170**

—— —— —— Crop and livestock insurance, 1937-1940: a selected list of references. Comp. by Mamie I. Herb. (Economic library list no. 23) Wash. D.C. June 1941. 38p. mim. **2170a**

—— —— —— Economic aspects of farm tractor operations; selected references, 1935-March 1941. Comp. by Nellie G. Larson. (Economic library list no. 26) Wash. D.C. 1941. 52p. mim. **2170b**

—— —— —— Factors affecting hog prices; a list of references. Comp. by Louise O. Bercaw. Wash. D.C. June 9, 1932. 7p. typ. **2171**

—— —— —— Farmers' response to price; a selected bibliography. Comp. by Oris V. Wells. Wash. D.C. 1932. 8p. typ. **2172**

—— —— —— Financing American cotton production and marketing in the United States. Comp. by Mildred C. Benton under the direction of Emily L. Day (Agricultural economics bibliog. no. 61) Wash. D.C. 1935. 45p. mim. **2173**

—— —— —— Food and cotton stamp plans; a selected list of references. Comp. by Mamie I. Herb (Economic library list, no. 18). Wash. D.C. 1940. 26p. mim. **2173a**

—— —— —— Foreign competition with American cotton; selected list of recent references (1932-1934) in English. Comp. by Emily L. Day. [Wash. D.C. March 29, 1934] 9p. typ. **2174**

—— —— —— Freight rates and agriculture; a list of references. Comp. by Minna Gill under the direction of Mary G. Lacy. Wash. D.C. Nov. 1927. 36p. mim. **2175**

—— —— —— Government control of cotton production in the United States, 1933-1935; a selected list of references. Comp. by Emily L. Day under the direction of Mary G. Lacy (Agricultural economics bibliog. no. 63) Wash. D.C. Jan. 1936. 59p. mim. **2176**

—— —— —— The grape industry; a selected list of references on the economic aspects of the industry in the United States, 1920-1931. Comp. by Vajen E. Hitz under the direction of Mary G. Lacy (Agricultural economics bibliog. no. 36) Wash. D.C. March 1932. 158p. mim. **2177**

—— —— —— Labor requirements of farm products in the United States; a list of references to material published since 1922. Comp. by Louise O. Bercaw under the direction of Mary G. Lacy (Agricultural economics bibliog. no. 26) Wash. D.C. 1929. 62p. mim. **2178**

—— —— —— Large scale and corporation farming; a selected list of references. Comp. by Margaret T. Olcott under the direction of Mary G. Lacy (Agricultural economics bibliog. no. 30) Wash. D.C. Nov. 1929. 85p. mim. **2179**

—— —— —— A list of international organizations interested in agriculture. Comp. by Katherine Jacobs under the direction of Mary G. Lacy (Agricultural economics bibliog. no. 22) Wash. D.C. Nov. 1927. 14p. mim. **2180**

—— —— —— Part-time farming; a brief list of recent references. Comp. by Esther M. Colvin under the direction of Mary G. Lacy (Agricultural economics bibliog. no. 43) Wash. D.C. Feb. 1933. 41p. mim. **2181**

—— —— —— The peach industry in the United States; a selected list of references on the economic aspects of the industry, including some references relating to Canada. Comp. by Louise O. Bercaw under the direction of Mary G. Lacy (Agricultural economics bibliog. no. 8) Wash. D.C. Oct. 1925. 35p. mim. **2182**

—— —— —— Price studies of the U.S. Department of Agriculture showing demand-price, supply-price, and price-production relationships. Comp. by Louise O. Bercaw under the direction of Mary G. Lacy (Agricultural economics bibliog. no. 58) Wash. D.C. Oct. 1935. 38p. mim. **2183**

—— —— —— Publications dealing with farm management, 1903-June 30, 1940. Comp. by M. A. Crosby, M. R. Cooper and D. E. Merrick. Wash. D.C. Dec. 1940. 133p. mim. **2183a**

—— —— —— Some references on types of farming in the United States. Comp. by Esther M. Colvin. Sept. 26, 1932. 5p. typ. **2184**

—— —— —— The soybean industry in the United States; a selected list of references on the economic aspects of the industry, 1920-1931. Comp. by Mamie I. Herb. Wash. D.C. Nov. 6, 1931. 19p. typ. **2185**

—— —— —— The strawberry industry in the United States; a selected list of references on the economic aspects of the industry. Comp. by Esther M. Colvin under the direction of Mary G. Lacy (Agricultural economics bibliog. no. 28) Wash. D.C. Oct. 1929. 50p. mim. **2186**

—— —— —— Uses for cotton; selected references in the English language. Comp. by Mildred C. Benton under the direction of Emily L. Day (Agricultural economics bibliog. no. 44) Wash. D.C. Nov. 1932. 43p. mim. **2187**

—— —— —— Vegetables; selected references on the marketing of vegetables. (Supplementary to bibliography on the marketing of agricultural products. U.S. Dept. of Agriculture. Miscellaneous publications no. 150) Comp. by Louise O. Bercaw. [Wash. D.C. Aug. 31, 1934] 14p. typ. **2188**

—— —— —— Wheat; cost of production, 1923-1930; references relating to the United States and some foreign countries. Comp. by Louise O. Bercaw under the direction of May G. Lacy (Agricultural economics bibliog. no. 33) Wash. D.C. 1931. 33p. mim. **2189**

U.S. Bureau of Agricultural Engineering. Current literature in agricultural engineering, Aug., 1931- . Wash. D.C. 1931- (Contents formerly included in Highways and rural engineering; current literature, June 23, 1926-April 13, 1927; Highways and agricultural engineering; current literature, April 20, 1927-June 24, 1931) **2190**

U.S. Bureau of Entomology. Bibliography of the more important contributions to American economic entomology. Comp. by Samuel Henshaw and Nathan Banks. Wash. Govt. Ptg. Off. 1889-1905. 8v. (Continued by Index to the literature of American economic entomology, issued by American Association of Economic Entomologists) **2191**

—— —— A bibliography on the use of airplanes in insect control to March 1, 1928. Comp. by Carlo Zeimet and Walker E. McBath. Wash. D.C. 1928? 17p. mim. **2192**

U.S. Bureau of Markets. Library. Selected list of publications on the marketing of farm products. [Wash. D.C.] 1918. 29p. mim. **2193**

U.S. Bureau of Public Roads. Library. Partial list of references on roadside development. Wash. D.C. 1930. 49p. **2194**

U.S. Department of Agriculture. Extension service. Office of cooperative extension work. Library. Boys' and girls' 4-H club work in the United States; a selected list of references. Comp. by Edith J. Webb. [Wash. D.C.] Jan. 1932. 217p. mim. **2195**

—— **Library.** Cotton literature; selected references, I- . [Wash. D.C.] Jan. 1931- **2196**

—— —— —— References on agricultural museums. By Everett E. Edwards. Wash. D.C. U.S. Dept. of Agriculture. 1936 **2197**

—— —— —— World food supply; a bibliography. Comp. by Margaret T. Olcott (Bibliog. contributions no. 9) Wash. D.C. June 1925. 68p. mim. **2198**

U.S. Federal Farm Board. Cooperation in agriculture; a selected and annotated bibliography, with special reference to marketing, purchasing, and credit. (Bul. no. 6) Wash. D.C. March 1931. 113p. **2199**

U.S. Federal Farm Board. Division of co-operative marketing. Publications issued by farmers' business associations. Wash. D.C. 1931. 16p. mim.   **2200**

U.S. Library of Congress. Division of bibliography. Brief list of references on the outlook for the farmer (method of marketing, increasing productivity of the soil, financing, labor supply and substitution of machinery, etc.). Jan. 26, 1921. 10p. mim.   **2201**

—— —— —— A list of recent documentary publications on sugar issued by the United States government. May 16, 1924. 8p. typ. (Supplement. Dec. 7, 1934. 11p. typ.)   **2202**

—— —— —— List of recent references on federal agricultural relief. Sept. 1, 1926. 13p. mim.   **2203**

—— —— —— List of recent references on the factors influencing the prices of staple agricultural products. Nov. 22, 1921. 11p. mim.   **2204**

—— —— —— List of references on abandoned farms in New England. Aug. 19, 1913. 6p. typ.   **2205**

—— —— —— List of references on blocs, with special reference to the agricultural bloc in Congress. April 26, 1922. 7p. typ.   **2206**

—— —— —— List of references on farm labor in the United States (With special reference to conditions of life and labor of farm workers). Feb. 2, 1921. 10p. mim.   **2207**

—— —— —— List of references on fur farming. Aug. 22, 1917. 5p. typ. (Supplements, Jan. 14, 1919. 3p.; Oct. 5, 1922. 2p.; Jan. 14, 1929. 3p.)   **2208**

—— —— —— List of references on government aid to farmers and immigrants. Special libraries. VI. p119-26 (Sept. 1915)   **2209**

—— —— —— List of references on rice and the rice industry. July 29, 1921. 14p. typ.   **2210**

—— —— —— List of references on the conservation, production and economic use of foods. June 19, 1917. 14p. typ. dup.   **2211**

—— —— —— List of references on the flax and linen industry. June 25, 1919. 15p. typ.   **2211a**

—— —— —— List of references on the flaxseed industry. March 14, 1917. 2, 3p. typ.   **2212**

—— —— —— List of references on the peanut industry. April 2, 1923. 12p. typ.   **2213**

—— —— —— List of speeches etc. on federal agricultural relief as printed in the Congressional Record, 69 Cong. 1st sess., v. 67 current file. Aug. 20, 1926. 17p. mim.   **2214**

—— —— —— Select list of references on agricultural implements, trade and manufacture. 1911. 9p. typ.   **2215**

—— —— —— Select list of references on conservation on the farm; prevention and utilization of waste; application of power; scientific management, etc. March 17, 1913. 6p. typ.   **2216**

—— —— —— Select list of references on government aid to farmers and immigrants. March 7, 1912. 13p. mim.   **2217**

—— —— —— Select list of references on government supervision of the food supply. Oct. 20, 1911. 9p. typ.   **2218**

—— —— —— Select list of references on grain, wheat, flour, etc. May 20, 1911. 64p. typ.   **2219**

—— —— —— Select list of references on sugar chiefly in its economic aspects. Comp. under the direction of H. H. B. Meyer. Wash. Govt. Ptg. Off. 1910. 238p. (Supplement. July 13, 1917. 25p. typ.)   **2220**

—— —— —— Select list of references on wool. March 20, 1913. 8p. typ.   **2221**

—— —— —— Select list of references on wool, with special reference to the tariff. Wash. Govt. Ptg. Off. 1911. 163p.   **2222**

—— —— —— A short list of references on the stabilization of prices of agricultural products in the United States. Oct. 31, 1923. 6p. typ.   **2224**

BUSINESS

General

American management index; a subject index to publications of the American Management Association, January, 1923-January, 1932, with appended list of these publications by series. N.Y. Am. Management Asso. 1932. 92p.   **2225**

Brentano's, New York. Business preparedness and efficiency; Brentano's list of books on modern business methods. N.Y. Brentano. 1917. 128p.   **2226**

Brown, Walter Vail. Scientific management; a list of references in the New York Public Library. N.Y. 1917. 81p.   **2227**

Business Book Bureau. What to read on business. Prepared expressly for Business Book Bureau. N.Y. 1912. 169p.   **2228**

Business Research Council. Economic and business research in American colleges and universities. N.Y. Business Research Council. 1932. 84p.   **2229**

Cleland, Ethel. Five hundred business books. Wash. D.C. Am. Lib. Asso. 1919. 72p.   **2230**

Crobaugh, Clyde J. The business man's library and the value of business reading; a select list of references for the business man, the young man contemplating a business career. [Babson Park, Mass. Babson Inst.] 1932. 31p.   **2231**

Dartmouth College. The Amos Tuck School of Administration and Finance. A reading list on business administration. Hanover, N.H. 1939. 51p.   **2232**

Davenport, Donald Hills and Scott, Frances V. An index to business indices. Chicago. Business Publications, Inc. 1937. 189p. **2232a**

Dixie Business Book Shop. Bibliography of 2700 business books. N.Y. Dixie Business Book Shop. 1922. 114p. **2233**

Fotts, F. E. The recent literature of business management. Harvard bus. rev. XVII. p117-24 (Autumn 1938) **2233a**

Gras, Norman Scott Brien and others. The literature of business history. Harvard bus rev. XVI. p105-25 (Autumn 1937) **2233b**

Harvard business review. Cumulative index, volumes I-XV, 1922-1937; index of authors; classified index of articles; subject index. (Cambridge. 1938) 56p. Harvard bus. rev. XVI. no. 2 **2233c**

Harvard University. Graduate School of Business Administration. Baker Library. A classification of business literature. N.Y. H. W. Wilson. 1937. 374p. planog. **2233d**

—— —— —— **Kress library of business and economics.** The Kress library of business and economics; catalog, covering material published through 1776, with data upon cognate items in other Harvard libraries. Boston, Mass. Baker Library, Harvard Graduate School of Business Administration. 1940. 414p. **2233e**

—— —— —— The Kress library of business and economics, founded upon the collection of books made by Herbert Somerton Foxwell, M.A., F.A.A. Boston. 1939. 53p. **2233f**

Hower, Ralph M. Recent articles on American business history. Bus. Hist. Soc. bul. X. p29-34. 1936 **2233g**

Manley, Marian C. Business information and its sources. Newark, N.J. Pub. Lib. 1939. 37p. **2234**

Meyer, H. H. B. Bibliography in relation to business and the affairs of life. Bibliog. Soc. of Amer. pap. X. no. 3. p103-18 (July 1916) **2235**

Nebraska University. College of Business Administration. What to read on business; a selected list of books covering every phase of business activity. n.p. n.d. n.p. 45p. **2236**

New York University. Book Store. Select business books; designed primarily to meet the needs of the student body of the New York University School of Commerce. N.Y. 1923. 24p. **2237**

Newark, N.J. Free Public Library. 1600 business books, arranged by authors, by titles and by subjects. Comp. by Sarah H. Ball under the direction of John Cotton Dana. N.Y. H. W. Wilson. 1917. 232p. **2238**

—— —— 2400 business books and guide to business literature. By Linda H. Morley and Adelaide C. Kight under the direction of John Cotton Dana. N.Y. H. W. Wilson. 1920. 456p. **2239**

—— —— The business branch. Business books: 1920-1926; an analytical catalog of 2600 titles. N.Y. H. W. Wilson. 1927. 592p. **2240**

Rogers, Bertha Harriet. Business morals; a bibliography. (Wisconsin Free Lib. Comn. Am. social questions no. 6) Madison, Wis. 1910. 37p. **2242**

Scovell, Wellington & Company. Selected professional and business books. Boston. 1922. 25p. **2243**

Selby, Paul Owen. Index to the teaching of general business, 1929-1938; junior business training, senior business training, introduction to business, consumer-business economics. Kirksville, Mo. Research Press. 1939. 48p. **2243a**

Selected books on business. (Nebraska stud. in business no. 43) Lincoln. Univ. of Nebraska. 1939. 50p. **2243b**

Smitley, Robert L. Bibliography of books on business economics. N.Y. Dixie Business Book Shop. 1925 **2244**

Special Libraries Association. Directories for the business man. Comp. by Laura A. Eales, of the Public business librarians group, with the cooperation of the Publications committee of the Special Libraries Association. N.Y. Special Libraries Asso. 1938. 66p. **2244a**

—— **Commercial technical group.** Guides to business facts and figures; an indexed and descriptive list emphasizing the less known business reference sources. N.Y. Special Libraries Asso. 1937. 59p. **2245**

U.S. Bureau of Foreign and Domestic Commerce. Division of business review. Business information section. Some references on prices. Comp. by Rachel Bretherton. Wash. D.C. 1938. 9p. mim. **2245a**

U.S. Library of Congress. Division of bibliography. Business cycles: a selected list of references. Comp. by Helen F. Conover. June 1939. 41p. mim. **2245b**

—— —— **Legislative reference service.** Small business bibliography. Wash. Govt. Ptg. Off. 1941. 18p. **2245c**

Wisconsin. Free Library Commission. Traveling library department. Books for your business; a selected list. Comp. by Anna R. Moore. Madison, Wis. 1929. 44p. **2246**

Wisconsin. University. Preliminary list of books on accounting, retailing, marketing, salesmanship and sales management, business correspondence, advertising. Madison. Univ. of Wisconsin. 1925. typ. **2247**

Accounting

Accountancy Library Association. Catalogue of accountancy library at recitation rooms of the School of Commerce, Accounts and Finance. Denver, Colo. 1910. 63p. **2248**

Accounting theses, June, 1940. Accounting rev. XV. p421-4 (Sept. 1940) **2248a**

American Institute of Accountants. Accountants' index; a bibliography of accounting literature to December, 1920. N.Y. Am. Inst. of Accountants. 1921. 1578p. (Supplements. 1923, 1928, 1936, 1940) **2249**
—— Library catalogue. N.Y. Jan. 1919. 237p. **2250**
American Telephone and Telegraph Co. Catalogue accounting library. N.Y. Am. Telephone and Telegraph Co. 1914. 75p. **2251**
Bentley, Harry C. and Leonard, Ruth S. Bibliography of works on accounting by American authors (1796-1934). Boston. Harry C. Bentley. 1934-35. 197, 408p. **2252**
Business Book Bureau. What to read on accounting; an impartial review of all the worth-while books (in English) on accounting theory and practice and on commercial law. N.Y. Kalkhoff. 1912. 47p. **2253**
Clevenger, Earl. Summary of research in bookeeping. Bus. educat. world. XIX. p565-7, 633-6. 1939 **2253a**
Columbia University. Library. A check list of books, printed before 1850, in the Montgomery Library of Accountancy at Columbia University. N.Y. Columbia Univ. Press. 1927. 46p. **2254**
—— A second check list of books, printed before 1850, in the Montgomery Library of Accountancy at Columbia University. N.Y. Columbia Univ. Press. 1930. 32p. **2255**
—— School of business. Montgomery library of accountancy. Exhibition of selected bocks and manuscripts from the Montgomery library of accountancy. South Hall, Columbia University, October, 1937. N.Y. 1937. 24p. **2255a**
Current literature. Jour. accountancy. I- . Nov. 1905- **2255b**
Dartnell Corporation. Sales executives' list of references to principal articles, books, reports and data published since 1916, relating to sales management and advertising. By Frances M. Cowan. Chicago. The Dartnell Corp. 1925. 108p. **2256**
Disbrow, Mary Ethel. Criticism of newspaper advertising in the United States since 1915; a selected bibliography. Madison. Univ. of Wisconsin Lib. School. 1931. 61p. typ. **2257**
Herwood & Herwood. The Herwood library of accountancy: a catalogue of books printed between 1494 and 1900 in the Herwood library of accountancy. N.Y. Herwood & Herwood. 1938. 233p. mim. **2257a**
The journal of accountancy. Index, vols. I-XVI, inclusive, November 1905-December 1913. N.Y. Ronald. 1914. 153p. Index, vol. 17-34, January 1914-December 1922. N.Y. 1923 **2257b**
Meixell, Granville. The trade catalog collection; a manual with source lists. N.Y. Special Libraries Asso. 1934. 53p. **2258**

National Committee on Municipal Accounting. Bibliography of municipal and state accounting. . . . Chicago. The Committee. 1937. 30p. **2258a**
—— Governmental accounting bibliography. (Bul. no. 13) Chicago. 1941. 61p. **2258b**
Sanders, T. H. Significant recent accounting literature. Harvard bus. rev. XV. p366-88 (Spring 1937) **2258c**
Special Libraries Association. Business and trade dictionaries; a classified guide to the sources of business terminology and definitions. N.Y. Special Libraries Asso. 1934. 39p. **2259**
U.S. Library of Congress. Division of bibliography. Advertising, with special reference to its social and economic effects; a bibliographical list of recent writings. Nov. 26, 1930. 13p. mim. **2260**
—— —— —— Community advertising; a bibliographical list of recent writings. Jan. 21, 1935. 7p. typ. **2261**
—— —— —— List of references on advertising. 1916. 35p. typ. (Also in Special libraries. VII. p61-76. April 1916) (Recent references. June 29, 1925. 28p. mim.) **2261a**
—— —— —— A list of references on billboards. Jan. 1915. 9p. mim. **2262**
—— —— —— List of references on scientific management and efficiency (Supplementary to list printed in Special libraries, May 1913). May 4, 1915. 24p. typ. (Supplement. March 9, 1917. 7p. typ.) **2263**
—— —— —— List of references on the management and care of office buildings and similar structures. April 6, 1923. 8p. mim. **2264**
—— —— —— List of references on the pension systems of corporations and firms. Jan. 21, 1931. 11p. mim. **2265**
—— —— —— Select list of references on negotiable instruments. Dec. 12, 1910. 9p. typ. (Supplement. 1919. 2p.) **2266**

Businesses

Advertising Federation of America. Bureau of Research and Education. Books for the advertising man; a classified bibliography on advertising, marketing, and related subjects. Prepared under the direction of Alfred T. Falk. N.Y. Advertising Federation of Amer., Bureau of Research and Education. 1935. 24p. Cumulative supplement for 1935-1939. N.Y. 1940. 12p. **2266a**
Blackett, O. W. The literature of business statistics; a bibliography. (Michigan business studies, vol. VIII, no. 1) Ann Arbor. Univ. of Michigan, Bureau of Business Research. 1936. 67p. **2266b**
Borden, N. H. Two years of advertising books. Harvard bus. rev. XVI. p247-53 (Winter 1938) **2266c**
Burpee, Lawrence J. A chapter in the literature of the fur trade. Bibliog. Soc. of Amer. pap. V. p45-60. 1910 **2268**

Cuthbertson, Stuart and Ewers, John C.
A preliminary bibliography on the American fur trade. St. Louis, Mo. U.S. Dept. of the Interior, National Park Service, Jefferson National Expansion Memorial. 1939. 191p. mim. **2268a**

Du Bois, Ayers James. Catalog of urban real estate appraisal data sources. Comp. for Joint committee on appraisal and mortgage analysis. Wash. D.C. 1937. 242p. mim. **2268b**

Institute of Distribution. Chain store bibliography, as of Jan. 2, 1940. N.Y. 1940. 35p. **2268c**

—— Telling the chain store story: a bibliography on chain stores, as of October 1, 1938. N.Y. The Inst. 1938. 23p. **2268d**

Larrabee, Carroll B. and Marks, Henry William. Check lists of advertising, selling and merchandising essentials. N.Y. McGraw-Hill Book Company. 1937. 396p. **2268e**

Monthly bibliography. Fuel in science and practice **2268f**

Nichols, John Peter. The chain store tells its story. N.Y. Inst. of Distribution. 1940. p233-65 **2268g**

Nute, Grace Lee. The papers of the American Fur Company; a brief estimate of their significance. Am. hist. rev. XXXII. p519-38 (April 1928) **2268h**

U.S. Bureau of Foreign and Domestic Commerce. Division of business review. Department stores (some selected basic information sources). (Business information service) Comp. by Rachel Bretherton. 1939. 11p. mim. **2268i**

—— —— **Business information section.** Retail hardware stores. Wash. D.C. The Section. 1938. 7p. mim. **2268j**

—— —— **Marketing research division. Marketing service section.** Some references on grocery wholesaling. Comp. by R. I. Whyte. Wash. D.C. The Section. 1938. 6p. mim. **2268k**

U.S. Department of Commerce. Domestic commerce division. Chain stores; a reading list. By T. S. Jackson. Wash. D.C. Aug. 1929 **2269**

U.S. Library of Congress. Division of bibliography. Chain stores; a bibliographical list. Sept. 14, 1937. 42p. mim. (Supplement. June 15, 1939. 33p. mim.) **2270**

—— —— —— List of references on co-operative stores. May 28, 1920. 12p. mim. **2271**

—— —— —— List of references on mortgage guaranty companies. Nov. 7, 1917. 3p. typ. **2272**

—— —— —— A list of references on the early fur trade in the United States and Canada. Comp. by Grace H. Fuller. Sept. 20, 1937. 13p. typ. **2272a**

—— —— —— List of references on the fur trade in the United States. Aug. 13, 1914. 7p. typ. **2273**

—— —— —— List of references on the grocery trade. Nov. 12, 1921. 13p. typ. **2274**

—— —— —— List of references on the mail order business. July 25, 1921. 7p. mim. **2275**

—— —— —— List of references on the real estate business. Special libraries. VII. p151-5 (Nov. 1916) **2276**

—— —— —— List of references on the real estate business. Sept. 24, 1923. 18p. mim. (Additional references. Nov. 30, 1927. 4p.) **2277**

—— —— —— List of references on the restaurant business including cafeterias and lunch-rooms. Feb. 17, 1923. 14p. typ. **2278**

—— —— —— List of references on the trading stamp business. Jan. 18, 1919. 7p. typ. **2279**

—— —— ——. References on department stores. Feb. 12, 1915. 6p. typ. (Supplements. Dec. 3, 1919. 6p. typ.; July 13, 1928. 2p.; March 7, 1935. 9p. typ.) **2280**

—— —— —— Select list of references on the furniture trade in the United States. March 6, 1913. 3p. typ. (Supplement. Jan. 19, 1917. 6p. typ.; 1923. 1p.) **2281**

—— —— —— A selected list of recent books and pamphlets on advertising including its economic and social effects. Comp. by Anne L. Baden. May 9, 1940. 38p. mim. **2281a**

—— —— ——. A selected list of recent references on the real estate business. Comp. by Helen F. Conover. Jan. 25, 1940. 22p. mim. **2281b**

Varney, Edith. Furs and fur bearers of the United States and Canada. St. Louis Pub. Lib. monthly bul. XXVII. p115-22 (March 1929) **2282**

Stocks and Trusts

Borden, Fanny. Monopolies and trusts in America, 1895-99. N.Y. State Lib. bul. 67. bibliog. III. Oct. 1901. 31, 33p. **2283**

Bullock, Charles J. Trust literature; a survey and criticism. *In* Trusts, pools, and corporations. Ed. by William Z. Ripley. Boston, N.Y., Chicago, London. Ginn. 1905. p428-73. (From Quar. jour. economics. XV. p167-217. Feb. 1901) **2284**

Bureau of Railway Economics. List of references on interlocking directorates. Wash. D.C. 1914. 9p. **2285**

—— List of references on regulation of the issuance of railroad stocks and bonds. Special libraries. VI. p16-18 (Jan. 1915) Same. 1919. 13p. mim. **2286**

—— Federal incorporation—a list of references. [Wash. D.C.] May 1933. 12p. typ. **2287**

Huebner, S. S. Bibliography on securities and stock exchanges. Am. Acad. Pol. and Social Sciences ann. XXXV. p699-714 (May 1910) **2287a**

Thompson, Laura A. A selected bibliography; employee stock ownership in the United States. Wash. Govt. Ptg. Off. 1927. p214-23 (From the Monthly labor rev. XXIV. p1366-73. June 1927) **2288**

U.S. Library of Congress. Division of bibliography. Books and pamphlets on investments, 1923-1931. April 27, 1932. 10p. typ. **2289**

—— —— —— List of books, (with references to periodicals), relating to trusts. Comp. under the direction of A. P. C. Griffin. Wash. Govt. Ptg. Off. 1907. 93p. **2290**

—— —— —— List of recent references on holding companies. July 6, 1936. 17p. typ. (Supplement. 1938. 15p. typ.) **2290a**

—— —— —— A list of recent references on investment trusts (supplementing previous lists). Wash. D.C. The Lib. May 3, 1939. 18p. photostat **2290b**

—— —— —— A list of recent references on the Securities Act of 1933, the Securities Exchange Act of 1934, and the Securities and Exchange Commission. Oct. 23, 1936. 12p. typ. **2290c**

—— —— —— List of recent references on speculation, stock exchanges, commodity exchanges, hedging and short selling. April 8, 1932. 22p. typ. **2291**

—— —— —— List of references on fraudulent practices in the promotion of corporations and the sale of securities. Nov. 8, 1915. 9p. typ. **2292**

—— —— —— A list of references on interlocking directorates. 1938. 10p. typ. **2292a**

—— —— —— List of references on investment trusts. May 21, 1932. 24p. typ. (Supplement. Dec. 12, 1935. 14p. typ.) **2293**

—— —— —— List of references on non-par value stock. Dec. 29, 1923. 4p. typ. **2294**

—— —— —— List of references on stock exchanges and speculation. July 12, 1923. 20p. mim. **2295**

—— —— —— List of references on trusts in the United States, including mergers (Supplementary to printed lists on federal control of commerce and corporations, 1913 and 1914). April 21, 1931. 31p. mim. (Supplement. April 14, 1938. 27p. reprod.) **2296**

—— —— —— A selected list of references on stocks and bonds. Dec. 21, 1933. 17p. typ. **2297**

U.S. Securities and Exchange Commission. Library. Bibliography; list of references on securities which are of general interest to S.E.C. Comp. under the direction of Lucile Donovan. Wash. D.C. Sept. 1, 1937. 586p. mim. **2297a**

—— —— —— Complete list of material. Revised to December 1, 1939. [Wash. D.C.] 1939. 341p. Supplement no. 1- . [Wash. D.C.] 1940- . mim. **2297b**

Miscellaneous

Boston. Public Library. Retail selling; a selected list of works in the public library of the city of Boston. Boston. 1929. 20p. **2298**

California. Bureau of Business Education. Bibliography on consumer education. [San Francisco. 1937] 426p. mim. **2298a**

Estey, Helen G. Select bibliography on cost of living in the United States. Special libraries. IX. p203-9 (Nov. 1918) **2299**

Fowell, Ruth Black. Educating the consumer. Part 1. Consumers in the modern market. Madison. W.P.A. Project, Univ. Extension Division, Univ. of Wisconsin. 1938. 72p. mim. **2299a**

Harvard University. Graduate School of Business Administration. George F. Baker Foundation. Harvard business reports. Cumulative index, volumes 1 to 10. N.Y. McGraw-Hill. 1932. 93p. **2300**

Hower, Ralph M. The Boston conference on business history. Jour. economic business hist. III. p463-80 (May 1931) **2301**

Illinois. University. Bureau of Business Research. Books about business cycles. (Bul. no. 22) Urbana. Univ. of Illinois. 1928. 53p. **2302**

Kyker, Benjamin Franklin. Bibliography: a list of books, pamphlets and publications on marketing, retailing, salesmanship, and merchandising, June 1938. (U.S. Office of Education. Misc. no. 2089) Wash. D.C. 1938. 77p. mim. **2302a**

Landis, Benson Young. A guide to the literature on consumer movements; books, pamphlets and articles on consumer cooperatives and other consumer movements. N.Y. Consumer Distribution Corporation. 1937. 4-11p. **2302b**

Leighton, Elmer Willard. Bibliography of works on commercial correspondence: 1870-1900. Brooklyn, N.Y. 1935. 29p. typ. **2302c**

Mann, George Carlisle. Bibliography on consumer education. Sponsored by Foundation for Consumer Education, Los Angeles, California. N.Y. Harper. 1939. 286p. **2302d**

New York University. Graduate School of Business Administration. Bureau of Business Research. Source book of research data; a list of reliable current sources of statistics of quantity and price for important commodities. N.Y. Prentice-Hall. 1923. 70p. **2303**

Niles & Niles. Review of published statistics relative to cost of merchandise distribution, rates of merchandise turnover, and fluctuations in manufacturing employments in the United States, 1913-1923. N.Y. 1925. 43p. **2304**

Parker, Florence E. The cooperative movement; a selective bibliography. Monthly labor rev. XX. p659-90 (March 1925) **2305**

Rossman, Joseph. Bibliography of trade-mark articles. Jour. Patent Off. Soc. XV. p553-65 (July 1933) **2305a**

Special Libraries Association. Trade association bureau. Trade associations in the United States; a reading and reference list. N.Y. 1934. 25p. **2306**

Thompson, Laura A. Children in street trades in the United States; a list of references. Monthly labor rev. XXI. p81-92 (Dec. 1925) **2307**

Tosdal, H. R. The consumer and consumption in recent literature. Harvard bus. rev. XVII. p508-14 (Summer 1939) **2307a**

U.S. Agricultural Adjustment Administration. Consumer services of government agencies. By Iris C. Walker. (Consumers' Counsel ser. Pub. I, rev.) Wash. Govt. Ptg. Off. 1937. 56p. (List of government publications of interest to consumers) **2307b**

—— —— Cooperative bookshelf; a bibliography of government publications on consumers' cooperation. (Consumers' counsel ser. Pub. 3) [Wash. Govt. Ptg. Off. 1937] 13p. **2307c**

U.S. Bureau of Agricultural Economics. Library. Factors affecting prices; a selected bibliography, including some references on the theory and practice of price analysis. Comp. by Louise O. Bercaw under the direction of Mary G. Lacy (Agricultural economics bibliog. no. 14) Wash. D.C. March 1926. 40p. mim. **2308**

—— —— —— Index to some sources of current prices. Comp. by Eva Thayer Shively (U.S. Dept. of Agriculture. Lib. Bibliog. contributions no. 5) Wash. D.C. April 1923. 124p. mim. **2309**

—— —— —— Price analysis; selected references on supply and demand curves and related subjects. Comp. by Louise O. Bercaw under the direction of Mary G. Lacy (Agricultural economics bibliog. no. 48) Wash. D.C. 1933. 98p. mim. **2310**

—— —— —— Price spreads; a selected list of references relating to analyses of the portion of the consumer's price accruing to various agencies. Comp. by Louise O. Bercaw under the direction of Mary G. Lacy (Agricultural economics bibliog. no. 4) Wash. D.C. March 1925. 20p. mim. **2311**

U.S. Bureau of Foreign and Domestic Commerce. Market research sources: a guide to information on domestic marketing. Prep. by Rachel Bretherton. Wash. Supt. of Doc. 1937. 273p. **2311a**

—— —— Division of business review. Some references to materials on house organs (basic information sources). By R. C. Leslie. Wash. D.C. April 1939. 5p. mim. **2311b**

—— —— —— Business information section. Some references to sources of data on industrial marketing. Comp. by T. J. Davis. 1938. 18p. mim. **2311c**

U.S. Department of Commerce. Library. Price sources, index of commercial and economic publications currently received in the libraries of the Department of Commerce which contain current market commodity prices. Comp. by Elizabeth M. Carmack. Wash. Govt. Ptg. Off. 1931. 320p. **2312**

U.S. Department of Labor. Library. Profit-sharing: selected references, 1923-1939. Comp. by Ruth Fine, under the direction of Laura A. Thompson. Wash. D.C. The Lib. 1939. 18p. mim. **2312a**

U.S. Library of Congress. Division of bibliography. Brief list of references on trade opportunities of the United States. Jan. 8, 1919. 6p. typ. **2313**

—— —— —— Business failures; a select list of references. May 10, 1932. 16p. typ. **2314**

—— —— —— Cooperation in the United States and foreign countries; a bibliographical list of references (Supplementary to the mimeographed list, June 1, 1923). Feb. 17, 1935. 29p. typ. **2315**

—— —— —— A list of recent books and pamphlets on cooperation in the United States and foreign countries. Comp. by Grace Hadley Fuller under the direction of Florence S. Hellman. Wash. D.C. 1939. 44p. mim. "Supplement to the mimeographed list of 1937" **2315a**

—— —— —— List of recent federal documents on cost of living and prices. Dec. 28, 1920. 9p. typ. **2316**

—— —— —— List of recent references on the mortgage situation in the United States, with references on governmental aid to housing. Jan. 5, 1934. 15p. typ. **2317**

—— —— —— A list of recent works on real estate mortgages. Feb. 14, 1924. 5p. typ. **2318**

—— —— —— A list of references on bonded and private warehouses in the United States. Dec. 11, 1923. 8p. typ. **2319**

—— —— —— List of references on business cycles. June 14, 1923. 9p. typ. (Additional references. 1931. 5p. typ.) **2320**

—— —— —— A list of references on business on the installment plan. Jan. 23, 1924. 6p. typ. (Supplement. Jan. 21, 1926. 3p. typ.; Additional references. Oct. 12, 1927. 3p.; Recent references. Jan. 28, 1928. 16p. mim.; Recent references. Oct. 15, 1929. 17p. mim.) **2321**

—— —— —— List of references on chambers of commerce and boards of trade. March 3, 1921. 15p. mim. (Supplement. March 2, 1926. 12p. mim.) **2322**

—— —— —— List of references on employers' associations. 1919. 10p. mim. (Additional references. May 25, 1927. 3p. typ.) **2323**

—— —— —— List of references on expositions in the United States and foreign countries, 1918-1928. Aug. 20, 1928. 16p. typ. **2324**

—— —— —— List of references on federal and state regulation of the prices of fuel. Oct. 28, 1921. 5p. mim. **2325**

—— —— —— **List of references on government regulation of prices.** July 3, 1917. 9p. dupl. (Supplement. July 12, 1918. 6p. typ.; July 15, 1918. dupl.; March 5, 1919. 7p. typ.; March 5, 1919. dupl.) **2326**

U.S. Library of Congress. Division of bibliography. List of references on options and futures. June 4, 1923. 17p. typ. **2327**

—— —— —— List of references on prices during the period, 1800-1850. Jan. 16, 1917. 4p. typ. **2328**

—— —— —— List of references on profit sharing and bonus systems. Feb. 12, 1920. 24p. mim. (Supplement. 1938. 54p. mim.) **2329**

teering. Aug. 25, 1921. 11p. typ. (Recent references. Aug. 2, 1922. 5p. typ.) **2330**

—— —— —— List of references on reciprocal or inter-insurance. Jan. 8, 1920. 4p. mim. **2331**

—— —— —— List of references on refrigeration and cold storage. Jan. 3, 1917. 19p. typ. **2332**

—— —— —— A list of references on the consumer, with special reference to recent economic conditions. May 23, 1934. 12p. typ. **2333**

—— —— —— List of references on the consumers' league. Jan. 30, 1923. 5p. mim. **2334**

—— —— —— List of references on the organization and work of trade associations (Exclusive of boards of trade and chambers of commerce). Aug. 3, 1922. 16p. mim. **2335**

—— —— —— List of references on the relations of government and business. May 10, 1923. 6p. mim. (Additional references. Nov. 10, 1931. 6p.) **2336**

—— —— —— List of references on trade acceptances. April 21, 1920. 10p. mim. **2337**

—— —— —— Mail-order business; a selected list of recent writings. Comp. by Anne L. Baden. Oct. 3, 1941. 21p. mim. **2337a**

—— —— —— Maintenance of resale prices in the United States; a bibliographical list. Dec. 26, 1930. 19p. mim. **2338**

—— —— —— Mortgage loan accounting; a bibliographical list. July 8, 1930. 6p. typ. **2339**

—— —— —— Price control, with special reference to price-cutting; a list of recent references. Sept. 3, 1935. 17p. mim. **2340**

—— —— —— References on department stores. Feb. 12, 1915. 6p. typ. (Supplements. Dec. 3, 1919. 6p. typ.; July 13, 1928. 2p.; March 7, 1935. 9p. typ.) **2341**

—— —— —— Salesmen and salesmanship; a list of books, 1925-1935. Aug. 8, 1935. 23p. mim. **2342**

—— —— —— Select list of references on credits, credit business and collecting of accounts. 1909. 7p. typ. (Additional references. Sept. 26, 1916. 3p.) **2343**

—— —— —— Select list of references on food adulteration 1907. 5p. typ. (Additional references. 1913. 1p.) **2344**

—— —— —— Select list of references on mortgages. May 11, 1912. 16p. typ. **2345**

—— —— —— Select list of references on the cost of living and prices. Comp. under the direction of H. H. B. Meyer. Wash. Govt. Ptg. Off. 1910. 107p. (Additional references. 1912. 120p.) **2346**

—— —— —— Select list of references on the premium system. Dec. 5, 1910. 11p. typ. **2347**

—— —— —— A selected list of references on fairs and expositions, 1928-1939. Comp. by Florence Hellman. 1938. 49p. typ. **2347a**

—— —— —— A selected list of references on profit sharing and bonus system. Comp. by Grace H. Fuller. June 21, 1938. 54p. mim. **2347b**

—— —— —— Short list of references on business and professional ethics. Dec. 6, 1924. 4p. typ. **2348**

—— —— —— Some recent references on retirement. April 2, 1926. 4p. typ. **2349**

—— —— —— Trade associations, including restraint of trade; a bibliographical list of recent writings (Exclusive of boards of trade and chambers of commerce). May 19, 1931. 26p. mim. **2350**

—— —— —— Unfair competition; a bibliographical list of recent writings. April 17, 1931. 6p. typ. **2352**

U.S. Works Progress Administration, New York (City). Literary development of cooperative principles and data; ser. A, pt. 1, Index of the laws pertaining to co-operation. Comp. under the supervision of J. Deutschman, Valery Tereshtenko and Bernhard Osterolenk. N.Y. The Admn. 1938. 42p. mim. **2352a**

Wilder, Ernestine. Consumer credit bibliography. N.Y. Prentice-Hall. 1938. p86-136 **2352b**

COMMERCE

Domestic

American Association of Port Authorities. Bibliographic notes on ports and harbors including lists by The Library of Congress. Comp. by Perry Young. New Orleans. Am. Asso. of Port Authorities. 1926. 188p. **2354**

—— Selected bibliography on ports and harbors and their administration, laws, finance, equipment and engineering. Comp. by William Joshua Barney. N.Y. Am. Asso. of Port Authorities. 1916. 144p. **2355**

Bureau of Railway Economics. Store door delivery; a list of references, chronologically arranged. Wash. D.C. Jan. 1933. 30p. mim. **2356**

Chicago. University. School of Commerce and Administration. Reading lists for students of commerce and business administration. Univ. jour. of business. p216-47 (March 1924) (Reprinted. Chicago. Univ. of Chicago. 1924. 32p.) **2357**

Greenwood, Edgar. Classified guide to technical and commercial books, a subject-list of the principal British and American works in print. London. Scott, Greenwood; N.Y. D. Van Nostrand. 1904. 216p. **2358**

Illinois. University. Bureau of Business Research. A market research bibliography. (Univ. of Illinois. Bul. no. 38) Urbana. Univ. of Illinois. 1931. 75p. **2359**

Johnson, Emory R. Bibliography. *In* History of domestic and foreign commerce of the United States. Wash. D.C. Carnegie Inst. of Wash. 1915. I. p112-17; II. p352-86 **2360**

New Bedford, Mass. Free Public Library. A collection of books, pamphlets, logbooks, pictures, etc., illustrating whales and the whale fishery . . . New Bedford, Mass. 1920. 24p. **2361**

Nystrom, Paul H. Bibliography of retailing; a selected list of books, pamphlets and periodicals. N.Y. Columbia Univ. Press. 1928. 87p. **2363**

Permanent International Association of Congresses of Navigation. Rivers, canals and ports; bibliographic notes, giving the list of the principal works which have appeared and of the articles published in periodicals of all countries. Brussels. Imprimerie des travaux publics. 1908. 729p. (Supplements. 1912, 1919, 1924) **2364**

Seattle. Public Library. Harbors and docks; a list of books and references to periodicals. . . (Reference list no. 5) Seattle. 1913. 40p. **2365**

Smith, George C. An outline for market surveys; prepared for manufacturers, distributors and communities. St. Louis. Industrial Club of St. Louis. 1930. 85p. **2366**

Special Libraries Association. Financial group. Handbook of commercial and financial services. N.Y. The Asso. 1939. 70p. **2366a**

U.S. Bureau of Agricultural Economics. Cooperative marketing of tobacco. A selected list of references. Comp. by Katherine F. Williams (Agricultural economics bibliog. no. 13) Wash. D.C. Feb. 1926. 5p. **2367**

—— —— **Library.** Bibliography of fruit and produce auctions; selected references. Wash. D.C. Sept. 25, 1931. 8p. typ. **2368**

—— —— —— Index to Summaries of cases and decisions on legal phases of cooperation [no. I-V] Prepared by H. M. Bain, Division of cooperative marketing. Wash. D.C. 1928. 32p. **2369**

—— —— —— Selected list of references on subjects relating to the grain trade in the United States and foreign countries. [Wash. D.C.] 1923. 19p. mim. **2370**

—— —— —— State trade barriers; selected references. Comp. by Louise O. Bercaw. (Economic library list no. 1, rev.) Wash. D.C. June 1940. 60p. processed **2370a**

U.S. Bureau of Foreign and Domestic Commerce. Barriers to interstate trade; bibliography. Chicago. Council of State Governments. 1939. 6p. mim. **2370b**

—— —— Sources of current trade statistics. (Market research series no. 13) Comp. by Jettie Turner. Wash. 1937. 47p. processed **2370c**

—— —— Suggested sources of information for teachers and students of commerce and economics. Wash. D.C. Oct. 1940. 6p. processed **2370d**

—— —— **Domestic commerce division.** Market research sources; a guide to information on domestic marketing. (Domestic commerce ser. no. 55) Wash. Govt. Ptg. Off. 1932. 277p. **2371**

U.S. Bureau of Labor Statistics. Cooperative movement; a selected bibliography. By J. J. Kunna. Monthly labor rev. XXXI. p782-801 (Sept. 1930) **2372**

U.S. Department of Agriculture. Agricultural cooperation; a selected and annotated reading list, with special reference to purchasing, marketing and credit, including only works printed in English, and exclusive of periodical references except reprints and proceedings of association. Comp. by Chastina Gardner. (Miscellaneous circular no. 11) Wash. D.C. 1923. 55p. **2373**

—— —— **Library.** Bibliography on the marketing of agricultural products. Comp. by Emily L. Day, Katherine Jacobs and Margaret T. Olcott. (Bibliog. contributions no. 7) Wash. D.C. June 1924. 133p. mim. **2374**

—— —— —— Bibliography on the preservation of fruits and vegetables in transit and storage with annotations contributed by the library of the Bureau of Markets and Crop Estimates. Comp. by Katherine G. Rice (Bibliog. contributions no. 4) Wash. D.C. June 1922. 76p. mim. **2375**

—— —— —— Refrigeration and cold storage; a selected list of references covering the years, 1915-1924 and the early part of 1925. Comp. by Louise O. Bercaw. (Bibliog. contributions no. 10) Wash. D.C. Oct. 1925. 58p. mim. **2376**

U.S. Federal Farm Board. Division of cooperative marketing. Cooperative marketing of tobacco; a selected list of references. Comp. by Chastina Gardner. Wash. D.C. Nov. 1931. 8p. **2377**

U.S. Library of Congress. Select list of books (with references to periodicals) relating to iron and steel in commerce. Wash. Govt. Ptg. Off. 1907. 25p. **2378**

—— —— **Division of bibliography.** Brief list of references on the marketing of manufactured products. June 9, 1923. 9p. mim. **2379**

—— —— —— Brief list of references on trade catalogues with emphasis on standardization. March 31, 1922. 6p. mim. **2380**

U.S. Library of Congress. Division of bibliography. Distribution of food. A list of recent books. July 27, 1928. 7p. typ. **2381**

—— —— —— Federal control of commerce and trade. Comp. under the direction of H. H. B. Meyer. Wash. D.C. Govt. Ptg. Off. 1913. 164p. **2382**

—— —— —— List of dictionaries of commercial commodities and other books descriptive of the materials used in the arts, manufacture and commerce. Nov. 15, 1923. 11p. typ. **2383**

—— —— —— List of recent references on ports and harbors (Supplementary to American Association of Port Authorities, selected bibliography 1916). Sept. 18, 1918. 13p. typ. (Supplementary lists. July 25, 1922. 26p. typ.; May 22, 1924. 22p. typ.; March 10, 1925. 23p. typ.; Feb. 4, 1926. 22p. typ.) **2384**

—— —— —— List of references on commercial arbitration. Jan. 8, 1914. 9p. mim. (Supplementary list. Aug. 7, 1922. 4p. mim.; March 26, 1932. 1p.) **2385**

—— —— —— List of references on co-operative distribution. March 10, 1913. 9p. typ. **2386**

—— —— —— List of references on farmers' elevators; coöperators, etc. March 30, 1922. 5p. mim. **2387**

—— —— —— List of references on the marketing of grain and grain exchanges. June 1, 1921. 12p. mim. **2388**

—— —— —— List of references on the whale industry. April 19, 1916. 4p. typ. (Supplement. Aug. 5, 1935. 10p. typ.) **2389**

—— —— —— A list of references on wholesaling. Aug. 30, 1935. 19p. typ. **2390**

—— —— —— Select list of references on abattoirs, markets, marketing and distribution of food products. Oct. 18, 1911. 9p. typ. **2391**

—— —— —— Select list of references on commerce. Oct. 3, 1910. 17p. typ. **2392**

—— —— —— Select list of references on cooperative distribution in the United States and foreign countries, June 1, 1923. 33p. mim. (Supplementary to the Bibliographie coopérative internationale, published by the International Cooperative Alliance, 1906) (Supplement. Feb. 17, 1933. 29p. typ.) **2393**

—— —— —— Select list of references on federal control of commerce and corporations, special aspects and applications. Comp. under the direction of H. H. B. Meyer. Wash. Govt. Ptg. Off. 1914. 104p. **2394**

U.S. Lighthouse Board. Index-catalogue of the library of the Lighthouse Board. Wash. Govt. Ptg. Off. 1886. 116p. **2394a**

Foreign

Allen, Joel A. Preliminary list of works and papers relating to the mammalian orders of cete and sirenia [whales]. (U.S. Geol. and geog. survey of the territories. Bul. no. 3. 1881) Wash. Govt. Ptg. Off. 1882. p399-562 **2395**

American Chamber of Commerce, Paris. Library. Catalogue of the library, 1905. Paris. 1905. 60p. **2396**

American Steamship Association. Bibliography of maritime literature. N.Y. Am. Steamship Asso. 1918. 14p. **2397**

Bibliographical lists of items in Commerce reports (of the Bureau of Foreign and Domestic Commerce on Latin America, Sept. 1918-April, 1922). Hispanic Am. hist. rev. I-V (Nov. 1918-Aug. 1922) **2398**

Boston Public Library. A selected list of books on the commercial relations of South America, principally with the United States in the public library of the City. (Brief reading lists no. 4. June 1918) Boston. The Trustees. 1918. 19p. **2399**

Chapin, Howard M. Bibliotheca Titanic. The Am. collector. I. p144-8 (Jan. 1926) **2400**

Haas, J. Anton de. Recent publications in the field of international economic relations. Harvard bus. rev. XVI. p491-8 (Summer 1938) **2400a**

Harvard University. Bureau for Economic Research in Latin America. The economic literature of Latin America; a tentative bibliography. Vol. I. Cambridge. Harvard Univ. Press. 1935. 315p. **2401**

Hesketh, Roger F. Selected bibliography on the international economic position of the United States. Internat. affairs. X. p103-9, 230-41 (Jan., March 1931) **2401a**

International Book Company, New York. A select list of export trade publications and other business books, 1915. N.Y. International Book Co. 1915. 24p. **2402**

Liverpool. Public Libraries, Museums and Art Gallery. Library. Commercial reference library; a guide to the contents of commercial books, directories, periodicals, reports, gazetteers, &c., ... Liverpool. Libraries, Museums & Arts Com. 1931. 86p. **2403**

Marine publications of American museums and institutions. Am. neptune. I. p196-8 (April 1941) **2403a**

National Foreign Trade Council. Selected bibliography of foreign trade. N.Y. National Foreign Trade Council. 1922. unpag. **2404**

Newark, N.J. Free Public Library. Ships and the ocean; a list of books on ships, commerce, and the merchant marine. Comp. for the United States Shipping Board by Miss M. L. Prevost. Wash. Govt. Ptg. Off. 1918. 7p. **2405**

Pan American Union. Columbus Memorial Library. A reference list on commerce, exporting and importing. Comp. by Charles E. Babcock. Wash. D.C. June 1919. 19p. **2406**

Pratt, E. E. Literature on foreign trade. Special libraries. X. p169-72 (Sept. 1919) **2407**

Shuey, Herbert Stanley. Bibliography of foreign trade publications. San Francisco. The Ten Bosch Co. 1918. 77p. **2408**

Snyder, James Wilbert. A bibliography for the early American China trade, 1784-1815. N.Y. Am. Hist. Co. 1940. 51p. (Reprinted from Americana, XXXIV, p553-72) **2408a**

U.S. Bureau of Foreign and Domestic Commerce. Indexed catalog of U.S. foreign trade; statistical statements for 1934. Approved by Committee on statistics. 3d ed. [Wash. D.C. 1934] 73p. mim. Same. 1935. 22p. **2409**

—— —— Training for foreign trade. (Miscellaneous ser. no. 97) Comp. by R. S. MacElwee and F. G. Nichols and others. Wash. Govt. Ptg. Off. 1919. 195p. **2410**

U.S. Library of Congress. Division of bibliography. The banana: culture-industry-commerce; a bibliographical list. July 7, 1927. 26p. typ. **2411**

—— —— —— Early American ships and shipping: a bibliographical list. Jan. 18, 1928. 7p. typ. **2412**

—— —— —— International free trade; a bibliographical list. Oct. 13, 1930. 13p. mim. **2413**

—— —— —— List of books (with references to periodicals) on mercantile marine subsidies. Comp. under the direction of A. P. C. Griffin. Wash. Govt. Ptg. Off. 1906. 140p. (Additional references. . Comp under the direction of H. B. Meyer. Wash. Govt. Ptg. Off. 1911. p143-64; supplements. April 21, 1914. 5p. typ.; Dec. 10, 1915. 9p. typ.; Dec. 28, 1915. 10p. typ.; List. 1915-22. 12p. mim.) **2414**

—— —— —— List of government publications containing current statistics on foreign commerce (including year books of statistical abstracts). Nov. 21, 1914. 26p. typ. **2415**

—— —— —— List of recent references on exporting. Dec. 31, 1929. 7p. typ. **2416**

—— —— —— List of recent references on the balance of trade, with special emphasis on invisible balance. Aug. 1, 1922. 8p. typ. **2417**

—— —— —— List of references on American shipping of to-day. Feb. 16, 1917. 13p. typ. **2418**

—— —— —— List of references on commerce between the United States and China. Dec. 11, 1916. 3p. typ. (Recent references. June 27, 1923. 8p. typ.) **2419**

—— —— —— List of references on dumping. Dec. 14, 1915. 10p. typ. (Recent references. Dec. 9, 1921. 9p. typ.) **2420**

—— —— —— List of references on embargoes. Comp. under the direction of H. H. B. Meyer. Wash. Govt. Ptg. Off. 1917. 44p. **2421**

—— —— —— List of references on marine salvage and wrecking operations. Oct. 18, 1922. 11p. typ. **2422**

—— —— —— List of references on ocean freight rates. Aug. 16, 1917. 4p. typ. **2423**

—— —— —— List of references on seamen in the merchant marine (in relation to the seamen's law of the United States, and safety at sea). Dec. 16, 1915. 14p. typ. **2424**

—— —— —— List of references on railways. July 21, 1922. 6p. typ. **2425**

—— —— —— List of references on shipping and shipbuilding. Comp. under the direction of H. H. B. Meyer. Wash. Govt. Ptg. Off. 1919. 303p. **2426**

—— —— —— List of references on shipping discrimination. Nov. 29, 1921. 13p. mim. **2427**

—— —— —— List of references on shipwrecks, collisions at sea: causes and prevention. Sept. 30, 1920. 25p. typ. **2428**

—— —— —— List of references on the American valuation plan for imports into the United States. Dec. 7, 1921. 4p. mim. **2429**

—— —— —— List of references on the commerce of the United States with the British West Indies. Nov. 18, 1916. 5p. typ. **2430**

—— —— —— List of references on the commercial relations between the United States and Australia. May 15, 1917. 4p. typ. **2431**

—— —— —— List of references on the depreciation of ships. Feb. 25, 1920. 4p. typ. **2432**

—— —— —— List of references on the export corporation plan (McNary-Haugen bill). Jan. 15, 1925. 7p. typ. **2433**

—— —— —— List of references on the history and development of maritime law. March 28, 1921. 8p. typ. **2434**

—— —— —— List of references on the Webb law (Combination in export trade). April 9, 1923. 4p. typ. **2435**

—— —— —— A list of references on tramp ships. Sept. 22, 1933. 5p. typ. **2436**

—— —— —— Select list of references on American registry for foreign ships. Nov. 19, 1912. 3p. typ. **2437**

—— —— —— Select list of references on the commercial relations between the United States and Germany. April 11, 1912. 8p. typ. **2438**

—— —— —— Select list of references on the Panama Canal in its commercial aspects. April 30, 1913. 15p. typ. **2439**

—— —— —— Select list of references on trade relations between Great Britain and the United States, 1783-1794. 1905? 8p. typ. **2440**

—— —— —— Select list of references relating to trade relations between the United States and Germany. Oct. 21, 1913. 4p. typ. **2441**

U.S. Library of Congress. Division of bibliography. Selected list of references on embargoes. Comp. by Helen F. Conover. Sept. 15, 1939. 8p. typ. **2441a**

—— —— —— Selected list of references on safety at sea. Comp. by Grace Hadley Fuller. 1940. 39p. reprod. typ. **2441b**

—— —— —— Selected list of writings on the American Merchant Marine, including subsidies. Jan. 18, 1936. 46p. mim. **2442**

—— —— —— Shipping finance; a list of recent references. Jan. 25, 1930. 6p. typ. **2443**

—— —— —— Shipping question: a list of recent writings. Jan. 27, 1928. 34p. mim. **2444**

—— —— —— Wooden shipbuilding on the Atlantic coast in the 18th and 19th centuries; a brief list of references. May 6, 1929. 3p. typ. **2445**

U.S. Tariff Commission. Library. Reciprocal trade: a current bibliography; selected list of references. Comp. as a W.P.A. project under the supervision of Cornelia Notz, with the assistance of Said Jarvinen and others. Wash. D.C. 1937. 282, 129p. photop. Supplement. 1940. 232p. **2446**

Velli, J. and Hasse, Adelaide R. Bibliography of export trade publications and business books. (Proceedings of The Second Pan Am. Scientific Cong. IV. pt. 1. p612-21) Wash. Govt. Ptg. Off. 1917 **2447**

FINANCE AND BANKING

American Numismatic and Archaeological Society. Catalogue of the numismatic books in the library of the . . . Society, with a subject index to the important articles in the American Journal of numismatics, and other periodicals, to the end of 1882. N.Y. T. R. Marvin; Boston. 1883. 31p. **2448**

Attinelli, Emanuel J. Numisgraphics, or a list of catalogues, in which occur coins or medals, which have been sold by auction in the United States, also, a list of catalogues or price lists of coins, issued by dealers, also a list of various publications of more or less interest to numismatologists which have been published in the United States. N.Y. 1876. 123p. **2449**

Bell, J. W. Recent literature on money and banking. Harvard bus. rev. XVII. p222-36 (Winter 1939) **2449a**

Blakey, R. G. Recent publications in public finance: with discussion. *In* National Tax Association. Proceedings of the 31st annual conference, 1938. Columbia, S.C. Tax Comm. The Asso. 1939. p51-86 **2449b**

Bogart, Ernest Ludlow and Rawles, William A. Trial bibliography and outline of lectures on the financial history of the United States. (Oberlin College Lib. bul. no. 5) Oberlin, Ohio. The News Ptg. Co. 1901. 49p. **2450**

Bogert, Henry. Catalogue of the extensive and valuable cabinet of coins and medals . . . together with a large collection of rare and valuable numismatic works. . . . N.Y. Bogert, Bourne & Outen. 1859. 93p. **2451**

Brannt, Willian T. Table of contents and index to the proceedings of the American Bankers Association from 1875 to 1892, inclusive. N.Y. 1893. 147p. **2452**

Brewington, Ann and Knisely, Verona B. The social concept of money; a bibliography. Chicago. Univ. of Chicago Press. 1935. 107p. **2453**

California. University. Bureau of Public Administration. Guaranty of bank deposits and the Federal Deposit Insurance Corporation: a reading list. Comp. by Dorothy Campbell Culver. Berkeley, Calif. 1933. 21p. mim. **2454**

—— —— —— Inflation: a selected bibliography, October, 1933. Comp. by Dorothy Campbell Culver. Berkeley, Calif. 1933. 13p. mim. **2455**

Crosby, W. Edgar, Jr. Recent books on bank management. Harvard bus. rev. XVII. p237-52 (Winter 1939) **2455a**

Day, Pearl M. The Federal Reserve banking system; a bibliography; supplement number one. N.Y. Pub. Lib. bul. XXXV. p229-38, 477-98 (April-July 1931) **2456**

Dewey, Davis Rich. Suggestions for students, teachers, and readers. *In* Financial history of the United States. N.Y. Longmans, Green. 1903. (Useful chapter references also included) p. ix-xxviii **2457**

Hillis, Madalene S. Concentrated wealth; a bibliography. Madison, Wis. Wisconsin Free Lib. Comm. 1909. 21p. **2457a**

Horton, Samuel Dana. A partial list of modern publications on the subject of money. *In* The International monetary conference of 1878. Proc. and exhibits (Senate executive document no. 58. 45 Cong. 3 sess. Ser. 1832) Wash. D.C. 1879. p737-73 **2458**

McLane, Clarke Joseph. Credit union bibliography. Wash. D.C. Riverford. 1936. 48p. **2459**

Masui, Mitsuzo. A bibliography of finance. [Kobe] The International Finance Seminar in the Kobe Univ. of Commerce. 1935. 1614, 116p. American books and articles p1285-614 **2459a**

New York. Public Library. Check list of American federal documents relating to finance in the New York Public Library. N.Y. Pub. Lib. bul. VI. p287-327 (Aug. 1902) **2460**

—— —— List of works in the New York Public Library relating to bimetallism, gold and silver standards, etc. N.Y. Pub. Lib. bul. IX. p344-87 (Sept. 1905) (Reprinted. N.Y. 1905. 44p.) **2461**

—— —— List of works in the New York Public Library relating to money and banking—United States. N.Y. Pub. Lib. bul. XII. p309-31, 346-99 (April-June 1908) **2462**

—— —— List of works in the New York Public Library relating to numismatics. N.Y. Pub. Lib. bul. XVII. p981-1049 (Dec. 1913) (Reprinted. N.Y. 1914. 195p.) **2463**

Robinson, Edward L. 1816-1916; one hundred years of savings banking, including comprehensive bibliography on thrift, co-operation and good management as it relates to thrift. Comp. by Marian R. Glenn and Ina Clement. N.Y. Am. Bankers Asso., Savings bank section. 1917. 89p. **2464**

Rossi, Diana I. International finance source book compiled for the Investment Bankers Association of America and the Institute of International Finance. Chicago. Investment Bankers Asso. of Amer., Education dept. 1928. 179p. **2465**

Sawyer, Rollin A., Jr. Federal banking system; a bibliography. N.Y. Pub. Lib. bul. XXXII. p34-48, 93-126, 180-94, 221-47 (Jan.-April 1928) **2466**

Shirley, William W. The world depression 1929—a list of books and pamphlets. N.Y. Pub. Lib. bul. XXXVII. p970-90, 1040-68 (Nov.-Dec. 1933) **2467**

Special Libraries Association. The bank library, why? when? where? how? n.p. 1930. 66p. **2468**

—— Exhibit committee. The bank library; a selected list of publications. Library exhibit, American Bankers Association, annual convention, Boston, 1937. [Boston? 1937] 36p. photop. **2468a**

—— —— Financial group. Sources of investment information compiled for the Investment Bankers Association of America. Chicago. Investment Bankers Asso. of Amer. 1930. 86p. **2469**

Thompson, Laura A. Labor banks in the United States; a list of references. Monthly labor rev. XXIII. p661-70 (Sept. 1926) **2470**

U.S. Bureau of Agricultural Economics. Library. Barter and script in the United States; selected references. Comp. under the direction of Mary G. Lacy (Agricultural economics bibliog. no. 40) Wash. D.C. Feb. 1933. 40p. mim. **2471**

U.S. Department of Commerce. Library. A list of bank publications issued periodically—foreign and domestic. Comp. by Elizabeth M. Carmack under the direction of Charlotte L. Carmody. Wash. D.C. June 1931. 20p. **2472**

U.S. Department of State. Library. List of books and periodical articles on silver and its relation to the current depression and to trade with China. [Wash. D.C.] 1931. 6p. **2473**

U.S. Federal Reserve Board. Select list of references on American finance and banking from 1894 to 1920. Wash. D.C. 1921. 24p. **2474**

U.S. Library of Congress. Division of bibliography. Annuities: a bibliographical list of writings. April 11, 1931. 13p. typ. **2475**

—— —— —— Bank consolidations: a bibliographical list. July 9, 1929. 6p. typ. **2476**

—— —— —— Branch, group, and chain banking: a list of recent writings. April 15, 1937. 30p. **2476a**

—— —— —— Brief list of books on corporation finance. (Investment, promotion, etc.). Jan. 29, 1921. 4p. typ. **2477**

—— —— —— Brief list of references on the Federal Reserve system. Sept. 25, 1918. 4p. typ. (Supplementary list. Jan. 6, 1923. 7p. typ.; List of recent references. June 23, 1926. 10p. typ.). **2478**

—— —— —— Brief list of references on the use of paper money in the Old Northwest. March 6, 1920. 4p. typ. **2479**

—— —— —— Capitalization (finance); a bibliographical list. Aug. 28, 1929. 12p. typ. **2480**

—— —— —— Currency question; a list of references to recent writings. Aug. 17, 1936. 3p. typ. **2481**

—— —— —— Federal and state control of banking, with special reference to guaranty of deposits; a bibliographical list of writings. Dec. 12, 1932. 32p. mim. **2482**

—— —— —— The gold standard and bimetallism; a bibliographical list. Oct. 16, 1931. 15p. typ. (Supplement. Sept. 25, 1936. 9p.) **2483**

—— —— —— Inflation and deflation of the currency; a list of references. Feb. 28, 1933. 20p. mim. (Supplement. Sept. 27, 1935. 22p. mim.) **2484**

—— —— —— Investment banking: a bibliographical list. March 15, 1928. 7p. typ. **2485**

—— —— —— List of books (with references to periodicals) relating to postal savings banks. Comp. under the direction of A. P. C. Griffin. Wash. Govt. Ptg. Off. 1908. 23p. **2486**

—— —— —— List of recent references on agricultural credit. Sept. 6, 1918. 8p. typ. **2487**

—— —— —— A list of recent references on investment banking. Comp. by Florence S. Hellman. April 12, 1940. 19p. typ. **2487a**

—— —— —— A list of recent references on investment trusts (supplementing previous lists). Comp. by Florence S. Hellman. May 3, 1939. 18p. typ. **2487b**

—— —— —— List of recent references on state banks and banking (supplementary to the section in printed select list of references on the monetary question, 1918). Sept. 1, 1922. 4p. typ. **2488**

—— —— —— A list of references on agricultural credit. Feb. 21, 1924. 14p. mim. **2489**

—— —— —— List of references on American investments in foreign countries. Dec. 13, 1922. 9p. mim. (American investments . . . bibliog. list. Oct. 23, 1928. 23p. mim.) **2490**

—— —— —— List of references on branch banking. Oct. 10, 1922. 13p. mim. **2491**

U.S. Library of Congress. Division of bibliography. A list of references on branch, group, and chain banking. Aug. 10, 1932. 15p. mim. **2492**

—— —— —— List of references on building and loan associations. Sept. 2, 1919. 20p. mim. (Supplements. Oct. 18, 1922. 13p. mim.; June 6, 1933. 14p. typ.) **2493**

—— —— —— List of references on cooperative and labor banks. Dec. 4, 1924. 12p. typ. **2494**

—— —— —— List of references on foreign exchange. 1905. 4p. typ. (Recent references. May 6, 1922. 17p. mim.; Dec. 18, 1933. 11p. typ.; April 17, 1935. 20p. typ.) **2495**

—— —— —— List of references on Freedman's Savings and Trust Company, and other Negro banks. Nov. 18, 1914. 4p. typ. **2496**

—— —— —— List of references on industrial banking. Dec. 15, 1921. 5p. typ. **2497**

—— —— —— List of references on mortgage banks. 1905. 5p. typ. **2498**

—— —— —— List of references on national banks. 1908. 8p. typ. **2499**

—— —— —— List of references on national banks and state banks. May 2, 1933. 9p. typ. **2500**

—— —— —— List of references on pawnbroking and usury (loan sharks). Jan. 28, 1919. 8p. typ. **2501**

—— —— —— A list of references on the banker in our economic system with sections on the National Credit Corporation and the Reconstruction Finance Corporation. March 4, 1932. 14p. typ. **2502**

—— —— —— List of references on the Federal Reserve Board; its organization, operation, etc. n.d. 11p. typ. **2503**

—— —— —— List of references on the financial and banking relations between the United States and Latin America. June 8, 1915. 10p. typ. **2504**

—— —— —— List of references on the manufacture of currency, metallic and paper. March 1, 1917. 4p. typ. **2505**

—— —— —— List of references on the resumption of specie payments. 1908. 7p. typ. **2506**

—— —— —— List of the more important works in the Library of Congress on banks and banking. Comp. under the direction of A. P. C. Griffin. Wash. Govt. Ptg. Off. 1904. 55p. **2507**

—— —— —— List of United States documents on agricultural credit banks. April 7, 1915. 10p. typ. **2508**

—— —— —— List of works relating to monetary commissions, United States and foreign. 1908. 13p. typ. **2509**

—— —— —— A list of works relating to the first and second banks of the United States, with chronological list of reports, etc., contained in the American state papers and in the Congressional documents. Comp. under the direction of A. P. C. Griffin. Wash. Govt. Ptg. Off. 1908. 47p. **2510**

—— —— —— Money; a list of recent books. Dec. 31, 1929. 6p. typ. (Additional references. Feb. 16, 1933. 1p.) **2511**

—— —— —— Select list of books relating to currency and banking, with special regard to recent conditions. Wash. Govt. Ptg. Off. 1908. 93p. **2512**

—— —— —— Select list of references on bank and mercantile credits in the United States. Nov. 3, 1910. 18p. typ. (Recent references. Aug. 1, 1923. 6p. typ.) **2513**

—— —— —— Select list of references on currency, mainly bond and asset currency. 1907. 10p. typ. **2514**

—— —— —— Select list of references on financial bubbles, paper money, inflation and depreciation, wildcat banking, etc. Feb. 27, 1913. 4p. typ. **2515**

—— —— —— Select list of references on the central bank question in the United States. 1910. 8p. typ. **2516**

—— —— —— Select list of references on the monetary question. Comp. by H. H. B. Meyer and William Adams Slade. Wash. Govt. Ptg. Off. 1913. 247p. (Select list. Aug. 24, 1914. 6p. typ.) **2517**

—— —— —— Select list of references on the New York safety-fund system. 1908. 8p. typ. **2518**

—— —— —— Select list of references on the panic of 1907. Feb. 1, 1910. 6p. typ. **2519**

—— —— —— Select list of references on the paper and metal money of the United States. n.d. 4p. typ. **2520**

—— —— —— Select list of works relating to government paper money. 1912. 11p. typ. **2521**

—— —— —— A selected list of recent books on the subject of money: United States and foreign countries. Comp. by Grace Hadley Fuller under the direction of Florence S. Hellman. Sept. 30, 1936. 22p. reprod. **2521a**

—— —— —— Selected list of references on bankruptcy in the United States with special reference to bankruptcy legislation, 1928-1939. Comp. by Grace H. Fuller. Jan. 2, 1940. 48p. mim. **2521b**

—— —— —— The silver question; a list of recent references. March 3, 1932. 8p. typ. (Supplement. Jan. 2, 1936. 14p. typ.) **2522**

—— —— —— Silver question; additional references. Aug. 27, 1936. 5p. typ. **2523**

Watkins, Marie O. Books on public and corporation finance and investment. St. Louis Pub. Lib. monthly bul. n.s. XV. p337-48 (Sept. 1917) **2524**

Westerfield, Ray B. Selected bibliography of money, credit, banking and business finance. Cambridge, Mass. Bankers Pub. Co. 1940. 136p. **2524a**

INDUSTRY

General

American Management Association. Industrial marketing data; sources of information, in the Department of Commerce, Bureau of the Census, Bureau of Foreign and Domestic Commerce, Bureau of Mines, Bureau of Standards. (Industrial marketing ser. no. 12) N.Y. The Asso. 1931. 56p. **2526**

American Society of Civil Engineers. Catalogue of the library of. . . Prepared by the Secretary under the direction of the Library committee. N.Y. 1900-02. 2v. **2527**

Baker, Helen. The office library of an industrial relations executive. [Princeton] Princeton Univ., Dept. of economics and social institutions, Industrial relations section. 1934. 21p. **2528**

Berg, R. M. Bibliography of management literature (up to February, 1927) N.Y. The Am. Soc. of Mechanical Engineers. 1927. 67p. **2529**

Boston. Public Library. Industrial problems, chiefly American; selected references to books and magazines in the public library of the city of Boston. (Brief reading lists no. 13. Dec. 1919) Boston. The Trustees. 1919. 18p. **2530**

Cannons, Harry George Turner. Bibliography of industrial efficiency and factory management (books, magazine articles, etc.) with many annotations and indexes of authors and of subjects. London. Routledge. 1920. 167p. **2531**

Chamberlain, Arthur Henry. Bibliography of the manual arts. Chicago. A. Flanagan. 1902. 100p. **2532**

Chicago. Public Library. Finding lists of the Chicago Public Library; useful arts. Chicago. 1908. p941-1132 **2533**

Clark, Victor S. Bibliography. *In* History of manufactures in the United States, 1860-1914. Wash. D.C. Carnegie Inst. of Wash. 1928. p841-57 **2534**

Columbia University. Teachers College. School of Industrial Arts. Annotated list of books relating to industrial arts and industrial education. (Technical education bul. no. 6) N.Y. 1911. 50p. **2535**

Hutchinson's technical and scientific encyclopedia. Ed. by C. F. Tweney and I. P. Shirshov. N.Y. Macmillan. 1936. IV. p2430-68 contain a Bibliography, a list of books and other sources of information on subjects of importance in practical and applied science, manufactures, and the skilled trades, to which is appended a list of publishers. **2535a**

John Crerar Library. A checklist of recent industrial surveys. Part I. General. Part II. Surveys of states, counties, or sections of the U.S. Part III. Surveys of cities. Comp. by Jerome K. Wilcox (Reference lists no. 14, 15) Chicago. 1931. 13, 41p. **2536**

—— A list of books on the history of industry and the industrial arts. Comp. by Aksel G. S. Josephson. Chicago. 1915. 486p. **2537**

National Association of Manufacturers of the United States of America. Bibliography of economic and social material available through the National Association of Manufacturers. . . . N.Y. 1940. 22p. **2537a**

New York. Public Library. Division of Science. List of book and periodical articles on the history of the industrial arts comprising 12,000 entries. MS. **2537b**

Newark, N.J. Free Public Library. American industries; a list of some American industries, with the names of books and papers in which short stories about them may be found. Newark, N.J. 1906? **2538**

Princeton University. Department of Economics and Social Institutions. Industrial relations section. The office library of an industrial relations executive. Comp. by Helen Baker. Princeton. Princeton Univ. 1938. 23p. **2538a**

—— —— Problems and policies in industrial relations in a war economy; a selected annotated bibliography. Princeton. Princeton Univ. 1940. 30p. Supplements. Nov. 15, 1940, March 1, 1941. 11, 14p. **2538b**

Smith, George C. Industrial surveys, an outline for communities and manufacturers. St. Louis. Industrial Club of St. Louis. 1930. 60p. **2539**

U.S. Federal Board for Vocational Education. Bibliography on foremen training; a selected and annotated list of references on recent books, pamphlets, and magazine articles. (Trade and industrial ser. no. 35. bul. no. 128) Wash. Govt. Ptg. Off. April 1928. 29p. **2540**

U.S. Library of Congress. Division of bibliography. List of recent references on location of industries including migration and decentralization. Aug. 10, 1933. 12p. mim. **2541**

—— —— —— List of references on art industries and trade. Aug. 11, 1921. 9p. typ. **2542**

—— —— —— List of references on arts and crafts. 1908. 12p. typ. **2543**

—— —— —— Select list of references on piece work versus time work in the trades. April 29, 1910. 6p. typ. **2544**

—— —— —— A short list of books on factory management. June 6, 1924. 6p. typ. **2545**

Worcester, Mass. Free Public Library. Selected list of industrial books, issued specially for the artisans and craftsmen of Worcester. Worcester, Mass. Belisle. 1912. 37p. **2546**

Domestic Science

Boston. Public Library. A list of books on domestic science in the public library of the city of Boston. Boston. Boston Pub. Lib. 1911. 78p. **2547**

Columbia University. Teachers College. School of Practical Arts. Annotated list of books relating to household arts. Prepared by the Teachers College, School of Practical Arts. (Technical education bul. no. 25) N.Y. 1916. 39p.   **2548**

Gourley, James E. Regional American cookery, 1884-1934; a list of works on the subject. N.Y. New York Pub. Lib. 1936. 36p. (Reprinted with additions from the New York Pub. Lib. bul. June-July 1935)   **2548a**

Langworthy, Charles Ford. U.S. government publications as sources of information for students of home economics. Wash. D.C. 1909. p227-52 (Reprinted from The Jour. of home economics. June 1909)   **2549**

Lincoln, Waldo. Bibliography of American cookery books, 1742-1860. Worcester, Mass. Am. Antiq. Soc. 1929. 145p. (Reprinted from the Am. Antiq. Soc. proc. n.s. XXXIX. p85-225. April 1929)   **2550**

Lyford, Carrie Alberta. Bibliography of home economics. (Bureau of Education. Bul. 1919. no. 46) Wash. Govt. Ptg. Off. 1919. 103p.   **2551**

Shaw, Robert Kendall. Bibliography of domestic economy in English. N.Y. State Lib. bul. 52. bibliog. II. p31-168 (Jan. 1901)   **2552**

U.S. Bureau of Education. List of references on home economics. (Lib. leaflet no. 21. June 1923) Wash. D.C. 1923. 21p.   **2553**

—— —— Titles of completed research from home economics departments in American colleges and universities, 1918 to 1923. (Home economics circular. no. 18) Wash. Govt. Ptg. Off. 1924. 14p.   **2554**

U.S. Department of Agriculture. Library. Agricultural and home economics extension in the United States; a selected list of references prepared in the Office of experiment stations library. Comp. by Cora L. Feldkamp (Bibliog. contributions no. 18) Wash. D.C. Sept. 1928. 56p. mim.   **2555**

Engineering

American Society of Civil Engineers. Index to transactions, volumes I to LXXXIII (1867 to 1920). Prepared under the direction of the Committee on publications by Elbert M. Chandler. N.Y. 1921. 272p. Same. 1921-1934. (Proc. of the Am. Soc. of Civil Engineers. LX. no. 9. pt. 2. Nov. 1934) [N.Y.] The Soc. 1934. 188p.   **2556**

—— **Construction division. Executive committee.** A selected bibliography on construction methods and plant applied to bridges, buildings, dams, hydroelectric plants, roads, sea-walls, sewers, tunnels, etc. Comp. under the direction of William Joshua Barney . . . . N.Y. The Soc. 1930. 117p.   **2557**

Atkins, Paul Moody. Bibliography of production engineering and factory cost accounting. Chicago. Soc. of Industrial Engineers. 1927. 96p.   **2558**

Cowing, Herbert L. One thousand technical books; a selected list with annotations emphasing especially elementary practical books. Wash. D.C. Am. Lib. Asso. June 1919. 123p.   **2559**

Jakkula, Arne Arthur. A history of suspension bridges in bibliographical form. . . . Ann Arbor, Mich. 1936. 587p. reprod.   **2559a**

New York. Public Library. New technical books; a selected list on industrial arts and engineering added to the New York Public Library, 1915-25 N.Y. N.Y. Pub. Lib. 1915-25   **2560**

Peddie, R. A. Engineering and metallurgical books, 1907-1911; a full title catalogue, arranged under subject headings, of all British and American books on engineering, metallurgy, and allied topics. N.Y. Van Nostrand. 1912. 206p.   **2561**

Pittsburgh. Carnegie Library. Technology department. Technical book review index, issued by the technology dept. of the Carnegie Library of Pittsburgh, 1915-28. Pittsburgh. 1915-29   **2562**

Shaw, Ralph. Engineering books available in America prior to 1830. N.Y. N.Y. Pub Lib. 1933. 67p. (Reprinted from the Bul. XXXVI. Jan.-June 1933)   **2563**

Society of Industrial Engineers. Buffalo chapter. Research committee. Bibliography of time study engineering or time study, motion study, wage incentives and fatigue in industry. N.Y. H. W. Wilson. 1933. 63p.   **2564**

U.S. Engineer School. Library. Breakwaters, a bibliography. Prep. by H. E. Haferkorn. Wash. Engineer Reproduction Plant, U.S. Army. 1932. 86p. **2564a**

—— —— —— Dams; a bibliography of books, periodicals, and society publications appearing from January 1924 through March 1936. Comp. by Alvan W. Clark. Fort Belvoir, Va. The Engineer School. 1936. 256p. Supplement. 1938. 110p.   **2564b**

U.S. Library of Congress. Division of bibliography. List of references on mechanical engineering. Aug. 5, 1918. 10p. typ.   **2565**

—— —— —— Machinery in industry; with special emphasis upon its effects on labor; a selected list of writings. Feb. 28, 1934. 28p. mim.   **2566**

—— —— —— Select list of works on the social and economic effects of the introduction of machinery. 1909. 4p. typ. **2567**

U.S. Office of Education. Bibliography on foreman improvement; a selected and annotated list of references, including books, pamphlets, and magazine articles. (Vocational education bul. no. 128. Trade and industrial ser. no. 35) Wash. Govt. Ptg. Off. 1935. 34p.   **2568**

Virginia. State Library. Finding list of books in . . . technology. . . . Va. State Lib. bul. IV. p310-55. 1912   **2569**

Health and Safety

Abstract of the literature of individual hygiene. Jour. of industrial hygiene. I. no. 1. May 1919- **2570**

American Association for Labor Legislation. Bibliography on industrial hygiene; trial list of references on occupational diseases and industrial hygiene. Am. labor legislation rev. II. p367-417 (June 1912) **2571**

American Public Health Association. Bibliography on industrial fatigue and allied subjects. Comp. by E. Gilfillan. (Rep. for meeting Sept. 30-Oct. 5, 1929) [Chicago. 1929] 38p. **2572**

National Bureau of Casualty and Surety Underwriters Library. Outline of source material on industrial safety, presented to the 19th annual conference of the Special Libraries Association held in Toronto, June, 1927. By Mildred B. Pressman. N.Y. 1927. 16p. autog. from typ. copy **2573**

—— A review of general literature on industrial accidents, factory management, hours of work, fatigue and rest periods, lighting, heating, ventilation, and sanitation and literature on these subjects in their relation to safety and production. Prepared by Mildred B. Pressman. N.Y. 1928. 43p. autog. from typ. copy **2574**

Pittsburgh. Carnegie Library. Industrial accidents; a select list of books. Pittsburgh. 1911. 12p. **2575**

U.S. Bureau of Labor Statistics. Bibliography: official state regulations, orders, advisory pamphlets, and labor laws relating to safety. Monthly labor rev. XXX. p481-94 (Feb. 1930) **2576**

—— —— **Library.** Books and periodicals on accident and disease prevention in industry in the library of the Bureau of Labor Industry. Wash. Govt. Ptg. Off. 1916. 23p. **2577**

U.S. Library of Congress. Division of bibliography. Brief list on legislation and court decisions protecting women workers. Sept. 28, 1916. 3p. typ. **2578**

—— —— —— List of references on the handling of accident cases among the civilian population. Oct. 14, 1919. 61p. typ. **2579**

—— —— —— Select list of references (in English) on industrial accidents and safety. Nov. 19, 1914. 3p. typ. **2580**

—— —— —— Select list of references on occupational injuries and diseases. Aug. 25, 1910. 10p. typ. **2581**

—— —— —— Select list of references on prevention of industrial accidents. 1911. 21p. mim. **2582**

Industries

Amalgamated Clothing Workers of America. Bibliography of the Amalgamated Clothing Workers of America. N.Y. Amalgamated Clothing Workers of Amer., Research dept. 1926. 20p. **2583**

American Society of Mechanical Engineers. Bibliography on the machining of wood. N.Y. The Soc. 1939. 74p. **2583a**

Ayer, Thomas Parker. Coal prices; a selected bibliography. Am. Acad. Pol. and Social Sciences ann. CXI. p344-62 (Jan. 1924) **2584**

Beck, Wilbert Bernard. Coal; its distribution, marketing, and transportation since 1918; a contribution to a bibliography. Madison. Univ. of Wisconsin Library School. 1938. 23p. typ. **2584a**

Briggs, Charles H. A bibliography of cerealiana; a list of books and pamphlets on cereal production and marketing, milling and baking, and insects and fungous infestations of cereals and cereal products, including publications of state, provincial and national agricultural experiment stations and boards of agriculture. Minneapolis, Minn. The Miller Pub. Co. 1938. 59p. **2584b**

Brooklyn. Public Library. A reading and reference list of books on building and building trades in the Brooklyn Public Library. Brooklyn, N.Y. 1910. 29p. **2585**

Burroughs, Elizabeth Harding. Bibliography of petroleum and allied substances. (U.S. Bureau of Mines. Bulletins 149, 165, 180, 189, 216, 290) Wash. Govt. Ptg. Off. 1918-29. (1922/23 by H. Britten) **2587**

Chamber of Commerce of the United States of America. Bibliography on building, housing and construction. Wash. D.C. Jan. 1933. 18p. mim. **2588**

—— Construction and civic development department. Bibliography on building, housing and construction. Wash. D.C. 1937. 34p. mim. **2588a**

Dalton, W. H. and others. Bibliography. *In* Petroleum; a treatise on the geographical distribution and geological occurrence of petroleum and natural gas. . . . By Sir Boverton Redwood. London. Charles Griffin. 1913. III. p187-349 **2589**

Fearing, Daniel Butler. Check list of books on angling, fish, fisheries, fishculture, etc., in the library of D. B. Fearing. N.Y. Printed for priv. distribution. 1901. 138p. **2590**

Goodwin, Helen Durrie. Bibliography—Shipbuilding in the Pacific Northwest. Wash. hist. quar. XI. p196-201 (July 1920) **2591**

Great Britain. Patent Office. Subject list of works on the textile industries and wearing apparel, including the culture and chemical technology of textile fabrics, in the library of the Patent Office. London. 1919. 329p. **2592**

Hardwicke, Robert Etter. Petroleum and natural gas bibliography. Austin, The Univ. of Texas. 1937. 167p. **2592a**

Hunter, Dard. Hand made paper and its water marks; a bibliography. Marborough-on-Hudson, N.Y. 1916. 22p. **2593**

Knit Goods Manufacturers of America. References on the Knit goods industry. Utica, N.Y. 1920. 34p. **2594**

Leidy, W. P. Shipbuilding and marine engines; a selected list of books and pamphlets. Booklist. XXXVII. p527-38. 1941
2594a

Los Angeles Public Library. A selected list of books for workers in the building and wood-working trades. Los Angeles. 1913. 31p.
2595

Louisiana. Dept. of Conservation. A selected list of periodicals, serials, and books dealing with petroleum and allied subjects and where this material may be found in some Oklahoma, Texas, and Louisiana libraries, together with a group of subject bibliographies on the petroleum industry obtained from the Technical department of the Tulsa Public Library. Comp. by Clarence P. Dunbar and Lucille M. Dunbar. New Orleans. 1939. 223p. mim.
2595a

National Association of Wool Manufacturers. A bibliography of wool and the woolen manufacture. National Asso. of Wool Manufacturers bul. XXI. p118-34 (June 1891)
2596

New York. Public Library. Check list of works on fish and fisheries in the New York Public Library, June 1, 1899. N.Y. Pub. Lib. bul. III. p296-312, 334-48 (July 1899)
2597

—— —— Chemistry and manufacture of writing and printing inks; a list of references in the New York Public Library. Comp. by William B. Gamble. N.Y. 1926. 105p. (Reprinted from the Bul. XXIX. p579-91, 625-77, 706-41 (Aug.-Sept. 1925)
2598

—— —— Hand-spinning and hand-weaving; a list of references in the New York Public Library. Comp. by William B. Gamble. N.Y. 1922. 41p. (Reprinted from the Bul. XXVI. p381-96 (May 1922)
2599

—— —— List of works in the library relating to fishing and fish culture. N.Y. 1909. 49p. (Reprinted from the Bul. XIII. p259-307. April 1909)
2600

—— —— List of works in the New York Public Library relating to illumination. N.Y. Pub. Lib. bul. XII. p686-734 (Dec. 1908)
2601

—— —— List of works in the New York Public Library, relating to the development and manufacture of typewriting machines. By William B. Gamble. N.Y. 1913. 18p. (Reprinted from the Bul. XVII. p697-712. Sept. 1913)
2602

Omaha. Technical High School. Library. The shop's library, material useful for elementary training. Booklist. XXXVII. p303-13. 1941
2602a

Phillips, William B. Bibliography of fuel oil. Am. Inst. of Mining Engineers bul. XC. p1040-70 (June 1914) (Prepared from the bibliography of petroleum in Sir Boverton Redwood's Treatise on petroleum, 1913, with many additions)
2603

Pittsburgh. Carnegie Institute. Institute of Technology. Glass manufacture; a bibliography of pertinent articles in periodicals and other literature issued in 1938. (Bul. no. 84) Pittsburgh, Pa. 1940. 251p. mim.
2603a

Pittsburgh. Carnegie Library. Brick manufacture and brick laying. Carnegie Lib. of Pittsburgh monthly bul. XVII. p8-33 (Jan. 1912)
2604

—— —— Literature of the coal industry for 1923; a classified list of the more important books, serials and trade publications during the year; with a few of earlier date, not previously announced. Pittsburgh. 1924. (Reprinted from "The Coal industry" Jan. 1924)
2605

Rose, Jennie Margaret. Potash production and control since 1910: a selected bibliography. Madison. Univ. of Wisconsin Lib. School. 1938. 50p. typ.
2605a

St. Louis. Public Library. Bibliography of the shoe industry, to which is added a selected list of books on leather manufacture. Comp. by Cecile Pajanovitch. St. Louis Pub. Lib. monthly bul. n.s. XXI. p243-51 (Sept. 1923)
2606

Special Libraries Association. Rubber committee. Bibliography on rubber technology, 1924-26. N.Y. 1926-30. 7 sections. mim.
2607

Surface, Henry E. Bibliography of the pulp and paper industries. (U.S. Forest Service. Bul. 123) Wash. Govt. Ptg. Off. 1913. 48p.
2608

Tulsa. Public Library. Subject card catalog of petroleum articles in magazines. Tulsa, Okla.
2608a

U.S. Bureau of Agricultural Chemistry and Engineering. Publications on production, properties, examination, marketing and uses of naval stores. Wash. D.C. 1941. 10p. mim.
2608b

U.S. Bureau of Agricultural Economics. Library. Economic development of the cotton-textile industry in the United States, 1910-1935; a selected bibliography. Comp. by Emily L. Day and Rachel P. Lane under the direction of Mary G. Lacy (Agricultural economics bibliog. no. 57) Wash. D.C. Sept. 1935. 137p. mim.
2609

—— —— —— Flour milling and bread making; a selected list of references. Comp. by C. Louise Phillips and J. H. Shollenberger (Agricultural economics bibliog. no. 2 revised) Wash. D.C. Feb. 1925. 20p. mim.
2610

—— —— —— The frozen food industry; selected references, January, 1937 to March, 1939. (Economic lib. list no. 2) By H. E. Hennefrund. Wash. D.C. The Bureau. April 1939. 14p. mim.
2610a

—— —— —— The peanut industry; a selected list of references on the economic aspects of the industry, 1920-1939. Comp. by H. F. Hennefrund. (Agricultural economics bibliog. no. 80) Wash. D.C. 1939. 238p. mim.
2610b

——— ——— ——— The tobacco industry: a selected list of references on the economic aspects of the industry, 1932-1938. Comp. by Louise O. Bercaw. (Agricultural economics bibliog. no. 75) Wash. D.C. Sept. 1938. 337p. mim. **2610c**

U.S. Bureau of Foreign and Domestic Commerce. The leather industry, 1935; a bibliography. Prepared by J. G. Schnitzer, Leather and rubber division. [Wash.] 1935. 22p. **2610d**

——— ——— Selected references on handicraft woodworking. Wash. D.C. 1938. 27p. lithog. **2610e**

——— ——— Some references to publications relating to the building and construction industry. Comp. by R. C. Leslie. Wash. D.C. May 1940. 16p. mim. **2610f**

——— ——— **Division of business review.** Some references to material on meat packing and distribution (basic information sources). Comp. by R. C. Leslie. Wash. D.C. June 1939. 9p. mim. **2610g**

——— ——— **Marketing research division. Marketing service section.** Building and construction (basic information sources). Comp. by R. C. Leslie. Wash. D.C. 1938. 24p. mim. **2610h**

——— ——— **Textile division.** Textile reading list; a partial bibliography on textile information. Prep. by Harry J. Robinson (Spec. bul. no. 634) [Wash.] 1938. 38p. **2610i**

U.S. Bureau of Mines. Recent articles on petroleum and allied substances. Comp. by the U.S. Bureau of Mines in cooperation with the American Petroleum Institute and the Special Libraries Association. Melissa Speer, bibliographer. San Francisco. Bureau of Mines, Petroleum field office. 1919-33. mim. **2611**

——— ——— **Petroleum Experiment Station. Library.** Author and subject card index of periodical articles on oil, gas and allied substances. Bartlesville, Okla. **2611a**

U.S. Department of State. International Fisheries Exposition, 1898, Bergen, Norway. Report of commissioner to exposition with bibliography of American fish and fisheries. Wash. Govt. Ptg. Off. 1901. 445p. **2612**

U.S. Geological Survey. Library. A suggestive list of references on federal regulation of the petroleum industry since August 19, 1933 with special reference to The Petroleum administration. Comp. by James T. Rubey and William H. Heers (Bibliog. list no. 3) [Wash. D.C.] 1935. 39p. reprod. typ. **2613**

U.S. Library of Congress. Division of bibliography. Automobile industry: selected list of recent writings. Comp. by Anne L. Baden. Oct. 6, 1938. 74p. mim. **2613a**

——— ——— ——— Brief list of references on cooperative building and housing projects. May 27, 1921. 4p. mim. **2614**

——— ——— ——— Brief list of references on government regulation of the packing industry. Oct. 21, 1919. 4p. mim. **2615**

——— ——— ——— Brief list of references on the lime industry. Jan. 21, 1919. 6p. typ. **2616**

——— ——— ——— Brief list of references on the piano and mechanical piano player industry. Dec. 20, 1921. 7p. typ. **2617**

——— ——— ——— Handicrafts: a selected list of recent books and pamphlets. Comp. by Helen F. Conover. April 28, 1939. 37p. mim. **2617a**

——— ——— ——— The laundry industry; a bibliographical list. Sept. 7, 1927. 19p. typ. **2618**

——— ——— ——— Leather and the leather industry; a list of recent books. Oct. 6, 1928. 10p. typ. **2619**

——— ——— ——— Leather and the leather industry; a list of recent references. Comp. by Helen F. Conover. Feb. 15, 1940. 15p. typ. **2619a**

——— ——— ——— List of books on the manufacture of alcholic beverages (beer, brandy, whisky, wine, etc.). May 1, 1935. 12p. typ. **2620**

——— ——— ——— A list of recent references on anthracite coal, with special reference to Pennsylvania. Comp. by Florence S. Hellman. July 7, 1938. 24p. typ. **2620a**

——— ——— ——— List of recent references on flour and grain milling. March 30, 1922. 10p. multig. **2621**

——— ——— ——— A list of recent references on the asbestos industry in the United States and foreign countries. June 12, 1933. 15p. typ. **2622**

——— ——— ——— A list of recent references on the coal industry of the United States (with special reference to production and labor condition). June 26, 1933. 27p. typ. **2623**

——— ——— ——— List of recent references on the coal situation in Congress. Feb. 12, 1927. 5p. typ. **2624**

——— ——— ——— List of recent references on the lumber industry in the United States. Feb. 18, 1921. 31p. typ. (Supplements. Dec. 4, 1923. 9p. mim.; Aug. 20, 1928. 37p. mim.; July 19, 1935. 24p. typ.) **2625**

——— ——— ——— List of references on dyestuffs, chemistry, manufacture, trade. Comp. under the direction of H. H. B. Meyer. Wash. Govt. Ptg. Off. 1919. 186p. **2626**

——— ——— ——— List of references on hat manufacture and trade. July 24, 1917. 4p. multig. (Additional references. 1921. 3p.) **2627**

——— ——— ——— List of references on labor in coal mining industries. March 27, 1917. 5p. typ. **2628**

——— ——— ——— List of references on marble and the marble industry. Dec. 12, 1922. 11p. mim. **2629**

——— ——— ——— List of references on oil-bearing shales and he oil-shale industry. Sept. 8, 1920. 6p. typ. **2630**

——— ——— ——— List of references on rubber tires, with special reference to manufacture. Oct. 11, 1919. 4p. typ. **2631**

U.S. Library of Congress. Division of bibliography. A list of references on sewing machines; trade and manufactures. Sept. 14, 1934. 8p. typ.   **2633**
—— —— —— List of references on textile machinery. Oct. 21, 1915. 16p. typ.   **2634**
—— —— —— List of references on the baking industry. March 19, 1921. 17p. typ.   **2635**
—— —— —— A list of references on the baking powder industry. July 19, 1924. 6p. typ.   **2636**
—— —— —— List of references on the boots and shoes industry including history. Aug. 9, 1922. 24p. typ.   **2637**
—— —— —— List of references on the brewing industry. July 17, 1917. 11p. typ.   **2638**
—— —— —— List of references on the by-products of the milk industry. June 16, 1917. 4p. typ.   **2639**
—— —— —— List of references on the canning industry. Feb. 18, 1914. 5p. typ.   **2640**
—— —— —— List of references on the carpet and rug industry of the United States. Aug. 16, 1922. 5p. typ.   **2641**
—— —— —— List of references on the clothing industry. 1916. 13p. typ.   **2642**
—— —— —— List of references on the confectionery industry of the United States and foreign countries. March 22, 1920. 9p. typ. (Additional references. July 5, 1929. 3p.)   **2643**
—— —— —— List of references on the cost of manufacture of cotton goods and prices. Oct. 25, 1921. 5p. typ.   **2644**
—— —— —— List of references on the economic and statistical aspects of shipbuilding in Great Britain and the United States, 1930-1940. Feb. 17, 1941. 24p. typ.   **2644a**
—— —— —— List of references on the foundry industry and foundry practice. Oct. 23, 1916. 6p. typ.   **2645**
—— —— —— List of references on the leather industry including history, production, uses, chemistry, and economics. June 28, 1918. 22p. typ.   **2646**
—— —— —— List of references on the machine tool industry, 1937-1939. Comp. by Florence S. Hellman. Aug. 8, 1939. 7p. typ.   **2646a**
—— —— —— List of references on the match industry. Aug. 29, 1923. 6p. mim.   **2647**
—— —— —— List of references on the meat packing industry. Jan. 9, 1920. 15p. mim.   **2648**
—— —— —— A list of references on the men's and boy's clothing industry. Oct. 5, 1935. 13p. typ.   **2649**
—— —— —— List of references on the milk industry. Nov. 6, 1916. 27p. typ. (Also in Special libraries. VIII. p10-22. Jan. 1917)   **2650**
—— —— —— List of references on the moving picture industry. Feb. 9, 1922. (Supplement. Jan. 12, 1936. 31p. mim.)   **2651**

—— —— —— List of references on the paper box industry. Oct. 23, 1919. 5p. typ.   **2652**
—— —— —— List of references on the paper industry and trade. Dec. 2, 1918. 15p. typ.   **2653**
—— —— —— List of references on the present coal situation in the United States. June 14, 1917. 3p. (List of references, 1917-20. Jan. 1920. 14p. mim.; List of recent references. July 15, 1920. 6p. mim.; List of references, 1921-22. Oct. 14, 1922. 16p. mim.; List of references, 1922-23. Jan. 4, 1924. 23p. mim.)   **2654**
—— —— —— List of references on the starch industry (manufacture and chemistry). July 23, 1914. 7p. typ. (Supplement. April 14, 1922. 5p. typ.)   **2655**
—— —— —— List of references on the storage of coal. June 30, 1920. 10p. mim.   **2656**
—— —— —— List of references on the straw industry and by-products of straw, with special reference to paper manufactures. Jan. 15, 1920. 6p. typ.   **2657**
—— —— —— List of references on the valuation of oil lands. Jan. 27, 1921. 3p. multig.   **2658**
—— —— —— List of references on the zinc industry. June 28, 1907. 8p. typ.   **2659**
—— —— —— List of recent references on toys and the toy industry. Jan. 15, 1931. 7p. typ.   **2660**
—— —— —— List of references on turpentine and the turpentine industry. Sept. 22, 1916. 5p. typ.   **2661**
—— —— —— Petroleum industry; a list of recent writings.' March 28, 1928. 7p. typ.   **2662**
—— ——. —— Rayon industry; list of recent references. June 1, 1929. 10p. mim.   **2663**
—— —— —— Select list of references on coal (1904 to date). Aug. 16, 1913. 14p. typ.   **2664**
—— —— —— Select list of references on salt; trade and manufacture. May 2, 1911. 14p. typ. (Supplement. Nov. 20, 1916. 5p. typ.; 1923. 3p.; June 6, 1935. 9p. typ.)   **2664a**
—— —— —— Select list of references on the aluminum industry (with special reference to the United States). Feb. 18, 1913. 4p. typ.   **2665**
—— —— —— Select list of references on the American Tobacco Company. 1909. 7p. typ.   **2666**
—— —— —— Select list of references on the federal regulation of the production and distribution of coal and oil. Dec. 14, 1923. 7p. typ.   **2667**
—— —— —— Select list of references on the silk industry. Jan. 24, 1913. 8p. typ. (Additional references. 4p.)   **2668**
—— —— —— Select list of references on the United States Steel Corporation. May 23, 1911. 10p. typ.   **2669**

—— —— —— Select list of references on water laws and legislation, water rights, government control of water power, etc. Oct. 4, 1912. 20p. dupl. **2670**

—— —— —— A selected list of recent references on the lumber industry of the United States and Canada. Comp. by Florence S. Hellman. May 16, 1939. 34p. mim. **2670a**

—— —— —— A selected list of recent references on the steel industry. May 5, 1924. 12p. mim. **2671**

—— —— —— Tobacco industry; a list of recent writings. April 20, 1929. 11p. typ. **2672**

Weaver, Gilbert Grimes and Ericcson, E. S. Bibliography of technical and industrial motion picture films and slides. N.Y. N.Y. State Dept. of Industrial Teacher-Training. [1934] p5-182 **2673**

West, Clarence J. Bibliography and patent list for 1937. N.Y. Technical Asso. of the Pulp and Paper Industry. 1938. 218p. **2673a**

—— Bibliography of paper making and United States patents on paper making and related subjects, 1931- . N.Y. Technical Asso. of the Pulp and Paper Industry. 1932- **2673b**

—— Bibliography of pulp and paper making 1900-1928. N.Y. Lockwood Trade Jour. Co. 1929. 982p. Bibliography. 1928-1935, 1936. 803p. **2674**

—— Reading list on paper-making materials. N.Y. Lockwood Trade Jour. Co. 1928. 239p. **2675**

White, W. C. Instructional methods in engineering—a bibliography. Jour. engineering educ. XXX. p761-88 (May 1940) **2675a**

Woodbury, Charles J. H. Bibliography of the cotton manufacture. Waltham, Mass. E. L. Barry. 1909. 213p. **2676**

Miscellaneous

John Crerar Library. The state industrial and manufacturing directories; a bibliography. By Jerome K. Wilcox (John Crerar Lib. Reference list no. 21) Chicago. 1932. 15p. **2677**

Lovell, Eleanor Cook and Hall, Ruth Mason. Index to handicrafts, modelmaking, and workshop projects. Boston. F. W. Faxon. 1936. 476p. **2678**

Manson, Grace Evelyn. Bibliography on psychological tests and other objective measures in industrial personnel. (Reprint and circular ser. of the Personnel Research Federation no. 1) N.Y. Personnel Research Federation. 1925. 28p. (Also in Jour. of personnel research. IV. p301-25. Nov.-Dec. 1925) **2679**

Mellon Institute of Industrial Research. A list of books, bulletins, journal contributions, and patents by members of Mellon Institute, 1911-1938. (Bibliographic series. Bulletin no. 4) Pittsburgh. [The Eddy Press Corporation] 1939. 242p. **2679a**

Mohrhardt, Charles M. Industrial training for national defense. Booklist. XXXVI. p445-56 (Aug. 1940) **2679b**

National Research Council. Division of engineering and industrial research. A bibliography on research; selected articles from the technical press, 1923-1924-1925. N.Y. 1926? 46p. **2680**

—— —— Five years of research in industry, 1926-1930; a reading list of selected articles from the technical press. Comp. by Clarence J. West. N Y. National Research Council. 1930. 91p. **2681**

Quoddy Regional Project. Library. An annotated bibliography of books & pamphlets on certain mechanical and allied trades. Quoddy Village, Me. 1940. 137p. reprod. **2681a**

Severance, Belknap. Select bibliography of inventions and inventors. Jour. Patent Off. Soc. XV. p42-57 (Jan. 1933) **2681b**

U.S. Library of Congress. Division of bibliography. Brief list of references on the three-shift system in continuous industries. June 2, 1921. 3p. typ. **2682**

—— —— —— Factory management; a list of recent references. Comp. by Anne L. Baden. Aug. 26, 1940. 15p. typ. **2682a**

—— —— —— Handicraft; a bibliographical list. July 22, 1930. 22p. typ. **2683**

—— —— —— List of recent references on industrial arbitration. Jan. 5, 1920. 9p. multig. (Supplement. Nov. 2, 1922. 9p. mim.) **2684**

—— —— —— List of references on industrial surveys. Jan. 13, 1916. 3p. typ. **2685**

—— —— —— List of references on limitations of output of industrial plants, mines, etc. Dec. 3, 1919. 3p. typ. **2686**

—— —— —— List of references on married women in industry. Feb. 26, 1920. 11p. typ. **2687**

—— —— —— List of references on suburban real estate development with special reference to industrial villages. June 9, 1925. 7p. mim. **2688**

—— —— —— A list of references on technocracy. Jan. 20, 1933. 7p. typ. **2689**

—— —— —— List of references on the industrial dependence and independence of the United States. July 31, 1918. 7p. typ. **2690**

—— —— —— Select list of references on industrial arbitration. Wash. Govt. Ptg. Off. 1903. 15p. (Supplement. Jan. 5, 1920. 9p. multig.; Nov. 2, 1922. 9p. mim.) **2691**

—— —— —— Select list of references on scientific management and industrial efficiency. April 12, 1912. 19p. typ. **2692**

—— —— —— Select list of references on the merit system for promotion of employees in industrial establishments. 1909. 4p. typ. **2693**

U.S. Tariff Commission. Raw materials bibliography: general references to selected raw materials and basic economic resources. Wash. D.C. Dec. 1939. 85p. mim. **2693a**

U.S. Works Progress Administration. Division of information. Industrial change and employment opportunity: a selected bibliography. Comp. by Alexander Gourvich and others. Wash. D.C. July 1939. 254p. mim.   **2693b**

Woerishoffer, Carola. A selected list of books and pamphlets in the English language on women in industry. Ed. by Helen Marot. Acad. Pol. Science proc. I. p188-93 (Oct. 1910)   **2694**

INSURANCE

Actuarial Society of America. Index to volumes XVI to XXV inclusive. Part I. General index. Part II. Index of legal notes. (A) Subject matter. (B) Parties. Part III. Subject-index of tables. N.Y. Printed for the Soc. by L. W. Lawrence. 1926. 166p.   **2695**

American Life Convention. Index to: 1. Proceedings, legal section, American Life Convention, 1906-1931. 2. Proceedings, Association of Life Insurance Counsel, 1913-1931. 3. Insurance law annotations in A.L.R. 4. Insurance law articles in various law journals. St. Louis. Am. Life Convention. 1932. 206p.   **2696**

Arizona University. Library. Unemployment insurance; a list of references in the University of Arizona Library. Comp. by Alvan W. Clark. Tucson, Ariz. Univ. of Arizona Lib. 1931. 17p. mim.   **2697**

Baltimore Life Underwriter's Association. Special report, Educational committee, including bibliography of insurance library books. Balt. 1938. 50p.   **2697a**

Bercaw, Louise O. Social insurance in the United States and foreign countries; a partial list of recent references. [Wash. D.C.] 1934. 54p.   **2698**

Currie, Gilbert Eggleson. Catalogue of the standard insurance works, etc., etc., etc. N.Y. Office U.S. insurance gazette. 1876. 40p. (With United States insurance gazette, Index, 1877)   **2699**

Detroit. Public Library. Unemployment insurance; a selected list of references. Detroit Pub. Lib. Civics division. 1931. 19p.   **2700**

Gummere, John S. A bibliography of American workmen's compensation commission reports. Law lib. jour. XXVIII. p42-50 (April 1935)   **2700a**

Hazard, Willis Hatfield. The literature of life insurance. Harvard bus. rev. XIX. p123-32 (Autumn 1940)   **2700b**

Hopkins, W. S. Social insurance and agriculture: a memorandum presenting suggestions for research and a bibliography. Wash. D.C. Social Science Research Council, Committee on Social Security. 1940. 93p.   **2700c**

Industrial Relations Counselors, Inc. New York. Library. Unemployment insurance; a classified bibliography of books, reports and periodical articles in English,

1928-1931, supplementing Unemployment compensation; a chronological bibliography of books, reports and periodical articles in English, 1891-1927. By Linda H. Morley. N.Y. 1932. 49p. mim.   **2701**

Institute of Actuaries, London. Library. Catalogue of the library of the Institute of Actuaries. London. [Cambridge. Printed by W. Lewis at Univ. Press] 1935. 202p.   **2702**

Insurance books reviews. Bulletin, no. 1- . 1933-   **2702a**

The **Insurance** law journal. Ten year index to volumes LXX-LXXXIX, 1928-1937. N.Y. L. A. Mack. 1938. 258p.   **2702b**

Insurance Library Association of Boston. A catalogue of the Insurance Library Association of Boston. To which is added a sketch of the history and work of the association together with other information. By Henry E. Hess. Boston. 1899. 268p.   **2703**

—— Index of current fire insurance and related subjects. Insurance Lib. Asso. bul. I-XIV (Nov. 1909-April 1924)   **2704**

Jenkins, William S. Social insurance and agriculture; a memorandum presenting suggestions for research and a bibliography. Wash. D.C. 1940. 93p.   **2704a**

Kachur, Nina Alberta. Health insurance, 1932-May 1938: a contribution to bibliography. Madison. Univ. of Wis. Lib. School. 1938. 92p. typ.   **2704b**

Metropolitan Life Insurance Company. Policyholders service bureau. Index of economic reports, October, 1931. N.Y. [1931] 72p.   **2705**

National Bureau of Casualty and Surety Underwriters. Library. Annual index to current literature, dealing with casualty, insurance, suretyship, and related subjects received in the library during the year, 1927-32. N.Y. 1928-33   **2706**

Princeton University. Department of Economics and Social Institutions. Industrial Relations Section. Selected list of references on unemployment, old age and health insurance. Prepared by Helen Baker. Princeton. Princeton Univ. 1936. 31p.   **2706a**

Special Libraries Association. Committee on insurance library manual. The creation and development of an insurance library. Text written by Daniel N. Handy. N.Y. 1932. 36p.   **2707**

Spectator Company, publisher. Catalogue of insurance publications, American and foreign; a comprehensive list of works upon all classes of insurance by well known authors of all countries. Chicago. 1922. 228p.   **2708**

Thompson, Laura A. Unemployment insurance and reserves in the United States: a selected list of recent references. (U.S. Bureau of Labor Statistics. Bul. no. 611. Employment and unemployment ser.) Wash. Govt. Ptg. Off. 1935. 54p.   **2709**

U.S. Bureau of Agricultural Economics. Library. Crop and livestock insurance; a selected list of references to literature issued since 1898. Comp. by Esther M. Colvin and Margaret T. Olcott. (Agricultural economics bibliog. no. 67) Wash. D.C. Nov. 1936. 264p. mim. **2709a**

U.S. Library of Congress. Division of bibliography. Brief list of references on life insurance. Feb. 8, 1922. 7p. typ. **2710**

————— Brief list of references on war risk insurance. May 12, 1921. 10p. typ. **2711**

————— Business life insurance; a bibliographical list. March 5, 1931. 8p. typ. **2712**

————— Government control of insurance in the United States and foreign countries: a selected list of recent writings. Comp. by Anne L. Baden. April 20, 1940. 49p. mim. **2712a**

————— Group insurance; a bibliographical list of recent writings. Nov. 27, 1935. 25p. mim. **2713**

————— Health insurance in the United States and foreign countries: a bibliographical list. Comp. by Helen F. Conover. April 23, 1938. 49p. mim. **2713a**

————— Industrial insurance; a brief bibliographical list. Aug. 26, 1927. 8p. typ. **2714**

————— Insurance advertising; a bibliographical list. March 22, 1929. 11p. typ. **2715**

————— Investments of life insurance companies of the United States; a bibliographical list. Nov. 6, 1930. 9p. typ. **2716**

————— List of recent references on industrial insurance with special reference to accident insurance. Oct. 9, 1915. 2-6p. typ. **2717**

————— A list of recent references on life insurance. May 25, 1934. 15p. typ. **2718**

————— A list of recent references on life insurance. Comp. by Florence S. Hellman. Oct. 26, 1938. 26p. typ. **2718a**

————— List of recent references on unemployment insurance. Dec. 5, 1921. 12p. mim. (Supplements. Nov. 7, 1923. 8p. typ.; May 12, 1928. 17p. mim.; Nov. 4, 1930. 10p. mim.; Sept. 26, 1931. 14p. mim.; Nov. 22, 1932. 17p. mim.; Sept. 27, 1933. 23p. mim.; Aug. 25, 1934. 22p. mim.; Sept. 14, 1935. 43p. mim.) **2719**

————— A list of references on automobile insurance. June 30, 1924. 9p. mim. **2720**

————— List of references on benefit societies with emphasis on fraternal insurance. May 5, 1923. 12p. typ. **2721**

————— A list of references on credit insurance. April 11, 1924. 7p. typ. **2722**

————— List of references on employers' liability insurance (especially mutual or cooperative). Sept. 11, 1915. 8p. typ. **2723**

————— List of references on government insurance of farm buildings, crops, etc. (Does not include live stock insurance). July 26, 1917. 4p. typ. **2724**

————— List of references on group insurance. Jan. 16, 1925. 9p. mim. **2725**

————— List of references on insurance of live stock. April 1, 1915. 9p. typ. (Additional references. 1920. 2p.) **2726**

————— List of references on title insurance. March 3, 1925. 4p. typ. **2727**

————— List of works relating to government regulation of insurance, United States and foreign countries. Wash. Govt. Ptg. Off. 1908. 67p. **2728**

————— Marine insurance; a bibliographical list. Aug. 21, 1927. 12p. typ. (Supplement. Jan. 25, 1930. 5p. typ.) **2729**

————— Select list of references on employers' liability and workmen's compensation. Comp. under the direction of H. H. B. Meyer. Wash. Govt. Ptg. Off. 1911. 195p. (Supplements. May 24, 1915. 19p. typ.; Nov. 12, 1919. 9p. typ.) **2730**

————— Select list of references on workingmen's insurance; general, United States, Great Britain, Germany, France, Belgium. Comp. by A. P. C. Griffin. Wash. D.C. Superintendent of Documents. 1908. 28p. **2731**

————— A selected list of recent books on insurance. Feb. 24, 1931. 5p. typ. **2732**

————— A short list of references on social insurance. Nov. 3, 1923. 9p. typ. (Additional references. 1932. 2p.) **2733**

LABOR

General

Abstracts of articles and reports. Human factor. I. pt. 1. Jan. 1922- **2734**

Allen, Frederick J. A guide to the study of occupations; a selected critical bibliography of the common occupations with specific references for their study. Cambridge. Harvard Univ. Press. London. Humphrey Milford, Oxford Univ. Press. 1921. 183p. **2735**

American federationist. Index to the contents of the American federationist for the years, 1894-1914. . . . Wash. D.C. 1914. 68p. **2736**

Bennett, Wilma. Occupations and vocational guidance; a source list of pamphlet material. N.Y. H.W. Wilson. 1938. 106p. **2736a**

Black, J. William. References on the history of labor and some contemporary labor problems. (Oberlin College Lib. Bul. I. no. 2) Oberlin, Ohio. May 1893. 43p. **2737**

Boston. Public Library. Occupations; short lists of books in the public library of the city of Boston. (Brief reading lists no. 9. June 1919) Boston. The Trustees. 1919. 28p. **2738**

California. Dept. of Education. Bureau of trade and industrial education. Occupational background for young people; a bibliography. Sacramento. The Dept. 1937. 41p. mim. rev. ed. **2738a**

Commons, John R. and others. Bibliography. *In* History of labour in the United States. N.Y. Macmillan. 1918-35. II. p541-87; III. 701-41; IV. 639-61 **2739**

Commonwealth College. Library. A basic list of books and pamphlets for a labor school library. Mena, Ark. 1939. 36p. mim. **2739a**

—————— Index to labor and radical publications. Mena, Ark. ms. **2739b**

Cowley, William H. The personnel bibliographical index. Columbus. Ohio State Univ. 1932. 433p. **2740**

Current periodicals. Personnel jour. I. no. 1. May 1922- **2741**

Edwards, Richard Henry. The labor problem. (Stud. in Am. social conditions. 4) Madison, Wis. April 1909. 49p. **2742**

Management index; abstracts and news items. Management rev. XII. no. 2. May 1923- **2743**

Marot, Helen. A handbook of labor literature; being a classified and annotated list of the more important books and pamphlets in the English language. Phila. Free Lib. of Economics and Pol. Science. 1899. 96p. **2744**

Massachusetts. Bureau of Statistics. Labor bibliography, 1912-1914. *In* Annual report on the statistics of labor, 1912, part II; 1913, part IV; 1914, part VIII. Boston. 1913-16 (Also in Labor bulletins) **2745**

Milwaukee. Public Library. Bibliographical list of books, essays and articles on political economy, with special reference to the labor question. Comp. by Theresa West. Milwaukee, Wis. 1887. p215-30 **2746**

Occupational index. v. I-II, 1936-37. N.Y. National Occupational Conference. 1936-37. v. 1-2 **2746a**

Parker, Willard E. Books about jobs; a bibliography of occupational literature. Chicago. Pub. for the National Occupational Conference by the American Lib. Asso. 1936. 402p. **2746b**

Price, Willodeen and Ticen, Zelma E. Index to vocations. N.Y. H.W. Wilson. 1938. 122p. 2d ed. **2746c**

Princeton University. Library. Periodical articles on labor; annotated and cumulated from the American journal of economics. Princeton. Princeton Univ. 1919. 102p. (Photostat in the Lib. of Cong.) **2747**

Rogers, Thomas Wesley and Marsh, Homer Ellsworth. Public employment offices and labor exchanges; an annotated bibliography and union list of books, pamphlets, periodical articles, and official documents. (Indiana stud. in business. special bul. June 15, 1935) Indiana Univ.,

School of Business Administration, Bureau of Business Research. 1935. 1210p. mim. **2748**

Rossi, William H. and Rossi, Diana I. Powers. Personnel administration; a bibliography. Balt. Williams & Wilkins. 1925. 365p. **2749**

Stone, Edna L. Recent books on labor in the United States. Special libraries. XIII. p147-56 (Nov. 1922) **2750**

Tanneyhill, Ann. Vocational guidance bibliography. N.Y. Dept. of Industrial Relations, National Urban League. 1939. 45p. mim. **2750a**

True, Ellen Isabel. The labor problem; a bibliography. (Wisconsin Free Lib. Comn. Am. social questions no. 3) Madison, Wis. 1909. 37p. **2751**

U.S. Bureau of Labor Statistics. Publications relating to labor. Monthly labor rev. I. no. 2. Aug. 1915- **2752**

U.S. Library of Congress. Division of bibliography. List of recent books on labor question. July 24, 1919. 9p. typ. **2753**

—————— A list of recent publications on various aspects of the labor problem. Dec. 31, 1923. 8p. typ. **2754**

—————— List of references on labor questions in the United States and foreign countries, 1700 to 1850. Feb. 17, 1920. 10p. typ. **2755**

U.S. Office of Education. 80 new books on occupations. Comp. by Walter J. Greenleaf. Wash. D.C. Aug. 1940. 25p. **2755a**

—————— Selected references on occupations for girls and women; excerpts from "References and related information on vocational guidance for girls and women." Wash. D.C. 1940. 56p. **2755b**

Wisconsin. State Historical Society. Collections on labor and socialism in the Wisconsin State Historical Library. Bul. of information no. 77. Nov. 1915. 14p. **2756**

Child Labor

Detroit. Public Library. List of references on federal regulation of child labor, including some references on states' rights and federal usurpation. Detroit. 1925. 19p. **2757**

National Child Labor Committee. Child labor selected bibliography, 1920-1927. N.Y. National Child Labor Com. March 1927. 27p. **2758**

Thompson, Laura A. Child labor, children in street trades in the United States; a list of references. Monthly labor rev. XXI. p1261-72 (Dec. 1925) **2759**

—— Federal control of child labor; a list of references. Monthly labor rev. XX. p71-101 (Jan. 1925) **2760**

—— References on child labor and minors in industry, 1916-24. (U.S. Children's Bureau. Publication no. 147) Wash. Govt. Ptg. Off. 1925. 153p. (Supplement to Bureau publication no. 18. List of references on Child labor) **2761**

U.S. Children's Bureau. List of references on child labor. Comp. under the direction of H. H. B. Meyer with the assistance of Laura A. Thompson (Publication no. 18) Wash. Govt. Ptg. Off. 1916. 161p. **2762**

U.S. Library of Congress. Division of bibliography. List of books (with references to periodicals) relating to child labor. Comp. under the direction of A. P. C. Griffin. Wash. Govt. Ptg. Off. 1906. 66p. **2763**

——— ——— ——— List of references on child labor in the United States and Great Britain. Oct. 15, 1923. 24p. mim. **2764**

——— ——— ——— Recent references on child labor in the South. July 16, 1914. 4p. typ. **2765**

Employers

Connecticut State Library. Employers' liability and workmen's compensation; list of references to material in the Connecticut State Library. (Bulletins of the Connecticut State Lib. no. 5. Legislative reference 1) Hartford, Conn. The Lib. 1913. 27p. **2766**

Talbot, Winthrop. A select bibliography of recent publications on the helpful relations of employer and employed. Cleveland. The author. 1912. 112p. **2767**

Thompson, Laura A. Injunctions in labor disputes; select list of recent references. Monthly labor rev. XXVII. p631-50 (Sept. 1928) **2768**

——— Profit sharing and labor copartnership; a list of recent references. Monthly labor rev. XVI. p859-71 (April 1923) **2769**

——— Recent literature on collective bargaining. Wash. U.S. Dept. of Labor Lib. 1919? 9p. mim. **2770**

U.S. Library of Congress. Division of bibliography. Brief list of books on capital and labor (particularly relating to disputes). Nov. 7, 1918. 5p. typ. **2771**

——— ——— ——— Brief list of references on collective bargaining. Wash. D.C. 1919. 5p. mim. **2772**

——— ——— ——— Brief list of references on railroad shopmen's strike, 1923 (really 1922). Nov. 22, 1922. 6p. mim. **2773**

——— ——— ——— List of references on individual and collective bargaining with special reference to the transportation industry. Oct. 30, 1923. 22p. typ. **2774**

——— ——— ——— List of references on the representation of labor on managerial boards. June 30, 1919. 6p. mim. **2775**

·——— ——— ——— List of references relating to injunctions in labor disputes. 1909. 24p. typ. **2776**

■——— ——— ——— Select list of books (with references to periodicals) on labor, particularly relating to strikes. Comp. under the direction of A. P. C. Griffin. Wash. Govt. Ptg. Off. 1903. 65p. **2777**

——— ——— ——— Select list of references on boycotts and injunctions in labor disputes. Comp. under the direction of H. H. B. Meyer. Wash. Govt. Ptg. Off. 1911. 69p. (Supplement. Sept. 6, 1912. 4p. typ.) **2778**

Unemployment

Brissenden, Paul F. Labor turnover; a selected bibliography. Monthly labor rev. XXIV. p842-57 (April 1927) **2779**

Chicago. University. Library. Unemployment and relief documents; a bibliography of source materials. Comp. by the Document section of the University of Chicago libraries (Pub. Administration Service, Chicago. Publication no. 39) Chicago. Pub. for the Am. Pub. Welfare Assoc. 1934. 18p. **2780**

Industrial Relations Counselors, Inc., New York. Library. Semi-annual review and unemployment benefits bibliography: 1928-1929. (Lib. bul. of Industrial Relations Counselors, Inc. no. 6. July 1930) N.Y. 1931. p17-36. mim. **2781**

——— ——— Unemployment compensation; a chronological bibliography of books, reports and periodical articles in English, 1891-1927. By Linda H. Morley. N.Y. 1928. 117p. mim. **2782**

Meriam, R. S. Unemployment; its literature and its problems. Quar. jour. economics. XLVI. p158-86 (Nov. 1931) **2783**

Schwenning, G. T. Dismissal compensation; a list of references. Monthly labor rev. XXXIV. p478-92 (Feb. 1932) **2784**

Select bibliography on unemployment; brief list of references on unemployment, employment exchanges and unemployment insurance. Prepared by the American Association for Labor Legislation, U.S. Bureau of Labor Statistics, Library of Congress. Am. labor legislation rev. IV. p403-20 (May 1914) **2785**

U.S. Department of Labor. Library. Recent literature on unemployment, with particular reference to causes and remedies. Comp. by Laura A. Thompson. [Wash. D.C. 1921] 35p. mim. **2786**

U.S. Library of Congress. Division of bibliography. Brief list of references on unemployment benefit funds of unions. June 7, 1922. 6p. mim. **2787**

——— ——— ——— A list of references on the unemployment situation in the United States, 1929-1930. Sept. 22, 1930. 11p. mim. (Supplements. Sept. 26, 1931. 26p. mim.; July 21, 1932. 34p. mim.; Aug. 14, 1934. 41p. mim.) **2788**

——— ——— ——— List of references on the utilization of public works to diminish unemployment. May 15, 1922. 14p. mim. (Supplementary. Sept. 22, 1931. 10p. mim.) **2789**

——— ——— ——— List of recent references on unemployment. Sept. 17, 1921. Wash. D.C. 1921. 24p. mim. **2790**

U.S. Library of Congress. Division of bibliography. Select list of references on unemployment and relief measures during industrial depressions. Sept. 23, 1914. 4p. typ.   **2791**

U. S. Social Security Board. Library. Selected list of references on unemployment compensation and related subjects. Wash. D.C. 1938. 75p. mim.   **2791a**

Wilcox, Jerome Kear. Unemployment relief documents; guide to the official publications and releases of F.E.R.A. and the 48 state relief agencies. N.Y. H.W. Wilson. 1936. 95p. (Contents: Checklist of the final state CWA reports; Checklist of the publications and releases of the F.E.R.A. and the Federal Surplus Relief Corporation; Checklist of the publications and releases of the National Youth Administration and the Works Progress Administration; Partial list of transient camp newspapers)   **2791b**

Unions

Barnett, George Ernest. A trial bibliography of American trade-union publications. (Johns Hopkins Univ. Stud. in hist. and pol. science. XXII ser. nos. 1-2) Balt. Johns Hopkins Univ. Press. 1907. 112p.   **2793**

Gearhart, Edna B. List of references on work shop committees. Special libraries. X. p203-8 (Oct. 1919)   **2794**

Murasken, Estelle and others. Picketing in labor disputes; a bibliography. Mervyn Crobaugh—project supervisor. Prep. under the auspices of the U.S. Works Progress Administration. Official project no. 165-97-6999; works project no. 6073-1040. N.Y. 1937. 156p. Reprod. **2794a**

Princeton University. Department of economics and social institutions. Industrial relations section. Selected book list, trade union history and policies and labor legislation, Industrial relations section, Princeton University, Princeton, N.J., July 1931. Ann Arbor, Mich. Edwards Bros., Inc. [1931] 17p. autog. from typ. copy   **2795**

—— —— —— A trade union library; selected book list and sources of current information for the trade union executive. Prep. by Helen Baker. (Report, no. 52) Princeton. Princeton Univ. 1938. 30p.
                                              2795a

Randall, Delia and Prussin, Jesse. The labor boycott; a bibliography. Emanuel Stein—director. Prep. under the auspices of the U.S. Works Progress Administration. Official project no. 165-97-6999; works project no. APN-6073-1040. N.Y. 1936. 5 pts. in 1v. Reprod.   **2795b**

U.S. Department of Labor. A select list of references on the legal aspect of trade unions, boycotts, injunctions, picketing, etc. Wash. D.C. 1916   **2795c**

U.S. Library of Congress. Division of bibliography. Brief list of books on trade unions in the United States with special reference to recent history. Jan. 24, 1923. 8p. mim.   **2796**

—— —— —— Brief list of references on collective bargaining. Nov. 7, 1919. 5p. multig.   **2797**

—— —— —— List of recent references on labor unrest with special reference to psychology. Jan. 5, 1921. 4p. multig. **2798**

—— —— —— List of references on the I.W.W. (Supplementary to Brissenden's "The launching of the I.W.W."). July 24, 1917. 5p. typ.   **2799**

—— —— —— List of references on the legal responsibility of trade unions. Nov. 25, 1924. 18p. mim.   **2800**

—— —— —— List of references on the open shop. Aug. 31, 1920. 17p. mim. **2801**

—— —— —— Select list of references on trade unions among railway employees. July 3, 1912. 7p. typ.   **2802**

Zimand, Savel. Representation in industry; a bibliography on workshop committees, Whitley councils, etc. N.Y. Pub. Affairs Information Service. 1919. 22p.
                                              2803

Work Hours

Bureau of Railway Economics. List of references relating to the eight-hour working day and to limitations of working hours in the United States with special reference to railway labor. Wash. D.C. Jan. 17, 1917. 30p.   **2804**

—— List of references to books and articles on the Adamson eight hour law of September, 1916. Wash. D.C. Sept. 19, 1919. 22p. mim.   **2805**

Thompson, Laura A. Five day week and other recent proposals for a shorter work week; a list of references. Monthly labor rev. XXXII. p501-18 (Feb. 1931)
                                              2806

—— The five day week in industry; a list of references. Monthly labor rev. XXIV. p237-41 (Jan 1927)   **2807**

U.S. Department of Labor. Library. Hours of work in relation to output; an annotated list of references. Comp. by Laura A. Thompson. Wash. D.C. 1920. 13p.
                                              2808

U.S. Library of Congress. Division of bibliography. List of books (with references to periodicals) relating to the eight-hour working day and to limitation of working hours in general. Comp. under the direction of A. P. C. Griffin. Wash. Govt. Ptg. Off. 1908. 24p. (Supplement. Aug. 27, 1911. 17p. typ.; June 10, 1919. 4p. typ.)   **2809**

—— —— —— List of references on state regulation of wages. Jan. 21, 1914. 7p. typ.   **2810**

—— —— —— List of references on the minimum wage question. Sept. 24, 1917. 12p. typ. (Recent references. March 24, 1923. 12p. mim.)   **2811**

—— —— —— Select list of references on a minimum wage for women. Oct. 1, 1913. 7p. typ. **2812**

—— —— —— Select list of references relating to night work for women. Oct. 10, 1913. 3p. typ. **2813**

—— —— —— A short list of references on wages of women in the United States. Dec. 22, 1923. 7p. typ. **2814**

Warren, Katherine. List of references on labor turn-over. Special libraries. X. p198-203 (Oct. 1919) **2815**

Miscellaneous

American labor legislation review. Index . . . volumes I-XX, 1911-1930. N.Y. Am. Asso. for Labor Legislation. 1931. 104p. **2816**

Bennett, Wilma. Occupations and vocational guidance; a source list of pamphlet material. N.Y. H. W. Wilson. 1936. 123p. **2817**

Bureau of Railway Economics. List of references on the right to strike. Comp. by Mary B. Ladd. Boston. 1919. 15p. (Reprinted from Special libraries. X. p255-68. Dec. 1919) **2818**

—— —— Memorandum: legislative history and list of discussions on "LaFollette's seamen's bill." Wash. D.C. Feb. 1928. 3p. **2819**

Gummere, John S. A bibliography of American Workmen's Compensation Commission reports and opinions; a preliminary list. Law lib. jour. XXVIII. p42-50 (April 1935) **2820**

Home Owners' Loan Corporation. A bibliography on employee relations; selected books, pamphlets, and magazine articles published in recent years. . . . Wash. D.C. 1939. 26p. photoprinted **2820a**

Hood, Robin. A bibliography on southern labor. Social forces. XIII. p133-7. 1934 **2820b**

Huber, Franz. A brief bibliography of the literature relating to changes in employment practices resulting from the operation of the Social security program. Wash. D.C. Committee on Social Security, Social Science Research Council. 1940. 9p. mim. **2820c**

Industrial Relations Counselors, Inc. Library. Job analysis and its allied activities; a classified and annotated bibliography. N.Y. 1932. 59p. **2821**

Lubin, Isador. Sources of labor legislation. Am. Acad. of Pol. and Social Science ann. CLXXXIV. p206-14 (March 1936) **2822**

Murasken Estelle and Deutsch, Rosa. Sympathetic strikes; a bibliography. Mervyn Crobaugh—project supervisor. Prep. under the auspices of the U.S. Works Progress Administration. Sponsoring agency—New York State Labor Dept.; cooperating agency—National Labor Relations Board. . . . Official project no. 165-97-6999; works project no. 6073-1040. N.Y. 1937. 90p. Reprod. **2822a**

National safety council. Library. Accident prevention—health and hygiene (industrial) (books and pamphlets); a selected reading list, January, 1932. [Chicago. National safety council lib. 1932] 28p. **2822b**

New York. Municipal Reference Library. Selected list of material on municipal strikes. N.Y. H.W. Wilson Co. 1920 **2822c**

—— **Public Library.** A check list of works in the New York Public Library on wages, etc. N.Y. Pub. Lib. bul. VI. p174-90 (May 1902) **2823**

Oklahoma. University. Bibliography on labor relations in the coal mining industry. Norman. CWA project **2823a**

Parker, Carlton H. Reading list on economic, psychological approach to labor problems. N.Y. H.W. Wilson Co. 1920 **2823b**

Rettengill, George Ewald. Sit-down strikes, a reading list. [N.Y. New York Pub. Lib. 1937] 5p. (Reprinted from the N.Y. Pub. Lib. bul. XLI. p480-4. June 1937) **2823c**

Shera, J. H. The age factor in employment; a classified bibliography. Bul. of bibliog. XIV. p100-1, 128-9, 154-6, 175-7, 193-5 (Jan.-Dec. 1932) **2825**

Spiegler, Samuel. An appraisal and abstract of available literature on the occupation of the bus and truck driver. N.Y. Occupational Index, Inc. 1939. 12p. **2825a**

Stone, Edna L. Recent references on convict labor. Monthly labor rev. XXI. p867-99 (Oct. 1925); XXVI. p1083-7 (May 1928) **2826**

Sullivan, James. A bibliography concerning vocations. N.Y. State Lib. Ninety-ninth annual rep. Bibliog. bul. 60. Jan. 1, 1917. 17p. **2827**

Thompson, Laura A. Bibliography; worker's leisure; a selected list of references. Monthly labor rev. XXIV. p637-47 (March 1927) **2828**

—— The older worker in industry; list of references. Monthly labor rev. XXIX. p237-342 (July 1929) **2829**

U.S. Adjutant General's Office. Personnel management; topical outline and bibliography. [Wash. D.C. 1919] 58p. **2830**

U.S. Bureau of Agricultural Economics. Library. Agricultural labor in the United States, 1915-1935; a selected list of references. Comp. by Esther M. Colvin and Josiah C. Folsom (Agricultural economics bibliog. no. 64) Wash. D.C. 1935. 493p. mim. **2831**

U.S. Bureau of Labor Statistics. Monthly labor review subject index, volumes I to XI, July, 1915 to December, 1920. Prep. by Karoline Klager and Elsie M. Pursglove. Wash. Govt. Ptg. Off. 1923. 176p. **2831a**

—— —— Personnel research agencies, with lists of publications. By Estelle M. Stewart. (Bureau of Labor Statistics. Bul. 518. Miscellaneous ser.) Wash. Govt. Ptg. Off. 1930. 197p. **2832**

U.S. Department of Labor. List of references on minimum wage for women in the United States and Canada. Comp. by Edna L. Stone (Bul. of the Women's Bureau no. 42) Wash. D.C. 1925. 42p. **2833**

—— —— Migration of workers; preliminary report of the Secretary of Labor pursuant to S. res. 298 (74th Congress) a resolution to make certain investigations concerning the social and economic needs of laborers migrating across state lines. Wash. D.C. The Dept. 1938. v. II, p250-96 **2833a**

U.S. Federal Board for Vocational Education. Bibliography of employment management. By Edward D. Jones (Federal Board for Vocational Education. Bul. no. 51. June 1920. Employment management ser. no. 9) [Wash. Govt. Ptg. Off. 1920] 119p. **2834**

U.S. Library of Congress. Division of bibliography. Brief list of references on labor in politics and labor parties. Dec. 16, 1922. 6p. typ. **2835**

—— —— List of references on prison labor. Comp. under the direction of H. H. B. Meyer. Wash. Govt. Ptg. Off. 1915. 74p. **2836**

—— —— List of references on public employment agencies. July 31, 1919. 10p. mim. **2837**

—— —— List of references on vacations with pay for office and factory workers. June 18, 1926. 5p. typ. **2838**

—— —— List of references on women's work and wages. 1909. 24p. typ. **2839**

—— —— List of speeches in Congress on the operation of Adamson labor law. Sept. 15, 1922. 4p. typ. **2840**

—— —— References on placement bureaus and related subjects. Dec. 12, 1923. 6p. typ. **2841**

—— —— Select list of references on home labor. Sept. 18, 1912. 9p. typ. (Supplementary. June 26, 1935. 21p. typ.) **2842**

—— —— Select list of references on vocations for women. Oct. 10, 1912. 18p. typ. (Recent references. Feb. 24, 1919. 16p. typ.) **2843**

U.S. Office of Governmental Reports. Selected list of references on the problem of the older worker. Prep. by the U.S. Information Service Division. Wash. D.C. Feb. 26, 1940. 13p. mim. **2843a**

U.S. Social Security Board. Library. Bureau of business management. Selected list of references on unemployment compensation and related subjects. Wash. D.C. The Bureau. 1938. 75p. mim. **2843b**

U.S. Soil Conservation Service. Personnel administration and personnel training; a selected list of references. Comp. by Mildred Benton and H. L. Buckhardt. (Soil conservation bibliography no. 2) Wash. D.C. Aug. 1940. 59p. processed **2843c**

U.S. Works Progress Administration. Careers and occupations. Evanston, Ill. Pub. Lib. 1936. 201p. mim. **2843d**

Virginia. State Board of Education. Occupational information; a source list of pamphlet material. [Richmond] 1935. 15p. mim. **2844**

MINING

Anthracite Operators Conference. A selected bibliography on anthracite, its preparation and utilization. N.Y. 1929. 50p. **2845**

Benkert, Helen. World production of silver since 1900: a selected bibliography. Madison. Univ. of Wisconsin Library School. 1938. 45p. typ. **2845a**

Brunken, David W. and Davis, John A. Bibliography. *In* Modern tunneling, with special reference to mine and water supply tunnels. N.Y. J. Wiley & Sons. 1914. p.360-419 **2845b**

Butte, Montana. Free Public Library. List of books on mining, geology, mineralogy, metallurgy, assaying, etc. (Bul. no. 2) Butte. 1917. 31p. **2846**

Columbia College. School of Mines. Library. Catalogue of the books and pamphlets in the library of the School of Mines of Columbia College, July 1st, 1875. N.Y. J. W. Amerman. 1875. 399p. **2847**

Crane, Walter R. Index of mining engineering literature, comprising an index of mining, metallurgical, civil, mechanical, electrical and chemical engineering subjects as related to mining engineering. N.Y. J. Wiley. 1909-12. 2v. **2848**

Darton, Nelson Horatio. Catalogue and index of contributions to North American geology, 1732-1891. (U.S. Geol. Survey. Bul. no. 127) Wash. Govt. Ptg. Off. 1896. 1045p. **2849**

Evans, Isabel F. Publications by survey authors on metals and nonmetals except fuels. (U.S. Geol. Survey. Bul. 580) Wash. Govt. Ptg. Off. 1915. p413-55 **2850**

Fleming, Russell Clark. Source book; a directory of public agencies in the United States engaged in the publication of literature on mining and geology. N.Y. Am. Inst. of Mining and Metallurgical Engineers. 1933. 128p. **2851**

Geological Society of America. Bulletin, index to volumes 1 to 10. Rochester, N.Y. 1900. 209p.; Volumes 21 to 30. N.Y. The Soc. 1920. 325p.; Volumes 31 to 40. N.Y. The Soc. 1930. 183p. **2852**

Great Britain. Patent Office. Library. Subject list of works on mineral industries in the library of the Patent Office, Parts I-III. London. Printed for H. M. Stationery Off. by Darling & Son. 1912. 295, 70, 133p. **2853**

Haferkorn, Henry E. Handy list of technical literature. Part IV. Mines and mining, assaying, metallurgy, analytical chemistry, minerals and mineralogy, geology, paleontology, etc. Milwaukee. Haferkorn; London. Gay & Bird. 1891. 87p. **2854**

Hess, Frank L. and Hess, Eva. Bibliography of the geology and mineralogy of tin. (Smithsonian miscellaneous colls. 58. no. 2) Wash. D.C. 1912. p19-408 **2855**

Jackson, Lucille. A guide to mineral industries literature. (Pennsylvania State College bul., Library stud., no. 2) State College, Pa. 1940. 18p. **2855a**

John Crerar Library. State mining directories and key indexes to the mineral resources of each state; a bibliography. Comp. by Jerome K. Wilcox (Reference list no. 32) Chicago. 1932. 39p. mim. **2856**

Journal of geology. A general index to the Journal of geology, volumes I to XXXV, 1893 to 1927. Ed. by Rollin T. Chamberlain; comp. by Dorothy S. Neff. Chicago. Univ. of Chicago Press. 1930. 279p. **2857**

Lee, Willis T. and Nickles, John M. Classified list of papers dealing with coal, coke, lignite, and peat contained in publications of U.S. Geological Survey, except those on Alaska. (U.S. Geol. Survey. Bul. 341) Wash. D.C. 1909. p419-36 **2858**

Mining world index of current literature, I-X, 1912-1916. Chicago. Mining World Co. 1912-16 **2859**

Nickles, John M. Bibliography of North American geology, 1908-30. (U.S. Geol. Survey. Bul. 372, 409, 444, 495, 525, 545, 584, 617, 645, 665, 684, 698, 731, 758, 802, 823) Wash. Govt. Ptg. Off. 1909-31 **2860**

—— Geologic literature on North America, 1785-1918. (U.S. Geol. Survey. Bulletins 746, 747) Wash. Govt. Ptg. Off. 1923-24. 1167, 658p. **2861**

Sawyer, Rollin A., Jr. Nationalization of coal mines; a list of references in the New York Public Library. N.Y. Pub. Lib. bul. XXIV. p297-305 (May 1920) **2862**

Thom, Emma M. Bibliography of North American geology, 1933/34-1935/36. (U.S. Geol. Survey. Bul. 869, 892) Wash. Govt. Ptg. Off. 1935, 1937. 389, 504p. **2863**

U.S. Bureau of Mines. Review of literature on conditioning air for advancement of health and safety in mines. (Information circular no. 7001) Comp. by D. Harrington and S. J. Davenport. Wash. D.C. March 1938. 38p. mim. **2863a**

—— —— Selected bibliography and map of manganese deposits of the United States by districts. By M. V. Healey and A. L. Johns. (Bureau of Mines. Information circular 6274) Wash. D.C. 1930. 19p. **2864**

U.S. Department of Agriculture. Library. Peat; a contribution towards a bibliography of the American literature through 1925. Comp. by Alice C. Atwood (Bibliog. contributions no. 12) Wash. D.C. Sept. 1926. 95p. mim. **2865**

U.S. Geological Survey. General index to mineral resources of the United States from 1882 to 1890. In Mineral resources of the United States, calendar years 1889 and 1890. Wash. D.C. 1892. p537-651 **2865a**

U.S. Library of Congress. Division of bibliography. Brief list of references on accidents in mines, with special regard to coal mines. Dec. 4, 1919. 3p. typ. **2866**

—— —— —— List of references on government ownership and control of mines in the United States and foreign countries. March 1, 1920. 23p. mim. **2867**

—— —— —— List of references on the marketing of minerals (exclusive of coal and petroleum). Dec. 31, 1921. 8p. typ. **2868**

—— —— —— Select list of books on mining and metallurgy. 1908. 27p. typ. **2869**

Wadleigh, Francis Rawle. A list of books and other sources of information regarding coal and coal products. Wash. D.C. W. F. Roberts. 1935. 63p. **2870**

Weeks, Fred Boughton. Bibliography and index of North American geology, paleontology, petrology, and mineralogy, 1892-1905. (U.S. Geol. Survey. Bul. 130, 135, 146, 149, 156, 162, 172, 188, 189, 203, 221, 240, 271, 301) Wash. Govt. Ptg. Off. 1902-07 **2871**

Weeks, Fred Boughton and Nickles, John M. Bibliography of North American geology for 1906 and 1907 with subject index. (U.S. Geol. Survey. Bul. 372) Wash. Govt. Ptg. Off. 1909. 317p. **2872**

PUBLIC UTILITIES

American Society of Civil Engineers. Bibliography on valuation of public utilities. Comp. by the library staff. N.Y. 1915. 2v. in 1. (Pt. I reprinted from the Trans. of the Am. Soc. of Civil Engineers. LXXVI. p2133-93. 1913. Pt. II Continuation to Dec. 23, 1915 prepared for the Am. Electric Asso.) **2873**

Boston Elevated Railway Company. Urban and interurban electric railways; a selected reference list of general literature. Supplement to reference list of literature on urban electric railways. Boston. 1930. 105p. **2874**

Brooklyn. Public Library. Books on municipal ownership. Brooklyn, N.Y. 1906. 27p. **2875**

California. University. Bureau of Public Administration. Milk—a public utility; a reading list. Comp. by Dorothy Campbell Culver. Berkeley. 1934. 12p. **2876**

Chicago. Municipal Reference Library. Proposed subways in the city of Chicago; a list of references to material on file in the Municipal Reference Library (chronologically arranged). Comp. by Frederick Rex. Chicago. 1932. 15p. mim.
2877

Cleveland. Municipal Reference Library. Selected bibliography on rapid transit subways, general and constructional features, 1896-1917, taken chiefly from the Engineering index. Cleveland. 1918. 38p. typ.
2878

Detroit. Bureau of Governmental Research. Select list of books on municipal affairs with special reference to municipal ownership. . . . Wash. Govt. Ptg. Off. 1900. 34p.
2879

Edison Electric Institute. Bibliography on government ownership of electric utilities and state regulation of electric utilities. N.Y. 1936. 19p.
2879a

Leininger, Grace Carr. A bibliography on utility holding companies. The jour. of land and public utility economics. XI. p419-24 (Nov. 1935)
2880

Milwaukee. Municipal Reference Library. Public utility, service at cost contracts; bibliography of material available at the Municipal Reference Library. 1924. 16p. mim.
2881

New York. State Library. Municipal ownership in the United States, with some reference to Great Britain. Comp. by James Hodgson. [Albany] 1918. 57p.
2882

Norman, Oscar Edward. Bibliography of rates for public utilities (1882-1934). (Rep. of the rate structure com. Appendix IV) [N.Y. Am. Gas Asso. 1934] 48p.
2883

Special Libraries Association. Committee on illumination. Technology group. Bibliography of illumination, 1924-1929/30. (Information bul. nos. 3, 5, 8, 9, 12) N.Y. 1926-31
2884

Stevens, Don Lorenzo. A bibliography of municipal utility regulation and municipal ownership. Cambridge. Harvard Univ. Press; London. Humphrey Milford, Oxford Univ. Press. 1918. 410p.
2885

U.S. Library of Congress. Division of bibliography. A brief list of references on government ownership of electric light and power utilities. Feb. 19, 1935. 6p. mim. (Additional references. Sept 1, 1936. 7p. mim.)
2886

—— —— —— Brief list of references on municipal ownership of public utilities. Feb. 26, 1923. 10p. mim. (Recent references. Jan. 4, 1928. 5p. typ.)
2887

—— —— —— Government ownership of public utilities; a bibliographical list. Dec. 16, 1930. 18p. mim. Same. March 12, 1935. 25p. mim.
2888

—— —— —— List of recent references on public service rates with special reference to regulation (cabs, gas, electricity, street railways, telephones, water). Nov. 2, 1915. 18p. typ. (Also in Special libraries. VII. p21-8. Feb. 1916)
2889

—— —— —— List of references on electric street railways of the United States (with special reference to construction). June 15, 1915. 5p. typ.
2890

—— —— —— List of references on government ownership and control in relation to their influence on business, politics and social life. Feb. 13, 1918. 6p. typ.
2891

—— —— —— List of references on government regulation and control of the natural gas industry in the United States. Jan 8, 1918. 7p. typ.
2892

—— —— —— List of references on the government ownership of the telegraph and the telephone. July 19, 1918. 15p. mim.
2893

—— —— —— List of references on the investigation of telephone companies in the United States. Feb. 4, 1920. 7p. mim.
2894

—— —— —— Public utilities; a list of recent references with special reference to rates and regulation (electric light and power, gas, motor vehicles, street railroads, water companies). Oct. 5, 1928. 68p. mim. (Supplement. May 26, 1931. 36p. mim.; Nov. 3, 1934. 47p. mim.)
2895

—— —— —— Recent references on rate regulation. Jan. 1930. 5p. typ.
2896

—— —— —— Select list of references on municipal ownership and operation of street railways (supplementing the printed list on municipal affairs, 1906). Oct. 28, 1912. 6p. typ.
2897

—— —— —— Select list of references on public service commissions. 1909. 6p. typ.
2898

—— —— —— Select list of references on public service rates in the United States and foreign countries (cabs, electricity, gas, street railways, telephones, water). Sept. 19, 1911. 7p. typ. Oct. 2, 1911. 7p. dupl.
2899

—— —— —— Speeches in Congress on government ownership of telegraph and telephone as printed in the Congressonal globe and the Congressional record. Feb. 16, 1916. 2p. typ.
2900

—— —— —— Urban transportation in the United States, street-railways, subways, taxis, trolley-buses, etc.; a bibliographical list. Oct. 16, 1933. 15p. mim.
2901

—— —— —— Water power in the United States; selected list of references. Oct. 4, 1927. 45p. mim. Same. Oct. 18, 1929. 40p. mim. (Supplement.) June 8, 1933. 28p. mim.)
2902

U.S. Securities and Exchange Commission. Library. List of references on public utilities. Wash. D.C. 1936
2902a

TARIFF

Shear, S. W. The tariff and agriculture in the United States. Berkeley. College of Agriculture. March 1926. 7, 6, 5p. mim.
2903

Taussig, Frank William. Topics and references in political economy VI, Harvard College: tariff legislation in the United States. Cambridge, Mass. 1893. 25p. **2904**

U.S. Library of Congress. Division of bibliography. Brief list of references on the tariff question, pro and con. May 9, 1922. 11p. mim. (Supplement. Jan. 21, 1928. 27p. mim.) **2905**

—— —— —— List of references on tariff commissions. Jan. 27, 1916. 16p. typ. **2906**

—— —— —— List of references on tariff for revenue only. May 11, 1920. 5p. typ. **2907**

—— —— —— List of references on the influence of the new tariff. March 13, 1914. 4p. typ. **2908**

—— —— —— List of references on the tariff act of 1922. Dec. 6, 1922. 10p. mim. (Recent writings. July 2, 1926. 6p. typ.) **2909**

—— —— —— List of references on the tariff relations between the United States and Canada. Feb. 14, 1931. 6p. typ. **2910**

—— —— —— Reports of special tariff commissions, United States (compiled by Bureau of Foreign and Domestic Commerce). Aug. 9, 1916. 4p. typ. **2911**

—— —— —— Select list of references on the tariff policy of free raw materials. Dec. 7, 1910. 9p. mim. **2912**

—— —— —— Selection of speeches on the Mills bill, 1888, as printed in the Congressional record, 50th Congress, 1st sess., v. 19. June 21, 1920. 3p. typ. **2913**

—— —— —— Selection of speeches on the Wilson tariff bill, 1894, as printed in the Congressional record, 53 Cong., 2d sess., v. 26. June 21, 1921. 2p. typ. **2914**

—— —— —— The tariff in its relation to the South, 1789-1923. Oct. 9, 1929. 12p. typ. **2915**

—— —— —— Tariff on hides. June 14, 1922. 4p. typ. **2916**

—— —— —— Tariff revision 1929; a bibliographical list. Aug. 13, 1929. 25p. mim. **2917**

U.S. Tariff Commission. The tariff; a bibliography; a select list of references. (Miscellaneous ser.) Wash. Govt. Ptg. Off. 1934. 980p. **2918**

—— —— Library. A list of books and pamphlets relating to the tariff. [Wash. D.C.] Feb. 1, 1932. 48p. mim. **2919**

TAXATION

Bureau of Railway Economics. The transportation tax; a list of references. Wash. D.C. 1921. 3p. (Also in Lib. jour. XLVI. p699-701. Sept. 1, 1921) **2920**

Crosman, Ralph. Single tax index; an exhaustive analytical and synthetical index. San Francisco. The Author. 1915 **2921**

Klemmedson, G. S. Reading references for the study of taxation. (Colorado Agricultural Experiment Station. Bul. 382) Fort Collins, Colo. 1931. 26p. **2922**

Massachusetts. State Library. Bibliography of works on taxation, January, 1898. Prepared by Ellen M. Sawyer (Special bul.) Boston. Wright & Potter. 1898. 25p. **2923**

National Tax Association. Digest and index, 1907-1925. (An index of the National Tax Assoc. proc. and bul. to 1925) By Roy G. Blakey and Gladys C. Blakey. N.Y. National Tax Asso. 1927. 519p. **2924**

U.S. Bureau of Agricultural Economics. Library. Homestead tax exemption in the United States; a selected list of references. Comp. by Margaret T. Olcott. (Economic library list no. 15) Wash. D.C. Oct. 1940. 23p. processed **2924a**

—— —— —— Incidence of the processing taxes under the agricultural adjustment act; a selected list of references. Comp. by Louise O. Bercaw. (Agricultural economics bibliog. no. 68) Wash. D.C. Jan. 1937. 46p. mim. **2924b**

—— —— —— Taxation and the farmer; a selected and annotated bibliography. Comp. by Margaret T. Olcott under the direction of Mary G. Lacy (Agricultural economics bibliog. no. 25) Wash. D.C. June 1928. 188p. **2925**

U.S. Department of the Treasury. Library. A bibliography of war taxation in the United States. Comp. by David R. Kessler. Wash. D.C. Sept. 28, 1939. 24p **2925a**

U.S. Library of Congress. Division of bibliography. Additional references relating to taxation of incomes. Wash. Govt. Ptg. Off. 1911. 144p. **2926**

—— —— —— Bibliography on forest taxation. 1910. 11p. typ. **2927**

—— —— —— Brief list of books on the theory of taxation. March 14, 1936. 5p. typ. **2928**

—— —— —— Brief list of references on federal taxation with special reference to power of taxation. Feb. 12, 1921. 6p. typ. **2929**

—— —— —— Brief list of references on state boards of equalization. Dec. 22, 1924. 2p. typ. **2930**

—— —— —— Brief list of references on state taxation of incomes. March 7, 1921. 2p. typ. **2931**

—— —— —— Brief list of references on the taxation of luxuries. April 19, 1920. 4p. mim. **2932**

—— —— —— Excess profits tax and capital stock tax: a selected list of references. Comp. by Anne L. Baden. June 5, 1940. 20p. typ. **2932a**

—— —— —— Federal income tax in the United States: a list of recent writings (supplementary to the mimeographed lists, Dec. 10, 1931 and July 9, 1934). June 8, 1937. 28p. **2932b**

—— —— —— List of recent references on excise or internal revenue taxation, with special reference to consumptive taxes (including sales tax). Aug. 9, 1921. 9p. typ. **2933**

U.S. Library of Congress. Division of bibliography. List of recent references on excise or internal revenue taxation with special reference to the sales tax. Feb. 2, 1926. 7p. typ.   **2934**

—— —— —— List of recent references on the income tax. Comp. under the direction of H. H. B. Meyer. Wash. Govt. Ptg. Off. 1921. 96p. (Supplements. Dec. 10, 1931. 36p. mim.; July 9, 1934. 21p. mim.; June 8, 1937. 28p. mim.)   **2935**

—— —— —— List of recent references on the sales tax, supplementary. Oct. 2, 1931. 9p. typ.   **2936**

—— —— —— A list of recent references on the taxation of business and corporations. Feb. 17, 1933. 14p. typ.   **2937**

—— —— —— List of references on "Excess profits" taxation. July 25, 1917. 5p. typ. (Same. Dec. 10, 1917. 8p. mim.)   **2938**

—— —— —— List of references on excise or internal revenue taxation in the United States (excluding taxation of incomes and inheritances) Jan. 9, 1913. 11p. typ.   **2939**

—— —— —— List of references on exemptions from taxation (exclusive of tax exempt securities). May 24, 1932. 13p. typ. (Supplement. Feb. 28, 1941. 31p. typ.) **2940**

—— —— —— List of references on income-tax evasion. Dec. 18, 1924. 4p. typ.   **2941**

—— —— —— List of references on lotteries in the United States and foreign countries, with emphasis on their use as a means of raising government revenue. 1934. 30p. reprod. from typ. copy   **2942**

—— —— —— List of references on progressive taxation with special reference to graduated land tax. Dec. 16, 1916. 3p. typ. Dec. 16, 1916. dupl.   **2943**

—— —— —— List of references on stamp taxation. May 4, 1917. 3p. typ.   **2944**

—— —— —— List of references on tax exemption of securities. Feb. 6, 1922. 4p. mim. (Supplement. Nov. 20, 1931. 6p. mim.; April 8, 1938. 15p. reprod.) **2945**

—— —— —— List of references on taxation in the United States, 1924-1926. July 29, 1926. 25p. typ.   **2946**

—— —— —— List of references on taxation of business. Jan. 9, 1914. 7p. typ.   **2947**

—— —— —— List of references on the commodities clause of the Hepburn act. March 24, 1914. 4p. typ.   **2948**

—— —— —— A list of references on the excess profits tax and the capital stock tax. July 16, 1934. 9p. typ.   **2949**

—— —— —— List of references on the exemption from taxation of property of churches and educational institutions. Feb. 24, 1916. 4p. typ.   **2950**

—— —— —— List of references on the Mellon plan of tax reduction. Jan. 19, 1924. 10p. typ.   **2951**

—— —— —— List of references on the "Mill tax" for education in the United States. Oct. 27, 1914. 5p. typ.   **2952**

—— —— —— List of references on the present tax situation. Nov. 21, 1930. 5p. typ.   **2953**

—— —— —— A list of references on the sales tax. May 1, 1932. 29p.   **2954**

—— —— —— List of references on the severance tax. Dec. 18, 1922. 3p. mim.   **2955**

—— —— —— List of references on the shifting and incidence of taxation. March 27, 1931. 6p. typ. (Supplementing the bibliography in Edwin R. A. Seligman's The shifting and incidence of taxation. 1927. p399-428)   **2956**

—— —— —— List of references on the taxation of automobiles. Sept. 28, 1922. 6p. typ.   **2957**

—— —— —— List of references on the taxation of corporations. 1907. 7p. typ.   **2958**

—— —— —— List of references on the taxation of farm property. March 10, 1923. 5p. typ.   **2959**

—— —— —— List of references on the taxation of gasoline, motor vehicles, accessories, etc. July 25, 1934. 19p. typ.   **2960**

—— —— —— A list of references on the taxation of inheritances. June 17, 1924. 25p. mim.   **2961**

—— —— —— List of references on the taxation of intangible property, with special reference to capital tax. April 24, 1918. 16p. dupl.   **2962**

—— —— —— List of references on the taxation of intangible property (with special reference to mortgages). June 22, 1916. 6p. typ.   **2963**

—— —— —— A list of references on taxation of intangibles. May 28, 1932. 11p. typ. mim.   **2964**

—— —— —— List of references on taxation of public utilities. Aug. 19, 1926. 6p. typ.   **2965**

—— —— —— List of references on the taxation of oil and gas properties. May 14, 1925. 8p. mim.   **2966**

—— —— —— List of references on the valuation of real property for taxation. June 21, 1916. 7p. typ.   **2967**

—— —— —— List of speeches, addresses, etc., on the sales tax as printed in the Congressional record. Jan. 10, 1933. 10p. mim.   **2968**

—— —— —— References on the relation between national and local taxation with special reference to capital cities. April 29, 1915. 11p. typ.   **2969**

—— —— —— References on the single tax (supplementing typewritten list of Feb. 21, 1925). March 27, 1925. 4p. typ. **2970**

—— —— —— Sales tax in the United States and foreign countries; a list of recent writings. Oct. 17, 1934. 29p. typ. (Same. Nov. 12, 1935. 27p. mim.; Same. Sept. 25, 1939. 34p. mim.)   **2971**

—— —— —— Select list of references on state tax commissions. Dec. 17, 1912. 4p. typ.   **2972**

—— —— —— Select list of references on the federal taxation of corporations. March 1, 1912. 4p. typ. **2973**

—— —— —— Select list of references on the single tax. Feb. 21, 1913. 15p. dupl. **2974**

—— —— —— Select list of references on the taxation of land values (unearned increment). April 4, 1913. 17p. dupl. **2975**

—— —— —— Select list of works relating to taxation of inheritance and of incomes, United States and some foreign countries. Wash. D.C. Superintendent of Documents. 1907. 86p. **2976**

—— —— —— A selected list of periodical references relating to Federal taxation, 1934-1939. Comp. by Florence S. Hellman. Aug. 5, 1939. 40p. typ. **2976a**

—— —— —— A selected list of recent references on inheritance taxation in the United States and foreign countries. Feb. 20, 1935. 47p. mim. **2977**

—— —— —— A selected list of references on inheritance taxation in the United States and foreign countries, supplementary to mimeographed list of 1935. Comp. by Ann D. Brown. June 25, 1940. 38p. mim. **2977a**

—— —— —— A selected list of references on the sales tax. Jan. 12, 1933. 27p. mim. **2978**

—— —— —— State income taxes; a bibliographical list of writings (supplementary to the printed list of recent references on the income tax, 1921, 46-60). Jan. 9, 1932. 19p. mim. (Supplement. July 16, 1934. 21p. mim.) **2979**

—— —— —— State taxation; a list of recent writings. Jan. 6, 1928. 13p. mim. (Recent writings. June 12, 1932. 52p. mim.) **2980**

—— —— —— Taxation; constitutional treatises. 1905. 5p. typ. **2981**

—— —— —— Taxation of natural resources, with special reference to severance taxes; a bibliographical list of writings. Comp. by Anne L. Baden. Aug. 30, 1940. 17p. mim. **2981a**

Washington. State Library. Select list of works relating to the income tax. Comp. by Josephine Holgate. Olympia, Wash. 1910. 28p. **2982**

Washington. University. University Extension Division. Bureau of Debate and Discussion. Taxation of land values; a bibliography. (Bul. no. 13. general ser. no. 85) Seattle. The Univ. 1914. 20p. **2983**

TRANSPORTATION AND COMMUNICATION

General

Baker, George P. Two years of books on transportation. Harvard bus. rev. XVI. p499-512 (Summer 1938) **2983a**

Bureau of Railway Economics. List of references on cost of transporting freight by water, trolley line and motor truck, with some comparison of cost of freight transportation by railroad. Wash. D.C. 1917. 3p. **2984**

—— Material collateral to the study of transportation employed by the library . . . in responding to inquiries from schools for material for use in class units. Wash. D.C. 1934. 16p. mim. **2985**

—— Some 1933-1934 books,—reports, and studies on transportation—memorandum. [Wash. D.C.] April 5, 1934. 8p. typ. **2986**

—— **Library.** Merchandising transportation—some references. Wash. D.C. March 1935. 12p. typ. **2986a**

—— —— School units on transportation in America; memorandum listing material for reference use usually available in the large libraries. Wash. D.C. Dec. 1, 1936. 45p. mim. **2986b**

Georgia. Dept. of Education. Source materials on transportation and communication. Atlanta. The Dept. 1938. p11-53, 61-94 **2986c**

Knowlton, D. C. Bibliography of transportation. The hist. teachers' mag. IV. p232-5 (Oct. 1913) **2987**

MacGill, Caroline E. and others. Bibliography. *In* History of transportation in the United States before 1860. Wash. D.C. Carnegie Inst. of Wash. 1917. p609-40 **2988**

Meyer, Balthasar Henry. Bibliography. *In* History of transportation in the United States before 1860. Wash. D.C. Carnegie Institution of Washington. 1917. p609-49 **2988a**

U.S. Bureau of Foreign and Domestic Commerce. History and development of transportation. Comp. by Ruth C. Leslie. (Basic information sources) Wash. D.C. May 1941. 28p. processed **2988b**

U.S. Library of Congress. Division of bibliography. Brief list of books on the history of communication in the United States (includes transportation). Dec. 2, 1919. 3p. typ. **2989**

—— —— —— List of references on horse-drawn transportation. April 21, 1923. 5p. typ. **2990**

—— —— —— List of references on individual and collective bargaining with special reference to the transportation industry. Oct. 30, 1923. 27p. typ. **2991**

—— —— —— List of references on transportation and communication in the United States since 1860. Jan. 15, 1924. 7p. typ. **2992**

—— —— —— A list of references on transportation, with a section on the problem of motor and rail competition and coordination in the United States. Oct. 19, 1933. 22p. mim. **2993**

Van Patten, Nathan. Hopkins transportation library. Stanford University, Calif. Stanford Univ. Press. 1937. 10p. **2993a**

Air

Brockett, Paul. Bibliography of aeronautics. (Smithsonian Inst. Miscellaneous colls. LV. Publication 1920) Wash. Govt. Ptg. Off. 1910. 940p.   **2994**

Bureau of Railway Economics. Library. Cost and development of commercial aviation; a list of references including material containing comparison of air & railroad services as to costs, speeds, safety, and historical development. Wash. D.C. 1925. 19p. mim.   **2995**

—— —— Air mail flights by Army flyers; memorandum [listing discussions chronologically]. Wash. D.C. 1940. 6p.   **2995a**

Carlson, R. H. A bibliography of books on the business and legal phases of commercial aviation. Seattle. Division of Transportation, Univ. of Washington. 1937. 19p. mim.   **2995b**

Culver, Dorothy Campbell. Civil and commercial aviation; a guide to federal legislation and administrative agencies. Berkeley, Calif. Univ. of California. 1940. 78p. mim.   **2995c**

Howard, Paul. Aeronautic training for national defense. Booklist. XXXVII. p101-9 (Nov. 1, 1940)   **2995d**

Index to current periodical literature. Air law rev., bibliog. section. II- no. 2- April 1931-   **2996**

Maggs Brothers. The history of flight; a descriptive catalogue of books, engravings and airmail stamps illustrating the evolution of the airship and the aeroplane. London. Maggs Brothers, Ltd. [1936] 232p.   **2996a**

National Bureau of Casualty and Surety Underwriters. Library. Selected list of books and articles on aeronautics for the insurance underwriter, covering: airplane construction, hazards and safeguards, laws and regulations. Prepared by Mildred B. Pressman. N.Y. 1928. 29p. **2997**

New York. Public Library. History of aeronautics; a selected list of references to material in the New York Public Library. By William B. Gamble. N.Y. N.Y. Pub. Lib. 1937. 254p. (Reprinted from the N.Y. Pub. Lib. bul. Jan. 1936-Sept. 1937)   **2998**

Renstrom, Arthur George. Principal U.S. investigations in aeronautics, 1918-37. N.Y. 1938. 8p., (Reprinted from Air law review, IX, no. 1. Jan. 1938) **2998a**

Ross, Raymond L. Mapping United States airways. Mil. engineer. XX. p476-8 (Nov.-Dec. 1928)   **2998b**

Seattle. Public Library. List of books on aeronautics in the Seattle Public Library. Seattle. 1931. 60p.   **2999**

Smithsonian Institution. Library. Langley Aeronautical Collection. A list of the books forming the Langley aeronautical collection deposited in the Library of Congress by the Smithsonian Institution, March, 1930. Wash. D.C. 1930. 69p. **2999a**

U.S. Bureau of Air Commerce. Bibliography on air transportation. [Wash. D.C.] May 1928. 46p.   **3000**

U.S. Engineer Department. A selected bibliography on airport design and construction, January 1930-July 1940. [Wash. 1940] 37p. reprod. from typ. copy **3000a**

U.S. Library of Congress. Maggs collection of aeronautics [purchased by the Library of Congress in 1930] [Wash. D.C. 1935] 203p. typ.   **3000b**

—— —— Division of bibliography. List of recent references on aircraft production in the United States. May 15, 1918. 3p. typ.   **3001**

—— —— —— List of references on commercial aeronautics. April 13, 1923. 11p. typ.   **3002**

—— —— —— List of references on the air service of the United States. Jan. 22, 1925. 11p. typ.   **3003**

—— —— —— List of references on the air service of the United States. Dec. 10, 1925. 14p. mim.   **3004**

U.S. National Advisory Committee for Aeronautics. Bibliography of aeronautics, 1909-1916- . Comp. by Paul Brockett. Wash. Govt. Ptg. Off. 1921-   **3005**

—— —— Technical publications of the Committee. *In* Annual reports, 1915- Wash. Govt. Ptg. Off. 1921-   **3006**

U.S. Office of the Chief of the Air Corps. Aeronautical book and magazine list, with references to principal documents, and papers of historical interest. (Air service information circular (Heavier-than-air) I. no. 21, March 29, 1920) Wash. Govt. Ptg. Off. 1920. 45p.   **3006a**

U.S. Works Progress Administration. Bibliography of aeronautics . . . pt. 1-. Comp. from the Index of aeronautics of the Institute of the Aeronautical sciences . . . [N.Y.] 1936- mim.   **3006b**

Washington, D. C. Public Library. Books on aeronautics; a reading list. Comp. by Alice Chace (Reference list no. 27) Wash. Govt. Ptg. Off. 1932. 59p. **3007**

Motor

American Automobile Association. Teacher's bibliography of safety materials; publications, legislation and regulations, films, lantern slides, transcriptions, for use with Sportsman-like driving series. Wash. D.C. American Automobile Association. 1937. 33p. mim.   **3007a**

American Electric Railway Association. Bibliography on modernization of electric railway (car and bus) equipment. (Bul. no. 269) N.Y. Aug. 1, 1929. mim. (Supplement to bibliography in report of its committee on essential features of modern cars, 1926)   **3008**

—— Bibliography on street and highway traffic. (Bul. no. 355. April 1, 1931) N.Y. 1931. 85p. (Revised edition of Bul. no. 305 issued April 1, 1930) (Supplement. 1932. 29p.)   **3009**

Automobile Manufacturers Association. Motor truck committee. Catalogue of pamphlets and material on motor truck and motor bus transportation. N.Y. Jacques & Co. 1937. 10p. **3009a**

Blessing, Arthur R. List of books on automobiles and motor cycles. N.Y. H. W. Wilson. 1918. 79p. **3010**

Boston Elevated Railway Company. Reference list of literature on urban electric railways indexed by cities, compiled from reports by railroad commissions, public service commissions, legislative commissions, investigating commissions, electric railway companies, transportation experts and others, with classified index. Boston. 1927. 151p. **3011**

Bureau of Railway Economics. List of references on the jitneys and jitney regulation. Wash. D.C. 1915. 11p. **3012**

—— Sources consulted in the preparation of "An economic survey of motor vehicle transportation in the United States." (Special ser. no. 60) Wash. D.C. Nov. 1933. 20p. **3013**

—— Library. Motor vehicle transportation in the United States; a brief list of discussions published since 1933. Wash. D.C. 1937. 11p. typ. **3013a**

Detroit. Public Library. Automobiles; selected list. Detroit. 1913. 20p. **3014**

General Motors Corporation. Dept. of public relations. Bibliography of traffic safety material and publications. N.Y. The Corporation Traffic and Safety Information Center, N.Y. World's Fair Highways and Horizons Exhibit. 1940. 35p. **3014a**

Harvard University. Bureau for Street Traffic Research. A bibliography on driving safety. Cambridge, Mass. 1937. 157p. mim. **3014b**

—— Street traffic; a selected and annotated bibliography of the literature of street traffic control and related subjects, 1920-1933. Cambridge, Mass. 1933. 223p. mim. **3015**

National Highway Users' Conference. Highways and motor transportation: a bibliography. Wash. D.C. The Conference. 1937. 100p. **3016**

National Research Council. Highway research board. Highway research, 1920-1940. Prep. by Committee on research activities, American association of state highway officials and Highway research board. Ed. by Ardery R. Rankin. [Wash. D.C.] 1940. 133p. **3016a**

—— Index to proceedings. Highway Research Board, volumes 1-12 (1921-1932). Prepared by W. V. McCown and Nellie McCormick, ed. by Roy W. Crum. Wash. D.C. 1933. 108p. **3017**

—— Committee on causes and prevention of highway accidents. Bibliography, street and highway safety. Prepared . . . by the staff of the library of the Bureau of Public Roads. Wash. D.C. Highway Education Board [1928?] 388p. autog. from typ. copy **3018**

New York (State) Public Service Commission. 1st district. Comprehensive bibliography on rapid transit taken from the library catalogue. N.Y. 1917. 100 blue printed p. **3019**

Permanent International Association of Road Congresses. Bibliographic index. Jan. 1932-June 1933 [Paris. 1932-33] (Cont. in the Association's bul.) **3019a**

United Railways and Electric Company of Baltimore. Traffic department. Bibliography of publications relating to vehicular traffic and traffic control. Balt. March 12, 1928. 29p. mim. **3020**

U.S. Bureau of Public Roads. Library. Bibliography on highway finance. Comp. by M. W. Helvestine. Wash. D.C. 1938. 95p. mim. **3020a**

—— —— Bibliography on highway safety. (U.S. Department of Agriculture, Miscellaneous publication 296) By Mildred A. Wilson. Wash. D.C. 1938. 136p. **3020b**

—— —— Highways, current literature. Wash. D.C. 1921- mim. (First title: Contents of new periodicals in Public Roads Library; later titles: Highways and rural engineering, Current literature, June 23, 1926-April 15, 1927; Highway and agricultural engineering current literature, April 20, 1927-June 24, 1931) **3022**

—— —— List of recent references on state aid to road-building in the United States. Dec. 5, 1919. 7p. typ. **3023**

—— —— List of references on earth roads. Sept. 3, 1925. 16p. typ. **3024**

—— —— List of references on highway transport. June 10, 1919. 15p. mim. **3025**

—— —— List of references on motor passenger transportation. June 12, 1925. 18p. mim. **3026**

—— —— List of references on motor truck transportation. Jan. 20, 1922. 19p. mim. **3027**

—— —— List of references on quarries for road making materials in the several states. July 24, 1915. 15p. typ. **3028**

—— —— List of references on the economic value of good roads. March 20, 1925. 9p. mim. **3029**

—— —— List of references on the old post roads and stage coach roads of Virginia. Jan. 19, 1921. 3p. typ. **3030**

—— —— List of speeches in Congress on national aid to road-building as published in the Congressional record, 1916-1921. March 29, 1921. 2p. typ. **3031**

—— —— Motor transport in the United States: a bibliographical list. Oct. 16, 1933. 21p. mim. **3032**

—— —— Select list of references on national aid to road-building in the United States. April 19, 1912. 9p. dupl. (Additional references. Nov. 5, 1914. 11p. typ.) **3033**

U.S. Library of Congress. Division of bibliography. Automobile trailers and trailer camps: a list of recent references. Comp. by Grace Hadley Fuller under the direction of Florence S. Hellman. April 23, 1937. 11p. Reprod.   3033a

U.S. Works Progress Administration, Massachusetts. A bibliography on driving safety. Boston. 1937. 157p. mim.   3033b

Washington. State Library. Roads; select list of references on roads. . . . Olympia, Wash. 1912. 41p.   3034

Wells, Fargo & Co. Catalogue Wells, Fargo and Company; historical exhibit, etc., at the World's Columbian exposition, Chicago, Illinois. San Francisco. H. S. Crocker. 1893. 32p.   3035

Wisconsin. Highway Commission. Highway safety bibliography. Prepared by Safety Department. Madison. The Commission. 1939. 33p. mim.   3035a

Wisconsin. Legislative Reference Library. Automobile accidents: causes and prevention, January 1930-May 1937; a selected bibliography. Comp. by E. B. Hage. Madison. 1937. 28p. typ.   3035b

Railroads

Adams, B. B. Select reading: railroad titles. Selected by railroad branch, Y.M.C.A. N.Y. 1895   3036

American Railway Association. Price list of publications issued by divisions and sections. . . . N.Y. 1933. 11,8p. mim. 3037

American Railway Engineering Association. General index to the Proceedings, volume 1-16 inclusive (1900-1915). Chicago. 1917. 271p.   3037a

—— **Committee XXII—economics of railway labor.** Bibliography of labor employed in the engineering and maintenance of way departments of railroads. Appendix A to its Report *in* American Railway Engineering Asso. bul. no. 202, XIX. p117-43 (Dec. 1917) (Reprinted in American Railway Engineering Asso. proc. XIX. p117-43. 1918)   3037b

American Society of Civil Engineers. Library. Railroads. (Index to the library of the American Society of Civil Engineers. Part I) N.Y. 1881. 188p.   3037c

—— —— Railroads. *In* Catalogue of the library. N.Y. 1900. p11-126   3037d

Association of American Railroads. Railroad histories and sources of historical information about railroads. Wash. D.C. April 25, 1940. 15p. processed   3037e

—— Railway literature for young people; a bibliography. Wash. D.C. 1940. 31p.   3037f

—— Streamline passenger trains in the United States listed in the order of their placement in regular scheduled service; with bibliography. Wash. D.C. 1940. 12p.   3037g

Baker, Edward. Railroadiana, consisting of books, pamphlets, maps, guides, time tables, etc., connected with the origin, rise and development of railways. . . . [Birmingham, (?) 1914?] 36p.   3038

Briggs, Samuel W. Regulation of interstate commerce; history of bills and resolutions introduced in Congress respecting federal regulation of interstate commerce by railways, etc., from the Thirty-seventh Congress to the Sixty-first Congress, inclusive, 1862-1911. Wash. Govt. Ptg. Off. 1912. 126p.   3038a

Broughton, Frederick. Catalogue of a collection of books on railway legislation, management, &c. . . . London, Ontario. Free Press Ptg. Co. 1883. 18p.   3039

Bureau of Railway Economics. Library. American railway accounting; a bibliography. *In* Railway Accounting Officers Association. Railway accounting procedure 1926 edition, p789-885; 1928 edition, p811-63; 1928 edition, p981-1016. Wash. D.C. Railway Accounting Officers Asso. 1926-28   3040

—— —— An annotated list of references to material discussing distribution of railroad construction and maintenance work throughout the year and over a period of years as a contribution towards preventing unemployment. Wash. D.C. Jan. 20, 1922. 46p. typ.   3041

—— —— Application of electricity to railways; bibliography of periodical articles appearing in a select list of periodicals covering the period . . . January, 1932- . Prepared by Edmund Arthur Freeman. (Jan. 1932-June 1933 in Am. Railway Engineering Asso. bul. XXV. no. 359. p3-22. Sept. 1933; 1933- reprinted from annual report of Am. Railway Asso. Electrical section)   3041a

—— —— Automatic train control in the United States; bibliography arranged chronologically. Wash. D.C. 1930. p160-90 (Reprinted from American Railway Association committee on automatic control. Automatic train control bul. no. 1)   3042

—— —— The Baltimore and Ohio Railroad Company and its subsidiaries; a bibliography. Comp. by Edward Arthur Freeman. Wash. D.C. Jan. 1927. 378p. mim. Supplement. April 1940. 17p. mim.   3043

—— —— Bibliographical memorandum of material discussing depreciation accounts prescribed for railroads by the Interstate Commerce Commission. Wash. D.C. April 1926. 8p. typ.   3043a

—— —— Bibliography of the Chicago and Alton railroad. Wash. D.C. March 17, 1921. 19p. typ.   3043b

—— —— Bibliography of the Nashville, Chattanooga & St. Louis Railway. Wash. D.C. April 7, 1922. 28p. mim.   3044

—— —— Bibliography of the Northern Pacific railway. Wash. D.C. Dec. 7, 1921. 68p. typ.   3044a

—— —— Bibliography on economics of railway labor. Am. Railway Engineering Asso. proc. XIX. p117-43 (March 1918) **3045**

—— —— Car ferries; a list of references. Wash. D.C. Oct. 1925. 24p. mim. **3046**

—— —— Carolina, Clinchfield and Ohio railway company; a list of references. Wash. D.C. Oct. 10, 1928. 8p. typ. **3046a**

—— —— Consolidation of railroads; a list of references to material discussing plans for consolidation of railroads in the United States, in connection with the Transportation act of 1920. Lib. jour. XLVI. p63-6 (Jan. 15, 1921) **3046b**

—— —— The coordination of transportation facilities; a list of references. Lib. jour. XLV. p737-41 (Sept. 15, 1920) **3046c**

—— —— Descriptive list of Bureau publications, 1910- . Wash. D.C. 1926- **3047**

—— —— Disaster relief by railroads, 1906-1930; a list of references (chronologically arranged). Wash. D.C. Oct. 1930. 30p. mim. **3048**

—— —— Early railroad lithographs in Henry E. Huntington Library and Art Gallery, San Gabriel, Calif. Wash. D.C. 1923. 20p. typ. **3048a**

—— —— Economies in labor to be effected through increased capital expenditures; a bibliographical memorandum. Wash. D.C. Oct. 26, 1935. 26p. typ. **3049**

—— —— Electrification of railroads; a list of references to material published 1926-March, 1929, inclusive. Wash. D.C. April 1929. 35p. mim. **3050**

—— —— Federal incorporation—a list of references. Wash. D.C. May 1933. 12p. typ. **3050a**

—— —— Financial structure of railroads in the United States, 1933-1935; a list of references chronologically arranged. [Wash. D.C.] April 1935. 20p. mim. **3051**

—— —— Government ownership of railways; a list of publications, 1917-1929. (Bul. no. 49. Supplement to Bul. no. 62. old ser. revised 1917) Wash. D.C. 1929. 98p. **3052**

—— —— Government ownership of railways; a list of publications, 1930-1937. Wash. D.C. 1938. 5,111p. mim. **3053**

—— —— Grade crossings; list of references to material published 1914-March 1927, supplementing list of references of 1915. Wash. D.C. 1927. 56p. **3054**

—— —— Holding companies; trial list of material with special reference to the Alleghany Corporation, Chesapeake Corporation, Delaware and Hudson Company and Pennroad Corporation. Comp. by Leonidas I. McDougle, Jr. [Wash. D.C. 1929] 20p. mim. **3055**

—— —— Increased use of the freight car; a bibliography. Wash. D.C. 1920. 24p. **3056**

—— —— A list of general references of recent material on railroad holding companies. Comp. by Leonidas I. McDougle, Jr. Wash. D.C. 1931. 20p. mim. **3057**

—— —— List of publications pertaining to government ownership of railways. (Bul. no. 62) Wash. D.C. 1914. 74p. **3058**

—— —— List of publications pertaining to government ownership of railways. (Bul. no. 62, revised) Wash. D.C. 1917. 100p. **3059**

—— —— A list of references of recent material on some railroad holding companies. Wash. D.C. 1931. 63p. mim. **3060**

—— —— List of references on American railway accounting. Wash. D.C. 1924. 159p. mim. **3061**

—— —— List of references on Delaware and Raritan Canal and Camden and Amboy Railroad and Transportation Company. Wash. D.C. Nov. 1934. 19p. typ. **3061a**

—— —— List of references on grade crossings. [Wash. D.C.] March 20, 1915. 27p. **3062**

—— —— List of references on maximum railway passenger fares. Wash. D.C. 1915. 13p. mim. **3063**

—— —— List of references on provisions of the Cummins bill regarding standards of rate-making and limitation of profits. Boston. 1920. 16p. (Reprinted from Special libraries. XI. p49-64. Feb. 1920) **3064**

—— —— List of references on railroad accounting. Wash. D.C. 1914. 14p. mim. **3065**

—— —— List of references on railroad terminals. [Wash. D.C.] 1916. 41p. mim. **3066**

—— —— List of references on railroads in war. Wash. D.C. Aug. 2, 1915. 34p. (Also in Special libraries. V. p134-43. Nov. 1914) **3067**

—— —— List of references on railway motor cars. Wash. D.C. Nov. 30, 1915. 37p. mim. **3067a**

—— —— List of references on railway dining cars. Wash. D.C. 1914. 5p. mim. **3068**

—— —— List of references on the Cummins railroad bill and the transportation act of 1920. Wash. D.C. 1920. 52p. typ. **3069**

—— —— List of references on the Delaware and Hudson Company. Wash. D.C. April 20, 1923. 45p. multig. **3070**

—— —— List of references on the Delaware and Raritan Canal and Camden and Amboy Railroad and Transportation Company. [Wash. D.C.] Nov. 1934. 19p. typ. **3071**

—— —— A list of references on the proposed consolidation of railroads. Wash. D.C. Aug. 14, 1923. 30p. (Supplements. Feb. 1925. 44p.; Jan. 1926. 21p.; Aug. 1927. 22p.; Aug. 1929. 31p.) **3073**

—— —— List of references on the question of giving to the Railroad Labor Board the power to enforce its decisions. Wash. D.C. 1922 **3074**

—— —— List of references on valuation of railways. Wash. D.C. Aug. 1, 1916. 130p. **3075**

—— —— List of references on valuation of steam railways. (Am. Railway Engineering Asso. bul. XVIII. no. 190. Oct. 1916) Chicago. 1916. 154p. **3076**

Bureau of Railway Economics. Library.
List of references: statistical methods in railway accounting and analysis of expenditures. Wash. D.C. 1919. 47p. mim.
3077

—— —— A list of references to articles on winter service on railroads. Wash. D.C. 1918
3078

—— —— List of references to articles relating to the employment of women on railroads and street railways. Special libraries. IX. p119-21 (Oct. 1917) (Separately printed 4p.; reprinted in Aera VI. p339-41. Nov. 1917)
3079

—— —— List of references to books and articles on Adamson law of September, 1916. Wash. D.C. 1917. 19p. mim.
3079a

—— —— List of references to legislation in the United States on minimum train crews and maximum length of trains. Wash. D.C. 1915. 20p. (Supplement. 1915. 20p.)
3080

—— —— List of references to literature on physical examination of railway employees. [Wash. D.C.] 1916. 17p.
3081

—— —— List of references to literature relating to the Union Pacific system. Wash. D.C. 1922. 229p. autog. from typ. copy
3082

—— —— List of references to publications pertaining to the government ownership of railways. Wash. D.C. March 1913. unpag.
3083

—— —— A list of references to recent material on some railroad holding companies. Wash. D.C. 1931. 64p. mim.
3083a

—— —— A list of references to the more important books and articles on government control and operation of railroads. Wash. D.C. Feb. 17, 1919. 22p.
3084

—— —— List of selected references to material emphasizing the economic aspects of electrification of railroads in the United States. Wash. D.C. April 17, 1924. 17p. mim.
3084a

—— —— A list of titles on railway pensions from the catalogue of the Bureau of Railway Economics. Wash. D.C. Oct. 30, 1929 14p. typ.
3085

—— —— Memorandum: references to material on some early sleeping car companies. Wash. D.C. 1927. 4p. typ.
3086

—— —— Memorandum: supplementary references on the Pennroad Corporation. Wash. D.C. 1930. 6p. typ.
3087

—— —— A memorandum: with references, on the history of standardization on the railroads of the United States of America. Jan. 18, 1923. 19p. typ.
3088

—— —— Minimum train crews and maximum length of trains—legislation in the United States. Special libraries. VI. p25-39 (Feb. 1915). Supplement. April 10, 1915. 6p. mim. Second supplement. Aug. 1, 1916. 14p. mim.
3088a

—— —— Missouri Pacific railway company; list of references. Wash. D.C. Dec. 27, 1922. 23p. typ.
3088b

—— —— Norfolk and Western Railway; a list of references. Wash. D.C. Dec. 1924. 52p. multig.
3089

—— —— "The O'Fallon case"; list of references, 1924-1929. Wash. D.C. 1929. 21p. mim. (Brief list. 1926-29. Wash. D.C. 1929. 11p.)
3090

—— —— Organization of railways; some material published from 1920-1929. [Wash. D.C.] 1929. 26p. reprod. from typ. copy
3091

—— —— The Pan-American Railway, 1879-1927; some references, chronologically arranged. Wash. D.C. Jan. 1928. 20p. mim.
3092

—— —— Pennroad corporation, supplementary references (to those in Holding companies; trial list. . . . 1929). Wash. D.C. 1929. 6p. typ.
3092a

—— —— Pensions in railway service; a list of references to material published 1932-May, 1935, supplementary to . . . references. . . comp. in February, 1932. . . [Wash. D.C.] June 1, 1935. 16p.
3093

—— —— Pensions in railway service; references, with notes. . . . Wash. D.C. 1932. 42p. mim. Supplementary list covering 1932-May 1935. 16,(2)p. typ.
3094

—— —— Pick-up and delivery service in the United States and Canada, 1933-1937, a list of references, chronologically arranged. . . . Wash. D.C. 1937. 32p. mim.
3095

—— —— Pooling, 1920-1939; a list of references with notes. [Wash. D.C.] Aug. 14, 1939. 81p. mim.
3096

—— —— Rail and air service, coordination, competition; a list of references. Wash. D.C. Sept. 1929. 24p.
3097

—— —— Railroad consolidation; a list of references. Wash. D.C. April 1930. 83p.
3098

—— —— Railroad history and political developments in the United States; memorandum listing some general discussions. Wash. D.C. June 29, 1937. 9p. typ.
3098a

—— —— Railroad labor relations, reports, etc. relating to, 1888-1930. Wash. D.C. 1931. 8p. typ.
3098b

—— —— Railroad land grants; a list of references (to material published 1831—February 1850). Wash. D.C. 1930? 16p. typ.
3098c

—— —— Railroad passenger service and traffic 1929-1935; a list of general references, arranged chronologically. Wash. D.C. Aug. 12, 1935. 19p. typ.
3099

—— —— Railroad pooling—a (bibliographical) memorandum. Wash. D.C. 1931. 69p. typ.
3099a

—— —— Railroads and geology in the United States; an exhibit of reports and other material in the library showing their inter-relations for 130 years . . . with notes by Elizabeth O. Cullen. Wash. D.C. Nov. 17, 1938. 30p. mim.
3099b

—— —— Railroads and national defense—some current material. Wash. D.C. July 24, 1940. 9p. mim.
3099c

—— —— Railroads and national defense in the United States—some discussions: a bibliography. Wash. D.C. Asso. of Am. Railroads. 1941. 62p. mim. **3099d**

—— —— The Railroads' war board; a brief list of references. Wash. D.C. 1925. 13p. typ. **3099e**

—— —— Railway economics; a collective catalogue of books in fourteen American libraries. Chicago. Pub. for the Bureau of Railway Economics by the Univ. of Chicago Press. 1912. 446p. **3100**

—— —— Railway motor cars; a list of references, revised to September, 1925, chronologically arranged. Wash. D.C. 1925. 62p. mim. Supplement. June 1, 1927. 7p. mim. **3101**

—— —— Railway traffic; some recent references. Wash. D.C. 1927. 18p. planog. **3102**

—— —— Recent accessions of interest, no. 1. March 13, 1935- . Wash. D.C. 1935- **3103**

—— —— References to articles on automobile accidents at railroad crossings. Wash. D.C. 1917. 7p. mim. **3104**

—— —— References, with notes, to material on railroad offices. [Wash. D.C.] Jan. 1925. 10p. typ. **3105**

—— —— Revised list of references on automatic train control. Wash. D.C. March 22, 1922. 32p. mim. **3106**

—— —— Select list of references on train crew legislation. Special libraries. IV. p121-5 (June 1913) **3107**

—— —— Some comments on the Plumb plan. Wash. D.C. Sept. 20, 1919, 20p. **3108**

—— —— Some references on the Atlantic coast line railway. Wash. D.C. Nov. 3, 1916. 3p. typ. **3108a**

—— —— Some references on the Southern railway. Wash. D.C. Dec. 23, 1916. 14p. typ. **3108b**

—— —— Some references on Wheeling and Lake Erie Railroad Company. Wash. D.C. 1916. 4p. typ. **3108c**

—— —— Some references to books and periodical articles on roadbeds of American railroads. Wash. D.C. 1920. 16p. typ. **3109**

—— —— Some references to material on arbitration of disputes between railroad companies and employees by government boards of arbitration. Wash. D.C. 1921. 21p. typ. **3110**

—— —— Some references to material on the cost of regulating the railroads of the United States. Wash. D.C. 1933. 7p. typ. **3111**

—— —— Some references to material on the development of relations between railroad managements and railroad employees that emphasize cooperation. Wash. D.C. April 22, 1924. 2,29,22p. mim. **3112**

—— —— Suburban service; brief list of references. Wash. D.C. 1928. 13p. mim. (Supplemental list. July 16, 1932. 2p. typ.) **3113**

—— —— Suggested list of works on railways (including material in Lafayette College Library). Wash. D.C. 1928. 16p. mim. **3114**

—— —— Survey of original sources of railway information. Wash. D.C. June 1924. 28p. mim. **3115**

—— —— Taxation of railroads; a brief list of references. Wash. D.C. July 7, 1926. 8p. typ. **3115a**

—— —— Trial bibliography of the Richmond, Fredericksburg and Potomac Railroad Company. Wash. D.C. Oct. 1934. 8p. typ. **3115b**

—— —— Trial bibliography on the New York, New Haven and Hartford Railroad. Wash. D.C. Nov. 30, 1915. 144p. typ. **3116**

—— —— Uses of wood by railroads; a list of references. Wash. D.C. 1925. 48p. **3117**

—— —— Ventilation of railroad tunnels; a list of references. Wash. D.C. 1925. 25p. **3118**

—— —— Wages, rules and working conditions on railroads in the United States; memorandum listing a few sources of material to indicate the scope of general material available. [Wash. D.C.] Nov. 6, 1933. 10p. typ. **3119**

—— —— Western Pacific railroad; list of references. Wash. D.C. 1922. 6p. typ. **3120**

Central Railway Club of Buffalo. Index of proceedings for the years 1893 to 1927, inclusive. Central Railway Club of Buffalo proc. XXXVI. p2568-80 (Feb. 1928) **3122**

Cleveland, Frederick A. and Powell, Fred W. Bibliography. *In* Railroad promotion and capitalization in the United States. N.Y. Longmans, Green. 1909. p295-342 **3123**

Cordz, Marian. Bibliography of railroads in the Pacific Northwest. Wash. hist. quar. XII. p91-114 (April 1921) **3124**

Cuba. Congreso Cámara de Representantes. Biblioteca. Catálogo de las obras que forman su biblioteca secciones de hacienda publica y de comercio y transporte. Havana. Imp. de Suarez, Carasa y ca. 1913. 272p. **3125**

Cullen, Elizabeth. Source material on railroad history. Special libraries. XVI. p44-8 (Feb. 1925) **3126**

Great Western Railway Institution, Swindon, England. Descriptive catalogue of the books in the central lending and reference libraries . . . 1917. Comp. by . . . W. Hildon Bagguley. Swindon, England. Morris Bros. 1917. 578p. **3127**

Haines, Donal Hamilton. The transportation library of the University of Michigan; its history and its needs. Ann Arbor, Mich. 1929. 14p. **3128**

Hammond, H. B. Catalogue of (his) railroad library, comprising the principal works on the construction and operation of railroads in the United States and Europe. N.Y. 1895. 28p. **3129**

Henry M. Sperry Library. List of books on railway signaling. N.Y. 1928. 13p. typ.　**3129a**

Hopkins, Timothy. Catalogue of the Hopkins Railway Library. Comp. by Frederick J. Teggart (Leland Stanford Junior Univ. Publications of the lib. I) Palo Alto, Calif. 1895. 231p.　**3130**

Illinois Railroad and Warehouse Commission. Library. Catalogue Railroad and Warehouse Commission Library. Springfield, Ill. 1912. 158p.　**3131**

Indiana. State Library. Street railways and railroads. (Indiana State Lib. bul. 3d ser. no. 7) Indianapolis. 1898. 26p.　**3131a**

Institution of Locomotive Engineers. List of papers read before the institution, 1916 to 1926 inclusive. Jour. Inst. of Locomotive Engineers. XVI. p77, 1035-40 (Nov.-Dec. 1926)　**3132**

International Railway Association. Monthly bibliography of railways. Bul. of the International Railway Asso. I. no. 1. July 1919- Brussels. M. Weissenbruch; London. P. S. King. 1919-　**3133**

Johnston, Richard H. Railroad libraries. Lib. jour. XLV. p259-65 (March 15, 1923)　**3134**

Lee, John W. M. A bibliography of the Baltimore and Ohio Railroad Company, 1827 to 1879. London. Priv. printed by the Chiswick Press, for the author. Balt. 1879. unpag.　**3135**

London University. Goldsmith's Company's Library of Economic Literature; list of manuscripts, maps and plans, and printed books and pamphlets mostly on railways and navigation, from the collections of John Urpeth Rastick, and his son Henry Rastick. . . . London. 1908. 16p.　**3136**

National Association of Railway and Utilities Commissioners. Select list of references on the valuation of public service corporations. Comp. by Mary M. Rosemond. n.p. 1912. 25p.　**3137**

National Liberal Club. Gladstone Library. Early railway pamphlets, 1825-1900. London. 1938. 60p.　**3137a**

New York. Public Library. List of works in the New York Public Library relating to government control of railroads, rates, regulation, etc. . . . N.Y. 1906. 26p. (Reprinted from Bul. X. p184-209. March 1906)　**3138**

New York Railroad Club. Index of the proceedings for the fiscal years 1895-1926, inclusive. N. Y. Railroad Club proc. XXXVII. p8195-216 (Dec. 1926)　**3139**

Norfolk and Western Railway Company. Transportation library; circulation list. Roanoke, Va. 1931-　**3140**

Peddie, R. A. Railway literature, 1556-1830; a handlist. London. Grafton. 1931. 79p.　**3141**

Perdonnet, Auguste (i.e. Jean Albert Vincent Auguste). Bibliographie raisonnée des chemins de fer. *In* Notions générales sur les chemins de fer. . . . Paris. Lacroix et Baudry. 1859. p371-445　**3142**

Princeton University. Pliny-Fisk Statistical Library. Catalogue of railroad mortgages. Prepared jointly by Pliny-Fisk Statistical Library of Princeton University and the Bureau of Railway Economics. Wash. D.C. 1919. 163p.　**3143**

Railway Accounting Officers' Association. American railway accounting: a bibliography. Wash. D.C. 1926. 96p. (Reprinted from Railway accounting procedure. 1926)　**3144**

Railway Signal Association. Index to signal literature, published by the Railway Signal Association, I. 1910. Bethlehem, Pa. Times Publishing Co. 1911　**3145**

Ripley, William Z. Railroads: recent books and neglected problems. Quar. jour. of economics. XL. p152-66 (Nov. 1925)　**3146**

Simmons-Boardman Publishing Co. A library of railway books. N.Y. 1922. 40p.　**3147**

Special Libraries Association. Committee on transportation. Railway transportation, some books, pamphlets, and other material published 1925-27. . . n.p. 1928. 60p. mim.　**3148**

Stone and Webster Management Association. Auditing department. Bibliography (of life of railway physical property). Am. Electric Accountants' Asso. proc. 1912. p194-226　**3149**

Taussig, Frank William. Topics and references in economics 5, [Harvard College, 1892-93], railways in the United States. Cambridge, Mass. 1892. 22p.　**3150**

Thomson, Thomas Richard. Check list of publications on American railroads before 1841. Part I. N.Y. Pub. Lib. bul. XLV. p3-68, 859-940 (Jan., Oct. 1941)　**3150a**

Traffic Club of Chicago. Historical collection of the Traffic Club of Chicago; a complete catalogue of documents, books, and pictures, articles in scrapbooks and articles in frame on display in the rooms of the club. Chicago. 1919. 36p.　**3151**

Tratman, E. E. R. Bibliography of railway stations, yards, marine terminals and air-ports. Am. Electric Railway Asso. bul. no. 350. XXXIV. p202-7 (Oct. 1932)　**3152**

United Engineering Society. Library service bureau. Bibliography on economics of railway operation. American Railway Engineering Association. Committee XXI—economics of railway operation. Report, Appendix A *in* American Railway Engineering Asso. bul. no. 203. XIX. p276-314 (Jan. 1918). (Reprinted in American Railway Engineering Asso. proc. XIX. p276-314. 1918)　**3153**

U.S. Bureau of Agricultural Economics. Library. Transportation of agricultural products in the United States, 1920-June 1939; a selected list of references relating to the various phases of railway, motor, and water carrier transportation. Comp. by Esther M. Colvin. (Agricultural economics bibliog. no. 81) Wash. D.C. Nov. 1940. 3pts.　**3153a**

U.S. Interstate Commerce Commission.
Recent accessions; a selected list. . . .
Wash. D.C. 1931- **3154**

U.S. Library of Congress. Division of bibliography. List of documents bearing on the Hepburn rate bill. 1908. 5p. typ. **3155**

—— —— —— List of periodicals in the Library of Congress which quote prices of American railroad securities, stocks and bonds. Nov. 22, 1917. 2p. typ. **3156**

—— —— —— List of recent discussions of the railroad situation. May 17, 1921. 3p. typ. **3157**

—— —— —— List of recent references on freight rates. March 23, 1929. 7p. typ. **3158**

—— —— —— List of recent references on the valuation of railroads (supplementary to list. . . . Bureau of Railway Economics, Chicago, 1916). June 5, 1926. 14p. mim. **3159**

—— —— —— List of references on anti-pass legislation. Jan. 31, 1914. 7p. typ. **3160**

—— —— —— List of references on government ownership and control of railroads, 1919-1924. Oct. 16, 1924. 10p. typ. **3161**

—— —— —— List of references on railroads in relation to the eight hour law. Oct. 11, 1916. 4p. typ. **3162**

—— —— —— List of references on the conflict of state and federal regulation of railroads. June 26, 1917. 7p. typ. **3163**

—— —— —— A list of references on the consolidation of railroads in the United States. Feb. 4, 1924. 11p. typ. **3164**

—— —— —— List of references on the performance of railroads since 1910. May 23, 1923. 17p. mim. **3165**

—— —— —— List of references on the Pullman Company. April 27, 1915. 6p. typ. **3166**

—— —— —— List of references on the railway clearing house. Feb. 8, 1918. 5p. typ. **3167**

—— —— —— List of references on the taxation of railroads. Aug. 1, 1924. 14p. typ. **3168**

—— —— —— List of speeches and debates on railroads in relation to eight hour law, as printed in Congressional record, 64 Cong., 1st sess. Oct. 12, 1916. 4p. typ. **3169**

—— —— —— List of works on land grants for railroads in the United States. n.d. 8p. typ. **3170**

—— —— —— List of works (with references to periodicals) on railroads in their relation to the government and the public, with appendix containing list of references on the Northern Securities Case. Comp. under the direction of A. P. C. Griffin. Wash. Govt. Ptg. Off. 1907. 131p. **3171**

—— —— —— Railways in the United States; a bibliographical list. Oct. 16, 1933. 38p. mim. **3172**

—— —— —— Select list of references on express companies. Nov. 22, 1910. 13p. typ. **3173**

—— —— —— Select list of references on government ownership of railroads. Comp. under the direction of A. P. C. Griffin. Wash. Govt. Ptg. Off. 1903. 14p. **3174**

—— —— —— Select list of references on government ownership of railroads. Jan. 28, 1914. 10p. typ. (Brief list. May 17, 1917. 4p. typ.; Brief list. March 8, 1918. 12p. dupl.; List of recent references. June 3, 1919. 10p. dupl.; Brief list. Nov. 11, 1924. 5p. mim.) **3175**

—— —— —— Select list of references on government regulation of railroad rates, with special reference to its constitutionality. March 1, 1911. 4p. typ. (Supplement. Aug. 16, 1912. 6p. typ.) **3176**

—— —— —— Select list of references on New York, New Haven and Hartford Railway system and the question of railway monopoly in New England. July 15, 1913. 14p. typ. **3177**

—— —— —— Select list of references on the relation between railways and waterways as agents of transportation. Aug. 19, 1910. 23p. typ. (Supplementary references. March 23, 1911. 4p.) **3178**

—— —— —— Select list of references on the valuation and capitalization of railroads. Comp. under the direction of H. H. B. Meyer. Wash. Govt. Ptg Off. 1909. 28p. (Supplement. Nov. 25, 1910. 16p.) **3179**

—— —— —— Select list of references on train crew legislation. May 10, 1913. 8p. dupl. **3180**

—— —— —— Speeches in Congress on government ownership and control of railroads as printed in the Congressional record. Jan. 20, 1919. 6p. dupl. **3181**

—— —— **Legislative reference service.** History of legislation governing the Northern Pacific land grants, 1866-1885. 1925. 30p. typ. **3181a**

—— —— —— Land grants to railroads. I. The Union Pacific. II. The Southern Pacific. 1929. 9p. typ. **3181b**

—— —— —— Legislative history of certain acts of Congress pertaining to the Pacific land grant. 1925. 13p. typ. **3181c**

—— —— —— Supreme Court decisions concerning railroad land grants. Dec. 18, 1930. 7p. typ. **3181d**

Water

Bureau of Railway Economics. Library. Inland waterway transportation in the United States; a brief list of discussions published since 1930. Wash. D.C. 1937. 7p. typ. **3181e**

—— —— The St. Lawrence seaway; an office transcript of cards in catalog of Bureau of Railway Economics Library, arranged chronologically. Wash. D.C. April 1, 1941. 61p. processed **3181f**

Chew, Anne C. and Churchill, Arthur C. References on the Great Lakes-Saint Lawrence waterway project. Wash. D.C. U.S. Dept. of Agriculture. Dec. 1940. 189p. mim. **3181g**

Pellett, Mirl Edison. Water transportation; a bibliography, guide, and union catalogue, with the cooperation of thirty-two North American libraries. Volume I. Harbors, ports, and port terminals. N.Y. H. W. Wilson. 1931. 685p. **3183**

Pittsburgh. Carnegie Library. Floods and flood prevention. Monthly bul. XIII. p417-58 (July 1908) **3184**

Shriver, Harry Clair. A bibliography and historical chronology relating to the proposed international Great Lakes-St. Lawrence deep waterway. Wash. D.C. 1939. 31p. typ. **3184a**

Thompson, S. A. Source material on water-ways. Special libraries. XVI. p49-51 (Feb. 1925) **3185**

U.S. Bureau of Agricultural Economics. Library. References on the Great Lakes-St. Lawrence River project. Comp. by Everett E. Edwards, Division of statistical and historical research. Wash. D.C. Nov. 1932. 53p. typ. **3186**

U.S. Dept. of Agriculture. Library. References on the Great Lakes-Saint Lawrence waterway project. By Everett E. Edwards and Mrs. Edith J. Lowe. (Bibliog. contributions no. 30) Wash. Oct. 1936. 185p. mim. **3186a**

U.S. Library of Congress. Division of bibliography. Bibliography on flood control (with special reference to Mississippi flood, 1927). Comp. by Florence S. Hellman (for the House flood control committee) House com. document no. 4. 70 Cong. 1 sess. 1928. 83p. **3187**

—— —— —— List of books on rivers of the United States. March 29, 1927. 7p. typ. **3188**

—— —— —— List of references on Atlantic intracoastal canals. July 25, 1918. 18p. typ. **3189**

—— —— —— List of references on Dismal Swamp canal. March 31, 1926. 5p. typ. **3190**

—— —— —— List of references on inland waterways of the United States. Feb. 15, 1918. 22p. dupl. (Recent writings. Feb. 17, 1928. 19p. mim.) **3191**

—— —— —— List of references on the Pacific Mail Steamship Company. July 24, 1916. 3p. typ. **3192**

—— —— —— List of references on the St. Lawrence River Ship Canal. Jan. 13, 1925. 11p. mim. (Supplements. Aug. 30, 1932. 31p. mim.; April 2, 1936. 16p. mim.) **3193**

—— —— —— List of speeches, etc., on waterways in the United States, as printed in the Congressional record, 1934-1938. Comp. by Anne L. Baden. May 26, 1938. 18p. mim. **3193a**

—— —— —— List of United States Congressional documents relating to the Chesapeake and Ohio Canal. n.d. 8p. typ. **3194**

—— —— —— List of works relating to deep waterways from the Great Lakes to the Atlantic Ocean, with some other related works, books, articles in periodicals, United States documents. Wash. Govt. Ptg. Off. 1908. 59p. **3195**

—— —— —— Literature on the Mississippi and other rivers dealing especially with flood conditions and the control of floods by levees and reservoirs. Feb. 11, 1914. 10p. typ. **3196**

—— —— —— The St. Lawrence navigation and power project: a list of recent references. Comp. by Ann D. Brown. March 12, 1940. 11p. mim. **3196a**

—— —— —— Select list of references on Atlantic coast-wise canals. 1909. 6p. typ. **3197**

—— —— —— Waterways in the United States; a bibliographical list. Oct. 16, 1933. 17p. mim. **3198**

—— —— —— Waterways in the United States: a selected list of recent references. Comp. by Grace H. Fuller. May 12, 1938. 40p. mim. **3198a**

Communication

Abstracts and references. Wireless engineer and experimental wireless. I. no. 1. Oct. 1923- **3199**

Detroit. Public Library. Civics division. Radio control: a list of references on the question resolved: that all radio broadcasting in the United States should be conducted in stations owned and controlled by the federal government. Detroit. 1933. 11p. **3200**

Isenburger, Herbert R. Bibliography on industrial radiography; a supplement to Industrial radiography, by Ancel St. John and H. R. Isenburger. Wash. D.C. Am. Documentation Inst. 1938. 52p. reprod. **3200a**

Stoddard, Edith M. Communication through the ages: a bibliography of materials for atmosphere and background for pupils in junior high school. N.Y. H.W. Wilson. 1938. 29p. **3200b**

U.S. Bureau of Foreign and Domestic Commerce. Electrical division. Radio references; a bibliography. By Lawrence D. Batson. [Wash.] 1935?- **3200c**

—— —— —— Current radio references; a bibliography. Comp. by Lawrence D. Batson. Wash. Sept. 1938. 61p. mim. **3200d**

—— —— —— Radio references; a bibliography. Comp. by Lawrence D. Batson. Wash. D.C. 1937. 33p. mim. **3200e**

U.S. Library of Congress. A list of recent references on communication, with special reference to the Federal Communications Commission. April 1, 1935. 9p. typ. **3201**

—— —— Division of bibliography. Bell Telephone system; a list of writings. April 21, 1930. 6p. typ. **3202**

—— —— —— List of references on government control of wireless telegraphy. Feb. 19, 1919. 5p. typ. **3203**

—— —— —— List of references on international communication. April 26, 1920. 18p. mim. (Supplement. April 12, 1924. 15p. mim.) **3204**

—— —— —— List of references on the American Telephone and Telegraph Company. June 10, 1924. 5p. typ. **3205**

—— —— —— List of references on the investigation of telephone companies in the United States. Feb. 4, 1920. 7p. mim. **3206**

—— —— —— Radio and radio broadcasting in the United States and foreign countries; a bibliographical list of recent references. July 24, 1935. 35p. mim. Recent references. April 18, 1939. 59p. mim. **3207**

—— —— —— The radio drama: a bibliographical list. 1937. 12p. typ. **3207a**

—— —— —— Recent references on radio laws and regulations. March 8, 1930. 9p. typ. **3208**

—— —— —— Select list of references on radio from the sociological, economic and legal standpoint. Oct. 6, 1924. 10p. mim. **3209**

—— —— —— A selected list of recent references on the telephone in the United States (with special reference to its economic and social conditions). Aug. 6, 1934. 36p. typ. (Supplement. Aug. 13, 1935. 13p. typ.) **3210**

—— —— —— Selected list of references on the regulation and control of radio broadcasting in the United States and foreign countries. May 20, 1933. 34p. mim. **3211**

—— —— —— Television; a bibliographical list. Jan. 7, 1929. 7p. typ. **3212**

—— —— —— Television: a selected list of recent writings. Comp. by Anne L. Baden. March 21, 1938. 25p. mim. **3212a**

Chapter VI

EDUCATION

GENERAL

Alexander, Carter. How to locate educational information and data; a text and reference book. N.Y. Columbia Univ., Teachers College. 1941. 439p. **3213**

Bardeen, Charles W. Catalogue of the School bulletin publications, author and subject in one alphabet. Syracuse, N.Y. Bardeen. 1908. 176p. **3214**

Bixler, Harold Hench. Check lists for educational research. N.Y. Columbia Univ., Teachers College, Bureau of publications. 1928. 118p. **3215**

Bolton, Frederick Elmer. A selected bibliography of books and monographs on education. Olympia, Wash. Superintendent of Public Instruction. 1921. 103p. **3216**

Burnham, William H. Bibliographies on educational subjects. (Publications of the Clark Univ. Lib. IV. no. 3. Dec. 1914) Worcester. Clark Univ. press. 1915. 45p. **3217**

—— Bibliographies on educational subjects; experimental and general pedagogy. (Publications of Clark Univ. Lib. IV. no. 5. Aug. 1915) Worcester. Clark Univ Press. 1915. 32p. **3218**

—— Bibliographies on educational subjects; the history of education. (Publications of Clark Univ. Lib. V. no. 6. Sept. 1917) Worcester. Clark Univ. press. 1917. 34p. **3219**

California. University. Department of pedagogy. Catalogue of books in the pedagogical section of the library of the University of California. Berkeley. 1895. 80p. **3220**

Chicago. University. Selected references in education, 1936- . Chicago. 1937- **3220a**

Columbia University. Books on education in the libraries of Columbia University. (Lib. bulletins no. 2) N.Y. Printed for the Univ. The Knickerbocker press. 1901. 435p. **3221**

Cubberley, Ellwᴏod P. Syllabus of lectures on the history of education, with selected bibliographies and suggested readings. N.Y. Macmillan. 1904. 361p. **3222**

Education in lay magazines. Educational research service. no. 7. June 1928- **3223**

Fletcher, Alfred Ewen. A select bibliography of education. *In* Sonnenschein's cyclopaedia of education. London. Swan Sonnenschein; N.Y. Macmillan. 1906. p531-61 **3224**

Good, Carter Victor, Barr, A. S. and Scates, Douglas E. The methodology of educational research. Ann Arbor Mich. Edwards Brothers. 1935. 303p **322⁵**

Hall, Granville Stanley and Mansfield John Melvin. Hints toward a select and descriptive bibliography of education arranged by topics and indexed by authors. Boston. D. C. Heath. 1886. 309p **322⁶**

International Institute of Intellectual Co operation. Bibliographie pédagogique internationale. International educational bibliography, 1936- . Paris. Société des Nations, Institut International de co opération intellectuelle. 1937- **3226**

Knight, Edgar W. Books on education 1938. Soc. educat. II. p564-73 (Nov 1938) **3226⁸**

—— Literature of education in the United States, 1935. The social stud. XXVII p103-19 (Feb. 1936) **322⁷**

Loyola Educational Digest. Current literature. Chicago [1925-28] **3227ª**

MacDowell, Lillian Ione. Board of Publi Education of the first school district of Pennsylvania, Philadelphia; catalog of the Pedagogical Library. Phila. Walther Ptg. House. 1907. 523p. **322⁸**

Monroe, Paul. Education. *In* The Cam bridge history of American literature Ed. by William P. Trent and others N.Y. G. P. Putnam's Sons. 1921. III p385-424; IV. p794 **322⁹**

Monroe, Walter S., Hamilton, Thomas T and Smith, V. T. Locating educational information in published sources. (Univ of Illinois. Bureau of educational re search. Bul. no. 50) Urbana, Ill. 1930 142p. **323⁰**

Monroe, Walter S. and others. Ten year of educational research, 1918-1927. (Univ of Illinois. Bul. v. 25. no. 51. Bureau of Educational Research. Bul. no. 42) Ur bana, Ill. 1928. p62-6 **323¹**

National Education Association of the United States. Educational policies com mission. A bibliography on education i the depression. Wash. D.C. 1937. 118p photop. **323²**

National Society for the Study of Educa tional Sociology. Bibliographies on edu cational sociology. First yearbook of The National Society for the Study of Educational Sociology, February 192⁸ Comp. by A. O. Bowden and Carroll D Champion. N.Y. N.Y. Univ. 1928. 154p **323³**

O'Rear, F. B. and Cottrell, Donald P. Bibliography of institutional publications in the field of education. N.Y. Columbia Univ. Teachers college. 1930. mim. (1437 items from 515 higher education institutions, including dissertations; covers 1914-29. May be borrowed) **3233**

Publishers' weekly. The American educational catalog for 1927-; an author index to text books in general use with names of publishers and price, with a subject index to the new school books of 1929-1930. N.Y. Publishers' weekly. 1929 **3234**

Research abstracts and bibliographies. Jour. of educational research. XVIII. no. 2. Sept. 1928- **3235**

Selected references in education, 1938; reprinted from the School review and the Elementary school journal for 1938. (Supplementary education monographs, no. 47) Chicago. Univ. of Chicago, Dept. of Education. 1939. 221p. **3235a**

Smith, Henry L. and O'Dell, Edgar Alvin. Bibliography of school surveys and of references on school surveys. (Bul. of the School of Education, Indiana univ. VIII. nos. 1 and 2. Sept. and Nov. 1931) [Bloomington, Ind.] Indiana Univ. School of Education, Bureau of cooperative research. 1931. 212p. **3236**

Touton, F. C. A selected and annotated bibliography on professional books in education. Calif. quar. of secondary education. I. p93-152 (Jan. 1925) **3237**

Townsend, M. E. and Stewart, A. G. Guides to study materials for teachers. N.Y. H. W. Wilson. 1936. 113p. **3238**

U.S. Commissioner of Education. Some recent educational bibliographies and lists of books designed more particularly for the use of educators and students. (Rep. of the Commissioner of Education. 1893-94. II) Wash. Govt. Ptg. Off. 1896. p1701-22 **3239**

U.S. Library of Congress. Want list of publications of educational institutions, 1909. Wash. D.C. 1909. 14p. **3240**

U.S. Office of Education. Bibliography of education for 1908/09-1911/12. (Bureau of Education bul. 1909. no. 9; 1911. no. 10; 1913. no. 59; 1915. no. 30) Wash. Govt. Ptg. Off. 1909-15 (A continuation of the nine annual summaries covering years 1899-1907 comp. by J. I. Wyer and others. Continued by the Monthly record of current educational publications) **3241**

—— —— Selected references in education, 1933-35; supplementary educational monographs published in conjunction with The School review and The Elementary school journal, numbers 41-42, January 1934, January 1935. Chicago. Univ. of Chicago Press. 1934, 1935. 190,189p. (Reprinted from The School review and The Elementary school journal for Jan. to Dec. 1933 and Jan. to Dec. 1934) **3242**

—— —— Library. Bibliography of research studies in education, 1926/27- . (Office of Education bul. 1928-) Wash. Govt. Ptg. Off. 1929- **3243**

—— —— —— Record of current educational publications. Jan. 1912-Jan./March 1932. Wash. Govt. Ptg. Off. 1912-32 (In Library circulars and bulletins. Beginning with 1913 this takes the place of the annual bibliography of education previously issued by the office. Continued in effect in Selected references in education, 1933- pub. by the Univ. of Chicago, 1934- Title from Jan. 1912-Oct. 1921: Monthly record of current educational publications) **3244**

Wheeler, J. L. and Hawes, M. E. Educational literature of 1937- . School and society. XLVII- . 1938- **3244a**

Whitney, Frederick L. Methods in educational research. N.Y., London. D. Appleton. 1931. 335p. **3245**

Witmer, Eleanor M. Educational research; a bibliography on sources useful in determining research completed or under way. Teachers College rec. XXXIII. p335-40 (Jan. 1932) **3246**

Wyer, James Ingersoll. A bibliography of the study and teaching of history. Am. Hist. Asso. rep. 1899. I. p561-612 **3247**

—— Recent educational bibliography. School rev. VI-XV (Oct. 1898-Oct. 1907) **3248**

—— A selected bibliography of some phases of education. Phila. Civic Club of Phila. 1899. 12p. **3249**

—— and others. Bibliography of education for 1899-1907. (1899-1906 in Educational rev. April 1900; April 1901; June 1902; 1903; 1904; 1905; Sept.-Oct. 1906; June 1907. 1907 in U.S. Bureau of Education. Bul. 1908. no. 3) **3250**

ADMINISTRATION

Alexander, Carter. Bibliography on educational finance, reviewed and presented by The Educational Finance Inquiry Commission under the auspices of The American Council on Education. Washington, D.C. N.Y. Macmillan. 1924. 257p. **3251**

—— and Covert, Timon. Bibliography on educational finance, 1923-1931. (U.S. Office of Education. Bul. 1932. no. 15) Wash. Govt. Ptg. Off. 1932. 343p. **3252**

Alexander, Thomas, Stratemeyer, Florence and Mead, A. R. A comprehensive bibliography on supervision. N.Y. Columbia Univ., Teachers College. 1930 **3253**

Baldwin, Bird T. and Mohr, Walter H. Bibliography of teachers' salaries. Wash. Govt. Ptg. Off. 1914. p440-61 (Reprinted from The Tangible rewards of teaching. . . Comp. by James E. Boykin and Roberta King. . . (U.S. Bureau of Education. Bul. 1914. no. 16) **3254**

Clark, Harold F. A cross-indexed bibliography on school budgets. (Bul. Indiana Univ. School of Education. II. no. 3) Bloomington, Ind. Bureau of Cooperative Research. Jan. 1926. 66p.   **3255**

Edson, Andrew Wheatley. A bibliography of a course on school administration, summer session, Teachers College, 1910. (Teachers College. Syllabi. no. 2) N.Y. Columbia Univ., Teachers College, 1910. 20p.   **3256**

Fowlkes, John Guy and Carlile, Amos B. Bibliography on school buildings. (Univ. of Wisconsin Bureau of Educational Research. Bul. no. 6. March 1925) Madison, Wis. [1925] 76p.   **3257**

Mathews, C. O. Bibliography on the honor system and academic honesty in American schools and colleges. (U.S. Office of Education. Pamphlet no. 16. Dec. 1930) Wash. D.C. 1931. 18p.   **3258**

Nelson, Charles A. Bibliography of teachers' salaries and pensions. Educational rev. XXXIII. p24-35 (Jan. 1907)   **3259**

Smith, Henry Lester. Bibliography of college and university buildings, grounds and equipment. (Bul. Indiana Univ. School of Education. X. no. 2. March 1934) Bloomington, Ind. 1934. 199p.   **3260**

Smith, Henry Lester and Chamberlain, Leo Martin. Bibliography of school buildings, grounds, and equipment. (Bul. Indiana Univ. School of Education. IV. no. 3. Jan. 1928; Pt. II. Bul. IX. no. 2. March 1933; Pt. III. Bul. IX. no. 3. June 1933; Pt. IV: Bul. XI. no. 2. March 1935) Bloomington. Indiana Univ., Bureau of Cooperative Research. 1928-35. 326, 182, 130, 216p.   **3261**

Strayer, George D. and Evenden, Edward S. Syllabus of a course in the principles of educational administration. (Teachers College. Syllabi. no. 11) N.Y. Columbia Univ., Teachers College. 1922. 166p.   **3262**

U.S. Office of Education. An annotated bibliography of studies pertaining to the county unit of school administration. By Timon Covert (Education Office. Circular no. 12) Wash. D.C. 1930. 16p. mim.   **3263**

—— —— List of references on student self-government and the honor system. Lib. leaflet no. 31. March 1925. 6p.   **3264**

HIGHER EDUCATION

American Association of University Professors. Bibliography of methods of increasing the intellectual interest and raising the standards of undergraduates. (Bul. IX. no. 8) Easton, Pa. 1923. p385-418   **3265**

American Association of University Women. Contributions towards a bibliography of the higher education of women. (Boston Pub. Lib. Bibliographies of special subjects no. 8) Boston. 1897. 42p. (Also pub. as Association of Col-

legiate Alumnae. Publications ser. 2. no. 61) (Supplement: Boston Public Library. Bibliographies of special subjects no. 9. Ed. by Edith E. Clarke. Boston. 1905. 57p. Also issued as Association of Collegiate Alumnae. Publications ser. 3. no. 2)   **3266**

Bartlett, Lester W. Bibliography on the professional growth of faculty members. Asso. of Am. Colleges bul. XII. p275-300 (Nov. 1926)   **3267**

Borden, Fanny. A list of references on college and university government and administration, 1819-1920 (Vassar College. Bul. X. no. 3) Poughkeepsie, N.Y. 1921. 39p.   **3268**

Columbia University. Teachers College. Annotated bibliography on academic freedom. Prepared under the direction of the staff in higher education by Marion C. Graves and others. [N.Y. 1931?] 9p. mim.   **3269**

—— —— Bibliographies on higher education. ERA project   **3269a**

Eells, Walter Crosby. Bibliography on junior colleges. (U.S. Office of Education. Bul. 1930. no. 2) Wash. Govt. Ptg. Off. 1930. 167p.   **3270**

—— Bibliography on surveys of higher education—Reference list of surveys of higher education, printed, mimeographed, manuscript. *In* Surveys of American higher education. N.Y. Carnegie Foundation for the Advancement of Teaching. 1937. p363-452   **3270a**

Engleman, Lois Eleanor and Eells, Walter Crosby. The literature of junior college terminal education. (Terminal education monograph no. 1) Wash. D.C. Am. Asso. of Junior Colleges. 1941. 322p.   **3270b**

Frazier, Benjamin W. Education of teachers: selected bibliography. Wash. D.C. Office of Education. 1936. 35p.   **3270c**

Good, Carter V. Bibliography on college teaching with special emphasis on methods of teaching. (The National Soc. of College Teachers of Education. Stud. in education. Yearbook XVI) Chicago. Univ. of Chicago Press. 1928. p66-95 **3271**

—— Bibliography on special method, the curriculum, and problems in twelve subject-matter fields, and miscellaneous references. *In* Teaching in college and university. Balt. Warwick and York. 1929. p436-519   **3272**

Hartson, L. D., Brentlinger, W. H. and Toops, H. A. The college student and his vocation; a selected bibliography (Ohio College Asso. Bul. no. 37) Columbus. Ohio State Univ. 1927. 17p. mim.   **3273**

Manson, G. E. Bibliography on methods for personal development of college students. Educational rec. II. p 1-42 (Jan. 1930)   **3274**

New York. State. University. College libraries in the United States; contributions toward a bibliography. By Hugh Williams. N.Y. State Lib. bul. bibliog. no. 19. p609-55 (Dec. 1899)   **3275**

Newland, T. E. and Toops, H. A. A selected bibliography on quantitative measurement in higher education. (National Soc. of College Teachers of Education. Yearbook no. XVIII) Chicago. Univ. of Chicago Press. 1930. p190-231 **3276**

O'Rear, F. B. Annotated bibliographies on selected topics of higher education, especially in the fields of staff problems, student personnel problems, and finance. N.Y. Columbia Univ., Teachers College. MS. **3277**

O'Rear, F. B. and Cottrell, Donald P. Bibliography of institutional publications in the field of education, compiled from data supplied from 502 higher educational institutions. N.Y. Columbia Univ., Teachers College. 1930. 72p. MS. **3278**

Peabody College. Bibliography of the history of higher education in the South. Nashville, Tenn. ms. **3278a**

Russell, J. D. and Hayes, D. T. Selected references on higher education. School rev. XLV. p781-8; XLVI. 777-85; XLVII. 775-84 (Dec. 1937, Dec. 1938, Dec. 1939) **3278b**

Stogdill, Z. L. Student maladjustment (a bibliography). (Ohio College Asso. Bul. no. 50) Columbus. Ohio State Univ. 1928. 49p. **3279**

Stowe, A. Monroe. Studies in collegiate education; a bibliography on recent literature on collegiate education. Lynchburg College bul. IV. no. 3. June 1930. (Continuation in V. no. 3. June 1931) 44,24p. **3281**

Sturtevant, Sarah M. and Hayes, Harriet. A partial bibliography for deans of women and girls. N.Y. Columbia Univ., Teachers College. 1929. 35p. **3282**

U.S. Library of Congress. Division of bibliography. List of references on the social value of higher education. 1917. 4p. typ. **3283**

U.S. Office of Education. List of references on higher education. By J. D. Wolcott (Lib. leaflet no. 35) Wash. Govt. Ptg. Off. 1927. 40p. **3284**

Vought, S. W. College catalog collection. *In* U.S. Office of Education. Library. Library facilities of the Office of Education. Wash. D.C. 1937. p14 (Also appeared in School life. XXII. p135-6. Jan. 1937) **3284a**

SECONDARY EDUCATION

Abel, J. F. An annotated list of official publications on consolidation of schools and transportation of pupils. (Rural school leaflet no. 9) Wash. Govt. Ptg. Off. 1923. 12p. **3285**

American educational catalog for 1940; revised to April 1940; an index to elementary and secondary schoolbooks, together with supplementary reading and pedagogical books in these fields, from data furnished by the textbooks publishers and compiled at the office of the Publishers' weekly. N.Y. Bowker. 1940. 150p. **3285a**

Beu, Frank Andrew. The junior high school; an annotated bibliography; an annotated classified bibliography of the periodical literature dealing with the junior high school, which was published from January 1, 1920 to June 1, 1930, inclusive. (Illinois State Teachers College. Teachers College bul. no. 113. July 1, 1933) Charleston. Eastern Illinois State Teachers College. 1931. 76p. **3286**

Brown, Elmer F. The history of secondary education in the United States—bibliography. School rev. V. p84-94, 139-47 (Feb.-March 1897) **3287**

Brueckner, Leo J. and others. Selected references on elementary school instruction. Element. school jour. XXXVI. p59-66, 129-46, 211-27. 1935 **3287a**

Burnham, William H. Bibliographies on educational subjects; secondary education. (Publications of Clark Univ. V. no. 1) Worcester. Clark Univ. Press. July 1916. 41p. **3288**

Heartman, Charles F. American primers, Indian primers, royal primers and thirty-seven other types of non-New-England primers, issued prior to 1830; a bibliographical checklist. Printed for Harry B. Weiss. Highland Park, N.J. 1935. 159p. **3289**

Heaton, Kenneth Lewis and others. Bibliography on secondary education. N.Y. Progressive Education Asso. 1940. 60p. **3289a**

New York. State. University. A selected, annotated bibliography on the general phases of secondary education for use by teachers and supervisors. Univ. of the State of N.Y. bul. no. 1024. July 15, 1933. 23p. **3290**

Odell, C. W. and Blough, J. H. An annotated bibliography dealing with extra-curricular activities in elementary and high schools. (Univ. of Illinois. Bul. XXIII. no. 24. Bureau of Educational Research. Bul. no. 29) Urbana. Univ. of Illinois. 1926. 40p. **3291**

Reeves, Stanley Newman. An annotated bibliography on the secondary school curriculum. (George Peabody College for Teachers. Master's thesis. 1929) Nashville, Tenn. 1929. 152p. MS. **3292**

U.S. Office of Education. An annotated bibliography of studies on consolidation and transportation, 1923-29. By Timon Covert. (Office of Education. Circular no. 9) Wash. D.C. 1930. 26p. mim. **3293**

—— —— An indexed list of city school reports. (Office of education. Circular no. 26-) Wash. D.C. Nov. 1930- . mim. **3294**

—— —— List of references on secondary education in the United States. (Lib. leaflet no. 22) Wash. D.C. June 1923. 10p. **3295**

U.S. Office of Education. List of references on the junior high school. (Lib. leaflet no. 27) Wash. D.C. 1924. 11p. (Earlier list in leaflet no. 5, 1919) **3296**

—— —— Research and investigations reported by city school systems, 1932-33. By Ruth A. Gray (Office of Education. Circular 128) Wash. Govt. Ptg. Off. 1934. 37p. Same. 1934-35. By Ruth A. Gray. (Circular 143) 33p. Same. 1935-36 (Circular 161) 24p. **3297**

—— —— A selected list of books on the education of early childhood. (Kindergarten circular. 1917. no. 1) Wash. D.C. 1917. 14p. **3298**

—— —— **Library.** List of educational research studies in city school systems, no. 1, Aug. 1930. By Edith A. Wright. (Office of Education. Circular no. 18) Wash. D.C. 1930. 85p. Same. no. 2. Oct. 1931. By Edith A. Wright (Circular no. 42) 71p. Same. no. 3. 1931-32. By Ruth A. Gray (Circular no. 72) 63p. **3299**

—— —— National committee on research in secondary education. Bibliography of current research undertakings in secondary education. By J. K. Norton. [Wash. D.C. 1926?] 47p. **3300**

Walkley, Raymond Lowrey. Bibliography of the relation of secondary schools to higher education. (U.S. Bureau of Education. Bul. no. 32. whole no. 606) Wash. Govt. Ptg. Off. 1914. 57p. **3301**

Windes, Eustace E. Bibliography of secondary education research, 1920-1925. (U.S. Bureau of Education. Bul. 1926. no. 2) Wash. Govt. Ptg. Off. 1926. 95p. **3302**

—— Bibliography of studies in secondary education (U.S. Bureau of Education. Bul. 1927. no. 27) Wash. Govt. Ptg. Off. 1927. 30p. **3303**

METHODS

American Federation of Teachers of the Mathematical and the Natural Sciences. Bibliography of science teaching. (U.S. Bureau of Education. Bul. 1911. no. 1) Wash. Govt. Ptg. Off. 1911. 27p. **3304**

Bardeen, Charles W. Clearance catalogue of books on teaching, no. 1, October 1914- . N.Y. Bardeen. 1914- **3305**

Barr, A. S. and Rudisill, Mabel. An annotated bibliography on the methodology of scientific research as applied to education. (Univ. of Wisconsin. Bul. of the Bureau of Educational Research. no. 13. June 1931) Madison, Wis. Univ. of Wisconsin. 1931. 129p. **3306**

Bibliography on methods of research in education. Rev. educ. research. IX. p591-646 (Dec. 1939) **3306a**

Branom, Frederick K. A bibliography of recent literature on the teaching of geography. Worcester. Clark Univ., Dept. of geography. 1930. 47p. **3307**

Brown, H. Emmett and Bird, Joy. Motion pictures and lantern slides for elementary visual education; Lincoln School research studies. Pub. by Columbia Univ. Bureau of publications of Teachers College,- for the Lincoln School of Teachers College. N.Y. 1931. 105p. **3308**

Burnham, William H. Bibliographies on educational psychology. (Publications of the Clark Univ. Lib. III. no. 5) Worcester. Clark Univ. Press. 1913. 44p. **3309**

—— Bibliographies on experimental pedagogy. (Publications of the Clark univ. Lib. III. no. 3) Worcester. Clark Univ. Press. 1912. 49p. **3310**

Bye, Edgar C. A bibliography on the teaching of the social studies. N.Y. H. W. Wilson. 1933. 104p. **3311**

Coleman, Algernon and Jacques, Agnes. An analytical bibliography of modern language teaching, 1927-1932. Chicago. Univ. of Chicago Press. 1933. 296p. **3312**

Engelhardt, N. L., Ganders, H. S. and Riefling, Jeannette. Bibliography of school records and reports. Teachers College Rec. XXVI. p765-81 (May 1925) **3313**

Glenn, Earl R. and Walker, Josephine. Bibliography of science teaching in secondary schools. (U.S. Bureau of Education. Bul. 1925. no. 13) Wash. Govt. Ptg. Off. 1925. 161p. **3314**

Harap, Henry. Annotated bibliography of curriculum objectives. Cleveland. Western Reserve Univ. 1931. 37p. MS. **3315**

—— Bibliography of curriculum making for teachers. Cleveland. Western Reserve Univ. 67p. MS. **3316**

Hildreth, Gertrude Howell. Bibliography of mental tests and rating scales. N.Y. The Psychological Corp. 1933. 242p. **3317**

Holmes, Henry W. A descriptive bibliography of measurement in elementary subjects. (Harvard bul. in education. V. June 1917) Cambridge. Harvard Univ. 1917. 46p. **3318**

Indiana University. School of Education. Bureau of Co-operative Research. Bibliography of educational measurements. (Bul. I. no. 5) Bloomington, Ind. 1925. 147p. **3319**

Kess, Edward Elmer. An annotated bibliography of methods of teaching history. (George Peabody College for Teachers. Master's thesis. 1929) Nashville, Tenn. 1929. 99p. MS. **3320**

Los Angeles, California. School District. An annotated bibliography on directed study. Los Angeles. City School District, Dept. of psychology and educational research. Jan. 1927. 15p. **3321**

Manahan, J. L. A bibliography of educational surveys and tests. (Univ. of Virginia rec. Extension ser. II. no. 3) Charlottesville. Univ. of Virginia. 1916. p50-92 **3322**

Mitchell, David and Ruger, Georgie J. Psychological tests; revised and classified bibliography. N.Y. The Bureau of Educational Experiments. 1918. 116p. **3323**

New York. State. University. Educational research division. Bibliography of objective tests in the vocational subjects. . . . Albany. Univ. of the State of N.Y. Press. 1932. 24p. **3324**

Odell, Charles W. An annotated bibliography dealing with the classification and instruction of pupils to provide for individual differences. (Univ. of Illinois. Bul. XXI. no. 12. Bureau of Educational Research. Bul. no. 16) Urbana. Univ. of Illinois. 1923. 50p. **3325**

—— A selected annotated bibliography dealing with examinations and school marks. (Univ. of Illinois. Bureau of Educational Research. College of Education. Bul. no. 43) Urbana. Univ. of Illinois. 1929. 42p. **3326**

Oliver, Thomas Edward. The modern language teachers handbook. Boston, N.Y. 1935. 706p. **3327**

—— Suggestions and references for modern language teachers. (Univ. of Illinois. School of Education. Bul. no. 12) Urbana. Univ. of Illinois. 1914. 52p. **3328**

Polatchek, Joseph. Present status of experimental studies. (College of the City of N.Y. Master's thesis. 1929) N.Y. 1929. 152p. MS. **3329**

Smith, David Eugene and Goldziher, Charles. Bibliography of the teaching of mathematics, 1900-1912. (U.S. Bureau of Education. Bul. 1912. no. 29) Wash. Govt. Ptg. Off. 1912. 95p. **3330**

Smith, Henry Lester and Wright, Wendell William. Second revision of the bibliography of educational measurements. (Bul. of Indiana Univ., School of Education. IV. no. 2. Nov. 1927) Bloomington. Indiana Univ. Bureau of Cooperative Research. 1927. 251p. **3331**

Talbot, Winthrop. Teaching English to aliens; a bibliography of textbooks, dictionaries and glossaries, and aids to librarians. (U.S. Bureau of Education. Bul. 1917. no. 39) Wash. Govt. Ptg. Off. 1918. 76p. **3332**

U.S. Library of Congress. Division of bibliography. List of references on the teaching of political science. May 18, 1914. 20p. typ. **3333**

U.S. Office of Education. Bibliography of educational and psychological tests and measurements. Comp. by Margaret Doherty and Josephine McLatchy under the direction of B. R. Buckingham (Bul. 1923. no. 55) Wash. Govt. Ptg. Off. 1923. 233p. **3334**

—— —— Bibliography of the work-study-play, or platoon, plan. (City school leaflet no. 10) Wash. D.C. July 1923. 7p. **3335**

—— —— Library. Bibliography of research studies in the training and professional status of teachers. Wash. Govt. Ptg. Off. 1931. p184-224 **3336**

White, W. T. Bibliography; the curriculum, sources and materials. Texas State Teachers Asso. 1930. 56p. **3337**

Woodring, Maxie Nave and Harold, Gil-Rachel Theresa. Enriched teaching of English in the high school; a source book for teachers of English, school librarians and directors of extra-curricular activities. . . . N.Y. Columbia Univ., Teachers College, Bureau of publications. 1927. 104p. **3338**

Woodring, Maxie Nave and Harold, Gilbert. Enriched teaching of commercial subjects in the high school; a source book for teachers of bookkeeping, shorthand, typewriting, commercial geography, and other commercial subjects. . . . N.Y. Columbia Univ., Teachers College, Bureau of publications. 1930. 339p. **3339**

Woodring, Maxie Nave and Sanford, Vera. Enriched teaching of mathematics in the high school; a source book for teachers of mathematics listing chiefly free and low cost illustrative and supplementary materials. N.Y. Columbia Univ., Teachers College, Bureau of publications. 1928. 128p. **3340**

Woodring, Maxie Nave and Schwendener, Norma. Enriched teaching of physical education in the high school; a source book for teachers of physical education, camp councillors, and recreation leaders. N.Y. Columbia Univ., Teachers College, Bureau of publications. 1929. 143p. **3341**

Woodring, Maxie Nave, Oakes, Mervin E. and Brown, Henry Emmett. Enriched teaching of science in the high school; a source book for teachers of general science, biology, physics, chemistry, and other sciences. . . . N.Y. Columbia Univ., Teachers College, Bureau of publications. 1928. 374p. **3342**

MISCELLANEOUS

About books. Jour. of adult education. I. no. 1. Feb. 1929- **3343**

Addis, Wellford. Bibliography of legal education. (Rep. of the Commissioner of Education. 1890-91) Wash. Govt. Ptg. Off. 1894. p565-78 **3344**

Affleck, G. B. Selected bibliography for 1937. Am. asso. health and phys. educ. res. quar. IX. p128-66 (Dec. 1938) **3344a**

—— Selected bibliography of physical training and hygiene. Am. physical education rev. XXXIII. p240-7, 520-30, 610-14 (March-Nov. 1928) **3345**

Alabama. Department of Education. A select list of references on temperance instruction in public schools. Montgomery. Dept. of Education of Alabama. 1910. 7p. **3346**

American Council on Education. Committee on motion pictures in education. Films on war and American neutrality; current bibliography no. 1, 16-mm. sound films. Wash. D.C. 1939. 44p. mim. **3346a**

—— —— Motion pictures in education; a summary of the literature; source book for teachers and administrators. Comp. by Edgar Dale and others. N.Y. H.W. Wilson. 1937. 472p. **3346b**

Ashley, T. W. Select bibliography of libraries and popular education. *In* Adams, Herbert Baxter. Public libraries and popular education. Univ. of the State of N.Y. Home education. bul. 31. p239-64 (May 1900)   **3347**

Bixler, Harold Hench and others. Bibliography of vocational guidance references for students. Atlanta. 1939. 134p. **3347a**

Boardman, Helen. Psychological tests; a bibliography. (Bureau of Educational Experiments. Bul. no. 6). N.Y. Bureau of Educational Experiments. 1917. [1918] 111p.   **3348**

Brewer, John M. and Kelly, Roy W. A selected critical bibliography of vocational guidance. (Harvard bulletins in education) Cambridge. Harvard Univ. Press. 1917. 76p.   **3349**

Brooklyn. Public Library. Choosing an occupation; a list of books and references on vocational choice, guidance and training in the Brooklyn Public Library. Brooklyn, N.Y. 1913. 63p.   **3350**

Brundage, H. D. and Richards, C. R. A selected bibliography on industrial education. National Education Asso. proc. Rep. of Com. on the place of industries in pub. education. 1910. p116-23 **3351**

Buehler, Ezra E. Federal aid for education; an exhaustive brief, questions and answers pertaining to analysis of the subject and a complete bibliography (p51-91) N.Y. Noble & Noble. 1934 **3352**

Burgess, W. R. and others. Military training in the public school; an annotated bibliography. Teachers College rec. XVIII. p141-60 (March 1917)   **3353**

Burnham, William H. Bibliography of school hygiene. National Education Asso. proc. 1898. p505-23   **3354**

Business education index; an author and subject index of business education articles, compiled from a selected list of periodicals and yearbooks published during the year 1940- . N.Y. The Business Education World. 1941-   **3354a**

Carnegie Endowment for International Peace. Library. History teaching and school text books in reation to international understanding; select list of books, pamphlets and periodical articles. Comp. by Mary Alice Matthews (Reading list no. 29) Wash. D.C. 1931. 14p.   **3355**

Carrigan, Margaret and others. Guide to guidance; an annotated bibliography of 1938 publications of interest to deans, counselors, and advisers. . . . Wash. D.C. Nat. Asso. of Deans of Women of the National Education Asso. 1939. 70p. mim. **3355a**

Child Study Association of America, Inc. Bibliography on parent education . . . selected from current magazines and pamphlets, Oct. 1932/Jan. 1934- . N.Y. Child Study Asso. of Amer. [1934-] **3356**

Congdon, Wray Hollowell and Henry, David D. Adult education; a bibliography with annotations and an introduction. [Lansing. Mich. School Service. 1934] 39p.   **3357**

Cook, Dorothy E. and Rahbek-Smith, Eva. Educational film catalog. N.Y. H. W. Wilson. 1939. 332p. 2d ed. Supplement. N.Y. H. W. Wilson. 1940. 126p. **3357a**

Cope, Henry F. A selected list of books on moral training and instruction in the public schools. Religious education. V. p718-32 (Feb. 1911)   **3358**

Detroit. Public Library. Federal aid to education; a selected list of references on the question, resolved: that the federal government should adopt a policy of equalizing educational opportunity, throughout the nation. Detroit. 1934. 10p. **3359**

Dunlop, Fanny and Johnson, Alice Sarah. Vocations for college women; a reading list. Chicago. Am. Lib. Asso. 1925. 16p. (Reprinted from the News-Bulletin of the Bureau of Vocational Information) **3360**

Eastern Manual Training Association. A selected bibliography relating to the theory and practice of manual training. Allegheny, Pa. 1902. 53p.   **3361**

Edge, Sigrid A. Books for self-education. Chicago. Am. Lib. Asso. 1938. 95p. **3361a**

Good, Carter V. Selected bibliography on techniques of educational research and related problems, 1931/1932- . Jour. of educational research. XXVI- (Oct. 1932-) **3362**

Gray, Rolland O. and Hunter, William L. Index to 2500 books on industrial arts education and vocational industrial education, 1820-1934. Ames. Iowa State College. 1935. 108p.   **3363**

Greenwood, James M. and Martin, Artemas. Notes on the history of American textbooks on arithmetic. Wash. Govt. Ptg Off. 1900. (Reprinted from the U.S. Commissioner of Education. Reports. 1897-98. p789-868; 1898-99. p781-837) **3364**

Harris, William T. and Richards, Zalmon. History of the National Educational Association of the United States; its organization and functions; historical sketch, list of meetings, places, dates and officers; chronological list of papers; and a classified list of subjects. Wash. D.C. 1892.   **3365**

Hartnett, Mary Rita, sister. A critically selected and annotated list of sources for research in nursing education. (Catholic Univ. of America. Studies in nursing education, V, fas. I) Wash. D.C. Catholic Univ. of America Press. 1940. 67p. **3365a**

Harvard Law School Association. Bibliography; the case system and other topics in legal education. *In* The Centennial history of the Harvard Law School. [Cambridge] The Harvard Law School Asso. 1918. p365-76   **3366**

Henry, T. W. Annotated bibliography on gifted children and their education. (Twenty-third yearbook of the National Soc. for the Study of Education. Pt. I) Bloomington, Ill. Pub. School Publishing Co. 1924. p389-443 **3367**

Henry E. Huntington Library and Art Gallery. Learning for ladies (1508-1895) a book exhibition at the Huntington Library. San Marino, Calif. 1936. 15p. **3367a**

Hunter, William Luther and Livingston, Everett G. A reader's guide to magazine articles on industrial arts education and vocational industrial education. Ames. Iowa State College, Industrial arts dept. 1934. 75p. mim. **3368**

Hutcherson, George Everett and others. Guidance; an annotated list of books helpful to pupils, teachers, librarians and counselors in secondary schools. Albany. Univ. of the State of New York. 1938. 63p. **3368a**

Indiana. State Library. Health education, an annotated bibliography. Selected and comp. by Marie J. LaGrange. Indianapolis. 1938. 25p. mim. **3368b**

Indiana. University. School of education. Bureau of cooperative research. Bibliography of school surveys and of references on school surveys. By H. L. Smith and E. A. O'Dell. Bloomington. Indiana Univ. Bookstore. 1938. 144p. **3368c**

Institute of Women's Professional Relations. Occupations for college women; a bibliography. By Chase Going Woodhouse and Ruth Frances Yeomans (North Carolina College for Women. Bul. no. 1. Oct. 1929) Greensboro, N.C. 1929. 290p. (Supplement no. 1. Feb. 1930. 86p. Supplement no. 2. Feb. 1931. 22p.) **3369**

International Council of Religious Education. Bureau of research. Christian religious education bibliography, 1931 through 1936. Chicago, Ill. 1938. 40p. **3369a**

John Crerar Library. The official state educational directories; a bibliography. Comp. by Jerome K. Wilcox (John Crerar Library. Reference list no. 12) Chicago. 1931. 15p. mim. **3370**

Kansas City Public Library. A reading list on vocational education. (Special lib. list no. 10) Kansas City, Mo. 1915. 44p. **3371**

Karpinski, Louis C. Colonial American arithmetics. *In* Bibliographical essays; a tribute to Wilberforce Eames. Cambridge. Harvard Univ. Press. 1924. p242-8. **3372**

Lingel, Robert. Educational broadcasting; a bibliography. Chicago. Univ. of Chicago Press. 1932. 162p. **3373**

Lomax, Paul Sanford and Toll, Lewis R. Annotated bibliography for course 232.3,4; evaluation of current literature in business education. N.Y. New York Univ. Bookstore. 1940. 64p. mim. **3373a**

McCabe, M. R. List of references on vocational guidance. (U.S. Bureau of Education. Lib. leaflet no. 36) Wash. Govt. Ptg. Off. 1929. 21p. **3374**

MacDonald, Arthur. Bibliography of exceptional children and their education. (U.S. Bureau of Education. Bul. 1912. no. 32) Wash. Govt. Ptg. Off. 1913. 46p. **3375**

McMillen, James Adelbert. The Gary system; a bibliography. Rochester, N.Y. 1917. 15p. **3375a**

McMurtrie, Douglas C. Bibliography of the education and care of crippled children; a manual and guide to the literature relating to cripples together with an analytic index. N.Y. Douglas C. McMurtrie. 1913. 99p. **3376**

Manson, Grace E. A bibliography of the analysis and measurement of human personality up to 1926. (National Research Council. Com. on scientific problems of human migration. Reprint and circular ser no. 72) Wash. D.C. 1926. 59p **3377**

Maverick, L. A. Bibliography. *In* The vocational guidance of college students. Cambridge. Harvard Univ. Press. 1926. p163-239 **3378**

Methodist Book Concern. Religious education catalog. N.Y. 1934- **3379**

Mias, C. S. Bibliography of religious education for schools and colleges. (China Christian Educational Asso. Bul. no. 13) Shanghai. 1926. 72p. **3380**

Michigan. University. Committee on vocational counsel and placement. Vocational information; a bibliography for college and high school students. (Official publication. XXX. no. 15. Oct. 13, 1928. Vocational ser. no. 1) Ann Arbor, Mich. 1928. 236p. **3381**

National Education Association of the United States. Index by authors, titles and subjects to the publications of the National Education Association for its first fifty years, 1857 to 1906. Comp. by Martha Furber Nelson. Winona, Minn. The Asso. 1907. 211p. **3382**

—— Titles of papers and discussions from 1857 to 1906, arranged by years and departments; bibliography of topics from 1857-1906. *In* Fiftieth anniversary volume 1857-1906. (Addresses and proc.) Winona, Wis. Pub. by the Asso. 1907. p561-730 **3383**

National Education Association of the United States. Research division. Dramatization in safety education: an annotated bibliography. Wash. D.C. 1940. 55p. **3383a**

—— —— Safety and safety education: an annotated bibliography. Wash. D.C. 1939. 64p. **3383b**

National Safety Council. Education Division. Bibliography of safety materials for the use of schools. N.Y. National Safety Council. 1935? 11p. **3383c**

Nelson, Charles Alexander. Analytical index to volumes 1 to 25, Educational review, January 1891 to May 1903. Rahway, N.J.; N.Y. Educational Rev. Publishing Co. 1904. 218p.   **3384**

New York. State. University. Selected bibliography of texts and references on immigrant education. (Univ. of the State of N.Y. Bul. no. 743. Oct. 1, 1921) Albany. Univ. of the State of N.Y. Press. 1921. 13p.   **3385**

Northrup, Clark S. A bibliography of the Phi Beta Kappa Society. N.Y. The Elisha Parmele Press. 1928. 328p.   **3386**

Perham, Philip D-B. Teaching by correspondence; an annotated bibliography. San Francisco. Calif. State Dept. of Education. Correspondence Extension Service. 1939. 106p. mim.   **3386a**

Peters, Iva L. An inclusive bibliography on vocational guidance, vocational training and vocational opportunities. Comp. under the direction of the Bureau of Municipal Research, Educational dept. N.Y. 1920. 45p. typ.   **3387**

Phelps, Edith M. Debate index, also bibliographies on inter-scholastic athletics, compulsory arbitration of industrial disputes, a new liberal party, government ownership of hydro-electric power. N.Y. H. W. Wilson. 1932. 144p. Rev. ed. 1939. 130p.   **3388**

Pierce, Anna E. Catalog of literature for advisers of young women and girls. N.Y. H. W. Wilson. 1923. 149p. (Supplement. 1930. 192p.)   **3389**

Pittsburgh. Carnegie Library. Choice of vocation; a selected list of books and magazine articles for the guidance of students. Pittsburgh. 1921. 54p.   **3390**

Price, Willodeen and Ticen, Zelma E. Index to vocations. N.Y. H. W. Wilson. 1936. 106p.   **3391**

Proctor, William Martin. Annotated bibliography on adult education. Los Angeles. Frank Wiggins Trade School, ptg. dept. 1935. 124p.   **3392**

Pugmire, D. R. A guide to the literature on penal education in the United States. Prepared for the Commission for the Study of the Educational Problems of Penal Institutions for Youth. N.Y. Oct. 1934. 11p. mim.   **3393**

Research abstracts and bibliographies. Jour. ed. research. I. Jan. 1920-   **3393a**

Richards, Charles Russell. Selected bibliography on industrial education. (National Soc. for the Promotion of Industrial Education. Bul. no. 2) [Asbury Park, N.J. Kinmouth Press] 1907. 32p.   **3394**

Russell, W. T. Historical textbooks published before 1861. Hist. teachers' mag. VI. p122-5 (April 1915)   **3395**

Ryan, Will Carson. The literature of American school and college athletics. (Bul. no. 24) N.Y. Carnegie Foundation for the Advancement of Teaching. 1929. 305p.   **3396**

Sargent, Porter Edward. Educational initiative; an analytical encyclopedic index, private school, summer camp, progressive and other educational enterprises under private instruction; bibliographies include Sargent publications, references to reviews of books of educational import, 1916-1933. Boston. Porter Sargent. [1934] 277p.   **3397**

Seeger, Ruth E. Orientation courses; an annotated bibliography. (Bibliographies in education no. 2) [Columbus] Ohio State Univ., Bureau of Educational Research. 1931. 39p.   **3398**

Shaffer, Velma Ruth. The Gary system: a bibliography, 1916-1935. N.Y. School of Lib. Service, Columbia Univ. 1935. 19p. mim.   **3398a**

Sheldon, Henry D. A select critical bibliography on student societies. *In* Student life and customs. N.Y. Appleton. 1901. p307-51   **3399**

Shryock, Richard H. Guide to the materials in the History teachers' magazine and the Historical outlook, volumes I-XVI, 1909-1925. Hist. outlook. XVI. p355-94 (Dec. 1925)   **3400**

Simons, Lao Genevra. Bibliography of early American textbooks on algebra published in the colonies and the United States through 1850. (The Scripta mathematica stud. no. 1) N.Y. Yeshiva College, Scripta mathematica. 1936. 68p.   **3401**

Smith, Faith Edith. A selected list of books, pamphlets and magazine articles on part-time education. N.Y. State Lib. bibliog. bul. 71. Univ. of the State of N.Y. bul. 746. Nov. 1921. 28p.   **3402**

Spieseke, Alice Winifred. The first textbooks in American history and their compiler, John M'Culloch. (Columbia Univ. Ph.D. thesis, 1938) N.Y. Teachers College, Columbia Univ. 1938. 135p. (Published also as Teachers College, Columbia Univ., Contributions to education, no. 744. Includes lists of books and almanacs published by M'Culloch)   **3402a**

Stebbing, Lucile Reiner. Child training and parent education; references to material in recent books. N.Y. H. W. Wilson. 1931. 51p.   **3403**

Thompson, Laura A. Recent references on adult workers' education. Monthly labor rev. XIX. p692-705 (Sept. 1924)   **3404**

Thompson, Olive. A guide to readings in civic education. (Univ. of Calif. Syllabus no. 157) Berkeley, Univ. of Calif. Press. 1924. 140p.   **3405**

Thonssen, Lester William and Fatherson, Elizabeth. Bibliography of speech education. N.Y. H.W. Wilson. 1939. 800p.   **3405a**

Townes, Mary Ella. Teaching with motion pictures; a guide to sources of information and materials. (Teachers College Library contributions, no. 1) N.Y. 1940. 29p.   **3405b**

U.S. Federal Board for Vocational Education. Bibliography on vocational guidance; a selected list of vocational guidance references for teachers, counselors and youths. (Bul. no. 66. Trade and industrial ser. no. 19) Wash. Govt. Ptg. Off. 1925. 85p. **3406**

U.S. Library of Congress. Division of bibliography. A list of recent books on vocational guidance. Sept. 9, 1932. 10p. typ. (Supplement. July 9, 1935. 8p. typ.) **3407**

—— —— —— List of references on correspondence schools. July 16, 1919. 4p. typ. **3408**

—— —— —— Select list of references on a national university. Oct. 8, 1910. 8p. typ. (Supplement. July 11, 1916. 5p. typ.) **3409**

—— —— —— Select list of references on compulsory education. Oct. 30, 1913. 6p. typ. **3410**

—— —— —— Select list of references on education and the state. 1908. 8p. typ. **3411**

—— —— —— Select list of references on industrial and technical education. Nov. 17, 1911. 28p. typ. **3412**

—— —— —— Select list of references on teachers' pensions. 1909. 8p. typ. **3413**

—— —— —— Select list of references on the history of American textbooks. 1909. 6p. typ. **3414**

U.S. Office of Education. Analytical index to Barnard's American journal of education, [thirty-one volumes, 1855 to 1881. Ed. by Henry Barnard] (U.S. Bureau of Education. A catalogue of educational literature. Pt. 1) Wash. D.C. 1892. 128p. **3415**

—— —— Annotated bibliography of medical inspection and health supervision of school children in the United States for the years, 1909-1912. (Bul. 1913. no. 16) Wash. Govt. Ptg. Off. 1913. 136p. **3416**

—— —— An annotated bibliography on the education and psychology of exceptional children. Comp. by Elsie H. Martens and F. E. Reynolds. Wash. Govt. Ptg. Off. 1937. 42p. **3417**

—— —— Bibliography of all-year schools and vacation schools in the United States. Lib. leaflet no. 23. Nov. 1923. 13p. **3418**

—— —— Bibliography of certain aspects of rural education (from January 1, 1920 to September 1, 1926). (Bul. 1927. no. 4) Wash. Govt. Ptg. Off. 1927. 56p. **3419**

—— —— Bibliography of education in agriculture and home economics. (Bul. 1912. no. 10) Wash. Govt. Ptg. Off. 1912. 62p. **3420**

—— —— Bibliography of industrial, vocational and trade education. (Bul. 1913. pt. 2. no. 22. whole no. 532) Wash. Govt. Ptg. Off. 1913. 92p. **3421**

—— —— A classified list of the principal subjects considered in the volumes of proceedings of The National Educational Association from 1870 to 1893 inclusive; author index to the volumes of addresses and proceedings of The National Educational Association. (U.S. Bureau of Education. Rep. 1892-93) Wash. Govt. Ptg. Off. 1895. p1513-33 **3422**

—— —— The education of native and minority groups; a bibliography, 1923-1932. By Katherine M. Cook and Florence M. Reynolds (Bul. 1933. no. 12) Wash. Govt. Ptg. Off. 1933. 57p. **3423**

—— —— Federal aid for education, 1935-36 and 1936-37, with a brief history and bibliography. (Leaflet no. 30) By Timon Covert. Wash. D.C. 1938. 24p. **3423a**

—— —— Good references on vitalizing rural education. Comp. by Walter H. Gaumnitz. (Bibliography no. 66) Wash. D.C. 1940. 17p. **3423b**

—— —— List of references on play and playgrounds. (Lib. leaflet no. 29. Nov. 1924) Wash. D.C. 1924. 13p. **3424**

—— —— List of references on the money value of education. (Lib. leaflet no. 24. July 1924) Wash. D.C. 1924. 7p. **3425**

—— —— List of references on vocational education. (Lib. leaflet no. 25) Wash. D.C. 1924. 20p. **3426**

—— —— List of references on vocational guidance. (Lib. leaflet no. 32, 33, 36) Wash. D.C. 1925, 1927, 1929. 11, 22, 21p. **3427**

—— —— Religious education bibliography. Jan./Dec. 1931- . Wash. Govt. Ptg. Off. 1932- **3428**

U.S. Office of Experiment Stations. List of publications of the Office of Experiment Stations on agricultural education. Wash. Govt. Ptg. Off. 1908. 13p. **3429**

U.S. Works Progress Administration. Books, pamphlets, and other materials recommended for teachers of workers' education. Rev. ed., incorporating supplements issued January and July 1935. April 1936. Prepared by Office of specialist in workers' education, Education division, Works Progress Administration. Wash. D.C. 1936. 58p. mim. **3429a**

Washington. University. Physical education bibliography. Comp. by physical education majors, class of 1929. Seattle. Univ. of Wash. Press. 1929. 31p. **3430**

Watson, Edna E. A source book for vocational guidance; choice selections and references for counselors, homeroom teachers, and others concerned with the guidance of youth. N.Y. H. W. Wilson. 1930. 241p. **3431**

Welch, Lila Merle and Lingenfelter, Mary Rebecca. Studies of home economics curriculum; an annotated bibliography. (Ohio State Univ. Bureau of Educational Research. Bibliographies in education no. 1) Columbus, Ohio. 1930. 46p. mim. **3432**

Wesley, Edgar B. A guide to the Commission report. Social stud. XXVII. p435-50 (Oct. 1936) (A guide to the "Conclusions and recommendations of the Commission on the social studies of the American Historical Association." N.Y. 1932-35. 13v.) **3432a**

Wilkinson, Ruth. Safety education, 1930-1938: a contribution to a bibliography. Madison. Univ. of Wisconsin Lib. School. 1938. 53p. typ. **3432b**

Wilson, Lewis A. A list of helpful publications concerning vocational instruction. Univ. of the State of N. Y. bul. no. 569. June 15, 1914. 41p. **3433**

Wood, Thomas Denison and Reesor, Mary. A bibliography on educational hygiene and physical education. N.Y. Columbia Univ. Teachers College. 1911. 41p. **3434**

CHAPTER VII

POLITICAL SCIENCE, CONSTITUTIONAL, LEGAL

GENERAL

Academy of Political Science. Political science quarterly, index to volumes I-XLV, 1886-1930. N.Y. Columbia Univ. 1931. 174p. **3435**

American Academy of Political and Social Science. The annals of the American Academy of Political and Social Science; cumulative index, [quinquennial] 25th-45th anniversary index [July 1890/Feb. 1916-Jan. 1931/Nov. 1935] Phila. 1916-36. 5v. **3435a**

—— The annals—Cumulative index 1931-1935, volumes 153-182; forty-fifth anniversary index. Phila. 1936. 169p. 1936-1940, volumes 183-212; fiftieth anniversary index. Phila. 1941. 179p. **3435b**

—— The Annals, twenty-fifth anniversary index; being an index to all publications of the American Academy of Political and Social Science from July 1890, up to and including January 1916. Phila. Am. Acad. of Pol. and Social Science. 1916. 156p.

The Annals, thirtieth anniversary index; . . . . published as a supplement to the March 1916 issue of the Annals. 1921. 79p. **3436**

Ammarell, Raymond Robert. Work book and study outline for problems of American democracy. Phila. McKinley Publishing Co. 1935. 64p. **3437**

Baker, George H., ed. Bibliography of political science, 1886. (Pol. science quar. I. supplement) Boston. Ginn; London. Henry Frowde. 1887. 55p. **3438**

Brookings Institution. Catalog of publications. Wash. D.C. 1930. 85p. **3439**

Burchfield, Laverne. Student's guide to materials in political science. Prepared under the direction of the Subcommittee on research of the Committee on policy of the American Political Science Association. N.Y. Henry Holt. 1935. 426p. **3440**

California. University. Bureau of Public Administration. Governmental research organizations in the western states; a directory of agencies and an index to their studies. By O. W. Campbell (Western states research activity ser. no. 1) Berkeley. Aug. 1935. 32p. mim. **3441**

—— Training for public service: a bibliography. Comp. by Dorothy Campbell Culver. Berkeley, Calif. 1937. 48p. mim. **3441a**

California Liquor Industries Association. Bibliography on liquor control; with a foreword by Margaret Rooney. Mida's criterion of the wine and liquor industries. XLII. p48-54, 120-3 (Sept. 1936); 86-92 (Oct. 1936); 48, 92-3 (Nov. 1936) (Cont.) **3441b**

Carpenter, Oliver Clinton. Debate outlines on public questions. N.Y. Minton, Balch. 1932. 329p. **3442**

Chicago. Joint Reference Library. Constructive economy in government; a source list. Chicago. 1933. 11p. mim. **3443**

—— Recent publications on governmental problems. . . Prepared for the Governmental Research Association, Sept. 7, 1932- Chicago. 1932- **3444**

Chicago. Public Library. Finding list of the Chicago Public Library; political science, social science, education. Chicago. Dec. 1893. p449-520 **3445**

Culver, Dorothy Campbell. Bibliography of inter-governmental relations in the United States. Ann. Am. Acad. CCVII. p219-28 (Jan. 1940) **3445a**

Galloway, George Barnes. American pamphlet literature of public affairs (a descriptive list of current pamphlets series) Wash. D.C. National Economic and Social Planning Asso. 1937. 16p. **3445b**

Greer, Sarah. A bibliography of civil service and personnel administration. (Commission of Inquiry on Public Service. Personnel Monograph I) N.Y. McGraw-Hill. 1935. 143p. **3446**

—— A bibliography of public administration. N.Y. National Inst. of Pub. Administration. 1926. 238p. **3447**

—— A bibliography of public administration. Part I. General literature. N.Y. Columbia Univ., Inst. of Pub. Administration. 1933. 90p. **3448**

Haddow, Anna. Political science textbooks and other publications, 1865-1900. *In* Political science in American colleges and universities, 1636-1900. N.Y. D. Appleton-Century. 1939. p235-56 **3448a**

Landis, Benson Young. Democracy: a reading list. Am. Lib. Asso. bul. XXXIV. no. 1. pt. II. p53-68 (Jan. 1940) **3448b**

Mathews, J. N. and Berdahl, C. A. Documents and readings in American government, national, state and local. N.Y. Macmillan. 1928 **3449**

Mulhauser, Roland and Huus, Randolph O. A bibliography on regional government. Cleveland. Western Reserve Univ. 1928. 59p. mim. **3450**

National Council for the Social Studies. Pamphlets on public affairs for use in social studies classes. Comp. by Henry Kronenberg and others. (Bul. no. 8) Cambridge, Mass. 1937. 80p. **3450a**

National Reform Association. Bibliography prepared by a committee of the National Reform Association; a list of works treating of the origin, nature, sphere and end of civil government. Pittsburgh. 1912. 35p.   **3451**

Nettlau, Max. Bibliographie de l'anarchie. Brussels. Bibliothèque des "Temps nouveaux." 1897. 294p.   **3452**

New Jersey. College. Library. Library of political science and jurisprudence; finding list. Princeton. Mutual Ptg. Co. 1893. 44p.   **3453**

Public Administration Clearing House. A directory of organizations in the field of public administration. Chicago. 1934. 178p.   **3454**

—— Public administration organizations; a directory of unofficial organizations in the field of public administration in the United States and Canada. Chicago. 1941. 187p.
3454a

Public Administration Service. Your business of government; a catalog of publications in the field of public administration. . . . Chicago. 1938. 20p.   **3454b**

Rosenthal, Clarice A. and others. Selected bibliography on civil liberties in the United States. N.Y. Am. Civil Liberties Union. 1937. p257-301 (Reprinted from the plates of the book You can't do that, by George Seldes)   **3454c**

Rugg, Harold Ordway. Teacher's guide for a history of American government and culture. Boston, N.Y. Ginn. 1931. 140p.
3455

Southern California. University. School of government. Institute of government. Committee of bibliographies. Legislative processes: selected bibliography. Comp. by Marguerite Seager. Los Angeles. The Univ. 1938. 17p. mim.   **3455a**

Special Libraries Association. Committee of the civic-social group. Public administration libraries; a manual of practice. Chicago. Pub. Administration Service. 1934. 67p.   **3456**

Stammhammer, Josef. Bibliographie der social-politik. Jena. Gustav Fischer. 1896-1912. 2v.   **3457**

—— Bibliographie des socialismus und communismus. Jena. Gustav Fischer. 1893-1909. 3v.   **3458**

Sumner, W. G. and others. Political economy and political science; a priced and classified list of books . . . (Economic tracts no. II. Ser. of 1880-81) N.Y. Soc. for Pol. Education. 1881. 36p.   **3459**

Texas. State Library. Finding-list of books on political science, law and allied topics. Prepared by John Boynton Kaiser. Austin, Texas. Austin Ptg. Co. 1911. 51p.
3460

U.S. Bureau of Efficiency. List of references on scientific management as the basis of efficiency, with special reference to the government service. Comp. by H. H. B. Meyer. Wash. Govt. Ptg. Off. 1920. 22p.
3461

U.S. Library of Congress. Catalogue of works relating to political economy and the science of government in the Library of Congress. Wash. Govt. Ptg. Off. 1869. 65p.   **3462**

—— —— **Division of bibliography.** Brief list of books on public debts. March 14, 1921. 5p. typ.   **3463**

—— —— —— Brief list of references on paternalism. Nov. 8, 1922. 8p. mim.   **3464**

—— —— —— Brief list of references on the rights of women. April 25, 1922. 5p. typ.   **3465**

—— —— —— List of books on the government and administration of the United States. Dec. 6, 1924. 8p. typ. (Brief list. March 11, 1937. 3p. typ)   **3466**

—— —— —— List of recent references on the budget system. Aug. 31, 1912. 5p. typ.   **3467**

—— —— —— List of references on bureaucracy. Aug. 14, 1922. 4p. typ. (Supplement. Nov. 27, 1931. 8p. typ.)   **3468**

—— —— —— List of references on comparative federal government. May 1, 1918. 6p. typ.   **3469**

—— —— —— List of references on federal, state, and municipal public work departments in the United States and foreign countries. Oct. 13, 1916. 15p. typ.
3470

—— —— —— List of references on governmental accounting and budgeting; national, state, county, municipal. Aug. 23, 1932. 25p. typ.   **3471**

—— —— —— List of references on one chamber and two chamber legislatures. (Supplementary to the list in Special libraries. March 1914) July 28, 1916. 3p. typ. Supplement. April 3, 1937. 15p.   **3472**

—— —— —— List of references on scientific management as the basis of efficiency with special reference to the government service. Oct. 23, 1919. 16p. typ.   **3473**

—— —— —— List of references on trade unions among government employees. Feb. 8, 1916. 6p. typ.   **3474**

—— —— —— List of references relating to public parks in the United States. 1904. 44p. typ.   **3475**

—— —— —— List of writings on political economy and theory, containing discussions of the functions of the state as regards public expenditure and welfare. 1906. 5p. typ. (Additional references. 1912. 2p)   **3476**

—— —— —— Recent books on American government and politics. Feb. 13, 1929. 7p. typ. (Additions. March 23, 1932. Jan. 21, 1933)   **3477**

—— —— —— Select list of foreign views of American institutions. April 22, 1910. 6p. typ.   **3478**

—— —— —— Select list of references on comparative legislation. 1908. 10p. typ.
3479

—— —— —— Select list of references on representative government. July 19, 1911. 6p. typ. (Supplement. March 29, 1920. 4p. typ.)   **3480**

—— —— Select list of recent references on the fee system of paying public officials. June 15, 1912. 6p. typ. **3481**

—— —— Select list of references on the recall. Nov. 2, 1911. 17p. typ. (Recent references. Feb. 27, 1913. 4p. typ.) **3482**

—— —— —— Select list of references on the removal of public officials exclusive of the recall. March 28, 1912. 4p. typ. **3483**

—— —— —— A selected list of references on the cost of government in the United States; federal, state, county and municipal. Oct. 10, 1934. 38p. mim. **3484**

U.S. Office of Education. Public affairs pamphlets; an index to inexpensive pamphlets on social, economic, political and international affairs. Wash. Govt. Ptg. Off. 1937. 95p. Supplement no. 1- Wash. Govt. Ptg. Off. 1938- **3484a**

Virginia. State Library. Political science (general), political theory, miscellaneous. Va. State Lib. bul. III. p128-213. 1910 **3485**

FEDERAL GOVERNMENT

Brookings Institution. Catalog of publications. Wash. D.C. 1937. 39p. **3485a**

California. University. Bureau of public administration. Sources for the study of federal administration. Prep. by Dorothy Campbell Culver. Berkeley. 1940. 25p. mim. **3485b**

Cam, Gilbert A. Reorganization of the administrative agencies of the United States government; a selected reading list. N.Y. New York Pub. Lib. 1937. 7p. (Reprinted from the N.Y. Pub. Lib. bul. XLI. p909-14 (Dec. 1937)) **3485c**

Brown, Everett S. Executive orders; a bibliographical note. Am. pol. science rev. XXIX. p246-9 (April 1935) **3487**

Foster, William Eaton. The literature of civil service reform in the United States Providence, R.I. Providence Press Co. 1881. 15p. **3488**

Griffin, A. P. C. List of references on civil service. (U.S. Civil service Com. Twenty-first rep. 1904) Wash. D.C. 1905. p133-53 **3489**

Institute for Government Research, Washington, D.C. Service monographs of the United States government. Balt. Johns Hopkins Univ. Press. 1918-34. nos. 1-66 (Each volume contains lengthy and useful bibliography) **3490**

St. Louis. Public Library. National parks, national monuments and national forests; a selective list of books, and articles. Comp. by students of the St. Louis Library School. St. Louis Pub. Lib. monthly bul. XXIX. p173-202 (July 1931) **3491**

Sheridan, James W. List of references on the reorganization of the executive departments. Supplementary to the mimeographed lists of November 10, 1925 and

February 1, 1932 of the Division of bibliography, Library of Congress, June 1, 1934. Wash. D.C. 1934. 38p. mim. **3492**

U.S. Bureau of Agricultural Economics. Library. Comment on the Agricultural adjustment administration; a short list of references. [Wash. D.C.] Feb. 14, 1935. 4p. typ. **3493**

U.S. Civil Service Commission. Civil service in periodical literature; a bibliography to and including 1898. (Fifteenth annual rep. 1898) Wash. Govt. Ptg. Off. 1899. p511-17 **3494**

—— —— List of references to history of the merit system. (Twenty-seventh annual rep. 1910) Wash. D.C. 1911. p164-8 **3495**

U.S. Department of Justice. Library and Lands Division. List of the references on the emergency powers of the President to expropriate property in time of war. Comp. by Philip Marcus and Nancy Phelps. Wash. D.C. Nov. 1939. 13p. typ. **3495a**

U.S. Department of the Interior. Magazine articles on national parks, reservations and monuments. Wash. Govt. Ptg. Off. 1911. 15p. **3496**

U.S. Geological Survey. Library. A list of references on the United States Geological Survey and its work. Comp. by James T. Rubey. Wash. D.C. 1934. 21p. mim. **3497**

U.S. Library of Congress. Division of bibliography. The appointing power of the president; a list of references. Nov. 26, 1928. 17p. typ. **3498**

—— —— —— Apportionment of members of the House of Representatives; a list of references. Sept. 17, 1928. 30p. typ. **3499**

—— —— —— Brief list of recent references on federal control. June 9, 1921. 8p. mim. **3500**

—— —— —— Brief list of references on prohibition in the United States. Oct. 28, 1926. 13p. mim. **3501**

—— —— —— Brief list of references on the separation of legislative and judicial powers in the United States; federal and state government. Aug. 4, 1920. 7p. typ. **3502**

—— —— —— Brief list of references on the war powers of Congress. June 9, 1917. 4p. typ. (Additional references. Oct. 1917. 2p.) **3503**

—— —— —— Centralization in the government of the United States, including state rights. Comp. by Ann D. Brown. May 17, 1940. 17p. mim. **3503a**

—— —— —— The Congress of the United States; a bibliographical list. Dec. 21, 1926. 42p. typ. **3504**

—— —— —— A critical bibliography on the vice-presidency of the United States. Jan. 21, 1941. 5p. typ. **3504a**

—— —— —— Federal Farm Board: a bibliographical list. July 31, 1931. 15p. typ. **3505**

U.S. Library of Congress. Division of bibliography. The federal judiciary; a list of recent writings. April 18, 1928. 8p. typ. **3506**

—— —— —— List of books, articles, etc., treating of the United States Senate. (Senate document no. 303. 59 Cong. 1 sess.) Wash. D.C. 1906. 11p. **3507**

—— —— —— List of books on the cabinets of England and America. Wash. Govt. Ptg. Off. 1903. 8p. (Supplement. Nov. 21, 1912. 4p. typ.; Aug. 11, 1922. 14p. mim.; Oct. 26, 1928. 6p.) **3508**

—— —— —— List of books on the rules and procedure of Congress. Dec. 3, 1921. 6p. typ. **3509**

—— —— —— List of books selected to illustrate the work of the Department of the Interior in developing the country. April 30, 1919. 9p. typ. **3510**

—— —— —— List of recent references on cloture with special reference to the Dawes proposition. Dec. 8, 1925. 5p. mim. **3511**

—— —— —— List of recent references on the classification of government positions, with special reference to salary standardization. July 10, 1923. 8p. typ. **3512**

—— —— —— List of recent references on the public lands of the United States (exclusive of public lands leasing and soldiers' settlement on the land). May 9, 1925. 6p. typ. **3513**

—— —— —— List of recent writings on the United States Senate. April 21, 1925. 4p. typ. **3514**

—— —— —— List of references on a national budget (supplementary to bibliography in Willoughby's "Problem of a national budget," 1918) Sept. 13, 1920. 9p. typ. **3515**

—— —— —— List of references on a proposed department of public works. Nov. 10, 1925. 2p. mim. **3516**

—— —— —— List of references on centralization in the government of the United States including state rights. March 4, 1926. 21p. mim. (Supplement. Aug. 14, 1930. 5p.; Additional references. Nov. 27, 1933. 2p.) **3517**

—— —— —— A list of references on civil service. Nov. 22, 1923. 8p. typ. **3518**

—— —— —— List of references on cloture. Nov. 17, 1915. 7p. typ. Dec. 6, 1915. mim. (Supplement. Aug. 8, 1922. 4p. mim.) **3519**

—— —— —— List of references on Congressional government and the electoral system. 1906. 5p. typ. **3520**

—— —— —— A list of references on governmental accounting and budgeting: national, state, county, municipal. Comp. by Florence S. Hellman. 1940. 33p. mim. **3520a**

—— —— —— A list of references on governmental purchasing. Nov. 22, 1923. 5p. typ. **3521**

—— —— —— List of references on leasing of public lands, 1911-1920. April 28, 1920. 8p. typ. **3522**

—— —— —— List of references on postal affairs. 1908. 10p. typ. **3523**

—— —— —— List of references on presidential term. April 10, 1920. 16p. mim. (Supplements. March 4, 1928. 10p. mim.; 1940. 10p. mim.) **3524**

—— —— —— List of references on presidential terms. Senate document no. 19. 70 Cong. 1 sess. 1927. Ser. 8870. p15-23 **3525**

—— —— —— List of references on pure food and drugs legislation in the United States. March 22, 1917. 3p. typ. **3526**

—— —— —— List of references on the administration of customs. Feb. 14, 1922. 14p. multig. **3527**

—— —— —— List of references on the cabinet and congress (This list includes references furnished by Prof. H. B. Learned). Oct. 17, 1917. 5p. typ. (Additional references. 1925. 1p.) **3528**

—— —— —— A list of references on the civil service and personnel administration in the United States: federal, state, and local. Comp. by Ann Duncan Brown under the direction of Florence S. Hellman. Nov. 6, 1936. 91p. reprod. Same. 1939. 55p. **3528a**

—— —— —— List of references on the classification of government positions. June 13, 1919. 8p. typ. **3529**

—— —— —— List of references on the educational activities of the U.S. government, exclusive of the Bureau of Education. Nov. 18, 1920. 3p. typ. **3530**

—— —— —— List of references on the expulsion of senators. Oct. 2, 1917. 2p. typ. **3531**

—— —— —— List of references on the federal civil service. April 28, 1922. 15p. mim. **3532**

—— —— —— List of references on the flag of the United States. July 6, 1922. 17p. typ. (Supplement. 1926. 1p.; Nov. 29, 1930. 9p. typ.) **3533**

—— —— —— List of references on the legislative caucus, chiefly in Congress. Nov. 26, 1913. 18p. mim. **3534**

—— —— —— List of references on the President's Commission on Economy and Efficiency. Oct. 28, 1919. 7p. typ. **3535**

—— —— —— A list of references on the procurement practices of the federal government. July 10, 1934. 14p. typ. **3536**

—— —— —— List of references on the recall of senators. Jan. 30, 1920. 3p. typ. **3537**

—— —— —— List of references on the reorganization of the executive departments. Nov. 10, 1925. 25p. mim. (Supplementary. Feb. 1, 1932. 21p. mim.; April 16, 1936. 46p. mim.) **3538**

—— —— —— List of references on the retirement system for federal employees of the United States. Aug. 15, 1934. 10p. typ. **3539**

—— —— —— List of references on the transfer of the maritime service bureaus to the Navy Department. Sept. 10, 1914. 4p. typ. **3540**

—— —— —— List of references on the United States Civil Service (supplementing the list of references in U.S. Civil Service report, 1904). Dec. 9, 1913. 10p. typ. (Additional references. Aug. 30, 1916. 3p.)   3541

—— —— —— A list of references on the United States Civilian Conservation Corps (supplementary to mimeographed list of June 1937) Comp. by Ann D. Brown. May 6, 1939. 14p. mim.   3541a

—— —— —— List of references on the United States Federal Trade Commission. Jan. 18, 1934. 15p. mim.   3542

—— —— —— List of references on the vice-presidency. July 19, 1916. 4p. typ.   3543

—— —— —— List of references on the war powers of the president. Sept. 24, 1919. 9p. typ.   3544

—— —— —— List of references on women in the federal Civil Service. April 15, 1922. 4p. typ.   3545

—— —— —— List of references relating to existing federal commissions. July 14, 1926. 10p. typ.   3546

—— —— —— List of text books for the use of those proposing to take civil service examination for the diplomatic and consular service. May 12, 1920. 8p. mim.   3547

—— —— —— List of works relating to second class mail matter (Report of the postal commission, 1906-07). Wash. Govt. Ptg. Off. 1907. p843-62 (Also printed as House document no. 608. 59 Cong. 2 sess. Ser. 5201)   3548

—— —— —— List of works relating to second class mail matter; books, articles in periodicals, congressional documents, reports, speeches, and articles in Publishers' weekly. 1906. 9, 5, 12, 2, 11, 6p typ. (List of recent references. Feb. 5, 1921. 9p. typ.)   3549

—— —— —— List of works relating to the House of Representatives. 1907. 24p. typ.   3550

—— —— —— Lobbying; a bibliographical list. Feb. 13, 1933. 18p. typ.   3551

—— —— —— Powers of Congress in investigations to compel the attendance of witnesses, and the production of papers and to punish for contempt. June 16, 1914. 7p. typ.   3552

—— —— —— Presidential term: references supplementing mimeographed list, March 4, 1928. Comp. by Grace H. Fuller. Jan. 10, 1940. 10p. mim.   3552a

—— —— —— Prohibition: a list of recent books. Oct. 2, 1928. 4p. typ.   3553

—— —— —— Secret sessions of the Senate; a bibliographical list. June 5, 1929. 4p. typ.   3554

—— —— —— Select list of references on civil service reform in American municipalities. July 6, 1910. 4p. typ.   3555

—— —— —— Select list of references on impeachment. Comp. under the direction of H. H. B. Meyer. Wash. Govt. Ptg. Off. 1912. 38p. (Supplement. June 11, 1931. 6p.)   3556

—— —— —— Select list of references on the commerce court. Nov. 11, 1912. 11p. typ.   3557

—— —— —— Select list of references on the departments of the United States government. Comp. under the direction of H. H. B. Meyer. Wash. Govt. Ptg. Off. 1911. 54p. (Supplement. May 19, 1915. 15p. typ.)   3559

—— —— —— Select list of references on the parcels post. Comp. under the direction of H. H. B. Meyer. Wash. Govt. Ptg. Off. 1911. 39p.
Same. Sept 2, 1911. 22p. typ. (Supplement. June 29, 1912. 9p. typ.)   3560

—— —— —— Select list of references on the pardoning power; federal and state. 1911. 7p. typ. (Also in Special libraries. III. p16-19. 1912)   3561

—— —— —— Select list of references on the postal service of the United States. Oct. 24, 1911. 31p. typ. (Supplement. May 17, 1923. 32p. typ.; March 9. 1931. 45p typ.)   3562

—— —— —— Select list of references on the public lands of the United States. April 1, 1910. 16p. typ. (Additonal references. March 3, 1915. 4p. typ.)   3563

—— —— —— Select list of references on the rules and procedure of the House of Representatives. Oct. 6, 1913. 13p. typ.   3564

—— —— —— Select list of references on the United States Secret Service. Dec. 24, 1910. 6p. typ. (Additional references. Jan. 14, 1928. 2p.)   3565

—— —— —— A selected list of recent references on federal and state grants-in-aid, including a section on education. Comp. by Grace H. Fuller. Sept. 4, 1940. 28p. mim.   3565a

—— —— —— A selected list of recent references on the cost of government in the United States: federal, state and local (supplement to the mimeographed list of 1934). Comp. by Grace H. Fuller. 1940. 40p. mim.   3565b

—— —— —— A selected list of references on the federal budget. Comp. by Grace H. Fuller. Aug. 21, 1940. 17p. mim.   3565c

—— —— —— The Senate's right to exclude senators elect from their seats, with special reference to corrupt practices; a bibliographical list. Nov. 7, 1930. 13p. typ.   3566

—— —— —— A short list of references on federal aid to specific activities ("dollar matching"). Jan. 8, 1924. 5p. multig. (Supplements. Oct. 7, 1926. 19p. mim.; Aug. 27, 1931. 5p.; Jan. 31, 1935. 44p. typ.)   3567

—— —— —— A short list of references on the proposed department of education. Feb. 19, 1924. 3p. typ.   3568

U.S. Library of Congress. Division of bibliography. Supplementary list of references on postal savings banks. 1909. 13p. typ.   **3569**

—— —— —— Women in the Congress of the United States; a list of references. Dec. 4, 1934. 11p. typ.   **3570**

—— —— —— Youth movements in the United States and foreign countries, including a section on the National Youth Administration. June 12, 1936. 46p. mim.
3571

U.S. National Archives. Card bibliography of the federal government. Wash. The National Archives. In progress   **3571a**

—— —— Card bibliography of the Navy Department and the naval shore establishment. Comp. by Henry P. Beers. Wash. The National Archives   **3571b**

—— —— Card bibliography of the War Department. Wash. The National Archives
3571c

U.S. National Resources Committee. Some recent references (since 1928) on national and state planning in the United States. Comp. by Harold Merrill, James T. Rubey and William Heers. Wash. D.C. Oct. 1935. 24p. mim. (Also U.S. Geol. Survey. Lib. Bibliog. list no. 5)   **3572**

U.S. President's Commission on Economy and Efficiency. Bibliographies of the United States government. [Wash. D.C. 1912?] 462p. typ. (Copy in Brookings Institution Library. Titles are monographic rather than bibliographic)   **3573**

—— Bibliography of congressional inquiries into the conduct of the business of executive departments other than by standing committees of Congress, 1789-1911. *In* Weber, Gustavus A. Organized efforts for the improvement of methods of administration in the United States. N.Y. D. Appleton and Company. 1919. p45-56 (Reprinted from The need for a national budget. (House doc. no. 854, 62 Cong. 2 sess.) Wash. Govt. Ptg. Off. 1912. p477-85)   **3573a**

—— Bibliography of the United States patent office, 1789-1912. *In* Report of the investigation of the United States patent office. (House document no. 1110. 62 Cong. 3 sess.) Wash. D.C. 1912. p519-35   **3574**

U.S. Works Progress Administration. Survey of Federal Archives. Bibliography of the Navy Department and the naval shore establishment. Comp. by Henry P. Beers. Wash. The National Archives. Jan. 30, 1937. 17p. typ.   **3574a**

Washington. State Library. Select list of references on conservation of natural resources. Comp. by Josephine Holgate. Olympia, Wash. 1911. 37p.   **3575**

Women's Auxiliary to the Civil Service Reform Association. Bibliography on civil service reform and related subjects. N.Y. Women's Auxiliary. 1913. 72p.   **3576**

STATE GOVERNMENT

Detroit. Public Library. Unicameral legislatures; a selected list of references on the question, resolved: That the several states should adopt a unicameral form of legislature. Detroit. 1937. 11p. mim.   **3576a**

Hale, Mrs. Carolyn Leavitt. Sources of current information on state government functions. (University of California. M.S. thesis) Berkeley, Calif.? 1939. 113p. typ.
3576b

Public Administration Service. Selected bibliography of materials concerning problems of state government. *In* The book of the states, 1939-40. volume III. Chicago. Council of State Governments. 1939. p313-29   **3576c**

U.S. Library of Congress. Division of bibliography. Additional references on state constitutions; provisions, methods of amendment, etc. April 30, 1914. 3p. typ.
3577

—— —— —— List of publications on publicity for the states. March 3, 1916. 11p. typ.   **3578**

—— —— —— A list of recent writings on state government and its reorganization, with a section on interstate compacts. Oct. 1, 1935. 44p. mim.   **3579**

—— —— —— List of references on commission and similar forms of government for states. June 15, 1922. 6p. mim. **3580**

—— —— —— List of references on state constitutions and their revisions. Aug. 26, 1920. 18p. mim.   **3581**

—— —— —— List of references on state government in the United States. (Emphasis has been placed on text-books). Nov. 2, 1920. 17p. typ.   **3582**

—— —— —— List of references on state police and similar law enforcing organizations. Nov. 17, 1922. 12p. mim.   **3583**

—— —— —— List of references on the admission of new states. 1904. 10p. typ.
3584

—— —— —— List of references on the budgets of the states. July 9, 1924. 13p. mim. (Supplementary to bibliography in W. F. Willoughby's The movement for budgetary reform in the states. N.Y. 1918)   **3585**

—— —— —— Repudiation of state debts; a bibliographical list. May 22, 1930. 10p. typ.   **3586**

—— —— —— Select list of recent references on federal intervention in the states. Nov. 27, 1912. 3p. typ.   **3587**

—— —— —— Select list of recent references state legislatures, with special references to their failure and reform. May 26, 1915. 7p. typ.   **3588**

—— —— —— Short list of references on state control of foreign corporations. Feb. 21, 1929. 4p. typ.   **3589**

COUNTY GOVERNMENT

Baker, Charles M. Select bibliography of American county government. June 1918. 14p. **3590**

California. State Library. Law and legislative reference section. County government bibliography. Sacramento. 1932. 6p. **3591**

New York. Municipal Reference Library. County government; an annotated list of references, June 1, 1915 to December 31, 1931. Comp. by M. Margaret Kehl. N.Y. 1932. 28p. (Reprint from Municipal Reference Lib. notes. XVIII. p17-39. Jan. 27-Feb. 10, 1932) **3592**

New York. Public Library. A list of works on county government, including county publications; references to material in the New York Public Library. Comp. by Rollin A. Sawyer, Jr. N.Y. 1915. 40p. (Reprinted from the Bul. XIX. p433-70. 1915) **3593**

Sawyer, Rollin A. A list of works on county government including county publications. N.Y. Pub. Lib. bul. XIX. p433-70 (May 1915) **3593a**

U.S. Bureau of Agricultural Economics. Land economics division. County planning and zoning; lists of enabling acts and commissions. By C. I. Hendrickson. Wash. D.C. 1936. 30p. mim. **3593b**

U.S. Library of Congress. Division of bibliography. County government and its reorganization in the United States; a bibliographical list of recent writings. Nov. 12, 1934. 31p. mim. (Supplement. June 16, 1937. 16p. mim.) **3594**

—— —— —— A list of recent references on county government in the United States. Comp. by Florence S. Hellman. July 31, 1940. 13p. mim. **3595**

—— —— —— List of references on county government. Aug. 6, 1914. 8p. typ. **3595a**

—— —— —— List of references on county unit. Jan. 30, 1935. 6p. typ. **3596**

CITY GOVERNMENT

Abstracts of water works literature. Am. Water Works Asso. jour. IX. no. 1. Jan. 1922- **3597**

American City Bureau. Selected list of municipal and civic books. N.Y. Am. City Bureau. 1913. 56p. **3598**

Betters, Paul V. List of publications of state leagues of municipalities. (Am. Municipal Asso. Rep. no. 10) Chicago. 1932. 39p. **3599**

Bibliography of municipal government and reform. National Conference for Good City Gov. proc. 1894. I. p341-81 **3600**

Bounds, Rogers J. A bibliography on the reorganization and consolidation of local government. Wash. D.C. 1932. 16p. reprod. from typ. copy **3601**

Brooks, Robert C. A bibliography of municipal problems and city conditions. (Municipal affairs. V. no. 1. March 1901) N.Y. Reform Club, Com. on city affairs. 1901. 346p. **3602**

Brown, Charles Harvey. List of titles on municipal government with special reference to city charters and to local conditions in Chicago. (Chicago City Club. Publication no. 3) Chicago. 1906. 51p. **3603**

Chicago. Municipal Reference Library. Catalogue of the Chicago Municipal Reference Library, 1908. Comp. and issued by Bureau of Statistics and Municipal Library. Chicago. 1908. 149p. **3604**

—— —— Index to municipal legislation: a cumulative, alphabetical subject index of municipal ordinances, proposed or adopted by city councils, boards of aldermen, city commissions and similar bodies, as recorded in their printed official proceedings and journals. Ed. by Frederick Rex. Chicago. 1937. 250p. mim. **3604a**

Chicago. Public Library. Check list of books and pamphlets on municipal government found in the free public libraries of Chicago. Chicago. 1911. 44p. **3605**

Conat, Mabel L. and Leatherman, Marian. Municipal documents and other publications on municipal government in the University of Illinois Library. Univ. of Illinois. bul. May 14, 1917. 49p. **3606**

Detroit. Public Library. Municipal affairs; books and articles in the Detroit Public Library. Detroit. 1902. 44p. **3607**

Hubbard, Theodora Kimball. A brief survey of recent city-planning reports in the United States. Harrisburg, Pa. Lay, Hubbard & Wheelright. 1915. 32p. (Reprint from Landscape architecture. Jan. 1915) **3608**

Meyer, Harold D. Town studies; a program for organizations interested in civic development. (Univ. of North Carolina. Extension bul. II. no. 4. Oct. 16, 1922) Chapel Hill. Univ. of North Carolina Press. 1922. 56p. **3609**

Municipal index; an index to all articles of importance on municipal subjects published between August 1912 and December 1917. . . . N.Y. Municipal jour. 1914-18 **3610**

Municipal index; a yearbook for city, town and county officials 1924. N.Y. The Am. city magazine. 1924- **3611**

Municipal index, in which are listed and classified all articles treating of municipal topics appearing in the leading periodicals. N.Y. Municipal jour. 1907 **3612**

Munro, William Bennett. A bibliography of municipal government in the United States. Cambridge. Harvard Univ. Press. London. Humphrey Milford, Oxford Univ. Press. 1915. 472p. **3613**

National Fire Protection Association. Publications on the subject of fire prevention and fire protection, available in the files and index to subjects covered in the printed records. Boston. 1926. 87p. **3614**

National Municipal League. Recent books reviewed. National municipal rev. I. Jan. 1912-   **3615**

National Resources Committee. Classified guide to material in the Library of Congress covering urban community development; a reference classification of subject headings used in the dictionary catalogues of the Library of Congress. Wash. D.C. March 1936. 102p. mim. **3616**

New York. Municipal Administration Service. Library. Selected list of recent municipal research reports. (Statistical ser. no. 4) N.Y. 1931. 8p.   **3617**

New York. Municipal Reference Library. Classified list of recent additions, current civic literature. Municipal reference lib. notes. I- 1914-   **3618**

—— List of works relating to public health in the Municipal Reference Library of the city of New York. N.Y. 1914   **3619**

New York. Public Library. Check list of American municipal official documents relating to finance in the New York Public Library. N.Y. Pub. Lib. bul. VI. p314-27 (Aug. 1902)   **3620**

—— List of works on city wastes and street hygiene in the New York Public Library. N.Y. Pub. Lib. bul. XVI. p731-83 (Oct. 1912)   **3621**

—— List of works relating to city charters, ordinances, and collected documents. N.Y. 1913. 383p. (Reprinted from Bul. XVI-XVII. 1912-13)   **3622**

—— Recent accessions of city documents. N.Y. Pub. Lib. bul. XVI-XVIII (Jan. 1912-Aug. 1914)   **3623**

New York. State Library. Legislative reference section. Bibliography of municipal ownership. Comp. by N. R. Levin. Albany. 1918. 50p. typ.   **3624**

Pittsburgh. Carnegie Library. Reference list: refuse and garbage disposal. By C. W. Holmes. Carnegie Lib. monthly bul. XIV. p3-34 (Jan. 1909)   **3625**

—— Sewage disposal and treatment, references to books and magazine articles. Pittsburgh. 1910. 96p. (Reprinted from the Monthly bul. XV. p488-578. Nov. 1910)   **3625a**

Rider, H. A. Direct labor versus contract system in municipal work; a bibliography. Special libraries. VIII. p101-4 (June 1916)   **3626**

Seattle. Public Library. Municipal government; a list of books and references to periodicals in the Seattle Public Library. (Reference list no. 4) Seattle. 1911. 31p.   **3627**

Special Libraries Association. Special committee on municipal documents. Basic list of current municipal documents; a check-list of official publications issued periodically since 1927 by the larger cities of the United States and Canada. N.Y. 1932. 71p.   **3628**

Sweeney, Helen B. Bibliography. *In* Zueblin, Charles. American municipal progress. N.Y. Macmillan. 1922. p429-95   **3629**

Syracuse. Public Library. List of books on municipal affairs and civic improvement in the Syracuse Public Library. Syracuse, N.Y. 1911. 64p.   **3630**

U.S. Library of Congress. Division of bibliography. Brief list of recent references on metropolitan areas. Feb. 13, 1932. 4p. typ.   **3631**

—— —— Community centers; a bibliographical list. July 15, 1930. 15p. mim.   **3632**

—— —— List of recent references on municipal home rule. Dec. 12, 1921. 6p. mim.   **3643**

—— —— List of references on city missions and relations of churches to city problems. Jan. 16, 1914. 4p. typ.   **3634**

—— —— List of references on community centers, their organization and application to war work. Feb 8, 1918. 8p. dupl. (Also in Special libraries. IX. p149-53. June 1918)   **3635**

—— —— List of references on condemnation of land with special reference to excess condemnation and municipal ownership. May 2, 1922. 13p. mim.   **3636**

—— —— List of references on fire prevention. (Supplementary to list printed in Special libraries, Feb. 1913). Aug. 20, 1915. 9p. typ. (Additional references. 1918. 3p.)   **3637**

—— —— List of references on fire protection. 1913. 19p. (Also in Special libraries. IV. no. 2. p28-42. Feb. 1913)   **3638**

—— —— List of references on mayoralty government of cities. May 19, 1920. 6p. mim.   **3639**

—— —— List of references on municipal accounting. June 24, 1914. 12p. typ. (Also in Special libraries. VI. p63-77. April 1915) (Recent references. Aug. 12, 1919. 3p. typ.)   **3640**

—— —— List of references on municipal auditoriums. March 11, 1926. 5p. typ.   **3641**

—— —— List of references on municipal finance and taxation. June 23, 1920. 25p. mim.   **3642**

—— —— List of references on municipal gas and water supply. n.d. 5p. typ.   **3643**

—— —— List of references on municipal markets. March 8, 1915. 5p. typ.   **3644**

—— —— List of references on municipal ownership of gas and electric lighting plants. June 23, 1915. 8p. typ.   **3645**

—— —— List of references on municipal pensions (exclusive of teachers' pensions). Oct. 29, 1922. 7p. typ. (Supplement. Aug. 13, 1934. 6p. typ.)   **3646**

—— —— List of references on sewage and sewage disposal. July 19, 1922. 16p. typ.   **3647**

—— —— —— List of references on special assessments for municipal improvements (supplementary to the typewritten list, Oct. 4, 1911). Nov. 16, 1916. 5p. typ. (Supplement. Nov. 16, 1916. 5p. typ.; additional references. Nov. 11, 1926. 3p.) **3648**

—— —— —— List of references on the city manager plan. Nov. 28, 1914. 4p. typ. (Supplementary lists. March 11, 1916. 10p. typ.; Jan. 24, 1919. 15p. typ.; Jan. 28, 1920. 13p. mim.; Jan. 20, 1927. 13p. mim) **3649**

—— —— —— List of references on the consolidation of city and county government. July 10, 1925. 10p. typ. **3650**

—— —— —— List of references on the budgets of cities. June 22, 1914. 12p. mim. (Same in Special libraries. VI. p49-56. March 1915) **3651**

—— —— —— List of references on the municipal police. Dec. 10, 1920. 16p. mim. **3652**

—— —— —— List of references on traffic control in cities. June 23, 1915. 9p. typ. (Also in Special libraries. VI. p163-70. Dec. 1915; Supplement. March 8, 1922. 14p. mim.) **3653**

—— —— —— List of references on traffic regulations (Supplementary to list printed in Special libraries. Nov. 15, 1915) March 8, 1922. 14p. mim. **3654**

—— —— —— Select list of books on municipal affairs with special reference to municipal ownership. Comp. under the direction of A. P. C. Griffin. Wash. Govt. Ptg. Off. 1906. 34p. **3655**

—— —— —— Select list of references on commission government for cities. Comp. under the direction of H. H. B. Meyer. Wash. Govt. Ptg. Off. 1913. 70p. (Supplements. Feb. 4, 1915. 5p. typ.; Oct. 8, 1917. 8p. typ.; Feb. 21, 1920. 13p. mim.) **3656**

—— —— —— Select list of references on fire prevention (typewritten). April 20, 1912. 18p. typ. **3657**

—— —— —— Select list of references on playgrounds. April 9, 1913. 11p. typ. **3658**

—— —— —— Select list of references on public playgrounds. 1909. 6p. typ. **3659**

—— —— —— Select list of references on the problems of city life. July 11, 1912. 8p. typ. **3660**

—— —— —— Select list of references on the work of women in civic reform. May 16, 1914. 4p. typ. **3661**

—— —— —— A selected list of references on municipal government in the United States. Comp. by Ann D. Brown. Nov. 12, 1938. 57p. mim. **3661a**

U.S. National Resources Committee. Classified guide to material in the Library of Congress covering urban community development; a reference classification of subject headings used in the dictionary catalogues of the Library of Congress. Comp. by Eric D. Bovet. Wash. D.C. 1936. 102p. mim. **3661b**

U.S. Work Projects Administration. District of Columbia. Bibliography of air raid precautions and civil defense. Wash. D.C. 1941. 343p. **3661c**

Upson, Lent D. A syllabus of municipal administration. Detroit. Bureau of Governmental Research, Inc. 1923. 66p. **3662**

CITY PLANNING AND IMPROVEMENT

Brooklyn. Public Library. City planning and beautifying; a selected list of books and of references to periodicals. Brooklyn, N.Y. 1912. 15p. **3663**

Chicago. Bureau of Social Surveys. Selected bibliography on housing, zoning and city planning in Chicago. Chicago. 1926. 19p. **3664**

Detroit. Public Library. Civics division. A selected list of references on slum clearance and low-cost housing. Detroit. 1935. 16p. mim. **3665**

Hayes, Zella M. Bibliography of regional planning. Bul. bibliog. XIII. p65-9 (Sept.-Dec. 1927) **3666**

Hubbard, Theodora K. and McNamara, Katherine. Planning information, up-to-date; a supplement 1923-1928 to Kimball's manual of information on city planning and zoning. Cambridge. Harvard Univ. Press. 1928. 103p. **3667**

Jenkins, F. W. Recent books and reports on housing and town planning. Housing betterment. IX. p60-71, 172-81 (Feb.-May 1920); X. 288-304 (Sept. 1921) **3668**

Kansas City. Public Library. Bibliography of municipal betterment. Kansas City Pub. Lib. quar. VIII. p21-71 (April 1908) **3669**

Kimball, Theodora. Bibliography; a selected list of references covering the field of city planning. *In* Manual of information on city planning and zoning including references on regional, rural, and national planning. Cambridge. Harvard Univ. Press. 1923. p53-188 **3670**

—— Classified selected list of references on city planning. Boston. National Conference on City Planning. 1915. 48p. **3671**

—— Streets; their arrangement, lighting and planning. Special libraries. VI. p42-8 (March 1915) **3672**

McClelland, Ellwood H. Bibliography of smoke and smoke prevention. (Univ. of Pittsburgh. Mellon Inst. of Industrial Research and School of Specific Industries. Smoke investigation bul. no. 2) Pittsburgh. 1913. 164p. **3673**

McNamara, Katherine. Bibliography of planning, 1928-1935; a supplement to manual of planning information, 1928 by Mrs. Theodora Kimball Hubbard and Katherine McNamara. (Harvard city planning stud. X) Cambridge. Harvard Univ. Press. 1936. 232p. **3674**

—— List of plan reports in the United States, 1928-1933. City planning. V-X (April 1929-April 1934) **3675**

National Housing Association. Recent books and reports on housing, zoning and town planning. (National Housing Asso. publication 59) N.Y. 1929. 33p. **3676**

New York. Public Library. Select list of works relating to city planning and allied subjects. N.Y. 1913. 35p. (Reprinted from Bul. XVII. p930-60. Nov. 1913) **3677**

Pittsburgh. Carnegie Library. Reference list; smoke prevention. Monthly bul. XII. p195-212 (May 1907) **3678**

Pray, James S. and Kimball, Theodora. City planning; a comprehensive analysis of the subject arranged for the classification of books, plans, photographs, notes and other collected material, with alphabetic subject index. Cambridge. Harvard Univ. press. 1913. 103p. **3679**

Rider. H. A. Bibliography on residential and industrial districts in cities. Special libraries. VII. p2-7 (Jan. 1916) **3680**

U.S. Library of Congress. Division of bibliography. Brief list of references on city planning. Jan. 12, 1917. 4p. typ. (Recent references. March 14, 1922. 12p. typ.) **3681**

—— —— —— **and Harvard university. Department of landscape architecture.** Check list of references on city planning. Special libraries. III. p61-123 (May 1912) **3682**

U.S. Work Projects Administration. Urban housing: a summary of real property inventories conducted as work projects, 1934-1936. By Peyton Stapp. Wash. Supt. of Doc. 1938. 326p. **3682a**

Walker, Ella K. City planning; bibliography of material in the University of California and Oakland and Berkeley public libraries. Berkeley City Club civic bul. March 14, 1914. p117-52 **3683**

ELECTIONS

Boston. Public Library. Presidential elections; selected titles of books in the public library of the city of Boston. (Brief reading list no. 17. Aug. 1920) Boston. 1920. 18p. **3684**

Detroit. Public Library. Preferential voting, Municipal ownership; selected bibliographies. Detroit. 1914. 14p. **3685**

Franklin, Margaret Ladd. The case for woman suffrage; a bibliography with an introduction by M. Carey Thomas. N.Y. Pub. by the National College Equal Suffrage League, sold by the National Am. Suffrage Asso. 1913. 315p. **3686**

John Randolph Haynes and Dora Haynes Foundation. Library. Initiative and referendum: a bibliography. Comp. by Josephine Ver Brugge Zeitlin. Los Angeles. 1940. 97p. photop. **3686a**

New York. State Library. Legislative reference bureau. Bibliography of books and articles on initiative, referendum and recall, 1912-1924. By Edith N. Snow. Albany. 1924. 13p. typ. **3687**

U.S. Library of Congress. Division of bibliography. A chronological conspectus of Congressional documents on the election of president of the United States, including documents on the presidential succession. Aug. 22, 1924. 17p. typ. **3688**

—— —— —— A chronological conspectus of debats (sic) in Congress on the election of president of the United States, including references to debates on the presidential succession. Aug. 16, 1924. 19p. typ. **3689**

—— —— —— Elections in the United States; a brief bibliographical list. Jan. 28, 1929. 4p. typ. **3690**

—— —— —— List of books (with references to periodicals) relating to proportional representation. Comp. under the direction of A. P. C. Griffin. Wash. Govt. Ptg. Off. 1904. 30p. (Supplement. 1905. 3p. typ.; 1910. 10p. typ.; 1914. 2p; List. . . 1910-1919. Feb. 17, 1920. 11p. typ.; List. . . 1920-1934. March 27, 1934. 9p. typ.) **3691**

—— —— —— List of discussions, etc., of property qualifications for voting. 1907. 3p. typ. **3692**

—— —— —— List of documents on contested elections in Congress. June 3, 1931. 7p. typ. **3693**

—— —— —— List of recent references on the selection of judges; election vs. appointment (supplementary to typewritten list of March 2, 1927). Jan. 17, 1939. 11p. photostat **3693a**

—— —— —— List of references on absent voting, including voting by proxy and voting by mail. July 3, 1915. 6p. typ. **3694**

—— —— —— List of references on ballot reform, exclusive of the short ballot. Oct. 16, 1915. 9p. typ. **3695**

—— —— —— List of references on compulsory voting. Oct. 5, 1925. 12p. mim. **3696**

—— —— —— List of references on primary election laws. Nov. 22, 1920. 9p. mim. (Supplements. Aug. 25, 1922. 4p. mim.; Sept. 13, 1926. 7p. mim.; Aug. 31, 1928. 9p. mim.) **3697**

—— —— —— List of references on primary elections, particularly direct primaries. Comp. under the direction of A. P. C. Griffin. Wash. Govt. Ptg. Off. 1905. 25p. **3698**

—— —— —— List of references on the educational qualifications for suffrage. April 14, 1925. 6p. typ. **3699**

—— —— —— List of references on the election versus appointment of judges. March 2, 1925. 8p. typ. **3700**

—— —— —— List of references on the electoral college, with emphasis on the substitution of direct vote by the people for the electoral college. Comp. by Grace Hadley Fuller. Jan. 18, 1937. 17p. **3701**

—— —— —— List of references on the popular election of senators. Comp. under the direction of A. P. C. Griffin. Wash. Govt. Ptg. Off. 1904. 39p. (Supplement. Sept. 9, 1910. 7p. typ.; 1911. p43-55)   **3702**

—— —— —— Select list of references on corrupt practices in elections. Comp. under the direction of A. P. C. Griffin. Wash. Govt. Ptg. Off. 1908. 12p.   **3703**

—— —— —— Select list of references on preferential voting and the transferable vote. Feb. 27, 1912. 10p. mim.   **3704**

—— —— —— Short list of references on the election of president of the United States. Aug. 19, 1924. 7p. mim.   **3705**

—— —— —— Select list of references on the initiative, referendum and recall. Comp. under the direction of H. H. B. Meyer. Wash. Govt. Ptg. Off. 1912. 102p. (Supplements. Jan. 30, 1914. 7p. typ.; Feb. 28, 1924. 4p. typ.; Oct. 28, 1926. 6p. typ.; July 16, 1934. 6p. typ.)   **3706**

—— —— —— List of references on the presidential primaries. Dec. 7, 1920. 7p. typ.   **3707**

—— —— —— Select list of references on the short ballot (Supplementing the select list of references on the short ballot printed in "Special libraries," May 1911). Nov. 23, 1914. 4p. (List of references. . . 1915-1926. Sept. 4, 1926. 4p. typ.)   **3708**

—— —— —— Select list of references on woman suffrage. Nov. 22, 1913. 18p. typ. (Recent references. Nov. 18, 1919. 7p. typ.)   **3709**

—— —— —— A selected list of references on primaries. June 17, 1931. 18p. typ.   **3710**

—— —— —— The short ballot; select list of references. By H. H. B. Meyer . . . with the co-operation of state libraries, state legislative reference departments and the Ohio State University Library. Columbus, Ohio. F. J. Heer. 1912. 8p.   **3711**

PUBLIC OPINION

American Civil Liberties Union. List of pamphlets, books, leaflets on civil liberty. N.Y. Am. Civil Liberties Union. 1927. 8p.   **3712**

Childs, Harwood L. A reference guide to the study of public opinion. Princeton University, School of Public and International Affairs. Princeton. Princeton Univ. press. 1934. 105p.   **3713**

Dale, Edgar and Vernon, Norma. Propaganda analysis: an annotated bibliography. (Ohio State University. Bur. of Educational Research. ser. 1, vol. 1, no. 2) Columbus, Ohio. 1940. 29p.   **3713a**

Lasswell, Harold D., Casey, Ralph D. and Smith, Bruce Lannes. Propaganda and promotional activities. Prepared under the direction of the Social Science Re-

search Council, advisory committee on pressure groups and propaganda. Minneapolis. Univ. of Minnesota Press. 1935. 450p.   **3714**

Schroeder, T. A. Free speech bibliography, including every discovered attitude toward the problem, covering every method of transmitting ideas and of abridging their promulgation upon every subject-matter. N.Y. H. W. Wilson; London. Grafton & Co. 1922. 247p.   **3715**

Smith, Bruce Lannes. Bibliography. [A continuation of: Lasswell, H.D. and others. Propaganda and promotional activities: an annotated bibliography. Minneapolis. 1935] Pub. opin. quar. I. Jan. 1937-   **3715a**

U.S. Library of Congress. Division of bibliography. Freedom of speech and the press; brief bibliography of recent writings. April 14, 1930. 8p. typ. (Additional references. Dec. 22, 1932. 2p.) Supplement. 1938. 27p. mim.   **3716**

—— —— —— List of references on extreme radicalism. April 24, 1920. 9p. typ. (Supplement. April 27, 1923. 3p. typ.)   **3717**

—— —— —— List of references on freedom of the press and speech, and censorship in time of war (with special reference to the European war). April 20, 1917. 8p. typ.   **3718**

—— —— —— List of references on liberty in the United States. March 13, 1935. 9p. typ.   **3719**

—— —— —— List of references on political and social psychology. Dec. 22, 1922. 7p. mim.   **3720**

—— —— —— List of references on publicity with special reference to press agents. Aug. 2, 1921. 5p. typ.   **3721**

—— —— —— List of references on the liberty of the press. 1906. 9p. typ. (Additional references. 1911. 2p.)   **3722**

—— —— —— Public relations: a selected list of references. Comp. by Helen G. Dudenbostel. 1940. 34p. typ.   **3722a**

—— —— —— Publicity and public opinion; a list of books. May 15, 1930. 9p. typ.   **3723**

—— —— —— A selected list of references on freedom of speech and the press. Supplement. Comp. by Grace H. Fuller. June 29, 1938. 27p. mim.   **3723a**

Young, Kimball and Lawrence, Raymond D. Bibliography on censorship and propaganda. (Univ. of Oregon Publication. March 1928. Journalism ser. I. no. 1) Eugene, Ore. The Univ. [1928] 133p.   **3724**

CONSTITUTIONAL

Barnwell, James G. Reading notes on the Constitution of the United States. Bul. of the Lib. Co. of Phila. n.s. no. 19. xv p. (July 1887) (Also separately printed. 1887)   **3725**

Carter, Edward W. and Rohlfing, Charles C. The Constitution of the United States; a bibliography. Am. Acad. of Pol. and Social Science ann. CLXXXV. p190-200 (May 1936)   **3726**

Ford, Paul Leicester. Bibliography and reference list of the history and literature relating to the adoption of the Constitution of the United States, 1787-1788. Brooklyn, N.Y. 1888. 61p. (Also in Ford, P. L. Pamphlets on the Constitution of the United States. Brooklyn, N.Y. 1888. p383-441; and in Curtis, George T. Constitutional history of the United States from their Declaration of Independence to the close of their Civil War. N.Y. Harper & Bros. 1897. p708-66)   **3727**

Foster, William E. References to the Constitution of the United States. (Economic tracts no. XXIX) N.Y. Soc. for Pol. Educ. 1890. 50p.   **3728**

Glasier, Gilson G. A bibliography on the constitutional aspects of the recovery program. Law lib. jour. XXVIII. p9-27 (Jan. 1935)   **3728a**

Griswold, Stephen B. List of constitutional convention journals, debates and proceedings, constitutions and ordinances, contained in the [New York state] law library, September 30, 1887. N.Y. State Lib. seventieth annual rep. 1887. p147-56   **3729**

Haines, Charles Grove. Histories of the Supreme Court of the United States written from the Federalist point of view. Reprinted from the Southwestern pol. and social science quar. IV. no. I. June 1923. 35p. Austin, Texas   **3730**

Henry E. Huntington Library and Art Gallery. The Constitution of the United States; an exhibition on the 150th anniversary of its formation. San Marino. The Lib. 1937. 25p.   **3730a**

Howard, George E. Comparative federal institutions; an analytical reference syllabus. (University of Nebraska. Dept. of pol. science and sociology. Publication no. 2) [Lincoln, Neb.] The Univ. 1907. 133p.   **3731**

Kimball, Reginald Stevens. A selected bibliography of works helpful in teaching the constitution of the United States. Hist. outlook. XVI. p211-16 (May 1925)   **3732**

Mead, Edwin D. The Constitution of the United States with bibliographical and historical notes, and outlines for study (Old South manuals). Boston. Old South Meeting House. 1887. 45p.   **3733**

Nicholson, Mrs. Dorothy (Campbell) and Graves, Richard P. Selective bibliography on the operation of the Eighteenth amendment. [Berkeley] Univ. of California, Bureau of Pub. Administration. 1931. 47p. mim.   **3733a**

Pennsylvania. Historical Commission. Constitution bibliography. Harrisburg. Dept. of Public Instruction. 1938. 14p.   **3733b**

Pennsylvania. Historical Society. The Constitution of the United States, its origin, formation, and adoption, as set forth in an exhibit of books, pamphlets, and documents from the collections of the Historical Society of Pennsylvania, display'd in commemoration of the one hundred and fiftieth anniversary of its signing on September 17, 1787. Phila. Hist. Soc. of Pennsylvania. 1937. 35p.   **3733c**

Perry, D. Bibliography on the constitutional aspects of the recovery program. Law lib. jour. XXVIII. p9-27 (Jan. 1935)   **3733d**

Philadelphia. Library Company. Exhibition of books and manuscripts in commemoration of the one hundred and fiftieth anniversary of the signing of the Constitution of the United States of America, September 17th, 1787. Phila. Library Company of Phila. 1937. 28p.   **3733e**

Reuschlein, H. G. A sesqui-centennial bibliography, some books about the Constitution, its makers and its interpreters. Georgetown law jour. XXVII. p1149-68 (June 1939)   **3733f**

Rosenbach, A. S. W. Historical documents commemorating the 150th anniversary of the Constitution of the United States, presented for public exhibition to S. Davis Wilson, mayor of the city of Philadelphia . . . Phila. Free Lib. of Phila. 1937. 28p.   **3733g**

Senior, Mildred R. The Supreme Court: its power of judicial review with respect to congressional legislation; selected references. (George Washington University. Publications of the Division of Library Science) Wash. D.C. 1937. 75p.   **3733h**

Snow, Freeman. A guide to the study of the constitutional and political history of the United States, 1789-1860; intended as the basis of a course of lectures or of a course of private study. Cambridge, Mass. W. H. Wheeler. 1882-83. 215, 43p.   **3734**

U.S. Library of Congress. Division of bibliography. The bill of rights; a bibliographical list. March 30, 1927. 6p. typ.   **3735**

—— —— —— Brief list of references on the religious test clause of the Constitution of the United States (Article VI, clause 3, and amendment I). Dec. 19, 1921. 7p. typ.   **3736**

—— —— —— List of books on secession and right of states to secede published during the last 15 years. April 21, 1914. 3p. typ.   **3737**

—— —— —— List of discussions of the fourteenth and fifteenth amendments with special references to Negro suffrage. Comp. under the direction of A. P. C. Griffin. Wash. Govt. Ptg. Off. 1906. 18p.   **3738**

—— —— —— List of references on amending the federal constitution by direct vote of the people. April 26, 1923. 3p. typ.   **3739**

—— —— —— List of references on judicial legislation by decisions of the United States Supreme Court declaring laws unconstitutional. Dec. 1, 1922. 11p. multig. (Supplement. Jan. 29, 1924. 10p. mim.) **3740**

—— —— —— List of references on proposed methods of amendment of the Constitution of the United States. March 7, 1925. 56p. typ. **3741**

—— —— —— List of references on the eighteenth amendment and its enforcement. Aug. 19, 1920. 8p. typ. (Same. Oct. 26, 1922. 14p. typ.; Supplement. Oct. 10, 1925. 8p. typ.) **3742**

—— —— —— List of references on the enforcement of the 18th amendment on the high seas within and without the three mile limit. May 10, 1923. 4p. typ. **3743**

—— —— —— List of references on the equal rights amendment proposed by the National Woman's Party. Nov. 15, 1923. 3p. typ. **3744**

—— —— —— List of references on the modification or repeal of the eighteenth amendment. Dec. 2, 1930. 16p. mim. (Supplement. Oct. 3, 1932. 18p. mim.) **3745**

—— —— —— List of references on the nineteenth amendment to the Constitution of the United States. Sept. 26, 1929. 12p. typ. **3746**

—— —— —— List of references on the popular election of supreme court judges, state and federal. Jan. 11, 1924. 5p. multig. **3747**

—— —— —— List of references on the proposed amendment to the Constitution of the U.S. giving Congress power to review decisions of the Supreme Court on constitutional questions. May 9, 1923. 4p. mim. **3748**

—— —— —— List of references on the revenue raising clause of the Constitution of the United States (Articles I, section 7, clause 1). Dec. 7, 1926. 7p. typ. **3749**

—— —— —— List of references on the Supreme Court of the United States with particular reference to the doctrine of judicial review. Nov. 26, 1935. 17p. mim. **3750**

—— —— —— List of speeches, etc., on the United States Supreme Court issue as printed in the Congressional Record, 75th Congress, first session, v. 81, current file. Comp. by Anne L. Baden. [Wash. 1937] 29p. reprod. **3750a**

—— —— —— List of works relating to the Supreme Court of the United States. Comp. under the direction of H. H. B. Meyer. Wash. Govt. Ptg. Off. 1909. 124p. (Supplement. Aug. 26, 1912. 7p. typ.; July 28, 1916. 6p. typ.; Dec. 14, 1922. 8p. multig.) **3751**

—— —— —— The proposed child labor amendment to the Constitution of the United States; a selected list of references. Feb. 19, 1934. 10p. typ. (Supplement. Nov. 1, 1935. 10p) **3752**

—— —— —— References on God and Jesus Christ in the Constitution of the United States. April 12, 1915. 2p. typ. **3753**

—— —— —— Select list of books on the Constitution of the United States. Comp. under the direction of A.P.C. Griffin. Wash. Govt. Ptg Off. 1903. 14p. (Supplement. March 24, 1920. 8p. typ.; Feb. 13, 1924. 2p. mim.; 1932. 2p.) **3754**

—— —— —— Select list of references on the constitutional law of the United States. June 6, 1913. 4p. typ. (Additional references. May 11, 1933. 2p.) **3755**

—— —— —— Select list of references on the revision of the Federal Constitution. Oct. 20, 1910. 7p. typ. **3756**

—— —— —— A selected list of recent references on the Constitution of the United States. Comp. by Grace H. Fuller. April 5, 1940. 50p. mim. **3756a**

—— —— —— A selected list of references on the Bill of Rights. Comp. by Grace H. Fuller. April 3, 1940. 21p. mim. **3756b**

—— —— —— A selected list of references on the Constitution of the United States, with special reference to present day problems. Sept. 25, 1935. 28p. mim. **3757**

—— —— —— A selected list of references on the constitutional powers of the president of the United States, including powers recently delegated. Nov. 15, 1933. 30p. mim. **3758**

—— —— —— Selected list on constitutional history. 1901. 7p. typ. **3759**

—— —— —— The Supreme Court issue: a selected list of references. Comp. by Florence S. Hellman. March 9, 1938. 42p. reprod. **3759a**

Washington, D.C. Public Library. Books on the Constitution of the United States; a selected list. (Reference list no. 25) Wash. Govt. Ptg. Off. 1930. 9p. **3760**

Wire, G. E. Index to memoirs, orders and rules of court, admissions to the bar and other interesting material found in United States Supreme Court reports, volumes one to two-hundred and ninety-one, inclusive. Law lib. jour. XXVIII. p27-39 (Jan. 1935) **3761**

Winsor, Justin. Editorial notes on the sources of information—The Constitution of the United States. *In* Narrative and critical history of America. Boston, N.Y. Houghton Mifflin. 1888. VII. p255-66 **3762**

POLITICAL

Adams, Frederick Baldwin. Radical literature in America; an address to which is appended a catalogue of an exhibition held at the Grolier club in New York city. Stamford, Conn. Overbrook. 1939. p39-62 **3762a**

American Political Science Association. Recent publications of political interest, books and periodicals. Am. pol. science rev. I. Nov. 1906- **3763**

Anderson Auction Co. Catalogue of a unique collection of pamphlets arranged to illustrate the progress and development of political history in the United States, Part I, 1685 to 1853. N.Y. Anderson Auction Co. 1903. 87p.   **3764**

Boon, Edward P. Catalogue of political pamphlets embracing the period between 1789 and 1879. N.Y. Holt Bros. 1880. 58p.   **3765**

Boyd, William Kenneth. Political writing since 1850. *In* The Cambridge history of American literature. Ed. by William P. Trent and others. N.Y. G. P. Putnam's. 1921. III. p337-66; IV. p782-4   **3766**

Bradley, Phillips. Literature of American politics and government, 1939 and 1940. Soc. educa. V. p118-27 (Feb. 1941) **3766a**
—— The literature of politics, 1934. The social stud. XXVI. p166-89 (March 1935)   **3767**

—— The literature of politics—1935 and 1936. Soc. educ. I. p190-200, 273-81 (March, April 1937)   **3767a**

Carpenter, Niles H. Literature of guild socialism. Quar. jour. econ. XXXIV. p763-75 (Aug. 1920)   **3767b**

Commonwealth College. Library. A list of recent references on a farmer-labor party. Comp. by students of the college under the direction of Henry Black. Mena, Ark. 1936. 8p. mim.   **3767c**

Griswold, William McCrillis. An alphabetical index to the political contents of "The Nation" (with occasional references to other works) forming a record of politics and politicians in the United States, 1865-1882. n.p. 1883. 40p.   **3768**

Hasse, Adelaide Rosalie. List of books and some articles in periodicals in the New York Public Library, relating to political rights, constitutions and constitutional law. N.Y. Pub. Lib. bul. VIII. p22-36 (Jan. 1904)   **3769**

Hayden, Ralston. Topical reading list on the political and constitutional history of the United States for the use of students in history, fourteen and fifteen, University of Michigan. Ann Arbor, Mich. G. Wahr. 1912. 151p.   **3770**

Howard, George E. Present political questions; an analytical reference syllabus. Lincoln, Neb. The Univ. [of Nebraska] 1913. 184p.   **3771**

Hyneman, C. S. Recent publications of political interest. Am. pol. sci. rev. XXXI. p. 580-609 (June 1937)   **3771a**

Indiana. University. Extension division. An outline for the study of current political, economic, and social problems, with bibliographies. (Indiana Univ. Bul. XII. no. 7) Bloomington, Ind. The Univ. 1914. 77p.   **3772**

Jameson, J. Franklin. Bibliographical— Proceedings, etc., of early party conventions. Am. hist. rev. I. p760-72 (July 1896) (Also reprinted. N.Y. Macmillan. 1896)   **3773**

Kerr, Charles H. What to read on socialism. Chicago. C. H. Kerr & Company. 1910. 60p.   **3773a**

Library Employees' Union of Greater New York. Industrial democracy, 1848-1919; a study help. [N.Y.] Am. Federation of Labor. 1919. 34p.   **3774**

McLaughlin, Andrew Cunningham. Publicists and orators, 1800-1850. *In* The Cambridge history of American literature. Ed. by William P. Trent. N.Y. G. P. Putnam's. 1918. II. p70-91, 468-80   **3775**

Malin, James C. Notes on the literature of Populism. The Kan. hist. quar. I. p160-4 (Feb. 1932)   **3776**

New York. Public Library. Political parties in the United States, 1800-1914; a list of references. By Alta Blanche Claflin. N.Y. N. Y. Pub. Lib. 1915. 74p. (Reprinted from the Bul. XIX. p646-718. Sept. 1915)   **3777**

—— Recent publications of political interest. Am. pol. sci. rev. I- . (Nov. 1906- .)   **3777a**

Ringwalt, Ralph Curtis. Briefs on public questions, with selected lists of references. N.Y. Longmans, Green and Co. 1911. 229p.   **3778**

Rosenbach, A. S. W. An exhibition to celebrate the Democratic national convention, opening June 23, 1936; great documents of the Democratic presidents from the collections of Dr. A. S. W. Rosenbach. [Phila.] The Free Lib. of Phila. 1936. 16p.   **3778a**

—— An exhibition to celebrate the Republican national convention, opening June 9, 1936; the Republican party; its history recorded by original documents from the collection of Dr. A. S. W. Rosenbach. [Phila.] The Free Lib. of Phila. 1936. 16p.   **3778b**

Rusk, Robert Leslie. Controversial writings [bibliography]. *In* The literature of the middle western frontier. N.Y. Columbia Univ. Press. 1925. II. p185-280   **3779**

Stephenson, Orland W. and Russell, Nelson Vance. Topical reading outline for a study of the political and constitutional history of the United States, 1760 to 1850. Ann Arbor, Mich. George Wahr. 1924. 188p.   **3780**

Sutton, Roberta Briggs. Speech index; an index to 64 collections of world famous orations and speeches for various occasions. N.Y. H. W. Wilson. 1935. 272p.   **3781**

U.S. Library of Congress. Division of bibliography. Brief list of books on political parties before 1865. Nov. 30, 1921. 4p. typ.   **3782**

—— —— —— A brief list of references on the Democratic and Republican parties. Jan. 22, 1924. 4p. typ. (Additional references. Feb. 11, 1932. 2p.)   **3783**

—— —— —— Democracy; a brief bibliographical list. March 19, 1927. 9p. typ.   **3784**

—— —— —— List of books on the native American party. n.d. 3p. typ.   **3785**

—— —— —— List of references on campaign expenses. Aug. 28, 1920. 4p. typ.   **3786**

—— —— —— List of references on Democracy as reflected in art and literature. Aug. 14, 1919. 4p. typ. **3787**

—— —— —— List of references on party government. March 29, 1920. 6p. typ. **3788**

—— —— —— List of references on Tammany. 1904. 8p. typ. **3889**

—— —— —— A list of references on the Communist Party in the United States. May 15, 1934. 9p. typ. **3790**

—— —— —— A list of references on the national committees of political parties. Jan. 31, 1924. 6p. typ. **3791**

—— —— —— List of references on the National Nonpartisan League. Nov. 1, 1918. 4p. typ. **3792**

—— —— —— A list of works in regard to comparative politics. 1910. 6p. typ. **3793**

—— —— —— List of works relating to party government in the United States. 1906. 21p. typ. **3794**

—— —— —— List of works relating to political parties in the United States. Comp. under the direction of A. P. C. Griffin. Wash. Govt. Ptg. Off. 1907. 29p. **3795**

—— —— —— Reports of the proceedings of party conventions, 1832-1904. 1904. 7p. typ. **3796**

—— —— —— Select list of references on political abuse, satire, "Muck-raking," etc. April 25, 1911. 6p. typ. **3797**

—— —— —— Select list of references on the Progressive Party. Feb. 4, 1913. 3p. typ. (Additional references. Jan. 7, 1919. 6p.) **3798**

—— —— —— Selected list of references on the convention system. Oct. 8, 1927. 8p. mim. **3799**

—— —— —— A selected list of references on the history of political parties in the United States. May 14, 1936. 43p. typ. Same. 52p. mim. **3800**

—— —— —— A selected list of references on the political history of the United States, immediately preceding and during the Civil War, as illustrated in Illinois, Kentucky, Maryland, Missouri, Tennessee and Virginia. June 19, 1933. 19p. typ. **3801**

—— —— —— Selection of delegates by the states to national presidential conventions. July 25, 1912. 8p. typ. **3802**

—— —— —— Short list of references to recent writings on American politics and political parties. Feb. 5, 1925. 3p. typ. **3803**

—— —— —— Third party movement; a bibliographical list. Sept. 17, 1928. 18p. mim. **3804**

Wilson, H. W. Company. The reference shelf; reprints of selected articles, briefs, bibliographies, debates, study outlines of timely topics. N.Y. H. W. Wilson. 1922- **3805**

Winsor, Justin. Critical essay on the sources of information—The history of political parties. *In* Narrative and critical history of America. Boston. N.Y. 1888. VII. p294-356 **3806**

LEGAL

Sources

American digest; decennial edition of the American digest; a complete digest of all reported cases from 1897 to 1906. St. Paul, Minn. West Publishing Co. 1908-12. 25v. (Vols. 21-25 contain tables of cases in the Century and Decennial digests) **3807**

—— —— descriptive-word index and table of cases affirmed, reversed or modified, covering current digest (American digest system) I, 1926- . St. Paul, Minn. West Publishing Co. 1927- **3808**

—— —— descriptive-word index to the first and second decennial digests; a means of finding the authorities in point through the words descriptive of the legal principles or of the facts in the case. St. Paul, Minn. West Publishing Co. 1924. 3070p. **3809**

—— —— descriptive-word index, 1926; third decennial digest supplementing descriptive-word index to the first and second decennial digests. St. Paul, Minn. West Publishing Co. 1928. 754p. **3810**

American Law Reports Annotated. Complete word index of annotations in American law reports, covering volumes 1-100 of A.L.R. with pocket supplement continuations . . . San Francisco, Calif. Bancroft-Whitney Company; Rochester, N.Y. The Lawyers Co-operative Publishing Company. 1937. 3v. **3810a**

Carter, Clarence Edwin. Zephaniah Swift and the Folwell edition of the laws of the United States. N.Y. Macmillan. 1934. p689-95 (Reprinted from the Am. hist. rev. XXXIX. July 1934) **3810b**

Check list of National reporter system revised to March 10, 1941. Law lib. jour. XXXIV. p69 (March 1941) **3810c**

Davis, Bancroft G. Fifty years of mining law. Harvard law rev. L. p897-908 (April 1937) **3810d**

Freeman, Abraham Clark. Digest of the American decisions, and index to the American decisions and the editor's notes thereto, with a table of the cases reported . . .[1760-1869]. San Francisco. A. L. Bancroft. 1882-86. 3v. **3811**

—— List of important notes in American decisions . . . 100 vols., American reports . . . 60 vols., American state reports, 120 vols., alphabetically arranged. San Francisco. Bancroft-Whitney Co. 1909. 81p. **3812**

Hart, Amos Winfield. Digest of decisions of law and practice in the Patent Office and the United States and state courts in patents, trade-marks, copyrights, and labels, 1886-1898. Chicago. Callaghan. 1898. 385p. Same. 1897-1912. By W. L. Pollard. Wash. D.C. 1912. 644p. Same. 1912-1919. 1920. 119p.   **3812a**

Hohenhoff, E. von. Bibliography of American and foreign journals which list and abstract patents. Patent Office Soc. jour. XVII. p808-25, 971-92 (Oct., Dec. 1935); XVIII. 49-67, 139-50 (Jan.-Feb. 1936)   **3812b**

Law, Stephen Dodd. Digest of American cases relating to patents for inventions and copyrights from 1789 to 1862, including numerous manuscript cases, decisions on appeals from the commissioners of patents and the opinions of the attorneys general of the United States under the patent and copyright laws, and embracing also the American cases in respect to trade-marks. N.Y. The Author. 1866. 697p.   **3812c**

Lowe, I. J. Key to the year of decision of any case in the United States Supreme Court reports. Law lib. jour. XXXIII. p142-7 (July 1940)   **3812d**

Lowery, Woodbury. Index-digest to the decisions of the Supreme Court of the United States in patent causes. Wash. D.C. 1897. 445p.   **3812e**

Lunden, Walter A. Systematic source book in juvenile delinquency. Pittsburgh, Pa. Univ. of Pittsburgh. 1938. 390p.   **3812f**

McLaughlin, Madge. Legal status of women in the United States since 1918; a contribution to a bibliography. Madison. Univ. of Wisconsin Lib. School. June 1924. typ.   **3813**

Morris, Richard B. Early American court records: a publication program. (Anglo-American legal history series) N.Y. N.Y. Univ. School of Law. 1941. 37p.   **3813a**

New York. Public Library. List of works in the New York Public Library relating to marriage and divorce. N.Y. 1905. 48p. (Reprinted from the Bul. IX. p466-513. Nov. 1905)   **3814**

Seegmiller, Keith I., Bowman, Helen L., and Donohoe, Sara A. Digest of Veterans' insurance cases. Wash. D.C. Bureau of War Risk Litigation. 1936. 371p.   **3814a**

Sherman, Henry. An analytical digest of the law of marine insurance, containing a digest of all the cases adjudged in this state that is, New York . . . with . . . an appendix of cases decided in the Supreme, Circuit, and District Courts of the United States. N.Y. Collins, Keese & Co. 1844. 315p.   **3814b**

Tucker, Charles Cowles. A chronological list of English and American reports from the earliest times down to the present, to which is added information concerning other useful legal publications . . . Wash. D.C. The National University (Law dept.) 1907. 57p.   **3814c**

U.S. Department of Justice. The federal antitrust laws with amendments, list of cases instituted by the United States and citations of cases decided thereunder or relating thereto. Wash. Govt. Ptg. Off. 1922. 158p.   **3814d**

U.S. Library of Congress. Division of bibliography. Baumes laws; a bibliographical list. Feb. 1, 1928. 4p. typ.   **3815**

——— ——— ——— List of books on mechanics' lien laws. April 27, 1925. 7p. typ.   **3816**

——— ——— ——— List of references on blue sky laws. June 26, 1922. 10p. mim.   **3817**

——— ——— ——— List of references on the legal status of woman. Nov. 3, 1914. 5p. typ.   **3818**

——— ——— ——— A list of references on uniform divorce laws. Feb. 14, 1925. 9p. typ.   **3819**

——— ——— ——— Select list of works relating to probate law. 1905. 7p. typ.   **3820**

——— ——— ——— Short list of references on oil and gas laws. Dec. 23, 1924. 4p. typ.   **3821**

——— ——— **Law Library.** Want and duplicate list of American statutes. . . . Wash. Govt. Ptg. Off. 1904. 29p.   **3822**

U.S. National Commission on Law Observance and Enforcement. Appendix 1: Check-list of printed reports containing criminal statistics. *In* Report on criminal statistics. (Publication no. 3, April 1, 1931) Wash. D.C. 1931. p91-140 **3822a**

Warner, A. B. Checklist of printed reports containing criminal statistics. *In* National Commission on Law Observance and Enforcement. Rep. on criminal statistics. Wash. Govt. Ptg. Off. 1931. p91-140   **3823**

Waterman, Thomas Whitney. The American chancery digest, being an analytical digested index of all the reported decisions in equity of the United States courts and of the courts of the several states. N.Y. Banks, Gould; Albany. Gould, Banks & Gould. 1851. 3v.   **3823a**

——— A digest of decisions in the criminal cases, contained in the reports of the federal courts and the courts of the several states, from the earliest period to the present time. N.Y. Baker, Voorhis. 1877. 816p.   **3823b**

General

American Library in Paris, Inc. American law; a finding list of books on this subject in public and private collections in Paris. Paris. 1929. 139p.   **3824**

Association of Practitioners before the Interstate Commerce Commission. Committee on education for practice. Selected reading list of books helpful in the study of the principal laws within the jurisdiction of the Interstate Commerce Commission. Wash. D.C. 1938. 63p.   **3824a**

Beale, Joseph H. The study of American legal history. West. Va. law quar. XXXIX. p95-103 (Feb. 1933)   **3824b**

Beardsley, Arthur Sydney. Legal bibliography and the use of law books. Chicago. Foundation Press, Inc. 1937. 514p. 3824c

Bibliographical section. N. Y. Univ. law quar. rev. VIII. no. 1. Sept. 1930- 3825

Bibliography of judicial councils. *In* Annual handbook of the National Conference of Judicial Councils, 1940- 3825a

Bradway, John S. A tentative bibliography of material on legal aid work. Rochester, N.Y. National Asso. of Legal Aid Organizations. 1940. 247p. mim. 3825b

Check list of new law books. Law lib. jour. 3825c

Chicago Law Institute. Library. Subject index, January 1, 1902-December 31, 1937. [Chicago. 1938] 409p. 3825d

Childs, Frank Hall. Where and how to find the law; a guide to the use of the law library. Chicago. LaSalle Extension Univ. 1923. 119p. 3826

Drummond, Forrest. American and British law book dealers and publishers. Law lib. jour. XXXIII. p148-55 (July 1940) 3826a

[Eldean, Fred August] How to find the law; a comprehensive treatment of the problems of legal research with illustrative pages from numerous publications, together with a legal bibliography for each state and the federal government. 3d ed. by Henry J. Brandt. . . A legal reference handbook. St. Paul, Minn. West Pub. Co. 1940. 923p. 3827

Federico, B. M. Bibliography of articles on American patent, trademark and copyright law, 1929-1938. Patent Office Soc. jour. XXI. p463-84 (June 1939) 3827a

Fisher, M. E. Recent literature in the field of patents, trade-marks and designs. Patent Office Soc. jour. XV. April 1933- 3827b

Friend, W. L., Jr. Law book review digest and current legal bibliography, I, no. 1-4, October 1931-Jan. 1932. Phila. Friend. 1931-32 3828

Gray, John Chipman. The nature and sources of the law. N.Y. Macmillan Co. 1921. 348p. 3828a

Hall, Margaret. Legal articles in general periodicals, fall-winter, 1939-40. Law lib. jour. XXXIII. p61-7 (March 1940) 3828b

Hendrickson, A. M. and Ames, Charles Lesley. The practitioners' manual of legal bibliography. St. Paul, Minn. 1910. 358p. 3829

Henry E. Huntington Library and Art Gallery. Legal manuscripts and printed books; a sequence illustrating the development of English and American law.... San Marino, Calif. 1935. 30p. 3830

—— A selection of legal manuscripts and printed books for the visit of the state bar of California. . . . San Marino, Calif. 1934. 26p. 3831

Hicks, Frederick C. Aids to the study and use of law books; a selected list, classified and annotated, of publications relating to law literature, law study and legal ethics. N.Y. Baker, Voorhis & Co. 1913. 129p. 3832

—— Materials and methods of legal research with bibliographical manual. Rochester, N.Y. The Lawyers Co-operative Publishing Co. 1923. 626p. 3833

—— Men and books famous in the law. Rochester, N.Y. The Lawyers Co-operative Publishing Co. 1921. 259p. 3834

—— Preliminary list of local law journals. Law lib. jour. XIII. p1-6 (April 1920) 3835

—— Technique of legal research for the practicing lawyer. Law lib. jour. XXXI. p1-12 (Jan. 1938) 3835a

Hoffman, David. A course of legal study, addressed to students and the profession generally. Balt. J. Neal. 1836. 876p. 3836

Internationale Vereinigung für Vergleichende Rechtswissenschaft und Volkswirtschaftslehre zu Berlin. Internationales und auslandisches recht; gesamtkatalog der bestande von 30 Berliner bibliotheken. Aus den mitteln der stiftung des herrn geheimen kommerzienrats dr. jur. et med. Eduard Simon in Berlin. Berlin. Franz Vahlen. 1914. 1466 col. p1469-1684 3837

Iowa. University. College of Law. Library. Catalogue of the Hammond historical law collection, in the law library of the State University of Iowa. Comp. by Frank H. Noble. Iowa City. 1895. 52p. 3837a

James, Eldon R. A list of legal treatises printed in the British colonies and the American states before 1801. *In* Harvard legal essays written in honor of and presented to Joseph Henry Beale and Samuel Williston. Cambridge. Harvard Univ. Press. 1934. p159-211 3838

Johns Hopkins University. Institute of Law. Current research in law for the academic year 1928/1929-. Balt. Johns Hopkins Univ. Press; London. Humphrey Milford, Oxford Univ. Press. 1929- 3839

Kaden, Erich-Hans. Bibliographie der rechtsvergleichenden literatur des zivil- und handelsrechtes in Zentral- und Westeuropa und in den Vereinigten Staaten von Amerika, 1870 bis 1928. Berlin. Franz Vahlen. 1930. 276 col [277-] 295p. 3840

Kaiser, John Boynton. Law, legislative and municipal reference libraries; an introductory manual and bibliographical guide. Boston. Boston Book Co. 1914. 467p. 3841

Keitt, Lawrence. Law library catalogues. *In* An annotated bibliography of bibliographies of statutory materials of the United States. Cambridge. Harvard Univ. Press. 1934. p158-75 3842

The **Lawyers'** confidential guide; complete list of legal directories, law list publishers, service bureaus and associations selling listings or memberships to the attorneys in the U.S.A. and Canada—with ratings. Chicago. 19? **3842a**

Lawyers' Co-operative Publishing Company. Law books and their use; a manual of legal bibliography, legal research and brief making for lawyers and students. Rochester, N.Y. 1936. 678p. **3843**

—— Legal research as applied to Ruling case law, American law reports, Lawyers reports annotated, U.S. Supreme Court reports, L. ed., and Rose's notes. Rochester, N.Y.; N.Y. Lawyers Co-operative Publishing Co.; San Francisco. Bancroft-Whitney Co. 1926. 170p. **3844**

—— Where to look for the law; a brief index of the standard textbooks and other useful legal textbooks and a catalogue of the books of The Lawyers Co-operative Publishing Co. Rochester, N.Y. 1911. 225p. **3845**

Legal periodical digest of current articles involving research in all law periodicals published in the English language, 1928-. N.Y. Commerce Clearing House, Inc. 1928- **3846**

Long, Marianna. A bibliographical check list of publications of the American Law Institute, including a list of pamphlets and articles about its work. Law lib. jour. XXXII. p159-200 (July 1939) **3846a**

Marvin, J. G. Legal bibliography, or a thesaurus of American, English, Irish, and Scotch law books; together with some continental treatises; interspersed with critical observations upon their various editions and authority. . . . Phila. T. & J. W. Johnson. 1847. 800p. **3847**

Miller, Clarence A. The value of legislative history of federal statutes. University of Pennsylvania Law Review. LXXIII. p158-70 (Jan. 1925) **3847a**

Moylan, Helen S. Selected list of books for the small law school library. Law lib. jour. XXXII. p399-425 (Nov. 1935) **3847b**

Myers, Denys P. Bibliography of aerial law, including magazine articles and references to general works. Special Libraries. V. p59-63 (April 1914) **3847c**

Page, William Herbert. Table of articles from legal periodicals arranged by titles. *In* Law of contracts. Cincinnati. W. H. Anderson. 1920-22. VI. p6479-546 **3848**

Park, Orville A. An index to the publications of the various bar associations of America. Atlanta, Ga. Franklin Ptg. & Publishing Co. 1899. 86p. **3849**

Philbrick, Francis S. Possibilities of American legal history. National Asso. of State Lib. proc. and pap. 1933-1934. p60-78 **3849a**

Pound, Roscoe. Fifty years of jurisprudence. Harvard law rev. L. p557-82 (Feb. 1937); II. p444-72, 777-812 (Jan., March 1938) **3849b**

Pruyn, A. P. Catalogue of books relating to the literature of the law. Albany, N.Y. 1901. 300p. **3850**

Recent local books, case books, treatises, indexes and services. Law lib. jour. **3850a**

Rosewater, Stanley M. The insurance lawyer's library. [Omaha. Cockle Ptg. Co. c1936] [31]p. **3850b**

Selected bibliography of aeronautical law. Jour. air law. VIII. p675-85 (Oct. 1937) **3850c**

Small, A. J. Bibliographical and historical check list of proceedings of bar and allied associations. Des Moines, Iowa. Issued under the auspices of the Am. Asso. of Law Libraries. 1923. 98p. **3851**

Soule, Charles C. The lawyer's reference manual of law books and citations. Boston. Soule and Bugbee. 1883. 497p. **3852**

Townes, John C. A partial legal bibliography. *In* Law books and how to use them. Austin, Texas. Austin Ptg. Co. [1909] p169-86 **3853**

U.S. Library of Congress. Division of bibliography. The lawyer and his relation to government; a brief bibliographical list. Jan. 11, 1928. 5p. typ. **3854**

—— —— —— A list of recent references on lynching and lynch law. Comp. by Ann Duncan Brown. 1940. 16p. mim. **3854a**

—— —— —— List of references on divorce. Jan. 1, 1915. 76p. typ. **3855**

—— —— —— List of references on divorce, submitted to the judiciary committee of the Senate, 63d Congress, 3d sess. in connection with S. J. res. 109, proposing an amendment to the constitution of the United States relating to divorce. Prepared under the direction of H. H. B. Meyer. Wash. D.C. 1915. 110p. **3856**

—— —— —— List of references on lawmaking, with special reference to the United States. May 24, 1922. 8p. mim. **3857**

—— —— —— List of references on lynch law. July 9, 1921. 17p. typ. **3858**

—— —— —— A list of references on lynching and lynch law. Feb. 12, 1934. 25p. typ. **3859**

—— —— —— List of references on marriage and divorce, with special reference to uniform legislation. Dec. 6, 1926. 9p. mim. **3860**

—— —— —— Marriage and divorce, with special reference to legal aspects: a selected bibliography. Comp. by Helen F. Conover. April 10, 1940. 55p. mim. **3860a**

—— —— —— Select list of references on reform in civil law and procedure. March 26, 1913. 16p. typ. **3861**

—— —— —— Select list of references on the legal relations of parents and children. Sept. 10, 1912. 7p. typ. **3862**

—— —— **Law library.** Index on constitutional law. Wash. D.C. **3862a**

—— —— —— Union lists of works on jurisprudence. Wash. D.C. **3862b**

Vance, John T. The law library of Congress. National Asso. of State Lib. proc. and pap. 1934-35. p29-37   **3862c**

White, A. V. Bibliography relating to the law of waters. Canadian law jour. XXXII. p549-60 (July 12, 1913)   **3863**

Courts

Arnold, John H. V. Catalogue of the library of trials and legal literature. . . comprising both civil and criminal trials in the courts of England and America. . . To be sold . . . by Bangs & Co. N.Y. 1900. 218p.   **3864**

Bates, Helen P. Selected bibliography on probation and juvenile courts. *In* New York State Probation Commission. First rep. 1907. Appendix H. Albany, N.Y. 1908. p189-214 (Supplements in Second rep. 1908. Appendix J. p135-47. and *ibid.* Appendix. p207-12)   **3865**

Connecticut. State Library. List of referdicial councils. Law lib. jour. XXIV. p25-39, 65-86 (Jan.-April 1931) (Revised, enlarged and completed by E. Hugh Behymer)   **3866**

Connecticut. State Library. List of references to material on juvenile courts. Compiled for the use of the committee of the Connecticut Prison Association. Hartford, Conn. 1918. 13p. typ.   **3867**

Leavitt, Julian. Bibliography of prosecution, including references to grand jury, legal aid, public defender, and related subjects. *In* United States National Commission on Law Observance and Enforcement. Rep. on prosecution. Wash. D.C. 1931. p223-318   **3868**

National Probation Association. A bibliography on probation, juvenile and domestic relations, courts, crime, psychiatric treatment, and related subjects. N.Y. 1926. 15p.   **3869**

Pound, Roscoe. A bibliography of procedural reform. Mass. law quar. V. p332-45. 1920   **3870**

—— A bibliography of procedural reform, including organization of courts. Illinois law rev. XI. p451-63. 1917   **3871**

Rolfer, Clara E. Juvenile courts and probation; a bibliography. Madison. Univ. of Wisconsin Lib. School. June 1916. 40p. multig.   **3872**

U.S. Children's Bureau. List of references on juvenile courts and probation in the United States and a selected list of foreign references. (Publication no. 124) Wash. D.C. 1923. 41p.   **3873**

U.S. Library of Congress. Division of bibliography. Brief list of references on women as jurors. Feb. 24, 1923. 2p. typ. (Additional references. Dec. 14, 1927. 1p.)   **3874**

—— —— —— The jury system; a bibliographical list. June 14, 1931. 3p. mim. (Supplement. May 29, 1935. 13p. mim.)   **3875**

—— —— —— List of recent references on the jury system. March 3, 1923. 5p. typ.   **3876**

—— —— —— List of references on contempt of court. Jan. 28, 1924. 4p. typ.   **3877**

—— —— —— List of references on jurisdiction of the courts in cases involving executive action and discretion. April 26, 1915. 13p. typ.   **3878**

—— —— —— List of references on probation and juvenile courts. Aug. 27, 1914. 23p. typ. (Recent references. Sept. 14, 1921. 10p. mim.)   **3879**

—— —— —— List of references on the recall of judges (supplementary to the printed list on the initiative, referendum and recall, 1912). Dec. 16, 1913. 9p. typ.   **3880**

—— —— —— Select list of references on the recall of judicial decisions. Oct. 1, 1913. 5p. typ.   **3881**

Willoughby, William Franklin. Bibliography. *In* Principles of judicial administration (Institute for government research. Principles of administration) Wash. D.C. The Brookings Inst. 1929. p607-52   **3882**

Wire, G. E. Index of celebrated cases, crimes, criminals, detectives, escapes, homicides, mysteries, swindles, trials, etc., described in general books (not in volumes specifically devoted to the particular case or person). Jour. of the Am. Inst. of Crime and Criminology. XXI. p339-63 (Nov. 1930)   **3883**

Wynn, Edmund B. Catalogue of the extraordinary collection of law trials. . . To be sold . . . by Banks & Co. 1893. 208p.   **3884**

Crime

American Institute of Criminal Law and Criminology. Cumulative index covering volumes one to twenty-four (1910-11 to 1933-34). [Jour. Am. crime and criminology] By George H. Weinmann. Chicago. 1934. 411p.   **3885**

Barron, A. M. Public defender; a bibliography. Jour. of criminal law and criminology. XIV. p556-72 (Feb. 1924)   **3886**

Bibliography and reader's guide on the general subject of delinquency, criminology, rehabilitation, and their psychological approaches. Iowa State Inst. bul. IV. p316-31. 1923   **3887**

Bibliography on criminology and penology. *In* Handbook of American prisons and reformatories. N.Y. The Osborne Asso. 1925-   **3887a**

Blackall, E. W. The social evil; a bibliography. Madison, Wis. Hist. Lib. 1914. 14p. typ.   **3888**

Bureau of Social Hygiene, Inc. Criminological research bulletin, I, 1931-. N.Y. 1931- (Concerns research in progress)   **3889**

California. University. Bureau of public administration. Bibliography of crime and criminal justice, 1932-1937. Comp. by Dorothy Campbell Culver. N.Y. H.W. Wilson. 1939. 391p.   **3889a**

Cantor, Nathaniel. Selected bibliography on crime, 1935-1940. Am. social. rev. V. p618-22 (Aug. 1940) **3889b**

Catalogue of works on criminal law, penology, and prison discipline. (National Cong. on penitentiary and reformatory discipline. Trans. 1870) Albany, N.Y. 1871. 642p. **3890**

Conner, Esther. Crime commissions and criminal procedure in the United States since 1920; a bibliography, January 1920-June 1927. Jour. of criminal law and criminology. XXI. p129-44 (May 1930) **3891**

Corson, M. Work of criminal laboratories; bibliography. Madison. Wisconsin Legislative Reference Lib. 1921 **3892**

Crafts, L. W. Bibliography of feeble-mindedness in relation to juvenile delinquency. Jour. of delinquency. I. p195-208 (Sept. 1916) (Reprinted Whittier, Calif. Whittier State School, Boys' ptg. instruction dept. 1916) **3893**

—— A bibliography on the relations of crime and feeble-mindedness. Jour. of criminal law and criminology. VII. p544-54 (Nov. 1917) **3894**

Criminal law magazine and reporter; an index digest of the leading articles, cases reported in full and in abstract, book reviews, news of general interest, and all other matters contained in the first sixteen volumes of the criminal law magazine and reporter, 1880-1894. By Rapalje Stewart. Jersey City, N.J. F. D. Linn. 1895. 227p. **3895**

Culver, Dorothy Campbell. Bibliography of crime and criminal justice, 1927-1931. Univ. of California, Bureau of Pub. Administration) N.Y. H. W. Wilson. 1934. 413p. **3896**

Cumming, John. A contribution towards a bibliography dealing with crime and cognate subjects. London. Metropolitan police district. 1935. 107p. **3896a**

Galbraeth, Charles Burleigh. Bibliography of capital punishment. Ohio State Lib. bul. I. no. 10. p1-16. 1906 **3897**

Gibson, Frances Patricia. The prevention of juvenile delinquency through coordinating councils and boys' clubs; a contribution to a bibliography. Madison. Univ. of Wisconsin Lib. School. 1938. 22p. typ. **3897a**

Glueck, Sheldon and others. Crime causation and housing. In Gr.es, J. M. and Ford, J. Housing and the community; home repair and remodeling, Appendix I. (The President's conference on home building and home ownership. Publications VIII) Wash. D.C. 1932. p105-200 **3898**

Grimsrud, Agnes Olea. Adult probation in the United States since 1925; a contribution to a bibliography. Madison. Univ. of Wis. Lib. School. 1938. 46p. typ. **3898a**

Kellogg, Angie L. Crime and sociology. Psychological bul. XI. p454-63 (Dec. 15, 1914); XII. p446-56 (Dec. 15, 1915); XIII. p454-60 (Dec. 15, 1916); XIV.

p379-87 (Nov. 1917); XVI. p75-82 (March 1919); XVII. p103-6 (March 1920) **3899**

Kuhlman, Augustus Frederick. A guide to material on crime and criminal justice. N.Y. H. W. Wilson. 1929. 633p. **3900**

Los Angeles Public Library. Municipal Library. The control of crime; selected list of recent books. Los Angeles. 1930. 15p. **3901**

Lunden, Walter A. A systematic outline of criminology, with selected bibliography. Pittsburgh. Univ. of Pittsburgh. 1935. 115p. **3902**

McCarthy, K. O'S. Racketeering; a contribution to a bibliography. Jour. of criminal law and criminology. XXII. p578-86 (Nov. 1931) **3903**

MacDonald, Arthur. Abnormal man, being essays on education and crime and related subjects, with digests of literature and a bibliography [205-434p.] (U.S. Bureau of Education. Circular of information no. 4) Wash. Govt. Ptg. Off. 1893 **3904**

—— Statistics of crime, insanity, and other forms of abnormality, and criminological studies, with a bibliography. Senate document no. 12. 58 Cong. Special sess. Ser. 4556 (Bibliog. on p109-95) **3905**

Meyer, H. H. B. List of references on sterilization of criminals and defectives. Special libraries. V. p23-32 (Feb. 1914) **3906**

National Probation Association, Inc. Selected reading for probation officers and others interested in delinquency, 1937. N.Y. The Asso. 1937. 12p. **3906a**

New York. Legislature. Children's court jurisdiction and juvenile delinquency committee. Annotated bibliography of studies in juvenile delinquency. In Report of the Joint legislative committee to investigate jurisdiction of the Children's courts, known as Children's court jurisdiction and juvenile delinquency committee. Albany. J.B. Lyon. 1939. p251-87 **3906b**

New York. Public Library. List of works in the New York Public Library relating to criminology. N.Y. 1911. 362p. (Reprinted from the Bul. XV. p259-317, 350-71, 379-446, 463-501, 515-57, 567-621, 635-714 (May-Nov. 1911) **3907**

Prison Association of New York. Catalogue of works on criminal law, penology and prison discipline. In Twenty-sixth annual report, 1870. Albany, N.Y. Argus. 1871. p588-622 **3908**

Randall, Dorothy Jean. Possible penalties for crime; a contribution to a bibliography. Jour. of criminal law and criminology. XX. p456-65 (Nov. 1929) **3909**

St. Louis. Public Library. Crime waves and criminals; an outline of social divergence and abnormality; a selected list of books to be found in the St. Louis Public Library. Comp. by Lucius H. Cannon. St. Louis. 1925. 24p. (Reprinted from the Monthly bul. n.s. XXIII. no. 4. p81-103. April 1925) **3910**

Sellin, Thorsten. A brief guide to penological literature. Am. Acad. Pol. and Social Science ann. CLVII. p225-32 (Sept. 1931)   3911
—— Science of criminology; bibliography. Jour. of criminal law and criminology. XVIII. p147-58, 295-318, 451-84, 629-39; XIX. p118-58, 290-320, 456-508, 656-91 (May 1927-Feb. 1929)   3912

Steinmetz, Richard Carlton. A selected bibliography for fire insurance company investigators and others engaged in the detection of arson and kindred crimes. Chicago, Ill. Mill Mutual Fire Prevention Bureau. [1940] 12p. mim.   3912a

U.S. Attorney General's Advisory Committee on Crime. Annotated bibliography in juvenile delinquency. Prepared by Mrs. Caroline Shurtleff Hughes. Wash. 1937. 31p. mim.   3912b

—— —— Bibliography on housing and crime. [Wash. 1936] 6p. mim.   3912c

U.S. Children's Bureau. List of references on juvenile delinquency. Comp. by Evangeline Kendall. Wash. D.C. 1939. 41p. mim. Supplementary list. March 1940. 15p. mim.   3912d

U.S. Federal Bureau of Investigation. Bibliography of crime and kindred subjects. Wash. D.C. 1937. 16p. mim.   3912e

U.S. Library of Congress. State law index. Crime control, state laws, 1935-1938, including 1940. (State law digest. Rep. no. 3) Wash. D.C. 1940. 77p.   3912f

—— —— Division of bibliography. Crime and criminal justice; a short list of books. April 11, 1930. 8p. mim. (Select list. Feb. 1935. 27p. mim.)   3913

—— —— —— List of recent references on the identification of criminals, with special reference to criminal identification bureaus. Nov. 15, 1922. 5p. typ.   3914

—— —— —— List of references on crime and criminology in the United States, with special reference to statistics. Feb. 23, 1922. 21p. mim.   3915

—— —— —— List of references on famous cases of great American detectives. June 17, 1922. 3p. typ.   3916

—— —— —— List of references on sterilization of criminals and defectives. Special libraries. V. p23-35 (Feb. 1914)   3917

—— —— —— List of references on the identification of criminals. Aug. 9, 1918. 7p. typ.   3918

—— —— —— List of references on women criminals. Oct. 28, 1916. 7p. dupl.   3919

—— —— —— Select list of references on capital punishment. Comp. under the direction of H. H. B. Meyer. Wash. Govt. Ptg. Off. 1912. 45p. (Supplement. Oct. 29, 1924. 10p. mim.; Nov. 4, 1926. 4p.; Nov. 21, 1930. 3p.; Feb. 16, 1931. 23p. mim.; June 3, 1935. p24-7. mim.)   3920

—— —— —— Select list of references on reform in criminal law and procedure. Jan. 15, 1912. 14p. mim. (List of references. Oct. 5, 1921. 6p. typ.)   3921

Wigmore, John H. A preliminary bibliography of modern criminal law and criminology. (Northwestern University Law School, Gary Library of Law. Bul. no. 1) Chicago. 1909. 128p.   3922

Law Enforcement

American journal of police science index to material published 1930-1941. Jour. crim. law. XXXI. p753-4 (March 1941)   3922a

American Prison Association. Index to the reports of the National Prison Association, 1870, 1873, 1874, 1883-1904. Comp. by Mary V. Titus, with introduction by Eugene Smith. (Senate document no. 210. 59 Cong. 1 sess.) Wash. Govt. Ptg. Off. 1906. 160p.   3923

Barry, A. G. Selected list of references for police school. Am. jour. of police science. II. p454-9 (Sept.-Oct. 1931)   3924

Campbell, Dorothy. Bibliography on training of police. Jour. of criminal law and criminology. XXIV. p591-7 (Sept.-Oct. 1933)   3925

Cochrane, Ava L. Some phases of prison reform. Madison. Univ. of Wisconsin Lib. School. June 1918. 77p. multig.   3926

Connecticut State Library. Legislative reference dept. List of references on reformatory work for women. [Hartford, Conn.] 1918. 5p. typ.   3927

Corcoran, Margaret May. State police in the United States; a bibliography. Jour. of criminal law and criminology. XIV. p544-55 (Feb. 1924)   3928

Goldberg, W. A. Bibliography: prisons and jails. Jour. criminal law. XXVIII. p380-95 (Sept. 1937)   3928a

Greer, Sarah. A bibliography of police administration and police science. N.Y. Columbia univ., Inst. of Pub. Administration. 1936. 152p.   3929

Hirst, Robert W. The policeman's and detective's guide to professional knowledge; an aid to police officers in searching for and selecting professional literature. New Bedford, Mass. 1923. 72p.   3929a

Johnsen, Julia E. Bibliography. *In* The problem of liquor control. N.Y. H. W. Wilson. 1934. p27-66   3930

—— Bibliography. *In* Selected articles on law enforcement. N.Y. H. W. Wilson. 1930. p13-49   3931

Munro, W. B. List of references on police administration. The Am. city. X. p362-4 (April 1914)   3932

Stone, Donald Crawford and Miles, Arnold. Selected bibliography of available police literature. Chicago, Ill. Police Chiefs News Letter. 1936. 11p. reprod. 3932a

U.S. Attorney General's Advisory Committee on Crime. Annotated bibliography on jails. Prepared by Mrs. Caroline Shurtleff Hughes. [Wash. 1937] 10p. mim.   3932b

U.S. Attorney General's Advisory Committee on Crime. Annotated bibliography on prisons (history, nature, and administration of). Prepared by Mrs. Caroline Shurtleff Hughes. [Wash. 1936] 36p. mim.   **3932c**

—— —— Annotated bibliography on probation. [Wash. 1937] 17p. mim.   **3932d**

—— —— Bibliography on recreation and delinquency. [Wash. 1936] 7p. mim.   **3932e**

U.S. Bureau of Prisons. Library. Convict labor; books and articles published, 1931-January 1935. (Reference list no. 1) Wash. D.C. 1935. 14p.   **3933**

U.S. Library of Congress. Division of bibliography. A list of manuals of justices of the peace, notaries and legal forms. July 10, 1922. 9p. multig.   **3934**

—— —— —— A list of references on policewomen. Oct. 21, 1924. 7p. mim.   **3935**

—— —— —— List of references on prison labor. Comp. by H. H. B. Meyer. Wash. Govt. Ptg. Off. 1915. 74p.   **3936**

—— —— —— List of references on respect for law, including public opinion as an aid to enforcement. March 4, 1922. 5p. multig   **3937**

—— —— —— List of references on state military police. Feb. 28, 1916. 3p. typ.   **3938**

—— —— —— List of references on state police and similar law enforcing organizations. Nov. 17, 1922. 12p. mim.   **3939**

—— —— —— List of references on the police power. Jan. 21, 1916. 5p. typ.   **3940**

—— —— —— List of references on the reformatory and probation systems. April 4, 1918. 6p. typ.   **3941**

—— —— —— A list of references on the "third degree." June 2, 1924. 4p. typ.   **3942**

—— —— —— Selected list of writings on the control of the liquor traffic in the United States and foreign countries. Nov. 9, 1932. 55p. mim.   **3943**

Vollmer, August. Bibliography on police organization and administration, criminal identification and investigation. Am. jour. of police science. II. p76-9 (Jan. 1931)   **3944**

Westcott, Allen P. A bibliography of firearms identification—"forensic ballistics." Jour. of criminal law and criminology. XXV. p992-1000 (March-April 1935)   **3945**

Will, Thomas E. Bibliography of prison reform. The Arena. X. p417-20 (Aug. 1894)   **3946**

CHAPTER VIII

ARMY AND NAVY

MILITARY

General

American Library Association. Engineering defense training; a booklist. Comp. by Harrison W. Craver and Harrison A. Von Urff. Chicago. 1940. 13p. **3946a**

Baker, Mary Ellen. Bibliography of lists of New England soldiers. (Register reprints. ser. A, no. 36) Boston. New England Hist. Geneal. Soc. 1911. 56p. (Reprinted from the New England hist. and geneal. register. LXIV. p61-72, 128-35, 228-37, 327-36; LXV. p11-19, 151-60. Jan. 1910-April 1911) **3947**

Bryant, Douglas Wallace. Bibliography of tanks and other military track-laying vehicles. (U.S. Library of Congress. Division of bibliography. Cooperative bibliographies, no. 1) Wash. D.C. 1941. 22p. **3947a**

Carter, William H. West Point in literature. Jour. of the Military Service Inst. of the U.S. XLIII. p378-83 (Nov.-Dec. 1908) **3947b**

Flick, Hugh M. The Harry A. Ogden collection. N.Y. Hist. Soc. bul. XXI. p3-11 (Jan. 1937) (Materials on civil and military costumes, particularly military uniforms of the colonial, revolutionary, and federal periods) **3947c**

Fort Eustis, Va. Library. The mechanized force—a bibliography. February 15, 1931. Fort Eustis, Va. 1931. 42p. mim. **3947d**

Ganoe, William A. Selected bibliography. *In* The history of the United States army. N.Y. Appleton. 1924. p531-65 **3948**

Guernsey, Rocellus Sheridan. Bibliography of the United States relating to military collective biography. N.Y. Geneal. and Biog. Soc. 1874 **3949**

Haferkorn, Henry E. and Heise, Paul. Handy lists of technical literature. Part II. Military and naval science, navigation, rowing, sailing, yachting; boat, ship and yacht building; ammunition, arms, tactics, and war. Milwaukee, Wis. National Publishing & Ptg. Co.; London. Stevens. 1890. 104p. **3950**

Hellman, Florence S. Military training for national defense. Booklist XXXVII. p337-48 (1941) **3950a**

Herring, Pendleton, ed. Civil-military relations; bibliographical notes on administrative problems of civilian mobilization. Prep. . . . for the Committee on Public Administration of the Social Science Research Council. Chicago. 1940. 77p. **3950b**

Hewitt, Edward W. and Coleman, W. E. Index of general orders and circulars affecting the Quartermaster's department, U.S. army, from 1865 to 1878, inclusive. Fort Leavenworth, Kans. H. Shindler, printer, 1879. 126p. interleaved **3950c**

Holden, Edward S. Bibliographies of West Point (1694-1902), of the U.S. Military Academy (1776-1902), and of the writings of the graduates of the U.S. Military Academy (1802-1902). *In* The Centennial of the United States Military Academy at West Point, New York. Wash. Govt. Ptg. Off. 1904. II. p1-397 **3951**

International military digest, annual; a review of the current literature of military science, 1915-1918. N.Y. Cumulative Digest Corp. 1916-19 **3952**

John Crerar library. A selected list of books on military medicine and surgery. Chicago. 1917. 58p. **3953**

Joint Committee on Library Research Facilities for National Emergency. Guide to library facilities for national defense. Ed. by Carl L. Cannon. Chicago. Am Lib. Asso. 1941. 448p. reprod. from typ. copy **3953a**

Lanza, Conrad H. List of books on military history and related subjects. Fort Leavenworth, Kan. General Service Schools Press. 1923. 19p. **3954**

The **military** library. Am. Mil. Inst. jour. I- 1937- **3954a**

New York. Public Library. Patriotism; a reading list. N.Y. 1917. 67p. **3955**

Ney, Virgil. Arms collectors of the United States, the who's who of the arms hobby. 2745 Browne St. Omaha, Neb. In progress **3955a**

Owen, Thomas M. Jr. Pensions: adjusted compensation and land bounties: a bibliography. Wash. The National Archives. In progress **3955b**

Pan American Union. Columbus Memorial Library. Selected list of books and magazine articles on hemisphere defense. (Bibliog. ser. no. 24) Wash. D.C. 1941. 14p. mim. **3955c**

Public Administration Service. Civil-military relations; bibliographical notes on administrative problems of civilian mobilization. Ed. by Edward P. Herring. Chicago. Pub. Admin. Service. 1940. 77p. **3955d**

Rodenbough, Theodore F. and Roberts, Thomas A. General index of The Journal of the Military Service Institution of the United States, vols. 1-34, 1880-1904. N.Y. 1904. 136p. (Continued for vols. XXXV

Rodenbough, T. F. and Roberts, T. A. General index of The Journal of the Military Service Institution—*Continued* to XLIX, 1904 to 1916 in Jour. of the Military Service Inst. of the U.S.; XLIX, LIII, LIX. 1911, 1913, 1916. 21, 69, 18p.) **3956**

Seaver, W. N. Economic and social aspects of war. N.Y. Pub. Lib. bul. XIX. p167-78 (Feb. 1915) **3957**

Soley, James Russell. Critical essay on the sources of information—editorial notes— The wars of the United States. *In* Narrative and critical history of America. Boston, N.Y. Houghton Mifflin. 1888. VII. p403-60 **3958**

Toomey, Noxon. Complete literature. *In* The history of the infantry drill regulations of the United States Army. St. Louis. 1917. p6-12. typ. **3959**

U.S. Adjutant General's Office. List of military publications, books, pamphlets, etc., received in the military information division, during 1897-1903. Wash. Govt. Ptg. Off. 1897-1903 **3960**

—— —— **Military information division.** Sources of information on military professional subjects; a classified list of books and publications. Wash. Govt. Ptg. Off. 1898. 501p. **3961**

U.S. Army. A.E.F., 1917-1920. General Staff Library. Catalogue of books and pamphlets in the library, General Staff, G-2. [Paris] Am. Expeditionary Forces, General headquarters. [1918?] 163p. **3962**

U.S. Army Service Schools. Fort Leavenworth. Library. Library catalog, 1927; The General service schools, Fort Leavenworth, Kansas; 55,650 books, pamphlets and documents, and 1,160 maps and atlases classified by subjects and countries, with alphabetic subject index. Fort Leavenworth, Kan. General Service Schools Press. 1927. 754p. **3963**

U.S. Army War College. Historical section. Bibliography of all posts garrisoned by United States troops. MS. **3964**

—— —— —— **Library.** Accession list of authors and titles from September 1, 1904 to January 1, 1905. Wash. Govt. Ptg. Off. 1905. 65p. (List from January 1 to July 1, 1905. Wash. Govt. Ptg. Off. 1905. 76p.) **3965**

—— —— —— —— Author and title list of accessions to the Army War College Library, including maps, and index of periodicals (from August 15, 1903 to) the fiscal year 1906. . . . Wash. Govt. Ptg. Off. 1904-06 **3966**

—— —— —— —— Card catalog on military affairs. Wash. D.C. **3966a**

—— —— —— —— List of authors and titles and catalogue of maps from August 15, 1903 to September 1, 1904. Wash. Govt. Ptg. Off. 1904. 179p. **3967**

—— —— —— —— Monthly list of military information carded from books, periodicals and other sources, nos. 1-67, Oct. 1915-May 1921. [Wash. Govt. Ptg. Off. 1915-21] **3968**

—— —— —— —— Notes on the catalogue or card index of books in the Army War College Library, including subject index for military books. [Wash. D.C. 1914] 39p. Autog. from typ. copy. **3969**

U.S. Bureau of Foreign and Domestic Commerce. Intelligence division. Some references to material on western hemisphere defense. Comp. by Ruth C. Leslie. Wash. D.C. Dec. 1940. 8p. processed **3969a**

U.S. Coast Artillery School. Index to current artillery literature. Jour. of the U.S. artillery. V. no. 1. Jan./Feb. 1896- **3970**

—— . **Library.** Analytical catalogue of the professional library of the United States Artillery School at Fort Monroe, Va. Comp. by Capt. James Chester. . . and 1st Lieut. Albert Todd. . . 1881 and 1885. Wash. Govt. Ptg. Off. 1886. 341p. **3971**

—— —— —— Library notes, 1926-. Fort Monroe, Va. Coast Artillery School Press. 1926- **3972**

U.S. Command and General Staff School, Fort Leavenworth. Book dept. Price list; military books, maps, and reconnaissance supplies. Fort Leavenworth, Kan. 1932. 22p. **3973**

—— —— **Library.** Quarterly review of military literature, I, Jan. 1922- **3974**

U.S. Engineer Department. Catalogue of the library of the Engineer Department, United States Army. Wash. D.C. 1881. 819p. **3975**

U.S. Engineer School. Library. Engineer troops; references to their organization, equipment, training and duties, together with a short list of books and pamphlets of interest to the Engineer service, Engineer school library. (Occasional pap. Engineer School, U.S. Army no. 47) Wash. D.C. Press of the Engineer School. 1911. 15p. (Printed as MS.) **3976**

—— List of accessions arranged under subject-headings in alphabetical order, from January 1910, to December 31, 1910, including donations received from various sources. (Occasional pap. Engineer School, U.S. Army no. 46) Wash. D.C. Press of the Engineer School. 1911. 59p. **3977**

U.S. General Service and Staff College, Fort Leavenworth. Library. Catalogue of the General Service and Staff College Library at Fort Leavenworth, Kans., May 1902. Fort Leavenworth. 1902. 160p. **3978**

U.S. Infantry Association. A selected list of literature on general military subjects. Wash. D.C. Oct. 1, 1935. 25p. processed **3979**

U.S. Information Service. Selected list of references on national defense. Wash. D.C. The Service. 1938. 21p. mim. **3979a**

U.S. Library of Congress. Division of bibliography. Brief list of books on national defense. Nov. 1, 1926. 7p. typ. **3980**

—— —— —— Brief list of references on a unified department of national defense. Oct. 31, 1925. 3p. typ. **3981**

—— —— —— Brief list of references on military and naval preparedness. Nov. 27, 1915. 4p. typ. Dec. 9, 1915. 4p. mim. (Supplement. Jan. 3, 1924. 5p. typ.) **3982**

—— —— —— A brief list of references on western hemisphere defense. Comp. by Helen F. Conover. Nov. 6, 1940. 15p. processed **3982a**

—— —— —— Compulsory military training, a selected list of references. Comp. by Ann D. Brown. July 30, 1940. 25p. mim. **3982b**

—— —— —— List of books on military law of the United States. Sept. 16, 1918. 2p. typ. **3983**

—— —— —— A list of recent references on military pensions of the United States. Comp. by Florence S. Hellman. Nov. 4, 1939. 19p. typ. **3983a**

—— —— —— List of recent references on railroads in war. June 5, 1917. 14p. dupl. **3984**

—— —— —— A list of recent references on traffic in arms, munitions, and implements of war and control of their manufacture. Oct. 15, 1934. 10p. typ. **3985**

—— —— —— A list of references on camouflage. Comp. by Grace H. Fuller. Nov. 13, 1940. 12p. mim. **3985a**

—— —— —— List of references on cantonment buildings, their construction, equipment, sanitation and care. April 12, 1918. 6p. dupl. **3986**

—— —— —— List of references on military education in schools, colleges, and universities. Sept. 20, 1915. 9p. typ. (Supplement. Nov. 17, 1916. 6p. typ.) **3987**

—— —— —— List of references on military tanks. Feb. 19, 1921. 8p. typ. **3988**

—— —— —— List of references on spies and spy systems. Jan. 1, 1918. 14p. dupl. **3989**

—— —— —— List of references on the army canteen question. 1904. 6p. typ. (Additional references. 1907. 1p.) **3990**

—— —— —— List of references on the defenses of the United States. Aug. 24, 1915. 6p. typ. **3991**

—— —— —— List of references on the manufacture, testing and transportation of explosives. May 22, 1916. 8p. typ. **3992**

—— —— —— List of references on the military academy at West Point. 1904. 7p. typ. **3993**

—— —— —— List of references on the militia. Aug. 17, 1917. 10p. typ. **3994**

—— —— —— List of references on the militia and national guard (supplementing list on the Militia, 1916). Comp. by Helen F. Conover. Sept. 14, 1940. 14p. typ. **3994a**

—— —— —— List of references on the use of gases in warfare. Nov. 13, 1917. 10p. typ. **3995**

—— —— —— List of references on voluntary enlistment in the army. Nov. 26, 1920. 4p. typ. **3996**

—— —— —— List of speeches, addresses, etc. on national defense as printed in the Congressional record, 1933-1940. Comp. by Anne L. Baden. Jan. 17, 1940. 39p. mim. **3996a**

—— —— —— List of works on contraband of war. 1904. 6p. typ. **3997**

—— —— —— National guard (supplementing 1916 list on militia). Aug. 1, 1933. 6p. typ. **3998**

—— —— —— References on the increase of the army of the United States. Dec. 30, 1914. 6p. typ. **3999**

—— —— —— Select list of references on the coast defenses of the United States. 1909. 4p. typ. **4000**

—— —— —— Selected list of recent references on American national defense (supplementary to typed list of June 1936). Comp. by Grace H. Fuller. Oct. 3, 1939. 40p. mim. **4000a**

—— —— —— Selected list of references on American national defense. June 16, 1936. 18p. typ. **4001**

—— —— —— Selected list of references on military pensions and bounties of the United States. Oct. 6, 1933. 51p. mim. **4002**

—— —— —— Selected list of references on the council of national defense. June 26, 1934. 7p. typ. **4003**

—— —— —— Selected list of references on the military and naval defense of colonies and dependencies. Dec. 12, 1901. 4p. typ. **4004**

U.S. Military Academy. Library. Catalogue of the library U.S. Military Academy, West Point, N.Y., 1873. Newburgh. Charles Jannicky. 1876. 723p. (Supplement to the catalogue of the library. . . . Poughkeepsie. A. V. Haight. 1882. p725-1027) **4005**

—— Library manual II. Manuscripts, rare books, memorabilia, and the like in the library, U.S.M.A. By Edward S. Holden (Bul. no. 2) West Point. 1908. 93p. **4006**

U.S. National Emergency Council. Information service division. Selected list of references on national defense. Wash. D.C. Dec. 1, 1938. 21p. mim. **4006a**

U.S. Ordnance Department. Library. Books and pamphlets catalogued during the months of Jan. 1929- . Wash. D.C. 1929- mim. **4007**

—— —— —— Catalogue of the Ordnance Office Library. Wash. Govt. Ptg. Off. 1875. 78p. **4008**

—— —— —— A selected list of articles in current periodicals of interest to the Ordnance Department. Wash. D.C. Jan. 2, April 1, July 1, Oct. 1, Nov. 15, 1940; Jan. 2, Feb. 15, 1941. mim. 7 pamphlets **4008a**

U.S. Signal Office. Library. Catalogue of the library, Office chief signal-officer, United States Army, Washington, June 30, 1932. Wash. Govt. Ptg. Off. 1872. 74p. **4009**

U.S. War Department. Announcements of army extension courses, 1936-1937. Wash. Govt. Ptg. Off. 1936. 24p. **4010**

U.S. War Department. Library. Alphabetical catalogue of the War Department Library. Wash. Govt. Ptg. Off. 1882. 325p. (Alphabetical list of additions . . . from June 1882 to May 1894. 3pts. 39, 114, 35p. Late additions . . . 1894. 30p.) **4011**

—— —— Author and title list of the most important accessions to the War Department Library, with subject entries in biography, military history and military science, and index of periodicals received during the calendar year 1904. Wash. Govt. Ptg. Off. 1905. 95p. **4012**

—— —— —— Check list of serial publications in the War Department Library, October 1, 1903. Wash. Govt. Ptg. Off. 1903. 42p. **4013**

—— —— —— Finding list of military biographies and other personal literature in the War Department Library (Subject catalogue no. 4) Wash. Govt. Ptg. Off. 1899. 145p. **4014**

—— —— —— Index to periodicals, annuals, and serials in the War Department Library (Subject catalogue no. 2) Wash. Govt. Ptg. Off. 1895. 36p. **4015**

—— —— —— Three finding lists issued by the War Department Library. 1, Serial publications. 2. Principal reference works. 3. Important accessions, 1898-1903. General A. W. Greely in supervisory charge, James W. Cheney, librarian. Wash. Govt. Ptg. Off. 1903. 3v in 1 **4016**

U.S. Work Projects Administration. District of Columbia. Bibliography of air raid precautions and civil defense. Wash. D.C. 1941. 343p. reprod. typ. **4016a**

Virginia. State Library. Finding list of books in . . . military science. Va. State Lib. bul. IV. p356-69. 1911 **4017**

Walworth, Arthur. School histories at war; a study of the treatment of our wars in the secondary school history books of the United States and in those of its former enemies. Cambridge, Mass. Harvard Univ. Press. 1938. 92p. **4017a**

WAR OF 1812

American Art Association. Illustrated catalogue of important Americana, rare books, tracts and broadsides including the William Bunker collection of historical books on the War of 1812. [N.Y. Lent & Graff. 1917] 198p. **4018**

Anderson Galleries, Inc. Choice books from private sources including a remarkable collection on the War of 1812. . . . N.Y. Anderson Auction Co. 1906. 72p. **4019**

Bibliography of the War of 1812. Bostonian Soc. proc. 1899. p57-64 **4020**

Bullard, Peter C. Bibliography of references concerning the campaign of Chancellorsville. [Ft. Leavenworth, Kan. The Command and General Staff School. 1936] 51p. typ. **4020a**

Grolier Club. Exhibition of naval and other prints, portraits and books relating to the War of 1812, November 7th to 23d, 1912. N.Y. 1912. 14p. **4021**

Louisville Public Library. Books and magazine articles on battle of Tippecanoe, battle of the River Raisin, battle of the Thames. Louisville, Ky. 1913. 11p. **4022**

Noble, Henry Harmon. A partial bibliography of printed works which contain records of service in the War of 1812, or which indicate where service records may be found. (General Soc. of the War of 1812. Proc. of the ninth biennial meeting . . .) Phila. The Soc. 1912. p48-54 **4022a**

Severance, Frank H. Notes on the literature of the War of 1812. Buffalo Hist. soc. publications. XVIII. p193-212. 1914 **4023**

U.S. Library of Congress. Division of bibliography. American prisoners of War of 1812 in Dartmoor prison; a list of references. Nov. 21, 1934. 5p. typ. **4024**

—— —— —— List of state rosters of soldiers in the War of 1812. Jan. 22, 1913. 4p. typ. **4025**

WAR WITH MEXICO

Aldine Book Company, Brooklyn, N.Y. Conquest of California, 1848, and historical material relating to the discovery, old settlements, adventures and narratives of events to 1928, with some allied matter of Pacific political and historical affairs; to which is added: railroad literature, 1828-1928. . . . Brooklyn, N.Y. 1928. 79p. **4026**

Haferkorn, Henry Ernest. The war with Mexico, 1846-1848; a select bibliography on the causes, conduct, and the political aspect of the war, together with a select list of books and other printed material on the resources, economic conditions, politics and government of the republic of Mexico and the characteristics of the Mexican people. . . . (Supplement no. 1. Professional memoirs. March-April 1914. VI. no. 26. Bibliog. contributions bul. no. 1) Wash. D.C. 1914. 93, xxviii p. **4027**

Lawson, William Thornton. Essay on the literature of the Mexican war (Columbia college. Senior class essay, 1882) [N.Y. 1882] 21p. **4028**

Mexico. Comisión de Estudios Militares. Biblioteca del Ejército. Apuntes para una bibliografía militar de México, 1536-1936, recopilación de fichas bibliográficas hecha por los del primer Congreso bibliográfico, convocado por el Ateneo nacional de ciencias y artes de México. Sección de estudios militares del Ateneo, mayor m.c. Néstor Herrera Gomez, mayor Silvino M. González. Mexico, D.F. [Talleres gráficos de la nación] 1937. 469p. **4028a**

Smith, Justin H. Sources for the history of the Mexican war, 1846-48. Military historian and economist. I. p18-32 (Jan. 1916) **4029**

U.S. Library of Congress. Division of bibliography. List of references on the war with Mexico, 1846-1848 (arguments justifying the cause of the U.S.). March 16, 1914. 3p. typ. **4030**

CIVIL WAR

Abbot, George Maurice. Contributions towards a bibliography of the Civil war. I. Regimental histories. Phila. Collins] 1886. 34p. (Reprinted from and continued in Bul. of the Lib. Co. of Phila., n.s. no. 16 appendix. xxx p. Jan. 1886; no. 17. appendix I. p53-9. July 1886; no. 18. p22-4. Jan. 1887; no. 19. p34-7. July-Sept. 1887; no. 20. p30-1. Jan. 1888; no. 21. p35-6. July 1888) **4031**

Adams, Charles Francis. Civil war literature. Nation. XCIX. p66-8, 97-9, 128-30, 159-61 (July 16, 23, 30, Aug. 6, 1914) **4031a**

American Art Association. The valuable collection of autographs, manuscripts and documents of persons intimately connected with the Civil War and Fort Sumter, formed by the late Major General Samuel Wylie Crawford, U.S.A. . . . N.Y. 1915. unpag. **4032**

Anderson Galleries, Inc. The fine library of John C. Burton, of Milwaukee, Wis. Part V. Civil war material. N.Y. 1916. 135p. **4033**

—— Library of the late Major William H. Lambert of Philadelphia. Part III. Civil war. N.Y. Metropolitan Art Asso. 1914. 127p. **4034**

Anderson Company, publishers. A catalog of books, maps, and pamphlets relating to the American Civil war. N.Y. 1904 **4035**

Anglim, James & Co. Catalogue of books and pamphlets relating to the late Civil war . . . and the reconstruction. Wash. D.C. 1886. 19p. **4036**

Bartlett, John Russell. The literature of the rebellion; a catalogue of books and pamphlets relating to the Civil war in the United States, and on subjects growing out of that event, together with works on American slavery, and essays from reviews and magazines on the same subjects. Boston. Draper and Halliday; Providence. S. S. Rider and Bro. 1866. 477p. **4037**

Boston. Public Library. A list of regimental histories and official records of the individual states in the Civil war in this library. Boston Pub. Lib. bul. IX. p289-314 (Aug. 1904) **4038**

Brigham, Clarence Saunders. Wall-paper newspapers of the Civil war. In Bibliographical essays; a tribute to Wilberforce Eames. Cambridge. Harvard Univ. Press. 1924. p203-10 **4039**

Clark, Arthur H. Catalogue of books relating to the American Civil war. Cleveland. 1917. 120p. **4040**

Columbia University. Library. The Townsend Library of national, state and individual Civil war records at Columbia University. N.Y. Styles & Cash. 1899. 15p. **4041**

Grant, S. H. Bibliography of the Civil war. Hist. mag. VI. p113-15, 146-9, 186-7, 206-8, 245-7, 342-6; VII. p54-8, 112-15 (April 1862-April 1863) **4042**

Harper, Francis P. Descriptive catalogue of an unusual collection of books and pamphlets relating to the rebellion and slavery including regimental histories, prison narratives, Confederate publications, biographies, poetry, etc., etc. N.Y. 1900. 65p. **4043**

Henkels, Stan V. Library of E. G. Blaisdell, esq. of Glassboro, New Jersey embracing history of the Civil war, Lincolniana and general American history. . . . Phila. 1917. 64p. **4044**

Hodgkins, William Henry. Catalogue of the . . . library of the late Major Wm. H. Hodgkins . . . comprising an extensive collection of Civil war literature. . . Boston. C. F. Libbie. 1906. 183p. **4045**

Irvine, Dallas D. The genesis of the official records [of the War of the Rebellion]. Miss. Valley hist. rev. XXIV. p221-9 (Sept. 1937) **4045a**

Lawrence, Samuel Crocker. Catalogue of the masonic library, masonic medals, Washingtoniana, ancient and honorable artillery company's sermons, regimental histories, and other literature relating to the late Civil war . . . Medford, Mass. Boston. C. H. Heintzemann. 1891. 320p. **4046**

Loyal Legion of the United States. Catalogue of the library of the commandery of the state of Illinois, Military Order of the Loyal Legion of the United States, January 1909. Chicago. 1909. 72p. **4047**

McCabe, James D. Literature of the war; Confederate publications in the sixties. South. Hist. Soc. pap. XLII. p199-203 (Oct. 1917) **4048**

Merwin Sales Co., New York. Catalogue of old books and pamphlets, including a long series of works on the Civil war in America, 1861-65. N.Y. 1914. 44p. **4049**

Military Order of the Loyal Legion of the United States. Ohio Commandery. Catalogue of the library. Prepared under the direction of Brevet Major A. M. Van Dyke, U.S.V., recorder, by Capt. William Holder. Cincinnati. 1901. 115p. **4050**

Morrison, Noah Farnham. Fiftieth anniversary catalog of books and pamphlets relating to the American civil war and slavery, offered for sale at the Sign of the ark . . . . Elizabeth, N.J. 1912. 106p. **4050a**

Newhall, Daniel H. A collection of books and pamphlets relating to the Civil war and Abraham Lincoln. N.Y. 1914. 44p. **4051**

Nicholson, John Page. Catalogue of library of Brevet Lieutenant-colonel John Page Nicholson . . . relating to the War of the rebellion, 1861-1866. Phila. J. T. Palmer. 1914. 1022p.   **4052**

Nicolay, John George. A rich collection of books and manuscripts mainly of the Civil war. . . . N.Y. Morse. 1905. 25p.   **4053**

Pennypacker, Isaac R. A library of Civil war literature. The nation. XCIX. p344-5 (Sept. 17, 1914) (Concerning the John P. Nicholson Library)   **4054**

Rosenbach Company. The surrender of Lee and the assassination of Lincoln, April, 1865; an exhibition of historical documents commemorating the seventy-fifth anniversary, April and May 1940. Phila. Rosenbach Company. 1940. 26p.   **4054a**

Tredwell, Daniel M. A catalogue of books and pamphlets, belonging to Daniel M. Tredwell, relating to the great Civil war between the North and the South, or the free and the slave states of the American Union. Brooklyn, N.Y. E. F. De Selding. 1874. 220p.   **4055**

Union League of Philadelphia. Catalogue of the Union League of Philadelphia. n.p. n.p. Oct. 1897. 254p.   **4056**

U.S. Army War College. Library. U.S. history—Civil war, 1861-1865. Bibliography. Comp. by Nancy Cramer Barndollar. n.p. 1932. 286p. typ.   **4056a**

U.S. Library of Congress. Division of bibliography. List of references on the battles of Franklin and Nashville, 1864. Oct. 20, 1922. 5p. typ.   **4057**

—— —— —— List of references on the Civil war mainly from the Confederate point of view. May 10, 1921. 11p. typ.   **4058**

—— —— —— A list of references on the siege and campaign of Vicksburg, 1863. Comp. by Florence S. Hellman. June 11, 1937. 10p. photostat   **4058a**

—— —— —— Select list of works on the Virginia campaigns of the Civil war. Aug. 14, 1912. 7p. typ.   **4059**

U.S. War Department. Library. Bibliography of state participation in the Civil war, 1861-1866 (Subject catalogue no. 6) Wash. Govt. Ptg. Off. 1913. 1140p.   **4060**

—— —— —— Military literature in the War Department Library relating to the campaign against Chattanooga, siege of Chattanooga, battle of Chickamauga, battle of Lookout Mountain, battle of Missionary Ridge, and the retreat of Bragg, comprising the period embraced from August 1863, to December 1863. (Catalogue no. 7) Wash. Govt. Ptg. Off. 1898. 75p.   **4061**

U.S. War Records Office. Report of the board of publications of the official records of the Union and Confederate armies. Wash. Govt. Ptg. Off. 1896. 11p.   **4062**

Wisconsin State Historical Society. Catalogue of books on the War of the rebellion and slavery, in the library. . . . Madison, Wis. Democrat Ptg. Co. 1887. 61p.   **4063**

SPANISH AMERICAN WAR

Grosvenor Library, Buffalo, N.Y. Reading list on Cuba and the present war with Spain. Buffalo, N.Y. 1898. 16p.   **4064**

Trelles, Carlos M. Bibliografía de la segunda guerra de independencia Cubana y de la Hispano-Yankee, publicado en la Revista illustrada "Cuba y America." Havana. 1902. 49p.   **4065**

U.S. Library of Congress. Division of bibliography. A list of books on the Spanish-American war, as they relate to Cuban campaign, 1898. Dec. 24, 1900. 11p. typ. (Supplement. Dec. 10, 1930. 10p. typ.)   **4066**

—— —— —— List of references on Sampson-Schley case. 1902. 2p. typ.   **4067**

WORLD WAR

Adams, Ephraim Douglass. The Hoover war collection at Stanford University, California; a report and an analysis. Stanford Univ. Stanford Univ. Press. 1921. 82p.   **4068**

Blakeslee, George H. A selected list of books on the present war. Worcester, Mass. 1917. p44-78. (Reprinted from Jour. of race development. VIII. July 1917)   **4069**

Boston. Public Library. A selected list of books on national defense, military and naval science and law in the Public Library of the city of Boston. (Brief reading lists no. 1. April 1917) Boston. Trustees. 1917. 25p.   **4070**

British Museum. Department of printed books. Subject index of the books relating to the European war, 1914-1918, acquired by the British Museum, 1914-1920. London. Printed by order of the Trustees. 1922. 196p.   **4071**

Brooklyn. Public Library. National defense; a select list of books in the Brooklyn Public Library. Brooklyn, N.Y. 1917. 27p.   **4072**

Brown, Mabel Webster and Williams, Frankwood E. Neuropsychiatry and the war; a bibliography with abstracts. N.Y. National Com. for Mental Hygiene, War work com. 1918. 292p.   **4073**

Bulkley, Mildred Emily. Bibliographical survey of contemporary sources for the economic and social history of the war. (Carnegie Endowment for International Peace. Division of economics and history. Economic and social history of the World War. British ser.) Oxford. Clarendon Press. 1922. 628 col. p629-48 **4074**

Clark University. Library. The war collection at Clark University Library. By Louis N. Wilson (Publications of the Clark Univ. Lib. VI. no. 1) Worcester. Clark Univ. Press. 1918. 53p. **4075**

Dutcher, George Matthew. A selected critical bibliography of publications in English relating to the World War. (War supplement to Hist. teachers' mag. March 1918. War reprint no. 3) Phila. McKinley Publishing Co. 1918. 34p. (Also in A. E. McKinley. Collected materials for the study of the war. Phila. McKinley Publishing Co. 1918. p105-36) **4076**

Fisher, H. H. The Hoover Library on War, Revolution and Peace. Bibliog. Soc. Am. pap. XXXIII. p107-15. 1939 **4076a**

Hanson, Joseph Mills. The historical section, Army war college. Am. Mil. Inst. jour. I. p70-4 (Summer 1937) **4076b**

Lange, F. W. T. Books on the great war; an annotated bibliography of literature issued during the European conflict with general indexes. London. Grafton. 1915-16. 4v. **4077**

Los Angeles. Public Library. Books in the Los Angeles Public Library relating to the European war. Los Angeles. 1917. 47p. **4078**

Lybyer, Albert Howe. The literature of the great war. Bibliog. Soc. Amer. pap. XI. p15-39 (Jan. 1917) **4079**

New York. Public Library. The European war; some works recently added to the library. N.Y. Pub. Lib. bul. XVIII-XXII, 1914-18 **4080**

Princeton University. Library. Books on the war, third list, books added to the British Museum Library, Jan. 1916 to March 1918 and not contained in the Library of Congress, New York Public Library or Princeton University Library. Princeton. 1918. 120p. photostat copy **4081**

—— —— European war collection; alphabetical author list; proof edition uncorrected. Princeton. Univ. Lib. 1918. 92p. **4082**

—— —— European war collection; classified list; proof edition uncorrected. Princeton. Univ. Lib. 1918. 97p. **4083**

Prothero, George W. A select analytical list of books concerning the great war. London. H.M. Stationery Off. 1923. 431p. **4084**

Richardson, Ernest Cushing. The bibliography of the war and the reconstruction of bibliographical methods. Bibliog. Soc. Amer. pap. XIII. p113-27. 1919 **4085**

Seymour, Charles. Re-fighting the war on paper. Yale rev. XVIII. p625-45 (June 1929) **4086**

U.S. Army Service Schools, Fort Leavenworth. Library. The World war. In Library catalog, 1927; The General service schools, Fort Leavenworth, Kansas, 55,650 books, pamphlets and documents . . . . Fort Leavenworth, Kan. General Service Schools Press. 1927. p445-571 mim. **4087**

U.S. Army war college. Historical section. List of regimental histories of U.S. troops in the European war. [n.p. n.d.] 58p. typ. **4087a**

U.S. Chief of Engineers Office. Partial list of histories of U.S. Army organizations (Regiments or larger, and special units) which participated in the World war, 1917-1919. Wash. D.C. May 20, 1923. 35p. mim. **4088**

U.S. Infantry Association. A selected list of literature on the World war, 1914-18. Wash. D.C. Oct. 1, 1935. 21p. processed **4089**

U.S. Library of Congress. Division of bibliography. Bibliography of the American field service in France. Aug. 26, 1918. 5p. typ. **4090**

—— —— A checklist of the literature and other material in the Library of Congress on the European war. Comp. under the direction of H. H. B. Meyer. Wash. Govt. Ptg. Off. 1918. 293p. **4091**

—— —— Classified list of magazine articles on the European war. n.d. 33p. dupl. **4092**

—— —— List of references on casualties in the European war, and strength of the armies in the field. Jan. 5, 1918. 22p. mim. **4093**

—— —— List of references on compulsory military service. March 29, 1917. 13p. mim. (Supplement. April 3, 1919. 17p. mim.) **4094**

—— —— List of references on German opinion of the preparedness of the United States. Feb. 11, 1920. 2p. typ. **4095**

—— —— List of references on motor transport in the European war. Nov. 30, 1917. 4p. typ. Dec. 20, 1917. 7p. dupl. **4096**

—— —— List of references on ordnance in the European war. Jan. 30, 1918. 14p. dupl. **4097**

—— —— List of references on recruiting. April 9, 1917. 7p. typ. **4098**

—— —— List of references on the work of the American Red Cross in the European war. April 3, 1917. 7p. typ. **4099**

—— —— A list of the histories of regiments and other units of the U.S. army in the European war. Aug. 4, 1919. 4p. typ. (Supplements. Aug. 30, 1919. 1p.; Nov. 10, 1919. 1p.; 1920. 4p.; Sept. 29, 1921. 19p. typ.; Mar. 30, 1922. 4p.; May 14, 1925. 1p.; Feb. 3, 1926. 1p.) **4100**

—— —— The United States at war, organzations and literature. Comp. under the direction of H. H. B. Meyer. Wash. Govt. Ptg. Off. 1917. 115p. **4101**

—— —— The World war; a list of the more important books published before 1934. Selected by Dr. Henry Eldridge Bourne. Wash. D.C. 1934. 20p. mim. (Supplement. June 28, 1936. 17p. mim. **4102**

Washington, D.C. Public Library. The World war (1914-1918) and its aftermath; a reading list. Comp. by Iva I. Swift (Reference list no. 26) Wash. Govt. Ptg. Off. 1931. 29p. **4103**

Washington. University. University Extension Division. Bureau of Debate and Discussion. Military training in the public school; a bibliography. (Bul. Univ. of Wash. Univ. extension ser. no. 20. General ser. no. 104) Seattle. The Univ. 1916. 13p. **4104**

Weitenkampf, Frank. War memorials; a list of references in the New York Public Library. N.Y. N.Y. Pub. Lib. 1919. 10p. (Reprinted from the Bul. XXIII. p499-506. Aug. 1919) **4105**

NAVAL

Anderson Galleries, Inc. Original printed records of American vessels captured by British men-of-war and privateers, 1803-1811, with incidental notes of captures by French and Spanish ships to which are appended a number of similar records relating to foreign captured vessels and five blockades, 1798-1810. N.Y. Am. Art Asso. 1926. unpag. **4106**

American Society of Naval Engineers. Journal of the American Society of Naval Engineers; general index, volumes I-XVI, 1889-1904. Wash. D.C. R. Beresford. 1905. 260p. **4107**

Barnes, John Sanford. Naval literature. Reprinted from Proc. of U.S. Naval Inst. XXIX. no. 2, whole no. 106. p333-55. Annapolis, Md. June 1903 **4108**

Browne, Margaret F. The rare collection of the Naval History Society with its wealth of priceless information regarding the wars of the United States. Naval Hist. Soc. ann. 13th year. p47-54. 1922. (Including MSS.) **4109**

Carnegie Endowment for International Peace. Library. Building up the U.S. Navy to treaty limits. M. Alice Matthews (Reading list. miscellaneous. no. 52) Wash. D.C. 1934. 4p. mim. **4110**

Edmunds, Albert J. Selected list of naval matter in the library of the Historical Society of Pennsylvania. Phila. 1903. 13p. (Reprinted from Pennsylvania mag. of hist. and biog. XXVII. p63-75. Jan. 1903) **4111**

Feipel, Louis N. Bibliography of literature concerning the U.S. Naval Academy to July 1, 1912. n.p. n.p. n.d. typ. **4111a**

—— The golden age of the U.S. Navy. N.Y. Brooklyn Pub. Lib. In progress **4111b**

—— Our rich but neglected old naval historical literature. U.S. Naval Inst. proc. XLVIII. p49-55 (Jan. 1922) **4112**

Harbeck, Charles Thomas. A contribution to the bibliography of the history of the United States Navy. Cambridge, Mass. Priv. printed at the Riverside Press. 1906. 247p. **4113**

Harvard University. Library. List of articles from periodicals relating to the United States Navy. Collected by Gardner W. Allen, and presented to the Harvard College Library. [n.p. 1916?] 133p. typ. **4114**

Hosmer, Helen R. Submarines in periodical literature from 1911 to 1917. Jour. Franklin Inst. CLXXXIV. p251-306 (Aug. 1917) **4115**

Jameson, Mary Ethel. Submarines; a list of references in the New York Public Library. N.Y. N.Y. Pub. Lib. 1918. 97p. (Reprinted with additions from the Bul. XXII. p18-69, 91-132. Jan.-Feb. 1918) **4116**

Knox, Dudley W. A new source of American naval history. U.S. Naval Inst. proc. LVI. p588-90 (July 1930) (Purchase of MS. letter book) **4117**

Krafft, Herman F. Catalogue of historic objects at the United States Naval Academy. Annapolis. U.S. Naval Inst. [Balt. The Industrial Ptg. Co.] 1925. 250p. (Contains material on MSS. Copy in Department of the Navy. Library has MS. additions and new accessions to Jan. 15, 1929 by Krafft) **4118**

Lincoln, C. H. Materials in the Library of Congress for a study of the United States naval history. Bibliog. Soc. Amer. pap. I. p84-95. 1906 **4119**

—— Naval manuscripts in national archives. Literary collector. VII. p65-8 (Jan. 1904) **4120**

Naval History Society, New York. Barnes Memorial Library. Catalogue of the books, manuscripts and prints and other memorabilia in the John S. Barnes Memorial Library of the Naval History Society. N.Y. Naval Hist. Soc. 1915. 377p. **4121**

Neeser, Robert Wilden. Statistical and chronological history of the United States Navy, 1775-1907. N.Y. Macmillan. 1909. 2v. (Volume 1 consists of bibliography and includes material on Department of the Navy archives. p3-12) **4122**

New York. Public Library. Naval architecture and shipbuilding; a list of references in the New York Public Library. Comp. by Rollin A. Sawyer, Jr. N.Y. N.Y. Pub. Lib. 1919. 59p. (Reprinted from the Bul. XXIII. p13-50, 73-91. Jan.-Feb. 1919) **4123**

—— —— A selected list of works in the library relating to nautical and naval art and science, navigation and seamanship, ship-building, etc. N.Y. N.Y. Pub. Lib. 1907. 151p. (Reprinted from the Bul. XI. June-Sept. 1907) **4124**

—— —— A selected list of works in the library relating to naval history, naval administration, etc. N.Y. Pub. Lib. bul. VIII. p261-95, 323-51, 369-93, 423-63, 560-75 (June-Nov. 1904) **4125**

—— Torpedoes; a list of references to material in the New York Public Library. Comp. by William A. Ellis. N.Y. N.Y. Pub. Lib. 1917. 85p. (Reprinted from the Bul. XXI. p657-715. Oct. 1917) **4126**

Nottingham, Loring. Ready-reference card system in use at Naval Hospital, Pensacola, Fla. Medicine and surgery bureau. Supplement to U.S. naval medical bul. V. no. 17. p48-56 (April 1921) **4126a**

Paltsits, Victor Hugo. Log books of the U.S. frigate *Congress*, 1845-1849, relating to the conquest of California and her voyages around the Horn. N.Y. Pub. Lib. bul. XXXVIII. p714-15 (Sept. 1934) **4126b**

Rushmore, David P. and others. Bibliography of the literature of submarines, mines and torpedoes. General electric rev. XX. p675-94 (Aug. 1917) **4127**

Society of Naval Architects and Marine Engineers, New York. Index to transactions for volumes 1-38, 1893-1930. N.Y. 1932. 135p. **4128**

U.S. Department of the Navy. Alphabetical catalogue of Navy Department Library—authors. Wash. Govt. Ptg. Off. 1891. 601p. (Supplement. 1892. 90p.; 1896. 105p.) **4129**

—— —— **Library.** Accessions to the Navy Department Library, author and titles entries, July-Dec. 1897-December 1910. Wash. Govt. Ptg. Off. 1898-1911. 26 nos. **4130**

—— —— —— Bibliographical catalogue of periodicals, Navy Department Library. Wash. Govt. Ptg. Off. 1897. 22p. **4131**

U.S. Library of Congress. Division of bibliography. A list of books on marine engineering, naval architecture and shipbuilding. Comp. by Florence S. Hellman. Aug. 5, 1940. 9p. typ. **4131a**

—— —— List of historical works and fiction relating to Annapolis and West Point. Sept. 10, 1915. 3p. typ. **4132**

—— —— —— List of references on naval operations in the European war. 1915. 10p. typ. (Additional references. Aug. 1918. 4p.) **4133**

—— —— —— List of references on sea power. Jan. 16, 1919. 10p. typ. **4134**

—— —— —— List of references on the increase of the navy. Jan. 26, 1914. 10p. typ.; Jan. 19, 1915. 10p. typ. **4135**

—— —— —— List of references on the navy in relation to national defense (including sea power and command of the sea, offensive and defensive operations, strategy, tactics, etc.). Feb. 17, 1915. 9p. typ. **4136**

—— —— —— Select list of references on America's contribution to sea literature (exclusive of fiction and the navy). March 11, 1922. 7p. typ. **4137**

—— —— —— Select list of references on submarine boats and warfare. Aug. 6, 1913. 5p. typ. (Supplement. May 21, 1917. 5p. typ.) **4138**

—— —— —— Select list of references on the United States Marine Corps. Aug. 5, 1913. 5p. typ. **4139**

—— —— —— A selected list of references on the expansion of the U.S. Navy, 1933-1939. Comp. by Grace H. Fuller. Dec. 7, 1939. 34p. mim. **4139a**

—— —— —— Selected list of references on the United States Navy. Dec. 23, 1924. 13p. mim. **4140**

U.S. Naval Academy. Library. Bibliography of naval literature in the United States Naval Academy Library. Comp. by Louis H. Bolander. Annapolis. U.S. Naval Acad. Lib. 1929. 42, 88, 151p. autog. from typ. copy **4141**

U.S. Naval Institute. Classified analytical index to the Proceedings, volume 28, no. 1, to volume 45, no. 10, serial numbers 101-200, March 1902-October 1919. Annapolis. The Inst. 1921. 173p. **4142**

—— General index of the Proceedings of the United States Naval Institute [I-XXVII, 1874-1901]. Prep. by Edward L. Beach. Balt. The Lord Baltimore Press, The Friedenwald Co. 1903. 266p. **4143**

U.S. Office of Naval Records and Library. Historical section. Digest catalogue of laws and joint resolutions, the Navy and the world war. (Publication no. 3) Wash. Govt. Ptg. Off. 1920. 64p. **4143a**

U.S. Superintendent of Documents. List of United States public documents and reports relating to construction of the new navy, also references to debates in Congress on the subject, 1880-1901. Wash. Govt. Ptg. Off. 1902. 18p. **4144**

—— —— Official documents relating to the navy of the United States of America. Wash. Govt. Ptg. Off. 1914. 22p. **4145**

United States Naval medical bulletin. Index, volumes I-XXVI, inclusive. U.S. Naval medical bul. XXVI. p1045-206 (Oct. 1928) **4145a**

Virginia State Library. Finding list of the books in . . . naval science. Comp. under the direction of Earl G. Swem. Va. State Lib. bul. IV. p369-77 (April-Oct. 1911) **4146**

Wright, N. H. Index, articles published or reprinted—Journal of the American Society of Naval Engineers, February 1913-May 1920. Jour. of the Am. Soc. of Naval Engineers. XXXIII. p69-97 (Feb. 1921) **4147**

Young, Lucien. Catalogue of works by American naval authors. Wash. D.C. Bureau of Navigation. 1888. 149p. **4148**

CHAPTER IX

RACES

INDIANS

Abel, Annie Heloise. A bibliographical guide to primary and secondary authorities. *In* The history of events resulting in Indian consolidation west of the Mississippi. Am. Hist. Asso. rep. 1906. I. p412-38 **4148a**

American Philosophical Society. Catalogue of manuscript works on the Indians and their languages presented to the American Philosophical Society, or deposited in their library. (Am. Philosophical Soc. trans. of the hist. and literary com. I. pxlvii-l) Phila. Abraham Small. 1819. (Reprinted in Buchanan, James. Sketches of the history, manners and cusoms of the North American Indians. London. p307-10) **4148b**

Arana, Enrique. Bibliografía de lenguas americanas. Buenos Aires, Imprenta de la Universidad, 1931. 13p. Del Boletín del Instituto de investigaciones históricas (de la Facultad de filosofía y letras, año x, t. XIII, nos. 49-50, p. 138-48, Buenos Aires, julio-diciembre 1931 **4148c**

Bancroft, Hubert Howe. Authorities quoted. *In* The native races of the Pacific states of North America. I. Wild tribes. N.Y. D. Appleton. 1874. p.xvii-xlix **4149**

Bandelier, Adolphe F. A. On the sources for aboriginal history of Spanish America. Am. Asso. Advancement Science proc. XVII p315-37. 1878 **4150**

Bangs & Co., New York. Catalogue of the books, pamphlets, autograph letters, original manuscripts & documents belonging to the late Henry R. Schoolcraft, the Indian historian and to Mrs. Schoolcraft. . . . N.Y. 1880. 34p. **4151**

Barba, Preston A. The American Indian in German fiction. German Am. ann. n.s. XI. p143-74. 1913 **4152**

Barnes, Nellie. American Indian verse; characteristics of style. (Bul. of the Univ. of Kansas. Humanistic stud. II. no. 4. Dec. 1921) Lawrence, Kans. The Univ. 1921. 63p. **4153**

Bissell, Benjamin. The American Indian in English literature of the eighteenth century. (Yale stud. in English. LXVIII) New Haven. Yale Univ. Press; London. Humphrey Milford, Oxford Univ. Press. 1925. 223p. **4154**

Blair, Emma H. Bibliography. *In* The Indian tribes of the Upper Mississippi Valley and region of the Great Lakes. Cleveland. Arthur H. Clark. 1912. II. p301-57 **4155**

Boyd, Julian, ed. Indian treaties printed by Benjamin Franklin, 1736-1762, with an introduction by Carl Van Doren and historical and bibliographical notes by Julian P. Boyd. Phila. Hist. Soc. of Pennsylvania. 1938. 340p. (Bibliographical notes and census, p301-8) **4155a**

Brinton, Daniel G. Aboriginal American authors and their productions; especially those in the native languages; a chapter in the history of literature. Phila. n.p. 1883. 63p. **4156**

Brown, Ruth R. George Catlin's portraits of North American Indians. *In* Papers in honor of Andrew Keogh librarian of Yale University. By the staff of the library 30 June 1938. New Haven. Priv. prints. 1938. p157-62 **4156a**

Butler, Ruth L. A bibliographical list of the Indian linguistics of the Americas. Chicago. Newberry Lib. In progress **4156b**

Byington, Rev. Cyrus. Choctaw bibliography; a list of books prepared and published in the Choctaw language by the missionaries of the American board of commissioners for foreign missions. (MS. in the lib. of the Bureau of Am. Ethnology) **4157**

Commission to the Five Civilized Tribes. Topical index to twelve annual reports of the Commission to the Five Civilized Tribes (1894-1905). Wash. Govt. Ptg. Off. 1906. 136p. **4157a**

Dennis, Elizabeth G. The Indians of America; a reference list for schools and libraries. St. Paul Public Library. Boston. F. W. Faxon. 1928. 67p. **4158**

Denver. Art museum. Department of Indian art. A guide to articles on the American Indians in serial publications. Comp. by Frederic H. Douglas. Denver. 1934. 332p. mim. **4158a**

Drake, Samuel Gardner. Catalogue of the private library of Samuel Gardner Drake. . . . Boston. Alfred Mudge & Son. 1876. 574p. **4159**

Dunbar, John Brown. Library of John B. Dunbar. . . . [N.Y. 1892] 151p. **4160**

Eames, Wilberforce. Rare Americana relating to the American Indians; being a portion of the library of Wilberforce Eames. . . . N.Y. Anderson Auction Co. 1915. 4pts. **4161**

Evan, Richard Xavier. The literature relative to Kateri Tekakwitha, the lily of the Mohawks, 1656-1680. Bul. recherches hist. XLVI. p193-209, 241-55 (juillet, août 1940) **4161a**

Fairchild, Hoxie Neale. The noble savage; a study in romantic naturalism. N.Y. Columbia Univ. Press. 1928. 535p. **4162**

Field, Thomas W. An essay towards an Indian bibliography; being a catalogue of books, relating to the history, antiquities, languages, customs, religion, wars, literature of the American Indians in the library of Thomas W. Field, with bibliographical and historical notes, and synopses of the contents of some of the works least known. N.Y. Scribner, Armstrong and Co. 1873. 430p. **4163**

Florida. University. Library. Bibliography on Seminole Indians. [Gainesville. 1940] 24p. mim. **4163a**

Foster, George E. Journalism among the Cherokee Indians. Mag. Am. hist. XVIII. p65-70 (July 1887) **4164**

—— Literature of the Cherokees; also bibliography and story of their genesis. Ithaca. N.Y. Muskogee, Indian Territory. Office of the Democrat. 1889. 69, 28p. **4165**

Gaines, Ruth. Books on Indian arts north of Mexico. N.Y. Exposition of Indian Tribal Arts, Inc. 1931. 15p. **4166**

Guide to references on Abnaki names. Maine Lib. bul. XVI. p82-6. 1931 **4166a**

Harding, Anne Dinsdale and Bolling, Patricia. Bibliography of articles and papers on North American Indian art. Wash. D.C. 1938. 365p. mim. **4166b**

Harper, Lathrop C. An interesting catalogue of books relating to the American Indians, their history, antiquities, languages, wars and captivities. . . . N.Y. Lathrop C. Harper. 1922. 41p. **4167**

Henkels, Stan V. & Son, Philadelphia. The collection of books from the library of the late William Ludwig Baker of Germantown consisting of books entirely relating to the North American Indians . . . many rare items of western travel and exploration. . . . Phila. Maurice H. Power. 1925. 48p. **4168**

Hiersemann, Karl W. Catalogue 396, America. III. American ethnology and lilinguistics. Leipzig. Buchhändler V. Antiquar Königstr. 1911. 48p. **4169**

Hodge, Frederick Webb. Bibliography. *In* Handbook of American Indians, north of Mexico. (Smithsonian Inst. Bureau of Am. Ethnology. Bul. no. 30) Wash. Govt. Ptg. Off. 1912. p1179-1221 (Reprinted as: Bibliography of American Indians north of Mexico. Wash. Govt. Ptg. Off. 1912) **4170**

Hoopes, Alban W. Bibliography of American Indians. Phila. (In progress) **4171**

Icazbalceta, Joaquin Garcia. Apuntes para un catálogo de escritores en lenguas indígenas de América. Mexico. Icazbalceta. 1866. 182p. **4172**

International Congress of Americanists, 15th, Quebec, 1906. Catalogue des manuscrits et des imprimés en langues sauvages ainsi que des reliques indiennes, exposés à Québec à l'occasion du XVᵉ congrès international des Américanistes, septembre, 1906. Quebec. Dussault & Proulx. 1906. 50p. **4173**

Jacobs, Melville. A survey of Pacific northwest anthropological research, 1930-1940. Pacific northw. quar. XXXII. p79-106 (Jan. 1941) **4173a**

Kate, Hermann Frederick Carel ten. The Indian in literature. (Smithsonian Inst. Annual rep. 1921) Wash. Govt. Ptg Off. 1922. p507-28 **4174**

Keiser, Albert. The Indian in American literature. N.Y. Oxford Univ. Press. 1933. 312p. **4175**

Kluckhohn, Clyde and Spencer, Katherine. A bibliography of the Navaho Indians. N.Y. J. J. Augustin. 1940. **4175a**

Knapp, Arthur Mason. The Indian question. Boston. Pub. Lib. bul. IV. p68-70 (April 1879) **4176**

Leechman, J. D. Bibliography of the anthropology of the Puget Sound Indians. Wash. hist. quar. XI. p266-73 (Oct. 1920) **4177**

Lesser, Alexander. Bibliography of American folklore, 1915-28. Jour. Am. folklore. XLI. p1-60 (Jan.-March 1928) **4178**

Littlefield, George E. Catalogue of books and pamphlets relating to the American Indians, selected from the stock of Geo. E. Littlefield. Boston. 1883. 24p. **4179**

Ludewig, Herman E. The literature of American aboriginal languages, with additions and corrections by Prof. W. W. Turner. Ed. by Nicholas Trübner. London. Trübner. 1858. 258p. **4180**

Lummis, Charles F. A reading list on Indians. Out west. XVIII. p357-65 (March 1903) (Also in St. Louis Pub. Lib. monthly bul. n.s. I. p107-11. Dec. 1903) **4181**

McLachlan, R. W. The first Mohawk primer. Canadian antiq. and numismatic jour. April 1908. p51-66 **4182**

Macleod, William Christie. Bibliography. *In* The American Indian frontier. N.Y. Knopf. 1928. p565-95 **4183**

Mitre, Bartolomé. Catálogo razonado de la sección lenguas Americanas, tomo I. Buenos Aires. Imp. de coni Hermanos. 1909. 409p. **4184**

[Muñoz y Manzano, C] Count de la Viñaza. Bibliografía española de lenguas indígenas de América. Madrid. 1892. 435p. **4184a**

Murchison, Kenneth S. Digest of decisions relating to Indian affairs, vol. I. judicial. (House doc. 538, 56th Cong. 2 sess.) Wash. D.C. 1901. 667p. **4184b**

New York. Museum of the American Indian, Heye Foundation. A series of publications relating to the American aborigines; list of publications of the Museum of the American Indian, Heye Foundation. (Indian notes and monographs no. 49) N.Y. Museum of the Am. Indian, Heye Foundation. 1933. 30p. **4185**

Newberry Library, Chicago. Narratives of captivity among the Indians of North America; a list of books and manuscripts on this subject in the Edward E. Ayer

Newberry Library. Chicago. Narratives of captivity—*Continued* collection of the Newberry Library. (Publications of the Newberry Lib. no. 3) Chicago. Newberry Lib. 1912. 120p. (Supplement I. By Clara A. Smith. 1928. 49p.)   **4186**

—— Notes on the historical source material in the Ayer collection on the North American Indian presented by Edward E. Ayer to the Newberry Library, Chicago. Chicago. Newberry Lib. 1927. 8p.   **4187**

Pilling, James Constantine. Bibliography of the Algonquian languages. (Bureau of Am. Ethnology. Bul. no. 13) Wash. Govt. Ptg Off. 1891. 614p.   **4188**

—— Bibliography of the Athapascan languages. (Bureau of Am. Ethnology. Bul. no. 14) Wash. Govt. Ptg Off. 1892. 125p.   **4189**

—— Bibliography of the Chinookan languages (including the Chinook jargon). (Bureau of Am. Ethnology. Bul. no. 14) Wash. Govt. Ptg. Off. 1893. 81p.   **4190**

—— Bibliography of the Eskimo language. (Bureau of Am. Ethnology. Bul. no. 1) Wash. Govt. Ptg. Off. 1887. 116p.   **4191**

—— Bibliography of the Iroquoian languages. (Bureau of Am. Ethnology. Bul. no. 6) Wash. Govt. Ptg. Off. 1888. 208p.   **4192**

—— Bibliography of the Muskhogean languages. (Bureau of Am. Ethnology. Bul. no. 9) Wash. Govt. Ptg Off. 1889. 114p.   **4193**

—— Bibliography of the Salishan languages. (Bureau of Am. Ethnology. Bul. no. 16) Wash. Govt. Ptg. Off. 1893. 86p.   **4194**

—— Bibliography of the Siouan languages. (Bureau of Am. Ethnology. Bul. no. 5) Wash. Govt. Ptg. Off. 1887. 87p.   **4195**

—— Bibliography of the Washashan languages. (Bureau of Am. Ethnology. Bul. no. 19) Wash. Govt. Ptg. Off. 1894. 70p.   **4196**

—— Catalogue of linguistic manuscripts in the library of the Bureau of American Ethnology. (Bureau of Am. Ethnology. Annual Rep. no. 1. 1879-80) Wash. Govt. Ptg. Off. 1881. p553-77   **4197**

—— Proof-sheets of a bibliography of languages of the North American Indians. (Bureau of Am. Ethnology) Wash. Govt. Ptg. Off. 1885. 1135p.   **4198**

Plume Trading & Sales Co., Inc. American Indian crafts, including suggestive outlines and bibliography of Indian lore. By Ralph Hubbard. N.Y. 1935. 64p. **4198a**

Powell, J. W. Literature relating to the classification of Indian languages. *In* Indian linguistic families. (Bureau of Am. Ethnology. Seventh annual rep. 1885-86) Wash. Govt. Ptg Off. 1891. p12-25   **4199**

Riverside, California. Public Library. Indians. (Bul. 136) Riverside, Calif. 1916. 29p.   **4200**

Roberts, R. B. Bibliography of the writings of American Indians. 7402 Bay Parkway, N.Y. In progress   **4200a**

Sabin, Joseph. Catalogue of the library belonging to Thomas W. Field. . . . N.Y. 1875. 393p.   **4201**

St. Louis. Public Library. Indians of North America; a list of books for children. Comp. by Louise P. Trask. St. Louis. 1921. 8p.   **4202**

Schmeckebier, Laurence F. Bibliography. *In* The office of Indian affairs; its history, activities and organization. (Inst. for Govt. Research. Service monographs of the U. S. govt. no. 48) Balt. Johns Hopkins Univ. Press. 1927. p537-80 **4203**

Schoolcraft, Henry Rowe. Literature of the Indian languages; a bibliographical catalogue of books, translations of the Scriptures, and other publications in the Indian tongues of the United States, with brief critical notices. *In* Information respecting the history, condition and prospects of the Indian tribes of the United States. Phila. Lippincott, Grambo & Co. 1854. IV. p523-54. (Reprint of his Bibliographical catalogue of books, etc., in the Indian tongues of the United States. Wash. D.C. C. Alexander. 1849. 27p.)   **4204**

Schuller, Rodolfo R. Lingüistica Americana; notas bibliográficas. De la Revista de archives, bibliotecas y museos. Madrid. 1912. 42p.   **4205**

Swadesh, M. Bibliography of American Indian linguistics, 1936-1937. Language. XIV. p318-23 (Oct. 1938)   **4205a**

Toomey, Thomas Noxon. Bibliographies of lesser North American linguistic families. (Hervas Laboratories of Am. Linguistics. Bul. 1) St. Louis. Hervas Laboratories. 1917. 20p.   **4206**

Trübner, N. A catalogue of works on the aboriginal languages of America. London. 1874   **4207**

Trumbull, J. Hammond. The Indian tongue and its literature as fashioned by Eliot and others. *In* The memorial history of Boston, including Suffolk county. Ed. by Justin Winsor. Boston. James R. Osgood. 1882. I. p465-80   **4208**

U.S. Department of Agriculture. Library. Agriculture of the American Indians; a classified list of annotated historical references with an introduction. Comp. by Everett E. Edwards. (Bibliog. contributions no. 23) Wash. D.C. 1932. 89p. mim.   **4209**

U.S. Library of Congress. Division of bibliography. Hopi Indians; a bibliographical list. Sept. 19, 1931. 5p. typ.   **4210**

—— —— —— List of books on Indians in North America. Aug. 4, 1932. 13p. typ.   **4211**

—— —— —— List of references on the relations of the Indians to the United States government. 1902. 35p. typ.   **4212**

—— —— —— The Pueblo Indians; a bibliographical list. Feb. 1, 1929. 10p. typ.   **4213**

—— —— —— References on Pocahontas supplementary to those in Hodge's Handbook of American Indians. June 4, 1932. 2p. typ.   **4214**

—— —— —— A selected list of books on the Indians of North America. Comp. by Helen F. Conover. Feb. 6, 1939. 25p. mim. **4214a**

U.S. Office of Indian Affairs. Bibliography of Indian affairs. (Bul. 2) Wash. D.C. 1923. 6p. **4215**

Vail, Robert W. G. Bibliography of American Indian captivities. Worcester, Mass. Am. Antiquarian Soc. In progress **4215a**

NEGRO AND SLAVERY

Book reviews—notes. Jour. negro hist. I-Jan. 1916- (includes periodical publications) **4215b**

Caliver, Ambrose and Greene, E. G. Education of negroes, 1931-1935. U.S. Office of Education bul. VIII. p1-63. 1937 **4215c**

Cardinall, Allan Wolsey. A bibliography of the Gold Coast; issued as a companion volume to the Census report of 1931. Accra, Gold Coast colony. Printed by the govt. printer. 1932. 384p. **4216**

Chicago Historical Society. Exhibition of objects illustrating the history and condition of the Republic of Liberia. 1914. n.p. n.p. 42p. **4217**

Clozel, Marie François Joseph. Bibliographie des ouvrages relatifs à la Sénégambie et au Soudan occidental. Paris. Ch. Delagrave. 1891. 60p. **4218**

Cook, P. A. W. A guide to the literature on Negro education. Teachers College rec. XXXIV. p671-7 (May 1933) **4219**

Cornell University. Library. May collection. Anti-slavery periodicals [authorship of tracts published by the American Anti-slavery Society]. Cornell Univ. Lib. bul. I. no. 8. p229-32 (Jan. 1884) **4220**

Damon, S. Foster. The Negro in early Amercan songsters. Bibliog. Soc. Amer. pap. XXVIII. pt. 2. p132-63. 1934 **4221**

Detweiler, F. E. The Negro press of the United States. Chicago. Univ. of Chicago Press. 1922. 274p. **4222**

Dubois, William E. B. Bibliography of the Negro folk song in America. Atlanta. (pub. ?) 1903 **4222a**

—— A select bibliography of the Negro American for general readers. (Atlanta Univ. Publications no. 10) Atlanta. Atlanta Univ. Press. 1905. 71p. **4223**

Dunlap, M. E. Special collections of Negro literature in the United States. Jour. of Negro education. IV. p482-9 (Oct. 1935) **4224**

Edwards, Richard Henry. The Negro problem; studies in American social conditions—2. Madison, Wis. Dec. 1908. 32p. **4225**

Eppse, Merl R. A guide to the study of the Negro in American history. Nashville, National Educational Pub. Co. 1937. 123p. **4225a**

Feipel, Louis N. Negro authors and their books. N.Y. Brooklyn Pub. Lib. In progress. **4225b**

Fisk University. Library. A select, classified, and briefly annotated list of two hundred fifty books by or about the negro, published during the past ten years. Comp. by S. E. Grinstead. Nashville, Tenn. 1939. 41p. mim. **4225c**

Fowler, Julian S. A classified catalogue of the collection of anti-slavery propaganda in the Oberlin College Library. Oberlin College Lib. bul. II. no. 3. 1932. 84p. **4226**

Funkhouser, Myrtle. Folk-lore of the American negro; a bibliography. Bul. of bibliog. XVI. p.28-9, 49-51, 72-3, 108-10, 136-7, 159-60 (Jan. 1937-Jan. 1939) **4226a**

Gay, Jean. Bibliographie des ouvrages relatifs à L'Afrique et à l'Arabie catalogue méthodique de tous les ouvrages français & des principaux en langues étrangères traitant de la géographie, de l'histoire, du commerce, des lettres & des arts de l'Afrique & de l'Arabie. San Remo. J. Gay & Fils. 1875. 312p. **4227**

Green, Elizabeth Lay. The Negro in contemporary American literature; an outline for individual and group study. Chapel Hill. Univ. of North Carolina Press. 1928. 94p. **4228**

Hampton, Va. Normal and Agricultural Institute. Collis P. Huntington library. A classified catalogue of the negro collection in the Collis P. Huntington Library, Hampton Institute. n.p. 1940. 255, [35]p. **4228a**

Howard University. Carnegie Library. Moorland foundation. A catalogue of books in the Moorland foundation. Comp. by workers on projects 271 and 328 of the Works Progress Administration, Margaret R. Hunton and Ethel Williams, supervisors, Dorothy B. Porter, director. Wash. D.C. 1939. 94, 166, 159, 23, 38, 19p. mim. **4228b**

Joucla, Edmond Antoine. Bibliographie de l'Afrique occidentale française. Paris. E. Sansot et cie. 1912. 275p. **4229**

Knox, Ellis O. Negroes as a subject of university research in 1932- . Jour. negro educ. II- . 1933- **4229a**

Lacy, Virginia. Bibliography of federal documents relating to the negro. Urbana. Univ. of Illinois Lib. School. In progress **4229b**

Lawson, Hilda Josephine. The negro in American drama (bibliography of contemporary negro drama). (Univ. of Illinois. Abstract of Ph.D. thesis, 1939) Urbana, Ill. 1939. 13p. **4229c**

Luke, Harry Charles Joseph. A bibliography of Sierra Leone, preceded by an essay on the origin, character and peoples of the colony and protectorate. London. Humphrey Milford, Oxford Univ. Press. 1925. 230p. **4230**

May, Samuel. Catalogue of anti-slavery publications in America. Am. Anti-slavery Soc. proc. at its third decade. Dec. 1863. p157-75. (Reprinted N.Y. 1864) **4231**

Murray, Daniel. Preliminary list of books and pamphlets by Negro authors for Paris exposition and Library of Congress. Wash. D.C. 1900. 8p. **4232**

National Urban League (for social service among Negroes). Dept. of research. Selected bibliography on the negro. N.Y. Nov. 1940. 58p. mim. **4232a**

—— —— Source materials on the urban negro in the United States, 1910-1938; a list of selected data. N.Y. The League. 1939. 71p. mim. **4232b**

New York. Public Library. List of works relating to the American colonization society, Negro colonization, etc., in the New York Public Library. N. Y. Pub. Lib. bul. VI. p265-9 (July 1902) **4233**

—— —— 135th street branch. The negro; a selected bibliography. N.Y. New York Pub. Lib. 1935. 21p. (Reprinted from the Branch library book news of April-May 1935) **4233a**

Phillips, M. R. and Miller, C. L. A selected annotated bibliography on relationship of the federal government to negro education. Jour. negro educ. VII. p468-74 (July 1938) **4233b**

Pier, Helen L. and Spalding, Mary Louisa. The Negro in industry; a selected bibliography. Monthly labor rev. XXII. p216-44 (Jan. 1926) **4234**

Porter, Dorothy Burnett. Afro-American writings published before 1835, with a list of imprints written by American Negroes, 1760-1835. (Columbia Univ. Thesis) [N.Y.] 1932 **4234a**

—— Library sources for the study of Negro life and history. Jour. of Negro education. V. p232-44 (April 1936) **4234b**

Reid, Ira De Augustine. Negro youth, their social and economic backgrounds; a selected bibliography of unpublished studies, 1900-1938. Wash. D.C. Am. Council on Education, Am. Youth Comm. 1939. 71p. mim. **4234c**

Ross, Frank Alexander and Kennedy, Louise Venable. A bibliography of Negro migration. N.Y. Columbia Univ. press. 1934. 251p. **4235**

Russell Sage foundation, New York. Library. Negro housing in towns and cities, 1927-1937. N.Y. Russell Sage foundation. 1937. 5p. **4235a**

St. Louis. Public Library. The American Negro; a selected list of books. Comp. by Norma Klinge and George-Anna Tod. St. Louis. St. Louis Pub. Lib. 1923. 14p. (Reprinted from St. Louis Pub. Lib. bul. n.s. XX. p282-93. Dec. 1922) (Similar titled list in ibid. XXVII. p237-54. Aug. 1929) **4236**

Schomburg, Arthur Alfonso. A bibliographical checklist of American Negro poetry (Bibliographical Americana; a series of monographs. Ed. by Charles F. Heartman, II). N.Y. C. F. Heartman. 1916. 57p. **4237**

Sieg, Vera. The Negro problem; a bibliography. (Wisconsin Free Lib. Comn. Am. social questions no. 1) Madison, Wis. Nov. 1908. 22p. **4238**

Spingarn, A. B. Collecting a library of negro literature. Jour. negro educ. VII. p12-18 (Jan. 1938) **4238a**

—— —— —— The negro; a selected list for school libraries of books by or about the negro in Africa and America. Nashville, Tenn. State Dept. of Education. 1941. 48p. **4238b**

Turner, Lorenzo Dow. Anti-slavery sentiment in American literature prior to 1865. (Univ. of Chicago. Ph.D. thesis) Wash. D.C. Asso. for the Study of Negro Life and Hist. Inc. 1929. 188p. **4239**

U.S. Bureau of Foreign and Domestic Commerce. Bibliography, the Negro in business. [Wash. 1935] 6p. mim. **4240**

U.S. Commissioner of Education. Bibliography of Negro education. (U.S. Commissioner of Education. Rep. 1893-94. I) Wash. Govt. Ptg. Off. 1896. p1038-61 **4241**

U.S. Library of Congress. Division of bibliography. List of books relating to the West coast of Africa (excepting Liberia and Nigeria) in the Library of Congress. 1908. 25p. **4242**

—— —— List of recent references on the Negro, with special reference to economic and industrial conditions. Sept. 30, 1935. 20p. typ. **4243**

—— —— —— A list of references on Negro migration. Dec. 20, 1923. 6p. typ. **4244**

—— —— —— List of references on Negro segregation in the United States. April 14, 1927. 7p. typ. **4245**

—— —— —— List of references on the Negro and the European war. Feb. 5, 1919. 3p. typ. **4246**

—— —— —— Select list of references on the Negro question. Comp. under the direction of A. P. C. Griffin. Wash. Govt. Ptg. Off. 1906. 61p. (Supplement. Oct. 30, 1911. 16p. typ.; Feb. 25, 1915. 9p. typ.; Feb. 3, 1926. 10p. typ.) **4247**

U.S. Office of Education. Bibliography on education of the Negro comprising publications from January 1928 to December 1930. Comp. by Ambrose Caliver and others. (U.S. Office of Education Bul. 1931. no. 17) Wash. Govt. Ptg. Off. 1931. 34p. **4248**

—— —— Good references on the life and education of negroes. Comp. by Ambrose Caliver and Ethel G. Greene. (Bibliog. no. 68) Wash. D.C. 1940. 13p. **4248a**

Viñaza, Cipriano Muñoz y Manzano, El conde de la. Bibliografía española de lenguas indígenas de América. Madrid. "Sucesors de Rivadeneyra." 1892. 427p. **4249**

Wauters, Alphonse Jules. Bibliographie du Congo, 1880-1895; catalogue méthodique de 3,800 ouvrages, brochures, notices et cartes relatifs à l'histoire, à la géographie et à la colonisation du Congo. Brussels. Administration du mouvement géographique. 1895. 356p. **4250**

Williamson, Harry A. The Negro in Masonic literature. Brooklyn, N.Y. 1922. 30p. **4251**

Woodson, Carter G. Ten years of collecting and publishing the records of the negro. Jour. negro hist. X. p598-606 (Oct. 1925) **4251a**

Work, Monroe N. A bibliography of the Negro in Africa and America. N.Y. H. W. Wilson. 1928. 698p. **4252**

—— A bibliography of the Negro in the United States. *In* Negro year book; an annual encyclopedia of the Negro, 1925-1926. Tuskegee Inst., Ala. Negro Year Book Publishing Co. 1925. p473-510 **4253**

—— A world bibliography of the negro, 1928-1938. Tuskegee Institute, Alabama. In progress (Supplement to his Bibliography of the negro in Africa and America) **4253a**

Wyeth, Ola M. Negro spirituals. Am. Lib. Asso. bul. XXVI. p520-4 (Aug. 1932) **4253b**

IMMIGRATION

Bogardus, E. S. The Mexican immigrant; an annotated bibliography. Los Angeles. Published by the Council on International Relations. June 1929. 21p. **4254**

Boston. Public Library. Americanization; a selected list of books in the public library of the city of Boston. (Brief reading lists no. 12. May 1919) Boston. The Trustees. 1919. 34p. **4255**

Edwards, Richard Henry. Immigration studies in American social conditions -3. Madison, Wis. Jan. 1909. 31p. **4256**

Grant, Madison. List of authoritative works on immigration [printed for the use of the Committee on immigration and naturalization, House of Representatives, December 24, 1928]. [Wash. Govt. Ptg. Off. 1928] 3p. **4257**

Janeway, William Ralph. Bibliography of immigration in the United States, 1900-1930. Columbus, Ohio. H. L. Hedrick. 1934. 132p. photolithographed **4258**

Lancour, A. Harold. Passenger lists of ships coming to North America, 1607-1825, a bibliography. N.Y. New York Pub. Lib. 1938. 26p. (Reprinted with revisions and additions from the New York Pub. Lib. bul. XLI. p389-410. May 1937) **4258a**

MacGeorge, Aileen Eleanor. Restriction of immigration, 1920 to 1925; a selected bibliography. Monthly labor rev. XXII. p510-26 (Feb. 1926) **4259**

Panunzio, Constantine. The immigrant portrayed in biography and story; a selected list with notes. N.Y. Foreign Language Information Service. 1925. 16p. **4260**

Pittsburgh. Carnegie Library. Foreign-born Americans; their contribution to American life and culture; a selected list. Pittsburgh. Carnegie Lib. 1920. 30p. **4261**

Ray, Mary Katherine. The immigration problem; a bibliography. (Wisconsin Free Lib. Comn. Am. social questions no, 2) Madison, Wis. 1909. 21p. **4262**

Talbot, Winthrop. Select bibliography on Americanization. *In* Americanization; principles of Americanization, essentials of Americanization, technic of race-assimilation; annotated bibliography. N.Y. H. W. Wilson. 1917. p.xiii-lii **4263**

U.S. Bureau of immigration. Catalogue of books and blanks used by the immigration service. January 1931. Wash. Govt. Ptg. Off. 1931. 12p. **4264**

U.S. Library of Congress. Division of bibliography. Brief list of recent references on immigration and the labor supply. Jan. 12, 1920. 5p. multig. **4265**

—— —— Citizenship; a list of books. March 16, 1933. 8p. mim. **4266**

—— —— Deportation of aliens; a bibliographical list. 1931. 11p. mim. **4267**

—— —— Immigration and its restriction in the United States; list of recent writings. April 12, 1930. 25p. mim. **4268**

—— —— Immigration and its restriction in the United States: a selected list of recent writings. Jan. 6, 1937. 86p. **4268a**

—— —— List of books (with references to periodicals) on immigration. Comp. under the direction of A. P. C. Griffin. Wash. Govt. Ptg. Off. 1907. 157p. **4269**

—— —— List of hearings held before the Senate committee on immigration and the House committee on immigration and naturalization together with compilations of immigration laws. Dec. 17, 1923. 8p. typ. **4270**

—— —— List of recent references on immigration in the United States, with special reference to the immigration act, 1924. Dec. 15, 1924. 9p. mim. **4271**

—— —— List of references on American immigration, including Americanization, effect of European war, etc. Sept. 16, 1918. 28p. dup. (Supplement. Jan. 13, 1920. 36p. mim.) **4272**

—— —— List of references on citizenship. April 15, 1926. 5p. mim. **4273**

—— —— List of references on immigration legislation 1911-1916. Oct. 12, 1916. 4p. typ. **4274**

—— —— List of references on intermarriage of races, with special emphasis on immigrants. March 8, 1920. 4p. multig. **4275**

—— —— List of references on naturalization and citizenship (exclusive of Americanization) 1910-1920. June 2, 1920. 30p. typ. **4276**

—— —— A list of references on naturalization in the United States, 1920-1931. June 5, 1931. 22p. typ. **4277**

—— —— List of references on recent immigration legislation in the United States. Feb. 9, 1923. 7p. multig. **4278**

—— —— A list of references on the citizenship and nationality of women. April 3, 1931. 6p. typ. **4279**

—— —— List of references on the immigrant in literature. July 1, 1921. 11p. mim. **4280**

U.S. Library of Congress. Division of bibliography. List of references on the "National origins" provision of the immigration act of 1924. June 26, 1926. 5p. typ. **4281**

—— —— —— List of references on the rights of aliens in the United States. March 25, 1924. 9p. typ. **4282**

—— —— —— Select list of references on Chinese immigration. Comp. under the direction of A. P. C. Griffin. Wash. Govt. Ptg. Off. 1904. 31p. (Supplement. 1905. 4p. typ.; Nov. 28, 1919. 6p. typ.; Nov. 26, 1929. 6p. typ.) **4283**

—— —— —— Select list of references on immigration restriction by an educational test. Jan. 13, 1913. 7p. typ. **4284**

MISCELLANEOUS

American Jewish Historical Society. Index to the publications of the American Jewish Historical Society, numbers 1 to 20. N.Y. The Soc. 1914. 600p. **4285**

American-Scandinavian Foundation. Union catalog of books on the Scandinavian countries, books in Scandinavian languages, and books by Scandinavian authors. N.Y. Cards **4285a**

Benson, Adolph B. The Scandinavian collection in the Yale University Library. Scandinavian stud. and notes. XIII. p33-47. 1934. MSS. **4285b**

Bibliographisches handbuch des auslanddeutschtums. Stuttgart. Deutsche Ausland-Institut. Ausland und Heimat-Verlags-A-G. 1932-33. 7 fasc. **4285c**

Brown, Francis J. and Roucek, J. S., eds. Selected bibliography. *In* Our racial and national minorities; their history, contributions, and present problems. N.Y. Prentice-Hall. 1937. p781-847 **4285d**

Čapek, Thomas. Padesát let českeho tisku v Americe od vydání "Slowana amerikánského" v Racine, dne I. ledna 1860 do I. ledna 1910. S doplňku do Začáku. 1911. N.Y. "Bank of Europe." 1911. 273p. (Bohemian American newspapers and literature) **4286**

Faust, Albert Bernhardt. Bibliography. *In* The German element in the United States. Boston, N.Y. Houghton Mifflin. 1909. II. p479-562 **4287**

Firkins, Ina Ten Eyck. Dutch in the United States. Bul. of bibliog. IX. p68-9 (July 1916) **4288**

—— Irish in the United States. Bul. of bibliog. IX. p22-4 (Jan. 1916) **4289**

—— Italians in the United States. Bul. of bibliog. VIII. p129-32 (Jan. 1915) **4290**

—— Japanese in the United States. Bul. of bibliog. VIII. p94-8 (Oct. 1914) **4291**

—— Scandinavians in the United States. Bul. of bibliog. VIII. p160-3 (April 1915) **4292**

—— Slavs in the United States. Bul. of bibliog. VIII. p217-20 (Oct. 1915) **4293**

Friedrich, Gerhard. A new supplement to Seidensticker's American-German bibliography. Pa. hist. VII. p213-24 (Oct. 1940) **4293a**

Greene, Amy Blanche. Handbook—bibliography on foreign language groups in the United States and Canada. N.Y. Council of Women for Home Missions and Missionary Education Movement. 1925. 160p. **4294**

Harvard College. Library. Union catalog of Scandinavian materials. Cambridge, Mass. Cards **4294a**

Helbig, Richard E. German American researches; the growth of the German American collection of the New York Public Library during 1906-1907; its importance for historical and literary studies. Reprinted from German-Am. ann. n.s. VI. no. 5. Sept. and Oct. 1908. p257-85 **4295**

Hodnefield, Jacob. Some recent publications relating to Norwegian-American history. Norwegian-Am. Hist. Soc. stud. V- . 1930- **4296**

Italian Library of Information. A selected list of bibliographical references and records of the Italians in the United States. N.Y. 1938. 19p. mim. **4296a**

Kenton, Alice M. Polish people in the United States; a selected bibliography. Monthly labor rev. XXII. p730-6 (March 1926) **4297**

Kohut, George A. Early Jewish literature in America. Am. Jewish Hist. Soc. publication no. 3. p103-47. 1895 **4298**

Mai, Richard. Auslanddeutsche quellenkunde, 1924-1933. Berlin. Weidmannsche buchhandlung. 1938 (Vereinigte Staaten, p353-68) **4298a**

Margoshes, Samuel. A list of books and articles on the Jews of New York. *In* The Jewish communal register of New York city, 1917-1918. Ed. by Kehillah (Jewish community) N.Y. 1918. p1503-24 **4299**

Meynen, Emil, ed. Bibliography on German settlements in colonial North America, especially on the Pennsylvania Germans and their descendants, 1683-1933. Leipzig. Otto Harrassowitz. 1937. 636p. **4299a**

Noé, Adolf C. von. A preliminary bibliography of German books on the United States since 1880. Bibliog. Soc. Amer. pap. IV. p102-19. 1909 **4300**

Pilcher, Margaret L. Racial elements in the United States. St. Louis Pub. lib. monthly bul. n.s. XVI. p389-402 (Oct. 1918) **4301**

Rosenbach, A. S. W. An American Jewish bibliography; being a list of books and pamphlets by Jews or relating to them published in the United States from the establishment of the press in the colonies until 1850. (Am. Jewish Hist. Soc. publication no. 30) Balt. [The Lord Baltimore Press] 1926. 486p. **4302**

Rosengarten, J. G. Sources of (German-American) history. A paper read before the German-American Historical Society of New York and the Pioneer-Verein of Philadelphia. Phila. Wm. F. Fell. 1892. 32p. **4303**

Seidensticker, Oswald. Deutsch-Americanische bibliographie bis zum schlusse des letzten jahrhunderts. Der Deutsche pioneer. IX. p178-83, 241-5, 264-8, 324-8, 348-51; X. 22-8, 62-6, 94-101, 133-6, 194-9, 224-30, 264-70, 309-16, 374, 422-9, 460-72; XII. 220-4 (Aug. 1877-Sept. 1880) **4304**

U.S. Bureau of Agricultural Economics. Division of statistical and historical research. References on Jewish agricultural communities in America. Comp. by Everett E. Edwards. [Wash. D.C. April 1934] 10p. typ. **4305**

—— —— —— References on the Filipinos in the United States. [Wash. D.C. Jan. 1935] 10p. typ. **4306**

U.S. Library of Congress. Division of bibliography. Brief list of references on Canadians in the United States. June 19, 1925. 5p. typ. **4307**

—— —— —— Brief list of references on racial migration. Nov. 9, 1922. 6p. typ. **4308**

—— —— —— List of references on Japanese in America. Dec. 18, 1916. 16p. typ. (Supplements. Nov 6, 1919. 4p. typ.; Nov. 20, 1920. 26p. mim.; Nov. 5, 1924. 10p. mim.) **4309**

—— —— —— List of references on Mexicans in the United States. Sept. 10, 1920. 2p. typ. **4310**

—— —— —— List of references on Scandinavians in America. June 29, 1916. 5p. typ. **4311**

—— —— —— List of references on Slavs in America. Nov. 15, 1920. 8p. mim. **4312**

—— —— —— List of references on the Chinese boycott. Feb. 25, 1932. 6p. typ. **4313**

—— —— —— List of references on the Italians in the United States (supplementary to printed list on immigration, 1907). Nov. 21, 1917. 7p. typ. **4314**

—— —— —— A list of works relating to the Germans in the United States. Comp. under the direction of A. P. C. Griffin. Wash. Govt. Ptg. Off. 1904. 32p. **4315**

—— —— —— Mexican labor in the United States; a brief bibliographical list. Jan. 11, 1928. 5p. typ. **4316**

—— —— —— Race problem in the United States; a brief bibliographical list. Jan. 29, 1929. 5p. typ. **4317**

—— —— **Reading room.** Y Cymry yn America; the Welsh in America; references to literature available in the Library of Congress. 1925. 18p. typ. **4318**

CHAPTER X

RELIGIOUS HISTORY

GENERAL

Ayer, Joseph Cullen. Yarnall Library of Theology of St. Clement's Church, Philadelphia; the Ellis Hornor Yarnall Foundation. Phila. n.p. 1933. 334p.　**4321**

Betten, Francis Sales. A short bibliography of church history for the use of teachers and students. Techny, Ill. Printed by the Mission Press. 1936. 32p.　**4321a**

Bodine, William Budd. Some hymns and hymn writers representing all who profess and call themselves Christians; short studies in the hymnal of the Episcopal church. Phila. Winston. 1907. 458p.　**4322**

Boston. Public Library. Catalogue of selected editions of the book of common prayer both English and American, together with illuminated missals in manuscript, early printed books of hours and other books of devotion, in the possession of private collectors in Boston or owned by the Boston Public and Harvard College libraries. . . . Boston. The Trustees. 1907. 52p.　**4323**

Bowerman, George Franklin. A selected bibliography of the religious denominations of the United States; with a list of the most important Catholic works of the world as an appendix compiled by J. H. McMahon. N.Y. Cathedral Lib. Asso. 1896. 94p.　**4324**

Bradshaw, Marion J. The war and religion; a preliminary bibliography of material in English, prior to January 1, 1919. N.Y. Associated Press. 1919. 136p.　**4325**

Case, Shirley Jackson and others. Christianity in the Americas; a bibliographical guide to the history of Christianity. (Univ. of Chicago. Publications in religious education. Handbooks of ethics and religion) Chicago. Univ. of Chicago press. 1931. 265p.　**4326**

Chicago. University. Library. Union catalog of manuscript and out-of-print sources for the history of Christianity on American frontiers. (In progress)　**4327**

Crum, Mason. A guide to religious pageantry. N.Y. Macmillan. 1923. 134p.　**4328**

Darling, James. Cyclopaedia bibliographica; a library manual of theological and general literature and guide to books, for authors, preachers, students and literary men; analytical, bibliographical and biographical. London. J. Darling. 1854-59. 3328p.　**4329**

Émery, Louis. Introduction à l'étude de la théologie protestante, avec index bibliographicus. Lausanne. 1904. 710p.　**4330**

General Theological Library. Catalogue of the General Theological Library, Boston, Massachusetts; a dictionary catalogue of religion, theology, sociology, and allied literature. Boston. Fort Hill Press. 1913. 313p.　**4331**

Goodenough, Caroline Louisa. High lights on hymnists and their hymns. Rochester, Mass. The author. 1931. 505p. (American hymnists treated p283-473　**4332**

Guilday, Peter. Guide to the materials for American church history in the Westminster diocesan archives (1675-1798). Catholic hist. rev. V. p382-401 (Jan. 1920)　**4333**

Hurst, John Fletcher. Literature of theology; a classified bibliography of theological and general religious literature. N.Y. Hunt & Eaton; Cincinnati. Cranston & Curts. 1896. 757p.　**4334**

International Council of Religious Education. Bureau of research. Abstracts in religious education; selected graduate theses in religious education, 1933- . Chicago. The Bureau. 1935- . 54p. mim.　**4334a**

International missionary bibliography. *In* Internat. rev. of missions. I. Jan. 1912-　**4334b**

International Missionary Council. Directory of foreign missions, missionary boards, societies, colleges, cooperative councils, and other agencies of the Protestant churches of the world. Ed. by Esther B. Strong and Abbé Livingston Warnshuis. N.Y., London. International Missionary Council. 1933. 278p. (Contains material on their publications)　**4335**

Jackson, Samuel Macauley. Bibliography of American church history, 1820-93. (Am. church history ser. XII) N.Y. Christian Literature Co.; Scribner. 1894. p441-513　**4336**

—— A contribution towards a missionary bibliography. *In* Report of the centenary conference on the Protestant missions of the world. . . Ed. by the Rev. James Johnston. London. J. Nisbet & Co. 1889. p489-538　**4337**

—— Works of interest to the student of church history which appeared in 1891 to 1894; a bibliography. Am. Soc. of Church Hist. pap. IV. p.xxv-lviii; V. xxv-lxxxii; VII. xxiii-cclviii. 1892-95　**4338**

Jackson, Samuel Macauley and Gilmore, G. W. Bibliography of foreign missions. N.Y. Funk & Wagnalls. 1891. p575-661 (Reprinted from Encyclopaedia of missions)　**4339**

Julian, John. Dictionary of hymnology; setting forth the origin and history of Christian hymns of all ages and nations . . . with biographical and critical notices of their authors and translations. London. J. Murray. 1892. 1616p. **4340**

Laurie, Thomas. List of publications of the several missions of the A.B.C.F.M. in the languages of the countries where they are situated. *In* The Ely volume; or, The contributions of our foreign missions to science and human well-being. Boston. Am. Board of commissioners for Foreign Missions. 1881. 532p. **4341**

Malcom, Howard. Theological index; references to the principal works in every department of religious literature. Boston. Gould & Lincoln. 1868. 487p. **4342**

Mampoteng, Charles. The Library [of the General Theological Seminary] and American church history. P. E. church hist. mag. V. p225-37. 1936 (Materials for American church history and Episcopal church periodicals) **4342a**

Mathews, Shailer and Smith, Gerald Birney. Bibliography. *In* A dictionary of religion and ethics. N.Y. Macmillan. 1921. p485-513 **4343**

Missionary Research Library, New York. Recommended titles on missions and related subjects. By Hollis W. Hering. N.Y. Com. of reference and counsel. 1925. 29p. **4344**

Mode, Peter G. Source book and bibliographical guide for American church history. Menasha, Wis. George Banta Publishing Co. 1921. 735p. **4345**

Murray, John Lovell. A selected bibliography of missionary literature. N.Y. Student Volunteer Movement. 1920. 58p. **4346**

New York. Public Library. List of periodicals in the New York Public Library, General Theological Seminary, and Union Theological Seminary, relating to religion, theology, and church history. N.Y. Pub. Lib. bul. IX. p9-31 (Jan. 1905) **4347**

Newberry Library. Religions, philosophy of religion, folk-lore, ethnic religions. Chicago. 1925. 237p. multig. as MS. **4348**

O'Callaghan, Edmund Bailey. A list of editions of the Holy Scriptures and parts thereof, printed in America previous to 1860, with introduction and bibliographical notes. Albany, N.Y. Munsell and Rowland. 1861. 415p. **4349**

Princeton Theological Seminary. Catalogue of the library of Princeton Theological Seminary. Pt. I. Religious literature. Princeton. C. S. Robinson & Co. 1886. 453p. **4350**

Religious Education Association. An index to all the publications of the Religious Education Association from February, 1903 to February, 1912. Chicago. Religious Education Asso. [1912?] 40p. **4350a**

Schaff, Philip and others. The American church history series. N.Y. The Christian Literature Co. 1893-94. 13v. (The volumes in the series contain bibliographies.) **4351**

U.S. Library of Congress. Division of bibliography. Brief list of references on Church unity and federation. Jan. 14, 1919. 4p. typ. **4352**

—— —— —— List of recent references on the effect of the European war on religion. June 16, 1922. 10p. typ. **4353**

—— —— —— List of references on church management and finance. Dec. 5, 1924. 7p. typ. **4354**

—— —— —— List of references on conscientious objectors. June 27, 1917. 3p. typ. **4355**

—— —— —— List of references on the country church in the life of the community (including the Church library). Jan. 3, 1919. 4p. typ. **4356**

—— —— —— List of references on the history of religious tolerance in the United States. Dec. 19, 1921. 9p. typ. **4357**

—— —— —— List of references on the Sunday-school. Jan. 28, 1915. 14p. typ. **4358**

—— —— —— List of yearbooks issued by the churches. July 15, 1926. 4p. typ. **4359**

—— —— —— Religion, historical and comparative; a short bibliographical list. Feb. 19, 1930. 5p. typ. **4360**

—— —— —— Select list of references on a weekly rest day and Sunday legislation. Nov. 6, 1912. 30p. dupl. **4361**

—— —— —— Select list of references on the evolution of religious liberty in the United States. 1907. 6p. typ. **4362**

Vernon, Ambrose White. Later theology. *In* The Cambridge history of American literature. Ed. by William P. Trent and others. N.Y. G. P. Putnam's. 1921. III. p201-5; IV. p742-51 **4363**

White, R. C. Writings pertaining to religion in eighteenth century American magazines. (Harvard Univ. thesis) **4363a**

Whitman, W. F. A church history bibliography for 1918-1920, inclusive. Cath. hist. rev. VIII. p333-59 (Oct. 1922) **4363b**

Wilson, Louis N. List of papers in the field of religious psychology. (Publications of Clark Univ. Lib. II. no. 8) Worcester. Clark Univ. Press 1911. 9p. **4364**

Wolff, Samuel Lee. Divines and moralists, 1783-1860. *In* The Cambridge history of American literature. Ed. by William P. Trent and others. N.Y. G. P. Putnam's. 1918. II. p196-223, 524-39 **4365**

Wright, John. Early Bibles of America; being a descriptive account of Bibles published in the United States, Mexico and Canada. N.Y. Thomas Whittaker. 1894. 483p. **4366**

—— Early prayer books of America; being a descriptive account of prayer books published in the United States, Mexico and Canada. St. Paul, Minn. Priv. printed. 1896. 492p. **4367**

—— Historic Bibles in America. N.Y. Thomas Whittaker. 1905. 222p. **4368**

Wylie, Alexander. Memorials of Protestant missionaries to the Chinese; giving a list of their publications and obituary notices of the deceased. . . Shanghai. Am. Presbyterian Mission Press. 1867. 331p. **4369**

Yale University. Divinity School. Day Missions Library. Catalogue of the foreign mission library of the Divinity School of Yale University. New Haven, Conn. no. 1-6. Jan. 1892-March 1902. New Haven. The Tuttle Morehouse & Taylor Press. 1895-1902. 6v. in 1 **4370**

Zion Research Library. Catalogue of the Zion Research Library, Brookline, Mass. Boston. T. O. Metcalf Co. 1930. 168p. (New books of the. . . ., 1930-32. 4 pamphlets) **4371**

BAPTIST

American Baptist Historical Society, Chester, Pa. Card index to Baptist history and biography. (Contains 30,000 cards) **4372**

—— **Library.** Catalogue of the books and manuscripts in the library of the American Baptist Historical Society, August 1874. [Phila. 1874] 108, 40p. **4373**

Crowell, William. Literature of American baptists, from 1814 to 1864. *In* American Baptist Missionary Union. The Missionary jubilee. . . . N.Y. Sheldon; Boston. Gould & Lincoln. 1865. p391-461 **4374**

Dexter, Henry Martyn. The true story of John Smyth, the Se-Baptist . . ., with collections toward a bibliography of the first two generations of the Baptist controversy. Boston. Lee & Shepard. 1881. (Bibliog. on p87-106) **4375**

Flory, John S. Appendix . . . work produced, either written or printed by the German Baptists in the eighteenth century. *In* Literary activity of the German Baptist brethren in the eighteenth century. Elgin, Ill. Brethren Publishing House. 1908. p291-327 **4376**

Haynes, T. W. Baptist cyclopaedia, or dictionary of Baptist biography, bibliography, etc. Charleston, N.C. 1848 **4377**

London. University. Regent's Park College. Angus Library. Catalogue of the books, pamphlets & manuscripts in the Angus Library at Regent's Park College, London. London. Kingsgate Press. 1908. 348p. **4378**

McIntyre, Willard E. Baptist authors; a manual of bibliography, 1500-1914. Montreal and Toronto. Industrial and Educational Press, Ltd. 1914. 192p. 30 nos. **4379**

Northern Baptist Convention. General Board of Promotion. Catalog of missionary literature, June 1922; a catalog of the missionary literature of the societies and boards of the Northern Baptist convention. N.Y. The General Board of Promotion of the Northern Baptist Convention [1922] 47p. **4379a**

Starr, Edward C. The Samuel Colgate Baptist historical collection. N.Y. hist. XIX. p263-8 (July 1938) (MSS. and published material at Colgate Univ.) **4379b**

Whitley, William Thomas. Baptist bibliography; being a register of the chief materials for Baptist history, whether in manuscript or print, preserved in Great Britain, Ireland, and the colonies. Comp. for the Baptist Union of Great Britain and Ireland. London. Kingsgate Press. 1916-22. 2v. **4380**

CATHOLIC

American Catholic Historical society. Index of the American Catholic historical researches, covering all its issues, volumes I-XXIX, July 1884-July 1912. Phila. Am. Catholic Hist. Soc. 1916. 320p. **4381**

—— Index to the Records of the American Catholic Historical Society, volumes I-XXXI, 1886-1920. Phila. Am. Catholic Hist. Soc. 1924. 515p. **4382**

—— A list of some early American publications (Catholic history). Am. Catholic hist. rec. XXXI. p248-56 (Sept. 1920) **4383**

American Catholic quarterly review; general index volumes I to XXV, January 1876-October 1900. Phila. [1901] 64p. **4384**

Bibliographia de historia S.J. *In* Archivum historicum Societatis Iesu. I. 1932- **4384a**

Billington, Ray Allen. Tentative bibliography of anti-Catholic propaganda in the United States (1800-1860). Catholic hist. rev. n.s. XII. p492-513 (Jan. 1933) **4385**

Bolton, Herbert E. The Jesuits in America: an opportunity for historians. Mid-America. XVIII. p223-33 (Oct. 1936) **4385a**

Brown, Stephen J. Catholic mission literature; a handlist. (Catholic bibliog. ser. no. 3) Dublin. Central Catholic Lib. 1932. 105p. **4386**

The **Catholic** bookman; international . . . survey of Catholic literature, I- Sept. 1937- Detroit. W. Romig. 1937- **4386a**

"**Catholic** encyclopedia" diocesan bibliography. Catholic hist. rev. IV. p264-73, 389-93, 542-6 (July 1918-Jan. 1919) (Books listed in the Catholic encyclopedia on the dioceses and archdioceses of the United States) **4387**

Catholic historical review. General index to volumes I-XX, April 1915 to January 1935. Comp. by Rev. Harold J. Bolton. Wash. D.C. 1938. 228p. **4387a**

Catholic School Book Co., New York. Catalogue of Catholic books published in the United States. [N.Y. 1893-97?] 96p. **4388**

Code, Joseph B. A selected bibliography of the religious orders and congregations of women founded within the present boundaries of the United States (1727-1850). Cath. hist. rev. XXIII. p331-51 (Oct. 1937); XXVI. p222-45 (July 1940) **4388a**

Dunne, Peter M. Jesuit annual letters in the Bancroft Library. Mid-America. XX. p263-72. 1938 **4388b**

English, Adrian T. The historiography of American Catholic history. Catholic hist. rev. n.s. V. p561-95 (Jan. 1926) **4389**

Finotti, Joseph M. Bibliographia Catholica Americana; a list of works written by Catholic authors, and published in the United States. N.Y. Catholic Publishing House. 1872. 318p. **4390**

Flynn, Thomas J. & Co. A complete catalogue of Catholic literature; containing all Catholic books published in the United States, together with a selection from the catalogue of the Catholic publishers of England and Ireland. Boston. T. J. Flynn. 1910. 218p. **4391**

Foik, Paul J. Pioneer efforts in Catholic journalism in the United States (1809-1840). Catholic hist. rev. I. p258-70 (July 1915) **4392**

—— Survey of source materials for the Catholic history of the Southwest. Catholic hist. rev. IX. p275-81 (Oct. 1929) **4393**

Guilday, Peter. Guide to the biographical sources of the American hierarchy. Catholic hist. rev. V. p120-8, 290-6; VI. p128-32, 267-71, 548-52 (April 1919-Jan. 1921) **4394**

—— Recent studies in American Catholic history. The Ecclesiastical rev. LXXXIV. p528-46 (May 1931) **4395**

—— The writing of parish histories. The Ecclesistical rev. XCIII. p236-57. (Sept. 1935) **4396**

Heimbucher, Max Joseph. Die orden und kongregationen der Katholischen kirche grossenteils neubearb. aufl. Paderborn. F. Schöningh. 1933-34. 2v. (With extensive bibliographical notes) **4397**

Holweck, F. G. The historical archives of the archdiocese of St. Louis. St. Louis Catholic hist. rev. I. p24-39 (Oct. 1918) **4398**

Lallou, William L. The archives of the American Catholic Historical Society [Philadelphia]. Catholic hist. rev. I. p193-5 (July 1915) **4399**

Meier, Joseph. The official Catholic directory. Cath. hist. rev. I. p299-304 (Oct. 1915) **4399a**

Parsons, Wilfrid. First American editions of Catholic Bibles. U.S. Cath. hist. soc. rec. XXVII. p89-98. 1937 **4399b**

Paschal, Robinson. A short introduction to Franciscan literature. N.Y. 1907. 55p. **4399c**

Periodical literature. Catholic hist. rev. I- April 1930- **4400**

Pittsburgh. Carnegie Library. Books by Catholic authors in the Carnegie Library of Pittsburgh; a classified and annotated list. Pittsburgh. Carnegie Lib. 1911. 240p. **4401**

Rommerskirchen, Giovanni and Dindinger, Giovanni, eds. Bibliografia missionaria... anno [I]- . 1933- . Isola del Liri. Soc. tip. A. Maciace & Pisani. 1935- **4401a**

St. Charles Seminary. Index of historical pamphlets in the library of St. Charles Seminary, Overbrook, Pa. Am. Catholic Hist. Soc. of Phila. rec. XIII. p60-119 (March 1902) (Roman Catholic church in Phila.) **4401b**

Schmitt, Edmund J. P. Bibliographia Benedictina; oder, Verzeichnis der schriftsteller des Benedictinerordens in den Vereinigten Statten Nord-Amerika's. Brunn. Raigerner Benedictiner-buchdruckerei. 1893. 66p. **4402**

Shea, John Gilmary. A bibliographical account of Catholic Bibles, Testaments, and other portions of Scripture, translated from the Latin Vulgate, and printed in the United States. N.Y. Cramoisy Press. 1859. 48p. (Reprinted from the N.Y. Freeman's jour.) **4403**

—— An essay on the bibliography of the councils, synods, statutes of the Catholic church in the United States. N.Y. 1890. 16p. **4404**

Streit, Robert. Americanische missionsliteratur. *In* Bibliotheca missionum. Veröffentlichungen des internationalen instituts für missionswissenschaftlichen forschung, vol. II-III. Aachen. Xaverius Verlagsbuchhandlung A.-G. 1924, 1929 **4405**

Stuart, Anna M. Catholic writers of Iowa. Iowa Catholic hist. rev. IV. p3-31 (April 1932) **4406**

Trenton. Public Library. Catholic catalogue, including Catholic authors and also certain works of Protestant authors which have some special interest for Catholics. Trenton council, no. 155, Knights of Columbus. 1908. 63p. **4407**

Université Catholique de Louvain. Revue d'histoire ecclesiastique, I- Louvain. 1900- **4408**

Washington, D.C. Public Library. Catalogue of Catholic and other select authors in the public library of the District of Columbia. Comp. by Julia H. Laskey. Wash. D.C. The Lib. 1915. 120p. **4409**

Willging, Eugene P. The Catholic directories. Cath. hist. rev. XX. p281-4 (Oct. 1934) **4409a**

—— The index to American Catholic pamphlets. St. Paul. Catholic Lib. Service. 1937. 128p. **4409b**

Willging, Eugene P. and Lynn, Dorothy E. A handbook of American Catholic societies. Scranton, Pa. Catholic Lib. Asso. 1940. 26p. **4409c**

CONGREGATIONAL

Dexter, Henry Martyn. Collections towards a bibliography of Congregationalism. *In* The Congregationalism of the last three hundred years, as seen in its literature. N.Y. Harper. 1880. Appendix. p5-308 **4410**

London, Congregational Library. A catalogue of the Congregational Library, Memorial Hall, Farrington Street, London, E.C. London, Plymouth. William Brendan and Son. 1895, 1910. 2v. **4411**

Monrad, Anna M. Catalogue of an exhibition . . . illustrating Congregationalism before 1800. New Haven. Yale Univ. Lib. 1915. 32p. **4411a**

Yale University, Library. Catalogue of an exhibition held in the Day Missions Library illustrating Congregationalism before 1800, held during the meeting of the National Council of Congregational Churches at New Haven, October 1915. Arranged by Anna M. Monrad. New Haven. 1915. 28p. **4412**

FRIENDS

Antiquarian researches among the early printers and publishers of Friends' books. Extracted from The American Friend, published in Philadelphia. Manchester, England? 1844. 63p. **4413**

Cadbury, Henry J. Quaker bibliographical notes. Friends' Hist. Asso. bul. XXIV. p83-93 (Autumn number, 1935); XXVI. p39-53. 1937 (This installment concerns anti-slavery writings) **4414**

Clark, Arthur H. Co. A catalogue of an extensive collection of books relating to the Quakers and Shakers. n.p. n.d. 12p. **4415**

Cox, John, Jr. Catalogue of the records in possession of, or relating to, the two New York yearly meetings of the religious society of Friends and their subordinate meetings, giving a detailed description of each volume, and its present location, and some historical notes concerning the establishment of meetings and the location of meeting-houses. (MS. Friends Seminary, N.Y.) **4416**

Cresson, Charles Caleb. Quakeriana; or, books relating to the Quakers, being rated as the most important collection in the country. . . Comp. by Stan V. Henkels. Phila. Bicking print. 1902. 52p. **4417**

Current literature—Periodicals. Friends' Hist. Asso. bul. **4417a**

Edmunds, A. J. Quaker literature in the libraries of Philadelphia. The Westonian. XIII. p182-203 (Eleventh month, 1907) **4418**

Franklin Bookshop. Quakeriana; out of print books, pamphlets, broadsheets, engravings, and manuscripts relating to The Society of Friends. (Catalog no. 19. season 1907-08. Quaker list no. 2) Phila. Franklin Bookshop. 1908. 50p. **4419**

Friends' Historical Association of Philadelphia. General index to Bulletin of Friends' Historical Association of Philadelphia, volumes I-X, 1906-1921. *With* Bulletin X, 1920-21. Phila. Friends' Hist. Asso. of Phila. 1922. 99p. Same. XI-XV. 1922-26. *With* special Logan-Story index appended 1927. With Bul. XV. 1926. 50p. p93-100
Same. XVI-XX. 1927-31. With Bul. XX. 1931. 92p. **4420**

Friends' Institute, London. Catalogue of books and pictures. London. 1907 **4421**

Friends' Library, Philadelphia. Catalogue of the books belonging to the library of the four monthly meetings of Friends of Philadelphia. Phila. Kite & Walton. 1853. 349p. (Supplement. 1853 to 1873. Phila. W. H. Pile. 1873. 73p.) **4422**

Grubb, Edward. The early Quakers. *In* The Cambridge history of English literature. Ed. by A. W. Ward and A. R. Waller. Cambridge, England. The Univ. Press. 1912. VIII. p101-14, 412-16 **4423**

Guilford College. Name index to the manuscript Quakeriana in the library. Guilford College, N.C. ms. **4423a**

Henkels, Stan V. Quakeriana; a remarkable collection of books relating to the Society of Friends. Phila. 1911. 95p. **4424**

Hewitt, Anna B. Quakers in the dictionary of American biography. Friends' Hist. Asso. bul. XXIV. p93-8 (Autumn number, 1935) **4425**

Littleboy, Anna L. A history of the Friends' Reference Library; with notes on early printers and printing in the Society of Friends. London. Soc. of Friends. 1921. 31p. **4426**

Mekeel, Joseph J. Glimpses into Haverford Quakeriana. Bul. of Friends' Hist. Asso. XXV. (Spring, 1936) **4426a**

Roberts, Charles. Illustrated catalogue of the private library of the late Charles Roberts of Philadelphia, comprising an extensive collection of noteworthy Quakeriana. . . . N.Y. Am. Art Asso. 1918. 138p. **4427**

Schulte's Book Store. A catalogue of Quakeriana and anti-Quaker literature. N.Y. Schulte's Book Store. 1917. 24p. **4428**

Smith, Joseph. Bibliotheca anti-Quakeriana; or a catalogue of books adverse to the Society of Friends, alphabetically arranged, with biographical notices of the authors together with the answers which have been given to some of them by Friends and others. London. Joseph Smith. 1873. 474p. **4429**

—— Bibliotheca Quakeristica; a bibliography of miscellaneous literature relating to the Friends (Quakers), chiefly written by persons not members of their society, also of publications by authors in some way connected, and biographical notices. London. Joseph Smith. 1883. 32p. **4430**

—— A descriptive catalogue of Friends' books; or books written by members of The Society of Friends, commonly called Quakers, from their first rise to the present time, interspersed with critical remarks, and occasional biographical notices, and including all writings by authors before joining, and by those after having left the Society, whether adverse or not as far as known. London. Joseph Smith. 1867. 2v. (Supplement. London. Edward Hicks. 1893. 364p.) **4431**

HUGUENOT

Swarthmore College. Friends' Historical Library. Catalogue of the Friends' Historical Library of Swarthmore College, Swarthmore, Pa. 1893. [Swarthmore, Pa. 1893] 62p. **4432**

Thomas, Allen C. Quaker books and Quakeriana in the library of Haverford College. Friends' Hist. Soc. of Phila. bul. IX. p27-32 (May 1919) **4433**

Wallace, H. E. List of Friends' meeting records, with names of those in charge. Pa. mag. hist. XXVII. p249-50. 1903 **4433a**

W(hiting), J(ohn). A catalogue of Friends books; written by many of the people called Quakers from the beginning or first appearance of said people. London. Sowle. 1708. 238p. **4434**

HUGUENOT

Bowdoin College. Library. MS. bibliography on Huguenots. **4435**

Huguenot Society of America. Catalogue of the books, pamphlets, and manuscripts belonging to the Huguenot Society of America, deposited in the library of Columbia College. . . Comp. by Elizabeth G. Baldwin. N.Y. The Soc. 1890. 107p. **4436**

—— **Library.** Catalogue or bibliography of the library of the Huguenot Society of America. Comp. by Julia P. M. Morand. N.Y. Priv. printed by Mrs. James M. Lawton. 1920. 351p. **4437**

U.S. Library of Congress. Division of bibliography. Select list of references on the Huguenots in America. April 24, 1911. 4p. typ. (Recent references. July 3, 1922. 3p. typ.) **4438**

JEWISH

American Jewish Historical Society. Index to the publications of the American Jewish Historical Society, numbers 1 to 20. [N.Y.] 1914. 600p. **4438a**

Boston. Public Library. Judaica; a selected reading list of books in the public library of the city of Boston. (Brief reading list no. 44. April 1934) Boston. The Trustees. 1934. 140p. **4439**

Central Conference of American Rabbis. Yearbook, index, vol. I-XL. Balt.? 1931. 175p. **4440**

Dropsie College. Classified index to volumes I-XX, 1909-1930 of The Jewish quarterly review. By P. Romanoff. Phila. Dropsie College for Hebrew and Cognate Learning. 1932. 226p. **4441**

Johns Hopkins University. Library. Catalogue of the Leopold Strouse Rabbinical Library, giving a list of the accessions by annual gift from Mr. Strouse during the years 1896, 1897, 1898, and 1899. Balt. 1900. 28p. **4442**

Journal of Jewish bibliography. I- Oct. 1938- **4442a**

Marcus, Jacob Rader. A brief introduction to the bibliography of modern Jewish history; a selected, annotated list of the standard books in several languages on the period from 1650 to modern times. (Hebrew Union College. Publication no. 16) Cincinnati. Hebrew Union College. 1935. 170p. mim. **4442b**

Schwab, Moïse. Répertoire des articles relatifs à l'histoire et à la littérature juives, parus dans les périodiques, de 1665 à 1900. Paris. P. Geunther. 1914-23. 539p. **4443**

U.S. Library of Congress. Division of bibliography. List of references on Zionism. Aug. 8, 1916. 12p. typ. **4444**

LUTHERAN

Augustana College and Theological Seminary. Denkmann Memorial Library. Bibliography of the catalogue books of the Augustana College Library. Comp. by Marcus Skarstedt (Augustana bul. ser. XIII. no. 1. March 1, 1917) Rock Island, Ill. 1917. 272p. **4445**

Beck, C. H. Bibliotheca Lutherana; eine sammlung von autotypen Luthers nebst den gesamtausgaben von Luthers werken und einer reichen auswahl von schriften der freunde und gegner der reformation über Luther bis auf die gegenwart. Nördlingen. 1883. **4446**

Concordia Publishing House. Catalog of Concordia Publishing House. St. Louis [1931-] 1030, [2], 24, 115, [1]p. **4446a**

Lutheran Historical Society. Catalogue of the Lutheran Historical Society's collection of books, pamphlets, photographs, etc. deposited in the Theological Seminary at Gettysburg, Pa. Phila. Lutheran Publishing House. 1890. 66p. **4447**

Morris, John G. Bibliotheca Lutherana; a list of publications of Lutheran ministers in the United States. Phila. Lutheran Publishing Soc. 1876. 139p. **4448**

Norlie, Olaf Morgan. Cumulative catalogue of Lutheran books in the English language. Decorah, Ia. 1924. 128p. **4449**

MENNONITE

Bender, Harold S. Two centuries of American Mennonite literature; a bibliography of Mennonitica Americana, 1727-1928. (Stud. in Anabaptist and Mennonite hist. no. 1) Goshen College, Goshen, Ind. The Mennonite Hist. Soc. 1929. 181p. (Reprinted from Mennonite quar. rev. I-II. Jan., Oct. 1927. Jan., April 1928) **4450**

Heatwole, Lewis J. List of American Mennonite books and periodicals. *In* Mennonite handbook of information. Scottdale, Pa. Mennonite Publishing House. 1925. p131-43 **4451**

Horsch, John. Buecher und schriften der taufgesinnten. *In* Kurzgefasste und lehren, sowie einem verzeichniss der literature der taufgesinnten. Elkhart, Ind. 1890. p107-33 **4452**

Horsch, John. Catalogue of the Mennonite Historical Library in Scottdale, Pennsylvania. Scottdale, Pa. Mennonite Publishing House. 1929. 88p.   **4453**

Vereenigde Doopsgezinde Gemeente te Amsterdam. Bibliotheek. Catalogus der werken over de doopsgezinden en hunne geschiedenis aanwezig in de bibliotheek der Vereenigde doopsgezinde gemeente te Amsterdam. Amsterdam. J. H. de Bussy. 1919. 357p.   **4454**

METHODIST

Archibald, Francis A. Methodism and literature; a series of articles from several writers on the literary enterprise and achievements of the Methodist Episcopal church with a catalogue of select books for the home, the church, and the Sunday school. Cincinnati. Walden & Stowe; N.Y. Phillips & Hunt. 1883. 427p.   **4455**

Ayres, Samuel Gardiner. A working conference on the union of American Methodism. N.Y. Methodist Book Concern. 1916. 30p.   **4456**

Cavender, Curtis H. Catalogue of works in refutation of Methodism, from its origin in 1729, to the present time; of those by Methodist authors on lay-representation, Methodist Episcopacy, etc., etc., and of the political pamphlets relating to Wesley's "Calm address to our American colonies." Phila. John Pennington. 1846. 54p.; N.Y. 1868. 56p. (Published under pseudonym H. C. Decanver)   **4457**

Green, Richard. Anti-Methodist publications issued during the eighteenth century; a chronologically arranged and annotated bibliography of all known books and pamphlets written in opposition to the Methodist revival during the life of Wesley; together with an account of replies to them, and some other publications; a contribution to Methodist history. London. Published for the author by C. H. Kelly. 1902. 175p.   **4458**

Methodist Book Concern. Authors' portrait catalogue [with their biographies] selected list of publications of the Methodist Book Concern. 1915. N.Y. Methodist Book Concern. 1915. 172p.   **4459**
—— Classified list of books of the general catalogue of the Methodist Episcopal church. N.Y. Carlton & Phillips. 1852. 100p.   **4460**
—— Selected list of publications of the Methodist Book Concern, founded 1789. Spring, 1913. N.Y. Methodist Book Concern. 1913. 122p.   **4461**

New England Methodist Historical Society. Library. List of some of the manuscripts, pamphlets, and newspapers in the archives of the society of use to students of Methodist church history. New England Methodist Hist. Soc. proc. 7th meeting. p26-37. 1887   **4462**

Osborn, George. Outlines of Wesleyan bibliography; a record of Methodist literature from the beginning in two parts; the first containing the publications of John and Charles Wesley, arranged in order of time; the second those of Methodist preachers alphabetically arranged. London. Wesleyan Conference Office. 1869. 220p.   **4463**

Wesleyan Methodist Church. Wesleyan conference office. Library. A catalogue of manuscripts and relics, engravings, and photographs, medals, books and pamphlets, pottery, medallions, etc. belonging to the Wesleyan Methodist conference . . . together with some of the principal books, mss., etc. in the possession of the United Methodist church. London. Methodist Publishing House. 1921. 217p.   **4464**

PRESBYTERIAN

Presbyterian Church. Board of Foreign Missions. Library. A catalogue of the books and maps belonging to the library of the Board of Foreign Missions of the Presbyterian church. N.Y. Mission house. 1861. 94p.   **4465**

Presbyterian Church. Board of Publications. Descriptive catalogue of the publications of the Presbyterian Board of publication, and Sabbath-school work. Phila. 1883. 551p.   **4466**
—— —— Numerical, alphabetical and descriptive catalogues of the publications of the Presbyterian Board of publication. Phila. Westcott & Thomson. n.d. 432p.   **4467**

Presbyterian Church. Synod of New Jersey. Report of the Committee on historical materials, Synod of New Jersey, for the year 1914. By the Rev. George H. Ingram. Presbyterian Hist. Soc. jour. VIII. p35-9 (March 1915) (Summary of records up to 1800 of early presbyteries and synods)   **4467a**

Presbyterian Historical Society. Library. Catalogue of books in the library of the Presbyterian Historical Society. Phila. J. B. Rodgers. 1865. 107p.   **4468**

Turner, Joseph Brown. A catalogue of manuscript records in the possession of the Presbyterian Historical Society. Presbyterian Hist. Soc. jour. VIII. p13-22 (March 1915)   **4469**

PROTESTANT EPISCOPAL

Morgan, John Pierpont. Catalogue of printed books illustrating the liturgy and history of the church, loaned by Mr. J. Pierpont Morgan and exhibited in the Avery Library, Columbia University on the occasion of the General convention of the Protestant Episcopal church, October 10-November 8, 1913. 27p.   **4470**

Perry, William Stevens. The bishops of the American church, past and present, sketches, biographical and bibliographical, of the bishops of the American church, with a preliminary essay on the historical Episcopate and documentary annals of the introduction of the succession into America. N.Y. Christian Literature Co. 1897. 397p. **4471**

—— Catalogue of valuable historical pamphlets and diocesan journals of the Protestant church . . . to be sold by Stan V. Henkels. . . . Phila. Bicking. 1899. 28p. **4472**

—— History of the American Episcopal church, 1587-1883. Boston. James R. Osgood. 1885. (Contains: The literary churchmen of the ante-revolutionary period, by Henry Coppee—Church literature since the revolution, by Julius H. Ward. II. p593-630) **4473**

—— Valuable historical library of the late right Rev. Wm. Stevens Perry, bishop of Iowa . . . to be sold . . . by Stan. V. Henkels. . . . Phila. Bicking. 1899. 130p. **4474**

Trinity College, Hartford. Library. A list of the early editions and reprints of the General convention journals, 1785-1814, in the library of Trinity College. Bul. n.s. V. no. II. (April 1908) 8p. **4475**

SWEDENBORGIAN

Eby, S. C. The story of the Swedenborg manuscripts. N.Y. The New-Church Press. 1926. 76p. **4476**

Hyde, James. A bibliography of the works of Emanuel Swedenborg, original and translated. London. Swedenborg Soc. 1906. 742p. **4477**

Stroh, Alfred H. and Ekelöf, Greta. An abridged chronological list of the works of Emanuel Swedenborg, including manuscripts, original editions, and translations prior to 1172. Uppsala, Stockholm. Almqvist & Wiksells. 1910. 54p. **4478**

Swedenborg Foundation. Swedenborg's writings and collateral New-church literature catalog. N.Y. Swedenborg Foundation. 1938? 32p. **4478a**

—— Who was Swedenborg, and what are his writings? With catalogue of the theological writings of Emanuel Swedenborg. N.Y. Am. Swedenborg Ptg. and Publishing. Soc. 1905. 21p. **4479**

Swedenborg Society. Bibliographical index to the published writings of Emanuel Swedenborg, original and translated, based upon the library of the Swedenborg Society and supplemented from England and foreign collections, public and private. London. Swedenborg Soc. 1897. 38p. **4480**

MISCELLANEOUS

Anderson, Rufus. Memorial volume of the first fifty years of the American Board of Commissioners for Foreign Missions. Boston. Pub. by the Board. 1861 (Lists of publications, p190-4, 339-45, 369-82, 435-46) **4480a**

Bardeen, C. W. Bibliography of the educational works of Comenius. *In* Laurie, S. S. John Amos Comenius, bishop of the Moravians, his life and educational works. Syracuse, N.Y. Bardeen. 1892. 272p. **4481**

Bay, J. Christian. Trappist library at Our Lady of Gethsemani, Kentucky. Am. collector. IV. p9-15 (April 1927) **4481a**

DeGroot, Alfred Thomas and Dowling, Enos Everett. The literature of the Disciples of Christ. Advance, Ind. Hustler Print. 1933. 78p. **4481b**

Dubbs, J. H. Early publications, literary activity as developed at Ephrata. Lancaster farmer, May 1880 (Also in Lancaster examiner and express, July 16, 1881) **4481c**

Eddy, Richard. Bibliography. *In* Universalism in America. Boston. Universalist Pub. House. 1886. II. p483-611 **4481d**

Esterquest, Ralph Theodore. Christian science; a selected bibliography. Evanston, Ill. 1937. 37p. photop. **4481e**

Gillett, E. H. Bibliography of the Unitarian controversy. Hist. mag. XIX. p316-24 (April 1871) **4482**

Hackensack, N.J. First Reformed Church. [List of records of ancient Dutch churches in New York and New Jersey, printed and manuscript.] *In* Records of the Reformed Dutch churches of Hackensack and Schraalenburgh, New Jersey, with the registers of members, marriages, baptisms, and the consistories, to the beginning of the nineteenth century. (Coll. of the Holland Soc. of New York, I) N.Y. Printed for the Soc. 1891. p[ix]-xv **4482a**

MacLean, J. P. Bibliography (Shakers). The Kentucky revival and its influence on the Miami valley. Ohio Arch. Hist. Soc. Publications. XII. p282-6 (July 1903) **4483**

—— A bibliography of Shaker literature. Columbus, Ohio. Pub. for the author by Fred J. Heer. 1905. 71p. **4484**

Malin, W. G. Catalogue of books relating to or illustrating the history of the Unitas fratrum, or United Brethren. Phila. Collins. 1881. 131p. **4485**

New York. Public Library. List of works in the New York Public Library relating to Shakers. N.Y. N.Y. Pub. Lib. 1904. 10p. (Reprinted from the Bul. VIII. p550-9. Nov. 1904) **4486**

New York (city). Union Theological Seminary. Library. Bibliography of Christian science literature and of books, pamphlets, and selected periodical articles concerning the life and work of Mary Baker Eddy and the cause of Christian science contained in the library of Union Theological Seminary, New York city. Comp. by Stella Hadden-Alexander. N.Y. 1934. 60p. carbon **4487**

Reichmann, Felix. History and bibliography of the Ephrata Brotherhood. 657 W. 161st St. N.Y. In progress   **4487a**

Richart, Genevieve. A list of authorized Christian science literature in the Library of Congress. Wash. 1923. 70p. typ. (Writings of Mary Baker Eddy and others)   **4487b**

Schroeder, Theodore A. The authorship of the book of Mormon. Am. jour. psychol. XXX. p66-72 (Jan. 1919)   **4488**

Shuey, William A. Historical catalogue of publications, 1834-1892. *In* Manual of the United Brethren Publishing House; historical and descriptive. Dayton, Ohio.

United Brethren Publishing House, W. J. Shuey, publisher. 1892. p303-21   **4489**

U.S. Library of Congress. Division of bibliography. List of references on the history of the primitive Christian church. Feb. 10, 1920. 6p. typ.   **4490**

—— —— —— Mormons and Mormonism; a list of books. Jan. 2, 1930. 4p. typ.   **4491**

Winter, E. C. Shaker literature in the Grosvenor Library; a bibliography. Grosvenor lib. bul. XXII. p66-119 (June 1940)   **4491a**

Zion Research Library. New books of the Zion Research Library. Brookline, Mass. 1930- (Religion)   **4491b**

CHAPTER XI

SOCIAL, CULTURAL, SCIENTIFIC

SOCIAL

General

Abstracts of periodical literature; Bibliography. Am. jour. sociol. **4491b**

American Folk-lore Society. Journal of American folk-lore—Index to volumes 1-40 (1888-1927). (Am. Folk-lore Soc. Memoirs. XIV. 1930) N.Y. G. E. Steckert & Co. 1930. 106p. **4492**

American Home Economics Association. Selected references on education for family life. Wash. D.C. The Asso. 1938. 32p. **4492a**

American journal of sociology. Classified index to the American journal of sociology, volumes I-XXV. Prepared by Ernest R. Mowrer. Chicago. Univ. of Chicago Press. 1922. 28p. **4493**

Bacon, Corinne, comp. Standard catalog; social sciences section; about 1300 titles of the most representative and useful books on social, economic and educational questions. (o.p. Replaced by Standard catalog for public libraries; ed. by M. E. Sears. 1934 edition) N.Y. H. W. Wilson. 1927. 160p. **4493a**

Barnes, Harry Elmer. History and social intelligence. N.Y. Alfred A. Knopf. 1926. 575p. **4493b**

—— The new history and social studies. N.Y. Century. 1925. 605p. **4493c**

Barnes, Harry Elmer and others. The history and prospects of the social sciences. N.Y. Alfred A. Knopf. 1925. 534p. **4493d**

Bernard, Jessie. The history and prospects of sociology in the United States. *In* Lundberg, George A., ed. Trends in American sociology. N.Y., London. Harper. 1929. p1-71 **4493e**

Bernard, L. I. A century of progress in the social sciences. Soc. forces. XI. p488-505 (May 1933) **4493f**

Bining, Arthur Cecil. A survey of textbooks and other teaching aids in the social studies published in 1933. Middle States Asso. Hist. Teachers Proc. no. 31. p115-51. 1933 **4494**

Bowers, Raymond V. Report of 1940 research census. Am. sociol. rev. V. p623-44 (Aug. 1940) **4494a**

Buros, Oscar Krisen. Research and statistical methodology, books and reviews, 1933-1938. New Brunswick, N.J. Rutgers Univ. Press. 1938. 100p. (Includes chapters on social science, education, geology and medicine) **4494b**

Chicago. Public Library. The social sciences; finding list. Chicago. Chicago Pub. Lib. 1914. 371p. **4495**

Eaton, Allen and Harrison, Shelby M. A bibliography of social surveys; reports of fact-finding studies made as a basis for social action, arranged by subjects and localities. N.Y. Russell Sage Foundation. 1930. 467p. **4496**

Ellwood, Charles A. and others. Recent developments in the social sciences. Phila. J. B. Lippincott. 1927. 427p. **4496a**

Fox, Dixon Ryan. A hundred years of the social sciences. Columbia univ. quar. XXVI. p64-85. 1934 **4496b**

Fry, Charles Luther. The technique of social investigation. N.Y., London. Harper. 1934. 315p. **4496c**

Greenberg, Emil. Social science references; thirty essential manuals, yearbooks, collections and indexes described for students. N.Y. New York Univ. Bookstore. 1940. 22, 3p. reprod. typ. **4496d**

Harvard University. A guide to reading in social ethics and allied subjects, lists of books and articles selected and described for the use of general readers by teachers in Harvard university. Cambridge. Harvard Univ. Press. 1910. 265p. **4497**

Hodgkins, George W. A guide to newer methods in teaching the social studies. (The National Council for the Social Studies. Bul. no., 7) Cambridge, Mass. Distributed by the National Council for the Social Studies. 1937. 75p. (Largely bibliographical in treatment) **4497a**

Howard, George Elliott. General sociology, an analytical reference syllabus. (Univ. of Nebraska. Dept. of political science and sociology. Publication no. 1) [Lincoln] The Univ. 1907. 86p. **4498**

—— Social psychology; an analytical reference syllabus. (Univ. of Nebraska. Dept. of political science and sociology. Publications) [Lincoln] The Univ. 1910. 88p. **4499**

Kaplan, Louis. Research materials in the social sciences; an annotated guide for graduate students. Madison. Univ. of Wis. Pr. 1939. 36p. **4499a**

London School of Economics and Political Science. A London bibliography of the social sciences. By B. M. Headicar and C. Fuller. London. The London School of Economics and Pol. Science. 1931-32. 4v. (First supplement. . . 1st June, 1929 to 31st May, 1931. Comp. by Marjorie Plant. 1934. 596p. Second supplement. June 1, 1931 to May 31, 1936. 1937. 1374p.) **4500**

Maunier, René. Manuel bibliographique des sciences sociales et économiques. Paris. Librairie de la Société du Recueil Serey, L. Tenin. 1920. 228p.   **4501**

National Council for the Social Studies. Bibliography of text-books in social studies for elementary and secondary schools. Comp. by W. F. Murra and others. (Bul. no. 12) Cambridge, Mass. The Council. 1939. 79p.   **4501a**

Nevins, Allan. Recent progress of American social history. Jour. econ. and bus. hist. I. p365-83 (May 1929)   **4501b**

Noa, Ernestine. Rural social science library of the University of North Carolina. N.C. lib. bul. IV. p46-8. 1919   **4501c**

Odum, Howard W. Type studies of literature and source materials. *In* Man's quest for social guidance; the study of social problems. N.Y. Holt. 1927. p567-631   **4502**

Omaha. University. Social science bibliography from 2500 selected newspapers and periodicals. Omaha, Neb. WPA project   **4502a**

Pittsburgh. Carnegie Library. Debate index [social problems]. Pittsburgh. Carnegie Lib. 1912. 84p. (Supplement to the 2d ed., 1912-1913. . . 1913. 23p.)   **4503**

Redman, Amabel. Classified catalogue of text books in the social studies for elementary and secondary schools. (Publication no. 2 of the National Council for the Social Stud.) Phila. McKinley Publishing Co. 1927. 41p.   **4504**

Seligman, Edwin R. A. and Johnson, Alvin. Encyclopedia of the social sciences. N.Y. Macmillan. 1930- (Bibliography with articles)   **4505**

Social Science Research Council. Social science abstracts, March 1929-Dec. 1932. N.Y. Social science abstracts. 1929-32. 4v.   **4506**

Tolman, William Howe and Hull, William Isaac. Bibliography of selected sociological references for the City Vigilance League, New York city. N.Y. City Vigilance League. 1893. 71p.   **4507**

U.S. Library of Congress. Division of bibliography. Brief list of references on recent social conditions and influences in the United States. March 31, 1923. 6p. typ.   **4508**

—— —— —— References on social problems of the American people. Nov. 25, 1931. 5p. typ.   **4509**

Wirth, Louis and Shils, Edward A. The literature of sociology, 1934. The Social stud., continuing the Hist. outlook. XXVI. p459-75, 525-46 (Nov., Dec. 1935)   **4511**

—— The literature of sociology—1935 and 1936. Soc. educ. I. p499-511, 575-85 (Oct.-Nov. 1937)   **4511a**

Children

Brooklyn. Public Library. The welfare of children; a reading list on the care of dependent children. Brooklyn, N.Y. 1907. 44p.   **4512**

Chicago. Public Library. Child welfare; a list of books and references to periodicals in the Chicago Public Library. Chicago. The Child Welfare Exhibit. 1911. 35p.   **4513**

Child Study Association of America, Inc. Books; a selected list for parents and teachers, selected and compiled by the Parents' bibliography committee. N.Y. Child Study Asso. of Amer. 1931. 86p.   **4514**

Child Welfare League of America, Inc. Child welfare bibliography. N.Y. 1937. 32p.   **4514a**

Furfey, Paul Hanly. A selected bibliography on child development. (The Catholic Univ. of Amer. Educational research bulletins. IV. no. 4) Wash. D.C. Catholic Education Press [1929] 51p.   **4515**

Hardin, Floyd, Chapman, Eulalia Dougherty and Hill, Letha Belle. Child psychology; a bibliography of books in English, annotated and classified. . . . (Bibliographical center for research. Rocky Mountain region. Regional checklist no. 4) Denver, Colo. 1938. 203p. reprod. typ.   **4515a**

Iowa. University. Child welfare research station. Publications of the Iowa child welfare research station, 1917-1935. (Bul. of the State Univ. of Iowa. n.s. no. 767. Nov. 24, 1934) Iowa City. State Univ. of Iowa. [1935] 101p.   **4516**

—— —— **Extension division.** Child welfare, surveys and bibliography. (The State of Iowa. Univ. extension bul. no. 16, Bul. of the State Univ. n.s. no. 111. March 15, 1916) Iowa City. The Univ. 1916. 8p.   **4517**

MacDonald, Arthur. Bibliography of child study. (U.S. Commissioner of education. Rep. 1897-98. II) Wash. Govt. Ptg Off. 1899. p1351-84   **4518**

Minnesota. University. Institute of Child Welfare. Annotated bibliography of the publications of the Institute of Child Welfare, 1925-1934. Minneapolis. Univ. of Minnesota. 1934. 82p.   **4520**

National Education Association. Research division. Preliminary bibliography on youth. Wash. D.C. 1935. 26p. mim.   **4521**

National Research Council. Committee on child development. Child development abstracts and bibliography, I, June 1927- . Wash. D.C. 1927-   **4522**

Rand School of Social Science, New York. Department of labor research. What shall I read? A book list for boys and girls emphasizing the progressive social spirit. Comp. by Grace Poole and Solon de Leon. N.Y. Issued by the Workmen's Circle, Educational dept. 1929. 285p.   **4523**

Rhoades, Lillian Ione. Bibliography of child study. Phila. Board of Education. 1902. 128p.   **4524**

St. Louis. Public Library. A list of books and articles on child welfare, and a reading list for use with the Junior civic league. Comp. by Effie L. Power and Frances E. Bowman. St Louis. 1912. 11p.   **4525**

U.S. Children's Bureau. Current index of references to articles and reports. (MS. index in the Bureau) **4527**

—— —— Foster home care for dependent children with lists of references [244-88p.] (Bureau publication 136, revised) Wash. Govt. Ptg. Off. 1926 **4528**

—— —— Illegitimacy as child welfare problem. Pt. 1. Brief treatment of prevalence and significance of birth out of wedlock, child's status, and state's responsibility for care and protection, with bibliographical material. By Emma O. Lundberg and Katherine F. Lenroot (Dependent, defective, and delinquent classes. ser. 9. Bureau publication 66) Wash. Govt. Ptg. Off. 1920. 105p. **4529**

—— —— References on physical growth and development of normal child. (Bureau publication no. 179) Wash. Govt. Ptg. Off. 1927. 353p. **4530**

—— —— References on the child, the family, and the court. (Children's Bureau. Publication no. 193) Wash. D.C. 1933. 44p. autog. from typ. copy **4531**

U.S. Library of Congress. Division of bibliography. A list of recent references on child welfare. Sept. 6, 1924. 13p. typ. **4532**

—— —— —— List of references on child placing and similar care of dependent children. Nov. 10, 1914. 8p. typ. **4533**

—— —— —— A list of references on the adoption of children. Sept. 23, 1924. 13p. typ. **4534**

—— —— —— A select list of references on the care and training of crippled children. Jan. 12, 1934. 9p. typ. and mim. **4535**

Veal, Ronald Tuttle and others. Classified bibliography of boy life and organized work with boys. N.Y. Asso. Press. 1919. 198p. **4536**

Waddle, Charles W. and Root, William T., Jr. A syllabus and bibliography of child study, with special reference to applied child psychology. (Los Angeles State Normal school. Bul. 1915) Sacramento. State Ptg. Off. 1915. 98p. **4537**

Wilson, Louis N. Bibliography of child study for the years [1898]-1910/11. Worcester. Clark Univ. Pr.; Wash. Govt. Ptg. Off. 1908-12. (1902-07 issued as Publications of the Clark Univ. Lib.; 1908/09-1909/10 as Bulletins of the U.S. Bureau of Education) **4538**

Housing

Beard, Belle Boone and others. Electricity in the home; being a list of books and articles with brief abstracts. Prepared in connection with a survey of the wider use of electricity in the home. N.Y. The Workers Education Press. 1927. 173p. **4539**

California. Library School. Selective list of articles on the housing problem in the United States, in the California State Library. N.Y. Gawne. 1917. 33p. typ. **4540**

Cam, Gilbert A. Slum clearance in the United States; a selected reading list. N.Y. pub. lib. bul. XLII. p551-60 (July 1938) **4540a**

Chicago School of Civics & Philanthropy. The housing problem; literature in central Chicago libraries. (Johnson extension fund publication. Bul. no. 16) Chicago. The School. July 1912. 40p. **4541**

Hoffman, E. A. Federal, state, and municipal aid to housing, 1918 to 1922; a selected bibliography. Monthly labor rev. XVI. p418-36 (Feb. 1923) **4542**

National Housing Association. Recent books and reports on housing, zoning and town planning, 1928- . (National Housing Asso. Publications no. 58-) N.Y. 1928- **4543**

New York (City). Housing Authority. Bibliographies on community planning with special reference to low cost housing. N.Y. CWA project **4543a**

New York. Municipal Reference Library. List of references on the housing problem on file in the New York Municipal Reference Library. Comp. by L. H. Bolander. N.Y. March 28, 1922. 45p. typ. **4544**

New York. Public Library. Municipal reference branch. An annotated list of references on industrial housing. Comp. by L. H. Bolander. 1921. 14p. typ. **4545**

Pittsburgh. Carnegie Library. Housing reference list. Carnegie Lib. monthly bul. XVI. p568-604 (Dec. 1911) **4546**

President's Conference on Home Building and Home Ownership, Washington, D.C., 1931. General index to the final reports of the President's conference on Home Building and Home Ownership. Prepared under the direction of Dan H. Wheeler, ed. by John M. Gries and James Ford. Wash, D.C. 1933. 114p. **4547**

—— Committee on farm and village housing. Housing in tourist camps; a bibliography. Comp. by Josiah C. Folsom. Wash. D.C. 1931. 23p. mim. **4548**

U.S. Bureau of Labor Statistics. Library. Bibliography on housing. Wash. D.C. 1913. 32p. mim. **4549**

U.S. Bureau of Standards. Division of building and housing. Bibliography on blighted areas and slums. Wash. D.C. 1931. 46p. **4550**

U.S. Library of Congress. Division of bibliography. List of references on home ownership in the United States. Dec. 6, 1924. 8p. typ. **4551**

—— —— —— A list of references on housing with special reference to housing projects and slum clearance. Sept. 1934. 35p. mim. (Supplement. May 18, 1935. 21p. typ. mim.) **4552**

—— —— —— List of references on landlord and tenant, with special reference to recent rent increases. Dec. 3, 1920. 9p. mim. **4553**

Social Reform

American Association for Labor Legislation. United States Bureau of Labor. Library of Congress. Select bibliography on social insurance; brief list of references on social insurance. Am. labor legislation rev. III. p285-92 (June 1913) **4557**

Boston. Public Library. A list of books on social reform. Boston Pub. Lib. bul. III. p159-84, 205-37 (May-June 1898) **4558**

Rugg, Harold Ordway and Krueger, Marvin. Social reconstruction; study guide for group and class discussion. N.Y. The John Day Co. 1933. 140p. **4559**

Stone, Edna L. Public old-age pensions in the United States; a list of references. Monthly labor rev. XXII. p1414-22 (June 1922); XXVIII. p1161-75 (May 1929); XXXIII. p738-46 (March 1932) **4560**

Syracuse. Public Library. Social betterment, part 3. (Bul. 20) Syracuse, N.Y. 1911. 35p. **4561**

U.S. Central Housing Committee. A catalog of United States public documents for use in housing research; a summary of 1936 publications, January-September, issued by the Central housing committee, sub-committee on research and statistics, Washington, D.C. . . . [Wash. D.C. 1936?] 40 numb. l. mim. **4561a**

—— —— Housing index-digest; a reference guide to current American and foreign housing literature, no. 1. Wash. D.C. June 15, 1936- **4561b**

U.S. Central Statistical Board. Construction, housing and real property, a survey of available basic statistical data. By Jean H. Williams. [Wash.] Govt. Ptg. Off. 1940. 169p. reprod. from typ. copy **4561c**

U.S. Department of Labor. Library. Public old-age pensions in the United States; references, 1932 to 1934. Wash. D.C. 1934. 10p. **4562**

U.S. Federal Emergency Relief Administration. Library. A selected list of references on old-age security—no. 3. The United States, Part I and II, Alabama-Minnesota, Mississippi-Wyoming. Comp. by Adelaide R. Hasse. [Wash. D.C.] 1935. 189p. mim. **4563**

—— **Library.** A selected list of references on old-age security, no. 2. The United States. Comp. by Adelaide R. Hasse. Wash. D.C. 1935. 44p. mim. **4564**

—— —— —— Social recovery plan, shifting of industry and population groups; a tentative list of references. Comp. by Adelaide R. Hasse. Wash. D.C. 1934. 23p. mim. (Supplement, Feb. 26, 1934. 9p. mim. **4565**

U.S. Library of Congress. Division of bibliography. List of recent references on mothers' pensions. April 12, 1926. 6p. typ. **4566**

—— —— —— List of references on Blue sky laws. June 26, 1922. 10p. mim. (Supplement. May 12, 1928. 8p. mim.) **4567**

—— —— —— Select list of references on dependency of widowhood, with special reference to widows' pensions. March 10, 1920. 8p. mim. **4568**

—— —— —— Select list of references on old age and civil service pensions. Wash. Govt. Ptg. Off. 1903. 18p. (Supplement. July 15, 1916. 20p. typ.; May 2, 1929. 4p. typ.) **4569**

—— —— —— Select list of references on pensions for mothers, motherhood insurance, etc. Nov. 20, 1912. 8p. dupl. (Supplement. Aug. 21, 1913. 6p. typ.) **4570**

—— —— —— Some recent references on retirement allowances. April 2, 1926. 5p. typ. **4571**

U.S. Social Security Board. Library. Housing for recipients of relief and public assistance; a bibliography with abstracts. Wash. D.C. Nov. 1939. 90(?)p. typ. **4571a**

Sports

Bartlett, John. The Bartlett collection; a list of books on angling, fishes and fish culture, in Harvard College Library. By Louise Rankin Albee (Harvard Univ. Lib. Bibliog. contribution no. 31) Cambridge, Mass. 1896. 180p. **4572**

Farquhar, Francis Peloubet. The literature of mountaineering. [Boston] Appalachian Mountain Club. [1940] p508-24, 72-95 (Reprinted from Appalachia, Dec. 1939, June 1940) **4572a**

Gee, Ernest R. Sporting books, comprising angling, big game, fox-hunting, racing, horses and horsemanship, shooting, surtees and nimrod, also many miscellaneous volumes, on various sports. N.Y. 1933. 66p. **4573**

—— The sportman's library being a descriptive list of the most important books on sport. N.Y. R.R. Bowker Co. 1940. 158p. **4573a**

Goodspeed, Charles E. Angling in America; its early history and literature. Boston. Houghton Mifflin Co. 1939. 381p. **4573b**

Greenwood, Frances Anderson. Swimming, diving and watersports; a bibliography and guide to equipment and supplies. [Tuscaloosa, Ala. Weatherford Ptg. Co.] 1935. 93p. **4573c**

Hargraves, Catherine Perry. History of playing cards and a bibliography of cards and gaming. Boston. Houghton Mifflin. 1930. (Bibliog. on p371-449) **4574**

Henderson, Robert W. Baseball and rounders, a bibliographical essay on the origins of baseball. N.Y. N.Y. Pub. Lib. 1939. 15p. **4574a**

—— Early American sport; a chronological check-list of books published prior to 1860. N.Y. Grolier Club. 1937. 134p. **4574b**

Jessel, Frederic. A bibliography of works in English on playing cards and gaming. London, N.Y. Longmans, Green. 1905. 312p. **4575**

Larsen, Selma P. Sporting magazines. Minn. hist. XVI. p187-91 (June 1935) **4575a**

Lottinville, A. J. Bibliography on boxing. Am. Asso. Health and Physical Education Research Quar. IX. p129-53 (Oct. 1938) **4575b**

McCurdy, Robert Morrill and Coulter, Edith Margaret. A bibliography of articles relating to holidays. Boston. The Boston Book Co. 1907. 55p. (Reprinted from Bul. of bibliog. V. April 1907-) **4576**

Mendenhall, Paul. Bibliography of studies on scouting. N.Y. Boy Scouts of Am. National Council. Research Service. 1938. 25p. **4576a**

New York. Public Library. List of works in the New York Public Library on sport in general, and on shooting in particular. N.Y. 1903. 57p. (Reprinted from the Bul. VII. p164-86, 201-34, May-June 1903) **4577**

—— —— The modern Olympics, a list of reference material in the New York Public Library. Comp. by Karl Brown. N.Y. New York Pub. Lib. 1939. 29p. (Reprinted from the N.Y. Pub. Lib. bul. XLIII. p405-31. May 1939) **4577a**

—— —— The Spalding baseball collection. N.Y. N.Y. Pub. Lib. 1922. 44p. (Reprinted from the N.Y. Pub. Lib. bul. XXVI. p86-127. Jan. 1922) **4578**

Phillips, John Charles. American game mammals and birds; a catalogue of books, 1582 to 1925, sport, natural history, and conservation. Boston. Houghton Mifflin. 1930. 638p. **4579**

Ranck, Wilson Marcy. Guide to sports and outdoor recreations; a selected list of books, 1918 to December 31, 1934. [Ann Arbor? Mich. Am. Physical Education Asso.? 1935] p[75]-151. (Reprinted from the Research quar. VI. no. 1. March 1935) **4580**

Raymond, George B. Catalogue of books on angling, shooting, field sports, natural history, the dog, gun, horse, racing and kindred subjects. N.Y. Printed for private distribution. 1904. 50p. **4581**

Russell Sage Foundation, New York. Sources of information on play and recreation. By Marguerita P. Williams. N.Y. Russell Sage Foundation. 1927. 94p. **4582**

Snow, E. T. Catalogue of the valuable and extensive library of books on angling, the property of the late Edward Snow, of Boston, Mass. . . . London. Sotheby, Wilkinson & Hodge. 1898. 48p. **4583**

U.S. Library of Congress. Division of bibliography. Brief list of references on commercial recreation (exclusive of moving pictures). Feb. 28, 1921. 9p. mim. **4584**

—— —— —— The circus; a bibliographical list. Feb. 11, 1928. 40p. typ. **4585**

—— —— —— List of references on the history of baseball. Nov. 13, 1924. 6p. typ. **4586**

—— —— —— Select list of references on dueling, particularly in Virginia. Oct. 30, 1914. 3p. typ. **4587**

U.S. National Park Service. Current bibliography. U.S. National Park Service. Yearbook, 1937- . Wash. Govt. Ptg. Off. 1938- (Includes state and local government publications) **4587a**

Van Sockum, C. M. Sport; attempt at a bibliography of books and periodicals published during 1890-1912 in Great Britain, the United States of America, France, Germany, Austria, Holland, Belgium and Switzerland. N.Y. Dodd & Livingston. 1914. 289p. **4588**

Westervelt, Leonidas. The circus in literature; an outline of its development and a bibliography with notes. N.Y. Priv. printed. 1931. 88p. **4589**

Wisconsin. Legislative reference Library. Gambling: its regulation, taxation, and legislation since 1920: a selected bibliography. Comp. by B. F. Cizon. Madison. June 1937. 19p. typ. **4589a**

Wright, Lyle H. Sporting books in the Huntington Library. San Marino, Calif. Huntington Library and Art Gallery. 1937. 132p. **4589b**

Welfare

Adams, Herbert Baxter. Notes on the literature of charities. (Johns Hopkins Univ. Stud. in hist. and pol. science. Vth ser. VIII) Balt. Johns Hopkins Univ. 1887. p277-324. (Also in Baltimore conference on charities. Rep. 1887) **4590**

Bassett, Lucy A. Transient and homeless persons; a bibliography. Jacksonville, Fla. Florida Emergency Relief Administration, Transient dept. Nov. 1934. 87p. mim. **4591**

Breckinridge, Sophonisba P. Public welfare administration, with special reference to the organization of state departments; outline and bibliography; supplementary to Public welfare administration in the United States: select documents. Chicago. Univ. of Chicago Press. [1934] 34p. **4592**

Burke, W. W. Administration of private social service agencies; a topical bibliography, with supplement. Chicago. Univ. of Chicago Press. 1927. 41p. **4593**

Chicago. Public Library. Community centers; select list of references in the Chicago Public Library. Comp. by Nathan R. Levin and Edith Kammerling. Chicago. 1917. 16p. **4594**

Farnam, Henry Walcott. Chapters in the history of social legislation in the United States to 1860. Ed. by Clive Day; with an introd. note by Victor S. Clark. (Monographic series, no. 488; Board of Research Associates in American Economic History) Wash. D.C. Carnegie Institution of Washington. 1938 (p271-322 contain bibliography by Miss Vera A. Timm) **4594a**

—— A short bibliography of poor relief, prepared in connection with a course of six lectures given in Yale University, 1894. New Haven, Conn. Priv. printed. 1894. 8p. **4595**

Johnson, F. Ernest. A bibliography of social service. N.Y. Federal Council of the Churches of Christ in America. 1918. 40p.
4596

Jones, Mary Katherine. Bibliography of college, social and university settlements. Phila. 1895. 54p.
4597

McBride, Christine and Kingsbury, S. M. Social welfare in time of war and disaster; a bibliography. The Survey. XXXIX. p94-6, 100-1, 287-9, 301, 441-3, 570-2, 682-4 (Oct. 27-Dec. 8, 1917, Jan. 19, Feb. 23. March 23, 1918)
4598

Montgomery, Caroline W. Bibliography of college, social, university and church settlements. Comp. for The College Settlements Association. Chicago. 1905. 147p.
4599

National Conference of Charities and Correction. Cumulative index of the Proceedings of the National Conference of Charities and Correction, volumes 1 to 33 inclusive. Comp. by Alexander Johnson. n.p. Pub. by the National Conference of Charities and Correction. 1907. 197p.
4600

National Conference of Social Work. Proceedings of the National Conference of Social Work [Formerly National Conference of Charities and Corrections] Index, 1874-1933. Chicago. Univ. of Chicago Press. 1935. 236p.
4601

Roethel, Emma. Social security, 1930-May 1938: a contribution to a bibliography. Madison. Univ. of Wisconsin Lib. School. 1938. 50p. typ.
4601a

Rushmore, Elsie Mitchell. A bibliography for social workers among foreign-born residents of the United States. N.Y. National Board of the Young Men's Christian Asso. 1920. 38p.
4602

—— Social workers' guide to the serial publications of representative social agencies, with an introduction by Frederick W. Jenkins. N.Y. Russell Sage Foundation. 1921. 174p.
4603

Tallet, Gladys M. Poverty; a bibliography. (Wisconsin Free Library Com. Am. social question no. 4) Madison, Wis. 1909. 21p.
4604

U.S. Federal Emergency Relief Administration. Library. Transients, recent studies, reports, etc., a reference list. . . Comp. by Adelaide Rosalie Hasse. Wash. D.C. 1934. 26p. mim.
4605

U.S. Library of Congress. Division of bibliography. Brief list of references on money-raising campaigns. May 19, 1920. 4p. typ.
4606

—— —— —— Brief list of references on the historical development of charity and social work. Aug. 13, 1921. 10p. (Supplement. Oct. 4, 1934. 20p. typ.)
4607

—— —— —— List of books on industrial welfare work. April 10, 1925. 11p. typ.
4608

—— —— —— List of references on medical social service. Jan. 20, 1921. 10p. typ.
4610

—— —— List of references on Red Cross societies. June 19, 1915. 22p. typ.
4611

—— —— List of references on social centers. Oct. 12, 1914. 8p. typ. (Supplement. Feb. 29, 1916. 4p. typ.)
4612

—— —— List of references on the care and control of mental defectives. March 31, 1917. 3p. typ.
4613

—— —— List of references on the John D. Rockefeller charities. Oct. 26, 1914. 4p. typ.
4614

—— —— List of references on the Salvation Army. July 26, 1920. 17p. typ.
4615

—— —— —— Select list of references on poverty. 1909. 20p. typ.
4616

—— —— —— Select list of references on state supervision and administration of charities and correction in the United States. Feb. 8, 1911. 3p. typ. (Recent references. Jan. 3, 1914. 3p.; supplement. Sept. 13, 1917. 4p.)
4617

—— —— Select list of references on welfare work for laborers. July 26, 1912. 16p. typ. (Supplement. Oct. 18, 1915. 12p. typ.)
4617a

U.S. Social Security Board. Library. Selected list of social security publications. (Circular no. 12) Wash. Govt. Ptg. Off. 1936. 8p.
4617b

—— —— —— Some basic readings in social security. Prepared in the library. Informational service, Social security board [Wash. 1937] 17p. photoprinted
4617c

Miscellaneous

American Council on Education. American youth: an annotated bibliography. Prep. by Louise A. Menefee and M. M. Chambers. Wash. D.C. 1938. 492p.
4617d

Book Group. New York chapter. A list of books on social reconstruction. N.Y. 1935
4618

Brooklyn. Public Library. Congestion of population; a partial list of books in the Brooklyn Public Library. Brooklyn, N.Y. 1908. 16p.
4619

—— Reading and reference list on costume. Brooklyn, N.Y. 1909. 64p.
4620

Carnegie Endowment for International Peace. Library. The youth movement; list of works on the youth movement; with selected references on student societies, and some account of youth-serving organizations. Comp. by Mary Alice Matthews. Wash. D.C. Feb. 15, 1940. 13p. mim.
4620a

Crafts, L. W. Bibliography of feeble-mindedness in its social aspects. (Jour. of psycho-asthenics. Monograph supplements. I. no. 3, March 1917) Faribault, Minn. School for Feebleminded and Colony for Epileptics. 1917. 73p.
4621

Federal Council of Churches of Christ in America. Committee on marriage and the home. Bibliography on education in family life, marriage, parenthood, and young people's relationships. N.Y. Federal Council of Churches; Chicago. International Council of Religious Education. 1935. 31p.   **4622**

Foreman, Paul Breck and Haraway, Albert H. A bibliography of recent fugitive studies in population. Jackson, Miss. State Planning Comm. and Works Progress Adm. ·1938. 8p. mim.   **4622a**

Hall, Willard. Bibliography of social dancing. Hastings-on-Hudson, N.Y. 1940. 105p. mim.   **4622b**

Harley, D. L. Surveys of youth: finding the facts. (Am. Council on Educational Studies, ser. 4, Am. Youth Comm. v. I, no. 1) Wash. D.C. 1937. 106p.   **4622c**

Hiler, Hilaire and Hiler, Meyer. Bibliography of costume, a dictionary catalog of about eight thousand books and periodicals. Ed. by Helen Grant Cushing and Adah V. Morris. N.Y. H.W. Wilson. 1939. 911p.   **4622d**

Howard, George Elliott. Bibliographical index. *In* A history of matrimonial institutions. Chicago. Univ. of Chicago Press. 1904. III. p263-402   **4623**

Komarovsky, Mirra. Selected bibliography on the family, 1935-1940. Am. sociol. rev. V. p558-65 (Aug. 1940)   **4623a**

(Krouse, Edna L.) Backgrounds of American culture. Pa. lib. notes. XIV. p542-8. 1935   **4623b**

Magriel, Paul David. A bibliography of dancing; a list of books and articles on the dance and related subjects. N.Y. H. W. Wilson. 1936. 229p. First supplement. 1936-1937. 1938. 41p.   **4623c**

Munro, Isabel Stevenson and Cook, Dorothy E. Costume index; a subject index to plates and illustrated text. N.Y. H.W. Wilson. 1937. 338p.   **4623d**

National Education Association. Research division. Bibliography on youth problems. Wash. D.C. Feb. 1938. 40p. mim.   **4623e**

New York. Public Library. Bibliography on the origin of dancing. N.Y. WPA project   **4623f**

Newark, N.J. Free Public Library. A subject index to about five hundred societies which issue publications relating to social questions. N.Y. H. W. Wilson. 1915. 20p.   **4624**

Nystrom, Paul H. Bibliography on fashion, costume, domestic architecture and home furnishings. N.Y. Columbia Univ. School of Business. 1937. 144p.   **4624a**

Ogg, Frederic Austin. Research in the humanistic and social sciences. (Rep. of a survey conducted for the Am. Council of Learned Societies) N.Y. Century. 1928. 454p.   **4625**

Quinn, James A. Topical summary of current literature on human ecology. Am. jour. sociol. XLVI. p191-226 (Sept. 1940)   **4625a**

Robertson, Annie Isabel. Guide to literature of home and family life; a classified bibliography for home economics with use and content annotations. Phila. Lippincott. 1924. 284p.   **4626**

Schmidt, Frederick Julius. Leisure time bibliography; a guide to books and magazine articles pertaining to leisure time and to avocational interests related to industrial arts education. Ames. Iowa State College, Industrial arts dept. [1935] 84p. mim.   **4627**

Schroeder, Theodore. List of references on birth control. N.Y. H. W. Wilson. 1918. 52p.   **4628**

Seligman, E. R. A. List of books on the social evil, including pamphlets and leaflets published in the United States and foreign countries. N.Y. Am. Vigilance Asso., Lib. dept. 1912. p261-90 (Reprinted from The Social evil, ed. by E. R. A. Seligman. N.Y. Putnam's)   **4629**

Stout Institute. Woman in social service; an outline . . . and bibliography for reference and class work. . . . Menomonie, Wis. The Stout Inst. 1914. 29p.   **4630**

Thurston, Flora M. A bibliography on family relationships. N.Y. The National Council of Parent Education. 1932. 273p.   **4631**

U.S. Bureau of Home Economics. Bibliography on studies of costs and standards of living in the United States. By Faith M. Williams . . . assisted by Helen Connolly. A preliminary report. [Wash. D.C. July 1930] 104p. (Supplementary bibliog. Jan. 1932. 111p. mim.)   **4632**

U.S. Extension Service. A selected list of references on family financial planning and money management. Comp. by Mary Rokahr. (Miscellaneous extension publication no. 44) Wash. D.C. Nov. 1939. 26p. processed   **4632a**

U.S. Library of Congress. Division of bibliography. Brief list of references on morality in the United States. June 21, 1923. 5p. typ.   **4633**

— — — List of recent books on feminism. Aug. 6, 1915. 4p. typ.   **4634**

— — — List of recent references on population (its decrease and increase with economic results). Aug. 2, 1920. 7p. mim.   **4635**

— — — List of recent references on social legislation. April 16, 1925. 5p. typ.   **4636**

— — — List of references on city and country life. June 28, 1921. 7p. typ.   **4637**

— — — List of references on communistic societies in the United States. Feb. 13, 1917. 5p. typ.   **4638**

— — — List of references on prison reform. April 15, 1916. 7p. typ. (Recent references. Dec. 12, 1927. 5p. typ.)   **4639**

— — — List of references on race track gambling. May 25, 1921. 7p. typ.   **4640**

U.S. Library of Congress. Division of bibliography. List of references on secret societies (exclusive of fraternities and the Ku Klux Klan). Dec. 4, 1922. 9p. typ.   **4641**

—— —— —— A list of references on social life in New York, Philadelphia, and Washington 1789 to 1812. March 12, 1935. 10p. typ.   **4642**

—— —— —— List of references on the drug habit and traffic. May 1, 1926. 35p. mim. (Supplement. June 12, 1929. 18p. mim.)   **4643**

—— —— —— Population and food supply; some recent writings. Nov. 29, 1927. 4p. typ.   **4644**

—— —— —— Prohibition: a list of recent books. Oct. 2, 1928. 4p. typ.   **4645**

—— —— —— White slave act; a list of bibliographical references. Jan. 17, 1930. 5p. typ.   **4646**

U.S. Work Projects Administration. Division of education projects. Bibliography on family life education. (Technical series Education circular no. 8) Wash. D.C. The Adm. 1938. 16p. mim.   **4646a**

Whitmore, Frank Hayden. Reading list on ethics. N.Y. State Lib. bul. 93. bibliog. 38. p469-98. 1905   **4647**

Williams, Faith Moors and Zimmerman, Carle C. Studies of family living in the United States and other countries: an analysis of material and method. (U.S. Dept. of Agriculture. Miscellaneous publications no. 223) Wash. Govt. Ptg. Off. 1935. 617p.   **4648**

Zimand, Savel. Modern social movements; descriptive summaries and bibliographies. N.Y. H. W. Wilson. 1921. 260p.   **4649**

EXPLORATION AND TRAVEL

American Geographical Society. Geographical publications. The Geog. rev. I. Jan. 1916-   **4651**

—— Index to the Bulletin of the American Geographical Society, 1852-1915. Comp. by Arthur A. Brooks. N.Y. 1918. 242p.   **4652**

—— Index to the Geographical review, volumes I-XV, 1916-1925. XVI-XXV, 1926-1935. By Arthur A. Brooks. N.Y. 1926, 1936. 432, 373p.   **4653**

American Historical Association. Bibliography of American travel and description, 1600-1900. (Worked upon by various members of the association. See Solon J. Buck. The bibliography of American travel: a project. Bibliog. Soc. of Amer. pap. XXII. p52-9. 1929. Now in the custody of Julian P. Boyd, Historical Society of Pennsylvania, Philadelphia; work being continued by Frank Monaghan)   **4654**

Babey, Anna M. Americans in Russia, 1776-1917; a study of the American travellers in Russia from the American revolution to the Russian revolution. N.Y. The Comet Press. 1938 (Bibliography p127-69)   **4654a**

Baird, Spencer F. List of the more important explorations and expeditions, the collections of which have constituted the principal sources of supply to the National Museum, with indication of the department of the government under which prosecuted (Annual report of the Board of regents of the Smithsonian Institution, for the year 1877). Wash. Govt. Ptg. Off. 1878. p105-17   **4655**

Bartlett, Harley Harris. The reports of the Wilkes expedition, and the work of the specialists in science. *In* Centenary celebration. The Wilkes exploring expedition of the United States Navy, 1838-1842, and symposium on American polar exploration. Am. Phil. Soc. proc. LXXXII. no. 5. p601-705. 1940   **4655a**

Bartlett, J. R. Bibliography of Carver's travels. Bookmart. IV. p17 (June 1886)   **4656**

Boston. Public Library. Arctic regions and Antarctic regions. Bost. Pub. Lib. bul. XIII, no. 1, whole no. 96, n.s. V. p21-49 (April 1894)   **4656a**

Brooks, John Graham. As others see us; a study of progress in the United States. N.Y. Macmillan. 1908. 365p.   **4657**

Cairns, William B. British criticisms of American writings, 1783-1815; a contribution to the study of Anglo-American literary relationships. (Univ. of Wisconsin. Stud. in language and literature no. 1) Madison, Wis. 1918. 97p.   **4658**

Chicago Historical Society. List of works on the Lewis and Clark expedition presented by Charles H. Conover. Chicago Hist. Soc. rep. 1910. p342-50 **4659**

Clark, David Sanders. American travelers and observers in the British Isles, a bibliography. Cleveland, Ohio. 1940- reprod. from typ. copy   **4659a**

Collins, Frank Shipley. The botanical and other papers of the Wilkes exploring expedition. Rhodora. XIV. p57-68 (April 1912)   **4659b**

Cooper, Lane. Travellers and observers, 1763-1846. *In* The Cambridge history of American literature. Ed. by William P. Trent, and others. N.Y. Putnam's. 1917. I. p185-214, 468-90   **4660**

Coues, Elliott. An account of the various publications relating to the travels of Lewis and Clark, with a commentary on the zoological results of their expedition. (U.S. Geol. and geog. survey of the territories. Bul. 1874-75. I. ser. 2. no 6) Wash. Govt. Ptg. Off. 1875. p417-44   **4661**

Cox, Edward Godfrey. A reference guide to the literature of travel, including voyages, geographical descriptions, adventures, shipwrecks and expeditions. Seattle. The Univ. of Washington. 1935-38. (Univ. of Washington publications in languages and literature. v. IX-X) 2v.   **4661a**

Curtiss, Frederic H. A little book on travel books. Boston. Priv. printed by T. O. Matcalfe Co. 1936   **4662**

Dellenbaugh, Frederick S. Travellers and explorers, 1846-1900. *In* The Cambridge history of American literature. Ed. by William P. Trent and others. N.Y. Putnam's. 1921. III. p131-70, 681-728 **4663**

Dondore, Dorothy Anne. The prairie and the making of middle America: four centuries of description. Cedar Rapids, Ia. The Torch Press. 1926. 472p. (Travel) **4663a**

Douglas, Antoinette. A selected list of original narratives of early western travel in North America. St. Louis Pub. Lib. monthly bul. n.s., XVII. p162-70 (May 1919) **4664**

Dunbar, Seymour. A contribution to a bibliography of the history of travel in America. *In* A history of travel in America. Indianapolis. Bobbs-Merrill. 1915. IV. p1447-81 **4665**

Engelmann, Wilhelm. Bibliotheca geographica; verzeichniss der seit mitte des vorigen jahrhunderts bis zu ende des jahres 1856 in Deutschland erschienen werke über geographie und reisen mit einschluss der landkarten, pläne und ansichten. Leipzig. Wilhelm Engelmann; Paris. Friedrich Klincksieck. 1858. 1225p. **4666**

Fanning, Clara Elizabeth. Travel in the United States, twenty-one programs and bibliography. N.Y. H. W. Wilson. 1916. 31p. **4667**

Feipel, Louis N. Following the circumnavigators around the globe through books. N.Y. Brooklyn Pub. Lib. In progress **4667a**

Gerber, Adolf. Beiträge zur auswanderung nach Amerika im 18 jahrhundert aus altwürttembergischen kirchenbüchern. Stuttgart. Steinkopf. [1928] 32p. **4668**

Gill, Theodore and Coues, Elliott. Material for a bibliography of the North American mammals. *In* Report of the United States Geological survey of the territories. F. V. Hayden. Wash. Govt. Ptg. Off. 1877. XI. p951-1081 **4669**

Haskell, Daniel C. The United States Exploring Expedition, 1838-1842 and its publications, 1844-1874: a bibliography. N.Y. Pub. Lib. bul. XLV. p69-89, 821-58·(Jan., Oct. 1941) **4669a**

Hasse, Adelaide Rosalie. Reports of explorations printed in the documents of the United States government. Wash. Govt. Ptg. Off. 1899. 90p. **4670**

James, Helen C. Select annotated bibliography on canoe trips, horseback trips and walking trips. Bul. of bibliog. XIII. p6-10 (Sept.-Dec. 1926). p30-1 (Jan.-April 1927). p49-52 (May-Aug. 1927). p71-3 (Sept.-Dec. 1927). p109-10 (May-Aug. 1928) **4671**

Jeffers, Le Roy. Selected list of books on mountaineering. N.Y. Pub. Lib. 1916. 46p. **4672**

Joerg, W. L. G. The geography of North America: a history of its regional exposition. N.Y. Am. Geog. Soc. 1936? (Reprinted from The Geographical Review, XXVI. no. 4. Oct. 1936) p640-63 **4672a**

Lawson McGhee Library. Calvin Morgan McClung historical collection of books, pamphlets, manuscripts, pictures and maps relating to early western travel and the history and genealogy of Tennessee and other southern states. Comp. by Laura Luttrell and Mary U. Rothrock. Knoxville, Tenn. Knoxville Lithographing Co. 1921. 192p. **4673**

Mesick, Jane Louise. The English traveller in America, 1785-1835. (Columbia Univ. Stud. in English and comparative literature) N.Y. Columbia Univ. Press 1922. 352p. **4674**

Mill, Hugh Robert. A bibliography of Antarctic exploration and research. *In* Royal Geographical Society. The Antarctic manual. London. Royal Geog. Soc. 1901. p521-80 **4674a**

Miner, W. H. The Lewis and Clark expedition; with a sketch of Meriwether Lewis and William Clark, and an annotated bibliography of the subject. Literary collector. III. p204-9; IV. p38-9 (March-April 1902) **4675**

Monaghan, Frank. French travellers in the United States, 1765-1932; a bibliography. N.Y. N. Y. Pub. Lib. 1933. 114p. (Reprinted from the Bul. March-July 1932) **4676**

Paltsits, Victor Hugo. Bibliographical data. *In* Thwaites, Reuben Gold. Original journals of the Lewis and Clark expedition. 1804-1806. N.Y. Dodd, Mead. 1904. I. p.lxi-xciii **4677**

Plympton, Charles W. Select bibliography on travel in North America. N. Y. State Lib. bul. bibliog. no. 3. May 1897. p35-60 **4678**

Rait, R. S. British writers on the United States. Quar. rev. no. 455. p357-71 (April 1918) **4679**

Rodd, Thomas. Catalogue of books, consisting of a collection of voyages and travels in various parts of the world, including an extensive series relating to the several countries of America. London. Compton and Ritchie. 1843. 116p. **4680**

Rusk, R. L. Travel and observation. *In* The literature of the middle western frontier. N.Y. Columbia Univ. Press. 1925. I. p79-130; II. p96-144 **4681**

Sears, Minnie Earl. Standard catalogue for public libraries; history and travel section; an annotated list of 1900 titles with a full analytical index. N.Y. H. W. Wilson. 1929. 285p. (o.p. Replaced by Standard catalog for public libraries; ed. by M. E. Sears, 1934 edition) **4682**

Smith, Charles C. Critical essay on the sources of information—Explorations to the north-west. *In* Narrative and critical history of America. Ed. by Justin Winsor. Boston, N.Y. Houghton Mifflin. 1884. III. p97-9 **4683**

Thwaites, Reuben Gold. Newly discovered personal records of Lewis and Clark. Scribner's mag. XXXV. p685-700 (June 1904) **4683a**

Thwaites, R. G. The story of Lewis and Clark's journals. Am. Hist. Asso. rep. 1903. I. p105-29   **4684**

Thwaites, Reuben Gold, ed. Early western travels, 1748-1846; v. XXXI-XXXII; analytical index to the series. Cleveland, Ohio. A. H. Clark. 1907. 334, 353p.
                                                        4684a

Towne, Jackson E. A bibliography of polar exploration. Bul. of bibliog. XV. p144-6, 167-8, 187-91; XVI. p12-15 (Sept. 1935-Sept. 1936)   **4684b**

Tuckerman, Henry T. America and her commentators with a critical sketch of travel in the United States. N.Y. Scribner. 1864. 460p.   **4685**

U.S. Library of Congress. Division of bibliography. Brief list of references on the Lewis and Clark expedition. June 2, 1925. 7p. typ.   **4686**

—— —— —— List of references on the geography of the United States, and its influence on the history and development of the country. May 11, 1922. 5p. typ.
                                                        4687

U.S. War Department. Surveys by the War Department; list of publications. House executive document no. 88. 45 Cong. 2 sess. 1878. Ser. 1809. 8p. **4688**

U.S. Works Progress Administration, New York (City) Annotated bibliography of the polar regions . . .N.Y. [1937?-] mim.
                                                        4688a

Venable, W. H. Some early travellers and annalists of the Ohio Valley. Ohio arch. hist. quar. I. p230-42 (Dec. 1887)   **4689**

Wagner, Henry Raup. Henry R. Wagner's The plains and the Rockies; a bibliography of original narratives of travel and adventure, 1800-1865. Revised and extended by Charles L. Camp. San Francisco. Grabhorn Press. 1937. 299p. **4690**

Wheeler, George M. Memoir upon the voyages, discoveries, explorations, and surveys to and at the west coast of North America and interior of the United States west of the Mississippi River, between 1500 and 1880, including later bibliographical and other references to determined latitudes, longitudes, and altitudes available for the basis of the permanent official topographic atlas of the United States. *In* U.S. War Department. Report upon United States geographical surveys west of the one hundredth meridian. Wash. Govt. Ptg. Off. 1889. I, appendix F. p481-745   **4690a**

Winship, George P. and Cowell, Maude E. C. Travellers and explorers, 1583-1763. *In* The Cambridge history of American literature. Ed. by William P. Trent. N.Y. Putnam's. 1917. I. p1-13, 365-80
                                                        4691

Winsor, Justin. Critical notes on the sources of information—Arctic exploration in the eighteenth and nineteenth centuries. *In* Narrative and critical history of America. Boston; N.Y. Houghton Mifflin. 1889. VIII. p104-30   **4691a**

FINE AND APPLIED ARTS

A. L. A. portrait index. Index to portraits contained in printed books and periodicals. Comp. with the cooperation of many librarians and others for the Publishing board of the American Library Association. Ed. by William Coolidge Lane and Nina E. Browne. Wash. Govt. Ptg. Off. 1906. 1600p.   **4691b**

Allen, Charles Dexter. American bookplates, a guide to their study with examples; with a bibliography by Eben Newell Hewins. N.Y. Macmillan. 1894. 437p.   **4691c**

American Antiquarian Society. An artist's index to Stauffer's "American engravers" by Thomas Hovey Gage. Worcester, Mass. 1921. 49p. (Reprinted from the Proc. of the Am. Antiq. Soc. for Oct. 1920)   **4692**

American architect. A classified list of books devoted to architecture and allied subjects. N.Y. Am. architect. 1912. 91p.
                                                        4693

American Association of Museums. Handbook of American museums. Wash. D.C. Am. Asso. of Museums. 1932. 779p. **4694**

American Ceramic Society. List of papers and discussions contained in the Transactions of the American Ceramic Society, volumes I to XVI (inclusive). Columbus, Ohio. Pub. for the Soc. by Edward Orton, Jr. 1915. 39p.   **4695**

American Institute of Architects quarterly bulletin, containing an index of literature from the publications of architectural societies and periodicals on architecture and allied subjects, I-XII, XIII, no. 1-3, Jan. 1, 1900-Oct. 1, 1912. Comp. and ed. by Glenn Brown. Wash. D.C. [1900-12]   **4696**

American Institute of Decorators. Interior architecture and decoration; a selected list of references compiled under the direction of the Committee on education. N.Y. N.Y. Pub. Lib. 1938. 37p.   **4696a**

Andrews, William Loring. Fragments of American history illustrated solely by the works of those of our own engravers who flourished in the 18th century. N.Y. Priv. Print. 1898. 68p.   **4696b**

Architectural record, I- . 1891- (Contains a list of publications on architecture)
                                                        4696c

Bach, Richard F. Bibliography of the literature of colonial architecture. The Architectural rec. XXXVIII. p382; XXXIX. p92-3, 388-9; XL. p188-9, 582-3; XLI. p189, 472-4; XLII. p88-91, 185-8 (Sept. 1915-Aug. 1917)   **4697**

—— Books on colonial architecture. The Architectural rec. XXXVIII. no. 2-XLII. no. 3 (Aug. 1915-Sept. 1917) Addenda for 1917. XLIV. p85-90, 175-80 (July-Aug. 1918)   **4698**

—— Early American architecture and the allied arts—a bibliography. The Architectural rec. LIX. p268-73, 328-34, 483-8, 525-32; LX. p65-70 (March-July 1926) Cont. in *ibid.* LXIII. p577-80; LXIV. p70-2, 150-2, 190-2 (June-Sept. 1928) **4699**

Baldwin, Muriel F. Plant forms in ornament; a selective list of references in the New York Public Library and other libraries of New York city. N.Y. N. Y. Pub. Lib. 1933. 59p. (Reprinted from the Bul. of the N.Y. Pub. Lib. June-Aug. 1933) **4700**

Baltimore. Peabody Institute. Books on architecture, decoration and furniture in the library of The Peabody Institute, Baltimore, Maryland, nineteen-twenty. [Balt. 1920] 23p. **4701**

Bibliography on interior architecture and decoration. N.Y. pub. lib. bul. XLIII. p89-112, 396-404 (Feb., May 1939) 4701a

Bolton, Charles Knowles. Checklist of American portraits to 1825. Shirley, Mass. In progress **4701b**

—— A descriptive catalogue of posters, chiefly American, in the collection of Charles Knowles Bolton, with biographical notes and a bibliography, May MDCCCXCV. Brookline, Mass. [Boston. W. B. Jones. 1895] [16]p. **4701c**

Bolton, Theodore. American book illustrators; bibliographic check lists of 123 artists. N.Y. R. R. Bowker. 1938. 290p. **4701d**

—— Check list of books illustrated by Thomas Nast. [N.Y. 1939] 10p. reprod. **4701e**

—— Early American portrait painters in miniature. N.Y. Sherman. 1921. 180p. **4702**

—— Index to American illustrators. [N.Y.] 1931. typ. **4702a**

Booth, Mary Josephine. Index to material on picture study. (Useful references ser. no. 26) Boston. F. W. Faxon. 1921. 92p. **4703**

Boston. Public Library. Applied art; a selected list of works in the Boston Public Library. (Brief reading list no. 39) Boston. 1929. 55p. **4704**

—— Catalogue of books relating to architecture, construction and decoration in the public library of the city of Boston. Second edition with an additional section on city planning. (Subject catalogue no. 10) Boston. Pub. by the Trustees. 1914. 535p. **4705**

—— List of books and magazine articles on American engraving, etching, and lithography. . . Boston. Pub. Lib. monthly bul. IX. no. 12. Dec. 1904. 7p. **4706**

Branner, John Casper. A bibliography of clays and the ceramic arts. Columbus, Ohio. Pub. by the Am. Ceramic Soc. Press of F. J. Heer. 1906. 451p. **4707**

Burroughs, Clyde H. Early American portraits at the Detroit Institute of arts. Art in America. XVII. p258-74 (Oct. 1929) **4707a**

California. State Library. Finding list of unclassified art and miscellaneous books. California State Library. Sacramento. A. J. Johnston, Superintendent of state ptg. 1892. 52p. **4708**

Carson, Hampton Lawrence. The Hampton L. Carson collection of engraved portraits of American naval commanders and early American explorers and navigators, also American sea and land battles. Catalogue comp. and sale conducted by Stan V. Henkels. [Phila. 1905] 80p. **4708a**

—— The Hampton L. Carson collection of engraved portraits of signers of the Declaration of independence, presidents and members of the Continental congress, officers in the American revolutionary war, views of Independence hall. Catalogue comp. and sale conducted by Stan V. Henkels. [Phila. 1904] 93, 5p. **4708b**

Chandler, Albert R. A bibliography of experimental aesthetics, 1865-1932. (Ohio State Univ. Bureau of education research. Mimeographs no. 1) Columbus, Ohio. 1933. 25p. **4709**

Chase, Frank H. A bibliography of American art and artists before 1835. *In* Dunlap, William. A history of the rise and progress of the arts of design in the United States. A new edition, illustrated, edited, with additions by Frank W. Bayley and Charles E. Goodspeed. Boston. Goodspeed. 1918. III. p346-77 **4710**

City Library Association, Springfield, Mass. Aids in drawing and design for teachers and students. Springfield, Mass. City Lib. Asso. 1914. 26p. **4711**

Clark, Marion E. and others. Art in home economics; a bibliography of costume design, history of costume, interior decoration, history of furniture, architecture, art principles and art appreciation. Chicago. Univ. of Chicago Press. 1925. 66p. **4712**

Colburn, Jeremiah. Catalogue of the Colburn collection of portraits and autographs. Boston. Bostonian Soc. 1901. 124p. **4712a**

Collections of historical photographs. Am. Mil. Inst. jour. I. p42-3 (Spring 1937) **4712b**

College Art Association of America. Committee on books for the College Art Library. Books for the College Art Library. The art bul. III. p3-60 (Sept. 1920) **4713**

Columbia College. Catalogue of the Avery Architectural Library; a memorial library of architecture, archaeology and decorative art. N.Y. 1895. 1139p. **4714**

Curtis, Nathaniel Cortlandt. The Ricker Library; a familiar talk to students of architecture in the University of Illinois. (Univ. of Illinois. Bul. XVII. no. 29) [Urbana. Univ. of Illinois] 1920. 77p. **4715**

Danvers Historical Society. Index of illustrations in the Historical collections of the Danvers Historical Society. Volumes I-XX, inclusive. Danvers hist. soc. coll. XXIII. p103-4. 1935 **4715a**

Detroit. Public Library. Fine arts department. Costume; a list of books. [Detroit] 1928. 56p. **4716**

—— —— Furniture; a list of books. [Detroit] 1929. 65p. **4717**

Ellis, Jessie Croft. General index to illustrations; 22000 selected references in all fields inclusive of nature. Boston. F. W. Faxon. 1931. 467p. **4717a**

—— Nature index; 5000 selected references to nature forms and illustrations of nature in design, painting and sculpture. Boston. F. W. Faxon. 1930. 319p. **4718**

—— Travel through pictures; references to pictures, in books and periodicals, of interesting sites all over the world. Boston. F. W. Faxon. 1935. 699p. **4718a**

Enoch Pratt Free Library. Etching and engraving; a list of books in the Enoch Pratt Free Library and in the library of the Peabody Institute relating to the art of engraving on metal, wood and stone. Baltimore, Md. Jan. 1923. 13p. **4719**

—— Union catalog of art books located in Baltimore. Baltimore, Md. Cards **4719a**

Essex Institute. Catalogue of portraits in the Essex Institute, Salem, Massachusetts, covering three centuries. Salem, Mass. 1936. 306p. **4719b**

Fansler, Roberta M. An index to the set of fine arts teaching and reference material for secondary schools. N.Y. Carnegie Corp. 1933. 225p. **4720**

Fielding, Mantle. American engravers upon copper and steel; biographical sketches and check lists of engravings; a supplement to David McNeely Stauffer's American engravers. Phila. n.p. 1917. 365p. **4721**

Fullerton, Pauline V. List of new books on architecture and the allied arts. The Architectural rec. LXIII. no. 1. Jan. 1928- **4722**

General Federation of Women's Clubs. Art division. Study outlines and bibliography of American art. Bridgewater, Mass. 1922 **4723**

Goelet, Robert. New York views, the important collection of seventeenth, eighteenth and early nineteenth century prints and drawings formed by Robert Goelet. ... N.Y. Am. Art Asso., Anderson Galleries, Inc. 1936. 54p. **4723a**

Goodspeed, Charles E. A collection of books and almanacs formed to illustrate the art of engraving in America. ... Boston. Goodspeed. 1909. 60p. **4724**

Grand Rapids Public Library. List of books on furniture with descriptive notes issued in connection with the hundredth furniture market in Grand Rapids, January 1928. [Grand Rapids, Mich.] Pub. by the Lib. Dec. 1927. 143p. **4725**

Graves, Mary de B. A study of American art and southern artists of note. (Univ. of North Carolina. Extension bul. IX. no. 2. Aug. 1929) Chapel Hill. Univ. of North Carolina Press. 1929. 34p. **4726**

Great Britain. Commissioners of Patents. Subject list of works on the fine and graphic arts (excluding photo-mechanical printing and photography) in the library of the Patent Office. (Patent Office Lib. Subject lists. n.s. BM-BZ) London. 1914. 224p. **4727**

Guth, Alexander C. Historic American buildings survey. Wis. archeol. n.s. XVIII. p121-6. 1938 **4727a**

Haferkorn, Henry Ernest. Handy lists of technical literature. . . Part V and VI. Fine arts and architecture, painting, sculpture, decoration, ornament, carpentry, building and art industries, etc. Milwaukee. Haferkorn; London. Gay & Bird. 1893. 336p. **4728**

Hamlin, Talbot F. A bibliography of American architecture. N.Y. Avery Lib. 1935. 100p. **4728a**

Hammond, William A. A bibliography of aesthetics and of the philosophy of the fine arts from 1900 to 1932. N.Y. Longmans. 1934. 205p. **4729**

Harshe, Robert B. A reader's guide to modern art. San Francisco. Wahlgreen Co. 1914. 40p. **4730**

Harvard University. Library. Catalogue of books relating to fine arts contained in the Harvard College Library, Fogg Museum of Art and the library of Paul Joseph Sachs. [Cambridge, Mass.] Jan. 1922. unpag. typ. **4731**

Haskell, Daniel C. American historical prints, early views of American cities, etc. N.Y. Pub. Lib. bul. XXXI. p991-1024 (Dec. 1927) **4731a**

Hind, Arthur Mayger. General bibliography—index of engravers and individual bibliography. *In* A history of engraving & etching, from the 15th century to the year 1914. London. Constable and Co. Ltd. 1923. p393-487 **4732**

Historic American Buildings Survey. Catalog of the measured drawings and photographs of the survey in the Library of Congress. Comp. and ed. by John P. O'Neill. Wash. Govt. Ptg. Off. 1938. 264p. **4732a**

Historic American Merchant Marine Survey. Catalogue of ship drawings and photographs produced by the Historic American Merchant Marine Survey for the Watercraft Collection of the Smithsonian Institution, U.S. National Museum. Wash. D.C. 1937. 24p. **4732b**

Historical Records Survey. American portrait inventory. In progress **4732c**

Historical Records Survey. New Jersey. American portrait inventory: 1440 early American portrait artists (1663-1860). Newark, N.J. Dec. 1940. 305p. mim. prelim. ed. **4732d**

—— —— Check list of 1439 American portrait artists. Newark, N.J. Dec. 1940. 167p. mim. **4732e**

Hitchcock, Henry Russell, Jr. American architectural books; a list of books, portfolios and pamphlets published in America before 1895 on architecture and related subjects. Middletown, Conn. 1938-39. 159p. mim. **4732f**

Hitchcock, Ripley. Etching in America, with lists of American etchers, and notable collections of prints. N.Y. White, Stokes & Alien. 1886. 95p. **4733**

Hunnewell, James Frothingham. Illustrated Americana, 1493-1889. [Worcester. C. Hamilton] 1890. 37p. (Reprinted from the Am. Antiq. Soc. proc. April 1889, April 1890) **4733a**

India House, New York. A descriptive catalogue of the marine collection to be found at India House. N.Y. Priv. print. 1935. 137p. **4733b**

Internationale bibliographie der kunstwissenschaft, 1902-1917/18. Berlin. B. Behr's verlag. 1903-20. 15v. **4734**

Kroch's Bookstores, Inc. Kroch's art manual; an annotated list of American and foreign books on fine and applied art. . . . Chicago. 1939. 94p. **4734a**

Lancour, A. Harold. American art catalogues. N.Y. Cooper Union. In progress **4734b**

Lawson, Mildred H. An annotated list of books on the arts for the teacher and student. Rev. by Royal B. Farnum. (Univ. of the State of N.Y. Bul. no. 633) Albany. Univ. of the State of N.Y. 1917. 87p. **4735**

Leland, Waldo G. The Lesueur collection of American sketches in the Museum of natural history at Havre, Seine-Inférieure. Miss. Valley hist. rev. X. p53-78 (June 1923) **4735a**

Levis, Howard C. Bibliography of American books relating to the prints and the art and history of engraving, also of catalogues of important sales and exhibitions of prints held in America, also of a few books and catalogues published in England relating to American prints. London. Chiswick Press. 1910. 79p. **4736**

—— A descriptive bibliography of the most important books in the English language relating to the art & history of engraving and the collecting of prints. London. Ellis. 1912. 571p. (Supplement and index. 1913. 141p.) **4737**

Lewis, John Frederick. Collection of John Frederick Lewis American portraits. . . . Phila. The Pennsylvania Academy of Fine Arts. 1934. 112p. **4737a**

Lincoln, Waldo. Checklist of portraits in the American Antiquarian Society. Worcester, Mass. 1923. 14p. **4737b**

List of recent publications. The Architectural rec. LVIII. no. 3-LXII. no. 6 (Sept. 1925-Dec. 1927) **4738**

Lucas, Edna Louise. Books on art; a foundation list. (Harvard-Radcliffe fine arts ser.) Cambridge, Mass. Fogg Museum of Art, Harvard Univ. 1936. 83p. **4738a**

McColvin, Eric Raymond. Painting; a guide to the best books with special reference to the requirements of public libraries. (A thesis accepted for the honours diploma of the Library Association) London. Grafton & Co. 1934. 261p. **4739**

McGill University. Library. A catalogue of books on art and architecture in McGill University Library and the Gordon Home Blackader Library of architecture. (McGill Univ. Publications. ser. VII. lib. no. 9) Montreal. McGill Univ. Lib. 1926. 192p. **4740**

McNamara, Katherine. Landscape architecture; a classified bibliography, with an author index. Cambridge. Harvard Univ., School of Landscape Architecture. 1934. 209p. mim. **4741**

Metropolitan Museum of Art. A short list of books on fine arts, with annotations. N.Y. 1937. 49p. **4741a**

Miersch, Ella Emilie. Reading list on house decoration and furnishing. (N.Y. State Lib. bul. bibliog. I. no. 20. Dec. 1899) Albany. Univ. of the State of N. Y. 1899. p661-76 **4742**

New York. Metropolitan Museum of Art. Index to the Bulletin of the Metropolitan Museum of Art, volumes I-XXII, 1905-1927. By Frances B. Hawley. N.Y. Gillis Press. 1928. 143p. **4743**

—— **Library.** Bibliography of museums and museology. Comp. by William Clifford. N.Y. 1923. 98p. **4744**

New York. Public Library. A handbook of the S. P. Avery collection of prints and art books in the New York Public Library. N.Y. N. Y. Pub. Lib. 1901. 81p. **4745**

—— —— List of works in the New York Public Library relating to ceramics and glass. N.Y. 1908. 38p. (Reprinted from the Bul. XII. p577-614. Oct. 1908) **4746**

—— —— List of works relating to furniture and interior decoration. N.Y. 1908. 32p. **4747**

—— —— **Art and prints division.** American historical prints; early views of American cities, etc. from the Phelps Stokes and other collections. By I. N. Phelps Stokes and Daniel C. Haskell. N.Y. N. Y. Pub. Lib. 1932. 327p. **4748**

Newark, N.J. Free Public Library and Newark Museum. Design in industry; the industrialist as an artist, I, no. 1, May 1930-III, no. 4, Dec. 1932. Newark. 1930-33 **4749**

Paine, Nathaniel. Early American engravings and the Cambridge Press imprints 1640-1692 in the library of the American Antiquarian Society. Worcester, Mass. 1906. 21p. (Reprinted from the Proc. of the Am. Antiq. Soc.) **4750**

Parsons, Arthur H. American political cartoons; a bibliography. N.Y. The Author, 509 W. 121st St. 1938. 19p. typ. **4750a**

Peabody Museum of Salem. Catalogue of portraits in the Peabody Museum of Salem. Essex Inst. hist. col. LXXIII. p170-94, 271-94, 363-94; LXXIV. p65-96, 165-96, 277-96. 1937-38   **4750b**

—— Portraits of shipmasters and merchants in the Peabody Museum of Salem. Salem. Peabody Museum. 1939. 185p.   **4750c**

Peters, Harry T. Currier & Ives, printmakers to the American people; a chronicle of the firm, and of the artists and their work, with notes on collecting; reproductions of 142 of the prints and originals, forming a pictorial record of American life and manners in the last century; and a checklist of all known prints published by N. Currier and Currier & Ives. Garden City, N.Y. Doubleday, Doran & Co., Inc. 1929. 331p. (Checklist on p209-331)   **4751**

Philadelphia. Museum of Art. Union catalog of art books in Philadelphia libraries. Phila. 1933- (In progress)   **4751a**

—— —— School of Industrial Art. Library. The library of the Pennsylvania Museum's School of Industrial Art. Catalogue, 1931. [Phila. 1931] 133p.   **4752**

Pittsburgh. Carnegie library. Catalogue of the J. D. Bernd department of architecture in the Carnegie Library. Pittsburgh. Carnegie Lib. 1898. 33p.   **4753**

—— —— Colonial architecture and other early American arts. Pittsburgh. Carnegie Lib. 1926. 28p.   **4754**

Rea, Paul Marshall. A directory of American museums. (Bul. of the Buffalo Soc. of Natural Sciences. X. no. 1) Buffalo. 1910. 360p.   **4755**

Robinson, John. The marine room of the Peabody Museum of Salem. Salem, Mass. Peabody Museum. 1921. 188p.   **4755a**

Sears, Minnie Earl. Standard catalog for public libraries; fine arts section; an annotated list of 1200 titles including books on costume and amusements with a full analytical index. N.Y. H. W. Wilson. 1928. 191p. (o.p. Replaced by Standard catalog for public libraries. 1934 edition. M. E. Sears, ed.)   **4756**

Seitz, Don C. Writings by and about James Abbott McNeill Whistler; a bibliography. Edinburgh. Otto Schulze. 1910. 181p.   **4757**

Shaw, Charles B. American painters. (North Carolina College for Women. Extension bul. III. no. 2. July 1927) Greensboro, N.C. 1927. 75p.   **4758**

Smith, George Campbell. Sporting and colored plate books illustrated by Alken, Rowlandson, Leech, the Cruikshanks, & others. N.Y. Am. Art Asso., Anderson Galleries, Inc. 1937. 192p.   **4758a**

Smith, Ralph Clifton. A bibliography of museums and museum work. Wash. D.C. Am. Asso. of Museums. 1928. 302p. **4759**

Solon, M. L. Ceramic literature; an analytical index to the works published in all languages on the history and technology of the ceramic art. London. Charles Griffin. 1910. 660p.   **4760**

Stauffer, David McNeely. American engravers upon copper and steel. Part II. Checklist of the works of the earlier engravers. N.Y. Grolier Club. 1907. 566p.   **4761**

Stohlman, W. Frederick. Special collections at Princeton. I. The Marquand art library. Princeton Univ. Lib. chron. I. p9-22 (Nov. 1939)   **4761a**

Stokes, Isaac Newton Phelps and Haskell, Daniel C. The Phelps Stokes collection of American historical prints, early views of American cities, etc. N.Y. Pub. Lib. bul. XXXV. p511-88, 619-57, 789-818 (Aug., Sept., Nov. 1931); XXXVI. 21-60, 101-23 (Jan., Feb. 1932)   **4761b**

Sturgis, Russell. Bibliography. In A dictionary of architecture and building, biographical, historical and descriptive. N.Y. Macmillan. 1902. III. col. 1141-1212   **4762**

Sturgis, Russell and Krehbiel, Henry Edward. Annotated bibliography of fine art; painting, sculpture, architecture, arts of decoration and illustration . . . music. . . . Ed. by George Iles (Am. Lib. Asso. Annotated lists) Boston. The Lib. Bureau. 1897. 89p.   **4763**

Taylor, Frank A. The Historic American merchant marine survey. Am. neptune. I. p63-79 (Jan. 1941)   **4763a**

—— The Historic American merchant marine survey. In Smithsonian Institution. Annual report, 1938. Wash. 1939. p595-9   **4763b**

Textile Foundation, Washington. D.C. Textile design; a bibliography and directory. Wash. D.C. Textile Foundation. 1932? 29p.   **4764**

Todd, Frederick P. The Huddy & Duval prints; an adventure in military lithography. Am. Mil. Inst. jour. III. p166-76 (Fall 1939) (American military forces, 1839-42)   **4764a**

Traphagen, Ethel. Costume design and illustration. N.Y. Wiley; London. Chapman & Hall. 1932. 248p. (Contains: A reading and reference list on costume. Pub. by the Brooklyn Pub. Lib. 1909. revised, 1932. p165-229)   **4765**

Tredwell, Daniel M. A monograph on privately illustrated books; a plea for bibliomania. N.Y. De Vinne Press. 1892. 501p.   **4765a**

U.S. Bureau of Foreign and Domestic Commerce. List of references on the glass industry. U.S. Bureau of Foreign and Domestic Commerce. Miscellaneous ser. no. 60. p405-23. 1917   **4766**

U.S. Copyright office. Catalog of copyright entries; pt. 4; works of art, reproductions of works of art, drawings, or plastic works of scientific or technical character, photography, prints, and pictorial illustrations. Wash. Govt. Ptg. Off. 1906-   **4766a**

U.S. Library of Congress. Division of bibliography. Collectors and collecting; a list of books. Aug. 12, 1931. 6p. typ.   **4767**

— — — List of references on pottery. April 25, 1921. 10p. typ. **4768**

— — — List of references on the glass industry. Oct. 17, 1916. 15p. typ. **4769**

— — — List of references on the hardware and cutlery industry. June 5, 1919. 7p. typ. **4770**

— — — A selected list of books on antique and period furniture. Jan. 30, 1936. 16p. typ. **4771**

— — Division of fine arts. Catalog of the Gardiner Greene Hubbard collection of engravings. Comp. by Arthur Jeffrey Parsons. Wash. Govt. Ptg. Off. 1905. 517p. **4771a**

U.S. National Park Service. Historic American buildings survey: catalogue of completed records, December 15, 1933 to December 31, 1935. [Wash. 1936] 156p. mim. **4771b**

Vail, Robert W. G. The American sketchbooks of a French naturalist, 1816-1837; a description of the Charles Lesueur collection, with a brief account of the artist. Am. Antiq. Soc. proc. XLVIII. p49-155 (April 1938) (Also reprinted Worcester, Mass. 1938. 109p.) **4771c**

Virginia. State Library. A list of portraits and pieces of statuary in the Virginia State Library. (Va. State Lib. bul. XIII. nos. 1, 2. Jan., April 1920) Richmond. Davis Bottom, Supt. Pub. Ptg. 1920. 29p. **4771d**

Walker Art Galleries. Illustrated catalogue of Indian portraits, followed by portraits of scouts, guides, generals, etc., all painted by Henry H. Cross; brief biographies by R. H. Adams. [Minneapolis] 1927. 120p. **4771e**

Wall, A. J. Books on architecture printed in America, 1775-1830. *In* Bibliographical essays; a tribute to Wilberforce Eames. Cambridge. Harvard Univ. Press. 1924. p299-311 **4772**

Washington, D.C. Public Library. Contemporary American painters. (Reference list no. 19) Wash. D.C. Public Lib. April 1926. unpag. **4773**

— — Reference list no. 11. Contemporary American artists. Wash. D.C. Pub Lib. Dec. 1912. 21p. **4774**

Washington, D.C. Society of Fine Arts. Reference list no. 9. History of painting; a selected list prepared to accompany a course of lectures given in the library hall under the auspices of the Washington society of the fine arts, 1911-1912. Wash. D.C. 1912. 15p. **4775**

Wehle, Harry B. Life in America: a special loan exhibition of paintings. N.Y. Metropolitan Museum of Art. 1939. 231p. (Catalogue of paintings displayed at the New York World's Fair) **4775a**

Weitenkampf, Frank. List of works in the New York Public Library relating to prints and their production. N.Y. Pub. Lib. bul. XIX. p847-935, 959-1002 (Nov., Dec. 1915) **4775b**

Whiting, Gertrude. Lace guide for makers and collectors; with bibliography and five-language nomenclature, profusely illustrated with half-tone plates and key designs. N.Y. Dutton. [c1920] 415p (Bibliog. on p243-401) **4776**

Worcester. Art Museum. XVIIIth century painting in New England; a catalogue of an exhibition held at the Worcester Art Museum in collaboration with the American Antiquarian Society, July and August 1934. Comp. by Louisa Dresser. Worcester, Mass. 1935. 187p. **4776a**

Worcester. Free Public Library. Arts and crafts selected list. Compiled by the reference department. Revised Nov. 1911. [Worcester, Mass.] 36p. **4777**

Young, Arthur Raymond. Art bibliography. N.Y. Columbia Univ., Teachers College. 1941. 78p. reprod. typ. **4777a**

LITERATURE

General

Aldred, Thomas. Sequel stories, English and American. 2d. ed. by W. H. Parker. [London] Asso. for Assistant Librarians. 1928. 91p. **4778**

Allibone, Samuel Austin. A critical dictionary of English literature and British and American authors living and deceased, from the earliest accounts to the latter half of the nineteenth century. Phila. v. 1 pub by Childs & Peterson. 1858; v. 2-3 pub. by J. B. Lippincott. 1870-71. (Supplement by John Foster Kirk in 2 v. Phila. J. B. Lippincott. 1902) **4779**

American Antiquarian Society. Bibliography of American literary first editions. (In progress; intended to replace Foley's American authors) **4780**

American Library Association. The "A.L.A." index; an index to general literature, biographical, historical and literary essays and sketches. Comp. by William I. Fletcher with the cooperation of many librarians. Boston; N.Y. Houghton Mifflin. 1901. 679p. Supplement, 1900-1910. Chicago. Am. Lib. Asso. 1914. 223p. **4780a**

Arnold. William Harris. A record of first editions of Bryant, Emerson, Hawthorne, Holmes, Longfellow, Lowell, Thoreau, Whittier. With an essay on book-madness by Leon H. Vincent. N.Y. Printed at the Marion Press. 1901. 101p. **4781**

Articles on American literature appearing in current periodicals. Am. literature. I. no. 3. Nov. 1929- **4782**

Atkeson, Mary Meek. A study of the local literature of the Upper Ohio Valley with special reference to the early pioneer and Indian tales, 1820-1840. (Ohio State Univ. Bul. XXVI. no. 3. Contributions in English 2) Columbus, Ohio. Sept. 1921. 62p. **4783**

Baugh, Albert C. and others. American bibliography for 1921- . Modern Language Asso. of Amer. publications. XXXVII. March 1922- **4784**

Blackmer, Alan Rogers. The Andover reading list Andover, Mass. Pub. under the direction of Phillips Acad. Dept. of English. 1931. 70p. **4785**

Bond, D. F. and others. Anglo-French and Franco-American studies: a current bibliography of significant books and articles of 1937 which deal with Anglo-French and Franco-American literary history, from the sixteenth century to the present. Roman rev. XXIX. p343-72 (Dec. 1938) **4785a**

Bonner, Paul Hyde. Sale catalogue of the private library of Paul Hyde Bonner as offered by Duttons, Inc. N.Y. 1931. 138p. **4786**

Brewer, Reginald Arthur. The delightful diversion; the whys and wherefores of book collecting. N.Y. Macmillan. 1935. 320p. **4787**

—— Six hundred American books worth money; a compilation of well known American first editions. . . . Detroit. Rare Book Information Bureau. 1933. 28p. **4788**

Brown, Stephen J. M. Libraries and literature from a Catholic standpoint. Dublin. Browne and Nolan, Ltd. 1937. 323p. **4788a**

—— Novels and tales by Catholic writers. Dublin. Central Catholic Lib. 1940. 24, 84p. **4789**

Brussel, I. R. Anglo-American first editions, 1826-1900; east to west, describing first editions of English authors whose books were published in America before their publication in England. With an introduction by Graham Pollard. (Bibliographia; studies in book history and book structure. . . . no. IX) London. Constable; N.Y. Bowker. 1935. 170p. (American literary piracy) **4789a**

Campbell, Killis. Recent additions to American literary history: a collective estimate. Stud. in philol. XXXIII. p534-43 (July 1936) **4789b**

Catholic Library Association. A reading list for Catholics. Ed. by John M. O'Loughlin. N.Y. The America Press. 1940. 124p. **4789c**

Catholic Unity League. Library list of 10,000 books and pamphlets. Comp. by Bertrand L. Conway. N.Y. Catholic Unity League. 1939. 108p. **4789d**

Cushing, William. Anonyms; a dictionary of revealed authorship. Cambridge, [Mass.] Cushing. 1889. 829p. **4790**

—— Initials and pseudonyms; a dictionary of literary disguises. N.Y. Crowell. [1885-88] 2v **4791**

Davidson, Levette J. Rocky Mountain life in literature; a descriptive bibliography. [Denver] Univ. of Denver Book Store. 1936. 25p. **4792**

De Menil, Alexander Nicolas. The literature of the Louisiana territory. St. Louis, St. Louis News Co. 1904. 354p. **4793**

Dickinson, Asa Don. The best books of the decade, 1926-1935; a later clue to the literary labyrinth. N.Y. H. W. Wilson. 1937. 194p. **4793a**

Donovan, F. P. The railroad in literature; a brief survey of railroad fiction, poetry, songs, biography, essays, travel and drama in the English language, particularly emphasizing its place in American literature. Boston. Railway & Locomotive Hist. Soc. 1940. 138p. **4793b**

Essay and general literature index. Comp. by Minnie Earl Sears and Marion Shaw. N.Y. H. W. Wilson. 1931- (Covers period since 1900) **4794**

Ferguson, John De Lancey. American literature in Spain. (Columbia Univ. stud. in English and comparative literature) N.Y. Columbia Univ. Press. 1916. 267p. (Bibliographies on p203-60) **4795**

Fitzgerald, John Arthur and Frank, Lawrence A. A list of 5,000 Catholic authors, alphabetically arranged. Ilion, N.Y. Continental Press. 1941. 101p. **4795a**

Flitcroft, John Ehret. Outline studies in American literature. N.Y. Prentice-Hall, Inc. 1930. 197p. **4796**

Foley, P. K. American authors, 1795-1895; a bibliography of first and notable editions chronologically arranged with notes. Boston. Printed for the subscribers. 1897. 350p. **4797**

Fullerton, Bradford Morton. Selective bibliography of American literature, 1775-1900; a brief estimate of the more important American authors and a description of their representative works. N.Y. W. F. Payson. 1932. 327p. **4798**

Graham, Bessie. The bookman's manual; a guide to literature. N.Y. R.R. Bowker. 1941. 829p. **4798a**

Grant, M. Series, sequels, sequences. Wilson bul. XI. p315-19 (Jan. 1937) **4798b**

The guide to Catholic literature, 1888-1940; an author-subject-title index in one straight alphabet of books and booklets, in all languages, on all subjects by Catholics or of particular Catholic interest. . . . Detroit. W. Romig [1940] 1239p. **4798c**

Hall, Alonzo C. A topical outline of American literature. Greensboro, N.C. Harrison Ptg. Co. 1925. 244p. **4799**

Harvey, Sir Paul. The Oxford companion to English literature. Oxford. Clarendon Press. 1932. 866p. **4800**

Hawley, Edith J. Roswell. Literary geography; a bibliography. (Bul. of bibliog. pamphlets no. 25) Boston. Boston Book Co. 1917. 28p. (Similar title in Bul. of bibliog. X. p34-8, 58-60, 76, 93-4, 104-5. April 1918-June 1919) **4801**

Hibbard, Addison. Studies in American literature. (Univ. of North Carolina. Extension bul. VI. no. 12) Chapel Hill. Univ. of North Carolina Press. 1927. 44p. **4802**

Hibbard, C. A. Studies in southern literature (Univ. of North Carolina. Extension bul. V. no. 10) Chapel Hill. Univ. of North Carolina Press. 1926. 42p. **4803**

Historical Records Survey. Pennsylvania. A description and analysis of the Bilbiography of American literature. Prep. by Edward H. O'Neill. Phila. Jan. 1941. 23p. **4803a**

Hodgkins, Louise Manning. A guide to the study of nineteenth century authors. Boston. D. C. Heath. 1898. 101,56p. **4804**

Johnson, Merle. American first editions; bibliographic check lists of the works of one hundred and five American authors. N.Y. R. R. Bowker. 1929. 242p. **4805**

—— High spots of American literature; a practical bibliography and brief literary estimate of outstanding American books. N.Y. Bennett Book Studios, Inc. 1929. 114p. **4806**

Knight, Lucian Lamar. Fifty reading courses—Bibliography—Analytical index. *In* Library of southern literature. Ed. by Edwin A. Alderman, Joel Harris and others. Atlanta, G. Martin & Hoyt. 1907. XVI. 226, 61, 212p. **4807**

Kunitz, Stanley J. and Haycraft, Howard, eds. American authors 1600-1900; a biographical dictionary of American literature. N.Y. H.W. Wilson. 1938 **4807a**

Leisy, Ernest E. Materials for investigations in American literature; a bibliography of dissertations, articles, research in progress and collections of Americana. Stud. in philology. XXIII-XXIV (Jan. 1926-July 1927) (Continued in different form in American literature.) **4808**

Manly, John Matthews and Rickert, Edith. Contemporary American literature; bibliographies and study outlines. Introduction and revision by Fred B. Millet. N.Y. Harcourt Brace. 1929. 378p. **4809**

Manly, Louise. List of southern writers. *In* Southern literature from 1579 to 1895. Richmond, Va. Johnson. 1895. p457-514 **4810**

Marble, Annie Russell. Pen names and personalities. N.Y., London. Appleton. 1930. 255p. **4811**

Middlebury College. Library. A check list, Abernethy Library of American literature, Middlebury College. Comp. by Viola C. White. Middlebury, Vt. Middlebury College Press. 1940. 291p. **4811a**

—— —— A check list of books in the Julian Willis Abernethy Library of American Literature, Middlebury College, Middlebury, Vermont. Comp. by Harriet Smith Potter (Middlebury College bul. XXV. no. 2. Oct. 1930) Middlebury, Vt. 1930. 238p. **4812**

Miller, James McDonald. An outline of American literature. N.Y. Farrar & Rinehart. 1934. 386p. **4813**

Miller, Leon. American first editions. n.p. Westport Press. 1933. 98p. **4814**

Millet, Fred B. Contemporary American authors: a critical survey and 219 bio-bibliographies. N.Y. Harcourt, Brace. 1940. 716p. **4814a**

Modern Humanities Research Association. Annual bibliography of English language and literature. . ., 1920-. Cambridge, England. Bowes & Bowes. 1921- **4815**

Modern Language Association of America. Publications. Index to volumes I-XXXIII. Comp. by William Kurrelmeyer. Balt. 1919. 99p. (Supplement to Modern Language Asso. of Amer Publications. XXXIV. no. 3) **4816**

Montgomery, Charles A. A selection of first editions of over one hundred and fifty representative American authors, from the library of Charles A. Montgomery, Brooklyn, N.Y. N.Y. Bangs & Co. 1895. 106p. **4817**

Morris, Adak V. Anonyms and pseudonyms. Chicago. Univ. of Chicago Press. 1933. 22p. **4818**

National Council of Women of the United States. The one hundred best books by American women during the past hundred years, 1833-1933, as chosen by the National Council of Women. Ed. by Anita Browne. Chicago. Associated Authors Service. 1933. 128p. **4819**

Peet, Louis Harman. Who's the author? A guide to the authorship of novels, stories, speeches, songs and general writings of American literature. N.Y. T. Y. Crowell. 1901. 317p. **4820**

Rue, Eloise. Subject index to readers. Chicago. Am. Lib. Asso. 1938. 192p. **4820a**

Rusk, Ralph Leslie. Bibliographies. *In* The literature of the Middle Western frontier. N.Y. Columbia Univ. Press. 1925. II. p39-363 **4821**

Rutherford, Mildred Lewis. The South in history and literature; a handbook of southern authors, from the settlement of Jamestown, 1607 to living writers. Atlanta, Ga. Franklin-Turner. 1907. 866p. **4822**

Schwartz, Jacob. 1100 obscure points; the bibliographies of 25 English and 21 American authors. London. Pub. by the Ulysses Bookshop. 1931. 95p. **4823**

Seton, Grace (Gallatin). Biblioteca femina. [n.p. 1940?] 41p. reprod. typ. **4823a**

Spaeth, John D. E. and Brown, Joseph E. American life and letters; a reading list. Princeton. Princeton Univ. Press. 1934. 56p. **4824**

Spargo, John Webster. A bibliographical manual for students of the language and literature of England and the United States; a short-title list. Chicago. Packard and Company. 1939. 191p. **4824a**

Standard catalog for public libraries: literature and philology section; an annotated list of 1600 titles with a full analytical index. Comp. by Minnie Earl Sears. N.Y. H.W. Wilson. 1931. 242p. **4824b**

Stanton, Theodore. A manual of American literature. N.Y., London. G. P. Putnam's. 1909. 493p. **4825**

Stone, Herbert Stuart. First editions of American authors; a manual for booklovers. Cambridge, Mass. Stone & Kimball. 1893. 223p. **4826**

Sypherd, Wilbur Owen. A bibliography on "English for engineers," for the use of engineering students, practicing engineers, and teachers in schools of engineering, to which are appended brief se-

Sypherd, W. O. A bibliography—*Cont.*
lected lists of technical books for graduates in civil, electrical, mechanical, and chemical engineering. Chicago, N.Y. Scott, Foresman and Co. 1916. 63p.   **4827**

Targ, William. Targ's American first editions and their prices. Chicago. William Targ. 1930. 114p.   **4828**

Taylor, Walter Fuller. A history of American letters with bibliographies by Harry Hartwick. Boston. American Book Co. 1936. p447-664   **4828a**

Texas. University. John Henry Wrenn Library. A catalogue of the library of the late John Henry Wrenn. Comp. by Harold B. Wrenn, ed. by Thomas J. Wise. Austin. Univ. of Texas. Priv. printed by E. T. Heron & Co. 1920. 5v.   **4829**

Trade prices current of American first editions, 1937- . N.Y. R. R. Bowker. 1937-   **4829a**

Traub, Hamilton. The American literary year book; a biographical and bibliographical dictionary of living North American authors. 1919- . Henning, Minn. P. Traub. 1919-   **4830**

Trent, William P. and others. Bibliographies. *In* The Cambridge history of American literature. N.Y. G. P. Putnam's. 1917-21. I. p363-566; II. p411-638; IV. p635-827   **4831**

Troxell, Gilbert McCoy. Bibliography of American literary first editions. A revision of P. K. Foley's bibliography. New Haven, Conn. Yale Univ. Lib. In progress   **4831a**

U.S. Library of Congress. Division of bibliography. List of references on the development of American literature. Sept. 17, 1914. 10p. typ.   **4832**

—— —— —— List of references on women in literature. June 1, 1922. 3p. typ.   **4833**

—— —— —— A list of some books on current American literature. Nov. 4, 1930. 6p. typ.   **4834**

—— —— —— A selected list of recent books on current American literature. 1938. 10p. typ.   **4834a**

Van Patten, Nathan. An index to bibliographies and bibliographical contributions relating to the work of American and British authors, 1923-1932. Stanford Univ. Stanford Univ. Pr. 1934. 324p.   **4835**

Wakeman, Stephen H. The Stephen H. Wakeman collection of nineteenth century American authors; the property of Mrs. Alice L. Wakeman, first editions, inscribed presentation and personal copies, original manuscripts and letters of nine American authors, Bryant, Emerson, Hawthorne, Holmes, Longfellow, Lowell, Poe, Thoreau, Whittier. N.Y. Am Art Asso. [1924] unpag.   **4836**

Williams, Stanley and Adkins, Nelson F. Courses of reading in American literature with bibliographies. N.Y. Harcourt, Brace. 1930. 163p.   **4837**

Children's Literature

American Library Association. Board on library service to children and young people. Subject index to children's plays. Chicago. Am. Lib. Asso. 1940. 277p.   **4937a**

—— **Section for library work with children.** Inexpensive books for boys and girls. Comp. by the Book evaluation committee of the Section for library work with children of the American Library Association. Chicago. Amer. Lib. Asso. 1936. 44p.   **4837b**

Andrews, Siri. Children's catalog; a dictionary of 4000 books with analytical entries for 1020 books and a classified list indicating subject headings. Comp. by Siri Andrews. N.Y. H.W. Wilson. 1936. 979p. Supplement. 1940. 202p.   **4837c**

Association for Childhood Education. Literature committee. Bibliography of books for young children. Wash. D.C. 1941. 76p.   **4837d**

Baker, Franklin T. A bibliography of children's reading. Teachers college rec. IX. p1-65 (Jan. 1908); IX. p1-45 (March 1908)   **4838**

Blanck, Jacob. Peter Parley to Penrod; a bibliographical description of the best loved American juvenile books. N.Y. Bowker. 1938. 153p.   **4838a**

Brown, Stephen James M. Catholic juvenile literature (Catholic bibliog. ser. no. 5) London. Burns, Bates and Washburne. 1935. 70p.   **4839**

Devereaux, Sister Mary Cecil. Children's literature; an annotated bibliography of books and periodical articles about children's literature and reading. Am. Lib. Asso. children's lib. yearbook. no. 4. 1932. p125-68   **4840**

Joint Committee of the American Library Association and the National Education Association. By way of introduction; a book list for young people. Chicago. Am. Lib. Asso. 1938. 130p.   **4840a**

Landrey, Kathleen Benedicta. A bibliography of books written by children of the twentieth century. Boston. Trustees of the Public Library. 1937. 13p.   **4840b**

Macpherson, Maud Russell. Children's poetry index. Boston. F. W. Faxon. 1938. 453p.   **4840c**

Mahony, Bertha E. and Whitney, Elinor. Five years of children's books; a supplement to Realms of gold. N.Y. Doubleday, Doran. 1936. 599p.   **4840d**

—— Realms of gold in children's books. N.Y. Doubleday, Doran. 1929. 796p.   **4840e**

Ohio. State University. Bibliography of children's books. Columbus. Hedrick. 1937. 156p.   **4840f**

Recommended children's books. Lib. jour.   **4840g**

Rosenbach, A. S. W. Early American children's books with bibliographical descriptions of the books in his private collection. Portland, Me. The Southworth Press. 1933. 354p.   **4841**

Shackleton, Clara Everett. Books for the younger generation in America, 1620-1820. N.Y. 600 West 116th St. In progress **4841a**

Smith, Elva S. The history of children's literature; a syllabus with selected bibliographies. Chicago. Am. Lib. Asso. 1937 244p. **4841b**

South Carolina. Dept. of Education. Elementary library catalog, 1938. Recommendations of Committee on selection of books for elementary schools, including delivered prices when purchased through Textbook commission. Issued by James H. Hope, state supt. of education. [Columbia. 1938] 98p. **4841c**

Terman, Lewis M. and Lima, Margaret. Children's reading. N.Y. D. Appleton. 1926. 363p. **4842**

Toronto. Public Library. Books for youth; a guide for teen-age readers. Ed. by Annie M. Wright, and others. [Toronto] 1940. 159p. **4842a**

U.S. Office of Indian affairs. Bibliography of Indian and pioneer stories for young folks (Bul. no. 13) Wash. Govt. Ptg. Off. 1931. 37p. **4843**

—— —— Bibliography of Indian stories for young folks. (Bul. no. 13) Phoenix, Ariz. Phoenix Indian School. 1927. 37p. **4844**

Wurzburg, D. A. Children's short story index for special holidays. Boston. F. W. Faxon. 1928. 116p. **4845**

Drama

American Dramatists Club. The American Dramatists Club list; a standard of reference for the protection of dramatic property, no. 1, 1895; a catalogue of plays and operas by American and foreign authors, produced in the United States. . . . N.Y. Am. Dramatists Club. 1895-1902. 6v. **4846**

American Pageant Association. A record list of American pageants, 1908-1915, and some English pageants. Boston. Am. Pageant Asso. 1908-15 **4847**

Anderson, John, Jr. Catalogue of the late Frank R. Burbank's collection of books, autographs and playbills (mainly relating to the drama). N.Y. John Anderson, Jr. 1902. 78p. **4848**

Baker, Blanch M. Dramatic bibliography; annotated list of books on the history and criticism of the drama and stage and on the allied arts of the theatre. N.Y. H. W. Wilson. 1933. 320p. **4849**

Boston. Public Library. British and American longer plays, 1900-1923; selected references to recent books in the public library of the city of Boston. (Brief reading list no. 26) Boston. 1923. 65p. (Reprinted from Quart. bul. of Jan.-March 1923) **4850**

—— —— **Allen A. Brown collection.** Catalogue of the Allen A. Brown collection of books relating to the stage in the public library of the city of Boston. Boston. The Trustees. 1919. 952p. **4851**

Brenner, Walter C. The Ford theatre Lincoln assassination play-bills; a study. Phila. The Author. 1937. 16p. **4851a**

Carson, Lionel. The stage yearbook. . . . London. Carson & Comerford. [1909]- (Gives American plays) **4852**

Carter, Jean. Annotated list of labor plays. N.Y. Labor Education Service of the Affiliated Schools for Workers, Inc. 1938. 18p. mim. **4852a**

Christeson, Frances Mary. A guide to the literature of the motion picture. Los Angeles. Univ. of Southern Calif. Pr. 1938. 76p. **4852b**

Colby, Elbridge. Early American comedy. N.Y. New York Pub. Lib. 1919. 11p. (Reprinted from the New York Pub. Lib. bul. July 1919) **4852c**

Davis, Harry. Roland Holt theatre collection. Carolina play-book. IX. p43-6. 1936 **4852d**

Drury, Francis K. Viewpoints in modern drama; an arrangement of plays according to their essential interest. (The Viewpoint ser. Josephine A. Rathbone, ed.) Chicago. Am. Lib. Asso. 1925. 119p. **4853**

Evanston, Illinois. Public Library. The drama; a catalogue of books on dramatic literature contained in the Evanston Public Library. Comp. by Gertrude L. Brown. Evanston, Ill. The Drama Club of Evanston. 1909. 32p. **4854**

Fellowship plays. Chicago. Methodist Episcopal Church. Div. of Plays and Pageants. 1937. 24p. **4854a**

Firkins, Ina Ten Eyck. Index to plays, 1800-1926. N.Y. H. W. Wilson. 1927. 307p. (Supplement. N.Y. H. W. Wilson. 1935. 140p.) **4855**

Fox Film Corporation. Catalogue of the stories and plays owned by Fox Film Corporation. Los Angeles. Times-Mirror Press. 1935. 326p. **4856**

Gilder, Rosamond and Freedley, George. Theatre collections in libraries and museums. N.Y. Theatre Arts. 1936. 182p. **4856a**

Graubel, George E. A decade of American drama. Thought (Fordham Univ. quar.) XV. p388-419 (Sept. 1940) **4856b**

Hartley, William H. Selected films for American history and problems. N.Y. Bur. of Publications, Teachers College, Columbia Univ. 1940. 275p. **4856c**

Haskell, Daniel C. List of American dramas in the New York Public Library. N.Y. Pub Lib. bul. XIX. p739-86 (Oct. 1915) **4857**

Hersey, Harold Brainerd. Pulpwood Editor: the fabulous world of the thriller magazines revealed by a veteran editor and publisher. N.Y. Frederick A. Stokes Company. 1937. 301p. **4857a**

Hill, Frank Pierce. American plays printed 1714-1830; a bibliographical record. Stanford Univ. Stanford Univ. Press. 1934. 152p. **4858**

Hyatt, Aeola L. Index to children's plays. Chicago. Am. Lib. Asso. 1931. 214p. **4859**

Logasa, Hannah and Ver Nooy, Winifred. An index to one-act plays. Boston. F. W. Faxon. 1924. 327p. (Supplement, 1924-31. 1932. 432p. 1932-40. 1941. 556p.) **4860**

Mantle, Robert Burns. Since nineteen hundred and nineteen; a list of playwrights and their plays. *In* Contemporary American playwrights. N.Y. Dodd, Mead. 1938. p303-28 **4860a**

—— **and Sherwood, Garrison P.** Plays produced in New York, June 15, 1909-June 15, 1919. *In* The best plays of 1909-1919 and the year book of the drama in America. N.Y. Dodd, Mead. 1933. p395-658 **4861**

Mason, Hamilton. French theatre in New York; a list of plays, 1899-1939. N.Y. Columbia Univ. Press. 1940. 442p. **4861a**

Motion picture review digest. N.Y. H.W. Wilson. 1936-January 22, 1940 **4861b**

Mulford, J. Bentley. Dramas and plays; an index to dramatic compositions published in English in the United States during 1921. Boston. F. W. Faxon. 1922. 85p. **4862**

New York. Public Library. Pageants in Great Britain and the United States; a list of references. Comp. by Caroline Hill Davis. N.Y. Pub. Lib. bul. XX. p753-91 (Oct. 1915) **4863**

Paulmier, Hilah. An index to holiday plays for schools. N.Y. H. W. Wilson. 1936. 59p. **4864**

Pence, James Harry. The magazine and the drama; an index. (Dunlap Soc. Publications. n.s. no. 2) N.Y. 1896. 190p. **4865**

Quinn, Arthur Hobson. General bibliography and list of American plays, 1860-1936. *In* A history of the American drama from the Civil war to the present day. N.Y. F. S. Crofts. 1936. p303-402 **4866**

—— A list of American plays. *In* A history of the American drama, from the beginning to the Civil war. N.Y., London. Harper. 1923. p417-62 **4867**

Rees, James. The dramatic authors of America. Phila. G. B. Zieber & Co. 1845. 144p. **4867a**

Rockwell, Ethel T. Historical pageantry; a treatise and a bibliography. (The State Hist. Soc. of Wisconsin. Bul. of information no. 84) [Madison] 1916. 19p. **4868**

—— A study course in American one-act plays. (Univ. of North Carolina. Extension bul. IX. no. 3) Chapel Hill. Univ. of North Carolina Press. 1929. 48p. **4869**

Roden, Robert F. Later American plays 1831-1900; being a compilation of the titles of plays by American authors published and performed in America since 1831. N.Y. The Dunlap Soc. 1900. 132p. **4870**

Shay, Frank. A guide to longer plays; a list of fifteen hundred plays for little theatres, professional and stock companies, art theatres, schools, amateurs and readers. N.Y. D. Appleton. 1925. 131p. **4871**

Silk, Agnes K. and Fanning, Clara E. Index to dramatic readings. Boston. F. W. Faxon. 1925. 303p. **4872**

Smith, Milton. Guide to play selection; a descriptive index of full-length and short plays for production by schools, colleges and little theaters. A publication of The National Council of Teachers of English. N.Y., London. 1934. 174p. **4873**

Tucker, Samuel Marion. Theatre books for the school library; a bibliography for the National Theatre Conference. N.Y. Theatre Arts, Inc. n.d. 31p. **4874**

U.S. Copyright office. Catalog of copyright entries. Pt. I, group 3; dramatic compositions and motion pictures. Wash. Govt. Ptg. Off. 1928- (The issues for 1920-27 were included in the main text of Part I of the catalog, and those for earlier years in Part 3) **4874a**

—— —— Dramatic compositions copyrighted in the United States 1870 to 1916. Wash. Govt. Ptg. Off. 1918. 2v. **4875**

U.S. Library of Congress. Division of bibliography. List of references on pageants, with separate section on Elizabethan pageants, pageants based on Shakespeare's plays and on costuming for pageants. 1916. 45p. typ. **4876**

—— —— —— List of references on the American drama. Nov. 21, 1918. 8p. typ. **4877**

—— —— —— Moving pictures in the United States and foreign countries; a selected list of recent writings. April 14, 1936. 72p. mim. **4878**

—— —— —— A partial list of war plays in the Library of Congress. Sept. 30, 1921. 4p. typ. **4879**

—— —— —— Select list of references on motion pictures. April 6, 1912. 7p. mim. (Supplement. Jan. 24, 1914. 5p. typ.) **4880**

Wegelin, Oscar. Early American plays, 1714-1830; a compilation of the titles of plays and dramatic poems written by authors born in or residing in North America previous to 1830. N.Y. Literary Collector Press. 1905. 94p. **4881**

Writers' Program. New York. The film index, a bibliography. N.Y. The Museum of Modern Art Film Lib. and The H.W. Wilson Company. 1941- **4881a**

Fiction

Admari, Ralph. Bibliography of dime novels. Am. Book Collector. V. p215-17 (July 1934) **4883**

Agnew, Janet Margaret. A southern bibliography; fiction, 1929-1938. (Louisiana State Univ. Lib. School. Bibliog. ser. no. 1) University, La. La. State Univ. Press. 1939. p9-63 **4883a**

—— A southern bibliography; historical fiction 1929-1938. (Louisiana State Univ. Lib. School. Bibliog. ser. no. 2) University, La. La. State Univ. Press. 1940. 80p. **4883b**

Allegheny, Pa. Carnegie Free Library. Catalogue of fiction, including folklore, mythology, and juvenile books in various classes. Authors—titles-subject-index. [Allegheny 1895] 192p. **4883c**

American Library Association. Replacement list of fiction. Comp. by the A.L.A. editorial staff from reports of practice in twelve representative libraries. Chicago Am. Lib. Asso. 1939. 101p. 2d ed. **4883d**

American rural fiction, 1937- U.S. Bureau of Agricultural Economics. Library. Agricultural economics literature **4883e**

Anderson, Eleanor Copenhaver. A list of novels and stories about workers. N.Y. Womans Press. 1938. 12p. **4883f**

Baechtold, Elsie Louise. Bibliography of American literature, especially fiction, having some phase of engineering as its theme. In progress **4883g**

Baker, Ernest Albert and **Packman, James.** A guide to the best fiction, English and American, including translations from foreign languages. London. George Routledge & Sons. 1932. 634p. **4884**

Bernbaum, E. Recent works on prose fiction before 1800. Mod. lang. notes. XLII. p580-93 (Dec. 1937) **4884a**

Bogart, E. L. Historical novels in American history. The Hist. teachers' mag. VIII. p226-30 (Sept. 1917) **4885**

Boston. Public Library. A chronological index to historical fiction, including prose fiction, plays and poems. Boston Pub. Lib. Bul. X-XIV (Jan. 1892-Jan. 1896) **4886**

Bragin, Charles. Bibliography of dime novels, 1860-1928. Brooklyn. C. Bragin. 1938. 5, 29p. mim. **4886a**

Brown, Herbert Ross. The sentimental novel in America, 1789-1860. Durham, N.C. Duke Univ. Press. 1940. 416p. **4886b**

Brown, Stephen James Meredith. Catalogue of novels and tales by Catholic writers. (Catholic bibliog. ser. no. 1) London. 1935. 84p. **4887**

Buck, Gertrude. American history in fiction for upper grades and high school. Hist. outlook. X. p384-7 (Oct. 1919) **4888**

Collmer, Clement. The American novel in Germany, 1871-1913. Phila. International Ptg. Co. 1918 **4888a**

Cummings, Ralph F. The Ralph F. Cummings standard dime and nickel catalogue of old weeklies, novels, and story papers of America, 1936-1937. Grafton, Mass. R. F. Cummings. 1936. 16p. **4889**

Dawson, Loleta I. and **Huntting, Marion Davis.** European war fiction and personal narratives; bibliographies. Boston. F. W. Faxon. 1921. 120p. **4890**

Dixson, Zella Allen. The comprehensive subject index to universal prose fiction. N.Y. Dodd, Mead. 1897. 421p. **4891**

Firkins, Ina Ten Eyck. Index to short stories. N.Y. H. W. Wilson. 1923. 537p. (Supplement. 1929. 332p.; Second supplement. 1936. 295p.) **4892**

Griswold, William McCrillis. Descriptive list of novels and tales dealing with American city life. Cambridge, Mass. W. M. Griswold. 1891. 120p. **4893**

—— Descriptive list of novels and tales dealing with American country life. Cambridge, Mass. W. M. Griswold. 1893. 51p. **4894**

—— Descriptive list of novels and tales dealing with the history of North America. Cambridge, Mass. W. M. Griswold. 1895. p101-83, 14 **4895**

—— Descriptive lists of American, international, romantic and British novels. Cambridge, Mass. W. M. Griswold. 1891. 617p. **4896**

Hannigan, Francis J. The standard index of short stories, 1900-1914. Boston. Small, Maynard & Co. 1918. 334p. **4897**

Heilman, Robert Bechtold. America in English fiction, 1760-1800; the influences of the American revolution. Baton Rouge. Louisiana State Univ. Press. 1937. 480p. **4897a**

Johnson, James Gibson. Southern fiction prior to 1860; an attempt at a first-hand bibliography. (Univ. of Virginia. Ph.D. dissertation) Charlottesville, Va. Michie Co. 1909. 126p. **4898**

Lenrow, Elbert. Reader's guide to prose fiction; an introductory essay, with bibliographies of 1500 novels selected, topically classified, and annotated for use in meeting the needs of individuals in general education. N.Y. D. Appleton-Century. 1940. 371p. **4898a**

Lingenfelter, Mary Rebecca. Vocations in fiction. Chicago. Am. Lib. Asso. 1938. 99p. **4898b**

Logasa, Hannah. Historical fiction and other reading references for history classes in junior and senior high schools. Phila. McKinley Publishing Co. 1934. 144p. **4899**

Loshe, Lillie Deming. The early American novel. (Columbia University stud. in English, ser. 2, vol. 2, no. 2) N.Y. Columbia Univ. Press. 1907. 131p. **4899a**

New York. Public Library. The Beadle collection of dime novels given to the New York Public Library by Dr. Frank P. O'Brien. N.Y. N. Y. Pub Lib. 1922. 99p. (Reprinted from the N.Y. Pub. Lib. bul. July 1922) **4900**

New York. State Library. Colonial New England in fiction. By Ellen F. Adams. Card bibliography in the library **4900a**

—— —— Contribution to a bibliography of civil war fiction. By Ethel A. Shields. Cards in the library **4900b**

Nield, Jonathan. A guide to the best historical novels and tales. London. Elkin Mathews & Marrot. 1929. 424p. **4900c**

Orians, G. Harrison. Censure of fiction in American romances and magazines, 1789-1810. Mod. lang. assoc. pub. LII. p195-214 (March 1937) **4900d**

Otis, D. S. and Ozanne, Jacques. American history through fiction; a guide to study for individuals and groups. (Reading and study for pleasure and profit; Adult study outlines, no.3) N.Y. Service Bureau for Adult Education, New York Univ. 1937. 64p.   **4900e**

Roos, Jean Carolyn. Background readings for American history; a bibliography for students, librarians and teachers of history. N.Y. H. W. Wilson. 1940. 59p.   **4901**

Russell, Percy. A guide to British and American novels; being a comprehensive manual of all forms of popular fiction in Great Britain, Australasia and America, from its commencement down to 1894. London. Digby, Long & Co. 1895. 314p.   **4902**

Schneider, Rebecca. Bibliography of Jewish life in fiction of America and England. Albany. N.Y. State Lib. School. 1916. 41p.   **4903**

Scribner's sons, Charles. American historical novels, fifteenth to nineteenth century; a collection of first editions. N.Y. Scribner Book Store [1937?] 96p.   **4903a**

Sherman, Caroline B. The development of American rural fiction. Agric. hist. XII. p67-76 (Jan. 1938)   **4903b**

Smith, Rebecca Washington. Catalogue of the chief novels and short stories by American authors dealing with the Civil war and its effects, 1861-1899. Bul. bib. XVI. p193-4 (Sept. 1939); XVII. p10-12, 33-5, 54-5 (Jan.-Sept. 1940)   **4903c**

—— The civil war and its aftermath in American fiction, 1861-1899. Chicago. Univ. of Chicago. 1937. 57p.   **4903d**

Smith, Veldren M. Small town life in American fiction. Bul. of bibliog. XIII. p113-14, 130-1 (May-Aug., Sept.-Dec. 1928)   **4904**

Standard catalog for public libraries: fiction section; an annotated list of 2100 novels with author and title entries. Comp. by Corinne Bacon. N.Y. H.W. Wilson. 1931. 207p.   **4904a**

Syracuse. Public Library. Gold star list of American fiction, 1823-1937; five hundred and sixty-five titles classified by subject, with notes. Syracuse, N.Y. Syracuse Public Lib. 1937. 32p.   **4904b**

Thiessen, N. J. An annotated bibliography of American historical fiction. (Kansas. State Teachers College, Emporia. Bul. of information. XVIII, no. 5) Topeka. Print. by Kansas State Ptg. Plant, W. C. Austin, State Printer. 1938. 65p.   **4904c**

U.S. Library of Congress. Reading room. A list of fiction in the Library of Congress by American authors or published in America 1775-1800. [Wash. D.C. 1936] 22p. typ. carbon   **4904d**

Van Nostrand, Jeanne. Subject index to high school fiction. Chicago. Am. Lib. Asso. 1938. 67p.   **4904e**

Wegelin, Oscar. Early American fiction, 1774-1830; a compilation of the titles of works of fiction by writers born or residing in North America . . . previous to 1831. N.Y. Smith. 1929. 37p.   **4905**

Wheeler, Harold L. Contemporary novels and novelists; a list of references to biographical and critical material. Rolla, Mo. Univ. of Missouri, School of Mines and Metallurgy. 1921. 140p.   **4906**

Wigmore, John Henry. A list of legal novels. Chicago. Northwestern Univ. Law Pub. Asso. 1908. p574-93 (Extract from the Illinois law rev. II. no. 9. April 1908)   **4907**

—— One hundred legal novels. Lib. jour. LII. p189-90 (Feb. 15, 1927)   **4908**

Wright, Lyle Henry. American fiction, 1774-1850; a contribution toward a bibliography. (Huntington lib. pub.) San Marino, Calif. 1939. 246p.   **4908a**

Poetry

Bruncken, Herbert. Subject index to poetry: a guide for adult readers. Chicago. Am. Lib. Asso. 1940. 201p. **4908b**

Ellinger, Esther Parker. The southern war poetry of the Civil war. (Univ. of Pennsylvania. Ph.D. dissertation) Phila. 1918. 192p.   **4909**

Frank, John C. Early American poetry, 1610-1820; a list of works in the New York public library. N.Y. N. Y. Pub. Lib. 1917. 58p. (Reprinted from the N.Y. Pub. Lib. bul. XXI. p517-72. Aug. 1917)   **4910**

Granger, Edith. Granger's index to poetry and recitations. Ed. by Helen Humphrey Bessey. Chicago. A. C. McClurg. 1940. 1549p.   **4910a**

—— An index to poetry and recitations; being a practical reference manual for the librarian, teacher, bookseller, elocutionist, etc. Chicago. A. C. McClurg. 1918. 1059p. (A supplement to Granger's index (1919-1928) Chicago. A. C. McClurg. 1929. 519p.   **4911**

Harris, Caleb Fiske. Catalogue of American poetry, comprising duplicates from the collection of the late C. Fiske Harris of Providence, R.I. . . . Providence. W. T. Tibbitts. 1883. 83p.   **4912**

—— Index to American poetry and plays in the collection of C. Fiske Harris. Providence, R.I. Printed for private distribution. 1874. 171p. (Same in Boston Pub. Lib. Bibliographies of special subjects no. 3. Boston. 1889)   **4913**

Johnson, Merle De Vore. You know these lines! A bibliography of the most quoted verses in American poetry. N.Y. G. A. Baker & Co. 1935. 195p.   **4913a**

McNaught, Rosamond Livingston. Who's who in poetry in United States. [Bloomington, Ill. Long & Fuller. 1931] 136p.   **4913b**

Manchester, Paul Thomas. A bibliography and critique of the Spanish translations from the poetry of the United States. (George Peabody College for Teachers. Contributions to education no. 41) Nashville, Tenn. George Peabody College for Teachers. 1927. 67p. **4914**

Morrison, Hugh A. Guide to the poetry of the World war. Wash. D.C. 1921. 376p. typ. **4915**

Stockbridge, John C. The Anthony memorial; a catalogue of the Harris collection of American poetry with biographical and bibliographical notes. Providence, R.I. 1886. 320p. **4916**

U.S. Library of Congress. Division of bibliography. List of collections of poetry relating to the European war. Oct. 21, 1922. 6p. typ. **4917**

—— —— —— List of references on southern poetry. May 9, 1916. 4p. typ. **4918**

Wegelin, Oscar. Early American poetry; a compilation of the titles of volumes of verse and broadsides by writers born or residing in North America north of the Mexican border (1650-1820). N.Y. Peter Smith. 1930. 239p. **4919**

Miscellaneous

Boston. Public Library. Finding list of fairy tales and folk stories in books at the branches of the public library of the city of Boston. Boston. Boston Pub. Lib. 1908. 48p. **4920**

Boyd, Julian P. The Princeton archives of American letters; a program to meet an obligation of future historians. Princeton Univ. Lib. chronicle. II. p20-2 (June 1941) **4920a**

Burke, W. J. The literature of slang. N.Y. Pub. Lib bul. XL. p1013-22 (Dec. 1936); XLI. p19-28, 113-24, 313-20, 681-95, 785-97, 851-74, 937-59 (Jan., Feb., April, Sept.-Dec. 1937); XLII. p333-42, 497-507, 564-74, 645-55 (April, June-Aug. 1938) **4920b**

Chandler, Frank W. The literature of roguery. Boston, N.Y. Houghton Mifflin. 1907. 2v **4921**

Davis, Caroline Hill. Pageants in Great Britain and the United States; a list of references. N.Y. Pub. Lib. bul. XX. p753-91 (Oct. 1916) **4921a**

Ditzion, Sidney. The history of periodical literature in the United States: a bibliography. Bul. bibliog. XV. p110, 129-33. 1935 **4921b**

Eastman, Mary H. Index to fairy tales, myths and legends. Boston. Faxon. 1926. 610p. Supplement. 1937. 566p. **4921c**

Faxon, Frederick Winthrop. Literary annuals and gift-books; a bibliography with a descriptive introduction. Boston. Boston Book Co. 1912. 140p. (Reprinted with changes and additions from the Bul. of bibliog. 1908 to 1911) **4922**

Ford, Edwin H. A bibliography of literary journalism in America. Minneapolis. Burgess Publishing Company. 1937 **4922a**

Goddard, Harold Clark. Transcendentalism. *In* The Cambridge history of American literature. Ed. by William P. Trent and others. N.Y. G. P. Putnam's. 1917. I. p326-48, 546-51 **4923**

Harlow, Victor Emmanuel. Bibliography and genetic study of American realism. Oklahoma City. Harlow Publishing Co. 1931. 110p. **4923a**

Hazard, Lucy Lockwood. The frontier in American literature. N.Y. Crowell. 1927. 308p. **4923b**

Hornor, Mrs. Marian S. Bibliography of books relating to Christmas in America to 1870. Stenton Ave. at Meadowbrook Lane, Chestnut Hill, Pa. In progress **4923c**

Ireland, Norma O. and Ireland, David E. An index to monologs and dialogs. Boston. F.W. Faxon. 1939. 127p. **4923d**

Klinefelter, Walter. A bibliographical list of Christmas books. Portland, Me. Southworth-Anthoensen Press. 1937. 114p. **4923e**

—— More Christmas books. Portland, Me. Southworth Press. 1938. p47-77 **4923f**

Lane, William Coolidge. Catalogue of English and American chap-books and broadside ballads in Harvard College Library. (Lib. of Harvard Univ. Bibliog. contributions no. 56) Cambridge, Mass. 1905. 171p. **4924**

Meine, Franklin Julius. American humor; an exhibition of books and prints from the collection of Franklin J. Meine, January 11 to March 31, 1939, the Newberry Library, Chicago. [Chicago. 1939] 20p. **4924a**

Mott, Howard S., Jr. Three hundred years of American humor (1637-1936). N.Y. H. S. Mott, Jr. 1937? 32p. **4924b**

New York. Public Library. A catalogue of the chapbooks in the New York Public Library. Comp. by Harry B. Weiss. N.Y. N. Y. Pub. Lib. 1936. 90p. (Reprinted with revisions and corrections from the N.Y. Pub. Lib. bul. of Jan.-March, Oct. 1935) **4925**

Nikolais, Alwin. Index to puppetry; a classified list of magazine articles published between 1910 and 1938. [Hartford. 1938] 60p. mim. **4925a**

Normano, J. F. Social Utopias in American literature. Internat. rev soc. hist. III. p287-99. 1938 **4925b**

Schmauck, Walter W. Christmas literature through the centuries. Chicago, Ill. W.M. Hill [1938] 418p. **4925c**

Starbuck, Edwin D. and Shuttleworth, Frank K. A guide to literature for character training. Volume I. Fairy tale, myth, and legend. Volume II. Fiction. N.Y. Macmillan. 1928, 1930. 389, 579p. **4926**

Thompson, Ralph. American literary annuals and gift books, 1825-1865. N.Y. H. W. Wilson. 1936. 183p. **4927**

Webb, Walter Preston. The literature of the Great Plains and about the Great Plains. *In* The Great Plains. Boston. Ginn. 1931. p453-83 **4927a**

Weiss, Harry B. Some comic histories of the United States. N.Y. Pub. Lib. bul. XLII. p303-14 (April 1938)   **4927b**

MEDICINE

Adelaide Nuting historical nursing collection. N.Y. Columbia Univ., Teachers College. 1929. 68p.   **4928**

Affleck, George Baird. Selected bibliography of physical training and hygiene, Sept. 1909-[1928]. *In* Am. physical education rev. XV-XXXIV. 1910-29   **4929**

American Medical Association. Bibliography on state medicine. Chicago. Am. Med. Asso. 1930. 22p. mim.   **4930**

—— Index to the transactions of the American Medical Association, v. 1-33. Prepared by William B. Atkinson. Phila. W. F. Fell & Co. 1883. 130p.   **4931**

—— The Journal of the American Medical Association. I, July 1883-. (Includes lists of current literature)   **4932**

American Public Health Association. Books for sanitarians; a bibliography on public health and allied topics. N.Y. Am. Pub. Health Asso. 1922-23. 2v.   **4933**

Bradford, Thomas Lindsley. Homeopathic bibliography of the United States from the year 1825 to the year 1891 inclusive. Phila. Boericke & Tafel. 1892. 596p.   **4934**

Burdett, Henry Charles. Asylum bibliography—Bibliography for British and foreign hospitals, including those in the United States. *In* Hospitals and asylums of the world. London. Churchill. 1893. II. p277-337; IV. p381-452   **4935**

Chayer, Mary Ella. Bibliography in health education for schools and colleges. N.Y. Putnam's. 1936. 100p.   **4936**

Child health literature. Child health bul. I. no. 1. March 1925-   **4937**

Davenport, James Henry. Literary doctors of medicine; a catalogue of the extra-professional writings of physicians and surgeons in the library of James Henry Davenport. Providence, R.I. Priv. printed. 1926. 306p.   **4938**

Dunbar, Helen Flanders. Emotions and bodily changes; a survey of literature on psychosomatic interrelationships, 1910-1933. N.Y. Columbia Univ. Press. 1935. 595p.   **4939**

Earle, Mabel L. Bibliographia eugenica. Supplement to Eugenical news issued quarterly volume I, part 1-16, 1927-1930. Cold Spring Harbor, Long Island, N.Y. n.p. n.d. 349p.   **4940**

Frankenberger, Charles. How to consult medical literature. Special libraries. XVII. p167-70 (May 1926)   **4941**

Garrison, Fielding Hudson. Bibliographic notes for collateral reading. *In* Introduction to the history of medicine with medical chronology, suggestions for study and bibliographic data. Phila. Saunders. 1929. p884-922   **4942**

Gross, Samuel David. History of American medical literature from 1776-1876. Phila. Collins. 1876. 85p.   **4943**

Himes, Norman Edwin. A guide to birth control literature; a selected bibliography on the technique of contraception and on the social aspects of birth control. London. N. Douglas. 1931. 46p.   **4944**

Holmes, Samuel Jackson. A bibliography of eugenics. (Univ. of Calif. Publications in zoology. XXV) Berkeley. Univ. of Calif. Press. 1924. 514p.   **4945**

Index medicus war supplement; a classified record of literature on military medicine and surgery, 1914-1917. Fielding H. Garrison, Frank J. Stockman, eds. Wash. D.C. Carnegie Inst. of Wash. 1918. 260p.   **4946**

John Crerar Library. Union catalog of medical works. Chicago, Ill. Cards   **4946a**

Kremers, Edward and **Urdang, George.** History of pharmacy: a guide and a survey. Phila. J. B. Lippincott. 1940. 466p. (The establishment of the literature, p224-92; Bibliography, p357-86)   **4946b**

Kydd, David Mitchell. Bibliography of rural medicine. *In* Conference on rural medicine, Cooperstown, New York, 1938. Rural medicine; proceedings of the conference. Springfield, Ill. C. C. Thomas. 1939. p245-68   **4946c**

McCurdy, J. H. A bibliography of physical training. Springfield, Mass. Physical Directors' Soc. of the Y.M.C.A. of North Amer. 1905. 369p.   **4947**

McMurtrie, Douglas C. and others. Index-catalogue of a library on rehabilitation of the disabled. Am. jour. of care for cripples. VIII. p191-295. 1919   **4948**

Malloch, Archibald. Catalogue of an exhibition of early and later medical Americana . . . [N.Y. Press of C. C. Morchand Co. 1927] [64]p.   **4949**

Marshall, Clara. Titles of medical papers written by the alumnae of the Women's medical college of Pennsylvania prior to January 1, 1897. *In* The Woman's Medical College of Pennsylvania. Phila. P. Blakiston Son & Co. 1897. p89-142   **4950**

Medical science abstracts and reviews, 1-12, Oct. 1919-Sept. 1925. London, N.Y. H. Milford, Oxford Univ. Press. 1919-25. 12v.   **4951**

National Health Council. Selected bibliography of books on public health. N.Y. 1923. 13p. mim.   **4952**

New York. State Board of Charities. A bibliography of eugenics and related subjects. (Eugenics and social welfare bul. no. 3) Albany, N.Y. State Board of Charities. 1913. 130p.   **4953**

New York. State Library. Books on health as related to the school child. N.Y. State Lib. bibliog. bul. 69. March 1, 1921. 37p.   **4954**

New York Academy of Medicine. Catalogue of an exhibition of early and later medical Americana. N.Y. Press of Charles C. Morchand. 1927. 64p.   **4955**

Packard, Francis Randolph. Pre-revolutionary medical bibliography. *In* History of medicine in the United States. Phila. Lippincott. 1901. p429-51 **4956**

Pilcher, Lewis Stephen. A list of books by some of the old masters of medicine and surgery together with books on the history of medicine and on medical biography in the possession of Lewis Stephen Pilcher; with biographical and bibliographical notes and reproductions of some title pages and captions. Brooklyn, N.Y. 1918. 201p. **4957**

Quarterly cumulative index to current medical literature, 1916-1926. Chicago. Am. Med. Asso. 1916-26. 11v. **4958**

Rockefeller Foundation. Bibliography of hookworm disease. (Publication no. 11) N.Y. The Rockefeller Foundation, International Health Board. 1922. 417p. **4959**

Shryock, Richard Harrison. Library collections in social medicine. [Chicago. 1936] p351-63. planog. (Reprinted from Public documents; papers presented at the 1936 conference of the American Library Association, edited by A.F. Kuhlman) **4959a**

—— Medical sources and the social historian. Am. hist. rev. XLI. p458-73 (April 1936) **4960**

Smith, Arthur W. Select bibliography of sanitary science and allied subjects. Boulder, Colo. Daily Camera. 1909. 37p. **4961**

Smith, Henry Hollingsworth. The principles and practice of surgery embracing minor and operative surgery, with a bibliographical index of American surgical writers from the year 1783 to 1860. Phila. J. B. Lippincott. 1863. I. p51-61 **4962**

Testerman, Mrs. Lulu. Bibliography of the history of medicine. Columbia, Mo. Univ. of Missouri. In progress **4962a**

U.S. Bureau of Animal Industry. Index catalogue of medical and veterinary zoology. Part I. By Albert Hassall and Margie Potter. Wash. Govt. Ptg. Off. 1932. 142p. **4963**

U.S. Department of Labor. Library. The national health program and medical care in the United States; selected recent references. Comp. by Ruth Fine. Wash. D.C. June 1940. 25p. mim. **4963a**

U.S. Library of Congress. Division of bibliography. Free medical service with special reference to state medicine; a bibliographical list. Nov. 12, 1930. 12p. mim. **4964**

—— —— —— List of references on the medical profession and war; past and present. Aug. 29, 1917. 6p. typ. **4965**

—— —— —— List of references since 1900 on the liquor question in its hygiene, economic and social phases. Nov. 15, 1915. 25p. typ. **4966**

—— —— —— Medical care in the United States and foreign countries, with special reference to socialization; selected list of recent writings. March 28, 1935. 45p mim. **4967**

—— —— —— Women as physicians in the United States; a selected list of books and pamphlets. Comp. by Ann D. Brown. Oct. 16, 1940. 32p. typ. **4967a**

U.S. Public Health Service. Bibliography of references to health legislation. Comp. by James A. Tobey. [Wash. D.C.] 1921. 8p. (Reprint 684 from Public health reports, Aug. 12, 1921) **4968**

—— —— Public health engineering abstracts. Wash. D.C. 1921- mim. **4969**

U.S. Surgeon General's Office. Library. Index-catalogue of the library, authors, and subjects. Wash. Govt. Ptg. Off. 1880-95. 16v. 2d ser. 1896-1916. 21v. 3d ser. 1918- **4970**

—— —— —— Index catalogue of the library. . . . (Army medical library, authors and subjects, 4th ser.) Wash. Govt. Ptg. Off. 1936- **4970a**

—— —— —— Texts illustrating the history of medicine in the library of the Surgeon general's office, U.S. Army, arranged in chronological order. Reprint from volume XVII, second series, Index catalogue of the library of the Surgeon General's Office. Wash. Govt. Ptg. Off. 1912. p89-178 **4971**

Viets, Henry R. The bibliography of medicine. Menasha, Wis. Banta. 1938. 15p. (Reprinted from the Medical Lib. Asso. bul. XXVII. 1938) **4971a**

Virginia. State Library. Finding list of books . . . medicine . . . Va. State Lib. bul. IV. p211-35. 1912 **4972**

Yandell, Lunsford Pitts. Address on American medical literature, delivered before the International Medical Congress. . . . Phila. 1876. 44p. (Extracted from the transactions) **4973**

MUSIC

Aldrich, Richard. A catalogue of books relating to music in the library of Richard Aldrich. N.Y. 1931. 435p. **4974**

Allen, Gardner Weld. Naval songs and ballads. Worcester, Mass. The Soc. 1926. 17p. (Reprinted from the Am. Antiq. Soc. proc. n.s. XXXV. p64-78) **4974a**

American Council of Learned Societies. Committee on musicology. Bibliography and abstracts of periodical publications relating to musicology; a directory of collectors of folk and primitive music with notes on their recordings; and lists of doctoral dissertations of interest to students of musicology. Planned **4974b**

Ayars, C. M. Contributions to the art of music in America by the music industries of Boston (1640-1936). N.Y. H. W. Wilson. 1937. 326p. **4975**

Bailey, Arthur Low. Bibliography of biography of musicians in English. N.Y. State Lib. Bul. bibliog. no. 17. p493-576 (Jan. 1899) **4976**

Benson, Louis F. The American revisions of Watt's Psalms. Phila. 1903 (Reprinted from the Jour. of the Presbyterian Hist. Soc. II. p18-34, 75-89. June-Sept. 1903)   **4977**

Blom, Eric. A general index to modern musical literature in the English language, including periodicals for the years 1915-1926. London, Phila. Curwen. 1927. 159p.   **4978**

Boardman, George Dana. Early printing in the middle colonies; address delivered before the Historical Society of Pennsylvania, December 11, 1885. . . . Phila. 1885. 20p.   **4978a**

Boston. Public Library. A list of books on the operas announced for production at the Boston opera house during the season of MCMXI-MCMXII in the public library of the city of Boston. Boston. Pub. by the Trustees. 1911. 49p.   **4979**

Bradley, Ruth E. Background readings in music. N.Y. H.W. Wilson. 1938. 32p.   **4979a**

Burrage, Henry Sweetser. Baptist hymn writers and their hymns. Portland, Me. Brown Thurston & Co. 1888. 682p. **4979b**

Carnegie Corporation of New York. Catalogue of the college music set. N.Y. Carnegie Corp. 1933. 117p.   **4980**

Child Study Association of America, Inc. Music and the child. Ed. by Doris S. Champlin. N.Y. Child Study Asso. of Amer. 1930. 87p.   **4981**

Cushing, Helen Grant. Children's song index; an index to more than 22,000 songs in 189 collections comprising 222 volumes. . . . N.Y. Wilson. 1936. 798p.   **4981a**

Dichter, Harry and Shapiro, Elliott. Early American sheet music; its lure and its lore, 1768-1889. N.Y. R.R. Bowker. 1941   **4981b**

Dickinson, Edward. Guide to the study of musical history and criticism. Oberlin, Ohio. Pearce & Randolph. 1895. 95p.   **4982**

—— The history of church music; syllabus with bibliographical references. (Oberlin College Lib. bul. I. no. 3) Oberlin, Ohio. 1896. 24p.   **4983**

Drexel, Joseph W. Catalogue of Jos. W. Drexel's musical library, consisting of musical writings, autographs of celebrated musicians, prints relating to music (including portraits of composers, etc.) and music for the church, theatre, concert room, &c. Phila. King & Baird. 1869. 48p.   **4984**

Dubbs, J. H. Early German hymnology of Pennsylvania. n.p. n.p. 1882? (Also in Quar. rev. Oct. 1888)   **4985**

Eames, Wilberforce. A list of editions of the "Bay Psalm Book," or the New England version of the Psalms. N.Y. 1885. 14p. (Reprinted from Sabin's Dictionary of books relating to America, XVI) **4986**

Early prayer books of America; being a descriptive account of prayer books published in the United States, Mexico and Canada. St. Paul, Minn. 1896. 492p.   **4986a**

Ewen, David. The man with the baton; the story of conductors and their orchestras. N.Y. Crowell co. 1937. p293-353, 355-62   **4986b**

Fisher, William Arms. One hundred and fifty years of music publishing in the United States; an historical sketch with special reference to the pioneer publisher, Oliver Ditson Company, Inc., 1783-1933. Boston. Oliver Ditson. 1933. 146p. **4986c**

Foote, Henry Wilder. Three centuries of American hymnody. Cambridge, Mass. Harvard Univ. Press. 1940. 427p.   **4986d**

Ford, Worthington Chauncey. The Isaiah Thomas collection of ballads. Am. Antiq. Soc. proc. n.s. XXXIII. pt. 1. p34-112 (April 1923)   **4987**

Henry, Mellinger Edward. A bibliography for the study of American folk-songs, with many titles of folk-songs (and titles that have to do with folk-songs) from other lands. . . . [London. Mitre Press. 1937] 142p.   **4987a**

Hipsher, Edward Ellsworth. American opera and its composers. Phila. Presser. 1927. 478p.   **4987b**

Historical Records Survey. Bibliography of music. Wash. D.C. In progress, 1936-   **4987c**

—— Guide to the study of music of America. By Keyes Porter. Wash. D.C. **4987d**

Hooper, Louisa M. Selected list of music and books about music for public libraries. Chicago. Am. Lib. Asso. 1909. 46p.   **4988**

Howard, John Tasker. A list of published orchestral and chamber music compositions by American composers—Bibliography. *In* Our American music; three hundred years of it. N.Y. Crowell. 1931. p625-69   **4989**

Howe, Mabel Almy. Music publishers in New York City before 1850: a directory. N.Y. Pub. Lib. bul. XXI. p589-604 (Sept. 1917)   **4990**

Lockwood, Albert. Notes on the literature of the piano. Ann Arbor. Univ. of Michigan Press. 1940. 257p.   **4990a**

Macdougall, Hamilton C. Early New England psalmody: an historical appreciation, 1620-1820. Brattleboro, Vt. Stephen Daye Press. 1940. 179p.   **4990b**

McKinney, Howard D. and Anderson, W. R. A list of phonograph records for use with Music in History [the evolution of an art, by the same authors]. N.Y. American Book Company. 1940. p xxxix   **4990c**

Mattfeld, Julius. The folk music of the western hemisphere; a list of references in the New York Public Library. N.Y. N. Y. Pub. Lib. 1925. 74p. (Reprinted from the Bul. of the N. Y. Pub. Lib. XXVIII. p799-830, 864-89. Nov., Dec. 1924)   **4991**

—— A selected bibliography of writings dealing with Grand Opera in New York. N. Y. Pub. Lib. bul. XXIX. p700-2, 803-14, 873-904 (Oct.-Dec. 1925) (Reprinted as: A hundred years of Grand Opera in New York, 1825-1925; a record of performances. N.Y. 1927. 107p.)   **4992**

Metcalf, Frank Johnson. American psalmody; or, titles of books, containing tunes printed in America from 1721-1820. Heartman's hist. ser. no. 27) N.Y. C. F. Heartman. 1917. 54p. **4993**

—— American writers and compilers of sacred music. N.Y. Abingdon. 1925 **4994**

—— List of sacred music including both hymn and tune books, printed in the United States from 1720 to 1880. Worcester, Mass. American Antiquarian Soc. MS. **4994a**

Minneapolis. Public Library. Music department. An index to folk dances and singing games. Chicago. Am. Lib. Asso. 1936. 202p. **4995**

Muller, Joseph. The Star Spangled Banner; words and music issued between 1814-1864; an annotated bibliographical list with some notices of different versions, texts, variants, musical arrangement, and notes on music publishers in the United States. N.Y. Baker. 1935. 223p. **4996**

Oathout, Melvin C. A bibliography of jazz. Durham, N.C. Duke Univ. Lib. In progress **4996a**

Quarterly booklist. The Music quar. XV. no. 2. April 1929- **4997**

National Association of Schools of Music. A musical literature list for music school libraries. Cincinnati. National Asso. of Schools of Music. 1935. 57p. **4998**

New York Public Library. List of works in the New York Public Library relating to folk songs, folk music, ballads, etc. N.Y. N. Y. Pub. Lib. 1907. 40p. (Reprinted from the Bul. XI. p187-226. May 1907) **4999**

—— Periodicals relating to music in the New York Public Library and the Columbia University Library. N. Y. Pub. Lib. bul. III. p232-8 (May 1899) **5000**

—— Selected list of works in the New York Public Library relating to the history of music. N.Y. N. Y. Pub. Lib. 1908. 36p. (Reprinted from the Bul. XII. p32-67. Jan. 1908) **5001**

Princeton University. Library. Finding list for the music library, 1909. Princeton. The Univ. Lib. 1909. 93p. **5002**

Reis, Claire Raphael. American composers, a record of works written between 1912 and 1932. N.Y. Internat. Soc. for Contemporary Music, United States Section. 1932. 128p. **5002a**

—— Composers in America; biographical sketches of living composers with a record of their works, 1912-1937. N.Y. Macmillan. 1938. 270p. **5002b**

Richardson, Alice Marion. Index to stories of hymns; an analytical catalog of twelve much-used books. Yardley, Pa. Cook & son, inc. 1929. 76p. **5003**

Rieck, Waldemar. Opera plots; an index to the stories of operas, operettas, etc., from the sixteenth to the twentieth century. N.Y. N. Y. Pub. Lib. 1927. 102p. **5004**

Sachse, Julius Frederick. The music of the Ephrata cloister . . . amplified with facsimile reproductions of parts of the text and some original Ephrata music of the Weyrauchs Hügel, 1739; Rosen und Lilen, 1745; Turtel Taube, 1747; Choral buch, 1754, etc. Lancaster, Pa. Printed for the author by The New Era Ptg. Co. 1903. 108p. **5005**

Sears, Minnie Earl and Crawford, Phyllis. Song index; an index to more than 12000 songs in 177 song collections comprising 262 volumes. N.Y. H.W. Wilson. 1926. 650p. Supplement. 1934. 366p. **5005a**

Sonneck, Oscar G. T. The bibliography of American music. Bibliog. Soc. of Amer. pap. I. pt. 1. p50-64. 1904-05 **5006**

—— Bibliography of early secular American music. Wash. D.C. Print. for the author by H. L. McQueen. 1905. 194p. **5006a**

Spivacke, Harold. The Archive of American folk-song in the Library of Congress: in its relationship to the folk-song collector. So. Folklore Quar. II. p31-5 (March 1938) **5006b**

Stringfield, Lamar. America and her music. (Univ. of North Carolina. Extension bul. X. no. 7. March 1931) Chapel Hill. Univ. of North Carolina Press. 1931. 74p. **5007**

Tuthill, Bernet C. Fifty years of chamber music in the United States. Reprinted from Music Teachers' National Asso. proc. 1928 **5008**

U.S. Copyright office. Catalog of copyright entries; pt. 3; musical compositions. Wash. Govt. Ptg. Off. 1906- **5008a**

U.S. Library of Congress. A list of books and pamphlets [collected] by Oscar G. Sonneck received in the Library of Congress. [Wash. D.C. 1929] 38, 3, 18p. **5009**

—— —— Division of music. Catalogue of the first editions of Stephen C. Foster (1826-1864). By Walter R. Whittlesey and Oscar G. Sonneck. 1915. 79p. **5009a**

—— —— —— Copy of typewritten lists on American folk song, furnished by Oliver Strunk. N.Y. 1936. 100p. typ. **5009b**

—— —— —— Report 1928/29-. Wash. Govt. Ptg. Off. 1929- **5010**

Upton, William Treat. Bibliography of early secular music. Revision of O.G.T. Sonneck's bibliography of 1905. 120 C. St., N.E. Wash. D.C. In progress **5010a**

Warrington, James. Short titles of books relating to psalmody in the United States, 1620-1820. Phila. Priv. printed. 1898. 96p. **5011**

PRINTING

Boston. Public Library. A list of books on the history and art of printing and some related subjects in the public library of the city of Boston and the libraries of Harvard College and the Boston Athenaeum. Boston. The Trustees. 1906. 38p. **5012**

Chicago. Public Library. Omnibus Project. List of periodicals to be included in cumulative index of printing periodicals. Chicago, Ill. 1940. 31p. typ. carbon
5012a

Green, Samuel Abbott. John Foster, the earliest American engraver and the first Boston printer. Boston. 1909. 149p. (Includes lists of printed titles and engravings)
5012b

—— Remarks on the early history of printing in New England. Boston. 1897. 16p.
5012c

Growoll, Adolf. American book clubs, their beginnings and history, and a bibliography of their publications. N.Y. Dodd, Mead. 1897. 423p.
5012d

Haas, Irvin. A bibliography of material relating to private presses. Chicago. Black Cat Press. 1937. 57p.
5012e

—— Bibliography of modern American presses. Chicago. Black Cat Press. 1935. 95p.
5013

—— A periodical bibliography of private presses. Bul. of bibliog. XV. p46-50 (Jan., April 1934)
5014

Hart, Horace. Bibliotheca typographica in usum eorum qui libros amant: A list of books about books. With an introduction by George Parker Winship. Rochester, N.Y. Leo Hart. 1933. 141p.
5015

Harvard University. Library. Index of all American imprints before 1800. MS.
5015a

Heartman, Charles F. Checklist of printers in the United States from Stephen Daye to the close of the War of independence, with a list of places in which printing was done. (Heartman's hist. ser. no.9) N.Y. 1915. 53p.
5016

Historical Records Survey. Illinois. A handlist of American publishers, 1876-1900 (compiled from the lists of publishers in Federick Leypoldt's American catalogue 1876-1900). Chicago, Ill. Nov. 1940. 43p. mim.
5016a

Lehmann-Haupt, Hellmut, Granniss, Ruth Shepard, and Wroth, Lawrence C. The book in America; a history of the making, the selling, and the collecting of books in the United States. N.Y. R.R. Bowker. 1939. 453p.
5016b

McCulloch, William. William McCulloch's additions to Thomas's history of printing. Am. Antiq. Soc. proc. XXXI. p89-247 (April 1921)
5017

McMurtrie, Douglas C. Books and pamphlets on the history of printing. Chicago. [1932] 14p.
5018

—— Further progress in the record of American printing. In Archives and libraries, 1940. Ed. by A.F. Kuhlman. Chicago. American Library Association. 1940. p36-43
5018a

—— Notes on the bibliography of the history of printing in the Americas. The Am. collector. V. p242-5 (March 1928); VI. p5-11 (April 1928), p68-77 (May-June 1928)
5019

—— The westward migration of the printing press in the United States, 1786-1836. Mayence [1930] 20p. (Offprint from Gutenberg jahrbuch 1930)
5019a

Marthens, J. F. Typographical bibliography; a list of books in the English language on printing and its accessories. Pittsburgh. Bakewell & Marthens. 1874. 43p.
5020

Michigan. University. William L. Clements library of American history. Historic examples of American printing and typography; a guide to an exhibition in the William L. Clements library at the University of Michigan (Bul. no. 32) Ann Arbor. 1940. 69p.
5020a

Moore, John W. Moore's historical, biographical, and miscellaneous gatherings in the form of disconnected notes relative to printers, printing, publishing, and editing of books, newspapers, magazines. Concord, Mass. Republican Press Asso. 1886. 604p.
5021

Munsell, Joel. Catalogue of books on printing and the kindred arts; embracing also works on copyright, liberty of the press, libel, literary property, bibliography, etc. Albany, N.Y. Munsell. 1868. 47p.
5022

New Bedford, Mass. Free Public Library. The William L. Sayer collection of books and pamphlets relating to printing, newspapers, and freedom of the press. New Bedford. Free Pub. Lib. 1914-20. 38, 24p.
5023

Newark, N.J. Free Public Library. Printing and allied industries; a list and periodicals. Newark. Free Pub Lib. 1911. 16p.
5024

Nichols, Charles Lemuel. Bibliography: a list of books, pamphlets, newspapers, & broadsides printed by Isaiah Thomas. In Isaiah Thomas, printer, writer & collector; a paper read April 12, 1911, before the Club of Odd Volumes. . . . Boston. Printed for the Club of Odd Volumes. 1912. p37-144
5025

Oswald, John Clyde. Printing in the Americas. N.Y. Gregg Pub. Co. 1937. 565p.
5025a

Peet, William. Bibliography of publishing and bookselling. In Mumby, F. A. Publishing and bookselling. London. Jonathan Cape. 1930. p419-59
5026

Rosenbach, A.S.W. One hundred and fifty years of printing in English America (1640-1790) an exhibition to celebrate the 300th anniversary of the establishment of the first press in this country from the collection by Dr. A.S.W. Rosenbach, with an introduction by Dr. George Parker Winship. [Phila.] Free Lib. 1940. 63p.
5026a

Rossiter, William S. Printing and publishing. In U.S. Twelfth census. Wash. D.C. U.S. Census Office. 1902. IX. p1037-119
5027

Shove, Raymond Howard. Cheap book production in the United States, 1870-1891. Urbana. Univ. of Illinois Lib. 1937. 166p.
5027a

Solberg, Thorvald. Copyright in Congress 1789-1904; a bibliography and chronological record of all proceedings in Congress in relation to copyright from April 15, 1789 to April 28, 1904, first Congress, 1st session, to fifty-eighth Congress, 2d session. (Copyright Off. bul. no. 8) Wash. Govt. Ptg. Off. 1905. 468p.   **5028**

Springer, John. An extended catalogue of a few books and pamphlets and scattered magazines in varied languages, and stages of English, treating on the history and mystery of printing, its appendages and dependencies. . . . Iowa City. Printed by J. Springer. 1878. 48p.   **5029**

Stevens, Henry, son and Stiles. A century of American printing, 1701 to 1800; a catalogue of books and pamphlets, with a few newspapers from that part of North America now called the United States. London. Henry Stevens, son and Stiles. 1916. 166p.   **5030**

Thomas, Isaiah. The history of printing in America, with a biography of printers and an account of newspapers. (Trans. of the Am. Antiq. Soc. V-VI) Albany, N.Y. Munsell. 1874. 2v.   **5031**

Thompson, John Smith. History of composing machines; a complete record of the art of composing type by machinery, . . . also lists of patents on composing machines, American and British, chronologically arranged. Chicago. Inland Printer. 1904. 200p.   **5031a**

Typothetae of the city of New York. Catalogue of the books in the library of the Typothetae of the city of New York, with a subject index. N.Y. Printed for the Typothetae at the De Vinne Press. 1896. 176p.   **5032**

U.S. Library of Congress. Division of bibliography. List of references on printing in America (supplementary to G. T. Watkins' bibliography, 1906). Jan. 25, 1917. 5p. typ.   **5033**

United Typothetae of America. Department of education. Research library. Graphic arts, October 1931; a classified list of the leading articles on printing from October (1931) printing trade journals and other periodicals on file at the U.T.A. research library, October 1931-March 1934. Wash. D.C. Nov. 1931-April 1934   **5034**

Virginia. State Library. A finding list of books relating to printing, book industries, libraries and bibliography in the Virginia State Library. Va. State Lib. bul. V. no. 2. p153-233. 1912   **5035**

Watkins, George Thomas. Bibliography of printing in America; books, pamphlets and some articles in magazines relating to the history of printing in the New World. Boston. The compiler. 1906. 31p.   **5036**

Winterich, John T. Early American books and printing. N.Y. Houghton Mifflin. 1935. 252p.   **5037**

SCIENCE

Academy of Natural Sciences of Philadelphia. An index to the scientific contents of the Journal and Proceedings of the Academy of Natural Sciences of Philadelphia (1817-1910). Phila. Acad. of Natural Sciences. 1913. 1419p.   **5038**

Agassiz, Louis. Bibliographia zoologiae et geologiae; a general catalogue of all books, tracts, and memoirs on zoology and geology. Cor. enl. and ed. by H. E. Strickland. London. Ray Soc. 1848-54. 4v.   **5039**

Allen, Francis Pitcher. A check list of periodical literature and publications of learned societies of interest to zoologists in the University of Michigan libraries. Univ. of Michigan, Museum of Zoology. Circular no. 2) Ann Arbor. Univ. of Michigan Press. 1935. 83p.   **5040**

Altsheler, Brent, comp. Natural history index-guide; an index to 3,365 books and periodicals in libraries; a guide to things natural in the field; where and how to find the most important objects of natural interest in all countries as described in the leading publications by the popular authors and well-known scientists and explorers of various nationalities. N.Y. H.W. Wilson. 1940. 583p.   **5040a**

American Association of Economic Entomologists. Index V to the literature of American economic entomology, January 1, 1930 to December 31, 1934. Comp. by Mabel Colcord, ed. by E. Porter Felt. (Special publication 5) College Park, Md. 1938. 693p.   **5040b**

American Chemical Society. Chemical abstracts. Pub. by the Am. Chemical Soc. I. Jan. 1907-   **5041**

—— List of periodicals abstracted by Chemical abstracts with a key to library files. Columbus, Ohio. Pub. by the Am. Chemical Soc. Ohio State Univ. 1931. p. cxlii   **5042**

American Library Association. Popular books in science; a reading list. Chicago. Am. Lib. Asso. 1929. 20p.   **5043**

American Mathematical Society. New York. Library. Catalogue of the library. Ed. by Raymond Clare Archibald. Am. Mathematical Soc. bul. XXXVIII. no. 1. pt. II. Jan. 1932. 126p.   **5045**

American Museum of Natural History. List of papers published in the Bulletin and Memoirs of American Museum of Natural History, 1881-1902. N.Y. 1902. 32p. **5045a**

American Philosophical Society. Classified index to the publications of the American Philosophical Society; a list of papers, monographs, treatises and books published by the Society, 1769-1940, classified according to subject. Phila. Am. Phil. Soc. 1940. 173p.   **5045b**

—— Proceedings . . . Index, volumes 51-75; 1912-1935. Phila. Am. Phil. Soc. 1937. 71p.   **5045c**

American Philosophical Society. Register of papers published in the transactions and proceedings of the American Philosopical Society. Comp. by Henry Phillips, Jr. Phila. McCalla & Stavely. 1881. 56p.   **5046**

Annotated bibliography of economic geology for 1937. Econ. geol. and Soc. econ. geol. bul. X. p235-446 (July 1938)   **5046a**

Annotated bibliography of economic geology for 1938. Prepared under the auspices of the Society of Economic Geologists. Econ. geol. XI. p1-208 (Feb. 1939)   **5046b**

Armstrong, Eva V. The story of the Edgar Fahs Smith memorial collection in the history of chemistry. [Phila.] Univ. of Pennsylvania. 1937. 21p.   **5046c**

Banks, N. A. A list of works on North American entomology. . . (U. S. Dept. of Agriculture. Division of entomology. Bul. no. 81. n.s.) Wash. D.C. Superintendent of Documents. 1910. 120p.   **5047**

Barrows, Frank E. Investigations of the chemical literature. Reprinted from Chemical & metallurgical engineering. XXIV. nos. 10, 11 and 12, March 9, 16 and 23, 1921. 40p.   **5048**

Berthold, Arthur. A selected bibliography on photographic methods of documentary reproduction. Jour. doc. reprod. I. p87-123 (Winter 1938)   **5048a**

Bibliography of philosophy, 1933- . Jour. of philosophy. XXXI- . 1934-   **5048b**

Bolton, Henry Carrington. A select bibliography of chemistry, 1492-1892 (Smithsonian Inst. Miscellaneous coll. no. 850) Wash. D.C. 1893. 1212p. (First supplement in Smithsonian Inst. miscellaneous colls. 1170. 1899. 489p. Second supplement. Smithsonian Inst. miscellaneous colls. part of v. XLIV. 1904. 462p.)   **5049**

Books received—Periodicals and reprints received. Jour. hist. ideas. I- Jan. 1940-   **5049a**

Bradley bibliography. A guide to the literature of the woody plants of the world published before the beginning of the twentieth century. Comp. at the Arnold Arboretum of Harvard University under the direction of Charles Sprague Sargent by Alfred Rehder. Cambridge, Mass. Riverside Press. 1911-18. 5v.   **5050**

California. University. Bibliograpical dictionary of philosophy. Berkeley. ERA project   **5050a**

Carruthers, Ralph Herbert. Microphotography; an annotated bibliography. N.Y. 1936. 28p. film reproduction of copy [Wash. D.C. Am. Documentation Inst., Offices of Science Service. 1937] Supplement by B.M. Johnson [Ann Arbor, Mich.] Law Lib., Univ. of Michigan. 1938. 9p. typ.   **5050b**

Cibella, Ross C. Directory of microfilm sources, including photostat service. N.Y. Special Libraries Asso. 1941. 56p. reprod. typ.   **5050c**

Cobb, Ruth. Periodical bibliographies and abstracts for the scientific and technological journals of the world. National Research Council bul. I. pt. 3. no. 3. p131-54 (June 1920)   **5051**

Colton, Harold Sellers. A list of selected readings for students in elementary college zoology. Phila., Univ. of Pennsylvania, Dept. of zoology. 1915. 40p.   **5052**

Columbia University. Department of Philosophy. Bibliography of philosophy. N.Y. 1933- In progress   **5052a**

—— **Library.** A catalogue of the Epstean collection on the history and science of photography. N.Y. Columbia Univ. Press. 1937. 109p.   **5052b**

Crane, E. J. and Patterson, Austin M. A guide to the literature of chemistry. N.Y. John Wiley. 1927. 438p.   **5053**

Critical bibliography of the history and philosophy of science and of the history of civilization. *In* Isis. International review devoted to the history of science and civilization; quarterly organ of the History of Science Society, 1913- Bruges, Belgium. 1913-   **5054**

Dana, James Dwight. Mineralogical bibliography. *In* System of mineralogy, comprising the most recent discoveries. N.Y., London. 1844. p594-616   **5055**

Dean, Bashford. A bibliography of fishes. Enlarged and ed. by Charles Rochester Eastman. N.Y. Pub. by the Am. Museum of Natural Hist. 1916-33. 3v.   **5056**

Dieserud, Juul. The scope and content of the science of anthropology; historical review, library classification and select, annotated bibliography; with a list of the chief publications of leading anthropological societies and museums. Chicago. Open Court Publishing Co. 1908. 200p.   **5057**

Emerson, Ralph Waldo, ed. Nature (1936); index concordance and bibliographical appendices. By Kenneth Walter Cameron. N.Y. Scholar's Facsimiles and Reprints. 1940. 94, 43p.   **5057a**

Estey, Helen Grace. A bibliography on psychology. Gardner, Mass. The author. 1926. 69p.   **5058**

Field Museum of Natural History. Catalogue of the Edward E. Ayer Ornithological Library. By John Todd Zimmer. (Field Museum of Natural Hist. Publication 239, 240. zoological ser. XVI) Chicago. 1926. 706p.   **5059**

Ford, Thomas H. The dawn of navigation and its books, theories, and instruments. U.S.N. inst. proc. XXXII. p209-84 (March 1906)   **5059a**

Gallatin, Frederic, Jr. Catalogue of a collection of books on ornithology in the library of Frederic Gallatin, Jr. N.Y. Priv. printed. 1908. 177p.   **5060**

Gamble, William Burt. Color photography; a list of references in the New York Public Library. N.Y. N. Y. Pub. Lib. 1924. 123p. (Reprinted Oct. 1924 from the Bul. of the N. Y. Pub. Lib. June-Sept. 1924)   **5061**

Gary, Ind. Public Library. Ten years of science and technology. [Gary, Ind.] Gary Pub. Lib. 1940. 61p.   **5061a**

Gaul, John J. A checklist of photography, listing the more important holdings in the Rocky Mountain Region, together with a few unlocated titles. (Bibliographical Center for Research, Rocky Mountain Region, Regional checklist no. 1) Denver. Dec. 1937. process print **5061b**

Gore, James Howard. A bibliography of geodesy. (U.S. Coast and Geodetic Survey. Rep. for 1902. Appendix no. 8) Wash. Govt. Ptg. Off. 1903. p427-787 **5062**

Habib, Nathan. Bibliography of anthropology, 1919-1939. 1407 Sheridan Ave. N.Y. Planned **5062a**

Haferkorn, Henry E. Aerial photography; bibliography of available material relating to the means, methods, experiments and results of aerial photography. . . . Wash. D.C. Press of the Engineer School. 1918. (Reprinted from Professional memoirs, Corps of engineers, U.S. Army and engineer department-at-large. X. no. 51, 52. May-June, July-Aug. 1918) **5063**

Hardin, Floyd and others. Child psychology, a bibliography of books in English. (Regional checklist, no. 4) Denver, Colo. Bibliog. Center for Research. 1938. 203p. mim. **5063a**

Harvard University. Museum of Comparative Zoology. Revised price list of the publications of the Museum of Comparative Zoology at Harvard College. Cambridge, Mass. 1930. 42p. **5064**

Henry E. Huntington Library and Art Gallery. Science and the new world (1526-1800) an exhibition. San Marino, Calif. 1937. 18p. **5064a**

Holland, Alma. Publication in the field of science from the University of North Carolina (1795-1934). *In* Journal of the Elisha Mitchell scientific society. L. Chapel Hill, N.C. 1934. p303-415 **5064b**

Holmes, Harry Nicholls. Bibliography of colloid chemistry . . . preliminary edition. Wash. D.C. National Research Council. 1923. 135p. mim. **5065**

House, Homer Doliver. A bibliography of the botany of New York state. *In* Report of the state botanist, 1915. (N.Y. State Museum. Bul. no. 188) Albany. Univ. State of N.Y. 1916. p66-105 **5066**

Hrdlička, Aleš. Physical anthropology in America; an historical sketch. Am. anthrop. n.s. XVI. p508-54 (Oct. 1914) **5066a**

Hume, Edgar Erskine. The foundation of American meteorology by the United States Army Medical Department. Bul. hist. med. VIII (Feb. 1940) **5066b**

Hurley, Richard James. Key to the out-of-doors, a bibliography of nature books and materials. N.Y. H.W. Wilson Co. 1938. 256p. **5066c**

Index to American botanical literature. Torrey Botanical Club bul. XIII. no. 1. Jan. 1886- **5067**

Indiana. University. Extension division. General science; a bibliography for general science teachers. By Harry Warren Wood (Bul. of the extension division. Indiana Univ. VI. no. 7) Bloomington, Ind. 1921. 20p. **5068**

International catalogue of scientific literature. Published for the International Council by the Royal Society of London. London. 1902-21. 254v. **5069**

Jackson, Benjamin Daydon. Guide to the literature of botany; being a classified selection of botanical works, including nearly 6000 titles not given in Pritzel's "Thesaurus." London. Longmans Green & Co. 1881. 626p. **5070**

John Crerar Library. A list of books, pamphlets and articles on cremation; including the collection of the Cremation Association of America. Ed. by H.E. Mose. Chicago. 1940. 65p. **5070a**

—— Sources of current reviews of scientific and technical books. Comp. by Jerome K. Wilcox. Chicago. 1930. 13p. typ. **5071**

—— Subject bibliography to histories of scientific and technical subjects: machinery, etc. Part 1. Comp. by J. K. Wilcox (Reference list no. 28) Chicago. 1933? 34p. mim. **5072**

Josephson, A. G. S. A list of books on the history of science, Chicago, John Crerar Library, January, 1911. Chicago. Printed by order of the Board of Directors. 1911. 297p. (Supplement. 1917. 139p.) **5073**

Karpinski, Louis Charles. Bibliography of mathematical works printed in America through 1850. With the cooperation for Washington libraries of Walter F. Shenton. Ann Arbor. Univ. of Michigan Press; London. H. Milford, Oxford Univ. Press. 1940. 697p. **5073a**

Kindle, Edward Martin and Miller, A. K. Bibliographic index of North American Devonian *Cephalopoda*. (Geological Soc. of Amer. Spec. pap. no. 23) [N.Y.] 1939. 179p. **5073b**

Little, Homer P. List of manuscript bibliographies in geology and geography. (National Research Council. Reprint and circular ser. no. 27) Wash. D.C. Feb. 1922. 17p. **5074**

Louttit, C. M. Bibliography of bibliographies on psychology, 1900-1927. (Bul. of the National Research Council no. 65, Nov. 1928) Wash. D.C. National Research council of the National Acad. of Sciences. 1928. 108p. **5075**

—— Handbook of psychological literature. (Publications of the Indiana Univ. psychological clinics. ser. II. no. 4) Bloomington, Ind. Principia Press. 1932. 273p. **5076**

Meisel, Max. A bibliography of American natural history; the pioneer century, 1769-1865. Brooklyn, N.Y. Premier Publishing Co. 1924-29. 3v. **5077**

Mellon, Melvin Guy. Chemical publications; their nature and use. N.Y. McGraw-Hill Co., Inc. 1928. 253p. **5078.**

Michigan. University. University extension division. Reference list of library books on science for high schools, junior colleges, and community centers. (Univ. bul. n.s. XXV. no. 2) Ann Arbor. The Univ. 1923. 54p.   **5079**

—— —— **William L. Clements Library of American History.** Ichthyologia et herpetologia americana; a guide to an exhibition in the William L. Clements Library illustrating the development of knowledge of American fishes, amphibians and reptiles; arranged for the nineteenth annual meeting of the American Society of Ichthyologists and Herpetologists. (Bul. XXV) Ann Arbor. Univ. of Michigan Press. 1936. 22p.   **5079a**

—— —— —— Mathematica americana; a guide to an exhibition in the William L. Clements library at the University of Michigan . . . (Bul. XXIII) Ann Arbor. n.p. 1935. 7p.   **5079b**

Miller, George Abram. Historical introduction to mathematical literature. N.Y. Macmillan. 1916. 302p.   **5079c**

Mottelay, Paul Fleury. Bibliographical history of electricity & magnetism. London. Charles Griffin. 1922. 673p.   **5080**

Munroe, Charles E. Index to the literature of explosives. Balt. Isaac Friedenwald. 1886-93. 195p.   **5081**

National Research Council. Handbook of scientific and technical societies and institutions of the United States and Canada. (Bul. no. 101, Oct. 1937) Wash. D.C. 1937. 283p.   **5081a**

—— **Research information service.** Classified list of published bibliographies in physics, 1910-1922. Comp. by Karl K. Darrow (Bul. VIII. pt. 5. July 1924. no. 47) Wash. D.C. National Research Council. 1924. 102p.   **5082**

—— —— List of manuscript bibliographies in astronomy, mathematics and physics. Comp. by Clarence J. West and Callie Hull (Reprint and circular ser. of the National Research Council no. 41) Wash. D.C. 1923. 14p.   **5083**

New books on science. Sci. news letter. I- . [19?-   **5083a**

New York. Public Library. List of works on the history of mathematics (including works printed before 1800) in the New York Public Library. N. Y. Pub. Lib. VII. p464-95 (Dec. 1903)   **5084**

Newberry Library. Philosophy, metaphysics, psychology, ethics. Chicago. 1922. 258p. multig. as MS.   **5085**

Pānchānana Mitra. A history of American anthropology. Calcutta. The Univ. of Calcutta. 1933. 239p.   **5085a**

Pittsburgh. Carnegie Library. Books by Pittsburgh authors—chemistry and metallurgy. Monthly bul. of the Carnegie Lib. of Pittsburgh. XXVII. p315-18 (July 1922)   **5086**

—— —— By-product coking; references to books and magazine articles. Pittsburgh, 1915. 40p. (Reprinted from the Bul. May 1915)   **5087**

—— —— List of technical indexes and bibliographies appearing serially. Monthly bul. of the Carnegie Lib. of Pittsburgh. XV. p292-301 (June 1910)   **5088**

Preston, Carleton Estey. Everyday science; an outline for schools and women's clubs. (Univ. of North Carolina extension bul. XIII. no. 4) Chapel Hill. Univ. of North Carolina Press [1933] 51p.   **5089**

Psychological abstracts, I, Jan. 1927- . Lancaster, Pa. Am. Psychological Asso. [1927-]   **5090**

Rand, Benjamin. Bibliography of philosophy, psychology and cognate subjects. N.Y. Macmillan. 1905. 542p.   **5091**

—— Selected works on the history of philosophy in the English language. Boston. Pub. by the Trustees. 1906. 13p. (Reprinted from the Boston Pub. Lib. Monthly bul. XI. p55-65. Feb. 1906)   **5092**

Rimbach, Richard. How to find metallurgical information. Phila. The Author. 1936. 32p.   **5092a**

Robinson, D. M. Bibliography of archaeological books, 1938. Am. jour. archaeol. XLIII. p371-7 (April 1939)   **5092b**

Rogers, Harriet C. Books in medicine, botany and chemistry printed in the American colonies and the United States before 1801 . . . with checklist of imprints (1668-1800). (Columbia Univ. Thesis) [N.Y.] 1932   **5092c**

Rosenbach Company. The sea; books and manuscripts on the art of navigation, geography, naval history, ship-building, voyages, shipwrecks, mathematics, including atlases, maps and charts. Phila., N.Y. Rosenbach Co. 1938. 224p.   **5092d**

Royal Photographic Society of Great Britain. Catalogue of books in the library of the Royal Photographic Society of Great Britain. London. 1907. 193p.   **5093**

Sears, Minnie Earl. Standard catalog for public libraries: philosophy, religion and general works section; an annotated list of 1000 titles with a full analytical index. N.Y. H. W. Wilson. 1932. 164p. (o.p. Replaced by the Standard catalog for public libraries. M. E. Sears, ed. 1934 ed.)   **5094**

—— Standard catalog for public libraries: science and useful arts section; an annotated list of 1800 titles with a full analytical index. N.Y. H. W. Wilson. 1931. 276p. (o.p. Replaced by the Standard catalog for public libraries. M. E. Sears, ed. 1934 ed.)   **5095**

Smith, Edgar F. Old chemistries. N.Y. McGraw-Hill. 1927. 89p.   **5096**

Smith, James Perrin. Catalogue of the library of Dr. James Perrin Smith on geology, paleontology and related subjects, mineralogy, zoology, conchology, biology and entomology. . . . Ann Arbor, Mich. Edwards Bros. [1933] 70p.   **5097**

Society for the Promotion of Engineering Education. A revised list of technical books suitable for public, industrial and school libraries and for both general and technical readers. Prepared by a committee of the Society for the Promotion of Engineering Education. Chicago. A. C. McClurg. [1906] 64p.   **5098**

Some new publications. Am. anthrop. XXX- . Jan./March 1928-   **5098a**

Sotheran, firm, bookseller, London. Bibliotheca chemico-mathematica: catalogue of works in many tongues on exact and applied science, with a subject-index. Comp. and annotated by H. Z. and H. C. S. London. H. Sotheran & Co. 1921. 2v. (First supplement. 1932. 496p.)   **5099**

Soule, Byron Avery. Library guide for the chemist. N.Y., London. McGraw-Hill. 1938. 302p.   **5099a**

Southern California. University. School of philosophy. Hoose library of philosophy. The Seeley Wintersmith Mudd foundation special collection in the Hoose Library of Philosophy, School of Philosophy. [Los Angeles] Univ. of Southern California. 1940. 39p.   **5099b**

Special Libraries Association. Electrical engineering committee. Commercial-technical group. A bibliography of bibliographies in electrical engineering, 1918-1929. Ed. by Katherine Maynard (Information bul. no. 11) Providence, R.I. Special Libraries Asso. 1931. 156p.   **5100**

—— —— Bibliography of electrical literature. (Information bul. no. 6) N.Y. Special Libraries Asso. 1928. 62p.   **5101**

Strong, Reuben Myron. A bibliography of birds; with special reference to anatomy, behavior, biochemistry, embryology, pathology, physiology, genetics, ecology, aviculture, economic ornithology, poultry culture, evolution, and related subjects. (Zoological ser. XXV, pts. 1-2; pub. nos. 442, 457) [Chicago. 1939] 2v.   **5101a**

Thayer, John E. Catalogue of a collection of books on ornithology in the library of John E. Thayer. Comp. by Evelyn Thayer and Virginia Keyes. Boston. Priv. printed. 1913. 186p.   **5102**

Tilley, Winthrop. The literature of science in the American colonies from the beginning to 1765. Providence, R.I. Brown Univ. In progress   **5102a**

Trenton, N.J. Public Library. Catalogue of works on science, useful arts, fine arts, February 1, 1903. Trenton. MacCrellish & Quigley. 1903. 54p.   **5103**

Trinity College, Hartford. Library. Sanitary science, a list of books in the Trinity College Library acquired chiefly through the J. Ewing Mears foundation on sanitary science. (Trinity College bul., n.s., v. XI) Hartford. Print. for the College. 1914. 33p.   **5103a**

U.S. Bureau of American Ethnology. Index to scientific publications in the United States. MS.   **5104**

U.S. Department of the Interior. National union catalog covering geology, mineralogy and related subjects. Wash. D.C. Cards   **5104a**

U.S. Geological Survey. Bibliography of photo-mapping and allied subjects. Comp. by Eric Haquinius and E. A. Shuster, Jr. [Wash. D.C.] 1929. 84p. mim.   **5105**

U.S. Government Printing Office. Permanence and durability of paper; an annotated bibliography of the technical literature from 1885 A.D. to 1939 A.D. Comp. by M. S. Kantrowitz and others. (Technical bul. no. 22) Wash. Govt. Ptg. Off. 1940. 114p.   **5105a**

U.S. Library of Congress. Division of bibliography. List of references on scientific research. March 7, 1917. 8p. typ.   **5106**

—— —— —— List of references on the development of science in the United States. Sept. 22, 1914. 5p. typ.   **5107**

U.S. Surgeon-General's Office. Library. Congresses: tentative chronological and bibliographical reference list of national and international meetings of physicians, scientists, and experts; 2d supplement, 4th ser., Index-catalogue, U.S. army (Army medical library) Wash. Govt. Ptg. Off. 1938. 288p. First addition. . . . Index-catalogue . . . 4th ser. Wash. Govt. Ptg. Off. 1939. IV. p29-51   **5107a**

Virginia. State Library. Finding list of books in science, medicine, agriculture, technology, military and naval science. Va. State Lib. bul. IV. p79-211. 1912   **5107b**

Watson, Sereno. Bibliographical index to North American botany; or citations of authorities for all the recorded indigenous and naturalized species of the flora of North America, with a chronological arrangement of the synonymy. (Smithsonian Inst. miscellaneous coll. no. 258) Wash. D.C. Smithsonian Inst. 1878. 476p.   **5108**

Weiss, Harry Bischoff. The pioneer century of American entomology. New Brunswick, N.J. 1936. 320p. mim.   **5109**

West, Clarence J. A realing list on scientific and industrial research and the service of the chemist to industry. (Reprint and circular ser. of the National Research Council no. 9) Wash. D.C. April 1920. 45p.   **5110**

West, Clarence J. and Berolzheimer, D.D. Bibliography of bibliographies on chemistry and chemical technology, 1900-1931. (Bulletins of the National Research Council. IX. pt. 3. no. 50. March 1925; no. 71. June 1929; no. 86. March 1932) 308, 161, 150p.   **5111**

West, Clarence J. and Hull, Callie. List of manuscript bibliographies in chemistry and chemical technology. (Reprint and circular ser. of the National Research Council no. 36) Wash. D.C. 1922. 17p. (Reprinted from the Jour. of industrial and engineering chemistry. XIV. no. 12. Dec. 1922)   **5112**

White, Charles Abiathar and Nicholson, H. Alleyne. Bibliography of North American invertebrate paleontology, being a report upon the publications that have hitherto been made upon the invertebrate paleontology of North America, including the West Indies and Greenland. (United States Geological Survey of the Territories. Misc. pub. no. 10) Wash. Govt. Ptg. Off. 1878. 132p.   **5112a**

Winlock, W. C. Account of progress in astronomy. *In* Smithsonian institution annual report, 1885-1894. Wash. Govt. Ptg. Off. 1886-95   **5113**

Wood, Casey Albert. An introduction to the literature of vertebrate zoology; based chiefly on the titles in the Blacker Library of Zoology, the Emma Shearer Wood Library of Ornithology, the Bibliotheca Osleriana and other libraries of McGill University, Montreal. (McGill Univ. publications. ser. XI (Zoology) no. 24) London. Oxford Univ. Press, Humphrey Milford. 1931. 643p.   **5114**

Wroth, Lawrence Counselman. The way of a ship; an essay on the literature of navigation science. Portland, Me. Southworth-Anthoensen Press. 1937. 91p.   **5114a**

Chapter XII

BIOGRAPHY AND GENEALOGY

BIOGRAPHY
General

Adams, Elizabeth L. The lives of the American pirates. More books. XV. p.315-30 (Oct. 1940) **5114b**

Alvord, Clarence Walworth. The study and writing of history in the Mississippi Valley. Miss. Valley Hist. Asso. proc. I. p98-110. 1907-08 **5114c**

American Antiquarian Society. Index of biographies in newspapers from 1875 to 1927. Worcester, Mass. (In progress) **5115**

—— Index to newspaper biographies and obituaries, 1875 to date. Worcester, Mass. In progress **5115a**

American Historical Association. Committee on the planning of research. Historical scholarship in America, needs and opportunities. . . . N.Y. R. Long & R.R. Smith. 1932. 146p. **5115b**

American Philological Association. Bibliographical record 1894- . Am. Philological Asso. trans. & proc. XXVII. 1896- (List of publications of members) **5116**

Andrews, Charles McLean. These forty years. Am. hist. rev. XXX. p225-50 (Jan. 1925) **5116a**

Barker, Eugene C. On the historiography of American territorial expansion. *In* The Trans-Mississippi west. Ed. by James F. Willard and Colin B. Goodykoontz. Boulder. Univ. of Colorado. 1930. p219-47 **1516b**

Bassett, John Spencer. The historians 1607-1783. *In* The Cambridge history of American literature. Ed. by William P. Trent and others. N.Y. Putnam's sons. 1917. I. p14-30, 380-5 **5117**

—— Later historians. *In* The Cambridge history of American literature. Ed. by William P. Trent and others. N.Y. G. P. Putnam's Sons. 1921. III. p171-200, 728-42p **5118**

—— The middle group of American historians. N.Y. Macmillan. 1917. 324p. **5118a**

—— The present state of history-writing. *In* J. J. Jusserand and others. The writing of history. N.Y. Scribner's. 1926. p91-141 **5118b**

—— Writers on American history, 1783-1850. *In* The Cambridge history of American literature. Ed. by William P. Trent and others. N.Y. G. P. Putnam's Sons. 1918. II. p104-22, 488-99 **5119**

Beard, Charles A. Historical interpretation in the United States. *In* An economic interpretation of the Constitution of the United States. N.Y. Macmillan. 1913. p1-18 **5119a**

Berlin. Preussische staatsbibliothek. Internationale personalbibliographie, 1850-1935 in der Preussischen staatsbibliothek. Bearbeitet von Max Arnim. Leipzig. K.W. Hiersemann. 1936. 572p. **5119b**

Bibliography—historians and historiography. Jour. mod. hist. I. March 1929- **5119c**

Bio[biblio]graphical sketches of rabbis and cantors officiating in the United States. *In* American Jewish year book, 5664. Phila. Jewish Publication Soc. of Amer. 1903. V. p40-108 **5120**

Boon, Edward P. Catalogue of biographical pamphlets. N.Y. 1878 **5121**

Boston. Public Library. Catalogue of the Galatea collection of books relating to the history of woman in the public library of the city of Boston. Boston. The Trustees. 1898. 34p. (Reprinted from the Monthly bul. III. no. 3. p67-102. 1898) **5122**

Brown, Stephen J. An index of Catholic biographies, Dublin, Central Catholic Library, 1930. 142p. **5123**

Callendar, Guy S. The position of American economic history. Am. hist. rev. XIX. p81-97 (Oct. 1913) **5123a**

Chicago. Public Library. Finding list of the Chicago Public Library—History and biography. Chicago. Chicago Pub. Lib. 1901. (Biography on p216-365) **5124**

Cole, Eva A. A check list of biographical directories and general catalogues of American colleges. N.Y. 1915. 7p. (Reprinted from N. Y. geneal. and biog. rec. XLVI, p51-7. Jan. 1915) **5125**

Cooper, Helen Margaret and Seely, Mary Louise. Biographical reference sources for personal name entries; an annotated bibliography of the more common American, English, French, German and Italian works for catalogers. [Urbana, Ill. Univ. of Illinois Lib. School. 1937] 17p. reprod. typ. **5125a**

Corr, Alys May. Bibliography of biographies and biographical sketches, supplemented by items of vocational interest. Classified. F.E.R.A. project . . . under the supervision of the Department of Sociology, University of Florida. Gainesville, 1935. 64p. mim. **5125b**

Current biography. I-. Jan. 1940-. N.Y. H.W. Wilson. 1940-. (Contains references) **5125c**

Day, G. P. The story of the Chronicles of America. Ohio hist. teach. jour. bul. no. 33. p425-32 (March 1924) **5125d**

Derby, George. A conspectus of American biography; being an analytical summary of American history and biography, containing also the complete indexes of the National cyclopaedia of American biography. N.Y. James T. White. 1906. 752p.   **5125e**

Dexter, Franklin Bowditch. Biographical sketches of the graduates of Yale College with annals of the college history. N.Y. Henry Holt. 1885-1912. 6v. (Contains authorities and writings for the various sketches)   **5126**

Dictionary of American biography, under the auspices of the American Council of Learned Societies. Ed. by Allen Johnson and Dumas Malone. N.Y. Scribner's. 1928-36. 20v. Index. 1937. 613p.   **5127**

Dunning, William Archibald. A generation of American historiography. Am. Hist. Asso. rep. 1917. p347-54   **5127a**

Elliott, Agnes M. Contemporary biography, references to books and magazine articles on prominent men and women of the time. Pittsburgh. Carnegie Lib. 1903. 171p.   **5128**

Elliott, Marian Grace. Buried bibliographies; a list of sources for biographical material which may easily be overlooked; a contribution to a bibliography. Wisconsin Lib. bul. XXVIII. p96-102, 137-45, 175-8 (April-June 1932)   **5128a**

Ely, Margaret. Some great American newspaper editors (Practical bibliographies). N.Y. H. W. Wilson. 1916. p9-33 (Contents: Samuel Bowles, G. W. Childs, H. W. Grady, Nathan Hale, W. Reid, C. Schurz, T. Weed)   **5129**

English, Adrian T. The historiography of American Catholic history (1785-1884). Cath. hist. rev. V. p561-98 (Jan. 1926)   **5129a**

Fitch, Elizabeth H. Autobiographies, memories, letters and journals in Case Library. Cleveland. 1910. 43p.   **5130**

Forbes, Harriette Merrifield. New England diaries, 1602-1800; a descriptive catalogue of diaries, orderly books and sea journals. Topsfield, Mass. Priv. printed. 1923. 439p.   **5131**

Ford, Paul Leicester. A partial bibliography of the writings of the members of the American Historical Association. Am. Hist. Asso. rep. 1889. p163-386 (Other lists in *ibid*. 1890. p115-60. by P. L. Ford and A. Howard Clark; 1891. p409-63; 1892, p211-303. by A. Howard Clark)   **5132**

Gooch, George Peabody. History and historians in the nineteenth century. London; N.Y. Longmans, Green. 1913. 600p. (The United States, p407-24)   **5132a**

Goodspeed's Book Shop. Personal narrative . . . some sources of American history. Boston. Goodspeed's Book Shop, Inc. 1938. 65p.   **5132b**

Gras, Norman Scott Brien. The rise and development of economic history. Econ. hist. rev. I. p12-34 (Jan. 1927)   **5132c**

Green, Fletcher Melvin. Studies in Confederate leadership; an outline for individual and group study. (Univ. of North Carolina. Extension bul. X. no. 8) Chapel Hill. Univ. of North Carolina Press. 1931. 39p.   **5133**

Green, Samuel A. List of memoirs printed in the collections of the Massachusetts Historical Society. 1891. 7p.   **5133a**

H., H. Naval history, Mahan and his successors. Mil. hist. and econ. III. p7-19 (Jan. 1918)   **5133b**

Harney, Martin P. Jesuit writers of history. Cath. hist. rev. XXVI. p433-46 (Jan. 1941)   **5133c**

Hefling, Helen and Dyde, Jessie W. Index to contemporary biography and criticism. Boston. F. W. Faxon. 1934. 229p. **5134**

Historical Records Survey. District of Columbia. A biobibliographical index of musicians in the United States of America from colonial times. Wash. D.C. Dec. 1940. 250p. mim.   **5134a**

Holt, W. Stull. The idea of scientific history in America. Jour. hist. ideas. I. p352-62 (June 1940)   **5134b**

Howard, George E. Biography of American statesmanship; an analytical reference syllabus. (Univ. of Nebraska. Dept. of political science and sociology. Publications) Lincoln. Univ. of Nebraska. 1909. 75p.   **5135**

Ireland, Norma Olin. Historical biographies for junior and senior high schools, universities and colleges; a bibliography. Phila. McKinley Publishing Co. 1933. 108p.   **5136**

Ives, George Burnham. General index to the American statesmen series, with an epitome of United States history. Boston, N.Y. Houghton Mifflin. 1917. 455p.   **5137**

Jameson, John Franklin. The history of historical writing in America. Boston; N.Y. Houghton Mifflin. 1891. 160p.   **5137a**

Jameson, John Franklin; MacMaster, John Bach; Channing, Edward. The present state of historical writing in America. Am. Antiq. Soc. proc. n.s. XX. p408-34 (Oct. 19, 1910)   **5137b**

Kelly, Howard A. and Burrage, Walter L. List of works chiefly consulted. *In* Dictionary of American medical biography; lives of eminent physicians of the United States and Canada, from the earliest times. N.Y., London. D. Appleton. 1928. ix-xxxp.   **5137c**

Kraus, Michael. A history of American history. N.Y. Farrar and Rinehart. 1937. 607p.   **5137d**

Logasa, Hannah. Biography in collections suitable for junior and senior high schools. N.Y. H. W. Wilson. rev. ed. 1940. 152p.   **5138**

Love, Cornelia Spencer. Other people's lives: a biographical round-up: current books, 1927/28-1932/33. (Univ. of North Carolina. Extension bul. VIII. no. 2; X. no. 6; XIII. no. 2) Chapel Hill. Univ. of North Carolina Press. 1928, 1930, 1933 **5139**

Maine. State Library. Annotated check list of biographies of persons of distinction born in Maine or resident there. Augusta, Me. MS. **5139a**

Mallet, Daniel Trowbridge. Mallet's index of artists; international-biographical, including painters, sculptors, illustrators, engravers and etchers of the past and the present. N.Y. Bowker. 1935. 493p. Supplement. 1940. 356p. **5140**

Merrill, Dana Kinsman. The development of American biography. Portland, Me. Southworth. 1932. 106p. **5140a**

Mervine, William M. Index to biographical sketches published in "The Friend," vols. 27 to 36. Pennsylvania Geneal. Soc. publications. III. p109-34 (Jan. 1907) **5141**

National Academy of Sciences. Biographical memoirs, I-[XV.] Wash. D.C. Pub. by the home secretary. 1877-[1934] (In progress. Contains useful bibliographies on scientists) **5142**

New York. Public Library. Card index to biographies of aviators and aeronautics. Comp. from books, periodicals and newspapers, by the staff of the Science and technology division. (4000 references in 1933) **5143**

—— List of works in the New York Public Library relating to women. N.Y. Pub. Lib. Bul. IX. p528-84 (Dec. 1905) **5144**

Oettinger, Edouard-Marie. Bibliographie biographique universelle; dictionnaire des ouvrages relatifs à l'histoire de la vie publique et privée des personnages célèbres de tous les temps et de toutes les nations depuis le commencement du monde jusqu'à nos jours. Brussells. J. J. Stienon. 1854. 2v. **5145**

O'Neill, Edward Hayes. Biography by Americans, 1658-1936; a subject bibliography. Phila. Univ. of Pennsylvania Press; London. H. Milford, Oxford Univ. Press. 1939. 465p. **5146**

—— A history of American biography 1800-1935. Phila. Univ. of Pennsylvania Press. 1935. 428p. **5147**

Pasquet, D. États-Unis. In Histoire et historiens depuis cinquante ans. Paris. 1927. II. p500-16 **5147a**

Pennypacker, Isaac R. Civil war historians and history. Pa. mag. hist. LI. p330-50. 1927 **5147b**

Pittsburgh. Carnegie Library. Lives and letters; a selected and annotated list. Rev. and enl. ed. of "List of one hundred entertaining biographies." Pittsburgh. Carnegie Lib. 1910. 36p. (Reprinted from the Monthly bul. March 1910) **5148**

—— —— Men of science and industry; a guide to biographies of scientists, engineers, inventors and physicians, in the Carnegie Library of Pittsburgh. Pittsburgh. Carnegie Lib. 1915. 189p. **5149**

Poggendorff, Johann Christian. Biographisch-literarisches handwörterbuch für mathematik, astronomie, physik mit geophysik, chemie, kristallographie und verwandte wissengebiete. . . . Leipzig. J.A. Barth. 1863-1904; Leipzig, Berlin. Verlag Chemie g.m.b.h. 1926- **5149a**

Porter, Kenneth W. Trends in American business biography. Jour. economic business hist. IV. p583-610 (Aug. 1932) **5150**

Preston, Wheeler. American biographies. N.Y. Harper. 1940. 1155p. (Dictionary of biographies of 5,257 well-known Americans, with a bibliography for each name) **5150a**

Riches, Phyllis M. An analytical bibliography of universal collected biography comprising books, published in the English tongue in Great Britain and Ireland, America, and the British Dominions. London. The Lib. Asso. 1934. 709p. **5151**

Root, W. T. American colonies and the British empire, colonial history, old style and new. Hist. teach. mag. VI. p281-6 (Nov. 1915) **5151a**

Ruschenberger, W. R. S. List of biographical notices of fellows and doctors of the College of Physicians of Philadelphia. In An account of the institution and progress of the College of Physicians of Philadelphia. Phila. W.J. Dornan. 1887. p292-304 **5151b**

Rusk, Ralph Leslie. Scholarly writings and schoolbooks. In The literature of the Middle Western frontier. N.Y. Columbia Univ. Press. 1925. I. p236-71; II. p281-350 **5152**

Russell Sage Foundation. Leaders in social adventure. (Bul. 102) N.Y. Aug. 1930. 11p. **5153**

Schlesinger, Arthur M. The American revolution reconsidered. Pol. sci. quar. XXXIV. p61-78 (March 1919) **5153a**

Seligman, Edwin R. A. Economists. In Trent, William Peterfield and others, eds. The Cambridge history of American literature. N.Y. Putnam's. 1921. IV. p425-43 **5153b**

Shaw, C. B. A reading list of biographies. (North Carolina College for Women. Extension bul. I. no. 1) Greensboro, N.C. 1922. 117p. **5154**

Shipton, Clifford K. Sibley's Harvard graduates, volume IV, 1690-1700; biographical sketches of those who attended Harvard College in the classes 1690-1700, with bibliographical and other notes. Cambridge. Harvard Univ. Press. 1933. 574p. **5155**

Sibley, John Langdon. Biographical sketches of graduates of Harvard University in Cambridge, Massachusetts. Cambridge, Mass. C. W. Sever. 1873-85. 3v. (Bibliography with sketches) **5156**

Smith, Ralph Clifton. A biographical index of American artists. Balt. Williams & Wilkins. 1930. 102p.   **5157**

Smith, Theodore Clarke. General index to the American statesmen series; with a selected bibliography. Boston, N.Y. Houghton Mifflin. 1900. 473p.   **5158**

—— The scientific historian and our colonial period. Atlantic mthly. XCVIII. p702-11 (Nov. 1906)   **5158a**

Stephens, H. Morse. Some living American historians. World's work. IV. p2316-27 (July 1902)   **5158b**

Stockett, Julia Carson. Masters of American journalism. (Practical bibliographies) White Plains, N.Y. H. W. Wilson. 1916. 40p. (Contents: J. G. Bennett, C. A. Dana, E. L. Godkin, H. Greeley, J. Pulitzer, H. J. Raymond)   **5159**

Stokes, Anson Phelps. Memorials of eminent Yale men; a biographical study of student life and university influences during the eighteenth and nineteenth centuries. New Haven. Yale Univ. Press. 1914. 2v. (Bibliography with sketches)   **5160**

Tappert, Katherine. Viewpoints in biography; an arrangement of books according to their essential interest. (Viewpoint ser. Ed. by Josephine A. Rathbone) Chicago. Am. Lib. Asso. 1921. 69p.   **5161**

Taylor, A. A. Historians of the reconstruction. Jour. negro hist. XXIII. p16-34 (Jan. 1938)   **5161a**

Tourscher, F. E. Catholic historical scholarship in the United States. Cath. hist. rev. VII. p470-9 (Oct. 1927)   **5161b**

Trent, William Peterfield and Erskine, John. The historians. *In* Great American writers. N.Y. Henry Holt. 1912. p169-86   **5161c**

Trenton, N.J. Free Public Library. List of entertaining autobiographies. Trenton. Trenton. Pub. Lib. 1910. 34p.   **5162**

Tyler, Moses Coit. New England: historical writers—New England: history and biography. *In* A history of American literature, 1607-1765. N.Y. Putnam's. 1878. I. p115-57; II. p131-58   **5162a**

U.S. Bureau of Education. List of publications by members of certain college faculties and learned societies in the United States, 1867-1872. (U.S. Bureau of Education. Circulars of information no. 4) Wash. Govt. Ptg. Off. 1873. 72p.   **5163**

U.S. Library of Congress. Division of bibliography. Biographies of presidents of the United States. June 10, 1937. 49p. mim.   **5163a**

—— —— —— List of biographies of Americans prominent since the Civil war. July 10, 1915. 11p. typ.   **5164**

—— —— —— List of biographies of men who made a success in spite of unusual difficulties or physical defects. Jan. 7, 1919. 6p. typ.   **5164a**

—— —— —— A list of books on prominent American business men. April 16, 1932. 19p. typ.   **5165**

—— —— —— List of references on some mayors who were reformers. Jan. 4, 1917. 7p. typ.   **5166**

—— —— —— List of references relating to notable American women. Comp. by Florence S. Hellman. March 25, 1931. 54p. typ. (Supplement. 1932. p54-75. mim. Supplement. 1937. 144p. mim. June 10, 1941. 122p. mim. Comprehensive index to notable American women 1932, 1937, 1941. June 19, 1941. 28p. mim.)   **5167**

—— —— —— Select list of references on eminent women. April 12, 1910. 15p. typ. (Additional references. 1916. 1p.)   **5168**

—— —— —— Women in the Congress of the United States; a list of references. Feb. 7, 1941. 22p. typ.   **5169**

Virginia. State Library. Finding list of biography. Va. State Lib. bul. I. no. 2. p37-131 (April 1908)   **5171**

Wade, Joseph Sanford. A bibliography of biographies of entomologists, with special reference to North American workers. Columbus, Ohio. 1928. p489-520. (Reprinted from the Ann. of the Entomological Soc. of Amer. XXI. no. 3)   **5172**

White's conspectus of American biography, a tabulated record of American history and biography. 2d ed. A revised and enlarged edition of A conspectus of American biography. Comp. by the editorial staff of the National cyclopaedia of American biography. N.Y. James T. White. 1937. 455p.   **5172a**

Who's who among North American authors. Los Angeles, Calif. Golden Syndicate Publishing Co. 1921-   **5173**

Who's who in America; a biographical dictionary of notable living men and women of the United States, 1899/1900- . Chicago. Marquis. 1899-   **5174**

Wilson, Florence H. and Wilson, Howard Eugene. Bibliography of American biography, selected and annotated for secondary schools. (Publications of the National Council for the Social Stud. no. 5) Phila. McKinley Publishing Co. 1930. 64p   **5175**

Personal—Writings by and about

Adams, Charles K. Smith, Charles Forster Charles Kendall Adams, a life sketch Madison. Univ. of Wisconsin. 1924. 150p (President Adams as writer, bibliography, p146-50)   **5175a**

Adams, Henry. Adams, James Truslow Bibliography of the writings of Henry Adams. *In* Henry Adams. N.Y. Boni 1933. p213-29   **5176**

—— Commager, Henry Steele. Henry Adams. *In* Hutchinson, William T. ed The Marcus W. Jernegan essays in American historiography. Chicago. Univ of Chicago Press. 1937. p191-206   **5176a**

Adams, Herbert B. Vincent, John Martin. Herbert B. Adams. *In* Odum, Howard Washington, ed. American masters of social science; an approach to the study of the social sciences through a neglected field of biography. N.Y. Holt. 1927. p99-131 **5176b**

Adams, James Truslow. McCracken, Mary Jane. Author biography of James Truslow Adams. Bul. of bibliog. XV. p65-8 (May-Aug. 1934) **5177**

Adams, John. Cronin, John W. and Wise, W. Harvey, Jr. A bibliography of John Adams and John Quincy Adams. (Presidential bibliog ser. no. 2) Wash. D.C. Riverford Publishing Co. 1935. 78p. **5178**

Adams, John Quincy. Cronin, John W. and Wise, W. Harvey, Jr. A bibliography of John Adams and John Quincy Adams. (Presidential bibliog. ser. no. 2) Wash. D.C. Riverford Publishing Co. 1935. 78p. **5179**

—— U.S. Library of Congress. Division of bibliography. John Quincy Adams, 1767-1848; a bibliographical list. Sept. 20, 1929. 15p. typ. **5179a**

Adams, Samuel. Krause, Dorothea Marie. Samuel Adams: patriot, September 27, 1722-October 2, 1803. Madison. Univ. of Wisconsin Lib. Sch. 1938. 37p. typ. **5179b**

Allen, Ethan. Pell, John. A bibliography of pamphlets and articles by Ethan Allen, 1737-1789. Bul. of the Ticonderoga Museum. I. no. 5. p31-4 (Jan. 1929) **5179c**

—— U.S. Library of Congress. Division of bibliography. Ethan Allen; a bibliographical list. May 19, 1928. 8p. typ. **5180**

Allen, Ira. Calendar of Ira Allen papers in the Wilbur Library, University of Vermont. Prep. by the Historical Records Survey. Montpelier, Vt. Historical Records Survey. 1939. 149p. **5180a**

Alvord. Buck, Solon J. Bibliography of the published works of C. W. Alvord. Miss. Valley hist. rev. XV. p385-90 (Dec. 1928) **5181**

—— Dargan, Marion, Jr. Clarence Walworth Alvord. *In* Hutchinson, William T. ed. The Marcus W. Jernegan essays in American historiography. Chicago. Univ. of Chicago Press. 1937. p323-38 **5181a**

Anderson. Haugen, Einar I. A critique and a bibliography of the writings of Rasmus B. Anderson. Wis. mag of hist. XX. p.255-69 (Mar. 1937) **5181b**

Andrews. Gipson, Lawrence H. Charles McLean Andrews and the re-orientation of American colonial historiography. Pa. mag. hist. LIX. p209-22 (July 1935) **5181c**

Arthur. U.S. Library of Congress. Division of bibliography. Chester Alan Arthur, 1830-1886; a bibliographical list. Feb. 21, 1930. 6p. typ. **5182**

Bache. Gould, Benjamin. A list of the published scientific papers of Alexander Dallas Bache. *In* Smithsonian Institution report, 1870. Wash. Govt. Ptg. Off. 1871. p108-16 **5182a**

Baldwin. Wright, George Frederick. Memorial of Charles Candee Baldwin, LL.D., late president of the Western Reserve Historical Society. (Western Reserve Hist. Soc. tracts, IV, no. 88) Cleveland. 1896 [125]-173p. **5182b**

Bancroft, George. Bassett, James Spencer. George Bancroft. *In* The Cambridge history of American literature. Ed. by William P. Trent and others. N.Y. G. P. Putnam's. 1918. II. p493-5 **5183**

—— Bassett, John Spencer. George Bancroft. *In* The middle group of American historians. N.Y. Macmillan. 1917. p138-210 **5183a**

—— Dubester, Nathan. George Bancroft, 1800-1891: a contribution to a bibliography. Madison. Univ. of Wisconsin Lib. School. 1938. 39p. typ. **5183b**

—— Stewart, Watt. George Bancroft. *In* Hutchinson, William T. ed. The Marcus W. Jernegan essays in American historiography. Chicago. Univ. of Chicago Press. 1937. p1-24 **5183c**

—— Strippel, Henry C. A bibliography of books and pamphlets by George Bancroft. *In* Howe, M. A. De Wolfe. The Life and letters of George Bancroft. N.Y. Scribner's. 1908. II. p329-41 **5184**

—— Bancroft, Hubert Howe. Literary industries; a memoir. San Francisco. Hist. Co. 1890. 808p. **5184a**

—— Bancroft, Hubert Howe. Methods of writing history. *In* Retrospection, political and personal. N.Y. Bancroft Co. 1912. p319-44 **5184b**

—— A brief account of the literary undertakings of Hubert Howe Bancroft. San Francisco. Bancroft; London. Trübner. 1882p. 12p. **5185**

Bancroft, Hubert Howe. Clark, George Thomas. Leland Stanford and H.H. Bancroft's "History," a bibliographical curiosity. Bibliog. Soc. Am. pap. XXVII, pt. 1. p12-23. 1933 **5186**

—— Hunt, Rockwell D. Hubert Howe Bancroft; his work and his method. Hist. Soc. South. Calif. annual publication. VIII. p158-73. 1911 **5187**

—— Morris, W. A. The origin and authorship of the Bancroft Pacific state publications; a history of a history. Oregon Hist. Soc. quar. jour. IV. p287-364 (Dec. 1903) **5188**

—— Oak, Henry Lebbeus. "Literary industries" in a new light; a statement on the authorship of Bancroft's Native races and History of the Pacific states, with comments on those works and the system by which they were written. . . . San Francisco. Bacon. 1893. 89p. **5189**

Bandelier. Hodge, F. W. Adolph Francis Alphonse Bandelier. Am. anthrop. XVI. p349-58 (Sept. 1914) **5189a**

Bandelier. Hodge, F. W. Biographical sketch and bibliography of Adolphe Francis Alphonse Bandelier. New Mexico hist. rev. VII. p353-70 (Oct. 1932)
5190

Barlow. U.S. Library of Congress. Division of bibliography. Joel Barlow, 1754-1812; a bibliographical list. May 15, 1935. 26p. typ.
5191

Barnard. Monroe, Will Seymour. Bibliography of Henry Barnard. Boston. New England Publishing Co. 1897. 10p. **5192**

Barnum. U.S. Library of Congress. Division of bibliography. List of references on Phineas Taylor Barnum. Oct. 13, 1921. 4p. typ.
5193

Beard. Blinkoff, Maurice. The influence of Charles A. Beard upon American historiography. (Univ. of Buffalo. Stud. XII, May 1926, Monographs in history, no. 4) [Buffalo, N.Y.?] [1936?] 84p.
5193a

Beecher. U.S. Library of Congress. Division of bibliography. List of references relating to Henry Ward Beecher. Dec. 23, 1921. 6p. typ.
5194

Beer, George Louis. George Louis Beer, a tribute to his life and work in the making of history and the moulding of public opinion. N.Y. Macmillan. 1924. 164p. (The historian, by C. M. Andrews, p7-43)
5194a

—— Scott, Arthur P. George Louis Beer. *In* Hutchinson, William T. ed. The Marcus W. Jernegan essays in American historiography. Chicago. Univ. of Chicago Press. 1937. p313-22
5194b

Beer, William. Hellman, Florence S. Writings of William Beer, 1849-1927. Bibliog. Soc. of Amer. pap. XX. p85-90. 1926 **5195**

Belknap. Marcou, Mrs. Jane. Life of Jeremy Belknap, D.D. the historian of New Hampshire, with selections from his correspondence. N.Y. Harper. 1847. 253p.
5195a

Bell. Historical Records Survey. District of Columbia. Calendar of Alexander Graham Bell correspondence in the Volta Bureau, Washington, D.C. Wash. D.C. 1940. 41p. reprod.
5195b

Benjamin. U.S. Library of Congress. Division of bibliography. Judah Philip Benjamin; a bibliographical list. Dec. 18, 1931. 6p. typ.
5196

Benton. U.S. Library of Congress. Division of bibliography. A list of references on Thomas Hart Benton (1782-1858). April 18, 1934. 16p. typ.
5197

Beveridge. Strevey, Tracy E. Albert J. Beveridge. *In* Hutchinson, William T. ed. The Marcus W. Jernegan essays in American historiography. Chicago. Univ. of Chicago press. 1937. p374-93 **5197a**

Beverley. H., F. Robert Beverley, the historian of Virginia. Va. mag. hist. XXXVI. p333-44 (Oct. 1928)
5197b

Blair. Descriptive list of the papers of Governor Austin Blair. Mich. hist. mag. I. p133-48 (Oct. 1917) (Burton Library, Detroit)
5197c

Boimare. Tinker, Edward L. Boimare, first and still foremost bibliographer of Louisiana. Bibliog. Soc. of Amer. pap. XXIV. p34-43. 1930
5198

Bolton. Ross, Mary. Writings and cartography of Herbert Eugene Bolton. *In* New Spain and the Anglo-American West. Lancaster, Pa. Lancaster Press. 1932. II. p245-52
5199

Boone. Jillson, Willard Rouse. A new Boone bibliography. *In* The Boone narrative; the story of the origin and discovery. Louisville, Ky. Standard Ptg. Co. 1932. p47-61
5200

—— Miner, W. H. Daniel Boone; contribution toward a bibliography of writings concerning Daniel Boone. N.Y. The Dibdin Club. 1901. 32p. (Reprinted from Publishers' weekly. LIX. p614-17, 938-40. March 2, April 6, 1901)
5201

—— U.S. Library of Congress. Division of bibliography. List of references on Daniel Boone (supplementary to W. H. Miner's Daniel Boone; contribution toward a bibliography. N.Y., 1901). Sept. 18, 1922. 5p. typ. (Additional references. July 11, 1931. 1p.)
5202

Boreman. Historical Records Survey. Calendar of the Arthur I. Boreman letters in the State Department of archives and history. Charleston, W. Va. 1939. 91p. mim.
5202a

Bouquet. U.S. Library of Congress. Division of bibliography. List of references on the life and services of Col. Henry Bouquet, and the battle of Bushy Run. Nov. 17, 1917. 2p. typ.
5203

Bourne. Hart, Albert Bushnell. The literary career of Edward G. Bourne. Yale alumni weekly. XVII. p641-4 (March 25, 1908)
5204

Bowditch. Peabody Museum of Salem, Salem, Mass. A catalogue of a special exhibit of manuscripts, books, portraits and personal relics of Nathaniel Bowditch. Portland, Me. Southworth-Anthoensen Press. 1937. 40p.
5204a

Boyd. Hamilton, William B., Jr. Bibliography of published writings. *In* In memoriam: William Kenneth Boyd, January 10, 1879-January 19, 1938. (Hist. pap. of the Trinity College hist. soc. ser. XXII) Durham. Duke Univ. Pr. 1938
5204b

Bozman. Harrison, Samuel Alexander. A memoir of John Leeds Bozman, the first historian of Maryland. Baltimore. J. Murphy. 1888. 69p.
5204c

Brackenridge. Heartman, Charles Frederick. A bibliography of the writings of Hugh Henry Brackenridge prior to 1825. (Heartman's hist. ser. no. 29) N.Y. Heartman. 1917. 37p.
5205

—— Newlin, Claude M. A chronological list of the published writings of Hugh Henry Brackenridge. *In* The life and writings of Hugh Henry Brackenridge. Princeton. Princeton Univ. Press. 1932. p316-22
5206

—— Newlin, Claude M. The writings of Hugh Henry Brackenridge. n.p. n.p. 1927. 33p. **5207**

Bradstreet. Lincoln, Charles Henry. A calendar of the manuscripts of Col. John Bradstreet in the library of the society. Am. Antiq. Soc. proc. n.s. XIX. p103-81 (April 15, 1908) **5207a**

Breckenridge. Breckenridge, James Malcom. William Clark Breckenridge, historical research writer and bibliographer of Missouri. St. Louis. The Author. 1932. 380p. **5207b**

Brewster. Brewster, Lyman Denison. Contributions to a bibliography of Elder William Brewster. New Eng. family hist. III. p411-21 (Oct. 1909) **5207c**

Brinton. Brinton, Daniel Garrison. Analytical catalogue of works and scientific articles by. . . . n.p. 1892. 14p. **5208**

—— Brinton, Daniel Garrison. A record of study in American aboriginal languages. Media. Printed for priv. distribution. 1898. 24p. **5209**

—— Culin, Stewart. Bibliography (of the works of D. G. Brinton). Am. Philosophical Soc. proc. memorial volume. I. p247-72. 1900 **5210**

Brown. Featherstonhaugh, T. A. Bibliography of John Brown. South. Hist. Asso. publications. I. p196-202 (July 1897); III. p302-6 (Oct. 1899) **5211**

—— Stutler, Boyd B. John Brown (1808-1859); a list of titles of books, pamphlets, and magazine articles to be used as a basis for a bibliography with historical and biographical notes. n.p. n.p. 1925. unpag. mim. **5212**

—— U.S. Library of Congress. Division of bibliography. List of works in the library of Congress relating to John Brown. 1910. 8p. typ. (Additional references. 1921. 5p.) **5213**

Browne. Lone, E. Miriam. Check list of first editions of the works of John Ross Browne, California pioneer, with a chronology, 1821-1872 (i.e. 1875). N.Y. Harper. 1930. 16p. **5214**

Bryan. Staples, Charles R. The Bryan family papers. Ky. Hist. Soc. reg. XXXIV. p196-200 (April 1936) **5214a**

Buchanan. Wise, W. Harvey, Jr. and Cronin, John W. A bibliography of Zachary Taylor, Millard Fillmore, Franklin Pierce, James Buchanan. (Presidential bibliog. ser. no. 7) Wash. D.C. Riverford Pub. Co. 1935. p53-62 **5214b**

Burgess. Burgess, John W. Reminisences of an American scholar. N.Y. Columbia Univ. Press. 1934. 430p. **5214c**

—— Shepherd, William R. John William Burgess. *In* Odum, Howard Washington, ed. American masters of social science; an approach to the study of the social sciences through a neglected field of biography. N.Y. Holt. 1927. p23-61 **5214d**

Burk. Campbell, Charles. Some material to serve for a brief memoir of John Daly Burk, author of a "History of Virginia," . . . . Albany, N.Y. J. Munsell. 1868. 123p. **5214e**

—— Wyatt, Edward Avery. John Daly Burk, patriot, playwright, historian. (Southern sketches, ser. 1, no. 7, ed. by J.D. Eggleston) Charlottesville, Va. Hist. Pub. Co. 1936. 32p. **5214f**

Burr. Tompkins, Hamilton Bullock. Burr bibliography; a list of books relating to Aaron Burr. Brooklyn, N.Y. Hist. Ptg. Club. 1892. 89p. **5215**

—— U.S. Library of Congress. Division of bibliography. List of references on Aaron Burr. Jan. 12, 1917. 5p. typ. **5216**

—— Wandell, Samuel H. Aaron Burr in literature; books, pamphlets, periodicals, and miscellany relating to Aaron Burr and his leading political contemporaries, with occasional excerpts from publications, bibliographical, critical and historical notes, etc. London. Kegan Paul, Trench, Trubner & Co., Ltd.; N.Y. Barnes & Noble, Inc. 1936. 302p. **5216a**

Burton. U.S. Library of Congress. Division of bibliography. Theodore Elijah Burton, 1851-1929; a bibliographical list. Jan. 4, 1932. 21p. typ. **5217**

Butler. Barker, Eugene C. The Butler papers and a supplement to the Austin papers. Texas State Hist. Asso. quar. XIV. p331-2 (April 1911) **5217a**

—— Barker, Eugene C. Private papers of Anthony Butler. Nation. XCII. p600-1 (June 15, 1911) **5217b**

Calhoun. U.S. Library of Congress. Division of bibliography. List of references on John C. Calhoun. March 2, 1910. 14p. typ. (Same. Dec. 15, 1920. 16p. typ.) **5218**

Carey. Finotti, Joseph Maria. Mathew Carey. *In* Bibliographica Catholica Americana; a list of books written by Catholic authors, and· published in the United States from 1784 to 1820 inclusive. N.Y. Catholic Publishing House. 1872. p268-91, 296-9 **5219**

Carnegie. U.S. Library of Congress. Division of bibliography. Select list of references relating to Andrew Carnegie. Sept. 23, 1913. 8p. typ. **5220**

Carroll. Storer, Agnes C. A list of publications relating to Charles Carroll of Carrollton (1737-1832). U.S. Catholic Hist. Soc. hist. rec. and stud. III. p226-42. 1903 **5221**

Carson. Publications of Hampton L. Carson, 1874-1913. The Pennsylvania Gazette, a weekly magazine of the Univ. of Pennsylvania. April 5, 1918. p723-4 **5222**

Carver. U.S. Library of Congress. Division of bibliography. List of references on John Carver. March 18, 1921. 4p. typ. **5223**

Catlin. Donaldson, Thomas. Bibliography of George Catlin, 1838-1871. (Smithsonian Inst. Annual rep. 1885) Wash. Govt. Ptg. Off. 1886. II. p779-93 **5224**

—— Miner, William Harvey. Bibliography of Catlin's works. Wyoming Hist. and Geol. Soc. proc. colls. XXI. p83-97. 1930 **5225**

Catlin. Miner, William Harvey. George Catlin; a short memoir of the man, with annotated bibliography of his writings. Literary collector. III. p23-7, 78-83 (Oct.-Dec. 1901) **5226**

Channing. Fahrney, Ralph Ray. Edward Channing. *In* Hutchinson, William T. ed. The Marcus W. Jernegan essays in American historiography. Chicago. Univ. of Chicago Press. 1937. p294-312 **5226a**

—— Fish, Carl Russell. Edward Channing, America's historian. Current hist. XXXIII. p862-7 (March 1931) **5226b**

—— Robinson, George W. Bibliography of Edward Channing. Cambridge. Harvard Univ. Press. 1932. 20p. **5227**

Chapman, Charles E. Chapman, Charles E. Bibliographical list (of Charles E. Chapman). Hispanic Am. hist. rev. VII. p394-400 (Sept. 1927) **5228**

Chapman, John. Edwards, Everett E. References on Johnny Appleseed. [John Chapman] Agric. lib. notes. XI. p270-9. 1936 **5228a**

—— U.S. Library of Congress. Division of bibliography. A list of references on John Chapman, 1775-1847, "Johnny Appleseed." July 3, 1935. 4p. typ. **5229**

Cheever. Shattuck, Frederick Cheever. Cheever papers. Mass. Hist. Soc. proc. LV. p286-9. 1923 **5229a**

Cheyney. Lingelbach, William E. ed. Portrait of an historian, Edward Potts Cheyney. Phila. Univ. of Pennsylvania Press. 1935. 46p. (As a writer, by Conyers Read, p14-24; and Bibliography, p37-46) **5229b**

Clark. Bibliography of George Rogers Clark. Sons of the Revolution in Indiana. bk. II. p69-88. 1903 **5229c**

—— Bodley, Temple. George Rogers Clark and the historians. Illinois State Hist. Soc. trans. 1935. Illinois State Hist. Lib. publications. no. 42. p73-109 **5229d**

—— Kellogg, Louise P. The early biographers of George Rogers Clark. Am. hist. rev. XXXV. p295-302 (Jan. 1930) **5230**

—— Swem, Earl G. Newly discovered George Rogers Clark material. Miss. Valley hist. rev. I. p95-7 (June 1914) (MSS. in Virginia State Lib.) **5231**

—— U.S. Library of Congress. Division of bibliography. Select list of references on George Rogers Clark and his Illinois campaign. 1907. 9p. typ. **5232**

Clay. U.S. Library of Congress. Division of bibliography. List of biographies in the Library of Congress relating to Henry Clay. Oct. 18, 1923. 6p. typ. (Supplement. Sept. 28, 1928. 6p.) **5233**

Cody. U.S. Library of Congress. Division of bibliography. Brief list of references on Buffalo Bill (William Frederick Cody, 1845-1917). Nov. 26, 1928. 3p. typ. **5234**

Cole, George Watson. List of the printed productions of George Watson Cole, 1870-1935; with comments by friends. Bul. bibliog. XVI. p32-5 (Jan.-April 1937) **5234a**

—— A list of the printed productions of George Watson Cole, 1870-1936. (Bul. of bibliog. pamphlets, no. 33) Boston. F.W. Faxon. 1936 **5234b**

Cook. Holmes, Maurice. An introduction to the bibliography of Captain James Cook, R.N. London. F. Edwards. 1936. 59p. **5234c**

—— Jackson, James. James Cook, 27 octobre-4 février 1779; cartographie et bibliographie. Société de géographie, [Paris] bul. 6 sér., t. 17, p[481]-538. 1879 **5234d**

—— New South Wales. Public Library. Bibliography of Captain James Cook, R.N., F.R.S., circumnavigator. Sydney. Alfred James Kent, govt. printer. 1928. 172p. **5234e**

Cooke. Beaty, John Owen. John Esten Cooke, Virginian. N.Y. Columbia Univ. Press. 1922. 173p. (Civil War soldier-historian, p73-109; Bibliography, p164-8) **5234f**

—— Wegelin, Oscar. A bibliography of the separate writings of John Esten Cooke. (Heartman's hist. ser. no. 43) Metuchen, N.J. 1925. 20p. **5234g**

Coolidge, Archibald Cary. Coolidge, Harold Jefferson and Lord, Robert Howard. Archibald Cary Coolidge, life and letters. Boston; N.Y. Houghton Mifflin. 1932. 368p. (Includes a Bibliography of the more important works of Archibald Cary Coolidge. p354-5) **5235**

—— Merriam, R. B. Archibald Cary Coolidge, a memoir. Mass. Hist. Soc. proc. LXIV. p394-403. 1930-32 **5235a**

Coolidge, Calvin. U.S. Library of Congress. Division of bibliography. Addresses of President Coolidge issued as government documents. March 22, 1930. 5p. typ. **5236**

Cotton. Tuttle, Julius H. Writings of Rev. John Cotton. *In* Bibliographical essays; a tribute to Wilberforce Eames. Cambridge. Harvard Univ. Press. 1924. p363-80 **5237**

Coues. Allen, J. A. List of principal works and papers—Biographical memoir of Elliott Coues, 1842-1899. (National Acad. of Sciences. Biog. memoirs. VI) Wash. D.C. 1909. p426-46 **5238**

Crittenden. U.S. Library of Congress. Division of manuscripts. Calendar of the papers of John Jordan Crittenden. Prep. from the original manuscripts in the Library of Congress by C.N. Feamster. Wash. Govt. ptg. off. 1913. 335p. **5238a**

Crockett. U.S. Library of Congress. Division of bibliography. List or references on David Crockett. Oct. 17, 1921. 6p. typ. **5239**

Custer. U.S. Library of Congress. Division of bibliography. List of references on General George Armstrong Custer. June 11, 1921. 12p. typ. (Later references. 1930. 2p.) **5240**

Dancey. Historical Records Survey. Michigan. Calendar of the John C. Dancey correspondence, 1898-1910. Detroit. April 1941. 23p. mim. **5240a**

Davis. U.S. Library of Congress. Division of bibliography. A list of books in the Library of Congress relating to Jefferson Davis. n.d. 7p. typ. (Additional references. 2p.) **5241**

De Bow. McMillen, James A. The works of James D. B. De Bow, a bibliography of De Bow's review with a check list of his miscellaneous writings, including contributions to periodicals and a list of references relating to James D. B. De Bow. (Heartman's hist. ser. no. 52) Hattiesburg, Miss. Book Farm. 1940. 36p. **5241a**

DeForest. Bemis, Samuel F. Papers of David Curtis DeForest and J. W. DeForest. Yale Univ. Lib. Gazette. XIV. p62-3 (April 1940) **5241b**

De Leon. Borden, Joseph Carleton, Jr. A bibliographical list of the writings of Daniel De Leon issued by the Socialist labor party of America from 1892 to 1936. N.Y. The School of Lib. Service, Columbia Univ. 1936. 45p. carbon copy **5241c**

De Peyster. Allaben, Frank. Bibliography. *In* John Watts de Peyster. N.Y. Frank Allaben Geneal. Co. 1908. II. p269-320 **5242**

—— **Wall, Alexander J.** De Peyster family papers. N. Y. Hist. Soc. bul. V. p105-6 (Jan. 1922) **5242a**

Douglass. Historical Records Survey. District of Columbia. Calendar of the writings of Frederick Douglass in the Frederick Douglass memorial home, Anacostia, D.C. Wash. D.C. Dec. 1940. 93p. mim. **5242b**

Drake, Daniel. Horine, Emmet Field. A bibliography of the Cincinnati physician, Daniel Drake. 523 Breslin Medical Bldg. Louisville, Ky. In progress **5242c**

Drake, Samuel G. Sheppard, John H. A memoir of Samuel G. Drake, A.M. Albany. J. Munsell. 1863 (A list of Mr. Drake's principal publications, p35-6) **5242d**

Draper. Anderson, Rasmus Bjorn. Biographical sketch of Lyman C. Draper, LL.D., secretary of the State Historical Society of Wisconsin. Cincinnati. P. G. Thomson. 1881. 31p. **5242e**

—— Thwaites, Reuben Gold. Bibliography. *In* Lyman Copeland Draper; a memoir. Wisconsin. hist. colls. p20-2. 1892 **5243**

Dunlap. Wegelin, Oscar. William Dunlap and his writings. Reprinted from The Literary collector. N.Y. 1904. 8p. **5244**

Dunn. Dunn, Caroline. Jacob Piatt Dunn: his Miami language studies and Indiana manuscript collection. (Indiana Hist. Soc. Prehistory research ser. I, no. 2) Indianapolis. 1937. p31-59 **5244a**

Dunning. Merriam, Charles Edward. William Archibald Dunning. *In* Odum, Howard Washington, ed. American masters of social science; an approach to the study of the social sciences through a neglected field of biography. N.Y. Holt. 1927. p131-45 **5244b**

Eames. Paltsits, Victor Hugo. Wilberforce Eames; a bio-bibliographical narrative. *In* Bibliographical essays; a tribute to Wilberforce Eames. Cambridge. Harvard Univ. Press. 1924. p1-34 **5245**

Ebeling. Landis, Charles I. Charles Daniel Ebeling, who from 1793 to 1816 published in Germany a geography and history of the United States in seven volumes. Pa. Ger. Soc. proc. XXXVI. p12-27. 1929 **5245a**

Eddy. U.S. Library of Congress. Division of bibliography. List of writings in the Library of Congress by Mrs. Mary Baker G. Eddy. 1907. 7p. typ. **5246**

Edison. U.S. Library of Congress. Division of bibliography. List of references on the life and inventions of Thomas A. Edison. April 24, 1916. 5p. typ. **5247**

Edwards. Faust, Clarence H. and Johnson, Thomas H. Jonathan Edwards, 1703-1758: representative selections, with introduction, bibliography, and notes. N.Y. American Book Company. 1935. 434p. **5247a**

—— Johnson, Thomas Herbert. The printed writings of Jonathan Edwards, 1703-1758; a bibliography. Princeton. Princeton Univ. Press; London. H. Milford, Oxford Univ. Press. 1940. 135p. **5247b**

—— More, Paul Elmer and Coss, John J. Edwards (Jonathan). *In* The Cambridge history of American literature. Ed. by William P. Trent and others. N.Y. G. P. Putnam's. 1917. I. p57-71, 426-38 **5248**

—— U.S. Library of Congress. Reading room. A list of printed materials on Jonathan Edwards, 1703-1758, to be found in the Library of Congress, including biographies, appreciations, criticisms, and fugitive references, with supplementary material not in the Library and with notes on his manuscripts and works. 1934. 29p. mim. **5249**

Egle. Aurand, A. Monroe, Jr. Notes and queries: historical, biographical and genealogical, relating chiefly to interior Pennsylvania 1878-1900; the works of Dr. William Henry Egle. Harrisburg, Pa. Priv. printed, The Aurand Press. 1934. 64p. **5250**

Ericsson. U.S. Library of Congress. Division of bibliography. List of references on John Ericsson. March 5, 1926. 6p. typ. **5251**

Evans. Stevens, Henry Newton. Lewis Evans, his map of the middle British colonies in America; a comparative account of eighteen different editions published between 1755 and 1814. London. H. Stevens, Son & Stiles. 1920. 58p. **5251a**

—— Wroth, Lawrence Counselman. The maps and geographical essays of Lewis Evans. *In* American bookshelf, 1755. Phila. Univ. of Pennsylvania Press. 1934. p148-66 **5251b**

Fairchild. Kellogg, Louise Phelps. The Fairchild papers. Wis. mag. hist. X. p259-81 (March 1927) (Fairchild family of Wisconsin)   **5251c**

Fewkes. Hough, Walter. Biographical memoir of Jesse Walter Fewkes. (National Acad. of Sciences. Biog. memoirs. XV) Wash. D.C. National Acad. of Sciences. 1934. p261-83   **5252**

Fillmore. Wise, W. Harvey, Jr. and Cronin, John W. A bibliography of Zachary Taylor, Millard Fillmore, Franklin Pierce, James Buchanan. (Presidential bibliog. ser. no. 7) Wash. D.C. Riverford Pub. Co. 1935. p27-32   **5252a**

Filson. Durrett, Reuben Thomas. John Filson, the first historian of Kentucky; an account of his life and writings, principally from original sources. (Filson Club publication no. 1) Louisville. The Filson club; Cincinnati. Robert Clarke & Co. 1884. 132p.   **5253**

Fink. Bureau of Railway Economics. Albert Fink, October 27, 1827-April 3, 1897; a bibliographical memoir of the father of railway economics and statistics in the United States. . . . Wash. D.C. 1927. 23p. mim.   **5254**

Fiske. Clark, John Spencer. The life and letters of John Fiske. Boston; N.Y. Houghton Mifflin. 1917. 2v.   **5254a**

—— Perry, Thomas Sergeant. John Fiske. Boston. Small, Maynard. 1906. 105p.   **5254b**

—— Pittsburgh. Carnegie Library. John Fiske. Carnegie Lib. monthly bul XXIII. p196-201 (April 1918)   **5255**

—— Sanders, Jennings B. John Fiske (1842-1901). Miss. Valley hist. rev. XVII. p264-77 (Sept. 1930) (*Also in* Hutchinson, William T. ed. The Marcus W. Jernegan essays in American historiography. Chicago. Univ. of Chicago Press. 1937. p144-70)   **5255a**

Fleming. Binkley, William C. The contribution of Walter Lynwood Fleming to southern scholarship. Jour. southern hist. V. p143-54 (May 1939)   **5255b**

—— Green, Fletcher, M. Walter Lynwood Fleming: historian of reconstruction. Jour. of south. hist. II. p497-521 (Nov. 1936)   **5255c**

Folwell. Folwell, William Watts. Historian. *In* William Watts Folwell; the autobiography and letters of a pioneer of culture. Ed. by Solon J. Buck. Minneapolis. Univ. of Minnesota Press. 1933. p266-73   **5256**

Force. Bassett, John Spencer. Peter Force. *In* The middle group of American historians. N.Y. Macmillan. 1917. p233-302   **5256a**

—— Historical Records Survey. District of Columbia. Calendar of the letters and documents of Peter Force and his son William Q. Force on the Mecklenburg declaration of independence in the Loomis collection, Washington, D.C. Wash. D.C. 1940. 35p. reprod. typ.   **5256b**

—— McGirr, Newman F. Bio-bibliography of Peter Force, 1790-1868. Hattiesburg, Miss. Charles F. Heartman. 1941. 30p.   **5256c**

Fox. Cadbury, Henry J. ed. Annual catalogue of George Fox's papers, compiled in 1694-1697. Phila. Friends Book Store; London. Friends Hist. Soc. 1939. 219p.   **5256d**

Franklin. Adams, Randolph G. A new imprint of the Passy press. General mag and hist. chron. Univ. of Pennsylvania. XXIX. p4-7 (Oct. 1926) (Reprinted. Phila. 1926. 4p.)   **5257**

—— Adams, Randolph G. Notes and queries. Colophon. II. p602-10 (Autumn 1937) (Bibliographical notes concerning Benjamin Franklin)   **5257a**

—— Boston. Public Library. Benjamin Franklin. (List of works by and about him. Boston. Pub. Lib. bul. V. p217-31 (Oct. 1882); p276-84 (Jan. 1883); p420-33 (Fall 1883)   **5258**

—— Campbell, William J. The collection of Franklin imprints in the museum of The Curtis Publishing Company, with a short-title check list of all the books, pamphlets, broadsides, &c, known to have been printed by Benjamin Franklin. Phila. Curtis Publishing Co. 1918. 333p.   **5259**

—— Craig, William Boyd. An annotated bibliography of Benjamin Franklin's autobiography with an historical introduction. n.p. n.p. n.d. carbon copy in Library of Congress   **5259a**

—— Crane, Verner W. Certain writings of Benjamin Franklin on the British Empire and the American colonies. Bibliog. Soc. of Amer. pap. XXVIII. pt. 1. p 1-27. 1934   **5260**

—— Crawford, Mary Caroline. An important Franklin discovery. Outlook. LXXXII. p117-21 (Jan. 20, 1906) (Franklin mss. now in the Univ. of Pennsylvania Lib.)   **5260a**

—— Dodd, Mead & Co. Books printed by Benjamin Franklin, born Jan. 17, 1706. . . . N.Y. Dodd, Mead. 1906. 29p.   **5261**

—— Dwight, Theodore F. Lost and found manuscripts of Benjamin Franklin. Mag. of Am. hist. IX. p428-39 (June 1883)   **5262**

—— Dwight, Theodore F. A report on the papers of Benjamin Franklin, offered for sale by Mr. Henry Stevens, and recommending their purchase by Congress, December 20, 1881. Senate miscellaneous document no. 21. 47 Cong. 1 sess. ser. 1993. 99p.   **5263**

—— Eddy, George Simpson. A ramble through the Mason-Franklin collection. Yale Univ. Lib. gazette. X. p65-90. 1936 (Library of Frankliniana collected by William Smith Mason)   **5263a**

—— Farrand, Max. Benjamin Franklin's memoirs. Huntington Lib. bul. no. 10. p48-78 (Oct. 1936)   **5263b**

—— Faÿ, Bernard. Benjamin Franklin; bibliographie et étude sur les sources historiques relatives à sa vie (Nouvelle collection historique). Paris. Colman-Lévy. 1931. 115p. **5264**

—— Ford, Paul Leicester. Franklin bibliography; a list of books written by, or relating to Benjamin Franklin. Brooklyn, N.Y. 1889. 467p. **5265**

—— Ford, Worthington Chauncey. List of the Benjamin Franklin papers in the Library of Congress. Wash. Govt. Ptg. Off. 1905. 322p. **5266**

—— The Franklin papers in the library of the American Philosophical Society. Popular sci. mthly. LXIII. p382-4 (Aug. 1903) **5266a**

—— Green, S. A. The story of a famous book; an account of Franklin's autobiography. Atlantic monthly. XXVII. p207-12 (Feb. 1871) (Reprinted separately) **5267**

—— Grolier Club. Catalogue of an exhibition commemorating the 200th anniversary of the birth of Benjamin Franklin. N.Y. De Vinne Press. 1906. 100p. **5268**

—— Hays, I. Minis. Calendar of the papers of Benjamin Franklin in the library of the American philosophical society (The Record of the celebration of the two hundredth anniversary of the birth of Benjamin Franklin. . . ., II-VI). Phila. Printed for the Am. phil. soc. New era print. co. Lancaster, Pa. 1908 **5268a**

—— Henkels, Stan V. Books printed by Benjamin Franklin, books from the library of Benjamin Franklin, letters written by Benjamin Franklin, books relating to Benjamin Franklin. . . . Phila. 1905. 90p. **5269**

—— Henkels, Stan V. Catalogue of the extraordinary collection of rare and valuable American history belonging to M. Polock, esq. of Philadelphia, embracing... Franklin imprints including fifty-two of the rarest and most valuable books printed and published by Benjamin Franklin. . . . Phila. Bicking print. 1895. 100p. **5270**

—— Livingston, Luther S. Benjamin Franklin's story of the Whistle, with an introductory note by L. S. Livingston and a bibliography to 1820 (Livingston reprints 3). Cambridge. Harvard Univ. Press. 1922. 34p. **5271**

—— Livingston, Luther S. Franklin and his press at Passy; an account of the books, pamphlets, and leaflets printed there, including the long-lost 'bagatelles.' N.Y. Grolier Club. 1914. 216p. **5272**

—— Michigan. University. William L. Clements Library of American History. An exhibition of books and papers relating to Dr. Benjamin Franklin, from the collections in this library and the library of William Smith Mason. (Univ. of Michigan. Bul. no. 12) Ann Arbor. 1926. 11p. **5273**

—— Michigan. University. William L. Clements Library of American History. Franklin's work as a printer. (Univ. of Michigan. William L. Clements Lib. bul. no. 3) Ann Arbor. Wm. L. Clements Lib. 1926 **5273a**

—— New York. Public Library. List of works in the New York Public Library by or relating to Franklin. N.Y. Pub. Lib. bul. X. p29-83 (Jan. 1906) **5274**

—— Rosenbach, Abraham Simon Wolf. The all-embracing Doctor Franklin, printer, bookseller, journalist, educator, politician, diplomat, patriot, statesman, wit, essayist, scientist, inventor, humanitarian, admirer of the ladies, moralist, philosopher; illustrated by books and manuscripts from the collection of Dr. A. S. W. Rosenbach. Phila. Free Lib. of Phila. 1938. 15p. **5274a**

—— Rosengarten, J. G. The Franklin papers in the American Philosophical Society. Am Philosophical Soc. proc. XLII. no. 173. p165-70 (Jan.-April 1903) **5275**

—— Rosengarten, J. G. Some new Franklin papers, a report. . . . [Phila.?] 1903. 7p. (Reprinted from Am. Phil. Soc. proc. XLII, no. 173) **5275a**

—— Sherman, Stuart P. Franklin. *In* The Cambridge history of American literature. Ed. by William P. Trent and others. N.Y. G. P. Putnam's. 1917. I. p90-110, 442-52 **5276**

—— Stevens, Henry. Benjamin Franklin's life and writings; a bibliographical essay on the Stevens collection of books and manuscripts relating to Doctor Franklin. London. Davy & Sons. 1881. 40p. **5277**

—— Stevens, Henry. Mr. Henry Stevens's Franklin collection of manuscripts and printed books all written by or in some way relating to Dr. Benjamin Franklin. *In* Stevens's Historical collections; catalogue of the first portion of the extensive & varied collections of rare books and manuscripts relating chiefly to the history and literature of America. . . . London. Sotheby, Wilkinson & Hodge. 1881. p159-76 **5278**

—— Swift, Lindsay. Catalogue of works relating to Benjamin Franklin, in Boston Public Library, including the collection given by Doctor Samuel Abbott Green with the titles of similar works not in the library. (Boston Public Library. Bibliographies of special subjects no. 1) Boston. Rockwell and Churchill. 1883. 42p. **5279**

—— U.S. Library of Congress. Division of bibliography. List of works relating to Benjamin Franklin published since the Franklin bicentenary. Aug. 7, 1924. 5p. typ. **5280**

—— U.S. Library of Congress. Division of manuscripts. List of the Benjamin Franklin papers in the Library of Congress. Comp. by John C. Fitzpatrick under the direction of Worthington C. Ford. Wash. Govt. Ptg. Off. 1905. 322p. **5280a**

Franklin. Witmer, Mrs. Lightner and Boggess, A.B. Calendar of the papers of Benjamin Franklin in the library of the University of Pennsylvania; being the appendix to the Calendar of the papers of Benjamin Franklin in the library of the American philosophical society. Phila. Univ. of Pennsylvania; Lancaster. New era print. co. 1908. p399-546 **5280b**

Fremont. U.S. Library of Congress. Division of bibliography. List of works relating to John C. Fremont. 1904. 12p. typ. (List. Nov. 10, 1915. 2p. typ.) **5281**

Freneau. Paltsits, Victor Hugo. A bibliography of the separate and collected works of Philip Freneau together with an account of his newspapers. N.Y. Dodd, Mead. 1903. 96p. **5282**

Fulton. Brooklyn. Public Library. List of books and magazine articles on Henry Hudson and the Hudson River, Robert Fulton and early steam navigation in the Brooklyn Public Library. Brooklyn. Brooklyn Pub. Lib. 1909. 12p. **5282a**

—— New York. Public Library. Catalogue of the William Barclay Parsons collection. N.Y. Pub. Lib. bul. XLV. p97-108, 585-658 (Jan., July 1941) MSS. of Robert Fulton and early publications of the Federal government) **5282b**

—— New York. Public Library. List of works in the New York Public Library relating to Henry Hudson, the Hudson River, Robert Fulton, early steam navigation, etc. N.Y. Pub. Lib. bul. XIII. p585-613 (Sept. 1909) **5282c**

Garfield. U.S. Library of Congress. Division of bibliography. Assassination of President Garfield and the Guiteau trial; a list of references. April 4, 1931. 5p. typ. **5283**

—— U.S. Library of Congress. Division of bibliography. List of references on James A. Garfield. Nov. 10, 1913. 29p. typ. **5284**

Gayarré. Beer, William. Contribution to pamphlet and periodical literature of Charles Gayarré. La. Hist. Soc. pubs. III, pt. 4. p42-5. 1906 **5284a**

—— Louisiana Historical Society. Gayarré memorial number. Louisiana Hist. Soc. publications. III. pt. 4. March 1907. 49p. **5285**

—— Tinker, Edward Larocque. Charles Gayarré, with a bibliographical list of his works. Bibliog. Soc. Amer. pap. XXVII. p24-64. 1933 **5286**

George. New York. Public Library. Henry George and the single tax; a catalogue of the collection in the New York Public Library. By Rollin A. Sawyer, Jr. N.Y. N. Y. Pub. Lib. 1926. 90p. (Reprinted from the Bul. XXX. p481-503, 571-98, 685-716, July-Sept. 1926) **5287**

Giddings. Historical Records Survey. Ohio. Calendar of the Joshua Reed Giddings manuscripts in the library of the Ohio State Archaeological and Historical Society, Columbus, Ohio—twenty-five sample pages. Columbus, Ohio. Dec. 1939. 29p. mim. **5287a**

Glass. U.S. Library of Congress. Division of bibliography. Hon. Carter Glass; a bibliographical list. Feb. 17, 1932. 12p. typ. **5288**

Golder. Fisher, H.H. Frank Golder. Jour. mod. hist. I. p253-5 (June 1929) **5288a**

Good. Richards, G.W. The Rev. James I. Good as a church historian. Am. Soc. Church Hist. pap. 2d ser. VIII. p199-209. 1928 **5288b**

Greeley, Horace. U.S. Library of Congress. Division of bibliography. List of references relating to Horace Greeley (exclusive of periodical articles) supplementary to bibliography in J. C. Stockett's Masters of American journalism. Dec. 28, 1921. 4p. typ. **5289**

Greely, Adolphus Washington. U.S. Library of Congress. Division of bibliography. List of references on Adolphus Washington Greely. Oct. 31, 1906. 9p. typ. **5290**

Gregg. Connelley, William E. Dr. Josiah Gregg, historian of the old Santa Fe trail. Miss. Valley Hist. Asso. proc. X. p334-48. 1919-20 **5290a**

—— Twitchell, Ralph Emerson. Dr. Josiah Gregg, historian of the Santa Fe trail. (Historical Soc. of New Mexico pub. no. 26) Santa Fe. Santa Fe New Mexican Pub. Corp. 1924? 45p. **5290b**

Hale. U.S. Library of Congress. Division of bibliography. List of references on Nathan Hale. Nov. 26, 1915. 4p. typ. **5291**

Hamilton. Ford, Paul Leicester. Bibliotheca Hamiltoniana; a list of books written by, or relating to Alexander Hamilton. N.Y. Printed for the author, The Knickerbocker Press. 1886. 159p. **5292**

Hand. Bowden, A. J. The unpublished revolutionary papers of Major-General Edward Hand of Pennsylvania, 1774-1784; the property of and offered for sale by George H. Richmond. N.Y. 1907. 30p. **5293**

Harding. U.S. Library of Congress. Division of bibliography. Addresses of President Harding issued as government documents. March 23, 1930. 5p. typ. **5294**

—— U.S. Library of Congress. Division of bibliography. References to biographical sketches of Warren Gamaliel Harding. Jan. 31, 1924. 2p. typ. **5295**

Harmar. The Harmar [Josiah] papers of the Clements library. W. Pa. hist. mag. XIX. p305-10 (Dec. 1936) **5295a**

—— University acquires the [Josiah] Harmar papers. Mich. alumnus. XLIII. p21-4 (Oct. 17, 1936) **5295b**

Harrison. Cronin, John W. and Wise, W. Harvey, Jr. A bibliography of William Henry Harrison, John Tyler, James Knox Polk. (Presidential bibliog. ser. no. 6) Wash. D.C. Riverford Publishing Co. 1935. 54p. **5296**

—— Martin, Dorothy V. William Henry Harrison and the campaign of 1840; a checklist of books and pamphlets in the Library. *In* Historical and Philosophical Society of Ohio. Annual report, 1940. Cincinnati, Ohio. 1940. p7-21 **5296a**

Harrisse. Adams, Randolph Greenfield. Three Americanists: Henry Harrisse, bibliographer; George Brinley, book collector; Thomas Jefferson, librarian. Phila. Univ. of Pennsylvania Press. 1939. 101p. **5296b**

—— Growoll, Adolf. Henry Harrisse; biographical and bibliographical sketch. N.Y. Didbin Club. 1899. 12p. **5296c**

Hayes. Ohio state archaeological and historical society. Hayes Memorial Library. Manuscript groups in the Hayes Memorial. *In* Annual report, 1939-40. Fremont, Ohio. 1940. p16-31 **5296d**

—— Ohio State Archaeological and Historical Society. An index and list of the letters and papers of Rutherford Birchard Hayes, nineteenth president of the United States; with notes on other source material at the Hayes Memorial Library, Spiegel Grove State Park, Fremont, Ohio. Columbus. Ohio State Arch. and Hist. Soc. 1933. 42p. **5297**

Hayne. U.S. Library of Congress. Division of bibliography. List of references on Robert Young Hayne. April 20, 1914. 4p. typ. **5298**

Hebard. In memoriam, Grace Raymond Hebard, 1861-1936. Laramie, Wyo. Univ. of Wyoming. 1937. 49p. **5298a**

—— Larson, Alfred. The writings of Grace Raymond Hebard. Wyo. ann. X. p151-4. 1938 **5298b**

Henry, the Navigator, prince of Portugal. U.S. Library of Congress. Division of bibliography. A list of references on Prince Henry the Navigator, 1394-1460. Comp. by Florence S. Hellman. Sept. 27, 1937. 7p. typ. **5298c**

Henry, Patrick. Henkels, Stan V. The Patrick Henry papers.... Phila. 1910. 104p. **5299**

—— U.S. Library of Congress. Division of bibliography. List of references on Patrick Henry. July 7, 1921. 10p. typ. **5300**

Higginson. Duck, Frances Ida. Thomas Wentworth Higginson, 1823-1911: a selected bibliography. Madison. Univ. Wisconsin Lib. School. 1938. 38p. typ. **5300a**

Hildreth. Kelly, Alfred H. Richard Hildreth. *In* Hutchinson, William T. ed. The Marcus W. Jernegan essays in American historiography. Chicago. Univ. of Chicago Press. 1937. p25-42 **5300b**

Hinsdale. Davis, Harold E. Burke Aaron Hinsdale. Ohio archaeol. and hist. quar. XLI. p241-83 (April 1932) **5300c**

—— Harris, W. T. Burke Aaron Hinsdale, 1837-1900. Educ. rev. XXI. p197-9 (Feb. 1901) **5300d**

Hoar. Speeches and addresses of George F. Hoar. Am. Antiq. Soc. proc. n.s. XVII. p159-66 (Oct. 21, 1905) **5300e**

Hodder. Malin, James C. Frank Heywood Hodder, 1860-1935. Kansas hist. quar. V. p115-21 (May 1936) **5301**

Hodge. Poast, Florence M. Bibliography of Frederick Webb Hodge, 1890-1916. Wash. D.C. 1917. 14p. **5301a**

Hodges. Muller, James Arthur. George Hodges popularizer of church history. P.E. Church hist. mag. IX. p78-89 (March 1940) **5301b**

Hoover. U.S. Library of Congress. Division of bibliography. List of references on Herbert C. Hoover. May 24, 1921. 9p. typ. (Recent references. Aug. 1, 1928. 9p. typ.) **5302**

Hough. Hickcox, John Howard. A bibliography of the writings of Franklin Benjamin Hough, Ph.D., M.D. (Univ. of the State of N.Y. Ninety-ninth annual rep.) Albany, N.Y. 1886. p321-47 **5303**

Houston. U.S. Library of Congress. Division of bibliography. General Samuel Houston; a bibliographical list. March 25, 1930. 9p. typ. **5304**

Howard. Todd, Arthur James. George Elliott Howard, 1849-1928. Am. jour. of sociology. XXXIV. p693-9 (Jan. 1929) **5305**

Howe. Smith, Joseph P. Henry Howe, the historian. Ohio archaeol. and hist. quar. IV. p311-37. 1895 **5305a**

Hrdlička. Borbolla, D. R. de la. Bibliografía del Dr. Aleš Hrdlička. Boletín bibliográfico de antropología americana. II. p53-76. 1938 **5305b**

Hudson. Brooklyn. Public Library. List of books and magazine articles on Henry Hudson and the Hudson River, Robert Fulton and early steam navigation in the Brooklyn Public Library. Brooklyn. Brooklyn Pub. Lib. 1909. 12p. **5306**

—— Murphy, Henry C. Bibliographical description of the various printed Dutch records concerning Hudson. *In* Henry Hudson in Holland; an enquiry into the origin and objects of the voyage which led to the discovery of the Hudson River, with bibliographical notes. Reprinted with notes, documents and a bibliography by Wouter Nijhoff. The Hague. 1909. p77-100 **5307**

—— New York. Public Library. List of works in the New York Public Library relating to Henry Hudson, the Hudson River, Robert Fulton, early steam navigation, etc. N. Y. Pub. Lib. bul. XIII. p585-613 (Sept. 1909) **5308**

Hulbert. Vermont. State Library Bibliography of the writings of Archer Butler Hulbert. Montpelier, Vt. 1929. 10p. **5309**

Hull. U.S. Library of Congress. Division of bibliography. References on General William Hull, 1753-1825. Dec. 15, 1930. 4p. typ. **5310**

Hutchinson. Deane, Charles. A bibliographical essay on Governor Hutchinson's historical publications. Boston. Priv. printed. 1857. 39p. (Also in Proc. of the Massachusetts Hist. Soc. III. p134-50. 1855-58) **5311**

Inman. Bibliography of the writings of Samuel Guy Inman. n.p. n.p. May 1934. unpag. mim.   **5312**

Irving. Burton, Richard. Washington Irving's services to American history. New England mag. XVI. p641-53 (Aug. 1897)   **5313**

—— Langfeld, William Robert. Washington Irving, a bibliography. N.Y. N.Y. Pub. Lib. 1933. 90p. (Reprinted with additions and revisions from the N.Y. Pub. Lib. bul. XXXVI. p415-22, 487-94, 561-71, 627-36, 683-9, 755-78, 828-41 (June-Dec. 1932)   **5313a**

—— Williams, Stanley Thomas and Edge, Mary Allen. A bibliography of the writings of Washington Irving: a check list. N.Y. Oxford Univ. Press. 1936. 200p.   **5313b**

Jackson. De Puy, Henry Farr. The library of the late Henry F. De Puy, Easton, Maryland; books from the libraries of the presidents of the United States; the most extensive collection of Andrew Jackson material ever offered. . . . N.Y. Anderson Galleries. 1925. 64p.   **5314**

—— MacDonald, William. The Jackson and Van Buren papers. Am. Antiq. Soc. proc. n.s. XVII. p231-8 (Oct. 1905)   **5315**

—— U.S. Library of Congress. Division of bibliography. List of references on Andrew Jackson. Dec. 15, 1914. 12p. typ.   **5316**

—— Wise, W. Harvey, Jr. and Cronin, John W. A bibliography of Andrew Jackson and Martin Van Buren. (Presidential bibliog. ser. no. 5) Wash. D.C. Riverford Publishing Co. 1935. 66p. **5317**

Jacob, John Jeremiah. Historical Records Survey. West Virginia. Calendar of the J. J. Jacob letters in West Virginia depositories. Charleston, W.Va. 1940. 251p. reprod. typ.   **5317a**

Jefferson. Berkeley, Francis L., Jr. Calendar of the Berkeley manuscripts in the Alderman Library, University of Virginia. Charlottesville, Va. Univ. of Virginia. In progress   **5317b**

—— Bullock, Mrs. Helen D. Catalogue and calendar of the Jefferson papers in the Alderman Library collection, University of Virginia. Charlottesville, Va. 1939. MS.   **5317c**

—— Clemons, Harry and Wyllie, John Cook. Bibliography of Jefferson's "Notes on the state of Virginia." Charlottesville. Univ. of Virginia. In progress   **5317d**

—— Hirsch, Rudolf. Mr. Jefferson; some bibliographical suggestions. Colophon. n.s. III. p134-9 (Winter 1938)   **5317e**

—— Johnston, Richard Holland. A contribution to a bibliography of Thomas Jefferson. *In* The writings of Thomas Jefferson. Ed. by Andrew A. Lipscomb. Wash. D.C. Thomas Jefferson Memorial Asso. 1904. XX. 73p. (Thirty copies reprinted)   **5318**

—— Peden, William H. Some aspects of Jefferson bibliography. Lexington, Va. Journalism Laboratory Press, Washington and Lee Univ. 1941. 24p.   **5318a**

—— Thomas, Charles M. Date inaccuracies in Thomas Jefferson's writings. Miss. Valley hist. rev. XIX. p87-90 (June 1932)   **5319**

—— Tompkins, Hamilton Bullock. Bibliotheca Jeffersoniana; a list of books written by or relating to Thomas Jefferson. N.Y., London. G. P. Putnam's Sons. 1887. 187p.   **5320**

—— U.S. Department of State. Calendar of the correspondence of Thomas Jefferson. (Bulletin of the Bureau of rolls and library of the Department of state no. 6) Wash. Dept. of state, 1894. 541p. (Supplementary bulletin no. 8. 1895. 593p.)   **5320a**

—— U.S. Library of Congress. Division of bibliography. Select list of references on Thomas Jefferson. April 2, 1919. 8p. typ. (Additional references. May 14, 1931. 2p.)   **5321**

—— Virginia. University. Alderman Library. Rare books and manuscripts division. Checklist of all known Jefferson letters. Charlottesville, Va. In progress   **5321a**

—— Wise, W. Harvey, Jr. and Cronin, John W. A bibliography of Thomas Jefferson. (Presidential bibliog. ser. no. 3) Wash. D.C. Riverford Publishing Co. 1935. 66p.   **5322**

Jesup. Letters of General Jesup. Cathedral age. XII. p67 (Winter 1937-38) (MS. letters of General Thomas S. Jesup)   **5322a**

Jillson. Norris, Pauline. Collected writings of Willard Rouse Jillson. Frankfort, Ky. State Jour. Co. 1933. 15p. (Separate revised issue from the April 1935 no. of The Register of the Kentucky State Hist. Soc. XXI. p133-45)   **5323**

—— Willis, George Lee. Willard Rouse Jillson, Kentuckian, geologist, author, public servant; a biographical sketch. Louisville, Ky. Standard Ptg. Co. 1930. 211p.   **5323a**

Johnson, Andrew. U.S. Library of Congress. Division of bibliography. List of references on Andrew Johnson (in addition to those appearing in the printed "Select list of references on impeachment"). March 13, 1917. 9p. typ.   **5324**

Johnson, Reverdy. Steiner, Bernard C. Reverdy Johnson papers in the Library of Congress. Md. hist. mag. XV. p42-55 (March 1920)   **5324a**

Johnson, Samuel. Schneider, Herbert W. A note on the Samuel Johnson papers. Am. hist. rev. XXXI. p724-6 (July 1926)   **5324b**

Johnson, William. Lincoln, Charles Henry. Calendar of the manuscripts of Sir William Johnson in the library of the [American Antiquarian] Society. Am. Antiq. Soc. proc. n.s. XVIII. p367-401 (Oct. 1907)   **5324c**

—— New York. State library. Calendar of the Sir William Johnson manuscripts in the New York state library. Comp. by Richard E. Day... (Bulletin, history no. 8) Albany, Univ. of the state of N.Y. 1909. 683p. **5324d**

Johnson family. Connecticut Historical Society. Johnson family letters and documents. *In* Annual report. . . 1914. Hartford. 1914. p16-20 **5324e**

—— Farrand, Max. The papers of the Johnson family of Connecticut. Am. Antiq. Soc. proc. n.s. XXIII. p237-46. 1913 **5324f**

Johnston, Joseph E. Swem, E. G. Joseph E. Johnston papers (and) John Marshall papers in the Library of William and Mary College. (Bulletin of the College of William and Mary in Virginia, vol. 33, no. 7) Williamsburg. 1939. 19p. **5324g**

Johnston, Richard Malcolm. Weeks, Stephen B. Bibliography of Richard Malcolm Johnston. South. Hist. Asso. pub. II. p318-27. 1898 **5324h**

Jones. U. S. Library of Congress. Division of manuscripts. Calendar of John Paul Jones manuscripts in Library of Congress. Comp. under the direction of Charles Henry Lincoln. Wash. Govt. Ptg. Off. 1903. 316p. **5324i**

Kelley. Davenport, W. T. Bibliography of Hall J. Kelley. Oregon Hist. Soc. quar. VIII. p375-86 (Dec. 1907) **5325**

Kelsey. Hewitt, Anna B. A bibliography of Rayner W. Kelsey's writings. Friends' Hist. Asso. bul. XXIV. p27-34 (Spring no. 1935) **5326**

Knox. Historical Records Survey. Massachusetts. Calendar of the General Henry Knox papers in the Chamberlain Collection, Boston Public Library. Boston. May 1939. 19p. mim. **5326a**

—— Williamson, Joseph. Bibliographical memoranda relating to General (Henry) Knox. Maine Hist. Soc. colls. 2d ser. I. p23-7. 1890. **5327**

Kohler. Coleman, Edward D. A bibliography of the writings of Max James Kohler. Am. Jew. Hist. Soc. pub. no. 34. p165-263. 1937 **5327a**

Lafayette. Blancheteau, Marcel. Le Général La Fayette; catalogue des livres, estampes, autographes et souvenirs. Paris, Pershing Hall. 1934. 200p. **5327b**

—— Gottschalk, Louis R. Lafayette. Jour. mod. hist. II. p281-7 (June 1930) (Critical bibliographical summary of biographical works) **5327c**

—— Monaghan, Frank. Franco-Americana in public and private collections. Franco-Am. rev. I. p378-80. 1937 (The Lafayette collection of Stuart W. Jackson of New York City) **5327d**

Lafitte. Orians, G. Harrison. Lafitte: a bibliographical note. Am. literature. IX. p351-3 (Nov. 1937) **5327e**

—— Rosenberg Library, Galveston. Magazines, books, newspapers, and manuscript articles; in the Rosenberg Library, pertaining to the life and history of Jean Lafitte in Louisiana and Texas. Galveston, Texas. 1927. 6p. photostat reprod. of typ. copy **5328**

La Follette. Stirn, Ernest William. An annotated bibliography of Robert M. La Follette, the man and his work. Chicago. Univ. of Chicago Press. 1937. 571p. photop. **5328a**

—— U.S. Library of Congress. Division of bibliography. List of references on Robert Marion La Follette. March 26, 1923. 7p. typ. (Supplement. May 19, 1937. 10p. typ.) **5329**

Lamar. West, Elizabeth Howard. Calendar of papers of Mirabeau Buonaparte Lamar, prepared from the original papers in the Texas State Library. Austin, Tex. Von Boeckmann-Jones Co. 1914. 355p. **5329a**

Larned. Larned, Joseph Nelson. Chronological list of the writings of J. N. Larned. Buffalo Hist. Soc. publications. XIX. p133-6. 1916 **5330**

Larson. Larson, Laurence Marcellus. The writings of Laurence Marcellus Larson. Northfield, Minn. Norwegian-Am. Hist. *In* The log book of a young immigrant. Asso. 1939. p305-8 **5330a**

Laurens. U.S. Library of Congress. Division of bibliography. List of writings by and relating to Henry Laurens. 1905. 7p. typ. **5331**

Law, John. Harsin, Paul. Étude critique sur la bibliographie des ouvrages de Law (John Law) (avec des mémoires inédits). Liége, Imp. H. Vaillant-Carmanne; Paris, Champion. 1928. 126p. **5331a**

Lea, Albert Miller. Powell, Clifford. The contributions of Albert Miller Lea to the literature of Iowa history. Iowa jour. hist. and politics. IX. p3-32 (Jan. 1911) **5332**

Lea, Henry Charles. Baumgarten, Paul Maria. Henry Charles Lea's historical writings; a critical inquiry into their method and merit. N.Y. J. F. Wagner. 1909. 200p. **5332a**

Lee, Arthur. Harvard university. Library. Calendar of the Arthur Lee manuscripts in the library of Harvard university. By Justin Winsor (Bibliographical contributions no. 8) Cambridge, 1882. 43p. (Reprinted from Harvard univ. bul. no. 23, 1878-82) **5332b**

Lee, Robert. Nicholson, John B. General Robert E. Lee, 1807-1870, a preliminary bibliography. 1936. ms. **5332c**

—— Washington and Lee University. A complete bibliography of printed books and articles on R. E. Lee in the hands of libraries and collectors. Lexington, Va. In progress **5332d**

Lee family. American philosophical society. Committee on historical manuscripts. Calendar of the correspondence of Richard Henry Lee and Arthur Lee. Am. phil. soc. proc. XXXVIII, p114-31, 1899 **5332e**

L'Enfant. Downing, Margaret B. The James Dudley Morgan collection of L'Enfant papers. U.S. Cath. Hist. Soc. rec. XIV. p112-19. 1920   **5332f**

Lieber. Harley, Lewis Reifsneider. Francis Lieber; his life and political philosophy. N.Y. Columbia Univ. Press. 1899. 213p.   **5332g**

—— Lieber, Francis. The writings of Francis Lieber. *In* The miscellaneous writings of Francis Lieber. II. Contributions to political science. Phila. J. B. Lippincott. 1881. p531-5   **5332h**

—— Perry, Thomas Sergeant. The life and letters of Francis Lieber. Boston. J. B. Lippincott. 1882. 439p.   **5332i**

—— Robson, Charles B. Papers of Francis Lieber. Huntington Lib. bul. no. 3. p135-55 (Feb. 1933)   **5332j**

Lincoln. Abraham Lincoln Association. [Index of] Bulletins of the Abraham Lincoln Association, 1923-1937, numbers 1 to 50. By Paul M. Angle, Benjamin P. Thomas and Harry E. Pratt. Springfield, Ill. 1938. 27p.   **5332k**

—— Anderson Auction Company. Broadsides, books and pamphlets on Abraham Lincoln. N.Y. 1907. p22-56   **5333**

—— Anderson Galleries, Inc. Catalogue of a collection of pamphlets relating to Abraham Lincoln with a few on John Brown and some Confederate imprints. . . . N.Y. 1904. 32p.   **5334**

—— Anderson Galleries, Inc. Catalogue of autographs, pamphlets, engravings, etc. relating to Abraham Lincoln. . . . N.Y. 1904. 36p.   **5335**

—— Anderson Galleries, Inc. Catalogue of Lincolniana; a remarkable collection of engravings, lithographs, books, eulogies, orations, pamphlets, etc., relating, wholly or in part, to Abraham Lincoln. N.Y. 1902. 22p.   **5336**

—— Anderson Galleries, Inc. The fine library of John C. Burton of Milwaukee, Wis. Part I. Lincolniana. N.Y. 1916. 138p.   **5337**

—— Anderson Galleries, Inc. The fine library of John C. Burton of Milwaukee, Wis. Part VI. Lincolniana and Civil war material. N.Y. 1916. 83p.   **5338**

—— Anderson Galleries, Inc. Library of the late Major William H. Lambert of Philadelphia. Part I. Lincolniana, first section. . . N.Y. 1914. 124p.   **5339**

—— Anderson Galleries, Inc. Library of the late Major William H. Lambert. Part IV. Lincolniana, second section. . . . N.Y. 1914. 132p.   **5340**

—— Anderson Galleries, Inc. The Lincoln collection formed by Emanuel Hertz. Part I. Autographs. Part II. Books, broadsides and medals. N.Y. 1927. 71, 58p.   **5341**

—— Angle, Paul M. Basic Lincolniana. Abraham Lincoln Asso. bul. June 1936   **5342**

—— Angle, P[aul] M. Famous Lincoln collections; the Illinois State Historical Library. Abraham Lincoln quar. I. p58-63 (March 1940)   **5342a**

—— Angle, Paul M. The Lincoln collection of the Illinois State Historical Library. Springfield. The Library. 1940. 21p.   **5342b**

—— Angle, Paul M. The Minor collection: a criticism. Atlantic mthly. CXLIII. p516-25 (April 1929)   **5342c**

—— Bangs & Co., New York. Lincolniana; a catalogue of scarce pamphlets on the election and administration of Abraham Lincoln . . . the great Civil war, 1860-1865. N.Y. 1902. 39p.   **5343**

—— Barton, William E. Abraham Lincoln and his books, with selections from the writings of Lincoln and a bibliography of books in print relating to Abraham Lincoln. Chicago. Marshall Field & Co. 1920. 108p.   **5344**

—— Barton, William E. The Lincoln of the biographers. Reprinted from the Trans. of the Illinois State Hist. Soc. publications no. 36. Springfield. Jour. Ptg. Co. 1930. 61p.   **5345**

—— Basler, Roy P. The Lincoln legend; a study in changing conceptions. Boston, N.Y. Houghton Mifflin. 1935. 335p.   **5346**

—— Booker, Richard. Check list of Lincolniana in the Journals and Publications of the Illinois State Historical Society, 1899-1938. Chicago. Home of Books, Inc. 1939. 17p.   **5346a**

—— Booth, Mary J. Partial bibliography of poems relating to Abraham Lincoln. Illinois. Hist. Soc. jour. I. p23-8 (Jan. 1909)   **5347**

—— Boyd, Andrew. A memorial Lincoln bibliography; being an account of books, eulogies and sermons, portraits, engravings, medals, etc., published upon Abraham Lincoln . . . comprising a collection in the possession of the compiler. Albany, N.Y. Boyd. 1870. 175p.   **5348**

—— Brooklyn. Public Library. Abraham Lincoln; a list of Lincoln's writings and works relating to Lincoln in the Brooklyn Public Library. Brooklyn. Brooklyn Pub. Lib. 1909. 23p.   **5349**

—— Brown University. Library. The McLellan Lincoln collection at Brown University, a sketch. By Esther Cowles Cushman, custodian. Providence. The Univ. Lib. 1928. 21p. (Also in the McLellan Lincoln collection. Publication. II) (Reprinted with some changes from The Am. collector for Sept. 1927)   **5350**

—— Chicago. Public Library. List of books and magazine articles on Abraham Lincoln. (Special bul. no. 7) Chicago. Chicago Pub. Lib. 1909. 43p.   **5351**

—— Cushman, Esther C. The McLellan Lincoln collection at Brown University. Am. collector. IV. p199-205 (Sept 1927)   **5351a**

—— Fish, Daniel. Lincoln bibliography; a list of books, and pamphlets relating to Abraham Lincoln. N.Y. Tandy. 1906. 135p.   **5352**

—— Fish, Daniel. Lincoln collections and Lincoln bibliography. Bibliog. Soc. of Amer. pap. III. p49-64. 1909   **5353**

—— Griffith, Albert H. Lincoln literature, Lincoln collections, and Lincoln collectors. Wisconsin. mag. hist. XV. p148-67 (Dec. 1931)   **5354**

—— Hart, Charles Henry. Bibliographia Lincolniana; an account of the publications occasioned by the death of Abraham Lincoln. Albany, N.Y. Munsell. 1870. 86p.   **5355**

—— Heartman, firm, auctioneers, New York. Two hundred and fifty-four sermons, eulogies, orations, poems and other pamphlets relating to Abraham Lincoln.... N.Y. C. F. Heartman. 1914. 32p.   **5356**

—— Heartman, firm, booksellers, New York. Two hundred and fifty-four sermons, orations, eulogies, poems and other pamphlets relating to Abraham Lincoln to be sold at unrestricted auction sale.... (Lancaster, Pa. Press of the Lancaster Ptg. Co. 1914) 30p.   **5356a**

—— Hertz, Emanuel. Bibliography of Abraham Lincoln, N.Y. In progress   **5356b**

—— Hertz, Emanuel. Notes on the Herndon-Weik collection of original Lincoln manuscripts, documents and other papers . . N.Y. Alexander Press. 1934. 24p.   **5357**

—— Illinois. State Historical Library. "Illinois" Lincoln exhibit, Illinois State Historical Library, Lincoln room, Illinois building. Phila. Sesqui-Centennial exposition. 1926. 32p.   **5358**

—— Lang, Frederick S. Catalogue of a Lincoln collection formed by Frederick S. Lang. Boston. C. F. Libbie. 1919. 129p.   **5359**

—— Libbie, C. F. & Co., Boston. Catalogue of an extensive private collection of books, pamphlets relating to Abraham Lincoln. Boston. C. F. Libbie. 1911. 115p.   **5360**

—— Lincoln Historical Research Foundation. Lincoln lore, no. 1-. Fort Wayne, Ind. 1929- (Leaflet describing Lincoln collection)   **5361**

—— Little, John Scripps. Abraham Lincoln, books and pamphlets, medals, portraits and autographs; the collection made by John Scripps Little of Rushville, Ill. Chicago. Chicago Book and Art Auctions, Inc. 1933. 66p.   **5362**

—— Madigan, Thomas F. A catalogue of Lincolniana, with an essay on Lincoln autographs by the Rev. Dr. William E. Barton. N.Y. Thomas F. Madigan. n.d. 88p.   **5363**

—— Mitchell, James Tyndale. The valuable collection of autographs and historical papers collected by Hon. Jas. T. Mitchell . . . Also the entire Lincoln memorial collection of Chicago. Catalogue comp. by Stan V. Henkels. Phila. T. Birch's Sons [1894] 111p.   **5363a**

—— Oakleaf, Joseph B. Lincoln bibliography; a list of books and pamphlets relating to Abraham Lincoln. Cedar Rapids, Ia. Torch Press. 1925. 424p. **5364**

—— Pratt, Harry E. Famous Lincoln collections; the Henry Horner collection. Abraham Lincoln quar. I. p106-11 (June 1940)   **5364a**

—— Pratt, Harry E. Recent Lincoln literature. Bul. Abraham Lincoln asso. no. 55, p5-9 (March 1939)   **5364b**

—— Randall, James G. Has the Lincoln theme been exhausted? Am. hist. rev. XLI. p270-94 (Jan. 1936)   **5364c**

—— Raney, McKendree Llewellyn. Famous Lincoln collections; the University of Chicago. Abraham Lincoln quar. I. p273-80 (March 1941)   **5364d**

—— Raney, McKendree L. and others. If Lincoln had lived [The William E. Barton collection of Lincolniana at the University of Chicago]. Chicago. Univ. of Chicago Press. 1934. p1-15   **5365**

—— Riverside, California. Public Library. Abraham Lincoln, 1809-1865; a bibliography. (Bul. no. 27) Riverside. Pub. Lib. 1912   **5366**

—— Russell, L. E. Abraham Lincoln; a contribution toward a bibliography. Cedar Rapids, Ia. Torch Press. 1910. 24p.   **5367**

—— Smith, George D. Abraham Lincoln, books, pamphlets, broadsides, medals, busts, personal relics, autograph letters, documents, unique life portraits. N.Y. George D. Smith. [191-] 171p.   **5368**

—— Smith, William H., Jr. A priced Lincoln bibliography. N.Y. Priv. printed. 1906. 70p.   **5369**

—— Starr, John W., Jr. A bibliography of Lincolniana not included in the compilation of Daniel Fish and Joseph Benjamin Oakleaf. Millersburgh, Pa. Priv. printed. 1926. 69p.   **5370**

—— Stephenson, Nathaniel Wright. Lincoln. In The Cambridge history of American literature. Ed. by W. P. Trent and others. N.Y. G. P. Putnam's Sons. 1921 III. p367-84; IV. p784-94   **5371**

—— U.S. Library of Congress. A list of Lincolniana in the Library of Congress. By George Thomas Ritchie. Wash. Govt. Ptg. Off. 1906. 86p.   **5372**

—— U.S. Library of Congress. Division of bibliography. Lincoln as a lawyer; a bibliographical list. Dec. 20, 1927. 3p. typ.   **5373**

—— Warren, Louis A. Famous Lincoln collections; the Lincoln national life foundation. Abraham Lincoln quar. I. p163-70 (Sept. 1940)   **5373a**

—— Wessen, Ernest James. Campaign lives of Abraham Lincoln, 1860; an annotated bibliography of Abraham Lincoln issued during the campaign year. . . Springfield, Ill. Illinois State Hist. Soc. 1938. 33p. (Also in the Ill. State Hist. Soc. pap. 1937)   **5373b**

—— Wessen, Ernest James. Check-list of contemporary broadsides relating to Abraham Lincoln. 20 North Foster St. Mansfield, Ohio. In progress   **5373c**

Lincoln. Wessen, Ernest James. Lincoln bibliography—its present status and needs. Bibliog. Soc. Amer. pap. XXXIV. p327-48. 1940   **5373d**

—— Worthington, Edna M. Famous Lincoln collections; Brown University. Abraham Lincoln quar. I. p210-15 (Dec. 1940)   **5373e**

Livingston. Nichols, Charles L. Papers of William Livingston. Mass. Hist. Soc. proc. LV. p225-8. 1923 (MSS. of William Livingston, governor of New Jersey, 1776-1790)   **5373f**

Long. U. S. Library of Congress. Division of bibliography. List of references relating to Huey Pierce Long, 1893-1935. Dec. 27, 1935. 11p. typ.   **5374**

Lossing. Paine, Nathaniel. A biographical notice of Benson John Lossing, LL.D. Worcester, Mass. Priv. print. 1892 (Bibliography, p7-8)   **5374a**

Lowell. Fuess, Claude. Some fogotten political essays by Lowell. Massachusetts Hist. Soc. proc. LXII. p3-12. 1928-29   **5375**

McDonogh. Swearingen, M. The John McDonogh papers. Southw. rev. XIX. p348-50. 1934   **5375a**

McMaster. Hutchinson, William T. John Bach McMaster, historian of the American people. Miss. Valley hist. rev. XVI. p23-49 (June 1929) (*Also in* Hutchinson, William T. ed. The Marcus W. Jernegan essays in American historiography. Chicago. Univ. of Chicago Press. 1937. p122-43)   **5375b**

—— Oberholtzer, Ellis Paxson. John Bach McMaster, 1852-1932. Phila. Hist. Soc. of Pennsylvania. 1933. 31p. (Reprint from the Pa. mag. hist. LVII. p1-31, Jan. 1933)   **5375c**

Macy. Noyes, Katherine Macy, ed. Jesse Macy: an autobiography. Springfield, Ill., Baltimore, Md. C.C. Thomas. 1933. 192p. (Contains: A list of publications by Jesse Macy. p184-6)   **5375d**

Madison. Cronin, John W. and Wise, W. Harvey, Jr. A bibliography of James Madison and James Monroe. (Presidential bibliog. ser. no. 4) Wash. D.C. Riverford Publishing Co. 1935. 45p.   **5376**

—— U.S. Department of State. Calendar of the correspóndence of James Madison. (Bureau of rolls and lib. bul. no. 4) Wash. Dept. of State. 1894. 739p. Index to the Calendar of the correspondence of James Madison. Wash. 1895. 70p.   **5376a**

—— U.S. Library of Congress. Division of bibliography. Life and writings of James Madison [a bibliographical list]. Nov. 2, 1926. 4p. typ.   **5377**

Mahan. [Kirkham, George Karbeek] The books and articles of Rear Admiral A. T. Mahan, U.S.N., General index. [N.Y. 1930]   **5378**

—— Pratt, Julius W. Alfred Thayer Mahan. *In* Hutchinson, William T. ed. The Marcus W. Jernegan essays in American historiography. Chicago. Univ. of Chicago Press. 1937. p207-26   **5378a**

—— Puleston, William D. Mahan; the life and work of Captain Alfred Thayer Mahan, U.S.N. New Haven. Yale Univ. Press. 1939. 380p.   **5378b**

—— Taylor, Charles Carlisle. The life of Admiral Mahan, naval philosopher, rear-admiral United States navy. N.Y. George H. Doran. 1920. 359p.   **5378c**

Mann, Horace. Federal Writers' Project. Massachusetts. Selective and critical bibliography of Horace Mann. Issued by Commissioner of Education James G. Reardon in cooperation with the Boston School Department. Roxbury, Mass. Roxbury Memorial High School Ptg. Dept. 1937. 54p.   **5378d**

—— Mann, B. Pickman. Bibliography [of Horace Mann.] (U.S. Commissioner of Education. Rep. 1895-96) Wash. Govt. Ptg. Off. 1897. I. p897-927 (Partly reprinted in Hinsdale, B.A. Horace Mann and the common school revival in the United States. N.Y. Scribner. 1898) **5379**

Marion. U.S. Library of Congress. Division of bibliography. General Francis Marion; a bibliographical list. July 10, 1928. 5p. typ.   **5380**

Marshall. Beveridge, Albert J. Some new Marshall sources. Am. Hist. Asso. rep. 1915. p203-5   **5380a**

—— Swem, Earl G. Joseph E. Johnston (and) John Marshall papers in the Library of William and Mary College. (Bulletin of the College of William and Mary in Virginia, v. 33, no. 7) Williamsburg. 1939. 19p.   **5380b**

—— U.S. Library of Congress. Division of bibliography. List of references relating to John Marshall. 1907. 13p. typ.   **5381**

—— U.S. Library of Congress. Writings of John Marshall. 1905. 5p. typ.   **5382**

Mather, Cotton. Holmes, Thomas J. Cotton Mather and his writings on witchcraft. Bibliog. Soc. of Amer. pap. XVIII. p31-59. 1924   **5383**

—— Holmes, Thomas J. Cotton Mather, a bibliography of his works. Cambridge, Mass. Harvard Univ. Press. 1940. 3v.   **5383a**

—— Holmes, Thomas J. The Mather bibliography. Bibliog. Soc. of Amer. pap. XXXI. p57-76. 1937   **5383b**

Mather, Increase. Holmes, Thomas J. Increase Mather; a bibliography of his works. Cleveland, Ohio. Printed at the Harvard Univ. Press. Cambridge. 1931. 2v.   **5384**

—— Holmes, Thomas J. Increase Mather his works, being a short title catalogue of the published writings that can be ascribed to him. Cleveland. For private distribution. 1930. 59p.   **5385**

Mather family. Holmes, Thomas J. The Mather literature. Cleveland. Priv. printed for William Gwinn Mather. 1927. 64p.   **5386**

—— Holmes, Thomas J. The minor Mathers, a list of their works. Cambridge, Mass. Harvard Univ. Press. 1940. 218p. (Includes an appendix: MSS. of the minor Mathers by William S. Piper. p189-204) **5386a**

—— Paine, Nathaniel. List of books received by the American Antiquarian Society from the sale of the first part of the Brinley Library; to which is added a catalogue [13-57p.] of the Mather publications previously in the society's library. Worcester, Mass. C. Hamilton. 1879. 62p. **5387**

Maury. Brown, Ralph Minthorne. Bibliography of Commander Matthew Fontaine Maury, including a biographical sketch. (Virginia Polytechnic Inst. Bul. XXIV. no. 2) [Blacksburg, Va. 1930] 61p. **5388**

—— Darter, L. J. Federal archives relating to Matthew Fontaine Maury. Am. neptune. I. p149-58 (April 1941) **5388a**

—— Hasse, Adelaide Rosalie. Tentative bibliography of Matthew Fontaine Maury. n.p. n.p. 1917. 36p. typ. **5389**

Meany. Todd, Ronald. Bibliography of the writings of Edmond Stephen Meany. Wash. hist. quar. XXVI. p176-91 (July 1935) **5390**

Meyer. Bureau of Railway Economics. A list of writings by Balthasar Henry Meyer. Wash. D.C. 1927. 5p. typ. **5391**

Mitchell. Carrier, Lyman. Dr. John Mitchell, naturalist, cartographer, and historian. Am. Hist. Asso. rep. 1918. I. p199-219 **5391a**

Monette. Riley, Franklin L. Life and literary services of Dr. John W. Monette. Mississippi Hist. Soc. publications. IX p199-237. 1906 **5392**

Monroe. Cronin, John W. and Wise, W. Harvey, Jr. A bibliography of James Madison and James Monroe. (Presidential bibliog. ser. no. 4) Wash. D.C. Riverford Publishing Co. 1935. 45p. **5393**

—— Jameson, J. Franklin. Bibliography of Monroe and the Monroe doctrine. *In* Gilman, Daniel C. James Monroe. Boston. Houghton Mifflin. 1883. p253-80 **5393a**

—— U.S. Department of State. Calendar of the correspondence of James Monroe. (Bureau of rolls and lib. bul. no. 2) Wash. Dept. of State. 1893. 371p. **5393b**

—— U.S. Library of Congress. Division of manuscripts. Papers of James Monroe, listed in chronological order from the original manuscripts in the Library of Congress. Comp. by W. R. Leech under the direction of Worthington C. Ford. Wash. Govt. Ptg. Off. 1904. 114p. **5393c**

Morgan. Gilchrist, Donald Bean. Lewis Henry Morgan; his gifts to the University of Rochester and a bibliography- of his works. Rochester, N.Y. 1923. 19p. (Reprinted from Publication fund ser. of the Rochester Hist. Soc. II. 1923) **5394**

Morris. Homes, Henry Augustus. Description and analysis of the remarkable collection of unpublished manuscripts of Robert Morris . . ., including his official and private diary and correspondence, in sixteen folio volumes, the property of General John Meredith Read. Albany, N.Y. J. Munsell. 1876. 19p. **5395**

Murphy. Stiles, Henry R. Memoir of the Hon. Henry C. Murphy, LLD., of Brooklyn, New York. N.Y. Trow's. 1883. 22p. **5395a**

Nilsson. Ristad, D. G. Svein Nilsson, pioneer Norwegian-American historian. Norwegian-Am. stud. and rec. IX. p29-37. 1936 **5395b**

Nimmo. Bureau of Railway Economics. Joseph Nimmo, Jr., 1837-1909; list of writings in the library. [Wash. D.C.] Oct. 14, 1933. 12p. typ. Revised ed. Dec. 18, 1936. 12p. mim. **5396**

O'Callaghan. Guy, Francis Shaw. Edmund Bailey O'Callaghan; a study in American historiography (1797-1880). (Catholic University of America. Stud. in Am. church hist. XVIII) Wash. D.C. 1934. 93p. **5396a**

—— Shea, John Gilmary. Edmund Bailey O'Callaghan, historian of New Netherland and New York. Mag. of Am. hist. V. p77-80 (July 1880) **5397**

Osgood. Beatty, E. C. O. Herbert Levi Osgood. *In* Hutchinson, William T. ed. The Marcus W. Jernegan essays in American historiography. Chicago. Univ. of Chicago Press. 1937. p271-93 **5397a**

—— Fox, Dixon Ryan. Herbert Levi Osgood, an American scholar. N.Y. Columbia Univ. Press. 1924. 167p. **5397b**

Parkman. Farnham, Charles Haight. A life of Francis Parkman. Boston. Little, Brown. 1900. 394p. (Bibliography of Francis Parkman's writings, p359-64) **5397c**

—— Leland, Waldo Gifford. Francis Parkman, 1823-1923, and the history of New France. Ex-libris. I. p227-36 (Feb. 1924) **5397d**

—— Lodge, Henry Cabot. Francis Parkman. Mass. Hist. Soc. proc. LVI. p319-35 (June 1923) **5397e**

—— Schramm, Wilbur L. Francis Parkman: representative selections, with introduction, bibliography, and notes. N.Y. American Book Co. 1938. 498p. **5397f**

—— Sedgwick, Henry Dwight. Francis Parkman. Boston; N.Y. Houghton Mifflin. 1904. 345p. **5397g**

—— Smith, Joe Patterson. Francis Parkman. *In* Hutchinson, William T. ed. The Marcus W. Jernegan essays in American historiography. Chicago. Univ. of Chicago Press. 1937. p43-59 **5397h**

—— Wrong, George M. Francis Parkman. Canad. hist. rev. IV. p289-403 (Dec. 1923) **5397i**

Parrington. Utter, William T. Vernon Louis Parrington. *In* Hutchinson, William T. ed. The Marcus W. Jernegan essays in American historiography. Chicago. Univ. of Chicago Press. 1937. p394-408 **5397j**

Peabody. Hidy, Muriel E. The George Peabody papers. Bus. Hist. Soc. pap. XII. p1-6 (Feb. 1938) **5397k**

Peary. U.S. Library of Congress. Division of bibliography. Robert Edwin Peary; a bibliographical list [exclusive of articles in periodicals]. May 29, 1931. 8p. typ. **5398**

Penn. Allen, Edward G. The Penn papers; description of a large collection of original letters, MS., documents, charters, grants, printed papers, rare books and pamphlets relating to the celebrated William Penn, to the early history of Pennsylvania . . . now the property of Edward G. Allen. London. Am. Lib. Agency. 1870. 24p. **5399**

—— Cadbury, Henry J. Notes on William Penn's letters to Holland. Quakeriana notes (Spring 1937) **5399a**

—— Hull, William Isaac. Eight first biographies of William Penn, in seven languages and seven lands (Swarthmore College Monographs on Quaker history, no. 3) [Swarthmore, Pa. Swarthmore College] 1936. 136p. **5399b**

—— Spence, Mary Kirk. William Penn; a bibliography; a tentative list of publications about him and his work. (Pennsylvania Hist. Comn. Bul. no. 1) Harrisburg, Pa. 1932. 19p. **5400**

Perkins. U.S. Department of Labor. Library. Frances Perkins: a bibliographical list. Wash. D.C. Aug. 1, 1937. 17p. mim. **5400a**

—— U.S. Library of Congress. Division of bibliography. Frances Perkins [Mrs. Paul Wilson]; a bibliographical list. Nov. 26, 1934. 4p. typ. **5401**

Perry. U.S. Library of Congress. Division of bibliography. Select list of references on Oliver Hazard Perry and the battle of Lake Erie. Oct. 26, 1910. 9p. typ. (Additional references. Nov. 18, 1935. 7p. typ.) **5402**

Phillips. Edwards, Everett E. A bibliography of the writings of Professor Ulrich Bonnell Phillips. Introduction by Fred Landon. Reprinted from Agricultural hist. VIII. p196-218 (Oct. 1934) **5403**

—— Gray, Wood. Ulrich Bonnell Phillips. *In* Hutchinson, William T. ed. The Marcus W. Jernegan essays in American historiography. Chicago. Univ. of Chicago Press. 1937. p354-73 **5403a**

—— Potter, David M., Jr. A bibliography of the printed writings of Ulrich Bonnell Phillips. Ga. hist. quar. XVIII. p270-82 (Sept. 1934) **5403b**

Pickering, Timothy. Massachusetts Historical Society. Historical index to the Pickering papers. (Mass. Hist. Soc. col. ser. 6, VIII) Boston. 1896. 580p. **5403c**

Pierce. U.S. Library of Congress. Division of manuscripts. Calendar of the papers of Franklin Pierce. Prep. from the original manuscripts in the Library of Congress by W. R. Leech. Wash. Govt. Ptg. Off. 1917. 102p. **5403d**

—— Wise, W. Harvey, Jr. and Cronin, John W. A bibliography of Zachary Taylor, Millard Fillmore, Franklin Pierce, James Buchanan. (Presidential bibliog. ser. no. 7) Wash. D.C. Riverford Pub. Co. 1935. p39-45 **5403e**

Pike, Albert. Boyden, William L. Bibliography of the writings of Albert Pike; prose, poetry, manuscript. Wash. D.C. The compiler? 1921. 71p. **5404**

Pike, Zebulon M. Bolton, Herbert Eugene. Papers of Zebulon M. Pike, 1806-1807. Am. hist. rev. XIII. p798-827 (July 1908) **5404a**

Poinsett. Historical Records Survey. Pennsylvania. Calendar of Joel R. Poinsett papers in the Henry D. Gilpin collection. Ed. by Grace E. Heilman and Bernard S. Levin. Phila. The Gilpin Library of the Historical Society of Pennsylvania. 1941. 264p. **5404b**

Polk. Cronin, John W. and Wise, W. Harvey, Jr. A bibliography of William Henry Harrison, John Tyler, James Knox Polk. (Presidential bibliog. ser. no. 6) Wash. D.C. Riverford Publishing Co. 1935. 54p. **5404c**

Pontiac. Michigan. University. William L. Clements Library of American history. Pontiac, chief of the Ottawas; a guide to an exhibition in the William L. Clements Library. (Bul. no. XXIX) Ann Arbor. Univ. of Michigan. 1939. 11p. **5404d**

—— U.S. Library of Congress. Division of bibliography. List of references on Pontiac. March 18, 1926. 4p. typ. **5405**

Powell. Warman, P. C. Catalogue of the published writings of John Wesley Powell. Wash. Acad. Science proc. V. p131-87. 1903 **5406**

Priest. Duncan, Winthrop H. Josiah Priest, historian of the American frontier; a study and bibliography. Am Antiq. Soc. proc. n.s. XLIV. pt. 1. p45-102. 1934 **5407**

Priestley. Fulton, John F. and Peters, Charlotte H. Works of Joseph Priestley, 1733-1804, preliminary short title list. New Haven, Conn. Laboratory of physiology, Yale Univ. School of Medicine. 1937. 20p. **5407a**

Randolph. U.S. Library of Congress. Division of bibliography. John Randolph of Roanoke, 1773-1833; a bibliographical list. Jan. 29, 1929. 10p. typ. **5408**

Rhodes. Howe, Mark A. D. James Ford Rhodes, American historian. N.Y. D. Appleton. 1929. 376p. **5408a**

—— Miller, Raymond Curtis. James Ford Rhodes. *In* Hutchinson, William T. ed. The Marcus W. Jernegan essays in American historiography. Chicago. Univ. of Chicago Press. 1937. p171-90 **5408b**

Romans. Phillips, Philip Lee. Notes on the life and works of Bernard Romans. (Florida State Hist. Soc. pub. no. 2) Deland, Fla. Florida State Hist. Soc. 1924. 128p. **5408c**

Roosevelt, Eleanor. Edelstein, Pauline. Bibliography of Eleanor Roosevelt, first lady of the land. Boston. Simmons College, School of Lib. Sci. 1940 **5408d**

Roosevelt, Franklin Delano. U.S. Library of Congress. Division of bibliography. A brief list of references on Franklin Delano Roosevelt, President of the United States, 1933-. Oct. 30, 1933. 6p. typ. **5409**

Roosevelt, Theodore. Thornton, Harrison John. Theodore Roosevelt. *In* Hutchinson, William T. ed. The Marcus W. Jernegan essays in American historiography. Chicago. Univ. of Chicago Press. 1937. p227-51 **5409a**
—— Vail, Robert W. G. Writings of Theodore Roosevelt. Albany. New York State Lib. In progress **5409b**
—— Wheelock, John Hall. A bibliography of Theodore Roosevelt. N.Y. Scribner's. 1920. 32p. **5410**

Ropes. A memoir of the life of John Codman Ropes, LL.D. . . . Boston. Priv. print. 1901. 114p. (Bibliography of the writings of John Codman Ropes, p111-15) **5410a**

Russell. Stearns, Raymond Phineas. A description of the Russell papers in the Historical Society of Pennsylvania. Pa. mag. hist. LXII. p205-12 (April 1938) (Papers relating to the business activities of William Russell (1740-1818), including his speculations in land, his colonizing efforts, his loans to American debtors, etc.) **5410b**

Sampson. Severance, Henry O. Francis Asbury Sampson. Bibliog. Soc. of Amer. pap. XII. p63-5. 1918 **5411**
—— Shoemaker, Floyd C. In memoriam Francis Asbury Sampson, 1842-1918. Missouri hist. rev. XII. p129-35 (April 1918) **5412**

Sanders. Rau, Louise. The Robert Sanders papers [in the Burton Historical Collection of the Detroit Public Library] Bus. Hist. Soc. bul. XII. p28-30 (April 1938) **5412a**

Schoolcraft. Streeter, Floyd D. Bibliography of the writings of Henry Rowe Schoolcraft. Am. collector. V. p2-8 (Oct. 1927) **5413**

Schouler. Ellis, Lewis Ethan. James Schouler. *In* Hutchinson, William T. ed. The Marcus W. Jernegan essays in American historiography. Chicago. Univ. of Chicago Press. 1937. p84-101 **5413a**

Scott. Carnegie Endowment for International Peace. Library. Bibliography of the writings of James Brown Scott. Wash. D.C. 1928. 25p. mim. (Supplement. March 9, 1932. 5,2p. mim) **5414**

Seidensticker. Evans, Lillian M. Oswald Seidensticker, bibliophile. Pa. hist. VII. p8-19 (Jan. 1940) **5414a**

Shea. Morrison, Noah Farnham. John Gilmary Shea; a memoir, with bibliography. *In* Charlevoix, P. F. X. History and description of New France. Ed. by John G. Shea. N.Y. Harper. 1900. I. p. v-xiv **5415**
—— Spillane, Edward. Bibliography of John Gilmary Shea. U.S. Catholic Hist. Soc. hist. rec. and stud. VI. pt. 2. p249-74 (Dec. 1912) **5416**

Sheridan. U.S. Library of Congress. Division of bibliography. Philip Henry Sheridan, 1831-1888; a bibliographical list. Aug. 12, 1935. 11p. typ. **5417**

Sherman. U.S. Library of Congress. Division of bibliography. List of works in the Library of Congress relating to Senator John Sherman including his writings. 1903. 10p. typ. **5418**

Simms. Salley, A. S., Jr. A bibliography of William Gilmore Simms. South. Hist. Asso. publications. I. p269-95 (Oct. 1897) **5419**

Smith, Alfred E. U.S. Library of Congress. Division of bibliography. Governor Alfred E. Smith; a bibliographical list. March 19, 1928. 6p. typ. (Additional references. Aug. 1, 1928. 1p.) **5420**

Smith, Gerrit. Historical Records Survey. New York (State). Calendar of the Gerrit Smith papers in the Syracuse University Library. General correspondence volume one, 1819-1846. Albany, N.Y. July 1941. 289p. mim. **5420a**

Smith, Jedediah Strong. Nasatir, A. P. A bibliography of sources relating to Jedediah Strong Smith. South. Calif. Hist. Soc. publications. XIII. pt. 3. 270-303. 1926 **5421**

Smith, John. Eames, Wilberforce. A bibliography of Captain John Smith. N.Y. 1927. 48p. (Reprinted from Sabin's Dictionary of books relating to America) **5422**
—— Morse, Jarvis M. John Smith and his critics; a chapter in colonial historiography. Jour. of south. hist. I. p123-37 (May 1935) **5423**

Smith, Thomas A. Manuscript collection of General Thomas A. Smith belonging to the Society. Mo. hist. rev. VI. p209 (July 1912) **5423a**

Sparks, Edwin Erle. Pennsylvania. State College. Memorial committee of the college senate. In memoriam Edwin Erle Sparks, president of Pennsylvania State College, 1908-1920. State College, Pa. 1925. 42p. **5423b**

Sparks, Jared. Adams, Herbert Baxter. The life and writings of Jared Sparks, comprising selections from his journals and correspondence. Boston; N.Y. Houghton Mifflin. 1893. 2v. (Bibliography of the writings of Jared Sparks, p596-617) **5423c**
—— Bassett, John Spencer. Jared Sparks. *In* The middle group of American historians. N.Y. Macmillan. 1917. p57-137 **5423d**

Sparks, Jared. Deane, William Reed. In memoriam, Jared Sparks, LL.D. n.p. n.d. (List of Mr. Sparks works, p29-32) **5423e**

Squier. Seitz, Don C. Letters from Francis Parkman to E. G. Squier, with biographical notes and a bibliography of E. G. Squier [p47-58]. Cedar Rapids, Ia. Torch Press. 1911 **5423f**

—— Squier, Ephraim George. A list of books, pamphlets, and more important contributions to periodicals, etc., with MS. notes by C. H. Berendt. N.Y. 1876. 8p. (*Also in* Squier, E. G. Catalogue of . . . [his] library *and in* Squier, Frank. A collection of books by Ephraim George Squier) **5424**

—— Squier, Frank. A collection of books by Ephraim George Squier, his own copies with some recently acquired additions and a few books by others. N.Y. 1939. 44p. mim. **5424a**

—— Valle, Rafael Heliodoro. Ephraim George Squire [Notas bio-bibliograficas]. Hispanic Am. hist: rev. V. p777-89 (Nov. 1922) **5425**

Stark. Gould, S. C. Bibliography on Major-General John Stark. Manchester Hist. Asso. colls. I. p205-11. 1896 **5426**

Steffens. U.S. Library of Congress. Division of bibliography. Bibliography of Lincoln Steffens. May 28, 1926. 6p. typ. **5427**

Stevens, Isaac I. Boening, Rose M. Bibliography of Isaac I. Stevens. Wash. hist. quar. IX. p174-96 (July 1918) **5428**

Stevens family. Historical Records Survey. New Jersey. Calendar of the Stevens family papers, Lieb Memorial Library, Stevens Institute of Technology, Hoboken, New Jersey. Newark, N.J. March 1940. 112p. mim. **5428a**

—— Historical Records Survey. New Jersey. Calendars of manuscript collections in New Jersey. Calendar of the Stevens family papers, Stevens Institute of Technology Library. . . . Hoboken, N.J. vol. 1, 1664-1760. Newark. 1940. 226p. **5428b**

Stevenson. Historical Records Survey. West Virginia. Calendar of the William E. Stevenson letters in the state Department of archives and history. Charleston, W. Va. 1939. 105p. mim. **5428c**

Stone. Carson, Hampton. The works of Frederick Dawson Stone. Pennsylvania mag. of hist. and biog. XXI. p. xxviii-xxx. 1897 **5429**

Stuyvesant. U.S. Library of Congress. Division of bibliography. Select list of references on Peter Stuyvesant. Oct. 28, 1910. 4p. typ. **5430**

Swanton. Nichols, Frances S. Bibliography of anthropological papers by John R. Swanton. *In* U.S. Smithsonian Institution. Essays in historical anthropology of North America. (Smithsonian miscellaneous collections. v. 100 (whole volume)) Wash. Smithsonian Institution. 1940. p593-600 **5430a**

Taylor, Alexander S. Cowan, Robert Ernest. Alexander S. Taylor, 1817-1876, first bibliographer of California. Calif. Hist. Soc. quar. XII. p18-24 (March 1933) **5431**

Taylor, Moses. Leech, Wilmer R. The Moses Taylor papers. N. Y. Pub. Lib. bul. XXXV. p259-61 (May 1931) (Merchant and banker) **5432**

Taylor, Zachary. U.S. Library of Congress. Division of bibliography. Select list of references on President Zachary Taylor. June 13, 1913. 7p. typ. (Additional references. Sept. 7, 1933. 8-13p. typ.) **5433**

—— Wise, W. Harvey, Jr. and Cronin, John W. A bibliography of Zachary Taylor, Millard Fillmore, Franklin Pierce, James Buchanan. (Presidential bibliog. ser. no. 7) Wash. D.C. Riverford Pub. Co. 1935. p7-19 **5433a**

Tecumseh. U.S. Library of Congress. Division of bibliography. List of references on Tecumseh, Shawnee chief. March 13, 1923. 4p. typ. **5434**

Thomas. U.S. Library of Congress. Division of bibliography. Select list of references on Major-General George Henry Thomas. June 14, 1913. 5p. typ. **5435**

Thompson. U.S. Library of Congress. Division of bibliography. Sir Benjamin Thompson, Count Rumford (1753-1814); a bibliographical list. Sept. 25, 1931. 6p. typ. **5436**

Thwaites. Alvord, Clarence Walworth. A critical analysis of the work of Reuben Gold Thwaites. Miss. Valley Hist. Asso. proc. VII. p321-33. 1914 **5436a**

—— Turner, Frederick J. Bibliography. *In* Reuben Gold Thwaites; a memorial address. Madison. State Hist. Soc. of Wisconsin. 1914. p63-94 **5437**

Tilden. U.S. Library of Congress. Division of bibliography. Select list of references on Samuel J. Tilden. June 2, 1911. 5p. typ. (Additional references. Dec. 13, 1923. 1p.) **5438**

Tilton. U.S. Library of Congress. Division of bibliography. Bibliography of Theodore Tilton, 1835-1907. Oct. 5, 1922. 5p. typ. **5439**

Troup. Hill, Robert W. The Robert Troup papers. N.Y. Pub. Lib. bul. XXXVII. p574-6 (July 1933) **5439a**

Trumbull. Wright, Arthur W. Biographical memoir of James Hammond Trumbull, 1821-1897. (National Acad. of Sciences. Biog. memoirs. VII) Wash. D.C. 1911. p143-69 **5440**

Turner. Becker, C. L. Frederick Jackson Turner. *In* American masters of social science. Ed. by H. W. Odum. N.Y. Holt. 1927. p273-321 **5441**

—— Craven, Avery. Frederick Jackson Turner. *In* Hutchinson, William T. ed. The Marcus W. Jernegan essays in American historiography. Chicago. Univ. of Chicago Press. 1937. p252-70 **5441a**

—— Edwards, Everett Eugene. The early writings of Frederick Jackson Turner; with a list of all his works. Madison. Univ. of Wisconsin Press. 1938. p231-72 **5441b**

—— Schafer, Joseph. Turner's early writings. Wis. mag. hist. XXII. p213-31 (Dec. 1938) **5441c**

Tyler, John. Cronin, John W. and Wise, W. Harvey, Jr. A bibliography of William Henry Harrison, John Tyler, James Knox Polk. (Presidential bibliog. ser. no. 6) Wash. D.C. Riverford Publishing Co. 1935 54p. **5441d**

Tyler, Moses Coit. Austen, Mrs. Jessica Tyler, ed. Moses Coit Tyler, 1835-1900; selections from his letters and diaries. N.Y. Doubleday, Page. 1911. 325p. (List of Tyler manuscripts and of published works by Tyler, p277-88) **5441e**

—— Jones, Howard Mumford. The life of Moses Coit Tyler. Ann Arbor. Univ. of Michigan Press. 1933. 354p. **5441f**

Van Buren. MacDonald, William. The Jackson and Van Buren papers. Am. Antiq. Soc. proc. n.s. XVII.p231-8 (Oct. 1905) **5441g**

—— U.S. Library of Congress. Division of manuscripts. Calendar of the papers of Martin Van Buren. Prep. by Elizabeth H. West. Wash. Govt. Ptg. Off. 1910. 757p. **5441h**

—— Wise, W. Harvey, Jr. and Cronin, John W. A bibliography of Andrew Jackson and Martin Van Buren. (Presidential bibliog. ser. no. 5) Wash. D.C. Riverford Publishing Co. 1935. 66p. **5441i**

Van Tyne. Davidson, Philip G. Claude Halstead Van Tyne. *In* Hutchinson, William T. ed. The Marcus W. Jernegan essays in American historiography. Chicago. Univ. of Chicago Press. 1937. p339-53 **5441j**

Vignaud. Cordier, Henri. Henry Vignaud. Soc. Amer. Paris jour. n.s. XV. p1-17. 1923 **5441k**

—— Dewey, Stoddard. The historical work of Henry Vignaud, an American of Louisiana and Paris (1830-1922). Ex libris. I. p360-4 (June 1924) **5441l**

Vilas. Nunns, Annie A. The Vilas papers. Wisconsin mag. of hist. XVII. p228-31 (Dec. 1933) (Papers of William F. Vilas) **5442**

Von Holst. Goldman, Eric. Hermann Eduard Von Holst: plumed knight of historiography. Miss. Valley hist. rev. XXIII. p511-32 (March 1937) **5442a**

Von Steuben. U.S. Library of Congress. Division of bibliography. A bibliography of General von Steuben. Dec. 24, 1912. 11p. typ. **5443**

Wagner. Published writings of Henry R. Wagner. n.p. n.p. 1934. unpag. **5444**

Walker, Francis A. Bibliography of the writings and reported addresses of Francis A. Walker. Am. Statistical Asso. publications. V. p276-90 (June 1897) **5445**

Walker, Robert James. U.S. Library of Congress. Division of bibliography. List of references on Robert James Walker, 1801-1869. April 17, 1925. 6p. typ. **5446**

Walker, William. Historical Records Survey. Louisiana. An inventory of the collections of the Middle American Research Institute. No. 1. Calendar I. Fayssoux collection of William Walker papers. New Orleans, La. May 1937. 28p. mim. **5446a**

—— U.S. Library of Congress. Division of bibliography. General William Walker (1824-1860); a bibliographical list. Sept. 3, 1929. 6p. typ. **5447**

Washington. American Library Association. Classified Washington bibliography. Comp. by a special committee of the American Library Association (Honor to George Washington and reading about George Washington. Pamphlet no. 16. Ed. by Albert Bushnell Hart) Wash D.C. U.S. George Washington bicentennial comn. 1931. 76p. (Also in History of the George Washington bicentennial celebration. v. I. Literature ser. Wash. D.C. 1932. p184-99) **5448**

—— Baker, William Spohn. Bibliotheca Washingtoniana; a descriptive list of the biographies and biographical sketches of George Washington. Wash. D.C. Robert M. Lindsay. 1889. 179p. **5449**

—— Binney, Horace. An inquiry into the formation of Washington's farewell address. Phila. Parry & McMillan. 1859. 250p. **5449a**

—— Boston Athenaeum. A catalogue of the Washington collection in The Boston Athenaeum, in four parts: I. Books from the library of General George Washington (1-234). II. Other books from Mount Vernon (234-273). III. The writings of Washington (274-340). IV. Washingtoniana (341-475). Comp. by A. P. C. Griffin and William Lane Coolidge. Boston. The Boston Athenaeum. 1897. 566p. (Index, by Franklin Osborn Poole. Cambridge, Mass. Univ. Press, John Wilson and Son, The Boston Athenaeum, 1900. 85p.) **5450**

—— Connecticut Historical Society. Washington letters in the library of the Connecticut Historical Society. Hartford, Conn. 1932. 53p. **5451**

—— Coulomb, Charles A. George Washington in recent biographies. Hist. outlook. XXIII. p70-80 (Feb. 1932) **5452**

—— Edwards, Everett E. George Washington and agriculture; a classified list of annotated references with an introductory note. (U.S. Dept. of Agriculture. Lib. Bibliog. contributions no. 22) Wash. D.C. 1936. 77p. mim. **5453**

—— Haraszti, Z. Washington bicentennial exhibit. More books. Bul. of the Boston Pub. Lib. VII. p79-97 (April 1932) **5454**

—— Henkels, Stan V. Catalogue of Washingtoniana; rare and scarce books relating to Washington, biographies, eulogies, histories, etc. and a choice collection of

Washington. Henkels, S. V. Catalogue —*Continued*
rare portraits of General Washington, American and foreign officers in the revolution, statesmen. . . . Phila. E. J. Bicking. 1898. 70p. **5455**

—— Henkels, Stan V. An extraordinary collection of Washington's letters, relics, revolutionary documents and the rarest works on American history. . . . Phila. 1891. 109p. **5456**

—— Henry E. Huntington Library and Art Gallery. George Washington 1732-1932; an exhibition at the Henry E. Huntington Library and Art Gallery, San Marino, California. San Marino, Calif. 1932. 25p. **5457**

—— Hough, Franklin Benjamin. Bibliographical list of books and pamphlets containing eulogies, orations, poems, or other papers, relating to the death of General Washington, or to the honors paid to his memory. *In* Washingtoniana; or, memorials of the death of George Washington, giving an account of the funeral honors paid to his memory. Roxbury, Mass. Printed for W. E. Woodward. 1865. II. p219-77 (Separately reprinted. Albany, N.Y. 1865. 59p.) **5458**

—— New York. Public Library. Calendar of Washington's copy-press letters in the New York Public Library. N.Y. Pub. Lib. bul. II. p202-26 (May 1898) **5458a**

—— Paltsits, Victor Hugo. Bibliography of the Farewell address. *In* Washington's Farewell address; in facsimile, with transliteration of all the drafts of Washington, Madison and Hamilton, together with their correspondence and other supporting documents. N.Y. N.Y. Pub Lib. 1935. p305-60 **5459**

—— Phillips, Philip Lee. Washington as surveyor and map-maker. D.A.R. mag. LV. p115-32 (March 1921) **5459a**

—— Pittsburgh. Carnegie Library. List of references on Washington's visits to Pittsburgh and the Ohio country. Monthly bul. of the Carnegie Lib. XIII. p79-93 (Feb. 1908) **5460**

—— Ruttenber, Edward Manning. Catalogue of manuscripts and relics in Washington's headquarters, Newburg, N.Y. Newburg, N.Y. E.M. Ruttenber. 1879. 75p. **5460a**

—— Stillwell, Margaret Bingham. Washington eulogies; a checklist of eulogies and funeral orations on the death of George Washington, December 1799-February 1800. N.Y. N.Y. Pub. Lib. 1916. 68p. (Reprinted from the Bul. of the N.Y. Pub Lib. May 1916) **5461**

—— Toner, J. M. Some account of George Washington's library and manuscript records, and their dispersion from Mount Vernon. Am. Hist. Asso. rep. 1892. p71-111 **5462**

—— U.S. Department of State. List indicating arrangement of the Washington papers. (Bureau of rolls and library bul. no. 3) Wash. D.C. 1894. p5-23 **5462a**

—— U.S. Library of Congress. Division of bibliography. List of addresses and speeches on George Washington. May 12, 1934. 7p. typ. **5463**

—— U.S. Library of Congress. Division of bibliography. List of references on George Washington, from 1903 to date. Feb. 18, 1914. 11p. typ. **5464**

—— U.S. Library of Congress. Division of manuscripts. Calendar of the correspondence of George Washington, commander-in-chief of the Continental army with the officers, June 17, 1775—January 4, 1784. Prep. by John C. Fitzpatrick. Wash. Govt. Ptg. Off. 1915. 4v. **5464a**

—— U.S. Library of Congress. Division of manuscripts. Calendar of the correspondence of George Washington, commander-in-chief of the Continental army with the Continental Congress. Prep. from the original manuscripts in the Library of Congress by John C. Fitzpatrick. Wash. Govt. Ptg. Off. 1906. 741p. **5464b**

—— U.S. Library of Congress. Division of manuscripts. A calendar of Washington manuscripts in the Library of Congress. Comp. under the direction of Herbert Friedenwald. Wash. Govt. Ptg. Off. 1901. 315p. **5464c**

—— U.S. Library of Congress. Division of manuscripts. List of the Washington manuscripts from the year 1592 to 1775 prepared from the original manuscripts in the Library of Congress by John C. Fitzpatrick. Wash. Govt. Ptg. Off. 1919. 137p. **5464d**

—— U.S. Library of Congress. Legislative reference service. The United States Congress on George Washington. Comp. by Myrtis Jarrell under the direction of H. H. B. Meyer. Wash. D.C. George Washington bicentennial comn. 1932. 66p. **5465**

—— U.S. Office of Education. Helps for schools in celebrating the George Washington bicentennial in 1932. Prepared by Florence C. Fox (Pamphlet no. 25) Wash. Govt. Ptg. Off. 1931. 23p. **5466**

—— Winsor, Justin. The portraits of Washington. *In* Narrative and critical history of America. Boston; N.Y. Houghton Mifflin. 1888. VII. p563-82 **5466a**

—— Wisconsin. State Historical Society. George Wsahington, 1732-1799; a list of manuscripts, books, and portraits in the library of the State Historical Society of Wisconsin. Prepared by Ruth Pauline Hayward (Bul. of information no. 98) Evansville, Wis. Antes Press. 1932. 70p. **5467**

Weare. Green, Samuel Abbott. Discovery of some Weare papers. Mass. Hist. Soc. proc. 3d ser. II. p17-22. 1909 (Weare family of New Hampshire) **5467a**

—— Hammond, Otis G. The Weare papers. Granite mthly. LI. p357-61 (Aug. 1919) (Papers of Meschech Weare, president of the Council and Chairman of the Committee of safety of New Hampshire during the Revolution) **5467b**

Webster, Daniel. Clapp, Clifford Blake. Analytical methods in bibliography applied to Daniel Webster's speech at Worcester in 1832. *In* Bibliographical essays; a tribute to Wilberforce Eames. Cambridge. Harvard Univ. Press. 1924. p211-21 **5468**

—— Clapp, Clifford Blake. The speeches of Daniel Webster; a bibliographical review. Bibliog. Soc. of Amer. pap. XIII. p3-63. 1919 **5469**

—— Hart, Charles Henry. Bibliographia Websteriana; a list of the publications occasioned by the death of Daniel Webster. Phila. 1883. 4p. (Extracted from the Bul. of the Mercantile Lib. Phila. July 1882) **5470**

—— Lodge, Henry Cabot. Webster. *In* The Cambridge history of American literature. Ed. by William P. Trent and others. N.Y. G. P. Putnam's Sons. 1918. II. p92-103, 480-8 **5471**

—— Webster, Fletcher. A chronological list of the writings and speeches of Daniel Webster embraced in the national edition. *In* The Writings and speeches of Daniel Webster, national edition. Boston. Little, Brown. 1903. XVIII. p579-619 **5472**

Webster, Noah. Skeel, Mrs. Roswell, Jr. Bibliography of Noah Webster. Bankers Trust Company, 529 Fifth Ave. N.Y. In progress **5472a**

—— Websteriana; a catalogue of books by Noah Webster collated from the library of Gordon L. Ford. Brooklyn, N.Y. The Hist. Ptg. Co. 1882. 20p. **5473**

Webster, Pelatiah. U.S. Library of Congress. Division of bibliography. Select list of references on Pelatiah Webster. Dec. 15, 1911. 3p. typ. **5474**

Weedon. American Philosophical Society. Committee on historical manuscripts. Calendar of the correspondence of Brigadier-General George Weedon, U.SA., with celebrated characters of the American Revolution. Am. Phil. Soc. trans. XXXVIII. p81-114. 1899 **5474a**

Weems. Ford, Paul Leicester. Mason Locke Weems; his works and ways. Part I. A bibliography left unfinished by Paul Leicester Ford. Ed. by Emily Ellsworth Ford Skeel. N.Y. 1929. 418p. **5475**

—— Wroth, Lawrence Counselman. Parson Weems; a biographical and critical study. Baltimore. Eichelberger. 1911. 104p. **5475a**

Weidensall. Historical Records Survey. Illinois. Calendar of the Robert Weidensall correspondence, 1861-1865 at George Williams College, Chicago, Illinois. Prep. by the Illinois Historical Records Survey project, Division of professional and service projects, Work projects administration. Chicago. 1940. 34p. reprod. **5475b**

Wesley. Green, Richard. The works of John and Charles Wesley; a bibliography containing an exact account of all the publications issued by The Brothers

Wesley, arranged in chronological order, with a list of the early editions and descriptive and illustrative notes. London. Methodist Publishing House. 1906. 291p. **5476**

Whistler. Seitz, Don Carlos. Writings by & about James Abbott McNeill Whistler; a bibliography. Edinburgh. O. Schulze and Co. 1910. 181p. **5476a**

Whitman. Bourne, Edward Gaylord. The legend of Marcus Whitman. Am. hist. rev. VI. p276-300 (Jan. 1901) *Also in* Essays in historical criticism. N.Y. Scribner's. 1901. p3-112 **5476b**

—— Smith, Charles Wesley. A contribution toward a bibliography of Marcus Whitman. (Bul. of the Univ. of Wash. Univ. stud. II) Seattle. 1909. 62p. (Reprinted from the Wash. hist. quar. III. no. 3-62. Oct. 1908) **5477**

Whitney. U.S. Library of Congress. Division of bibliography. List of references on Eli Whitney. June 16, 1926. 5p. typ. **5478**

Whittier. Currier, Thomas Franklin. A bibliography of John Greenleaf Whittier. . . . Cambridge, Mass. Harvard Univ. Press. 1937. 692p. **5478a**

Whittlesey. Baldwin, C. C. Bibliography of Colonel Whittlesey's publications. Western Reserve Hist. Soc. tracts. II. no. 67. p428-34 (May 1886) **5479**

Williams, Otho Holland. Historical Records Survey. Maryland. Calendar of the General Otho Holland Williams papers in the Maryland Historical Society. Baltimore, Md. 1940. 454p. **5479a**

Williams, Roger. Chapin, Howard M. List of Roger Williams' writings. (Contributions to Rhode Island bibliog. no. IV) Providence, R.I. Preston & Rounds. 1918. 7p. **5480**

—— Guild, R. A. An account of the writings of Roger Williams. [Providence] Lib. of Brown Univ. Dec. 10, 1862. 11p. **5481**

Williamson. Williamson, William Cross. Memoir of Joseph Williamson. Boston. D. Clapp. 1903. 9p. (Reprinted from the New Eng. hist. and geneal. reg.) **5481a**

Wilson, James. U.S. Library of Congress. Division of bibliography. List of references relating to James Wilson, 1792-1798. May 23, 1925. 4p. typ. **5482**

Wilson, Woodrow. Brown, George Dobbin. An essay towards a bibliography of the published writings and addresses of Woodrow Wilson, 1910-1917. Princeton. Princeton Univ. Lib. 1917. 52p. **5483**

—— Clemons, Harry. An essay toward a bibliography of the published writings and addresses of Woodrow Wilson, 1875-1910. Princeton. Princeton Univ. Lib. 1913. unpag. **5484**

—— Daniel, Marjorie L. Woodrow Wilson —historian. Miss. Valley hist. rev. XXI. p361-74 (Dec. 1934) **5484a**

Wilson, Woodrow. Leach, Howard Seavoy. Bibliography of the published writings and addresses of Woodrow Wilson, March 4, 1913 to 1927. *In* Baker, Ray Stannard and Dodd, William E. The public papers of Woodrow Wilson. The new democracy. II. p437-83. War and peace. III. p543-636. N.Y., London. Harper's. 1926-27   **5485**

—— Leach, Howard Seavoy. An essay towards a bibliography of the published writings and addresses of Woodrow Wilson, March 1917 to March 1921. Princeton. Princeton Univ. Lib. 1922. 73p. **5486**

—— McKean, Dayton D. Notes on Woodrow Wilson's speeches. Quar. jour. of speech. XVI. p176-84 (April 1930) **5487**

—— Sears, Louis Martin. Woodrow Wilson. *In* Hutchinson, William T. ed. The Marcus W. Jernegan essays in American historiography. Chicago. Univ. of Chicago Press. 1937. p102-21 **5487a**

—— Tigert, J. J. Woodrow Wilson's history of the American people. Meth. quar. rev. LII. p227-53 (April 1903) **5487b**

—— U.S. Library of Congress. Division of bibliography. Woodrow Wilson; a short bibliographical list. June 13, 1927. 8p. typ. **5488**

Winchell. Upham, Warren. Bibliography of N. H. Winchell (1861-1914). Geol. Soc. of Amer. bul. XVI. p31-46. 1915 **5489**

Winsor. Yust, William F. A bibliography of Justin Winsor, 1877, superintendent of the Boston Public Library, 1868, librarian of Harvard University, 1877-1897. (Lib. of Harvard Univ. Bibliog. contributions no. 54) Cambridge, Mass. 1902. 32p. **5490**

Winthrop. Winthrop, Robert Charles, Jr. A memoir of Robert C. Winthrop. Boston. Little, Brown. 1897. 358p. **5490a**

Wright. Bibliography of the writings of Hon. Carroll D. Wright, 1874-1908. Am. Statistical Asso. publications. XI. p550-61 (Sept. 1909) **5491**

Yancey. Historical Records Survey. North Carolina. A calendar of the Bartlett Yancey papers in the Southern historical collection of the University of North Carolina. Raleigh, N.C. 1940. 48p. reprod. **5491a**

GENEALOGY

American Antiquarian Society. Check list locating genealogies. (In progress) **5492**

Bibliographical Society of America. Consolidated genealogical card index. In progress **5492a**

Boston. Public Library. Catalogue of family histories, with many works containing genealogical information in the Boston Public Library. By Arthur Mason Knapp (Bibliographies of special subjects no. 7) Boston. Boston Pub. Lib. 1891. 16p. **5493**

—— A finding list of genealogies and town and local histories containing family records, in the public library of the city of Boston. Boston. Pub. by the Trustees. 1900. 80p. **5494**

Brackett, T. State library bulletin board. N.H. Pub. Lib. bul. XXXIII. p114-15 (June 1937) (Includes notice of the card index of the Library's genealogical collection) **5494a**

Cincinnati. Public Library. Card index of genealogical material. (On deposit in the library) **5495**

Daughters of the American Revolution. Index of the Rolls of honor (ancestor's index) in the lineage books of the National Society of the Daughters of the American Revolution, volumes 1 to 40. Pittsburgh. Press of Pierpont, Siviter & Co. 1916. 424p. Vols. 41 to 80, 81 to 120. Wash. D.C. Judd and Detweiler. 1926, 1939. 450, 432p. **5496**

—— Library. Catalogue of genealogical and historical works, library of the National Society, Daughters of the American Revolution. [Washington, D.C. 1940] 352p. **5496a**

Doane, Gilbert Harry. Searching for your ancestors; the why and how of genealogy. N.Y. McGraw-Hill. 1937 (Appendices A-D: Bibliographies, States whose offices of vital statistics have records dating before 1900, Census records [on file at the Bureau of the Census, Washington, D.C.], A bibliography of lists, registers, rolls, and rosters of Revolutionary war soldiers. p205-42) **5496b**

Durrie, Daniel S. Index to American genealogies and to genealogical material contained in all works such as town histories, county histories, local histories, historical society publications, biographies, historical periodicals, and kindred works, alphabetically arranged. Albany. Munsell. 1900. 352p. **5497**

Eno, Joel N. American genealogical sources and genealogical limitations. Reprinted from Americana. XXII. no. LV. Oct. 1928. 13p. **5498**

Gatfield, George. Guide to printed books and manuscripts relating to English and foreign heraldry and genealogy. London, Mitchell and Hughes. 1892 (America p522-39) **5498a**

Glenn, Thomas Allen. A list of some American genealogies which have been printed in book form, arranged in alphabetical order. Phila. Henry T. Coates. 1897. 71p. **5499**

Goodspeed, Charles E. & Co. Goodspeed's catalogue, genealogies and town histories containing genealogies. . . . Boston. Goodspeed. 1919. 128p. **5500**

Goodspeed's Book Shop. Genealogy and local history . . . Boston. Goodspeed's Book Shop. 1936. 185p. **5500a**

Illinois. State Historical Library. A list of the genealogical works in the Illinois State Historical Library. By Georgia L. Osborne (Publication no. 18) Springfield. The Lib. 1914. 163p. (Supplement. 1919. 182p.) **5501**

Index to genealogical periodicals. American genealogist and New Haven geneal. mag. IX. no. 4. April 1933- **5502**

Institute of American Genealogy. Library. Library catalogue of the Institute of American Genealogy. Chicago. Inst. of Am. Geneal. [1934] 79p. **5503**

—— —— Library catalogue of the Institute of American Genealogy. Chicago. 1939. 111p. **5503a**

Jacobus, Donald L. Index to genealogical periodicals. New Haven, Conn. D. L. Jacobus. 1932. unpag. (Cont. in Am. genealogist and New Haven geneal. mag. IX. April 1933-) **5504**

Keller, Alton H. Index to the names of families mentioned in a series of genealogical articles published in 1903-1908 in the Baltimore Sun newspaper. n.p. n.p. n.d. 11p. **5505**

Larson, Cedric. The rising tide of genealogical publications in America. N.Y. 1938. p100-12 (Overrun from The Colophon, n.s. III, no. 1) **5505a**

Long Island Historical Society. Library. Catalogue of American genealogies in the library of the Long Island historical society. Brooklyn. The Society. 1935. 660p. **5505b**

McIlwaine, Henry Read. Material in the Virginia State Library of genealogical value. National Geneal. Soc. quar. XXIX. p25-33. 1931 **5506**

Michigan. State Library. Genealogy and American local history in the Michigan State Library. Lansing, Mich. 1915. 169p. **5507**

Moody, Katherine T. Material for genealogical research in the St. Louis Public Library. St. Louis Pub. Lib. monthly bul. XIII. p225-54 (Aug. 1915) **5508**

Morris, Seymour. A list of genealogies being compiled. Chicago. 1896. 17p. **5509**

Munsell, Joel and Sons. The American genealogist, being a catalogue of family histories, a bibliography of American genealogy, or a list of the title pages of books and pamphlets on family history published in America from 1771 to date. Albany, N.Y. Munsell. 1900. 406p. **5510**

—— Index to American genealogies; and to genealogical material contained in all works such as town histories, county histories, local histories, historical society publications, biographies, historical periodicals and kindred works, alphabetically arranged. Albany, N.Y. Munsell. 1900. 352p.
Same. Albany, N.Y. Munsell. 1933. 40p. **5511**

—— List of titles of genealogical articles in American periodicals and kindred works, giving the name, residence and earliest date of the first settler of each family. Albany, N.Y. Munsell. 1899. 165p. **5512**

National Society of Colonial Dames of New York. Catalogue of the genealogical and historical library of the Colonial Dames of New York. N.Y. The Soc. 1912. 518p. **5513**

New York. Public Library. American genealogies. N. Y. Pub Lib. bul. I. p247-56, 280-8, 316-22, 343-50 (Sept.-Dec. 1897) **5514**

Onderdonk, Henry. Names of persons and places, with a bibliography. Jamaica, N.Y. 1866. MS. unpag. **5515**

St. Louis. Public Library. Genealogical material and local histories in the St. Louis Public Library. Revised edition by Georgia Gambrill. [St. Louis.] 1941. 219p. reprod. typ. **5516**

Scranton, Helen Love. Cross-index to New Haven Genealogical Magazine volumes I-VIII, inclusive, Families of ancient New Haven, by Donald Lines Jacobus. [New Haven] 1939. 301p. photo. **5516a**

Shepard, Charles. Genealogical bibliographies and handbooks. Nation. Geneal. Soc. quar. XII. p25-7 (June 1923) **5516b**

Smith, Philip M. Directories in the Library of Congress. Am. Genealogist and New Haven geneal. mag. XIII. p46-53. 1936 (City, town and county directories) **5516c**

Syracuse. Public Library. List of books on genealogy and heraldry in the Syracuse Public Library, including parish registers, visitations, history of names and allied subjects. Syracuse, N.Y. The Lib. 1910. 119p. (Genealogies added to Syracuse Public Library since 1911. 1926. unpag. typ.) **5517**

U.S. Library of Congress. American and English genealogies in the Library of Congress. Comp. under the direction of the chief of the catalogue division. Wash. Govt. Ptg. Off. 1919. 1322p. **5518**

—— —— **Division of bibliography.** List of libraries and societies having genealogical collections. July 20, 1916. 3p. typ. **5519**

—— —— —— List of references on personal names. Jan. 12, 1920. 6p. typ. (Additional references. 1922. 2p. typ.) **5520**

U.S. Veterans' Administration. Custodians of public records; information respecting custodians of established records of births, marriages, divorces and deaths in the several states, Canada, Canal Zone, Cuba, Hawaii, Newfoundland, Porto Rico, and the Philippine Islands. . . . Wash. D.C. 1932. 77p. **5521**

Virginia. State Library. Provisional list of works on genealogy and works helpful in genealogical research in the Virginia State Library (Fourth annual report, 1906-1907). Richmond. Davis Bottom. 1907. p102-32 (Also Va. State Lib. bul. I. Jan. 1908) **5522**

Virkus, Frederick A. The handbook of American genealogy. Chicago. Inst. of Am. Geneal. 1932- **5523**

CHAPTER XIII

TERRITORIES, POSSESSIONS, DEPENDENCIES

GENERAL

U.S. Congress. House. Committee on Printing. Territorial papers of the United States ... Report [and Supplemental report] [To accompany S. 2242] ... Wash. Govt. Ptg. Off. 1937. 6p. **5523a**

U.S. Congress. House. Committee on Printing. Official papers. Hearings before the committee on printing, House of representatives, Seventy-fifth Congress, first session on S. 2242, a bill to further amended[!] an act entitled "An act to authorize the collection and editing of official papers of the territories of the United States now in the National archives," approved March 3, 1925, as amended ... Wash. Govt. Ptg. Off. 1937. 55p. **5523b**

U.S. Library of Congress. Division of bibliography. Brief list of references on the insular possessions of the United States, including the Panama Canal Zone. June 27, 1922. 11p. typ. **5524**

—— —— List of books (with references to periodicals) relating to the theory of colonization, government of dependencies, protectorates, and related topics. By A. P. C. Griffin. Wash. Govt. Ptg. Off. 1900. 156p. (Also in U.S. Bureau of Statistics. Colonial administration, 1800-1900. . . . From the Summary of commerce and finance for October 1901. Wash. Govt. Ptg. Off. 1901. p1567-626) **5525**

—— —— Select list of references on the administration of justice in our insular possessions. Feb. 21, 1913. 5p. typ. **5526**

—— —— Select list of references on the Federal supervision of the territories. July 20, 1914. 10p. typ. **5527**

ALASKA

Alaska. Agricultural Experiment Stations. List and analytical index of publications of Alaska Agricultural Experiment Stations, Jan. 1898 to July 1931. By Elizabeth H. Langdale (Alaska Agricultural Experiment Stations. Circular 3) ? April 1932. 56p. **5528**

Alaska. Historical Library and Museum, Juneau. Descriptive booklet on the Alaska historical museum, issued by the Alaska historical Association. Edited by Rev. A. P. Kashevaroff, curator. Juneau, Alaska. Daily Alaska Empire Print. 1936. 52p. **5528a**

Andrews, C. L. Some Russian books on Alaskan history. Pacific Northwest quar. XXVIII. p75-87 (Jan. 1937) **5528b**

Basanoff, V. Archives of the Russian church in Alaska in the Library of Congress. Pacific hist. rev. II. p72-84 (March 1933) **5529**

Dall, William Healey and Baker, Marcus. Partial list of charts, maps and publications relating to Alaska and the adjacent region, from Puget Sound and Hakodadi to the Arctic ocean, between the Rocky and the Stanovoi mountains. *In* U.S. Coast and Geodetic Survey. Pacific coast pilot. Wash. D.C. 1892. p165-223 **5530**

Morrison, Hugh A. Alaskan newspapers and periodicals; preliminary check list prepared for the use of Hon. James Wickersham, delegate from Alaska. Wash. D.C. 1915. 28p. **5531**

Smith, Philip S. Selected list of Geological survey publications on Alaska. (U.S. Geol. Survey. Bul. 824) Wash. Govt. Ptg. Off. 1932. p. 1a-14a **5532**

Taylor, Alexander S. Bibliography of Alaska (1600-1867). *In* Browne, J. Ross. Resources of the Pacific slope. N.Y. Appleton. 1869. p598-604 **5533**

U.S. Department of the Interior. Office of the Secretary. Government publications on Alaska. Wash. D.C. [1909] 10p. **5534**

U.S. Library of Congress. Division of bibliography. List of references on Alaska. May 7, 1923. 7p. mim. **5535**

—— —— List of references on the reindeer industry. April 18, 1916. 4p. typ. **5536**

—— —— List of speeches on Alaska appearing in the Congressional record during the last few years. Aug. 4, 1914. 2p. typ. **5537**

—— —— Select list of references on railroads in Alaska. Dec. 30, 1913. 4p. typ. **5538**

—— —— Division of maps. Alaska and the north-west part of North America, 1588-1898, maps in the Library of Congress. Comp. by Philip Lee Phillips. Wash. Govt. Ptg. Off. 1898. 119p. **5538a**

U.S. Superintendent of Documents. Partial reference list of United States government publications on Alaska. Wash. Govt. Ptg. Off. 1898. p63-76 (Reprinted from the Monthly catalogue of U.S. public documents, Jan. 1898) **5539**

Wickersham, James. A bibliography of Alaskan literature, containing the titles of all histories, travels, voyages, newspapers, periodicals, public documents, etc., printed in English, Russian, German, French, Spanish, etc., relating to, descriptive of, or published in Russia, America or Alaska, from 1724 to and including 1924. (Miscellaneous publications of the Alaska Agricultural College and School of Mines. I) Cordova. Cordova daily times. 1927. 635p. **5540**

HAWAIIAN ISLANDS

Ballou, Howard Malcolm and Carter, George Robert. Bibliography of books in the native Hawaiian language. Boston, Honolulu. 1908. 346p. typ. **5541**

—— —— The history of the Hawaiian Mission Press, with a bibliography of the earlier publications. *In* Gilman, G. D. Journal of a canoe voyage along the Kauai Palis. (Hawaiian Hist. Soc. Pap. XIV) Honolulu. Paradise of the Pacific print. 1908. p9-44 **5542**

Boston. Public Library. Finding list of books in the library relating to the Hawaiian Islands. Boston Pub. Lib. bul. n.s. IV. p86-8 (April 1893) **5543**

Bryan, E. H., Jr. The contributions of Thomas G. Thrum to Hawaiian history and ethnology. Hawaiian Hist. Soc. rep. 1932. p13-22 **5544**

Carter, George Robert. Preliminary catalogue of Hawaiiana in the library of George R. Carter. . . Collected largely by Howard Malcolm Ballou. Part I. Boston. Heintzemann. 1915. 191p. **5545**

A check list of books printed in the Hawaiian and other Pacific island dialects in the library of Sir R. L. Harmsworth. London. Printed for private distribution only. 19? 28p. **5545a**

Hawaii. Board of Commissioners of Public Archives. Report of the Board of Commissioners of Public Archives. . . 1928. Honolulu. 1928. 18p. **5546**

Hawaii. Historical Commission of the Territory of Hawaii. Reports of the Historical Commission, I, nos. 1-5, 1922-1928. Honolulu. Honolulu star-bul. Ltd. 1923-29 (Contain information on MS. material) **5547**

Hawaii. Legislature. Special report of the Committee on Foreign Relations in re an appropriation for the preservation and arrangement of the Government archives and the preparation of a bibliography of the Hawaiian Kingdom. Honolulu. 1892. 33p. **5548**

—— —— Committee on foreign relations. Special report of the Committee on foreign relations in reference to an appropriation for the preservation and arrangement of the government archives and the preparation of a bibliography of the Hawaiian kingdom. Honolulu. Elele Pub. Co. 1892. 33p. **5548a**

Hawaii. University. University of Hawaii books. Honolulu. Univ. of Hawaii. 1937. 31p. **5548b**

Hawaiian annual. Index to Hawaiian annual, 1875-1932. By Margaret Fitcomb and Anita Ames (Bernice Bishop Museum. Special publication 24) Honolulu. The Museum. 1934. 59p. **5549**

Hawaiian Club. A catalogue of works published at, or relating to, the Hawaiian Islands. Copied from Hawaiian Club papers of October 1868. Boston. A. A. Kingman. 1868. 81p. typ. **5550**

Hawaiian Historical Society. Catalogue of bound books in the library of the Hawaiian Historical Society. By C. M. Hyde. Honolulu. Robert Grieve. 1897. 29p. **5551**

—— List of books on the Hawaiian Islands. Honolulu. 1928. 9p. **5552**

Hawaiian Mission Children's Society. Voyages to Hawaii before 1860; a study based on historical narratives in the library of the Hawaiian Mission Children's Society. Honolulu. Pub. by the Soc. 1929. 108p. (Bibliog. on p85-108) **5553**

Hoes, R. R. Librarian's report [on collection of papers and periodicals printed in Honolulu]. Hawaiian Hist. Soc. rep. I p10-13. 1893 **5554**

Hunnewell, James Frothingham. Bibliography of the Hawaiian Islands. Boston. A. A. Kingman. 1869. 75p. **5555**

Kuykendall, Ralph Simpson. Hawaiian diplomatic correspondence in the Bureau of Indexes and Archives of the Department of State, Washington, D.C. (Publications of the Hist. Comn. of the Territory of Hawaii. I. no. 3) Honolulu. Honolulu star-bul. Ltd. 1926. 56p. **5556**

Leebrick, K. C. A brief statement of the opportunities for historical research in Hawaii. Am. Hist. Asso. rep. 1920. p119-21 **5557**

Libbie, C. F. & Co. Catalogue of books and pamphlets relating to Hawaii and the South Sea Islands; early voyages, narratives, travels, history, shipwrecks, pirates, whaling, etc., historical and biographical discourses, legislative, territorial and government reports. Boston. C. F. Libbie. 1918. 30p. **5558**

Lydecker, Robert C. The archives of Hawaii. Hawaiian Hist. Soc. pap. no. 13. p5-23. 1906 **5559**

MacCaughey, Vaughn. The one hundred most important books and files relating to The Hawaiian Islands. Bul. of bibliog. X. p71-3 (Oct., Nov., Dec. 1918) **5560**

Martin, William. Catalogue d'ouvrages relatifs aux îles Hawaii; essai de bibliographie Hawaiiene. Paris. Challamel Ainé. 1867. 92p. **5561**

Pease, W. Harper. A catalogue of works relating to the Hawaiian Islands. Honolulu. H. M. Whitney. 1862. 24p. **5562**

Peters, Woods. Rare national treasures in Hawaiian archives. Americana. XXXII. p58-63. 1938 **5562a**

Phillips, James Tice. A preliminary check list of the printed reports and correspondence of the Minister of Foreign Relations of the government of the Hawaiian Islands, 1845 to 1862, inclusive, together with a list of the printed government documents referred to or quoted therein. Honolulu. Printed for private circulation by the Hawaiian Hist. Soc. 1928. 16p.   **5563**

Stearns, Mrs. Norah Dowell. Annotated bibliography and index of geology and water supply of the Island of Oahu, Hawaii. (Territory of Hawaii. Division of hydrography. Bul. no. 3) [Honolulu. Porter Ptg. Co.] 1935. 74p.   **5563a**

U.S. Department of Agriculture. Hawaii Agricultural Experiment Station. Index to publications of the Hawaii Agricultural Experiment Station (July 1, 1901 to December 31, 1926). Prepared by Elizabeth H. Langdale. Wash. Govt. Ptg. Off. 1927. 28p.   **5564**

U.S. Library of Congress. Division of bibliography. The Hawaiian Islands; a bibliographical list. Feb. 2, 1931. 13p. typ.   **5565**

—— —— —— List of books relating to Hawaii (including references to collected works and periodicals). By A. P. C. Griffin. Wash. Govt. Ptg. Off. 1898. 26p.   **5566**

Yzendoorn, Reginald. A study in Hawaiian cartography prior to Cook's rediscovery. Hawaiian Hist. Soc. rep. XXI. p23-32. 1913   **5566a**

PHILIPPINE ISLANDS

Alvarado, Eduardo R. Philippine agricultural bibliography. Manila. Bur. of Agriculture. 1926-   **5566b**

Bach, John. Philippine maps from the time of Magellan. Mil. engineer. XXII. p351-9 (July 1930)   **5566c**

Barrantes, Vicente. Apunte bibliográfico de algunos libros y papeles volantes relacionados con las guerras piráticas. *In* Guerras piráticas de Filipinas contra Mindanaos y Joloanas. Madrid. Imp. de Manuel G. Hernandez. 1878. p351-92   **5567**

—— Colección de corridos presentado por el excmo Sr. D. V. Barrantes. *In* Catálogo de la exposición general de las Islas Filipinas celebrada en Madrid inaugurada por S.M. la reina regente el 30 de junio de 1887. Madrid. 1887. p713-32   **5568**

Becker, George F. List of books and papers on Philippine geology. (U.S. Geol. Survey. Twenty-first annual rep.) Wash. Govt. Ptg. Off. 1901. p595-605   **5569**

Blumentritt, Ferdinand. Vocabular einzelner ausdrücke und redensarten, welche dem Spanischen der Philippinischen Inseln eigenthümlich sind. Mit einem anhange: Bibliotheca Philippina. Alphabetisch geordnete sammlung einer anzahl von druckschriften und manuscripten linguistischen, geographischen, ethnographischen, historischen und naturwissenschaftlichen inhalts, die auf die Philippinen bezug haben. Leitmeritz. 1882-85. 131,64p.   **5570**

Carnegie Endowment for International Peace. Library. Philippine independence; select list of books and articles on independence of the Philippine Islands, published since 1930. Comp. by Mary Alice Matthews. (Select bibliographies, no. 9) Wash. D.C. The Endowment. 1939. 8p. mim.   **5570a**

España. Archivo de Indias de Sevilla. Catálogo de los documentos relativos a las islas Filipinas existentes en el Archivo de Indias de Sevilla. Por D. Pedro Torres y Lanzas y D. Francisco Navas (Obra editada por la Compañia general de tabacos de Filipinas, t. I-) Barcelona. Imp. de la Viuda de Luis Tasso. 1925-   **5571**

Lara, C. B. Bibliography on leprosy and related subjects in the Philippine Islands. *In* Leprosy research in the Philippines; a historical-critical review (Philippine Islands. National Research Council. Bul. no. 10) Manila. 1936. p27-48   **5571a**

LeRoy, James A. The Philippines, 1860-1898; some comment and bibliographical notes. *In* The Philippine Islands, 1493-1898. Ed. by Emma Helen Blair and James Alexander Robertson. Cleveland. Clark. 1907. LII. p112-207   **5572**

Llorens Asensio, Vicente. Cátalogo de los documentos referentes al viaje de Magallanes y del Cano que se conservan en el Archivo general de Indias. *In* La primera vuelta al mundo; relacion documentado del viaje de Hernando de Magallanes y Juan Sebastian del Cano, 1519-1922. Sevilla. Imp. de la "Guia Comercial." 1903. p89-179   **5573**

Malcolm, George A. The Philippines; a glance at Philippine legal sources and institutions. Am. Bar Asso. jour. VIII. p252-4 (April 1922)   **5574**

Manila. University of the Philippines. Library. List of references on Philippine-American trade and economic relations which are available in the University of the Philippines library. Manila. 1937. 135p.   **5574a**

Marin y Morales, Valentin. Ensayo de una síntesis de los trabajos realizados por las corporaciones religiosas españolas de Filipinas. Manila. Imp. de Santo Tomas. 1901. 2v.   **5575**

Martinez, Vigil Ramón. La orden de Predicadores; sus glorias en santidad, apostolado, ciencias, artes y gobierno de los pueblos, seguidas del ensayo de una biblioteca de dominicos españoles. Madrid. [Imp. de Antonio Perez Dubrull] 1884. (Bibliography on p229-430)   **5576**

Medina, José Toribio. Bibliográfia Española la de las Filipinas (1523-1810). Santiago de Chile. Imp. Cervantes. 1898. 556p.   **5577**

—— La imprenta en Manila desde sus orígenes hasta 1810. Santiago de Chile. Autor. 1896. 280p. (Adiciones y ampliaciones. Santiago de Chile. Impreso y grabado en casa del autor. 1904. 203p.) **5578**

Middleton, Thomas Cooke. Some notes on the bibliography of the Philippines. Free Lib. of Phila. bul. no. 4. Dec. 1900. 58p. **5579**

New York. Public Library. Works relating to the Philippine Islands in the New York Public Library. N.Y. Pub. Lib. bul. IV. p19-29 (Jan. 1900) **5580**

Pardo de Tavera, Trinidad Hipolito. Biblioteca Filipina ó sea catálogo razonado de todos los impresos, tanto insulares como extranjeros, relativos á la historia, la etnografía, la lingüistica, la botánica, la fauna, la flora, la geología, la hidrografía, la geografía, la legislacion, etc., de las Islas Filipinas, de Joló y Marianas. Wash. Govt. Ptg. Off. 1903. 439p. (Also in Senate document no. 74. 57 Cong. 2 sess. pt. II) **5581**

—— Noticias sobre la imprenta y el grabado en Filipinas. Madrid. Hernandez. 1893. 48p. **5582**

Perez, Angel and Güemes, Cecelio. Adiciones y continuación de "La imprenta en Manila" de D. J. T. Medina, ó Rarezas y curiosidades, bibliográficas filipinas de las bibliotecas de esta capital. Manila. Santos y Bornal. 1904. 620p. **5583**

Pérez, Elviro Jorde. Catálogo bio-bibliográfico de los religiosos Agustinos de la Provincia del Santísimo Nombre de Jésus de las Islas Filipinas desde su fundación hasta nuestros días. Manila. Colegio de Sto. Tomás. 1901. 875p. **5584**

Philippine Islands. Bureau of Science. Library. Bibliography on mines and mining in the Philippines. Comp. by Cirilo B. Perez and L. Estrella-Villanueva. Manila. Bur. of Ptg. 1937. 100p. **5584a**

—— —— —— Philippine bibliography of the minor crops of the Philippines. Comp. by Basilio Hernandez and Laureana Estrella. [Manila] Sept. 1, 1934. 162p. mim. **5585**

—— —— —— Philippine bibliography of the nine major crops of the Philippines: rice, sugar cane, abaca, coconut, tobacco, corn, maguey, coffee and cacao. Basilio Hernandez, reference librarian. Manila. Feb. 1933. 131p. mim. **5586**

Philippine Islands. Department of Agriculture and Natural Resources. Bureau of agriculture. Philippine agricultural bibliography. Part. I. Check list of bulletins, circulars, and miscellaneous publications of the Bureau of agriculture with index thereto. By Eduardo R. Alvarado. Manila. Bureau of Ptg. 1926. 38p. **5587**

Philippine Library. List of works in the Filipiniana division relating to the study of the bibliography of the Philippine Islands, Parts I-IV. Philippine Lib. bul. I. p14-16, 27-32, 44-8, 61-4, 93-6, 115-16 (Sept.-Dec. 1912) **5588**

Philippine Library and Museum. Legislative reference division. Check list of publications of the government of the Philippine Islands, September 1, 1900, to December 31, 1917. Comp. by Emma Osterman Elmer. Manila. Bureau of Ptg. 1918. 288p. **5589**

Retana y Gamboa, Wenceslao Emilio. Aparato bibliográfico de la historia general de Filipinas deducido de la colección que posee en Barcelona la Compañia general de tabacos de dichas islas. Madrid. Imprenta de la sucesora de M. Minuesa de los Rios. 1906. 3v. **5590**

—— Archivo del bibliófilo filipino; recopilación de documentos historicos, científicos, literarios y políticos, y estudios bibliograficos. Madrid. Imp. de la viuda de M. Minuesa de los Rios. 1895-1905. 5v. **5591**

—— Bibliografía de Mindanao (epítome). Madrid. Imp. de la viuda de M. Minuesa de los Rios. 1894. 69p. **5592**

—— Catálogo abreviado de la biblioteca Filipina. Madrid. [Imp. de la viuda de M. Minuesa de los Rios] 1898. 652p. **5593**

—— Catálogo de obras filipinas que ofrece en venta W. E. Retana. Madrid. Claudio Coello. [1902] 160p. **5594**

—— La imprenta en Filipinas, (1593-1810) con una demonstracion grafico de la originalidad de la primitiva; adiciones y observaciones a la Imprenta en Manila de D. J. T. Medina. Madrid. Imp. de la viuda de M. Minuesa de los Rios. 1899. 276col. **5595**

—— El periodismo Filipino; noticias para su historia (1811-1894); apuntes bibliográficos, indicaciones biográficas, notas críticas, semblancas, anécdotas. Madrid. En la imp. viuda de M. Minuesa de los Rios. 1895. 646p. **5596**

—— Tablas cronológica y alfabética de imprentas é impresores de Filipinas (1593-1898). Madrid. V. Suárez. 1908. 114p. **5596a**

Robertson, James Alexander. Bibliography of the Philippine Islands, printed and manuscript; preceded by a descriptive account of the most important archives and collections containing Philippina. Cleveland. Clark. 1908. 437p. (Issued as a separate from The Philippine Islands, 1493-1898, vol. LIII, ed. by Emma Helen Blair and James A. Robertson) **5597**

—— Notes on the archives of the Philippines. Am. Hist. Asso. rep. 1910. p421-5 **5598**

Robertson, James Alexander, trans. and ed. Magellan's voyage around the world, by Antonio Pigafetta; the original text of the Ambrosian MS. with English translation. notes, bibliography, and index. Cleveland. Clark. 1906. 3v. (Bibliography of Pigafetta manuscripts and printed books in II. p241-313) **5599**

Streit, Robert and Dindinger, P. Johannes.
Missionsliteratur der Philippinen. 1800-
1909. *In* Bibliotheca missionum; veroffent-
lichungen des internationalen instituts für
missionswissenschaftliche forschung. vol.
IX. Aachen. Franziskus Xaverius Mis-
sionsverein. 1936. 996p. (Volumes IV-VI
1928-31 have sections on the Philippines)
5600

Taylor, Carson. History of the Philippine
press. The Philippine revolutionary press
by Epifanio de los Santos. List of Philippine publications registered as second
class matter on February 1, 1927. Man-
ila. 1927. 61p.   **5601**

**U.S. Library of Congress. Division of bib-
liography.** A list of books (with references to periodicals) on the Philippine Islands in the Library of Congress. By
A. P. C. Griffin . . . with chronological
list of maps in the Library of Congress
by P. Lee Phillips. Wash. Govt. Ptg.
Off. 1903. 397p. (Reprint of Pt. I. of
Senate document no. 74. 57 Cong. 2 sess.
Ser. 4423) (Recent references. June 7,
1924. 8p. typ.; Selected list. July 3, 1935.
43p. mim.)   **5602**

—— —— List of references on Philippine independence. Dec. 13, 1921. 13p.
mim. (Recent writings. Jan. 14, 1931. 25p.
mim.)   **5603**

—— —— List of references on the influence of the friars on the economic
life and thought of the Philippine Islands. Oct. 3, 1922. 3p. typ.   **5604**

—— —— List of works relating to
the American occupation of the Philippine Islands, 1898-1903. By A. P. C. Griffin. Reprinted from the list of books
(with references to periodicals) on the
Philippine Islands, 1903. With some additions to 1905. Wash. Govt. Ptg. Off.
1905. 100p.   **5605**

U.S. Philippine Commission. Report of
the chief of the bureau [or division] of
archives. *In* Annual reports of the Philippine Commission, 1902-1912. Wash.
Govt. Ptg. Off. 1903-13   **5606**

Valenzuela, Jesús. History of journalism
in the Philippine Islands. Manila. The
Author. 1933. 217p.   **5607**

Vidal y Soler, Sebastian. Memoria sobre
el ramo de montes en las Islas Filipinas.
Madrid. Imp. de Aribau y C.ª 1874. (Contains: Lista de algunas obras y articulos
importantes referentes á los países del
extremo oriente; p249-96 on the Philippines)   **5608**

Vindel, Pedro. Biblioteca ultramarina;
manuscritos muchos de ellos originales
e inéditos referentes a América, China,
Filipinas, Japón y otras países. . . .
Madrid. 1917. p169-324   **5609**

—— Catálogo sistemático é ilustrado de la
Biblioteca Filipina reunida y puesta en
venta. Madrid. 1904. 444p.   **5610**

PUERTO RICO

America Foreign Law Association. Porto
Rico. (Bibliographies of foreign law ser.
5) N.Y. 1928. 10p.   **5611**

Ayala Duarte, C. Historia de la literatura
en Puerto Rico. Boletin de la Academia
venezolana. I. p310-44 (Caracas. 1934)
5611a

**Geigel y Zenón, José and Ferrer, Abelardo
Morales.** Bibliografía. Puertorriqueña.
Barcelona. Editorial Araluce. 1934. 453p.
5612

Indice de reales cédulas (Copia de un Cua-
derno apolillado, que encontré en los
Archivos de Santa Catalina cuando siendo Secretario Civil recibí orden del
Governador General Geo. W. Davis para
remitir porte de los documentos de la
Fortaleza á la Librería del Congreso en
Washington; y otro guardarlos en la Intendencia) Boletín historico de Puerto
Rico. año 1. número 1-2. p11-74 (enero-
febrero, marzo, abril 1914) (Cover period
1646-1808)   **5613**

Pedreira, Antonio S. Bibliografía Puertorriqueña (1493-1930). (Monografias de la
Universidad de Puerto Rico. serie A. estudios hispanios. num. 1) Madrid. Imp.
de la Libreria y casa editorial Hernando
(s.a.) 1932. 707p.   **5614**

—— Libros puertorriqueños de 1936. El
mundo. enero 17, 1937   **5614a**

**Puerto Rico. Agricultural Experiment Sta-
tion.** List and analytical index of publications of Porto Rico Agricultural Experiment Station (July 1900 to Mar.
1930). By Elizabeth H. Langdale (Puerto
Rico. Agricultural Experiment Station.
Circular 21) Wash. Govt. Ptg. Off. 1930.
42p.   **5615**

Rivera, Guillermo. A tentative bibliography of the belles-lettres of Porto Rico.
Cambridge. Harvard Univ. Press. 1931.
61p.   **5616**

Russell, Charles W. Report to the United
States evacuation commission—Archives
of Porto Rico—Land title papers. *In*
Military government of Porto Rico from
October 18, 1898 to April 30, 1900. Brig.
Gen. Geo. W. Davis. Wash. Govt. Ptg.
Off. 1902. p468-75   **5617**

Sama, Manuel M. Bibliografía Puerto-
Riqueña. Mayagüez. Tipografia comer-
cial-marina. 1887. 159p.   **5618**

Trelles, Carlos M. Ensayo de bibliografía
Cubana de los siglos XVII y XVIII seguido de unos apuntes para la bibliografía Dominicana y Portorriqueña. Matanzas. Imp. "El escritorio." 1907. 228p.
5619

**U.S. Library of Congress. Division of bib-
liography.** A list of books (with references to periodicals) on Porto Rico. By
A. P. C. Griffin. Wash. Govt. Ptg. Off.
1901. 55p.   **5620**

—— —— Puerto Rico: a selected list
of references. Comp. by Ann D. Brown.
Oct. 5, 1939. 50p. typ.   **5620a**

MISCELLANEOUS

Guam museum notes. Guam recorder. XIV. p19, 24, 30-1, 23, 36, 20, 34 (July-Nov. 1937) (Describes materials, including documents) **5620b**

Larson, Harold. Some recent books on the Virgin Islands. Jour. negro hist. XXIV. p467-72 (Oct. 1939) **5620c**

Lenson, R. H. The Department of Records and Accounts. [Guam] Guam recorder. XIV. p16-17, 32 (July 1937) **5620d**

Reid, Charles F. and others. Bibliography of the island of Guam. Prep. with the assistance of the Federal Works Agency, Work Projects Administration, Official project number 465-97-3-18, sub phase "American possessions," Division of professional and service projects for the city of New York. N.Y. H.W. Wilson. 1939. 102p. **5620e**

Reid, Charles F. and others. Bibliography of the Virgin Islands. Prep. with the assistance of the Federal Works Agency, Work Projects Administration . . . sub phase "American possessions," Division of professional and service projects for the city of New York. N.Y. H.W. Wilson. 1941 **5620f**

U.S. Library of Congress. Division of bibliography. A list of books (with references to periodicals) on Samoa and Guam. Comp under the direction of A. P. C. Griffin. Wash. Govt. Ptg. Off. 1901. 54p. (Supplements. July. 20, 1911. 16p. typ. Additional references. Jan. 8, 1931. 4p.) **5621**

—— —— —— A list of books (with references to periodicals) on the Danish West Indies. Comp. under the direction of A. P. C. Griffin. Wash. Govt. Ptg. Off. 1901. 18p. **5622**

—— —— —— Select list of references on Guam. June 27, 1911. 4p. typ. (Additional references. Jan. 9, 1931. 2p.) **5623**

—— —— —— Select list of references on the Panama Canal; administration, commercial aspects, etc. July 16, 1912. 18p. typ. **5624**

—— —— —— The Virgin Islands of the United States: a list of references, 1922-1936. Comp. by Helen F. Conover, under the direction of Florence S. Hellman. April 10, 1937. 12p. reprod. **5624a**

Virgin Islands of the United States. A bibliography of the Virgin Islands of the United States, formerly The Danish West Indies. St. Thomas. Govt. Ptg. Off. 1922. 11p. (Reprinted in the Governor's report for 1928.) **5625**

CHAPTER XIV

STATES

SOURCES

American Legislators' Association. Legislative digests and indexes. Chicago. The Asso. 1934. 3p. mim. **5626**

—— Publications of resolutions. Comp. by Raymond E. Manning. Chicago. The Asso. March 31, 1934. 3p. mim. **5627**

—— State manuals. Chicago. The Asso. July 7, 1934. 8p. mim. **5628**

American State Reports. Table of cases reported in volumes 1-72, inclusive, of the American state reports, with an index to the principal notes embraced in those volumes. San Francisco. Bancroft-Whitney. 1900. 243p. **5628a**

Ames, Herman V. Résumé of the archives situations in the several states in 1907. Am. Hist. Asso. rep. 1907. I. p163-87 **5629**

—— State documents on federal relations; the states and the United States. Phila. Univ. of Pennsylvania. 1911. 320p. (Issued in pamphlets, 1900-1906; contains numerous lists of references) **5630**

Anderson Galleries, Inc. American library of W. H. Winters; a remarkable collection of early acts, journals, laws, etc. of Arkansas, California, Connecticut, etc.... N.Y. 1923. 125p. **5631**

Bowker, Richard R. State publications; a provisional list of the official publications of the several states of the United States from their organization. N.Y. Publishers' weekly. 1899-1908. 4v. **5632**

Bradley, Phillips. Legislative recording in the United States. Am. pol. science rev. XXIX. p74-83 (Feb. 1935) **5633**

Campbell, D. W. and Pollock, W. C. A digest of the decisions of the Supreme Courts of the states and territories of the arid region and of the United States Circuit and Supreme Courts in cases including questions relative to the use and control of water in that region. Wash. D.C. 1889. 59p. **5633a**

Check list of current American state reports and session laws exclusive of side reports. Law lib. jour. XXXIII. p162-6 (July 1940) (Revised from time to time) **5633b**

Chicago. Joint Reference Library. State tax surveys: a bibliography. Chicago. 1935. 10p. mim. **5633c**

Chicago. University. Library. Official publications relating to American state constitutional conventions. N.Y. H. W. Wilson. 1936. 97p. **5633d**

Columbia University. Legislative drafting research fund. Index digest of state constitutions. Prepared for the New York State Constitutional Convention Commission. N.Y. State Constitutional Convention Comn. 1915. 1546p. **5634**

Dersheim, Elsie. An outline of American state literature. Lawrence. Kansas World Co. 1921. 187p. **5635**

Durrell, Harold Clarke. The centralization of vital records in the various states. New Eng. hist. geneal. reg. XC. p9-31 (Jan. 1936) **5635a**

Dutcher, George Matthew. Bibliography of contemporary editions of the constitutions of the original thirteen states together with the Declaration of Independence and the Articles of Confederation, as authorized for publication by the Congress of the Confederation in 1783. 77 Home Avenue, Middletown, Conn. In progress **5635b**

Gates, Charles M. The administration of state archives. Am. archivist. I. p130-41 (July 1938) *Also in* Pacific northw. quar. XXIX. p27-39 (Jan. 1938) **5635c**

Gill, Theodore. Bibliography of reports of [state] fishery commissions. Senate miscellaneous document no. 74. 42 Cong. 3 sess. 1874. Ser. 1547. p774-84 **5636**

Griffith, William. Law books of the several states. *In* Annual law register of the United States. Burlington, N.J. David Allinson. 1822. IV. p1448-51 **5637**

Hale, Mrs. Carolyn Leavitt. Sources of current information on state government functions. (Univ. of California. M.S. thesis) [Berkeley, Calif.] 1939. 113p. typ. **5637a**

Hodgson, James Goodwin. The official publications of American counties: a union list; with an introduction on the collecting of county publications. Fort Collins, Colo. Colorado State College. 1937. 594p. mim. **5637b**

Holbrook, Franklin F. The collection of state war service records. Am. hist. rev. XXV. p72-8 (Oct. 1919) **5638**

John Crerar Library. Bibliography of official rosters, state manuals, state yearbooks, etc., currently issued. Comp. by Jerome K. Wilcox. Chicago. The Lib. 1930. 29p. typ. **5639**

Kahn, Herman. Digest of state laws pertaining to the protection and preservation of historical and archaeological sites and historical records. Wash. D.C. National Park Service, Branch of historic sites and buildings. 1937. ms. **5639a**

Kuhlman, Augustus Frederick. The need for a checklist-bibliography of state publications. *In* American Library Association. Committee on public documents. Public documents; state, municipal, federal, foreign; policies concerning issuance, distribution and use. Chicago. Am. Lib. Asso. 1934. p65-80 (*Also in* Lib. quar. V. p31-58. 1935) **5640**

McKinley, Albert E. Progress in the collection of war records by state war history organizations. Am. Hist. Asso. rep. 1920. p145-54 **5641**

Magee, Ernest De Los. A digest of the decisions of the courts of last resort of the several states, from the year 1896 to the year 1900, contained in American state reports, volumes 49 to 72, inclusive, to which is prefixed an alphabetical index to the notes therein contained, and a table of cases reported in vols. 1 to 72, inclusive. San Francisco. Bancroft-Whitney. 1900. 1536p. **5641a**

—— Index-digest to the monographic notes in the American state reports, volumes 1 to 91. San Francisco. Bancroft-Whitney Co. 1903. 267p. **5641b**

Massachusetts. State Library. Hand-list of legislative sessions and session laws, statutory revisions, compilations, codes, etc., and constitutional conventions of the United States and its possessions and of the several states to May 1912. Pub. by the trustees. Prepared by Charles J. Babbitt under direction of Charles F. D. Belden. Boston. Wright & Potter Ptg. Co. 1912. 634p. **5642**

Morse, Lewis Wilbur. A check list of judicial council reports from their beginning through 1935. [N.Y. 1936] 7p. (Reprinted with additions to Illinois, New Jersey, New York and Oregon, from Law Lib. jour. XXIX. Jan. 1936) **5643**

—— Historical outline and bibliography of attorneys general reports and opinions from their beginning through 1936. Law lib. jour. XXX. p37-247 (April 1937) (Includes states, territories, United States) **5643a**

National Association of State Libraries. Public document clearing house committee. Check-list of collected state documents. (To be prepared) **5644**

—— —— Check-list of constitutional conventions and journals. (To be prepared) **5645**

—— —— Check-list of legislative journals of states of the United States of America. Comp. by Grace E. MacDonald. Providence. Oxford Press. 1938. 274p. **5645a**

—— —— Check-list of Senate and House journals. (To be prepared) **5646**

—— —— Check-list of session laws. Comp. by Grace E. MacDonald. N.Y. H. W. Wilson. 1936. 266p. **5647**

—— —— Check-list of state departmental publications. (To be prepared) **5648**

—— —— Check-list of statutes of states of the United States of America including revisions, compilations, digests, codes and indexes. Comp. by Grace E. MacDonald. Providence. Oxford Press. 1937. 147p. **5648a**

—— —— Preliminary check-list of legislative journals. Comp. by Grace E. MacDonald. Providence. Oxford Press. 1937. 245p. **5648b**

—— —— Preliminary check-list of session laws, 1850-1933. Comp. by Grace E. MacDonald. N.Y. H.W. Wilson. 1934. 39p. **5648c**

—— —— Preliminary check-list of statutes and compilations. (In preparation) **5649**

National Bureau of Casualty and Surety Underwriters. Library. Official state regulations, orders, advisory pamphlets, and labor laws relating to safety. Monthly labor rev. XXX. p481-94 (Feb. 1930) **5650**

National Education Association of the United States. Research division. State school legislation—bibliography (important publications issued. . . January 1, 1934-) [Wash. D.C. 1934-] **5650a**

New Jersey State Bar Association. Catalogue of an exhibit of the early laws of the several states in the Union, consisting of the colonial laws, the first territorial laws, and the first laws of each of the states represented. . . . n.p. n.p. [1931] 16p. **5651**

New York. Public Library. Check list of United States state documents in the New York Public Library relating to finance. N.Y. Pub. Lib. bul. VI. p293-314 (Aug. 1902) **5652**

New York. State Library. Comparative summary and index of state legislation in 1890-1908. N.Y. State Lib. bul. legislation no. 1-38 (Feb. 1891-Sept. 1909) **5653**

Official cumulative index to state legislation; a complete record and a numerical and subject index of all bills introduced in all state legislatures. N.Y. National Asso. of State Lib. and Am. Asso. of Law Lib. 1915. 658p. **5653a**

Reece, Ernest J. State documents for libraries. Urbana. The Univ. of Illinois. 1915. 163p. **5654**

Review of judicial council reports. American Judicature Society jour. XIV- (June 1930-) **5654a**

Sampson, F. A. States publications of archives. Mo. hist. rev. VII. p38-40 (Oct. 1912) **5654b**

Shearer, Augustus H. A list of official publications of American state constitutional conventions, 1776-1916. Comp. for use in the Newberry Library (Publication no. 6) Chicago. Newberry Lib. 1917. 39p. (Earlier edition in Publication no. 4) **5655**

Singewald, Karl. Progress in the collection of war records by state war history associations. Am. Hist. Asso. rep. 1920. p135-45 **5655a**

State publications . . . 1884 [- 1895]. *In* American catalogue . . . 1884-1890, 1890-1895. Comp. by R.R. Bowker and others. N.Y. Publishers' Wkly. 1891, 1896. p265-94, 63-100   **5655b**

State unemployment compensation reports received; complete list of published annual reports of state unemployment compensation agencies received by the Social Security Board. Soc. security bul. II. p90-2 (Aug. 1939); III. p84-6 (Oct. 1940) **5655c**

Swan, R. T. Summary of present state of legislation of states and territories relative to custody and supervision of public records. Am. Hist. Asso. rep. 1906. II. p13-21   **5656**

Thompson, Violet M. E. State planning board publications. Planning forum. II. p19-26 (June 1938)   **5656a**

Torbert, William S. Table of cases alphabetically arranged as to the several states in the American decisions, 100 vols.; American reports, 60 vols.; American state reports, 100 vols., showing the cases to which notes are appended . . . also list of notes in the above vols. . . . by A. C. Freeman. San Francisco. Bancroft-Whitney. 1905. 754p.   **5656b**

U.S. Bureau of Agricultural Economics. Library. List of state official serial publications containing material on agricultural economics. Comp. by Esther M. Colvin under the direction of Mary G. Lacy (Agricultural economics bibliog. no. 38) Wash. D.C. July 1932. 219p. mim.   **5657**

—— —— —— State and federal publications dealing with the marketing of agricultural products; a list of references to the printed publications of state and federal departments of agriculture, markets, etc., issued since 1924. Comp. by Louise O. Bercaw. Wash. D.C. April 26, 1930. 61p.   **5658**

U.S. Bureau of labor statistics. Bibliography: official state regulations, orders, advisory pamphlets, and labor laws relating to safety. Monthly labor rev. XXX. p481-94 (Feb. 1930)   **5658a**

U.S. Congress. House of Representatives. Perpetuation and preservation of the archives and public records of the several states and territories and of the United States. House rep. no. 1767. 56 Cong. 1 sess. 1900. Ser. 4027. 6p.   **5659**

U.S. Department of Justice. Library. Want list of session laws (state and territorial). Wash. Govt. Ptg. Off. 1912. 10p.   **5660**

U.S. Library of Congress. Report from the librarian of Congress, transmitting in compliance with a resolution of the Senate, a catalogue of all the laws, and of all the legislative and executive journals and documents, of the several states and territories, now in the library, December 27. 1839. Senate document no. 16. 26 Cong. 1 sess. Ser. 355. 14p.   **5661**

—— —— **Division of accessions.** Duplicate session laws and state reports available for exchange, January 1912. Wash. Govt. Ptg. Off. 1912. 53p.   **5662**

—— —— —— Want list; session laws and state reports, 1912. Wash. Govt. Ptg. Off. 1911. 27p.   **5663**

U.S. Library of Congress. Division of bibliography. List of the corporation laws of the states. Nov. 21, 1910. 9p. typ. **5664**

—— —— **Division of documents.** Duplicate list of state and territorial session laws, journals and collected documents. Wash. Govt. Ptg. Off. 1903. 14p.   **5665**

—— —— —— Monthly check-list of state publications, 1910-. Wash. Govt. Ptg. Off. 1912-   **5666**

—— —— —— Tentative check list of state publications relating to the European war, 1917-1919. *In* Monthly list of state publications. Wash. Govt. Ptg. Off. 1920. X. p579-648   **5667**

—— —— —— Want list of state and territorial session laws, journals and collected documents. Wash. Govt. Ptg. Off. 1903. 28p.   **5668**

—— —— **Law library.** List of session laws (1800-1899) in the law Library of Congress. n.d. 95p. typ.   **5669**

—— —— —— List of session laws prior to 1800 in the Law Library of Congress. n.d. 69p. typ.   **5670**

—— —— **Legislative reference bureau.** State law index; an index and digest to the legislation of the states of the United States enacted during the bienniums, 1925/26- . Wash. Govt. Ptg. Off. 1929-   **5671**

—— —— **Legislative reference service.** Digest of outstanding state legislation on agriculture, 1935-39. Wash. Govt. Ptg. Off. 1940. 113p.   **5671a**

—— —— **State law index.** Current ideas in 1938 State legislatures; a review of reported bills introduced between January 1 and March 31, in legislatures meeting in 1938. Comp. by Margaret W. Stewart. (State law digest, Report no. 1) Wash. Govt. Ptg. Off. 1938. 26p.   **5671b**

—— —— —— Digest of outstanding state legislation on agriculture, 1935-1939. (State law digest rep. no. 4) Wash. D.C. 1940. 113p.   **5671c**

—— —— —— Sources of information on legislation of 1937-1938; a bibliographical list of published material reporting legislative bills and enactments of 1937 and 1938. Comp. by Jacob Lyons. (State law index, special report, no. 1) Wash. Govt. Ptg. Off. 1938. 38p.   **5671d**

U.S. National Resources Board. Bibliography of state planning reports in the library of the National Resources Board. *In* National resources committee. State planning; a review of activities and progress, June 1935. Wash. Govt. Ptg. Off. 1935. p294-305 (Reprinted in Plan Age. I. p21-8)   **5672**

U.S. National Resources Committee. Library. Bibliography of reports by state and regional planning organizations received in the Library of the National Resources Committee. Wash. D.C. 1937- . no. 1- **5672a**

Washington (state). Department of social security. Studies and reports in the field of social welfare conducted by state-wide and local agencies in the 48 states, 1932-1939. Comp. by E. M. Cull. (Monograph no. 35) Olympia. 1940. 52p. mim. **5672b**

Wire, George E. Reprints of colonial, territorial or state session laws. Worcester County Law Lib. annual rep. 1910. p13-19 (Reprinted in large part in Law lib. jour. IV. p31-5. Jan. 1912) **5673**

SECONDARY

Alvord, Clarence W. The relation of the state to historical work. Minnesota hist. bul. I. p3-25 (Feb. 1915) **5674**

American Antiquarian Society. Memorandum of local histories in the library of the American Antiquarian Society. [Worcester. Hamilton. 1869] 15p. **5675**

American Legislators' Association. Interstate Legislative Reference Bureau. Recent publications on legislative problems. Chicago. Interstate Legislative Reference Bureau. 1932- mim. **5676**

Bradford, Thomas Lindsley. Bibliographer's manual of American history, containing an account of all state, territory, town and county histories relating to the United States. . . . Revised by S. V. Henkels. Phila. Henkels. 1907-10. 5v. **5677**

Bradley, Phillips. Opportunity and challenge, a discussion of state year-books. State governments. IX. p122-5 (June 1936) **5677a**

Carnegie Endowment for International Peace. Library. Interstate compacts. M. Alice Matthews, librarian (Brief references list no. 2) Wash. D.C. 1938. 8p. mim. **5678**

Clark, Arthur H., Co. The United States; a catalogue of books relating to the history of its various states, counties and cities and territories arranged alphabetically by states. . . . Cleveland. Arthur H. Clark. 1928. 411p. **5679**

Council of State Governments. State tax surveys; bibliography. Prepared for the Council of State Governments by the Joint reference library. [Chicago. 1935] 10p. mim. **5680**

Ebeling, Christoph Daniel. Erdbeschreibung und geschichte von Amerika; die Vereinigten Staaten von Nordamerika. Hamburg. C.E. Bohn. 1793-1816. 7v. (Lists of maps precede the descriptions of the states) **5680a**

Federal Writers' Project. American guide series. Published variously, different publishers. 1937- (Guides to states, cities, regions, trails, etc., containing bibliographies) **5680b**

—— Catalog: American guide series. Wash. Govt. Ptg. Off. 1938. 31p. **5680c**

Fox, Dixon Ryan. State history. Pol. science quar. XXXVI. p572-85 (Dec. 1921); XXXVII. p99-118 (March 1922) **5681**

Graves, William Brooke. Reference list on interstate compacts and interstate cooperation. Chicago? 1938. 11p. **5681a**

Griffin, Appleton Prentiss Clark. Index of articles upon American local history, in historical collections in the Boston Public Library. (Bibliographies of special subjects no. 2) Boston. The Trustees. 1889. 225p. (Originally in the Boston Public Library bulletin, V-VIII, 1883-89) **5682**

—— Index of the literature of American local history, in collections published in 1890-95 (with some others). Boston. C. H. Heintzemann. 1896. 151p. **5683**

Grosvenor Library. An index-catalogue of books in the department of local history and genealogy. Buffalo. The Lib. 1908. 67p. **5684**

Harper, Francis Perego. Catalogue of a remarkable collection of books on the middle states; state, county and town, with other historical works relating to New York, New Jersey and Pennsylvania. . . . N.Y. 1906 **5685**

Laurent, Eleanore V. Legislative reference work in the United States. Chicago. Council of State Governments. 1939. p26-35. mim. **5685a**

Ludewig, Herman E. The literature of American local history; a bibliographical essay. N.Y. R. Craighead. 1846. 180p. (Supplement in Literary world, Feb. 19, 1848, from which it was extracted) **5686**

National Society of the Colonial Dames of America. Book guide to the separate states of these United States of America. . . May 1933. [Providence, R.I. E. A. Johnson] 1933. [51]p. **5687**

New York. Public Library. Check list of American county and state histories in the New York Public Library. N.Y. Pub. Lib. bul. V. p434-40 (Nov. 1901) **5688**

Perkins, Frederic Beecher. Check list for American local history. Reprinted with additions from the Bulletins of the Boston Public Library [III-IV. Jan. 1876-Jan. 1879] Boston. Rockwell & Churchill. 1876. 198p. **5689**

Peterson, Clarence Stewart. Bibliography of county histories of the 2982 counties in the 48 states. N.Y. 1935. [39]p. typ. **5690**

Pfankuchen, L. Doctoral disserations in political science: American state and local government and politics. Am. pol. sci. rev. XXXIV. p772-4 (Aug. 1940) **5690a**

Read, William A. Research in American place names, 1920-1926. Zeits. ortsnamenforschung. IV. p185-91. 1928 **5690b**

Recent publications on legislative problems, April 11, 1938- . Chicago. Council of State Governments. 1938- **5690c**

Sparlin, Estal Earnest. The administration of public printing in the States. (University of Missouri. Ph.D. thesis, 1937) [Columbia. 1937] 120p. (*Also in* Univ. of Missouri stud. XX, 4, Oct. 1937)   **5690d**

Stose, G. W. and LaForge, Laurence. List of geologic maps of states. *In* National Research Council. Division of geology and geography. Annual report, 1928-29. Wash. Govt. Ptg. Off. 1929. appendix S, exhibit A, 6p.   **5690e**

Tanner, Henry S. Geographical memoir. *In* A new American atlas. Phila. H. S. Tanner. 1823. p1-18 (Early state maps of the United States)   **5690f**

Thornton, Ella May. State author collections. Am. lib. asso. bul. XXIII. p398-400 (1929)   **5690g**

U.S. Bureau of Agricultural Economics. Library. State measures for the relief of agricultural indebtedness in the United States 1932 and 1933. Comp. by Louise O. Bercaw, Margaret T. Olcott and Mary F. Carpenter under the direction of Mary G. Lacy (Agricultural economics bibliog. no. 45) Wash. D.C. 1933. 64p. mim.   **5691**

—— —— —— State measures for the relief of agricultural indebtedness in the United States, 1933 and 1934. Comp. by Margaret T. Olcott and Louise O. Bercaw under the direction of Mary G. Lacy. (Agricultural economics bibliog. no. 53) Wash. D.C. June 1934. 402p. mim.   **5692**

U.S. Federal Emergency Relief Administration. Library. Non-institutional relief measures of the states and territories. Comp. by Adelaide R. Hasse. [Wash. D.C. 1934] unpag. mim.   **5693**

U.S. Library of Congress. Division of bibliography. Brief list of references on defaulted state, county, township and municipal bonds. March 3, 1922. 4p. mim.   **5694**

—— —— —— List of official state historical departments and offices. April 9, 1920. 4p. typ.   **5695**

U.S. Office of Education. Library. Research and investigations reported by state departments of education and state education associations, 1932-33. By Ruth A. Gray (Circular 127) Wash. Govt. Ptg. Off. 1934. 24p.; Same. 1934-35 (Circular 141) 21p.; Same. 1935-36 (Circular 160) 21p.   **5696**

—— —— —— List of educational research studies of state departments of education and state education associations, 1930-33. By Edith A. Wright and Ruth A. Gray (Office of Education. Circular 31, 44, 63, 127) Wash. Govt. Ptg. Off. 1931-34. 40, 43, 44, 24p. (Circular 127 by R. A. Gray)   **5697**

U.S. Office of Experiment Stations. Library. List of extension publications of the state agricultural colleges. Wash. D.C. 1919-31. mim. Monthly, discontinued)   **5698**

Wilcox, Jerome Kear. Publications of new state agencies and sources of information concerning these new state functions. *In* American Library Association. Committee on public documents. Public documents, 1937. Chicago. Am. Lib. Asso. 1937. p54-139   **5698a**

Wilcox, Jerome Kear, ed. Manual on the use of state publications. Sponsored by the Committee on public documents of the American Library Association. Chicago. Am. Lib. Asso. 1940. 342p.   **5698b**

Woodward, Charles L. American topographs "locals" books and pamphlets relating to places. N.Y. Charles L. Woodward. n.d. 65p.   **5699**

SOCIETIES

American Council of Learned Societies. A catalogue of publications in the humanities by American learned societies, Jan. 1932- . Wash. D.C. 1932-   **5700**

American Council of Learned Societies and the Social Science Research Council. Survey of activities of American agencies in relation to materials for research in the social sciences and the humanities. Comp. by Franklin F. Holbrook. Wash. D.C. N.Y. Pub. by the cooperating councils. 1932. 184p. planog.   **5701**

American Historical Association. Classified list of publications of the American Historical Association, 1884-1912. Am. Hist. Asso. Rep. 1912. p305-39   **5702**

—— Report of Committee on methods of organization and work on the part of state and local historical societies. Reuben G. Thwaites, chairman, Benjamin F. Shambaugh, Franklin L. Riley. Am. Hist. Asso. rep. 1905. I. p249-325   **5703**

Bowker, Richard Rogers. Publications of societies; a provisional list of the publications of American scientific, literary, and other societies from their organization. N.Y. Publishers' weekly. 1899. 181p.   **5704**

Boyd, Julian P. State and local historical societies of the United States. Am. hist. rev. XL. p10-37 (Oct. 1934)   **5705**

Carnegie Institution of Washington. Handbook of learned societies and institutions: America. Comp. by David Thompson. (Carnegie Inst. of Wash. Publication no. 39) Wash. D.C. 1908. 592p.   **5706**

Clark, A. Howard. List of publications of the American Historical Association, 1885-1902, and of the American Society of Church History, 1888-1897, contents of American historical review, 1895-1902. Am. Hist. Asso. rep. 1902. I. p575-639   **5707**

Conference of Historical Societies. Historical societies in the United States and Canada; a handbook. Indianapolis. Conference of Hist. Societies. 1936. 136p.   **5708**

Griffin, A. P. C. Bibliography of American historical societies (The United States and the Dominion of Canada). Am. Hist. Asso. rep. 1905. 1374p.   **5709**

Homes, Henry A., Fletcher, W. I. and others. Historical societies in the United States. *In* U.S. Bureau of Education. Public libraries in the United States of America; their history, condition and management. Wash. Govt. Ptg. Off. 1876. p312-77 **5710**

Kelly, James. Learned societies and other literary associations, with a list of their publications, 1861-1871. *In* The American catalogue of books published in the United States from Jan. 1861 to Jan. 1871. N.Y. John Wiley & Son. 1871. I. p283-303; II. p466-88 **5711**

Publications of societies... 1884-1895. *In* American catalogue... 1884-1890, 1890-1895. Comp. by R. R. Bowker and others. N.Y. Publishers' Wkly. 1891, 1896. p297-310, 103-30 **5711a**

Rhees, William J. Manual of public libraries, institutions, and societies in the United States and British provinces of North America. Phila. J. B. Lippincott. 1859. 687p. **5712**

U.S. Office of Education. Library. A handbook of educational associations and foundations in the United States. (Bul. 1926. no. 16) Wash. Govt. Ptg. Off. 1926. 82p. **5713**

Weeks, Stephen B. A preliminary list of American learned and educational societies. *In* U.S. Commissioner of Education. Rep. 1893-94. II. p1493-661 **5714**

SECTIONS

Confederate States of America

Bauer, Ignacio. Lista cronologica de documentos en contrados en la cartera C.S.A., iniciales que significan 'Confederate States of America', y abandonados por el delegado del presidente Jefferson Davis en España, Mr. P. A. Rost. Real Acad. Hist. bol. LXXVI. p161-2 (1920) **5715**

Boston Athenaeum. Confederate literature; a list of books and newspapers, maps, music and miscellaneous matter printed in the South during the Confederacy, now in the Boston Athenaeum. Prepared by Charles N. Baxter and James M. Dearborn. Boston. Boston Athenaeum. 1917. 213p. **5716**

Bruce, Kathleen. Confederate and reconstruction archives unearthed in Richmond by the Survey of Federal Archives in Virginia. The W.P.A. record in Virginia, Feb. 1937, p3, 14 **5716a**

Callahan, J. Morton. The Confederate diplomatic archives—The Pickett papers. So. Atlantic quar. II. p1-9 (Jan. 1903) **5717**

Campbell, Albert H. The lost war maps of the Confederates. Century. XXXV. p479-81 (Jan. 1888) **5717a**

Cappon, Lester J. A note on Confederate ordnance records. Am. Mil. Inst. jour. IV. p94-102 (Summer 1940) **5717b**

Christian, George L. General Lee's headquarters records and papers—the present location of some of these. Sou. Hist. Soc. pap. n.s. VI. p229-31. 1923 **5717c**

Confederate Memorial Literary Society, Richmond, Va. Southern Historical Manuscripts Commission. A calendar of Confederate papers, with a bibliography of some Confederate publications; preliminary report of the Southern Historical Manuscripts Commission. Prepared under the direction of the Confederate Memorial Literary Society by Douglas Southall Freeman. Richmond, Va. Confederate Museum. 1908. 620p. **5718**

Confederate States of America. Laws, statutes, etc. A list of the titles of the several editions of the session laws and statutes at large. *In* Laws and joint resolutions of the last session (Nov. 7, 1864-Mar. 18, 1865) together with the secret acts of previous congresses. Ed. by Charles W. Ramsdell. Durham, N.C. Duke Univ. Press. 1941. p. xx-xxiii **5718a**

Dauber and Pine Bookshops, Inc. The Confederacy, including southern poetry, general literature, first editions. [etc.] Zorn collection (Catalogue no. 190) [N.Y. 1936] 70p. **5718b**

Freeman, Douglas Southall. The South to posterity; an introduction to the writings of Confederate history. N.Y. C. Scribner's Sons. 1939. 235p. **5718c**

Hamer, Philip M. Records of the Confederacy located by the Survey of Federal Archives. Paper read before the Southern Historical Association, Nashville, November 20, 1936 [Wash. D.C. The National Archives] ms. **5718d**

Harwell, Richard B. Confederate collection. Emory alumnus. XVII (Jan. 1941) (The Keith M. Read imprints) **5718e**

Henkels, Stan V. Rare Confederate books and pamphlets; publications on Confederate history. . . . Phila. [1913] 41p. **5719**

Hesseltine, William B. The propaganda literature of Confederate prisons. Jour. of south. hist. I. p56-66 (Feb. 1935) **5720**

Historical Records Survey. Massachusetts. A calendar of the Ryder collection of Confederate archives at Tufts College. Boston, Mass. 1940. 168p. reprod. typ. **5720a**

Irvine, Dallas D. The fate of Confederate archives. Am. hist. rev. XLIV. p823-41 (July 1939) **5720b**

Leiter, Levi Ziegler. Confederate States of America. *In* The Leiter library; a catalogue of the books, manuscripts and maps relating principally to America, collected by the late Levi Ziegler Leiter. With collations and bibliographical notes by Hugh Alexander Morrison. Wash. Priv. printed. 1907. p241-341 **5721**

London, Lawrence. A bibliography of Confederate publications, omitting Confederate States of America and publications of the individual states. Univ. of North Carolina. Chapel Hill, N.D. In progress **5721a**

Mohrhardt, Foster Edward. Official publications of the Confederate states. Washington and Lee Univ. Lexington, Va. In progress   **5721b**

Morrison, Hugh Alexander. A bibliography of the official publications of the Confederate States of America. Bibliog. Soc. of Amer. pap. III. p92-132. 1908 **5722**

Publication of Confederate rosters by the Federal government. Southern Hist. Asso. pub. VII. p149-58, 410-13 (May, Sept. 1903)   **5722a**

Randolph, J. W., Company. Catalogue of scarce Confederate publications (new and second-hand) and books relating to the war between the states. . . . Richmond, Va. 1897. 17p.   **5723**

Robinson, William M., Jr. Confederate judicial records. Am. archivist. IV. p117-21 (April 1941)   **5723a**

—— The second congress of the Confederate States of America; enactments at its second and last session. Am. hist. rev. XLI. p306-17 (Jan. 1936)   **5724**

Snowden, Yates. War time publications (1861-1865) from the press of Walker, Evans & Cogswell Co., Charleston, S.C.; an addendum to one hundred years of Wecco. Charleston, S.C. Walker Evans & Cogswell Co. 1922. 30p. photostat **5725**

Southern Historical Society, Richmond, Va. Records of the Confederate armies in possession of the Southern Historical Society, at Richmond, Va. Printed from catalogue furnished by Rev. Wm. Jones. . . . Wash. D.C.. War Records Publication Off. 1880. 58p.   **5726**

Sumner, John Osborne. Materials for the history of the government of the Southern Confederacy. Am. Hist. Asso. pap. IV. p331-45. 1890   **5726a**

U.S. Library of Congress. List of books in the Library of Congress published in the Confederate States, 1860-1865. (MS. in longhand in the Rare book room, undated) 18p.   **5727**

U.S. Office of Naval Records and Library. List of Confederate documents, papers, and logs lent . . . by individuals—Papers of the Confederate State Department— Confederate State Department correspondence—Proclamations, appointments, etc., of President Davis, February 12, 1861 to January 28, 1865—State Department correspondence with diplomatic agents, 1861-1865. *In* Official records of the Union and Confederate Navies in the War of the Rebellion. Wash. Govt. ptg. off. 1922. Series II, vol. 3, p18-89 **5727a**

Virginia. State Library, Richmond. A list of the official publications of the Confederate States government in the Virginia State Library and the library of the Confederate Memorial Literary Society. Va. State Lib. bul. IV. no. 1 (Jan. 1911) 45p.   **5728**

Waters, Willard O. Confederate imprints in the Henry E. Huntington Library, unrecorded in previously published bibliographies of such material. Bibliog. Soc. of Amer. pap. XXIII. p18-109. 1929 (Also reprinted in 1930)   **5729**

Weeks, Stephen Beauregard. Confederate text-books (1861-1865); a preliminary bibliography. Wash. Govt. Ptg. Off. 1900. (Reprinted from the U.S. Bureau of Education. Report of the commissioner of education for 1898-99. p1139-55)   **5730**

District of Columbia

Baker, Marcus. Surveys and maps of the District of Columbia. Nation. geog. mag. VI. p149-78 (Nov. 1894)   **5730a**

Brigham, Clarence S. District of Columbia—bibliography of the American newspapers, 1690-1820. Am. Antiq. Soc. proc. n.s. XXIII. p343-691 (Oct. 1913)   **5731**

Bryan, William Bogart. Bibliography of the District of Columbia; being a list of books, maps, and newspapers, including articles in magazines and other publications to 1898. Prepared for the Columbia Historical Society. Wash. Govt. Ptg. Off. 1900. 211p. (Senate document. no. 61. 56 Cong. 1 sess. Ser. no. 3848) **5732**

Columbia Historical Society. Index to authors and titles of the Records of the Columbia Historical Society, District of Columbia, volumes 1 to 33-34 inclusive, 1897-1932. Comp. by Ella J. Morrison. Wash. D.C. Roberts. 1933. 18p.   **5733**

Griffin, A. P. C. Issues of the District of Columbia press in 1800, '01-'02. Columbia Hist. Soc. rec. IV. p32-74. 1901 **5734**

—— —— Inventory of the church archives of the District of Columbia: The Protestant Episcopal Church, Diocese of Washington: vol. I-II. Wash. D.C. Dec., April 1940. 309, 122p. mim.   **5734a**

—— —— Inventory of the municipal archives of the District of Columbia. Wash. D.C. 1940- . mim. Board of Accountancy, Board of Examiners and Registrars of Architects, Board of Barber Examiners, Board of Cosmetology. April 1940. 31p. **5734b**

McMurtrie, Douglas C. The beginnings of printing in the District of Columbia. Somerville, N.J. Priv. printed. 1933. (Extract from Americana, XXVII. p265-89. Third quarter. 1933)   **5735**

—— History of the District of Columbia press up to 1815. (Photostat in the Library of Congress. Periodical division) **5736**

Meyers, William Frederick. The comprehensive general index of the laws of the District of Columbia in force January 1, 1912. Wash. D.C. L.G. Kelly. 1912. 421p. **5736a**

Millington, Yale O. A list of newspapers published in the District of Columbia, 1820-1850. Bibliog. Soc. of Amer. pap. XIX. pt. 1-2. p43-65. 1927 **5737**

Phillips, Philip Lee. List of maps and views of Washington and District of Columbia in the Library of Congress. Wash. Govt. Ptg. Off. 1900. 77p. **5737a**

Slausson, Allan B. District of Columbia newspapers compiled from all available sources. 1904. (MS. in the Library of Congress. Periodical division) **5738**

Torbert, William Sydenham. A comprehensive index to the amended code of laws for the District of Columbia, with a table indicating sections repealed and amended. Wash. D.C. 1903. 86p. **5738a**

U.S. Library of Congress. Division of bibliography. History and description of Washington, D.C.; a bibliographical list. March 10, 1927. 8p. typ. (Supplement. Feb. 21, 1936. 17p. typ.) **5739**

—— —— —— List of documents relating to the District of Columbia (Its relation to the Federal government with special reference to the half-and-half system, and finance). March 16, 1915. 10p. typ. **5740**

—— —— —— List of references on the District of Columbia (Its relations to the federal government, with special reference to the half-and-half system and finance). March 15, 1915. 6p. typ. **5741**

—— —— —— A list of references on the White House. Nov. 20, 1924. 4p. typ. **5742**

—— —— —— Politics and government in the District of Columbia with special reference to suffrage: a bibliographical list. 1940. 14p. typ. **5743**

—— —— —— Social life in Washington: a bibliographical list. March 17, 1930. 17p. typ. **5744**

—— —— —— The White House: a bibliographical list. Comp. by Ann Duncan Brown under the direction of Florence S. Hellman. Wash. 1939. 42p. mim. **5744a**

—— —— Division of maps. A descriptive list of maps and views of Washington and District of Columbia including Mount Vernon. By Philip Lee Phillips. [Wash. 1916]. typ. **5744b**

Vedel, Carina Annette. Historic and picturesque Washington with its environs; a contribution to a bibliography. (Univ. of Wisconsin. Lib. School) [Madison, Wis.] June 1923. 28p. typ. (carbon) **5745**

Washington, D.C. Public Library. Index to The Rambler; a series of articles on Washington and vicinity contributed to the Evening star by John Harry Shannon. 4 volumes 1912-1927. Wash. D.C. Pub. Lib. 1930. 73p. typ. (carbon) (Citations in this index refer to volume and page in scrap books in charge of the Washingtoniana section of the District of Columbia Public Library—note from cover) **5746**

Mississippi Valley

Blegen, Theodore C. Some aspects of historical work under the New Deal. Miss. Valley hist. rev. XXI. p195-206 (Sept. 1934) (Historical surveys) **5746a**

Buck, Solon J. The progress and possibilities of Mississippi Valley history. Chron. Oklahoma. I. p227-43 (June 1923) **5747**

—— Some materials for the social history of the Mississippi Valley in the nineteenth century. Miss. Valley Hist. Asso. Proc. IV. p139-51 (1910-11) **5748**

Davis, William Morris. Maps of the Mississippi River. By the Mississippi River Commission. Jour. school geog. V. p379-82. 1901 **5748a**

Gregory, Winifred. Improvement of the Upper Mississippi river; a bibliography. Bul. of the Affiliated Engineering Societies of Minnesota. III. p218-40 (Dec. 1918) **5749**

Historical news and comments. Miss. Valley hist. rev. I- . June 1914- (Includes notices of publications) **5749a**

Lynch, William O. The Mississippi Valley and its history. Miss. Valley hist. rev. XXVI. p3-20 (June 1939) **5749b**

Mississippi Valley Historical Association. The Mississippi Valley historical review; an index to volumes I-XV, 1914-1929. Miss. Valley Hist. Asso. [Cedar Rapids, Ia. Torch Press] 1932. 137p. **5750**

—— A topical guide to The Mississippi Valley historical review, Volumes I-XIX, 1914-1932 and The Mississippi Valley Historical Association proceedings, volumes I-XI, 1907-1924. Comp. by Charles H. Norby and Walker D. Wyman under the direction of Louis Pelzer. n.p. The Miss. Valley Hist. Asso. 1934. 88p. **5751**

Mississippi Valley historical review; a journal of American history; cumulative index to volumes XVI-XXV, June 1929 through March 1939. Comp. by Bertha E. Josephson. Cedar Rapids, Ia. Torch Press. 1940. 209p. **5751a**

St. Louis. Public Library. A list of books upon Louisiana territory to 1821. St. Louis Pub. Lib. monthly bul. n.s. I. p3-9 (March 1903) **5752**

U.S. Engineer School. Library. Geology of the Mississippi Valley south of Cairo, the climate of the Mississippi Valley, its change in the past and predictions for the future; a bibliography of books and articles on the subjects in English. Prep. by Henry E. Haferkorn. [Wash.] Army War College. 1927 **5752a**

—— —— —— The Mississippi River and Valley; a bibliography of books, pamphlets and articles in periodicals, together with an index. Prepared under the direction of the Chief of Engineers, U.S. Army, by Henry E. Haferkorn. Fort Humphreys, Va. Engineer School. 1931. 116p. **5753**

New England

Ham, Edward Billings. Journalism and the French survival in New England. New Eng. quar. XI. p89-107 (March 1938) **5753a**

—— The library of the Union St-Jean Baptiste d'Amérique. Franco-Am. rev. I. p271-5. 1937 (Books, periodicals and manuscripts in the library at Woonsocket, R.I., with special reference to New England) **5753b**

Harte, Charles Rufus. Booklets and newspaper supplements on the hurricane of September 21, 1938. 28 West Elm St. New Haven, Conn. In progress **5753c**

Martin, Thomas P. New England on the western seas. Harvard Alumni bul. XIX. p477-9 (March 22, 1917) (MSS. relating to the early activities of Yankee traders on the Pacific Ocean) **5753d**

New England quarterly. General index vols. I-X, 1928-1937. Prep. by Waldo Palmer. In progress **5753e**

New England Regional Planning Commission. Connecticut River valley water resources bibliography. (Pub. no. 40) [Boston. 1936] **5753f**

Salem Press Co. New England history; preface: the writing habit of the New England Yankee; list of Americana pertaining to New England. Salem, Mass. Salem Press Co. 1911. 30p. **5753g**

Old Northwest

Bradley, Isaac S. Available material for the study of the institutional history of the Old Northwest. Am. Hist. Asso. rep. 1896. I. p296-319 **5754**

Buck, Solon J. Historical activities in the Old Northwest and eastern Canada, 1913-1914, 1914-1915. Miss. Valley hist. rev. I. p57-94. II. p74-105 (June 1914, June 1915) **5755**

Buffalo. Public Library. Card bibliography of the Great Lakes. **5756**

Clements, William L. Source books for the history of the Lake region. Bibliog. Soc. Am. pap. XVI. pt. 1. p1-5. 1923 **5756a**

Cole, Arthur C. Historical activities in the Old Northwest. Miss. Valley hist. rev. III. p50-76; IV. p64-88; V. p51-77; VI. p74-98; VII. p127-41 (June 1916; June 1917; June 1918; June 1919; Sept. 1920) **5757**

Edwards, Everett Eugene. Some sources for Northwest history: agricultural periodicals. Minn. hist. XVIII. p407-14 (Dec. 1937) **5757a**

Knox College. Library. An annotated catalogue of books belonging to the Finley collection on the history and romance of the Northwest. . . Supplemented by a Bibliography of the discovery and exploration of the Mississippi Valley by A. P. C. Griffin. Galesburg, Ill. Knox College. 1924. 67p. (Second edition includes maps but not Griffin's list, pub. 1928) **5758**

—— —— Some recent additions to the Finley collection on the history and romance of the Northwest. Collected and contributed by Edward Caldwell. [Galesburg? Ill. 1937?] 30p. photoprinted **5758a**

Lapham, Julia A. A glimpse of maps of the northwest territory. Am. antiq. XXVII. p121-6. 1905 **5758b**

McMurtrie, Douglas C. Beginnings of printing in the Middle West. Chicago. 1930. 14p. **5759**

Newhall, Daniel H. Books and pamphlets relating to the Middle West, No. 86. N.Y. 1915. 34p. **5760**

Nute, Grace Lee. Some sources for northwest history. Minn. hist. XV. p194-9 (June 1934) (County archives) **5760a**

O'Leary, H. A. Catalogue of new and second-hand books, maps and pamphlets relating to the Middle West and Northwest. Brooklyn, N.Y. 1909. 28p. **5761**

Phillips, Philip Lee. The rare map of the Northwest, 1785, by John Fitch...; a bibliographical account, with facsimile reproduction including some account of Thomas Hutchins and William McMurray. Wash. D.C. W.H. Lowdermilk and Co. 1916. 43p. **5761a**

Stephenson, George M. Some sources for northwest history, Swedish immigration material. Minnesota hist. XVIII. p69-75 (March 1937) **5761b**

Thwaites, Reuben Gold. Publishing activities of the historical societies of the Old Northwest. Am. Hist. Asso. rep. I. p188-200. 1905 **5762**

Vocelle, Mary Dolores. Archaeological excavations, 1900-1938, in Illinois, Indiana, Michigan, Ohio, and Wisconsin: a contribution to a bibliography. Madison. Univ. of Wisconsin Lib. School. 1938. 57p. typ. **5762a**

Wisconsin. State Historical Society. Suggestive outlines for the study of the history of the Middle West, Kentucky and Tennessee. Prepared in conjunction with the Univ. of Wisconsin, School of Hist. (Bul. of information no. 15) Madison. Democrat Ptg. Co. 1901. 29p. **5763**

Wood, Edwin O. Bibliography. *In* Historic Mackinac. II. p681-740. N.Y. Macmillan. 1918 **5764**

South

Alabama, Mississippi and Tennessee newspaper files in the library of the society. Am. Antiq. Soc. proc. n.s. XVII. p274-9 (1906) **5765**

Beale, Howard K. On rewriting reconstruction history. Am. hist. rev. XLV. p807-27 (July 1940) **5765a**

Beer, William. Bibliographical notes on material relating to the history of the gulf states. Gulf states hist. mag. I. p419-22 (May 1903) **5766**

Berea College. Bibliography of material on Southern mountain life and people. Berea, Ky. ms. **5766a**

Birmingham. Public Library. Department of southern history and literature. *In* Birmingham Public Library. Report, 1935-1937. Birmingham. 1937. p15-17 **5766b**

Bowers, Claude G. Rediscovering the Old South. Chapel Hill. Univ. of North Carolina. 1930. 14p. (Southern Historical Collection in the University of North Carolina Library) **5766c**

Boyd, William K. and Brooks, Robert T. A selected bibliography and syllabus of the history of the South, 1584-1876. (Bul. of the Univ. of Georgia. XVIII. no. 6) Athens, Ga. The McGregor Co. 1918. p7-133 **5767**

Chapman, Lila May. The southern collection of books in the Birmingham Public Library. Southeastern Lib. Asso. pap. 1930. p44-52 **5768**

Cole, Fred C. Research projects in southern history. Jour. southern hist. IV. p544-58 (Nov. 1938); V. p581-6 (Nov. 1939) **5768a**

Cole, Fred C. and Higginbotham, Sanford W. Research projects in southern history. Jour. southern hist. VII. p431-47 (Aug. 1941) **5768b**

Cole, Theodore Lee. Bibliography of the statute law of Alabama, Arkansas and Florida. South. Hist. Asso. publications. I. p61-75, 113-26, 211-25 (Jan.-July 1897) **5769**

Coulter, E. Merton. Historical activities on southern subjects. Georgia. hist. quar. XIV. p58-65 (March 1930) **5770**

—— What the South has done about its history. Jour. south. hist. II. p3-28 (Feb. 1936) **5771**

Cremer, Henry. Available sources for the study of American history, written from the southern point of view. Indiana, Pa. Grosse. 1931. 11p. **5772**

Cumming, W. P. A checklist of early maps of the Southeast in eastern libraries. Davidson, N.C. Davidson College. In progress **5772a**

Downs, Robert Bingham. Resources of southern libraries; a survey of facilities for research. Chicago. Am. Lib. Asso. 1938. 370p. **5772b**

Duke University. Library. The centennial exhibit of the Duke University Library, consisting of material from the George Washington Flowers memorial collections of books and documents relating to the history and literature of the South, April 5-June 5, 1939. Durham, N.C. 1939. 60p. **5772c**

Edwards, Everett E. References on the mountaineers of the southern Appalachians. (U.S. Dept. of Agriculture. Library. Bibliog. contributions no. 28) Wash. D.C. Dec. 1935. 148p. mim. **5773**

George Peabody College for Teachers. Bibliography of literary societies in the South before 1860. Nashville, Tenn. ms. **5773a**

Hamer, Philip M. The records of southern history. Jour. southern hist. V. p3-17 (Feb. 1939) **5773b**

Hamilton, J. G. de R. A national southern collection at the University of North Carolina. Chapel Hill. Univ. of North Carolina. n.d. 14p. **5773c**

Historical news and notices. Jour. southern hist. I- . Feb. 1935- **5773d**

Hunter, Paul. Catalogue of Americana and Tennesseeana, principally of the southern states. Nashville, Tenn. Paul Hunter. 1914. 36p. **5774**

Jackson, David K. The contributors and contributions to the Southern literary messenger (1834-1864). Charlottesville, N.C. Hist. Publishing Co. 1936. 192p. **5775**

McMurry, Donald L. Recent historical activities in the South and the Trans-Mississippi Southwest. Miss. Valley hist. rev. III. p478-512 (March 1917) **5776**

New York Southern Society. Library. Catalogue of the New York Southern Society "Garden library" of southern Americana. Comp. by John F. P. Lillard. N.Y. The Soc. 1891. 143p. **5777**

North Carolina. University. Card bibliography of Southern Americana. Chapel Hill, N.C. **5777a**

Phillips, Ulrich B. Documentary collections and publications of the older states of the South. Conference of state and local historical societies. Am. Hist. Asso. rep. 1905. I. p200-4 **5778**

Ramsdell, Charles W. Materials for research in the agricultural history of the Confederacy. Agric. hist. IV. p18-22 (Jan. 1930) **5778a**

Sioussat, St. George L. Historical activities in the Old Southwest. Miss. Valley hist. rev. I. p400-17 (Dec. 1914) **5779**

Sondley Library. Card file of imprints of southern states, arranged by states, and imprints of non-southern states before 1820. Asheville, N.C. **5779a**

The South in the building of the nation; a history of the southern states designed to record the South's part in the making of the American nation; ... v. XIII; index and reading courses, by J. Walker McSpadden. Richmond, Va. Southern Pub. Soc. 1913. 454p. **5779b**

Southern Historical Society papers. An author and subject index to the Southern Historical Society papers, vols. 1-38. Comp. by Kate Pleasants Minor under the direction of Earl G. Swem. Va. State Lib. bul. VI. No. 3, 4 (July-Oct. 1913) 139p. **5780**

Stockbridge, Helen Elvira. A bibliography of the southern Appalachian and White mountain regions. Wash. D.C. Judd & Detweiler. 1912. p173-254 (Reprinted from the Proc. of the Soc. of Am. Foresters. VI. no. 2. 1911) **5781**

Stone, Robert C. Appalachiana. Norfolk County, Mass. Blue Hill Meteorological Observatory (Card bibliography pertaining to the southern Appalachians) **5781a**

Thompson, Edgar T. A bibliography of the plantation. Duke University, Durham, N.C. In progress **5781b**

Trent, William P. Historical studies in the South. Am. Hist. Asso. pap. IV. p383-91. 1890 **5781c**

U.S. Library of Congress. Division of bibliography. List of references on regional, city and town planning. with special reference to the Tennessee Valley. Aug. 28, 1933. 46p. mim. **5782**

—— —— —— List of references on the mountain whites. Sept. 12, 1935. 26p. typ. **5783**

—— —— —— List of references on the Muscle Shoals nitrate plant. March 1, 1923. 8p. mim. **5784**

—— —— —— List of references on the Muscle Shoals project. Jan. 23, 1926. 19p. mim. **5785**

—— —— —— List of references on "The South." Feb. 26, 1923. 4p. typ. **5786**

—— —— —— List of references relating to debts of southern states incurred for railroads and internal improvements. 1910. 28p. typ. **5787**

—— —— —— Muscle Shoals; a bibliographical list of recent references. Aug. 21, 1931. 31p. mim. (Additional references. Aug. 21, 1931. 31p. mim. (Additional references. Oct. 11, 1933. 4p.; Recent references. Dec. 5, 1933. 9p. typ.) **5788**

—— —— —— Select list of references on recent and prospective development of the southern states. 1909. 8p. typ. **5789**

—— —— —— A selected list of recent books and pamphlets on the South. Comp. by Ann D. Brown. June 13, 1940. 24p. mim. **5789a**

Weeks, Stephen B. On the promotion of historical studies in the South. South. Hist. Asso. publications. I. p13-34 (Jan. 1897) **5790**

Wilson, Louis Round and Downs, R. B. Special collections for the study of history and literature in the Southeast. Bibliog. Soc. of Am. pap. XXVIII. pt 2. p97-131. 1934 (Printed and MS.) **5791**

West

Anderson, Alexander Dwight. The authorities. *In* The silver country; or, the great Southwest; a review of the mineral and other wealth. N.Y. Putnam's. 1877. p130-87 **5792**

Anderson Galleries, Inc. Far West and gateway literature; rare California broadsides, western laws and history, rare books on Mormonism, California acquisition, overland railroad and travel, western bandits, pioneers and adventurers, etc., etc. . . . N.Y. Anderson Galleries. 1923. 111p. **5793**

—— A great collection of original source material relating to the early West and the Far West. . . . N.Y. Anderson Galleries. 1922. 212p. **5794**

—— Rare books on California and other western states, general Americana. . . . N.Y. Anderson Galleries. 1916. 60p. **5795**

—— The West, its history and romance; rare curious and important books, pamphlets, broadsides, and maps relating to the Western states . . . including the original manuscripts of Sutter's fort, 1846, 1847. . . . N.Y. Anderson Galleries. 1921. 121p. **5796**

—— Western Americana; an extraordinary collection dealing with the local history and march of events in the regions lying within the Ohio and Mississippi Valleys and westward to the Pacific Ocean. . . . N.Y. Anderson Galleries. 1923. 250p. **5797**

Appleton, John Bargate. The Pacific Northwest, a selected bibliography covering completed research in the natural resource and socio-economic fields, an annotated list of in-progress and contemplated research, together with critical comments thereon, 1930-39. Portland, Ore. Northwest Regional Council. 1939. 454p. **5797a**

Babcock, Willoughby M. Some sources for northwest history; cataloguing pictorial source material. Minn. hist. XV. p439-44 (Dec. 1934) **5797b**

Bancroft, Hubert Howe. Authorities consulted. *In* History of Nevada, Colorado and Wyoming. San Francisco. Hist. Co. 1890. p.xix-xxxii **5798**

—— Authorities consulted. In History of Washington, Idaho, and Montana, 1845-1889. San Francisco. Hist. Co. 1890. p.xvii-xxvi **5799**

—— Authorities quoted. *In* History of the North Mexican states and Texas. San Francisco. Bancroft. 1884. I. p.xix-xlviii **5800**

—— Authorities quoted in the history of the Northwest Coast. *In* History of the Northwest Coast. San Francisco. Hist. Co. 1890. I. p.xvii-xxiii **5801**

Bay, Jens Christian. A handful of western books. Cedar Rapids, Ia. Torch Press. 1935. 44p. **5802**

—— A second handful of western books. Cedar Rapids, Ia. Priv. printed for the friends of the Torch Press. 1936. 56p. **5802a**

—— A third handful of western books. Cedar Rapids, Ia. Priv. print. for the friends of the Torch Press. 1937. 58p. **5802b**

Bepler, Doris W. Descriptive catalogue of western historical materials in California periodicals, 1854-1890. (Univ. of California. MS. M.A. thesis. 1920) **5803**

Blaine, Harold A. The great west as revealed in the magazines, from the Louisiana purchase to the building of the Union Pacific Railroad. (Western Reserve Univ. thesis) **5803a**

Book shelf. The Frontier; a magazine of the Northwest, I, May 1920- . **5804**

Buley, R. Carlyle. A guide to the study of the West (Appalachian to Pacific Coast) 1763 to the present. Univ. of Indiana, Bloomington. In progress **5804a**

California. University. Bibliography of literature dealing with the trans-Mississippi West. Berkeley. WPA project **5804b**

Camp, Charles L. Western history—a check list of recent publications. Cal. Hist. Soc. quar. IX. Dec. 1930- **5804c**

Claremont College. Library. Materials on the Pacific area. Claremont, Calif. 1939. 141p. mim. **5804d**

Clark, Dan Elbert. Historical activities in the Trans-Mississippi Northwest. Miss. Valley hist. rev. II. p384-406; III. p347-67; IV. p342-61 (Dec. 1915; Dec. 1916; Dec. 1917) **5805**

—— Historical activities in the Trans-Mississippi Northwest and western Canada. Miss. Valley hist. rev. I. p240-56 (Sept. 1914) **5806**

Coman, Katherine. Bibliography. In Economic beginnings of the Far West. N.Y. Macmillan. 1912. I. p399-418; II. p387-414 **5807**

Comment and historical news. Pacific hist. rev. I- . 1932- (Includes bibliography) **5807a**

Davidson, George. Maps of the northwest coast of North America. In The Alaska boundary. San Francisco. Alaska Packers Asso. 1903. p49-53, 149-82 **5807b**

Dennis, William. Sources of North-Western history. Manitoba Hist. and Scientific Soc. trans. no. 6. (1882-83) 4p. **5808**

Edwards, Everett E. References on the significance of the frontier in American history. (U.S. Dept. of Agriculture. Lib. Bibliog. contributions no. 25) Wash. D.C. Oct. 1939. 99p. mim. **5809**

Ellis, George E. Critical essay on the sources of information—editorial note—The Hudson Bay company. In Narrative and critical history of America. Ed. by Justin Winsor. Boston. N.Y. Houghton Mifflin. 1889. VIII. p65-80 **5810**

Fleming, Walter L. Recent historical activities in the Trans-Mississippi Southwest. Miss. Valley hist. rev. II. p529-60 (March 1916) **5811**

Hamilton, Raphael N. The early cartography of the Missouri Valley. Am. hist. rev. XXXIX. p645-62 (July 1934) **5811a**

Hodder, Frank H. Books on the Louisiana purchase. Dial. XXXIII. p35-7 (July 16, 1902) **5811b**

Howay, F. W. The early literature of the Northwest Coast. Royal Soc. of Canada proc. 3d ser. XVIII. section II. p1-31 (May 1924) **5812**

Hudson's Bay Company. Hudson's Bay Company; a selected bibliography. Winnipeg. Hudson's Bay House. 1936. 7p. **5812a**

Hussey, Roland Dennis. Pacific history in Spanish American historical reviews, 1935-1937. Pacific hist. rev. VII. p343-62 (Dec. 1938) **5812b**

Iowa. State Historical Society. Some publications—western Americana. Iowa jour. hist. pol. VI. Jan. 1908- **5813**

Judson, Katherine Berry. Subject index to the history of the Pacific Northwest and of Alaska as found in the United States government documents, congressional series, in the American state papers, and in other documents, 1789-1881. Olympia Wash. Lamborn. 1913. 341p. **5814**

Lewis, William S. A contribution towards a bibliography of the camel, with particular reference to the introduction of camels into the United States and the camel pack trains in the western mining camps. Calif. Hist Soc. quar. IX. p336-44 (Dec. 1930) **5814a**

McMurtrie, Douglas C. Pioneer printers of the Far West. San Francisco. Red Tower Press. 1933. 12p. **5815**

Major, Mabel and others. Southwest heritage; a literary history with bibliography. Albuquerque, N. Mex. Univ. of N. Mex. Pr. 1938. p135-58 **5815a**

New York Historical Society. Library. Early newspapers, with a list of the society's collection of papers published in California, Oregon, Washington, Montana, and Utah. Comp. by Alexander J. Wall. N.Y. Hist. Soc. quar. bul. XV. p39-66 (July 1931) **5816**

Newhall, Daniel H. Some books and pamphlets relating to the Far West. N.Y. Daniel H. Newhall. [?] 36p. **5817**

Northwest Regional Council. Selected bibliography of publications dealing with Northwest resources suitable for school use. In Pacific Northwest problems and materials; an introduction. Portland, Ore. 1940. p121-90 **5817a**

Outram, James. Bibliography of the Rocky Mountains and Selkirk ranges. Appalachia. X. p179-86. 1903 **5818**

Pacific Coast Branch of the American Historical Association. Reviews of books. The Pacific hist. rev. I. March 1932- **5819**

Pacific Northwest Americana. Wash. hist. quar. XIII- . Jan. 1922- **5819a**

Pacific Northwest Library Association. Committee on bibliography. Union card catalog of Pacific Northwest Americana. Seattle. Univ. of Washington Lib. In progress, 1937- **5819b**

Pacific Northwest Regional Planning Commission. Pacific Northwest water resources: bibliography. Portland, Ore. 1936. [46]p. typ. **5819c**

Parish, John C. Historical activities in the Trans-Mississippi Northwest, 1917-1919. Miss. Valley hist. rev. VI. p360-80; VII. p242-60 (Dec. 1919; Dec. 1920) **5820**

Paxson, Frederic. A generation of the frontier hypothesis: 1893-1932. Pacific hist. rev. II. p34-51 (March 1933) **5821**

Reid, R. L. British Columbia: a bibliographical sketch. Bibliog. Soc of Amer. pap. XXII. p20-44. 1928 **5822**

Riverside, California. Public Library. The Colorado River and its tributaries; a bibliography of books, magazine articles and government documents in the Riverside public library. Comp. by Bertha L. Walsworth. Riverside, Calif. Riverside Pub. Lib. 1922. unpag. mim.   5823

Rockwood, Eleanor Ruth. Books on the Pacific Northwest for small libraries. N.Y. H. W. Wilson. 1923. 55p.   5824

Rogers, James Grafton. The mining district governments of the West: their interest and literature. National Asso. of State Lib. proc. and pap. 1934-35. p58-65 5824a

St. Louis. Public Library. Furs and fur bearers of the United States and Canada; a list of books and articles on the technology and romance of the subject. Comp. by Edith Varney. St. Louis. St. Louis Pub. Lib. 1929. 10p. (Reprinted from the monthly bul. n.s. XXVII. no. 4. p115-22. April 1929) 5825

Smith, Charles C. Critical essay on the sources of information—Explorations to the north-west. In Winsor, Justin. Narrative and critical history of America. Boston; N.Y. Houghton Mifflin. 1884. III. p97-104   5825a

Smith, Charles Wesley. Pacific Northwest Americana; a checklist of books and pamphlets relating to the history of the Pacific Northwest. N.Y. H. W. Wilson; London. Grafton. 1921. 329p.   5826

—— Pacific Northwest bibliography. Pacific Northw. lib. asso. quar. II. p9-11 (Oct. 1937) (Concerns the union catalog of Pacific Northwest Americana in process of compilation at the University of Washington Library)   5826a

Todd, J. R. Progress on the union catalogue of books and pamphlets relating to the Pacific northwest. Pacific northw. lib. asso. quar. II. p28-9 (Oct. 1937)   5826b

Toronto. Public Library. The Canadian North West: a bibliography of the sources of information in the public reference library of the city of Toronto in regard to the Hudson's Bay Company, the fur trade and the early history of the Canadian North West. Toronto. Toronto Pub. Lib. 1931. 52p.   5827

Tucker, Mary. Books of the Southwest. N.Y. J. J. Augustin. 1937   5827a

Turner, Frederick J. The West as a field for historical study. Am. Hist. Asso. rep. 1896. I. p281-96   5828

Turner, Frederick J. and Merk, Frederick. List of references on the history of the West. Cambridge. Harvard Univ. Press. 1922. 156p.   5829

U.S. Library of Congress. Division of bibliography. Select list of writings on the military history of the West. 1907. 20p. typ.   5830

U.S. National Park Service. A concise history of scientists and scientific investigations in Yellowstone National Park, with a bibliography of the results of research and travel in the park area. By Carl P. Russell. [Wash. D.C. 1934] 144p. mim.   5831

U.S. National Resources Planning Board. Annotated bibliography of social and economic research studies—Inventory of research resources relating to social and economic problems. In Northern great plains problems. Omaha, Neb. Field Office, National Resources Planning Board. 1940. 2v.   5831a

Voth, Mrs. Hazel Hunt. National parks and monuments west of the Mississippi River; a bibliography. Berkeley, Calif. Western Museum Laboratories, National Park Service. In progress   5831b

Voth, Mrs. Hazel Hunt and Russell, Carl P. Yellowstone National Park: a bibliography. [Berkeley, Calif.?] Western Museum Laboratories, National Park Service. 1940. 200p.   5831c

Winsor, Justin and Channing, Edward. Territorial acquisitions and divisions. In Narrative and critical history of America. Boston, N.Y. Houghton Mifflin. 1888. VII. p527-62   5832

Winther, Oscar O. Guide to periodical literature pertaining to the Trans-Mississippi West. Bloomington. Indiana Univ. In progress   5832a

Winton, Harry N. M. A Pacific Northwest bibliography, 1940. Pacific northw. quar. XXXII. p203-14 (April 1941)   5832b

ALABAMA

Alabama. Department of Archives and History. Alabama newspapers and periodicals. In Alabama official and statistical register, 1915. Comp. by Thomas M. Owen. Montgomery. Brown. 1915. p271-307   5835

—— —— Checklist of newspapers and periodical files in the Department of Archives and History of the state of Alabama. Comp. by Thomas M. Owen. (Bul. no. 3) Montgomery. 1904. 65p.   5836

—— —— Constitutional conventions of Alabama. In Alabama official and statistical register, 1903. Comp. by Thomas M. Owen. Montgomery. Brown. 1903. p118-46   5837

—— —— The establishment, organization, activities and aspirations of the Department of Archives and History of the state of Alabama. Comp. by the director T. M. Owen (Alabama. Dept. of Archives and Hist. Bul. no. 1) Montgomery. Brown Ptg. Co. 1904. 48p.   5838

Alabama. Geological Survey. Complete list of publications of the Geological Survey of Alabama to February 1, 1931. Montgomery, Ala. Wilson Ptg. Co. 1931. 15p.   5838a

Alabama. History Commission. An account of manuscripts, papers and documents pertaining to Alabama in official repositories beyond the state . . . within the state . . . in private hands. War records of Alabama. *In* Report of the Alabama History Commission, 1900. Ed. by Thomas M. Owen. Montgomery. Brown. 1901. I. p45-369 **5839**

Boyd, Minnie Clare. Alabama newspapers to 1860. Mississippi State College for Women (In progress) **5839a**

Cole, Theodore Lee. Bibliography of the statute law of the southern states. Part I: Alabama. Southern Hist. Asso. pubs. I. p61-75 (Jan. 1897) **5839b**

Darden, David L. The care and custody of Alabama historical materials. Ala. hist. quar. II. p152-7 (Summer 1940) **5839c**

Engstfeld, Caroline P. Bibliography of Alabama authors. (Howard College. Bul. 81. March 1923. special issue) Birmingham. Howard College. 1923. 48p. **5840**

Garrett, Mitchell B. The preservation of Alabama history. North Carolina hist. rev. V. p3-19 (Jan. 1928) **5841**

Historical Records Survey. Alabama. Check list of Alabama imprints, 1807-1840. (American imprints inventory, no. 8) Birmingham, Ala. 1939. 159p. mim.
5841a

—— —— Inventory of the church archives of Alabama: Protestant Episcopal Church. Birmingham, Ala. Nov. 1939. 106p. mim.
5841b

—— —— Inventory of the county archives of Alabama. Birmingham, Ala. 1938- . mim. No. 17. Colbert. May 1939. 333p.; No. 18. Conecuh. May 1938. 127p.; No. 33. Hale. July 1940. 147p.; No. 43. Lowndes. Nov. 1939. 401p.; No. 46. Marengo. Aug. 1940. 205p.; No. 60. Sumter. Aug. 1940. 204p.; No. 61. Talladega. April 1940. 435p.
5841c

Jones, Walter Bryan. Complete list of publications of the geological survey of Alabama to November 1, 1934. *In* History and work of geological surveys and industrial development in Alabama. . . . (Geol. survey of Alabama. Bul. no. 42). Univ. of Alabama. Jan. 1935. p50-103 **5842**

McMurtrie, Douglas C. A brief history of the first printing in the state of Alabama. Birmingham. Priv. printed. 1931. (Reprinted from Typo-Talk for May 1931. p5-8) **5843**

Owen, Thomas M. Alabama archives. Am. Hist. Asso. rep. 1904. p487-553 **5844**

—— A bibliography of Alabama. Am. Hist. Asso. rep. 1897. p777-1248 **5845**

—— State departments of archives and history. Am. Hist. Asso. rep. 1904. p235-53 **5846**

—— The work of William Henry Fowler as Superintendent of Army Records, 1863-1865. Ala. Hist. Soc. trans. II. p178-91. 1897-98 **5846a**

Screws, W. W. Alabama journalism. *In* Memorial record of Alabama. Brant and Fuller, compilers. Madison, Wis. Brant and Fuller. 1893. p158-235 **5847**

Smith, Eugene Allen. Geological surveys in Alabama. Jour. of geology. II. p275-87. 1894 **5847a**

Survey of Federal Archives. Alabama. Inventory of federal archives in the states. Birmingham, Ala. 1939- . mim. The Federal Courts. June 1940. 85p.; The Department of the Treasury. Sept. 1940. 174p.; The Department of War. Dec. 1940. 150p;. The Department of Justice. June 1940. 45p.; The Department of the Navy. April 1939. 10p.; The Department of Commerce. Dec. 1940. 32p.; The Farm Credit Administration. June 1940. 17p. The Veterans' Administration. March 1941. 45p. **5847b**

U.S. Bureau of Agricultural Economics. Library. Alabama—An index to the state official sources of agricultural statistics. Comp. by Margaret T. Olcott under the direction of Mary G. Lacy (Agricultural economics bibliog. no. 15) Wash. D.C. March 1926. 96p. mim. **5848**

ARIZONA

Alliot, Hector. Bibliography of Arizona, being the record of literature collected by Joseph Amasa Munk, M.D., and donated by him to The Southwest Museum of Los Angeles, California. Los Angeles. Southwest Museum. 1914. 431p. **5849**

Arizona. Historian. Report of the Arizona historian from Oct. 1909 to Dec. 1911. (Bibliog. of Arizona) n.p. n.p. n.d. 32p. **5850**

Arizona. State Library. Bibliography and checklist. Publications, reports and public documents of Arizona state agencies, issued or received during the period July 1, 1931 to June 30, 1933- . State Lib. news letter, no. 1- . July 1933- **5850a**

—— —— Check-list of annual reports, Arizona law, and other current publications issued by or under the authority of the State of Arizona for the fiscal year, 1915/16-1930/31. Phoenix. 1917-32. 16v. **5850b**

—— —— State library news letter, no. 1- . July 1933- (Includes Check list of Arizona state reports and publications 1931/33-) **5850c**

Arizona. University. Library. Check list of University of Arizona official announcements & publications. Arizona Univ. rec. XI. no. 2. Lib. bibliog. no. 4. pt. II. p23-46. 1918 **5851**

Favour, Alpheus H. A four-foot shelf of Arizona laws. Prescott. Prescott Hist. Soc. 1930. 24p. **5852**

Historical Records Survey. Arizona. A check list of Arizona imprints, 1860-1890. (American imprints inventory, no. 3) Chicago. 1938. 41p. mim. **5852a**

—— —— Inventory of the county archives of Arizona. Phoenix, Ariz. 1938- . mim. No. 7. Maricopa. Aug. 1940. 438p.; No. 10. Pima. July 1938. 207p. **5852b**

Jenkins, Olaf P. and Wilson, Eldred D.
List of United States geological survey publications relating to Arizona. (Univ. of Arizona. Bul. no. 104. Geol. ser. no. 1) Tucson. Univ. of Arizona, Bureau of Mines. 1919-20. 40p.   **5853**

Leonard, Ida R. Preliminary survey of the more important archives of the territory and state of Arizona. Comp. for the Am. Hist. Asso. 1935. MS.   **5854**

Lutrell, Estelle. A bibliographical list of books, pamphlets and articles on Arizona in the University of Arizona Library. Tucson, Ariz. n.p. 1913. 60p.   **5855**

—— Bibliography of Arizona mining, metallurgy and geology. (Univ. of Arizona. Bul. 23. Economics ser. 7) Tucson, Ariz. 1915-16. 49p.   **5856**

—— Check list of Arizona publications. Tucson. Univ. of Arizona Lib. (In progress)   **5856a**

McMurtrie, Douglas C. The beginnings of printing in Arizona, with a preliminary check-list of Arizona book and pamphlet imprints, 1860-1875. Phoenix, Ariz. Priv. printed. 1932. p173-87 (Extract from the Arizona hist. rev. Oct. 1932)   **5857**

—— The beginnings of printing in Arizona, with an account of the early newspapers and a bibliography of books, pamphlets, and broadsides printed in Arizona, 1860-1875. Chicago. Black Cat Press. 1937. 44p.   **5857a**

Munk, Joseph Amasa. Arizona bibliography; a private collection of Arizoniana. Los Angeles. 1908. 98p.   **5858**

—— Bibliography of Arizona books, pamphlets and periodicals in the library of Dr. J. A. Munk. Los Angeles. 1900. 28p.   **5859**

—— History of Arizona literature; an address delivered at the annual meeting of the Arizona Federated Women's Clubs in Flagstaff, Arizona, April 1, 1925. Flagstaff? 1925? 24p.   **5860**

—— Story of The Munk Library of Arizoniana. Los Angeles. Times-Mirror Press. 1927. 78p.   **5861**

Southwest Society of the Archaeological Institute of America. The Lummis Library and collections. (Munk Lib. Seventh bul.) Los Angeles. 1910. p3-34 **5862**

Survey of Federal Archives. Arizona. Inventory of federal archives in the states. Tucson, Ariz. 1938- . mim. The Federal Courts. Sept. 1938. 29p.; The Department of the Treasury. March 1938. 41p.; The Department of War. Sept. 1938. 33p.; The Department of Justice. Sept. 1938. 18p.; The Post Office Department. March 1939. 36p.; The Department of the Navy. Sept. 1938. 2p.; The Department of the Interior. March 1939. 148p.; The Department of Agriculture. Jan. 1938. 202p.; The Department of Commerce. Aug. 1938. 11p.; The Department of Labor. Sept. 1938. 66p.; The Veterans' Administration. Aug. 1938. 15p.; The Civil Works Administration. Oct. 1938. 21p.; The Emergency Relief Administration. Nov.

1938. 50p.; The Works Progress Administration. Nov. 1938. 72p.; The Farm Credit Administration. Aug. 1938. 3p.; Miscellaneous Agencies. April 1939. 165p. **5862a**

U.S. Library of Congress. Division of bibliography. List of references on Arizona (With special reference to Arizona before 1893). Feb. 5, 1915. 5p. typ. **5863**

—— —— —— List of references on the Salt River project (Roosevelt dam). April 12, 1924. 3p. typ.   **5864**

Wilson, E. D. Bibliography of the geology and mineral resources of Arizona. Arizona. Bureau of Mines. Geological ser. no. 13, bul. no. 146. 164p. 1939 **5864a**

ARKANSAS

Allsopp, Frederick William. History of the Arkansas press for a hundred years and more. Little Rock. Parke-Harper. 1922. 684p.   **5865**

Arkansas. History Commission. Arkansas history catalog. By Dallas T. Herndon. Ft. Smith. Calvert-McBride. 1923. 164p.   **5866**

—— —— Bibliography of historical and literary writings of Arkansas. (Bul. of information no. 4. Dec. 1912) Little Rock. n.p. n.d. p73-87   **5867**

—— —— Biographical index. Dallas T. Herndon, secretary (Bul. of information nos. 13, 14, 15, 16) Little Rock. 1915? 164p.   **5868**

—— —— Catalogue by authors of texts mentioned in topical outline—Arkansas constitutional conventions. (Bul. of information nos. 21 and 22. Jan. to June 1917. Constitutional convention number) Little Rock. n.p. n.d. p28-54 **5869**

—— —— Catalogue. Arkansas State History Museum. By Dallas T. Herndon. Ft. Smith. Calvert-McBride. 1923. 53p. (Some manuscripts listed)   **5870**

—— —— Classified catalogue historical information. (Bul. of information nos. 17, 18, 19, 20. Jan. to Dec. 1916) Dallas T. Herndon, secretary. Little Rock. [1917] 181p. (Index to material in newspapers)   **5871**

—— —— Index to biographical material in state newspapers. Little Rock, Ark.   **5871a**

—— —— The Kie Oldham papers (1860-1875). Dallas T. Herndon, secretary (Bul. of information no. 5. March 1913) Little Rock. 1913? p107-73 (Manuscript collection on the Civil war and aftermath in Ark.)   **5872**

—— —— [List of state papers in the collections of L. C. Gulley, Samuel W. Williams and John E. Knight in the custody of the commission] Dallas T. Herndon, secretary (Bul. of information no. 2. June 1912) Little Rock. [Democrat Ptg. Co. 1912] p17-51   **5873**

Arkansas. State Planning Board. Compendium of maps and charts; progress report. [Little Rock] 1937. 60p. processed   **5873a**

Arkansas. University. Index of all centennial issues of Arkansas newspapers. Fayetteville, Ark.   **5873b**
—— —— **Library.** Union catalog of Arkansiana in libraries in the state. Fayetteville, Ark. Cards   **5873c**
Branner, John C. Bibliography of the geology of Arkansas. *In* Annual report of the Geological survey of Arkansas for 1891. Little Rock, Ark. Brown Ptg. Co. 1894. II. p319-40   **5873d**
—— Bibliography of the geology of Arkansas. *In* Purdue, A. H. The slates of Arkansas. (The Geological Survey of Arkansas, 1909) Fayetteville, Ark. 1909. p99-164   **5873e**
Cole, Theodore Lee. Bibliography of the statute law of the southern states. Part II: Arkansas. Southern Hist. Asso. pubs. I. p113-26 (April 1897)   **5873f**
Gaither, Mrs. Zella Hargrove. Some living Arkansas writers. Arkansas Hist. Asso. publications. I. p324-9. 1906   **5874**
Historical Records Survey. Arkansas. Inventory of the county archives of Arkansas. Little Rock, Ark. 1939- . mim. No. 12. Cleburne. March 1939. 217p.; No. 13. Cleveland. April 1941. 113p.; No. 19. Cross. July 1940. 114p.; No. 23. Faulkner. Dec. 1939. 251p.; No. 30. Hot Spring. March 1940. 121p.   **5874a**
Matthews, Jim P. A bibliographical study of Arkansas state publications. (Univ. of Illinois. M.A. thesis) [Urbana] 1933. typ. (carbon) 335p.   **5875**
Matthews, Jim P. and Jones, Virgil L. Arkansas books. Univ. of Arkansas. Bul. XXV. no. 8 (July 15, 1931) 31p. **5876**
Reynolds, John Hugh. Public archives of Arkansas. Am. Hist. Asso. rep. 1906. II. p23-51   **5877**
Reynolds, John H. and others. An account of books, manuscripts, papers and documents concerning Arkansas in public repositories beyond the state, . . . within the state, . . . in private hands. Arkansas Hist. Asso. publications. I. p43-273. 1906 **5878**
Shinn, Josiah H. Early Arkansas newspapers. Arkansas Hist. Asso. publications. I. p395-403. 1906   **5879**
Survey of Federal Archives. Arkansas. Inventory of federal archives in the states. New Orleans, La. 1938- . mim. The Federal Courts. Jan. 1940. 52p.; The Department of the Treasury. June 1939. 25p.; The Department of War. Aug. 1938. 126p.; The Department of Justice. Oct. 1938. 15p.; The Department of the Navy. Aug. 1938. 6p.; The Department of the Interior. 1941. 8p.; The Department of Agriculture. Oct. 1939. 165p.; The Department of Commerce. Oct. 1938. 8p.; The Department of Labor. March 1940. 6p.; The Veterans' Administration. Oct. 1940. 40p.; The Farm Credit Administration. 1941. 8p.; The Works Progress Administration. 1941. 68p.   **5879a**

Thomas, David Y. The preservation of Arkansas history. North Carolina hist. rev. V. p263-74 (July 1928)   **5880**
U.S. Library of Congress. Division of bibliography. Early Arkansas: a list of books. Feb. 8, 1929. 6p. typ.   **5881**

CALIFORNIA

American Art Association—Anderson Galleries, Inc. The pioneer and mining days of California. N.Y. Publishers' Press Co. 1930. 68p.   **5882**
Anderson Galleries. California and the Far West, books, pamphlets and broadsides. N.Y. Anderson Galleries. 1920. 2pts. 48,55p.   **5883**
—— California: books, pamphlets and broadsides (Sale number 1468). N.Y. 1920. 48p.   **5884**
—— Catalogue of the library of Mr. Charles Howard Shinn, the well-known writer on California. . . N.Y. Anderson Galleries. 1917. 68p.   **5885**
Apponyi, Flora Haines. The libraries of California, containing descriptions of the principal private and public libraries throughout the state. San Francisco. A.L. Bancroft and Company. 1878. 304p. **5885a**
Baker, C. C. A list of newspapers in the Los Angeles City Library. Hist. Soc. South. Calif. annual publications X. pts. 1-2. p80-5. 1916   **5886**
Bancroft, Hubert Howe. Authorities quoted. *In* History of California, 1542-1890. San Francisco. Bancroft. 1884. I. p. xxv-lxxxviii   **5887**
—— Bibliography of pastoral California. *In* California pastoral, 1769-1848. San Francisco. Hist. Co. 1888. p751-92 **5888**
—— Early California literature. *In* Essays and miscellany. San Francisco. Hist. Co. 1890. p591-668   **5889**
—— Index of the builders of the commonwealth. San Francisco. History Co. 1892. 113p.   **5889a**
Barr, Louise Farrow. Presses of northern California and their books, 1900-1933. Berkeley. Univ. of Calif. Book Arts Club. 1934. 276p.   **5890**
Bayle, Constantine. Cartología del P. Kino—sus continuadores. Razón y fe. LXI. p34-45 (Sept. 1921)   **5890a**
Bibliography relating to the Russians in California. Calif. Hist. Soc. quar. XII. p210-16. 1933   **5890b**
Bolton, Herbert E. Father Kino's lost history; its discovery and its value. Bibliog. Soc. Amer. pap. VI. p9-34. 1911   **5890c**
Bruncken, Ernest. A bibliography of forestry in California. Comp. in the California State Library. Sacramento. Shannon. 1908. 16p.   **5891**
Bunje, E. T. H., Irish, J. H., Hagin, R. and Flaherty, M. Cultural contributions of California: California viticulture. Section I: Annotated bibliography. Berkeley. Univ. of California. 1937. 88p. typ. **5891a**

California. Agricultural Experiment Station. Publications of the Agricultural Experiment Station, University of California from 1877 to 1918. Rep. 1918. p102-18 **5892**

California. Attorney General's Office. Index of opinions of the attorney general of the state of California. [Sacramento. California State Ptg. Off. 1940. 116p. **5892a**

California. Bureau of Printing. Division of documents. Official catalog of documents—reports, maps. Published by agencies of the state of California. Comp. and distributed by supervisor of documents, Bureau of printing, Department of finance. Sacramento, Calif. [1940] 1v. photop. **5892b**

California. Department of Finance. Division of service and supply. Bureau of printing. Division of documents. California state publications and documents distributed by supervisor of documents. Sacramento. April 1, 1934. 3p. **5893**

California. Historical Survey Commission. Guide to the county archives of California. By Owen C. Coy (Publication of the Calif. Hist. Survey Comn.) Sacramento. State Ptg. Off. 1919. 622p. **5894**

—— —— Preliminary report of the California Historical Survey Commission, February 1917. Sacramento. State Ptg. Off. [1917] 71p. **5895**

California. Legislative Counsel Bureau. Index to the laws of California, 1850-1920, including the statutes, the codes, and the constitution of 1879, together with amendments thereto, prepared in accordance with an act of the legislature approved May 24, 1919. Sacramento. State Ptg. Off. 1921. 1288p. (Supplement . . . 1921-1932. . . . 1933. 1207p.) **5896**

California. Secretary of State. California newspapers. *In* California Blue book or state roster, 1932. Sacramento. State Ptg. Off. 1932. p295-308 **5897**

California. State Library. Alien ownership of land; select list of references to material in the California State Library. News notes of Calif. lib. IX. p683-6. 1914 (Japanese in California) **5897a**

—— —— California city publications received during 1914- . News notes of Calif. libraries. IX. no. 1. Jan. 1914- **5898**

—— —— California newspapers in state library, 1911. Sacramento. W. W. Shannon, Superintendent state ptg. 1911. 6p. **5899**

—— —— California state publications received during 1906- . News notes of Calif. libraries. I. no. 4. Aug. 1906- **5900**

—— —— Card index of vital statistics. **5901**

—— —— Card index to California newspapers. **5902**

—— —— Catalogue of state publications of California, 1850 to July 1894. (Calif. State Lib. rep. 1892-94) Sacramento. A. J. Johnston, superintendent of state ptg. 1894. p31-72 **5903**

—— —— Catalogue of the California State Library, general department, authors. Comp. by Talbot H. Wallis. Sacramento. Young. 1889. 1172p. (Supplement. San Francisco. Caxton Ptg. Co. 1898. 980p.) **5904**

—— —— Fiction in the State Library having a California coloring. News notes of Calif. lib. IX. p228-42. 1914 (Supplementary list, ibid. XIII. p874-8. 1918) **5904a**

—— —— A list of books, tracts, pamphlets and other publications, together with maps, charts and plans now in the state library, relating to California, and, incidentally, to the adjoining states and territories from the earliest period of discovery to the present time. *In* Bibliotheca Californiae; a descriptive catalogue of books in the State Library of California, Volume II, General library. Comp. by Ambrose P. Dietz. Sacramento. D. W. Gelwicks. 1870. p687-789 **5905**

—— —— List of printed maps contained in the map department. (California State Library. Spec. bul. no. 1) Sacramento. A.J. Johnston, Supt. State Ptg. 1899. 43p. **5905a**

—— —— Manuscript index of material in California newspapers, 1846- . **5906**

—— —— News notes of California libraries, I- . (May-Dec. 1906-) (Lists California state publications) **5906a**

—— —— Union catalog of accessions in county libraries of the state, city libraries, university libraries. MS. **5907**

—— —— Union catalog of books and periodicals in libraries in the States. Sacramento, Calif. Cards **5907a**

—— —— **Sutro branch.** Maps showing the Californias in the Sutro branch, California State Library; list of maps and authors and list of all localities indicated in lower and upper California. Comp. by Charles B. Turrill [San Francisco] 1917. 217p. photostat **5907b**

California. State Mining Bureau. Bibliography, index, map and catalog of minerals in California. San Francisco. WPA project **5907c**

California. State Mining Bureau. Catalogue of books, maps, lithographs, photographs, etc. in the library of the State Mining Bureau at San Francisco. Sacramento. 1884. 19p. **5907d**

—— —— Catalogue of the library of California state mining Bureau, San Francisco, Cal., September 1, 1892. Sacramento. A. J. Johnston, superintendent state ptg. 1892. 149p. **5908**

—— —— Catalogue of the publications of the California State Mining Bureau, 1880-1917. Comp. by Edwin Snow Boalich (Calif. State Mining Bureau bul. 77) Sacramento. 1918. 44p. **5909**

—— —— General index to publications of the California State Mining Bureau. (Calif. State Mining Bureau bul. 46) Sacramento. 1907. 54p. **5910**

California. Supervisor of Documents. California state publications and documents. . . July 1, 1938. Sacramento. 1938 (A price list issued from time to time) **5910a**

California. Surveyor General. Corrected report of Spanish and Mexican grants in California, complete to February 25, 1886. Sacramento, Calif. James J. Ayers, Supt. State Ptg. 1886. 19p. **5910b**

California. University. Library. List of printed maps of California. Comp. by Joseph C. Rowell. (Univ. of California Lib. bul. no. 9) Berkeley. 1887. 33p. **5910c**

California Historical Society. The twenty rarest and most important works dealing with the history of California; a symposium. Calif. Hist. Soc. quar. X. p79-83 (March 1931) **5911**

California Library Association. A union list of newspapers in offices of publishers and in libraries of Southern California. Comp. under the direction of the Newspaper section of the Coordinating committee for the union list of serials in the libraries of Southern California. (Pub. no. 2) [Los Angeles] Sixth district, California Lib. Asso. 1936. 200p. mim. **5911a**

—— Sixth district. Local documents committee. A union list of local documents in libraries of southern California. (Publication no. 1) n.p. Calif. Lib. Asso. 1935. 166p. mim. **5912**

California Library School. Cattle and dairying in California; a selective list of articles on cattle and dairying in California in the California State Library. Comp. by V. Clowe. Sacramento Lib. School. 1917. 24p. **5913**

Casarin, Manuel Jimeno. Jimeno's index of land concessions, from 1830 to 1845, and the "Toma de razon," or registry of titles for 1844-45, in the archives of the office of the surveyor general of the United States for California. San Francisco. Lee & Carl (1858) 13,30p. **5913a**

Cate, Chester March. The first California laws printed in English. *In* Bibliographical essays; a tribute to Wilberforce Eames. Cambridge. Harvard Univ. Press. 1924. p331-6 **5914**

Caughey, John Walton. A commentary on Californiana. *In* California. N.Y. Prentice-Hall. 1940. p607-49 **5914a**

Chandler, Katherine. List of California periodicals issued previous to the completion of the trans-continental telegraph (Aug. 15, 1846-Oct. 24, 1861). Lib. Asso. Calif. publications. no. 7 (March 1905) 20p. **5915**

Chapman, Charles E. The literature of California history. Southwest hist. quar. XXII. p318-52 (April 1919) (Revised and issued as appendix to the author's History of California (N.Y. Macmillan. 1921) 487-509p.) **5916**

Chavez, Alberto N. Bibliografía antropológica californiana. Ethnos (Mexico) I. p100-6. 1920; 238-40. 1922 **5916a**

Cole, George Watson. Missions and mission pictures; a contribution towards an iconography of the Franciscan missions of California. California library association. Handbook and proceedings of the annual meeting, 1910. Sacramento. 1910. p44-66 (Reprinted from News notes of Calif. libraries. V. p390-412. July 1910) **5917**

Cooley, Laura C. Selected list of source material in the Los Angeles public library, California from the discovery to the end of the Spanish period. Hist. Soc. of South. Calif. annual publications. XI. p91-101. 1918 **5918**

Cowan, Robert Ernest. Bibliographical notes on early California. Am. Hist. Asso. rep. 1904. p267-78 **5919**

—— A bibliography of the history of California and the Pacific west, 1510-1906. San Francisco. Bookclub of Calif. 1914. 318p. **5920**

—— A bibliography of the Spanish press of California, 1833-1845. San Francisco. 1919. 31p. **5921**

Cowan, Robert Ernest and Cowan, Robert Granniss. A bibliography of the history of California, 1510-1930. San Francisco. John Henry Nash. 1933. 3v. **5922**

Crocker, Charles Templeton. Catalogue of the library of Charles Templeton Crocker. Hillsborough, Calif. 1918. 314p. **5923**

Díaz Mercado, Joaquín. Bibliografía sumaria de la Baja California. (Bibliografías mexicanas. no. 2) México, D.A.P.P. 1937. 179p. **5923a**

Drake, Eugene B. Jimeno's and Hartnell's indexes of land concessions, from 1830 to 1846; also toma de razon or registry of titles, for 1844-'45; approvals of land grants by the territorial deputation and departmental assembly of California, from 1835 to 1846, and a list of unclaimed grants. Comp. from the Spanish archives in the U.S. Surveyor-general's office. San Francisco. Kenny & Alexander. 1861. 17, 68p. **5923b**

Du Bois, Eugene. Two maps of the gold regions of California in 1849; a bibliography. [Cambridge] Harvard College. 1932. 6p. typ. **5923c**

Duniway, David C. The California Food Administration and its records in The National Archives. Pacific hist. rev. VII. p228-38 (Sept. 1938) **5923d**

—— Note on records of the California Food Administration in the Bancroft Library. Pacific hist. rev. VIII. p104 (March 1939) **5923e**

Eakle, Arthur S. Bibliography of California minerals. *In* Minerals of California. (Calif. State Mining Bureau bul. no. 91) Sacramento. Calif. State Mining Off. 1923. p306-21 **5924**

Eldredge, Zoeth Skinner. The Spanish archives of California; paper read before the California Genealogical Society, July 13, 1901. San Francisco. Murdoch. 1901. 8p.   5925

Engelhardt, Zephyrin. The sources of California mission history. *In* The Missions and missionaries of California. San Francisco. James H. Barry Company. 1912. II, pxxxi-xlvi   5925a

Essig, E. O. Bibliography relating to the Russians in California. Calif. Hist. Soc. quar. XII. p210-16 (Sept. 1933)   5926

Fitch, George Hamlin. California books and authors. *In* Eldredge, Zoeth S. History of California. N.Y. Century Company. 1915. V, p487-502   5926a

Gaer, Joseph. Bibliography of California literature; fiction of the gold-rush period, drama of the gold-rush period, poetry of the gold-rush period. (Calif. literary research project. Monograph no. 8 (Gc-d) SERA project 2-F2-132) n.p. 1935. 123p. mim.   5927

—— Bibliography of California literature, pre-gold rush period. (Calif. literary research project. Monograph no. 7 (G-a) Abstract from the SERA project 2-F2-132 (3-F2-197) n.p. 1935. 69p. mim. 5928

—— California in juvenile fiction. (Calif. literary research project. Monograph no. 12. SERA project 2-F2-132 (3F2-197) Calif. literary research) n.p. 1935. 61p. mim.   5929

—— The theatre of the gold rush decade in San Francisco. (Calif. literary research project. Monograph no. 5 (G-f) Abstract from the SERA project 2-F2-132 (3F2-197) Calif. literary research) n.p. 1935. 99p. mim.   5930

[Guillén y Tato, Julio Fernando.] Repertorio de los mss., cartas, planos y dibujos relativos a las Californias, existentes en este museo. (Publicaciones del Museo naval. I) [Madrid] 1932. 127p.   5931

Guinn, J. M. The old pueblo archives. Hist. Soc. South. Calif. annual publications. IV. p37-42. 1897. (Los Angeles archives)   5932

Hanna, Phil Townsend. Libros Californianos; or, five feet of California books. Los Angeles. J. Zeitlin. 1931. 74p. 5933

Harding, George L. A check list and census of California Spanish imprints, 1833-1845. Calif. Hist. Soc. quar. XII. p130-6 (June 1933)   5934

Hasse, Adelaide Rosalie. Index of economic material in documents of the states of the United States: California, 1849-1904. (Carnegie Inst. of Wash. Publication no. 85) Wash. D.C. Carnegie Inst. of Wash. 1908. 316p.   5935

Head, Edwin L. Report on the archives of the state of California. Am. Hist. Asso. rep. 1915. p277-309   5936

Heartman, Charles Frederick. The pioneer press of the golden gate; California newspapers 1850-1874. over 2700 individual numbers. . . . Metuchen, N.J. 1926. 11p.   5937

Heller, Elinor Raas and Magee, David. Bibliography of the Grabhorn Press, 1915-1940. San Francisco. David Magee. 1940. 198p.   5937a

Henry E. Huntington Library and Art Gallery. California from legendary island to statehood; an exhibition at the Huntington Library. San Marino, Calif. 1933. 27p.   5938

—— Card catalogue of printed materials on California. San Marino, Calif.   5938a

—— Los Angeles: the transition decades, 1850-70; an exhibition at the Huntington library. San Marino, Calif. 1937. 25p.   5938b

Hinkel, Edgar Joseph, ed. Bibliography of California fiction, poetry, drama in three volumes . . . produced on a Works Progress Administration Project, administration project 165-03-7308, area serial 0803-1008, work project 6463, sponsored by the Alameda County Library, Oakland, California. Prep. under the direction of Edgar J. Hinkel, ed., William E. McCann, assistant ed., Marie Holden, cataloguer. Oakland, Calif. 1938. 3v.   5938c

Historical Records Survey. Guide to public vital statistics records in California. Vol. I. Birth records. June 1941. 72p.; Vol. II. Death records. July 1941. 62p. mim.   5938d

Historical Records Survey. Northern California. Inventory of the county archives of California. San Francisco, Calif. 1937- . mim. No. 10. Fresno. July 1940. 624p.; No. 22. Marin. Dec. 1937. 136p.; No. 27. Mono. April 1940. 139p.; No. 20. Napa. March 1941. 619p.; No. 36. San Benito. Feb. 1940. 585p.; No. 39. San Francisco. vol 2. May 1940. 418p.; No. 41. San Luis Obispo. Nov. 1939. 524p.; No. 42. San Mateo. June 1938. 184p.; No. 44. Santa Clara. April 1939. 330p.   5938e

—— —— Inventory of the state archives of California. San Francisco, Calif. 1941- . mim. Department of Industrial Relations: Division of Immigration and Housing. April 1941. 47p.   5938f

Historical Records Survey. Southern California. Inventory of the county archives of California. Los Angeles, Calif. 1940- . mim. Title-line inventory. No. 7. Ventura. 1940. 155p.; No. 20. Los Angeles. Tax Collector's office. Jan. 1940. 172p.; Assessor's office. Jan. 1941. 288p.; No. 38. San Diego. Vol. III. Tax and financial offices. Jan. 1941. 238p.; Title-line inventory of the county archives of California: San Bernadino. Aug. 1940. 132p.; Title-line inventory of the county archives of California: Santa Barbara. Jan. 1941. 187p.   5938g

Historical Society of Southern California. General index to annual publications, volumes I-XI, 1884-1920. Prepared by Robert C. Gillingham. Hist. Soc. South. Calif. annual publications. XII. (1921) 86p.   5939

Hopkins, Rufus C. The Spanish archives of California. *In* Dwinelle, John W. The colonial history of the city of San Francisco. San Francisco. Towne & Bacon. 1866. p v-ix **5939a**

Hotaling, Anson Parsons. Catalogue of the private library of Anson Parsons Hotaling. San Francisco. 1897. 88p. **5940**

Kemble, Edward C. A history of California newspapers; being a contemporary chronicle of early printing and publishing on the Pacific Coast; reprinted for the first time from the Sacramento Daily Union of December 25, 1858; being the account of early American printing and publishing written soonest after the events it chronicles. Ed. by Douglas C. McMurtrie. N.Y. Plandome Press. 1927. 281p. (The editor's introduction, inadvertently omitted, appeared in Calif. Hist. Soc. quar. VII. p277-81. 1928; from which it was reprinted in 1931) **5941**

Kuykendall, Ralph Simpson. History of early California journalism. (Univ. of Calif. MS. thesis) Berkeley. 1918 **5942**

Lesley, Lewis Burt-King. California and Pacific coast history materials. Grizzly bear. XXXIV. p8-9 (Nov. 1923) (Materials for the period of British interest in London archives) **5942a**

Lombardi, John. Lost records of the surveyor-general in California. Pacific hist. rev. VI. p361-71 (Dec. 1937) **5942b**

Lounsbury, Ralph G. Records pertaining to California land claims and titles of Spanish and Mexican origin, deposited in The National Archives and in other governmental agencies of the United States in Washington, D.C. MS. in The National Archives. 1939 **5942c**

Lundy, F. A. Cowan library of Californiana. School and soc. XLV. p234-5 (Feb. 13, 1937) **5942d**

M. H. De Young Memorial Museum. Bibliographical data pertaining to California artists of the San Francisco region. San Francisco. WPA project **5942e**

McConnell, Winona. California Indians; annotated list of material in the California state library. News notes of Calif. libraries. X. p484-522 (July 1915) **5943**

McCorkle, Julia N. A history of Los Angeles journalism. Hist. Soc. South. Calif. annual publications. X. pts. 1-2. p24-43. 1915-16 **5944**

MacDonald, A. S. Per mare, per terras; a list of books, California and the Pacific in the library of Augustin S. MacDonald. Oakland, Calif. Enquirer Publishing Co. 1903. 76p. **5945**

McMurtrie, Douglas C. Pioneer printing in California. (Reprinted from National printer journalist. July 1932. 4p.) **5946**

—— The Third historical record of printing in California. San Pedro. San Pedro High School Print Shop. 1935. p7-12 **5947**

Mighels, Ella Sterling. A classified list of California writers—poets, prose-writers, historians, orators, divines, journalists, publishers, etc. *In* Literary California, poetry, prose and portraits. San Francisco. Harr Wagner Pub. Co. 1918. p382-423 **5947a**

—— The story of the files: a review of California writers and literature. N.Y. Westermann; San Francisco. Co-operative Ptg. Co. 1893. 460p. **5948**

Parish, John C. California books and manuscripts in the Huntington Library. The Huntington Lib. bul. no. 7. p1-58 (April 1935) **5949**

Parma, Rosamund and Armstrong, Elizabeth. The codes and statutes of California: a bibliography. Law lib. jour. XXII. p41-56 (Jan. 1929) **5950**

Pomona College. Catalog of Californiana and western Americana. Claremont, Calif. In progress **5951**

Richman, Irving Berdine. Notes with lists of sources. *In* California under Spain and Mexico, 1835-1847. Boston, N.Y. Houghton Mifflin. 1911. p359-500 **5952**

San Francisco Women's Literary Exhibit. A list of books by California writers; issued by the San Francisco women's literary exhibit, Columbian exposition, 1893, under the auspices of the San Francisco world's fair association. San Francisco. Raveley Ptg. Co. 1893. 52p. **5953**

Save-the-Redwoods League. Bibliography of the redwoods; reading-list of articles, pamphlets and books on the sequoia sempervirens. . . . Berkeley. Save-the-Redwoods League. 1935. 15p. **5954**

Scanland, J. M. Some aspects of pioneer California journalism. Bookman. XXIII. p40-8 (March 1906) **5955**

Shedd, Solon. Bibliography of the geology and mineral resources of California to December 31, 1930. (Calif. Dept. of Natural Resources. Division of mines and mining. Bul. no. 104. March 1932) Sacramento. State Ptg. Off. 1933. 376p. **5956**

Shuck, Oscar T. ed. California law books—complete list. *In* History of the bench and bar of California. Los Angeles. Commercial Ptg. House. 1901. p1131-3 **5956a**

Skaife, Alfred C. Early California law books. San Francisco bar. I. no. 1. p12-16; no. 3. p7-13; no. 5. p8-10; no. 6. p5-8; II. no. 2. p11-15; no. 4. p6-10. 1937-38 **5956b**

Stone, T. P. California law books, complete list. *In* History of the bench and bar of California. Ed. by Oscar T. Shuck. Los Angeles. Commercial Ptg. House. 1901. p1131-3 **5957**

Survey of Federal Archives. California. Inventory of federal archives in the states. San Francisco, Calif. 1939- . mim. The Federal Courts. May 1939. 103p.; The Department of the Treasury. Parts I-IV. 1940. 869p.; The Department of the Interior. 1941. 2v.; The Department

Survey of Federal Archives. California. Inventory—*Continued*
of Justice. May 1940. 108p.; The Department of Agriculture. June 1940. 728p.; The Department of Commerce. May 1939. 139p.; The Department of Labor. June 1940. 331p.   **5957a**
—— —— Lists of maps in the Spanish and Mexican land claims cases in the United States District Court for the Northern District of California. San Francisco. 1940. unpag. typescript in The National Archives   **5957b**

Taylor, Alexander S. Bibliografa Californica; or, notes and materials to aid in forming a more perfect bibliography of those countries anciently called "Californica," and lying within the limits of the Gulf of Cortez to the Arctic Seas, and west of the Rocky Mountains to the Pacific Ocean. n.p. n.p. n.d. 113p. (First published in the Sacramento Daily Union of June 25, 1863, with additions in the same paper of March 13, 1866)   **5958**

Thornton, Crittenden. The laws of California. *In* Eldredge, Zoeth S. History of California. N.Y. Century. 1915. v. V. p397-420   **5958a**

Touton, Frank C. Graduate degrees, with major field in education; given during the academic year in California, 1929/1930-[1933/1934]. Calif. quar. of secondary education. VI. p34-49; VII. p112-28; VIII. p94-110; IX. p77-94; X. p58-67 (1930-34)   **5958b**

Underhill, Leslie. Historical and reminiscent articles in the first twenty volumes of the Grizzly Bear magazine. Grizzly bear. XX. p22-4 (April 1917)   **5958c**

U.S. Bureau of Agricultural Economics. Library. Imperial County, California; a selected list of references. Comp. by Howard B. Turner. (Economic library list no. 27) Wash. D.C. June 1941. 77p. mim.   **5958d**
—— —— —— California; an index to the state sources of agricultural statistics. Part I. Fruits, vegetables and nuts. Part II. Crops other than fruits, vegetables and nuts. Part III. Livestock and livestock products. Part IV. Land, farm property, irrigation, and miscellaneous items—An index to official sources. Part V. An index to some unofficial sources. Comp. by Louise O. Bercaw under the direction of Mary G. Lacy. (Part V comp. under the direction of M. J. Abbott, University of California library) (Agricultural economics bibliog. no. 31) Wash. D.C. 1930-31. mim.   **5959**

U.S. General Land Office. List of original documents in cases presented to the United States land commission, now on file in the office of the United States surveyor-general for California—Catalogue of the original espedientes or records in relation to land claims in upper California under the Spanish and Mexican governments, with references to registries of the same, arranged in alphabetical order, now on file in the Spanish archives of the office of the United States surveyor-general for California. *In* Annual report, 1880. Wash. Govt. Ptg. Off. 1880. p395-454, 455-520. *Also in* Report of the surveyor-general of California made to the Secretary of Interior for the year 1880. Wash. Govt. Ptg. Off. 1881. p113-72, 173-238   **5959a**

U.S. Library of Congress. Division of bibliography. List of references on the Panama-Pacific exposition. Feb. 2, 1914. 6p. typ. (Additional references. 1915. 2p.)   **5960**
—— —— —— Lower California; a bibliographical list. Aug. 15, 1931. 13p. typ. Supplement. Dec. 23, 1938. 9p. photo.   **5960a**

U.S. Works Progress Administration. History of journalism in San Francisco. . . San Francisco. 1939- .reprod. typ. **5960b**

Venable, Reid. Selected list of references relating to irrigation in California. (Calif. Agricultural Experiment Station. Circular no. 260) Berkeley. 1923. 62p   **5961**

Vodges, Anthony W. A bibliography relating to the geology, paleontology and mineral resources of California. (Calif. State Mining Bureau bul. no. 30) Sacramento. 1904. 290p.   **5962**
—— A calatogue of the official geological surveys in the state of California. Calif. Acad. of Sciences. 2d ser. III. p325-37 (May 3, 1893)   **5963**

Wagner, Henry Raup. California imprints, August 1846-June 1851. Berkeley. The Author? 1922. 97p.   **5964**
—— The Templeton Crocker collection of Californiana. Calif. hist. quar. XIX. p79-81 (March 1940) (Books and mss. in the California Historical Society)   **5964a**

Wallis, Talbot H. List of digests, indexes, citations and reports; also, the statute law, journals, and appendices of the California legislature. n.p. n.p. n.d. 2p.   **5965**

Waterson, Robert C. Letter written from San Francisco, Cal., to the Massachusetts Historical Society. Reprinted from the proceedings of the society. Cambridge, Mass. John Wilson and Son. 1870. 10p. (The Proceedings XI. p347-54. 1869-70) (Spanish and Mexican archives of California)   **5965a**

Wheat, Carl Irving. Pioneers; the engaging tale of three early California printing presses, and their strange adventures. Los Angeles. Priv. print. 1924. 29p.   **5965b**
—— The Schweitzer collection of Californiana. Calif. Hist. Soc. quar. XI. p184-7 (June 1932) (Books on the Sonoma valley)   **5966**

Wheeler, Alfred. Land titles in San Francisco, and the laws affecting the same, with a synopsis of all grants and sales of land within the limits claimed by the city. San Francisco. Alta California Steam Ptg. Establishment. 1852. 127p.   **5966a**

Winans, Joseph W. Catalogue of the library of Jos. W. Winans. San Francisco. H. S. Crocker & Co. 1887. 160p.   **5967**

Young, John P. Journalism in California Pacific Coast and exposition biographies. San Francisco. Chronicle Publishing Co. 1915. 362p.   **5968**

COLORADO

Allison, Edith Mary. Bibliography and history of Colorado botany. [Boulder, Colo. 1908?] p51-76. (Reprinted from Univ. of Colorado stud. VI, no. 1. Dec. 1908)   **5968a**

Budd, Montgomery R. Index to Colorado School of Mines publications. Colorado School of Mines quar. XXIII. no. 3. 1928. 44p.   **5969**

Chapman, Eulalia, Bishop, Amie Louise, and Van Male, John. Comprehensive checklist of books and articles on Colorado. Denver, Colo. Bibliographical Center for Research. In progress **5969a**

Colorado. State Board of Library Commissioners. Check list of Colorado public documents. Denver. Smith-Brooks. 1910. 203p.   **5970**

Colorado. State Planning Commission. Annotated catalogue of unpublished engineering and geological reports on mineral resources of Colorado. Denver. Colorado State Planning Comm. Dec. 1936. 91p. mim.   **5971**

Colorado Social Science Association. Preliminary report on the archives of Colorado. May 1929. 31p. multig.   **5971a**

Davidson, L. J. Books concerning Colorado, 1859-1869. Colorado mag. V. p64-75 (April 1928)   **5972**

Historical Records Survey. Colorado. Inventory of the county archives of Colorado. Denver, Colo. 1938- . mim. No. 3. Arapahoe. Feb. 1939. 174p.; No. 6. Bent. July 1938. 175p.; No. 11. Conejos. Oct. 1938. 179p.; No. 12. Costilla. May 1938. 122p.; No. 22. Fremont. Jan. 1938. 146p.; No. 27. Hinsdale. Oct. 1939. 230p.; No. 38. Logan. April 1940. 302p.; No. 44. Morgan. Sept. 1939. 292p.; No. 57. San Miguel. Jan. 1941. 139p.; No. 63. Yuma. Feb. 1941. 163p.   **5972a**

Hoyt, Mary Elizabeth. Bibliography and index of the mines, mining companies and mills of Gilpin County, Colorado, beginning with the discovery of gold in 1859. (Colorado School of Mines quar. XXXII, no. 3) Golden, Colo. 1937. 113p.   **5972b**

Johnson, Jesse Harlan. Bibliography of the geology and related subjects of northwestern Colorado (revised to June 1, 1926). (Colorado School of Mines quar. XXI, no. 3) [Golden 1926] 52p.   **5972c**

Jones, Olive M. Bibliography of Colorado geology and mining with subject index from the earliest explorations to 1912. (Colorado geol. survey. Bul. 7) Denver. 1914. 493p.   **5973**

MacDowd, Kennie. Bibliography of Colorado authors. Denver. Bibliographical Center for Research. Cards   **5973a**

McMurtrie, Douglas C. The public printing of the first territorial legislature of Colorado. Denver, Colo. 1936. p72-8 (Extract from the Colo. mag. March 1936)   **5973b**

McMurtrie, Douglas C. and Allen, Albert H. Early printing in Colorado, with a bibliography of the issues of the press, 1859 to 1876, inclusive, and a record and bibliography of Colorado territorial newspapers. Denver. A. B. Hirschfeld Press. 1935. 305p.   **5974**

Marshall, Thomas M. The miners' law of Colorado. Am. hist. rev. XXV. p426-39 (April 1920)   **5975**

Paxson, Frederic Logan. A preliminary bibliography of Colorado history. Univ. of Colorado stud. III. p101-14, (June 1906)   **5976**

—— The public archives of the state of Colorado. Am Hist. Asso. rep. 1903. I. p415-37   **5977**

Rex, Wallace Hayden. Colorado newspapers, 1859-1933. Published by the Denver Public Library and the State Department of Education as a report on official project no. 665-84-3-59, work project no. 3787, conducted under the auspices of the Works Progress Administration, Women's and professional division. Denver. Bibliographical Center for Research, Rocky Mountain Region. 1939. 775p. photop.   **5977a**

Stone, Wilbur Fiske. The press of Colorado. In History of Colorado. Chicago. S. J. Clarke. 1918. I. p781-815   **5978**

Survey of Federal Archives. Colorado. Inventory of federal archives in the states. Denver, Colo. 1938- . mim. The Federal Courts. Oct. 1939. 36p.; The Department of the Treasury. May 1939. 149p.; The Department of War. May 1939. 90p.; The Department of Justice. Oct. 1939. 22p.; The Department of the Navy. Dec. 1938. 9p.; The Department of Agriculture. Parts I-III. Aug. 1940. 538p.; The Department of Labor. Sept. 1940. 29p.   **5978a**

U.S. Bureau of Agricultural Economics. Library. Delta County, Colorado; a selected list of references. Comp. by Howard B. Turner. (Economic library list no. 21) Wash. D.C. April 1941. 11p. mim.   **5978b**

U.S. National Park Service. Bibliography, Mesa Verde National Park, Colorado. (Occasional pap. no. 1, Mesa Verde National Park. Colorado) n.p. [1935] 20p.   **5979**

Willard, James F. The public archives of Colorado. Am. Hist. Asso. rep. 1911. I. p365-92   **5980**

CONNECTICUT

Andrews, Charles M. [Introductory essay on the colonial laws of Connecticut] *In* Reports on the laws of Connecticut by Francis Fane. (Twelfth publication of the Acorn Club) New Haven. Tuttle, Morehouse and Taylor Press. 1915. p1-54 **5981**

Bacon, William Plumb. Bibliography of class books and class records, 1792-1910, Yale University. [New Britain?] 1910. 21p.   **5981a**

Bates, Albert Carlos. Bibliography of Connecticut broadsides to 1800. Hartford. Connecticut Hist. Soc. In progress **5981b**

—— Check list of Connecticut almanacs, 1709-1850. Am Antiq. Soc. Proc. n.s. XXIV. pt. 1. p93-215 (April 1914) **5982**

—— Connecticut statute laws; a bibliographical list of editions of Connecticut laws from the earliest issues to 1836. (Third publication of the Acorn Club) Hartford. Hartford Press. 1900. 120p.   **5983**

—— Fighting the Revolution with printers ink in Connecticut; the official printing of that colony from Lexington to the Declaration. New Haven. 1918. p129-60 (Reprinted from pap. of the New Haven Colony Hist. Soc. IX) **5984**

—— A list of official publications of Connecticut, 1774-1788 as shown by the bills for printing. (Acorn Club of Connecticut. Publication no. 14) Hartford. Hartford Ptg. Co. 1916. 54p. **5985**

—— Report on the public archives of Connecticut. Am. Hist. Asso. rep. 1900. II. p26-36 **5986**

—— Supplementary list of books printed in Connecticut, 1709-1800. Hartford. Acorn Club. 1938. 91p.. (Supplement to James Hammond Trumbull's List of books. . . .) **5986a**

—— Thomas Green. New Haven Colony Hist. Soc. pap. VIII. p289-309. 1914. (Hartford printer) **5987**

—— The work of Hartford's first printer. *In* Bibliographical essays; a tribute to Wilberforce Eames. Cambridge. Harvard Univ. Press. 1924. p345-61 (Thomas Green, 1764-68) **5988**

Brigham, Clarence S. Connecticut—Bibliography of American newspapers, 1690-1820. Am. Antiq. Soc. Proc. XXIII. p254-330 (Oct. 1913) **5989**

Casey, Marcus A. A typographical galaxy. The Connecticut quar. II. p25-42 (Jan., Feb., March 1896) (Printing at Hartford) **5990**

Clark, David Sanders. Journals and orderly books kept by Connecticut soldiers during the French and Indian war, 1755-1762. New Eng. hist. geneal. reg. XCIV. p225-30 (July 1940) A supplementary list. *ibid.* XCV. p18-20 (Jan. 1941) **5990a**

Connecticut. Examiner of public records. Connecticut town records, June 30, 1930. Comp. under the direction of Lucius B. Barbour (Bul. of the Connecticut State Lib. no. 15) Hartford. The Lib. 1930. 53p.   **5992**

Connecticut. Laws, Statutes, etc. A general index to the private laws and special acts of the state of Connecticut. Comp. by Samuel A. Eddy. Bridgeport, Conn. Marigold Ptg. Co. 1897. 322p. **5992a**

—— —— An index to the general statutes of the state of Connecticut, and to the public acts of 1889 to 1893, both inclusive. Hartford, Conn. Case, Lockwood & Brainard. 1894. 413p. **5992b**

Connecticut. Secretary of State. Report of the Secretary of State and State librarian to the general assembly (of Connecticut) on Ancient court records. By L. M. Hubbard and C. J. Hoadley. Hartford. Case, Lockwood & Brainard. 1889. 35p. **5993**

Connecticut. State Library. Connecticut state publications, their binding and distribution. By George S. Godard. (Bul. no. 11) Hartford, Conn. 1925. 27p. (Reprinted from the report of the state librarian, 1922) **5993a**

—— —— Connecticut state publications, town and municipal publications. *In* Connecticut State Library. Rep. 1908. Hartford. Pub. by the State. 1909. p17-29 (Also issued as Bulletins of the Connecticut State Lib. no. 3) **5994**

—— —— (81) probate districts deposited in the Connecticut State Library, Hartford. [Hartford, Conn. 1934?] **5994a**

—— —— Instructions for care of archives in the Connecticut State Library. By Effie M. Prickett. (Bulletins of the Connecticut State Lib. no. 8) Hartford. The Lib. 1920. 14p. **5995**

—— —— Public documents of the state of Connecticut. . . (Bul. no. 14) Hartford. 1929. 13p. **5995a**

—— Select list of manuscripts in the Connecticut State Library. (Connecticut State Lib. Bul. no. 9. *In* Report of the state librarian, 1916, Appendix II) Hartford. The Lib. 1920. 32p. **5996**

Connecticut. Temporary examiner of public records. Reports, 1904, 1906, 1908. Hartford. Hartford Press. 1904-09. 3v. in 1 **5996a**

Connecticut. Tercentenary Commission. Exhibition of maps of Connecticut, past and present. . . . [Hartford, Conn. 1935] [13]p. **5996b**

—— —— The Tercentenary pamphlet series and its contributors. [New Haven] 1936. 22p. **5996c**

Connecticut Historical Society. Connecticut local histories in Connecticut Historical Society and Watkinson Library. Connecticut Hist. Soc. pap. and rep. 1895. p22-38 **5997**

—— Examples of Connecticut imprints of the eighteenth century, exhibited by the Connecticut Historical Society and the Watkinson library. Hartford. The Soc. 1935. 32p. **5997a**

—— List of bound newspapers in the Connecticut Historical Society. Connecticut Hist. Soc. pap. and rep. 1893. p30-4 **5998**

—— List of family genealogies in the library of the Connecticut Historical Society, corrected to August 31. Hartford. The Soc. 1911. 42p. **5999**

—— Manuscripts of Connecticut interest exhibited by the Connecticut Historical Society and the Watkinson Library. Hartford. 1935. 23p. **6000**

—— Publications by Connecticut authors exhibited by the Connecticut Historical Society and the Watkinson Library. Hartford. 1935. 28p. **6001**

—— Some of the manuscript collections in the Connecticut Historical Society. Connecticut Hist. Soc. pap. and rep. 1893. p26-30 **6002**

Connecticut. State Planning Board. A bibliography on the land and water resources of Connecticut. Hartford, Conn. 1934. 27p. typ. **6002a**

Crofut, Florence S. Bibliography. *In* Guide to the history and the historic sites of Connecticut. New Haven. Yale Univ. Press. 1937. II. p877-913, also *passim* **6002b**

Cushman, Alice Burrington. An index of material concerning Connecticut. Prepared for elementary and junior high school grades. Hartford. Connecticut State Dept. of Education. 1935. 32p. **6003**

Fisher, Samuel H. The publications of Thomas Collier, printer 1784-1808. Litchfield. Litchfield Hist. Soc. 1933. 98p. **6004**

Flagg, Charles Allcott. (Reference list on Connecticut local history. N. Y. State Lib. Bul. 53. Dec. 1900. Bibliog. II, no. 23) Albany. Univ. of the State of N.Y. 1900. p175-283 **6005**

Gay, Frank B. Bibliography of the society. *In* Connecticut Historical Society. Historical documents and notes; genesis and development of the society and associated institutions in the Wadsworth Athenaeum. Hartford. Case, Lockwood & Brainard. 1889. p81-4 **6006**

Godard, George S. Archives of Connecticut. National Asso. of State Libraries. Lib. proc. and pap. 1926-27. p12-17 (Also in Am. Lib. Asso. bul. XXI. p441-5. Oct. 1927) **6007**

—— Connecticut state publications; their binding and distribution. (Bul. of the Connecticut State Lib. no. 11) Hartford. The Soc. 1925. 27p. **6008**

—— History and progress of collecting material for a bibliography of Connecticut. Bibliog. Soc. of Amer. pap. II. p84-94. 1907-08 **6009**

Gregory, H. E. Bibliography of the geology of Connecticut. (Connecticut Geological Survey bul. VIII) Hartford, Conn. 1907. 123p. **6009a**

Gummere, J. S. Some noted trials in Connecticut; a bibliography. Law lib. jour. XXX. p529-39 (Nov. 1937) **6009b**

Hartford, Connecticut. General index of the land records, 1639-1839, volumes 1 and 61, inclusive. Hartford. Wiley, Waterman & Eaton. 1873. 613p. **6010**

Hasse, Adelaide Rosalie. Index of economic material in documents of the states of United States: Connecticut, 1789-1904. Prep. for the Department of Economics and Sociology of the Carnegie Institution of Washington. (Unpublished manuscript on cards in the Connecticut State Library) **6010a**

Historical Records Survey. Connecticut. Inventory of the church archives of Connecticut. New Haven, Conn. 1940- . mim. Protestant Episcopal. Sept. 1940. 309p.; Lutheran. 1941. 188p. **6010b**

—— —— Inventory of the town and city archives of Connecticut. New Haven, Conn. 1938- . mim. No. 1. Fairfield County: vol. 21. Weston. May 1940. 108p.; No. 2. Hartford County: vol. 1. Avon, Berlin, Bloomfield. July 1939. 299p., vol. 17. Newington. Dec. 1939. 98p.; No. 5. New Haven County: vol. 8. North Branford, North Haven, Orange, Oxford, Prospect, Seymour, Southbury. June 1938. 189p. **6010c**

—— —— Preliminary check list of American portraits, 1620-1825 found in Connecticut. Hartford, Conn. 1939. 37p. mim. **6010d**

Kilbourn, Dwight C. Catalogue of the American library of Dwight C. Kilbourn, Part I, Litchfield, Conn., 1908. Pittsfield, Mass. Sun Ptg. Co. 1908? 85p. **6011**

King, John Hamilton. Index to the general statutes of Connecticut, revision of 1930. Orange, Conn. 1932. p2041-515 **6011a**

Litchfield Historical Society. Catalogue of books, papers and manuscripts of the Litchfield Historical Society, Noyes Memorial Building. Litchfield, Conn. 1906. 115p. **6012**

McMurtrie, Douglas C. Pioneer printing in Connecticut. Springfield, Ill. 1932. 4p. (Reprinted from the National printer journalist, June 1932) **6013**

Maltbie, William Mills and Townshend, Henry H. Index-digest of the Connecticut reports, volumes 64 to 97, inclusive [1894-1922] including a table of cases reported from Kirby to volume 98 inclusive [1785-1923.] Hartford? Published by the state of Connecticut. 1924. 765p. **6013a**

Mead, Nelson P. Public archives of Connecticut. Am. Hist. Asso. rep. 1906. II. p53-127 **6014**

National Society of the Colonial Dames of America. Connecticut. Connecticut houses; a list of manuscript histories of early Connecticut homes. (Bul. of the Connecticut State Lib. no. 16. *In* Report of the state librarian, 1930) Hartford. Pub. by the state. 1931. p79-117 (Earlier list in Report of the state librarian for 1922) **6014a**

Paltsits, Victor Hugo. The almanacs of Roger Sherman, 1750-1761. Worcester. Davis Press. 1907. 48p. (Reprinted from the Am. Antiq. Soc. proc. n.s. XVIII. p213-58) **6015**

Perry, Frederick L. A general index to the private laws and special acts of the state of Connecticut. Rockville, Conn. 1922. 266p.   6015a

Porter, William S. Archives of Connecticut. New Eng. hist. geneal. reg. III. p167-8 (April 1849)   6015b

Survey of Federal Archives. Connecticut. Inventory of federal archives in the states. Hartford, Conn. 1939- . mim. The Federal Courts. June 1939. 29p.; The Department of the Treasury. Pt. 1. 1941. 296p.; The Department of War. May 1939. 63p.; The Department of Justice. March 1940. 17p.; The Department of the Navy. May 1939. 76p.; The Department of the Interior. Dec. 1939. 13p.; The Department of Agriculture. June 1940. 199p.; The Department of Commerce. June 1940. 24p.; The Veterans' Administration June 1940. 42p.; The Department of Labor. Dec. 1940. 25p.; The Civil Works Administration. Dec. 1939. 12p.; Miscellaneous Agencies. March 1940. 84p.
6015c

Thompson, Edmund. Maps of Connecticut before the year 1800; a descriptive list. Windham, Conn. Hawthorn House. 1940. 66p.   6015d

Trumbull, James Hammond. List of books printed in Connecticut, 1709-1800. (Acorn Club publication no. 9) Hartford. Case, Lockwood & Brainard. 1904. 251p. 6016

U.S. Library of Congress. Division of bibliography. Select list of references on the "Blue laws" of Connecticut. 1908. 4p. typ.   6017

Wegelin, Oscar. A bibliographical list of books and pamphlets relating to or printed in Stamford, Fairfield County, Connecticut. Bibliog. Soc. of Amer. pap. VII. p22-32. 1913   6018

Yale University. Library. List of Connecticut and New Haven imprints. MS. 6018a

DELAWARE

American Swedish Historical Museum. New Sweden historical exhibit, 1638-1938; official catalog, June-July, nineteen hundred thirty-eight. Phila., N.Y. Aquatone Presses of E. Stern & Company, Inc. 1938. 70p.   6018b

Brigham, Clarence S. Delaware—Bibliography of American newspapers, 1690-1820. Am. Antiq. Soc. proc. n.s. XXIII. p331-42 (Oct. 1913)   6019

Conrad, Henry C. Newspapers and books. In History of the state of Delaware. Wilmington. The Author. 1908. III. p1085-116   6020

Dawson, Edgar. Public archives of Delaware. Am. Hist. Asso. rep. 1906. II. p129-48   6021

Delaware. Public archives commission. Calendar of records in the custody of the public archives commission of the state of Delaware, December 1, 1932. Dover? 4p. (Reprod. from typ. copy)
6022

Delaware. State Portrait Commission. Catalogue of Delaware portraits collected by the Delaware State Portrait Commission in the capitol buildings, Dover, Delaware. Dover, Dela. 1941. 64p. 6022a

Delaware Historical Society. Price list of publications of the Historical Society of Delaware. . . Wilmington, Del. [Wilmington] 1940. 11p.   6022b

Gilpin Library of the Historical Society of Pennsylvania. New Sweden, 1638-1938; being a catalogue of rare books and manuscripts relating to the Swedish colonization on the Delaware River. Phila. 1938. 51p.   6022c

Hasse, Adelaide Rosalie. Index of economic material in documents of the states of the United States: Delaware, 1789-1904. (Carnegie Inst. of Wash. Publication no. 85) Wash. D.C. Carnegie Inst. of Wash. 1910. 137p.   6023

Hawkins, Dorothy Lawson. A checklist of Delaware imprints up to and including 1800; a contribution to the history of printing in Delaware. (Columbia Univ. Master's essay) 1928. 74p. typ.   6024

—— James Adams; the first printer of Delaware. Bibliog. Soc. of Amer. pap. XXVIII. pt. 1. p28-63. 1934   6025

Historical Records Survey. Delaware. Inventory of the church archives of Delaware: Preprint of sections 22. Lutheran Church, and 29. Protestant Episcopal Church. Wilmington, Del. June 1938. 43p. mim.   6025a

Jacobowsky, C. Vilh. Litteraturen om Nya Sverige. Ymer, 1937. p272-98 (A bibliographical study of the literature dealing with New Sweden on the Delaware)
6025b

Johnson, Amandus. Bibliography. In The Swedish settlements on the Delaware; their history and relation to the Indians, Dutch and English. N.Y. Appleton. 1911. II. p767-812   6026

Keen, Gregory B. Critical essay on the sources of information—New Sweden, or the Swedes on the Delaware. In Narrative and critical history of America. Ed. by Justin Winsor. Boston, N.Y. Houghton Mifflin. 1884. IV. p488-502   6027

McMurtrie, Douglas C. The Delaware imprints of 1761. Metuchen, N.J. Priv. printed. 1934. 8p.   6028

Michigan. University. William L. Clements Library of American History. New Sweden, 1638-1938; a guide to an exhibition of rare books and maps in the William L. Clements library arranged in commemoration of the tercentenary of the Swedish settlements on the Delaware. (Bulletin no. XXVIII) Ann Arbor. Univ. of Michigan. 1938. 12p.   6028a

National Society of Colonial Dames of America. Delaware. A calendar of Delaware wills, New Castle County, 1682-1800. Abstracted and compiled by the Historical research committee of the Colonial Dames of Delaware. N.Y. H. F. Hitchcock. 1911. 218p.   6029

Ryden, George Herbert. Bibliography of Delaware history. Univ. of Delaware. [1927] 25p. mim.   6030

Survey of federal archives. Delaware. Inventory of federal archives in the states. Wilmington, Del. 1941- . mim. The Farm Credit Administration. March 1941. 9p.   6030a

U.S. Library of Congress. Books, maps and prints relating to New Sweden; tercentenary commemorating the first settlement of the Swedes and the Finns on the Delaware, 1638-1938. Wash. Govt. Ptg. Off. 1938. 51p.   6030b

FLORIDA

Beer, William. List of original authorities on the history of the British province of West Florida, in the Record Office, London. In The capture of Fort Charlotte, Mobile. La. hist. soc. pub. I, pt. 3. p34. 1896   6030c

Beeson, Eleanor. The St. Augustine Historical Restoration. Fla. hist. quar. XVI. p110-18 (Oct. 1937)   6030d

Buckingham-Smith collection. Transcripts and bibliography of material in the sixteenth, seventeenth and eighteenth centuries relating to Florida. (In the N. Y. Hist. Soc.)   6031

Chatelain, Verne E. The St. Augustine historical program. Carnegie Institution of Washington. Yearbook. XXXVI. p372-7. 1936-37; XXXVII. p389-91. 1937-38   6031a

Cole, Theodore Lee. Bibliography of the statute law of the southern states. Part III: Florida. Southern Hist. Asso. pubs. I. p211-25 (July 1897)   6031b

Colonial land claims in East and West Florida. Fla. hist. quar. XVII. p243-4 (Jan. 1939) (Historical Records Survey work upon the records of the Boards of Commissioners 1822-26)   6031c

A digest of Florida material in Niles' register (1811-1849). Fla. hist. quar. XVIII. p227-8 (Jan. 1940)   6031d

Emig, Elmer J. A check-list of extant Florida newspapers, 1845-1876. Florida Hist. Soc. quar. IX. p77-87 (Oct. 1932) 6032

Florida. Agricultural Experiment Station. Catalog of the official publications of the Florida Agricultural experiment station and Florida Agricultural extension service, 1888-1937. Comp. by Ida Keeling Cresap. Gainesville, Fla. Univ. of Fla. 1938. 97p.   6032a

Florida. State Library. Florida material in the volumes of Niles' register, National intelligencer, and De Bow's review in Florida State Library. Tallahassee. State Lib. 1932. 19p. mim.   6032b

────── Florida material in U.S. Congressional documents in Florida State Library. Tallahassee. State Lib. 1932. 15p. mim.   6032c

Florida. University. Department of journalism. Bibliography of newspapers in Florida from 1830 to 1876. MS.   6033

Florida Historical Society. The quarterly periodical; index, volumes VII-XIV. In Fla. hist. soc. quar. XIV. p283-95. 1936 6033a

Florida Library Association. Preliminary check list of Floridiana, 1500-1865, in the libraries of Florida. Comp. by Pattie Porter Frost. Florida lib. bul. II. p2-16 (April 1930)   6034

Hanna, Alfred Jackson. The union catalog of Floridiana. N.Y. 1939. p67-74 (Reprinted from the Proceedings of the second convention of the Inter-American Bibliographical and Library Association, 1939)   6034a

Harley, A. F. Bernard Romans's map of Florida engraved by Paul Revere, and other early maps in the library of the Florida Historical Society. Fla. Hist. Soc. quar. IX. p47-57 (July 1930)   6034b

Hasbrouck, Alfred. A union catalog of Floridiana. Fla. hist. soc. quar. XVI. p119-26 (Oct. 1937)   6034c

Historical Records Survey. Florida. Check list: records required by law in Florida counties (revised). Jacksonville, Fla. 1939. 89p. mim.   6034d

────── Guide to depositories of manuscript collections in the United States: Florida. Jacksonville, Fla. April 1940. 28p. mim.   6034e

────── Guide to public vital statistics records in Florida. Jacksonville. 1941. 70p.   6034f

────── Inventory of the church archives of Florida: Baptist bodies. Jacksonville, Fla. 1939- . mim. No. 3. Black Creek Baptist Association. July 1940. 20p.; No. 12. Lake County Baptist Association. April 1940. 33p.; No. 17. Northeast Florida Baptist Association. April 1940. 21p.; No. 18. Northwest Baptist Association. Oct. 1940. 25p.; No. 19. Okaloosa Baptist Association. May 1940. 21p.; No. 20. Orange Blossom Baptist Association. June 1940. 40p.; No. 21. Palm-Lake Baptist Association. July 1940. 16p.; No. 25. Pinellas County Baptist Association. June 1940. 28p.; No. 30. Seminole Baptist Association. June 1940. 42p.; No. 32. Southwest Baptist Association. Sept. 1939. 29p.; Florida State Association of Old Line Baptists, composed of missionary Baptist churches. July 1940. 14p.; Digest of the Roman Catholic records in Florida: St. Augustine parish, white baptisms, 1784-1792. 1941. 162p. 6034g

────── Inventory of the county archives of Florida. Jacksonville, Fla. 1938- . mim. No. 8. Charlotte. Nov. 1938. 149p.; No. 10. Clay. Jan. 1941. 478p.; No. 11. Collier. March 1938. 134p.; No. 16. Duval. Feb. 1938. 185p.; No. 18. Flagler. Aug. 1938. 126p.; No. 25. Hardee.

Historical Records Survey. Florida. Inventory of county archives—*Continued* June 1939. 250p.; No. 26. Hendry. June 1938. 141p.; No. 46. Okaloosa. May 1939. 179p.; No. 54. Pinellas. June 1940. 380p.; No. 58. Sarasota. May 1939. 217p. **6034h**
—— —— A preliminary short-title check list of books, pamphlets, and broadsides printed in Florida, 1784-1860. Comp. by Douglas C. McMurtrie. (American imprints inventory. Imprints memoranda, no. 1) Jacksonville. 1937. 3, 15p. mim. **6034i**

The **Historical** Records Survey and State Archives Survey of Florida. Fla. hist. quar. XVII. p59-63 (July 1938) **6034j**

Jacksonville, Florida. Public Library. Genealogical material, local and state history in the Jacksonville Public Library. Comp. by Pattie Porter Frost. Jacksonville. Arnold Ptg. Co. 1929. 15p. **6035**

Karpinski, Charles L. Mapping Florida. Print connoisseur. IX. p291-310. 1929 **6035a**

Julien C. Yonge Library, Pensacola, Florida. Catalogue. . . . Copy prepared by Historical Records Survey and State Archives Survey, WPA State Office. Jacksonville. 1937 **6035b**

Kimber, Sidney A. The "relation of a late expedition to St. Augustine," with biographical and bibliographical notes on Isaac and Edward Kimber. Bibliog. Soc. of Amer. pap. XXVIII. pt. 2. p81-96. 1934 **6036**

Knauss, James Owen. Territorial Florida journalism. (Publications of the Florida State Hist. Soc. no. 6) Deland. Florida State Hist. Soc. 1926. 250p. **6037**

McMurtrie, Douglas C. The first printing in Florida. Atlanta, Ga. Priv. printed. 1931. 18p. (Reprinted with additions from the Southern printer for March 1931) **6038**

Manning, Mabel M. The East Florida papers in the Library of Congress. Hispanic Am. hist. rev. X. p392-7 (April 1930) **6039**

Marchman, Watt. The Florida Historical Society, 1856-1861, 1879, 1902-1940. Fla. hist. quar. XIX. p3-65 (July 1940) **6039a**
—— History of the Florida archives from 1513 to date. St. Augustine, Fla. In progress **6039b**

Mowat, Charles L. Material relating to British East Florida in the Gage papers and other manuscript collections in the William L. Clements Library. Fla. hist. quar. XVIII. p46- (July 1939) **6039c**

Robertson, James Alexander. The archival distribution of Florida manuscripts. Florida Hist. Soc. quar. X. p35-50 (July 1931) **6040**
—— Bibliography of Florida to 1821; and An annotated checklist of Florida books and pamphlets, 1821 to date. (In progress) **6041**
—— The preservation of Florida history. North Carolina hist. rev. IV. p351-65 (Oct. 1927) **6042**

—— The Spanish manuscripts of the Florida State Historical Society. Worcester, Mass. Am. Antiq. Soc. 1929. 24p. (Reprinted from the Am. Antiq. Soc. proc. for April 1929) **6043**

Saunders, Harold Rinalden. English books written by Floridians, residents and visitors. (Univ. of Florida. Master's thesis) August 1929. 119p. typ. **6044**

Sellards, E. H. Bibliography of Florida geology. *In* Florida Geological Survey. Annual report. I, 1907-08. Tallahassee. 1908. p73-108 **6044a**

Survey of Federal Archives. Florida. Inventory of federal archives in the states. Jacksonville, Fla. 1940- . mim. The Federal Courts. May 1940. 67p.; The Department of the Treasury. May 1941. 240p.; The Department of War. May 1940. 176p.; The Department of the Navy. March 1941. 177p.; The Department of Justice. April 1941. 43p.; Department of Agriculture. 1941. 203p.; The Department of Commerce. 1941. 35p.; The Veterans' Administration. Feb. 1941. 28p. **6044b**

T. T. Wentworth, Jr. Library, Pensacola, Florida. Catalogue. . . . Copy prepared by Historical Records Survey and State Archives Survey, WPA State Office. Jacksonville. 1936 **6044c**

Thomas, David Y. Report on the public archives of Florida. Am. Hist. Asso. rep. 1906. II. p149-58 **6045**
—— Report upon the historic buildings, monuments and local archives of St. Augustine, Florida. Am. Hist. Asso. rep. 1905. I. p339-52 **6046**

Typoscripts of manuscripts made by Florida Historical Records Survey. Fla. hist. quar. XVIII. p216-24 (Jan. 1940) **6046a**

U.S. Library of Congress. Division of bibliography. List of books relating to Florida. Nov. 30, 1921. 7p. typ. (Supplement. July 24, 1933. 19p. typ.) **6047**

U.S. National Archives. The Spanish archives of Florida, 1821-1938. By Irene A. Wright. 1938 (MS. in The National Archives) **6047a**

Wroth, Lawrence C. Source materials of Florida history in the John Carter Brown University. Fla. hist. quar. XX. p3-46 (July 1941) **6047b**

GEORGIA

Banks, E. M. and Phillips, Ulrich B. Early newspaper files in the library of Emory College, Georgia. Gulf states hist. mag. II. p194-5 (Nov. 1903) **6048**

Bibliography of the Georgia Historical Society. Ga. Hist. Soc. ann. 1916. p27-37 **6048a**

Brantley, Rabun Lee. Georgia journalism of the Civil war period. (Contributions to education of George Peabody College for Teachers no. 58) Nashville. George Peabody College for Teachers. 1929. 134p. **6049**

Brigham, Clarence S. Georgia—Bibliography of the American newspaper, 1690-1820. Am. Antiq. Soc. proc. n.s. XXIII. p370-94 (Oct. 1913) **6050**

Brooks, Robert P. A preliminary bibliography of Georgia history. (Univ. of Georgia bul. X. no. 10A. ser. no. 127) Athens, Ga. McGregor. 1910. 45p. **6051**

Cobb, Maud B. Check list of the Georgia archival material in certain offices of the capitol. Georgia Hist. Asso. proc. I. p49-63. 1917 **6052**

—— The condition of Georgia's archives. Georgia Hist. Asso. proc. I. p32-5. 1917 **6053**

Crane, Verner W. The promotion literature of Georgia. In Bibliographical essays; a tribute to Wilberforce Eames. Cambridge. Harvard Univ. Press. 1924. p281-98 **6054**

De Renne, Wymberley Jones. Books relating to the history of Georgia in the library of Wymberley Jones De Renne, of Wormsloe, Isle of Hope, Chatham County, Georgia, 1905. Savannah. Savannah morning news. 1905. 74p. **6055**

Emory University. Indexes to the City Builder (Atlanta), Methodist Magazine, and Atlanta Journal Magazine. Emory University, Ga. **6055a**

Flanders, Bertram H. Finding list of Georgia newspapers, 1763-1860. Duke University, Durham, N.C. In progress **6055b**

—— Finding list of Georgia periodicals, 1802-1865. Duke University, Durham, N.C. In progress **6055c**

—— Georgia literary periodicals to 1865. Duke University, Durham, N.C. In progress **6055d**

Flanders, Ralph B. Newspapers and periodicals in the Washington Memorial library, Macon, Ga. North Carolina hist. rev. VII. p220-3 (April 1930) **6056**

Flisch, Julia A. Report on the local records of Georgia. Am. Hist. Asso. rep. 1906. II. p159-64 **6057**

Georgia. Office of Compiler of State Records. Report of Allen D. Candler, compiler of state records, to the governor, June 16, 1903. Atlanta, Ga. G.W. Harrison, State Printer [Franklin Ptg. and Pub. Co.] 1903. 14p. **6057a**

Georgia. State Department of Archives and History. Revolutionary soldiers' receipts for Georgia bounty grants. Issued by Georgia State Dept. of Archives and History. Ruth Blair, state historian and director. Atlanta. Foote and Davies Co. 1928. 85p. (Longhand MS. in the Lib. of Cong.) **6058**

Georgia. State Library. Card index to Georgia items appearing in the Atlanta Constitution. Atlanta, Ga. **6058a**

—— —— Trial checklist of Georgia state documents. Comp. by Ella May Thornton. [Atlanta] 1940. 70p. typ. **6058b**

Georgia. University. A history of journalism and newspapers in Georgia, 1820-1932. Athens, Ga. ERA project **6058c**

Georgia Historical Society. Bibliography of the Georgia Historical Society. Georgia Hist. Soc. ann. 1916. p27-37 **6059**

—— General index Georgia historical quarterly, volumes I through XV. Comp. by Eva W. Martin. Savannah. 1931. 28p. **6060**

—— List of publications of the Georgia Historical Society. Georgia hist. quar. XII. p61-70 (March 1928) **6061**

Georgia Historical Society. Name index to newspapers. Savannah, Ga. ms. **6061a**

Georgia State Library. The De Renne gift. By John Milledge. Atlanta. Geo. H. Harrison, state printer. 1894. 20p. **6062**

Hart, Bertha Sheppard. Introduction to Georgia writers. Macon. J. W. Burke. 1930. 322p. **6063**

Historical Records Survey. Georgia. Classified inventory of Georgia maps. Atlanta, Ga. April 1941. 149p. mim. **6063a**

—— —— Inventory of the church archives of Georgia. Atlanta, Ga. 1941- . mim. Atlanta association of Baptist church, affiliated with Georgia Baptist convention. April 1941. 92p. **6063b**

—— —— Inventory of the county archives of Georgia. Atlanta, Ga. 1938- . mim. No. 25. Chatham. March 1938. 160p.; No. 32. Clinch. Sept. 1940. 52p.; No. 37. Cook. Aug. 1941. 114p.; No. 47. Dougherty. Jan. 1941. 254p.; No. 50. Echols. Sept. 1940. 46p.; No. 81. Jefferson. May 1940. 231p.; No. 106. Muscogee. Jan. 1941. 319p.; No. 121. Richmond. April 1939. 152p. **6063c**

Jack, Theodore H. Historiography in Georgia. Proc. of the first annual session of the Georgia Hist. Asso. 1917. p21-32 **6064**

—— The preservation of Georgia history. North Carolina hist. rev. IV. p239-51 (July 1927) **6065**

Jone·, Charles C. Critical essay on the sources of information—The English colonization of Georgia. In Narrative and critical history of America. Ed. by Justin Winsor. Boston, N.Y. Houghton Mifflin. 1887. V. p392-405 **6066**

Knight, Lucian Lamar. Shall our records be lost? Georgia's most vital need: a department of archives. Report of . . . compiler of state records, to the governor, June 30, 1917. Atlanta, Ga. Byrd Ptg. Co. 1917. 34p. **6066a**

Lamar, Joseph R. Georgia law books. Georgia Bar Asso. rep. 1898. p118-46 **6067**

Lanning, John Tate. A descriptive catalogue of some legajos on Georgia in the Spanish archives. Georgia hist. quar. XIII. p410-21 (Dec. 1929) **6068**

Mackall, Leonard L. The Wymberley Jones De Renne Georgia Library. Georgia hist. quar. II. p63-86 (June 1918) **6069**

McMurtrie, Douglas C. The first printing in Georgia. Metuchen, N.J. Printed for Charles F. Heartman. 1927. 8p. **6070**

Murtrie, Douglas C. James Johnston, first printer in the royal colony of Georgia. The Lib. 4th ser. X. no. 1. p73-83. 1930 (Also in Trans. of the Bibliog. Soc. second ser. X. p78-80. 1929. Reprinted from this, London. 1929) **6071**
—— Located Georgia imprints of the eighteenth century not in the De Renne catalogue. Savannah. Priv. printed. 1934. 44p. (Also in the Georgia hist. quar. XVIII. p27-65. March 1934) **6072**
—— The pioneer printer of Georgia. Chicago. Eyncourt Press. 1930. 11p. (Reprint from the Southern printer for June 1929) **6073**
—— Pioneer printing in Georgia. Savannah. Priv. printed. 1932. 39p. (Reprint from the June 1932 issue of the Georgia hist. quar.) **6074**
Milledge, John. The De Renne gift. Atlanta, Ga. 1894. 20p. (Georgia and the South) **6074a**
Phillips, Ulrich Bonnell. Georgia local archives. Am. Hist. Asso. rep. 1904. p555-96 **6075**
—— The public archives of Georgia. Am. Hist. Asso. rep. 1903. I. p439-74 **6076**
Savannah, Ga. Public Library. Index of historical source materials on Chatham County and Savannah, Georgia. Savannah, Ga. ERA project **6076a**
Survey of Federal Archives. Georgia. Inventory of federal archives in the states. Atlanta, Ga. 1939- . mim. The Federal Courts. Jan. 1941. 113p.; The Department of the Treasury. June 1939. 161p.; The Department of War. Feb. 1941. 404p.; The Department of Justice. Aug. 1939. 130p.; The Department of the Navy. May 1939. 21p.; The Department of Agriculture. 1941. The Farm Credit Administration. Feb. 1941. 33p. **6076b**
Thornton, Ella May. Finding list of books and pamphlets relating to Georgia and Georgians. Atlanta. 1928. 129p. **6077**
—— The legal literature of Georgia. Law Lib. jour. XXV. p201-8 (July 1932) **6078**
U.S. Library of Congress. Division of bibliography. List of references on the history and government of Georgia (State, county, local and municipal). Nov. 6, 1920. 11p. typ. **6079**
Wymberley Jones De Renne Library. Catalogue of the Wymberley Jones De Renne Georgia Library at Wormsloe, Isle of Hope, near Savannah, Georgia. Comp. by Azalea Clizbee. Wormsloe. Priv. printed. 1931. 3v. **6080**

IDAHO

Historical Records Survey. Idaho. A check list of Idaho imprints, 1839-1890. (American imprints inventory, no. 13) Chicago. 1940. 74p. reprod. typ. **6080a**
—— —— Inventory of the county archives of Idaho. Boise, Idaho. 1937- . mim. No. 11. Boundary. Feb. 1939. 139p.; No. 17. Clark. March 1940. 115p.; No. 28. Kootenai. Oct. 1939. 199p.; No. 30.

Lemhi. May 1938. 66p.; No. 34. Minidoka. Sept. 1937. 51p.; No. 35. Nez Perce. June 1939. 194p.; No. 39. Power. April 1941. 144p.; No. 41. Teton. Dec. 1940. 123p. **6080b**
—— —— A short-title check list of books, pamphlets, and broadsides printed in Idaho, 1839-1890. Comp. by Douglas C. McMurtrie (American imprints inventory. Imprints memoranda, no. 2) Chicago, Ill. 1938. 45p. mim. **6080c**
Idaho. State Historical Society, Boise. Manuscript index of Idaho newspapers. **6081**
McMurtrie, Douglas C. The beginnings of printing in Idaho. Mainz. 1932. p234-45 (Sonderabzug aus dem Gutenberg-Jahrbuch. 1932) **6082**
Marshall, Thomas M. Report on the public archives of Idaho. Am. Hist. Asso. rep. 1917. p137-72 **6083**
Rees, John E. Idaho chronology, nomenclature, bibliography. Chicago. W. B. Conkey. 1918. 125p. **6084**
Survey of Federal Archives. Idaho. Inventory of federal archives in the states. Ogden, Utah. 1939- mim. The Department of Justice. June 1939. 16p.; The Department of Agriculture. Sept. 1939. 316p.; The Department of Commerce. June 1939. 22p. **6084a**
U.S. Library of Congress. Division of bibliography. Brief list of references on Idaho: its history, resources and industries. May 29, 1919. 4p. typ. **6085**
Varley, Thomas and others. A preliminary report on the mining districts of Idaho. (U.S. Bureau of Mines. Bul. 166) Wash. Govt. Ptg. Off. 1919. 113p. (Bibliographies on counties through the text compiled by A. C. Stewart and D. C. Livingston) **6086**

ILLINOIS

Advertising Federation of America. A subject-index to market research information on Chicago and Cook County, Illinois. Prepared by the Bureau of research and education of the Advertising Federation of America in cooperation with the Local community research committee of the University of Chicago. 1929. 66p. **6087**
Alvord, Clarence Walworth. Eighteenth-century French records in the archives of Illinois. Am. Hist. Asso. rep. 1905. I. p353-66 **6088**
—— The finding of the Kaskaskia records. Illinois State Hist. Soc. trans. 1906. publication no. 11. p27-31 **6089**
—— Bibliography. In The centennial history of Illinois. Chicago. McClurg. 1920-22. 5v. **6090**
—— Sources of early Catholic history in Illinois. Ill. Cath. hist. rev. I. p73-8 (Nov. 1918) **6090a**
Alvord, Clarence Walworth and Pease, Theodore Calvin. The archives of the state of Illinois. Am. Hist. Asso. rep. 1909. p379-463 **6091**

Angle, Paul McClelland. Suggested readings in Illinois history; with a selected list of historical fiction. Springfield, Ill. 1935. 26p. **6092**

Bay, Jens Christian. Scarce and beautiful imprints of Chicago. Bibliog. Soc. of Amer. pap. XV. pt. 2. p88-102. 1922 (Also reprinted) **6093**

Bibliography of Illinois medical history. Illinois medical jour. XLIX. p389-99. 1926 **6094**

Blood, Kenneth. The Macon County Recorder's office. Ill. lib. XXII. p27-8 (March 1940) **6094a**

Bonney, Charles C. Bibliography of World's Congress publications. *In* U S. Commissioner of Education. Rep. 1893-94. Wash. Govt. Ptg. Off. 1896. II. p1754-60. (Reprinted from The Dial. XX. p7-10. Jan. 1, 1896) **6095**

Boss, Henry Rush. Early newspapers in Illinois; read before the Franklin Society of the city of Chicago, January 20, 1870. (Franklin Soc. publications. II) Chicago. Franklin Soc. 1870. 48p. **6096**

Buck, Solon Justus. Travel and description, 1765-1865; together with a list of county histories, atlases, and biographical collections and a list of territorial and state laws. (Coll. of the Illinois State Hist. Lib. v. IX. Bibliog. ser. v. II) Springfield. Illinois State Hist. Lib. 1914. 514p. **6097**

Chicago. City Council. Index to the journal of the proceedings of the city council, 1927/28. [Chicago. 1928-] **6097a**

Chicago. Municipal reference library. Checklist of publications issued by local governing bodies in Chicago and Cook County. Chicago. 1936-37. 2v. reprod. **6097b**

—— —— Check-list of publications issued by local governing bodies in Chicago and Cook County. Chicago. 1940. 3p. mim. **6097c**

Chicago. University. Library. Newspapers in libraries of metropolitan Chicago; a union list prepared by the University of Chicago libraries, document division. Chicago. 1931. 89p. **6098**

—— —— Private civic and social service agencies of Chicago; a union list of their reports and publications. Chicago. Univ. of Chicago Bookstore. 1936. 243p. **6099**

Chicago and Cook county; a union list of their official publications, including the semi-official institutions. The University of Chicago libraries, Document section. Chicago. 1934. 231p. mim. **6100**

Conover, James F. A digested index of all the reported decisions in law and equity of the Supreme Courts of the states of Ohio, Indiana and Illinois [1819-30]. Phila. Key & Biddle. 1834. 512p. **6100a**

Federal Writers' Project. Illinois. Selected bibliography; Illinois, Chicago, and its environs. Chicago. American Guide Series. 1937. 58p. photop. **6100b**

Field, Alston G. The Historical Records Survey in Illinois. Ill. State Hist. Soc. jour. XXX. p264-9. 1937 **6100c**

Fleming, Herbert Easton. Magazines of a market-metropolis; being a history of the literary periodicals and literary interests of Chicago. (Univ. of Chicago. Ph.D. dissertation) Chicago. Univ. of Chicago Press. 1906. (Reprinted from Am. jour. of sociology. XI. p377-408, 499-531, 784-816; XII. p68-118. Nov. 1905-July 1906) **6101**

Greene, Evarts B. The plans of the Illinois State Historical Library with special reference to the care of the public archives. Illinois State Hist. Soc. jour. VI. p206-13 (July 1913) **6102**

Gross, Eugene L. and Gross, William L. An index to all the laws of the state of Illinois, both public and private, which are not printed at large in Gross's statutes of 1869. . . 1818 to 1869. Springfield, Ill. E.L. and W.L. Gross. 1869. 140p. **6102a**

Hasse, Adelaide Rosalie. Index of economic material in documents of the states of the United States: Illinois, 1809-1904. (Carnegie Inst. of Wash. Publication no. 85) Wash. D.C. Carnegie Inst. of Wash. 1909. 393p. **6103**

Heinl, Frank J. Newspapers and periodicals in the Lincoln-Douglas country, 1831-1832. Illinois State Hist. Soc. jour. XXIII. p371-438 (Oct. 1930) **6104**

Historical Records Survey. Check list of Chicago ante-fire imprints, 1851-1871. (American imprints inventory, no. 4) Chicago. 1938. 727p. mim. **6104a**

Historical Records Survey. Illinois. Calendar of the Ezekiel Cooper collection of early American Methodist manuscripts, 1785-1839, at Garrett Biblical Institute, Evanston, Illinois. Chicago, Ill. Jan. 1941. 97p. mim. **6104b**

—— —— Guide to depositories of manuscript collections in Illinois. Chicago. June 1940. 55p. mim. prelim. ed. **6104c**

—— —— Guide to public vital statistics records in Illinois. Chicago. May 1941. 138p. **6104d**

—— —— Inventory of the county archives of Illinois. Chicago, Ill. 1937- . mim. No. 1. Adams. April 1939. 210p.; No. 5. Brown. Feb. 1938. 93p.; No. 8. Carroll. Dec. 1937. 103p.; No. 10. Champaign. Jan. 1938. 118p. (printed); No. 12. Clark. June 1938. 132p.; No. 18. Cumberland. April 1938. 105p.; No. 21. Douglas. Nov. 1939. 282p.; No. 25. Effingham. Sept. 1940. 254p.; No. 26. Fayette. Sept. 1939. 165p. (plano.); No. 28. Franklin. Jan. 1941. 200p.; No. 39. Jackson. March 1939. 206p.; No. 43. Jo Daviess. Feb. 1938. 122p.; No. 48. Knox. Sept. 1938. 220p.; No. 53. Livingston. June 1940. 250p.; No. 54. Logan. July 1938. 207p.; No. 56. Macoupin. July 1939. 212p.; No. 68. Montgomery. Oct. 1939. 230p. (printed); No. 69. Morgan. June 1939. 213p.; No. 71. Ogle. July 1940. 310p.; No. 74. Piatt. Aug. 1940. 266p.; No. 75. Pike. March 1938. 121p.; No 81.

Historical Records Survey. Illinois. Inventory of county archives—*Continued*
Rock Island. Dec. 1939. 274p.; No. 83. Sangamon. April 1939. 228p.; No. 85. Scott. May 1938. 121p.; No. 86. Shelby. Jan. 1940. 236p.; No. 88. St. Clair. Sept. 1939. 345p.; No. 89. Stephenson. June 1938. 143p.; No. 92. Vermilion. March 1940. 364p.   **6104e**

Illinois. Department of Agriculture. Library. Catalogue of the library of the Illinois Department of Agriculture, 1884. Springfield. H. W. Rokker. 1884. 59p.
6105

Illinois. Geological Survey. List of publications on the geology of Illinois, with appended index. Urbana, Ill. 1933. 83p.
6105a

Illinois. Legislative Reference Bureau. Constitutional convention; index to debates of constitutional convention of 1869-70. Comp. and pub. by the Legislative Reference Bureau. Printed by authority of the State of Illinois. Springfield. Schnepp & Barnes. 1919. 31p. **6106**

—— —— General statement of work of Legislative Reference Bureau and a consolidated index to constitutional convention bulletins nos. 1-15. Comp. and pub. by the Legislative Reference Bureau. Printed by authority of the State of Illinois. Springfield. Schnepp & Barnes. 1919. 20p.   **6107**

—— —— Illinois party platforms, 1914, with select bibliographies of available material on file in the Legislative Reference Bureau, relating to the subjects enumerated therein. Legislative Reference Bureau, State of Illinois, Finley F. Bell, secretary. Springfield. Schnepp & Barnes. 1914. 43p.   **6108**

Illinois. Secretary of State. The Illinois archives division. By Margaret Cross Norton. *In* Blue book, 1925-26. Springfield. Illinois State Jour. Co. 1925. p436-43   **6109**

—— —— Index to former Blue books. *In* Blue book, 1931-1932. Springfield. Jour. Ptg. Co. 1931. p917-75   **6110**

—— —— List of documents published by the State of Illinois. For distribution by . . . Secretary of State. Springfield. n.p. 1912, 1914?, 1918   **6111**

—— —— Newspapers of Illinois. *In* Blue book of the state of Illinois, 1931-1932. By H. L. Williamson. Springfield. Jour. Ptg. Co. 1931. p608-20   **6112**

Illinois. State Geological Survey. Publications on the geology, mineral resources, and mineral industries of Illinois, with appended index, September 1, 1933. Urbana. Printed by authority of the State of Illinois. 1933. 83p.   **6113**

Illinois. State Historical Library. Alphabetic catalog of the books, manuscripts, maps, pictures, and curios of the Illinois State Historical Library; authors, titles, subjects, 1900. Comp. by Jessie Palmer Weber. Springfield. Phillips Bros. 1900. 363p.   **6114**

—— —— Card bibliography of Illinois history.   **6115**

—— —— General index to collections, journals, publications, 1899-1928. Comp. by Juliet G. Sager. Quincy. Royal Ptg. Co. 1930. 95p.   **6116**

—— Important purchase of books by the Illinois State Historical Library. Ill. Hist. Soc. jour. II. p49-70 (Jan. 1910)
6116a

—— —— An outline for the study of Illinois state history, with a reference list from the books, and other historical material in the Illinois State Historical Library. Comp. by Jessie Palmer Weber and Georgia L. Osborne (Illinois State Hist. Lib. Circular I. no. 1. Nov. 1905) Springfield. H. W. Rokker. [1906?] 94p.
6117

Illinois. State Library. Catalog of the Illinois State Library. Comp. under the direction of James A. Rose. Danville. Illinois Ptg. Co. 1903. 712p.   **6118**

—— —— Check list of Illinois documents. Springfield. In progress   **6118a**

—— —— Archives division. The archives division of the Illinois State Library. By William J. Stratton, Secretary of State. Springfield. Jour. Ptg. Co. 1930. 32p.   **6119**

—— —— —— Biennial report, 1922-. *In* Illinois. Secretary of State. Biennial rep. 1922-   **6120**

Illinois Press Association. Illinois newspaper directory; history of Illinois Press Association. [Springfield, Ill. Hartman-Jefferson Ptg. Co.] 1934. 744p.   **6120a**

Illinois state documents received by the State Library. Ill. lib.   **6120b**

The J. Nick Perrin collection. Ill. lib. XXII. p22-4 (Oct. 1940) (Early Cahokia and St. Clair County records period 1737 to 1850, recently given to the State Archives)   **6120c**

James, Edmund J. A bibliography of newspapers published in Illinois prior to 1860. Illinois State Hist. Soc. publications. no. 1. 1899. 94p.   **6121**

—— Information relating to the territorial laws of Illinois passed from 1809-1812. Illinois State Hist. Lib. publications. no. II. 1899. 15p.   **6122**

—— The territorial records of Illinois. I. The executive register, 1809-1818 II. Journal of the executive council, 1812. III. Journal of the House of Representatives, 1812. Illinois State Hist. Lib. publications. no. II. 1901. 170p. (Lists and indexes)   **6123**

Jamison, Isabel. Literature and literary people of early Illinois. Illinois State Hist. Soc. publications. IX. no. 13. p123-39. 1908   **6124**

John Crerar Library. Checklist of the official publications of the Century of progress international exposition and its exhibitors, 1933. Comp. by J. K. Wilcox (Reference list no. 27) Chicago. 1933. 51p. mim. (Supplements. 1933, 1934) **6125**

Johnson, G. E. and Ochs, Robert D. The historical source material in the Illinois and Michigan canal office, Lockport, Ill. Comp. under the auspices of the National Park Service **6125a**

Josephson, Aksel G. S. The Chicago Literary Club—bibliography. Bibliog. Soc. of Amer. pap. XI. p93-116. 1917 **6126**

Leland, Waldo Gifford. Report on the public archives and historical interests of the State of Illinois, with special reference to the proposed education building. *In* Illinois state education building commission. Rep. to the forty-eighth general assembly. 1913. p11-57 **6127**

McMurtrie, Douglas C. A bibliography of Peoria imprints, 1835-1860. Springfield. Priv. printed. 1934. 30p. **6128**

—— Books and pamphlets printed in Chicago, 1835-1850. Chicago Hist. Soc. bul. I. p9-23, 57-64, 88-100, 120-32 (Nov. 1934-Aug. 1935) **6129**

—— The contribution of the pioneer printers to Illinois history. Ill. State Hist. Soc. pap. 1938. p20-38 **6129a**

—— Early Illinois copyright entries, 1821-1850. Chicago Hist. Soc. bul. II. p50-61 (June 1936); III. p92-101 (March 1937) **6130**

—— The first printers of Chicago; with a bibliography of the issues of the Chicago Press, 1836-1850. Chicago. Cuneo Press. 1927. 42p.
Notes in supplement to "The first printers of Chicago." Chicago. Priv. printed. 1931. 14p. **6131**

—— The first printers of Illinois. Springfield. Priv. printed. 1933. (Extract from the Jour. of the Illinois State Hist. Soc. for Oct. 1933. p202-21) **6132**

—— The first printing in Peoria, Illinois. Chicago. Ludlow Typography Co. 1929. 30p. **6133**

—— Pioneer printing in Illinois. Springfield, Ill. 1931. 4p. (Reprint from Dec. 1931 issue of the National printer journalist) **6134**

—— The rise of printing in Mount Morris, Illinois. Mount Morris, Ill. Priv. printed. 1933. 3p. **6135**

Maynard, Glenn R. Newspapers of Ogle County, Illinois; with bibliographical and other notes. (Univ. of Illinois. M.A. thesis) 1935. 154p. **6136**

Miller, Carl R. Journalism in Illinois before the thirties. Illinois State Hist. Soc. jour. II. p149-56 (April 1918) **6137**

New York Historical Society. A catalogue of Illinois newspapers in the New York Historical Society. By Thomas O. Mabbott and Philip D. Jordan. Springfield, Ill. 1931. 58p. (Reprinted from the Jour. of the Illinois State Hist. Soc. XXIV. p187-242. July 1931) **6138**

Norton, Margaret C. The archives of Illinois. Ill. lib. (Notes on material in the archives) **6138a**

—— Correspondence of Illinois governors. Ill. lib. XXI. p14-16 (Sept. 1939) **6138b**

—— County archives. Ill. lib. XXII. p27 (March 1940) **6138c**

—— County archives. Ill. lib. XXIII. p24-7 (June 1941) (Probate court records) **6138d**

—— The General Assembly and its records. Ill. lib. XXII. no. 1. p25-9 (Jan. 1940); no. 4. p17-22 (April 1940); no. 5. p22-8 (May 1940); no. 6. p23-8 (June 1940) **6138e**

Pease, Theodore Calvin. The county archives of the state of Illinois. (Collections of the Illinois State Hist. Lib. v. XII. Bibliog. ser. v. III) Springfield. Illinois State Hist. Lib. 1915. 730p. **6139**

—— The county records of Illinois. Illinois State Hist. Soc. jour. VII. p374-8 (Jan. 1915) **6140**

Pennsylvania. State Library. World's fair literature. *In* Report of the State librarian, 1893. Harrisburg? Busch. 1894. p60-157 **6141**

Scott, Franklin William. Newspapers and periodicals of Illinois, 1814-1879. (Coll. of the Illinois State Hist. Lib. VI. Bibliog. ser. I) Springfield. Illinois State Hist. Lib. 1910. 610p. **6142**

Smith, Charles Wesley. A contribution toward a bibliography of Morris Birkbeck and the English settlement in Edwards County, Illinois founded by Morris Birkbeck and George Flower, 1817-1818. Ill. State Hist. Lib. pub. X. p165-77. 1906 **6142a**

Snively, E. A. Newspapers and newspaper men of Illinois. Illinois State Hist. Soc. trans. V. p205-13. 1904 **6143**

Stites, Katherine. Card calendar of source material for the study of Illinois history. Chicago, Ill. 1747 North Mason Avenue (Manuscript and published sources) **6143a**

Survey of Federal Archives. Illinois. Inventory of federal archives in the states. Chicago, Ill. 1939- . mim. The Federal Courts. March 1940. 139p.; The Department of the Treasury. March 1940. 283p.; The Department of War. Vols. A-B. 1941. 2v.; The Department of Justice. June 1940. 60p.; The Department of the Navy. March 1940. 177p.; The Department of the Interior. 1941. 110p.; The Department of Agriculture. Parts I-II. Jan. 1939. 344p.; The Department of Commerce. Jan. 1939. 26p.; The Department of Labor. May 1941. 69p.; The Farm Credit Administration. 1941. 12p. **6143b**

U.S. Federal Emergency Relief Administration. Library. Non-institutional relief measures of the states and territories: Illinois. Comp. by Adelaide R. Hasse. Wash. D.C. 1934. 77p. mim. **6144**

U.S. General Land Office. Index to the Illinois military patent book. By G. C. Bestor. Peoria. Woodcock. 1853. 113p. **6145**

Ward, Arnold. Early editors and newspapers of Vermilion County. Illinois State Hist. Soc. jour. XXV. p261-70 (Jan. 1933) **6146**

Weber, Mrs. Jessie. Publications of the Illinois State Historical Library and Society. [Springfield State Register. 1925] 16p. (Reprinted from the Jour. of the Ill. State Hist. Soc. XVII. no. 2. Oct. 1924) **6146a**

Wilkin, Ralph H. Index to the proceedings of the Illinois State Bar Association from 1877 to 1910. Ill. State Bar Asso. proc. XXXV. p485-526. 1911 **6146b**

Windsor, Elizabeth. Illinois imprints (omitting Chicago). Urbana. Univ. of Illinois Lib. School. In progress **6146c**

Wirick, Harriet P. A checklist and study of Illinois imprints through 1850. (Univ. of Illinois. Thesis) [Urbana] 1932 **6146d**

Wood, Charles H. and Long, Joseph D. A digest of the Illinois reports, from the earliest period to the year [1863-1866]; embracing all the decisions of the Supreme Court of the state. Chicago. 1872 **6146e**

INDIANA

Arbaugh, Dorothy. Indiana Department of Public Instruction checklist of bulletins 1903-Oct. 1937. Lib. occurrent. XII. p275-92 (Jan.-March 1938) **6146f**

Bibliography of Indiana local history contained in county histories, atlases and collected biographies. Ind. State Lib. bul. V. p3-8 (March 1910) **6146g**

Books and newspaper articles. Ind. hist. bul. **6146h**

Boswell, Jessie Partridge. A descriptive list of Indiana Senate and House journals, 1816-1933, and documentary journals, 1835/36-1912/13. (MS. on cards in the Indiana Historical Bureau, Indianapolis) **6146i**

Brown, Austin H. The first printers in Indianapolis, George Smith and Nathaniel Bolton. Indiana quar. mag. hist. II. p121-6 (Sept. 1906) **6147**

Brown, Edna. Indiana state publications. (Univ. of Illinois. M.A. thesis) 1930 **6148**

Colton, J. H. Catalogue of maps, charts, books, etc. In Fisher, R.S. Indiana. N.Y. J.H. Colton. 1852. 18p. **6148a**

Cottman, George S. The early newspapers of Indiana; beginnings and development of journalism. Indiana quar. mag. hist. II. p107-21 (Sept. 1906) **6149**

—— The Indiana magazine of history, a retrospect. Ind. mag. hist. XXV. p281-7 (Dec. 1929) **6149a**

Esarey, Logan. Checklist and history of Indiana newspapers. (MS. in his possession) **6150**

—— Indiana local history; a guide to its study, with some bibliographical notes. (Indiana Univ. Extension division. Bul. I. no. 7) Bloomington, Ind. 1916. 19p. **6151**

Greene, Evarts B. Our pioneer historical societies. Ind. Hist. Soc. pub. X. p83-97. 1931 **6151a**

Henley, Lillian E. Bibliography of Indiana local history contained in county histories, atlases and collected biographies. Indiana quar. mag. hist. VI. p43-54 (March 1910) **6152**

—— Bibliography of town and city histories in the Indiana State Library. Indiana quar. mag. hist. VI. p91-5 (June 1910) **6153**

Historical Records Survey. Indiana. Inventory of the county archives of Indiana. Indianapolis, Ind. 1936- . mim. No. 2. Allen. Sept. 1939. 380p. (mult.); No. 5. Blackford. 1936. 76p. (prelim. ed.); No. 6. Boone. 1937. 143p. (printed); No. 11. Clay. June 1939. 404p. (mult.); No. 18. Delaware. March 1940. 387p.; No. 28. Greene. Oct. 1938. 204p. (mult.); No. 34. Howard. Sept. 1939. 152p. (printed); No. 38. Jay. July 1940. 399p. (printed); No. 46. La Porte. May 1939. 189p. (printed); No. 49. Marion. June 1938. 219p. (printed); No. 53. Monroe. July 1940. 433p. (mult.); No. 55. Morgan. Feb. 1941. 436p. (mult.); No. 65. Posey. June 1940. 378p.; No. 71. St. Joseph. April 1939. 248p. (printed); No. 73. Shelby. July 1940. 415p.; No. 79. Tippecanoe. April 1941. 516p. (mult.); No. 82. Vanderburgh. Feb. 1939. 269p. (mult.); No. 87. Warrick. Jan. 1940. 379p. (mult.) **6153a**

Hopkins, Thomas C. Contents of the published volumes [and] General index to all the publications of the Indiana Geological Survey, the Department of Geology and Natural History, and the Department of Geology and Natural Resources. In Indiana. Department of Geology and Natural Resources. Twenty-eighth annual report, 1903. Indianapolis. 1904. p487-553 **6153b**

Howe, Daniel W. Catalogue of the laws of the Indiana territory and the state of Indiana. In Indiana State Library. Biennial report, 1885-1886. Indianapolis. W. B. Burford. 1886. p47-51 **6154**

—— A descriptive catalogue of the official publications of the territory and State of Indiana from 1800 to 1890. (Indiana Hist. Soc. Publications. II. no. 5) Indianapolis. Bowen-Merrill. 1890. p135-229 **6155**

Hurst, Roger A. The New Harmony manuscript collection. Ind. mag. hist. XXXVII. p[45]-49 (March 1941). (Describes a collection of 14,000 pieces in the library of the Workingmen's Institute of New Harmony, Ind.) **6155a**

Indiana. Constitutional Convention, 1850-1851. Index to the Journal of Debates of the Indiana Constitutional convention, 1850-1851. Comp. by Jessie P. Boswell. Pub. by the Indiana Historical Bureau, Indianapolis. [Indianapolis. Wm. B. Burford Ptg. Co.] 1938. 136p. **6155b**

Indiana. Department of Public Welfare. Check list of DPW bulletins issued to date, March 1, 1937. [Indianapolis. 1937] 24p. mim. **6155c**

—— —— **Division of public assistance.** List of public and semi-public records available for the verification of age in the respective counties of the state of Indiana. [Indianapolis. 1938] 99p. **6155d**

Indiana. Historical Bureau. Books and newspaper articles. Indiana hist. bul. I. no. 11-12. Sept. 1924- **6156**

—— —— Check list of bulletins issued by the Indiana Historical Commission and the Indiana Historical Bureau. Indiana hist. bul. IX. p557-60 (July 1932) **6157**

Indiana. Historical Bureau. Publications of the Indiana Historical Bureau and the Indiana Historical Society. [Indianapolis. 1938] (Reprinted from the Ind. hist. bul. XV. no. 5, May 1938) p217-27. *See also* Ind. hist. bul. XVII. p187-200 (April 1940) **6157a**

Indiana. Laws, Statutes, etc. A general index of the Indiana statutes contained in Burns' annotated Indiana statutes of 1914 . . . also an appendix containing an index to private acts adopted prior to 1852. By Harrison Burns. Indianapolis. Bobbs-Merrill. 1914. 408p. **6157b**

Indiana. State Library. Bibliography of cities and towns, May 1, 1898. Indiana State Lib. bul. 3d ser. no. 2. 1898. 55p. **6158**

—— —— Catalogue. 1903. Indianapolis. Burford. 1904. 523p. (Supplement. April 1, 1905. 177p.) **6159**

—— —— County histories. Indiana State Lib. bul. XI. p17-25 (Sept. 1916) **6160**

—— —— Index to documentary journal of Indiana to 1899. *In* Indiana. State Library. Twenty-third biennial report, 1899-1900. Indianapolis. Burford. 1900. p293-326 **6161**

—— —— Index to Indiana governors' messages, 1816-1851. Comp. by Mary H. Roberts. *In* Indiana. State Library. Legislative reference department. Bul. no. 2. Indianapolis. 1908. 13p. **6162**

—— —— Indiana documents received at the State Library. Library occurent. VII- . 1925- **6162a**

—— —— A list of Indiana newspapers available in the Indiana State Library, the Indianapolis Public Library, the Library of Indiana University, and the Library of Congress, Washington, D.C. Indiana State Lib. bul. XI. no. 4. Dec. 1916. 31p. **6163**

—— —— List of Indiana newspapers on file in the Indiana State Library at this date. Indiana quar. mag. hist. I. p42-5 (First quar. 1905) **6164**

—— —— Reading list on Indiana in the Civil war, May 1902. Indiana State Lib. bul. 3d ser. no. 9. 1902. 12p. **6165**

—— —— A select bibliography of Indiana historical material in the Indiana State Library. Indiana State Lib. bul. X. p2-16 (Sept. 1915) **6166**

—— —— State documents and publications distributed by the state library. *In* Indiana. State library. Biennial reports, 1907-1908- . Indianapolis. Burford 1909- **6167**

—— —— State documents received. Bul. IV-X (1909-15) **6167a**

Indiana. Supreme Court. Law Library. Catalogue and subject index of Indiana Supreme Court library. [Indianapolis] 1940. 645p. **6167b**

Indiana Historical Society. List of publications, 1897-1928. Indianapolis? 1928 **6168**

Indiana Historical Society publications. Ind. hist. bul. XVII. p194-9 (April 1940) **6168a**

Indiana magazine of history. [General index] Indiana magazine of history, volumes I-XXV, 1905-1929. By Dorothy Riker. Bloomington. Indiana Univ. Press. 1930. 200p. **6169**

Indianapolis. Public Library. A consolidated index to thirty-two histories of Indianapolis and Indiana. Indianapolis, Ind. 1939. 363p. mim. **6169a**

—— —— Indexes and bibliographies of source materials in Indianapolis history. Indianapolis, Ind. WPA project **6169b**

Karpinski, Robert W. Indiana on early maps. Ind. hist. bul. XV. p110-17. 1938 **6169c**

Lapp, John A. The public documents of Indiana. Indiana quar. mag. hist. VI. p105-13 (Sept. 1910) **6170**

—— The public documents of Indiana. Library occurrent. II. nos. 6-7. p108-11, 130-3 (March-June 1910) **6171**

Lilly, Eli. Bibliography on Indiana archaeology. Indiana hist. bul. IX. p445-79 (May 1932) **6172**

Lindley, Harlow. Indiana archives and history. Indiana quar. mag. hist. IV. p55-62 (June 1908) **6173**

—— Indiana history and archives. Indiana State Lib. bul. VIII. p2-3 (July-Sept. 1913) **6173a**

—— Report on the archives of the state of Indiana. Am. Hist. Asso. rep. 1910. p315-30 **6174**

McMurtrie, Douglas C. The first printing in Indiana. Metuchen, N.J. 1934. (Reprinted with revisions and additions from the May-June 1934 issue of the Am. book collector. p3-6) **6175**

—— Indiana imprints, 1804-1849; a supplement to Mary Alden Walker's "Beginnings of printing in the state of Indiana," published in 1934. . . . (Indiana Historical Society. Publications. XI, no. 5) Indianapolis. Indiana Hist. Soc. 1937. p307-93 **6175a**

Marsters, Vernon Freeman and Kindle, Edward Martin. Geological literature of Indiana, stratigraphic and economic. Ind. Acad. Sci. proc. 1893. p156-91 **6175b**

Moses, John F. The newspapers of Rush County (Ind.). Indiana quar. mag. hist. X. p53-62 (March 1914) **6176**

National Library of Wales. A bibliography of Robert Owen, the socialist, 1771-1858. Aberystwyth. Pub. by the National Lib. of Wales in association with the Press board of the Univ. of Wales. 1925. 90p. **6177**

New Harmony. Workingmen's Institute Library. List of books and pamphlets (relating to the early history of New Harmony and to Robert Owen and his disciples, with early New Harmony prints) in a special collection in the Library of the Workingmen's Institute. New Harmony, Ind. Comp. and annotated by Rena Reese. New Harmony, Ind. 1909. 21p. **6178**

Packard, Jasper. Newspapers. *In* History of La Porte County, Indiana, and its townships, towns, and cities. La Porte. S. E. Taylor. 1876. p459-64 **6179**

Publications of the Indiana Historical Bureau. Ind. hist. bul. XVII. p187-93 (April 1940) **6179a**

Rauch, John G. and Armstrong, Nellie C. A bibliography of the laws of Indiana, 1788-1927. (Indiana hist. publications. XVI) Indianapolis. Hist. Bureau of the Indiana Lib. and Hist. Dept. 1928. 77p. **6180**

Researches relating to Indiana history. Ind. hist. bul. XVII. p236-9 (May 1940) **6180a**

South Bend, Indiana. Public Library. Books about Indiana in the Public library of South Bend with a list of Indiana writers represented in the Public library. South Bend, Ind. 1920. 28p. **6181**

Stoler, Mildred C. Indiana Historical Society manuscript collections. Ind. mag. hist. XXX. p267-9 (Sept. 1934) **6181a**

—— Manuscript accessions. Indiana mag. hist. XXIX. p44-7 (March 1933) **6182**

—— Manuscripts in Indiana State Library. Indiana mag. hist. XXVII. p236-9 (Sept. 1931) **6183**

Survey of Federal Archives. Indiana. Inventory of federal archives in the states. Indianapolis, Ind. 1938- . mim. The Federal Courts. March 1939. 44p.; The Department of the Treasury. Nov. 1938. 65p.; The Department of War. Jan. 1939. 143p.; The Department of Justice. Oct. 1938. 20p.; The Department of the Navy. Feb. 1939. 9p.; The Department of the Interior. April 1939. 24p.; The Department of Agriculture. March 1939. 393p.; The Department of Commerce. Oct. 1939. 20p.; The Department of Labor. March 1939. 47p.; The Veterans' Administration. Feb. 1939. 51p.; The Civil Works Administration. July 1939. 97p.; The Emergency Relief Administration. Oct. 1939. 115p.; The Farm Credit Administration. April 1939. 21p.; The Works Progress Administration. Pt. I-II 1941. 425p.; Miscellaneous Agencies. Paris I-II. Oct. 1940. 261p. **6183a**

U.S. Library of Congress. Division of bibliography. A list of books on the history of Indiana. March 2, 1931. 8p. typ. **6184**

Van Schreeven, William J. Indiana Food Administration papers. Ind. mag. hist. XXXIII. p422-7 (Dec. 1937) **6184a**

Venn, Florence. Index of historical articles in Indianapolis newspapers. Indiana quar. mag. hist. V. no. 3-VII. no. 2 (Sept. 1909-June 1911) **6185**

Walker, Mary Alden. The beginnings of printing in the state of Indiana; comprising a brief analysis of the literary production, and a list of items printed to 1850. Crawfordsville. R. E. Banta. 1934. 124p. **6186**

Wish, Harvey. New Indiana archival documents. Indiana mag. of hist. XXXII. p360-9 (Dec. 1936) **6187**

Woodburn, James A. The Indiana historical society: a hundred years. Indiana hist. soc. publications. X. no. 1. p5-46. 1930 **6188**

—— The public archives of Indiana. Am. Hist. Asso. rep. 1900. II. p37-8 **6189**

Yohn Brothers. Catalogue of a collection of books relating to the history and geography of Indiana and books by Indiana authors. Indianapolis. Yohn Brothers. 1878. 16p. **6190**

IOWA

Aldrich, Charles. Journalism of Northwest Iowa. Ann. Iowa. 3d ser. XIII. p509-28 (Jan. 1923) **6191**

Brigham, Johnson. A general survey of the literature of Iowa history. Iowa jour. hist. I. p77-104 (Jan. 1903) **6192**

Brigham, Johnson and others. A book of Iowa authors, by Iowa authors. Des Moines. Iowa State Teachers Asso. 1930. 247p. **6193**

Budington, Margaret and Fitzpatrick, T. J. A bibliography of Iowa state publications for 1898-[1905]. Iowa jour. hist. I-V (July 1903-July 1907) **6194**

Clark, Dan Elbert. One hundred topics in Iowa history. (State Hist. Soc. of Iowa. Bul. of information ser. no. 7) Iowa City. Iowa State Hist. Soc. 1914. 39p. **6195**

Coffey, Wilbur John. A list of books and pamphlets written by Cedar Rapids authors. Dubuque. Columbia College Lib. 1930. 42p. **6196**

Cole, Theodore Lee. Historical bibliography of the statute law of Iowa. (Iowa State Univ. Law bul. no. 2) Iowa City. 1891. p38-48 **6197**

Cook, Luella E. Histories of Iowa counties. Ia. jour. hist. XXXVI. p115-51 (April 1938) **6197a**

Fitzpatrick, T. J. Bibliography of the Iowa territorial documents. Iowa jour. hist. V. p234-69 (April 1907) (Reprinted Iowa City. 1907) **6198**

Garver, Frank H. Bibliography of Sioux City authors. Acad. of Science and Letters of Sioux City, Iowa. 1903/04. I. p185-91 **6199**

Historical Records Survey. A check list of Iowa imprints, 1838-1860, in supplement to those recorded by Alexander Moffit in the Iowa Journal of History and Biography for January, 1938. (American imprints inventory, no. 15) Chicago, Ill. 1940. 84p. **6199a**

Historical Records Survey. Iowa. Guide to depositories of manuscript collections in the United States: Iowa. Des Moines, Ia. June 1940. 47p. mim. **6199b**

—— —— Guide to manuscript collections in Iowa. Vol. I. Des Moines, Ia. Sept. 1940. 57p. mim. **6199c**

—— —— Inventory of the county archives of Iowa. Des Moines, Ia. 1938- . mim. No. 14. Carroll. July 1940. 141p.; No. 18. Cherokee. May 1939. 180p.; No. 25. Dallas. Aug. 1938. 168p.; No. 31. Dubuque. Feb. 1938. 172p.; No. 47. Ida. May 1938. 154p.; No. 50. Jasper. Dec. 1938. 183p.; No. 81. Sac. July 1940. 164p.; No. 97. Woodbury. May 1940. 371p. **6199d**

Iowa. Agricultural Experiment Station. List of publications. Agricultural Experiment Station . . . and Extension Service . . . Iowa State College of Agriculture and Mechanic Arts. Ames, Ia. 1937. 15p. **6199e**

Iowa. Commission to the Louisiana purchase exposition. List of books by Iowa authors. Collected by the Auxiliary committee of the Iowa commission, Louisiana purchase exposition, for the exhibit of books by Iowa authors in the Iowa state building. St. Louis, 1904. Des Moines. Iowa Lib. Com. 1904. 30p. **6200**

Iowa. Historical, Memorial and Art Department. Annals of Iowa, Third Series. Index, volumes I-VIII, April 1893-January 1909. Des Moines. Hist. Dept. of Iowa. 1912. 225p.

Second index, volumes IX-XVI, April 1909-April 1929. Des Moines. Hist. Dept. of Iowa. 1931. 144p. **6201**

—— —— Biennial report. Des Moines, Ia. 1894- (Lists state documents) **6201a**

—— —— Archives division. Public archives; a manual for their administration in Iowa. By Cassius C. Stiles. Des Moines. 1928. 181p. (Reprinted from Ann. of Iowa. 3d ser. XVI. p241-308, 331-94, 448-66. April-Oct. 1928) **6202**

Iowa. Library Commission. Check list of the publications of the State of Iowa; with an index to the Iowa documents. Comp. by Lavinia Steele. Des Moines. B. Murphy, state printer. 1904. 65p. **6203**

Iowa. Secretary of State. Report . . . to the governor of Iowa of the number of documents and publications on hand Jan. 1, 1907-Dec. 31, 1913. Des Moines, 1907-14 **6203a**

Iowa. State documents editor. Iowa publications: report of the State Document Department for the biennial period ended Dec. 31, 1916: June 30, 1918: June 30, 1920. Des Moines. 1917-21. 3v. **6204**

Iowa. State Historical Society. Some publications—Iowana. Iowa jour. hist. I. Jan. 1903- **6205**

Iowa. State Library. The laws, journals, documents, etc., published by Iowa, 1838-90. *In* Biennial report of the state librarian, 1891. Des Moines. G. H. Ragsdale, state printer. 1891. p164-203 **6206**

Iowa. State Planning Board. Abstracts of excerpts from public documents regarding crime and delinquency in Iowa. Ames. Sept. 1935. 384p. typ. **6206a**

—— —— Bibliography. Iowa State Planning Board, July, 1937. [Des Moines. 1937] 14p. mim. **6206b**

Iowa. Superintendent of printing. Newspapers for Iowa. *In* State of Iowa, 1933-1934; official register. Des Moines. State of Iowa. 1934? p279-99 **6207**

Johnson, Jack T. Guides to Iowa Territory. Palimpsest. XX. p65-76 (March 1939) **6207a**

Keyes, Charles Rollin. Annotated bibliography of Iowa geology and mining. (Iowa geol. survey. XXII) Des Moines. 1913. p157-908 **6208**

—— Bibliography of Iowa geology. *In* Iowa. Geological Survey. First annual report for 1892. Des Moines, Ia. 1893. I. p209-464 **6208a**

Lees, James H. Bibliography of Iowa coals. (Iowa geol. survey. Annual rep. 1908. XIX) Des Moines. Iowa geol. survey. 1909. p659-87 **6209**

McMurtrie, Douglas C. The beginnings of printing in Iowa. Des Moines. Priv. printed. 1933. (Extract from the Ann. of Iowa. XIX. p3-22. July 1933) **6210**

—— Directories of Iowa newspapers, 1850-1869. Des Moines. Priv. print. 1935. p11-25 (Extract from the Ann. of Iowa. July 1935) **6210a**

—— The first printers at Council Bluffs. Excerpt from Ann. of Iowa. July 1931. p2-11 **6211**

—— Pioneer printing in Iowa. Springfield, Ill. 1932. 4p. (Reprinted from the Dec. 1932 issue of the National printer journalist) **6212**

Macy, Katherine Young. Notes on the history of Iowa newspapers, 1836-1870 (Univ. of Iowa. Extension bul. no. 175. July 1, 1927) Iowa City. Pub. by the Univ. 1927. 114p. **6213**

Marple, Alice. Iowa authors and their works; a contribution toward a bibliography. Des Moines. Hist. Dept. of Iowa. 1918. 359p. **6214**

Moffit, Alexander. A checklist of Iowa imprints, 1837-1860. Ia. jour. hist. XXXVI. p3-95 (Jan. 1938) **6214a**

—— Iowa imprints before 1861. Ia. jour. hist. XXXVI. p153-205 (April 1938) **6214b**

Mott, David C. Early Iowa newspapers; a contribution toward a bibliography of the newspapers established in Iowa before the Civil war. Ann. of Iowa. 3d ser. XVI. p161-233 (Jan. 1928) **6215**

Mott, Frank Luther. Literature of pioneer life in Iowa, with a partially annotated bibliography. Iowa City. State Hist. Soc. of Iowa. 1923. 89p. **6216**

Moylan, H. S. Bradford's Iowa reports. Ia. law rev. IV. p104-6 (May 1938) **6216a**

Parvin, Theodore Sutton. Earliest maps of Iowa. Mag. Am. hist. XXIII. p416-17. 1890 **6216b**

Petersen, William John. Two hundred topics in Iowa history. (Iowa Hist. Soc. Bul. of information. ser. no. 15. ed. by Benjamin F. Shambaugh) Iowa City. State Hist. Soc. of Iowa. 1932. 96p. **6217**

Reilly, Eugene Harold. A list of books and pamphlets written by Dubuquers. Dubuque. Columbia College Lib. 1928. 29p. **6218**

Schmidt, Louis B. The activities of the State Historical Society of Iowa. Hist. teachers' mag. VI. p75-81 (March 1915) **6219**

Shambaugh, Benjamin F. The public archives of Iowa. Am. Hist. Asso. rep. 1900. II. p39-46 **6220**

—— A report on the public archives. Ann. of Iowa. 3d ser. VII. p561-91 (Jan. 1907) **6221**

—— A second report on the public archives. Des Moines. Hist. Dept. of Iowa. 1907. 364p. **6222**

—— Statute law-making in Iowa. (Applied history ser. III) Iowa City, Ia. State Hist. Soc. of Iowa. 1916. 718p. **6222a**

Shipton, W. D. Bibliography of the driftless area. Ia. Acad. Sci. proc. XXIV. p67-81. 1917 **6222b**

Springer, John. Memoranda relating to the early press of Iowa. Iowa City. Iowa State Ptg. Off. 1880. 17p. **6223**

Stewart, Helen. Iowa state publications. (Univ. of Illinois. Master's thesis) 1937. MS. 360p. (Being prepared for publication) **6223a**

Stiles, Cassius C. Public archives division. Ann. of Iowa. 3d ser. XVI. p107-30 (Oct. 1927) **6224**

—— Public archives of Iowa. Ann. of Iowa. 3d ser. X. p273-319 (Jan.-April 1912) **6225**

Survey of Federal Archives. Iowa. Inventory of federal archives in the states. Des Moines, Ia. 1938- . mim. The Federal Courts. May 1940. 69p.; The Department of the Treasury. Feb. 1939. 74p.; The Department of War. July 1940. 92p.; The Department of Justice. June 1939. 15p.; The Department of the Navy. June 1939. 13p.; The Department of the Interior. Oct. 1940. 22p.; The Department of Agriculture. May 1940. 327p.; The Department of Commerce. Nov. 1938. 32p.; The Department of Labor. March 1939. 47p.; The Farm Credit Administration. Jan. 1940. 39p.; The Veterans' Administration. Feb. 1939. 51p.; The Civil Works Administration. July 1939. 97p.; The Emergency Relief Administration. Oct. 1939. 115p.; The Works Progress Administration. April 1941. 425p.; Miscellaneous agencies. Oct. 1940. 417p. **6225a**

Torch Press Book Shop. Contribution toward a priced bibliography of books referring to the state of Iowa. Cedar Rapids, Iowa. 1910 **6226**

KANSAS

Becker, Carl. Public archives of Kansas. Am. Hist. Asso. rep. 1904. p597-601 **6227**

Bibliography of Kansas statute law. *In* Revised statutes of Kansas, 1923. Supplement 1933. Topeka. Kansas State Print. Plant. 1934. p684-6 **6227a**

Callahan, James. P. Kansas in the American novel and short story. Kansas State Hist. Soc. colls. XVII. p139-88. 1926-28 **6228**

Gaeddert, G. Raymond. First newspapers in Kansas counties, 1854-1864. Kans. hist. quar. X. p3-33, 124-49, 299-323, 380-411 (Feb., May, Aug., Nov. 1941) **6228a**

Green, Paul G. An annotated bibliography of the history of education in Kansas. (Kansas State Teachers College of Emporia. Bul. of information, v. XV, no. 9, Sept. 1935) Topeka, Kan. State Ptg. Plant. 1935. 33p. **6228b**

Hay, Robert. A bibliography of Kansas geology with some annotations. Kan. Acad. Sci. trans. XIV. p261-78. 1893-94 **6228c**

Hill, Esther Clark. The Pratt collection. Kansas hist. quar. I. p83-8 (Feb. 1932) (MSS. relating to the activities of John G. Pratt, missionary printer and Indian agent in Kansas, 1837-70) **6229**

Historical Records Survey. Kansas. Checklist of Kansas imprints, 1854-1876. (American imprints inventory, no. 10) Topeka, Kans. 1939. 387p. **6229a**

—— Inventory of the county archives of Kansas. Topeka, Kans. 1937- . mim. No. 6. Bourbon. July 1940. 423p.; No. 11. Cherokee. April 1940. 334p.; No. 30. Franklin. Aug. 1939. 249p.; No. 33. Graham. Dec. 1939. 224p.; No. 35. Gray. Aug. 1939. 269p.; No. 37. Greenwood. May 1938. 156p.; No. 46. Johnson. July 1937. 115p.; No. 63. Montgomery. Sept. 1938. 168p.; No. 70. Osage. April 1941. 243p. mim.; No. 88. Seward. Dec. 1938. 186p.; No. 89. Shawnee. Dec. 1940. 645p. **6229b**

Holt, Beatrice H. Kansas state publications since 1898. (Univ. of Illinois. M.A. thesis) Urbana, Ill. 138p. autog. from typ. copy **6230**

Kansas. State Library. Kansas books (20th biennial report of the state librarian). Topeka. Kansas State Ptg. Plant. 1916. p11-14 **6231**

Kansas. State Teachers College. An author index to the research work of Kansas educators in recent years. The Techne. XIV. no. 3. 40p. (Jan.-Feb. 1931) **6232**

Kansas history as published in the press. Kans. hist. quar. I- . (Nov. 1931-) **6232a**

Kansas State Historical Society. Library.
Bound newspapers and periodicals . . . in
the library of the society. . .—Kansas
newspapers and periodicals now received.
Kansas State Hist. Soc. trans. III. p144-
78. 1883-85. (Similar lists in Kansas
State Hist. Soc. 4th (p60-84), 11th (p68-
122), 14th (p119-46), biennial reports, and
in 29th annual meeting proc. p21-48. 1900)
6233

—— —— A catalog of Kansas constitutions,
and territorial and state documents in the
historical society library. Kansas State
Hist. Soc. trans. VI. p383-475. 1897-1900
6234

—— —— Catalog of the Kansas territorial
and state documents in the library of the
State historical society, 1854-1898. Prep.
by Zu Adams. Topeka. W.Y. Morgan,
State Printer. 1900. 93p. (Originally
printed in the Transactions of the Kansas
State Historical Society, 1897-1900. VI.
p383-475. Revised and reissued in 1905
in Bowker's State publications) **6234a**

—— —— History of Kansas newspapers;
a history of the newspapers and magazines published in Kansas from the organization of Kansas Territory, 1854, to
January 1, 1916; together with statistical
information of the counties, cities and
towns of the state. W. E. Connelley,
secretary. Topeka. Kansas State Ptg.
Plant, W. R. Smith, state printer. 1916.
373p. **6235**

—— —— Kansas books; a typical selection
of books and pamphlets from the Kansas
section of the library of the Kansas State
Historical Society. Kansas State Hist.
Soc. 14th biennial rep. p99-117. 1904 **6236**

—— —— Kansas history as published in
the state press. Kansas hist. quar. I.
Nov. 1931- **6237**

—— —— List, by counties, of newspapers
and periodicals published in Kansas,
March 1, 1884. By F. G. Adams. Topeka.
Kansas Publishing House. 1884. 23p.
(Similar lists appeared in 1889 and 1894)
6238

—— —— List of duplicate Kansas state and
miscellaneous publications, for exchange
by the Kansas State Historical Society.
Topeka. Kansas State Ptg. Plant. 1917.
26p. **6239**

—— —— A list of Kansas newspapers and
periodicals received by the Kansas State
Historical Society, June 1931- . Kirke
Mechem, secretary. Topeka. Kansas
State Ptg. Plant. 1931- **6240**

—— —— A list of Kansas newspapers received by the Kansas State Historical
Society. Topeka. State Ptg. Off. 1913-30
6241

—— —— A list of the books indispensable to
a knowledge of Kansas history and literature, issued as an aid to librarians
and students. Topeka. Kansas State Ptg.
Plant. 1916. 16p. **6242**

—— —— Recent additions to the library.
Kans. hist. quar. I- (Nov. 1931-) (Annual
list of additions to the library of the
Kansas State Hist. Soc.) **6242a**

Kansas State Teachers Association. Research studies in Kansas; brief abstracts
of theses developed at the graduate
schools of the state. Kansas teacher and
western school jour. XLII. p24-5. 1936
6242b

Long, A. L. History of early Kansas literature. (Univ. of Kansas. Thesis) 1916
6243

McMurtrie, Douglas C. Pioneer printing
of Kansas. Kansas hist. quar. I. p3-16
(Nov. 1931) **6244**

**McMurtrie, Douglas C. and Allen, Albert
H.** A forgotten pioneer press of Kansas.
Chicago. John Calhoun Club. 1930. 30p.
(Ioway and Sac Mission Press) **6245**

—— —— Jotham Meeker, pioneer printer
of Kansas, with a bibliography of the
known issues of the Baptist Mission
Press at Shawanoe, Stockbridge and
Ottawa, 1834-1854. Chicago. Eyncourt
Press. 1930. 169p. **6246**

Ruppenthal, J. C. A bibliography of the
statute law of Kansas. Law Lib. jour.
XXIII. p79-103 (July 1930) **6247**

Shafer, J. D. An index to the laws of
Kansas, comprising all general, special
and private acts contained in the original
authorized editions of the laws from the
organization of the Territory of Kansas,
in 1855, to the close of the XVII annual
session of the state legislature in 1877.
Leavenworth. Ketcheson & Durfee. 1877.
315p. **6248**

Survey of Federal Archives. Kansas. Inventory of federal archives in the states.
Topeka, Kans. 1938- . mim. The Federal Courts. Feb. 1939. 22p.; The Department of the Treasury. Dec. 1938.
48p.; The Department of War. Feb. 1939.
45p.; The Department of Justice. May
1939. 15p.; The Department of the Navy.
May 1939. 8p.; The Department of Agriculture. Feb. 1940. 182p.; The Department
of Commerce. Aug. 1940. 11p.; The
Department of Labor. 1941. 39p. **6248a**

U.S. Department of Labor. Library. List
of references on the Kansas court of industrial relations. Comp. by Laura A.
Thompson. Wash. D.C. 1921. 10p. autog.
from typ. copy. (A revision of the list
published in the Library journal, Nov. 1,
1920. Supplementary list. 1922. 5p.) **6249**

Wright, Purd B. Bibliography of books
printed in Kansas City, Missouri to 1910.
Kansas City, Kansas City Pub. Lib. In
progress **6249a**

KENTUCKY

Baylor, Orval W. Kentucky history in old
depositions. Ky. Hist. Soc. reg. XXXVII.
p177-83 (July 1939) **6249b**

Brigham, Clarence S. Kentucky—Bibliog-
raphy of American newspapers, 1690-1820.
Am. Antiq. Soc. proc. n.s. XXIV. p363-403
(Oct. 1914) **6250**

Clark, Thomas D. Travelers' accounts as a source of Kentucky history. Filson Club hist. quar. XIV. p205-23 (Oct. 1940)
6250a

Hasse, Adelaide Rosalie. Index of economic material in documents of the states of the United States—Kentucky, 1792-1904. (Carnegie Inst. of Wash. Publication no. 85) Wash. D.C. Carnegie Inst. of Wash. 1910. 452p.   **6251**

Historical Records Survey. Kentucky. Check list of Kentucky imprints, 1787-1810. (American imprints inventory, no. 5) Chicago, Ill. 1939. 103p. mim.
6251a

—— —— Check list of Kentucky imprints, 1811-1820 (American imprints inventory, no. 6) Chicago, Ill. Nov. 1939. 118p. mim.
6251b

—— —— Guide and check list of county governmental organization and county record system, past and present, of Kentucky counties. Louisville, Ky. March 1937. 77p. mim.   **6251c**

—— —— Inventory of the county archives of Kentucky. Louisville, Ky. 1937- . mim. No. 14. Breckenridge. Sept. 1940. 391p.; No. 20. Carlisle. June 1938. 166p.; No. 34. Fayette. Aug. 1937. 121p.; No. 57. Jessamine. Feb. 1940. 331p.; No. 61. Knox. Dec. 1937. 149p.; No. 63. Laurel. Dec. 1938. 244p.; No. 74. McCreary. Feb. 1938. 82p.; No. 82. Meade. Jan. 1941. 377p.   **6251d**

Hovey, Horace C. and Call, Richard E. Bibliographie chronologique et analytique de Mammoth Cave, Kentucky (États-Unis d'Amérique) 1815 à 1914, Traduite et ordonnée par E. A. Martel. Spelunca, bulletin et mémoires de la Société de Spéléologie. IX. no. 73. p3-49 (Sept. 1913)
6252

Jillson, Willard Rouse. The Beauchamp-Sharp tragedy in American literature. Ky. Hist. Soc. reg. XXXVI. p54-60 (Jan. 1938)   **6252a**

—— Bibliography of Lincoln County, chronologically and historically arranged and annotated. Ky. State Hist. Soc. reg. XXXV. p339-59 (Oct. 1937)   **6252b**

—— Early Kentucky history in manuscript —a brief account of the Draper and Shane collections. Ky. Hist. Soc. reg. XXXIII. p137-50 (April 1935)   **6252c**

—— Early Kentucky literature, 1750-1840. Frankfort. Kentucky State Hist. Soc. 1932. 121p.   **6253**

—— Early maps and plats of Kentucky. In Pioneer Kentucky. Frankfort, Ky. State Jour. Co. 1934. p19-55   **6253a**

—— The first printing in Kentucky; some account of Thomas Parvin and John Bradford and the establishment of the Kentucky gazette in Lexington in the year 1787, with a bibliography of some seventy titles. Louisville. C. T. Dearing print. company. 1936. 55p.   **6253b**

—— Geological research in Kentucky; a summary account of the several geological surveys of Kentucky, including a complete list of their publications and a general bibliography of 806 titles pertaining to Kentucky geology. (Kentucky. Geological Survey 1920-1932. Geologic reports, XV) Frankfort, Ky. 1923. 228p.
6253c

—— Kentucky acts and legislative journals 1792-1800; a preliminary locating index. Ky. Hist. Soc. reg. XXXV. p196-7. 1937
6253d

—— Kentucky geography: an historical sketch—1909-1937. Ky. Hist. Soc. reg. XXXV. p277-85. 1937   **6253e**

—— Kentucky history; a check and finding list of the principal published and manuscript sources of the general, regional, and county history of the commonwealth, 1729-1936. Louisville, Ky. The Standard Ptg. Co. 1936. 87p.   **6253f**

—— The Kentucky land grants; a systematic index to all of the land grants recorded in the state land office at Frankfort, Kentucky, 1782-1924. (Filson Club publications no. 33) Louisville. Standard Ptg. Co. 1925. 1844p.   **6253g**

—— Old Kentucky entries and deeds; a complete index to all of the earliest land entries, military warrants, deeds and wills of the commonwealth of Kentucky. (Filson Club publications no. 34) Frankfort, Ky. Standard Ptg. Co. 1926. 571p. **6253h**

—— Rare Kentucky books, 1776-1926; a check and finding list of scarce, fugitive, curious and interesting books and pamphlets, with annotations and prices current appended. Louisville, Ky. Standard Ptg. Co. 1939. 199p.   **6253i**

Johnson, Mrs. Augusta (Phillips). A century of Wayne county, Kentucky, 1800-1900. Louisville, Ky. Standard Ptg. Co. 1939. p197-266   **6253j**

Kentucky. Geological Survey, 1920-1932. A bibliography of the several books, reports, papers and maps relating to geology written and prepared by Willard Rouse Jillson. Frankfort, Ky. 1920-26 (ser. VI. pamphlet nos. 1, 2, 3, 4, 11; 7, 11, 14, 17, 22p.)   **6253k**

Kentucky. Land Office. A calendar of the warrants for land in Kentucky, granted for service in the French and Indian war. Abstracted by the late Philip Fall Taylor. In Society of Colonial Wars. Kentucky year book. n.p. 1917. pt. II, p63-136 **6253l**

Kentucky. Library Commission. Handbook of Kentucky libraries. (Kentucky Library Commission. Bulletin no. 1) Frankfort. 1911. 49p.   **6253m**

Kentucky. Secretary of State. Catalogue records, documents, papers, etc. Kentucky governors, 1792-1926. Comp. by Emma Guy Cromwell, Secretary of State. Frankfort. State Jour. Co., printer to the commonwealth. 1926. 185p.   **6254**

Kentucky. State Library. Catalogue. Frankfort. 1928. 474p.   **6254a**

Kentucky. University, Lexington. Department of history and the Library. Union catalog of materials relating to Kentucky and western history in Lexington and vicinity. (Deposited with the Hist. dept.) **6255**

Kentucky Library Association. Check list of Kentucky newspapers contained in Kentucky libraries. Prepared by the Kentucky Library Association, Ludie Kinkead, editor, and the Kentucky newspaper checklist, T. D. Clark . . . editor of Kentucky division. Lexington, Ky. 1935. 42,10p. mim. **6256**

Kentucky State Historical Society. Card index of Kentucky military pay rolls and certificates of service, 1787-1794. Frankfort, Ky. **6256a**

—— Card index to early Kentucky newspapers. Frankfort, Ky. **6256b**

—— Catalogue no. 5 of Kentucky State Historical Society, from 1914 to 1917. Comp. by the librarian, Miss Sally Jackson. Frankfort, Ky. 1917. (Supplement to catalogue no. 5. 1919. 37p.) **6257**

—— Catalogue of books, magazines, manuscripts, newspapers, etc., in the rooms of the Kentucky State Historical Society. By the secretary-treasurer, Mrs. Jennie C. Morton. Louisville. Globe Ptg. Co. 1909. 48p. **6258**

Louisville. Public Library. Card index of the Louisville Courier-Journal, 1917-1920, 1924 to date. Louisville, Ky. **6258a**

McElroy, Robert McNutt. A critical bibliography of Kentucky history. *In* Kentucky in the nation's history. N.Y. Moffat, Yard. 1909. p547-77 **6259**

McMurtrie, Douglas C. A bibliography of eighteenth century Kentucky broadsides. Filson Club hist. quar. X. p23-31 (Jan. 1936) **6260**

—— A bibliography of Kentucky statute law, 1792-1830. Filson Club hist. quar. IX. p95-120 (April 1935) **6261**

—— A check-list of Kentucky almanacs, 1789-1830. Kentucky State Hist. Soc. reg. XXX. p237-59 (July 1932) **6262**

—— Check list of Kentucky imprints, 1811-1820, with notes in supplement to the Check list of 1787-1810 imprints. Louisville. Historical Records Survey. 1939. 235p. mim. (American imprints inventory, no. 6) **6262a**

—— Early Kentucky medical imprints, with a bibliography to 1830. Frankfort, Ky. Priv. printed. 1933 **6263**

—— Notes on printing in Kentucky in the eighteenth century, with special references to the work of Thomas Parvin, first journeyman printer in Kentucky. Filson Club hist. quar. X. p261-80 (Oct. 1936) **6264**

—— Proof sheets of a bibliography of Kentucky imprints, 1787-1822, unrevised; printed as manuscripts, subject to corrections and additions. Chicago. 1932. [1934] [113p.] **6265**

—— Unlocated early Kentucky imprints. Louisville. 1931. p16-34 (Extract from the Filson Club hist. quar. for Jan. 1931) **6266**

McMurtrie, Douglas C. and Allen, Albert H. Check list of Kentucky imprints, 1787-1810. (American imprints inventory, no. 5) Louisville. Historical Records Survey. 1939. 205p. mim. **6266a**

Miller, A. M. Bibliography of literature referring to the geology of Kentucky, 1809-1919. *In* Kentucky Geological Survey, Series V. Bulletin 2. Frankfort, Ky. State Jour. Co. 1919. p359-92 **6266b**

Myers, Irene T. Report on the archives of the state of Kentucky. Am. Hist. Asso. rep. 1910. p331-64 **6267**

Perrin, William Henry. The pioneer press of Kentucky, from the printing of the first paper west of the Alleghenies, Aug. 11, 1787 to the establishment of the daily press in 1830. (Filson Club publications. no. 3) Louisville. Filson Club. 1888. 93p. **6268**

Phillips, Philip Lee. The first map of Kentucky by John Filson; a bibliographical account with facsimile reproduction from the copy in the Library of Congress. Wash. D.C. W.H. Lowdermilk. 1908. 22p. **6268a**

Rawings, Kenneth W. Trial list of titles of Kentucky newspapers and periodicals before 1860. Ky. Hist. Soc. reg. XXXVI. p263-87 (July 1938) **6268b**

Rothert, Otto A. Brief sketches of the Filson Club's publications and its History quarterly with a general index to their chief topics. The Filson Club hist. quar. II. p1-59, 79-107 (Jan. 1937) **6269**

—— The Filson Club and its activities, 1884-1922; a history of The Filson Club, including lists of Filson Club publications and papers on Kentucky history. Prepared for the club, also names of members (Filson Club publications. no. 32) Louisville, Ky. 1922. 64p. **6269a**

—— The Filson Club and its activities in geneaology. Ind. hist. bul. XVII. p100-8 (Feb. 1940) **6269b**

—— General index—The Register of the Kentucky State Historical Society, Frankfort, Kentucky, vol. 1 to 20, no. 1 to 60, 1903-1922. Supplement to the Reg. X. no. 60. 40p. (Sept. 1922) **6270**

—— Local history in Kentucky literature; a manuscript read before the Louisville literary club, September 27, 1915. 30p. typ. **6271**

Shaler, Nathaniel S. Description of the preliminary topographical and geological maps of Kentucky, edition of 1877. *In* Kentucky. Geological Survey, 1873-1891. Reports of progress. . . . n.s. Frankfort. Yeomen Press. 1877. III. p347-64 **6271a**

Shearin, Hubert G. and Combs, Josiah H. A syllabus of Kentucky folk-songs. (Transylvania Univ. Stud. in English. II) Lexington. Transylvania Ptg. Co. 1911. 43p. **6272**

Smith, W. T. A complete index to the names of persons, places and subjects mentioned in Littell's laws of Kentucky; a genealogical and historical guide. Lexington. Bradford Press Club. 1931. 213p. **6273**

Smith, Z. F. Introductory—Part I. Historians and histories of Kentucky. Part II. Other works containing Kentucky history. *In* The history of Kentucky. Louisville. Courier-Jour. 1886. p. vii-xxi **6274**

Staples, Charles R. New discoveries amongst old records. Ky. Hist. Soc. reg. XXXIII. p307-25 (Oct. 1935) (Kentucky archives) **6274a**

Sulzer, Elmer G. Geological research in Kentucky—addenda. Ky. Hist. Soc. reg. XXX. p322-34 (Oct. 1932) (Publications of the Geological Survey of Kentucky) **6274b**

Survey of Federal Archives. Kentucky. Inventory of federal archives in the states. Louisville, Ky. 1938- . mim. The Federal Courts. Nov. 1939. 89p.; The Department of the Treasury. June 1939. 131p.; The Department of War. 1941. 124p.; The Department of Justice. Sept. 1938. 16p.; The Department of the Navy. Jan. 1939. 9p.; The Department of Agriculture. Oct. 1940. 125p.; The Farm Credit Administration. Nov. 1938. 20p. **6274c**

Tenney, S. M. Materials on Kentucky history in the library of historical foundation of the Presbyterian and Reformed churches, Montreat, North Carolina. Filson Club hist. quar. V. p99-111 (April 1931) (Manuscript and printed material) **6275**

Townsend, John Wilson. A history of Kentucky literature since 1913. Filson Club hist. quar. XIII. p21-36 (Jan. 1939) **6275a**

—— Kentuckians in history and literature. N.Y., Wash. D.C. Neale. 1907. 189p. **6276**

—— Kentucky in American letters, 1784-1912. Cedar Rapids. Torch Press. 1913. 2v. **6277**

Transylvania College. Card bibliography of Kentucky imprints prior to 1830 in its own collection. Lexington, Ky. **6277a**

—— Index catalog of Transsylvania documents, 1783-1851. Lexington, Ky. ms. **6277b**

U.S. Army War College. Library. References, Newport Barracks, Ky. Comp. by Nancy Cramer Barndollar. n.p. n.p. 1933. 2p. typ. **6277c**

U.S. Library of Congress. Division of bibliography. List of books relating to Kentucky. March 23, 1925. 26p. typ. (Supplementary to bibliog. in Robert McElroy's Kentucky in the nation's history, 1909) **6278**

—— —— —— Select list of references on the Scotch-Irish in the South and the Ohio Valley, with special reference to Kentucky. Oct. 25, 1913. 5p. typ. (Additional references. 1918. 2p) **6279**

Wisconsin. State Historical Society. Calendar of the Kentucky papers of the Draper collection of manuscripts (Publications of the State Hist. Soc. of Wis. Calendar series, II). Madison, Pub. by the Soc. 1925. 624p. **6279a**

Yandell, Lunsford. Medical literature of Kentucky. Read before the Kentucky State Medical Society, 1874. Louisville. J. P. Morton. 1874. 52p. **6280**

LOUISIANA

Beer, William. Louisiana history in government documents. Gulf state hist. mag. I. p184-93. 1902 **6280a**

—— "Moniteur de la Louisiane" New Orleans, 1794. Bibliog. Soc. of Am. pap. XIV, pt. 2. p127-31. 1920 (French newspapers in the United States before 1800) **6280b**

—— Some points in Louisiana cartography. *In* International Congress of Americanists. Reseña de la segunda sesión del XVII Congreso internacional de americanistas efectuada en la ciudad de México durante el mes de septiembre de 1910. México. Imp. del Museo n. de arqueología, historia y etnología. 1912. p436-40 **6280c**

Bond, Frank. Historical sketch of "Louisiana" and the Louisiana purchase... with a statement of other acquisitions. Wash. Govt. Ptg. Off. 1912. 14p. (Early maps of Louisiana) **6280d**

Brigham, Clarence S. Louisiana—Bibliography of American newspapers—1690-1820. Am. Antiq. Soc. proc. n.s. XXIV. p404-16 (Oct. 1914) **6281**

Butler, Pierce. Report on the transcripts of documents in the Ministère des colonies, Paris, France copied for The Society, by M. Victor Tantet. Louisiana Hist. Soc. publications. IV. p156-9. 1908 **6282**

Caulfeild, Ruby Van Allen. The French literature of Louisiana. N.Y. Columbia Univ., Inst. of French Stud. 1929. 282p. (Appendix containing bibliographies on p190-277) **6283**

Chambon, Celestin M. Notes gathered from the Archives of the Cathedral-Church of St. Louis, New Orleans, Louisiana. (Publication of the Howard Memorial Lib.) New Orleans. 1908. 10p. (Reprinted from The Morning Star, March 7, 14, 21, 1908) **6283a**

—— The Saint Louis Cathedral archives. *In* In and around the old St. Louis Cathedral of New Orleans. New Orleans. Philippes Printery. 1908. p91-104 **6283b**

Cruzat, Heloise H. and Lugano, Gaspar. Records of the Superior Council of Louisiana. La. hist. quar. I- . (Jan. 1917-) **6283c**

Dart, Henry Plauche. The archives of Louisiana. Louisiana hist. quar. II. p349-67 (Oct. 1919) **6284**

—— Cabildo archives. La. hist. quar. III. p71-99 (Jan. 1920) **6284a**
—— Index to the publications of the Louisiana Historical Society, 1895-1917. Louisiana hist. quar. V. p431-46 (July 1922) **6285**
—— The law library of a Louisiana lawyer in the 18th century Louisiana State Bar Asso. rep. XXV. p12-29. 1924. (Reprinted in Am. Bar. Asso. jour. XI. p107-12. Feb. 1925) **6286**
Dart, Henry Plauche, ed. Gayarré's report on Louisiana archives in Spain. La. hist. quar. IV. p464-80 (Oct. 1921) (Originally published in House misc. doc. 22, 46 Cong. 2 sess.) **6286a**
Deiler, John Hanno. Geschichte der New Orleanser deutschen presse; nebst anderen denkwürdigkeiten der New Orleanser Deutschen. New Orleans. Im selbstverlage des verfassers. 1901. 40p. **6287**
Dienst, Alex. The New Orleans newspaper files of the Texas revolutionary period. Southw. hist. quar. IV. p140-51 (Oct. 1900) **6287a**
Dunbar, Clarence P. A list of some of the available publications dealing with the geology and mineral resources of Louisiana and related areas. (Louisiana. Dept. of Conservation. General bul. handbook... pt. III) New Orleans. Louisiana Dept. of Conservation. 1933. p235-69 **6288**
Foote, Lucy B. Official publications of the state of Louisiana, 1898-1934. (Univ. of Illinois, Master's thesis) 1935. 555p. MS. (A revision of this is in progress; it is to cover 1803-1934.) **6288a**
Forstall, Edmond J. An analytical index of the whole of the public documents relative to Louisiana, deposited in the archives of the department "de la marine et des colones [sic]" et "Bibliothèque du roi" at Paris. *In* French, Benjamin F. Historical collections of Louisiana. Phila. Daniels & Smith. 1850. II. p41-87 (Also published in DeBow's rev. I. p357-68, 437-43, 519-27 (April-June 1846) **6288b**
Fortier, Alcée. Old papers of colonial times. La. Hist. Soc. pubs. I, pt. 2. p6-25. 1895 (MS. papers of the French Superior Council and the Spanish Cabildo) **6288c**
—— Report of Prof. Fortier. La. Hist. Soc. pubs. I, pt. 1. p3-9. 1895 (MSS. in the Louisiana Historical Society relating to the French province of Louisiana) **6288d**
Griffin, Max L. A bibliography of New Orleans magazines. La. hist. quar. XVIII. p491-556. 1935 **6289**
Harris, G. D. and Veatch, A. C. Historical review [of geological literature of Louisiana] Louisiana state experiment station, pt. V, p11-44. 1899 **6289a**
Heartman, Charles F. The "Blue Book"; a bibliographical attempt to describe the guide books to the houses of ill fame in New Orleans. By Semper Idem. (Heartman's hist. ser. no. 50) 1936. 77p. **6289b**

Historical Records Survey. Louisiana. Calendar of manuscript collections in Louisiana. University, La. State Univ. 1938- . Ser. 1. The Department of Archives: No. 1. Taber collection. May 1938. 12p. **6289c**
—— —— Guide to depositories of manuscript collections in Louisiana. La. hist. quar. XXIV. p305-53 (April 1941) **6289d**
—— —— Guide to the manuscript collections in Louisiana, the Department of Archives, Louisiana State University. Vol. I. Ed. by William Ransom Hogan. University, La. The Dept. of Archives, Louisiana State Univ. Aug. 1940- . 55p. mim. **6289e**
—— —— Inventory of the parish archives of Louisiana. New Orleans, La. 1938- . mim. No. 2. Allen. June 1938. 91p.; No. 6. Beauregard. Oct. 1940. 105p.; No. 8. Bossier. Aug. 1940. 295p.; No. 10. Calcasieu. March 1938. 113p.; No. 22. Grant. April 1940. 110p.; No. 26. Jefferson. Jan. 1940. 437p.; No. 28. LaFayette. Feb. 1938. 118p.; No. 35. Natchitoches. Sept. 1938. 180p.; No. 36. Orleans: Preliminary inventory of notarial records. June 1939. 172p.; No. 38. Plaquemines. Aug. 1939. 228p.; No. 44. St. Bernard. Dec. 1938. 166p.; No. 45. St. Charles. Nov. 1937. 117p.; No. 55. Terrebonne. May 1941. 169p.; No. 59. Washington. March 1940. 365p. **6289f**
—— —— Inventory of the state archives of Louisiana. New Orleans, La. 1941- . mim. Series II. The Judiciary: No. 2. The Supreme Court of Louisiana. April 1941. 59p. **6289g**
King, Grace. The preservation of Louisiana history. North Carolina hist. rev. V. p363-71 (Oct. 1928) **6290**
Louisiana. Laws, statutes, etc. Index and concordance of the Civil code of Louisiana: with references to the revised statutes of 1856. Prep. by Byron F. Cook. New Orleans. J.B. Steel. 1857. 221p. **6290a**
Louisiana. State museum. Biennial report, 1906/08- . New Orleans, La. 1908- **6290b**
—— —— Louisiana State Museum, New Orleans. Handbook of information, concerning its historic buildings and the treasures they contain. Prep. by Robert Glenk. New Orleans. 1941. 400p. **6290c**
—— —— Department of Louisiana history and archives. Archives of Louisiana. (Fifth biennial rep. of the board of curators, 1914-15) New Orleans. 1916. p33-40 **6290d**
Louisiana. State University. A partial list of maps dealing with Cameron and Vermilion parishes. By James H. McGuirt. *In* Reports on the geology of Cameron and Vermilion parishes. (Louisiana Department of Conservation geological bul. no. 6) New Orleans. T.J. Moran Sons. 1936. p199-203 **6290e**
—— —— Department of archives. Name and place index to the manuscript collection. University, La. Louisiana State Univ. In progress **6291**

Louisiana. State University. Library. Card catalog of Louisiana historical materials. Baton Rouge, La.   6292

—— —— —— Manuscript checklist of newspaper files.   6293

Louisiana Historical Society. A catalogue of the colonial exhibit of the Louisiana Historical Society and loan exhibit of members and friends, consisting of books, pamphlets, documents, maps, charts, views, pictures, plans, etc., New Orleans, December 20th 1903, centennial transfer of Louisiana. [New Orleans. 1903] 32p.   6294

McCain, William D. The papers of the Food Administration for Louisiana, 1917-1919 in The National Archives. La. hist. quar. XXI. p869-74 (July 1938)   6294a

McGrath, John. The salvation of the parish records in 1862. East and West Baton Rouge hist. soc. proc. I. p24-5. 1916-17   6294b

McMurtrie, Douglas C. Denis Braud, imprimeur du roi à la Nouvelle Orléans. Paris. 1929. 14p. (Extrait du Bulletin du bibliophile)   6295

—— Early printing in New Orleans, 1764-1810, with a bibliography of the issues of the Louisiana press. New Orleans. Searcy and Pfaff. 1929. 151p.   6296

—— The French press of Louisiana. [New Orleans. 1935] 19p. (Reprinted from the Louisiana hist. quar. XVIII. no. 4. Oct. 1935)   6297

—— The pioneer printer of New Orleans. Chicago. Eyncourt Press. 1930. 17p. (Reprinted from The Southern printer. Jan.-Feb. 1929)   6298

McVoy, Lizzie Carter and Campbell, Ruth Bates. A bibliography of fiction by Louisianians and on Louisiana subjects. (Louisiana State Univ. Stud. no. XVIII) Baton Rouge. Louisiana State Univ. Press. 1935. 87p.   6299

Marr, Robert Hardin. Index to the acts of Louisiana, indexing all statutes adopted in 1870 and thereafter, inclusive of the regular session of 1930, and such local and special laws of date prior to 1870, as seemed of any present interest. New Orleans. F. F. Hansell & Bro., Ltd. 1931. 652p.   6300

New Orleans Library Club. Libraries in the city of New Orleans. New Orleans. The Club. 1936. 13p. mim.   6300a

Porteous, Laura L. Index to the Spanish judicial records of Louisiana. La. hist. quar. VI- . (Jan. 1923-)   6300b

Price, William. Work of indexing Louisiana Black Boxes. Louisiana Hist. Soc. publications. VIII. p7-20. 1914-15. (French archives)   6301

Robinson, Elrie. Old newspapers . . . collection of Elrie Robinson . . . [St. Francisville, La.] St. Francisville democrat. 1936. 19p.   6301a

Roussève, Charles Barthelemy. The negro in Louisiana; aspects of his history and his literature. New Orleans. Xavier Univ. Press. 1937. 212p.   6301b

Scroggs, William O. The archives of the state of Louisiana. Am. Hist. Asso. rep. 1912. p275-93   6302

Survey of Federal Archives. Louisiana. Inventory of federal archives in the states. New Orleans, La. 1938- . mim. The Federal Courts. Nov. 1939. 56p.; The Department of the Treasury. Dec. 1938. 361p.; The Department of War. Sept. 1939. 232p.; The Department of Justice. Oct. 1938. 23p.; The Department of the Navy. July 1938. 49p.; The Department of Agriculture. July 1938. 308p.; The Department of Commerce. June 1939. 92p.; The Department of Labor. June 1940. 23p.; The Veterans' Administration. June 1940. 44p.; The Farm Credit Administration. April 1941. 13p.; The Emergency Relief Administration. June 1941. 14p.; The Works Progress Administration. June 1941. 103p.   6302a

Thomassy, Marie Joseph Raymond. Cartographie de l'ancienne Louisiane. In Géologie pratique de la Louisiane. Nouvelle-Orleans. Chez l'auteur. 1860. p205-26   6302b

Thompson, Thomas P. Catalogue of Americana, consisting principally of books relating to Louisiana and the Mississippi Valley (Louisiana purchase). . . . New Orleans. Priv. printed. 1903. 52p.   6303

—— Index to a collection of Americana, relating principally to Louisiana art and miscellanea; all included in the private library of T. P. Thompson. New Orleans. Perry & Buckley. 1912. 203p.   6304

—— Louisiana writers, native and resident, including others whose books belong to a bibliography of that state; to which is added a list of artists. Comp. for Louisiana state commission, Louisiana purchase exposition. New Orleans. 1904. 64p. 6305

Tinker, Edward Larocque. Bibliography of the French newspapers and periodicals of Louisiana. Worcester. Am. Antiq. Soc. 1933. 126p. (Reprinted from Am. Antiq. Soc. proc. n.s. XLII. p247-370. Oct. 1932)   6306

—— Les écrits de langue française en Louisiane au XIX⁰ siècle; essais biographiques et bibliographiques. Paris. H. Champion. 1932. 502p.   6307

Tucker, John H., Jr. Source books of Louisiana law; pt. I, Civil code; pt. II, The code of practice; pt. III, Spanish laws; pt. IV, Constitution, statutes, reports and digests. Tulane law rev. VI, p280-300 (Feb. 1932); VII. 82-95 (Dec. 1932); VIII. 396-405 (April 1934); IX. 244-67 (Feb. 1935)   6308

Tulane University. Theses on Louisiana. Louisiana Lib. Asso. bul. I. no. 3 (Dec. 1932)   6309

MAINE

Ayer, Harry B. Index to the probate records of the county of York, Maine, from January 1, 1901, to January 1, 1911. [Biddeford, Me.] Press of the Biddeford Jour. 1911. 134p.   **6309a**

Babb, Cyrus Cate. Bibliography of Maine geology. Maine State Water Storage Comn. annual rep. III. 1913. p185-242. (Reprinted, Waterville Sentinel Publishing Co. 1913. 68p.)   **6310**

Boardman, Samuel L. Agricultural bibliography of Maine; biographical sketches of Maine writers on agriculture, with a catalogue of their works and an index to the volumes on the Agriculture of Maine from 1850 to 1892. Augusta. Boardman. 1893. 117p. (Also in Maine. Dept. of Agriculture. Agriculture of Maine. Thirty-fifth annual rep. 1892) **6311**

—— Descriptive sketches of six private libraries of Bangor, Maine. Bangor. Printed for the Author. 1900. 161p. (Reprinted from the columns of the Bangor daily commercial. Contains titles on Maine, Daniel Webster, Indians)   **6312**

—— A general index to the principal articles and leading subjects in the volumes of the Agriculture of Maine, from 1850 to 1875. Annual reports of the Agricultural societies, 1875-76. Augusta, Me. 1876. p257-74   **6313**

Boston. Public Library. The Popham colony. Boston Pub. Lib. bul. III. p272-3 (Oct. 1877)   **6314**

Bowdoin College Library, Brunswick. Manuscript bibliography on Maine supplementary to Williamson.   **6315**

Brigham, Clarence S. Maine—Bibliography of American newspapers, 1690-1820. Am. Antiq. Soc. proc. n.s. XXIV. p417-49 (Oct. 1914)   **6316**

Bryant, H. W. A catalogue of miscellaneous books, comprising local history and genealogy with many items of interest to collectors of Maine books. [Portland. 1896] 8p.   **6316a**

—— A check list of Maine town histories for the use of librarians and collectors. [Portland. 1904] 8p.   **6316b**

Drummond, Josiah H. Bibliographic memorandum of the laws of Maine. Maine Hist. Soc. colls. and proc. second ser. II. p391-402. 1891. (Printed also in the 25th rep. of the Librarian of the Maine State Lib. 1891-92. p34-41)   **6317**

—— Bibliography of Maine laws. *In* Maine State Library, Biennial report, 1891-92. p34-41   **6317a**

Fassett, Frederick Gardiner. A history of newspapers in the District of Maine, 1785-1820. The Maine bul. XXXV. no. 3. Nov. 1932 (Univ. of Maine. Stud. 2d ser. no. 25) Orono. Univ. Press. 1932. 242p.   **6318**

—— A history of newspapers in the state of Maine, 1820-1860. Massachusetts Inst. Technology. In progress.   **6319**

Folsom, George. A catalogue of original documents in the English archives relating to the early history of the state of Maine. N.Y. Priv. printed by G. B. Teubner. 1858. 137p.   **6320**

Griffin, Joseph. Bibliography of Maine. *In* History of the press of Maine. Brunswick. J. Griffin. 1872. p215-72 **6321**

—— Supplement to the History of the press in Maine, with complete indexes. Brunswick. J. Griffin. 1874. p289-320 **6322**

Hall, Drew B. Reference list on Maine local history. N.Y. State Lib. bul. 63. bibliog. 28. p775-917 (June 1910) **6323**

Hasse, Adelaide Rosalie. Index of economic material in documents of the states of the United States—Maine, 1820-1904. (Carnegie Inst. of Wash. Publication no. 85) Wash. D.C. Carnegie Inst. of Wash. 1907. 95p.   **6324**

Historical Records Survey. Maine. Inventory of the town and city archives of Maine. Portland, Me. 1938- . mim. No. 4. Franklin County: vols. 1 and 2. Avon and Berlin. May 1939. 104p., vol. 4. Chesterville. June 1939. 77p., vols. 5 and 6. Coplin, Dallas. 1939. 74p., vol. 7. Eustis. 1939. 75p. ; No. 5. Hancock County: vol. 1. Towns of Mt. Desert: Mount Desert, Bar Harbor, Cranberry Isles, Seaville, Tremont, Southwest Harbor. March 1938. 236p., vol. 1-2. Index to vol. 1. Towns of Mt. Desert. March 1940. 66p. **6324a**

Huston, Almer J. A check list of Maine local histories. Portland, Me. 1915. 44p.   **6325**

—— List of Maine material in the library of the Maine Historical Society at Portland which is not in the Maine State library. n.p. n.p. n.d.   **6325a**

Johnson, Allen. Report on the archives of the state of Maine. Am. Hist. Asso. rep. 1908. I. p261-318   **6326**

McMurtrie, Douglas C. A history of Maine imprints. Springfield, Ill. n.d. 4p. **6326a**

—— Maine imprints, 1792-1820; an open letter to R. Webb Noyes. Chicago. Priv. printed. 1935. 12p.   **6327**

—— Pioneer printing in Maine. Springfield, Ill. 1932. 4p. (Reprinted from the National printer journalist. March 1932) **6328**

Maine. State historian. Report of the State historian, 1909-1910. Henry S. Burrage, state historian. Augusta. Kennebec Jour. print. 1910. 18p. (Summary of work of the state historian since 1907, and account of MSS. and records relating to Maine history)   **6329**

—— —— Executive, legislative and judicial departments of Maine (and their publications). (27th rep. of the Maine state librarian. 1895-96) Augusta. Kennebec Jour. print. 1897. p23-32   **6330**

—— —— Guide to references on Abnaki names. Maine State Lib. bul. XVI. p82-6 (April 1931)   **6330a**

—— —— Index of Maine state publications, 1904-1934. typ.   **6330b**

Maine. State historian. Index to Maine public documents, 1834-1867. (32d rep. of the Maine state librarian. 1905-06) Augusta. Kennebec Jour. print. 1907. p26-90 **6331**

—— —— Maine Indians; selected list of references available at the Maine State Library. n.p. n.p. n.d. 5p. mim. **6331a**

—— Maine public and legislative documents. Maine State Lib. bul. II. p5-6 (July 1917) **6332**

—— —— Manuscript bibliographies on Maine history. **6333**

—— —— Sources for a maritime history of Maine. Maine State Lib. bul. XVII. p34-40 (Oct. 1931) **6333a**

—— —— [Bibliography of the] State of Maine. (Maine state librarian rep. 1891-92) Augusta. Burleigh & Flynt. 1892. p19-33 **6334**

—— —— State publications, 1912-1933. Maine lib. bul. II-XVIII **6334a**

Maine. University. Union list of serials in Maine libraries. Comp. by Dorothy Smith. (Bulletin, v. 39. no. 8) Orono. 1937. 257p. **6334b**

—— —— **Department of History and Government.** A reference list of manuscripts relating to the history of Maine. Parts I-II-III (Maine bul. Aug. 1938, Aug. 1939) Orono. Univ. of Maine Press. 1938-41. 427, 261, 211p. Pt. II contains an introduction on Maine maps, by Fanny Hardy Eckstorm. Pt. III is an index.) **6334c**

—— —— —— A reference list of manuscripts relating to the history of Maine, conducted under the auspices of the University of Maine with funds provided by the Federal Emergency Relief Administration. Orono. 1935. 699p. ms. **6334d**

Maine Genealogical Society. List of family histories in the library of the Maine Genealogical Society. Maine Geneal. Soc. rep. 1911. p14-42 **6335**

Nichols, Charles Lemuel. Checklist of Maine, New Hampshire and Vermont almanacs. Worcester. Am. Antiq. Soc. 1929. 103p. (Reprinted from the Am. Antiq. Soc. proc. n.s. XXXVIII. p63-163. April 1928) **6336**

Norton, Charles B. The bibliography of the state of Maine, and other papers of interest; together with a catalogue of a large collection of works upon bibliography and America. (Norton's literary letter. no. 4) N.Y. 1859. 72p. **6337**

Noyes, Reginald Webb. A bibliography of Maine imprints to 1820. Stonington, Me. Printed by Mrs. and Mr. R. W. Noyes. 1930. unpag. (Supplement. 1934. 11p.) **6338**

—— The development of printing in the District of Maine, with an appended bibliography of Maine imprints to 1820. (Columbia Univ. Master's essay) 1929. 186p. typ. **6339**

—— A guide to the study of Maine local history. Ann Arbor? Mich. 1936. 87p. mim. **6339a**

Ring, Elizabeth. A bibliography of the state of Maine, 1892-1940. Maine Univ. In progress **6340**

Smith, Edgar Crosby. Maine map-makers and their maps. Sprague's jour. Me. hist. II. p3-9 (May 1914) **6340a**

—— Maps of the state of Maine; a bibliography of the maps of the state of Maine. Bangor, Me. Priv. print. C. H. Glass and Co. 1903. 29p. **6340b**

—— Moses Greenleaf, Maine's first map-maker, a biography: with letters, unpublished manuscripts and a reprint of Mr. Greenleaf's rare paper on Indian place-names, also a bibliography of the maps of Maine. (The De Burians, Pub. no. 2) Bangor, Me. 1902. 165p. **6340c**

Smith, Edward S. C. and Avery, Myron H. An annotated bibliography of Katahdin. Wash. D.C. Appalachian Trail Conference. 1937 **6340d**

Sprague, John Francis. A bibliography of Piscataquis County, Maine. Dover. Observer Publishing Co. 1916. p34-43 (Reprinted from Piscataquis County Historical Society, its by-laws and membership, etc., and a bibliography of Piscataquis county, 1916) **6341**

Survey of Federal Archives. Maine. Inventory of federal archives in the states. Rockland, Me. 1938- . mim. The Federal Courts. Jan. 1939. 23p.; The Department of the Treasury. May 1939. 417p.; The Department of War. Jan. 1940. 172p.; The Department of Justice. Jan. 1939. 5p.; The Department of the Interior. Feb. 1940. 26p.; The Department of the Navy. Feb. 1941. 395p.; The Department of the Interior. Feb. 1940. 26p.; The Department of Agriculture. Oct. 1938. 90p.; The Department of Commerce. Oct. 1938. 77p.; The Department of Labor. Oct. 1940. 71p.; The Veterans' Administration. May 1939. 53p.; The Farm Credit Administration. April 1939. 14p.; The Civil Works Administration. 1941. 15p.; The Works Progress Administration. 1941. 42p.; Miscellaneous agencies. 1941. 123p. **6341a**

Twinem, Joseph Conrad. Bibliography of Maine geology from 1836 to 1930. *In* Maine. State geologist. Report on the geology of Maine. Augusta. 1932. p17-86 **6341b**

U.S. National Youth Administration. Maine. An annotated bibliography of books and pamphlets on certain mechanical and allied trades. By Charles J. Boorkman. Quoddy Village, Me. March 1940. 137p. **6341c**

Williamson, Joseph A. A bibliography of the state of Maine, from the earliest period to 1891. Portland. Thurston. 1896. 2v. **6342**

—— Historical review of literature in Maine. Maine Hist. Soc. col. 2d ser. II. p113-27. 1891 **6342a**

Willis, William. A descriptive catalogue of books and pamphlets relating to the history and statistics of Maine, or portions of it. Hist. mag. VII. second ser. p145-82 (March 1870) **6343**

Wood, Richard G. A bibliography of travel in Maine, 1783-1861. New England quar. VI. p426-39 (June 1933) **6344**

MARYLAND

Alexander, John Henry. Index to the calendar of Maryland state papers. Balt. J. S. Waters. 1861. 66p. **6345**

Allen, Ethan. Report of the Rev. Dr. Ethan Allen, in relation to the records of the Executive department; and letter from John H. Alexander . . . in reference to calendar of Domestic state papers. [Annapolis? 1861] 8p. **6346**

—— Report on the condition of the public records. Annapolis. T. J. Wilson. 1860. 5p. **6347**

Baldwin, Jane and Henry, Roberta Bolling. The Maryland calendar of wills, from 1635-1743. Balt. Dulany; Kohn & Pollock. 1901-28. 8v. **6348**

Baltimore. City Library. Catalogue (Baltimore and Maryland section) City Library, City Hall, Baltimore, Maryland. Issued by Wilbur F. Coyle, city librarian, May 1909. [Balt. Meyer & Thalheimer. 1909] 68p. **6349**

Brantly, William T. Critical essay on the sources of information—The English in Maryland, 1632-1691. In Narrative and critical history of America. Ed. by Justin Winsor. Boston, N.Y. Houghton Mifflin. 1884. III. p553-62 **6350**

Brigham, Clarence S. Maryland—Bibliography of American newspapers, 1690-1820. Am. Antiq. Soc. proc. n.s. XXV. p128-92 (April 1915) **6351**

Catholic University of America. Library. The Michael Jenkins collection of works on the history of Maryland. Wash. D.C. Catholic Univ. of Amer. 1913. 28p. **6352**

Clark, W. B. Publications of the Maryland Geological Survey, Maryland State Weather Service, and Maryland Forestry Bureau. Johns Hopkins Univ. cir. 1907, no. 7. p5-20 **6352a**

Cotton, Jane Baldwin. The Maryland calendar of wills 1635-1738. Baltimore. 1901-25. 7v. **6352b**

Garrett, John W. Seventeenth century books relating to Maryland. Md. hist. mag. XXXIV. p1-39 (March 1939) **6352c**

Giddens, Paul H. Bibliography of Maryland during the time of Governor Horatio Sharpe, 1753-1769. Maryland hist. mag. XXXI. p6-15 (March 1936) **6353**

Gilmer, Gertrude. Maryland newspapers—ante-bellum, 1793 to 1861. Maryland hist. rev. XXIX. p120-31 (June 1934) **6354**

Hambleton & Co. Old maps, prints, lithography, engravings of Baltimore City, points therein and nearby. Baltimore. 1936? 51p. **6354a**

Historical Records Survey. Maryland. Inventory of the church archives of Maryland. Baltimore, Md. 1940- . mim. Protestant Episcopal: Diocese of Maryland. Nov. 1940. 310p. **6354b**

—— Inventory of the county archives of Maryland. Baltimore, Md. 1937- . mim. No. 1. Allegany. Sept. 1937. 101p.; No. 6. Carroll. March 1940. 273p.; No. 11. Garrett. June 1938. 128p.; No. 13. Howard. March 1939. 181p.; No. 15. Montgomery. Feb. 1939. 319p.; No. 21. Washington. Dec. 1937. 153p.; No. 22. Wicomico. Sept. 1940. 222p. mim. **6354c**

Holbein, M. Clotilde, Sister. Maryland tercentenary, 1634-1934; a bibliography of early colonial Maryland history. [Mt. Washington, Md.] 1932. 9p. **6355**

Hoyt, William D., Jr. Logs and papers of Baltimore privateers. Md. hist. mag. XXXIV. p165-74 (June 1939) **6355a**

—— The papers of the Maryland State Colonization Society. Md. hist. mag. XXXII. p247-71 (Sept. 1937) **6355b**

Keidel, George Charles. Catonsville articles by George C. Keidel. [Balt. 1920] 3p. (Reprinted Feb. 1920 from the Maryland hist. mag. XIV. p400-2. 1919) **6356**

—— Early Maryland newspapers: a list of titles. Maryland hist. mag. XXVIII. p119-37, 244-57, 328-44; XXIX. p25-34, 132-44, 223-36, 310-22; XXX. p149-56 (June 1933-June 1935) **6357**

Kilty, William. Index to the laws of Maryland, from the year 1818 to 1825, inclusive. Annapolis. Jeremiah Hughes. 1827. unpaged **6357a**

Lee, John Westley Murray. A hand list of laws, journals, and documents of Maryland to the year 1800. Balt. Priv. printed. 1878. 16p. **6358**

—— Newspapers in the Maryland Historical Society. Mag. of Am. hist. VI. p469-71 (June 1881) **6359**

Litsinger, Elizabeth C. Check list of the official publications of Maryland (state, county, city). Enoch Pratt Free Library, Baltimore (In progress) **6359a**

—— Maryland department. In Enoch Pratt Free Library. Reorganization of a large public library. Baltimore. 1937. mim. **6359b**

McMurtrie, Douglas C. Pioneer printing in Maryland. Springfield, Ill. 1932. 4p. (Reprinted from the Aug. 1932 National printer journalist) **6360**

Magruder, James M. Index of Maryland colonial wills, 1634-1777, at land office. Annapolis, Md. 1933. 3v. mim. **6361**

—— Magruder's Maryland colonial abstracts —wills, accounts and inventories, 1772-1777. Annapolis, Md. 1934-39. 5v. mim. **6361a**

Maryland. Court of Appeals. Catalogue of manuscripts and printed matter in the possession of the court of appeals of Maryland, November 1926. Balt. Daily Rec. Co. 1926. 29p. **6362**

Maryland. Geological Survey. [Series of reports dealing with the systematic geology of Maryland, containing bibliographies] Baltimore. Johns Hopkins Press. 1901-26 **6362a**

Maryland. Hall of Records. Annual report, 1939/1940- . Annapolis, Md. 1941- **6362b**

—— —— List and analysis of the index holdings. **6362c**

—— —— Preliminary guide to the materials in the Hall of Records. Annapolis, Md. In progress **6362d**

Maryland. Laws, Statutes, etc. Index to the laws and resolutions of the state of Maryland, from 1800 to 1813, inclusive. Annapolis. 1815. 228p.; Same. 1826-1831. Annapolis. William M'Neir. 1832. [344]p.; Same. 1832-1837. Annapolis. W. M'Neir. 1838 [538]p.; Same. 1838-1845. Annapolis. Riley & Davis. 1846. 754p. **6363**

Maryland. Public Records Commission. Condensed report . . . for the years, 1904-05. [Balt.? 1905?] 15p. (Condensed account of a 2000 page report on MSS. in state and county archives) **6364**

Maryland. State Library. Check list of Maryland publications in that library. Annapolis, Md. MS. **6364a**

—— —— Report of D. Ridgely (State librarian) to the executive of Maryland, in relation to the collection of documents, papers, &c., &c., ordered to be deposited in the council chamber. Also, a second and third report joined with this. Annapolis. W. M'Neir. 1836. 13,17,8p. **6365**

Maryland Historical Society. Calendar of the Calvert papers. (Fund publication. no. 28) Balt. 1889 **6366**

—— Catalogue of the manuscripts, maps, medals, coins, statuary, portraits and pictures; and an account of the library of the Maryland historical society. By Lewis Mayer. (Maryland hist. publications. III. no. 4) Baltimore. John D. Toy. 1854. 49p. **6367**

——· **Publication committee.** Archives of Maryland; calendar and report. Baltimore. 1883. liv p. **6368**

Mathews, Edward B. Bibliography and cartography of Maryland including publications relating to the physiography, geology and mineral resources. (Maryland Geol. Survey) Balt. 1897. I. p229-401 **6369**

—— The maps and mapmakers of Maryland, including a history of cartographic progress in Maryland. (Maryland Geol. Survey. Spec. pub. v. 2, pt. IIIb) Baltimore. Johns Hopkins Press. 1898. p337-488 (Also published in v. II of the Survey, p337-488) **6369a**

Miller, Anna Irene. Suggested readings in Maryland literature. Balt. n.p. 1924. 15p. **6370**

Minick, Amanda Rachel. History of printing in Maryland, 1791-1800. Enoch Pratt Free Lib. Baltimore, Md. In progress **6370a**

Morris, John G. Bibliography of Maryland. Hist. mag. XVII. p240-2, 328-30 (April-May 1870) **6371**

Passano, Mrs. Eleanor Phillips. An index of the source records of Maryland, genealogical, biographical, historical. Balt. Priv. print. [Waverly Press, Inc.] 1940. 478p. **6371a**

Quinlan, J. R. Medical annals of Baltimore, 1608 to 1880. Balt. 1884 **6372**

Radoff, M. L. Early Annapolis records. Md. hist. mag. XXXV. p74-8 (March 1940) **6372a**

—— Notes on Baltimore County land records. Md. hist. mag. XXXIII. p183-8 (June 1938) **6372b**

Rede, Kenneth. Bibliography of Maryland imprints, 1777-1820. Enoch Pratt Free Library, Baltimore. typ. **6372c**

Richardson, Mrs. Hester D. Report of the public records commission of Maryland. Am. Hist. Asso. rep. 1905. I. p367-8 **6373**

Ringgold, J. T. Index to Maryland decisions from first Harris & McHenry to sixty-first Maryland, including Bland & Johnson. Baltimore. 1886 **6374**

Scisco, Louis Dow. Baltimore county records of 1665-1667. Md. hist. mag. XXIV. p342-8 (Dec. 1929) (Digest of court records) **6374a**

—— Colonial records of Ann Arundell. Md. hist. mag. XXII. p62-7 (March 1927) **6374b**

—— Colonial records of Baltimore County. Md. hist. mag. XXII. p245-58 (Sept. 1927) **6374c**

—— Colonial records of Cecil County. Md. hist. mag. XXIII. p20-5 (March 1928) **6374d**

—— Colonial records of Charles county. Maryland Hist. mag. XXI. p261-70 (Sept. 1926) **6375**

—— Colonial records of Dorchester County. Md. hist. mag. XXIII. p243-6 (Sept. 1928) **6375a**

——· Colonial records of Frederick County. Md. hist. mag. XXV. p206-8 (June 1930) **6375b**

——· Colonial records of Kent County. Md. hist. mag. XXI. p356-61 (Dec. 1926) **6375c**

—— Colonial records of Prince George's County. Md. hist. mag. XXIV. p17-23 (March 1929) **6375d**

—— Colonial records of Queen Anne's County. Md. hist. mag. XXIV. p224-8 (Sept. 1929) **6375e**

—— Colonial records of Somerset County. Md. hist. mag. XXII. p349-98 (Dec. 1927) **6375f**

—— Colonial records of Talbot County. Md. hist. mag. XXII. p186-9 (June 1927) **6375g**

Shepherd, H. E. The representative authors of Maryland, from the earliest time to the present day, with biographical notes and comments upon their work. N.Y. Whitehall. 1911. 234p. **6376**

Society for the History of the Germans in Maryland. Catalog of the library of the Society. . . Balt. Schneidereith & Sons. 1907. 47p. **6377**

—— List of books contained in the library of the Society for the History of the Germans in Maryland, alphabetically arranged according to subjects and authors. (6th-10th annual reports. 1891/2-96) Balt. 1892-96 **6378**

Steiner, Bernard C. Descriptions of Maryland. (Johns Hopkins Univ. Stud. in hist. and pol. science. XXII. nos. 11-12) Balt. 1904. p567-651 **6379**

—— Some unpublished manuscripts from Fulham Palace. Md. hist. mag. XII. p115-63 (June 1917) **6379a**

Strahorn, John Sentman. Index of Maryland statutes and cases on criminal law . . . College Park, Md. 1937. 63 numb. 1., A38 numb. 1. 3d ed. **6379b**

Survey of Federal Archives. Maryland. Inventory of federal archives in the states. Baltimore, Md. 1938- . mim. The Federal Courts. Feb. 1939. 45p.; The Department of the Treasury. Feb. 1939. 272p.; The Department of War. June 1939. 336p.; The Department of Justice. Aug. 1938. 16p.; The Department of the Navy. Dec. 1938. 70p.; The Department of the Interior. Feb. 1939. 19p.; The Department of Agriculture. Oct. 1938. 177p.; The Department of Commerce. Dec. 1938. 62p.; The Department of Labor. Aug. 1938. 25p.; The Veterans' Administration. Aug. 1939. 79p.; The Farm Credit Administration. Aug. 1939. 27p.; Miscellaneous Agencies. Parts I-II. March 1940. 335p. **6379c**

Terwilliger, W. Bird. A history of Baltimore literary magazines, 1790-1940. College Park, Md. Univ. of Maryland. In progress **6379d**

Thompson, Henry F. The parish records of Maryland. Md. hist. mag. II. p126-33 (June 1907) **6379e**

Toner, J. M. Medical bibliography of Maryland chiefly prior to 1880. Trans. of Medical and Chirurgical Faculty of Maryland. LXXXIII. p358-92. 1881 **6380**

U.S. Library of Congress. Division of bibliography. A selected list of references on Maryland (with special reference to its government, finance, economic and social conditions). Nov. 4, 1933. 18p. typ. **6381**

Wheeler, Joseph Towne. Booksellers and circulating libraries in colonial Maryland. Md. hist. mag. XXXIV. p1-137 (June 1939) **6381a**

—— The Maryland press, 1777-1790. Baltimore. Maryland Hist. Soc. 1938. 226p. **6381b**

Williams, George H. Maps of the territory included within the state of Maryland, especially the vicinity of Baltimore. Johns Hopkins Univ. cir. XII. no. 103. p37-44 (Feb. 1893) **6381c**

Wroth, Lawrence Counselman. A history of printing in colonial Maryland, 1686-1776. Balt. Typothetae of Balt. 1922. 275p. **6382**

—— The Maryland colonization tracts, 1632-1646. *In* Essays offered to Herbert Putnam by his colleagues and friends on his thirtieth anniversary as Librarian of Congress, 5 April 1929. New Haven. Yale Univ. Press. 1929. p539-55 **6383**

—— The St. Mary's City press; a new chronology of American printing. Colophon. n.s. I. p333-57. 1936 (Also extracted) **6383a**

MASSACHUSETTS

Sources

Bell, Charles Upham. Index, or summary digest of the Massachusetts reports, vol. 128 to 132. Boston. 1883 **6384**

—— Index to penalties for crime and criminal evidence, pleading and practice, prescribed in the general statutes of Massachusetts 1920, and acts and resolves of 1921. Boston. Mass. Digest Asso., Inc. 1922. 276p. **6385**

—— Index to penalties for crime, prescribed in chapters 212 to 220 of the revised laws of Massachusetts. Boston. Boston Book Co. 1903. 139p. **6386**

Boston. City Council. Index to the City Council minutes from July 16, 1868 to Jan. 3, 1880. Comp. by William H. Lee. Boston. 1885. **6387**

Boston. City Council. Index to the city documents, 1834-1897; with an appendix containing a list of city publications not included among the numbered documents. Boston. 1897. 142p. **6388**

—— —— List of by-laws and ordinances and of the special acts relating to Boston. Comp. by C. W. Ernst. Boston. 1890 **6389**

—— —— List of private and special acts relating to the city of Boston. Comp. by Thomas Dean. Boston. 1881. **6390**

—— —— A list of the documents not serially numbered, published by the town or city of Boston, prior to A.D. 1891. Boston. 1894. 40p. **6391**

Clark, David S. Journals and orderly books kept by Massachusetts soldiers during the French and Indian wars. N.E. hist. and geneal. reg. XCV. p118-22 (April 1941) **6391a**

Davis, Andrew McFarland. Calendar of the papers and records relating to the Land bank of 1740, in the Massachusetts archives and Suffolk court files. Col. Soc. Mass. pub. IV. p1-121. 1910 **6391b**

—— Report on the public archives of Massachusetts. Am. Hist. Asso. rep. 1900. II. p47-59 **6392**

Edmonds, John H. The Massachusetts archives. Am. Antiq. Soc. proc. n.s. XXXI. p18-60 (April 1921) **6393**

Essex Institute. Ship registers of the District of Newburyport, Massachusetts, 1789-1870. Salem, Mass. 1937. 279p. mim.
6393a

Ford, Worthington Chauncey. Bibliography of the Massachusetts house journals, 1715-1776. Colonial Soc. of Massachusetts publications. IV. p201-89. 1910 **6394**

Ford, Worthington Chauncey and Matthews, Albert. Bibliography of the laws of the Massachusetts Bay, 1641-1776. Colonial Soc. Massachusetts publications. IV. p291-480 (1910) (Also priv. printed. Cambridge. Harvard Univ. Press. 1907. 186p.)
6395

Goodell, Abner C., Jr. A chronological sketch of the legislation from 1752 to 1884 on the subject of printing the acts and resolves of the Province of Massachusetts Bay, with a table showing the progress of work done by the present commission, etc. Boston. 1889. 47p. **6396**

Green, Samuel A. Remarks, in calling attention to a collection of manuscript plans by Jonathan Danforth. Mass. Hist. Soc. proc. 2d ser. IX. p193-5. 1895 **6396a**

Hasse, Adelaide Rosalie. Index of economic material in documents of the states of the United States: Massachusetts, 1789-1904. (Carnegie Inst. of Wash. Publications. no. 85) Wash. D.C. Carnegie Inst. of Wash. 1908. 310p. **6397**

Henkels, Stan V. Rare and scarce Americana . . . a collection of early laws and resolves of Massachusetts. . . . Phila. Henkels. 1916. 44p. **6398**

Hilkey, Charles J. The unpublished sources for early American legal history. W. Va. law quar. XL. p224-9 (April 1934) (Relates to Massachusetts) **6398a**

Historical Records Survey. Massachusetts. Abstract and index of the records of the inferior court of pleas (Suffolk County Court), held in Boston, 1680-1698. Boston, Mass. 1940. 224p. mim. **6398b**

—— —— A description of the manuscript collections in the Massachusetts Diocesan Library. Boston. Feb. 1939. 81p. mim. **6398c**

—— —— Guide to depositories of manuscript collections in Massachusetts. Boston. May 1939. 160p. mim. **6398d**

—— —— Index to Proclamations of Massachusetts issued by governors and other authorities, 1620-1936. Boston, Mass. 1937. 2v. **6398e**

—— —— Inventory of the city and town archives of Massachusetts. Boston, Mass. 1939- . mim. No. 6. Franklin County: vol. 1. Ashfield. 1940. 108p., vol. 2. Bernardston. 1941. 93p.; vol. 3. Buckland. 1940. 78p.; No. 7. Hampden County: vol. 1. Agawam. 1941. 74p.; vol. 5. Chicopee. Oct. 1939. 296p.; No. 10. Middlesex County: vol. 5. Ayer. 1941. 148p. (mult.); vol. 29. Maynard. 1941. 146p. (mult.); No. 11. Norfolk County: vol. 1. Avon. May 1939. 83p., vol. 2. Bellingham. Aug. 1939. 76p., vol. 4.

Brookline. 1940. 348p., vol. 11. Holbrook. 1941. 179p. (mult.); No. 13. Suffolk County: vol. 1. Boston. Part 5. Feb. 1940. 349p., vol. 2. Athol. 1941. 231p. (mult.); No. 14. Worcester County: vol. 3. Auburn. Feb. 1940. 99p., vol. 4. Barre. 1940. 132p., vol. 5. Berlin. 1941. 108p., vol. 11. Clinton. 1941. 117p. (mult.) **6398f**

—— Inventory of the county archives of Massachusetts. Boston, Mass. 1937. mim. No. 5. Essex. Dec. 1937. 370p. **6398g**

Hitchings, A. Frank. Ship registers of the District of Salem and Beverley, 1789-1900. Essex Inst. hist. col. XXXIX. p185-208; XL. 49-72, 177-200, 217-40, 321-36; XLI. 141-64, 309-32, 357-80; XLII. 89-110. 1903-06 **6398h**

Homes, Henry Augustus. An account of the manuscripts of Gen. Dearborn, as Massachusetts commissioner in 1838 and 1839 for the sale of the Seneca Indian lands in the state of New York. Read before the Albany Institute October 12, 1880. Albany. Weed, Parsons. 1881. 11p. **6399**

Kellen, W. V. An index to the public statutes of the Commonwealth of Massachusetts and to the public acts of 1882 to 1887, both inclusive. Boston. Wright & Potter. 1888. 559p. **6400**

Massachusetts. Geodetic Survey. Publications available for distribution, Massachusetts Geodetic Survey, June, 1938. Boston. The Survey. 1938. 8p. **6400a**

Massachusetts. Laws, statutes, etc. The index to the general laws of the commonwealth of Massachusetts and . . .the constitution. Boston. 1923. 1108p. **6400b**

—— —— The index to the revised laws of the commonwealth of Massachusetts. Boston. 1902. 570p. **6400c**

Massachusetts. Record Commission. First—thirty-second report of the Commissioner of public records. . . 1888-1919. Boston. Wright & Potter Ptg. Co., state printers. 1889-1920. 32v. **6401**

—— —— Report on the custody and condition of the public records of parishes, towns and counties. Boston. 1889-1902. 14v. **6402**

Massachusetts. Secretary of the Commonwealth. Division of public records. Annual reports. Boston. 1921- **6403**

—— —— **Public documents division.** List of annual reports of state departments, boards and commissions. Boston. 1926. 4p. **6404**

Massachusetts. Supreme Judicial Court. Catalogue of records and files in the office of the clerk of the Supreme Judicial Court for the county of Suffolk. Boston. 1890. 169p. (Revised. 1896. Boston. 1897. p171-81) **6405**

Massachusetts Historical Society. [Memorandum on the printing of provincial and colonial laws in Massachusetts]. Massachusetts Hist. Soc. proc. 1835-55. II. p575-80 **6406**

Matthews, Albert. Notes on the Harvard College records 1636-1800. Reprinted from the Publications of The Colonial Soc. Massachusetts. vol. XIV. Cambridge, Mass. John Wilson and Son, Univ. Press. 1913. p312-18   **6407**

Matthews, Nathan. Early files of the county courts of Massachusetts. Mass. law quar. X. p46-52 (Feb. 1925) (Reprinted from the Mass. Hist. Soc. proc. Oct. 1923)   **6407a**

Middlesex County, Massachusetts. Index to the probate records, first series, 1648-1871. Cambridge, Mass. 1914. 552p. **6408**

Morison, Samuel Eliot. The custom-house records in Massachusetts, as a source of history. Mass. Hist. Soc. proc. LIV. p324-31. 1922   **6408a**

Noble, John. The records and files of the Superior Court of Judicature, and of the Supreme Judicial Court, their history and places of deposit. Col. Soc. Mass. pubs. V. p5-26. 1897-1898   **6408b**

Pierce, H. B. and others. Report to the legislature of Massachusetts upon the condition of the records, files, papers, and documents in the Secretary's department, January 1885. Boston. 1885. 42p.   **6409**

Salem and Boston custom house records of the pre-Revolutionary period. Essex Inst. hist. col. XXXIX. p159-67 (April 1903)   **6409a**

Savary, A. W. The pre-revolutionary Boston custom house records. New Eng. hist. geneal. reg. LXVII. p222 (April 1903)   **6409b**

Scott, Henry Edwards. The publication of vital records of Massachusetts towns. New Eng. hist. and geneal. reg. LXXIII. p52-62 (Jan. 1919)   **6409c**

Seybolt, Robert Francis. The town officials of colonial Boston, 1634-1775. Cambridge. Harvard Univ. Press. 1939. 416p. (Constitutes an index to the Boston records)   **6409d**

Stebbins, Howard L. Outline of Massachusetts statute law publications. Law Lib. jour. XX. p72-84 (Oct. 1927)   **6410**

Suffolk County, Massachusetts. Probate index, 1636-1893. Boston. 1895. 3v. **6411**

Survey of Federal Archives. Massachusetts. Alphabetical list of ship registers, District of Barnstable, Massachusetts, 1814-1913. Comp. from original documents stored in the New Bedford Custom House. Boston. 1938. 163p. mim.   **6411a**

—— —— Inventory of federal archives in the states. Boston, Mass. 1938- . mim. The Federal Courts. July 1938. 44p.; The Department of the Treasury. Parts I-III. Jan. 1939. 734p.; The Department of War. May 1939. 466p.; The Department of Justice. Sept. 1938. 26p.; The Department of the Navy. July 1938. 171p.; The Department of the Interior. July 1938. 14p.; The Department of Agriculture. July 1938. 115p.; The Department of Commerce. Aug. 1938. 83p.; The Department of Labor. June

1939. 84p.; The Farm Credit Administration. May 1939. 15p.; The Veterans' Administration. Dec. 1940. 46p.; The Emergency Relief Administration. April 1941. 141p.; Miscellaneous agencies. Aug. 1940. 128p.   **6411b**

—— —— Ship registers of Dighton-Fall River, Massachusetts, 1789-1938. Boston, Mass. 1939. 178p. mim.   **6411c**

—— —— Ship registers of New Bedford, Massachusetts. Boston, Mass. 1940- . mim.   **6411d**

—— —— Ship registers of the district of Plymouth, Massachusetts, 1789-1908. Boston, Mass. 1939- . Part I, 209p. mim.   **6411e**

Swan, Robert Thaxter. The Massachusetts Public Record Commission and its work. Am Hist. Asso. rep. 1901. p97-112   **6412**

Whitman, Benjamin. An index to the laws of Massachusetts: from the adoption of the Constitution to the year MDCCXCVI. Worcester. Libbie & Co. 1797. 152p.   **6412a**

Whitmore, William H. A bibliographical sketch of the laws of Massachusetts colony from 1630 to 1686 in which are included The Body of Liberties of 1641, and the Records of the Court of assistants, 1641-1644, arranged to accompany the reprints of the laws of 1660 and of 1672. Boston. Rockwell and Churchill. 1890. 150p.   **6413**

Williams, C. H. S. Index to Massachusetts decisions in the Massachusetts reports from 1860 to 1877 inclusive. [Relating to] the constitution, the general statutes and the acts and resolves of the general court since 1860. Boston. 1878. 138p.   **6414**

General

Beebe Town Library, Wakefield, Massachusetts. Histories of the commonwealth of Massachusetts, its counties, cities and towns, in the Lucius Beebe Memorial Library, Wakefield, Massachusetts. [Wakefield] 1930. [8p.]   **6415**

Board of Jamestown exposition managers for Massachusetts. 1607-1907; a descriptive catalogue of the Massachusetts exhibit of colonial books at the Jamestown ter-centennial exposition. Boston. Priv. printed. 1907. 78p.   **6416**

Boston. Public Library. Boston and the Bay Colony; a tercentenary exhibit of rare books, broadsides and manuscripts shown in the treasure room of the Boston Public Library during the summer of 1930. Boston. The Trustees. 1930. 31p. (Reprinted from the June 1930 issue of More books, the Bul. of the Boston Pub. Lib.)   **6417**

Boston. Public Library. The Pilgrims; a selected list of works in the public library of the city of Boston; a contribution to the Tercentenary celebration. Comp. by Mary Alice Tenney (Brief reading lists no. 15. June 1930) Boston. The Trustees. 1920. 43p. **6418**

—— —— Tercentenary celebration, 1630-1930. The Massachusetts Bay Colony and Boston; a selected list of works in the Public library of the city of Boston. (Brief reading lists no. 43. May 1930) Boston. The Trustees. 1930. 165p. **6419**

Cambridge. Public Library. List of books in the Cambridge Public Library relating to the Pilgrim fathers and the settlement of Plymouth, Mass., in 1620. Cambridge, Mass. Tribune Composition Co. 1920. 16p. **6420**

Colburn, Jeremiah. Bibliography of the local history of Massachusetts. Boston. W. P. Lunt. 1871. 119p. (Reprinted from the New England Hist. and Geneal. Soc. reg. XXI-XXV. Jan. 1867-April 1871) **6421**

Davis, Andrew McFarland. Historical work in Massachusetts. Cambridge. John Wilson. 1893. 57p. (Reprinted from The Publications of the Colonial Soc. Massachusetts. I. p21-71) **6422**

Dexter, Franklin B. Critical essay on the sources of information—The Pilgrim church and Plymouth colony. *In* Narrative and critical history of America. Ed. by Justin Winsor. Boston, N.Y. Houghton Mifflin. 1884. p283-94 **6423**

Flagg, Charles Allcott. A guide to Massachusetts local history; being a bibliographic index to the literature of the towns, cities, and counties of the state, including books, pamphlets, articles in periodicals and collected works, books in preparation, historical manuscripts, newspaper clippings, etc. Salem. Salem Press Co. 1907. 256p. **6424**

—— Some articles concerning Massachusetts in recent magazines. Mass. mag. II. p43-4, 99-100, 162-4, 228-9 (Jan.-Oct. 1909); III. p62-70, 117-20, 178-9, 257-9 (Jan.-Oct. 1910) **6424a**

Gee, Clarence Stafford. The Bradford manuscript. Church hist. VI. p136-44 (June 1937) (William Bradford's History of Plymouth Plantation) **6424b**

Jaques, Mrs. F. W. Bibliographical index to periodical literature bearing on Massachusetts services during the Civil war. *In* Higginson, Thomas Wentworth. Massachusetts in the army and navy during the war of 1861-65. Boston. Wright & Potter. 1895. II. p609-733 **6425**

Jones, Matt Bushnell. Thomas Maule, the Salem Quaker, and free speech in Massachusetts Bay, with bibliographical notes. Essex Inst. hist. col. LXXII. p1-42 (Jan. 1936) **6425a**

McCombs, Charles F. The Massachusetts Bay exhibition. N.Y. Pub. Lib. bul. XXXV. p465-71 (July 1931) **6426**

Massachusetts. Board of Jamestown exposition managers. The Massachusetts colonial loan exhibit at the Jamestown ter-centennial exposition, 1607-1907. Boston. Wright and Potter. 1907. 107p. **6427**

Massachusetts. State Library. Catalogue of the State Library of Massachusetts. Boston. Rand, Avery. 1880. 1048p. **6428**

Massachusetts archives. N.E. hist. geneal. reg. II. p105-7 (Jan. 1848) (Catalogue of volumes in the library of the State House, 1622-1787) **6428a**

Massachusetts Historical Society. Catalogue of the books, pamphlets, newspapers, maps, charts, manuscripts, &c. in the library of the Massachusetts Historical Society. Boston. John Eliot. 1811. 96p. **6429**

New York. Public Library. Massachusetts Bay; the founding and early years of the colony; a brief guide to an exhibition held at The New York Public Library. N.Y. 1931. 9p. **6430**

Pittsburgh. Carnegie Library. The Pilgrims; selected material for use in connection with the Pilgrim tercentenary celebration. [Pittsburgh] 1920. 13p. **6430a**

Providence, Rhode Island. Public Library. Reference lists no 45: William Bradford and the Plymouth colony. Providence Pub. Lib. bul. III. p103-5 (May 1897) **6431**

Sullivan Brothers & Libbie. Americana; catalogue of the valuable private library of J. G. Smith, esq. of Worcester, Mass., comprising a valuable collection of state and town histories, historical pamphlets, and tracts, mostly relating to Massachusetts. . . . Boston. W. F. Brown & Co. 1883. 94p. **6432**

Winsor, Justin. The earliest maps of Massachusetts bay and Boston harbor. *In* The memorial history of Boston. Boston. J.R. Osgood & Co. 1880. I. p37-67 **6432a**

Local

American Antiquarian Society. Index to obituary notices in the Boston transcript, 1875-1930. [Worcester, Mass. 1938?]-40. 5v. (This index also covers the Boston advertiser from 1875 to 1884) **6432b**

Bolton, Charles Knowles. Some works relating to Brookline, Massachusetts, from its settlement to the year 1900, with notes and corrections. Brookline. Riverdale Press. 1900. p91-179 (Reprinted from the Brookline Hist. Publication Soc. publications. nos. 19-20) **6433**

Boston. Index to city documents, from 1834 to 1897. Boston. 1897. 142p. **6433a**

Boston. Engineering Department. List of maps of Boston published between 1600 and 1903, copies of which are to be found in the possession of the city of Boston or other collectors of the same. Boston Municipal Ptg. Off. 1903. 248p. (Reprint of Appendix I, annual report of the city engineer, Feb. 1, 1903) **6433b**

Boston. Public Library. Bibliography of Boston. Boston Pub. Lib. bul. III. p42-7 (Feb. 1898) **6435**

—— —— The Harvard tercentenary; an exhibit of rare books, manuscripts, maps & engravings relating to the history of Harvard College, in the Treasure room of the Boston Public Library, August-October, 1936. Boston, Mass. 1936. 22p. **6435a**

—— —— A list of maps and views of Boston and Boston harbor, 1633-1899. Bost. Pub. Lib. bul. IV. p295-313 (Oct. 1899) **6435b**

—— —— Literature of the history of Boston during the Revolutionary period. Boston Pub. Lib. bul. II. p382-92 (July 1875) **6436**

Boston Authors Club. A bibliography of the Boston Authors Club. Plainfield, N.J. Recorder Press. 1904. 42p. **6436a**

Cambridge. Public Library. Selected list of books, pamphlets, etc., relating to Cambridge. Cambridge, Mass. Monk & Bordley. 1905. 31p. **6437**

Cutter, William R. Contributions to a bibliography of the local history of Woburn, Mass. n.p. n.p. [1890?] p179-219 **6438**

Ford, Worthington Chauncey. The Boston book market, 1679-1800. Boston. Club of Odd Volumes. 1917. 198p. **6439**

Foster, W. E. The founding of Boston; references accompanying the 250th anniversary, Sept. 17, 1880. Lib. jour. V. p288-90 (Sept./Oct. 1880) **6440**

Goddard, Delano A. The pulpit, press and literature of the Revolution. *In* The memorial history of Boston, including Suffolk County, Massachusetts, 1630-1880. Ed. by Justin Winsor. Boston. Ticknor. 1881. III. p119-48 **6441**

Goss, Elbridge Henry. Bibliography of Melrose. Melrose. L. F. Williams. 1889. (Reprinted from the Melrose jour. May 12; June 2, 16, 20; July 14; Aug. 4; Oct. 13, 20, 27; Nov. 10; Dec. 1, 9, 1888) **6442**

Gray, Francis C. Remarks on the early laws of Massachusetts. Mass. Hist. Soc. col. ser. 3. VIII. p191-215. 1843 **6442a**

Green, Samuel Abbott. Bibliography of Groton (1673-1888) maps, plans, etc. Groton hist. ser. II. no. VII. p173-226; II. no. XIV. p450-4. 1888, 89 **6443**

Griffin, A. P. C. Bibliography—A list of books, etc., relating to the history of the Old South Church, society, and meeting-house, arranged according to date of publication. *In* Hill, Hamilton Andrews. History of the Old South Church (Third church) Boston, 1669-1884. Boston, N.Y. Houghton Mifflin. 1890. II. p581-655 **6444**

Harvard Law School Association. Bibliography of the Harvard Law School. *In* The centennial history of the Harvard Law School, 1817-1917. Cambridge. Harvard Law School Asso. 1918. p344-64 **6445**

Harvard University Press. A list of books, &c about Harvard for sale at the prices affixed. Cambridge. Harvard Univ. Press. 1933. 14p. **6446**

Historical Records Survey. Massachusetts. Index to local news in the Hampshire Gazette, Northampton, Massachusetts, 1786-1937. Boston, Mass. 1939. 3v. **6446a**

Hunnewell, James F. Bibliography of Charlestown, Mass., and Bunker Hill. Boston. James R. Osgood. 1880. 100p. **6447**

—— A bibliography of Charlestown and Bunker Hill. *In* A century of town life; a history of Charlestown, Massachusetts, 1775-1887. Boston. Little, Brown. 1888. p261-300 **6448**

Littlefield, George Emery. Early Boston booksellers, 1642-1711. Boston. Club of Odd Volumes. 1900. 256p. **6448a**

Lowe, John Adams. Williamsiana; a bibliography of pamphlets & books relating to the history of Williams College, 1793-1911. Williamstown, Mass. Pub. by the Trustees. 1911. 37p. **6449**

[Mann, Moses W.] Medford on the map. Medford hist. reg. XXI. p32-7 (April 1918) (Maps) **6449a**

Massachusetts. Agricultural College. Bibliography of the college. Part I. The institution. (Semi-centennial publications no. 2) Amherst. The College. 1917. 69p. **6450**

Massachusetts Historical Society. Library. Bibliography of Cambridge, Mass. imprints. Planned **6450a**

Matthews, Albert. Bibliography of the Plymouth discourses (1769-1895). Colonial Soc. Massachusetts publications. XVII. p384-91 (Dec. 1914) **6451**

Nichols, Charles Lemuel. Bibliography of Worcester: a list of works, pamphlets, newspapers, and broadsides printed in the town of Worcester, Mass. from 1775 to 1848, with historical and explanatory notes. Worcester. Priv. printed. 1899. 216p. **6452**

Nourse, Henry S. Lancastriana: II. A bibliography compiled for the public library of Lancaster. Lancaster, Mass. W. J. Coulter. 1901. 46p. **6453**

Paine, Nathaniel. Bibliography of Worcester history. comp . . . for the account of the celebration of the two hundredth anniversary of the naming of Worcester, Mass. Worcester. Priv. printed. 1885. 18p. (Reprinted from Celebration of the two hundredth anniversary of the naming of Worcester, Oct. 14 and 15, 1884. p167-76) **6454**

Sargent, Lucius M. Notices of the histories of Boston by Sigma [pseud.] Boston. A. Williams. 1857. 7p. **6455**

Shurtleff, Nathaniel Bradstreet. A topographical and historical description of Boston. Boston. City Council. 1891. 720p. **6455a**

Walton, Clarence Eldon. An historical prospect of Harvard College, 1636-1936; Harvard University archives: tercentenary exhibition. Boston. Soc. for the Preservation of New Eng. Antiq. 1936. 48p. **6455b**

Winsor, Justin. Introduction [The sources of Boston's history]. *In* The memorial history of Boston. Boston. Osgood. 1880. I. p. xiii-xxiii   **6456**

Young, Malcolm Oakman. Amherstiana; a bibliography of Amherst College. Amherst. Amherst College. 1921. 40p. **6457**

Newspapers

Ayer, Mary Farwell. Check list of Boston newspapers, 1704-1780, with bibliographical notes by Albert Matthews. (Publications of the Colonial Soc. Massachusetts. IX. coll.) [Boston. The Soc.] 1907. 527p.   **6458**

Brigham, Clarence S. Massachusetts—Bibliography of American newspapers 1690-1820. Am. Antiq. Soc. proc. n.s. XXV. p396-501 (Oct. 1915)   **6459**

—— Massachusetts [Boston]—Bibliography of American newspapers, 1690-1820. Am. Antiq. Soc. proc. n.s. XXV. p193-293 (April 1915)   **6460**

Cummings, Charles A. The press and literature of the last hundred years. *In* The memorial history of Boston including Suffolk county, 1630-1880. Boston. Ticknor. 1881. III. p617-82   **6461**

Davis, Andrew McFarland. The Cambridge Press. Am. Antiq. Soc. proc. n.s. V. p295-301 (April 1888) (Also reprinted)   **6462**

Gilman, Alfred. The newspaper press of Lowell. Old Residents' Hist. Asso. contributions. II. p233-67. 1883   **6463**

Goddard, Delano A. The press and literature of the provincial period. *In* The memorial history of Boston including Suffolk county, Massachusetts 1630-1880. Boston. James R. Osgood. II. p387-436   **6464**

Green, Samuel Abbott. Bibliographical list of titles printed by Foster. *In* John Foster, the earliest American engraver and the first Boston printer. Pub. by the Massachusetts Hist. Soc. at the charge of the Waterston fund no. 2. Boston. 1909. p55-134   **6465**

Harris, Rendel and Jones, Stephen R. The Pilgrim press; a bibliographical and historical memorial of the books printed at Leyden by the Pilgrim fathers with a chapter on the location of the Pilgrim press by Dr. Plooÿ. Cambridge, England. W. Heffer & Sons, Ltd. 1922. 89p.   **6466**

Homer, Thomas Johnston. A guide to serial publications founded prior to 1918 and now or recently current in Boston, Cambridge and vicinity. Boston. Trustees of the Pub. Lib. 1922-32. 5pts.   **6467**

Littlefield, George Emery. The early Massachusetts press, 1638-1711. Boston. Club of Odd Volumes. 1907. 2v.   **6468**

Mangan, John J. The newspapers of Lynn. Lynn Hist. Soc. reg. XIII. p131-68. 1909   **6469**

Massachusetts. State Library. Newspapers in the State Library of Massachusetts, 1911. *In* Second annual report of the . . . State Library for . . . 1911. Boston. Wright & Potter, state printers. 1912. p25-8   **6470**

Moore, George Henry. The first folio of the Cambridge Press, memoranda concerning the Massachusetts laws of 1648. N.Y. Printed for the author. 1889. 16p.   **6471**

Paradise, Scott H. A history of printing in Andover, Massachusetts, 1798-1931. [Andover] Andover Press. 1931. 37p. **6472**

Roden, Robert F. The Cambridge Press, 1638-1692; a history of the first printing press established in English America, together with a bibliographical list of the issues of the press. N.Y. Dodd, Mead. 1905. 193p.   **6473**

Starbuck, Alexander. Nantucket's newspapers. Nantucket Hist. Asso. proc. VIII. p11-20 (July 15, 1902)   **6474**

Streeter, Gilbert L. Account of the newspapers and other periodicals, published in Salem, from 1768 to 1856. Essex Inst. proc. I. p157-87. 1856   **6475**

Tapley, Harriet Silvester. Salem imprints, 1768-1825; a history of the first fifty years of printing in Salem, Massachusetts, with some account of the bookshops, booksellers, bookbinders and the private libraries. Salem. Essex Inst. 1927. 512p.   **6476**

Weeks, Lyman H. and Bacon, Edwin M. Massachusetts periodicals. *In* An historical digest of the provincial press. Massachusetts, series I. Boston. Soc. for Americans, Inc. 1911. p4-10   **6477**

Miscellaneous

Colonial Society of Massachusetts. Index to (The publications) volumes I-XXV, 1892-1924. Boston. Pub. by the Soc. 1932. 293p.   **6479**

Danvers Historical Society. Historical collections; index to volumes VI-XX. Under direction of the committee on publications. (Hist. coll. of the Danvers Hist. Soc. XXI) Danvers, Mass. The Soc. 1933. 135p.   **6480**

—— Index to the historical collections of the Danvers Historical Society, volumes I-V. Danvers, Mass. The Soc. 1919. 68p.   **6480a**

—— Subject index to the Historical collections of the Danvers Historical Society, vols. I-XX, inclusive. [Danvers Hist. Soc. col. XXIII] Danvers, Mass. 1935. p105-12   **6481**

Essex Institute. The Essex Institute historical collections. Subject index to volumes I-LXVII, 1859-1931. Ed. by Harriet Silvester Tapley. Salem, Mass. Printed for the Essex Inst. 1932. 153p.   **6482**

Flagg, Charles Alcott. Massachusetts in literature. Mass. mag. IV. p49-57, 99-103, 174-8, 213-15 (Jan.-Oct. 1911) **6482a**

Ford, Worthington Chauncey. Broadsides, ballads, &c printed in Massachusetts, 1639-1800. Massachusetts Hist. Soc. colls. LXXV. 1922. 483p. **6483**

Gettemy, Charles F. Publications of the Massachusetts Bureau of Statistics, 1869-1915. *In* The Massachusetts Bureau of Statistics, 1869-1915; a sketch of its history, organization and functions. Boston. Wright & Potter. 1915. p45-59 **6484**

Green, Samuel A. Bibliography of the Massachusetts Historical Society. Boston. John Wilson and Son. 1871. 10p. (Reprinted from the Proc. of the Massachusetts Hist. Soc. 1871) **6485**

—— Centennial bibliography of the historical society. Massachusetts Hist. Soc. proc. second ser. VI. p203-49, 343-9. 1890-91. (Also printed separately, Cambridge, 1891. p3-56) **6486**

Historical Records Survey. Massachusetts. American portraits, 1620-1825, found in Massachusetts. . . . Boston. 1939. 2v. **6486a**

Lane, William Coolidge. Early Harvard broadsides. Am. Antiq. Soc. proc. n.s. XXIX. p264-304 (Oct. 1914) **6487**

Massachusetts. State board of agriculture. Agriculture of Massachusetts; synoptical and analytical index, 1837-1892. Prepared and arranged by Frederick H. Fowler. Boston. Wright & Potter. 1893. 301p. **6488**

—— —— General index of the twenty-five annual reports of the Secretary of the Massachusetts State Board of Agriculture, 1853-1877 (Twenty-fifth annual report of the Secretary of the Massachusetts State Board of Agriculture for 1877). Boston. Rand, Avery. 1878. xcv p. **6489**

—— —— Library. Classification and catalogue of the library of the Massachusetts State Board of Agriculture. Prepared and arranged by Frederick H. Fowler. . . . Boston. Wright & Potter. 1899. 125p. **6490**

Massachusetts. State Planning Board. Index of studies and statistical compilations relating to economic conditions in Massachusetts. Boston. n.d. 47p. mim. **6490a**

Massachusetts Historical Society. Handbook of the publications and photostats, 1792-1933. Collections: 77 volumes, proceedings: 64 volumes, special publications. Boston. 1934. 144p. **6491**

—— Index to the Collections of the Massachusetts Historical Society. (In every tenth volume) **6492**

—— Index to the first twenty volumes of the proceedings of the Massachusetts Historical Society, 1791-1883. Boston. Pub. by the Soc. 1887. 521p. **6493**

—— Index to the second series of the Proceedings of the Massachusetts Historical Society, 1884-1907. Boston. Pub. by the Soc. 1909. 490p. **6494**

Massachusetts Housing Association. Bibliography on Massachusetts Housing conditions, April 1931, second run, June 1931. Comp. by Doris E. Skedd. [Boston. Massachusetts Housing Asso. 1931] 17p. autog. from typ. copy **6495**

Moore, George H. Bibliographical notes on witchcraft in Massachusetts. Worcester. Am. Antiq. Soc. 1888. 31p. (Reprinted from the Proc. of the Am. Antiq. Soc. n.s. V. p245-73. April 1888) **6496**

Nichols, Charles L. Notes on the almanacs of Massachusetts. Am. Antiq. Soc. proc. n.s. XXII. p15-134 (April 1912) (Reprinted Worcester. 1912. 122p.) **6497**

Page, Alfred Baylies. John Tulley's almanacks, 1687-1702. [Boston. 1910] p207-23 (Separate from Trans. of the Colonial Soc. Massachusetts. Dec. 1910) **6498**

Stickney, Matthew A. Almanacs and their authors. Essex Inst. hist. colls. VIII-XIV (March 1866-Oct. 1877) **6499**

Swift, Lindsay. The Massachusetts election sermons; an essay in descriptive bibliography. Cambridge, Mass. J. Wilson and Son. 1897. 68p. (Reprinted from the Colonial Soc. of Massachusetts publications. I. p388-451) **6500**

Tuttle, Julius Herbert. List of historical societies in Massachusetts. Old-time New Eng. XII. p19-23 (July 1921) **6500a**

MICHIGAN

Applegate, Thomas S. A history of the press of Michigan. Prepared for the Centennial, by order of Gov. John J. Bagley. Adrian. Times Steam Presses. 1876. 64p. **6501**

Bayley, William Shirley. Geological explorations and literature. *In* The Marquette and iron-bearing district of Michigan. (U.S. Geol. Survey monograph. XXVIII) Wash. Govt. Ptg. Off. 1897. p5-148 **6502**

Brower, Leone I. Bibliography of fiction with Michigan setting. Minneapolis. Minnesota Hist. Soc. To be published **6502a**

Burton, Clarence M. The Burton historical collection of the public library, Detroit. Bibliog. Soc. Am. pap. XVI. pt. 1. p10-16. 1922 **6502b**

Conger, John L. Report on the public archives of Michigan. Am. Hist. Asso. rep. 1905. I. p369-76 **6503**

Detroit. Public Library. Father Gabriel Richard [Issues from his press]. Detroit Pub. Lib. Burton hist. colls. leaflet. I. p81-4 (March 1923) **6504**

—— —— Michigan biography. Indexed on cards **6504a**

Doelle, J. A. Historical materials owned by the Keweenaw Historical Society, Houghton, Michigan; bibliography. Michigan hist. mag. I. p129-55 (July 1917) **6505**

Dority, Ione E. Municipal reporting in Michigan since 1930. *In* American Library Association. Committee on public documents. Public documents 1937. Chicago. Am. Lib. Asso. 1937. p146-67   **6505a**

Farmer, Silas. The history of Detroit and Michigan. Detroit. 1884 (Maps, p32-6, 697-9)   **6505b**

Foster, Bernice M. Michigan novelists. Ann Arbor. George Wahr. 1928. 30p. **6506**

Fuller, George N. Historical work in Michigan. Mich. hist. mag. VII. p232-47 (July 1923)   **6506a**

Goodrich, Mrs. Marge Knevels. A bibliography of Michigan authors. Richmond. Richmond Press, Inc. 1928. 222p.   **6507**

Graphic Arts Association of Grand Rapids. One hundred years of printing in Grand Rapids, written and published in connection with the centennial celebration and exhibition conducted by the Graphic Arts Association of Grand Rapids, Michigan, at the Civic Auditorium, April 14-17, 1937. Grand Rapids. 1937. 52p.   **6507a**

Historical Records Survey. Michigan. Calendar of the Baptist collection of Kalamazoo college, Kalamazoo, Michigan. Detroit, Mich. Dec. 1940. 194p. mim. **6507b**

—— —— Guide to manuscript depositories in the United States: Michigan. Detroit, Mich. May 1940. 75p. mim. **6507c**

—— —— Guide to public vital statistics records in Michigan: Birth records. Detroit, Mich. 1941. 166p. mim. **6507d**

—— —— Inventory of the church and synagogue archives of Michigan. Detroit, Mich. 1940- . mim. Dearborn churches. July 1940. 54p.; Jewish bodies. March 1940. 65p.; Protestant Episcopal bodies, Diocese of Michigan. March 1940. 126p.; Protestant Episcopal bodies, Diocese of Western Michigan. June 1940. 46p.; Protestant Episcopal Churches: Diocese of Northern Michigan. Dec. 1940. 41p.; African Methodist Episcopal Church: Michigan Conference. Sept. 1940. 24p.; Presbyterian Church in U.S.A.: Presbytery of Detroit. Aug. 1940. 64p.; Evangelical Church, Michigan Conference. March 1941. 58p.; Evangelical and Reformed Church. April 1941. 45p.; Roman Catholic Church: Archdiocese of Detroit. July 1941. 186p.; Church of God, Michigan Assemblies. May 1941. 62p.   **6507e**

—— —— Inventory of the county archives of Michigan. Detroit, Mich. 1937- . mim.; No. 2. Alger. March 1941. 271p.; No. 4. Alpena. May 1938. 72p.; No. 7. Baraga. Nov. 1937. 46p.; No. 9. Bay. Nov. 1940. 339p.; No. 13. Calhoun. May 1941. 327p.; No. 16. Cheboygan. Dec. 1938. 115p.; No. 25. Genesee. March 1940. 224p.; No. 35. Iosco. May 1938. 81p.; No. 36. Iron. June 1938. 84p.; No. 38. Jackson. June 1941. 360p.; No. 52. Marquette. May 1940. 297p.   **6507f**

—— —— Inventory of the town and municipal archives of Michigan. Detroit,

Mich. 1940- . mim. City of Detroit: No. 10. City Treasurer. Dec. 1940. 72p.; No. 31. Arts Commission. March 1941. 38p.; No. 32. Department of Recreation. Dec. 1940. 49p.; No. 82. Wayne County: City of Hamtramck, Office of Engineer. May 1940. 36p (prelim. inv.)   **6507g**

—— —— Vital statistics holdings by government agencies in Michigan. Detroit, Mich. 1941. 166p. mim.   **6507h**

Holmes, J. C. Some notes respecting the pioneer newspapers of Michigan. Michigan Pioneer and Hist. Soc. colls. I. p385-95. 1877   **6508**

Index to newspapers on file in Michigan. Mich. Lib. bul. XVIII (Feb. 1927) **6508a**

Irving, Roland Douglas and Van Hise, Charles Richard. Geological explorations and literature. *In* The Penokee iron-bearing series of Michigan and Wisconsin. (U.S. Geol. Survey monograph no. 19) Wash. Govt. Ptg. Off. 1892. p5-102   **6509**

Jenks, William I. The "Hutchins" map of Michigan. Mich. hist. mag. X. p358-73 (July 1926)   **6509a**

—— The Michael Shoemaker collection of maps. Mich. hist. col. XXXIX. p297-300. 1915   **6509b**

—— Michigan copyrights. Mich. hist. mag. XI. p110-43, 271-87, 445-58, 630-52 (Jan.-Oct. 1927); XII. p108-24, 584-9, 740-3 (Jan., July-Oct. 1928); XIII. p121-6, 555-9 (Jan., July 1929); XIV. p150-5, 311-13 (Jan.-Apr. 1930)   **6509c**

—— Some early maps of Michigan. Mich. Hist. Soc. col. XXXVIII. p627-37. 1912   **6509d**

Karpinski, Louis Charles. Bibliography of the printed maps of Michigan, 1804-1880, with a series of over one hundred reproductions of maps constituting an historical atlas of the Great Lakes and Michigan. Lansing, Mich. Michigan Hist. Comm. 1931. 539p.   **6509e**

Kolehmainen, John I. Finnish newspapers and periodicals in Michigan. XXIV. p119-28 (Winter 1940)   **6509f**

Legler, Henry E. King Strang's press; a bibliographical narrative. Literary collector. VIII. p33-40 (June 1904)   **6510**

Loomis, Frances. Card index of biographical sketches in Michigan histories and biographies. Detroit. Detroit Public Library. In progress   **6510a**

McMurtrie, Douglas C. Early printing in Michigan, with a bibliography of the issues of the Michigan press, 1796-1850. Chicago. John Calhoun Club. 1931. 351p.   **6511**

—— Pioneer printing in Michigan. Springfield, Ill. 1933. 4p. (Reprinted from the National printer journalist. Oct. 1932)   **6512**

Marquette County Historical Society, Marquette. Catalog [of the library]. Ishpeming. 1928. 45p.   **6513**

Michigan. Geological and Biological Survey. Catalog and table of contents of the publications of the Michigan Geological and Biological Survey with a list of publications of the United States Geological Survey relating to Michigan, 1838-1920. R. A. Smith, state geologist. [Lansing. 1921] 35p.   **6514**

Michigan. Historical Commission. Michigan bibliography; a partial catalogue of books, maps, manuscripts and miscellaneous materials relating to the resources, development and history of Michigan from earliest times to July 1, 1917, together with citation of libraries in which the materials may be consulted, and a complete analytic index by author and subject. Comp. by Floyd Benjamin Streeter. Lansing. Michigan Hist. Comn. 1921. 2v. (A supplement to this bibliography is being prepared)   **6515**

—— —— The Michigan Historical Commission; its inception, organization, administration, and aims. Prepared by George N. Fuller (Bul. no. 1) Lansing, Mich. 1913. 41p.   **6516**

—— —— Report on the archives in the Department of state, State capitol, Lansing. Michigan hist. mag. II. p437-54 (July 1918)   **6517**

—— —— Report on the archives in the Executive department, State capitol, Lansing. Michigan hist. mag. II. p238-56 (April 1918)   **6518**

Michigan. Laws, Statutes, etc. Index to the statutes. *In* Howell's annotated statutes of the state of Michigan. . . . Comp. by Colin P. Campbell. Chicago. Callaghan. 1914. VI. p6097-755   **6518a**

Michigan. Secretary of State. List of publications [newspapers] in Michigan. *In* Michigan official directory and legislative manual, 1935/36. Lansing. Pub. by the State of Michigan. [1935] p173-84   **6519**

Michigan. State Board of Agriculture. General index of Michigan agricultural reports, including the Transactions of the State Agricultural Society, 1849 to 1859 and the annual reports of the State Board of Agriculture, 1862-1888. Lansing, Mich. 1889. 370p.   **6520**

Michigan. State Library. Documents received from the State of Michigan for distribution and exchange, 1904-16. *In* Report of the State Librarian for year June 30, 1902 to July 1, 1904. June 30, 1914 to July 1, 1916   **6520a**

—— —— List of publications of the territory and state of Michigan, 1806-1891. (Michigan State Lib. Biennial rep. 1890-92) Lansing. Robert Smith & Co. 1892. p65-71   **6521**

Michigan. University. William L. Clements Library. Michigan through three centuries; a guide to an exhibition of books, maps, and manuscripts in the William L. Clements Library. (Bul. no. XXVII) Ann Arbor. Univ. of Michigan. 1937. 20p.   **6521a**

Michigan news index; a master-key to the state news, 1-2, Jan. 1925-Dec. 1926. Adrian. Adrian daily telegram. 1925-26   **6522**

Michigan Pioneer and Historical Society. Index to the reports and collections of the Michigan Pioneer and Historical Society, vols. I-XV, 1874-1890. Lansing. Smith. 1904. 612p.

Same. Vols. 16-30, 1890-1906. Lansing. Wynkoop, Hallenbeck Crawford Co., state printers. 1907. 554p.   **6523**

—— List of subjects and authors, Michigan historical collections, volumes 1 to 39. Michigan Pioneer and Hist. Soc. colls. XXXIX. p459-582. 1915   **6524**

Pearson, Alice L. The Upper Peninsula in fictional literature. Mich. hist. mag. XXIV. p329-38 (Spring 1940)   **6524a**

Person, Harlow Stafford. Report on the public archives of Michigan. Am. Hist. Asso. rep. 1900. p60-3   **6525**

Shaw, Wilfred Bryon. A bibliography of the University of Michigan. (Univ. of Michigan Official pub. XXXVII. no. 49) Ann Arbor [1936] 11p.   **6525a**

Smith, Harlan Ingersoll. Memoranda towards a bibliography of the archaeology of Michigan. *In* Michigan Geological Survey. Pub. 10, biological ser. 3. Lansing. Wynkoop Hallenbeck Crawford. 1912. p167-80   **6525b**

Streeter, Floyd Benjamin. The Burton historical collection. Am. collector. I. p123-34 (Jan. 1926)   **6525c**

Survey of Federal Archives. Michigan. Inventory of federal archives in the states. Lansing and Detroit, Mich. 1938- . mim. The Federal Courts. June 1938. 51p.; The Department of the Treasury. July 1939. 298p.; The Department of War. Parts I-II. Dec. 1939. 286p.; The Department of Justice. June 1938. 41p.; The Department of the Navy. Dec. 1939. 34p.; The Department of Agriculture. Dec. 1939. 205p.; The Department of Commerce. Dec. 1939. 87p.; The Department of Labor. Dec. 1939. 100p.; The Farm Credit Administration. June 1940. 38p.; The Veterans' Administration. Aug. 1940. 50p.   **6525d**

U.S. Library of Congress. Division of bibliography. List of Michigan authors and their works. March 4, 1915. 11p. typ.   **6526**

—— —— —— List of references on Michigan regiments in the War of the rebellion. 1908. 5p. typ.   **6527**

—— —— —— List of references on the Sault Ste. Marie canal. Jan. 27, 1919. 6p. typ.   **6528**

MINNESOTA

Ackermann, Gertrude W. Home missionary records. Minn. hist. XVI. p313-18 (Sept. 1935) (Archives of the American Home Missionary Society)   **6528a**

Blegen, Theodore Christian. The Minnesota Historical Society in 1937. Minn. hist. XIX. p43-62 (March 1938) **6528b**

—— The Minnesota Historical Society in 1936. Minn. hist. XVIII. p42-60 (March 1937) **6528c**

—— Recent progress of the Minnesota Historical Society. Minn. hist. XV. p56-68 (March 1934) **6528d**

—— Some sources for St. Croix Valley history. Minn. hist. XVII. p385-95 (Dec. 1936) **6528e**

Blegen, Theodore Christian and Beeson, Lewis. Minnesota, its history and its people; a study outline with topics and references. Minneapolis. Univ. of Minnesota Press. 1937. 237p. **6529**

Brown, Genevieve R. and Richards, Carmen. Bibliography of Minnesota authors. 4337 Wooddale Ave. Minneapolis, Minn. In progress **6529a**

Buck, Solon J. The Minnesota Historical Society in 1930. Minnesota hist. XII. p21-33 (March 1931) **6530**

Gates, Charles M. Some sources for northwest history; account books. Minn. hist. XVI. p70-5 (March 1935) **6530a**

—— Some sources for northwest history; probate records. Minn. hist. XVII. p189-93 (June 1936) **6530b**

Gregory, Winifred. Bibliography of Minnesota mining and geology. (Minnesota School of Mines. Experiment station. Bul. 4) Minneapolis. Univ. of Minnesota. 1915. 157p. (Supplement. Minnesota School of Mines. Experiment station. Bul. 8. 1920. 43p.) **6531**

Historical Records Survey. Minnesota. Check list of Minnesota imprints, 1849-1865. (American imprints inventory no. 2) St. Paul, Minn. May 1938. 110p. mim. **6531a**

—— —— Guide to depositories of manuscript collections in the United States: Minnesota. St. Paul. 1941. 84p. mim. **6531b**

—— —— Guide to public vital statistics records in Minnesota. St. Paul, Minn. July 1941. 142p. mim. **6531c**

—— —— Inventory of the county archives of Minnesota. St. Paul, Minn. 1937- . mim. No. 5. Benton. March 1940. 293p.; No. 7. Blue Earth. Aug. 1937. 76p.; No. 11. Cass. Feb. 1941. 152p.; No. 12. Chippewa. Sept. 1940. 177p.; No. 19. Dakota. May 1940. 158p.; No. 21. Douglas. March 1941. 142p.; No. 22. Faribault. Oct. 1938. 256p.; No. 24. Freeborn. Aug. 1937. 91p.; No. 25. Goodhue. Aug. 1941. 198p.; No. 26. Grant. Nov. 1939. 301p.; No. 29. Hubbard. April 1941. 157p.; No. 32. Jackson. April 1940. 329p.; No. 33. Kanabec. May 1941. 630p.; No. 41. Lincoln. June 1941. 119p.; No. 45. Marshall. Dec. 1939. 308p.; No. 46. Martin. Oct. 1939. 291p.; No. 47. Meeker. Nov. 1940. 119p.; No. 49. Morrison. April 1940. 323p.; No. 52. Nicollet. May 1938. 195p.; No. 53. Nobles. Dec. 1939. 273p.; No. 55. Olmsted. April 1939. 292p.; No. 56. Otter Tail. Nov. 1940. 184p.; No. 59. Pipestone. Aug. 1939. 279p.; No. 65. Renville. Dec. 1940. 132p.; No. 66. Rice. Sept. 1940. 128p.; No. 67. Rock. July 1940. 120p.; No. 70. Scott. Jan. 1939. 307p.; No. 71. Sherburne. Sept. 1940. 172p.; No. 73. Stearns. May 1940. 171p.; No. 78. Traverse. Oct. 1938. 235p.; No. 79. Wabasha. April 1939. 326p.; No. 82. Washington. Oct. 1938. 284p.; No. 86. Wright. Sept. 1940. 118p. **6531d**

Historical Society has many business records. Minn. hist. news. Oct. 1940. no. 226 **6531e**

Holbrook, Franklin F. The Neill papers in the manuscript collection of the Minnesota Historical Society. Minn. Hist. bul. I. p369-77 (Aug. 1916) (Papers of E. D. Neill relating to the history of Minnesota) **6531f**

—— War history work in Minnesota. Minnesota hist. bul. III. p126-36 (Aug. 1919) **6532**

Jerabek, Esther. Almanacs as historical sources. Minn. hist. XV. p444-9 (Dec. 1934) **6532a**

Johnston, Daniel S. B. Minnesota journalism in the territorial period, 1849-1854. Minnesota Hist. Soc. colls. X. pt. 1. p247-351. 1900-04 **6533**

—— Minnesota journalism from 1858 to 1865. Minnesota Hist. Soc. colls. XII. p183-262. 1905-08 **6534**

Kellar, Herbert A. The Minnesota state archives, their character, condition and historical value. Minnesota hist. I. p37-53 (May 1915) **6535**

—— A preliminary survey of the more important archives of the territory and state of Minnesota. Am. Hist. Asso. rep. 1914. I. p385-476 **6535a**

Kiekenapp, Marian R. Conservation in Minnesota. (Univ. of Minnesota bibliog. projects no. 3) [Minneapolis] 1936. 18p. reprod. typ. **6535b**

Larsen, Arthur J. The Minnesota Historical Society in 1939. Minn. hist. XXI. p33-46 (March 1940) **6535c**

Loehr, Rodney C. Business history material in the Minnesota Historical Society. Bus. Hist. Soc. bul. XIV. p21-8 (April 1940) **6535d**

—— Some sources for Northwest history; Minnesota farmers' diaries. Minn. hist. XVIII. p284-97 (Sept. 1937) **6535e**

McMurtrie, Douglas C. Pioneer printing in Minnesota. Springfield, Ill. 1932. 4p. (Reprinted from National printer journalist for Feb. 1932) **6536**

Martin, Mamie Ruth. Check list of Minnesota imprints, 1849-1865. (American imprints inventory, no. 2) Chicago. Historical Records Survey. 1938. 219p. mim. **6536a**

Minnesota. Department of Education. Library division. Minnesota authors. [St. Paul, Minn. 1934] 10p. mim. **6537**

Minnesota. **Laws, statutes.** An analytical index to the general and special laws of the territory and state, from 1849 to 1875 By John C. Shaw and J. B. West. St. Paul. 1876. 121,63p.   **6538**

Minnesota. **Public Library Commission.** Minnesota state publications. Minnesota Pub. Lib. Comn. lib. notes and news. IV. p61-4 (Dec. 1913)   **6539**

—— —— Minnesota writers. Minnesota Pub. Lib. Comn. lib. notes and news. II. p114-17 (May 1908)   **6540**

Minnesota. **Resources Commission.** Bibliography of research publications available at the Minnesota Resources Commission. St. Paul, Minn. 1939. 22p. photop.   **6540a**

Minnesota. **Secretary of State.** List of Minnesota newspapers and their publishers arranged by counties, published by Mike Holm, corrected to January 1, 1927. 15p.   **6541**

—— —— Minnesota newspapers by counties. *In* The legislative manual of the state of Minnesota, 1931. [Minneapolis. 1930] p413-27   **6542**

Minnesota. **State Planning Board.** List of maps and charts. [St. Paul. 1937] 52p. mim.   **6542a**

Minnesota. **University. Division of library instruction.** Mesabi iron range Lake Superior region, Minn. Comp. by Margaret Briggs. (Bibliog. project no. 4) Minneapolis. 1937. 37p. mim.   **6542b**

Minnesota. **War Records Commission.** Third biennial report, including a descriptive catalog of the manuscript material comprising nearly a million and a half items assembled by the Commission [relating to State's participation in the Spanish-American and World wars] St. Paul. 1925. 31p.   **6543**

Minnesota Historical Society. Bibliography of Minnesota newspapers. MS. **6544**

—— A bibliography of Minnesota territorial documents. Comp. by Esther Jerabek. (Publications of the Minnesota Hist. Soc. Special bul. III) St. Paul. Minn. Hist. Soc. 1936. 157p.   **6545**

—— Catalogue of the library of the Minnesota Historical Society. St. Paul. The Pioneer Press. 1888. 2v.   **6546**

—— Check list of Minnesota public documents issued from July 1, 1923- . (Publications of the Minnesota Hist. Soc.) St. Paul. Minnesota Hist. Soc. 1923-   **6547**

—— History and index of Minnesota newspapers, 1849-1934. St. Paul, Minn. ERA project   **6547a**

Minnesota weather records among the first. Minn. hist. news. no. 226 (Oct. 1940)   **6547b**

Niemi, Signa. Mesabi iron range of Minnesota; a bibliography. Madison. Univ. of Wisconsin Lib. School. 1920. 18p. **6548**

Nute, Grace Lee. Some sources for northwest history: Minnesota county archives. Minn. hist. XV. p194-9 (June 1934) **6548a**

St. Paul. Public Library. Material descriptive of Minnesota. Minnesota Pub. Lib. Comn. lib. notes and news. IV. p169-72 (March 1915)   **6549**

Schmid, Calvin Fisher and others. Guide to studies of social conditions in the twin cities; an annotated bibliography. Published as a report on Minnesota Works Progress Administration, research project 5209, sponsored by the University of Minnesota. Minneapolis. Bureau of Social Research, Minneapolis Council of Social Agencies. 1938. 474p. **6549a**

Survey of Federal Archives. Minnesota. Inventory of federal archives in the states. St. Paul, Minn. 1938- . mim. The Federal Courts. June 1939. 55p.; The Department of the Treasury. Dec. 1938. 173p.; The Department of War. March 1940. 133p.; The Department of Justice. May 1939. 32p.; The Department of the Navy. Dec. 1938. 21p.; The Department of Agriculture. Parts I-II. Sept. 1938. 366p.; The Department of Commerce. May 1939. 24p.; The Department of Labor. Aug. 1940. 101p.; The Veterans' Administration. May 1940. 55p.; The Farm Credit Administration. April 1939. 67p.; Miscellaneous agencies. Jan. 1941. 221p.   **6549b**

Virtue, Ethel B. The Pond papers. Minn. hist. bul. III. p82-6 (May 1919) (Papers of Samuel W. and Gideon H. Pond (1833-1850) missionaries to the Sioux in Minnesota)   **6549c**

Wadsworth, M. E. List of papers and works on Lake Superior. Bul. of the Museum of Comparative Zoology at Harvard College in Cambridge. VII. p133-57 (July 1880)   **6550**

Williams, John Fletcher. Bibliography of Minnesota from the Minnesota Historical Society collections, III, part 1. St. Paul. Press Ptg. Co. 1870. 65p.   **6551**

—— History of the newspaper press of St. Paul, Minnesota. St. Paul. n.p. 1871. 13p.   **6552**

Winchell, Newton Horace. Historical sketch and list of publications relating to the geology and natural history of Minnesota. (The Geol. and Natural Hist. Survey of Minnesota. The first annual rep. for the year 1872) Minneapolis. Johnson, Smith & Harrison. 1884. p22-37   **6553**

Winchell, Newton Horace and Winchell, H. V. Bibliography of the origin of iron ores. *In* The iron ores of Minnesota. (Minnesota Geol. and Natural Hist. Survey. Bul. no. 6) Minneapolis. 1891. p258-334   **6554**

MISSISSIPPI

Brigham, Clarence S. Mississippi—Bibliography of American newspapers, 1690-1820. Am. Antiq. Soc. proc. n.s. XXVI. p83-92 (April 1916)   **6555**

Cole, Theodore L. Statute laws of Mississippi. St. Louis. F. H. Thomas Law Book Co. 1892. 4p. **6556**

—— Statute laws of Mississippi. Mississippi. Secretary of State. Biennial rep. 1896-97) Jackson. Clarion-Ledger print. 1897. p107-9 **6557**

Development of historical work in Mississippi. Southern Hist. Asso. pub. VI. p335-40 (July 1902) **6557a**

Hamilton, William B., Jr. The sources of history of the Mississippi Territory. Jour. Miss. hist. I. p29-36 (Jan. 1939) **6557b**

Heartman, Charles F. Mississippi copyright entries, 1850-1870. Jour. Miss. hist. II. p. 79-87 (April 1940) **6557c**

Historical Records Survey. Mississippi. Inventory of the church archives of Mississippi. Jackson, Miss. 1940- . mim. Jewish congregations and organizations. Nov. 1940. 41p.; Protestant Episcopal Church, Diocese of Mississippi. June 1940. 146p. **6557d**

—— —— Inventory of the county archives of Mississippi. Jackson, Miss. 1937- . mim. No. 3. Amite. Sept. 1937. 85p.; No. 18. Forrest. June 1938. 140p.; No. 22. Grenada. April 1940. 172p.; No. 27. Humphreys. Aug. 1941. 179p.; No. 37. Lamar. July 1939. 329p.; No. 55. Pearl River. Feb. 1938. 127p. **6557e**

Humphreys, Rena and Owen, Mamie. Index of Mississippi session acts, 1817-1865. Jackson, Miss. Tucker Ptg. House. c. 1937. 345p. **6557f**

McCain, William D. Mississippiana for public, high school, and junior college libraries. Jackson, Miss. Hederman Bros. 1941. 25p. **6557g**

McMurtrie, Douglas C. Preliminary check list of Mississippi imprints, 1798-1810. Printed as manuscript subject to revision. Chicago. 1934. p7-53 **6558**

—— A short-title list of books, pamphlets and broadsides printed in Mississippi 1811 to 1830. Chicago. 1936. 47p. printed & mim. as MS. **6559**

Mississippi. Department of Archives and History. A checklist of Mississippi government publications. Comp. by William D. McCain. Jackson, Miss. In progress **6559a**

—— —— A checklist of Mississippi newspapers in the Mississippi Department of Archives and History. Comp. by William D. McCain. Jackson, Miss. In progress **6559b**

—— —— A guide to the manuscript collections of the Mississippi Department of Archives and History. Comp. by William D. McCain. In progress **6559c**

—— A library of Mississippi history; publications of the Mississippi Dept. of Archives and History and publications of the Mississippi Historical Society. Jackson, Miss. 1926. 19p. **6560**

—— —— [Lists of documents in England, France, and Spain, 1540-1798, of value for Mississippi history]. *In* Fifth annual report of the Director of the Mississippi Department of Archives and History. Rowland Dunbar. Nashville. Brandon Ptg. Co. 1907. p32-177 **6561**

—— —— Mississippi Supreme Court reports and digests—Statute laws of Mississippi. *In* The Official and statistical register of the state of Mississippi, 1908. By Dunbar Rowland. Nashville. Brandon Ptg. Co. 1908. p268-74 **6562**

—— —— Newspaper files. (Sixth annual report of the director of archives and history of the state of Mississippi, 1906-07) Nashville. Brandon Ptg. Co. 1908. p32-7 **6563**

—— —— An official guide to the historical materials in the Mississippi Department of Archives and History. *In* Eleventh-[twelfth] annual report of the director of the Department of archives and history of the state of Mississippi, 1911-13. Dunbar Rowland, director. Nashville. Brandon-Craig-Dickerson. 1914. p43-147 **6564**

Mississippi. Historical Commission. An account of manuscripts, papers, and documents pertaining to Mississippi in public repositories beyond the state . . . within the state of Mississippi . . . in private hands. Mississippi Hist. Soc. publications. V. p49-293. 1902 **6565**

Mississippi. Secretary of State. Mississippi reports. Comp. by J. L. Powers, Secretary of State—Statute laws of Mississippi. Comp. by T. L. Cole. Mississippi. Secretary of State. Biennial rep. 1896-97. p104-9 **6566**

Mississippi. State Library. Catalogue of the Mississippi State Library. By Mrs. Mary Morancy. Jackson. Power & Barksdale. 1877 **6567**

Mississippi. State Planning Commission. A bibliography of recent fugitive studies in population. Jackson. June 15, 1938. 8p. mim. **6567a**

Mississippi Historical Society. Complete contents of the publications of the Mississippi Historical Society arranged by volumes, vols. I-XIV. Mississippi Hist. Soc. publications. XIV. p301-6. 1914 **6568**

—— Complete contents . . . topically arranged, author index . . . complete contents . . . arranged by volumes, general index of volumes I-X of the Publications of the Mississippi Historical Society. Mississippi Hist. Soc. publications. X. p483-579. 1909 **6569**

Owen, Thomas McAdory. A bibliography of Mississippi. Am. Hist. Asso. rep. 1899. I. p633-828 **6570**

Rainwater, Percy L. The Historical Records Survey in Mississippi. Jour. Miss. hist. I. p77-81 (April 1939) **6570a**

Riley, Franklin L. The Department of Archives and History of the state of Mississippi. Am. Hist. Asso. rep. 1903. I. p475-8 **6571**

Robinson, Mary. Mississippi newspaper files in the library of the American Antiquarian Society, Worcester, Mass. Gulf States hist. mag. II. p50-3 (July 1903) **6572**

Rowland, Dunbar. The importance of preserving local records illustrated by the Spanish archives of the Natchez district. Am. Hist. Asso. rep. 1905. I. p204-10 **6573**

Schilling, George E. The Survey of Federal Archives in Mississippi. Jour. Miss. hist. I. p207-16 (Oct. 1939) **6573a**

Survey of Federal Archives. Mississippi. Inventory of federal archives in the states. New Orleans, La. 1938- . mim. The Federal Courts. Jan. 1940. 59p.; The Department of the Treasury. March 1940. 49p.; The Department of War. Oct. 1938. 99p.; The Department of Justice. Oct. 1939. 17p.; The Department of the Navy. Aug. 1938. 4p.; The Department of Agriculture. Dec. 1939. 240p.; The Department of Commerce. Oct. 1938. 10p.; The Department of Labor. June 1940. 32p.; The Veterans' Administration. June 1940. 35p.; The Farm Credit Administration. June 1940. 9p.; The Works Progress Administration. June 1941. 81p. **6573b**

Sydnor, Charles Sackett. Historical activities in Mississippi in the nineteenth century. Jour. of south. hist. III. p139-60 (May 1937) **6573c**

—— The beginning of printing in Mississippi. Baton Rouge. Franklin Press. 1935. p49-55 (Reprinted from the Jour. of south. hist. I. Feb. 1935) **6574**

Thompson, Robert H. Mississippi codes. Mississippi State Bar Asso. proc. 1926. p44-75 **6575**

U.S. Bureau of Agricultural Economics. Library. Leake and Union Counties, Mississippi; a selected list of references. Comp. by Howard B. Turner. (Economic library list no. 27) Wash. D.C. June 1941. 15p. mim. **6575a**

U.S. Library of Congress. Division of bibliography. List of Mississippi authors and their works. March 8, 1915. 6p. typ. **6576**

—— —— —— A list of references relating to Mississippi. Oct. 29, 1935. 17p. typ. **6577**

Weathersby, William H. The preservation of Mississippi history. North Carolina hist. rev. V. p141-50 (April 1928) **6578**

White, James M. and Riley, Franklin L. Libraries and societies. Miss. Hist. Soc. pub. V. p169-227 (1902) **6578a**

MISSOURI

Belden, H. M. A partial list of song ballads and other popular poetry known to Missouri. ? 1910 **6579**

Boatman, Mildred. The Ozark region; a list of books and articles. St. Louis Pub. Lib. monthly bul. XXVII. p151-4 (May 1929) **6580**

Breckenridge, William Clark. Bibliography of medicine in St. Louis and Missouri—Partial bibliography of Doniphan expedition—Bibliography of material relating to Missouri in the Kansas struggle—Bibliography of slavery and Civil war in Missouri. In Breckenridge, James Malcolm. William Clark Breckenridge, historical research writer and bibliographer of Missouri. St. Louis. Pub. by the author. 1932. p300-2, 303-4, 305-8, 309-49 (The Bibliography of slavery and Civil war in Missouri is also pub. in the Missouri hist. rev. II. p233-48. April 1908, and separately printed) **6581**

Breckenridge, William Clark and Sampson, Francis Asbury. Bibliography of early Missouri imprints, 1808-1850. In Breckenridge, James Malcolm. William Clark Breckenridge, historical research writer and bibliographer of Missouri. St. Louis. Pub. by the author. 1932. p249-99 **6582**

Brown, Dorothy Grace. Early St. Louis newspapers, 1808-1850. (Wash. Univ. thesis) June 1931. MS. **6583**

Byars, William Vincent. A century of journalism in Missouri. Missouri hist. rev. XV. p53-73 (Oct. 1920) **6584**

Cole, Theodore L. Laws of Missouri. St. Louis. F. H. Thomas Law Book Co. 1890. 3p. **6585**

De Menil, Alexander Nicolas. A century of Missouri literature. Missouri hist. rev. XV. p74-125 (Oct. 1920) **6586**

—— The St. Louis book authors. St. Louis. Wm. Harvey Miner Co. 1925. 69p. **6587**

Garland, J. S. An index to the statute laws of Missouri . . . from the inauguration of the territorial government to . . . 1868. St. Louis. St. Louis Books & News Co. 1868. 421p. **6588**

Garraghan, Gilbert Joseph. Some newly discovered Missouri maps. Mo. Hist. Soc. col. V. p256-64 (June 1928) **6588a**

Historical Records Survey. Missouri. Inventory of the church archives of Missouri. St. Louis, Mo. 1940- . mim. No. 1. Baptist bodies, Tebo Baptist Association. Oct. 1940. 55p. **6588b**

—— —— Inventory of the county archives of Missouri. St. Louis, Mo. 1937- . mim. No. 19. Cass. April 1941. 142p.; No. 26. Cole. Nov. 1938. 150p.; No. 30. Dallas. Nov. 1940. 109p.; No. 42. Henry. Oct. 1940. 114p.; No. 58. Linn. Dec. 1938. 114p.; No. 64. Marion. Jan. 1941. 230p.; No. 73. Jasper. Jan. 1940. 269p.; No. 80. Pettis. June 1939. 212p.; No. 82. Pike. Nov. 1937. 85p.; No. 90. Reynolds. June 1938. 117p.; No. 91. Ripley. May 1938. 92p.; No. 102. Shelby. March 1939. 168p. **6588c**

—— —— A preliminary check list of Missouri imprints, 1808-1850. (American imprints inventory, no. 1) Wash. D.C. 1937. 225p. mim. **6588d**

Hunter, W. and Myer, W. G. Index to volumes 1-50 of the Missouri reports. St. Louis. 1873 **6589**

Hyde, William. Newspapers (of St. Louis) and newspaper people of three decades. Missouri Hist. Soc. publications. no. 12. p5-24. 1896   **6590**

Kansas City. Public Library. Bibliography—Missouri. Kansas City Pub. Lib. quar. I. p69-100 (July 1901)   **6591**

Keyes, Charles Rollin. Bibliography of Missouri geology. (Missouri Geol. Survey. X. 1896) Jefferson City. Tribune. 1896. p219-523   **6592**

Lawson, John D. A century of Missouri legal literature. Missouri hist. rev. XV. p595-610 (July 1921)   **6593**

Lefler, Grace. Missouri documents for the small public library. Missouri hist. rev. IV. p321-7 (July 1910) (Also separate. 1909)   **6594**

McCain, William D. The papers of the Food Administration for Missouri, 1917-1919, in The National Archives. Mo. hist. rev. XXXII. p56-61 (Oct. 1937)   **6594a**

McDermott, John Francis. Louis Richard Cortambert and the first French newspapers in Saint Louis, 1809-1854. Bibliog. Soc. Amer. pap. XXXIV. p221-53. 1940   **6594b**

McMurtrie, Douglas C. Early Missouri book and pamphlet imprints, 1808-1830. Am. book collector. I. p96-103, 159-62, 231-4 (Feb.-April 1932) (Republished. Chicago. 1937. 17p. mim.)   **6595**

—— Joseph Charless, pioneer printer of St. Louis. Chicago. Ludlow Typograph Co. 1931. 39p.   **6596**

Missouri. State Department. Newspapers of Missouri. *In* State of Missouri, 1931-1932. Official manual. Jefferson City. Botz Ptg. and Stationery Co. 1931? p691-711   **6597**

Missouri. State Historical Society. Book notices. Missouri hist. rev. I. Oct. 1906-   **6598**

—— —— Card index of biographical references to Missourians in county histories and other works. (On deposit in the Society)   **6599**

—— —— Card index to subject and biographical matter in Missouri newspapers, 1836- . (On deposit in the Society)   **6600**

—— —— The Missouri historical review; index, volumes I-XXV, October 1906-July 1931. Comp. by the Columbia Library Club. Columbia. State Hist. Soc. of Missouri. 1934. 353p. planog.   **6601**

—— —— Old newspaper files (in the library of the State Historical Society of Missouri). Missouri hist. rev. V. p34-43 (Oct. 1910) (Also reprinted)   **6602**

Missouri. State Library. Law Dept. Catalog of the Law department of the Missouri State Library. Comp. by George E. Smith and A. J. Menteer. Jefferson City. 1915. 436p.   **6602a**

Organ, Minnie. History of the county press of Missouri. Missouri hist. rev. IV. p111-33, 149-66, 252-308 (Jan.-July 1910)   **6603**

St. Louis. Mercantile Library. Chronological list of Missouri and Illinois newspapers, 1808-1897, in the St. Louis Mercantile Library. (Lib. reference list no. I. pt. 1) St. Louis. 1898. p1-17 **6604**

St. Louis. Public Library. Books on St. Louis: history, government, institutions. St. Louis Pub. Lib. monthly bul. n.s. XXIII. p330-1 (Sept. 1925)   **6605**

—— —— An index to the publications of the Missouri Geological Survey. St. Louis Pub. Lib. mthly bul. n.s. XII. p120-32 (May 1914)   **6605a**

—— —— Library School. Missouri; a selected list of books and articles. Comp. by the class of 1926, St. Louis Library School. St. Louis Pub. Lib. monthly bul. n.s. XXIV. p129-58 (Lib. School no. June 1926)   **6606**

Sampson, Francis Asbury. Bibliography of books of travel in Missouri. Missouri hist. rev. VI. p64-81 (Jan. 1912) (Reprinted separately)   **6607**

—— A bibliography of Missouri authors. Sedalia, Mo. 1901. 58p. (Reprinted from Conard, Howard Louis. An encyclopedia of the history of Missouri; a compendium of history and biography for ready reference. N.Y., Louisville, St. Louis. South. Hist. Co. Haldeman, Conard & Co., proprietors. 1901. I. p215-70)   **6608**

—— Bibliography of Missouri biography. Missouri hist. rev. II. p131-57 (Jan. 1908) (Also reprinted)   **6609**

—— A bibliography of Missouri state publications for 1905-1909. Missouri hist. rev. I. p85-99 (Oct. 1906); II. p303-18 (July 1908); IV. p182-201 (April 1910)   **6610**

—— A bibliography of the geology of Missouri. (Geol. Survey of Missouri. Bul. no. 2) Jefferson City. Tribune. 1890. 168p.   **6611**

—— Bibliography of the Missouri Press Association. Missouri hist. rev. IX. p155-76 (April 1915)   **6612**

—— A catalogue of publications by Missouri authors and periodicals of Missouri of 1903, in World's fair exhibit, in Missouri building. Columbia. E. W. Stephens. 1904. 47p.   **6613**

—— History and publications of the Missouri State Horticultural Society. (The thirty-third annual rep. of the State Horticultural Soc. of Missouri. 1890) Jefferson City, Mo. 1891. p437-49   **6614**

—— Official publications of Missouri bibliography. Columbia, Mo. 1905. p313-56 (Reprinted from Bowker's State publications)   **6615**

Saylor, Corilla E. Check list of Missouri documents. Univ. of Illinois Lib., Urbana, Ill. In progress   **6615a**

Scharf, John Thomas. List of Missouri authors and their contributions to literature. *In* History of St. Louis city and county. Phila. Everts. 1883. II. p1609-15   **6616**

Shoemaker, Floyd C. Historical articles in Missouri newspapers. Missouri hist. rev. IX. Oct. 1914-   **6617**

Survey of Federal Archives. Missouri. Inventory of federal archives in the states. St. Louis, Mo. 1938- . mim. The Federal Courts. Dec. 1938. 65p.; The Department of the Treasury. Dec. 1938. 164p.; The Department of War. Dec. 1938. 125p.; The Department of Justice. Dec. 1937. 46p.; The Department of the Navy. Dec. 1938. 17p.; The Department of the Interior. Dec. 1938. 31p.; The Department of Agriculture. Dec. 1938. 230p.; The Department of Commerce. Dec. 1938. 23p.; The Department of Labor. Dec. 1938. 69p.; The Veterans' Administration. Dec. 1938. 38p.; The Civil Works Administration. Dec. 1938. 18p.; The Emergency Relief Administration. Dec. 1938. 58p.; The Works Progress Administration. Dec. 1938. 137p.; The Farm Credit Administration. Dec. 1938. 19p.; Miscellaneous Agencies. Dec. 1938. 177p.   **6617a**

U.S. Children's Bureau. References to Missouri statutes relating to children; an annotated and classified reference list of all statutes and constitutional provisions in Missouri relating to children. Supplement to the report of the Missouri Children's Code Commission. n.p. 1917. 67p.   **6618**

U.S. Library of Congress. Division of bibliography. List of books on the history of Missouri. Jan. 20, 1925. 8p. typ.   **6619**

—— —— —— A list of references on the Ozarks. March 24, 1936. 16p. typ.   **6620**

Usher, Roland G. A bibliography of sanitary work in St. Louis during the Civil war. Missouri Hist. Soc. colls. IV. p73-81. 1912   **6621**

Viles, Jonas. The archives at Jefferson City. Missouri hist. rev. II. p284-95 (July 1908)   **6622**

—— Report on the archives of the state of Missouri. Am. Hist. Asso. rep. 1908. I. p319-64   **6623**

Violette, E. M. The preservation and dissemination of Missouri history. Mo. hist. rev. XXXII. p327-39 (April 1938)   **6623a**

Winslow, A. Geological surveys in Missouri. Jour. of geology. II. p207-21. 1894   **6623b**

MONTANA

Adams, Winona. Check list of Montana documents. Univ. of Montana, Missoula, Mont. MS.   **6623c**

Blankenship, Joseph William. A century of botanical exploration in Montana, 1805-1905: collectors, herbaria and bibliography. *In* Montana Agricultural College. Sci. stud. botany. Bozeman, Mont. 1905. I. p1-31   **6623d**

Garver, Frank Harmon. Montana as a field for historical research. Miss. Valley Hist. Asso. proc. VII. p99-112. 1913-14   **6623e**

Cole, Theodore L. Montana laws. St. Louis. F. H. Thomas Law Book Co. 1890. 2p.   **6624**

Historical Records Survey. Montana. Guide to public vital statistical records in Montana. Bozeman, Mont. March 1941. 85p. mim.   **6624a**

—— —— Inventory of the county archives of Montana. Bozeman, Mont. 1938- . mim. No. 1. Beaverhead. Nov. 1939. 203p.; No. 28. Madison. May 1940. 208p.; No. 32. Missoula. Sept. 1938. 190p.; No. 47. Silver Bow. July 1939. 231p.; No. 51. Toole. Oct. 1938. 123p.   **6624b**

McMurtrie, Douglas C. Montana imprints, 1864-1880; bibliography of books, pamphlets and broadsides printed within the area now constituting the state of Montana. Chicago. The Black Cat Press. 1937. 82p.   **6624c**

—— Pioneer printing in Montana. Iowa City, Ia. Priv. printed. 1932. 16p. (Reprinted from Journalism quar. June 1932)   **6625**

Montana. Department of Agriculture, Labor and Industry. Division of publicity. Directory of Montana newspapers, revised to October 1, 1931. Helena, Mont. 1927. [4]p.   **6626**

Montana. Historical Society. Catalogue of the library of the society. Prepared by William F. Wheeler. Helena. Wells. 1892. 57p.   **6627**

Montana. University. Library. Check list of Montana historical material. MS. **6628**

Phillips, Paul C. The archives of the state of Montana. Am. Hist. Asso. rep. 1912. p295-303   **6629**

Survey of Federal Archives. Montana. Inventory of federal archives in the states. Butte, Mont. 1939- . mim. The Federal Courts. Jan. 1941. 31p.; The Department of War. Jan. 1941. 72p.; The Department of Agriculture. July 1939. 155p.; The Department of Commerce. July 1939. 9p.; The Veterans' Administration. Nov. 1940. 24p.; The Farm Credit Administration. July 1939. 11p.   **6629a**

NEBRASKA

Barbour, Erwin H. and Fisher, Cassius A. The geological bibliography of Nebraska. (Nebraska State Board of Agriculture. Annual rep. 1901, 1902) Lincoln. State Jour. Co. 1902. p248-66   **6630**

Baumer, Bertha. Nebraska material in the Omaha Public Library. 1931. mim. **6630a**

Caldwell, Howard W. Report on the public archives of Nebraska. Am. Hist. Asso. rep. 1900. II. p64-6   **6631**

Cole, Theodore L. Nebraska [laws]. St. Louis. F. H. Thomas Law Book Co. n.d. 1p.   **6632**

Gilmore, Sylvia. The official publications of Nebraska. (Univ. of Illinois. Master's Thesis) [Urbana] 1935. 206p. typ.   **6632a**

Harvey, Alice G. Nebraska writers. Omaha. Citizen Ptg. Co. 1934. 110p.   **6633**

Historical Records Survey. Nebraska. Guide to depositories of manuscript collections in the United States: Nebraska. Lincoln, Neb. June 1940. 32p. mim. **6633a**

Historical Records Survey. Nebraska. Inventory of the county archives of Nebraska. Lincoln, Neb. 1939- . mim. no. 37. Gosper. June 1940. 174.; no. 39. Greeley. May 1941. 211p.; no. 58. Loup. May 1941. 127p.; no. 80. Seward. June 1939. 216p.   **6633b**

History in Nebraska newspapers. Neb. hist. I- . Feb. 1918-   **6633c**

Lammers, Sophia J. A provisional list of Nebraska authors. (Bibliog. contributions from the lib. of the Univ. of Nebraska. V) Lincoln, Neb. 1918. 60p. **6634**

McMurtrie, Douglas C. Pioneer printing in Nebraska. Springfield, Ill. 1932. 4p. (Reprinted from National printer journalist for January 1932)   **6635**

Miller, George L. Newspapers and newspaper men of the territorial period. Nebraska State Hist. Soc. proc. and colls. 2d ser. V. p31-47. 1902   **6636**

Morton, Julius Sterling. Nebraska territorial press. *In* Illustrated history of Nebraska. Lincoln. Jacob North. 1906. II. p336-78   **6637**

—— Territorial journalism. Nebraska State Hist. Soc. proc. and colls. 2d ser. V. p11-30. 1902   **6638**

Nebraska. Legislative reference bureau. Bibliography; a partial list of more recent printed material about Nebraska. *In* The Nebraska blue books, 1934. Lincoln. Dec. 1934. p501-8   **6639**

—— List of newspapers and periodicals published in Nebraska, July 1934. *In* The Nebraska blue book, 1934. Lincoln. Dec. 1934. p395-406   **6640**

—— —— Subject index of legislative bills with other legislative information. Lincoln, Neb. 1937. 59p.   **6640a**

—— —— Subject index of Senate and House bills with other legislative information, February 21, 1935. Lincoln. Nebraska Legislative Reference Bureau. 1935. 88p.   **6641**

Nebraska. State Historical Society. Know Nebraska first; shelf of Nebraska Historical Society publications, 1885-1929. [Lincoln. 1929] 14p.   **6642**

—— —— Nebraska newspapers; the State Historical Society collection of twenty thousand files. Nebr. hist. mag. XV. p67-75 (April-June 1934)   **6642a**

Omaha. Public Library. Bibliographical material on the history of Nebraska. MS. **6642b**

—— —— Nebraska material in the Omaha Public Library. Comp. by Bertha Baumer, October 1931. [Omaha. 1931] 21p. reprod. from typ. copy   **6643**

Sheldon, Addison E. Report on the archives of the state of Nebraska. Am. Hist. Asso. rep. 1910. p365-420   **6644**

Shotwell, Margaret B. Nebraska authors. *In* First national authors' week, Oct. 22-29, 1923. Omaha. Kieser's Bookstore. 1923. p23-37   **6645**

Survey of Federal Archives. Nebraska. Inventory of federal archives in the states. Lincoln, Neb. 1938- . mim. The Federal Courts. June 1939. 29p.; The Department of the Treasury. April 1939. 56p.; The Department of War. May 1940. 96p.; The Department of Justice. June 1939. 13p.; The Department of the Navy. May 1939. 7p.; The Department of the Interior. June 1939. 20p.; The Department of Agriculture. March 1940. 165p.; The Department of Commerce. Nov. 1938. 16p.; The Veterans' Administration. June 1939. 10p.; The Farm Credit Administration. Feb. 1940. 54p.; Miscellaneous agencies. April 1941. 69p.   **6645a**

Writers' Program. Nebraska. Printing comes to Lincoln. Written and compiled by workers of the Writers' Program, Work Projects Administration in the state of Nebraska. Sponsored by the Ben Franklin club of Lincoln. Lincoln, Neb. Woodruff Ptg. Co. 1940. 80p. **6645b**

NEVADA

Angel, Myron. History of journalism. *In* History of Nevada. Oakland. Thompson & West. 1881. p291-332   **6646**

Drury, Wells. Journalism. *In* Davis, Sam Post. The History of Nevada. Reno, Los Angeles. Elms Publishing Co. 1913. I. p459-502   **6647**

Hicks, Charles R. Report on the archives of Nevada completed for the Public Archives Commission in 1934. MS.   **6648**

Historical Records Survey. Nevada. A check list of Nevada imprints, 1859-1890. (American imprints inventory, no. 7) Chicago. 1939. 127p. mim.   **6648a**

—— —— Inventory of the church archives of Nevada. Reno, Nev. 1939- . mim. Roman Catholic Church. Aug. 1939. 49p.; Protestant Episcopal. Jan. 1941. 69p. mim. **6648b**

—— —— Inventory of the county archives of Nevada. Reno, Nev. 1937- . mim. No. 3. Douglas. Nov. 1937. 72p.; No. 4. Elko. Dec. 1938. 178p.; No. 6. Eureka. Oct. 1939. 201p.; No. 12. Nye. Dec. 1940. 216p.; No. 13. Ormsby. March 1940. 178p.; No. 16. Washoe. Sept. 1938. 115p. **6648c**

McMurtrie, Douglas C. A bibliography of Nevada newspapers, 1858 to 1875 inclusive. Mainz. Gutenberg-Jahrbuch. 1935. p292-312 (Reprinted from the Gutenberg jahrbuch, 1935)   **6649**

Nevada. Superintendent of State Printing. Biennial reports, 1899/1900-1921/1922. Carson City. State Ptg. Off. 1901-23 (Also issued in the Appendix to Journals of Senate and Assembly . . . of the legislature of the state of Nevada. Include statements of printing for the various departments of the government)   **6650**

Survey of Federal Archives. Nevada. Inventory of federal archives in the states. Reno, Nev. 1940- . mim. The Federal Courts. April 1940. 25p.; The Department of the Treasury. March 1940. 22p.; The War Department. 1941. 10p.; The Department of Justice. May 1940. 15p.; The Department of the Navy. March 1940. 21p.; The Department of the Interior. July 1940. 178p.; The Department of Agriculture. Feb. 1941. 125p.; The Department of Labor. Reno. 1941. 26p.; The Farm Credit Administration. 1941. 5p. **6650a**

U.S. Library of Congress. Division of bibliography. A selected list of references on Nevada. March 13, 1934. 33p. typ. **6651**

NEW HAMPSHIRE

Alden, Timothy. The glory of America; a century sermon delivered at the South Church in Portsmouth, New Hampshire IV January, MDCCCI, together with a number of historical notes, and an appendix, containing an account of the newspapers printed in the state. Portsmouth, N.H. 1801. 47p. **6652**

Balcom, George L. Catalogue of the valuable private library of the late George L. Balcom, esq. of Claremont, N.H., comprising an extensive collection of historical books relating to New Hampshire, including nearly complete set of New Hampshire town, county and regimental histories, genealogies, rare pamphlets of local interest, newspapers, etc. . . . Boston. Press of the Libbie Show print. 1901. 226p. **6653**

Bangs and Co. Catalogue of a valuable library, specially relating to New Hampshire. . . . N.Y. 1883. 64p. **6654**

Batchellor, Albert S. [Bibliographical memoranda on the early New Hampshire laws]. *In* Laws of New Hampshire, province period, 1702-1745. Concord, N.H. Rumford Ptg. Co. 1913. II. p. xi-1, 38-44, 240-5, 515-17, 655-65, 759-61 **6655**

—— Historical and bibliographical notes on the military annals of New Hampshire. A reprint of a chapter from the History of the seventeenth regiment. Concord. Rumford Press. 1898. 50p. **6656**

—— A list of documents in the public record office in London, England (1606-1771), relating to the province of New Hampshire. (New Hampshire Hist. Soc. colls. X) Manchester, N.H. 1893. 557p. **6657**

—— The revolutionary archives of New Hampshire; a reprint of the introduction to volume 30 of the New Hampshire state papers. Manchester. J. B. Clarke Co. 1910. xvii p. **6658**

Bent, Allen H. A bibliography of the White Mountains. Boston. Pub. for the Appalachian Mountain Club by Houghton Mifflin, Riverside Press. 1911. 114p. **6659**

Brackett, Thelma. New Hampshire documents. Bul. of the New Hampshire libraries. n.s. XXXIII. p121-7 (Sept. 1937) **6659a**

Brigham, Clarence S. New Hampshire—Bibliography of American newspapers, 1690-1820. Am. Antiq. Soc. proc. n.s. XXVI. p96-184 (April 1916) **6660**

Chase, F. Bibliography of Dartmouth College. Granite monthly. V. p321-4 (July 1882) **6661**

Dover. Public Library. A list of books and pamphlets in the Dover Public Library relating to New Hampshire. Dover. H. E. Hodgdon. 1903. 172p. **6662**

Farmer, John. Author list of New Hampshire, 1685-1829, as published in the New Hampshire register of 1829. Manchester. J. B. Clarke. 1890. 18p. (From rep. of the librarian. New Hampshire State Lib. 1890) **6663**

Fitzpatrick, John T. Notes on New Hampshire statute law, to supplement the Hand-list of American statute law. Law Lib. jour. XIII. p51-6 (July 1920) **6664**

Gould, Sylvester C. Bibliography of Manchester, N.H. (New Hampshire State Lib. rep. no. 24) Concord. Pearson. 1894. p217-331 **6665**

Ham, John R. Bibliography of Dover, N.H., containing titles of (1) works on Dover, (2) works written by residents of Dover, while residents, (3) works bearing the publication imprint of Dover. (Rep. of the state librarian. 1892) Concord. Evans. 1892. p193-266 **6666**

Hammond, Otis G. Bibliography of the newspapers and periodicals of Concord, N.H., 1790-1898. Concord. Evans. 1902. 32p. (Reprinted from the Rep. of the state librarian. 1901-02) **6667**

—— Checklist of New Hampshire local history. Concord. New Hampshire Hist. Soc. 1925. 106p. **6668**

—— Index to the Granite monthly, volumes one to thirty-four. New Hampshire Pub. Lib. bul. n.s. IV-V. p29-135. 1903-04 **6669**

—— The Weare papers. Granite monthly. LI. p357-61 (Aug. 1919) (Papers of Meschech Weare, president of the Council and chairman of the Committee of safety of New Hampshire during the Revolution) **6669a**

Harris, Mary Bartlett. Bibliography of Warner. (Rep. of the . . . state librarian [New Hampshire] 1902-1904. VIII. pt. V) [Concord. Rumford Ptg. Co. 1905?] **6670**

Hasse, Adelaide Rosalie. Index of economic material in documents of the states of the United States—New Hampshire, 1789-1904. (Carnegie Inst. of Wash. Publication no. 85) Wash. D.C. Carnegie Inst. of Wash. 1907. 66p. **6671**

Historical Records Survey. New Hampshire. Guide to depositories of manuscript collections in the United States: New Hampshire. Manchester, N.H. Aug. 1940. 44p. mim. **6671a**

Historical Records Survey. New Hampshire. Inventory of the church archives of New Hampshire. Manchester, N.H. 1938- . mim. Inventory of the Roman Catholic Church records in New Hampshire. April 1938. 127p. **6671b**

—— —— Inventory of the county archives of New Hampshire. Manchester, N.H. 1938- . mim. No. 1. Belknap. June 1938. 64p.; No. 2. Carroll. Feb. 1939. 160p.; No. 3. Cheshire. Aug. 1939. 196p.; No. 4. Coos. Feb. 1940. 238p.; No. 5. Grafton. April 1940. 152p.; No. 7. Merrimack. Dec. 1936. 25p. (prelim. ed.) **6671c**

—— —— Inventory of the town archives of New Hampshire. Manchester, N.H. 1939- . mim. No. 1. Belknap County: vol. 8. New Hampton. April 1941. 84p.; No. 7. Merrimack County: vol. 6. Canterbury. Feb. 1941. 79p.; No. 8. Rockingham County; vol. 1. Atkinson. Oct. 1939. 67p., vol. 2. Auburn. Dec. 1939. 77p., vol. 4. Candia. Aug. 1940. 82p., vol. 5. Chester. May 1940. 83p., vol. 11. Exeter. Nov. 1940. 100p., vol. 13. Greenland. July 1941. 80p. **6671d**

Hitchcock, C. H. The geology of New Hampshire. Jour. of geology. IV. p44-62. 1896 **6671e**

—— Topographical maps of the State. *In* The geology of New Hampshire. Concord. E. A. Jenks. 1874. pt. I, p227-47 **6671f**

Hoyt, Albert H. Historical and bibliographical notes on the laws of New Hampshire. Am. Antiq. Soc. proc. XXVI. p89-104 (April 26, 1876) **6672**

Libbie, C. F. & Co. Catalogue of the library of the late Hon. Charles H. Bell of Exeter, N.H., consisting of a valuable collection of Americana, New Hampshire town histories, acts and laws, constitutions, New Hampshire. . . . Boston. Libbie Show print. 1895. 164p. **6673**

McClintock, J. N. Bibliography of New Hampshire. Granite monthly. IV. p286-91 (April 1881) **6674**

McFarland, Asa. Early history of the Concord press. Granite monthly. II. p164-71 (March 1879) **6675**

McMurtrie, Douglas C. The beginnings of printing in New Hampshire. The Lib. 4th ser. XV. p340-63 (Dec. 1934) **6676**

Moore, J. W. Bibliography of Manchester, N.H.; a collection of books, pamphlets and magazines from 1743-1885. . . . Manchester, N.H. 1885. 52p. (Addenda. 1886? p53-60) **6677**

New Hampshire (Colony). Assembly. House of Representatives. Index to the Journals of the House of Representatives, province of New Hampshire, in the office of the Secretary of State, 1711-1784. v. 1. Manchester. John B. Clarke. 1890; v.2. Concord. E. N. Pearson. 1894 **6678**

New Hampshire (Colony). Governor and Council. Index to records of the Council of New Hampshire, from November 17, 1631 to April 17, 1784 in the office of the Secretary of State. Concord, N.H. 1896. (Index to MS. records) **6679**

New Hampshire. Forestry Commission. Bibliography of the White Mountains. (New Hampshire Forestry Comn. Second annual rep. 1894) Concord. Edward N. Pearson. 1894. p111-15 **6680**

New Hampshire. General Court. Index to the journals of the House of Representatives of New Hampshire from April 21, 1775 to April 17, 1784, in the office of the Secretary of State. Concord. Edward N. Pearson. 1894. 503p. **6681**

—— —— Index to the records of the council of New Hampshire from Nov. 17, 1631 to April 17, 1784 in the office of the Secretary of State. Concord. Edward N. Pearson. 1896. 540p. **6682**

New Hampshire. Library Commission. New Hampshire local history. New Hampshire Lib. Comn. bul. n.s. II. p121-8 (Dec. 1901) **6683**

—— —— New Hampshire state publications. New Hampshire Lib. Comn. bul. III. p148-54 (June 1902) **6684**

New Hampshire. State Library. Author list of New Hampshire, 1685-1829. (Rep. of the state librarian. 1890) Manchester. J. B. Clarke. 1890. p163-78 **6685**

—— —— Author list of the New Hampshire State Library, June 1, 1902. Manchester. J. B. Clarke. 1904. 2v (Supplement. 1904. 594p. 1906. 432p.) **6686**

—— —— Check list of New Hampshire laws, 1789-1889. (Rep. of the state librarian. 1890) Manchester. J. B. Clarke. 1890. p145-52 (Reprinted with additions in Reports of the state librarian. 1891. p121-8; 1892. p111-17) **6687**

—— —— Check list of New Hampshire laws, 1789-1891, public acts, 1789-1834, public and private acts, 1835-1891. (Rep. of the state librarian. 1892) Concord. Evans. 1892. p105-17 **6688**

—— —— A check-list of New Hampshire state documents received at the State Library, Jan. 1938- . Comp. by B. Ruth Jeffries. Concord. 1938- . mim. mthly. **6688a**

—— —— Condensed list of reports of departments and some other state publications of New Hampshire. (Rep. of the state librarian. 1892) Concord. Evans. 1892. p77-125 **6689**

—— —— A descriptive list of the historical and statistical publications of New Hampshire published prior to 1860; with additions, comprising some works historical and descriptive, published since that time. Prepared by Samuel C. Eastman. (Rep. of the state librarian. 1891) Concord. Evans. 1891. p181-226 (Reprinted from Norton's literary letter) **6690**

—— —— Index list of reports of departments of the state of New Hampshire and other documental matter published in the appendices to legislative journals, 1822-1869, and in the "annual reports," 1870-90. (Rep. of the state librarian. 1891) Concord. Evans. 1891. p85-119 **6691**

—— —— A list of official publications, state of New Hampshire, issued from October 1, 1892 to October 1, 1894, also special publications of departments for the same period. (Rep. of the state librarian. no. 24) Concord. Pearson. 1894. p101-12 **6692**

—— —— List of reports of departments, state of New Hampshire, and other documental matter as found in appendices of legislative journals, and subsequently in the "annual reports." (Rep. of the state librarian. 1890) Manchester. J. B. Clarke. 1890. p95-137 **6693**

—— —— New Hampshire official publications, 1889-1890. (Rep. of the state librarian. 1890) Manchester. J. B. Clarke. 1890. p89-94 **6694**

—— —— Some publications, historical and descriptive issued during the period, 1859-1891, with a few works of an earlier date. (Rep. of the state librarian. 1891) Concord. Evans. 1891. p227-73 **6695**

New Hampshire. Statutes. Acts and laws of the state of New Hampshire, 1780-1789. Reprinted in photo-facsimile, with a bibliographic note, from the copy collected by Hon. Timothy Walker, now in the Library of Congress. Wash. D.C. Statute Law Book Co. 1907. p201-452 **6696**

—— —— Index to the laws of New Hampshire, recorded in the office of the Secretary of State, 1679-1883. Manchester. J. B. Clarke. 1886. 594p. **6697**

New Hampshire Library Association. Bibliography of Dartmouth College and Hanover, N.H. Comp. by James Thayer Gerould (Rep. of the state librarian. 1894) Concord. Pearson. 1894. p149-216 (Reprinted. Concord. Pearson. 1894. 69p.) **6698**

Norton, Charles B. New series, no. 1, Norton's literary letter, comprising the bibliography of the state of New Hampshire and other papers of interest; together with a catalogue of a large collection of works upon bibliography and America. N.Y. Charles B. Norton. 1860. 45, 23p. **6699**

Rugg, Harold G. The Dresden press. Dartmouth alumni mag. XII. p796-814 (May 1920) **6700**

Sargent, George H. The centenary of the Andover press; the work of a pioneer printer whose imprints now rank among the rarities sought by book collectors (Ebenezer Chase). Granite monthly II. p287-95 (July 1919) **6701**

Stevens, Henry & Son. A catalogue of books and pamphlets relating to New Hampshire. . . London. Henry Stevens & Son. 1885. 40p. **6702**

Stickney, Joseph A. The ante-revolutionary publications in New Hampshire. Granite monthly. V. p390-4 (Sept. 1882) **6703**

—— A collection of New Hampshire registers, with note and comment thereon. Great Falls, N.H. Fred L. Shapleigh. 1887. 37p. **6704**

Survey of Federal Archives. New Hampshire. Inventory of federal archives in the states. Manchester, N.H. 1938- . mim. The Federal Courts. ser. II. June 1941. 8p.; The Department of the Treasury. July 1938. 41p.; The Department of War. Oct. 1938. 42p.; The Department of Justice. Sept. 1938. 8p.; The Department of the Navy. Sept. 1939. 5p.; The Department of the Interior. 1941. 4p.; The Department of Agriculture. June 1938. 71p.; The Department of Commerce. Sept. 1938. 11p.; The Department of Labor. Feb. 1941. 19p.; The Veterans' Administration. Oct. 1938. 10p.; The Works Progress Administration. April 1939. 32p.; The Farm Credit Administration. Dec. 1938. 5p. **6704a**

Towle, Dorothy S. Bibliography of New Hampshire imprints, 1756-1850. Durham, N.H. In progress **6704b**

Walker, Joseph B. An index of the historical matter contained in The New Hampshire registers from 1772 to 1892, in The Political manuals from 1857 to 1872, and in The People hand-books for 1874, 1876 and 1877. (Rep. of the state librarian. 1891) Concord. Evans. 1891. p291-331 (Also separately printed. Concord. Evans. 1892) **6705**

Whittemore, Caroline. A checklist of New Hampshire imprints, 1756-1790, with an introductory essay on the history of printing in New Hampshire, 1756-1790. (Columbia Univ. Master's essay) 1929. 137p. typ. **6706**

NEW JERSEY

Andrews, Frank De Witte. A bibliography of Vineland, its authors and writers. Vineland, N.J. 1916. 21p. **6707**

A[nkenbrand], F[rank], Jr. A bibliography of Vineland maps, published and originals in the possession of the Vineland Historical Society. Vineland hist. mag. XXIII. p134-40. 1938 **6707a**

Bergen County Historical Society. Index to historical papers and their authors, which have appeared in the Bergen County Historical Society "Papers and proceedings," 1902-1922. Bergen County Hist Soc. pap. and proc. no. 14. p87-92. 1922. (Separately printed. 1922. 15p.) **6708**

Bibliography of session laws [of New Jersey state library]; guide for the collection of the early laws of New Jersey (1) Table of sittings of colonial assembly from 1702-76; (2) Table of sittings of legislature from 1776-1884. Somerville, N.J. 1899. 8p.   **6709**

Black, George F. List of works in the New York Public Library relating to the geology, mineralogy, and paleontology of New Jersey. N.Y. N. Y. Pub. Lib. 1916. 36p. (Reprinted from the Bul. XX. p501-25. June 1916)   **6710**

Boyer, Charles Shimer. History of the press in Camden county, New Jersey. Camden. Sinnickson Chew & Sons. 1921. 64p.   **6711**

Brigham, Clarence S. New Jersey—Bibliography of American newspapers, 1690-1820. Am. Antiq. Soc. proc. n.s. XXVI. p413-60 (Oct. 1916)   **6712**

Brown, Elizabeth S. An examination of old maps of northern New Jersey, with reference to the identification of the Nutley area, Washington's route across it, and to the boundary dispute between Newark and Acquackanonk. Paterson, N.J. The Press Ptg. and Pub. Co. 1907. 12p. (Also in N.J. Hist. Soc. proc. n.s. IV. p65-74 (Jan.-April 1907)   **6712a**

Catalogue of the "New Jersey archives." N.J. Hist. Soc. proc. LI. p234-5. 1933   **6712b**

A checklist of Monmouth County (N.J.) newspapers in the Monmouth County Historical Association. Monmouth Co. Hist. Asso. bul. I. p12-34. 1935   **6712c**

Colles, Julia Keese. Authors and writers associated with Morristown, N.J., with a chapter on historic Morristown. Morristown. Vogt Bros. 1895. 454p.   **6713**

Collins, Varnum Lansing. Early Princeton printing. Princeton. Princeton Univ. Press. 1911. 47p.   **6714**

Cremer, Henry. Available sources for the study of the economic history of New Jersey. Indiana, Pa. Grosse Ptg. Shop. 1932. 10p.   **6715**

Dunham, Charles B. A reference approach to New Jersey history. N.J. Hist. Soc. proc. LV. p21-42. (Jan. 1937)   **6715a**

Fannan, Mary E. New Jersey state publications on history, geology, geography, climate, resources, industries and other topics. Newark. Pub. for the Free Pub. Lib. 1907. 15p.   **6716**

Gaskill, Nelson B. and others. Report on the condition of the public records of the state of New Jersey. Am. Hist. Asso. rep. 1916. I. p165-99   **6717**

Hasse, Adelaide Rosalie. Index of economic material in documents of the states of the United States: New Jersey, 1789-1904. (Carnegie Inst. of Washington. Publication no. 85) Wash. D.C. Carnegie Inst. of Wash. 1914. 706p.   **6717a**

Heartman, Charles F. Preliminary checklist of almanacs printed in New Jersey prior to 1850. Metuchen, N.J. Printed for the compiler. 1929. 39p.   **6718**

Hill, Frank Pierce and Collins, Varnum Lansing. Books, pamphlets and newspapers printed at Newark, New Jersey, 1776-1900. Newark. Priv. printed. 1902. 296p.   **6719**

Historical Records Survey. New Jersey. Calendar of the New Jersey State Library manuscript collection in the cataloguing room, State Library, Trenton, New Jersey. Newark, N.J. July 1939. 168p. mim.   **6719a**

—— —— Check list of New Jersey imprints, 1784-1800. (American imprints inventory no. 9) Newark, N.J. Sept. 1939. 95p. mim.   **6719b**

—— —— Guide to depositories of manuscript collections in the United States: New Jersey. Newark, N.J. Jan. 1941. 62p. mim.   **6719c**

—— —— Inventory of the church archives of New Jersey. Newark, N.J. 1938- . mim. Baptist bodies. Dec. 1938. 289p.; Baptist bodies: Seventh Day Baptist supplement. Aug. 1939. 161p.; Protestant Episcopal: Diocese of New Jersey and Diocese of Newark. Feb. 1940. 434p.; The Salvation Army—Jersey City. April 1940. 34p.; Unitarian Church. June 1940. 32p.; Presbyterians. Aug. 1940. 562p.; Baha'i Assemblies. Dec. 1940. 26p.; United Brethren. Feb. 1941. 191p.; Christian Reformed. Feb. 1941. 39p.; Congregational Christian. March 1941. 99p.   **6719d**

—— —— Inventory of the county archives of New Jersey. Newark, N.J. 1937- . mim. No. 2. Bergen. 1939. 279p.; No. 14. Morris. Sept. 1937. 135p.; No. 15. Ocean. Dec. 1940. 240p.; No. 16. Passaic. Jan. 1940. 228p.   **6719e**

—— —— Inventory of the municipal archives of New Jersey. Newark, N.J. 1939- mim. No. 7. Essex County: vol. 17. City of Orange. May 1941. 202p.; No. 9. Hudson County. vol. 2. Boro of East Newark. May 1941. 106p. (printed); No. 13. Monmouth County: vol. 7. Boro of Belmar. May 1941. 145p. (printed).; No. 14. Morris County: vol. 8. Township of Denville. May 1941. 150p. (printed); vol. 38. Wharton. 1939. 65p. (printed)   **6719f**

—— —— The Historical Records Survey in New Jersey. Description of its purpose, account of its accomplishments, bibliography of its publications. Newark, N.J. 1941. 66p. reprod. typ.   **6719g**

Honeyman, A. Van Doren. Index-analysis of the statutes of New Jersey, 1896-1909, together with references to all acts, and parts of acts, in the "General statutes" and pamphlet laws expressly repealed; and the statutory crimes of New Jersey during the same period. Plainfield. New Jersey Law Jour. Publishing Co. 1910. 338p.   **6720**

Hood, John. Index of colonial and state laws, between the years 1663 and 1903 inclusive. Camden. Sinnickson Chew & Sons. 1905. 1353p.   **6721**

Humphrey, Constance H. Check-list of New Jersey imprints to the end of the revolution. Bibliog. Soc. of Amer. pap. XXIX. pts. 1-2. p43-149. 1930 **6722**

[Johnston, Elma Lawton]. Trenton's newspapers, 1778-1932. [Trenton] Trenton times newspapers. 1932. 66p. **6723**

Kemmerer, Donald I. Neglected source material on colonial New Jersey. N.J. Hist. Soc. proc. LVII. p29-34 (Jan. 1939) (MSS. in libraries outside of the state) **6723a**

Lee, Francis B. The bibliography of the colonial law books of New Jersey. The New Jersey law jour. XIV. p326-9 (Nov. 1891) **6724**

McMurtrie, Douglas C. A bibliography of Morristown imprints, 1798-1820. New Jersey Hist. Soc. proc. LIV. p129-54 (April 1936) **6725**

Morrison, Noah Farnham. A catalog of a collection of books relating to New Jersey for sale by Noah Farnham Morrison. [Elizabeth, N.J. 1903] 24p. **6726**

Morsch, Lucile M. Check list of New Jersey imprints, 1784-1800. (American imprints inventory, no. 9) Baltimore. Historical Records Survey. 1939. 189p. mim. **6727**

Nelson, William. Bibliography of the printed proceedings of the Provincial assembly [of New Jersey] 1707-1776 [and of the printed acts of the legislature of New Jersey, 1703-1800, and ordinances of the governors]. (New Jersey. Public Rec. Comn. rep. 1899) Somerville, N.J. 1899. p31-93 **6728**

—— Check-list of the issues of the press of New Jersey, 1723, 1728, 1754-1800. Paterson. Call Ptg. and Publishing Co. 1899. 42p. **6729**

—— Church records in New Jersey; notices of the character, extent and condition of the original records of about one hundred and fifty of the older churches and Friends' meetings, with other data. Paterson. Paterson Hist. Club. 1904. 32p. **6730**

—— Fifty years of historical work in New Jersey. *In* Semi-Centennial celebration of the founding of The New Jersey Historical Society. New Jersey Hist. Soc. colls. VIII. p15-167. 1900. (Also in Proc. of the New Jersey Hist. Soc. 2d ser. XIII. p201-353. 1894-95) **6731**

—— Illustrated catalogue of New Jersey memorabilia and rare and valuable books and documents comprising the extensive library of the late William Nelson of New Jersey. N.Y. Lent & Graff Co. 1915. 246p. **6732**

—— Official records of Bergen county in the clerk's office. New Jersey Hist. Soc. proc. 2d ser. III. p174-81. 1873 **6733**

—— The public archives of New Jersey. Am. Hist. Asso. rep. 1903. I. p479-541 **6734**

—— Some New Jersey printers and printing in the eighteenth century. Worcester. Am. Antiq. Soc. 1911. 44p. (Reprinted from the Proc. of the Am. Antiq. Soc. n.s. XXI. p15-56 April 1911) **6735**

—— Sources of history of revolutionary events in New Jersey. Paterson. "Press" Ptg. and Publishing Co. 1900. 12p. **6736**

—— Sources of revolutionary history. New Jersey Hist. Soc. proc. 3d ser. II. p91-4 (May 1897) **6737**

New Brunswick Historical Club. List of readers and subjects of papers, 1870-1914. (New Brunswick Hist. Club. Publications IV) Comp. by the Secretary, Richard Morris. New Brunswick, N.J. [1914] 14p. **6738**

New Jersey. Agricultural Experiment Station. Agricultural publications of the New Jersey Agricultural College, experiment station, and extension service, Rutgers University. New Brunswick, N.J. 1934- **6739**

New Jersey. Archives. Calendar of records in the office of the Secretary of State, 1664-1703. Ed. by William Nelson. (Documents relating to the colonial history of the state of New Jersey, vol. XXI) Paterson, N.J. The Press Ptg. and Pub. Co. 1899. 770p. **6739a**

New Jersey. Department of Agriculture. Author and subject index of Department of Agriculture publications (July 1916-Dec. 1930). (Circular no. 192) Trenton, N.J. 1931. 111p. **6740**

New Jersey. Department of Institutions and Agencies. Division of statistics and research. Publications relating to public welfare work in New Jersey. Trenton, N.J. Nov. 1934. 21p. mim. **6741**

New Jersey. Department of Public Instruction. New Jersey, its history, resources and life; a bibliography of curriculum source materials for elementary schools. [Trenton] 1940. 90p. **6741a**

New Jersey. Department of State. Index of wills, inventories, etc., in the office of the Secretary of State prior to 1901. [Trenton] 1912-13. 3v. **6742**

New Jersey. Laws, Statutes. A guide for the collection of the early laws of New Jersey, giving a table of the sittings of the colonial assembly from 1702 to 1776, and of the state legislature from 1776 to . . . 1844. Trenton, N.J. 1881. 8p. **6743**

—— —— The New Jersey statutory cumulative index, 1925- . Newark. Soney & Sage. [1926-] **6744**

New Jersey. Public Library Commission. State documents. New Jersey lib. bul. II. p6-9 (June 1913) **6745**

New Jersey. Public Record Commission. Acts of the general assembly of the state of New Jersey under the constitution of New Jersey, 1776-1800. (First rep. of the Pub. Rec. Comn. 1899) Somerville. Unionist-Gazette. 1899. p77-93 **6746**

New Jersey. Public Record Commission.
Bibliography of the printed acts of the legislature of New Jersey, 1703-1800, and ordinances of the governors. Comp. by William Nelson (First rep. of the Pub. Rec. Comn. 1899) Somerville. Unionist-Gazette. 1899. p49-76 **6747**

—— —— Bibliography of the printed proceedings of the Provincial assembly, 1707-1776. Comp. by William Nelson (First rep. of the Pub. Rec. Comn. 1899) Somerville. Unionist-Gazette. 1899. p31-48 **6748**

—— —— Description of records in the office of the Secretary of State. (First rep. of the Pub. Rec. Comn. 1899) Somerville. Unionist-Gazette. 1899. p5-17 **6749**

—— —— New Jersey legislative proceedings. (First rep. of the Pub. Rec. Comn. 1899) Somerville. Unionist-Gazette. 1899. p19-29 **6750**

New Jersey. Public Record Office. Condition of the public records in the state of New Jersey. Special rep. of the director of the Pub. Rec. Office, State of New Jersey. Trenton? Pub. Rec. Office. 1921. 18p. **6751**

New Jersey. State Library. Check list of annual reports and other current publications issued by or under the authority of the state of New Jersey, July 1, 1915. Comp. by John P. Dullard. Trenton, N.J. 1915. 12p. **6752**

—— —— New Jersey books and pamphlets in the general library. (New Jersey State Lib. Annual rep. 1900) Trenton. John L. Murphy Publishing Co. 1900. p13-71 **6753**

—— —— Legislative reference department. Descriptive list of laws and joint resolutions enacted by the state of New Jersey, legislative session, 1916- . [Trenton?] 1916- **6754**

New Jersey. State Revenue Department. Index of titles of corporations chartered under general and special laws by the legislature of New Jersey, between the years 1693 and 1870, inclusive; giving the dates of acts of incorporation and the several supplements thereto, with a reference to the pages of the pamphlet laws. By John Hood. Trenton. Printed at the True Am. Office. 1871. 196p. **6755**

New Jersey Historical Society. Bibliography [of the publications of the society]. New Jersey Hist. Soc. proc. n.s. XIII. p339-53. 1895 **6756**

—— Books and pamphlets relating to New Jersey history and biography, published in 1892-1900. New Jersey Hist. Soc. proc. 2d ser. XIII. p35-9, 146-8; 3d ser. I. p145-9; II. p186-91; III. p108-17 (Jan. 1894-April 1906) **6757**

—— Calendar of New Jersey wills, administrations, etc. Ed. by A. Van Doren Honeyman. (Documents relating to the colonial history of the state of New Jersey, XXIII, XXX, XXXII-XXXIV. Archives of the state of New Jersey, 1st ser.) Somerville, N.J. The Unionist-Gazette Asso. 1901-31. 5v. **6757a**

—— Documents relating to the colonial history of New Jersey. Calendar of records in the office of the Secretary of State. Ed. by William Nelson (Archives of New Jersey. ser. 1. XXI) Paterson. Press Ptg. & Publishing Co. 1890. 770p. **6758**

—— [List of] original documents deposited with the Society by Mrs. Charlotte L. Rutherford. New Jersey Hist. Soc. proc. 2d ser. III. p110-14. 1873. (MSS. on colonial period) **6759**

—— Subject-index to the thirty-six volumes (1845-1919) of the Proceedings of the New Jersey Historical Society. By A. Van Doren Honeyman. New Jersey Hist. Soc. proc. n.s. V. p1-71 (Jan. 1920) **6760**

—— Library. Genealogical index to books, pamphlets, MSS., etc. in the New Jersey Historical Society Library. Newark, N.J. 1923. 45p. (Reprinted from its Proc. n.s. VIII. p83-123. April 1923) **6761**

New Jersey law journal. . . Index to subjects and cases, volumes I-XXIII (1878-1900). Prep. by S. M. Burlingame. Plainfield, N.J. New Jersey Law Jour. Pub. Co. 1901. 468p. Vol. II, indexing volumes XXIV-XXXVIII, 1901-1915. Plainfield, N.J. New Jersey Law Jour. Pub. Co. 1916. 348p. **6761a**

New Jersey Library Association. Junior members' round table. Union catalog committee. Survey of special collections in New Jersey libraries. N.Y. H.W. Wilson. 1940. 113p. **6761b**

Newark, N.J. Free Public Library. Newark-in-print; references to Newark in books, pamphlets, reports, newspapers and in records which tell the story of the growth of Newark from 1666 through 1930. Newark. The Lib. 1931. 24p. **6762**

Osborn, George Augustus. A bibliography of Rutgers College. New Brunswick. Rutgers College Lib. 1900. 11p. **6763**

Pomfret, John E. and Dunham, Charles P. Bibliography of New Jersey history prior to 1789. Princeton Univ. MS. (Comprises 20,000 items) **6764**

Ricord, Frederick W. General index to the documents relating to the colonial history of the state of New Jersey, First series in ten volumes. Newark. Daily Advertiser Ptg. House. 1888. 198p. **6765**

Roome, William. The early days and early surveys of East New Jersey. Morristown. "The Jerseyman" Print. 1883. 56p. **6765a**

Sheppard, F. A. New Jersey union catalog. N.J. lib. bul. VI. p12-15. 1937 **6765b**

Speer, Peter T. The searchers' guide to records of real estate, Essex County, N.J. Newark, N.J. L.J. Hardham. 1889 **6765c**

Stevens, Henry and Whitehead, William A.
An analytical index to the colonial documents of New Jersey, in the State paper offices of England. New Jersey Hist. Soc. colls. V. p 1-476. 1858 **6766**

Survey of Federal Archives. New Jersey. Inventory of federal archives in the states. Newark, N.J. 1939- . mim. The Department of the Treasury. Nov. 1939. 271p.; The Department of War. Sept. 1940. 209p.; The Department of the Navy. April 1940. 154p.; The Department of the Interior. Oct. 1940. 23p.; The Department of Agriculture. July 1939. 221p.; The Department of Commerce. Oct. 1940. 51p.; The Department of Labor. Oct. 1940. 67p.; The Veterans' Administration. Sept. 1940. 38p.; The Farm Credit Administration. Feb. 1941. 10p. **6766a**

Traver, Clayton L. Early Trenton imprints and maps. *In* Trenton Historical Society. A history of Trenton, 1679-1929, two hundred and fifty years of a notable town with links in four centuries. Princeton. Princeton Univ. Press. 1929. II, p1041-9 **6766b**

Trenton. Free Public Library. The city of Trenton, N.J.; a bibliography. Trenton, N.J. 1909. 27p. **6767**

Union catalog of Jerseyana. Lib. V. p83-4 (April 1937) **6767a**

U.S. Library of Congress. Division of bibliography. List of references on Princeton University. Feb. 15, 1915. 6p. typ. **6768**

Whitehead, William A. Catalogue of books, pamphlets, and other publications referring in whole, or in part, to New Jersey during the colonial period, exclusive of the public documents of the state. New Jersey Hist. Soc. colls. V. p477-93. 1858 **6769**

—— Critical essay on the sources of information—Editorial notes—The English in East and West Jersey, 1664-1689. *In* Narrative and critical history of America. Ed. by Justin Winsor. Boston, N.Y. Houghton Mifflin. 1884. III. p449-56 **6770**

—— Titles of the several editions of the laws of New Jersey, including revisions, compilations, and digests. New Jersey Hist. Soc. colls. V. p497-9. 1858 **6771**

NEW MEXICO

Bancroft, Hubert Howe. Bibliography of early New Mexican history. *In* History of Arizona and New Mexico, 1530-1888. San Francisco. The History Company. 1889. p19-26 **6771a**

Bandelier, Adolph F. A. Documentary history of the Rio Grande pueblos of New Mexico. I. Bibliographic introduction. Archaeological Institute of America. Papers of the School of American Archaeology, no. 13. p1-28. 1910 **6771b**

Bibliography of New Mexican ethnology, and ethnography, 1936 and 1937, with résumé of southwestern field work. N. Mex. anthropologist. II. p52-62 (Jan.-Feb. 1938) **6771c**

Cole, Theodore L. Statute laws of New Mexico. St. Louis. F. H. Thomas Law Book Co. 1892. 2p. **6772**

Historical Records Survey. New Mexico. Inventory of the county archives of New Mexico. 1937- . mim. No. 1. Bernalillo. Sept. 1938. 255p.; No. 4. Colfax. Nov. 1937. 94p.; No. 7. Dona Ana. Nov. 1940. 261p.; No. 8. Eddy. May 1939. 213p.; No. 18. Otero. Oct. 1939. 202p.; No. 23. Sandoval. Jan. 1939. 180p.; No. 29. Torrance. April 1939. 181p.; No. 30. Union. June 1940. 202p.; No. 31. Valencia. July 1940. 236p. **6772a**

Keyes, C. R. Bibliography of New Mexico geology and mining. MS. **6772b**

McMurtrie, Douglas C. The first printing in New Mexico. Chicago. John Calhoun Club. 1929. 16p. **6773**

—— The history of early printing in New Mexico, with a bibliography of the known issues of the New Mexican press, 1834-1860. Santa Fe, N.M. 1929. (Extract from New Mexico hist. rev. IV. p372-410. Oct. 1929) (Some supplementary New Mexican imprints, 1850-1860. Santa Fe. 1932. (Extract from New Mexico hist. rev. VII. p165-75. April 1932) **6774**

New Mexico. University. Library. A check list of New Mexico newspapers. (The University of New Mexico bul. Sociological series v. II, no. 2; whole no. 277) Albuquerque, N.M. Univ. of New Mexico Press. 1935. 31p. **6774a**

New Mexico Historical Society. Book reviews. New Mexico hist. rev. I. Jan. 1926- **6775**

—— Catalogue of books in English in the library of the Society relating to New Mexico and the Southwest, January 1910. (Hist. Soc. of New Mexico. Publication no. 15) Santa Fe. New Mexico Ptg. Co. 1910. 49p. **6776**

Raines, Lester Courtney. More New Mexico writers and writings. Las Vegas. New Mexico Normal Univ., Dept. of English and speech. 1935. 90p. mim. **6777**

—— Writers and writings of New Mexico. Las Vegas. New Mexico Normal Univ. Dept. of English. 1934. 142p. mim. **6778**

Scholes, France V. Manuscripts for the history of New Mexico in the National Library in Mexico City. New Mexico hist. rev. III. p301-23 (July 1928) **6779**

Shelton, Wilma Loy. Check list of the official publications of New Mexico. Univ. of New Mexico, Albuquerque, N. Mex. In progress **6779a**

Standley, Paul C. A bibliography of New Mexican botany. *In* U.S. Nat. Herbarium contributions. XIII. pt. 6. p229-46. Wash. D.C. 1910 **6779b**

Survey of Federal Archives. New Mexico. Inventory of federal archives in the states. Albuquerque, N. Mex. 1940- . mim. The Department of the Treasury. 1941. 41p.; The Department of War. Jan. 1941. 13p.; The Department of the Navy. Dec. 1940. 7p.; The Federal Courts. April 1941. 14p.; The Veterans' Administration. Dec. 1940.. 25p.; The Civil Works Administration. Jan. 1941. 10p.   **6779c**

Twitchell, Ralph E. Reports, documents, etc., published by the United States government relating to New Mexico, 1847-1874. Palacio. VII. p159-67 (Nov. 1919)   **6780**

—— The Spanish archives of New Mexico. Cedar Rapids, Ia. The Torch Press. 1914. 2v.   **6780a**

U.S. General Land Office. List of documents relating to grants of land by the Spanish and Mexican governments in the archives of the office of the surveyor-general of New Mexico, June 30, 1885. *In* Annual report, 1885. Wash. Govt. Ptg. Off. 1885. p383-400   **6780b**

—— —— Schedule of documents relating to grants of land by the Spanish and Mexican governments, forming the archives of the surveyor general of New Mexico; Abstract of the grants of lands selected from the public records of the Territory, found in the archives of Santa Fe, New Mexico. *In* Annual report, 1856. (House ex. doc. 1, 34th Cong. 3 sess.) Wash. D.C. 1856. p413-32, 433-9   **6780c**

Vaughan, John H. A preliminary report on the archives of New Mexico. Am. Hist. Asso. rep. p465-90. 1909   **6781**

Wagner, Henry R. New Mexico Spanish press. New Mexico hist. rev. XII. p1-40 (Jan. 1937)   **6781a**

Wootton, Thomas Peltier. Geologic literature of New Mexico. (New Mexico. State Bureau of Mine and Mineral Resources. Bul. no. 5) Socorro, N.M. 1930. 127p.   **6782**

NEW YORK

Archives

Ackerly, Orville B. Long Island town records. N.Y. geneal. and biog. rec. XLVIII. p75-6 (Jan. 1917)   **6782a**

Albany County, N.Y. Index to the public records of the county of Albany. Albany. 1902-16. 27v.   **6782b**

—— Board of supervisors. Index to the public records of the county of Albany, state of New York, 1630-1894; grantees. Comp. under the direction of Wheeler B. Melius. Albany. Argus Co. 1908-11. 12v.   **6782c**

—— —— Index to the public records of the county of Albany, state of New York, 1630-1894; grantors. Comp. under the direction of Wheeler B. Melius. Albany. Argus Co. 1902-07. 14v.   **6782d**

—— —— Index to the public records of the county of Albany, state of New York, 1630-1894; lis pendens. Comp. under the direction of Wheeler B. Melius, and Frank H. Burnap. Albany. Argus Co. 1915-17. 4v.   **6782e**

—— Index to the public records of the county of Albany, state of New York, 1630-1894. Maps. Comp. under the direction of Wheeler B. Melius. Albany. Argus Co. 1905. cccclxxviii p.   **6782f**

—— Surrogate's Court. Index to wills and to letters of administration; index to wills from 1780 to Dec. 1, 1895; index to administrations from 1794 to Dec. 1. 1895. Albany. J. B. Lyon. 1895. 240p.   **6782g**

Banta, Theodore Melvin. Index to Dutch records (in the City clerk's office, New York). N.Y. 1900. (From Yearbook of the Holland Soc. of N. Y. 1900. p110-82, 190-203; 1901. p121-76)   **6783**

Brodhead, John Romeyn. The final report of John Romeyn Brodhead, agent of the state of New-York, to procure and transcribe documents in Europe, relative to the colonial history of said state made to the governor, 12th February, 1845. (Senate document no. 47) Albany. E. Mack, printer to the Senate. 1845. 374p.   **6784**

—— List of documents relating to the colony of New York, found in the archives in London from 1664 to 1718. Senate document 106 C; Assembly document 195 C. Paris. July 12, 1842. p31-113   **6785**

Colonial commissions, 1680-1772. N.Y. Hist. Soc. bul. VII. p123-7 (Jan. 1924); VIII. p26-31, 53-5, 84-7 (April-Oct. 1924); VIII. p116-18 (Jan. 1925); IX. p32-5, 68-71, 99-103 (April-Oct. 1925)   **6785a**

Comstock, Frederick H. Index to wills, deeds, and other instruments and to litigations affecting the titles to real property, which have been judicially considered by the courts of the state of New York. N.Y. Lawyers Title Insurance Co. 1896. 247p.   **6785b**

Corwin, Edward Tanjore. Recent researches in Holland and ecclesiastical records of the state of New York. Read Dec. 28, 1906. Am. Soc. of Church Hist. pap. ser. II, I. p43-66. 1908. (Also issued separately and in the reprint of the papers. 1913. p51-78)   **6786**

Dutch West India company manuscripts. Yearbook of the Holland Soc. of N.Y. 1900. p150-2   **6787**

Eardeley, William Applebie. Queens County, L.I., surrogate records at Jamaica, N.Y.; indices and abstracts of wills, 1787-1835. Brooklyn, N.Y. 1913. (Typ. MS. in N.Y. Pub. Lib.)   **6788**

—— Records in the office of the county clerk at Jamaica, L.I., 1680-1781; Wills and administrations, guardians and inventories. Brooklyn, N.Y. 1918. (Typ. MS. in N.Y. Pub. Lib.)   **6789**

Fernow, Berthold. The archives of the state of New York. N.Y. geneal. and biog. rec. XX. p106-13 (July 1889) **6790**

—— Calendar of wills on file and recorded in the offices of the clerk of the court of appeals, of the county clerk of Albany and of the Secretary of State 1626-1836. Comp. under the auspices of the Colonial Dames of the State of New York and published by the Society. N.Y. Knickerbocker Press. 1896. 657p.   **6791**

Grim, Charles Frederick. An essay towards an improved register of deeds; city and county of New York to December 31, 1799, inclusive. N.Y. Gould, Banks & Co. 1832. 371p.   **6792**

Gritman, C. T. An index to the land records of Queens County, Long Island, N.Y. N.Y. 1920. I:A-H. (Typ. MS. in N.Y. Pub. Lib)   **6793**

Gummere, Amelia M. Manuscripts concerning the Otsego purchase of 1769. Friends Hist. Asso. bul. XX. p21-4 (Spring no. 1931) (Papers of Samuel Allison, attorney and surveyor-general of West Jersey)   **6794**

Historical Records Survey. New York. Guide to ten major depositories of manuscript collections in New York state (exclusive of New York City). Ed. by Harry B. Yoshpe. Middle States Asso. of Hist. and Soc. Sci. Teachers proc. XXXVIII, no. 2, 1941   **6794a**

—— —— Inventory of the church archives of New York state. Albany, N.Y. 1939- . mim. Protestant Episcopal Church, Diocese of Western New York. May 1939- . mim. Protestant Episcopal Church: Diocese of Western New York. May 1939. 69p.; Diocese of Rochester. June 1941. 266p.   **6794b**

—— —— Inventory of the county archives of New York. Albany, N.Y. 1937- . mim. No. 1. Albany. Oct. 1937. 170p.; No. 3. Broome. July 1938. 87p.; No. 4. Cattaraugus. Feb. 1939. 84p.; No. 6. Chautauqua. Oct. 1938. 85p.; No. 7. Chemung. Jan. 1939. 84p.; No. 51. Ulster. Part II. Oct. 1940. 434p.   **6794c**

Holland Society of New York. Inventory and digest of early church records in the library of The Holland Society of New York. *In* Holland Society of New York. Yearbook. 1912. p1-50, 206-7. N.Y. 1916   **6795**

Homes, Henry A. On the correspondence of Governor D. D. Tompkins, lately acquired by the state. Albany Inst. trans. XI. p223-40. 1885   **6796**

Jacobsen, Edna L. Manuscript treasures in the New York State Library. N.Y. hist. XX. p265-76 (July 1939)   **6796a**

Kings County, New York. Commissioner of records. Report of the commissioner of records, Kings County, 1910. [N.Y. M. B. Brown Ptg. & Binding Co. 1911] 131p. (Contains brief inventories)   **6797**

Larson, Henrietta M. The records of a flour milling firm of Rochester, New York. Bus. Hist. Soc. bul. XI. p108-10. 1937 (Papers of the Moseley and Motley milling company of Rochester, now in the collections of the Bus. Hist. Soc.)   **6797a**

Melius, W. B. and Burnap, F. H. Index to the public records of the county of Albany, 1630-1894; maps, grantors, grantees, mortgagors, lis pendens. Albany, N.Y. 1915-17. 4v.   **6798**

Morris, Richard B. The federal archives of New York city. Am. hist. rev. XLII. p256-72 (Jan. 1937)   **6798a**

New York (Colony). Calendar of New York colonial commissions, 1680-1770: abstracted by the late Edmund B. O'Callaghan. (New York Hist. Soc. The John Divine fund ser. of histories and memoirs, VII) N.Y. N.Y. Hist. Soc. 1929. 108p.   **6798b**

—— Names of persons for whom marriage licenses were issued by the Secretary of the province of New York, previous to 1784. Albany. Weed, Parsons and Company. 1860. 480p. (Other licenses were issued later under the title: Supplementary list of marriage licenses, as State Lib. bul., hist. no. 1, April 1898. 48p.   **6798c**

—— New York marriage licenses; originals in the archives of the New York Historical Society. Contributed by Robert H. Kelby. N.Y. 1916? 44p. (Reprinted from the N.Y. Geneal. and biog. rec. July 1915- . Additions and corrections to the volume published by the state in 1860)   **6798d**

—— **Council.** Calendar of council minutes, 1668-1783. By Berthold Fernow and Arnold J. T. Van Laer. (New York. State Library. Bul. 58, March 1902, Hist. 6) Albany. Univ. of the State of New York. 1902. 720p.   **6798e**

New York. Education Department. Division of public records. Condition of the public records in the state of New York. Report of the Chief of the division of public records to the commissioner of education. Albany. State of N. Y. Education Dept. 1912. 8p.   **6800**

New York. Forest Commission. Catalogue of maps, field notes, surveys, and land papers of patents, grants, and tracts situate within the counties embracing the forest preserve of the state of New York. Comp. by J. B. Koetteritz, C. E. (N.Y. Forest Comn. Annual rep. 1890) Albany. J. B. Lyon, state printer 1891. p165-317   **6801**

New York (State) Governor. List of letters received by the late Gov. Tompkins, between the years 1807 & 1817 together with names of the places from which they were written. n.p. 188? 47p.   **6802**

New York (State) Historian. Historical account and inventory of records of the city of Kingston. (N. Y. state local hist. City records. Prepared by the Division of archives and hist.) Albany Univ. of the State of N.Y. 1918. 48p.   **6803**

—— Historical account and inventory of the records of Suffolk County, James F. Richardson, County clerk. (N. Y. state local hist. County records. Prepared by the Division of archives and hist.) Albany. Univ. of the State of N.Y. 1921. 34p.   **6804**

—— The records of Ballston Spa, Saratoga County (N. Y. state local hist. Village records. Prepared by the Division of archives and hist.) Albany Univ. of the State of N.Y. 1921. 11p.   **6805**

—— The records of Huntington, Suffolk County. Romanah Sammis, local historian. (N.Y. state local hist. Town records, prepared by the Division of archives and hist.) Albany. Univ. of the State of N.Y. 1921. 17p.   **6806**

—— The records of Smithtown, Suffolk County. (N.Y. state local hist. Town records. Prepared by the Division of archives and hist.) Albany. The Univ. of the State of N.Y. 1917. 6p.   **6806a**

—— The records of the village of Marcellus, Onondaga County. Elmer P. Clark, village clerk. (N.Y. state local hist. Village records. Prepared by the Division of archives and hist.) Albany. Univ. of the State of N.Y. 1922. 11p. **6807**

New York. Secretary of State. Calendar of historical manuscripts in the office of the Secretary of State. Ed. by Edmund B. O'Callaghan. Albany. Weed, Parsons. 1865-66. 2v.   **6808**

—— —— Calendar of historical manuscripts relating to the War of the revolution in the office of the Secretary of State. Albany. Weed, Parsons. 1868. 2v.   **6809**

—— —— Catalogue of maps and surveys in the offices of the Secretary of State, State Engineer and Surveyor, and Comptroller, and the New York State Library. Prep. under the direction of David E. E. Mix. Albany. C. Van Benthuysen. 1859. 375p.   **6809a**

New York. State Department. Calendar of New York colonial manuscripts, indorsed land papers; in the office of the Secretary of State of New York, 1643-1803. Albany. Weed, Parsons. 1864. 1087p.   **6810**

—— —— Catalogue of the records of the office of Secretary of State with information pertaining to the office. Comp. by F. G. Jewett under direction of John Palmer. Albany. Brandow. 1898. 142p.   **6811**

—— —— Index to volumes one, two and three of translations of Dutch manuscripts in the office of the Secretary of State. By E. B. O'Callaghan. Albany. Weed, Parsons. 1870. 118p.   **6812**

—— —— Report of the Secretary relative to the records, etc. in his office. n.p. 1820. 43p.   **6813**

New York. State Engineer and Surveyor. Catalogue of maps and field books in the Land bureau of the Department of the State Engineer and Surveyor. N.Y. 1920   **6813a**

New York. State Engineer and Surveyor. Catalogue of maps and papers in the Land bureau of the Department of the State Engineer and Surveyor, New York, 1910. Comp. by Merritt Peckham, Jr. Albany. J. B. Lyon, state printer. 1911. p229-75, 731-42 (Reprinted from the annual report of the State Engineer and Surveyor, 1910)   **6813b**

New York. State Library. Annotated list of the principal manuscripts in the New York State Library. N.Y. State Lib. bul. hist. no. 3. p209-37 (June 1899) **6814**

—— —— Catalogue of historical papers and parchments received from the office of the Secretary of State, and deposited in the New York State Library. Made by the Regents of the university, Feb. 13, 1849. Albany. Weed, Parsons. 1849. 55p.   **6815**

—— —— Church records, originals or typewritten copies added to the New York State Library to June 30, 1921. *In* New York State Library. One hundred and fourth annual report. . . 1921 (Bul. no. 760) Albany. The Univ. of the State of New York. 1922. p85-97   **6815a**

—— —— Report of the director [on the condition of the manuscripts after the fire of 1911]. (N.Y. State Lib. 94th annual rep. 1911) Albany. Univ. of the State of N.Y. 1913. p7-36   **6816**

—— —— **Manuscripts and history section.** An inventory of New York state and federal census records. Prep. by Edna L. Jacobsen. [Albany. 1937] 2p.   **6816a**

—— —— —— Reports. *In* New York. State Library. Annual reports, 1890- . Albany. 1891-   **6816b**

New York County. Register. Index of conveyances in the office of register of the city and county of New York. Prepared under the direction and supervision of . . . commissioners of records. William Miner, register. Grantors, corporations. N.Y. McSpedon & Baker. 1858. 262p.   **6817**

—— —— Index of conveyances recorded in the office of register of the city and county of New York. Prepared under the direction and supervision of . . . commissioner of records . . . Grantees, A-Z. N.Y. C. W. Baker. 1858-64. 24v.   **6818**

—— —— Index of conveyances recorded in the office of register of the city and county of New York. Prepared under the direction and supervision of . . . commissioner of records. Grantors A-Z. N.Y. McSpedon & Baker. 1857-58. 26v.   **6819**

—— —— Index of conveyances recorded in the office of Register of the city and county of New York. Prepared under the direction and supervision of . . . Commissioner of records, William Miner, register. Grantors, masters in chancery and sheriffs. N.Y. McSpedon & Baker. 1858. 265p. **6820**

Old New York inventories of estates, 1717-1800. N.Y. Hist. Soc. bul. VIII. p43-6 (July 1924) **6820a**

Osgood, Herbert L. Report on the public archives of New York. Am. Hist. Asso. rep. 1900. II. p67-250 (Also separately printed) **6821**

Paltsits, Victor Hugo. Inventory of the Rensselaerswyck manuscripts. Edited from the original manuscripts in the New York Public Library. N.Y. N.Y. Pub. Lib. 1924. 54p. (Reprinted from the Bul. of the N.Y. Pub. Lib. XXVIII. p359-68, 453-70, 524-47. May-July 1924) **6822**

—— Some manuscript sources for the history of central and western New York in the New York Public Library. N.Y. hist. XIX. p58-63 (Jan. 1938) **6822a**

—— Tragedies in New York's public records. Am. Hist. Asso. rep. 1909. p369-78 **6823**

Peterson, A. E. New York's Common Council minutes, 1784-1831. Am. city. XIX. p99-101 (Aug. 1918) **6823a**

Purple, S. S. Index to marriage records, from 1639 to 1801, of the Reformed Dutch church in New Amsterdam and New York. N.Y. Priv. printed. 1891. 87p. **6824**

Records of the Tontine coffee house association. N.Y. hist. soc. bul. XVIII. p11-12 (1934) **6824a**

Report of John Lewin to the Duke of York, in 1681: custom house records. N.Y. colonial documents. III. p302-9 **6825**

Roach, George. The Historical Records Survey in New York. N.Y. hist. XXI. p187-92 (April 1940) **6825a**

Sawyer, Ray Cowen. Abstract of wills for New York County. N.Y. 1934-39. 12v. **6825b**

—— Abstract of wills of Greene County, New York. N.Y. 1933-34. 3v. **6825c**

—— Index of New York state wills, 1662-1850 on file at the office of the surrogate for New York County in the hall of records, New York City. **6825d**

Stokes, Isaac Newton Phelps. The Dutch grants. *In* The iconography of Manhattan Island, 1498-1909. N.Y. Robert H. Dodd. 1916. II. p355-411 **6825e**

Survey of Federal Archives. New York. Inventory of federal archives in the states. New York. 1939- . mim. The Federal Courts. Nov. 1939. 174p.; The Department of the Treasury. Parts I-III. June 1940. 1482p.; The Department of Justice. Nov. 1939. 119p.; The Department of the Navy. Sept. 1940. 546p.; The Department of Agriculture. June 1939. 446p. **6825f**

Thomas, Milton H. and Shepard, Charles, II. Index to the wills, administrations and guardianships of Kings County, New York, 1650 to 1850. (Shepard geneal. ser. no. 18) Wash. D.C. Charles Shepard, II. 1926. 93p. **6826**

Vail, Robert W. G. The Sherman and Fassett collections of political papers. N.Y. Pub. bul. XXXIII. p7-8 (Jan. 1929) (James Schoolcraft Sherman manuscripts concerning national and New York politics, 1906-12; J. Sloat Fassett's scrapbooks relating to New York politics, 1887-1910) **6826a**

Van Laer, Arnold J. T. The translation and publication of the manuscript Dutch records of New Netherland, with an account of previous attempts at translation. N.Y. State Lib. bul. bibliog. 46. 1910. 28p. **6827**

Vosburgh, Royden Woodward. Early New York church records; a report and digest of the records transcribed by the New York Genealogical and Biographical Society, 1913 to 1920. N.Y. Geneal. and Biog. Soc. rec. XLIX. p11-16; LII. p152-7 (Jan. 1918, April 1921) **6828**

Wyer, Malcom Glenn and Groves, Charlotte Elizabeth. Index of New York governors' messages, 1777-1901. N.Y. State Lib. bul. 100. legislation no. 26. yearbook of legislation. II. 1905. unpag. **6829**

Printed Sources

Archer, Ornon. General index to the documents of the state of New York from 1777 to 1865 inclusive. Albany. Weed, Parsons. 1866. 544p. **6830**

Birdseye, Clarence Frank. A full and complete analytical index of the code of civil procedure and the statutory construction law of the state of New York. N.Y. Baker, Voorhis & Co. 1900. 477p. **6831**

—— Supplementary index to the session laws of the state of New York, with all changes and modifications noted, and under a single alphabet from session of 1897 down to session of 1901. Albany. Banks & Co. 1901. 316p. **6832**

—— A table, chronologically arranged, of the statutes of the state of New York, amended, repealed, continued, or otherwise modified or affected covering the laws passed from the session of 1777 to the close of the session of 1886. N.Y. L. K. Strouse. 1887. 2v. (Supplement. 1894. 371p.) **6833**

Bogart, William H. Index to the documents of the legislature of New York, from 1842 to 1854, inclusive. (Senate document 33. I. 1855) Albany. C. Van Benthuysen. 1855. 278p. **6834**

—— Index to the laws of the state of New York, 1842 to 1855. (State of New York. Documents of the Senate, 1856, no. 110) Albany. 1856. 296p. **6834a**

Brodhead, John Romeyn. General introduction. *In* Documents relating to the colonial history of the state of New York. Albany. Weed, Parsons. 1856. I. p. v-xlv   **6835**

Cole, Harry E. Department reports of the state of New York, containing the messages of the governor and the decisions, opinions and rulings of the state officers, departments, boards and commissions, volume 44, index—volumes 1-41. Albany. J. B. Lyon. 1933. 607p.   **6836**

Cook, Walter A. General index to the documents of the state of New York from 1777 to 1871. Albany. 1871. 575p.   **6836a**

Edmonds, John W. An index to and an analysis of the New York statutes at large, comprising the contents of the first seven volumes. Albany. Weed, Parsons. 1872. 313p.   **6837**

Fitzpatrick, John T. The revised statutes of New York. Law lib. jour. XIX. p72-9 (Oct. 1926)   **6838**

—— Revisions and compilations of the laws of New York. Law lib. jour. XII. p21-31 (July 1919)   **6839**

—— The session laws of New York. Law lib. jour. XIII. p80-6 (Jan. 1921)   **6840**

Foley, Janet Wethy. Index [to] volumes I, II, and III; names of New York state pioneers, whose births, marriages, deaths, residences, were published from July, 1934 to June 30, 1937 in Early settlers of New York state, their ancestors and descendants. [Akron, N.Y. T. H. Foley. 1937?] [102]p. [With Early settlers of New York state, their ancestors and descendants, v. I-III]   **6840a**

Fowler, Robert Ludlow. Facsimile of the laws and acts of the General Assembly for their majesties province of New York, etc., etc., at New York, printed and sold by William Bradford, printer to their majesties King William and Queen Mary 1694, together with an historical introduction, notes on the laws, and appendices. N.Y. Grolier. 1894. clxiii, 84,3,4,11p.   **6841**

Gillett, T. S. General index to the laws of the state of New York. Albany. 1859. 745p.   **6841a**

Hasse, Adelaide Rosalie. The first published proceedings of an American legislature. Bibliographer. II. p240-2 (April 1903)   **6842**

—— Index of economic material in documents of the states of the United States —New York, 1789-1904. (Carnegie Inst. of Wash. Publication no. 85) Wash. D.C. Carnegie Inst. of Wash. 1908. 553p. **6843**

—— Some materials for a bibliography of the official publications of the General Assembly of the colony of New York, 1693-1775. N.Y. N.Y. Pub. Lib. 1903. 73p. (Reprinted from the Bul. of the N.Y. Pub. Lib. VII. p51-79, 95-116, 129-51, Feb.-April 1903)   **6844**

Hannan, William Everett. Indexes to reports of the special tax investigation commissions, 1916-1938. *In* New York. Legislature. Legislative documents, no. 96, 1938. Albany. Lyon. 1938. 579p. **6844a**

Hastings, Hugh and Noble, Henry Harmon. Military minutes of the Council of appointment of the state of New York, 1783-1821; volume IV (index). Albany. James B. Lyon, state printer. 1902. p2451-3038   **6844b**

Havens, Henry H. General index of the laws of the state of New York. [1858-65] Albany. 1866. 335p.   **6844c**

Hildeburn, Charles R. Bibliographical note. *In* New York. Facsimile of the laws and acts of the General Assembly for their majesties province of New York, etc Printed and sold by William Bradford. . . 1694. Together with an historical introduction. N.Y. Grolier Club. 1894. p.cliii-clviii   **6845**

Jewett, Alice Louise. Official publications of the state of New York relating to its history as colony and state. Submitted for graduation. . . New York State Library School class of 1914. Univ. of the State of N.Y. bul. no. 635. March 15, 1917. N.Y. State Lib. bibliog. bul. 59. 62p. (Also in N.Y. State Lib. 99th annual rep.)   **6846**

Legislative Index Publishing Company. New York legislative index, constituting a complete record of all bills introduced in the Senate and Assembly during the 135th annual session of the legislature of the state of New York, beginning January 3, 1912. Albany. Legislative Index Publishing Co. 1912. 443p. **6847**

New York (City) Common council. Index —Minutes of The Common Council of the City of New York, 1675-1776. N.Y. Dodd, Mead. 1905. VIII. p157-478   **6848**

—— Minutes of the Common Council of the City of New York, 1784-1831 (v. I-XIX). Analytical index. Prepared by David M. Matteson. Pub. by the City of N. Y. N.Y. M. B. Brown Ptg. and Binding Co. 1930. 2v.   **6849**

New York (State) Adjutant and Inspector General's Office. Index of awards on claims of the soldiers of the War of 1812, as audited and allowed by the Adjutant and inspector generals, pursuant to chapter 176, of the laws of 1859. Albany. Weed, Parsons. 1860. 576p.   **6850**

New York (State) Governor, 1777-1795. Analytical index—Public papers of George Clinton, first governor of New York, 1777-1795, 1801-1804. N.Y. J. B. Lyon. 1911, 1914. v. 9-10 (Vol. 10 contains: List of papers of Gov. George Clinton, 1773-1815, in collections, other than the New York State Library, p1029-33) **6850a**

New York (State). Laws. General index to the laws of the state of New York, 1777-1901, both dates, inclusive. Prepared pursuant to resolution of the Assembly, April 23, 1901, under direction of Archie E. Baxter, clerk of the Assembly. . . Albany. J. B. Lyon, state printers. 1902. 3v.   **6851**

New York (State) Legislature. Bibliography of codification and statutory revision. Prep. under authority of the special joint committee of the legislature of New York on statutory revision commission bills. 1900. 44p.   **6851a**

—— —— General index to the documents of the state of New York [1777-1857]. Prep. by T. S. Gillett. Albany, N.Y. Weed, Parsons. 1860. 520p.   **6851b**

—— —— General index to the legislative documents of the state of New York from 1777 to 1888 inclusive. Albany, N.Y. 1891. 975p.   **6852**

—— —— Assembly. Index to Assembly bills, 1860-1870. By Cornelius W. Armstrong. Albany, N.Y. 1870. 279p. Same. 1871-1875. By H. Calkins. Albany, N.Y. 1875. 146p.   **6853**

—— —— —— Index to Assembly journals, 1777-1795. Albany, N.Y. 1814. 178p.   **6854**

—— —— —— List of all the incorporations in the state of New York, except religious incorporations. By Aaron Clark. Albany. Jesse Buel. 1819. 106p.   **6855**

—— —— Senate. Catalogue of petitions and papers presented to the Senate; also classified index to bills introduced into the Senate during the session of 1871. Albany. Argus Co., printers. 1871. 70p.   **6856**

—— —— —— Index to Senate bills, 1862-1871. Comp. under the supervision of C. W. Armstrong. Albany. Argus Co., printers. 1871. 266p.   **6857**

—— —— —— Index to Senate journals, 1777-1799. Albany, N.Y. 1814. 143p. **6858**

New York (State). Secretary of State. General index to corporations from 1811 to January 1st, 1898. Comp. and arranged under the direction of John Palmer, Secretary of State. Albany. Brandow. 1898. 2v.   **6859**

—— —— General index to foreign corporations from June 11, 1892 to January 1, 1912. Comp. under the direction of Edward Lazansky, Secretary of State. Albany. J. B. Lyon, state printers. 1912. 191p.   **6860**

New York. State Library. List of official court reports of New York, latest digests, indexes and citations, and of laws, journals and documents of the legislature. ? 1889   **6861**

—— —— List of official publications of the state of New York relating to the history of New York as a colony and state. Card bibliography in the New York State Library   **6861a**

New York. State University. Recent New York state publications of interest to libraries, 1907-17. New York libraries. I-V   **6861b**

—— —— The State dept. of education. Division of archives and history. Ecclesiastical records of the state of New York. Volume VII. Index. Prep. by E. T. Corwin under the auspices of the state historian, James A. Holden. Albany, The Univ. of the state of N.Y. 1916. 382p.   **6861c**

O'Callaghan, Edmund B. General index to the Documents relative to the colonial history of the state of New York. Albany. Weed, Parsons. 1861. 686p.   **6862**

—— Origin of legislative assemblies in the state of New York, including titles of laws passed previous to 1691. Albany. Weed, Parsons. 1861. 39p.   **6863**

Weaks, Mabel C. Calendar of the messages and proclamations of General George Clinton, first governor of the state of New York; with some legislative responses, August, 1777, to September 1781. N.Y. Pub. Lib. bul. XXXI. p539-67 (July 1927)   **6863a**

General

Asher, G. M. A bibliographical and historical essay on Dutch books and pamphlets relating to New-Netherland and to the Dutch West-India Company and to its possessions in Brazil, Angola, etc. Amsterdam. Frederik Muller. 1854-67. 234p.   **6864**

Bangs & Co. Catalogue of the library of the late E. B. O'Callaghan M.D., LL.D., the historian of New York, extremely rich in early New York history and rare Americana. . . . N.Y. 1882. 223p. (Also appears under names of E. W. Nash. N.Y. Douglas Taylor. 1882)   **6865**

Bibliography and cartography of the battle [of Lake George]. (Soc. for the Preservation of Scenic and Hist. Places and Objects. Annual rep. 1900) Albany. James B. Lyon. 1900. p65-8   **6866**

City History Club. Bibliography of the Dutch period. N.Y. 190? 5p.   **6867**

Fernow, Berthold. Critical essay on the sources of information—Editorial notes—New Netherland or the Dutch in America. *In* Narrative and critical history of America. Ed. by Justin Winsor. Boston, N.Y. Houghton Mifflin. 1884. IV. p409-42   **6868**

Flagg, Charles A. and Jennings, Judson T. Bibliography of New York colonial history. Submitted for graduation. . . New York state library school, class of 1897. N.Y. State Lib. bul. 56. bibliog. II. p289-558 (Feb. 1901)   **6869**

Flick, Alexander C. ed. Select bibliography [at end of chapters]. *In* History of the state of New York. Pub. under the auspices of N.Y. State Hist. Asso. N.Y. Columbia Univ. Press. 1933- I-   **6870**

Griffin, Appleton Prentiss Clark. Index to articles in historical collections relating to New York colony and state. Boston. 1887. 8p. (From the Boston Pub. Lib. bul.)   **6871**

Hasse, Adelaide Rosalie. New York state—boundaries, references and other papers in the New York Public Library relating to the boundaries of the state of New York. N.Y. Pub. Lib. bul. IV. p359-78 (Nov. 1900)   **6872**

Henkels, Stan V. Unique collection of broadsides gathered by Gerard Bancker . . . embracing the largest collection of pre-revolutionary and revolutionary broadsides relating to New York city and state. . . . Phila. E. J. Bicking. 1898. 36p.   **6873**

Holden, James A. A bibliography of Oriskany and Herkimer. N.Y. State Hist. Asso. proc. XI. p42-5. 1912   **6874**

—— Bibliography of the campaign of 1758. N.Y. State Hist. Asso. proc. X. p337-49. 1911   **6875**

—— Jane McCrea bibliography. N.Y. State Hist. Asso. proc. XII. p295-310. 1913 **6876**

New York. Public Library. Publications relating to New York affairs under Governor Cosby. N.Y. Pub. Lib. bul. II. p249-55 (July 1898)   **6876a**

—— —— Works relating to the state of New York in the New York Public Library. N.Y. Pub. Lib. bul. IV. p163-78, 199-220 (May-June 1900)   **6876b**

New York. State Library. Catalogue of the New York State Library, January 1, 1850. Albany. C. Van Benthuysen. 1850. 1058p.   **6877**

—— —— Catalogue of the New York State Library, 1872; subject-index of the general library. Albany. Van Benthuysen Ptg. House. 1872. 651p. (First supplement. 1872-1882. Albany. Weed, Parson. 1882. 414p.)   **6878**

—— —— New York colonial history; a contribution to a bibliography of publications, 1899-1915. Comp. by Beulah Bailey. Card bibliography in the New York State Library   **6878a**

New York. State University. School libraries division. A list of books relating to the history of the state of New York. Reprinted from the twelfth annual rep. of the State Dept. of Education. Albany. Univ. of the State of N.Y. 1916. 40p. **6879**

New York Historical Society. Catalogue of printed books in the library of the New York Historical Society. N.Y. Hist. Soc. colls. 2d ser. IV. 1859. 653p.   **6880**

New York State Historical Association. Publications, articles and manuscripts [relating to New York]. N.Y. State Hist. Asso. proc. XXIII- Quar. jour. VI. 1925-   **6883**

—— and **New York Library Association.** Union card catalog of printed and manuscript materials on New York history. Ticonderoga, N.Y. 1926-   **6884**

Paltsits, Victor Hugo. The New York tercentenary; an exhibition of the history of New Netherland. N. Y. Pub. Lib. bul. XXX. p655-84, 759-92 (Sept.-Oct. 1926)   **6885**

Stevens, John Austin. Critical essay on the sources of information—Editorial notes—The English in New York. *In* Narrative and critical history of America. Ed. by Justin Winsor. Boston, N.Y. Houghton Mifflin. 1884. III. p411-20 **6886**

Stockum, Wilhelmus Petrus Van, Jr. A catalogue of rare Dutch pamphlets relating to New-Netherland and to the Dutch West- and East-Indian companies, and to its possessions in Brazil, Angolo, etc. . . . The Hague. Van Stockum's Antiquariat. 1911. 42p.   **6887**

Winters, William Hoffman. Three hundredth anniversary of the settlement on Manhattan Island, 1614-1914; a literary and legal bibliography of the old Dutch province of Nieuw Netherlandt (New Netherland) and the city of Nieuw Amsterdam (New Amsterdam). N.Y. 1914. 34p.   **6888**

New York City

Anderson Galleries, Inc. New York City books, maps, views, plans, broadsides and general Americana from the collection of John D. Crimmens. N.Y. Anderson Galleries. 1916. 61p.   **6890**

Andrews, William Loring. Check list of maps and atlases relating to the city of New York in the New York Public Library. N.Y. Pub. Lib. bul. V. p60-73 (Feb. 1901)   **6890a**

—— The iconography of the Battery and Castle Garden. N.Y. C. Scribner's Sons. 1901. 43p.   **6890b**

—— New Amsterdam, New Orange, New York; a chronologically arranged account of engraved views of the city from the first picture published in MDCLI until the year MDCC. N.Y. Dodd, Mead & Co. 1897. 131p.   **6890c**

Archives of the City (New York). Municipal Reference Lib. notes. XXVI. p82-5 (Oct. 16, 1940)   **6890d**

Brady, Mary F. New York city, yesterday, today and tomorrow; a bibliography of materials. . . . N.Y. H.W. Wilson. 1939. 26p.   **6890e**

Brooklyn. Public Library. List of books on greater New York. Brooklyn. Brooklyn Pub. Lib. 1906. 33p.   **6891**

Bureau of Railway Economics. Library. Railroads in New York City, 1813-1899; a list of references, chronologically arranged. Wash. D.C. Dec. 1939. 74p. mim. **6891a**

—— —— Railroads in New York City, 1900-1939; a list of references, chronologically arranged. Wash. D.C. Dec. 1939. 56p. mim.   **6891b**

Cannon, Carl L. A small library about a great city. N. Y. Pub. Lib. bul. XXVII. p23-6 (Jan. 1923)   **6892**

Chamber of Commerce of the State of New York. Classified list of trade and allied associations and publications in the City of New York, with appendix of governmental offices. N.Y. 1931. 50p. **6893**

Cole, George Watson and others. Libraries of greater New York; manual and historical sketch of the New York Library Club. N.Y. 1902. 185p. **6894**

Colonial Order of the Acorn. New York chapter. Views of early New York, with illustrative sketches prepared for the New York chapter of the Colonial Order of the Acorn. N.Y. DeVinne Press. 1904. 142p. **6894a**

Couillard, Ada S. Bridging the Hudson River at New York City; annotated bibliography. Municipal Reference Lib. notes. pts. 1-3. p25-40 (Feb. 13, 20, 27, March 5, 1924) **6895**

Crimmins, John D. New York city books, maps, views, plans, broadsides and general Americana, from the collection of John D. Crimmins. [N.Y. D. Taylor. 1916] 62p. **6895a**

Demarest, Benjamin S. Catalogue of maps of New York city and vicinity. [N Y. 1908?] 12p. **6895b**

Dengler, Adolf. Descriptive index of the maps on record in the office of the register of city and county of New York. N.Y. Diossy. 1875. 119p. **6895c**

Dubois, Florence. Guide to statistics of social welfare in New York City. (Study 3 of the Research bureau of the Welfare Council) N.Y. Welfare Council of N. Y. City. 1930. 313p. **6896**

Edmonds, John H. The Burgis views of New York and Boston. Bostonian Soc. proc. XXXIV. p29-50. 1915 **6896a**

Fridenberg, Robert. Illustrated catalogue of the notable collection of views of New York and other American cities formed by Mr. Percy R. Pyne, 2d. N.Y. 1917 **6896b**

Griffin, A. P. C. New York City. Boston. 1887. 11p. (Photostat bibliography) **6897**

Grolier Club. A catalogue of the plans and views of New York city from 1651 to 1860 exhibited at the Grolier Club from December 10 to December 25 MDCCCXCVII. N.Y. DeVinne Press. 1897. 38p. **6897a**

Guernsey, Rocellus Sheridan. Living authors at the New York bar; being a catalogue of the books they have written and edited. N.Y. McDivitt, Campbell & Co. 1875. p6-47 **6898**

Harrison, Shelby M. and Eaton, Allen. Welfare problems in New York City which have been studied and reported upon during the period from 1915 through 1925. N.Y. Pub. by the Welfare Council of New York City. 1926. 84p. **6899**

Haskell, Daniel C. Manhattan maps—a cooperative list. N.Y. Pub. Lib. bul. XXXIV. p241-56, 328-45, 541-56, 593-627, 653-75, 725-42 (April, May, July-Oct. 1930) **6899a**

Hemstreet, Charles. Literary New York; its landmarks and associations. N.Y., London. Putnam's. 1903. 271p. **6900**

Historical Records Survey. New York (City). Guide to manuscript depositories in New York City. N.Y. 1941. 149p. mim. **6900a**

—— —— Inventory of the church archives of New York City. N.Y. 1939- . mim. Eastern Orthodox Churches and the Armenian Apostolic Church in America. Dec. 1940. 178p.; Lutheran. Dec. 1940. 152p.; The Methodist Church. Dec. 1940. 216p.; Presbyterian Church in the United States of America. March 1940. 160p.; Protestant Episcopal Church in the United States of America: Diocese of Long Island, Brooklyn and Queens, vol. 1. Feb. 1940. 58p.; vol. 2. Sept. 1940. 67p.; Reformed Church in America. Aug. 1939. 95p.; Society of Friends. 1940. 224p.; Roman Catholic Church, Archdiocese of New York. July 1941. 181p. **6900b**

—— —— Inventory of the county and borough archives of New York City. N.Y. 1939- . mim. No. 1. Bronx. Feb. 1940.; 336p.; No. 5. Richmond. Aug. 1939. 411p. **6900c**

Holmes, John B. List of maps of estates in the city of New York, published by John B. Holmes. Hist. mag. 3d ser. II. p260-4. 1873 **6900d**

Jordan, Joshua Hawkins. Catalogue of a loan exhibition of rare views of old New York city exhibited by Lawyers Title Insurance and Trust Company. New Rochelle [?] N.Y. 1909. 53p. **6900e**

Lawrence, Richard Hoe. Catalogue of the engravings issued by the Society of Iconophiles of the city of New York, MDCCCXCIV-MCMVIII. N.Y. 1908. 87p. **6900f**

McKay, George L. A register of artists, booksellers, printers and publishers in New York City, 1781-1800. N. Y. Pub. Lib. bul. XLV. p387-95, 483-99 (May, June 1941) **6900g**

—— A register of artists, booksellers, printers and publishers in New York City, 1811-1820. N.Y. Pub. Lib. bul. XLIV. p351-7, 415-28, 475-87 (April-June 1940) **6900h**

Meehan, Thomas F. Catholic literary New York, 1800-1840. Catholic hist. rev. IV. p399-414 (Jan. 1919) **6901**

Nelson, Charles Alexander. Columbiana; a bibliography of manuscripts, pamphlets and books relating to the history of King's College, Columbia College, Columbia University. N.Y. Columbia Univ. 1904. 47p. **6902**

New York (City). Board of Aldermen. Special committee to investigate police department. Index to the Record and reports of the committee. . . . N.Y. 1914. 29p. **6903**

New York. Municipal Reference Library. Monographs and reports on municipal problems; some recent reports of exceptional interest published by the city of New York. N.Y. Municipal Reference Lib. 1917. 8p. **6904**

New York. **Municipal Reference Library.** Monthly list of New York City publications. Municipal Reference Lib. notes. I. Feb. 10, 1915- **6905**

—— Subways in the city of New York; an annotated list of selected references, 1910-1927. Municipal Reference Lib. notes. May 18, 1927. **6906**

—— What to read on New York City government; a list of references. By Dorsey W. Hyde, Jr. (Special rep. no. 1) N.Y. Municipal Reference Lib. 1918. 8p. **6907**

New York. **Public Library.** Check list of engraved views of the city of New York in the New York Public Library. N.Y. Pub. Lib. bul. V. p222-6 (June 1901) **6907a**

—— —— Check list of maps in the New York Public Library relating to the city of Brooklyn and to Kings County. N.Y. Pub. Lib. bul. VI. p84-8 (March 1902) **6907b**

—— —— Lists of works relating to New York City. N. Y. Pub. Lib. bul. V. 1901. (Lists on numerous phases of the city's history in this volume, including a list of maps) **6908**

—— New York City and the development of trade; a reading list. N.Y. N.Y. Pub. Lib. 1914. 39p. **6909**

—— Selected list of references bearing on the city plan of New York. N.Y. Pub. Lib. bul. XVII. p396-408 (May 1913) **6910**

New York Historical Society. Guide to the manuscript collections. Comp. by Dorothy C. Barck. N.Y. In progress **6910a**

Newmann, Felix J. A brief description of New York, formerly called New Netherland by Daniel Denton. With a bibliographical introduction by Felix Neumann. Cleveland. Burrows. 1902. p5-32 **6911**

Paltsits, Victor Hugo. Bibliography [of New York City archives, unprinted, documents and manuscripts, printed sources, secondary sources]. *In* Stokes, I. N. Phelps. The Iconography of Manhattan Island, 1498-1909. N.Y. Robert H. Dodd. 1928. VI. p181-281 **6912**

Reynolds, James Bronson. A civic bibliography for Greater New York. N.Y. Russell Sage Foundation. 1911. 296p. **6913**

Stokes, Isaac Newton Phelps. The iconography of Manhattan Island, 1498-1909, compiled from original sources and illustrated by photo-intaglio reproductions of important maps, plans, views and documents in public and private collections. N.Y. R. H. Dodd. 1915-1928. 6v. **6913a**

Valentine, David Thomas. Historical index to manuals of the corporation of the city of New York (Valentine's manuals) 1841 to 1870. N.Y. Francis P. Harper. 1900. 95p. **6914**

Wall, Alexander J. The printing of the records of the city of New York in the days of William M. Tweed by the "ring." N.Y. Hist. Soc. bul. VII. p88-97 (Oct. 1923) (Concerns 15 volumes of the minutes of the Common council of the city of New York, 1675-1776 in the New York Hist. Soc.) **6914a**

Walter, Henrietta R. Investigations of industries in New York city, 1905-1921; a revision of a list of published reports, compiled in 1916 and reprinted with the permission of the Russell Sage Foundation. Revised and comp. by Mary E. Brown. N.Y. Vocational Guidance and Employment Service for Juniors. 1921. 35p. **6915**

Weitenkampf, Frank. The Eno collection of New York city views. N.Y. Pub. Lib. bul. XXIX. p327-54, 385-414 (May-June 1925) (Also issued separately) **6915a**

Wilson, James Grant. The Knickerbocker authors. *In* The memorial history of the City of New York. N.Y. N.Y. Hist. Co. 1893. IV. p54-77 **6916**

Local

Albany **Institute and Historical and Art Society. Library.** Albany authors; a list of books written by Albanians, contained in the collection of the Albany Institute and Historical and Art society, 1902, with biographical data. Librarian, Cuyler Reynolds. [Albany? 1902?] 107p. **6917**

Anderson, John. Bibliography of books printed on Long Island before 1831. Queens Borough Pub. Lib. 89-14 Parsons Blvd. Jamaica, N.Y. In progress **6917a**

Beal, Minnie M. Bibliography of New York canals and navigable waterways. *In* Whitford, Noble E. History of the canal system of the state of New York, together with brief histories of the canals of the United States and Canada. Albany. Brandow Ptg. Co. 1906. II. p1173-366 (Supplement to the Annual report of the State engineer and surveyor of the state of New York for 1905) **6918**

Bestor, Arthur Eugene, Jr. Chautauqua publications; an historical and bibliographical guide. Chautauqua, N.Y. Chautauqua Press. 1934. 67p. **6919**

Chase, Franklin H. Where to find it; bibliography of Syracuse history. Pub. by the Onondaga Hist. Asso. Syracuse. Dehler Press. 1920. 219p. **6920**

Chautauqua; a bibliography of the lake and vicinity. Bul. of bibliog. I. p86-7 (July 1898) **6921**

Clark, Edith. Niagara Falls, a partial bibliography. Bul. of bibliog. III. p85-90 (July 1903) **6922**

Cornell University. **Library.** References for the history of the settlement of western New York. Cornell Univ. Lib. bul. I. p181-2 (July 1883) **6923**

Donaldson, Alfred L. Bibliography. *In* A history of the Adirondacks. N.Y. Century. 1921. II. p299-363 **6924**

Dow, Charles Mason. Anthology and bibliography of Niagara Falls. Albany. Pub. by the state of N.Y., J. B. Lyon. 1921. 2v. **6925**

Dutchess County Historical Society. Index to the Year books of the Dutchess County Historical Society, 1914-1927. [Poughkeepsie?] 1927. 31p. Index . . . volume 13 (1928)-volume 18 (1933). [n.p. 1933] p69-78 **6925a**

East Hampton, N.Y. Free Library. Why the Long Island collection? East Hampton. East Hampton Star Press. 1937? 14p. **6925b**

Foreman, Edward R. Proposed bibliography of Rochester publications, together with check list of Rochester publications, 1816-1860. Rochester. Pub. by Rochester Hist. Soc. 1926. 80p. (Reprinted from vol. V. publications fund ser. of the Rochester Hist. Soc.) **6926**

Fryer, Thomas T. A catalogue of books, pamphlets, engravings, etc., relating to Niagara Falls. Buffalo, N.Y. T. T. Fryer. 1894 **6927**

Grabau, Amadeus W. Partial bibliography of the geology of Niagara and the Great Lakes. Annual rep. of the Commissioners of the State Reservation at Niagara. XVIII. p130-9. 1900 **6928**

Hall, C. R. Critical bibliography of Long Island. Garden City, N.Y. Adelphia College. In progress **6928a**

Haskell, Daniel C. A partial bibliography of Niagara Falls. Annual rep. of the Commissioners of the State Reservation at Niagara. XXIX. p49-98. 1913 **6929**

Historical Records Survey. New York (State). A check list of the imprints of Sag Harbor, Long Island, 1791-1829. (American imprints inventory, no. 12) Albany, N.Y. 1939. 20p. mim. **6929a**

Holden, Edward S. Maps of West Point and vicinity, 1769-1902. *In* The Centennial of the United States Military Academy at West Point, New York. Wash. Govt. Ptg. Off. 1904. II. p40-4 **6929b**

Hufeland, Otto. A check list of books, maps, pictures, and other printed matter relating to the counties of Westchester and Bronx. (Publications of the Westchester County Hist. Soc. VI) White Plains. Pub. for Westchester County by the Westchester County Hist. Soc. 1929. 320p. **6930**

Kemp, James Furman. A review of work hitherto done on the geology of the Adirondacks. N.Y. Acad. Sci. trans. XII. p19-24 (Nov. 1892) **6930a**

Long Island Historical Society. Library. Catalogue of the library of the Long Island Historical Society, 1863-1893. Brooklyn. Printed for the Soc.; Balt. Press of Deutsch Lithographing & Ptg. Co. 1893. 801p. **6931**

Ludewig, Hermann E. The literature of the local history of New York. Literary world. III. p46-50 (Feb. 19, 1848) **6932**

McMillen, James A. Card bibliography of the Adirondacks supplementing C. A. Sherrill's bibliography, 1898. MS. in the New York State Lib. (1915) **6932a**

McMurtrie, Douglas Crawford. A bibliography of books and pamphlets printed at Ithaca, N.Y., 1820-1850. (Grosvenor lib. bul. XIX, no. 4) Buffalo, N.Y. Grosvenor Lib. 1937. p45-105 **6932b**

—— A bibliography of books, pamphlets and broadsides printed at Auburn, N.Y., 1810-1850. (Grosvenor Lib. bul. XX, no. 4) Buffalo, N.Y. Grosvenor Lib. 1938. p69-152 **6932c**

—— A bibliography of books, pamphlets and broadsides printed at Canandaigua, New York, 1799-1850. Grosvenor lib. bul. XXI. p61-107. 1939 **6932d**

—— A check list of books, pamphlets, and broadsides printed at Schenectady, N.Y., 1795-1830. Chicago. 1938. 35p. mim. **6932e**

—— A check list of eighteenth century Albany imprints. (N.Y. State Lib. bibliog. bul. 80) Albany. Univ. of the State of New York Press. 1939. 83p. **6932f**

—— A check list of the imprints of Sag Harbor, L.I., 1791-1820. (American imprints inventory, no. 12) Chicago. The WPA Historical Records Survey Project. 1939. p23-61. **6932g**

—— The first guides to Niagara Falls. Chicago. Priv. printed. 1934. 12p. **6933**

—— Issues of the Brooklyn press; a list of books and pamphlets printed in Brooklyn, New York, from 1799 through 1820, in supplement to Wegelin's bibliography . . . (Brooklyn Public Library. Dick S. Ramsay Fund publication, no. 1) Brooklyn Pub. Lib. 1936. 22p. **6933a**

—— Rochester imprints, 1819-1850, in libraries outside of Rochester; an informal check-list. Chicago. A.H. Allen. 1937. 46p. mim. **6933b**

Munsell, Frank. Bibliography of Albany; being a catalogue of books and other publications relating to the city and county of Albany in the state of New York. Albany. J. Munsell's Sons. 1883. 72p. **6934**

Nethercut, Mary Bell. Niagara Falls; a bibliography. Madison. Univ. of Wisconsin Lib. School. June 1913 **6935**

New York. Public Library. List of works relating to Brooklyn in the New York Public Library. N.Y. Pub. Lib. bul. VI (Jan.-March 1902) **6936**

—— **State Library.** Bibliography of the Niagara frontier, 1812-1837. Cards in the library **6936a**

Onderdonk, Henry, Jr. The bibliography of Long Island. Jamaica, L.I. 1866. 56p. (Also in Furman, Gabriel. Antiquities of Long Island. N.Y. J. W. Bouton. 1875. p435-69) **6937**

Porter, Peter Augustus. A catalogue of books, pamphlets, engravings, etc. relating largely to Niagara Falls. n.p. n.p. n.d. 40p. **6938**

Remington, Cyrus K. [Bibliography of Niagara Falls]. Annual rep. of the Commissioners of the State Reservation at Niagara. X. p72-107. 1894 **6939**

Remington, Cyrus K. List of publications [relating to Niagara Falls]. Annual rep. of the Commissioners of the State Reservation at Niagara. XI. p75-83. 1895.   **6940**

Rochester. Museum of Arts and Sciences. Almanacs now in the possession of the Rochester Museum of Arts and Sciences. Rochester, N.Y. Sept. 1935 [Rochester. 1935] 24,11p. typ.   **6940a**

Rochester. University. Department of Sociology. Annotated bibliography of periodical references on Rochester, New York, January 1925-September 1936. Comp. by R. B. Goodman. Rochester. The Univ. 1937. 49p. mim.   **6940b**

—— —— Bibliography of published and unpublished social studies on Rochester, N.Y., 1917-1937. Comp. by S. C. Steele. Rochester. The Univ. 1937. 29p.   **6940c**

Rochester Historical Society. Publication fund series, general index . . . Comp. by Dr. Blade McKelvey, under the authority of Professor Dexter Perkins, . . . and J. Arthur Jennings. (Publication fund ser. XV. General index to volumes I-XIV) Rochester, N.Y. Pub. by the Soc. 1937. 198p.   **6940d**

Roger, H. A. Niagara Falls, bibliography. N.Y. State Lib. 1904. MS.   **6941**

Scarsdale, New York. Public Library. A union list of Westchester County books in Westchester County libraries. Scarsdale. Scarsdale Pub. Lib. 1934. 27p.   **6942**

Sealock, Richard B. and Seely, Pauline A. Long Island bibliography. Baltimore. 1940. 338p. reprod. typ.   **6942a**

Severance, Frank H. Early literature of the Niagara region. *In* Studies of the Niagara frontier. Buffalo Hist. Soc. publications. XV. p9-24. 1911   **6943**

—— 19th century visitors who wrote books. *In* Studies of the Niagara frontier. Buffalo Hist. Soc. publications. XV. p25-76. 1911   **6944**

—— Random notes on the authors of Buffalo. Buffalo Hist. Soc. pub. IV. p339-79. 1896   **6944a**

—— The story of Phinney's almanack, with notes on other calendars and weather forecasters of Buffalo. Buffalo Hist. Soc. publications. XXIV. p343-58. 1920   **6945**

U.S. Library of Congress. Division of bibliography. Brief list of references on the Hudson River. Jan. 3, 1913. 4p. typ.   **6946**

—— —— —— Select list of references on federal control of the Niagara River. March 12, 1912. 4p. typ. (Additional references. July 9, 1919. 3p. typ.)   **6947**

Utica. Public Library. A bibliography of the history and life of Utica; a centennial contribution. Utica. Goodenow Ptg. Co. 1932. 237p.   **6948**

Vassar College. Library. Vassar college, 1860-1877; a list of books and articles about Vassar printed between 1860 and 1877. Comp. by students in "Bibliography 2," 1927. Poughkeepsie, N.Y. 1927. 8p.   **6949**

Newspapers

Brayman, J. C. and others. The periodical press of Buffalo; a few reminiscences and a bibliography. Buffalo Hist. Soc. publications. XIX. p153-9. 1914   **6950**

Brigham, Clarence S. New York—Bibliography of American newspapers, 1690-1820. Am. Antiq. Soc. proc. n.s. XXVII. p177-274 (April 11, 1917); XXVIII. p63-133 (April 10, 1918)   **6951**

—— New York City—Bibliography of American newspapers, 1690-1820. Am. Antiq. Soc. proc. n.s. XXVII. p375-513 (Oct. 1917)   **6952**

Brooklyn. Public Library. Union list of periodicals and newspapers currently received. Brooklyn. Brooklyn Pub. Lib. 1937- . Reprod. typ. Prepared annually   **6952a**

Brooklyn Daily Eagle. Index, 1891-1902. Brooklyn, N.Y. 1891-190?   **6953**

Fitch, Charles Elliott. The press of Onondaga; a lecture delivered before the Onondaga Historical Association. Syracuse. Daily Standard Print. 1868. 16p.   **6954**

Follett, Frederick. History of the press in western New York from the beginning to the middle of the nineteenth century, with a preface by Wilberforce Eames. (Heartman's hist. ser. no. 34) N.Y. Heartman. 1920. 65p. (Originally pub. Rochester. Jerome & Bros. 1847)   **6955**

Fox, Louis H. New York city newspapers, 1820-1850; a bibliography. Chicago. Univ. of Chicago Press. 1928. 131p. (Reprinted from Bibliog. Soc. of Amer. pap. XXI. pts. 1-2. 1927)   **6956**

Gavit, Joseph. A tentative list of Albany County newspapers, 1820-1880. 1930. (MS. in the N. Y. Pub. Lib.)   **6957**

Halsey, Francis W. The beginnings of daily journalism in New York City. N.Y. State Hist. Asso. proc. XVII. p87-99. 1919   **6958**

Hildeburn, Charles R. A list of the issues of the press in New York, 1693-1752. Phila. J. B. Lippincott. 1889. 28p. (Reprinted from Pennsylvania mag. hist. and biog. XII. p475-82; XIII. p90-8, 207-15. 1888-89)   **6959**

L.O.P. Sketches of the character of the New York press. N.Y. 1844. 47p.   **6960**

McMurtrie, Douglas C. Issues of the Brooklyn press; a list of books and pamphlets printed in Brooklyn, New York, from 1790 through 1820, in supplement to Wegelin's bibliography. Brooklyn. Brooklyn Pub. Lib. 1936. 22p.   **6961**

Martin, Charlotte M. and Martin, B. E. The New York press and its makers in the eighteenth century. *In* Historic New York. (Half moon ser. no. 4, ed. by Maud W. Goodwin and others) N.Y. Putnam. 1898. p119-62 **6962**

Mudge, Isadore G. Student periodicals at Columbia, 1813-1911. Columbia Univ. quar. XIII. p430-6 (Sept. 1911) **6963**

New York. Public Library. Check list of newspapers published in New York City contained in the New York Public Library, December 31st, 1900. N. Y. Pub. Lib. bul. V. p20-30 (Jan. 1901) **6964**

Salisbury, Guy H. Early history of the press of Erie County. Buffalo Hist. Soc. publications. II. p199-217. 1880 **6965**

Severance, Frank H. Contributions towards a bibliography of Buffalo and the Niagara region. *In* The periodical press of Buffalo, 1811-1915. Buffalo Hist. Soc. publications. XIX. p177-312. 1915; XXIV. p383-6. 1920. **6966**

Stokes, Isaac Newton Phelps. Early New York newspapers 1725-1811. *In* The iconography of Manhattan Island, 1498-1909. N.Y. Robert H. Dodd. 1916. II. p413-52 **6966a**

Stone, William L. Newspapers and magazines. *In* The Memorial history of New York. Ed. by James Grant Wilson. N.Y. N.Y. Hist. Co. 1893. IV. p133-64 **6967**

Storke, Elliot G. History of the press in Cayuga County, from 1798 to 1877. Cayuga County Hist. Soc. colls. III. p49-88 1889 **6968**

Wegelin, Oscar. The Brooklyn, New York, press, 1799-1820. Bibliog. Soc. of Amer. bul. IV. p37-49. 1912 **6969**

Printing

Benton, Joel. Some early Hudson River imprints. Literary collector. III. p119-22; IV. p38 (Jan., April 1902) **6970**

Eames, Wilberforce. The first year of printing in New York, May 1693-April 1694. N. Y. Pub. Lib. bul. XXXII. p3-24 (Jan. 1928) (Reprinted. N.Y. 1928. 25p.) **6971**

Ford, Paul Leicester. Bibliography of the issues of Hugh Gaine's Press, 1752-1800. *In* The Journals of Hugh Gaine. N.Y. Dodd, Mead. 1902. I. p85-174 **6972**

Granniss, Ruth Shepard. The New York printers and the celebration of the French revolution of 1830. *In* Bibliographical essays; a tribute to Wilberforce Eames. Cambridge. Harvard Univ. Press. 1924. p193-202 **6973**

Grolier Club, New York. Catalogue of books printed by William Bradford and other printers in the Middle Colonies. . . . N.Y. De Vinne Press. 1893. 100p. **6974**

Hamilton, Milton W. The country printer, New York State, 1785-1830. (New York State Hist. Asso. ser. IV) N.Y. Columbia Univ. Press. 1936. 360p. **6974a**

Hildeburn, Charles R. Printing in New York in the seventeenth century. *In* The Memorial history of the city of New York. Ed. by James Grant Wilson. N.Y. N.Y. Hist. Co. 1892. I. p570-603 **6975**

—— Sketches of printers and printing in colonial New York. N.Y. Dodd, Mead. 1895. 189p. **6976**

Hill, William Henry. A brief history of the printing press in Washington, Saratoga and Warren counties state of New York; together with a check list of their publications prior to 1825, and a selection of books relating particularly to this vicinity. Fort Edward. Priv. printed. 1930. 117p. **6977**

McMurtrie, Douglas C. Additional Buffalo imprints, 1812-1849. Chicago. A. H. Allen. 1937 (Reprinted from Grosvenor Lib. bul. XVIII. p69-91. 1936) **6977a**

—— Additional Geneva imprints, 1815-1849. Chicago. A. H. Allen. 1937 (*Also* Grosvenor Lib. bul. XVIII. p93-9. 1936) **6977b**

—— A bibliography of books and pamphlets printed at Geneva, N.Y., 1800-1850. Buffalo. Grosvenor Lib. 1935. p82-112 (Being vol. 17. no. 4 of the Grosvenor Lib. bul.) **6978**

—— Imprints advertised in the Whitestown gazette, 1796-1798. Chicago. Priv. printed. 1935. 6p. **6979**

—— Pamphlets and books printed in Buffalo prior to 1850; being a supplement to the list compiled by Dr. F. H. Severance and published in the Buffalo Historical Society publications, VI, Appendix A, 1903. [Being vol. 16. no. 4 of the Grosvenor Lib. bul.] Buffalo. Grosvenor Lib. 1934. 107p. **6980**

—— Pioneer printing in New York. Reprinted from the January 1933 issue of the National printer journalist. 5p. **6981**

—— A preliminary check list of books and pamphlets printed in Geneva, N.Y., 1800-1850. Buffalo. Grosvenor Lib. 1935. 25p. printed and mim. as MS. **6982**

—— Rochester imprints, 1819-1850. Chicago. A. H. Allen. 1937 **6982a**

—— A short-title list of books, pamphlets, and broadsides printed in Auburn, N.Y., 1810 to 1850. Chicago. Chicago Hist. Soc. 1936. 79p. Printed and mim. as MS. **6983**

—— A short-title list of books, pamphlets and broadsides printed in Ithaca, N.Y., 1811 to 1850. Buffalo. Grosvenor Lib. 1936. 55p. **6983a**

Moore, George H. Typographiae neoeboracensis primitiae; historical notes on the introduction of printing into New York, 1693. N.Y. Printed for the Author. 1888. 18p. **6984**

Munsell, Joel. Bibliotheca Munselliana; a catalogue of the books and pamphlets issued from the press of Joel Munsell, from the year 1828 to 1870. Albany. Priv. print. 1872. 191p. **6984a**

New York. Public Library. New York broadsides, 1762-1779. N.Y. Pub. Lib. bul. III. p23-33 (Jan. 1899)   **6985**

Sargent, George H. James Rivington, the Tory printer; a study of the Loyalist pamphlets of the Revolution. Am. collector. II. p336-41 (June 1926)   **6986**

Severance, Frank H. Pamphlets and books printed in Buffalo prior to 1850; contributions towards a bibliography of the Niagara region. Buffalo Hist. Soc. publications. VI. p547-605. 1903   **6987**

W.B. Catalogue of works printed by William Bradford. Hist. mag. III. p173-6 (March 1859)   **6988**

Williams, John Camp. An Oneida County printer; William Williams, printer, publisher, editor; with a bibliography of the press at Utica, Oneida County, New York, from 1803-1838. N.Y. Scribner's. 1906. 26,211p.   **6989**

Miscellaneous

Asher, George Michael. A list of maps and charts of New-Netherland, and of the views of New-Amsterdam, being a supplement to his bibliographical essay on New-Netherland. Amsterdam. Frederik Muller; N.Y. Charles B. Norton. 1855. 22, 23p.   **6989a**

Brodhead, John Romeyn. Observations respecting the two ancient maps of New Netherland found in the royal archives of the Hague in 1841, by J. Romeyn Brodhead. N.Y. Hist. Soc. proc. 1845. p183-92   **6989b**

Clarke, John Mason. A list of publications relating to the geology and paleontology of the state of New York, 1876-1893. *In* New York. State Geologist. Thirteenth annual report, 1893. Albany. James B. Lyon. 1894. I. p561-97 (Reprinted from N.Y. State Museum rep. XLVII. p753-91. 1893)   **6989c**

Ellis, Mary. Index to publications of the New York State Natural History Survey and New York State Museum, 1837-1902; also including other New York publications on related subjects. N.Y. State Museum bul. no. 66, misc. no. 2. p239-653 (June 1903)   **6989d**

Gannett, Henry. The mapping of New York state. Am. Geog. Soc. bul. XXVII. p21-9. 1895   **6989e**

Heawood, Edward. The earliest maps of the New York region. Geog. jour. LIII. p276-9 (April 1919)   **6989f**

Kelby, Robert H. Bibliography of the publications of the Society. *In* New York Historical Society, 1804-1904. N.Y. 1905. p135-60   **6990**

Leighton, Henry. One hundred years of New York State geologic maps, 1809-1909. N.Y. State Mus. bul. CXXXIII. p115-55. 1909   **6990a**

Moore, Kay Kirlin. A checklist and index for the University of the State of New York bulletins, numbers 255-1094, June 1902 to June 1936. (N.Y. State lib. Bibliog. bul. 79) Albany. Univ. of the State of N.Y. 1938. 373p.   **6990b**

Neumann, Felix. Daniel Denton's brief description of New York, formerly called New Netherlands; a bibliographical essay. N.Y. Publishers' Wkly. 1902. 7p. (Reprinted from the Publishers' wkly. LXI; *also in* Denton, Daniel. A brief description of New York. Cleveland. 1902. p5-32)   **6990c**

New York. Department of Agriculture. Index to the first twenty-five annual reports of the New York Agricultural Experiment Station, 1882-1906. (N.Y. State Agricultural Experiment Station. Annual rep. XXVI. pt. 1) Albany, N.Y. 1908. p355-456   **6991**

New York (State). Historian. Handbook of historical and patriotic societies in New York state, including list of local historians. Albany. Univ. of the State of N.Y. 1926. 63p.   **6991a**

New York. State Education Department. Bibliography of research studies in education (New York) completed since September 1929. Albany, N.Y. 1930. 23p. MS.   **6992**

New York. State Library. Catalogue of New York State Library: 1856. Maps, manuscripts, engravings, coins, &. Albany. C. Van Benthuysen. 1857. 224p. (v. III of the Catalogue of the library)   **6992a**

New York. State University. Bibliography of research studies in education pertaining to New York state. Prepared by New York Education Department, Educational research division. Albany Univ. of the State of N.Y. Press. 1932. 30p.   **6993**

—— Needed educational research in New York state and research studies in progress, 1931-1932. Albany. Univ. of the State of N.Y. Press. 1932   **6993a**

—— —— The State dept. of education. Handbooks of historical and patriotic societies in New York state, including list of local historians. Prepared by the State Department of education, Division of archives and history. Albany. Univ. of the State of N.Y. Press. 1926. 63p.   **6994**

New York (City). Municipal Reference Library. Constitutional revision: a list of references selected for a preliminary study of the problem of revision of the New York state constitution. Comp. by M. M. Kehl. N.Y. March 4, 1937. 5p. mim.   **6994a**

New York City manuals (Valentine's). An index to the illustrations in the Manuals of the corporation of the city of New York, 1841-1870. N.Y. Soc. of Iconophiles. 1906. 107p. (The manuals were compiled chiefly by David Thomas Valentine; the index was prepared by Richard H. Lawrence)   **6994b**

New York. Public Library. Bulletin; index to volumes 1-40, 1897-1936. Comp. and ed. by Daniel C. Haskell. N.Y. N.Y. Pub. Lib. 1937. 197p. 6994c

New York Genealogical and Biographical Society. Subject index of the New York genealogical and biographical record, volumes I-XXXVIII. Comp. by Florence E. Youngs. N.Y. N. Y. Geneal. and Biog. Soc. 1907. 47p. 6995

New York history. Index to proceedings, volumes XXIV to XXXIII, quarterly journal, volumes VII to XII, New York history, volumes XIII to XVI. N.Y. hist. XVI. p502-48 (Oct. 1935) 6995a

New York State Historical Association. Index to proceedings, volumes I to XXIII, Quarterly journal, volumes I to VI. N.Y. State Hist. Asso. proc. XXIII. Quar. jour. VI. p421-66. 1925 6996

Sherman, Louis R. List of publications of New York State Public Service Commission, first district. [N.Y.] Pub. Service Comn. Lib. June 1910. [15]p. typ. 6997

Vail, Robert W. G. Bibliography of promotion literature of New York State, 1790-1850. Albany. New York State Lib. In progress 6997a

Valentine, David Thomas. List of maps and other illustrations which have appeared in the manual from its commencement to the present time. N.Y. 1857 6997b

Wall, Alexander J. A list of New York almanacs, 1694-1850. N.Y. N.Y. Pub. Lib. 1921. 122p. (Reprinted from the N.Y. Pub. Lib. bul. XXIV. p287-96, 335-55, 389-413, 443-60, 508-19, 543-59, 620-41. May-Nov. 1920) 6998

NORTH CAROLINA

Bassett, John S. Report on the public archives of North Carolina. Am. Hist. Asso. rep. 1900. II. p251-66; 1901. II. p342-52 6999

Bassett, John S., Raper, Charles Lee and Vaughan, J. H. North Carolina county archives. Am Hist. Asso. rep. 1904. p603-27 7000

Boyd, William K. and Hamilton, J. G. A syllabus of North Carolina history, 1584-1876. Durham. Seeman Printery. 1913. 101p. 7001

Brigham, Clarence S. North Carolina— Bibliography of American newspapers 1690-1820. Am. Antiq. Soc. proc. n.s. XXVIII. p293-322 (Oct. 1918) 7002

Connor, R. D. W. Index to North Carolina articles in the North Carolina review, the North Carolina booklet, and the North Carolina day program. North Carolina Lib. bul. I. p91-8 (Sept. 1911) 7003

Corbitt, D. L. A guide to the archives of the North Carolina Historical Commission. Raleigh, N.C. In progress 7003a

Crittenden, Charles Christopher. North Carolina newspapers before 1790. (Univ. of North Carolina. James Sprunt hist. stud. XX. no. 1) Chapel Hill. Univ. of North Carolina Press. 1928. 83p. 7004

Edwards, Mattie Erma. Report on Survey of Federal Archives in North Carolina through June 30, 1937. N.C. hist. rev. XV. p389-99 (Oct. 1938) 7004a

Hamilton, J. G. de Roulhac. The preservation of North Carolina history. North Carolina hist. rev. IV. p3-21 (Jan. 1927) 7005

Hill, D. H. North Carolina bibliography for the years 1902-1905. In Literary and historical activities in North Carolina, 1900-1905. (Publications of The North Carolina Hist. Comn. I) Raleigh. E. M. Uzzell & Co. 1907. (Bibliography for 1903 by R. F. Beasley) 7006

—— North Carolina bibliography of the year. North Carolina Hist. Comn. publications. bul. no. 11. p29-31, 98-9. 1912 7007

Historical Records Survey. North Carolina. Guide to depositories of manuscript collections in the United States: North Carolina. Raleigh, N.C. July 1940. 18p. 7007a

—— —— The historical records of North Carolina: the county records. Edited by Charles Christopher Crittenden and Dan Lacy. Raleigh. North Carolina Hist. Comm. 1938-39. 3v. 7007b

—— —— Inventory of the church archives of North Carolina. Raleigh, N.C. 1940- . mim. Southern Baptist Convention: Alleghany Association. March 1940. 12p.; Brunswick Association. 1941. 23p.; Central Association. 1941. 40p.; Flat River Association. 1941. 39p.; Southern Baptist Convention: Raleigh Association. July 1940. 56p.; Stanly Association. 1941. 33p. 7007c

—— —— Inventory of the state archives of North Carolina. Raleigh, N.C. 1939- . mim. Ser. 2. Agencies of fiscal control. no. 4. Local government commission. March 1941. 30p.; Ser. 4. Regulatory agencies: No. 3. Insurance Department. Aug. 1940. 69p.; No. 4. State Board of Alcoholic Control. Nov. 1939. 12p.; No. 5-27. Licensing Board. May 1941. 123p.; Ser. 9. Miscellaneous agencies: No. 1. North Carolina Historical Commission. Sept. 1940. 13p.; No. 5. Board of Advisors of Veterans' Loan Fund. Aug. 1940. 22p.; No. 10. North Carolina Rural Electrification Authority. Jan. 1940. 9p.; Social service agencies: No. 20. Stonewall Jackson Manual Training and Industrial School. 1941. 12p. 7007d

House, Robert B. Preservation of North Carolina's World war records. North Carolina booklet. XIX. p81-8 (Jan. 1920) 7008

—— Preserving North Carolina war records as a state enterprise. So. Atlantic quar. XIX. p109-17 (April 1920) 7009

—— World war records. North Carolina Hist. Comn. publications. bul. no. 27. p13-25. 1921 7010

Hussey, Mrs. M. M. North Carolina folklore, a bibliography. North Carolina Lib. bul. VII. p288-93. 1930 **7010a**

Jarvis, Thomas J. North Carolina must preserve its historical records. N.C. State Literary and Hist. Asso. proc. XI-XII. p19-28. 1912 **7010b**

Lacy, Dan. Records in the offices of registers and deeds in North Carolina. N.C. hist. rev. XIV. p213-29 (July 1937) 7010c

Laney, Francis B. and Wood, Katharine H. Bibliography of North Carolina geology, mineralogy and geography, with a list of maps. (North Carolina. Geol. and Economic Survey. Bul. no. 18) Raleigh, N.C. 1909. 428p. **7011**

—— —— List of maps of North Carolina. *In* North Carolina. Geological Survey, 1891-1925. Bibliography of North Carolina geology, mineralogy and geography, with a list of maps. . . . Raleigh. 1909. p271-362 (Bul. no. 18) **7011a**

Leatherman, Minnie W. North Carolina bibliography for 1912-1917. North Carolina Hist. Comn. publications. bul. no. 12. p43-6; no. 15. p80-2; no. 18. p116-21; no. 20. p98-101; no. 22. p86-8; no. 23. p124-7. 1913-18 **7012**

Litton, Gaston. Enrollment records of the Eastern Band of Cherokee Indians. N.C. hist. rev. XVII. p199-230 (July 1940) (Also reprinted) **7012a**

McCain, William D. The papers of the Food Administration for North Carolina, 1917-1919 in The National Archives. N.C. hist. rev. XV. p34-40 (Jan. 1938) **7012b**

McCoy, George William. A bibliography for the Great Smoky Mountains. Asheville, N.C. 1932. 31p. mim. **7013**

McMurtrie, Douglas C. A bibliography of North Carolina imprints, 1761-1800. N.C. hist. rev. XIII. p47-86, 143-66, 219-54 (Jan.-July 1936) **7014**

—— Eighteenth century North Carolina imprints, 1749-1800. Chapel Hill. Univ. of North Carolina Press. 1938. 198p. **7014a**

—— The first twelve years of printing in North Carolina, 1749-1760. North Carolina hist. rev. X. p214-34 (July 1933) (Also separately printed. Raleigh, N.C. 1933. 23p.) **7015**

—— Pioneer printing in North Carolina. Springfield, Ill. 1932. (Reprinted from the Nov. 1932 issue of the National printer journalist) 4p. **7016**

Mason, Robert L. and Avery, Myron H. A bibliography for the Great Smokies. Reprinted from Appalachia. XVIII. no. 3. p271-7 [Boston. 1931] **7017**

Moore, Hight C. The poetic literature of North Carolina; a bibliography. Univ. mag. XXXVIII. no. 1. n.s. XXV. Oct. 1907. 17p. **7018**

North Carolina. General Assembly. Indexes to documents relative to North Carolina during the colonial existence of said state, now on file in the offices of the Board of Trade and State Paper Office in London, transmitted in 1827.

Raleigh. T. Loring. 1843. 120,76p. (Also in Univ. of North Carolina mag. no. 11. I. 1845) **7019**

North Carolina. Historical Commission. Biennial reports. Raleigh. Edwards & Broughton. 1904- (Contain material on bibliography and archives) **7020**

—— —— Calendars of manuscript collections. v. I. Prepared from original manuscripts in the collections of the North Carolina Historical Commission by D. L. Corbitt. (Publications of the North Carolina Hist. Comn.) Raleigh. Edwards & Broughton. 1926. 351p. **7021**

—— —— Check list of North Carolina newspaper files, 1751-1876. MS. **7022**

—— —— Classification and arrangement of collections. North Carolina Hist. Comn. publications. bul. no. 24. p6-16. 1919 **7023**

—— —— Handbook of county records deposited with the North Carolina Historical Commission. By D. L. Corbitt (Publications of the North Carolina Hist. Comn. Bul. no. 32) Raleigh. Edwards & Broughton. 1925. 45p. **7024**

—— Index to North Carolina items in the colonial and revolutionary newspapers of South Carolina. MS. **7025**

—— North Carolina books in the state library. *In* Literary and historical activities in North Carolina, 1900-1905. (Publications of the North Carolina Hist. Comn. I) Raleigh. E. M. Uzzell & Co. 1907. p613-23 **7026**

North Carolina. State Library. A bibliography of newspapers in the North Carolina state library. (Biennial rep. of the state librarian) Raleigh, N.C. 1923. p30-84 **7027**

—— —— A bibliography of North Carolina. *In* Biennial reports of the state librarian, 1918, 1920, 1922, 1924, 1926. Raleigh. Edwards & Broughton Ptg. Co. 1919-26 **7028**

—— —— Complete bibliography of bound newspapers. (Biennial rep. of the state librarian. 1924-26. Appendix C) Raleigh. Edwards & Broughton. 1926. p8-131 **7029**

—— —— Genealogical material in the North Carolina State Library. By Carrie L. Broughton and Pauline Hill (Biennial rep. of the state librarian. 1926-28) Raleigh. Edwards & Broughton. 1928. p11-71 **7030**

—— —— Index to the Raleigh News and Observer, 1922 to date. Raleigh, N.C. **7030a**

North Carolina booklet. Index to volumes 1-20 (May 1901-April 1921) of the North Carolina booklet. Comp. by Grace Stowell. (North Carolina College for Women. Extension bul. I. no. 7) Greensboro. The College. 1923. 27p. **7031**

Olds, F. A. The development of North Carolina records. North Carolina hist. and geneal. rec. I. p47-52. 1932. **7032**

Palmer, Mary B. North Carolina bibliography, 1917-1921/1922. (Publications of the North Carolina Hist. Comn. Bul. no. 26, 28, 30) Raleigh. Edwards & Broughton. 1920-23 **7033**

Rumph, L. V. Bibliography of North Carolina history and literature in 1928. North Carolina Lib. bul. VII. p122-4, 167-73. 1928-29   **7033a**

Survey of Federal Archives. North Carolina. Inventory of federal archives in the states. Raleigh, N.C. 1939- . mim. The Federal Courts. April 1940. 102p.; The Department of the Treasury. June 1939. 151p.; The Department of War. June 1940. 91p.; The Department of Justice. Oct. 1939. 32p.; The Department of the Navy. June 1939. 12p.; The Department of the Interior. July 1940. 36p.; The Department of Agriculture. Parts I-III. June 1939. 423p.; The Department of Commerce. Dec. 1939. 32p.; The Department of Labor. Aug. 1940. 10p.; The Farm Credit Administration. Aug. 1940. 26p.; The Civil Works Administration. March 1941. 16p.; The Works Progress Administration. March 1941. 158p. **7033b**

Swain, Mary G. The press of Guilford County. Guilford County Literary and Hist. Asso. publications. I. p24-7. 1908   **7034**

Thornton, Mary Lindsay. Bibliography of the official publications of North Carolina. Univ. of North Carolina Lib. Chapel Hill, N.C. In progress   **7034a**

—— North Carolina bibliography, 1934/1935-1938/1939. North Carolina hist. rev. XIII. p167-72 (April 1936); XV. p162-9 (April 1938); XVI. p201-12 (April 1939); XVII. p167-79 (April 1940)   **7035**

—— North Carolina, a classified list of books. Raleigh. Library Commission of North Carolina. 1929. 7p.   **7035a**

—— North Carolina collection at the University. North Carolina Lib. bul. VI. p11-14 (Dec. 1924)   **7036**

—— North Carolina state publications. North Carolina lib. bul. IV. p173-8 (Sept. 1921)   **7036a**

Weeks, Stephen B. A bibliography of the historical literature of North Carolina. (Harvard Univ. Lib. Bibliog. contributions no. 48) Cambridge, Mass. 1895. 79p.   **7037**

—— Historical review of The Colonial and state records of North Carolina. *In* North Carolina. Index to the colonial and state records of North Carolina, IV, The state records of North Carolina, XXX. Goldsboro, N,C. Nash Bros.; Charlotte. Observer Ptg. House. 1914. (Reprinted. Raleigh. E. M. Uzzell & Co. 1914. 169p.)   **7038**

—— Index to the colonial and state records of North Carolina covering volumes I-XXV. *In* North Carolina. The Colonial and state records of North Carolina, XXVII-XXX. Goldsboro, N.C. Nash Bros.; Charlotte. The Observer Ptg. House. 1909-14. 4v.   **7039**

—— Libraries and literature in North Carolina in the eighteenth century. Am. Hist. Asso. rep. 1895. p169-267   **7040**

—— The North Carolina historians. North Carolina Hist. Comn. publications. bul. no. 18. p71-86. 1915   **7041**

—— The pre-revolutionary printers of North Carolina: Davis, Steuart and Boyd. North Carolina booklet. XV. p104-21 (Oct. 1915)   **7042**

—— The press of North Carolina in the eighteenth century, with biographical sketches of printers, an account of the manufacture of paper, and a bibliography of the issues. Brooklyn. Hist. Ptg. Club. 1891. 80p.   **7043**

—— A select bibliography of North Carolina; list of books for schools, libraries and amateurs. Raleigh. North Carolina Lib. Comn. 1913. 23p.   **7044**

—— The Weeks collection of Caroliniana *In* Literary and historical activities in North Carolina, 1900-1905. (Publications of the North Carolina Hist. Comn. I) Raleigh. E. M. Uzzell & Co. 1907. p575-603 (Reprinted. Raleigh. E. M. Uzzell & Co. 1907. 31p.)   **7045**

Wheeler, J. H. Press of North Carolina from 1749 to 1851. *In* Historical sketches of North Carolina. Phila. Lippincott, Grambo. 1851. p112-16   **7046**

Woody, Robert H. The public records of South Carolina. Am. archivist. II. p244-63 (Oct. 1939)   **7046a**

—— Report on the archives of South Carolina submitted to the Public Archives Commission of the American Historical Association. 1933. ms.   **7046b**

Worthington, Samuel Wheeler. Ancient and rare North Caroliniana; a brief résumé of some of the early and rare publications on North Carolina from 1524 to 1929. Wilmington, N.C. Wilmington Stamp and Ptg. Co. 1939. 12p.   **7046c**

NORTH DAKOTA

Crawford, Lewis F. The North Dakota State Historical Society—its collections, aims and purposes. Univ. of North Dakota quar. jour. XIV. p55-9 (Nov. 1923)   **7048**

Davis, Mrs. Florence H. (North Dakota State Historical Society). Report on the archives of North Dakota completed for the Public archives commission in 1934. MS.   **7049**

Historical Records Survey. North Dakota. Abstract and check list of statutory requirements for county records. Bismarck, N.D. Jan. 1939. 151p. mim. **7049a**

—— —— Inventory of the county archives of North Dakota. Bismarck, N.D. 1938- . mim. No. 29. Mercer. March 1941. 125p.; No. 53. Williams. April 1938. 119p.   **7049b**

McMurtrie, Douglas C. Pioneer printing in North Dakota. Bismarck. Priv. printed. 1932. (Extract from North Dakota hist. quar. April 1932. p221-30) **7050**

Mathys, Della. Check list of North Dakota publications. Univ. of North Dakota Lib. Grand Forks. In progress **7050a**

North Dakota State Historical Society. [Newspapers]. (Bul. no. 1. Museum and lib. of the State Hist. Soc. of North Dakota) Bismarck, N.D. 1917. unpag. **7051**

Survey of Federal Archives. North Dakota. Inventory of federal archives in the states. Bismarck, N.D. 1941- . mim. The Federal Courts. April 1941. 23p.; The Department of the Treasury. Feb. 1941. 62p.; The Department of War. March 1941. 17p.; The Department of Justice. April 1941. 7p.; The Department of the Navy. May 1941. 5p. **7051a**

U.S. Library of Congress. Division of bibliography. List of references on Rupert's land and the Red River of the North prior to 1870. Oct. 24, 1922. 10p. typ. **7052**

Wallace, W. S. The literature relating to the Selkirk controversy. Canadian hist. rev. XIII. p45-50 (March 1932) **7053**

OHIO

Baldwin, Charles Candee. Early maps of Ohio and the west. (Western Reserve and northern Ohio Hist. Soc. [hist. and archaeol. tracts] no. 25) [Cleveland] 1875. 25p. **7053a**

—— The geographical history of Ohio. Western Reserve and Northern Ohio Hist. Soc. tract no. 63. p319-32. 1884 **7053b**

Brigham, Clarence S. Ohio—Bibliography of American newspapers, 1690-1820. Am. Antiq. Soc. pap. n.s: XXIX. p129-80 (April 1919) **7054**

Carter, Clarence E. Ohio historiography since the civil war. Ohio hist. teach. jour. no. 8. p274-7 (Jan. 1918) **7054a**

—— Some Ohio historians. Ohio hist. teach. jour. no. 3. p124-7 (Nov. 1916) **7054b**

Cole, Frank T. Private collections of manuscripts. Ohio Archaeol. and Hist. Soc. pub. XVIII. p399-401 (Oct. 1909) (*Also in* Ohio Valley Hist. Asso. rep. II. p18-19) **7054c**

Covert, John C. The pioneer press of Cleveland. Early Settlers' Asso. of Cuyahoga County .ann. III. p861-72 1897 **7055**

Curwen, Maskell E. A revising index to the statute law of the state of Ohio, showing the present state of the law by indicating the changes that have been made since the publication of Swan's statutes. Dayton. 1849. 91p. **7055a**

Feuchter, Clyde E. Journalism in the Western Reserve during the civil war. Cleveland. Western Reserve Univ. In progress **7055b**

Hanna, Charles Augustus. Historical collections of Harrison County, the state of Ohio; with lists of the first landowners, early marriages (to 1841), will records (to 1861), burial records of the early settlements, and numerous genealogies. N.Y. Priv. print. 1900. 636p. **7055c**

Hasse, Adelaide Rosalie. Index of economic material in the documents of the states of the United States: Ohio, 1787-1904. (Carnegie Inst. of Wash. Publication no. 85) Wash. D.C. Carnegie Inst. of Wash. 1912. 2v. **7056**

Hayes, Rutherford Platt. Publications of the state of Ohio, 1803-1896; together with an index to the executive documents. Norwalk. Laning Ptg. Co. 1897. 71p. (Also in the Fifty-second Annual rep. of the . . . Ohio State Lib. for . . . 1897) **7057**

Historical and Philosophical Society of Ohio. A partial list of books in its library relating to the state of Ohio. Cincinnati. 1893. 108p. **7058**

—— Library. Catalogue of the Torrence papers. Cincinnati. 1887. 21p. (Private papers and letters relating to the early history of Cincinnati) **7058a**

Historical Records Survey. Ohio. Bibliography of Ohio. Columbus, Ohio. In progress **7058b**

—— —— Inventory of business records. The D. Connelly Boiler Company. The J. B. Savage Company. Cleveland, Ohio. May 1941. 104p. reprod. typ. (A steamboiler and a printing business whose records are in the collections of Western Reserve University) **7058c**

—— —— Inventory of the county archives of Ohio. Columbus, Ohio. 1936- . mim. No. 1. Adams. Dec. 1938. 237p.; No. 2. Allen. Dec. 1936. 114p.; No. 5. Athens. May 1939. 275p.; No. 8. Brown. June 1938. 204p.; No. 18. Cuyahoga. Vol. I. April 1937. 347p.; No. 24. Fayette. July 1940. 297p.; No. 31. Hamilton. Oct. 1937. 311p.; No. 42. Knox. April 1939. 308p.; No. 48. Lucas. April 1937. 148p.; No. 71. Ross. June 1939. 307p.; No. 73. Scioto. Aug. 1938. 236p.; No. 76. Stark. Jan. 1940. 345p.; No. 78. Trumbull. April 1937. 128p.; No. 84. Washington. April 1938. 330p. **7058d**

—— —— Inventory of the municipal archives of Ohio. Columbus, Ohio. 1938- . mim. No. 18. Cuyahoga County: vol. 5. Cleveland: records. Dec. 1939. 538p. (printed); Guide to records of Cuyahoga County municipalities other than Cleveland: vol. 2. Municipal archives. Dec. 1938. 669p. **7058e**

—— —— Inventory of the state archives of Ohio. Columbus, Ohio. 1940- . mim. Secretary of State. July 1940. 71p. **7058f**

Hooper, Osman Castle. History of Ohio journalism, 1793-1933. Columbus. The Spahr Glenn Co. 1933. 190p. **7059**

Janeway, William Ralph. A selected list of Ohio authors, and their books. Columbus. H. L. Hedrick, mim. publications. 1933. 248p. **7060**

Kohlehmainen, John I. Finnish newspapers in Ohio. Ohio archaeol. and hist. quar. XLVII. p123-8. 1938 **7060a**

Kyle, Eleanor Rachael. Early Ohio imprints. (Univ. of Illinois. Thesis) [Urbana] 1932 **7060b**

Lawyers Cooperative Publishing Company. General index to Ohio jurisprudence, volumes 1-17, by the publisher's editorial staff. Rochester, N.Y. Lawyers Cooperative Publishing Co. 1931. 231p. **7061**

—— Index to new Probate code of Ohio, with parallel references to Ohio jurisprudence. Rochester, N.Y. Lawyers Cooperative Publishing Co. 1932. 102p. **7062**

McMullen, Charles H. The publishing activities of Robert Clarke & Co., of Cincinnati, 1858-1909. Bibliog. Soc. Amer. pap. XXXIV. p315-26. 1940 **7062a**

McMurtrie, Douglas C. Early printing in Dayton, Ohio. Dayton. Ptg. House Craftsmen's Club of Dayton and Vicinity. 1935. 30p. **7063**

Miami University, Oxford, Ohio. Library. The Samuel F. Covington Library of Ohio Valley history, with a sketch of Samuel Fulton Covington. By S. J. Brandenburg. (Miami Univ. bul. ser. XIII. no. 2) Oxford. Miami Univ. 1914. 75p. **7064**

Ohio. Agricultural Experiment Station. Fifty-year index to personnel and publications of the Ohio Agricultural Experiment Station. (Ohio. Agricultural Experiment Station. Bul. 301) Wooster, Ohio. April 1932. 188p. **7065**

Ohio. Geological Survey. A bibliography of Ohio geology: a subject index of the publications of the Geological Survey of Ohio, from its inception to and including bulletin eight of the fourth series, by Alice G. Derby [and] a bibliography of the publications relating to the geology of Ohio, other than those of the State geological survey, by Mary W. Prosser. (Bul. no. 6) Columbus, Ohio. 1906. 332p. **7065a**

Ohio. Laws, Statutes, etc. Index 112 Ohio laws, regular session, 87th General Assembly, January 3rd to May 11th, 1927. Comp. under the direction of Thomas E. Bateman . . by O. B. Parsons. . Columbus. F. J. Heer. 1927. 47p. **7066**

—— —— —— An index to all the laws and resolutions of the state of Ohio; including the laws adopted and enacted by the governor and judges and the Territorial legislature, from the commencement of the territorial government to the year 1844-45, inclusive. Prepared by Zechariah Mills. Columbus. Scott & Co's Steam Power Press. 1846. 181p. **7067**

—— —— —— Index to laws in force in acts [of] general nature from 1869 to 1876; with table containing acts and sections in Swan and Critchfield's and Swan and Sayler's statutes, and acts which are no longer in force. Prepared by authority. [Bound with general and local laws, 1st session, 1876] Columbus, Ohio. 1876. 367,249p. **7068**

—— —— —— Index to Ohio laws, general and local, and to the resolutions of the General Assembly, from 1845-6 to 1857, inclusive; with an appendix, containing an index to the documents in the journals of the House and Senate from 1802 to 1836. By William T. Coggeshall. Columbus. R. Nevin. 1858. 302p. **7069**

—— —— —— An index to the statutes of Ohio; contained in volumes XL, XLI, XLII, XLIII, XLIV, XLV, of the General laws. Printed by authority of the General Assembly. Columbus, Ohio. 1847. 95p. **7070**

Ohio. Secretary of State. Check list of Ohio public documents, I, no. 1, Sept. 1933- . Columbus, Ohio. 1933- **7071**

Ohio. State Library. Catalogue of manuscript papers, deposited in the State Library from the governor's office. [Columbus, Ohio. 191?] 23p. **7072**

—— —— Catalogue of the Ohio State Library. Comp. by William Holden. Columbus. Nevins & Meyers. 1875. 727p. (Supplement no. 1. 1875-82. Comp. by Mary C. Harbaugh. Columbus. G. J. Brand & Co. 1882. 296p.) **7073**

—— —— Checklist of Ohio public documents. Columbus. Ohio State Lib. 1930. 6p. **7074**

—— —— List of newspapers and periodicals in Ohio State Library, other libraries of the state, and list of Ohio newspapers in the Library of Congress. (Fifty-fifth annual rep. of the Ohio State Lib. . . . 1900. Appendix) Columbus F. J. Heer. 1900. p116-279 **7075**

—— —— List of works relating to Ohio canals. Comp. by C. B. Galbreath (Sixty-fourth annual rep. of the Ohio State Lib. . . 1909) Springfield. Springfield Publishing Co. 1910. p35-43 (Reprinted Springfield. 1910. 16p.) **7076**

—— —— Newspapers and periodicals in Ohio State Library, other libraries of the state, and lists of Ohio newspapers in the Library of Congress and Historical Society of Wisconsin. Comp. by C. B. Galbreath. Columbus. F. J. Heer. 1902. 268p. **7077**

—— —— Publications of the state of Ohio, 1929. Comp. by E. W. Hartley. Columbus, Ohio. 1930. 12p. **7078**

Ohio. State Supervisor of Public Printing. Official list of newspapers published in Ohio. Columbus. F. J. Heer. 1916. 60p. **7079**

Ohio. State University. Botany and Zoology Library. Bibliography of Ohio botany (1755-1931). Comp. by Ethel Melsheimer Miller. (Ohio State Univ. bul. XXXVII. no. 5. Nov. 15, 1932. Ohio Biological Survey. Bul. 27 (v. V. no. 4) Columbus. The Univ. 1932. p283-376 **7080**

Ohio. State University. Library. State document list, no. 1-41, Oct. 1915-March 1917. Columbus, Ohio. 1915-17   **7081**

Ohio. Supreme Court. Library. Index-catalogue of the law library of the Supreme Court of Ohio, May 1, 1914. By Edward Antrim. Columbus, Ohio. The F. J. Heer Ptg. Co. 1914. 592p.   **7081a**

Ohio State Archaeological and Historical Society. Ohio archaeological and historical quarterly; supplement to vol. XI, including index for vols. I-XI, inclusive. Ohio arch. and hist. quar. XI. p263-486. 1903   **7082**

—— List of publications with table of contents. n.p. n.p. 1903? 27p.   **7083**

—— **Library.** County historical material in the Ohio State Archaeological and Historical Society. Comp. by Clarence L. Weaver and Helen Mills. Ohio archaeol. and hist. quar. XLV. p95-150. 1936 **7083a**

Osborn, Herbert. Bibliography of Ohio zoology. *In* Ohio. Biological Survey. Bul. no. 23, IV, no. 8. Columbus. 1930. p353-410   **7083b**

Overman, William D. Index to materials for the study of Ohio history. Ohio arch. and hist. quar. XLIV. p138-55 (Jan. 1935)   **7084**

—— Research projects in Ohio history. Ohio archaeol. and hist. quar. XLVIII. p338-40 (Oct. 1939)   **7084a**

—— Select list of materials on Ohio history in serial publications. Columbus, Ohio. The Ohio State Arch. and Hist. Soc. 1941. 36p. (Reprinted from Ohio arch. and hist. quar. L. p137-70. April-June 1941)   **7084b**

—— Some experiences in making a state historical survey. Ohio archaeol. and hist. quar. XLIII. p307-14 (April 1934) (C.W.A. and F.E.R.A. surveys of county archives)   **7084c**

Paul, Hosea. Maps and atlases of the Fireland's counties and cities. Firelands pioneer. n.s. XX. p2059-62. 1918   **7084d**

Peet, Stephen Denison. The discovery of Ohio; early maps of the great west. Am. antiq. and oriental jour. I. p21-35. 1878   **7084e**

Phillips, Philip Lee. The first map and description of Ohio, 1787, by Manaseh Cutler; a bibliographical account, with reprint of the "Explanation." Wash. D.C. Lowdermilk & Co. 1918. 41p. **7085**

Rodabaugh, James H. The accomplishments and future program of the Ohio Historical Records Survey project. Ohio arch. and hist. quar. L. p277-92 (July-Sept. 1941)   **7085a**

Ryan, Daniel Joseph. The Civil war literature of Ohio; a bibliography with explanatory and historical notes. Cleveland. Burrows. 1911. 518p.   **7086**

Schlesinger, Arthur Mier. Bibliography of the Ohio-Michigan boundary dispute. (Michigan Geol. and Biological Survey. Publication 22. Geol. ser. 18. Biennial

rep. of the director and report on retracement and permanent monumenting of the Michigan-Ohio boundary). Lansing, Mich. 1916. p91-118   **7087**

Shepard, Frederick J. A Johnson's Island bibliography. Grosvenor Lib. bul. IX. p33-44 (March 6, 1927) (Prison for Confederate officers in Sandusky Bay, Lake Erie)   **7087a**

Shera, Jesse H. A check-list of Oxford imprints, 1827-1841. Ohio arch. and hist. quar. XLIV. p128-37 (Jan. 1935)   **7088**

Sherman, Christopher E. Miscellaneous data, being volume IV, final report, Ohio Cooperative Topographic Survey. [Columbus] Ohio State Univ. Press. 1933. 327p.   **7088a**

Stevenson, Richardson T. A preliminary report on the Ohio archives. Am. Hist. Asso. rep. II. p165-96. 1906   **7089**

Stump, Vernon Caradine. Early newspapers of Cincinnati. Ohio arch. and hist. quar. XXXIV. p169-83 (April 1925)   **7090**

Survey of Federal Archives. Ohio. Inventory of federal archives in the states. Columbus, Ohio. 1939- . mim. The Federal Courts. Sept. 1940. 96p.; The Department of the Treasury. 1941. 2v.; The Department of Justice. June 1940. 55p.; The Department of the Navy. Feb. 1939. 32p.; The Department of the Interior. 1941. 7p.; The Department of Commerce. March 1939. 30p.; The Farm Credit Administration. April 1939. 14p.   **7090a**

Taylor, James W. Old maps and Indian trails. *In* History of the state of Ohio. Cincinnati. 1854. p156-65   **7090b**

Thomas, Mrs. Cyrus. Bibliography of the earthworks of Ohio. Ohio arch. and hist. quar. I. p69-78, 191-200, 272-83. 1887-88   **7091**

Thomson, Peter Gibson. A bibliography of the state of Ohio; being a catalogue of the books and pamphlets relating to the history of the state, with collations and bibliographical and critical notes. . . . Cincinnati. The Author. 1880. 436p. **7092**

—— Catalogue of books relating to the state of Ohio, the West and North-west. Cincinnati. 1890. 108p.   **7093**

Trautwein, George C. Ohio courts and their reports of their decisions. Univ. of Cincinnati law rev. VII. p60-9 (Jan. 1933)   **7093a**

Union catalog of the libraries of Cleveland and vicinity. *In* Western Reserve University. Annual reports, 1936-1937. Western Reserve Univ. bul. n.s. XI. p69-70 (Dec. 15, 1937)   **7093b**

U.S. Library of Congress. Division of bibliography. List of references on Senators from Ohio. May 31, 1922. 29p. typ.   **7094**

—— —— —— Select list of references on the history of Western Reserve in Ohio. 1908. 6p. typ.   **7095**

Venable, W. H. Beginnings of literary culture in the Ohio Valley; historical and biographical sketches. Cincinnati. Robert Clarke. 1891. 519p.   **7096**

—— Ohio literary men and women; an address prepared for the Ohio centennial celebration at Chillicothe, Ohio, May 20, 1903. Reprinted from the Ohio Arch. and Hist. Soc. publications. Columbus. F. J. Heer. 1904. p582-663 **7097**

—— Ohio literary men and women. *In* Randall, Emilius O. and Ryan, Daniel J. History of Ohio. N.Y. Century hist. co. 1912. V. p1-84 **7098**

Weaver, Clarence L. and Mills, Helen. County historical material in the Ohio State Archaeological and Historical Society Library. Ohio arch. and hist. quar. XLV. p95-150 (April 1936) **7099**

Weisenburger, Francis Phelps. A half century of the writing of history in Ohio. Ohio archaeol. and hist. quar. XLIV. p326-52 (July 1935) **7099a**

Wessen, Ernest J. Bibliography of Ohio almanacs to 1850. 20 North Foster St. Mansfield, Ohio. In progress **7099b**

Western Reserve Historical Society. Partial list of manuscripts, field notes and maps. Cleveland. July 1885. 16p. **7100**

Whayman, Horace W. A complete list of newspapers in the Ohio State Library. Old Northwest geneal. quar. II. p24-7. 1899 **7101**

Wilkie, Florence. Early printing in Ohio, 1793-1820, with checklist of Ohio imprints for that period. (Columbia Univ. Thesis) [N.Y.] 1933 **7101a**

Wilson, Marion Frances. Cleveland's union catalogue. Lib. Jour. LXI. p801-2 (Nov. 1, 1936) **7101b**

Wright, Almon R. Sources for Ohio world war history in the papers of the Food Administration in The National Archives. Ohio archaeol. and hist. quar. XLVII. p355-62 (Nov. 1938) **7101c**

OKLAHOMA

Ash, Lee, Jr. and Wright, Icelle E. Check list of the official publications of the territory and state of Oklahoma from 1890 to date. Oklahoma Agricultural and Mechanical College, Stillwater, Okla. In progress **7101d**

Foreman, Carolyn Thomas. Oklahoma imprints, 1835-1907; a history of printing in Oklahoma before statehood. Norman. Univ. of Oklahoma Press. 1936. 499p. **7102**

Foreman, Grant. Report of Grant Foreman, a director of the Oklahoma Historical Society to the board. Chron. Oklahoma. XIV. p3-8 (March 1936) (MS. material on Oklahoma) **7103**

—— Sources of Oklahoma history. Chron. Oklahoma. V. p42-57 (March 1927) **7104**

Gleason, Elsie Cady. Newspapers of the Panhandle of Oklahoma, 1886-1940. Chron. Okla. XIX (June 1941) **7104a**

Hill, James J. Bibliography of Indian Territory documents. Univ. of Oklahoma, Norman, Okla. In progress **7104b**

—— Bibliography of Oklahoma and Indian Territory. In progress **7105**

—— Report on the archives of Oklahoma completed for the American Historical Association, Public Archives Commission. [Norman, Okla. Univ. of Oklahoma] 1934. ms. **7105a**

Historical Records Survey. Oklahoma. Check list of various records required or permitted by law in Oklahoma. Oklahoma City, Okla. Jan. 1937. 67p. mim. **7105b**

—— —— Guide to public vital statistics records in Oklahoma. Oklahoma City. June 1941. 85p. mim. **7105c**

—— —— Inventory of the church archives of Oklahoma. Oklahoma City, Okla. 1937. mim. No. 7. Bryan County. Oct. 1937. 24p. **7105d**

—— —— Inventory of the county archives of Oklahoma. Oklahoma City, Okla. 1937- . mim. No. 3. Atoka. Feb. 1941. 125p.; No. 5. Beckham. March 1939. 238p.; No. 11. Cherokee. Aug. 1941. 156p.; No. 13. Cimarron. Jan. 1938. 104p.; No. 31. Haskell. July 1940. 113p.; No. 41. Lincoln. Jan. 1940. 128p. (prelim. ed.); No. 46. McIntosh. June 1938. 183p.; No. 49. Mayes. May 1937. 127p.; No. 51. Muskogee. Dec. 1937. 18ip.; No. 61. Pittsburg. May 1940. 182p.; No. 64. Pushmataha. May 1938. 173p. **7105e**

—— —— Inventory of records in Muskogee County court house. (Muskogee) 1936. mim. **7105f**

—— —— Inventory of the state archives of Oklahoma. Oklahoma City, Okla. 1938- . mim. A list of records of the state of Oklahoma. Dec. 1938. 272p. **7105g**

—— —— Report on the accomplishments and activities of the Oklahoma Historical Records Survey (February 18, 1936 to January 20, 1940) Oklahoma City, Okla. Oklahoma Hist. Soc. 1940. 13p. reprod. **7105h**

Iben, Icko. A survey of research materials in Oklahoma libraries. Stillwater. A. and M. College. 1937. 44p. **7105i**

McMurtrie, Douglas C. Pioneer printing in Oklahoma. Springfield, Ill. 1932. 3p. (Reprinted from the May 1932 issue of National printer journalist) **7106**

Marable, Mary Hays and Boylan, Elaine. A handbook of Oklahoma writers. Norman, Univ. of Oklahoma Press, 1939. 308p. **7106a**

Oklahoma. Library Commission. Oklahoma libraries, 1900-1937; a history and handbook. Oklahoma City. The Commission. 1937. 276p. **7106b**

—— —— Union card catalog of books in the state on Oklahoma history. Oklahoma City, Okla. **7106c**

—— —— Union catalog of Oklahomiana in libraries in the state. Oklahoma City, Okla. Cards **7106d**

Oklahoma. State Planning Board. A compendium of maps and charts pertaining to state planning in Oklahoma. Oklahoma City. 1936. 132p. lithog. **7106e**

Oklahoma. University. Bibliographies on the political and journalistic history of Oklahoma. Norman, Okla. CWA project
7106f
—— —— Bibliography on regional geography. Norman, Okla. CWA project
7106g
Oklahoma Historical Society. Index and catalog of newspapers and other historical archives in Oklahoma. Oklahoma City. WPA project **7106h**
—— Manuscript sources for the history of Oklahoma. Comp. by James W. Moffitt. In progress **7106i**
—— **Library.** Biographical index. Oklahoma City, Okla. In progress **7106j**
—— —— Index to the manuscript collections. Oklahoma City, Okla. In progress
7106k
—— —— Index to Oklahoma newspapers. Oklahoma City, Okla. In progress **7106l**
Ray, Grace Ernestine. Early Oklahoma newspapers; history and description of publications from earliest beginnings to 1889. (Univ. of Oklahoma bul. n.s. no. 407. Stud. no. 28) Norman. Univ of Oklahoma. [1928] 119p. **7107**
Survey of Federal Archives. Oklahoma. Inventory of federal archives in the states. Oklahoma City, Okla. 1938- . mim. The Federal Courts. June 1939. 60p.; The Department of the Treasury. June 1938. 60p.; The Department of War. June 1938. 158p.; The Department of Justice. May 1939. 97p.; The Department of the Navy. May 1939. 11p.; The Department of Agriculture. Nov. 1938. 313p.; The Department of Commerce. May 1940. 6p.; The Department of Labor. Nov. 1938. 35p.; The Veterans' Administration. May 1940. 34p.; The Works Progress Administration. Nov. 1939. 89p.; The Farm Credit Administration. Sept. 1938. 41p.; The Emergency Relief Administration. Dec. 1940. 36p.; Miscellaneous agencies. Oct. 1940. 110p. **7107a**
Thomas, Sister Ursula. The Catholic church on the Oklahoma frontier; a critical bibliography. Mid-America. XX. p186-207. 1938 **7107b**
Trout, L. E. and Myers, G. H. Bibliography of Oklahoma geology with subject index. (Oklahoma Geol. Survey bul. 25) Norman. 1915. 105p. **7107c**
U.S. Bureau of Agricultural Economics. Library. Okfuskee County, Oklahoma· a selected list of references. Comp. by Howard B. Turner. (Economic library list no. 28) Wash. D.C. June 1941. 13p. mim. **7107d**
U.S. Bureau of Agricultural Economics. Library. Oklahoma—an index to the state official sources of agricultural statistics. Comp. by Icelle E. Wright under the direction of Mary G. Lacy. Including a list of the unofficial sources of Oklahoma agricultural statistics. Comp. by Margaret Walters (Agricultural economics bibliog. no. 21) Wash. D.C. Aug. 1927. 460p. **7108**
U.S. Library of Congress. Division of bibliography. Select list of references on

Oklahoma. Feb. 1, 1910. 8p. typ. (Additional references. 1915. 1p.) **7109**
Ursula, Sister M. Sources for the study of Oklahoma Catholic missions; a critical bibliography. Chron. Okla. XVI. p346-77 (Sept. 1938) **7109a**

OREGON

Bagley, Clarence B. Pioneer papers of Puget Sound. Oregon Hist. Soc. quar. IV. p365-85 (Dec. 1902) **7110**
Bancroft, Hubert Howe. Authorities quoted. *In* History of Oregon. San Francisco. Hist. Co. 1886. p.xix-xxxix
7111
Barry, J. Neilson. First local government, 1841: index to primary sources. Ore. hist. quar. XLI. p195-202 (June 1940) **7111a**
—— Primary sources to early government. Wash. hist. quar. XXV. p139-47 (April 1934) (Oregon country and the Willamette Valley) **7111b**
Cole, Theodore Lee. Statute law of Oregon. St. Louis. F. H. Thomas Law Book Co. 1891. 3p. **7112**
Dixon, Dorothy E. Bibliography of the geology of Oregon. (Univ. of Oregon publication. Geol. ser. I. no. 1) Eugene. The Univ. 1926. 125p. **7113**
Fairbrook, Glenn. A brief sketch of the early Oregon session laws and codes. Law lib. jour. VIII. p1-4 (April 1915)
7114
Henderson, C. W. and Winstanley, J. B. Bibliography of the geology, paleontology, mineralogy, petrology, and mineral resources of Oregon, with subject index by Graham J. Michael. Univ. of Oregon bul. n.s. 10. no. 4. 1912. 49p. **7115**
Himes, George H. History of the press of Oregon, 1839-1850. Oregon Hist. Soc. quar. III. p327-70 (Dec. 1902) **7116**
Historical Records Survey. Oregon. A guide to the Angelus studio collection of historic photographs. Prep. by the Oregon Historical Records Survey project, Division of professional and service projects, Work projects administration. Sponsored by the University of Oregon. Portland, Ore. 77p. reprod. **7116a**
—— —— Guide to the depositories of manuscript collections in the United States: Oregon-Washington. Portland, Ore. Dec. 1940. 42p. mim. **7116b**
—— —— Guide to the manuscript collections of the Oregon Historical Society. Portland, Ore. 1940. 133p. reprod. typ.
7116c
—— —— Inventory of the county archives of Oregon. Portland, Ore. 1937- . mim. No. 4. Clatsop. Sept. 1940. 273p.; No. 14. Hood River. Dec. 1939. 203p.; No. 17. Josephine. Nov. 1939. 192p.; No. 22. Linn. May 1939. 181p.; No. 25. Morrow. Oct. 1937. 57p.; No. 26. Multnomah. Vol. I-II. June, May. 1940. 222, 218p.; No. 29. Tillamook. April 1940. 240p.; No. 33. Wasco. Feb. 1941. 332p.; No. 34. Washington. Nov. 1940. 300p. **7116d**

Historical theses on Oregon. Ore. hist. quar. XLI. p236 (June 1940) **7116e**

Hughes, Katherine Whipple. A contribution toward a bibliography of Oregon botany, with notes on the botanical explorers of the state. (Oregon State College. Thesis ser., no. 14; U.S. Work Projects Admin. O.P. no. 665-94-3-51) [Corvallis] 1940. 93p. processed **7116f**

Hulbert, Herman. The WPA Historical Records Survey in Oregon. Commonwealth rev. XIX. p251-60. 1937 **7116g**

Jillson, Willard Rouse. A bibliography of the geology and paleontology of the John Day Region, Oregon. Frankfort, Ky. 1923. 13p. **7116h**

Ludington, Flora Belle. The newspapers of Oregon, 1846-1870. Oregon hist. quar. XXVI. p229-62 (Sept. 1925) **7117**

McArthur, Lewis A. Earliest Oregon post offices as recorded at Washington. Ore. hist. quar. XLI. p53-71 (March 1940) (Includes some data on records) **7117a**

McMurtrie, Douglas C. Check list of Oregon imprints. Chicago. n.p. n.d. 59p **7118**

Oregon. State College. List of blue print county maps of Oregon [on file, Room 206 Mines Building, Oregon State College. Comp. under the direction of George C. Martin, May, 1935] 15p. typ. **7118a**

—— —— List of mine and property maps on file room 206 Mines Building, Oregon State College. [Comp. under the direction of George C. Martin, May 1935] 17p. typ. **7118b**

Oregon. State Library. Reports of state officers, 1908-13. (Biennial rep. of the state librarian, 1908-1912) **7118c**

Oregon. State Planning Board. Bibliography of the geology and mineral resources of Oregon with digests and index to July 1, 1936. Prepared by Ray C. Treasher, . . . [and] Edwin T. Hodge. With assistance of W.P.A. project 498-(3)-A. Issued by the Oregon State Planning Board. Portland, Ore. Conger Printing Co. 1936. 224p. lithog. **7118d**

Oregon. University. Portland Extension Division. Bibliography of literary and historical data on Multnomah County, Oregon. Portland. ERA project **7118e**

Parker, Jamieson. Historic American buildings survey. Ore. hist. quar. XXXV. p31-41, 176-9 (March, June 1934) **7118f**

Parrish, Philip H. Oregon literature 1930-31. Oregon hist. quar. XXXIII. p156-9 (June 1932) **7119**

Portland. Library Association. Check list of Oregon state documents through 1925. MS. **7120**

Powers, Alfred. Early printing in the Oregon country. Portland. Portland Club of Ptg. House Craftsmen. 1933. 16p. **7121**

—— History of Oregon literature. Portland, Oregon. 1935. 809p. **7122**

Rockwood, E. Ruth. Check list of Oregon state documents. Lib. Asso. of Portland, Portland, Ore. In progress **7122a**

Scott, L. M. Oregon history writers and their materials. Oregon hist. quar. XXV. p284-93 (Sept. 1924) **7123**

Sheldon, Henry Davidson. A critical and descriptive bibliography of the history of education in the state of Oregon. (Univ. of Oregon publication. Education ser. II. no. 1) Eugene. The Univ. 1929. 16p. **7124**

Survey of Federal Archives. Oregon. Inventory of federal archives in the states. Portland, Ore. 1939- . mim. The Federal Courts. June 1939. 37p.; The Department of the Treasury. March 1941. 330p.; The Department of War. July 1940. 263p.; The Post Office Department. 1941. 887p.; The Department of Justice. June 1939. 28p.; The Department of the Navy. April 1940. 29p.; The Department of the Interior. Feb. 1941. 446p.; The Department of Labor. Feb. 1939. 108p.; The Veterans' Administration. March 1940. 67p.; The Farm Credit Administration. April 1940. 10p.; The Civil Works Administration. April 1941. 15p.; The Emergency Relief Administration. 1941. 26p.; The Works Progress Administration. March 1941. 102p.; Miscellaneous agencies. 1941. 258p. **7124a**

—— —— Inventory of the records of the Provisional and Territorial Governments of Oregon, 1843-1859. Portland, Ore. 1936. 168p. MS. **7124b**

Turnbull, George S. History of Oregon newspapers. Portland, Ore. Binfords & Mort. 1939 560p. **7124c**

U.S. Bureau of Agricultural Economics. Library. Oregon; a preliminary list of the sources of agricultural and related statistics of the state. Comp. by Lucia Haley . . . in cooperation with the library, Bureau of Agricultural Economics. Wash. D.C. 1927. 12p. mim. **7125**

Young, F. G. Report on the archives of Oregon. Am. Hist. Asso. rep. 1902. I. p337-55 (*Also in* Ore. hist. quar. III. p371-88 (Dec. 1902) **7126**

—— State historical activities. Ore. hist. quar. XVIII. p305-10 (Dec. 1917) **7126a**

PENNSYLVANIA

Archives

Ames, Herman V. and McKinley, Albert E. Report on the public archives of the city and county of Philadelphia. Am. Hist. Asso. rep. 1901. II. p231-344 (Reprinted Wash. Govt. Ptg. Off. 1902) **7127**

Ames, Herman V. and Shimmell, Lewis S. The public archives of Pennsylvania. Am. Hist. Asso. rep. 1900. II. p267-93 **7128**

Bethlehem. Public Library. Collection of historical data in Bethlehem. Pa. Lib. & Mus. notes. XVI. p19-20 (April 1937) (MS. copies and transcriptions of early records) **7128a**

Braderman, Eugene Maur and Levin, Bernard Shaw. Pennsylvania and her archives. Pa. hist. VIII. p59-64 (Jan. 1941)
7128b

Burchard, Edward L. and Mathews, Edward B. Manuscripts and publications relating to the Mason and Dixon line and other lines in Pennsylvania, Maryland, and the Virginias involving the charter rights of the Baltimores and the Penns. *In* Report on the resurvey of the Mason and Dixon line, part IV. Harrisburg. Harrisburg Publishing Co. 1909. p209-403
7129

Bureau of Municipal Research, Philadelphia. Index of Philadelphia ordinances; an index of the more important ordinances and resolutions of City council of Philadelphia, with citations of pertinent city solicitors' opinions and court decisions. Phila. Philadelphia Bar Association. 1937. 62p.
7129a

Calhoun, Gertrude L. Collections of the Union county Historical Society. Union Co. Hist. Soc. proc. II. p212-21. 1934 (Description of mss., books, and artifacts)
7129b

Chester county wills and administrations. Chester co. col. no. 1. p34-40; no. 2. 76-80; no. 3. 116-20; no. 4. 156-60; no. 5. 196-200; no. 6. 236-40; no. 7. 276-80; no. 8. 310-20 (Oct., Nov. 1936; Jan., Feb., April, June, Aug., Oct. 1937)
7129c

Coleman, James. Catalogue of original deeds, charters, copies of royal grants, petitions, original letters, proclamations, old maps and plans in manuscripts and printed of the great William Penn and his family, extra 518 items. London. Coleman. 1870. 32p. (Supplement. cir. 1870. 12p.)
7130

Connor, R. D. W. The National Archives and Pennsylvania history. Pa. hist. VII. p63-78 (April 1940)
7130a

Field, Alston G. The collection of business records in western Pennsylvania. Bus. hist. soc. bul. VIII. p57-63 (June 1934)
7130b

Fisher, Joshua F. A list of the instructions, letters, etc. from Thomas and Richard Penn, proprietaries and governors of Pennsylvania, to James Hamilton, esq. Hist. Soc. of Pennsylvania memoirs II. p225-38. 1827
7131

Fulton, Eleanore Jane and Mylin, Barbara Kendig. An index to the will books and intestate records of Lancaster County, Pa., 1729-1850. Lancaster. Priv. printed. 1936
7131a

Garrison, Curtis W. The C.W.A. survey of historical source material in Pennsylvania. Pennsylvania hist. I. p217-31 (Oct. 1934)
7132

—— Dispersal of Butler County records. Western Pa. hist. mag. XVII. p189-90 (Sept. 1934)
7132a

—— Economic material in the Pennsylvania archives and other depositories. Bus. Hist. Soc. bul. VIII. p97-101 (Dec. 1934)
7132b

—— Recent accessions of various depositories. Pa. hist. I. p48-50 (Jan. 1934) (Accession of manuscripts)
7132c

Gates, Thomas S. The possibilities of Philadelphia as a center for historical research. Pa. mag. hist. LXII. p121-9 (April 1938)
7132d

Genealogical Society of Pennsylvania. List of manuscripts in the collections. Pennsylvania Geneal. Soc. publications. VI. p309-18 (March 1917)
7133

Godecke, Karl. Accomplishments and future program of the Pennsylvania Historical Records Survey. Pa. hist. VII. p236-42 (Oct. 1940)
7133a

Hildeburn, Charles R. Index to Philadelphia wills and administrations, 1681-1825. (MS. in the Historical Society of Pennsylvania) 3v.
7134

Historical Records Survey. Pennsylvania. Descriptive catalogue of the Du Simitière papers in the Library Company of Philadelphia. Philadelphia. 1940. 196p. mim.
7134a

—— —— Guide to depositories of manuscript collections in Pennsylvania. Comp. by Margaret Sherburne Eliot and Sylvester K. Stevens. (Pennsylvania Historical Commission, no. 4, Bul. 774) Harrisburg. Pennsylvania Hist. Com. 1939. 136p.
7134b

—— —— Guide to the manuscript collections in the Historical Society of Pennsylvania. Comp. by Paul Bleyden, ed. by Bernard S. Levin. Phila. Hist. Soc. of Pennsylvania. 1940. 350p.
7134c

—— —— Inventory of the county archives of Pennsylvania. Harrisburg, Pa. 1938- . mim. No. 1. Adams. May 1941. 313p.; No. 7. Blair. May 1941. 294p.; No. 23. Delaware. Aug. 1939. 254p.; No. 25. Erie. Aug. 1940. 374p.; No. 26. Fayette. May 1939. 291p.; No. 27. Forest. Oct. 1940. 201p.; No. 30. Greene. Nov. 1940. 259p. (mult.); No. 36. Lancaster. Feb. 1941. 294p.; No. 40. Luzerne. Dec. 1938. 239p.; No. 63. Washington. May 1941. 400p.; No. 64. Wayne. July 1939. 207p.
7134d

Holbrook, Franklin F. The Survey in retrospect. Western Pa. hist. mag. XIX. p293-304 (Dec. 1936) (Western Pa. Hist. Survey)
7134e

Hulbert, Archer Butler. The Moravian records [library at Bethlehem, Pa.] Ohio arch. and hist. quar. XVIII. p199-226. 1909
7134f

Hussey, Miriam. Business manuscripts in the library of the Historical Society of Pennsylvania. Bus. Hist. Soc. bul. X. p48-51. 1936
7134g

James, Alfred P. Opportunities for research in early western Pennsylvania history. Western Pa. hist. mag. XVI. p125-37 (May 1933) Discussion of published and ms. materials)
7134h

Johnston, Louis W. H. The government-supported historical survey of Pennsylvania in the western counties. Western Pennsylvania hist. mag. XVIII. p209-22 (Sept. 1935) (Civil Works Administration survey)
7135

Kuczynski, V. Fr. Catalogue of papers relating to Pennsylvania and Delaware deposited at the State Paper Office London. Phila. Sherman. 1850. 167p. (Also in Hist. Soc. of Pennsylvania memoirs. IV. pt. 2. p225-385. 1850) **7136**

Levin, Bernard S. Business records in the Historical Society of Pennsylvania. Pa. mag. hist. LXIV. p430-5 (July 1940) **7136a**

Long, Amelia Reynolds. Manuscript collections on early jurisprudence and legislation in Pennsylvania. Pa. hist. II. p190-3 (July 1935) **7136b**

McClurkin, A. J. Summary of the Bank of North America records. Pa. mag. hist. LXIV. p88-96 (Jan. 1940) **7136c**

Pennsylvania. Archives. The propriety manors [list]. *In* Draughts of the propriety manors in the Province of Pennsylvania, as preserved in the Land department of the commonwealth. Ed. by William Henry Egle. (Pennsylvania archives, 3d ser.) Harrisburg. Clarence M. Busch. 1894. IV. [3]p. **7136d**

Pennsylvania. Historical society. List of Penn manuscripts, purchased by the Historical Society of Pennsylvania, Dec. 27, 1882 from Colonel Stewart Forbes, administrator in England of the estate of Thomas Gordon Penn, deceased, and designated "Penn manuscripts, Forbes collection." Pennsylvania mag. of hist. and biog. XXVIII. p155-68 (April 1904) **7137**

—— —— Table of contents of volumes I and II of papers relating to, or formerly the property of Colonel William Bradford, of Philadelphia, now in the possession of the Historical Society of Pennsylvania. Phila. 1878. 35p. **7138**

Pennsylvania. State Library. Index of the Paper books of the Supreme and superior courts of the state of Pennsylvania. *In* Catalogue of the law books of the Pennsylvania State Library. [Harrisburg] 1899. p733-963 **7139**

Pilcher, James Evelyn. The Pennsylvania archives as they apply to Cumberland County. Read before the historical meeting of the Hamilton Library Association, Carlisle, Pa. and reprinted for the historical department. n.p. 190? 18p. **7139a**

Puttick & Simpson. Catalogue of books, manuscripts, maps, charts and engravings, from the libraries of William Penn and his descendants. . . . London. Puttick & Simpson. 1872. 151p. **7140**

Selsam, J. Paul. The survey of manuscript source material in Pennsylvania. Pa. hist. I. p98-100 (April 1934) (The C.W.A. historical survey in Pennsylvania) **7140a**

Spofford, Ernest. Some of the manuscript resources of the Historical Society of Pennsylvania. Pa. hist. I. p88-97 (April 1934) **7140b**

Survey of Federal Archives. Pennsylvania. Inventory of federal archives in the states. Phila. 1940- . mim. The Federal Courts. March 1940. 71p.; The Department of the Treasury. Pts.1-2. Philadelphia. 1941. 184, 213p.; The Department of War. Pts.1-2. Philadelphia. 1941. 241, 235p.; The Department of Justice. March 1940. 38p.; The Department of the Navy. June 1940. 243p.; The Department of the Interior. April 1941. 49p.; The Department of Agriculture. June 1941. 341p.; The Department of Commerce. May 1940. 37p.; The Veterans' Administration. March 1941. 43p.; The Farm Credit Administration. April 1941. 12p. **7140c**

Whitehead, James L. The survey of Federal Archives in Philadelphia, with particular emphasis on the records of the Mint and the district court. Pa. mag. hist. LXII. p162-74 (April 1938) **7140d**

Printed Sources

Ames, Herman V. and Keller, Luther R. Public archives of Pennsylvania. Am. Hist. Asso. rep. 1904. p629-49 (List of the contents of the Pennsylvania archives, 2d and 3rd series) **7141**

Ford, Worthington Chauncey. Some London broadsides and issues on Pennsylvania. Pennsylvania mag. of hist. and biog. XXIX. p65-9. 1905 **7142**

Good, D. Clare. An index to cases construing the statutes of Pennsylvania, 1664-1908, the constitution of Pennsylvania and the British statutes. Phila. Johnson. 1908. 705p. (Supplement. 1912. 240p.) **7143**

Hasse, Adelaide Rosalie. Index of economic material in documents of the states of the United States—Pennsylvania, 1790-1904. (Carnegie Inst. of Wash. Publication no. 85) Wash. D.C. Carnegie Inst. of Wash. 1919-22. 3pts. **7144**

Hazard, Samuel. General index to the Colonial records, in 16 volumes and to the Pennsylvania archives, in 12 volumes. Phila. Joseph Severns & Co. 1860. 653p. **7145**

Henkels, Stan V. Historical notes on the laws and legal practice of Pennsylvania as a colony. . . . Phila. 1902. 12p. **7146**

—— Rare and scarce Americana; embracing an unique collection of manuscripts of the laws of Pennsylvania and papers relating to the legal practice of the colony, from 1682-1744; broadsides, historical letters and slave deeds. . . . Phila. 1902. 92p. **7147**

Lamberton, James McCormick. A list of special acts of assembly relating to Harrisburg, Pennsylvania. [Harrisburg? Telegraph Ptg. Co. 1906?] 50p. **7148**

Martin, John Hill. The bibliography of the laws of Pennsylvania. Legal intelligencer. XXXIX. p366-7 (Oct. 6, 1882) (Reprinted in the author's Bench and bar of Philadelphia. Phila. Rees Welsh. 1883. p185-91) **7149**

Matlack, Samuel Dreher and Bur, Lawrence J. Index and concordance to Pepper and Lewis's digest of decisions and encyclopaedia of Pennsylvania law, volumes 1 to 23 and volumes 1 and 2 cross reference annals, 1682-1906; together with tables of acts of assembly, acts of Congress and British statutes construed and applied in the Pennsylvania cases and an alphabetical index to the acts. Phila. Welsh. 1908. 863p.   **7150**

Montgomery, Thomas Lynch. Index to fifth series—Pennsylvania archives. *In* Sixth series, XV, pt. 1 and 2. Harrisburg. Harrisburg Printing Co. 1907   **7151**

—— Index to sixth series—Pennsylvania archives. *In* Seventh series, I-V. Harrisburg. C. E. Aughinbaugh. 1914   **7152**

Pennsylvania. Commission on Laws. Brief statement of facts regarding the Commission for the Compilation of the Laws of Pennsylvania prior to 1800. n.p. 1897. 14p.   **7153**

Pennsylvania. Department of Property and Supplies. Bureau of publications. Index to digest of election laws of Pennsylvania. *In* The Pennsylvania manual, 1933. Harrisburg, Pa. 1933. p579-613   **7154**

—— —— —— **Division of documents.** List of state publications..., no. 1-   (Feb. 1937-) (Price list)   **7154a**

Pennsylvania. State Library. Check list of laws and statutes of Pennsylvania from 1714 to 1801 (Rep. of the State librarian. 1904) [Harrisburg] Ray. 1905. p103-20   **7155**

—— —— Checklist of the laws, minutes, journals, and documents published by Pennsylvania, 1682-1898. (Rep. of the State librarian of Pennsylvania. 1900) [Harrisburg] Ray. 1901. p314-407 (With additions appears also in Reports for 1901, 1902, 1903. Earlier list (1682-1889) in Rep. for 1888-89)   **7156**

Pittsburgh. Carnegie Library. Official documents of the city of Pittsburgh; tentative list. Pittsburgh. Carnegie Lib. 1903. 16p.   **7157**

Price, Giles D. Index to local legislation in Pennsylvania, 1700-1892; together with an index to the titles of corporations organized by special acts, and to all laws relating thereto. Phila. T. & J. W. Johnson & Co. 1894. 1032p.   **7158**

Schlegel, Marvin W. The Pennsylvania archives. Pa. hist. VIII. p219-27 (July 1941) (Account of the published Pennsylvania archives)   **7158a**

Shearer, Augustus Hunt. Bibliographical and descriptive notes on the issues of the Journal of the Pennsylvania assembly, 1776-1790. Pennsylvania mag. of hist. & biog. XLI. p359-64 (July 1917)   **7159**

Western Pennsylvania Historical Survey. Calendar of published and unpublished documents relating to the history of Western Pennsylvania. (Cards in the Historical Society of Western Pennsylvania)   **7160**

Wright, R. E. Alphabetical and analytical index to the Supreme Court reports from 1st Dallas to (29th) Smith, (1754-1874). Phila. 1874-77. 2v.   **7161**

General

Aurand's Book Store. Catalog of Pennsylvaniana (new and second-hand); a bibliography of the Keystone state (listing more than 1000 items). Harrisburg. Aurand's Book Store. Feb. 1928. 64p.   **7162**

Bining, Arthur C. Bibliography of works on Pennsylvania history. (In progress)   **7163**

—— A selected bibliography of secondary works on Pennsylvania history. Pennsylvania Lib. notes. XIII. p355-71 (Oct. 1933) (Reprinted separately. 1933)   **7164**

Branch, West. Histories of Pennsylvania. Williamsport, Pa. Daily gazette and bulletin, Jan. 12, 1871   **7164a**

Dunaway, Wayland F. A brief bibliography of Pennsylvania history for high school teachers. Pennsylvania hist. I. p38-46 (Jan. 1934)   **7165**

Gates, Paul W. Research projects in Pennsylvania history. Pennsylvania hist. I. p15-27 (Jan. 1934)   **7166**

Pennsylvania. Department of Public Instruction. Pennsylvania bibliography; articles published by societies belonging to the Pennsylvania Federation of Historical Societies. Pennsylvania Hist. Com. bul. no. 2. 1933. 102p.   **7167**

Pennsylvania. State Library. Accessions relating to Pennsylvania. (Reports of the State librarian of Pennsylvania. 1903-21/22) Harrisburg, Pa. 1904-23   **7168**

Pennsylvania Federation of Historical Societies. Historical publications relating to Pennsylvania. Pennsylvania Federation of Hist. Societies. acts & proc. 1913. p51-65; 1914. p58-71; 1915. p61-71; 1916. p64-72; 1917. p59-66; 1918. p63-9; 1919. p78-82; 1920. p73-8; 1921. p79-83; 1923. p38-55; 1931. p19-24   **7169**

Pennsylvania Society. Pennsylvania books, 1900-1923. *In* Pennsylvania society year book, 1902-1923. N.Y. The Pennsylvania Soc. 1902-23   **7170**

Sewickley, Pa. Public Library. Alexander C. Robinson collection. An annotated catalog of the Alexander C. Robinson collection of western Pennsylvania. Ed. by Lowell W. Nicols. [Sewickley] Lib. Soc. of Sewickley, Pa. 1940. 229p.   **7170a**

Stone, Frederick D. Bi-centennial reading. Phila. Lib. Co. bul. n.s. no. 9. p65-76 (July 1882)   **7171**

—— Critical essay on the sources of information—The founding of Pennsylvania. *In* Narrative and critical history of America. Ed. by Justin Winsor. Boston, N.Y. Houghton Mifflin. 1884. III. p495-516   **7172**

Williams, James A. Pennsylvania German bibliography. Phila. In progress   **7172a**

Local

Bausman, Lottie M. A bibliography of Lancaster County, 1745-1912. (Publications of the Pennsylvania Federation of Hist. Societies) Phila. Patterson & White. 1916. 460p. **7173**

Bibliographical Planning Committee of Philadelphia. Philadelphia libraries and their holdings. . . . [Phila.] Univ. of Pennsylvania Press. 1941. 45p. photoprint **7173a**

Camp, Gertrude Helmbold. Views of old Philadelphia and vicinity, portraits, maps. The Hayloft, Whitemarsh, Montgomery County, Pennsylvania. 1927. 35p. **7173b**

City History Society of Philadelphia. Philadelphia history; index to volume I (publications 1 to 13). Comp. by William J. Campbell. Phila. 1917. p405-54 **7173c**

Croll, Philip C. Lebanon County imprints and bibliography. Lebanon County Hist. Soc. pap. IV. p153-99 (Feb. 21, 1908) **7174**

Crumrine, Boyd. The bibliography of Washington County (so completed up to December 25, 1907) under the auspices of the Washington County Historical Society. (Pennsylvania Federation of Hist. Societies. Pennsylvania bibliographies no. 1) [Harrisburg. Pennsylvania Federation of Hist. Societies. 1909] 29p. **7175**

Edmunds, Albert J. Bibliography of Lancaster County; being a chronological list of books and pamphlets printed therein and belonging to the library of the Historical Society of Pennsylvania, together with a few printed elsewhere. Phila. 1905. (MS. in the Hist. Soc. of Pennsylvania) **7176**

Fortenbaugh, Robert. Bibliography of Adams County. Historical Society of Gettysburg College. (MS. card bibliography on printed materials and newspaper items) **7177**

Hayden, Horace Edwin. A bibliography of the Wyoming Valley, Pennsylvania; being a catalogue of all books, pamphlets, and other ephemera in any way relating to its history, with bibliographical and critical notes. Wyoming Hist. & Geol. Soc. proc. & colls. II. pt. 1. p86-131. 1886 **7178**

Henry, Frederick P. Medical literature of Philadelphia. *In* Standard history of the medical profession of Philadelphia. Chicago. Goodspeed Bros. 1897. p479-544 **7179**

Hexamer, E. & Son. Alphabetical index to Hexamer's insurance maps of Philadelphia, 1889, 1893, 1898. Phila. E. Hexamer & Son. 1889-1898. 3v. **7179a**

Index of personal and place names, Northumberland County Historical Society publications I to X, 1929 to 1938 inclusive. Northumberland Co. Hist. Soc. proc. X. p25-194. 1938 **7179b**

Jackson, Joseph. The iconography of Philadelphia. Pa. mag. hist. LIX. p57-73. (Jan. 1935) **7179c**

Lancaster County Historical Society. Historical papers and addresses. Index of personal names appearing in volumes XI to XX inclusive of the Proceedings of the Lancaster County Historical Society. Prep. by Gilbert H. Yeager and William Frederic Worner. Lancaster. 1934. 128p. **7179d**

—— Maps and pictures of old Lancaster. Lancaster Co. Hist. Soc. pap. XXVI. p127-32 (June 1922) **7179e**

Martin, John Hill. The miscellaneous legal literature of the Philadelphia bar. Legal intelligencer. XL. p486-7 (Dec. 21, 1883) **7180**

Morgan, George. A bibliography of Philadelphia, with annotations, as well as directions for finding the books, pamphlets and manuscripts listed. *In* The city of the firsts, being a complete history of the city of Philadelphia from its founding, in 1682, to the present time. Phila. Hist. Publication. Soc. 1926. p485-522 **7181**

Parkinson, Sarah Woods. Local history; a few early Carlisle publications. Carlisle? 1910. 23p. **7182**

Pendleton, Marguerite L. Bibliography on Pittsburgh housing conditions 1904 to February 1929. Revised to May 9, 1930. Issued by The Pittsburgh Housing Association. 1930. 9p. mim. **7183**

Pennsylvania. State Library. Bibliography of Pennsylvania history—state, county, town and township in The Pennsylvania State Library. (Rep. of the State librarian of Pennsylvania. 1901) [Harrisburg. Ray] 1902. p253-85 **7184**

—— —— Check-list of Pennsylvania county, town and township histories, 1794-1892. (Rep. of the State librarian. 1891) Harrisburg. Meyers. 1892. 24p. **7185**

Pennsylvania book reviews. Pa. arts and sciences. I- . 1935- **7185a**

The Perkiomen region. Index to Perkiomen region, December 1, 1921-July 1932. Prep. by Sara Bond. Perkiomen region. X. p147-202 (Oct. 1932) **7185b**

Philadelphia Athenaeum. Catalogue of first volumes of periodicals on display in honor of the 200th anniversary of the founding of the University of Pennsylvania. [Phila. 1940] 24p. **7185c**

Phillips, Philip Lee. A descriptive list of maps and views of Philadelphia in the Library of Congress, 1683-1865. (Geographical Society of Philadelphia. Special pub. no. 2) n.p. 1926. 91p. **7185d**

Pittsburgh. Carnegie Library. Pennsylvania; a reading list for the use of schools, with special reference to Indian warfare and the local history of Pittsburgh. Carnegie Lib. 1911. 83p. **7186**

Sauer, Ethel M. Chester county periodicals. Chester county col. VII. p270-5 (Aug. 1937) **7186a**

Stearns, Bertha Monica. Early Philadelphia magazines for ladies. Pa. mag. hist. LXIV. p479-91 (Oct. 1940) **7186b**

Trautwine, William. Some old maps of Philadelphia. Phila. 1881 **7186c**

Tubbs, Charles. Bibliography of Tioga County, 1804-1903. Wellsboro. Agitator Print. 1904. 20p. **7187**

U.S. Library of Congress. Division of bibliography. List of references on Germantown, Pa. Feb. 28, 1917. 4p. **7188**

—— —— —— List of references on Valley Forge. March 11, 1926. 5p. typ. **7189**

Washington County Historical Society. Bibliography of Washington County; in our early days, number 1 of volume I. Wash. Pa. Wash. County Hist. Soc. 1908. 16p. **7190**

Western Pennsylvania Historical Society. Bibliography and location list of publications relating to the history of Western Pennsylvania. (Cards in the Society building) **7191**

Witmer, Aimee F. Bibliography on Hershey, the chocolate town. Boston. Simmons College, School of Lib. Sci. 1940. 115p. typ. **7191a**

Wyoming Historical and Geological Society. History of the Wyoming Historical and Geological Society, Wilkes-Barre, Pa., 1858-1913. [Wilkes-Barre] Printed for the Soc. 1913. 43p. (Publications of the Soc. p17-30) **7192**

Newspapers

Bell, Edwin C. Notes on journalism; history of the Morning herald and other Titusville papers. Titusville. Morning Herald Print. 1910. 53p. **7193**

Berks County. Historical Society. List of bound newspapers in the possession of the Historical Society of Berks County, Reading, Pa. [Reading, Pa.] 1933. 5p. typ. **7194**

Bowman, Charles M. Lebanon County— a story of its newspapers. Lebanon County Hist. Soc. Hist. pap. and addresses. I. p393-403. 1902 **7195**

Brigham, Clarence S. Pennsylvania—Bibliography of American newspapers, 1690-1820. Am. Antiq. Soc. proc. XXX. p81-150. 1920; XXXII. p346-79. 1922 **7196**

—— Pennsylvania [Philadelphia]—Bibliography of American newspapers, 1690-1820. Am. Antiq. Soc. proc. n.s. XXXII. p81-214. 1922 **7197**

Church, E. F. The newspapers of Bucks County, Pa. Bucks County Hist. Soc. colls. I. p118-25. 1908 **7198**

Diffenderffer, F. R. The newspapers of Lancaster County. Lancaster County Hist. Soc. hist. pap. & addresses. VI. p103-13. 1902 **7199**

Field, Alston G. The press in Western Pennsylvania to 1812. Western Pa. hist. mag. XX. p231-64 (Dec. 1937) **7199a**

Freeze, John G. [List of newspapers published in Columbia Co., Pa.] *In* A history of Columbia County, Pennsylvania. Bloomsburg. Elwell & Bittenbender. 1883. p187-94 **7200**

Hause, Nathan E. Annotated catalogue of newspaper files in the Pennsylvania State Library. (Rep. of the state librarian. 1900) Harrisburg. Ray. 1901. p185-308 **7201**

Historical Records Survey. Pennsylvania. Bibliography of Pennsylvania newspapers. Henry F. Marx, director. Easton, Pa. In progress **7201a**

—— —— Checklist of Philadelphia newspapers available in Philadelphia. Harrisburg, Pa. 1937. mim. **7201b**

Knauss, James Owens. Table of German American newspapers of the eighteenth century. *In* Social conditions among the Pennsylvania Germans in the eighteenth century as revealed in German newspapers published in America. [Lancaster. New Era Ptg. Co. 1922] (Reprinted from the Proc. of the Pennsylvania-German Soc. XXIX) **7202**

McClure, A. K. Pennsylvania journalism. *In* Jenkins, Howard M. Pennsylvania, colonial and federal. Phila. Pennsylvania Hist. Publishing Asso. 1903. III. p185-207 **7203**

Miller, Daniel. Early German American newspapers. Pennsylvania-German Soc. proc. & addresses. XIX. 1908. 107p. **7204**

—— The German newspapers of Berks County. Berks County Hist. Soc. trans. III. p4-22. 1912 **7205**

Munday, Eugene H. The press of Philadelphia in 1870-71. *In* The Proof-sheet, March 1870-March 1872. Phila. Collins & M'leester. 1870-72. (Photostat copy in the Free Lib. of Phila.) **7206**

Pennsylvania. Department of Property and Supplies. Bureau of publications. Miscellaneous journals and magazines [published in Pennsylvania]. *In* The Pennsylvania manual, 1933. Harrisburg, Pa. 1933. p961-5 **7207**

—— —— —— Newspapers published in Pennsylvania. *In* The Pennsylvania manual, 1933. Harrisburg, Pa. 1933. p951-61 **7208**

Pennsylvania. Historical Commission. Bibliography of Pennsylvania newspapers—1820-1920. Pa. Hist. Comm. rep. VI. p28-30. 1937 (Report on the progress of the check list of local and state newspaper files) **7208a**

Pennsylvania. University. Library. Checklist of newspapers in the University of Pennsylvania Library. By Emily M. Smith. [Phila.] 1931. 19p. typ. **7209**

Philadelphia papers. Bibliog. Soc. of Amer. pap. XIV. pt. 1. p92-126. 1922 **7210**

Reader, Francis Smith. History of the newspapers of Beaver County, Pennsylvania. New Brighton. F. S. Reader & Son. 1905. 176p. **7211**

Sauer, Ethel M. Chester County newspapers. Chester co. col. no. 1. p3-7; no. 2. 45-50; no. 3. 91-5; no. 4. 150-5; no. 5. 191-5; no. 6. 224-31 (Oct. 1936-April, June 1937) **7211a**

Scharf, John Thomas and Wescott, Thompson. The press of Philadelphia. *In* History of Philadelphia, 1609-1884. Phila. L. H. Everts & Co. 1884. p1958-2062   **7212**

Steinmetz, Mary Owen. Berks County Historical Society—List of newspapers in the society's collection. 1934. (MS. in the Hist. Soc. of Pennsylvania) 5,7p.   **7213**

U.S. Works Progress Administration. Historical records survey. Project 6102. A checklist of Philadelphia newspapers in libraries of Philadelphia. Phila. 1936. 115p. multig.   **7214**

Young, J. R. Weekly newspapers and the magazines. *In* Memorial history of the city of Philadelphia from its first settlement to the year 1895. N.Y. N.Y. Hist. Soc. 1898. II. p268-84   **7215**

Printing

Barnsley, Edward Roberts. Presses and printers of Newtown before 1868; a paper presented before the Bucks County Historical Society at Newtown, Pennsylvania, on September 22, 1934. Newtown, Pa. 1935. 61p.   **7216**

Bridenbaugh, Carl. The press and the book in eighteenth century Philadelphia. Pa. mag. hist. LXV. p1-30 (Jan. 1941)   **7216a**

Brotherhead, William. Bibliography of William Bradford's books. *In* Forty years among the old booksellers of Philadelphia. Phila. A. P. Brotherhead. 1891. p103-15   **7217**

Diffenderffer, Frank Ried. Early German printers of Lancaster and the issues of their presses. Lancaster. Reprinted from the New Era. 1904. p53-93 (Papers read before the Lancaster County Hist. Soc. Jan. 1, 1904. VIII. no. 3)   **7218**

Hildeburn, Charles R. A century of printing; the issues of the press of Pennsylvania, 1685-1784. Phila. Matlack & Harvey. 1885. 2v. (Part previously pub. in the Phila. Lib. Co. bul. n.s. no. 8. p44-55 (Jan. 1882); no. 10. p75-100 (Jan. 1883); no. 11. p97-119 (July 1883); no. 14. p. i-xxx (Jan. 1885))   **7219**

Kent, Henry W. Chez moreau de St.-Méry, Philadelphia, with a list of imprints enlarged by George Parker Winship. *In* Bibliographical essays; a tribute to Wilberforce Eames. Cambridge. Harvard Univ. Press. 1924. p66-78   **7220**

McMurtrie, Douglas Crawford. The first printers of York, Pennsylvania, including the text of some of the imprints of the York press during the early days of the revolutionary war. York, Pa. The Maple Press Co. 1940. 48p.   **7220a**

Metzger, Ethel. Supplement to Hildeburn's Century of printing, 1685-1775, with an introductory essay. (Columbia Univ. Master's essay) [N.Y.] 1930. 127p. typ.   **7221**

Miner, William Penn. The progress of printing in Luzerne County. Wyoming Hist. and Geol. Soc. proc. & colls. VI. p106-12. 1901   **7222**

Nolan, J. Bennett. Bibliography of the first decade of printing in Reading, Pennsylvania. *In* The first decade of printing in Reading, Pennsylvania. Reading. Reading National Bank and Trust Co. 1930. p21-32   **7223**

Publications of Christopher Sower. n.p. n.p. 1876? 16p.   **7224**

Sachse, Julius Frederick. The Ephrata press. *In* The German sectarians of Pennsylvania 1742-1800; a critical and legendary history of the Ephrata cloister and the Dunkers. Phila. Printed for the Author, P. C. Stockhausen. 1900. III. p222-54   **7225**

Sealock, Richard Burl. Publishing in Pennsylvania, 1785-1790, with a list of imprints not included in Evans' American bibliography. . . (Columbia University. Master's thesis) N.Y. 1935. 150p. Photo.   **7225a**

Seidensticker, Oswald. Die deutsch-amerikanischen incunabeln. Der Deutsche pionier. VIII. p475-84 (Feb. 1877)   **7226**

—— The first century of German printing in America, 1728-1830, preceded by a notice of the literary work of F. D. Pastorius. Phila. Schaefer & Korade. 1893. 253p.   **7227**

Thompson, David Wilson. Bibliography of Carlisle imprints for the first half century, 1786-1835. *In* Early publications of Carlisle, Pennsylvania, 1785-1835. Carlisle. Sentinel Press. 1932. p78-128   **7228**

Wallace, John William. Books printed by Bradford. *In* An old Philadelphian, Colonel William Bradford, the patriot printer of 1776; sketches of his life. Phila. Sherman. 1884. p349-62   **7229**

Miscellaneous

Armor, William C. Scotch-Irish bibliography of Pennsylvania. Scotch-Irish Soc. of Amer. proc. & addresses 8th cong. 1896. p253-89   **7230**

Aurand, Ammon Monroe, Jr. The Germans in Pennsylvania; a bibliography—A Pennsylvania German library; or, the pleasures of "riding" a hobby. Harrisburg. Priv. printed, Aurand Press. 1930. 62p.   **7231**

Brinton, Hugh P., Jr. Family and child welfare studies in Pennsylvania, 1921-1926; a bibliography compiled through the co-operation of the Department of sociology, University of Pennsylvania and the Child welfare division, Public Charities Association of Pennsylvania. Phila. Com. on philanthropic labor. Phila. yearly meeting of Friends. 1927. 43p.   **7232**

Cremer, Henry. Available sources for the study of industrial and social history of Western Pennsylvania. Indiana, Pa. Grosse. 1930. 19p.   **7233**

—— Available sources for the study of problem economics in Western Pennsylvania. Indiana, Pa. Grosse. 1930. 8p.   **7234**

Federation of Social Agencies of Pittsburgh and Allegheny County. Bureau of social research. A bibliography of studies of social conditions in the Pittsburgh area, 1929-1930. Pittsburgh. [Tonat Press Co.] 1931. 85p.
Same. 1930-1935. Pittsburgh. 1936. 111p.
7235

Fisher, Joshua Francis. Catalogue of political tracts relating to the history of the colony of Pennsylvania from 1681 to 1777. cir. 1838. (MS. in the Am. Philosophical Soc., Phila.)
7236

Ford, Worthington Chauncey. The first separate map of Pennsylvania. Mass. Hist. Soc. proc. LVII. p172-83. 1924
7236a

Garrison, Hazel Shields. Cartography of Pennsylvania before 1800. Pa. mag. hist. LIX. p255-83 (July 1935)
7236b
—— List of 1543 maps of Pennsylvania. (Mim. list in Library of Congress, Division of maps)
7236c

Giddens, Paul. Beginnings of the oil industry in Pennsylvania: sources and bibliography. In progress
7236d

Haldy, Gertrude Hensel and Worner, William Frederic. Index of authors whose papers or addresses have appeared in volumes I to XXXV, inclusive, of the proceedings of the Lancaster County Historical Society. Lancaster County Hist. Soc. hist. pap. & addresses. XXXVI. p1-38. 1932
7237
—— —— Index of personal names appearing in volumes XXI to XXVI inclusive of the Proceedings of the Lancaster County Historical Society. Lancaster County Hist. Soc. publications. XXVII-XXXII. 1930-31. 67, 69p.
7238

Harpster, John W., ed. Selective bibliography of travel and description in western Pennsylvania. In Pen pictures of early western Pennsylvania. Pittsburgh. Univ. of Pittsburgh Press. 1938. p299-327
7238a

Helbig, R. E. German-American genealogies chiefly Pennsylvania, found in New York Public Library. The Pennsylvania-German. VIII. p303-7 (Oct. 1906)
7239

Hildeburn, Charles R. An index to the obituary notices published in the "Pennsylvania gazette": 1728-1791. Pennsylvania mag. of hist. and biog. X. p334-49. 1886
7240

Historical Records Survey. Pennsylvania. Checklist of maps pertaining to Pennsylvania up to 1900. Harrisburg, Pa. 1935. mim. Supplement 1936. mim. **7240a**

Holcomb, Richmond C. The early Dutch maps of upper Delaware valley. N.J. Hist. Soc. proc. n.s. XI. p18-45 (Jan. 1926)
7240b

Hornor, Mrs. Marian S. Bibliography of Pennsylvania almanacs to 1850. Stenton Ave. at Meadowbrook Lane, Chestnut Hill, Pa. In progress
7240c

Hunter, William Luther. Abstracts of graduate theses and dissertations in industrial arts education and vocational-industrial education accepted by institutions of higher learning in Pennsylvania, 1921-1933. Ames. Iowa State College, Industrial arts dept. 1934. mim.
7240d

Ingham, William A. A list of and brief guide to the publications of the Pennsylvania Geological Survey, 1874-1891. n.p. Busch. 1896. xxx p.
7240e

Kane, Hope Frances. Notes on early Pennsylvania promotion literature. Pa. mag. hist. LXIII. p144-68 (April 1939)
7240f

Long, Harriet C. A select bibliography (of the Pennsylvania-Germans) submitted in partial fulfillment of the requirements for the degree of B.L.S., N.Y. State Library School, 1910. The Pennsylvania-German. XI. p460-76 (Aug. 1910)
7241

Manwiller, Charles E. An educational index of the Pennsylvania school journal, 1852-1875. (Univ. of Pittsburgh. M.A. thesis) 1927
7242

Mulhern, James. Bibliography. In A history of secondary education in Pennsylvania. Ph. D. thesis) Phila. The Author. 1933. p611-84
7243

Nead, Daniel Wunderlich. Index to proper names mentioned in the proceedings and addresses of the Pennsylvania-German Society, vols. I-VI. Pennsylvania-German Soc. proc. and addresses. VIII. 1898. 91p.
7244

Pennsylvania. Department of Public Instruction. Checklist of maps pertaining to Pennsylvania up to 1900. Ed. by Hazel Shields Garrison. [Harrisburg, Pa.] 1936. 89p. mim.
7244a

Pennsylvania. Geological Survey. The publications of the Second Geological Survey of Pennsylvania. Harrisburg, Pa. 1885. 12p.
7244b

Pennsylvania. Historical Society. Index to the Pennsylvania magazine of history and biography. In progress
7244c

Pennsylvania. State Department of Welfare. Division of research and statistics. Bibliography of references on adult and juvenile probation in Pennsylvania. Prepared for the Pennsylvania committee on probation by William Wallace Weaver of the University of Pennsylvania. [Harrisburg, Pa. 1934] 11p. mim.
7245

Pennsylvania. State Library. Bibliography of the Scotch-Irish of Pennsylvania. (Rep. of the State librarian of Pennsylvania. 1901) [Harrisburg] Ray. 1902. p287-324 (Based on Armor's bibliography)
7246

Pennsylvania. State Planning Board. An analysis of the status of mapping in Pennsylvania. Prep. by George R. Copeland and James A. Patterson. Harrisburg, Pa. 1936. 56p. mim.
7246a

Pennsylvania. Topographic and Geological Survey. Publications of the United States Geological Survey relating to Pennsylvania. Harrisburg, Pa. 1914. 10p. **7246b**

Pennsylvania Federation of Historical Societies. Statistics [publications] of its members. Pennsylvania Federation of Hist. Societies. acts and proc. 1907-32. Harrisburg, Pa. 1908-33 **7247**

Pennsylvania Historical Survey. A partial bibliography of the archaeology of Pennsylvania and adjacent states. Ed. by Claude E. Schaeffer and Leo J. Roland. Harrisburg, Pa. Pennsylvania Hist. Comm. Comm. 1941. 45p. mim. **7247a**

Pennsylvania History Club. List of members with their historical bibliographies; a contribution to Pennsylvania historical bibliography. Pennsylvania Hist. Club publications. I. p19-58 (Feb. 1909) **7248**

Pennsylvania-German Society. Publications of the Pennsylvania German Society; a descriptive list. Norristown. Norristown Press. 1929. 19p. (Also in Pennsylvania-German Soc. proc. and addresses. XXXIV. p115-31. 1929) **7249**

Phillips, Henry, Jr. Certain old almanacs published in Philadelphia between 1705 and 1744. Phila. 1881. 7p. (Reprinted from Am. Phil. Soc. proc. XIX) **7250**

Pittsburgh. Carnegie Library. List of references on the whisky insurrection in Western Pennsylvania in 1794. Carnegie Lib. monthly bul. XI. p344-53 (July 1906) **7251**

Reichard, Harry Hess. Books, magazines and newspapers cited. *In* Pennsylvania-German dialect writings and their writers; a paper prepared at the request of the Pennsylvania-German Society. Pennsylvania-German Soc. proc. and addresses. XXVI. p321-400. 1918 **7252**

Rosenbach, A. S. W. Retrospect. Pa. mag. hist. LX. p305-8 (Oct. 1936) (Hist. of the Pennsylvania magazine of history and biography) **7252a**

Sachse, Julius Friedrich. Title-pages of books and pamphlets that influenced German emigration to Pennsylvania, reproduced in facsimile. Pennsylvania-German Soc. proc. and addresses. VII. p199-256. 1897 **7253**

Society news and accessions. Pa. mag. hist. **7253a**

Union index of Pennsylvania maps. Pa. mag. hist. LIX. p182. April 1935) (Compilation undertaken by the Pennsylvania State Archives) **7253b**

U.S. Library of Congress. Division of bibliography. List of references on the Pennsylvania Germans. Dec. 8, 1921. 14p. typ. **7254**

Vanderbilt, Paul. Philadelphia union catalog. *In* Wilson, Louis Round, ed. Library trends; papers presented before the Library Institute at the University of Chicago, August 3-15, 1936. Chicago. Univ. of Chicago Press. 1937. p200-24 **7254a**

Warrington, James. A bibliography of church music books issued in Pennsylvania, with annotations. Penn Germania. n.s. I. p170-7, 262-8 (March-April 1912) **7255**

RHODE ISLAND

Bartlett, John Russell. Bibliography of Rhode Island; a catalogue of books and other publications relating to the state of Rhode Island, with notes, historical, biographical and critical. Printed by order of the General Assembly. Providence. A. Anthony. 1864. 287p. **7257**

Bongartz, J. Harry. Check list of Rhode Island laws, containing a complete list of the public laws and acts and resolves of the state of Rhode Island to date, with notes and pagings. Providence. J. A. and R. A. Reid. 1893. 8p. (Supplement through 1902 in Annual rep. of the Rhode Island state librarian. 1903. p8-10) **7258**

Brigham, Clarence Saunders. Bibliography of Rhode Island history. Boston, Syracuse. Mason Publishing Co. 1902. p653-81 (Reprinted from Field, Edward. State of Rhode Island and Providence Plantations at the end of the century; a history. [Boston, Syracuse. Mason Publishing Co. 1902] **7259**

—— A bibliography of the Narragansett country. Bul. bibliog. IV. p116-17. 1906 **7259a**

—— List of books upon Rhode Island history. (Rhode Island educational circulars. Hist. ser. I) State of Rhode Island, Dept. of Education. 1908. 8p. **7260**

—— Report on the archives of Rhode Island. Am. Hist. Asso. rep. 1903. I. p543-644 **7261**

—— Rhode Island—Bibliography of American newspapers, 1690-1820. Am. Antiq. Soc. proc. n.s. XXXIV. p79-127 (April 1924) **7262**

Brigham, Herbert O. Check-list of serial publications of Rhode Island. 1931. mim. 36p. **7262a**

Brown University. Bibliography, 1756-1898. Issued by the librarian. Providence. Remington Ptg. Co. 1898. 20p. **7263**

Chalmers, George. Catalogue of his papers relating to Rhode Island. (In the N.Y. Pub. Lib.) **7264**

Chapin, Howard M. Ann Franklin of Newport, printer, 1736-1763. *In* Bibliographical essays; a tribute to Wilberforce Eames. Cambridge. Harvard Univ. Press. 1924. p337-46 **7265**

—— Cartography of Rhode Island. (Contributions to Rhode Island bibliog. no. III) Providence. Preston & Rounds. 1915. 11p. **7265a**

—— Check list of Rhode Island almanacs, 1643-1850; with introductions and notes. Am. Antiq. Soc. proc. n.s. XXV. p19-54 (April 1915) (Reprinted. Worcester, Mass. 1915. 38p.) **7266**

—— Checklist of maps of Rhode Island [in the Rhode Island Historical Society Library]. (Contributions to Rhode Island bibliog. no. V) Providence. Preston & Rounds. 1918. 48p. (*Also in* Rhode Island Hist. Soc. col. XII. p26-32, 58-64, 89-95 (Jan.-July 1919) **7266a**

Early Rhode Island maps. R.I. Hist. Soc. news sheet. no. 48. pl (Jan. 1, 1915) **7266b**

Hammett, Charles E., Jr. A contribution to the bibliography and literature of Newport, R.I., comprising a list of books published or printed in Newport, with notes and additions. Newport. Hammett; Providence. Rider. 1887. 185p. **7267**

Hasse, Adelaide Rosalie. Index of economic material in documents of the states of the United States: Rhode Island, 1789-1904. (Carnegie Inst. of Wash. Publication no. 85) Wash. D.C. Carnegie Inst. of Wash. 1908. 95p. **7268**

Historical Records Survey. Rhode Island. Inventory of the church archives of Rhode Island. Providence, R.I. 1939- . mim. Society of Friends. May 1939. 80p. **7268a**

—— —— Preliminary check list of American portraits, 1620-1825 found in Rhode Island. Providence, R.I. 1939. 17p. mim. **7268b**

—— —— Summary of legislation concerning vital statistics in Rhode Island. Providence, R.I. July 1937. 18p. mim. **7268c**

International Typographical Union No. 33, Providence. Printers and printing in Providence, 1762-1907. Prepared by a committee of Providence Typographical Union Number Thirty-three, as a souvenir of the fiftieth anniversary of its institution. Providence. Allied Ptg. Co. 1907. 212, xcvi p. **7269**

John Carter Brown Library. A list of books, pamphlets, newspapers, and broadsides printed at Newport, Providence, Warren between 1727 and 1800. Providence. Print. for the Rhode Island Hist. Soc. 1915. 88p. **7269a**

Libbie, C. F. & Co. Catalogue of rare books from . . . a Rhode Island collector, including many books relating to New England. Boston. C. F. Libbie. 1914. 139p. **7270**

MacDonald, Grace E. Check-list of legislative documents in the Rhode Island state archives. (R.I. Secretary of State. State Bureau of Information. Annual bul. no. 1) Providence, Oxford Press. 1928. 24p. **7270a**

McMurtrie, Douglas C. The beginning of printing in Rhode Island. Somerville, N.J. 1935. p607-29 (Extract from Americana. fourth quarter. XXXIX. no. 4. 1935) **7271**

—— Pioneer printing in Rhode Island. Reprint from the September, 1932, National printer journalist. 4p. **7272**

New publications of Rhode Island interest. R.I. hist. soc. col. **7272a**

Perry, Amos. New England almanacs, with special mention of those published in Rhode Island. Narragansett hist. reg. IV. p27-39 (July 1885) **7273**

—— Rhode Island Historical Society, sketch of its history, with list of papers read at its stated meetings. Providence. Snow & Farnham. 1890. p17-37 (Reprinted from the Proc. of the Soc. 1889-90) **7274**

—— The town records of Rhode Island; a report. R.I. Hist. Soc. publications. n.s. I. p[99]-182 (July 1893) **7275**

Preston, Howard W. List of Rhode Island books entered for copyright, 1790-1816. Rhode Island Hist. Soc. colls. XIII. p69-72, 95-101 (April-July 1920) **7276**

Providence. City Library. Catalogue of the City Library in the mayor's office, Providence. Comp. by the mayor's clerk. Providence. Providence Ptg. Co., city printers. 1886. 62p. **7277**

Providence. City Registrar. Alphabetical index of the births, marriages, and deaths, recorded in Providence, R.I., 1636-1870. Providence. Sidney S. Rider. 1879-82. 4v. **7278**

Providence. Franklin Society. Index of publications bearing upon the geology and mineralogy of Rhode Island, chronologically arranged. *In* Report on the geology of Rhode Island. Providence. 1887. p2-57 **7278a**

Providence. Municipal Court. Index to the probate records of the Municipal Court of the city of Providence, Rhode Island, from 1646 to . . . 1899. Prepared under the direction of Edward Field. Providence. Providence Press, Snow & Farnham. 1902. 333p. **7279**

Rhode Island. Laws, Statutes, etc. Check list of Rhode Island laws, containing a complete list of the public laws and acts and resolves of the state of Rhode Island to date. Providence, R.I. 1873-1921 **7279a**

—— —— Index to general laws of Rhode Island, revision of 1909. Prepared by Bertram S. Blaisdell. Providence. E. L. Freeman. 1909. 1622p. **7279b**

—— —— Index to the printed acts and resolves of, and of the petitions and reports to the General Assembly of the State of Rhode Island and Providence Plantations, from 1758 to 1850. By John Russell Bartlett. Providence. Knowles, Anthony & Co. 1856. 424p.
Same. 1850 to 1862. By John Russell Bartlett. Providence. Anthony & Co. 1863. 104p.
Same. 1863 to 1873. By Joshua M. Addeman. Providence. Providence Ptg. Co. 1875. lxviii, 131p.
Same. 1873 to 1899. By Charles P. Bennett. Providence. E. L. Freeman. 1907. 460p. **7279c**

Rhode Island. Secretary of State. Report of the Secretary of State on the public archives and records. (Fourth annual rep. state rec. commissioner. 1898. Appendix A) Providence. E. L. Freeman. 1898. p15-21 **7280**

Rhode Island. State Library. Check list of legislative documents in the Rhode Island state archives. By Grace E. MacDonald (Rhode Island Office of the Secretary of State. State Bureau of Information, Annual bul. no. 1) Providence. Oxford Press. 1928. 24p.   7281

—— —— Check list of state documents of Rhode Island, annual departmental publications. Providence. Rhode Island State Lib. Aug. 1931. 36p.   7282

Rhode Island. State Record Commissioner. Annual reports of the State Record Commissioner, 1898-1912? Providence. E. L. Freeman. 1898-1912?   7283

—— —— Church records, abstract from returns of custodians of records on file in State Record Commissioner's office. (Ninth annual rep. of the State Rec. Commissioner. 1906. Appendix) Providence. E. L. Freeman. 1906. p13-92 7284

—— —— Revolutionary military papers. (Eighth annual rep. of the State Rec. Commissioner. 1905. Appendix) Providence. E. L. Freeman. 1905. p13-64 7285

—— —— Vital records of Rhode Island, 1639-1850. Comp. and pub. by James N. Arnold (Fourth annual rep. of the State Rec. Commissioner. Appendix C) Providence. E. L. Freeman. 1898. p23-8 7286

Rhode Island Historical Society. Rhode Island imprints; a list of books, pamphlets, newspapers and broadsides printed at Newport, Providence, Warren, Rhode Island, between 1727 and 1800. Providence. Printed for the Rhode Island Hist. Soc., Standard Ptg. Co. 1915. 88p. Addenda to Rhode Island imprint list. Rhode Island Hist. Soc. colls. XIV. p87-96. July 1921)   7290

Rider, Sidney S. A bibliographical and historical introduction to the digest of Rhode Island laws of 1719 and incidentally to all other folio laws. *In* The charter and acts of His Majesties colony of Rhode Island and Providence Plantations in America, 1719. Providence. Sidney S. Rider and Burnett Rider. 1895. p3-18   7291

Smith, Joseph Jencks. New index to the civil and military lists of Rhode Island. Providence, R.I. Joseph J. Smith. 1907. 182p.   7291a

Survey of Federal Archives. Rhode Island. Inventory of federal archives. Providence, R.I. 1938- . mim. The Federal Courts. May 1938. 40p.; The Department of the Treasury. Dec. 1938. 377p.; The Department of War. Dec. 1938. 277p.; The Department of Justice. Aug. 1938. 13p.; The Department of the Navy. March 1939. 335p.; The Department of the Interior. May 1938. 11p.; The Department of Agriculture. Feb. 1939. 125p.; The Department of Commerce. April 1938. 59p.; The Department of Labor. Nov. 1938. 54p.; The Veterans' Administration. Jan. 1939. 31p.; The Farm Credit Administration. April 1938. 5p.   7291b

—— —— Ship registers and enrollments of Newport, R.I., 1790-1939   7291c

Winship, George Parker. Newport newspapers in the eighteenth century. Newport Hist. Soc. bul. XIV. p1-19 (Oct. 1914)   7292

SOUTH CAROLINA

Charleston Library Society. A catalogue of the portraits, books, pamphlets, maps and manuscripts presented to the Charleston Library Society, May 12, 1906 by Hon. Wm. Ashmead Courtenay. Columbia. Priv. printed. 1908. 148p.   7293

College of Charleston. Index to the first fifteen volumes of South Carolina Historical and Genealogical Magazine. Charleston, S.C. ms.   7293a

Courtney, William A. The public records of South Carolina. Va. mag. hist. I. p466-7 (April 1894)   7293b

Duke University. Index to The State, Columbia, South Carolina, 1882-1911. Durham, N. C. (Newspaper)   7293c

Easterby, J. H. Guide to the reading and study of South Carolina history. Charleston. In progress   7293d

English, Elizabeth D. Author list of Caroliniana in the University of South Carolina Library. (University of South Carolina bulletin, Dec. 15, 1932, no. 134) Columbia. 1932. 337p.   7293e

Ford, Worthington Chauncey. Early maps of Carolina. Geog. rev. XVI. p264-73 (April 1926)   7293f

Gee, Wilson. South Carolina botanists; biography and bibliography. (Univ. of South Carolina. Bul. 72) Columbia, S.C. 1918. 52p.   7293g

Historical Records Survey. South Carolina. Inventory of the county archives of South Carolina. Columbia, S.C. 1937- . mim. No. 1. Abbeville. April 1938. 106p.; No. 2. Aiken. Dec. 1938. 115p.; No. 3. Allendale. Aug. 1938. 64p.; No. 4. Anderson. Aug. 1939. 169p.; No. 11. Cherokee. Feb. 1941. 176p.; No. 17. Dillon. Dec. 1938. 78p.; No. 21. Florence. Aug. 1938. 106p.; No. 27. Jasper. Oct. 1938. 72p.; No. 31. Lee. Jan. 1937. 46p.; No. 35. McCormick. June 1940. 135p.; No. 37. Oconee. June 1939. 133p.; No. 39. Pickens. June 1941. 257p.; No. 40. Richland. April 1940. 239p.; No. 41. Saluda. Oct. 1940. 168p.   7293h

Hoole, William Stanley. Check-list and finding list of Charleston periodicals, 1732-1864. Durham. Duke Univ. Press. 1936. 84p.   7293i

Kendall, Henry Plimpton. Early maps of Carolina and adjoining regions from the collection of Henry P. Kendall. . . Prep. by Louis Charles Karpinski on the basis of the 1930 catalogue comp. by Priscilla Smith. [Charleston, S.C. 1937] 67p. 7293j

King, William L. The newspaper press of Charleston; a chronological and biographical history, embracing a period of one hundred and forty years. Charleston. Edward Perry. 1872. 192p. **7294**

List and abstracts of papers in the State Paper Office, London, relating to South Carolina. S.C. Hist. Soc. col. I. p87-307.; II. p118-326; III. p272-343. 1857-1859. 3v. **7294a**

McMurtrie, Douglas C. A bibliography of South Carolina imprints, 1731-1740. Charleston. Priv. printed. 1933. 23p. (Also in South Carolina hist. and geneal mag. XXXIV. p117-37. July 1933) **7295**

—— The first decade of printing in the royal province of South Carolina. The Lib. 4th ser. XIII. no. 4. p425-52. 1933 (Reprinted. London. Bibliog. Soc. 1933) **7296**

Presbyterian College. Union catalog of South Caroliniana. Clinton, S.C. **7296a**

Rice, William. A digested index of the statute law of South Carolina, from the earliest period to the year 1836, inclusive. Charleston. 1838. 396p. **7296b**

Salley, Alexander S., Jr. A bibliography of the women writers of South Carolina. South. Hist. Asso. publications. VI. p143-57 (March 1902) **7297**

—— The first presses of South Carolina. Bibliog. Soc. of Amer. pap. II. p28-69. 1908 **7298**

—— Preservation of South Carolina history. North Carolina Hist. rev. IV. p145-57 (April 1927) **7299**

—— South Carolina's records of the Revolution. Daughters of the Am. Revolution, mag. LXXI. p283-5 (April 1937) **7299a**

Shearer, James F. French and Spanish works printed in Charleston, South Carolina. Bibliog. Soc. Am. pap. XXXIV. p137-70. 1940 **7299b**

Smiley, W. W. Official publications of the state of South Carolina. Urbana. Univ. of Illinois Lib. School. In progress **7299c**

Smith, W. Roy. Literature for the study of the colonial history of South Carolina. South Atlantic quar. I. p162-70 (April 1902) **7300**

South Carolina. Codes. General index to 1922 code . . . including the state and federal constitutions and rules of court and also 1922-25 session laws. Comp. by the editorial staff of the American digest system under direction of the Committee for reindexing the Code of South Carolina. St. Paul, Minn. 1927. 486p. **7301**

South Carolina. Historical Commission. [Legislative records in the custody of the commission]. *In* Report of the Historical Commission of South Carolina, 1906. [Raleigh] Gonzales & Bryan. 1905-06. p13-19 **7302**

South Carolina. Laws, Statutes, etc. Digested index of statute law from earliest period to 1836 incl. By William Rice. Charleston, S.C. 1938. 396p. **7303**

South Carolina. Public Record Commission. Report . . . to the General Assembly of South Carolina. Columbia, S.C. 1893- **7304**

South Carolina. University. Library. Author list of Caroliniana in the University of South Carolina Library. Comp. by Elizabeth D. English. . . ed. by Robert M. Kennedy (Univ. of South Carolina. Bul. no. 134. Dec. '15, 1923) Columbia, S.C. 1923. 337p. **7305**

Survey of Federal Archives. South Carolina. Inventory of federal archives in the states. New York, N.Y. and Albany, N.Y. 1939- . mim. The Department of the Treasury. July 1939. 111p.; The Department of Justice. June 1939. 18p. **7305a**

U.S. Library of Congress. Division of bibliography. List of references on reconstruction in South Carolina. Aug. 17, 1920. 4p. typ. **7306**

Webber, Mabel L. South Carolina almanacs, to 1800. S. C. hist. mag. XV. p73-81 (April 1914) **7306a**

Whitney, Edson Leone. Bibliography of the colonial history of South Carolina. Am. Hist. Asso. rep. 1894. p563-86 **7307**

Woody, Robert H. The republican newspaper press of South Carolina, 1860-1880. Durham, N.C. Duke Univ. In progress **7307a**

SOUTH DAKOTA

Coursey, Oscar William. Literature of South Dakota. Mitchell. Educator Supply Co. 1925. 393p. **7308**

Fox, Lawrence K. Survey of state archives of South Dakota to be published by the state. 1934 **7309**

Goodfellow, Ferd J. South Dakota state publications. South Dakota hist. colls. II. p83-5. 1904 **7310**

Historical Records Survey. South Dakota. Inventory of the county archives of South Dakota. Mitchell, S.D. 1937- . mim. No. 3. Bennett. Oct. 1940. 89p.; No. 8. Buffalo. Dec. 1937. 42p.; No. 12. Clark. March 1941. 132p.; No. 27. Haakon. Jan. 1941. 106p.; No. 47. Mellette. Dec. 1940. 86p.; No. 48. Miner. July 1941. 133p. **7310a**

Krueger, Ruth. South Dakota state documents. (Univ. of Illinois. Master's thesis) Univ. of Illinois, Urbana. 1936. 180p. MS. **7310b**

McMurtrie, Douglas C. The beginnings of the press in South Dakota. Iowa City. Priv. printed. 1933. p125-31 (Extract from the Journalism quar. June 1933) **7311**

Morford, Lee. Newspapers of the Black Hills. Black Hills engineers. XVIII. p61-6 (Jan. 1930) **7312**

O'Harra, Cleophas C. A bibliography of the geology and mining interests of the Black Hills region. (South Dakota School of Mines. Bul. no. 11. Dept. of geol.) Rapid City, S.D. May 1917. 216p. **7313**

Robinson, Doane. South Dakota literature. South Dakota hist. colls. VI. p84-106. 1912   7314

South Dakota. State Historical Society. Catalogue [of] books, pamphlets and newspapers in the South Dakota division of the South Dakota State Library, July 1, 1908. South Dakota hist. colls. IV. p16-57. 1908   7315

—— A catalogue of the bound books produced by South Dakota authors. South Dakota hist. colls. II. p79-82. 1904   7316

—— —— Newspapers in the State Historical Society. South Dakota hist. colls. II. p15-19. 1904   7317

—— —— Newspapers of South Dakota. South Dakota hist. colls. XI. p411-18. 1922   7318

South Dakota. State Planning Board. Bibliography of South Dakota state planning board publications. Brookings, S.D. South Dakota State Planning Board. 1939. 12p. photop.   7318a

—— —— Master index to South Dakota State Planning Board publications. Brookings, S.D. Central Office. 1937. 16p. Reprod.   7318b

South Dakota historical collections. Index to South Dakota historical collections, vols. I-XVI. Comp. by Ethel Collins Jacobsen. Pierre, S.D. 1935. 138p. mim.   7318c

TENNESSEE

Baker, Mary E. Tennessee serials, together with the holdings of Tennessee libraries; a tentative list prepared with the assistance of the Tennessee Library Association. Knoxville, Tenn. Univ. of Tennessee. 1937. 57p.   7318d

Brigham, Clarence S. Tennessee—Bibliography of American newspapers, 1690-1820. Am. Antiq. Soc. proc. n.s. XXXV. p79-97 (April 1925)   7319

Cheney, Frances Neel (Mrs. B. B. Cheney). Bibliography of official publications of Tennessee. International House. N.Y. In progress   7319a

Cockrill, Elizabeth. Bibliography of Tennessee geology, soils, drainage, forestry, etc., with subject index. (Tennessee Geol. Survey. Bul. 1-B) Nashville, Tenn. 1911. 119p.   7320

Foster, A. P. Tennessee department of library, archives and history. Tennessee hist. mag. VI. p266-78 (Jan. 1921) 7321

Ganier, A. F. Bibliography of Tennessee archaeology. Arrow points. X. p6-8 (Jan. 1925)   7321a

Giddings, Frederick. Early Tennessee surveys and maps. Tenn. law rev. IV. p115-24 (March 1926)   7321b

Goodpasture, A. V. An account of the compilations of the statute laws of Tennessee. Am. hist. mag. VII. p69-79 (Jan. 1902)   7322

Halley, R. A. The preservation of Tennessee history. Am. hist. mag. and Tennessee Hist. Soc. quar. VIII. p49-63 (Jan. 1903)   7323

Historical Records Survey. Tennessee. Check list of acts and codes of the state of Tennessee, 1792-1939. Nashville, Tenn. June 1940. 21p. mim.   7323a

—— —— Check list of records required or permitted by law in Tennessee. Nashville, Tenn. Aug. 1937. 51p. mim. 7323b

—— —— Guide to collections of manuscripts in Tennessee. Nashville, Tenn. 1941. 38p.   7323c

—— —— Guide to depositories of manuscript collections in Tennessee. Nashville, Tenn. Dec. 1940. 27p.   7323d

—— —— Guide to public vital statistics in Tennessee. Nashville, Tenn. June 1941. 146p. mim.   7323e

—— —— Inventory of the church archives of Tennessee. Nashville, Tenn. 1939- . mim. Tennessee Baptist Convention: Nashville Baptist Association. Dec. 1939. 69p.; Jewish Congregations. July 1941. 55p.   7323f

—— —— Inventory of the county archives of Tennessee. Nashville, Tenn. 1937- . mim. No. 1. Anderson. July 1941. 89p.; No. 5. Blount. April 1941. 89p.; No. 6. Bradley. Jan. 1941. 137p.; No. 17. Crockett. Aug. 1940. 115p.; No. 2. Bedford. May 1940. 152p.; No. 33. Hamilton. Nov. 1937. 130p.; No. 38. Haywood. March 1939. 161p.; No. 53. Loudon. March 1941. 128p.; No. 84. Tipton. July 1941. 166p.; No. 75. Rutherford. March 1938. 138p.; No. 95. Wilson. Sept. 1938. 177p.   7323g

Lewis, Charles Lee. Robert Thomas Quarles and the archives of Tennessee. Tenn. hist. mag. IX. p3-8. 1926   7323h

Luttrell, Laura E. Historical activities in and respecting Tennessee, 1923-1929. East Tennessee Hist. Soc. publications. I. no. 2. p94-106. 1930   7324

—— Writings on Tennessee history. East Tennessee Hist. Soc. publications. III. p127-33 (Jan. 1931); IV. p116-21 (Jan. 1932); cont.   7325

McMurtrie, Douglas C. Early printing in Tennessee, with a bibliography of the issues of the Tennessee press, 1793-1830. Chicago. Chicago Club of Ptg. House Craftsmen. 1933. 141p.   7326

—— Pioneer printing in Tennessee. Springfield, Ill. 1931. 2p. (Reprinted from the Nov. 1931 issue of National printer journalist)   7327

Mellen, George F. Calvin Morgan McClung and his library. Tennessee hist. mag. VII. p3-26 (April 1921)   7328

Moore, Mrs John Trotwood. The Division of Library and Archives in Tennessee. National Asso. State Lib. proc. and pap. 1937-38. p16-20   7328a

Nashville. Public Library. Card bibliography of Tennessee history. Nashville, Tenn.   7328b

—— Card bibliography of Tennessee writers. Nashville, Tenn.   7328c

Ochs, George W. The press of East Tennessee. *In* East Tennessee, historical and biographical. Chattanooga. A. D. Smith. 1893. p157-69 **7329**

Paul, George Hurst. Tennessee newspaper directory. n.p. 1929. 8p. mim. **7330**

Scates, Silas Erwin. A classification of some historical material in Nashville, Tennessee. (George Peabody College for Teachers. M.A. thesis) 1926. MS. **7331**

Shoup, Charles Samuel. An annotated bibliography of the zoology of Tennessee. Nashville, Tenn. The Joint Univ. Lib. 1939. p583-623 (Reprinted from the American midland naturalist. XXI. no. 3. May 1939) **7331a**

Sioussat, St. George Leakin. A preliminary report upon the archives of Tennessee. Am. Hist. Asso. rep. 1906. II. p197-238 **7332**

Skeffington, Mary. Catalogue—Tennesseana. (Tennessee State Lib. rep. 1911-12) Nashville. Brandon Ptg. Co. 1913. p96-121 **7333**

Some early maps of Tennessee. Am. hist. mag. II. p183-5. 1897 **7333a**

Springer, Patricia. Bibliography of Tennessee historical material in Nashville libraries. (George Peabody College for Teachers. Master's thesis) Nashville, Tenn. 1930. 246p. MS. **7334**

Survey of Federal Archives. Tennessee. Inventory of federal archives in the states. New Orleans, La. 1938- . mim. The Federal Courts. April 1940. 96p.; The Department of the Treasury. July 1939. 98p.; The Department of War. July 1938. 91p.; The Department of the Interior. Feb. 1941. 53p.; The Department of Justice. Nov. 1939. 37p.; The Department of the Navy. July 1938. 9p.; The Department of Agriculture. Sept. 1938. 187p.; The Department of Commerce. June 1940. 10p.; The Department of Labor. 1941. 25p.; The Farm Credit Administration. June 1941. 36p.; Miscellaneous agencies. May 1941. 85p. **7334a**

Tennessee. Historical Committee. Tennessee department of library, archives and history. Nashville. Tennessee Industrial School, Ptg. dept. 1922. 18p. **7335**

Tennessee. State Library. Bibliography of writers, artists, musicians, etc. relating to Tennessee. Nashville, Tenn. **7335a**

—— —— Card catalog of Tennessee state publications. Nashville, Tenn. **7335b**

—— Catalogue—Tennesseana. (Biennial rep. of the State librarian. 1911-12) Nashville, Tenn. 1913. p31-133 **7336**

Tennessee. University. Card catalog of Tennessee state publications. Knoxville, Tenn. (Supplementary to similar list at the Tennessee State Library) **7336a**

—— —— Inventory of official records preceding 1860 in the archives of certain Tennessee counties. Knoxville, Tenn. **7336b**

—— —— Union list of Tennessee serials in the libraries of Tennessee. Knoxville, Tenn. **7336c**

Turner, H. H. and Ogden, E. L. Author and title index to papers and index to portraits in the proceedings of the Bar Association of Tennessee, sessions 1-50, 1882-1931. Tenn. law rev. X. p193-216 (April 1932) **7336d**

U.S. Library of Congress. Division of bibliography. The Tennessee Valley area; a list of fiction. Aug. 18, 1933. 10p. typ. **7337**

Wiley, Edwin. Eighteenth century presses in Tennessee. Bibliog. Soc. of Amer. pap. II. p70-83. 1907-08 **7338**

Williams, Samuel C. A history of codification in Tennessee. Tennessee law rev. X. p165-79 (April 1932) **7339**

Wisconsin. State Historical Society. Calendar of the Tennessee and King's Mountain papers of the Draper collection of manuscripts. (Publications of the State Hist. Soc. of Wisconsin, Calendar ser., III) Madison. The Soc. 1929. 698p. **7339a**

TEXAS

Agatha, Sister M. Texas prose writings; a reader's digest. Dallas. Banks Upshaw. 1936. 168p. **7341**

Barker, Eugene C. Notes on early Texas newspapers, 1819-1836. Southwestern hist. quar. XXI. p127-44 (Oct. 1917) **7342**

—— The public archives of Texas. Am. Hist. Asso. rep. 1901. II. p353-8 **7343**

—— Report on the Bexar archives. Am. Hist. Asso. rep. 1902. I. p357-63 **7344**

Barns, Florence Elberta. Texas writers of today. Dallas. Tardy Publishing Co. 1935. 513p. **7345**

Bentley, Imogen. A history of Texas magazines. Nashville, Tenn. Peabody. In progress **7345a**

Bolton, Herbert Eugene. Records of the mission of Nuestra Señora del Refugio. Southw. hist. quar. XIV. p164-6 (Oct. 1910) **7345b**

—— Spanish mission records at San Antonio. Southw. hist. quar. X. p297-307 (April 1907) **7345c**

Castañeda, Carlos E. and Martin, Early, Jr. Three manuscript maps of Texas by Stephen F. Austin; with biographical and bibliographical notes. Austin, Tex. Priv. print. 1930. 55p. **7345d**

Cole, Theodore L. Laws of Texas. St. Louis. F. H. Thomas Law Book Co. n.d. 3p. **7346**

Fort Worth. Public Library. Card index to Fort Worth newspapers, 1870 to date. Fort Worth, Tex. **7346a**

Goodwin, John E. Special collections in the University of Texas Library. Bibliog. Soc. of Amer. pap. XVII. p63-9. 1923 **7347**

Gray, A. C. History of the Texas press. *In* Wooten, Dudley G. A comprehensive history of Texas, 1685 to 1897. Dallas. Scarff. 1898. II. p368-423 **7348**

Gutsch, Milton R. Texas and the preservation of war history materials. Miss. Valley Hist. Asso. proc. X. pt. 1. p95-107. extra no. (July 1920) **7349**

Haggard, J. Villasana. Spanish archives handbook. (Austin) Univ. of Texas. 1938. 95p. typ. (Spanish archives of Texas) **7349a**

Harrison, Guy Bryan. The Texas collection of Baylor University. (Baylor University historical publications, ser. 1, the Baylor bul. XLIV, no. 4, Dec. 1940) Waco, Tex. Baylor Univ. Press. 1940. 75p. **7349b**

Historical materials in the Rosenberg library (Galveston). Southw. hist. quar. XXVII. p168-9 (July 1923) **7349c**

Historical Records Survey. Texas. Check list of records required or permitted by law in Texas. San Antonio, Texas. Jan. 1937. 86p. mim. **7349d**

—— —— Inventory of the colonial archives of Texas, 1821-1837. No. 3. Municipality of Brazoria, 1832-1837 (Brazoria County Courthouse, Angleton, Texas) San Antonio, Texas. 1937. 120p. mim. **7349e**

—— —— Inventory of the county archives of Texas. San Antonio, Texas. 1937- . mim. No. 10. Bandera. June 1940. 113p.; No. 11. Bastrop. June 1941. 128p.; No. 25. Brown. May 1940. 147p.; No. 29. Calhoun. Jan. 1941. 115p.; No. 61. Denton. Aug. 1937. 125p.; No. 62. De Witt. Jan. 1940. 123p.; No. 75. Fayette. Dec. 1940. 167p.; No. 92. Gregg. Aug. 1940. 179p.; No. 94. Guadalupe. Dec. 1939. 393p.; No. 105. Hays. Jan. 1940. 105p.; No. 111. Hood. March 1940. 69p.; No. 120. Jackson. Dec. 1940. 103p.; No. 158. Marion. March 1940. 118p.; No. 166. Milam. June 1941. 131p.; No. 167. Mills. April 1940. 78p.; No. 198. Robertson. March 1941. 140p.; No. 199. Rockwall. Feb. 1940. 73p.; No. 202. Sabine. June 1939. 217p.; No. 213. Somervell. March 1940. 63p.; No. 232. Uvalde. May 1941. 143p.; No. 247. Wilson. Nov. 1939. 100p. **7349f**

—— —— Texas newspapers, 1813-1939; a union list of newspaper files available in offices of publishers, libraries, and a number of private collections. San Antonio, Tex. 1941. 293p. mim. **7349g**

Holden, W. C. Frontier journalism in West Texas. Southwestern hist. quar. XXXII. p206-21 (Jan. 1929) **7350**

McMurtrie, Douglas C. Pioneer printing in Texas. Austin, Texas. 1932. 28p. (Reprint with additions from Southwestern hist. quar. XXXV. p173-93. Jan. 1932) **7351**

Meyer, H. H. B. List of references on county government. *In* James, Herman G. County government in Texas. (Univ. of Texas. Bul. no. 2525. July 1, 1925) Austin. The Univ. 1925. p121-35 **7352**

Montgomery, Vaida Stewart. A century with Texas poets and poetry. Dallas. Kaleidograph Press. 1934. 120p. **7353**

Moore, Ike. The Texas press, 1813-1846. San Jacinto. San Jacinto Museum of History. In progress **7353a**

Norton, A. B. History of the early newspapers of Texas. *In* Baillio, F. B. and Edwards, Henry. History of the Texas Press Association. Dallas. Southwestern Ptg. Co. 1916. p318-80 **7354**

Payne, Leonidas Warren. A survey of Texas literature. Chicago. Rand, McNally. 1928. 76p. **7355**

Pillsbury, Stanley R. Texas, 1836-1936, an exhibition. N.Y. Pub. Lib. bul. XLI. p71-94 (Feb. 1937) **7355a**

Raines, Cadwell Walton. Analytical index to the laws of Texas, 1823-1905. Austin. Von Boeckmann-Jones. 1906. 559p. **7356**

—— A bibliography of Texas; being a descriptive list of books, pamphlets, and documents relating to Texas in print and manuscript since 1536. Austin. Gammel. 1896. 268p. (Reprinted 1934) **7357**

Ramsdell, Charles W. The preservation of Texas history. North Carolina hist. rev. VI. p1-16 (Jan. 1929) **7358**

Rannick, Selina M. A survey of German literature in Texas. Southwestern hist. quar. XXXIII. p134-59 (Oct. 1929) **7359**

Rogers, John William. Finding records on the Texas plains, with a representative bibliography of books on the Southwest by J. Frank Dobie. Dallas. Southwest press. 1931. 57p. **7360**

Rosenberg Library. Henry Rosenberg, 1824-1893. Galveston, Tex. (N.Y. Devinne Press) 1928. 226p. (p139-226 on the Rosenberg Library) **7360a**

Simonds, Frederic William. A record of the geology of Texas for the decade ending December 31, 1896. Texas Acad. Sci. trans. III. p17-296. 1899 **7360b**

Smither, Harriet. The archives of Texas. Am. archivist. III. p187-200 (July 1940) **7360c**

Spell, Lota M. Samuel Bangs; the first printer in Texas. Hispanic Am. hist. rev. XI. p248-58 (May 1931) **7361**

Streeter, Thomas W. Bibliography of Texas for the period 1795-1845. Morristown, N.J. In progress **7361a**

—— Bibliography of Texas imprints through 1845. Morristown, N.J. In progress **7361b**

Survey of Federal Archives. Texas. Inventory of federal archives in the states. San Antonio, Texas. 1939- . mim. The Federal Courts. Parts I-IV. June 1939. 275p.; The Department of the Treasury. Parts I-IV. June 1939. 384p.; The Department of War. Parts I-XII. June 1939. 1364p.; The Department of Justice. June 1939. 70p.; The Department of the Navy. June 1939. 24p.; The Department of the Interior. Jan. 1941. 114p.; The Department of Agriculture. Parts I-IX. June 1940. 1815p.; The Department of Commerce. June 1939. 75p.; The Department of Labor. Parts I-II. Oct. 1940. 539p.; The Veterans' Administration. Dec. 1940. 97p.; The Farm Credit Administration. June 1940. 81p.; Miscellaneous agencies. Parts I-II. Oct. 1940. 482p. **7361c**

Texas. Agricultural Experiment Station. Subject list of Texas agricultural experiment station publications as of September 1, 1933- for the use of libraries and station workers. [College Station. 1933-] mim. **7362**

Texas. Laws, Statutes, etc. Vernon's annotated civil and criminal statutes of the state of Texas revision of 1925. General index and tables. Kansas City, Mo. Vernon Law Book Co. 1927. 628p. (Cont.) **7362a**

Texas. Library and Historical Commission. Biennial reports, 1909/1910- . Austin. Austin Ptg. Co. 1911- (Reports include material on archives and MSS. in the library) **7363**

—— —— Texas documents. Texas libraries. I. p12-14 (Nov. 1909) **7363a**

—— —— Transcripts from British Public Record Office. Transcripts from the archives of Mexico. (Second biennial rep. 1911-12) Austin. Von Boeckmann-Jones. 1914. p27-63 (Cover period 1820-30) **7364**

Texas. State Library. Index to some miscellaneous Texas history questions answered at the Texas State Library. n.p. 1926. 82p. mim. **7365**

Texas. University. Library. The archives. Austin. Univ. of Texas. n.d. 8p. **7365a**

—— —— —— Index to Texas biography. Austin, Tex. ms. **7365b**

—— —— —— Name index to all Texas newspapers before 1845. Austin, Tex. ms. **7365c**

—— —— —— Union catalog of books, periodicals, pamphlets, etc. in Texas libraries relating to Texas and the Southwest. Austin, Texas. In progress, 1921- **7365d**

Texas State Historical Association. Book reviews and notices. Southwestern hist. quar. II. July 1898- **7366**

Texas State-wide Records Project. Index to probate cases of Texas. San Antonio, Tex. 1940- reprod. typ. **7366a**

Tullis, Coral H. Publications of the Texas State Historical Association, July, 1897, through April, 1937. Southw. hist. quar. XLI. p3-82 (July 1937) **7366b**

U.S. Library of Congress. Division of bibliography. List of references on the diplomatic relations of the republic of Texas. Aug. 12, 1920. 3p. multig. **7367**

—— —— —— Texas; a bibliographical list. Feb. 23, 1929. 25p. typ. **7368**

Webb, Mrs. Margaret. Bibliography on Texas municipal government. [Austin. 1939] 33p. mim. **7368a**

Whatley, W. A. The historical manuscript collection of the University of Texas. Texas hist. teachers bul. IX. p19-25 (Nov. 1920) **7369**

Whitmore & Smith, firm, booksellers. Check-list of books on and about Texas and the great Southwest, and other works. Comp. and pub. by Whitmore & Smith. Dallas. [1935] 28p. **7370**

Wilcox, Fannie M. Texas state author collection. Am. Lib. Asso. bul. XXIV. p561-2 (Sept. 1930) (*Also in* National Asso. of State Lib. pap. and proc. 1930. p42-3) **7370a**

Winkler, Ernest W. Collections of the Archive and History Department of the Texas State Library. Southw. hist. quar. XX. p406-9 (April 1917) **7370b**

—— Destruction of historical archives of Texas. Texas State Hist. Asso. quar. XV. p148-55 (Oct. 1911) **7371**

—— First-[third] annual reports of the classifier and translator of manuscripts in the Texas State Library. *In* Twenty-ninth and thirty-first annual reports of commissioner of agriculture. . . Part 2. Austin. Von Boeckmann-Jones Co. 1904; Houston. State Ptg. Co. 1906. (General account of MSS. in the library and of archives; calendar of Manuel de Salcedo correspondence, 1810-1812, and of the Yoakum papers, 1845-57) **7372**

—— Some historical activities of the Texas Library and Historical Commission. Southw. hist quar. XIV. p294-304 (April 1911) **7372a**

UTAH

Alter, J. Cecil. Early Utah journalism: a half century of forensic warfare waged by the West's most militant press. Salt Lake City. Utah Hist. Soc. 1938. 405p. **7372b**

Bancroft, Hubert Howe. Authorities consulted in the History of Utah. *In* History of Utah, 1540-1887. San Francisco. Hist. Co. 1890. p. xxi-xlvii **7373**

Berrian, William. Catalogue of books, early newspapers, and pamphlets, on Mormonism collected by the late William Berrian. [N.Y. V. H. Everson print. 1898] 48p. **7374**

Deseret News Office. Catalogue of publications of the Church of Latter-Day Saints. Salt Lake City. Nov. 1884. 8p. **7375**

Federal Writers' Project. Utah. A partial bibliography of source material on Weber County and Ogden City, Utah. Ogden, Utah. Ogden Hist. Soc. 1938. 3, 27p. mim. **7375a**

Genealogical Society of Utah. Catalogue of family histories in the library of the Genealogical Society of Utah. Utah geneal. and hist. mag. IX. p83-96, 139-44, 184-92 (April-Oct. 1918); X. p41-8, 87-96, 136-44 (Jan.-July 1919) **7375b**

Historical Records Survey. Utah. Check list of newspapers and magazines published in Ogden. Ogden, Utah. May 1938. 5p. mim. **7375c**

—— —— History and bibliography of religion. Ogden, Utah. June 1940. 121p. mim. **7375d**

—— —— Inventory of the church archives of Utah. Ogden, Utah. 1940- . mim. Vol. 2. Baptist Church. Aug. 1940. 71p. mim. Smaller denominations. Feb. 1941. 73p. **7375e**

—— —— Inventory of the county archives of Utah. Ogden, Utah. 1937- . mim. No. 2. Box Elder. Dec. 1938. 160p.; No. 4. Carbon. July 1940. 261p.; No. 5. Daggett. Aug. 1939. 133p.; No. 8 Emery. March 1941. 179p.; No. 10. Grand. April 1938. 89p.; No. 15. Morgan. Aug. 1937. 39p.; No. 23. Tooele. June 1939. 259p.; No. 24. Uintah. Nov. 1940. 254p.; No. 25. Utah. Sept. 1940. 329p.; No. 26. Wasatch. July 1938. 95p.; No. 29. Weber. Jan. 1940. 236p. (prelim. ed.) **7375f**

—— —— Inventory of the state archives of Utah. Ogden, Utah. 1940- . The State of Deseret. 1940. 187p. (Reprinted from the Utah State Historical Society. VIII. p65-251. April, July, Oct. 1940) **7375g**

—— —— Records required of county officers, State of Deseret, March 15, 1849 to April 5, 1851. Ogden, Utah. Aug. 1937. 3p. mim. **7375h**

McMurtrie, Douglas C. The beginnings of printing in Utah, with a bibliography of the issues of the Utah press, 1849-1860. Chicago. John Calhoun Press. 1931. 91p. **7376**

—— Notes on early printing in Utah outside of Salt Lake City. Los Angeles. Press of the Frank Wiggins Trade School. 1938. 9p. (Reprinted with some revisions, from the Utah hist. quar. V. p83-7. July 1932) **7376a**

—— Pioneer printing in Utah. Springfield, Ill. 1933. 3p. (Reprinted from the June 1933 issue of the National printer journalist) **7377**

Neff, Andrew L. (University of Utah). Report on the territorial archives of Utah completed for the Public archives commission in 1934. Utah state archives, 1896-1935, completed in 1935. MSS. **7378**

New York. Public Library. List of the works in the New York Public Library relating to the Mormons. N.Y. Pub. Lib. bul. XIII. p183-239 (March 1909) **7379**

Survey of Federal Archives. Utah. Inventory of federal archives in the states. Salt Lake City, Utah. 1939- . mim. The Federal Courts. Oct. 1939. 17p.; The Department of the Treasury. Oct. 1939. 80p.; The Department of War. June 1940. 46p.; The Department of Justice. Oct. 1939. 20p.; The Department of the Navy. Feb. 1940. 9p.; The Department of the Interior. Sept. 1940. 146p.; The Department of Commerce. May 1940. 34p.; The Department of Labor. Sept. 1940. 46p.; The Veterans' Administration. April 1940. 30p.; The Farm Credit Administration. May 1940. 24p. **7379a**

U.S. Library of Congress. Division of bibliography. A list of recent references on Utah, with special references to economic and social conditions. 1938. 8p. typ. **7379b**

—— —— —— A list of references on the economic development of Utah with special reference to Mormonism. Feb. 19, 1924. 6p. typ. **7380**

Utah. State Planning Board. Index of maps. Salt Lake City. 1936. 16p. mim. **7380a**

Woodward, Charles L. Bibliotheca Scallawagiana; catalogue of a matchless collection of books, pamphlets, autographs, pictures, &c., relating to Mormonism and the Mormons . . . to be sold . . . Bangs & Co. [N.Y. 1880] 50p. **7381**

VERMONT

Benedict, G. G. Early Vermont bibliography of the eighteenth century. The Vermonter. V. p171-7 (May 1900) **7382**

—— The recovery of the Fay records. Mag. of hist. VI. p166-70 (Sept. 1907) (Records of the early general conventions which formed the commonwealth of Vermont) **7382a**

Brigham, Clarence S. Vermont—Bibliography of American newspapers, 1690-1820. Am. Antiq. Soc. proc. n.s. XXXV. p99-160 (April 1925) **7383**

Conant, Harrison J. The admission of Vermont to the union; a bibliography. Vt. Hist. Soc. proc. n.s. VIII. p210-13 (June 1940) **7383a**

—— The legislation of Vermont. Law lib. jour. XXI. p82-5 (Oct. 1928) **7384**

Cooley, Elizabeth Frances. Vermont imprints before 1800; an introductory essay on the history of printing in Vermont, with a list of imprints, 1779-1799. Montpelier, Vt. Vt. Hist Soc. 1937. 133p. **7384a**

Early Vermont newspapers. Vt. Hist. Soc. proc. 1882. p xv-xix **7384b**

The First conference of Lake Champlain historians. Collections of historical material in and around Burlington, by Leon W. Dean; The Pliny Moore collection, by Hugh McLellan; The Sheldon Museum, by Florence A. Allen; Summary of address by Doctor Dixon Ryan Fox; The Champlain Valley Archaeological Society, by John H. Bailey; Notes on the Vermont Historical Society's collections relating to Lake Champlain, by Agnes K. Lawson; Some miscellaneous historical material, by C. Eleanor Hall. Vt. Hist. Soc. proc. VII. n.s. p185-204 (Sept. 1939) **7384c**

Flanders, Helen Hartness. Index of ballads and folk-songs in the archive of Vermont folk-songs at Smiley Manse, Springfield, Vermont. Vt. Hist. Soc. proc. n.s. VIII. p214-51 (June 1940) **7384d**

—— List of folk-songs recorded in Vermont in November, 1939. Vt. Hist. Soc. proc. n.s. VIII. p302-11 (Sept. 1940) **7384e**

—— The quest for Vermont ballads: index of ballads and folk-songs in the archive of Vermont folk-songs at Smiley Manse, Springfield, Vermont. Vt. Hist. Soc. proc. n.s. VII. p73-98 (June 1939). First Supplement. Ibid. 279-85 (Dec. 1939) **7384f**

Gilman, Marcus Davis and others. The bibliography of Vermont; or a list of books and pamphlets relating in any way to the state, with biographical and other notes. Burlington. Free Press Asso. 1897. 350p. (Also in Montpelier Argus and Patriot, Jan. 29, 1879-Sept. 22, 1880) **7385**

Goodrich, J. E. Vermont literature. The Vermonter. IX. p69-83 (Oct. 1903) **7386**

Hamilton, Milton W. Rural journalism in Vermont, 1781-1850. Reading, Pa. Albright College. In progress **7386a**

Hasse, Adelaide Rosalie. Index of economic material in documents of the states of the United States—Vermont, 1789-1904. (Carnegie Inst. of Wash. Publication no. 85) Wash. D.C. Carnegie Inst. of Wash. 1907. 71p. **7387**

Historical Records Survey. Vermont. Index to the Burlington free press in the Billings library, University of Vermont. Montpelier, Vt. 1940- . reprod. **7387a**

—— —— Inventory of the church archives of Vermont. Montpelier, Vt. 1939- .mim. No. 1. The Diocese of Vermont—Protestant Episcopal. 1940. 253p.; Preprint of Churches of Hinesburg, 1789-1939. May 1939. 13p. **7387b**

—— —— Inventory of the town, village and city archives of Vermont. Montpelier, Vt. 1938- . mim. No. 1. Addison County: vol. 2 Bridport. 1939. 60p.; No. 4. Chittenden County: vol. 1. Bolton. May 1939. 56p., vol. 3. Charlotte. 1939. 72p., vol. 5. Essex. Aug. 1940. 102p.; No. 6. Franklin County: vol. 4. Fairfax. 1940. 72p.; No. 7. Towns of Grand Isle County: Alburgh, Grand Isle, Isle LaMotte, North Hero, South Hero, Two Heroes, Alburgh Village. Dec. 1939. 259p.; No. 8. Lamoille County: vol 1. Belvidere. Oct. 1940. 58p., vol. 2. Cambridge. June 1941. 96p., vol. 3. Eden. Dec. 1940. 58p., vol. 4. Elmore. Feb. 1941. 62p., vol. 5. Hyde Park. Dec. 1940. 76p., vol. 6. Johnson. July 1941. 88p., vol. 7. Town of Morristown and Sterling, Village of Morrisville. 1940. 121p., vol 8. Stowe and Mansfield. Aug. 1940. 130p., vol. 9. Waterville. July 1939. 53p., vol. 10. Wolcott. Oct. 1939. 68p.; No. 10. Orleans County: vol. 1. Albany. 1940. 75p., vol. 5. Coventry. Aug. 1940. 64p., vol. 7. Town of Derby, Villages of Derby, Derby Line. 1939. 103p., vol. 7. supplement. Town of Salem. 1781-1880. April 1941. 40p.; No. 11. Rutland County: vol. 1. Benson. April 1941. 62p.; vol. 3. Castleton. March 1941. 104p., vol. 8. Hubbardton. Nov. 1940. 56p., vol. 13. Mt. Tabor. March 1941. 60p., vol. 25. Wallingford. April 1940. 87p., vol. 22. Shrewsbury. 1940. 59p.; No. 13. Windham County: vol. 6. Grafton. 1940. 87p., vol. 9. Jamaica. Jan. 1941. 74p.; No. 14. Windsor County: vol. 6. Cavendish. Jan. 1941. 100p., vol. 12. Plymouth. 1940. 65p. **7387c**

Jones, Matt Bushnell. List of additions to Gilman's Bibliography of Vermont. Boston. 1926. 69p. (Photostat of typewritten original made by New York Public Library) **7388**

Libbie, C. F. & Co. Catalog of an important collection of books carefully selected from several private libraries and attics in Vermont, by Charles E. Tuttle of Rutland, Vermont . . . including nearly 1000 items of Vermontiana. . . . Boston. C. F. Libbie. 1918. 233p. **7389**

Norton, Charles B. New series no. 2; Norton's literary letter, comprising the bibliography of the state of Vermont and other papers of interest, together with a catalogue of rare and early printed works upon America. N.Y. C. B. Norton. 1860. 41p. **7390**

Perry, Merrill C. The Historical Records Survey and its progress in Vermont. Vt. Hist. Soc. proc. VII. p161-77 (Sept. 1939) **7390a**

Rugg, Harold Goddard. Isaac Eddy, printer-engraver. In Bibliographical essays; a tribute to Wilberforce Eames. Cambridge. Harvard Univ. Press. 1924. p313-29 **7391**

Shearer, Augustus Hunt. Report on the archives of the state of Vermont. Am. Hist. Asso. rep. 1915. p311-55 **7392**

Spargo, John. Anthony Haswell, printer-patriot-ballader; a biographical study with a selection of his ballads, and an annotated bibliographical list of his imprints. Rutland. Tuttle Co. 1925. 293p. (Bibliog. p243-93) **7393**

Survey of Federal Archives. Vermont. Inventory of federal archives in the states. Rutland, Vt. 1938- . mim. The Federal Courts. Dec. 1939. 17p.; The Department of the Treasury. Sept. 1939. 129p.; The Department of War. Dec. 1938. 114p.; The Department of Justice. Dec. 1938. 14p.; The Department of the Navy. March 1939. 4p.; The Department of Agriculture. Oct. 1939. 141p.; The Department of Commerce. April 1940. 25p.; The Department of Labor. Feb. 1941. 90p.; The Veterans' Administration. Dec. 1939. 11p. **7393a**

U.S. Library of Congress. Division of bibliography. List of writings on the history of Vermont. 1908? 13p. typ. **7394**

Vermont. Council. Some old maps touching Vermont. In Records of the Governor and Council of the state of Vermont. Montpelier, Vt. Joseph Poland. 1880. VIII, appendix J. p431-6 **7394a**

Vermont. Free Library Commission. Recent Vermont documents. Bul. XXIV- (Sept. 1928-) **7394b**

Vermont. Secretary of State. Index to the papers of the surveyors-general, published by authority of number 221, acts of 1906. (State papers of Vermont, I) Rutland, Vt. The Tuttle Co. 1918. 170p. **7394c**

Vermont historical gazetteer. Index to the contents of the Vermont historical gazetteer. Comp., ed. and pub. by Abbie M. Hemenway. Rutland, Vt. The Tuttle Co., Marble City Press. 1923. 1118p. **7394d**

Vermonter. Index to the Vermonter, volumes 1-17. Index published by the Vermont Historical Society, through the courtesy of the compiler, Mr. E. Lee Whitney. Vermont Hist. Soc. proc. 1911-12. p115-62 **7395**

Wilbur, James Benjamin. A note on the laws of the republic of Vermont. *In* Bibliographical essays; a tribute to Wilberforce Eames. Cambridge. Harvard Univ. Press. 1924. p277-80 **7396**

VIRGINIA

Bibliography of Virginia and West Virginia legal publications in library of College of Law, West Virginia University. West Virginia law quar. XXVI. p43-57 (Nov. 1919) **7397**

Boston. Public Library. Early history of Virginia. Boston Pub. Lib. bul. III. p269-71 (Oct. 1877) **7398**

Brigham, Clarence S. Bibliography of Winchester newspapers printed prior to 1820. Winchester Hist. Soc. pap. I. p233-9. 1930 **7399**

Brock, Robert A. Critical essay on the sources of information—Virginia 1606-1689. *In* Narrative and critical history of America. Ed. by Justin Winsor. Boston, N.Y. Houghton Mifflin. 1884. III. p153-66 **7400**

Brown, Kirk. Memorandum on the state of preservation of sundry records in Virginia and Maryland. *In* Moffat, R. Burnham. The Barclays of New York. N.Y. R.G. Cooke. 1904. p403-15 **7400a**

Bruce, Kathleen. Materials for southern agricultural history: materials for Virginia agricultural history. Agric. hist. IV. p10-14 (Jan. 1930) **7400b**

Bryan, John S. [Virginia statutes prior to the twentieth century]. Virginia State Bar Asso. trans. XI. p55-70. 1898; XII. p58-70. 1899 **7401**

Cappon, Lester Jesse. Bibliography and finding list of Richmond, Virginia, periodicals. University of Virginia, Charlottesville, Va. In progress **7401a**

—— Bibliography of Virginia history since 1865. Under the direction of Dumas Malone (Univ. of Virginia. Inst. for Research in the Social Sciences. Inst. monograph no. 5) [Charlottesville] Univ. of Virginia, Inst. for Research in the Social Sciences. 1930. 900p. **7402**

—— A checklist of Henkel (New Market, Va.) imprints. Charlottesville, Va. Alderman Lib. In progress **7402a**

—— Guide to manuscript sources and collections in Virginia. Univ. of Virginia. (In preparation) **7403**

—— The making and preserving of Virginia history. Univ. of Virginia news letter. VIII (April 15, 1932) **7403a**

—— Virginia newspapers, 1821-1935; a bibliography with historical introduction and notes. N.Y., London. Appleton-Century for the Univ. of Virginia, Inst. of Research in the Social Sciences. 1936. 209p. **7404**

—— The Yankee press in Virginia, 1861-1865. William and Mary quar. XV. p81-8 (Jan. 1935) **7405**

Casey, Joseph J. Personal names in Hening's statutes at large of Virginia, and Shepherd's continuation. N.Y. [Piser & Russell] 1896; Bridgewater, Va. Green Bookman. 1933] 159p. **7406**

Chapman, Mrs. Blanch (Adams). Wills and administrations of Elizabeth City County, Virginia, and other genealogical and historical items, 1610-1800. [Smithfield? Va.] 1941. 302p. reprod. typ. **7406a**

Clemons, Harry. A survey of research materials in Virginia libraries 1936-37. Charlottesville, Va. Univ. of Virginia Lib. 1938. 79p. mim. **7406b**

Clemons, William Montgomery. Virginia wills before 1799 . . . register of all names mentioned in over six hundred recorded wills. . . . Copied from the court house records of Amherst, Bedford, Campbell, Loudoun, Prince William and Rockbridge counties. Pompton Lakes, N.J. 1924. 107p. **7407**

Complete library of Virginia statutes of a general and permanent nature which have at any time been in force between the years 1619 and 1906, both inclusive. Virginia law reg. XI. p1048-50 (April 1906) **7408**

Cunningham, Mrs. Anna Payne and others. Analytical index and list of publications of the Virginia Agricultural experiment station, 1888-1938. [Blacksburg] 1938. 118p. **7408a**

Davis, Richard Beale. A checklist of Petersburg, Virginia, imprints. 916 Mortimer Ave. Fredericksburg, Va. In progress **7408b**

Eckenrode, H. J. List of manuscripts exhibited by the Virginia State Library and the Virginia Historical Society at the Jamestown Exposition. Va. State Lib. annual rep. 1907. p66-100 **7408d**

Edmonds, Albert Sydney. The Henkels, early printers in New Market, Virginia, with a bibliography. Wm. and Mary quar. XVIII. p174-95 (April 1938) **7408e**

Fisk University. Index to the Norfolk Journal and Guide. Nashville, Tenn. **7408f**

Flagg, C. A. and Waters, W. O. Virginia's soldiers in the Revolution; a bibliography of muster and pay rolls, regimental histories, etc., with introductory and explanatory notes. Virginia mag. of hist. and biog. XIX. p402-14 (Oct. 1911); XX. p52-63, 181-94, 267-81 (Jan.-July 1912); XXI. p337-46 (Oct. 1913); XXII. p57-67 (Jan. 1914) **7409**

Fleet, Beverley. Virginia colonial abstracts. Richmond, Va. 1937- . mim. **7409a**

Ford, Worthington Chauncey. Captain John Smith's map of Virginia, 1612. Geog. rev. XIV. p433-43 (July 1924)
7409b

—— **Tyndall's map of Virginia** [1608]. Mass. Hist. Soc. proc. LVIII. p244-7. 1925
7409c

Foster, James W. Maps of the first survey of the Potomac River, 1736-1737. Wm. and Mary quar. XVIII. p149-59 (April 1938)
7409d

—— Potomac River maps of 1737 by Robert Brooke and others. Wm. and Mary quar. XVIII. p406-18 (Oct. 1938)   **7409e**

Frick, Bertha Margaret. A history of printing in Virginia, 1750-1783, with a list of imprints for that period. (Columbia Univ. Thesis) [N.Y.] 1933
7409f

Hall, Wilmer L. A bibliography of taxation in Virginia since 1910. Virginia State Lib. bul. XVI. no. 1. Nov. 1925. 38p.
7410

—— The public records of Virginia: their destruction and preservation. Va. lib. IV. p2-22. 1931
7410a

Harris, William H. Hening and the statutes at large. Virginia law reg. n.s. XIII. p25-37 (May 1927)   **7411**

Harrison, Fairfax. The maps and map makers of Virginia—The manuscript source records. *In* Landmarks of Old Prince William. Richmond. Priv. print. The Old Dominion Press. 1924. II. p601-52, 677-709
7411a

—— The Northern Neck maps of 1737-1747. Wm. and Mary quar. 2d ser. IX. p1-15 (Jan. 1924)   **7411b**

Hemphill, W. Edwin. A bibliography of the unprinted official records of the University of Virginia. *In* Virginia. University. Library. Sixth annual report of the Archivist, University of Virginia library, for the year 1935-36. [Charlottesville, Va.] Univ. of Virginia. 1936. p9-30 **7411c**

Hiden, Martha Woodroof. Preservation of county court records in Virginia. D.A.R. mag. LXIX. p84-5 (1935)   **7411d**

Historical manuscripts in the library of the College of William and Mary. Wm. and Mary quar. 2d ser. XX. p388-90 (July 1940)
7411e

Historical Records Survey. Virginia. Guide to the manuscript collections of the Virginia Baptist Historical Society. Supplement no. 1- Index to obituary notices in the Religious herald, Richmond, Virginia, 1828-1938. Richmond, Va. Dec. 1940. 386p. mim.
7411f

—— —— Inventory of the church archives of Virginia. Richmond, Va. 1939- . mim. Dover Baptist Association. Nov. 1939. 56p.; Negro Baptist Churches in Richmond. June 1940. 59p.   **7411g**

—— —— Inventory of the county archives of Virginia. Richmond, Va. 1938- . mim. No. 4. Amelia. Feb. 1940. 251p.; No. 21. Chesterfield. Aug. 1938. 299p. (printed); No. 27. Dinwiddie. July 1939. 207p.; No. 47. Isle of Wight. April 1940. 289p.; No.

60. Middlesex. May 1939. 147p.; No. 73. Powhatan. Aug. 1939. 202p.; No. 88. Southampton. March 1940. 265p. **7411h**

Hopkins, Garland Evans. A list of petitions from York County to the General Assembly from 1776 to 1861. Wm. and Mary quar. XVIII. p119-24 (Jan. 1938)
7411i

Hughes, Robert M. Some notes on material relating to William and Mary College and its alumni, in the Southern literary messenger. Wm. and Mary quar. 2d ser. III. p95-7 (April 1923)   **7411j**

King, Junie E. S. Abstracts of wills, inventories, and administration accounts of Albemarle County, Virginia (1748-1800); Amherst County, Virginia (1761-1800). Beverly Hills, Calif. 1940. 57, 49p. reprod. typ.
7411k

—— Abstracts of wills, inventories, and administration accounts of Loudoun County, Virginia, 1757-1800. Beverly Hills, Calif. 1940. 135p. reprod. typ. **7411l**

Kingsbury, Susan Myra. An introduction to the records of the Virginia Company of London, with a bibliographical list of extant documents. Wash. Govt. Ptg. Off. 1905. 214p. (Also in The records of the Virginia Company of London, the court book, from the manuscript in the Library of Congress. Wash. Govt. Ptg. Off. 1906)
7412

Lassiter, Francis R. Prince George County records. Va. mag. hist. IV. p272-81 (Jan. 1897)   **7412a**

List of manuscript sources for Bacon's rebellion which have been printed. Va. mag. hist. XIV. p296-301 (Jan. 1907)
7412b

Lukens, R. R. Captain John Smith's map. Mil. engineer. XXIII. p435-8 (Sept.-Oct. 1931)   **7412c**

McDonald, A. W. Virginia's claim to the Potomac River. Report. Hist. mag. IX. p13-24. 1865   **7412d**

McMurtrie, Douglas C. The beginnings of printing in Virginia. Lexington. [Printed in the journalism laboratory of Washington and Lee Univ.] 1935. 48p.
7413

Martin, William H. Some Virginia law books in a Virginia law office. Virginia law reg. n.s. XII. nos. 1-8. p13-19, 74-84, 141-51, 193-202, 279-89, 321-30, 385-400, 478-90 (May-Dec. 1926)   **7414**

Minor, Kate Pleasants and Harrison, Susie B. A list of newspapers in the Virginia State Library, Confederate Museum and Valentine Museum. Virginia State Lib. bul. V. no. 4. p279-425 (Oct. 1912) **7415**

Morrison, Samuel Eliot. Exhibition of Virginiana in the Widener library treasure room. Harvard alumni bul. XXXVII. p159-61, 197-9 (Nov. 2,9, 1934)   **7415a**

Nelson, Thomas Forsythe. Report on the Chalkley manuscripts. . . . Wash. D.C. The McQueen Press. 1912. 24p. (Judge Chalkley's copy of the Augusta County records at Staunton)   **7415b**

New York. Public Library. List of works in the New York Public Library relating to Virginia. N.Y. Pub. Lib. bul. XI. p64-83, 99-125, 143-68 (Feb.-April 1907) **7416**

Newman, Carol M. Virginia literature. (Univ. of Virginia. Ph.D. thesis) n.p. n.p. 1903. 69p. (Contains a checklist of Virginia writers, 1607-1901) **7417**

Norfolk. Public Library. Newspapers in the Norfolk Public Library. (Appendix E, Fifteenth annual report, 1908) Norfolk, Va. Burk & Gregory. 1909. p18-25 **7417a**

Nugent, Nell Marion. Cavaliers and pioneers; abstracts of Virginia land patents and grants, 1623-1800. Richmond. The Dietz Ptg. Co. 1934- . I- . **7417b**

Paul, Katherine S. A partial list of Virginia authors and their works. Compiled for the use of the Committee on Virginia authors of the Board of World's fair managers. n.p. n.p. [1892] 60p. **7418**

Phillips, Philip Lee. The rare maps of Virginia and Maryland by Augustine Herrman, first lord of Bohemia manor, Maryland; a bibliographical account with facsimile reproduction from the copy in the British Museum. Wash. D.C. Lowdermilk and Co. 1911. 23p. **7418a**

—— Some early maps of Virginia and the makers, including plates relating to the first settlement of Jamestown. Va. mag. hist. XV. p71-81 (July 1907) **7418b**

—— Virginia cartography, a bibliographical description. (Smithsonian miscellaneous collection. v. 37, no. 1039) Wash. D.C. Smithsonian Inst. 1896. 85p. **7418c**

Roberts, Joseph K. and Bloomer, Robert O. Catalogue of topographic and geologic maps of Virginia. Richmond. The Dietz Press. 1939. 246p. **7418d**

Robins, Sally Nelson. Virginia vestrybooks and parish registers. Va. mag. hist. III. p85-6 (July 1895) **7418e**

Robinson, Morgan Poitiaux. Bibliography —Virginia counties: those resulting from Virginia legislation. Virginia State Lib. bul. IX. pt. VII. p209-76. 1916 **7419**

Ross, William E. History of Virginia codification. Virginia law reg. XI. p79-101 (June 1905) **7420**

Shepard, Charles. Genealogical bibliographies relating to Virginia. National Geneal. Soc. quar. XIX. p33-7 (March 1931) **7421**

Smith, Glenn Curtis. A checklist of Charlottesville imprints. Charlottesville, Va. Alderman Lib. In progress **7421a**

—— Index to the Richmond Enquirer, 1816-1820. Charlottesville, Va. Univ. of Virginia. In progress **7421b**

Stanard, William G. The Virginia archives. Am. Hist. Asso. rep. 1903. I. p645-64 **7422**

Stewart, Robert Armistead. Index to printed Virginia genealogies, including key and bibliography. Richmond. Old Dominion press. 1930. 265p. **7423**

Survey of Federal Archives. Virginia. Inventory of federal archives in the states. Richmond, Va. 1941- . mim. The Department of Justice. Jan. 1941. 37p.; The Department of Agriculture. June 1941. 436p. **7423a**

Swem, Earl G. An analysis of Ruffin's Farmers' register, with a bibliography of Edmund Ruffin. Virginia State Lib. bul. XI. nos. 3, 4. p39-144 (July, Oct. 1918) **7424**

—— A bibliography of the conventions and constitutions of Virginia, including references to essays, letters, and speeches in the Virginia newspapers. Virginia State Lib. bul. III. no. 4. p354-431. 1910 **7425**

—— A bibliography of Virginia. Part I. Containing the titles of books in the Virginia State Library which relate to Virginia and Virginians, the titles of those books written by Virginians, and of those printed in Virginia. Part II. Containing the titles of the printed official documents of the commonwealth, 1776-1916. Part III. The acts and the journals of the General Assembly of the colony, 1619-1776. Virginia State Lib. bul. VIII. nos. 2-4. p31-767 (1915); X. nos. 1-4 (Jan.-Oct. 1917) 1404p.; XII. nos. 1-2 (Jan.-April 1919) 71p. **7426**

—— A contribution to the bibliography of agriculture in Virginia. Virginia State Lib. bul. XI. nos. 1-2 (Jan., April 1918) 35p. **7427**

—— A list of manuscripts recently deposited in the Virginia State Library by the state auditor. Virginia State Lib. bul. VII. no. 1 (Jan. 1914) 32p. **7428**

—— A list of manuscripts relating to the history of agriculture in Virginia. collected by N. F. Cabell, and now in the Virginia State Library. Virginia State Lib. bul. VI. no. 1 (Jan 1913) 20p. **7428a**

—— Maps relating to Virginia in the Virginia State Library and other departments of the commonwealth, with the 17th and 18th century atlas-maps in the Library of Congress. (Virginia. State Lib. bul. VII, 1914, no. 2/3) Richmond. D. Bottom. 1914. p37-263 **7428b**

—— Virginia historical index. Roanoke. Stone Ptg. and Manufacturing Co. 1934, 1936. 2v. **7429**

Thomas, Ella Marshall. Virginia women in literature; a partial list. Richmond. B. F. Johnson. 1902. 61p. **7430**

Torrence, William Clayton. A trial bibliography of colonial Virginia; special report of the Department of bibliography. *In* Fifth-[Sixth] annual report of the Library board of the Virginia State Library, 1907-1908, 1908-1909. Richmond. D. Bottom. 1908, 1909. 154, 94p. **7431**

Trimble, K. W. Some old Yorktown maps. Mil. engineer. XXIII. p439-43 (Sept.-Oct. 1931) **7431a**

Tyler, Lyon G. London Company records. Am. Hist. Asso. rep. 1901. I. p543-51 **7431b**

—— Preservation of Virginia history. North Carolina hist. rev. III. p529-38 (Oct. 1926) **7432**

U.S. Library of Congress. Division of bibliography. List of references on the Potomac River, including the canal. Aug. 11, 1922. 6p. typ. **7433**

—— —— —— References on the boundary controversies between Virginia (and West Virginia) and Maryland. Sept. 14, 1914. 9p. typ. **7434**

Virginia. Calendar of Virginia state papers and other manuscripts . . . preserved in the capitol at Richmond. . . . Richmond. 1875-93. 11v. **7434a**

Virginia. House of Delegates. Index to enrolled bills of the General Assembly of Virginia, 1776-1910. Comp. by John W. Williams. Richmond. Davis Bottom, Superintendent pub. ptg. 1911. 1155p. **7435**

Virginia. State Library. A bibliography of Virginia. Part IV. Three series of sessional documents of the House of Delegates: extra session, January 7-April 4, 1861; called session, September 15-October 6, 1862; and adjourned session, January 7-March 31, 1863. Virginia State Lib. bul. XVIII. no. 2. p61-96 (June 1932) **7436**

—— —— Calendar of transcripts in the Virginia State Library. Richmond. D. Bottom, Supt. Pub. Ptg. 1905. 638p. **7436a**

—— —— Catalogue of portraits and statuary in the Virginia State Library. By Edward S. Evans. Richmond. D. Bottom, Supt. of Pub. Ptg. 1906. 8p. **7436b**

—— —— Checklist of Virginia state publications. 1926: Virginia State Lib. bul. XVI. no. 4 (Oct. 1927); 1927: XVII. no. 2 (Dec. 1928); 1928: XVII. no. 4 (Feb. 1930); 1929: XVIII. no. 1 (Aug. 1931); 1930, 1931: XVIII. nos. 3-4 (Dec. 1933) **7437**

—— —— Index to obituary notices in the Richmond Enquirer from May 9, 1804 through 1828, and the Richmond Whig from January 1824 through 1838. Virginia State Lib. bul. XIV. no. 4 (Oct. 1921) 237p. **7438**

—— —— Jamestown exhibit [Virginia historical manuscript exhibit at the Jamestown exposition]. (Virginia State Lib. Fourth annual rep. 1906-07) Richmond. Davis Bottom, Superintendent of pub. ptg. 1907. p66-100 **7439**

—— —— **Department of archives and history.** A calendar of legislative petitions, arranged by counties, Accomac-Bedford. (Virginia State Lib. Fifth annual rep. 1908) Richmond, Davis Bottom, Supt. of Pub. Ptg. 1908. 302p. **7439a**

—— —— —— Calendar of transcripts, including the annual report of the Department of archives and history. Richmond. Davis Bottom. 1905. 658p. **7439b**

Virginia. University. Library. Bibliography of Albemarle County, Virginia. Charlottesville, Va. In progress **7439c**

—— —— —— The Byrd Library; a collection of Virginiana in the library of the University of Virginia, founded on the Alfred Henry Byrd gift. Comp. by John S. Patton. . . . Charlottesville. Univ. of Virginia Press. 1914. 45p. **7440**

—— —— —— Card bibliography of Virginiana. Charlottesville, Va. **7440a**

—— —— —— First-third annual reports of the archivist [Lester J. Cappon], University of Virginia library, 1930-1933. Charlottesville. Univ. of Virginia. 1931-34 **7441**

—— —— —— Handbook of manuscripts in the Alderman Library, University of Virginia. Charlottesville, Va. In progress **7441a**

—— —— —— Index to the University of Virginia publications. Charlottesville, Va. In progress **7441b**

—— —— —— **Archives.** Annual report of the archivist. . . 1930- [Charlottesville Va.] 1931- **7441c**

—— —— —— —— Bibliography of original Baptist church records in the Virginia Baptist Historical Society, University of Richmond. *In* Seventh annual report of the Archivist, University of Virginia Library, 1936-37. Charlottesville, Va. Univ. of Va. 1937 **7441d**

—— —— —— —— General index to the first ten annual reports of the Archivist. [Charlottesville. 1941] 34p. **7441e**

Virginia. War History Commission. Index to source material—First Virginia council of defense. *In* Virginia war agencies selective service and volunteers. (Publications of the Virginia War Hist. Comn. Source vol. IV. ed. by Arthur K. Davis) Richmond. Pub. by order of the executive com. 1926. p393-486 **7442**

—— —— Supplement no. 1, 2, 3, Source material from Virginia counties, cities, calendar of military histories, narratives and reports, lists and calendars of source materials. Virginia mag. of hist. and biog. XXIX. p65-96, 193-224, 305-36, 449-96 (Jan.-Oct. 1921) **7443**

—— —— Virginia war history in newspaper clippings. (Publications of the Virginia War Hist. Comn. ed. by Arthur Kyle Davis. Source vol. II) Richmond. Pub. by the order of the executive com. 1924. 453p. **7444**

—— —— Virginia war letters, diaries and editorials. (Publications of the Virginia War Hist. Comn. ed. by Arthur Kyle Davis. Source vol. III) Richmond. Pub. by order of the executive com. 1925. 528p. **7445**

Virginia Historical Society. Catalogue of the manuscripts in the collection of the Virginia Historical Society, and also of some printed papers. Richmond. William Ellis Jones. 1901. 120p. **7446**

—— A list of the portraits, engravings, &c., in the library of the Virginia Historical Society. Richmond, Va. 1894. 7p. **7446a**

—— Virginia newspapers in public libraries; annotated list of Virginia newspapers in the Library of Congress, Virginia Historical Society, and Virginia State Library. Virginia mag. of hist. and biog. VIII. p337-46; IX. p1-11, 130-8, 289-97, 411-14; X. p225-9, 421-3 (April 1901-April 1903) **7447**

Virginia Library Association. Handbook of Virginia libraries. Charlottesville. Univ. of Virginia. 1936. 92p. mim. **7447a**

Virginia Military Institute. Bibliography on the history of Virginia Military Institute. Lexington, Va. ERA project **7447b**

Virginia State Bar Association. Virginia local public records; housing conditions in the offices of the clerks of county and city court of record, 1921. Report of a special committee . . . to cooperate with the State Library Board. Richmond. 1930. 15p. (Reprint from Annual rep. of the Bar Asso. 1929) **7448**

Watson, Thomas L. A bibliography of the geological, mineralogical and paleontological literature of the state of Virginia. (Cornell Univ. Bulletins of Am. paleontology. II. no. 7) Ithaca. Harris Co. 1897. 109p. **7449**

William and Mary College. Card bibliography of Virginiana. Williamsburg, Va. **7449a**

William and Mary College quarterly. Index to genealogic data in sixteen volumes and one number (I to XVI, no. 1, inclusive), July 1892 to July 1908, inclusive, of William and Mary College quarterly. Williamsburg, Va. [Richmond? 1908?] xii p. **7449b**

William L. Clements Library. A brief account of Ralegh's [sic] Roanoke colony of 1585; being a guide to an exhibition upon the three hundred fiftieth anniversary. (Bul. of the William L. Clements Lib. Univ. of Michigan. XXII) Ann Arbor, Mich. n.p. 1935. 18p. **7450**

Williams, John W. Index to enrolled bills of the General Assembly of Virginia, 1776 to 1862, original parchments. Richmond. Davis Bottom, Supt. of Pub. Ptg. 1908. 941p. **7450a**

Winsor, Justin. Notes on the maps of Virginia, etc. *In* Narrative and critical history of America. Boston; N.Y. Houghton Mifflin. 1886. III. p167-8. 1884 **7450b**

Wisconsin. State Historical Society. The Preston and Virginia papers of the Draper collection of manuscripts. (Publications of the State Hist. Soc. of Wisconsin, Calendar ser., I) Madison. The Soc. 1915. 357p. (The William Preston papers cover 1731 to 1791, and like the Virginia papers concern the western Virginia frontier) **7450c**

Worthington, M. B. Virginia genealogy; list of the old parish registers and vestry books in the library of the theological seminary, Fairfax County, Va. 1902 **7451**

Wynne, Thomas Hicks. Catalogue of the library collected by the late Hon. Thos. H. Wynne, of Richmond, Va. . . rich in works relating to the history of Virginia. Richmond. Richmond Dispatch Steam Press. 1875. 158p. **7452**

WASHINGTON

Arnold, Ralph. Bibliography of the literature referring to the geology of Washington. *In* Washington. Geological Survey. Annual report, 1901-02. Olympia, Wash. 1902-03. II. p321-38 **7452a**

Avery, Mary. Survey of Seattle church archives. Pacific Northwest quar. XXVIII. p163-91 (April 1937) **7453**

Babb, James E. While Idaho was a part of Washington. Pacific northw. quar. XV. p285-8 (Oct. 1924) (MS. records of the period, 1859-62) **7453a**

Barry, J. Neilson. Primary sources to early government. Wash. hist. quar. XXV. p139-47 (April 1934) **7454**

Beardsley, Arthur S. The codes and code makers of Washington, 1889-1937. Pacific northw. quar. XXX. p3-50 (Jan. 1939) **7454a**

—— Compiling the Territorial Codes of Washington. Pacific Northwest quar. XXVIII. p3-54 (Jan. 1937) **7454b**

Bennett, William A. G. Bibliography and index of geology and mineral resources of Washington, 1814-1936. (Washington. Department of Conservation and Development. Division of Geology. Bul., no. 35) Olympia, Wash. State Ptg. Plant. 1939. 140p. **7454c**

Blinn, Harold E. W.P.A. prepares tools for historical research in Washington state. Pacific northw. quar. XXX. p387-98 (Oct. 1939) **7454d**

Bowman, Jacob N. Report on the archives of the state of Washington. Am. Hist. Asso. rep. 1908. I. p365-98 **7455**

—— The state archives at Olympia. Wash. hist. quar. II. p241-9 (April 1908) **7456**

Cole, Theodore L. Washington laws. St. Louis. F. H. Thomas Law Book Co. 1890. 2p. **7457**

Deutsch, Herman J. Survey of Spokane church archives. Pacific northw. quar. XXVIII. p383-403 (Oct. 1937) **7457a**

Douglas, Jesse S. Guide to The Washington historical quarterly and The Pacific northwest quarterly, 1906-1938. Pacific northw. quar. XXIX. p339-416 (Oct. 1938) **7457b**

Grim, Mrs. Alta B. Federal, Washington state, and other states' documents in Washington State Library. Washington State lib., Lib. news bul. I. p4-7 (Oct. 1932) **7457c**

Hassell, Susan W. A hundred and sixty books by Washington authors. Seattle. Lowman & Hanford Co. 1916. 40p. **7458**

Historical Records Survey. Washington.
Guide to depositories of manuscript collections in the United States: Oregon-
Washington. Spokane, Wash. Dec. 1940.
42p. mim.   **7458a**

—— —— Inventory of the county archives
of Washington. Spokane, Wash. 1938- .
mim. No. 1. Adams. June 1939. 275p.;
No. 2. Asotin. Dec. 1938. 209p.; No. 3.
Benton. June 1939. 258p.; No. 21. Lewis.
April 1940. 346p.; No. 26. Pend Oreille.
Sept. 1937. 82p.; No. 29. Skagit. March
1938. 133p.; No. 39. Yakima. July 1940.
435p.   **7458b**

—— —— A survey of Everett, Yakima,
and Wenatchee church archives. Pacific
northw. quar. XXX. p417-26 (Oct. 1939)
                                              7458c

Hitt, J. M. Care of archives in the state
of Washington. Am. Lib. Asso. bul. XVI.
p392-4 . 1922 (*Also in* National Asso.
State Lib. proc. and add. 1922. p4-6)
                                              7458d

McMurtrie, Douglas C. Pioneer printing
in Washington. Springfield, Ill. 1932. 4p.
(Reprint April 1932. National printer
journalist)   **7459**

—— Washington newspapers, 1852-1890, inclusive; a supplement to Professor
Meany's list. Wash. hist. quar. XXVI.
p34-64, 129-43 (Jan.-April 1932)
Same. Chicago. A. H. Allen. 1936 **7460**

Meany, Edmond S. Newspapers of Washington Territory. Wash. hist. quar. XIII.
p181-95, 251-68 (July, Oct. 1922); XIV.
p21-9, 100-7, 186-200, 269-90 (Jan.-Oct.
1923)   **7461**

Meany, Edmond S., Jr. Food administration papers for Washington, Oregon and
Idaho, deposited in The National Archives. Pacific northw. quar. XXVIII.
p373-82 (Oct. 1937)   **7461a**

Nelson, Herbert B. The literature of the
Oregon Territory. Seattle. Univ. of
Wash. In progress   **7461b**

O'Donnell, Gretchen. Bibliography of
Washington geology and geography.
(Wash. Geol. Survey. Bul. no. 12) Olym-
pia, Wash. 1913. 63p.   **7462**

Oliphant, J. Orin. Additions to Professor
Meany's newspapers of Washington Ter-
ritory. Wash. hist. quar. XVIII. p33-54
(Jan. 1927)   **7463**

Pipes, Nellie B. Articles in the Oregon
historical quarterly relating to the Columbia River, settlement of Astoria,
Lewis and Clark Expedition. Oregon
hist. quar. XXVII. p214-20 (June 1926)
                                              7464

Pollard, Lancaster. A check list of Washington authors. Seattle, Wash. Camas
Pr. 1940. 96p. (Reprinted from the
Pacific Northw. quar. XXXI. p3-96 (Jan.
1940))   **7464a**

—— Washington literature: a historical
sketch. Pacific northw. quar. XXIX.
p227-54 (July 1938)   **7464b**

Survey of Federal Archives. Washington.
Inventory of federal archives in the
states. Portland, Wash. 1940- . mim.
The Federal Courts. March 1940. 91p.;
The Department of Justice. March 1940.
47p.; The Farm Credit Administration.
May 1940. 38p.; The Civil Works Ad-
ministration. April 1941. 21p.   **7464c**

**U.S. Library of Congress. Division of bib-
liography.** List of references on the
names Rainier and Tacoma. Jan. 8, 1925.
9p. typ.   **7465**

—— —— List of works relating to
the history of the state of Washington
and of the Oregon country. 1908. 25p. typ.
                                              7466

Washington. State Historical Society. The
Washington historical quarterly. Index
to volumes I-X. Wash. hist. quar. X.
p243-88 (Oct. 1919) Same. I-XX [should
be XI-XX]. By Ethel M. Christoffers.
Wash. hist. quar. XX. p243-87 (Oct.
1929)   **7467**

Washington. State Library. Card index of
genealogical material in the Boston
Transcript and the D.A.R. magazine.
Olympia, Wash.   **7468**

—— —— A reference list of public documents, 1854-1918, found in the files of the
state library. Olympia. Frank M. Lam-
born. 1920. 51p.   **7469**

Washington. University. Library. Check
list of the official publications. Univ. of
Washington. Seattle, Wash. In progress
                                              7469a

WEST VIRGINIA

Brown, Samuel B. A bibliography of works
upon the geology and natural resources
of West Virginia, from 1764-1901; and
also a cartography of West Virginia,
from 1737-1901. (West Virginia Geol.
Survey. Bul. no. 1) Morgantown. Acme
Publishing Co. 1901. 85p.   **7470**

Historical Records Survey. West Virginia.
A checklist of West Virginia imprints,
1791-1830. (American imprints inventory,
no. 14) Chicago. 1940. 62p. mim.   **7470a**

—— —— Guide to public vital statistics
records in West Virginia. Charleston,
W. Va. March 1941. 75p. mim.   **7470b**

—— —— Inventory of the church archives
of West Virginia. Charleston, W.Va.
1939- . mim. The Protestant Episcopal
church. June 1939. 119p.   **7470c**

—— —— Inventory of the county archives
of West Virginia. Charleston, W.Va.
1937- . mim. No. 12. Grant. May 1938.
127p.; No. 22. Lincoln. March 1938. 136p.;
No. 24. Marion. Feb. 1941. 310p.; No. 28.
Mineral. Jan. 1941. 120p.; No. 31. Monroe.
Nov. 1938. 200p.; No. 36. Pendleton.
Jan. 1939. 201p.; No. 38. Pocahontas. Dec.
1937. 112p.; No. 40. Putnam. April 1941.
125p.; No. 42. Randolph. Nov. 1938. 179p.;
No. 43. Ritchie. Sept. 1938. 160p.; No. 44.
Rome. Aug. 1941. 109p.; No. 46. Taylor.
April 1939. 173p.   **7470d**

—— —— List of maps stored in Kanawha County Court House, Charleston, W.Va. (Copy in Library of Congress, Division of maps) **7470e**

—— —— A preliminary bibliography relating to churches in West Virginia, Virginia, Kentucky, and southern Ohio. Charleston, W.Va. 1940. 15p. reprod. typ. **7470f**

Kellogg, Louise Phelps. West Virginia material in the Draper manuscripts. W.Va. hist. II. p5-11 (Oct. 1940) **7470g**

Lewis, Virgil A. Newspapers and periodicals of West Virginia. Charleston, W.Va. 1904 **7471**

Lucke, John Becker. Bibliography and index of West Virginia geology and natural resources to July 1, 1937. (W.Va. Geological Survey bul. no. 4) Morgantown. 1937. 84p. **7471a**

McMurtrie, Douglas C. The beginnings of printing in West Virginia, with notes on the pioneer newspapers and early book and pamphlet imprints. Charleston. Press of Charleston High School. 1935. 20p. **7472**

—— West Virginia imprints; being a first list of books, pamphlets, and broadsides printed within the area now constituting the state of West Virginia—1791-1830. Charleston, W.Va. Charleston High School Print Shop. 1936. 24p. **7473**

Quenzel, Carrol H. West Virginia University collection of manuscripts. Business hist. soc. bul. VIII. p21-3 (March 1934) (Economic and business materials) **7473a**

Recent accessions to the State Department of Archives and History. W.Va. hist. I- . (July 1940- .) **7473b**

Recent publications of interest to West Virginians. W.Va. hist. I- . (Oct. 1939- .) **7473c**

State history as featured by the press. W.Va. hist. I- . (Oct. 1939- .) **7473d**

Survey of Federal Archives. West Virginia. Inventory of federal archives. Charleston, W.Va. 1938- . mim. The Department of the Treasury. Dec. 1938. 65p.; The Department of War. March 1939. 77p.; The Department of the Navy. July 1939. 12p.; The Department of Agriculture. Feb. 1939. 149p. **7473e**

U.S. Library of Congress. Division of bibliography. A list of references on the Monongahela Valley, West Virginia (Historical, industrial, agricultural and social development). April 11, 1934. 13p. typ. **7474**

—— —— List of works on the formation of the state of West Virginia from the commonwealth of Virginia and their ensuing relations. Nov. 1, 1913. 13p. typ. **7475**

U.S. Works Progress Administration. List of miscellaneous maps stored in basement of Kanawha County Court House, Charleston, West Virginia. [193?] 21p. typ. **7475a**

West Virginia. Department of Archives and History. Bibliography in Virginia and West Virginia. West Virginia. Dept. of Archives and Hist. Third biennial rep. 1911) Charleston, W.Va. 1911. p.x-xxxi **7476**

—— —— A bibliography of the journals and public documents of West Virginia, which have been issued since the formation of the state. (West Virginia. Dept. of Archives and Hist. Second biennial rep. 1908. Virgil A. Lewis, state historian and archivist) Charleston, W.Va. 1908. p13-71 **7477**

—— —— A bibliography of West Virginia, parts I and II. Comp. by Innis C. Davis, Emily Johnston, and others. (Biennial report, 1936/38) [Charleston. 1939] 143,392p. **7477a**

—— —— Early newspapers in West Virginia—Files and copies in this department—Newspapers published in West Virginia in 1860. (West Virginia. Dept. of Archives and Hist. First biennial. rep. 1906. Virgil A. Lewis, state historian and archivist) [Charleston, W.Va. 1906] p58-61 **7478**

—— —— Legislative archives. Public documents and state papers relating to the period of the reorganized government [of West Virginia]. Public documents and state papers of Virginia relating to West Virginia (West Virginia. Dept. of Archives and Hist. First biennial rep. 1906. Virgil A. Lewis, state historian and archivist) [Charleston, W.Va. 1906] p36-55 **7479**

West Virginia. Geological Survey. List of publications, July 1, 1937- . Morgantown, W.Va. 1937- **7479a**

West Virginia. State Library. Index catalogue of the West Virginia State Library, law books only. B. H. Oxley, state librarian. [Charleston, W.Va. Tribune Ptg. Co.] 1920. 567p. **7479b**

West Virginia. University. Bibliography of West Virginia. Morgantown, W.Va. (In progress) **7480**

—— —— Division of documents. First report of the archivist of the Division of documents of the West Virginia University, 1935-1936. Morgantown. West Virginia Univ. 1936. (Contains a list of manuscript collections) **7481**

Wood, Warren. Representative authors of West Virginia. Ravenswood. Worthwhile Book Co. 1926. 322p. **7482**

WISCONSIN

Baker, Florence Elizabeth. A bibliographical account of the Wisconsin constitutional conventions. Madison. State Hist. Soc. of Wisconsin. 1898. 37p. (Reprinted from the Proc. of the State Hist. Soc. of Wisconsin. XLV. p123-59. Dec. 1897 **7483**

Berryman, John R. Wisconsin bibliography. *In* History of the bench and bar of Wisconsin. Chicago. H. C. Cooper, Jr. & Co. 1898. I. p281-314 **7484**

Blake, William Phipps. The progress of geological surveys in the state of Wisconsin—a review and a bibliography. Wis. Acad. Sci. arts and letters trans. IX. pt. 1. p225-31. 1893 **7484a**

Blegen, Theodore C. A report on the public archives. (State Hist. Soc. of Wisconsin. Bul. of information no. 94) Madison. Democrat Ptg. Co. Nov. 1918. 115p. **7485**

Bradley, Isaac Samuel. Bibliography of Wisconsin's participation in the war between the states, based upon material contained in the Wisconsin Historical Library. Madison. Wisconsin Hist. Com., May 1911. 9,42p. **7486**

—— Check-list of Wisconsin public documents to 1912. Wisconsin State Hist. Soc. Madison, Wis. MS **7486a**

Buck, Solon J. Recent activities of the Wisconsin Historical Society. Minn. hist. I. p94-108 (Aug. 1915) **7486b**

Durrie, Daniel Steele. A bibliography of the state of Wisconsin. Hist. mag. 2d ser. VI. p29-41 (July 1869) **7487**

Fish, Carl Russell. Report on the public archives of Wisconsin. Am. Hist. Asso. rep. 1905. I. p377-419 **7488**

Gaebler, Hans D. The printing of Wisconsin session laws, 1836-1838. Law lib. jour. XXXIII. p56-9 (March 1940) **7488a**

Hazeltine, Mary Emogene. One hundred years of Wisconsin authorship, 1836-1937; a contribution to a bibliography of books by Wisconsin authors. Madison. Wis. Lib. Asso. 1937. 149p. mim. **7488b**

Historical Records Survey. Wisconsin. Abstract and check list of statutory requirements for county records. Madison, Wis. Feb. 1937. 72p. mim. **7488c**

—— —— Guide to depositories of manuscript collections in the United States: Wisconsin. Madison. Jan. 1941. 36p. mim. **7488d**

—— —— Inventory of the church archives of Wisconsin. Madison, Wis. 1938- . mim. Church of the United Brethren in Christ. April 1940. 136p.; Moravian Church. Nov. 1938. 57p. **7488e**

—— —— Inventory of the county archives of Wisconsin. Madison, Wis. 1937- . mim. No. 3. Barron. March 1939. 387p.; No. 6. Buffalo. Sept. 1940. 277p.; No. 9. Chippewa. April 1941. 204p.; No. 10. Clark. July 1941. 164p.; No. 17. Dunn. June 1941. 168p.; No. 32. La Crosse. June 1939. 324p.; No. 37. Marthon. Aug. 1940. 387p.; No. 41. Monroe. Feb. 1941. 184p.; No. 43. Oneida. April 1941. 231p.; No. 54. Rusk. June 1939. 293p.; No. 55. St. Croix. Oct. 1940. 256p.; No. 59. Sheboygan. Dec. 1937. 113p.; No. 61. Trempealeau. Sept. 1940. 480p.; No. 69. Waushora. Feb. 1941. 212p. **7488f**

Kellogg, Louise Phelps. The Fairchild papers. Wis. mag. hist. X. p259-81 (March 1927) **7489**

—— Search for Wisconsin manuscripts in Canada. State Hist. Soc. of Wisconsin proc. LIX. p36-42. 1912 (MSS. concerning the fur trade, country of the Upper Lakes before 1836) **7489a**

Legler, Henry Edward. Early Wisconsin imprints, with bibliography, 1836-50. State Hist. Soc. of Wisconsin proc. LI. p118-38 (Oct. 1903) **7490**

—— Narratives of early Wisconsin travellers, prior to 1800. State Hist. Soc. of Wisconsin proc. LIII. p157-93 (Nov. 1905) **7491**

—— A Wisconsin group of German poets, with a bibliography. Wisconsin acad. of Sciences, Arts and Letters trans. XIV. p471-84 (Aug. 1914) **7492**

Libby, Orin G. Report on the public archives of Wisconsin. Am Hist. Asso. rep. 1900. II. p294-7 **7493**

McMurtrie, Douglas C. Early printing in Milwaukee. Milwaukee, Wis. Cuneo press. 1930. 79p. **7494**

—— Early printing in Wisconsin, with a bibliography of the issues of the press, 1833-1850. Seattle, Wash. Pub. and printed by F. McCaffrey. 1931. 220p. **7495**

Martin, Lawrence. Wisconsin maps; chronological list of federal and state survey reports, with a few other early papers on the geology and physical geography of Wisconsin. *In* The physical geography of Wisconsin. (Wisconsin. Geological and Natural History Survey. Bul. no. 36, Educational ser. no. 4) Madison. 1932. p494-513, 525-47 **7495a**

Merrill, Julia W. Wisconsin documents. Wisconsin lib. bul. I. p85-7 (Nov. 1905) **7495b**

Milwaukee. State Teachers College. Bibliography on Milwaukee history compiled from newspapers of the period, 1880-90. Milwaukee. WPA project **7495c**

Niendstedt, Joyce Elizabeth. Wisconsin in periodical literature, 1926-1938: a selected bibliography of social progress in the state. Madison. Univ. of Wisconsin Lib. School. 1938. 22p. typ. **7495d**

Nordlie, Anna Elizabeth. German and Scandinavian authors of Wisconsin; a supplement to Hazeltine's One hundred years of Wisconsin authorship. Madison. Univ. of Wisconsin Lib. School. 1938. 24p. typ. **7495e**

Survey of Federal Archives. Wisconsin. Inventory of federal archives in the states. Madison, Wis. 1939- . mim. The Federal Courts. Oct. 1939. 37p.; The Department of the Treasury. May 1939. 186p.; The Department of War. Jan 1939. 66p.; The Department of Justice. March 1939. 24p.; The Department of the Navy. Jan. 1939. 14p.; The Department of the Interior. Oct. 1939. 110p.; The Department of Agriculture. May 1939. 328p.; The Department of Commerce. March 1939. 57p.; The Veterans' Administration. Jan. 1939. 51p.; The Civil Works Administration. Oct. 1939. 23p. **7495f**

Wegelin, Oscar. Wisconsin verse; a compilation of the titles of volumes of verse written by authors born or residing in the state of Wisconsin. Bibliog. Soc. of Amer. pap. VII. p90-114. 1914 **7496**

Wisconsin. Free Library Commission. Check list of the journals and public documents of Wisconsin. Madison. Democrat Ptg. Co. 1903. 179p. **7497**

Wisconsin. Laws, statutes. Index of laws [1879-1897, inclusive] with appendixes showing revised statutes expressly amended or repealed, and expressed amendments or repeals of general and private and local laws. [Appended to session laws, 1895] 220p. **7498**

Wisconsin. Legislative Reference Library. Wisconsin's historical manuscripts. By Alice E. Smith. *In* The Wisconsin blue book, 1933. Madison. Democrat Ptg. Co. 1933. p 1-17 **7499**

Wisconsin. State Historical Society. Bibliography of Wisconsin authors; being a list of books and other publications, written by Wisconsin authors, in the library of the State Historical Society of Wisconsin. Prepared under the direction of Reuben Gold Thwaites and Isaac Samuel Hammond, by Emma Alethea Hawley. Madison. Democrat Ptg. Co. 1893. 263p. **7500**

—— —— Check-list of publications of the Society, 1850-1913. By Reuben Gold Thwaites and Annie Amelia Nunns (Bul. of information no.67) Madison, Wis. July 1913. 55p. (Earlier list appeared in the Proc. of the State Hist. Soc. of Wisconsin. L. p102-26. 1902) **7501**

—— —— Check-list of Wisconsin public documents issued during 1917-18. (Bulletin of information, nos. 91, 95) Madison. 1918-19 **7502**

—— —— Index to the Proceedings of the State Historical Society of Wisconsin, 1874-1901. Prepared by Mary Elizabeth Haines under the direction of Reuben Gold Thwaites. Madison. The Soc. 1904. 399p. **7503**

—— —— Index to volumes I-XX, of the Wisconsin historical collections. (State Hist. Soc. of Wisconsin. Colls. XXI) Madison, Wis. 1915. 573p. (Index to volumes I-X appeared in the Colls. X. 1883-85. p511-58) **7504**

—— —— The Keyes and Civil war manuscript collections in the Wisconsin Historical Library. (Bul. of information no. 81) Madison, Wis. March 1916. 20p. **7505**

—— —— List of books by Wisconsin authors exhibited by the State Historical Society of Wisconsin in the Wisconsin state building, World's Columbian exposition, 1893. Madison. Democrat Ptg. Co. 1893. 14p. **7506**

—— —— Periodicals and newspapers currently received at the Wisconsin Historical Library. (Bul. of information no. 82) Madison, Wis. June 1916. 27p. **7507**

—— —— A selected list of printed material relating to the history of Wisconsin. (Bul. of information no. 11) Madison, Wis. Dec. 1899. 18p. **7508**

—— —— Strong and Woodman manuscript collections in the Wisconsin State Historical Library. (Bul. of information no. 78) Madison, Wis. Nov. 1915. 22p. **7509**

—— —— Suggestive outlines for the study of Wisconsin history. (Bul. of information no. 10) Madison, Wis. Nov. 1899. 13p. **7510**

—— —— **Library.** Catalogue of the library of the State Historical Society of Wisconsin. Prepared by Daniel S. Durrie and Isabel Durrie. Madison. Pub. by order of the state. 1873-87. 7v. **7513**

Wisconsin Academy of Sciences, Arts and Letters. Subject and author index to the papers published by the Academy, 1870-1932. Comp. by Lowell E. Noland. Wisconsin Acad. of Sciences, Arts and Letters trans. XXVII. p573-606. 1932 **7514**

Wisconsin Archaelogical Society. The Wisconsin archeologist quarterly. Table of contents, volumes 1-20, volumes 1-7, new series, 1901-1928. Milwaukee. 1928. 17p. **7515**

The **Wisconsin magazine of history.** Index, volumes I-XV, 1917-31. Prep. by Lillian Krueger. (Madison, State Hist. Soc. of Wisconsin, 1934) 292p. **7515a**

Wisconsin documents. Wisconsin lib. bul. X. p71-2 (April 1914) **7515b**

WYOMING

Bovee, Gladys G. Bibliography and index of Wyoming geology, 1823-1916. (Wyoming state geol. Bul. 17) Cheyenne, Wyo. 1918. p315-446 **7516**

Chaplin, W. E. Some of the early newspapers of Wyoming. Wyoming Hist. Soc. miscellanies. 1919. p7-24 **7517**

Chatterton, F. Index to all the statutes of Wyoming, including session laws of 1927. Sheridan, Wyo. Mills Co. 1928. 402p. **7518**

Hayden, F. V. Bibliography of the Yellowstone National Park. *In* . U.S. Geological and geographical survey of the territories. Twelfth annual rep. 1878. Wash. Govt. Ptg. Off. 1883. p427-32 **7519**

Historical Records Survey. Wyoming. Inventory of the county archives of Wyoming. Cheyenne, Wyo. 1938- . mim. No. 8. Goshen. June 1940. 178p.; No. 11. Laramie. July 1938. 115p.; No. 16. Platte. Dec. 1939. 172p.; No. 19. Sweetwater. March 1939. 171p. **7519a**

McMurtrie, Douglas C. Pioneer printing in Wyoming. Cheyenne. Priv. printed. 1933. 16p. (Reprinted from the Ann. of Wyoming. Jan. 1933) **7520**

Survey of Federal Archives. Wyoming. Inventory of federal archives in the states. Denver, Colo. 1939- . mim. The Department of the Treasury. Feb. 1939. 21p.; The Department of War. June 1939. 153p.; The Department of Justice. Jan. 1939. 10p.; The Department of the Navy. Jan. 1939. 6p.; The Department of Agriculture. June 1939. 151p.; The Department of Labor. Oct. 1940. 30p.   **7520a**

U.S. Library of Congress. Division of bibliography. Wyoming; a bibliographical list. Jan. 23, 1936. 98p. typ.   **7521**

Wheeler, Eva Floy. A bibliography of Wyoming writers. Univ. Wyo. pub. VI. p12-37 (Feb. 1939)   **7521a**

Willard, James F. The public archives of Wyoming. Am. Hist. Asso. rep. 1913. I. p275-317   **7522**

Wyoming. University. Agricultural experiment station. Index bulletin E, March 1915, indexing bulletins no. one to ninety-eight and reports no. one to twenty-three inclusive. By John E. Anderson. Laramie. Boomerang Ptg. Co. 1915. 94p.   **7523**

CHAPTER XV

CARTOGRAPHY

American Geographical Society. Bibliography of regional geography of the United States. N.Y. MS. **7524**
—— A catalogue of maps of Hispanic-America including maps in scientific periodicals and books, and sheet and atlas maps with articles on the cartography of the several countries and maps showing the extent and character of existing surveys. N.Y. Am. Geog. Soc. 1930-32. 4v. **7525**

Anville, Jean B. B. d'. Inventaire de la collection geographies de M. d'Anville. 710p. MS. in Library of Congress **7526**

Bacon, Mary R. Pictorial maps useful in the study of U.S. history. Wilson bul. VII. p121-3 (Oct. 1932) **7527**

Bailey, Alfred Goldsworthy. The John Clarence Webster collection, an address. (New Brunswick Museum col. no. I) Saint John, N.B. 1936. 15p. (Collection in the New Brunswick Museum including maps, portraits, paintings, etc., relating to the French and Indian wars, American revolution, and early relations between the American colonies and Canada) **7528**

Baker, Marcus. A century of geography in the United States. Phil. Soc. Wash. bul. XIII. p223-39. 1898 **7529**

Baker, Oliver Edwin. Agricultural maps. *In* U.S. Department of Agriculture. Yearbook, 1928. Wash. Govt. Ptg. Off. 1929. p640-65 **7530**

Beer, William. Hand list of maps, showing the development of the cartography of the north shore of the Gulf of Mexico, and specially of the coast line of Louisiana. [New Orleans. 1904] 4p. **7531**

Bibliotheca geographica; jahresbibliographie der geographischen literatur; herausgegeben von der Gesellschaft für erdkunde zu Berlin. bd. 1-19, jahrg. 1891/92-1911/12. Berlin. W.H. Kuhl. 1895-1917. 19v. **7532**

Bliss, Richard. Classified index to the maps in Petermann's Mitteilungen, 1855-81. (Harvard Univ. Lib. Bibliog. contributions, no. 16) Cambridge, Mass. Univ. Press. 1884. 55p. (Republished from the Bul. of Harvard Univ. no. 22-7, 1882-84) **7533**

Boatman, Mildred. Maps in the St. Louis Public Library. St. Louis. 1931. 16p. **7534**

British Museum. Department of manuscripts. Catalogue of the manuscript maps, charts, and plans, and of the topographical drawings in the British Museum. London. Print. by order of the trustees. 1844-61. 3v. **7535**

British Museum. Department of printed books. Map room. Catalogue of the printed maps, plans, and charts in the British Museum. London. 1885. 2v. **7536**

Brown, Horace. Maps pertaining to early America (collection of Horace Brown) the Fleming museum, University of Vermont, October 5 to October 21, 1935. Burlington? 1935. 15p. **7537**

Brown, Lloyd A. Notes on the care and cataloguing of old maps. Windham, Conn. Hawthorn House. 1940. 110p. (List of references, p91-110) **7538**

Brown, Ralph Hall. De Brahm charts of the Atlantic Ocean, 1772-1776. Geog. rev. XXVIII. p124-32 (Jan. 1938) **7539**
—— Early maps of the United States: the Ebeling-Sotzmann maps of the northern seaboard states. Geograph. rev. XXX. p471-9 (July 1940) **7540**
—— Materials bearing upon the geography of the Atlantic seaboard, 1790 to 1810. Asso. Am. Geog. ann. XXVIII. p201-31 (Sept. 1938) **7541**

Buffière, Pierre. Exposition cartographique à la Bibliothèque Nationale de Paris. Nature. II. p187-90, 219-22. 1892 **7542**

Burrage, Henry Sweester. The cartography of the period. Maine Hist. Soc. col. 2d ser. VIII. p398-415. 1897 (15th-16th centuries) **7543**

Canada. Archives. Catalogue of maps, plans and charts in the map room of the Dominion Archives. Classified and indexed by H. R. Holmden. (Publications of the Canadian Archives, no. 8) Ottawa. Govt. Ptg. Bur. 1912. 685p. **7544**

Canada. Geographic Board. Catalogue of maps in the collection of the Geographic Board. Ottawa. J. de L. Tache. 1918. 50p. **7545**

Carey, Charles H. Some early maps and myths. Ore. hist. quar. XXX. p14-32 (March 1929) (North America) **7546**

Cutter, Louis F. Some maps of northern peaks. Appalachia. XIII. p167-70 **7547**

De Costa, Benjamin Franklin. Early cartography of America. *In* Bardsen, Ivar. Sailing directions of Henry Hudson. Albany. J. Munsell. 1869. p44-7 **7548**

Des Barres, Joseph Frederick Wallet. Surveys of North America, entitled Atlantic Neptune; published by command of government, for the use of the Royal Navy of Great Britain. London. Sold by W. Babbs. 1781. 16p. (Contains lists of maps in the Atlantic Neptune) **7549**

Dow, George Francis. Early American maps published in New England. *In* Arts and crafts in New England, 1704-1775. Topsfield, Mass. Wayside Press. 1927. p xv, 14-37, 300 **7550**

Faden, William. Catalogue of a curious and valuable collection of original maps and plans of military positions held in the old French and Revolutionary wars; with plans of the different cities and maps of the country. Comp. by Edward Everett Hale. Boston. [J. Wilson & Son, printers] 1862. 13p. **7551**

Fite, Emerson D. and Freeman, Archibald, eds. A book of old maps, delineating American history from the earliest days down to the close of the Revolutionary war. Cambridge. Harvard Univ. Press. 1926. 299p. (References accompany each map) **7552**

Froidevaux, Henri. La Société de géographie et l'étude géographique de continent américain (1821-1821). France-Amérique. XII⁰ ann. no. 115. p158-62 (July 1921) **7553**

Gallois, L. La cartographie du moyen âge et la carte attribuée à Christophe Colomb. Revue historique. CLIII. p40-81 (Sept. 1926) **7554**

Gannett, Henry. A graphic history of the United States. Am. Geog. Soc. bul. XXVIII. p251-72. 1896 **7555**

Grande, Stefano. Le carte d'America di Giacomo Gastaldi; contributo all storia della cartografia del secolo XVI. Torino. C. Clausen. 1905. 166p. **7556**

Hale, Edward Everett. Early maps [of America] in Munich. [also] Notes on Robert Dudley, duke of Northumberland, and his Arcano del mare. Am. Antiq. Soc. proc. LXI. p84-96 (Oct. 21, 1873) **7557**

Harrisse, Henry. Découverte et évolution cartographique de Terre Nueve et des pays circonvoisins, 1497-1501-1769 . . . essais de géographie historique et documentaire. London. H. Stevens, Son & Stiles; Paris. H. Welter. 1900. 420p. **7558**

—— The early cartography of the New World [and] Cartographia Americana vetustissima [1461-1536]. *In* Harrisse, Henry. The discovery of North America. London. H. Stevens & Son. 1892. p253-314, 363-648 **7559**

Hartshorne, Richard. Racial maps of the United States. Geog. rev. XXVIII. p276-88. 1938 **7560**

Harvard University. Library. A catalogue of the maps and charts in the library of Harvard University. (Catalogue of the Library of Harvard University, III, pt. 2) Cambridge. E. W. Metcalf. 1831 (America, p183-212) **7561**

Heawood, Edward. Reproductions of notable early maps. Geog. jour. LXXVI. p240-8 (Sept. 1930) (Maps of the world pre-Columbian and post-Columbian periods) **7562**

Henry E. Huntington Library and Art Gallery. A catalogue of rare maps of America from the sixteenth to nineteenth centuries. London. Museum Book Store. 1927. 92p. **7563**

Hitchcock, C. H. The geological map of the United States. Am. Inst. of Mining Engineers trans. XV. p465-88. 1886 **7564**

Hoffman, Frederick L. An inventory of the collections of the Middle American Research Institute. No. 3. Maps in the Frederick L. Hoffman Collection. Prep. by the Historical Records Survey. New Orleans. Middle American Research Institute. 1939. 146p. **7565**

Hulbert, Archer Butler. The Crown collection of photographs of American maps; a collection of original photographs, carefully mounted, of maps important historically yet hitherto unpublished, contained in the British Museum and other foreign archives, especially chosen and prepared to illustrate the early history of America. Index. Cleveland, Ohio. Priv. print. by the A.H. Clark Company. 1909. 43p. **7566**

Imago mundi: a periodical review of early cartography. I- . 1935- (Includes bibliographies) **7567**

Ispizúa, Segundo de. Historia de la geografía y de la cosmografía en las edades antigua y media con relación a los grandes descubrimientos marítimos realizados en los siglos XV y XVI por españoles y portuguese. Madrid. Gráficas reunidas. s.a. 1922-26. 2v. **7568**

Karpinski, Louis Charles. Cartographical collections in America. Imago mundi. I. p62-4. 1935 **7569**

—— Catalogue of manuscript maps relating to America, found in libraries of France, Spain, and Portugal. n.p. 191? 34p. photostat reprod. **7570**

—— Maps relating to America in various Paris libraries. n.p. 1928. 37p. photostat **7571**

Keuning, J. Vroegste Kartografie van Amerika. Tijdschrift v. gesch. XXXI. p158-72. 1916 (Early charts of the world) **7572**

Kohl, Johann Georg. Asia and America; an historical disquisition concerning the ideas which former geographers had about the geographical relation and connection of the old and new world. Am. Antiq. Soc. proc. n.s. XXI. p284-338. 1911 **7573**

—— A descriptive catalogue of those maps, charts and surveys relating to America, which are mentioned in vol. III of Hakluyt's great work. Wash. D.C. H. Polkinhorn. 1857. 86p. **7574**

—— Lost maps. Littell's living age. LI. 2d ser. XV. p251-4 (Oct. 25, 1856) (From the National intelligencer) (Early America) **7575**

Latorre y Satén, Germán. La cartografía colonial Americana. Bol. centro estud. Am. Sevilla, año III. no. 6. p3-10; no. 9-10. p3-14; no. 15. p1-17. 1915 **7576**

—— La cartografía colonial Americana; cartas geograficas mas antiquas referentes al Nuevo Mundo contenidas en el Archivo general de Indias de Sevilla. Sevilla. Guía oficial. 1916. 79p. **7577**

Le Gear, Clara Egli and Platt, Elizabeth. Checklist of map lists. Wash. D.C. Library of Congress; N.Y. Am. Geographical Soc. In progress **7578**

Libbey, William. Bibliography of political and physical geography. Princeton, N.J. Princeton Univ. MS. **7579**

Lingel, Robert. The Atlantic Neptune. N.Y. Pub. Lib. bul XL. p571-603 (July 1936) **7580**

Lobeck, A. K. Bibliography of the physiography of the United States. Madison. Univ. of Wisconsin. MS. **7581**

MacFadden, Clifford Herbert. A bibliography of Pacific area maps. San Francisco. N.Y. Am. Council, Inst. of Pacific Relations. 1941. 107p. **7581a**

McLennan, John Stewart. Maps, plans and views [of Louisbourg, Nova Scotia]. *In* Louisbourg from its foundation to its fall, 1713-1758. London. Macmillan. 1918. p429-35 **7582**

McNeill, John M. Historical maps and charts. Reprinted from The Scientific mthly. L. p435-47 (May 1940) (Description of the collection of the U.S. Coast and Geodetic survey) **7583**

Maps of America: I. United States. II. British America. III. Latin America. N.Y. Argosy Bookstore. 1937. 46p. **7584**

Marcel, Gabriel. Quatrième centenaire de la découverte de l'Amérique. Catalogue des documents géographiques exposés à la section des cartes et plans de la Bibliothèque National. Paris. J. Maisonneuve. 1892. 77p. **7585**

Marcou, Jules and Marcou, John Belknap. Mapoteca geologica Americana; a catalogue of geological maps of America (north and south) 1752-1881, in geographic and chronologic order. (U.S. Geological Survey bul. II, no. 7) Wash. Govt. Ptg. Off. 1884. 184p. **7586**

Martin, Lawrence. Notice sur les cartes anciennes de l'Amérique du Nord exposées au pavillon des Etats-Unis. *In* France. Comité des travaux historiques et scientifiques. Bulletin de la section de géographies. Paris. Impr. nationale. 1932. XLVII. p99-111 **7587**

Martin, Lawrence, Fitton, Edith, and Johnson, Clarence G. Hispanic-American map exhibition at the Library of Congress at Washington: a selection of Hispanic-American maps representative of four centuries of historical, diplomatic and cartographic progress in the two Americas. Pan Amer. Inst. Geog. Hist. proc. 1937. p243-54 **7588**

Michigan. University. William L. Clements Library of American History. An exhibition of maps engraved within the present limits of the United States, mostly prior to 1800. (William L. Clements Lib. bul. XX) Ann Arbor. 1933. 15p. **7589**

Múñoz Maluschka, Dora. Cartografía primitiva americana. Rev. Chilena hist. y geog. LV. p311-14 (Oct. 1927); LVI. p344-70 (Jan. 1928); LVII. p267-88 (April 1928) **7590**

National Research Council. Committee on tectonics. Catalogue of small-scale geologic maps useful for broader regional studies (with emphasis on modern maps). Wash. D.C. 1933. 132p. **7591**

New England History Teachers' Association. A catalogue of the collection of torical material. Boston; N.Y. Houghton Mifflin. 1912. 33p. (Maps, charts, atlases, pictures, etc.) **7592**

Paltsits, Victor Hugo. Maps illustrating early discovery and exploration in America, 1502-1530. Reproduced by photography from the original manuscripts. Issued under the direction of Edward Luther Stevenson. (New Brunswick, N.J. 1903-1905) Am. hist. rev. X. p863-7 (July 1905) **7593**

Paullin, Charles Oscar. Atlas of the historical geography of the United States. Ed. by John K. Wright. Wash.; N.Y. Pub. jointly by the Carnegie Inst. of Wash. and the Am. Geog. Soc. of N.Y. 1932. 162p. (Includes lists of sources) **7594**

Power, J. L. Catalogue of maps in the Intelligence Division, War Office; America, West Indies and Oceania. London? 1891. 301p. **7595**

Raisz, Erwin Josephus. American cartography. *In* General cartography. N.Y., London. McGraw-Hill. 1938. p57-70 **7596**

—— Outline of the history of American cartography. Isis. XXVI. p373-89. 1937 **7597**

[Rico y Sinobas, Manuel] Mapoteca de Amèrica. [Madrid. Imprenta y Fundición Tipográfica de los Hijos de J. A. Garcia. 1899] 109p. **7597a**

Royal Geographical Society. Library. Map room. Catalogue of map room of the Royal Geographical Society. London. J. Murray. 1882. 404p. **7598**

Ruge, Sophus. The development of the cartography of America up to the year 1570. (Smithsonian Institution. Annual report, 1894) Wash. Govt. Ptg. Off. 1896. p281-96 **7599**

Santa Cruz, Alonso de. Islario general de todas las islas del mundo. Madrid. Impr. del Patronato de huérfanos de intendencia é intervención militares. 1918. 559p. **7600**

—— Die karten von Amerika in dem Islario general de Alonso de Santa Cruz. . . . Innsbruck. Wagner. 1908. 59p. **7601**

Scaife, Walter B. America: its geographical history, 1492-1892. Six lectures delivered to graduate students of the Johns Hopkins University. . . . (Johns Hopkins Univ. studies in hist. and pol. sci. Extra vol. XIII) Balt. Johns Hopkins Univ. Press. 1892. 176p. **7602**

Schuller, Rodolfo. Literature concerning the different early American maps. Cards in the Division of Maps, Library of Congress **7603**

Stevens, Henry. Catalogue of the American maps in the library of the British Museum. London. C. Whittingham. 1866. 17p. **7604**

Stevenson, Edward Luther. A description of early maps, originals and facsimiles (1452-1611) being a part of the permanent wall exhibition of the American Geographical Society. . . . N.Y. Am. Geog. Soc. 1921. 20p. **7605**

—— Early Spanish cartography of the new world, with special reference to the Wolfenbüttel-Spanish map and the work of Diego Ribero. Worcester, Mass. The Davis Press. 1909. 52p. (Reprinted from Am. Antiq. Soc. proc. n.s. XIX. p369-419 (April 1909)) **7606**

—— Portolan charts; their origin and characteristics with a descriptive list of those belonging to the Hispanic Society of America. (Publications of Hispanic Society of America, no. 82) N.Y. [The Knickerbocker Press] 1911. 76p. **7606a**

Thiele, Walter. Official map publications; a historical sketch, and a bibliographical handbook of current maps and mapping services in the United States, Canada, Latin America, France, Great Britain, Germany, and certain other countries. Chicago. Am. Lib. Asso. 1938. 356p. **7607**

Thorington, Christine R. Early maps of America. Antiquarian. X. p66-70 (April 1928) **7608**

Tillinghast, William H. and Winsor, Justin. The geographical knowledge of the ancients considered in relation to the discovery of America—Critical essay on the sources of information—Notes. *In* Winsor, Justin, Ed. Narrative and critical history of America. Boston; N.Y. Houghton Mifflin. 1889. I, p33-58 **7609**

Toronto. Public Reference Library. Map collection of the public reference library of the city of Toronto, Canada. Toronto. Pub. Lib. 1923. 111p. **7610**

Tryon, R. M. Maps in forty-four textbooks in American history for the junior high school grades. School rev. XXXIII. p428-43 (June 1925) **7611**

U.S. Board of Surveys and Maps. Map collections in the District of Columbia. Comp. by the Map information office, January 1930. Revised and reprinted July 1932 and September 1938. Printed in cooperation with the National Resources Committee. Wash. D.C. 1938. 50p. mim. **7612**

U.S. Bureau of Foreign and Domestic Commerce. Some references to map producers and sellers. Comp. by G. A. West. Wash. D.C. Oct. 1940. 6p. processed **7613**

U.S. Coast and Geodetic Survey. Catalogue of maps of the United States and territories, coast survey, and northern and northwestern lakes, 1862. Wash. D.C. H. Polkinhorn. 1862. 74p. **7614**

U.S. Copyright Office. Catalog of copyright entries; pt. 1. . . maps and charts. Wash. Govt. Ptg. Off. 1906- **7615**

U.S. Department of Commerce. Aeronautics branch. Air navigation maps. (Aeronautics bul. no. 10) Wash. Govt. Ptg. Off. 1931. 13p. **7616**

U..S. Library of Congress. Division of maps. An account of the activities and the more important accessions of the Division of maps. . . 1932/33- . Wash. Govt. Ptg. Off. 1934- **7617**

—— —— Annual report. *In* Report of the librarian of Congress. Wash. Govt. Ptg. Off. 1899- **7618**

—— —— Author list of the geographical atlases in the Library of Congress. Enl. and rev. ed. comp. under the direction of Philip Lee Phillips. Wash. Govt. Ptg. Off. 1920. clxiii p. **7619**

—— —— A bibliography of cartography. *In* A list of maps of America in the Library of Congress. Comp. by Philip Lee Phillips. Wash. Govt. Ptg. Off. 1901. p5-90 (Also published separately) **7620**

—— —— Catalogue of an exhibition in the Division of maps comprising some 200 Hispanic-American maps, atlases, geographies, globes, and portraits of historical, diplomatic, and cartographic interest, ranging through four centuries. Comp. by Lawrence Martin and others. [Wash.] Govt. Ptg. Off. 1935. 20p. **7621**

—— —— Disturnell's map. By Colonel Lawrence Martin. Wash. Govt. Ptg. Off. 1937. p339-70 (Reprinted from Hunter Miller's Treaties and other international acts of the United States of America. V. 1937) **7622**

—— —— A list of atlases and maps applicable to the world war. Comp. under the direction of Philip Lee Phillips. Wash. Govt. Ptg. Off. 1918. 202p. **7623**

—— —— A list of geographical atlases in the Library of Congress, with bibliographical notes. Comp. under the direction of Philip Lee Phillips. Wash. Govt. Ptg. Off. 1909-20. 4v. **7624**

—— —— —— A list of maps of America in the Library of Congress. Comp. by Philip Lee Phillips. Wash. Govt. Ptg. Off. 1901. 113p. **7625**

—— —— —— Noteworthy maps, no. 1- ; accessions with acknowledgement of sources of gifts, exchanges, and transfer, 1925/26- . Wash. Govt. Ptg. Off. 1927- **7626**

—— —— —— Lowery collection. The Lowery collection; a descriptive list of maps of the Spanish possessions within the present limits of the United States, 1502-1820. By Woodbury Lowery. Ed. by Philip Lee Phillips. Wash. Govt. Ptg. Off. 1912. 567p. **7627**

Uricoechea, Ezecquiel. Mapoteca Colombiana; coleccion de los títulos de todos los mapas, planos, vistas, etc., relativos á la América española, Brasil é islas adyacentes, arreglada cronologicamente i precedida de una introduccion sobre la historia cartográfica de América. Lóndres. Trűbner. 1860. 215p. **7628**

Wagner, Henry Raup. The cartography of the northwest coast of America to the year 1800. Berkeley, Calif. Univ. of California Press. 1937. 543p. **7629**

—— The manuscript atlases of Battista Agnese. [Chicago. Univ. of Chicago Press. 1931] 110p. (Reprinted from the Bibliog. Soc. Am. pap. XXV. 1931) **7630**

—— The portolan atlases of American interest in the Henry E. Huntington Library and Art Gallery. *In* Essays offered to Herbert Putnam. . . . New Haven, Conn. Yale University Press. 1929. p498-509 **7630a**

Warren, Gouverneur Kemble. Memoir to accompany the map of the territory of the United States from the Mississippi River to the Pacific Ocean. . . . *In* U.S. War Department. Reports of explorations and surveys to ascertain the most practicable and economical route for a railroad from the Mississippi River to the Pacific Ocean. Wash. D.C. B. Tucker. 1855. XI. p17-91 **7631**

Webster, John Clarence. Joseph Frederick Wallet des Barres and the Atlantic Neptune. Royal Soc. Canad. proc. 3d ser. XXI. sec. 2. p21-40. 1927 (Surveys of the coasts and harbors of North America, 1777-1784) **7632**

Wieder, Frederik Caspar. Onderzoek naar de oudste kaarten van de omgeving van New York. K. Ned. Aardrijkskundig Genootschap, tijdschrift. ser. 2. XXXV. pt. 2. p235-60. 1918 **7633**

Wieder, Frederik Caspar and Stokes, Isaac Newton Phelps. Cartography: an essay on the development of knowledge regarding the geography of the east coast of North America; Manhattan Island and its environs on early maps and charts. *In* Stokes, Isaac Newton Phelps. The iconography of Manhattan Island, 1498-1909. N.Y. Robert H. Dodd. 1916. II. p3-179 **7634**

Wilgus, Alva Curtis. Maps relating to Latin America in books and periodicals. (Pan American Union. Columbus Memorial Library. Bibliographic series, no. 10) Wash. D.C. 1933. 103p. mim. **7635**

Winsor, Justin. Baptista Agnese, and American cartography in the sixteenth century. Cambridge. J. Wilson & Son. 1897. 167p. (Reprint from Mass. Hist. Soc. proc. May 1897) **7636**

—— Bibliographical notes, early maps of New England. *In* Narrative and critical history of America. Boston; N.Y. Houghton Mifflin. 1884. III. p380-4 **7637**

—— The earliest maps of the Spanish and Portuguese discoveries. *In* Narrative and critical history of America. Boston; N.Y. Houghton Mifflin. 1886. II. p93-128 **7638**

—— The early cartography of the Gulf of Mexico and adjacent parts. *In* Narrative and critical history of America. Boston; N.Y. Houghton Mifflin. 1886. II. p217-30 **7639**

—— The general atlases and charts of the sixteenth and seventeenth centuries. *In* Narrative and critical history of America. Boston; N.Y. Houghton Mifflin. 1884. IV. p369-77 **7640**

Winsor, Justin, ed. The Kohl collection of maps relating to America. (Harvard College Library. Bibliog. contributions, 1886, I, no. 19) Cambridge, Mass. Harvard Univ. Lib. 1886. 70p. (Republished from Harvard Univ. bul. nos. 26-35, 1883-86. Collection transferred from the Department of State to the Library of Congress in 1903. Reprinted with index by Philip Lee Phillips, Library of Congress. Wash. Govt. Ptg. Off. 1904. 189p.) **7641**

ADDENDA

American Geographical Society. Current geographical publications; additions to the Research catalogue of the American Geographical Society. I- . Jan. 1938- **7643**

American poetry: 1930-1940; a record of poetry publication in the United States during the last decade. Accent. I. p213-28 (Spring 1941) **7644**

Anderson, R. R. Preliminary check list of the laws of the Indian tribes. Law lib. jour. XXXIV. p126-48 (July 1941) **7645**

Baron, Salo Wittmayer. Bibliography of Jewish social studies, 1938-39. (Jewish social studies publications, no. 1) N.Y. Conference on Jewish Relations. 1941. 291p. **7647**

Beals, Ralph A. and Brody, Leon. The literature of adult education. N.Y. Am. Asso. for Adult Education. 1941. 493p. **7648**

Bibliography of waterworks literature. Public works (See monthly numbers) **7649**

Boggs, R. S. Folklore bibliography for 1940. Southern folklore quar. V. p39-76 (March 1941) **7650**

Booker, Richard. Abraham Lincoln in periodical literature, 1860-1940. Chicago. Compiler, 1252 N. Clark St. 1941. 67p. **7651**

Brigham, Clarence S. James Franklin and the beginnings of printing in Rhode Island. Mass. Hist. Soc. proc. LXV. p536-44. 1940. **7652**

Brown, Karl. Materials of maritime interest in the New York Public Library. Am. neptune I. 381-90 (Oct. 1941) (Printed and manuscript) **7653**

Brown, Ralph H. The first century of meteorological data in America. Monthly weather rev. LXVIII. p130-3 (May 1940) **7654**

Bullock, Helen D. The papers of Thomas Jefferson. Am. archivist. IV. p238-49 (Oct. 1941) **7655**

Bureau of Railway Economics. Library. Railroads and national defense in the United States, some current discussions of. Wash. D.C. 1941. 62p. reprod. typ. **7656**

Burke, William Jeremiah and Howe, Will D. American authors and books, 1640-1940. N.Y. Scribner's. 1941. 858p. **7657**

Buros, Oscar Krisen, ed. The second yearbook of research and statistical methodology: books and reviews. Highland Park, N.J. Gryphon Press. 1941. 383p. **7658**

California. State Planning Board. Surveys and maps in California. Sacramento. 1940. **7659**

Cameron, Kenneth Walter. Collections of Episcopal church manuscripts. P. E. church hist. mag. X. p402-9 (Dec. 1941) **7660**

Carroll, H. Bailey. Texas county histories. Southw. hist. quar. XLV p74-98, 164-87 (July, Oct. 1941) (To be cont.) **7661**

Castañeda, Carlos E. Bibliography: printed works—manuscripts. In Our Catholic heritage in Texas, 1519-1936; the mission era. Austin, Tex. Von Boeckmann-Jones. 1936-39. I. p379-401; II. 349-68; III. 411-39; IV. 357-78 **7662**

Chamberlin, E. H. Supplementary bibliography on monopolistic competition. Quar. jour. econ. CVI. p160-9 (Nov. 1941) (Supplements *his* The theory of monopolistic competition, 1938) **7663**

Chicago. University. Press. The University of Chicago Press catalogue of books and journals, 1891-1941. [Chicago. Univ. of Chicago Press] 1941. 432p. **7664**

Clark, H. H. Literary criticism in the North American review, 1815-1835; summaries of out-standing critical essays. Wis. Acad. Sci. trans. XXXII. p301-50 (1940) **7665**

Clemons, Harry. A survey of research materials in Virginia libraries, 1936-37. (University of Virginia bibliog. ser., no. 1) Charlottesville, Va. Alderman Lib. 1941. 100p. **7666**

Coan, Otis W. and Lillard, Richard G. America in fiction; an annotated list of novels that interpret aspects of life in the United States. Stanford University, Calif. Stanford Univ. Press. 1941. 141p. **7667**

College of the Pacific. Library. Theses accepted by the college in partial fulfillment of the requirements for the degree of master of arts, presented to the library, 1912-1939. Stockton, Calif. 1940. 26p. reprod. typ. **7668**

Colorado. State College of Education. Abstracts of field studies for the degree of doctor of education submitted to the Colorado State College of Education in partial fulfillment of the requirements for the degrees of doctor of education and doctor of philosophy, 1939- Ann Arbor, Mich. Univ. Microfilms. 1940- lithop. **7669**

Coolidge, Guy Omeron. Bibliographical index to the French occupation of the Champlain Valley from 1609 to 1759. Montpelier. Vermont Hist. Soc. 1941. 40p. **7670**

Davis, Charles S. Extension Service records in Alabama. Am. archivist. IV. p275-80 (Oct. 1941) **7671**

Delaware. University. Faculty. University of Delaware staff bibliography, 1930/40. *In* Delaware. University. Delaware notes; fourteenth series, 1941. (Bul. v. 36, n.s., no. 3) Newark, Dela. 1941. p105-33 **7672**

Demaree, A. L. The farm journals, their editors, and their public, 1830-1860. Agric. hist. XV. p182-8 (Oct. 1941) **7673**

Detroit Bureau of Governmental Research, Inc. A bibliography of reports, memoranda and publications of the Detroit Bureau of Governmental Research, Inc., March, 1916 to September, 1932. Detroit, Mich. 1932. 15p. **7674**

Drury, Clifford M. Walker collection. Ore. hist. quar. XLII. p269-71 (Sept. 1941) (MSS. concerning the Northwest in the custody of Washington State College at Pullman) **7675**

Duvivier, Ulrick. Bibliographie générale et méthodique d'Haïta. Port-au-Prince, Haïta. Imprimerie de l'état. 1941. 2v. **7676**

Eales, Laura A. National defense; basic books for industrial training. [Bridgeport, Conn.] Bridgeport Pub. Lib. 1941. 57p. mim. **7677**

Eberstadt, Edward, & Sons. The northwest coast; a century of personal narratives of discóvery, conquest & exploration from Bering's landfall to Wilkes' surveys, 1741-1841; books, maps & manuscripts offered for sale by Edward Eberstadt & Sons. N.Y. [1941] 127p. **7678**

Emory University. Catalog of manuscripts in the Keith Read Confederate Collection. Atlanta, Ga. ms. **7679**

Farmer, F. Bibliographical data about codes of Virginia. Law lib. jour. XXXIV. p234-41 (Sept. 1941) **7680**

The **Forbes** collection of whaling prints at the Francis Russell Hart Nautical Museum. Cambridge. Massachusetts Inst. of Technology. 1941. 14p. **7681**

Friedmann, Robert. Dutch Mennonite devotional literature from Peter Peters to Joannes Deknatel, 1625-1753. Menn. quar. rev. XV. p187-207 (July 1941) **7682**

Friends, Society of. American Friends service committee. Index, unnumbered bulletins and publications of the American Friends service committee . . . from 1914 to Jan. 1940. [Phila. 1940] 15p. reprod. typ. **7683**

[**Garrison, Fielding Hudson**] Available sources and future prospects of medical biography. [N.Y. Press of Charles C. Morchand Co. 1928] p585-607. (Reprinted from the Bul. of the New York Academy of Medicine. IV, May 1928) **7684**

Georgia. State Department of Archives and History. Index of sixteen volumes of unpublished colonial records of Georgia. Atlanta, Ga. ms. **7685**

Georgia. State Library. Trial checklist of Georgia state documents. Comp. by Ella May Thornton. [Atlanta] 1940. 70p. typ. **7686**

Gibson, William Hamilton. American book illustrators; a checklist. Publishers weekly. CXL. p484-5 (Aug. 16, 1941) **7687**

Goldenweiser, Alexander. Recent trends in American anthropology. Am. anthrop. XLIII. 151-63 (April-June 1941) **7688**

Goldman, Eric F. Historiography and urbanization; essays in American history in honor of W. Stull Holt. Baltimore. Johns Hopkins Press. 1941. **7689**

Grier, Mary Catharine. Oceanography of the north Pacific Ocean, Bering Sea and Bering Strait: a contribution toward a bibliography. (Univ. of Washington pub. Lib. ser., 2) Seattle, Wash. 1941. 290p. **7690**

Grismer, Raymond Leonard. A new bibliography of the literatures of Spain and Spanish America, including many studies on anthropology, archaeology, art, economics, education, geography, history, law, music, philosophy and other subjects. Minneapolis. Perine. 1941. 2v. **7691**

Gropp, Arthur Eric. Guide to libraries and archives in Central America and the West Indies, Panama, Bermuda, and British Guiana, supplemented with information on private libraries, bookbinding, bookselling and printing. (Tulane University of Louisiana. Middle American Research Institute. Middle American research series. pub. 10) New Orleans. 1941. 721p. **7692**

Haggin, Bernard H. Music on records; a new guide to the music, the performances, the recordings. N.Y. Knopf. 1941. 253p. **7693**

Harwell, Richard Barksdale. Confederate belles-lettres; a bibliography and finding list of the fiction, poetry, drama, songsters and miscellaneous literature published in the Confederate States of America. (Heartman's hist. ser. no. 56) Hattiesburg, Miss. Book Farm. 1941. 79p. **7694**

Hastings, William Thomson. Syllabus of American literature. Chicago. Univ. of Chicago Press. 1941. 141p. **7695**

Hauch, Charles C. Fuentes en los Estados Unidos relativas al proyecto de anexión de la República Dominicana, 1869-1871. Dominican Republic. Archivo General de la Nación. Boletin. IV. p[183]-87 (Aug. 1941) **7696**

Heckman, Oliver S. A selected bibliography of Pennsylvania history for secondary schools. Pa. hist. VIII. p167-80 (April 1941), 337-42 (Oct. 1941) **7697**

Henry E. Huntington Library and Art Gallery. American manuscript collections in the Huntington Library for the history of the seventeenth and eighteenth centuries. Comp. by Norma B. Cuthbert. (Huntington Library lists, no. 5) San Marino, Calif. 1941. 93p. **7698**

Hinkel, Edgar Joseph and McCann, William E. eds. Criticism of California literature; fiction, poetry, drama; a digest and bibliography. Published by the Alameda County Library, Oakland, California, as a report of official project no. 665-08-3-85, conducted under the auspices of the Work Projects Administration. Oakland, Calif. 1940-   **7699**

Historic American Buildings Survey. A list of published writings of special interest in the study of historic architecture of the Mississippi Valley. St. Louis. U.S. Dept. of the Interior. National park service. Nov. 1940. 29p. mim.   **7700**

Historical Records Survey. Louisiana. An inventory of the collections of the Middle American Research Institute, no. 4: maps in the Library of the Middle American Research Institute. New Orleans, La. Nov. 1941. 279p. mim.   **7701**

—— —— Louisiana newspapers, 1794-1940; a union list of Louisiana newspaper files available in offices of publishers, libraries, and private collections in Louisiana. University, La. Hill Memorial Library, Louisiana State University. Oct. 1941. 292p. mim.   **7702**

Historical Records Survey. Massachusetts. Guide to the manuscript collections in the Worcester Historical Society. Boston. 1941. 54p.   **7703**

Historical Records Survey. Missouri. Early Missouri archives. St. Louis. 1941. 98p. (Lists Ste. Genevieve archives, 1761-1854 and St. Charles archives, 1790-1806)   **7704**

Historical Records Survey. New Jersey. Index of the Official register of the officers and men of New Jersey in the Revolutionary War. Newark. 1941. 142p. (Indexes William S. Stryker's compilation published at Trenton, 1872)   **7705**

Historical Records Survey. Tennessee. The Historical Records Survey in Tennessee: a review of five years. [Knoxville] 1941 (Reprint from East Tennessee Hist. Soc. pub., no. 13, p91-101, 1941)   **7706**

—— —— List of Tennessee imprints, 1793-1840, in Tennessee libraries. (American imprints inventory, no. 16) Nashville, Tenn. 1941. 97p.   **7707**

Historical Records Survey. West Virginia. Calendar of the Henry Mason Mathews letters and papers in the State Department of Archives and History. Charleston, W. Va. 1941. 327p.   **7708**

—— —— Calendar of wills in West Virginia. Charleston, W. Va. 1941- reprod. typ.   **7708a**

Historical Records Survey. Wisconsin. An index to governors' messages. Madison, Wis. 1941. 186p. reprod. typ.   **7709**

Hoyt, William D. The Warden papers. Md. hist. mag. XXXVI. p302-14 (Sept. 1941). (Describes the papers of David B. Warden, American consul in Paris, 1810-14)   **7710**

Hussey, Minnie M. The women's collection: a bibliography of material in all matters pertaining to women's interests added to the Woman's College Library of the University of North Carolina, 1937-40. Greensboro, N.C. Univ. of North Carolina. 1941. 55p. lithop.   **7711**

Hussey, Roland D. Some articles in Spanish American historical reviews, 1938-1940. Pacific hist. rev. X. p327-42 (Sept. 1941)   **7712**

Hutchinson, Edward Prince. Preliminary report of the population collection in the Library of Congress. [Wash. D.C.] 1940. 12p. reprod. typ.   **7713**

Index bibliographicus Societatis Iesu, 1937 [-1938] Romae. 1938-40. 2v.   **7714**

Index to early American periodical literature, 1728-1870. Sponsored by New York city, Board of education, New York University, English department, and New York University libraries. N.Y. Pamphlet Distributing Co. 1941-   **7715**

Indiana. State Library. Guide to genealogical material in Pennsylvania archives, series 1-6, published 1852-1914. [Indianapolis] 1937. 16p.   **7715a**

Joline, John F., Jr. Special collections at Princeton: VI. The Pierson civil war collection. Princeton Univ. Lib. chron. II. p105-10 (April 1941)   **7716**

Jones, Claude E. Collected biographies to 1825. Bul. bibliog. XVII. p90-2 (May-Aug. 1941) (To be cont.)   **7717**

Jordan, Philip D. Some bibliographical and research aids to American medical history. Ohio arch. hist. quar. L. p305-25 (Oct.-Dec. 1941)   **7718**

Kansas. University. School of education. Abstracts of doctoral dissertations in education, completed in 1940- Lawrence. Univ. of Kansas. 1941-   **7719**

Kefauver, G. N. and others. Selected references on the organization and administration of secondary education. School rev. XLV. p621-6, 702-8 (Oct.-Nov. 1937); XLVI. 623-6, 701-6 (Oct.-Nov. 1938); XLVII. 622-6, 702-6 (Oct.-Nov. 1939); XLVIII. 624-8, 704-7 (Oct.-Nov. 1940); XLIX. 622-8, 704-8 (Oct.-Nov. 1941) **7720**

Kenney, James F. Public records of the Province of Quebec, 1763-1791. Reprinted from the Trans. of the Royal Soc. of Canada. 3 ser. sect. II. v. XXXIV. 1940.   **7721**

Kentucky. University. Department of library science. Books with Kentucky background for high school libraries. Comp. by Azile Wofford. Lexington, Ky. 1941. 12p. reprod. typ.   **7722**

Ker, Annita Melville. Mexican government publications; a guide to the more important publications of the national government of Mexico, 1821-1936. (Publications of the Library of Congress) Wash. Govt. Ptg. Off. 1940. 333p. **7723**

Kopf, Edwin William. Bibliography section of the paper entitled "Origin, development and practices of livestock insurance." N.Y. L. W. Lawrence. 1928. p367-72. (Reprinted from the Proceedings of the Casualty Actuarial Soc. XIV, May 25, 1928) **7724**

LaFuze, G. Leighton. The Puerto Rico Food Administration: its organization and papers. *Hisp. Am. hist. rev.* XXI. p499-504 (Aug. 1941) **7725**

Lambert, R. E. National defense source book. Freeport, N.Y. Readers' Reference and Research Bureau. 1941. **7726**

Lanctot, Gustave. Past historians and present history in Canada. Canad. hist. rev. XXII. p241-53 (Sept. 1941) **7727**

Lewis, Charles Lee. American short stories of the sea. U.S. Naval Inst. proc. LXVII. p371-7 (March 1941) **7728**

Lunn, A. J. E. Bibliography of the history of the Canadian press. Canad. hist. rev. XXII. p416-33 (Dec. 1941) **7729**

Lyons, P. W. America in story; a regional bibliography. Elementary English rev. XVIII. p217-24 (Oct. 1941) (To be cont.) **7730**

McCarthy, Stephen A. America in eighteen-eighties; a bibliographical study of intellectual and cultural development. Chicago. Univ. of Chicago. 1941. p327-35. typ. **7731**

McLemore, Richard Aubrey. An outline for Mississippi history. Hattiesburg, Miss. The Author. 1941. 46p. (Bibliography included) **7732**

Maggs Brothers. Bibliotheca nautica. London. Maggs Brothers. 1928-38. 4 pts. **7733**

Mariners' Museum. Catalogue of the Robert L. Hague collection. (Museum pub. no. 9) Newport News, Va. 1941. 61p. (Naval art and science, ships, ship models) **7734**

Medina, José Toribio. La imprenta en México (1859-1831). Santiago de Chile. Impreso en casa del autor. 1907-12. 8v. **7736**

Meserve, Frederick Hill. The photographic portraits of Abraham Lincoln; a descriptive list of the portraits in the Meserve collection, copies of which were presented to Lincoln Memorial University by Carl W. Schaefer. . . . [N.Y.] Priv. print. [Charles J. Amm Co., Inc.] 1941. 21p. **7737**

New York. Public Library. Catalogue of the William Barclay Parsons collection. By Karl Brown. N.Y. N.Y. Pub. Lib. 1941. 108p. (Reprinted from the N.Y. Pub. Lib. Bul. XL. p95-108, 585-658, Jan., July 1941) (Engineering) **7738**

—— A guide to reference collections of the New York Public Library. Comp. by Karl Brown. N.Y. N.Y. Pub. Lib. 1941. 430p. **7739**

New York (State) Laws, statutes, etc. (Erie county) Index of consolidated and general laws affecting Erie County, New York. Research conducted under auspices of the Works Progress Administration Project #50359, state of New York. [n.p.] Erie County Board of Supervisors. 1938. 2v. in 1. reprod. typ. **7740**

Nichols, Madaline W. Selected list of Latin American periodicals regularly containing bibliographies or bibliographical sections. Inter-Am. bibliog. rev. I- . 1941- **7741**

Norris, Henry H. and LeBlanc, Blanche. Bibliography on employee relations, with references to books and periodicals covering all phases of personnel activities. N.Y. Am. Electric Railway Asso. 19-? **7742**

North Carolina. University. Documents department. Monthly checklist of official North Carolina publications. I- . Jan. 1941- **7743**

Norton, Margaret C. The archives of Illinois: The circuit court and its records. Ill. lib. XXIII. p22-8 (Nov. 1941) **7744**

Ohio Social Planning Committee. Bibliography of current publications of official and unofficial state agencies in Ohio working in the social fields of education, health and public welfare. Columbus. 1941. 13p. mim. **7745**

Orata, Pedro Tamesis and Cookingham, Waldo B. Occupational information and guidance bibliography, 1937-38. (U.S. Office of Education. Vocational division bul. no. 212; Occupational information and guidance ser. no. 5) Wash. Govt. Ptg. Off. 1941. 521p. **7746**

Pan American Union. Division of intellectual cooperation. Latin American journals dealing with the social sciences and auxiliary disciplines. Comp. by Edmundo Lassalie. Wash. D.C. 1941. 73p. reprod. typ. **7747**

Pennsylvania. Historical Society. Guide to the manuscript collections in the Historical Society of Pennsylvania. Pa. mag. hist. LXV- . Oct. 1941- (Supplements the Guide listed under item 7134c) **7748**

Pennsylvania State College. Library. Pennsylvania author headings. Comp. by Olive S. Holt. (Lib. stud. no. 3, Pa. State Col. bul. XXXV) State College, Pa. 1941. 54p. **7749**

Penrose, Boies. Prints and drawings in the collections of the Historical Society of Pennsylvania. Pa. mag. hist. LXVI. p140-60 (Jan. 1942) **7751**

Ragatz, Lowell Joseph. Early French West Indian records in the Archives Nationales. Inter-Am. bibliog. rev. I. p151-90 (Fall 1941) **7752**

Report of research census of 1937 [-1941] conducted by the American Sociological Society. Am. sociol. rev. II. p518-30 (Aug. 1937); III. 553-67 (Aug. 1938); IV. 543-59 (Aug. 1939); V. 623-44 (Aug. 1940); VI. 542-62 (Aug. 1941) **7753**

Richie, Eleanor Louise. An annotated bibliography on housing for use in home economics education; references selected chiefly from the housing literature of 1938, 1939, and the first quarter of 1940 exclusive of state and local housing literature; socioeconomic research abstract series of the Home economics education service, August 1940. Wash. U.S. Office of Education. 1940. 41p. mim.   **7754**

Robinson, Charles N. and Leyland, John. The literature of the sea from the origins to Hakluyt—Seafaring and travel, the growth of professional text books and geographical literature. *In* Ward, A. W. and Waller, A. R. The Cambridge history of English literature. Cambridge, England. The Univ. Press. 1909. IV. p66-108, 453-62   **7755**

Rosenthal, Clarice A. et al. Selected bibliography on civil liberties in the United States. *In* Seldes, George. You can't do that; a survey of the forces attempting, in the name of patriotism, to make a desert of the bill of rights. N.Y. Modern Age Books. 1938. p255-301   **7756**

Rowse, Edward F. The archives of New York. Am. archivist. IV. p267-74 (Oct. 1941)   **7757**

St. Louis University graduate theses relating to Missouri, 1935/1936 [-1938/1939] Mo. hist. rev. XXXII. p240-1 (Jan. 1938); XXXIII. p115-17 (Oct. 1938); XXXIV. p108-10 (Oct. 1939); XXXV. p283 (Jan. 1941)   **7758**

Schaaf, William Leonard. A bibliography of mathematical education; a classified index of the periodical literature since 1920, containing over 4000 references. Forest Hills, N.Y. Stevinus Press. [1941] 144p. lithop.   **7759**

Schwarz, Sanford. Research in international economics by federal agencies. (Carnegie Endowment for International Peace. Division of economics and history. International economics handbook, no. 2, ed. by Eugene Staley) N.Y. Columbia Univ. Press. 1941. 357p.   **7760**

Schwegmann, George A., Jr. Preliminary checklist of newspapers on microfilm. Jour. doc. reprod. IV. p122-34 (June 1941)   **7761**

Scudder, R. E. Current bibliographical sources for government document acquisition; an annotated list. College and research lib. II. p270-6 (June 1941)   **7762**

Siebert, Wilbur H. Sources of the history of the underground railroad—Bibliography. *In* The underground railroad from slavery to freedom. N.Y. Macmillan. 1898. p1-16, 380-402   **7763**

Smith, G. Hubert. Some sources for northwest history: The archives of military posts. Minn. hist. XXII. p297-301 (Sept. 1941) (Fort Ridgely)   **7764**

Special Libraries Association. Special library resources: I. United States and Canada. Ed. by Rose L. Vormelker. N.Y. 1941. 764p.   **7765**

——. Southern California chapter. Union list of periodicals in libraries of southern California. Los Angeles. University of California at Los Angeles, Bureau of Governmental Research. 1941. 589p.   **7766**

Spivacke, Harold. The Archive of American folksong in the Library of Congress. Pittsburgh 1941 p123-7. (Reprinted from the Proc. of the Music Teachers National Asso. for 1940)   **7767**

Stanford University. Library. University bibliography for the academic year 1938/39. Stanford University, Calif. 1939. 67p.   **7768**

Steinmetz, R. C. Investigation of arson; a selected bibliography. Jour. crim. law. XXXII. p233-40 (July-Aug. 1941)   **7769**

Survey of Federal Archives. California. Ship registries and enrollments, port of Eureka, California, 1859-1920. San Francisco. 1941. 167p.   **7770**

Survey of Federal Archives. Louisiana. Ship registers and enrollments of New Orleans, Louisiana: vol. 1, 1804-1820. University, La. 1941. 171p.   **7771**

Survey of Federal Archives. Rhode Island. Ship registers and enrollments of Providence, Rhode Island, 1773-1939: vol. 1, A-M. Providence, 1941. 766p.   **7772**

Texas. University. Classified list of master of arts dissertations in history, 1895-1940 inclusive. Prep. by Charles Cumberland. [Austin? 1941] 63p. reprod. typ.   **7773**

Thompson, Lawrance. The printing and publishing activities of the American Tract Society from 1825 to 1850. Bibliog. Soc. Amer. pap. XXXV. p81-114. 1941.   **7774**

Tilley, Nannie M. The Trinity College Historical Society, 1892-1941. Durham. Duke Univ. Press. 1941. 133p.   **7775**

Torres Lanzas, Pedro. Independencia de América; fuentes para su estudio; catálogo de documentos conservados en el Archivo General de Indias de Sevilla, la serie. Madrid. 1912. 6v.   **7776**

Tucker, Sara Jones. Archival materials for the anthropologist in the National Archives, Washington, D.C. Reprinted from Am. anthrop. XLIV. p617-44 (Oct.-Dec. 1941)   **7777**

U.S. Bureau of Agricultural Economics. Library. Economic aspects of farm tractor operation; selected references, 1935-March 1941. Comp. by Nellie G. Larson. (Economic library list, no. 26) Wash. D.C. 1941. 52p. mim.   **7778**

U.S. Bureau of Foreign and Domestic Commerce. List of selected publications, corrected to May 15, 1938 [-Nov. 1, 1938, Jan. 1, 1940, March 31, 1941] Wash. Govt. Ptg. Off. 1938-41. 4v.   **7779**

—— —— Industrial reference service. The Negro press; its size, scope, coverage and distribution. (Business ser. no. 8) Wash. D.C. 1941. 12p.   **7780**

U.S. Department of Agriculture. List of the agricultural periodicals of the United States and Canada published during the century, July 1810 to July 1910. Comp. by Stephen Conrad Stuntz, edited by Emma B. Hawks (Miscellaneous publication no. 398) Wash. Govt. Ptg. Off. 1941. 190p. **7781**

U.S. Information Service. Library. National defense and neutrality; proclamations, executive orders, military orders and presidential administrative orders and regulations, July 1, 1939 through March 19, 1941. Wash. D.C. [1941] [37]p. reprod. typ. **7782**

U.S. Library of Congress. Division of bibliography. The effect of war on the cost of living; a selected list of references. Comp. by Anne D. Brown. 1941. 17p. mim. **7783**

—— —— —— A list of recent references on bankruptcy in the United States (supplementing list of Jan. 2, 1940). Comp. by Grace H. Fuller. 1941. 23p. mim. **7784**

—— —— A selected list of references on the copper industry, 1914-1941. Comp. by Helen F. Conover. 1941. 29p. typ. **7785**

—— —— Hispanic foundation. Latin American periodicals current in the Library of Congress. Prep. by Murray M. Wise and others. Wash. D.C. 1941. 137p. reprod. typ. **7786**

U.S. National Archives. Tentative bibliography on the conservation of cultural resources in times of war. Wash. D.C. April, 1941. 7p. mim. Supplement. June 1941. p8-9. mim. **7787**

U.S. Patent Office. Index of patents issued from the United States Patent Office, 1940. Wash. Govt. Ptg. Off. 1941. 1255p. **7788**

U.S. Public Health Service. Public Health Service publications; a list of publications issued during the period July/Dec. 1936-. Pub. health rep. LII- . March 26, 1937- **7789**

—— —— Division of sanitary reports and statistics. Selected bibliography on health and medical services in the United States and related subjects, with special reference to the National health conference of 1938. Comp. by Elizabeth G. Pritchard and Margaret T. Prince. [Wash. D.C.] 1939. 37p. reprod. typ. **7790**

U.S. Work Projects Administration. Annals of Cleveland: bibliographical series; index to Cleveland periodicals. Cleveland. 1939- reprod. typ. (Authors) **7791**

University of Missouri graduate theses relating to Missouri, 1935/1936 [-1938/1939] Mo. hist. rev. XXXII. p242-3 (Oct. 1938); XXXIII. 114-15 (Oct. 1938); XXXIV. 107-8 (Oct. 1939); XXXV. 284-5 (Jan. 1941) **7792**

Vermont. Dept. of education. Bibliography of professional books on education, 1932-1939. Montpelier, Vt. State Dept. of Education. 1940. 32p. **7793**

Virginia. University. Abstracts of dissertations accepted in partial fulfillment of the requirements for the degree of doctor of philosophy, 1937[-1940] Charlottesville. [1937-40] 4v. **7794**

Wade, K. C. Articles relating to inter-American affairs published in English in 1941- . Inter-Am. bibliog. rev. I- . 1941- **7795**

Ward, A. W. and Waller, A. R. The Cambridge history of English literature. Cambridge, England. The Univ. Press. 1907-27. 15v. **7796**

Washington University graduate theses relating to Missouri, 1935/1936[-1938/1939] Mo. hist. rev. XXXII. p243-4 (Jan. 1938); XXXIII, 117-18 (Oct. 1938); XXXIV. 111 (Oct. 1939); XXXV. 285-6 (Jan. 1941) **7797**

Weber, Friedrich. Beiträge zur charakteristik der älteren geschichtsschreiber über Spanisch-Amerika; eine biographical-bibliographische skizze. Leipzig. R. Voigtländer. 1911. 338p. **7798**

Wesley, Edgar B. Reading guide for social studies teachers. Wash. D.C. National Council for the Social Studies. 1941. 158p. **7799**

Wilcox, Jerome Kear. Official defense publications; guide to state and federal publications. Berkeley, Calif. Bur. of Pub. Admin., Univ. of California. Sept. 1941. 106p. mim. **7800**

Wilgus, Alva Curtis. Bibliographical essay on leading works in various languages dealing with Hispanic America printed since the year 1800. *In* The development of Hispanic America. N.Y. Farrar & Rinehart. 1941. p856-911 **7801**

—— Recent publications in English dealing with Latin American affairs and related fields, 1941-. Inter-Am. bibliog. rev. I- . 1941- **7802**

Wilson, Nancy. The library of the Department of Archives and History. W. Va. hist. III. p147-55 (Jan. 1942) **7803**

Wisconsin. University. College of Agriculture. American regional literature; study of the literature of rural life based on a course given by August Derleth in 1940 for students in the Farm folk school-College of Agriculture, University of Wisconsin. [Madison. 1941] 28p. reprod. typ. **7804**

The **writings** of Augustus Hunt Shearer. Grosvenor lib. bul. XXIII. p93-5 (June 1941) **7805**

Zimmerman, Fred L. and Read, Phyllis R., comps. Numerical list of current publications of the United States Department of Agriculture. (U.S. Department of Agriculture. Miscellaneous publication no. 450) Wash. Govt. Ptg. Off. 1941. 934p. **7806**

INDEX